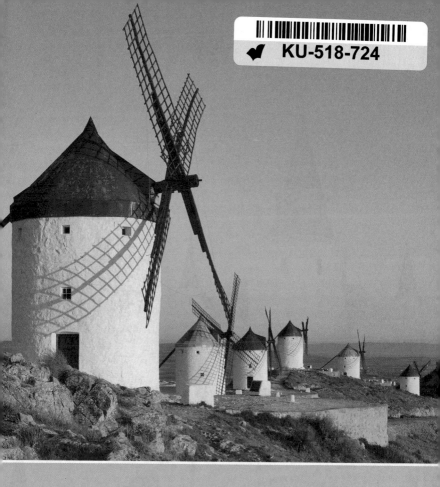

THE ROUGH GUIDE TO

Spain

written and researched by

Simon Baskett, Jules Brown, Mark Ellingham, John Fisher, Geoff Garvey, AnneLise Sorensen and Greg Ward

with additional contributions by

Jen Foster

ROUGH GUIDES

roughguides.com

Contents

Introduction to
Spain

If you're visiting Spain for the first time, be warned: this is a country that fast becomes an addiction. You might intend to come just for a beach holiday, a walking tour or a city break, but before you know it you'll find yourself hooked by something quite different – the wild celebration of some local fiesta, perhaps, or the otherworldly architecture of Barcelona. Even in the best-known destinations – from the capital, Madrid, to the *costas*, from the high Pyrenees to the Moorish cities of the south – there are genuinely surprising attractions at every turn, whether it's hip restaurants in the Basque country, the wild landscapes of the central plains, or cutting-edge galleries in the industrial north. Soon, you'll notice that there is not just one Spain but many – and indeed, Spaniards themselves often speak of Las Españas (the Spains).

Partly, this is down to an almost obsessive regionalism, stemming from the creation in the late 1970s of seventeen *comunidades autonomías* – autonomous regions – with their own governments, budgets and cultural ministries, even police forces. You might think you are on holiday in Spain – your hosts may be adamant that you're actually visiting Catalunya, and will point to a whole range of differences in language, culture and artistic traditions, not to mention social attitudes and politics. Indeed, the old days of a unified nation, governed with a firm hand from Madrid, seem to have gone forever, as the separate kingdoms that made up the original Spanish state reassert themselves in an essentially federal structure.

Does any of this matter for visitors? As a rule – not really, since few tourists have the time or inclination to immerse themselves in contemporary Spanish political discourse. Far more important is to look beyond the clichés of paella, matadors, sangría and siesta if you're to get the best out of a visit to this amazingly diverse country.

Even in the most over-touristed resorts of the Costa del Sol, you'll be able to find an authentic bar or restaurant where the locals eat, and a village not far away where an age-old bullfighting tradition owes nothing to tourism. The large cities of the north,

ABOVE LA PEDRERA, BARCELONA **RIGHT** CADAQUÉS, COSTA BRAVA >

from Barcelona to Bilbao, have reinvented themselves as essential cultural destinations (and they don't all close down for hours for a kip every afternoon). And when the world now looks to Spain for culinary inspiration – the country has some of the most acclaimed chefs and innovative restaurants in the world – it's clear that things have changed. Spain, despite the current economic uncertainty, sees itself very differently from a generation ago. So should you – prepare to be surprised.

Where to go

Spain's cities are among the most vibrant in Europe. Exuberant **Barcelona**, for many, has the edge, thanks to Gaudí's extraordinary *modernista* architecture, the lively promenade of the Ramblas, five kilometres of sandy beach and the world's best football team. The capital, **Madrid**, may not be as pretty, but it claims as many devotees – immortalized in the movies of Pedro Almodóvar, and shot through with a contemporary style that informs everything from its major-league art museums to its carefree bars and summer cafés. Then there's **Seville**, home of flamenco and all the clichés of southern Spain; **Valencia**, the vibrant capital of the Levante, with a thriving arts scene and nightlife; and **Bilbao**, a not-to-miss stop on Spain's cultural circuit, due to Frank Gehry's astonishing Museo Guggenheim.

AVE High-speed Line
F.E.V.E. Private Railway
Standard Motorway
Toll Motorway

0   150
kilometres

Not only are Spain's modern cities and towns lively and exciting, they are monumental – literally so. History has washed over the country, adding an architectural backdrop that varies from one region to another, dependent on their occupation by Romans, Visigoths or Moors, or on their role in the medieval Christian Reconquest or in the later Golden Age of imperial Renaissance Spain. Touring **Castilla y León**, for example, you can't avoid the stereotypical Spanish image of vast cathedrals and hundreds of *reconquista* castles, while the gorgeous medieval university city of Salamanca captivates all who visit. In northerly, mountainous **Asturias** and the **Pyrenees**, tiny, almost organically evolved, Romanesque churches dot the hillsides and villages, while in **Galicia** all roads lead to the ancient, and heartbreakingly beautiful cathedral city of Santiago de Compostela. **Andalucía** has the great mosques and Moorish palaces of Granada, Seville and Córdoba; **Castilla-La Mancha** boasts the superbly preserved medieval capital of Toledo; while the harsh landscape of **Extremadura** cradles ornate *conquistador* towns built with riches from the New World.

The Spanish **landscape**, too, holds just as much fascination and variety as the country's urban centres. The evergreen estuaries of Galicia could hardly be more different from the high, arid plains of Castile, or the gulch-like desert landscapes of Almería. In particular, Spain has some of the finest **mountains** in Europe, with superb walking – short hikes to week-long treks – in a dozen or more protected ranges or *sierras* – especially the Picos de Europa and the Pyrenees. There are still brown bears and lynx in the wild, not to mention boar, storks and eagles, while a near-five-thousand-kilometre coastline means great opportunities for fishing, whale-watching and dolphin-spotting.

Agriculture, meanwhile, makes its mark in the patterned hillsides of the wine- and olive-growing regions, the baking wheat plantations and cattle

ranches of the central plains, the *meseta*, and the rice fields of the eastern provinces of Valencia and Murcia, known as the Levante. These areas, although short on historic monuments and attractions, produce some of Spain's most famous exports, and with the country now at the heart of the contemporary European foodie movement, there's an entire holiday to be constructed out of simply exploring Spain's rich **regional cuisine** – touring the Rioja and other celebrated wine regions, snacking your way around Extremadura and Andalucía in search of the world's best *jamón serrano* (cured mountain ham), or tucking into a paella in its spiritual home of Valencia.

And finally, there are the beaches – one of Spain's greatest attractions, and where modern tourism to the country began in the 1960s. Here, too, there's a lot more variety than the stereotypical images might suggest. Long tracts of coastline – along the **Costa del Sol** in Andalucía in particular – have certainly been massively and depressingly over-developed, but

SPANISH TIME

Spanish time is notionally one hour ahead of the UK – but conceptually Spain might as well be on a different planet. Nowhere else in Europe keeps such late hours. Spaniards may not take a traditional midday **siesta** as much as they used to, but their diurnal rhythms remain committedly nocturnal. They'll saunter out around 8 or 9pm in the evening for a **paseo**, to greet friends and maybe have a drink and tapas, and if they're eating out, they'll commonly start at 10 or 11pm, often later in Madrid, where it's not unusual for someone to phone around midnight to see if you're going out for the evening.

Like everything else, practices differ somewhat by region. Madrid – its inhabitants nicknamed **los gatos** or "the cats" for their nocturnal lifestyle – is famed for staying up the latest, with Andalucía a close second. In the north, particularly in Catalunya, they keep more northern European hours. And, of course, **summer nights** never seem to really end.

Author picks

Our hard-travelling authors have visited every corner of Spain – from the Rías of Galicia to the white towns of Andalucía – to bring you some unique travel experiences. These are some of their own, personal favourites.

In-your-face fiestas La Tomatina (p.815) puts the pulp in people (literally); or do battle with wine, not tomatoes, in Haro (p.413).

Gourmet treats Spain tickles the taste-buds, from L'Escala anchovies (p.724) to Jijona *turrón* (p.835), washed down with Asturian cider (p.529).

Classic journeys Legendary pilgrim hike, the Camino de Santiago (p.558), is a life must-do, but for train thrills the Catalan Cremallera (p.752) is a blast.

Delightful towns Not famous, no fanfares, but thoroughly lovely – Cudillero in Asturias (p.540), El Burgo de Osma in Castilla y León (p.403) and Andalucía's Zahara de la Sierra (p.261).

Amazing views The go-on-twist-our-arm choices are the views from the walls of Ávila (p.154) and Barcelona from the cross-harbour cable-car (p.663).

Hip and hot nightlife That's *Maumau* in Barcelona (p.696), *Potemkin* in Granada (p.347) and *Macumba Clubbing* in Madrid (p.116).

Best beaches Top of a very crowded field – Conil in Andalucía (p.290), Águilas in Murcia (p.845) Ibiza's Cala D'Hort (p.860).

Urban art Chillida in San Sebastián (p.456), Gaudí's Parc Güell (p.678) or the vertical garden in Madrid's Caixa Forum (p.86) – eye-popping, urban masterworks all.

Our author recommendations don't end here. We've flagged up our favourite places – a perfectly sited hotel, an atmospheric café, a special restaurant – throughout the guide, highlighted with the ★ symbol.

LEFT GRANADA'S ALHAMBRA **RIGHT FROM TOP** LA TOMATINA; ZAHARA DE LA SIERRA, ANDALUCÍA; SARDINES AND ANCHOVIES delightful pockets remain, even along the biggest, concrete-clad *costas*. Moreover, there are superb windsurfing waters around Tarifa and some decidedly low-key resorts along the **Costa de la Luz**. On the **Costa Brava**, in the northeast in Catalunya, the string of idyllic coves between Palamos and Begur is often overlooked, while the cooler Atlantic coastline boasts the **surfing beaches** of Cantabria and Asturias, or the unspoilt coves of Galicia's estuaries. Offshore, the **Balearic Islands** – Ibiza, Formentera, Mallorca and Menorca – also have some superb sands, with party-fuelled Ibiza in particular offering one of the most hedonistic backdrops to beachlife in the whole Mediterranean.

Hedonism, actually, brings us full-circle, back to one of the reasons why Spain is pretty much irresistible and infectious. Wherever you are in the country, you can't help but notice the Spaniards' wild – often over-bearing – enthusiasm for **having a good time**. Festival time is a case in point – these aren't staid, annual celebrations, they are raucous reaffirmations of life itself, complete with fireworks, fancy dress, giants, devils, bonfires, parties, processions and sheer Spanish glee. But even outside *fiesta* time there's always something vibrant and noisy happening – from local market to late-night bar, weekend football match to beachside dance club. Meals are convivial affairs – not for most Spaniards the rushed sandwich or chain-restaurant takeaway – and long lunches and late dinners are the norm throughout the country. And with family at the heart of Spanish society, there's a genuine welcome for, and interest in, you and yours, whether at resort hotel or rustic guest house. "*A pasarlo bien!*" (Have a good time!), as the Spanish say.

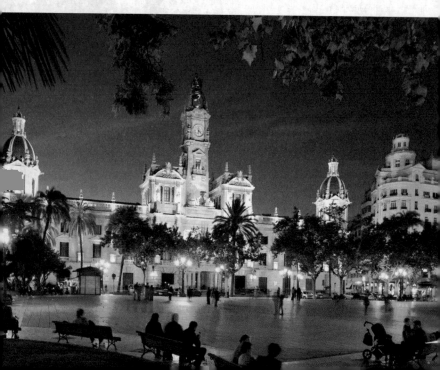

ON THE TAPAS TRAIL

Everyone thinks they know tapas – the little nibbles served up in bars – yet nothing can prepare you for the variety available on their home soil. If all you've ever encountered is deep-fried squid and spicy potatoes, then a treat awaits. That's not even to say that those dishes aren't authentic – but the truth is that your first beachfront plate of Andalucían **calamari** or **patatas bravas** in back-street Barcelona really make you sit up and take notice. The proper way to eat tapas is to wander from one bar to another to sample a particular speciality, since the best bars tend to be known for just one or two dishes... and the locals wouldn't dream of ordering anything else. So you might duck into one place for **jamón serrano** (cured ham), another for **pulpo gallego** (pot-cooked octopus), a third for **pimientos de Padrón** (small green peppers – about one in ten being fiery-hot), and then maybe on to a smoky old bar that serves just **fino** (dry sherry) from the barrel along with slices of **mojama** (dried, pressed roe). And that's not counting the creative, new-wave bars where sculpted **montaditos** (canapés), yucca chips, samosas, sushi-fusion titbits or artisan-produced cheese and meat are all vying for your attention before you sit down later to the serious business of dinner.

When to go

If Spain is a country of many regions, it's also a country of many **climates** (see p.51). The high central plains (which include Madrid) suffer from fierce extremes – stiflingly hot in summer, bitterly cold and swept by freezing winds in winter. The Atlantic coast, in contrast, has a tendency to be damp and misty, with a relatively brief, humid summer. The Mediterranean south is warm virtually all year round, and in parts of Andalucía it's positively subtropical – it's often pleasant enough to take lunch outside, even in the winter months. On a general holiday or city break, in most regions spring, the early part of summer and autumn are the best times to visit. Temperatures will be fairly clement, sites and attractions open, and tourist numbers relatively low – worth considering, especially if your destination is one of the beach resorts or cultural attractions. Spain is one of the most visited countries on the planet – it plays host to about sixty million tourists a year, rather more than the entire population – and all main tourist destinations are packed in high summer. Even the Pyrenean mountains aren't immune, swapping winter ski crowds for summer hikers and bikers. August is Spain's own holiday month – when the *costas* are at their most crowded, though inland cities (including Madrid) are, by contrast, pretty sleepy, since everyone who can, leaves for their annual break.

28

things not to miss

It's not possible to see everything that Spain has to offer in one trip – and we don't suggest you try. What follows, in no particular order, is a selection of the country's highlights, including spectacular architecture, outstanding natural wonders, flamboyant local festivals and a few culinary treats. Each entry has a page reference to take you straight into the Guide, where you can find out more.

1 FLAMENCO IN SEVILLE
Page 282
The stamp of heels and heart-rending lament of a *cante jondo* encapsulate the soul of the Spanish south.

2 LAS ALPUJARRAS
Page 350
Drive over lemons and walk old mule paths in this picturesque region of mountain villages nestled in the southern folds of the Sierra Nevada.

3 BURGOS CATHEDRAL
Page 418
Perhaps Spain's finest Gothic cathedral dominates the likeable small city of Burgos, destined to be European City of Culture in 2016.

4 IBIZA AND FORMENTERA'S HIDDEN COVES
Page 859
The islands' little-developed beaches range from gem-like coves to sweeps of white sand.

5 GOURMET SNACKS IN SAN SEBASTIÁN
Page 458

Pintxos are kings of the tapas in the Basque region's culinary capital.

6 CLUBBING IN IBIZA
Page 858

Forget sleep, and experience everything else to excess, on Ibiza – the ultimate party island.

7 SEGOVIA
Page 159

At eight hundred metres long the extraordinary Roman aqueduct of Segovia is one of Spain's most breathtaking ancient monuments.

8 TEATRE-MUSEU DALÍ, FIGUERES
Page 739

The Dalí museum in Figueres is as surreal as its creator – who lies in a mausoleum within.

9 TOLEDO
Page 126

The capital of medieval Spain, Toledo has changed little since its depiction in El Greco's paintings.

10 LA MEZQUITA, CÓRDOBA
Page 312

Nothing can prepare you for the breathtaking Grand Mosque of Córdoba – one of the world's most beautiful buildings

11 PARADORES
Page 747

Converted castles and monasteries – such as this one in Cardona – provide many of Spain's most atmospheric hotels.

12 BODEGAS YSIOS
Page 83

Rioja region's amazing designer temple of wine.

13 THE ALHAMBRA, GRANADA
Page 30

The legendary Moorish palace complex is a monument to sensuality and contemplative decoration.

14 SEMANA SANTA
Page 28

Easter week sees processions of masked penitents, with the biggest events in Seville and Málaga.

15 FUNDACIÓ JOAN MIRÓ
Page 67

The instantly recognizable colours, shapes and forms of Joan Miró's life's work in Barcelona's museum.

16 SANTIAGO DE COMPOSTELA
Page 49

The pilgrim route to Santiago de Compostela left a swathe of Gothic and Renaissance churches, not least the great cathedral.

17 PARQUE NACIONAL COTO DE DOÑANA
Page 304

Doñana's unique habitats host myriad birds and other wildlife, including the Iberian lynx.

18

19

20

18 UNIVERSIDAD DE SALAMANCA
Page 378
Spain's most famous and historic university sits at the heart of the gorgeous honey-coloured city.

19 PICOS DE EUROPA
Page 524
Take a hike along the stunning Cares Gorge, the most popular walk in glorious Picos de Europa National Park.

20 MUSEO DEL PRADO, MADRID
Page 76
Spain's greatest art museum is an obligatory visit on any trip to the capital.

21 SITGES
Page 772
Sitges is Spain's biggest gay resort and throws simply spectacular parties, especially at Carnival time.

22 ROMAN RUINS OF MÉRIDA
Page 211
Wander at will around the ancient Roman ruins of Mérida, the most extensive such remains in the country.

23 MUSEO GUGGENHEIM, BILBAO
Page 469
Frank Gehry's flagship creation of undulating titanium has become one of the iconic buildings of our age.

24 SEVILLE
Page 263
The quintessential Andalucian city with sun-drenched plazas, winding alleyways, Moorish monuments and more bars than seems remotely feasible.

25 SAGRADA FAMILIA, BARCELONA
Page 673
One of Spain's truly essential sights – Antoni Gaudí's unfinished masterpiece, the church of the "Sacred Family".

26 SHERRY TASTING IN JEREZ
Page 302
There are few greater pleasures than a chilled glass of fino or manzanilla, and there's no better place to sample them than in the sherry heartland of Jerez.

27 LAS FALLAS
Page 804
In March, Valencia erupts in festivities as giant models are burnt and fireworks crackle across town to celebrate San José.

28 A NIGHT ON THE TILES, MADRID
Page 115
Delight in the capital's most traditional of rituals – a night of bar-hopping and clubbing rounded off by a dawn reviver of *chocolate con churros*.

27

28

Itineraries

Spain is a vast and varied country, and you can't cover all of it in a single trip. Our Grand Tour concentrates on Spain's major cities and outstanding sights, while our other suggested routes focus on two fascinating regions, one in the south, one in the north. Each itinerary will take a packed two weeks to cover; with only a week to spare you can cover part of one, and get a flavour of the whole country or one of the regions that make Spain special.

GRAND TOUR OF SPAIN

Two weeks in Spain and no idea where to start? Our "Grand Tour" puts you on the right track.

❶ **Madrid** The vibrant capital is at the heart of all that makes modern Spain tick, from world-class art collections to a buzzing café society and a wild nightlife. **See p.58**

❷ **Toledo** With time for just one side-trip from Madrid, it has to be the old rock-bound capital of Toledo, the home of El Greco and packed with magnificent buildings. **See p.126**

❸ **Seville** You could spend weeks exploring Andalucía (see opposite) – but for a taster, Seville combines gorgeous buildings with a vibrant flamenco and tapas scene. **See p.263**

❹ **Valencia** The rapidly changing city of Valencia – cultural hub of the east, not to mention the spiritual home of paella – makes a natural break on the journey up the long Mediterranean coast. **See p.796**

❺ **Barcelona** Leave Spain – as the locals would have you believe – for the cool Catalan capital, with its Art Nouveau architecture, designer shops, and stylish bars and clubs. **See p.640**

❻ **Figueres** The two-hour side-trip towards the French border is made with only one destination in mind – the extraordinary Teatre-Museu Dalí. **See p.739**

❼ **Logroño** This handsome city sits at the heart of the Rioja region, and while it's only small there's nothing modest about its superb tapas and wine bars. From here, you could detour along the northern coast (see opposite). **See p.410**

❽ **Valladolid** Re-live Spain's Golden Age in the capital of Castilla y León, whose majestic Plaza Mayor has no equal. **See p.392**

❾ **Salamanca** The most beautiful city in Spain, its buildings fashioned from a honey-coloured stone that glows as the sun sets. **See p.374**

THE BEST OF ANDALUCÍA

❶ **Málaga** This transport hub is the obvious place to start, but it's also worth lingering for a day to enjoy this vibrant coastal city. **See p.229**

❷ **Ronda** Sited astride a towering gorge is the queen of Andalucía's white towns. **See p.256**

❸ **Seville** The essence of all things *andaluz*, with a stunning cathedral, Moorish Alcázar and atmospheric old quarter. **See p.263**

❹ **Córdoba** A must-see destination, featuring one of the world's greatest Moorish buildings, the Mezquita, at its heart. **See p.312**

❺ **Baeza and Úbeda** These twin Renaissance architectural jewels are filled with a wealth of monuments in honey-tinted stone. **See p.325**

ABOVE LA CIUDAD DE LAS ARTES Y LAS CIENCIAS, VALENCIA

❻ Cazorla Natural Park A stunning array of wildlife inhabits the rugged mountains, gorges and forested valleys of Cazorla. **See p.329**

❼ Granada Overlooked by the seductive Alhambra, the historic city of Granada is one of Spain's most compelling attractions. **See p.330**

❽ Almuñécar The Costa Tropical's main resort has great beaches and plenty of places to eat, drink and dance the night away. **See p.243**

NORTHERN SPAIN, ALONG THE ATLANTIC COAST

❶ Bilbao Revitalized by the success of its Guggenheim Museum, the energetic city of Bilbao is set amid the spectacular green hills of the Basque Country. **See p.468**

❷ San Sebastián This elegant seaside resort boasts one of Europe's best city beaches; its superb cuisine is at its most affordable in the *pintxos* bars of the old quarter. **See p.452**

❸ Pamplona An intriguing destination, which comes alive during the bull-running of July's San Fermín festival. **See p.484**

❹ Santillana del Mar Often hailed as Spain's prettiest village, Santillana is an exquisite

medieval ensemble with some gorgeous hotels. **See p.509**

❺ Picos de Europa Just a few kilometres back from the sea, the snowy peaks are interspersed with lush meadows and ancient settlements, and offer superb hiking. **See p.515**

❻ Llanes Delightful seaside towns dot the Asturian coast, but bustling little Llanes, close to superb beaches and soaring mountains, is perhaps the finest of all. **See p.529**

❼ Oviedo Ravishing little Visigothic churches pepper the hills here – though you'll have to tear yourself away from the city's cider-houses to see them. **See p.536**

❽ The Rías of Galicia The fjord-like estuaries that slice into Galicia cradle dramatic scenery and splendid beaches, with the wild Rías Altas in the north and the busier, gentler Rías Baixas to the south. **See p.561**

❾ Santiago de Compostela For over a thousand years, this magnificent cathedral city has welcomed footsore pilgrims; its historic core, bursting with bars and restaurants, remains irresistible. **See p.546**

FERIA DE ABRIL, SEVILLE

Basics

Getting there

Madrid and Barcelona are the two main Spanish airports, though the summer holiday trade to the costas and the Balearics, and the rapid growth of European budget airlines, has opened up regional airports right across Spain. Taking the train to Spain is a greener option and has much to recommend it – there's a lot to be said for waking up refreshed in Madrid or Barcelona after the quick Eurostar service to Paris and the comfortable overnight journey on the "train-hotel". Driving is more of an adventure, but there are several routes that can save you time, like the direct ferry services from Portsmouth and Plymouth to Santander and Bilbao.

Flights from the UK and Ireland

Flight time to Spain is two to three hours, depending on the route, and usually the cheapest flights are with the no-frills **budget airlines** such as bmibaby (Wbmibaby.com), easyJet (Weasyjet.com), flybe (Wflybe.com), Jet2 (Wjet2.com) and Ryanair (Wryanair.com), who between them fly from over twenty regional UK airports direct to **destinations all over Spain** – not just Madrid and Barcelona, but also to smaller regional Spanish airports like Málaga, Alicante, Bilbao, Valencia and in the Balearics. Note that London flights tend to depart from Stansted or Luton, while it's always worth double-checking the exact Spanish airport used – Ryanair (and others') "Barcelona" flights, for example, are actually to Girona (1hr to the north) or Reus (1hr 15min to the south). **Fares** for flights on all routes start at around £9.99 each way. However, book last minute in the summer and you can expect to pay considerably more, up to £100 each way depending on the route.

For flights **to the costas and Balearics**, you can also check with holiday and charter companies such as Monarch (Wmonarch.co.uk), First Choice (Wfirstchoice.co.uk), Thomas Cook (Wflythomascook.com) and Thomson (Wthomsonfly.com). You might not get the rock-bottom deals of the budget airlines, as schedules and prices are geared towards the summer holiday season, but flights depart from convenient regional airports right around the UK.

The widest range of **scheduled flights** is with the now-merged Iberia (Wiberia.com) and British Airways (Wba.com), with direct services from London Gatwick or Heathrow to half a dozen Spanish cities (most frequently to Madrid and Barcelona, but also Valencia, Málaga and Alicante) and connections on to most other airports in Spain. You'll also be able to arrange add-on sections to London from regional English airports such as Manchester or Newcastle or from Scotland. Special offers start at around £100 return, though a typical late-booking summer rate will be more like £200 return.

From Ireland, you can fly with Iberia from Dublin to Madrid, or with Aer Lingus (Waerlingus.com) from Dublin or Cork to up to eight Spanish airports (including Barcelona, Bilbao, Málaga and Alicante). Ryanair also connects Dublin and Shannon with most of the same destinations, plus places like Seville, Valencia and Murcia. Prices start at around €39.99 each way, though these rise sharply for last-minute bookings or to popular summer destinations.

Flights from the US and Canada

The widest choice of scheduled flights **from the United States** to Spain is with Iberia (Wiberia.com), which flies direct, nonstop from New York to Madrid or Barcelona, and from Miami and Chicago to Madrid. Journey time (typically overnight) is between seven hours ten minutes and eight hours thirty minutes, depending on the route. Fares start at around $1000 return. The advantage of flying with Iberia is that it offers connecting flights to almost anywhere in Spain, which can be very good value if booked with your transatlantic flight.

Other airlines offering Spain routes (some on a code-share basis with Iberia or other airlines) include American Airlines (Waa.com), Delta (Wdelta.com), Continental (Wcontinental.com), Spanair (Wspanair.com) and United (Wunited.com). Or you can fly to Spain with airlines such as Air France, KLM, Lufthansa, TAP or British Airways, for example, which tend to fly via their respective European hubs – in which case, you can add three to four hours to your total travel time, depending on the connection.

From Canada, there are routes from Toronto and Montréal to Madrid and Barcelona with Air Canada (Waircanada.com), with onward connections across Spain with their partner Spanair. Or fly with one of the major European airlines via their respective hubs – fares in all cases start from around Can$1100 return.

Flights from Australia, New Zealand and South Africa

There are no direct flights to Spain **from Australia or New Zealand**, but many airlines offer through-tickets

A BETTER KIND OF TRAVEL

At Rough Guides we are passionately committed to travel. We feel that travelling is the best way to understand the world we live in and the people we share it with – plus tourism has brought a great deal of benefit to developing economies around the world over the last few decades. But the growth in tourism has also damaged some places irreparably, and climate change is exacerbated by most forms of transport, especially flying. All Rough Guides' trips are carbon-offset, and every year we donate money to a variety of charities devoted to combating the effects of climate change.

with their partners via their European or Asian hubs. Flights via Asia are generally the cheaper option, but fares don't vary as much between airlines as you might think, and in the end you'll be basing your choice on things like flight timings, routes and possible stop-offs on the way. If you're seeing Spain as part of a wider European trip, you might want to aim first for the UK, since there's a wide choice of cheap flights to Spain once there. Or consider a Round-the-World fare, with most basic options able to offer Madrid or Barcelona as standard stopovers.

From **South Africa**, there are direct flights with Iberia (W iberia.com) from Johannesburg to Madrid, which take around ten hours; or it's around fifteen hours if you fly via London.

Package holidays, tours and city breaks

The basic, mass-market **package holidays** to the traditional resorts on the Costa del Sol, Costa Brava, Costa Blanca and others are not to everyone's taste, but bargains can be found online or at any UK high-street travel agent, from as little as £99 for a seven-night flight-and-hotel package. There are often really good deals for families, either in hotels or in self-catering apartments, though the time of year you visit can increase prices significantly (school holidays are always most expensive).

A huge number of **specialist tour operators** offer a wider range of activity holidays or tours, from hiking in the Pyrenees to touring the artistic highlights of Andalucía. We've given a flavour of what's available in the listed reviews at the end of this section, but the options are almost endless. Prices vary wildly depending on the quality of accommodation offered and whether the tours are

fully inclusive or not. Many hiking or bicycle tours, for example, can either be guided or done on a more independent (and cheaper) self-guided basis. Spanish-based tour operators offer some of the more interesting, off-the-beaten-track options, but for these you'll usually have to arrange your own flights to Spain, while many foreign-based operators also tend to quote for their holidays exclusive of airfares.

Some operators and websites specialize in **city breaks**, with destinations including Barcelona, Madrid, Seville and Granada. UK prices start at around £200 for three-day (two-night) breaks, including return flights, airport transfer and B&B in a centrally located one-, two- or three-star hotel. Adding extra nights or upgrading your hotel is possible, too, usually at a fairly reasonable cost. The bigger US operators, such as American Express and Delta Vacations, can also easily organize short city breaks to Spain on a flight-and-hotel basis, while from Australia Iberian specialist Ibertours (W ibertours.com.au) can arrange two- or three-night packages in most Spanish cities.

Other deals worth considering are fly-drive offers, where you'll get a **flight, accommodation and car rental** arranged through your tour operator. Some companies specialize in villas and apartments, or off-the-beaten-track farmhouses and the like, while on other holiday packages you can tour the country's historic paradores, with car rental included.

Specialist tour operators

ADVENTURE

Adventure Center US ☎ 1 800 228 8747, W adventurecenter .com. Active vacations in the Picos de Europa, Pyrenees, Catalunya, Andalucía and the Sierra Nevada – self-guided trekking to rustic family adventures, starting at $1000 (excluding airfares).

Alto-Aragon UK ☎ 0208 398 1321, W altoaragon.co.uk. An established English-run company offering summer hiking and activity holidays (from around £500, land-only), and winter cross-country skiing programmes (from £300, land-only) in the high Pyrenees.

Exodus Travels UK ☎ 0845 805 9418, W exodus.co.uk. Walking and cycling in Andalucía, Mallorca, the Picos de Europa and the Pyrenees (and most minor mountain ranges), as well as cycling or multi-adventure (climbing, caving, rafting, etc), cultural and sightseeing trips. There's a big range of trips at all prices, but typical is a week's walking in the Sierra Nevada, from £769 including flights.

Spirit of Adventure UK ☎ 01822 880 277, W spirit-of -adventure.com. Multi-activity holidays in Catalunya, Andalucía, Galicia and the Picos de Europa. There's trekking, climbing and sea-kayaking, with some activity holidays specifically aimed at families (from £600 per person).

BACKPACKER TRAVEL

Busabout UK ☎ 0845 0267 514, W busabout.com. The European backpacker bus service also offers a seven-day Spain/Portugal bus tour (basically Andalucía and the Algarve; from £449) plus special annual Fallas, Running of the Bulls and La Tomatina trips, all aimed at a young, party crowd.

CYCLING

Bravobike Spain ☎ 917 582 945, W bravobike.com. Offers a variety of cycle tours from one day in Madrid, Segovia or Toledo, for example, to themed week-long tours in *conquistador* country, La Rioja wine country or along the Camino de Santiago. Prices are variable, but from €25 for a short half-day trip, €800 self-guided per week and from €1000 guided.

Easy Rider Tours US ☎ 1 800 488 8332, W easyridertours.com. Guided cycling and sightseeing tours in Andalucía, Castilla y León, and along the pilgrims' way to Santiago de Compostela. Tours are all-inclusive and fully supported, from around $3500 for a week, though airfares are extra.

Iberocycle Spain ☎ 942 581 085, W iberocycle.com. An English-run, Spain-based company specializing in supported or self-guided cycling tours of northern Spain in particular (Cantabria, Asturias, Basque Country, Catalunya). Short five-night trips start at around €510.

FOOD AND DRINK

Arblaster & Clarke UK ☎ 01730 263111, W arblasterandclarke .com. The most notable wine-tour specialist, with quality trips to all Spain's wine-producing regions, including agreeable accommodation and tastings at both famous and little-known wineries. From £1500, excluding flights.

A Taste of Spain Spain ☎ 856 079 626, W atasteofspain.com. Organizes gourmet culinary tours of Catalunya, the Basque region/La Rioja, Andalucía and central Spain, with tastings, meals and cookery lessons. From around €300 for a day's excursion to taste Iberico ham to €3000 for a week following La Mancha's saffron route.

HISTORY, ART AND CULTURE

Abercrombie and Kent UK ☎ 0845 618 2200, W abercrombiekent .co.uk; US ☎ 1 800 554 7016, W abercrombiekent.com. Upmarket independent or fully escorted tailor-made tours, with the ten-day "Signature Spain" trip (Córdoba, Granada, Seville, from $8500) typically providing high-speed train travel, luxury hotels and a private guide for monument visits.

Madrid and Beyond Spain ☎ 917 580 063, W madridandbeyond.com. Classy customized holidays and special experiences, from private gallery tours to expert-led walks through Gaudí's Barcelona. Variable prices.

Martin Randall Travel UK ☎ 020 8742 3355, W martinrandall .com. The leading cultural-tour specialists, offering small-group, expert-led trips to Catalunya, Madrid, Toledo, Aragón and Seville, among others. Departures several times a year on various trips and themes, from around £1300 for a five-day Madrid art trip to £3000 for eight nights' gourmet wining and dining in Catalunya.

HORSERIDING

Fantasia Adventure Holidays Spain W fantasiaadventure holidays.com. British-run company offering riding breaks on the Costa de la Luz, from full-board weekends to week-long holidays (from £525, excluding flights). Contact is best by email.

SURFING

Surf Spain UK W surfspain.co.uk. Surf camps and tailor-made surfing holidays in the north and south of Spain, with six-night breaks from £409 per person (excluding flights). Contact is best by email.

WALKING

ATG-Oxford UK ☎ 01865 315678, W atg-oxford.co.uk. Sustainable-tourism outfit with off-the-beaten-track walking holidays in La Rioja or the volcanic countryside around Girona, plus the Pyrenees, Catalunya and the Camino de Santiago. Five-day holidays start from £475.

Inntravel UK ☎ 01653 617722, W inntravel.co.uk Self-guided walking tours in Galicia, Andalucia; the Pyrenees, Balearics and Catalunya. Each night's destination is a small family-run hotel where your baggage is waiting. A typical seven-day walking holiday starts at around £600.

Olé Spain US ☎ 1 888 869 7156, W olespain.com. Small-group cultural walking tours in Catalunya, Andalucía and Extremadura, with prices starting at $3300 for an eight-day tour (excluding airfares).

Ramblers Worldwide Holidays UK ☎ 01707 331 133, W ramblersholidays.co.uk. Long-established walking-tour operator, with hiking holidays in most Spanish mountain regions, as well as vineyard rambles and tours of classical Andalucía. From around £725 for an all-inclusive week in the Sierra Nevada.

Walk Alpujarras Spain ☎ 958 858 580, W walkalpujarra.com. Group and individual self-guided walking tours organized by experienced guide and author Jeremy Rabjohns. From around £400 for a seven-night holiday.

Trains

Travelling **by train from the UK to Spain** is a viable – and fun – option, with total journey times from London of around sixteen hours to Barcelona, eighteen hours to Madrid. You take the afternoon **Eurostar** (W eurostar.com) from London St Pancras International via the Channel Tunnel to Paris and change there for the overnight "train-hotel" for either Barcelona (via Figueres and Girona) or Madrid (via Burgos and Valladolid). **Fares** start at £69 return for the Eurostar to Paris (through-tickets available from UK towns and cities), plus from £130 return for the cheapest sleeper accommodation on the overnight train. You'll have to book well in advance on all services to get the lowest prices. There are alternative daytime services through France and Spain, though they don't save you any money. If you don't mind the journey to Spain taking a whole lot longer, there are also minor routes that cross the central Pyrenees (via Canfranc or Puigcerdà), though you may have to spend the night at either of the border towns if you want to see the mountains in daylight.

The best first stop for information about train travel to Spain is the excellent ⓦ**seat61.com**, which provides full route, ticket, timetable and contact information. You can book the whole journey online with **Rail Europe** (ⓦraileurope.co.uk) or contact a specialist rail agent like Ffestiniog Travel (ⓦffestiniogtravel.co.uk) or the Spanish Rail Service (ⓦspanish-rail.co.uk). If you live outside the UK, you can book Eurostar and "train-hotel" tickets through the websites ⓦraileurope.com, ⓦraileurope.ca and ⓦraileurope.com.au. These agencies can also advise about **rail passes** (principally InterRail and Eurail), which have to be bought before leaving home (see opposite).

Buses

You can reach most major towns and cities in Spain by bus from the UK with **Eurolines** services (ⓦeurolines.co.uk). The main routes are from London (though inexpensive add-on fares are available from any British city) to Barcelona (25hr), Madrid (27hr) and Valencia (30hr), with connections on to other Spanish destinations, but it's a long time to spend cooped up in a bus. Standard return fares are £125 to Barcelona, £150 to Madrid, though there are advance deals and special offers – it's always cheapest to book online.

Eurolines also has a **Eurolines Pass**, which allows unlimited travel on Eurolines routes between forty-odd cities, but only between Madrid, Barcelona and Alicante within Spain, so it's not much use for a Spanish tour. Better value is the **Busabout Explorer** (ⓦbusabout.com), a seasonal (May–Oct) hop-on, hop-off backpacker bus service whose routes begin in Paris (add-ons from London available) and take in Barcelona, Valencia, Madrid, Pamplona and San Sebastián (from £329; pass valid for the entire season; other options available).

Driving to Spain

Driving to Spain from the UK is an interesting way to get there, but with fuel, road toll and overnight costs it doesn't compare in terms of price with flying or taking the train. It's about 1600km from London to Barcelona, for example, which, with stops, takes almost two full days to drive, and another 600km on to Madrid.

Many people use the conventional **cross-Channel ferry links**, principally Dover–Calais,

though services to Brittany or Normandy might be more convenient depending on where you live (and they cut out the trek around Paris). However, the quickest way of crossing the Channel is to use the **Eurotunnel** (ⓦeurotunnel.com), which operates drive-on, drive-off shuttle trains between Folkestone and Calais/Coquelles. The 24-hour service runs every twenty minutes throughout the day; though you can just turn up, booking is advised, especially at weekends and in summer holidays, or if you want the best deals (from £53 one way).

The best way to cut driving time is to use one of the direct **UK–Spain ferry crossings**, especially if you're heading for the Basque region, Galicia, Castilla y León or even Madrid. Brittany Ferries (ⓦbrittany-ferries.co.uk) operates car and passenger ferry services **from Portsmouth and Plymouth to Santander** (3 weekly; 20–24hr) or **Bilbao** (2 weekly; 24hr). Fares start at around £200 return per person (includes the car), but it costs significantly more in summer, particularly August – it's cheaper for foot-passengers, though everyone has to book some form of seating or cabin accommodation.

Any ferry company or travel agent can supply up-to-date schedules and ticket information, or you can consult the encyclopedic ⓦdirectferries.com, which has details about, and links to, every European ferry service.

Getting around

Most of Spain is well covered by public transport. The rail network reaches all the provincial capitals and the main towns along the inter-city lines, and there's an expanding high-speed network that has slashed journey times on major cross-country routes from Madrid. Inter-city bus services are often more frequent and cheaper than the regular trains, and will usually take you closer to your destination, as some train stations are a few kilometres from the town or village they serve. Driving a car, meanwhile, will give you the freedom to head away from the major tourist routes and take in some of the spectacular scenery at your own pace.

One important point to remember is that all public transport, and the bus service especially, is drastically reduced on **Sundays and public holidays** – don't even consider travelling to out-of-the-way places on these days. The words to look out for on timetables are *diario* (daily), *laborables* (workdays, including Sat), and *domingos y festivos* (Sun and public hols).

By train

Spanish trains, operated by **RENFE** (☎ 902 320 320, ⓦ renfe.com), tend to be efficient and comfortable, and nearly always run on time. There's a confusing array of services, though the website has a useful English-language version on which you can check timetables and even buy tickets with a credit card (printing them out at home before you travel).

Cercanías are local commuter trains in and around the major cities, while **media distancia** (regional) and **larga distancia** (long-distance) trains go under a bewildering number of names, including Avant, Alaris, Intercity (IC), Regional and Talgo services. The difference is speed, service and number of stops, and you'll always pay more on the quickest routes (sometimes quite a lot more).

The premier services are the high-speed trains, such as the **Euromed** from Barcelona to Alicante, or the fast-expanding **AVE** (Alta Velocidad Española) network from Madrid to Seville, Málaga, Valencia, Segovia/Valladolid, Zaragoza, Barcelona and Huesca; and from Barcelona to Seville and Málaga. The AVE trains have cut travelling times dramatically, with Madrid to Seville, for example, taking two

and a half hours compared with six to nine hours on the slower trains. The AVE network is set to expand right across the peninsula over the next decade, northeast to the French border, northwest to Castilla y León, the Basque Country and Asturias, and west to Lisbon in Portugal.

Tickets, fares and rail passes

Although you can just turn up at the station for short hops, **advance booking** is essential (and seat reservations obligatory) for long-distance journeys. Advance tickets can be bought at the stations between sixty days and five minutes before departure, but don't leave it to the last minute, as there are usually long queues (and often separate windows for the different types of train). Automatic **ticket machines** at main stations take some of the hassle out of queuing.

The best deals are always available **online** on the RENFE website, where "Web" and "Estrella" fares offer discounts of up to sixty percent on the full fares. Otherwise, **return fares** (*ida y vuelta*) are discounted by ten to twenty percent, depending on the service – you can buy a single, and so long as you show it when you buy the return, you'll still get the discount. There's also a whole range of other **discounted fares** of between 25 and 40 percent for those over 60 or under 26, the disabled, and children aged 4 to 11 years.

Actual fares vary wildly, but as an example, you'll pay around €19 on the regional service from Madrid to Salamanca (2hr 40min trip), while on the Madrid to Barcelona route you could pay €45 for the overnight "Estrella" service (9hr 30min) or €120 on the high-speed AVE service (around 3hr).

The major pan-European **rail passes** (InterRail and Eurail) are only worth considering if you're visiting the country as part of a wider European tour. Both schemes also have single-country Spain rail passes available, which might be better value depending on your Spanish itinerary. The **InterRail Spain Pass** (ⓦ interrailnet.com) is only available to European residents and allows three, four, six or eight days' train travel within one month, with under-26, second- and first-class versions available. For anyone else, **Eurail** (ⓦ raileurope.com) has various Spain passes available, typically offering three days' travel in two months, again in various classes. You can check current prices on the websites, but bear in mind that it often works out cheaper to buy individual tickets in Spain as you need them, and it's certainly more convenient to be free to choose long-distance buses on some routes. All passes have to be bought before you

---

ALL ABOARD

As well as the main Spanish rail system, there are also several private and regional train lines offering a different view of some spectacular parts of the country, mainly in the north.

The best is probably the narrow-gauge **FEVE line** (see p.500), which runs right across the wild northwest, from Santander in Cantabria, through Asturias to Ferrol in Galicia. Catalunya has its own local commuter line, the **FGC** (see p.703), which operates the mountain rack-railway to **Montserrat**, as well as the **Cremallera**, the "Zipper" (see p.752), another rack-and-pinion line that slinks up a Pyrenean valley to the sanctuary and ski station of Núria.

In the Sierra Guadarrama, just north of Madrid, the narrow-gauge line from **Cercedilla** to the ski station at Puerto de Navacerrada and then on to Cotos is a great way to see the mountains (see p.149).

leave home, and you'll still be liable for supplements and seat reservations on long-distance and high-speed trains.

By bus

Buses will probably meet most of your transport needs, especially if you're venturing away from the larger towns and cities. Many smaller villages and rural areas are only accessible by bus, almost always originating in the capital of their province. Services are pretty reliable, whether it's the two-buses-a-day school or market run or the regular services between major cities (the latter often far more conveniently scheduled than the equivalent train services). **Fares** are very reasonable, too: Madrid to León (3hr 30min), for example, costs around €23, Madrid to Santander (6hr) around €28. On inter-city runs, you'll usually be assigned a seat when you buy your ticket. Some destinations are served by more than one **bus company**, but main bus stations have posted timetables for all services (and, sometimes, someone who can speak English). Or you can check timetables on the company websites, which, while not always up-to-date, do at least give an idea of available services. Major companies like Alsa (@alsa.es) and Avanzabus (@avanzabus.com) have nationwide services, and both have English-language versions of their websites.

There are only a few cities in Spain (Madrid, Barcelona and Valencia, for example) where you'll need to use the **local bus** network, and all the relevant details are given in the accounts. You'll also sometimes need to take a local bus out to a campsite or distant museum or monastery; fares are very cheap, rarely more than a euro or two.

By car

Spain has an extensive system of highways, both free and with tolls. The **autopistas** are the most comfortable and best-kept roads. The second-grade roads, **autovías**, often follow similar routes, but their speed limits are lower. Many *autopistas* and some *autovías* are toll roads, relatively expensive by local standards but worth paying for the lighter traffic encountered. You can usually pay with a credit card, although it's wise to have enough cash just in case. Toll roads are usually designated by an "AP" or "R" or the word "*peaje*".

The Spanish **drive on the right**, and **speed limits** are enforced throughout the country. On most *autopistas* it is 120kph, on the *autovía* 90kph, and in towns and villages 50kph. Police have the power to fine drivers on the spot for speeding or any other transgressions, and if you don't have any cash, they will escort you to the nearest cash machine and issue you with a receipt there and then. You can pay by credit card at most petrol stations for **fuel** (*gasolina*), the main companies being Cepsa and Repsol.

An EU **driver's licence** is sufficient to drive in Spain. US, Canadian, Australian and New Zealand licences should also be enough, though you may want to get an International Driver's Licence as well, just to be on the safe side. If you are bringing your own car, you will need your vehicle registration and insurance papers – and check with your

---

THE SPANISH DRIVING EXPERIENCE

If it's your first time out on a Spanish road, especially in one of the bigger cities, you could be forgiven for thinking you've stumbled upon the local chapter of *Mad Max* devotees, out for a burn-up. In fact, those wild-eyed, dangerously speeding, non-signalling, bumper-hogging, mobile-talking, horn-sounding road warriors are normal law-abiding Spanish citizens on their way to work. **Traffic lights** and **pedestrian crossings** in particular present a difficult conceptual challenge – if you are going to stop at either, make sure you give plenty of warning to avoid another vehicle running into the back of you, and keep an eye out for cars crossing your path who have jumped the lights. **Signposting** is universally poor (yes, *that* was the turn you wanted), even on main roads and highways, while joining and exiting **autopistas/ autovías** can be particularly dangerous, as it's almost a point of honour not to let anyone in or out. Many of the worst **accidents** are on the N roads, which have only a single carriageway in each direction, so take particular care on these. Major roads are generally in good **condition**, though some minor and mountain roads can be rather hairy and are little more than dirt tracks in the more remote regions. Sheep, goats and cattle are also regular hazards. Having said all this, things are (slowly) improving and drivers are a bit more careful because of increased use of radar and speed controls. The police are also setting up more **drink-driving** controls than before, though you have to remember that this is a country where it's considered a good idea to have bars in motorway service stations.

SPAIN'S TEN BEST DRIVES

There are some fantastic driving routes in this land of big scenery, big horizons and big surprises – here's our choice of Spain's best drives.

Alt Empordà Track the coastline in northern Costa Brava as you take in Greek and Roman ruins at Empúries and Salvador Dalí's former home outside the picturesque town of Cadaqués. See p.724.

Cañón de Río Sil Gaze upon Galicia's most arresting landscape along this dramatic canyon that is also home to one of the country's foremost wine-producing regions. See p.590.

The Cincó Villas Lose yourself in small-town Aragón on the 80km drive linking the historic "five towns," from Tauste to Sos del Rey Católico. See p.609.

El Escorial to Ávila The most scenic route out of Madrid province, an hour's drive from Felipe II's colossal monastery and over the hills to the historic walled city of Ávila. See p.151.

Gipuzkoa Head inland from San Sebastián and immerse yourself in Basque culture at Tolosa's lively carnival and historic Oñati, with its distinctive *casas torres*. See p.461.

Inland from Calpe It's the juxtaposition between hedonistic sun-and-sand and quiet, rural inland Valencia that marks this leisurely 55km excursion, from Calpe to Alcoy. See p.828.

Puerto de las Palomas to Zahara de la Sierra One of the most dramatic descents in Andalucía starts from the "Pass of the Doves" and corkscrews dizzily downwards to the ancient Moorish village of Zahara, with spectacular views across the sierras. See p.260.

Sierra de la Demanda Mountain monasteries, verdant valleys and bare upland vistas on the two-hour drive (LR113) from La Rioja to the Castilla y León heartland. See p.416.

Through the Valle de Jerte Track the Río Jerte for 70km (N110 out of Plasencia towards Barco de Ávila) on one of the most picturesque drives in Spain – carpeted in cherry blossom every spring. See p.193.

Vielha to Esterri d'Aneau Snowy peaks, thickly forested slopes and, above all, utter mountain stillness – this 42km drive over the Bonaigua Pass (2072m) is pure Pyrenees. See p.768.

---

insurers that you are covered to drive the car abroad. It's also compulsory to carry two hazard triangles, reflective jackets in case of accident or breakdown, an official first-aid kit and a set of spare bulbs. Rear seat belts are also compulsory, as are child seats for infants.

Parking can be a big pain in the neck, especially in big cities and old-town areas. Metered parking zones usually have stays limited to a couple of hours, though parking between 8pm and 8am, on Saturday afternoons and all Sundays tends to be free. Green or blue bays signify pay-parking areas in most cities, but it's always worth double-checking that you're allowed to park where you've just left your car, as any illegally parked vehicle will be promptly towed. Some cities (like Granada) have also introduced old-town **congestion charges**, which you might unwittingly trigger as a casual visitor. It's nearly always best to pay extra for a hotel with parking or use a pay car park, for which you'll need to budget anything from €12 to €20 a day.

Car rental

Car rental is cheapest arranged in advance through one of the large multinational agencies (Avis, Budget, EasyCar, Europcar, Hertz, Holiday Autos, National or Thrifty, for example). There are hundreds of pick-up offices in Spain, including regional airports and major train stations. Rates start from around £140/$200 a week for a two-door Renault Clio or similar, more for larger vehicles and in peak holiday periods. Local Spanish companies (such as Pepecar; ⓦ pepecar.com) can sometimes offer better value for money.

You'll need to be 21 or over (and have been driving for at least a year) to rent a car in Spain. It's essential to check that you have adequate **insurance cover** for your rental car, and that all visible damage on a car you're picking up is duly marked on the rental sheet. It's definitely worth considering paying the extra charge to reduce the "excess" payment levied for any damage, but these waiver charges (by the day) soon add up. However, you can avoid **excess charges** in the event of damage by taking out an annual insurance policy (from £37.99) with ⓦ insurance4carhire.com, which also covers windscreen and tyre damage.

By bike

Bike rental is not common, save in resort areas or in tourist-oriented cities such as Barcelona and Madrid, where you can expect to pay up to €20 a day, or around €25 for a half-day bike tour. Barcelona, Seville and some other cities also have bike-transit schemes, where you join (by paying a deposit) and then pick up bikes (free or low-cost) to ride around the city from one depot to another. However, dedicated cycle paths are rare (again, Barcelona is an exception), and cycling around most major Spanish cities can be a hair-raising, if not downright dangerous business.

Outside towns and cities, cycling is a great way to see parts of the country that might otherwise pass

DISTANCE CHART (KM)

	Alicante	Barcelona	Bilbao	Burgos	Córdoba	Granada	Jaén	León	Madrid
Alicante	–	552	814	645	513	372	417	762	420
Barcelona	552	–	609	629	893	889	840	818	630
Bilbao	814	609	–	160	795	820	730	350	400
Burgos	645	629	160	–	640	664	581	178	245
Córdoba	513	893	795	640	–	238	110	736	404
Granada	372	889	820	664	238	–	98	761	424
Jaén	417	840	730	581	110	98	–	677	342
León	762	818	350	178	736	761	677	–	349
Madrid	420	630	400	245	404	424	342	349	–
Málaga	480	1022	930	776	168	125	211	871	543
Murcia	82	602	785	634	482	297	342	749	408
Pamplona	723	490	152	210	841	869	791	404	456
Salamanca	630	835	398	248	604	634	543	208	219
San Sebastián	769	525	249	300	924	949	854	489	534
Santander	837	715	103	186	820	856	762	280	428
Santiago de Compostela	1033	1165	596	526	1009	1032	949	364	607
Seville	606	1055	861	711	149	261	300	674	537
Toledo	439	710	472	317	391	413	326	412	78
Valencia	183	365	651	590	536	510	454	702	361

you by, though bear in mind that Spain is one of the most mountainous countries in Europe and there are often searing high-summer temperatures with which to contend. You also need to be extremely careful on the road (single file only, at all times), since Spanish drivers don't generally expect to see cyclists and don't take much care when they do. Off-road biking is a far better idea, and increasing numbers of mountain-bikers are taking to the trails in national parks or following long-distance routes like the Camino de Santiago.

Ferries and planes

Anyone heading from the Spanish mainland to the Balearic Islands will probably do so by **ferry** or **catamaran** express ferry (from Alicante, Barcelona, Dénia or Valencia) – all the details are in the relevant city and island chapters. However, there's also an extensive network of internal Spanish **flights**, including to and between the Balearics, with Iberia (ⓦiberia.com), Spanair (ⓦspanair.com) and other smaller operators. These can be worth it if you're in a hurry and need to cross the entire peninsula, or if you can snap up a bargain web fare, but otherwise tourists rarely use flights to get

around Spain. The main exception has always been Europe's busiest air route, that between Madrid and Barcelona, though this is now facing stiff competition from the high-speed AVE train, which is comparable in overall centre-to-centre journey time, and often cheaper.

Accommodation

There's a great variety of accommodation in Spain, ranging from humble family-run pensions to five-star luxury hotels, often in dramatic historic buildings. The mainstay of the coastal resort is the typical beachfront holiday hotel, though renting an apartment or a villa gives you more freedom, while farm stays, village B&Bs, rural guesthouses and mountain inns are all increasingly popular possibilities.

Compared with other European countries, accommodation in Spain is still pretty good value. In almost any town, you'll be able to get a no-frills double room in a *pensión* or small hotel for around €50, sometimes even less, especially out in the sticks. As a

Málaga	Murcia	Pamplona	Salamanca	San Sebastián	Santander	Santiago de Compostela	Seville	Toledo	Valencia
480	82	723	630	769	837	1033	606	439	183
1022	602	490	835	525	715	1165	1055	710	365
930	785	152	398	249	103	596	861	472	651
776	634	210	248	300	186	526	711	317	590
168	482	841	604	924	820	1009	149	391	536
125	297	869	634	949	856	1032	261	413	510
211	342	791	543	854	762	949	300	326	454
871	749	404	208	489	280	364	674	412	702
543	408	456	219	534	428	607	537	78	361
–	414	993	674	1065	967	1124	231	527	649
414	–	772	604	812	817	1015	531	420	233
993	772	–	453	97	264	742	924	529	524
674	604	453	–	554	370	437	467	273	573
1065	812	97	554	–	350	836	2022	631	612
967	817	264	370	350	–	499	896	508	769
1124	1015	742	437	836	499	–	901	672	970
231	531	924	467	2022	896	901	–	507	684
527	420	529	273	631	508	672	507	–	378
649	233	524	573	612	769	970	684	378	–

rule, you can expect to pay from €100 for something with a bit of boutique styling, and from €150–200 for five-star hotels, historic paradores and luxury beach-front resorts. However, the trend is bucked by Madrid and Barcelona, in particular, and some fashionable coastal and resort areas, where rooms are often appreciably more expensive in all categories.

Advance reservations are essential in major cities and resort areas at peak holiday, festival or convention times. Local festivals and annual events also tend to fill all available accommodation weeks in advance. That said, as a general rule, if you haven't booked, all you have to do is head for the cathedral or main square of any town, which is invariably surrounded by an old quarter full of *pensiones* and hotels. You don't always pay more for a central location; indeed, the newer three- and four-star properties tend to be located more on the outskirts. **Families** will find that most places have rooms with three or even four beds at not a great deal more than the double-room price; however, **single travellers** often get a comparatively bad deal, and can end up paying sixty to eighty percent of the price of a double room.

Accommodation prices are **seasonal**, but minimum and maximum rates should be displayed at reception. In high season on the costas, many hotels only take bookings for a minimum of a week, while some also require at least a half-board stay. However, it's worth noting that high season isn't always summer, in ski resorts for example, while inland cities such as Madrid tend to have cheaper prices in August, when everyone heads for the coast.

Where possible, **website** bookings nearly always offer the best deals, especially with the larger **hotel groups** that have made big inroads into Spain – it's always worth checking NH Hoteles (W nh-hotels .com), Accor (W accorhotels.com) and Sol Meliá (W solmelia.com) for current deals. Organizations like **Bancotel** (W bancotel.es; deals available online or through vouchers available in Spain from travel agents and other outlets) also offer good discounted rates on accommodation.

Private rooms and B&Bs

The cheapest beds are usually in **private rooms**, in someone's house or above a bar or restaurant. The signs to look for are *habitaciones* (rooms) or *camas* (beds), or they might be touted at resort bus and train stations in summer as you arrive. The

ACCOMMODATION PRICES

We give a room price for all establishments reviewed in this guide. Unless otherwise stated, this represents the price for the **cheapest available double or twin room in high season** (ie usually Christmas/New Year, Easter, and June–September, though local variations apply – summer prices might be high-season on the Costa del Sol but will be low-season in scorching inland Andalucía, for example). Consequently, at many times of the year, or during special promotions, you'll often find a room for a lower price than that suggested. For **youth hostels** and anywhere else with **dorm beds**, we also give the per-person overnight rate. Note that **eight percent tax** (IVA) is added to all accommodation bills, which might not be specifically stated until it is time to pay, so always ask if you're uncertain.

rooms should be clean, but might well be very simple and timeworn; you'll probably share a communal bathroom.

The number of private "**bed-and-breakfast**" establishments (advertised as such) is on the increase, and while some are simply the traditional room in someone's house, others – especially in the major cities – are very stylish and pricey home-from-homes.

Pensiones, hostales and hotels

Guesthouses and hotels in Spain go under various anachronistic names – *pensión*, *fonda*, *residencia*, *hostal*, etc – though only **hotels and pensiones** are recognized as official categories. These are all star-rated (hotels, one- to five-star; *pensiones*, one- or two-star), but the rating is not necessarily a guide to cost or ambience. Some smaller, boutique-style *pensiones* and hotels have services and facilities that belie their star rating; some four- and five-star hotels have disappointingly small rooms and an impersonal feel.

At the budget end of the scale are **pensiones** (marked P), **fondas** (F) – which traditionally had a restaurant or dining room attached – and **casas de huéspedes** (CH), literally an old-fashioned "guest-house". In all such places you can expect straightforward rooms, often with shared bathroom facilities (there's usually a washbasin in the room), while occasionally things like heating, furniture (other

than bed, chair and desk) and even external windows might be too much to hope for. On the other hand, some old-fashioned *pensiones* are lovingly cared for and very good value, while others have gone for a contemporary, boutique style.

Next step up, and far more common, are **hostales** (Hs) and **hostal-residencias** (HsR), which are not hostels, in any sense, but budget hotels, generally offering good, if functional, rooms, usually with private bathrooms and – in the better places – probably heating and air-conditioning. Many also have cheaper rooms available without private bathrooms. Some *hostales* really are excellent, with good service and up-to-date furnishings and facilities.

Fully-fledged **hotels** (H), meanwhile, have a star-rating dependent on things like room size and staffing levels rather than any intrinsic attraction. There's often not much difference in price between a one-star hotel and a decent *hostal*, for example, and the *hostal* might be nicer. At three and four stars, hotel prices start to increase and you can expect soundproofing, an elevator, an English-language channel on the TV and a buffet breakfast spread. At five stars, you're in the luxury class, with pools, gyms, jacuzzis, and prices to match, and some hotels differentiate themselves again as five-star "deluxe" or "gran classe" (GL).

You can pick up lists of local accommodation from any Spanish tourist office, and there are countless websites to look at, too, including the excellent **Rusticae** (Ⓦ rusticae.es), which highlights scores of stylish rural and urban hotels across the country.

Paradores

Spain has over ninety superior hotels in a class of their own, called **paradores** (Ⓦ parador.es), which are often spectacular lodgings converted from castles, monasteries and other Spanish monuments (although some are purpose-built). They can be really special places to stay, sited in the most beautiful parts of the country, or in some of the most historic cities, and prices are very good when compared with the five-star hotels with which they compete. Overnight rates depend on location and popularity, and start at around €110 a night, though €150–180 is more typical. That said, a whole host of special offers and web deals (through the official website) offer discounted rates for the over 60s, the 20s to 30s, or for multi-night stays.

A popular approach is to take a fly-drive holiday based around the paradores. There is no end of routes you could choose, but good options include the area around Madrid and through the Sierra de Gredos;

along the Cantabrian coast, past the Picos de Europa; or along the French–Spanish border and through the foothills of the Pyrenees. Another popular route takes you through Galicia, and on to one of the most sumptuous paradores of all in Santiago de Compostela. Three-night **packages**, where you stay in a different parador every night, start at €159 per person (based on two sharing, car rental not included). All the details are on the website, or contact the official parador **agents**, Keytel in the UK (W keytel.co.uk) or Petrabax in the US (W petrabax.com).

Villas, apartments and rural tourism

Most UK and European tour operators can find you a self-catering **villa** or **apartment**, usually on one of the costas or in the Balearics. They are rented by the week, and range from simple town-centre apartments to luxury coastal villas with private pools. Prices, of course, vary wildly, but the best deals are often packages, including flights and car rental, with endless **villa agencies** including First Choice (W firstchoice .co.uk/villas) or Iglu Villas (W igluvillas.com).

Casas rurales (rural houses), or *casas de pagès* in Catalunya, are where many Spanish holidaymakers stay. It's a wide-ranging concept, from boutique cave dwellings to restored manor houses, many with pools and gardens. You can rent by the room, or by the property, either on a B&B basis or self-catering, depending on the accommodation. Many places also offer outdoor activities such as horseriding, walking, fishing and cycling. They are generally excellent value for money, starting at around €30 per person, even cheaper if you're in a group or staying for longer than a night or two.

ASETUR (W ecoturismorural.com), the association for rural tourism in Spain, has an excellent website where you can search thousands of properties by region, while many Spanish tourist-office websites also carry information on *casas rurales*. Holiday companies in your own country may also have Spanish rural properties available, or contact Spain-based **agencies** like Ruralia (Cantabria and Asturias; W ruralia.com), Rustic Blue (Andalucía; W rusticblue .com), Agroturisme (Catalunya; W agroturisme .org), Casas de Gredos (W casasgredos.com; Ávila and Gredos area), and Top Rural (Spain-wide; W toprural.com).

Youth hostels

There are around 250 youth hostels (*albergues juveniles*) in Spain under the umbrella of the **Red Española de Albergues Juveniles** (REAJ; W reaj .com), the Spanish youth hostel association that is affiliated to the international organization, Hostelling International (HI; W hihostels.com). There are full details of each hostel on the REAJ website (English-language version available), and we've included some of the best in the Guide.

However, many hostels are only open in the spring and summer, or tend to be inconveniently located in some cities; they also can be block-booked by school/youth groups. You'll also need an HI membership card, though you can buy one at most hostels on your first night. And at €16–25 a night in high season (less for under-26s, and out of season) for a bunk bed with shared facilities, they're no cheaper than a basic double room in a *hostal* or *pensión*. That said, hostels are good places to meet other travellers, and there are some really

---

PICK OF THE PARADORES

Nearly all Spain's **paradores** have a quirky history, a story to tell or a magnificent location – here's our choice of the best, from former palaces to pilgrims' hospitals.

Hostal dos Reis Católicos, Santiago de Compostela Apparently the oldest hotel in the world, impressively set in a fifteenth-century hospital at the end of the Camino de Santiago. See p.559.

Parador Carlos V, Jarandilla Majestic former imperial palace, set in the verdant Vera valley. See p.194.

Parador Castillo de Santa Catalina, Jaén Occupying a stunning, crag-bound thirteenth-century Moorish fortress, this is one of the most spectacular locations in Spain. See p.324.

Parador Condes de Alba y Aliste, Zamora Occupying a grand palace in the middle of a quiet town, Zamora's parador is gentility defined. See p.391.

Parador Hostal San Marcos, León One of León's major historic buildings, once a pilgrims' hostel, later a very grand sixteenth-century monastery. See p.437.

Parador de Lerma, Lerma A remarkable ducal palace facing a broad plaza of elegant beauty. See p.426.

Parador Marqués de Villena, Alarcón Just fourteen rooms in this characterful Arabic castle perched on the rocky promontory above the Río Júcar. See p.184.

Parador Nacional Castell de la Suda, Tortosa Tortosa's highest point, the splendid Castillo de la Suda, looms majestically over the lush Ebre valley. See p.786.

TEN UNUSUAL PLACES TO STAY

Take ancient buildings, magnificent locations, historic charms, designer flair and sheer Spanish style – and the result is enough **unusual places to rest** your head for a whole lifetime's worth of holidays.

La Casa Azul, Valencia Boutique rooms inspired by the antique brooches and necklaces of local jeweller Vicente Gracia. See p.809.

Casa Madrid, Madrid More grandee's mansion than hotel, with its hand-painted frescoes, classical statues and aristocratic furnishings. See p.100.

Hosteria del Monasterio, Castilla y León Classy hotel rooms within a sprawling monastery hidden high in the Riojan hills. See p.416.

Hotel Castell d'Empordà, Catalunya Eight-hundred-year-old hilltop castle that Salvador Dalí once tried to buy. See p.722.

Hotel España, Barcelona Boutique hotel, yes, but also a peerless *modernista* artwork. See p.687.

Hotel El Mudayyan, Aragón Venture into the medieval tunnels (as far as you dare) under this Moroccan-style boutique hotel. See p.616.

Hotel Toruño, Andalucía Spot flamingos, herons, avocets and more without leaving your bed. See p.306.

Jallambau Rural, Galicia Enjoy expansive views over Ría de Muros from this spectacularly perched, stone B&B. See p.572.

Posada San José, Castilla-La Mancha Precariously perched on the edge of the gorge in one of Cuenca's famous "hanging houses". See p.182.

Refugio Marnes, Valencia Sleep like a sultan in this sumptuous Bedouin tent in the middle of the Valencian countryside. See p.827.

gorgeously located ones, especially in Andalucía and in the hiking regions of northern Spain.

Some cities and resort areas also have a wide range of **independent backpacker hostels**. Prices are similar, they tend to be far less institutional, and open all year round, and you won't need a membership card. Also, many are brand-new, often with private rooms as well as dorms, and with excellent facilities (en-suite rooms, cafés, wi-fi, bike rental, tours, etc).

Mountain refuges, monasteries and pilgrim accommodation

In mountain areas and some of the national parks, climbers and trekkers can stay in **refugios**, simple dormitory huts, generally equipped only with bunks and a very basic kitchen. They are run by local mountaineering organizations, mostly on a first-come-first-served basis, which means they fill up quickly in high summer, though you can book in advance at some (or bring a tent and camp outside). Overnight prices start around €15 per person (or €30–40 with a meal included).

It is sometimes possible to stay at Spanish **monasterios** or **conventos**, which may let empty cells for a small charge. You can just turn up and ask – many will take visitors regardless of sex – but if you want to be sure of a reception, it's best to approach the local *turismo* first, or phone ahead. There are some particularly wonderful monastic locations in Galicia, Castilla y León, Catalunya and Mallorca. If you're following the Camino de Santiago, you can take full advantage of monastic accommodation specifically reserved for **pilgrims** along the route (see p.558).

Camping

There are literally hundreds of authorized campsites in Spain, mostly on the coast and in holiday areas. They work out at about €5 or €6 per person plus the same again for a tent, and a similar amount for each car or caravan. The best-located sites, or the ones with top-range facilities (restaurant, swimming pool, bar, supermarket), are significantly more expensive. If you plan to camp extensively, buy the annual *Guía de Campings*, which you can find in large bookshops, or visit ⓦ vayacamping.net.

In most cases, **camping outside campsites** is legal – but there are certain restrictions. You're not allowed to camp "in urban areas, areas prohibited for military or touristic reasons, or within 1km of an official campsite". What this means in practice is that you can't camp on the beach, while in national parks camping is only allowed in officially designated areas. Aside from these restrictions, however, and with a little sensitivity, you can set up a tent for a short period almost anywhere in the countryside. Whenever possible, ask locally first.

Food and drink

Spanish cuisine has come a long way in recent years, and Spanish chefs are currently at the forefront of contemporary European cooking. You know a power-shift has taken place when Restaurant magazine's annual "World 50 Best Restaurants" list regularly cites three or four Spanish eateries in the top

ten, and when there are more gourmet places in the Basque Country worth making a special trip for than in Paris. There's some fantastic food to be had in every region, and not just the fancy new-wave stuff either – the tapas, gazpacho, tortilla and paella that you may know from home are simply in a different league when made with the correct ingredients in their natural surroundings.

Of course, not every restaurant is a gourmet experience and not every dish is a classic of its kind. Tourist resorts – after all, where many people go – can be disappointing, especially those aimed at a foreign clientele, and a week on one of the costas can just as easily convince you that the Spanish national diet is egg and chips, *sangría*, pizza and Guinness. However, you'll always find a good restaurant where the locals eat, and few places in Europe are still as good value, especially if you have the *menú del día*, the bargain fixed-price lunch that's a fixture across the country.

Breakfast, snacks and sandwiches

The traditional Spanish **breakfast** (*desayuno*) is *chocolate con churros* – long, extruded tubular doughnuts served with thick drinking chocolate or coffee. Some places specialize in these but most bars and cafés also serve cakes and pastries (*bollos* or *pasteles*), croissants and toast (*tostadas*), or crusty sandwiches (*bocadillos*) with a choice of fillings (try one with omelette, *tortilla*). A "sandwich", incidentally, is usually a less-appetizing ham or cheese sandwich in white processed bread. Other good places for snacks are **cake shops** (*pastelerías* or *confiterías*) or the local bakery (*panadería*), where they might also have savoury pasties and turnovers.

Bars, tapas and raciones

One of Spain's glories is the phenomenon of **tapas** – the little portions of food that traditionally used to be served up free with a drink in a bar. (The origins are disputed but the word is from *tapar*, "to cover", suggesting a cover for drinks' glasses, perhaps to keep the flies off in the baking sun.) Tapas can be anything – a handful of olives, a slice or two of cured ham, a little dish of meatballs or *chorizo*, spicy fried potatoes or battered squid. They will often be laid out on the counter, so you can see what's available, or there might be a blackboard menu. Most bars have a speciality; indeed, Spaniards will commonly move from bar to bar, having just the one dish that they consider each bar does well. Conversely, if you're in a bar with just some pre-fried potatoes and day-old Russian salad on display, and a prominent microwave, go somewhere else to eat.

Aside from a few olives or crisps sometimes handed out with a drink, you pay for tapas these days (the cities of Granada and León are honourable exceptions), usually around €1.50–4 a portion.

IT'S FOOD, JIM, BUT NOT AS WE KNOW IT

King of molecular gastronomy, and godfather of Spanish contemporary cuisine, **Ferran Adrià**, started it all, with his liquid-nitrogen-frozen herbs, seafood-reduction Rice Krispies and exploding olive-oil droplets. His multi-Michelin-starred *El Bulli* restaurant on the Costa Brava might now be gone, with plans underway to turn it into a cookery foundation and "centre for creativity" (see p.728), but the influences of Spain's best-known chef have shaken the restaurant scene, as his former employees, acolytes and disciples have gone on to make the country one of the most exciting places to eat in the world.

The style-city of Barcelona, not surprisingly, is at the forefront of this innovative form of cooking, with **Carles Abellán**'s *Comerç 24* (see p.691) typical of the breed, while the **Roca brothers**' celebrated *El Celler de Can Roca* in Girona (see p.738) keeps Catalunya firmly in the vanguard of new-wave cuisine. However, it's in the Basque Country that many of the hottest chefs are currently in action: **Andoni Aduriz** at *Mugaritz*, Errenteria, San Sebastián (see p.460), father-and-daughter team **Juan Mari and Elena Arzak** at *Arzak*, San Sebastián (see p.459), and **Martín Berasategui** at *Restaurante Martín Berasategui*, Lasarte-Oria, San Sebastián (see p.460), are all cooking sensational food in restaurants that regularly feature in lists of the world's best. Maybe it's a northern thing, but there's less fuss in the south of the country about the so-called *cocina de autor*; in the capital, perhaps only **Sergi Arola** cuts the new-wave mustard with his *Sergi Arola Gastro* in Madrid (see p.110), while **Dani García** is making waves by the sea at *Calima*, Marbella (see p.246).

Raciones (around €6–12) are simply bigger plates of tapas, perfect for sharing or enough for a meal – you're sometimes asked if you want a *tapa* or a *ración* of whatever it is you've chosen.

There are big regional variations in tapas. They are often called **pinchos** (or *pintxos*) in northern Spain, especially in the Basque provinces, where typically tapas come served on a slice of baguette, held together with a cocktail stick. When you've finished eating, the sticks are counted up to arrive at your bill. This kind of tapas can be as simple as a cheese cube on bread or a far more elaborately sculpted concoction; they are also known as **montaditos** (basically, *canapés*). Famously good places across Spain for tapas-tasting include Madrid, León, Logroño, San Sebastián, Granada, Seville and Cádiz.

Most cafés and bars have some kind of tapas available, while you'll also find a decent display in **tascas**, **bodegas** and **tabernas** (kinds of taverns) and **cervecerías** (beer-houses). It's always cheapest to stand at the bar to eat; you'll pay more to sit at tables and more again to sit outside on a terrace.

SPANISH CUISINE

There really is no such thing as traditional "Spanish" cuisine, since every region claims a quite separate culinary heritage. That said, lots of dishes crop up right across the country, whatever their origin, while typical Mediterranean staples are ubiquitous – olive oil, tomatoes, peppers, garlic, onions and lemons and oranges.

It's usual to start your meal with a **salad** or a plate of cold cuts, while **soups** might be fish or seafood or, in the north especially, hearty broths such as the Galician cabbage-and-potato *caldo gallego*. Boiled potatoes with greens, or a thick minestrone of vegetables, are also fairly standard starters, while depending on the season you might be offered grilled asparagus or artichokes, or stewed beans with chunks of sausage.

Anywhere near the coast, you really should make the most of what's on offer, whether it's the fried fish of Málaga, Basque shellfish or the seafood specialities in Galicia, notably octopus (*pulpo*). Fish stews (*zarzuelas*) can be memorable, while seafood rice dishes range from *arroz negro* ("black rice", cooked with squid ink) to the better-known **paella**. This comes originally from Valencia (still the best place for an authentic one), though a proper paella from there doesn't include fish or seafood at all but things like chicken, rabbit, beans and snails.

Meat is most often grilled and served with a few fried potatoes. Regional specialities include *cordero* (lamb) from Segovia, Navarra and the Basque Country, as well as *cochinillo* (suckling pig) or *lechal* (suckling lamb) in central Spain. **Cured ham**, or *jamón serrano*, is superb, produced at its best from acorn-fed Iberian pigs in Extremadura and Andalucía, though it can be extremely expensive. Every region has a local **sausage** in its locker – the best known is the spicy *chorizo*, made from pork, though others include *morcilla* (blood sausage; best in Burgos, León and Asturias), and *butifarra*, a white Catalan sausage made from pork and tripe. **Stews** are typified by the mighty *fabada*, a fill-your-boots Asturian bean-and-meat concoction.

Cheeses to look out for include Cabrales, a tangy blue cheese made in the Picos de Europa; Manchego, a sharp, nutty cheese made from sheep's milk in La Mancha; Mahon, a cow's-milk cheese from Menorca, often with paprika rubbed into its rind; Idiazábal, a smoked cheese from the Basque Country; and Zamorano, made from sheep's milk in Castilla y León.

In most restaurants, **dessert** is nearly always fresh fruit or *flan*, the Spanish *crème caramel*, with the regions often having their own versions such as *crema catalana* in Catalunya and the Andalucian *tocino de cielo*. There are also many varieties of *postre* – rice pudding or assorted blancmange mixtures – and a range of commercial ice-cream dishes.

If you want to know more about the food in the region where you're travelling, turn to the special **features**:

Restaurants

The simplest kind of restaurant is the **comedor** (dining room), often a room at the back of a bar or the dining room of a *hostal* or *pensión*. Traditionally, they are family-run places aimed at lunching workers, usually offering a straightforward set meal at budget prices. The highway equivalent are known as **ventas** or **mesones** (inns), dotted along the main roads between towns and cities. These have been serving Spanish wayfarers for centuries – some of them quite literally – and the best places are immediately picked out by the line of cars and trucks outside. Proper restaurants, **restaurantes**, come in a myriad of guises, from rustic village restaurants to stylish Michelin-starred eateries; **asadores** specialize in grilled meats, **marisquerías** in fish and seafood.

Almost every restaurant serves a weekday, fixed-price lunchtime meal, the **menú del día**, generally three courses including wine for €8–15, occasionally even cheaper, depending on where you are in Spain. This is obviously a terrific deal; the *menú del día* is only sporadically available at night, and sometimes prices are slightly higher (and the menu slightly fancier) at weekends. The very cheapest places are unlikely to have a written menu, and the waiter will tell you what the day's dishes are. In smarter restaurants in bigger cities and resorts, there will still be a *menú del día*, though it might be a shadow of the usual à la carte menu, and drinks may be excluded. Even so, it's a way of eating at a restaurant that might normally cost you three or four times as much. Top city restaurants often also feature an upmarket *menú* called a **menú de degustación** (tasting menu), which again can be excellent value, allowing you to try out some of the country's finest cooking for anything from €50 to €100 a head.

Otherwise, in bars and so-called *cafeterías*, meals often come in the form of a **plato combinado** – literally a combined dish – which will be a one-plate meal of something like steak, egg and chips, or *calamares* and salad, often with bread and a drink included. This will generally cost in the region of €5–9.

If you want a menu in a restaurant, ask for **la carta**; *menú* refers only to the fixed-price meal. In all but the most rock-bottom establishments it is customary to leave a small **tip**, though five percent of the bill is considered sufficient and service is normally included in a *menú del día*. IVA, the eight-percent **tax**, is also charged, but it should say on the menu if this is included in the price or not.

Spaniards generally eat very late, with **lunch** served from around 1pm (you'll be the first person there at this time) until 4pm, and **dinner** from 8.30pm or 9pm to midnight. Obviously, rural areas are slightly earlier to dine, but making a dinner reservation for 10.30pm or even later is considered perfectly normal in many cities in Spain. Most restaurants **close one day a week**, usually Sunday or Monday.

Vegetarians

Vegetarians generally have a fairly hard time of it in Spain, though there's an increasing number of veggie restaurants in the bigger cities (including some really good ones in Madrid and Barcelona). In more rural areas, there's usually something to eat, but you may get weary of fried eggs and omelettes. However, many tapas favourites, especially in the south, are veggie (like fried aubergine, or spinach-and-chickpeas in Seville), while superb fresh fruit and veg, and excellent cheese, is always available in the markets and shops.

In restaurants, you're faced with the extra problem that pieces of meat – especially ham, which the Spanish don't regard as real meat – and tuna are often added to vegetable dishes and salads. You'll also find chunks of *chorizo* and sausage turning up in otherwise veg-friendly soups or bean stews. The phrases to get to know are *Soy vegetariano/a. Como sólo verduras. Hay algo sin carne?* ("I'm a vegetarian. I only eat vegetables. Is there anything without meat?"); you may have to add *y sin marisco* ("and without seafood") and *y sin jamón* ("and without ham") to be really safe.

Some salads and vegetable dishes are strictly **vegan**, but they're few and far between. Fruit and nuts are widely available, nuts being sold by street vendors everywhere.

Coffee, tea and soft drinks

Café (coffee) is invariably an espresso (*café solo*); for a large cup of weaker, black coffee, ask for an *americano*. A *café cortado* is a *café solo* with a drop of milk; a *café con leche* is made with lots of hot milk. Coffee is also frequently mixed with brandy, cognac or whisky, all such concoctions being called *carajillo*. Iced coffee is *café con hielo*. **Chocolate** (hot chocolate) is a popular breakfast drink, or for after a long night on the town, but it's usually incredibly thick and sweet. For a thinner, cocoa-style drink, ask for a brand name, like Cola Cao.

Spaniards usually drink **té** (tea) black, so if you want milk it's safest to ask for it afterwards, since ordering *té con leche* might well get you a glass of warm milk with a tea bag floating on top. Herbal teas (*infusions*) are widely available, like *manzanilla* (camomile), *poleo* (mint tea) and *hierba luisa* (lemon verbena).

Local soft drinks include **granizado** (crushed-ice) or **horchata** (a milky drink made from tiger nuts or almonds), available from summer street stalls, and from milk bars (*horchaterías*, also known as *granjas* in Catalunya) and ice-cream parlours (*heladerías*). Although you can drink the **water** almost everywhere, it tastes revolting in some cities and coastal areas – inexpensive *agua mineral* comes either sparkling (*con gas*) or still (*sin gas*).

Wine

One of the great pleasures of eating out in Spain is the chance to sample some of the country's excellent **wines**. Over fifty percent of the European Union's vineyards lie in Spain and *vino* is the invariable accompaniment to every meal. At lunchtime, a glass or small pitcher of the house wine – often served straight from the barrel – is usually included in the *menú del día*; otherwise, restaurant wine starts at around €5–10 a bottle, although the sky's the limit for the really good stuff. And there's plenty of that, since in recent years Spanish wine has enjoyed an amazing renaissance, led largely by the international success of famous wine-producing regions like La Rioja and Ribera del Duero. Other regions – not perhaps so well-known abroad – are also well worth investigating, like Galicia or the Priorat in Catalunya, and every wine-producing area is set up for *bodega* (winery) visits, tastings and tours. In Andalucía, meanwhile, the classic wine is **sherry** – *vino de jerez* – while champagne in Spain means the Catalan sparkling wine, **cava**.

The festival and tourist drink is, famously, **sangría**, a wine-and-fruit punch that's often deceptively strong; a variation in Catalunya is *sangría de cava*. *Tinto de verano* is a similar red-wine-and-soda or -lemonade combination; variations on this include *tinto de verano con naranja* (red wine with orangeade) or *con limón* (lemonade).

Beer

Beer (*cerveza*) is nearly always lager, though some Spanish breweries also now make stout-style brews, wheat beers and other types. It comes in 300ml bottles (*botellines*) or, for about the same price, on tap – a *caña* of draught beer is a small glass, a *caña doble* larger, and asking for *un tubo* (a tubular glass) gets you about half a pint. Mahou, Cruz Campo, San Miguel, Damm, Estrella de Galicia and Alhambra are all decent beers. A **shandy** is a *clara*, either with fizzy lemon (*con limón*) or lemonade (*con casera* or *con blanca*).

Spirits and shots

In mid-afternoon – or, let's face it, even at breakfast – Spaniards take a *copa* of liqueur with their coffee, such as *anís* (similar to Pernod) or *coñac*, the local **brandy**, which has a distinct vanilla flavour. Most brandies are produced by the great sherry houses in Jerez (like Lepanto, Carlos I and Cardinal Mendoza), but two good ones that aren't are the Armagnac-like Mascaró and Torres, both from Catalunya. Instead of brandy, at the end of a meal many places serve **chupitos** – little shot glasses of flavoured schnapps or local fire-water, such as Patxarán in Navarra and the Basque Country, Ratafía in Catalunya or Orujo in Galicia. One much-loved Galego custom is the *queimada*, when a large bowl of *aguardiente* (a herb-flavoured fiery liqueur) with fruit, sugar and coffee-grains is set alight and then drunk hot.

You should order **spirits** by brand name, since there are generally less expensive Spanish equivalents for standard imports, or simply specify *nacional*. Larios gin from Málaga, for instance, is about half the price of Gordon's. Measures are staggeringly generous – bar staff generally pour from the bottle until you suggest they stop. Long drinks include the universal Gin-Tónic and the Cuba Libre (rum and Coke), and there are often Spanish Caribbean rums (*ron*) such as Cacique from Venezuela or Havana Club from Cuba.

SPAIN'S TOP 6 BODEGA VISITS

Bodegas Codorníu Penedès. Spain's first producers of cava, located in outstanding Catalan Art Nouveau premises. See p.771.

Bodegas Marqués de Riscal La Rioja Alavesa. Terrific wine, and an extraordinary Frank O. Gehry-designed building to boot. See p.483.

Bodegas Ysios La Rioja Alavesa. Located in a stunning building by Santiago Calatrava. See p.483.

Condes de Albarei Galicia. Co-operative *bodega* turning out excellent Albariño wines. See p.575.

González Byass Jerez. One of the biggest sherry producers, makers of the Tio Pepe brand. See p.302.

Costers del Siurana Priorat. Investigate the up-and-coming Priorat region wires in deepest Catalunya. See p.785.

The media

The ubiquitous Spanish newspaper kiosk is your first stop for regional and national newspapers and magazines, though hotels and bars nearly always have a few kicking around for customers. The bigger cities, tourist towns and resorts will also have foreign newspapers available (some of which are actually published in Spain), generally on the day of issue or perhaps a day late. Television is all-pervasive in bars, cafés and restaurants, and you're going to find yourself watching more bullfighting, basketball and Venezuelan soap operas than perhaps you'd bargained for. Most hotel rooms have a TV, too, though only in the fancier places will you get any English-language programming, and then probably only the BBC News, CNN or Eurosport satellite channels.

Newspapers

Of the Spanish **national newspapers** the best are the Madrid-based centre-left *El País* (Ⓦelpais.es) and the centre-right *El Mundo* (Ⓦelmundo.es), both of which have good arts and foreign news coverage, including comprehensive regional "what's on" listings and supplements every weekend. The **regional press** is generally run by local magnates and is predominantly right of centre, though often supporting local autonomy movements. Nationalist press includes *Avui* in Catalunya, printed in Catalan, and the Basque papers *El Correo*, *Deia* and *Gara*, the last of which has close links with ETA. All that said, the paper with the highest circulation is *Marca* (Ⓦmarca.com), the country's top **sports daily**, mainly football-dominated; there's also *As* (Ⓦas.com), *El Mundo Deportivo* (Ⓦelmundodeportivo.es) and *Sport* (Ⓦsport.es). The main cities are also awash with **free newspapers**, which are dished out at bus and metro stops.

Magazines

There's a bewildering variety of **magazines** specializing in celebrity gossip (known collectively as *la prensa rosa*), ranging from the more traditional *Hola* to the sensationalist *QMD! (Qué Me Dices)*. *El Jueves* ("The Thursday" – strapline: "The magazine that comes out on Wednesdays") is a weekly comic-strip-style satirical magazine, while the online daily *El Confidencial* (Ⓦelconfidencial.com) gives the inside track on serious economic and political stories. There are also various **English-language magazines** and papers produced by and for the expatriate communities in the main cities and on the costas, such as *InMadrid* (Ⓦin-madrid.com), *Barcelona Metropolitan* (Ⓦbarcelona-metropolitan.com), and – for southern Spain – *Sur in English* (Ⓦsurinenglish.com) and *The Olive Press* (Ⓦtheolivepress.es).

Radio

There are hundreds of local radio channels, broadcasting in Spanish and regional languages, alongside a handful of national ones. The state-run Radio Nacional de España, or **RNE** (Ⓦrtve.es/radio), covers five stations: Radio Nacional, a general news and information channel; Radio Clásica, broadcasting mainly classical music and related programmes; the popular music channel Radio 3; Radio 4, in Catalan; and the rolling news and sports channel Radio 5. Radio Exterior is RNE's international shortwave service. Other **popular channels** include Cadena Ser and Onda Cero (news, talk, sports and culture), the Catholic Church-run COPE, 40 Principales (for the latest hits, Spanish and otherwise) and Cadena 100 (music and cultural programming). Radio Marca (dedicated sports radio) is also very popular.

Television

RTV (Ⓦrtve.es/television) provides the main, state-run channels, namely La 1 (ie, "Uno"), a general entertainment and news channel, and its sister La 2 ("Dos"). Private national stations are Antena 3, Cuatro (ie Four), Telecinco (Five) and La Sexta (Sixth). There are also plenty of **regional channels**, the most important being Catalunya's TV3 and Canal 33, both broadcast in Catalan, and the Basque Country's ETB channels (in Basque), though there are also stations in Galicia (TVG), Andalucía (Canal Sur) and Valencia (Canal Nou) with local programming. The main satellite channel is Canal+.

Festivals

It's hard to beat the experience of arriving in some small Spanish village, expecting no more than a bed for the night, to discover the streets decked with flags and streamers, a band playing in the plaza and the entire population out celebrating the local fiesta. Everywhere in Spain, from the tiniest hamlet to the

great cities, devotes at least a couple of days a year to partying, and participating in such an event propels you right into the heart of Spanish culture.

Local saints' days aside, Spain has some really major events worth planning your whole trip around, from the great Easter processions of Semana Santa (Holy Week) to the famous bull-running during July's Fiesta de San Fermín in Pamplona. There are also fiestas celebrating deliverance from the Moors, safe return from the sea, or the bringing in of the grapes – any excuse will do. One thing they all tend to have in common is a curious blend of religious ceremony and pagan ritual – sombre processions of statuary followed by exuberant merrymaking – in which fire plays a prominent part.

The **annual festival calendar in this section** concentrates on the country's most notable fiestas. For more regional and local fiestas turn to the **feature boxes** found in each chapter.

Outsiders are always welcome at fiestas, the only problem being that it can be hard to find a hotel, unless you book well in advance. The other thing to note is that while not every fiesta is a national **public holiday** (see p.56), or vice versa, you may well get stuck if you arrive in town in the middle of an annual event, since pretty much everything will be closed.

JANUARY

5: Cabalgata de Reyes When the "Three Kings" (reyes) arrive to bring the children their presents for Epiphany. Most cities stage a spectacular cavalcade as the Three Kings are driven through the streets throwing sweets to the crowds.

16–17: Sant Antoni Bonfires and saint's day processions, especially on the Balearic Islands.

FEBRUARY

Week preceding Ash Wednesday and Lent: Carnaval An excuse for wild partying and masques, most riotous in Cádiz (Andalucía), Sitges, Catalunya and Águilas (Valencia).

MARCH

12–19: Las Fallas Valencia holds the biggest of the bonfire festivals held for San José, climaxing on the Nit de Foc (Night of Fire) when enormous caricatures are burnt, and firecrackers let off in the streets. See p.804.

TOP 5 FIESTAS

Semana Santa Andalucía p.228
Feria de Abril Seville. See p.263
Fiesta de San Fermín Pamplona. See p.486
Las Fallas Valencia. See p.804
La Tomatina Buñol. See p.815

EASTER

March/April: Semana Santa Holy Week is celebrated across Spain, most theatrically in Seville, Málaga, Murcia and Valladolid, where *pasos* – huge floats of religious scenes – are carried down the streets, accompanied by hooded penitents atoning for the year's misdeeds. Maundy Thursday and Good Friday see the biggest, most solemn processions.

APRIL

22–24: Fiestas de Moros y Cristianos Mock battle between Moors and Christians in Alcoy, Valencia. See p.829.

23: Sant Jordi A day of celebration across the region, especially Barcelona (see p.646) for Catalunya's patron saint – Sant Jordi, St George. Being the birth date of Cervantes, it's also celebrated as National Book Day throughout Spain.

Last week: Feria de Abril Spectacular week-long fair in Seville, with a major bullfighting festival.

MAY

Early May: Horse Fair Jerez (Andalucía). Horsey hi jinks – show-jumping, parades and the famous "dancing Andalusian horses" – turn Jerez into equine heaven.

15: San Isidro Madrid's patron saint's day sees a two-week fiesta either side of the actual date.

Seventh Sunday after Easter: Pentecostés Pentecost is celebrated by the Romería del Rocío – the great pilgrimage-fair – at El Rocío, near Huelva (Andalucía). See p.305.

Thursday after Trinity Sunday: Corpus Christi Religious processions accompanied by floats and penitents, notably in Toledo, Granada and Valencia, plus the spectacular costumed events of Berga's Festa de la Patum, Catalunya (see p.753).

Last week: Feria de la Manzanilla The big annual sherry festival celebrates the famous tipple of Sanlúcar de Barrameda (Andalucía).

JUNE

2nd or 3rd week: Sónar Europe's biggest electronic music and multimedia bleep-fest, held over three days in Barcelona. See p.646.

23–24: San Juan Midsummer's eve is celebrated with bonfires and fireworks all over Spain, marking a hedonistic welcome to the summer – particularly in San Juan de Alicante and in Barcelona.

JULY

7–14: San Fermín The famed "Running of the Bulls" at Pamplona. See p.486.

25: Santiago Spain's patron saint, St James, is honoured at Santiago de Compostela, with fireworks and bonfires.

Last 3 weeks: Pirineos Sur World music festival on a floating stage at Lanuza, near Sallent de Gállego, in the Pyrenees.

AUGUST

10–11: Misteri d'Elx Elche, Valencia (see p.836) hosts mock battles between Christians and Moors, ending with a centuries-old mystery play.

Last week: Los Santos Niños Gigantones (giant puppets) are paraded in Alcalá de Henares, near Madrid.

Last Wednesday: La Tomatina Buñol, near Valencia, hosts the country's craziest fiesta, a one-hour tomato fight. See p.815.

SEPTEMBER

First week: Vendimia The grape harvest is celebrated wildly in Valdepeñas (Castilla-La Mancha), Jerez (Andalucía) and many other wine towns.

21: San Mateo The annual Rioja wine harvest bash coincides with the local saint's day in Logroño (La Rioja).

Third Week: Festa de Santa Tecla Human castles (*castells*) and processions of *gegants* (giant puppets) in Tarragona.

24: La Mercè Barcelona's biggest annual party (either side of the saint's day, 24th) sees a week's worth of giants' parades, fireworks and human-castle-building.

OCTOBER

1: San Miguel Villages across the country celebrate their patron saint's day.

12: La Virgen del Pilar Honouring the patron saint of Aragón is an excuse for bullfights, dancing and celebrations in Zaragoza and elsewhere.

DECEMBER

24: Nochebuena Christmas Eve is particularly exuberant, with parties and carousing early in the evening before it all suddenly stops in time for family dinner or Mass.

31: Nochevieja New Year is celebrated by eating a grape for every stroke of the clock in Plaza del Sol in Madrid, Plaça de Catalunya in Barcelona, and main squares and bars throughout the country.

Culture and etiquette

Spain is a fantastically welcoming, vibrant country, characterized by its love of life. With a population of over 44 million it's a diverse place, too, with regional identities as characteristic as their local landscapes: the Basques, Galicians and Catalans all adding their own languages and cultures to the mix. No matter where you decide to visit though, many of the clichés of Spanish life, such as the siesta, busy bars and restaurants open late into the night, and towns celebrating lively festivals, still pretty much ring true.

Social life and etiquette

One of the most important aspects of Spanish life is the family; no celebration would be complete without an extended gathering, although this is more common away from the busy cities where modern life takes its toll. Even so, the elderly are respected, and it's not uncommon to have older relatives being cared for in the family home. Likewise, children are absolutely adored, and included in everything.

Food plays an important part in Spanish family life, with lunch (*la comida*) the biggest meal of the day, often lasting from 2 to 4pm. It's common for shops and whole villages to come to a standstill for the afternoon meal and **siesta**, especially in more out-of-the-way places. Evening meals, which often start as late as 10pm, are usually preceded by a leisurely stroll, or **paseo**, when you may take in an aperitif in a bar or two.

Friends are more likely to meet in restaurants for meals, but if you are **invited to someone's house** for dinner, you should take a small gift for any children, along with chocolates, a bottle of wine, or some flowers (though avoid dahlias, chrysanthemums and flowers in odd numbers as these would only be given at funerals). Also bear in mind that **drinking** too much isn't common, and despite the fact there seems to be a bar on every corner, this is more for coffee and socializing than heavy boozing.

The Spanish are among the biggest **smokers** in Europe, with an estimated thirty percent of the population smoking regularly. Attitudes are changing, however, and the law now bans smoking in all public places, including shops, public transport, bars and restaurants.

Tipping is common in Spain, although not always expected, but locals are small tippers and twenty cents on a bar table or five percent in a restaurant is usually enough. It is also common practice to tip taxi drivers, hotel porters and the like in small change.

If you are planning to indulge in any topless **sunbathing**, consider local feelings first, and try to stick to beaches where people are already doing it. You also need to make sure you are properly covered if you enter a **church**; shorts and sleeveless tops should be avoided.

Greetings

If you're **meeting someone** for the first time, you should shake their hand. If you become friends, you may well move on to hugging (men) or kisses on each cheek (women), starting with the left. Men are also more likely to kiss women hello and goodbye, than to shake their hand. To say **hello**, use *Buenos días* before lunch and *Buenos tardes* after that. Bear in mind that in Spain the sense of time is somewhat elastic, so unless you're meeting for business (when being late is very bad form) don't be offended if you are left waiting for a good ten or twenty minutes.

Sports and outdoor activities

Spain is nothing if not enthusiastic about sport, with football and basketball all but national obsessions, and bullfighting – whether or not you agree it's a "sport" – one of its cultural highlights. There are also plenty of opportunities to get out and enjoy the country's stunning outdoors, whether it's ambling around a golf course, skiing in the southern slopes, chasing surf off the Basque Country coast or canyoning in the Pyrenees.

Basketball

Basketball (*baloncesto*) comes second only to football in national interest, and the 2014 World Championships (W spain2014.org) will be held in Spain, the second time the country has hosted the world's biggest basketball tournament. Domestically, there are eighteen professional teams competing in the national league, **ACB** (W acb .com), whose season runs from September to June; while other big competitions include the Copa del Rey and the Europe-wide Euroleague. The two biggest teams are, not entirely coincidentally, owned by the two most successful football teams, Barcelona and Real Madrid, and have won the ACB (until 1983 known as the Liga Nacional) dozens of times between them. There's more basketball information on the Federacion Española de Baloncesto website (W feb.es). Games are broadcast on TV, or match tickets cost from around €15.

Bullfighting

The **bullfight** is a classic image of Spain, and an integral part of many fiestas. In the south, especially, any village that can afford it will put on a *corrida* for an afternoon, while in big cities such as Madrid or Seville, the main festival times are accompanied by a season of prestige fights. However, with the exception of Pamplona, bullfighting is far more popular in Madrid and all points south than it is in the north or on the islands. Indeed, many northern cities don't have

> ## BASQUE GAMES AND SPORTS
> It's a whole different ballgame in the Basque Country, where sporting obsessions are of a very distinct kind. **Pelota** (a version of which is known as **jai alai**, Basque for "happy party") is played all over Spain, but in Euskal Herria even the smallest village has a *pelota* court or *fronton*, and betting on the sport is rife. **Rowing** is also hugely popular, and regattas are held every weekend in summer. During local fiestas, you'll also see other unique Basque sports including **aizkolaritza** (log-chopping), **harri-jasotzea** (stone-lifting), **soka-tira** (tug-of-war) and **segalaritza** (grass-cutting). The finest exponents of the first two in particular are popular local heroes (the world champion stone-lifter Iñaki Perurena's visit to Japan resulted in the sport being introduced there – he remains the only lifter to surpass the legendary 315kg barrier).

bullrings, while the regional governments of both Catalunya and the Canary Islands have gone so far as to **ban bullfighting**. Spain's main opposition to bullfighting is organized by **ADDA** (Asociación Defensa Derechos Animal; W addaong.org), whose website has information (in English) about international campaigns and current actions.

Los Toros, as Spaniards refer to bullfighting, is certainly big business, with the top performers, the matadors, on a par with the country's biggest pop and sports stars. To aficionados (a word that implies more knowledge and appreciation than mere "fan"), the bulls are a culture and a ritual – with the emphasis on the way man and bull "perform" together – in which the *arte* is at issue rather than the cruelty. If pressed on the issue of the slaughter of an animal, they generally fail to understand. Fighting bulls are, they will tell you, bred for the industry; they live a reasonable life before they are killed, and, if the bullfight went, so, too, would the bulls.

If you decide to attend a *corrida*, try to see a big, prestigious event, where star performers are likely to despatch the bulls with "art" and a successful, "clean" kill. There are few sights worse than a matador making a prolonged and messy kill, while the audience whistles and chucks cushions. The most skilful events are those featuring mounted matadors, or *rejoneadores*; this is the oldest form of *corrida*, developed in Andalucía in the seventeenth century.

The **bullfight season** runs from March to October, and **tickets** for *corridas* start from around €5 – though you can pay much more (up to €150) for the prime seats and prestigious fights. The cheapest seats are *gradas*, the highest rows at the back, from where you can see everything that happens without too much of the detail; the front rows are known as the *barreras*. Seats are also divided into *sol* (sun), *sombra* (shade) and *sol y sombra* (shaded after a while), though these distinctions have become less crucial as more and more bullfights start later in the day, at 6pm or 7pm, rather than the traditional 5pm. The *sombra* seats are more expensive, not so much for the spectators' personal comfort as the fact that most of the action takes place in the shade.

The corrida

The **corrida** begins with a procession, to the accompaniment of a *pasodoble* by the band. Leading the procession are two *alguaciles*, or "constables", on horseback and in traditional costume, followed by the three matadors, who will each fight two bulls, and their *cuadrillas*, their personal "team", each comprising two mounted *picadores* and three *banderilleros*.

Once the ring is empty, the first bull appears, to be "tested" by the matador or his *banderilleros* using pink and gold capes. These preliminaries conducted (and they can be short, if the bull is ferocious), the **suerte de picar** ensues, in which the *picadores* ride out and take up position at opposite sides of the ring, while the bull is distracted by other *toreros*. Once they are in place, the bull is made to charge one of the horses; the *picador* drives his short-pointed lance into the bull's neck, while it tries to toss his padded, blindfolded horse, thus tiring the bull's powerful neck and back muscles. This is repeated up to three times, until the horn sounds for the *picadores* to leave. For many, this is the least acceptable stage of the *corrida*, and it is clearly not a pleasant experience for the horses, who have their ears stuffed with oil-soaked rags to shut out the noise, and their vocal cords cut out to render them mute.

The next stage, the **suerte de banderillas**, involves the placing of three sets of *banderillas* (coloured sticks with barbed ends) into the bull's shoulders. Each of the three *banderilleros* delivers these in turn, attracting the bull's attention with the movement of his own body rather than a cape, and placing the *banderillas* while both he and the bull are running towards each other.

Once the *banderillas* have been placed, the **suerte de matar** begins, and the matador enters the ring alone, having exchanged his pink-and-gold cape for the red one. He (or she) salutes the president and then dedicates the bull either to an individual, to whom he gives his hat, or to the audience by placing his hat in the centre of the ring. It is in this part of the *corrida* that judgements are made and the performance is focused, as the matador displays his skills on the (by now exhausted) bull. He uses the movements of the cape to attract the bull, while his body remains still. If he does well, the band will start to play, while the crowd *olé* each pass. This stage lasts around ten minutes and ends with the kill. The matador attempts to get the bull into a position where he can drive a sword between its shoulders and through to the heart for a *coup de grâce*. In practice, they rarely succeed in this, instead taking a second sword, crossed at the end, to cut the bull's spinal cord; this causes instant death.

If the audience is impressed by the matador's performance, they will wave their handkerchiefs and shout for an award to be made by the president. He can award one or both ears, and a tail – the better the display, the more pieces he gets – while if the matador has excelled himself, he will be carried out of the ring by the crowd, through the *puerta grande*, the main door, which is normally kept locked.

Popular current **matadors** include the veteran Enrique Ponce, Julián "El Juli" López, and Granada's David "El Fandi" Fandila, Francisco Rivera Ordoñez and Manuel Jesús Cid Sala "El Cid"; currently the top female matador is María Paz Vegá from Málaga. But the *torero* who sets most male aficionados' hearts aflutter (and many female ones, too) is the moody, quixotic and media-shy José Tomás Román Martín; fighting under the name José Tomás, his fans claim that his courageous, high-risk style – he has been seriously gored on numerous occasions – has taken the art back to its roots.

Football

Spanish **fútbol** is indisputably hot at present – after decades of habitual underperformance, the national team became European champions in 2008, world champions in 2010, and Under-21 European champions in 2011, while the current Barcelona club side – mercurial *tiki-taka* (pass-and-move) masters – have been hailed as the world's best team. Certainly, if you want the excitement of a genuinely Spanish sporting event, watching a Sunday-evening game in **La Liga** (🌐 lfp.es) usually produces as much passion as anything you'll find in the bullring.

For many years, the country's two dominant teams have been big-spending **Real Madrid** and **FC Barcelona**, and these two have shared domestic league and cup honours more often than is healthy. Opposition in recent years has been from **Valencia**, the Andalucian powerhouse of **Sevilla** and the emerging force of **Villarreal**, who have experienced a rags-to-riches success story under president and ceramics tycoon Fernando Roig. Other significant teams include **Athletic Bilbao**, who only draw on players from Euskal Herria (the Basque Country in both Spain and France and Navarra) or who came through the club's youth ranks, while Real Madrid and Barcelona's respective local rivals are **Atlético Madrid** (the third-biggest team in terms of support) and **Espanyol**.

The league **season** runs from late August until May, and most games kick off at 5 or 7pm on Sundays, though live TV usually demands that one key game kicks off at 10pm on Saturday and 9pm on Sunday. With the exception of local derbies, major European games, and the so-called *clásicos* between Real Madrid and Barcelona, **tickets** are not too hard to get. They start at around €30 for La Liga games, with the cheapest in the *fondo* (behind the goals); *tribuna* (pitchside stand) seats are much pricier, while to see an average Real Madrid (see p.95) or Barcelona (see p.679) game could easily cost you up to €100.

Golf

When Cantabria boy Severiano "Seve" Ballesteros died in 2011, aged just 54, the whole nation mourned. He and his fellow golfers, like José María Olazábal, Sergio García and Miguel Ángel Jiménez, have raised the country's golf profile immeasurably in recent years, while with around three hundred **golf courses** Spain is one of the best European destinations for the amateur golfer too. Temperatures, especially favourable in the south, mean that you can play more or less year-round on the Costa del Sol, while a number of courses have built away from the traditional centres, for example along the Costa de la Luz and the Atlantic coast, which, while not as nice in winter, tend to be a little cheaper. There are increasing concerns, however, about the amount of water used by courses in a country that is experiencing a severe water crisis.

Plenty of tour operators can arrange golf-holiday packages, while for more information visit the very useful **Golf Spain** website (Ⓦgolfspain.com), which details all the country's golf courses and golf schools, plus green fees and golf-and-resort packages.

Hiking and mountain sports

Spain is one of the most mountainous countries in Europe, and as such is hugely popular with walkers. Aside from the classic long-distance routes, there are fantastic day-hikes, climbs and circuits possible almost everywhere, though you'll need to be properly equipped with map, compass or GPS, hiking boots and mountain gear.

In Andalucía, the **Sierra Nevada** mountain range and national park offers spectacular walking among the highest peaks in Europe after the Alps. It can be pretty hard going, but there are less-challenging hikes in the foothills, particularly the lush valleys of Las Alpujarras. For the best trekking in central Spain, head for the **Sierra de Gredos**, two hours' drive from Madrid, where there are lots of excellent one- and two-day hikes in the shadow of the highest peak, Almanzor (2592m). To the north, in the Pyrenees, the largest concentration of peaks lies in the eastern half of the range, particularly in Catalunya's **Parc Nacional d'Aigüestortes i Estany de Sant Maurici**, where there are walks of all levels, from afternoon rambles to multi-day expeditions. Further challenges abound to the west, where the **Aragonese Pyrenees** are home to the two highest peaks in the range, Aneto (3404m) and Posets (3375m), while in Aragón's **Parque Nacional de Ordesa** there are both rewarding day-hikes and more intensive climbs. If asked to choose just one corner of Spain, though, many would plump for the rugged **Picos de Europa** in Cantabria and Asturias, which, although only 40km or so across, offers a surprising diversity, from easy day-treks to full-blown expeditions.

Rafting and canyoning

There's **rafting** (see p.759) in various rivers across Spain, though the fast-flowing Noguera Pallaresa in the eastern Pyrenees is the most popular choice for expeditions. The season runs roughly from March to October, during which time you can fling yourself down the rapids in an inflatable raft from around €35 for a two-hour trip, and more like €70–80 for an all-day trip with lunch.

The Parque Natural Sierra de Guara (Ⓦguara.org) and the Parque Nacional de Ordesa (Ⓦordesa.net) provide some of the best locations in Europe for **canyoning** (*barranquismo*) – hiking, climbing, scrambling and abseiling in caves, gorges and rivers. Operators in most of the local villages (including Alquézar and Torla) offer equipment and guides, with prices starting from around €70 for a

SPAIN'S CLASSIC HIKES

The country's **major footpaths** are known as GR (Grande Recorrido) or PR (Pequeño Recorrido), some of which make up part of the trans-European walking routes that extend across the entire continent. GR paths are the longest, and are marked by red-and-white stripes, while the smaller PR routes (yellow-and-white) can usually be done in a day. The best-known routes are the GR11, which crosses the Pyrenees from coast to coast, via Andorra; the GR65 and its variants, the Camino de Santiago; and the GR7, which starts from Tarifa in Andalucía, heads through the Sierra Nevada and up the Catalan coast before reaching the Pyrenees.

Baixa Garrotxa A 28-kilometre loop through the spectacular Garrotxa volcanic region of northeastern Catalunya. See p.742.

Camino de Santiago The legendary, month-long pilgrimage route runs from the Pyrenees to Santiago de Compostela, by way of Romanesque architecture in Navarra, mighty Gothic cathedrals in Castilla y León, fine wines in La Rioja and beautiful green Galicia scenery (see p.558); also features on the regional sections in Castilla y León (see p.426), Navarra (see p.491) and Galicia (see p.558).

Cañón de Añisclo Much less visited and wilder than its neighbour Ordesa, this spectacular river gorge is overlooked by wedding-cake palisades. See p.637.

Carros de Foc The trans-park circuit takes in the most scenic corners

of the Parc Nacional d'Aigüestortes i Estany de Sant Maurici, a challenging route linking nine overnight refuges. See p.763.

Circo de las Cinco Lagunas A scintillating one-day walk in the Sierra de Gredos, with sparkling mountain lakes and the half-tame Gredos ibex to see. See p.157.

Circo de Soaso The best sampling of Aragón's Parque Nacional de Ordesa – upstream along the valley to a superb waterfall, and back via a spectacular corniche route called the Faja de Pelay. See p.635.

Desfiladero de Cares The classic Picos de Europa hike – through the Cares Gorge – is a dramatic twelve-kilometre route along a path hewn out of the cliff face. See p.524.

Pedraforca One of the most revered peaks in Catalunya is a relatively easy one to bag, with a variety of routes up. See p.754.

full day's expedition. The park websites have more information on routes and local organizations.

Skiing and snowboarding

Spain offers a decent range of slopes, and often at lower prices than its more mountainous European neighbours. It is also home to the southernmost skiing in Europe, in the form of the Sol y Nieve resort in the **Sierra Nevada** (Andalucía), which has the longest season in Spain, running from November to April and sometimes even May, allowing you to ski in the morning and head to the beach in the afternoon – really, the only thing the resort's got going for it. Much more challenging skiing is to be had in the north of the country in the Pyrenees. The **Aragonese Pyrenees** are home to a range of resorts catering for beginners to advanced skiers, while the resorts in the **Catalan Pyrenees**, to the east, encompass Andorra; the biggest resort here is Soldeu/El Tarter. Other options include the more intimate **Alto Campoo**, near Santander, and, for a day's excursion, easy-to-intermediate skiing just outside Madrid at **Valdesqui** and **Navacerrada**.

There are ski deals to Spain from tour operators in your home country, though it often works out cheaper if you go through a local Spanish travel agent or even arrange your trip directly with local providers. Many local hotels offer ski deals, and we've covered some options in the Guide. Equipment rental will set you back around €20–30 a day as a general

rule, and daily lift-passes around €25–40, although the longer you rent or ski for, the cheaper it will be.

Watersports

Spain offers a vast range of watersports, especially along the Mediterranean coast where most resorts offer **pedalo and canoe rental** (from €10/hour), sailing tuition, and **boat rental** (€40/hour) and **waterskiing** (from €30/15min).

Surfing is best on the Atlantic coast, backed up by the fact that the area plays regular host to a number of prestigious competitions such as the Billabong Pro, Ferrolterra Pantín Classic and the Goanna Pro. Breaks such as the legendary Mundaka (Costa Vasca), considered by many as the best left-hander in Europe, along with a superb run of beaches with waves for all abilities, make the region's reputation. The surfing season runs roughly from September to April, meaning that a full wet suit is a basic requirement in the cold Atlantic waters. If you prefer to surf in warmer waters, the Andalucian coastline has a few decent spots. For more information, Ⓦ beachwizard .com is an excellent website giving full details of all the best spots in Spain, along with reviews, maps and travel information.

Tarifa on the Costa de la Luz is *the* spot in Spain – indeed, in the whole of Europe – for **windsurfing and kitesurfing**, with strong winds almost guaranteed, and huge stretches of sandy beach to enjoy. You'll also find schools dotted around the rest of the coast, with another good spot being the rather colder option of the Atlantic coast in Galicia. Prices are around €25 for an hour's board and sail rental, and €10 for wet suits, while lessons start at €35 an hour including board rental.

Travelling with children

Spain is a good country to travel with children of any age; they will be well received everywhere, and babies and toddlers, in particular, will be the centre of attention. You will probably have to change your usual routine, since young children stay up late in Spain, especially in the summer. It's very common for them to be running around pavement cafés and public squares after 10 or 11pm, and yours will no doubt enjoy joining in. It's expected that families dine out with their children, too, so it's not unusual to see up to four generations of the same family eating tapas in a bar, for example.

Holidays

Many holiday hotels and self-contained club-style resorts offer things like kids' clubs, babysitting, sports and entertainment. The only caveat is that, of course, you're unlikely to see much of Spain on these family-oriented holidays. The two best cities to take children, hands down, are Madrid and Barcelona, which have loads of child-friendly attractions. Otherwise, Spain has various theme parks and leisure activities specifically aimed at kids, while the long Spanish coastline has a bunch of popular **water parks**.

Museums, galleries and sights throughout Spain either offer **discounts** or **free entry** for children (it's often free for under-4s or even under-7s), and it's the same on trains, sightseeing tours, boat trips and most other usual tourist attractions.

Accommodation

If you're travelling independently, finding **accommodation** shouldn't be a problem, as *hostales* and *pensiones* generally offer rooms with three or four beds. Bear in mind that much budget accommodation in towns and cities is located on the upper storeys of buildings, often without lifts. It's also worth noting that some older-style *pensiones* don't have heating systems – and it can get very cold in winter. If you want a cot provided, or baby-listening or **baby-sitting** services, you'll usually have to pay the price of staying in a more expensive hotel – and even then, never assume that these facilities are provided, so always check in advance. **Self-catering accommodation** offers the most flexibility; even in major cities, it's easy to rent an apartment by the night or week and enjoy living like a local with your family.

Products, clothes and services

Baby food, disposable nappies, formula milk and other standard items are widely available in pharmacies and supermarkets, though not necessarily with the same range or brands that you will be used to at home. Organic baby food, for example, is hard to come by away from the big-city supermarkets, and most Spanish non-organic baby foods contain small amounts of sugar or salt. Fresh milk, too, is not always available; UHT is more commonly drunk by small children. If you require anything specific for your baby or child, it's best to bring it with you or check with the manufacturer about equivalent brands. Remember the airline restrictions on carrying liquids in hand luggage if you're planning to bring industrial quantities of Calpol to see you through the holiday.

For **babies' and children's clothing**, Prénatal (Ⓦprenatal.es) and Chicco (Ⓦchicco.es) are Spain's market leaders, with shops in most towns and cities. Or you can always try the local El Corte Inglés department store.

Families might eat out a lot, but things like **highchairs and special children's menus** are rare, except in the resorts on the costas and islands. Most bars and cafés, though, will be happy to heat milk bottles for you. **Baby-changing areas** are also relatively rare, except in department stores and shopping centres, and even where they do exist they are not always up to scratch.

Attitudes

Most establishments are **baby-friendly** in the sense that you'll be made very welcome if you turn up with a child in tow. Many museum cloakrooms, for example, will be happy to look after your pushchair as you carry your child around the building, while restaurants will make a fuss of your little one. However, **breast-feeding** in public is not widespread, though it's more acceptable in big resorts and the main cities; the local village café is probably not the place to test rural sensibilities. **Noise** is the other factor that often stuns visiting parents. Spain is a loud country, with fiesta fireworks, jackhammers, buzzing mopeds and clamouring evening crowds all adding to the mix. Babies sleep through most things, but you might want to pick and choose accommodation with the location of bars, clubs, markets, etc firmly in mind.

Travel essentials

Addresses

Addresses are written as: c/Picasso 2, 4° izda. – which means Picasso Street (*calle*) no. 2, fourth floor, left- (*izquierda*) hand flat or office; dcha. (*derecha*) is right; cto. (*centro*) centre. Other confusions in Spanish addresses result from the different spellings, and sometimes words, used in Catalan, Basque and Galician – all of which are replacing their Castilian counterparts; for example, *carrer* (not *calle*) and *plaça* (not *plaza*) in Catalan.

Climate

Overall, spring, early summer and autumn are ideal times for a Spanish trip – though the weather varies enormously from region to region. Note that the chart below shows **average temperatures** – and while Seville, the hottest city in Spain, can soar high into the 90s at midday in summer, it is a fairly comfortable 23–27°C (75–80°F) through much of the morning and late afternoon. Equally, bear in mind that temperatures in the north or west, in Extremadura or León for example, can approach

freezing at night in winter, while mountainous regions can get extremely cold much of the year.

Complaints

By law, all establishments (including hotels) must keep a *libro de reclamaciones* (**complaints book**). If you have any problems, you can usually produce an immediate resolution by asking for the book, since most establishments prefer to keep them empty, thus attracting no unwelcome attention from officialdom. If you do make an entry, English is acceptable but write clearly and simply; add your home address, too, as you are entitled to be informed of any action, including – but don't count on it – compensation. Or take your complaint to any local *turismo*, which should attempt to resolve the matter while you wait.

Costs

Prices in Spain have increased considerably over the last ten years or so, but in general there are still few places in Europe where you'll get a better deal on the cost of simple meals and drinks, while public transport remains very good value.

It's difficult to come up with **a daily budget** for the country, as your sixty-cent glass of wine and €30 *pensión* room in rural Andalucía might be €3 and €60, respectively, in Madrid or Barcelona. However, as a very rough guide, if you always stay in the cheapest hotels, use public transport and stick to local restaurants, you could get by on between €50 and €80 a day. Stay somewhere a bit more stylish or comfortable, eat in fancier restau-

AVERAGE TEMPERATURES

	Jan	Mar	May	Jul	Sep	Nov
Alicante, Costa Blanca						
°C/°F	16/61	20/68	26/78	32/90	30/86	21/70
Barcelona, Catalunya						
°C/°F	13/56	16/61	21/70	28/83	25/77	16/61
Madrid, Castile						
°C/°F	9/49	15/59	21/70	31/88	25/77	13/56
Málaga, Costa del Sol						
°C/°F	17/63	19/67	23/74	29/84	29/84	20/68
Mallorca, Balearics						
°C/°F	14/58	17/63	22/72	29/84	27/80	18/65
Pontevedra, Galicia						
°C/°F	14/58	16/61	20/68	25/77	24/75	16/61
Santander, Cantabria						
°C/°F	12/54	15/59	17/63	22/72	21/70	15/59
Seville, Andalucía						
°C/°F	15/59	21/70	26/78	35/95	32/90	20/6

rants, and go out on the town, and you'll need more like €100–150 a day, though, of course, if you're holidaying in Spain's paradores or five-star hotels, this figure won't even cover your room.

Visiting museums, galleries, churches and monasteries soon adds up – if you visited every site we cover in Salamanca alone, for example, you'd be out of pocket by €30 or so. Accordingly, it pays to take along any **student/youth or senior citizen cards** you may be entitled to, as most attractions offer discounts (and make sure you carry your passport or ID card). Some museums and attractions are **free** on a certain day of the week or month (though note that this is sometimes limited to EU citizens only; you'll need to show your passport). Any **entrance fees** noted in this guide are for the full adult price; children (as well as seniors) usually get a discount, and the under-4s are often free.

Crime and personal safety

The police in Spain come in various guises. The **Guardia Civil**, in green uniforms, is a national police force, formerly a military organization, and has responsibility for national crime, as well as roads, borders and guarding public buildings. There's also the blue-uniformed **Policía Nacional**, mainly seen in cities, who deal with crime, drugs, crowd control, identity and immigrant matters, and the like. Locally, most policing is carried out by the **Policía Municipal**, who wear blue-and-white uniforms, and these tend to be the most approachable if you're reporting a crime for example. In certain of the autonomous regions, there are also regional police forces, which are gradually taking over duties from the Guardia Civil and Policía Nacional. The **Mossos d'Esquadra** in Catalunya (blue uniforms with red-and-white trim) and the Basque **Ertzaintza** (blue and red, with red berets) have the highest profile, though you're most likely to encounter them on traffic and highways duty.

In the unlikely event that you're robbed, go straight to the police, where you'll need to make an official statement known as a **denuncia**, not least because your insurance company will require a police report. Expect it to be a time-consuming and laborious business – you can do it online (details on Ⓦpolicia.es), but you'll still have to go into the station to sign it. If you have your passport stolen, you need to contact your embassy or consulate.

Avoiding trouble

Pickpocketing and **bag-snatching** is, unfortunately, a fact of life in major Spanish cities and

---

EMERGENCY NUMBERS

- ☏ **112** All emergency services
- ☏ **061** Ambulance
- ☏ **080** Fire service
- ☏ **062** Guardia Civil
- ☏ **091** Policía Nacional

---

tourist resorts, though no more so than anywhere else in Europe. You need to be on guard in crowded places and on public transport, but there's no need to be paranoid. Drivers shouldn't leave anything in view in a **parked car**; take the SatNav or iPod with you. **On the road**, be cautious about accepting help from anyone other than a uniformed police officer – some roadside thieves pose as "good Samaritans" to persons experiencing car and tyre problems, some of which, such as slashed tyres, may have been inflicted at rest stops or service stations in advance. The thieves typically attempt to divert your attention by pointing out a problem and then steal items from the vehicle while you are looking elsewhere.

Incidentally, if you are stopped by a proper police officer for a **driving offence**, being foreign just won't wash as an excuse. They'll fine you on the spot, cash or card.

Sexual harassment

Spain's macho image has faded dramatically, and these days there are relatively few parts of the country where **women travelling alone** are likely to feel intimidated or attract unwanted attention. There is little of the pestering that you have to contend with in, say, the larger Italian cities, and the outdoor culture of terrazas (terrace bars) and the tendency of Spaniards to move around in large, mixed crowds, help to make you feel less exposed. *Déjame en paz* ("leave me in peace") is a fairly standard rebuff, and if you are in any doubt, take a taxi, always the safest way to travel late at night.

The major **resorts** of the costas have their own artificial holiday culture, where problems are more likely to be caused by other alcohol-fuelled holidaymakers. You are actually more vulnerable in isolated, **rural regions**, where you can walk for hours without coming across an inhabited farm or house, though it's rare that this poses a threat – help and hospitality are much more the norm. Many single women happily tramp the long-distance pilgrim footpath, for example, though you are always best advised to stay in rooms and *pensiones* rather than camping wild.

STAYING SAFE IN SPANISH CITIES

Certain Spanish cities – Madrid, Barcelona and Seville particularly – have a bad rep as far as petty crime is concerned. While it's easy to get spooked by lurid tales of local thievery (hoteliers often go to great pains to warn guests of the dangers), taking the usual sensible **precautions** should help make your stay safe.

Know where your belongings are at all times (eg, don't leave **bags** unattended, even if you're looking at rooms upstairs in a *hostal*). Carry handbags slung across your neck, not over your shoulder; don't put wallets in your back pocket; leave passport and tickets in the hotel safe; and keep a photocopy of your passport, plus notes of your credit card helplines and so on.

On the street, beware of people standing unusually close at street kiosks or attractions, or of those trying to distract you for any reason (pointing out "bird shit" – in reality, planted shaving cream – on your jacket, shoving a card or paper to read right under your nose). Next thing you know, your purse has gone.

Electricity

The current in most of Spain is 220v – bring an adaptor (and transformer) to use UK and US laptops, cellphone chargers, etc.

Entry requirements

EU citizens (and those of Norway, Iceland, Liechtenstein and Switzerland) need only a valid national-identity card or passport to enter Spain. Other Europeans, and citizens of the **United States**, **Canada**, **Australia** and **New Zealand**, require a passport but no visa, and can stay as a tourist for up to ninety days. Other nationalities (including South Africans) will need to get a visa from a Spanish embassy or consulate before departure. Visa requirements do change, and it's always advisable to check the current situation before leaving home.

Most EU citizens who want to stay in Spain for longer than three months, rather than just visit as a tourist, need to register at a provincial **Oficina de Extranjeros** (Foreigners' Office), where they'll be issued with a residence certificate; you'll find a list of offices (eventually) on the Ministry of Interior website (🅦 mir.es). You don't need the certificate if you're an EU citizen living and working legally in Spain, or if you're legally self-employed or a student (on an exchange programme or otherwise). US citizens can apply for one ninety-day extension, showing proof of funds, but this must be done from outside Spain. Other nationalities wishing to extend their stay will need to get a special visa from a Spanish embassy or consulate before departure.

Health

The **European Health Insurance Card (EHIC)** gives EU citizens access to Spanish state public-health services under reciprocal agreements. While this will provide free or reduced-cost medical care in the event of minor injuries and emergencies, it won't cover every eventuality – and it only applies to EU citizens in possession of the card – so travel insurance is essential.

No **inoculations** are required for Spain, and the worst that's likely to happen to you is that you might fall victim to an upset stomach. To be safe, wash fruit and avoid tapas dishes that look as if they were prepared last week. Water at public fountains is fine, unless there's a sign saying "*agua no potable*", in which case don't drink it.

For minor complaints, go to a **farmacia** – pharmacists are highly trained, willing to give advice (often in English) and able to dispense many drugs that would be available only on prescription in other countries. They keep usual shop hours (Mon–Fri 9am–1.30pm & 5–8pm), but some open late and at weekends, while a rota system (displayed in the window of every pharmacy) keeps at least one open 24 hours in every town.

If you have special medical or dietary requirements, it is advisable to carry a letter from your doctor, translated into Spanish, indicating the nature of your condition and necessary treatments. With luck, you'll get the address of an English-speaking **doctor** from the nearest *farmacia*, police station or tourist office – it's obviously more likely in resorts and big cities. Treatment at **hospitals** for EU citizens in possession of the EHIC card is free; otherwise, you'll be charged at private-hospital rates, which can be very expensive.

In **emergencies**, dial ☎ 112 for an ambulance.

Insurance

You should take out a comprehensive **insurance**

ROUGH GUIDES TRAVEL INSURANCE

Rough Guides has teamed up with WorldNomads.com to offer great travel insurance deals. Policies are available to residents of over 150 countries, with cover for a wide range of adventure sports, 24hr emergency assistance, high levels of medical and evacuation cover and a stream of travel safety information. Roughguides.com users can take advantage of their policies online 24/7, from anywhere in the world – even if you're already travelling. And since plans often change when you're on the road, you can extend your policy and even claim online. Roughguides.com users who buy travel insurance with WorldNomads.com can also leave a positive footprint and donate to a community development project. For more information go to Ⓦ roughguides.com/shop.

policy before travelling to Spain, to cover against loss, theft, illness or injury. A typical policy will provide cover for loss of baggage, tickets and – up to a certain limit – cash or travellers' cheques, as well as cancellation or curtailment of your journey. When securing baggage cover, make sure that the per-article limit will cover your most valuable possession. Most policies exclude so-called **dangerous sports** unless an extra premium is paid: in Spain, this can mean most watersports are excluded (plus rafting, canyoning, etc), though not things like bike tours or hiking.

If you need to make a claim, you should keep receipts for medicines and medical treatment, and in the event you have anything stolen, you must obtain an official statement from the police.

Internet

Wireless internet access (wi-fi, pronounced "wee-fee" in Spain) is widespread in cafés, bars, hotels and other public "hotspots" – Barcelona city council, for example, operates Spain's largest free public wi-fi network. Otherwise, you can get online at computer shops and phone offices (*locutorios*), where you'll pay as little as €1 an hour, though it can cost two or three times as much.

Laundry

You'll find a few coin-op self-service laundries (*lavanderías automáticas*) in the major cities, but you normally have to leave your clothes for a service wash and dry at a *lavandería*. A dry cleaner is a *tintorería*. Note that by law you're not allowed to leave laundry hanging out of windows over a street, and many *pensiones* and *hostales* expressly forbid washing clothes in the sink. To avoid an international incident, ask first if there's somewhere you can wash your clothes.

Mail

Post offices (*Correos*; Ⓦcorreos.es) are normally open weekdays from 8am to 2pm and again from 5 to 7.30pm, though branches in bigger places may have longer hours, may not close at midday and may open on Saturday mornings. There's an office-finder on the website, which also gives exact opening hours and contact details for each post office in Spain. As you can also pay bills and buy phonecards in post offices, queues can be long – it's often easier to buy **stamps** at tobacconists (look for the brown-and-yellow *estanco* sign).

Outbound mail is reasonably reliable, with letters or cards taking around three days to a week to the UK and the rest of Europe, a week to ten days to North America, New Zealand and Australia, although it can be more erratic in the summer. There's also a whole host of express-mail services (ask for *urgente* or *exprés*).

Maps

In addition to the maps in this guide, virtually indestructible, waterproof **Rough Guide maps** are available covering Andalucía and the Costa del Sol, Barcelona, Madrid, Mallorca and Northern Spain. You'll also find a good selection of **road maps** in most Spanish bookshops, street kiosks and service stations. Most widely available are the regional Michelin maps (1:400,000), covering the country (including the Balearics) in a series of nine maps, though there are also whole-country maps and atlas-format versions available. Other good country and regional maps are those published by Distrimapas Telstar (Ⓦdistrimapas-telstar.es), which also produces reliable indexed **street plans** of the main cities. Any good book or travel shop in your own country should be able to provide a decent range of Spain maps, or buy online from specialist stores such as ⓦstanfords.co.uk or ⓦrandmcnally.com.

You can buy **hiking/trekking maps** from specialist map/travel shops in Spain, including La Tienda Verde in Madrid (ⓦtiendaverde.es), and Librería Quera (ⓦllibreriaquera.com) or Altaïr (ⓦaltair.es) in Barcelona. These and other bookshops stock the full range of **topographical maps** issued by two government agencies – the Instituto Geográfico Nacional and the Servicio Geográfico del Ejército – available at scales of 1:200,000, 1:100,000, 1:50,000 and occasionally 1:25,000. The various SGE series are considered to be more up to date, although neither agency is hugely reliable. A Catalunya-based company, Editorial Alpina (ⓦeditorialalpina.com), produces useful 1:40,000 or 1:25,000 map/booklet sets for most of the Spanish **mountain and foothill areas** of interest, and these are also on sale in many bookshops.

Money

Spain's currency is the **euro** (€), with notes issued in denominations of 5, 10, 20, 50, 100, 200 and 500 euros, and coins in denominations of 1, 2, 5, 10, 20 and 50 cents, and 1 and 2 euros. Up-to-the-minute currency **exchange rates** are posted on ⓦoanda.com.

By far the easiest way to get money is to use your bank debit card to withdraw cash from an **ATM**, found in villages, towns and cities all over Spain, as well as on arrival at the airports and major train stations. You can usually withdraw up to €300 a day, and instructions are offered in English once you insert your card. Make sure you have a personal identification number (PIN) that's designed to work overseas, and take a note of your bank's emergency contact number in case the machine swallows your card. Some European debit cards can also be used directly in shops to pay for purchases; you'll need to check first with your bank.

All major **credit cards** are accepted in hotels, restaurants and shops, and for tours, tickets and transport, though don't count on being able to use them in every small *pensión* or village café. You can also use your credit card in an ATM to withdraw cash, though remember that these advances will be treated as loans, with interest accruing daily from the date of withdrawal. If you use a foreign credit card in some shops, you may also be asked for photo ID, so be prepared to show a driving licence or passport. Make sure you make a note of the number for reporting lost or stolen cards to your credit card company.

Spanish **bancos** (banks) and **cajas de ahorros** (savings banks) have branches in all but the smallest villages. **Banking hours** are usually Monday to Friday 8.30am to 2pm, with some city branches open Saturday 8.30am to 1pm (except June–Sept when all banks close on Sat), although times can vary from bank to bank. Outside these times, it's usually possible to change cash at larger hotels (generally with bad rates and low commission) or with travel agents – useful for small amounts in a hurry.

In tourist areas, you'll also find specialist **casas de cambio**, with more convenient hours (though rates vary), while some major tourist offices, larger train stations and most branches of El Corte Inglés department store have exchange facilities open throughout business hours.

Opening hours

Almost everything in Spain – shops, museums, churches, tourist offices – closes for a **siesta** of at least two hours in the middle part of the day. There's a lot of variation (and the siesta tends to be longer in the south), but you'll get far less aggravated if you accept that the early afternoon is best spent asleep, or in a bar, or both.

Basic **working hours** are Monday to Friday 9.30am to 2pm and 5 to 8pm. Many **shops** open slightly later on a Saturday (at 10am) and close for the day at 2pm, though you'll still find plenty of places open in cities, and there are regional variations. Moreover, department and chain stores and shopping malls tend to open a straight Monday to Saturday 10am to 9 or 10pm.

Museums and galleries, with very few exceptions, also have a break between 1 or 2pm and 4pm. On Sundays, most open mornings only, and on Mondays many close all day (museums are also usually closed Jan 1 & 6, May 1, Dec 24, 25 & 31). Opening hours vary from year to year, though often not by more than half an hour or so. Some are also seasonal, and usually in Spain, "summer" means from Easter until September, and "winter" from October until Easter.

The most important **cathedrals, churches and monasteries** operate in the same way as museums, with regular visiting hours and admission charges. Other churches, though, are kept locked, generally opening only for worship in the early morning and/or the evening (between around 6 and 9pm).

Public holidays

Alongside the Spanish **national public holidays**

(see box, below) there are scores of regional holidays and local fiestas (often marking the local saint's day), any of which will mean that everything except hotels, bars and restaurants locks its doors.

In addition, **August** is traditionally Spain's own holiday month, when the big cities are semi-deserted, with many shops and restaurants closed for the duration. In contrast, it can prove nearly impossible to find a room in the more popular coastal and mountain resorts at these times; similarly, seats on planes, trains and buses in August should if possible be booked in advance.

Shopping

The great city **markets** of Spain are attractions in their own right – bustling, colourful and hugely photogenic – but even so they are emphatically not "just for tourists". Local people still do their daily shop in places like La Boqueria in Barcelona, Valencia's Mercado Central or Madrid's refurbished Mercado de San Miguel, while a visit to any town's local market is a sure way to get a handle on regional produce and specialities. Independent **food shops** thrive too, from traditional bakeries to classy delis serving the finest cured meats, while the bigger cities support whole enclaves of foodie shops – in Barcelona's La Ribera neighbourhood, for example, you can flit from alley to alley to buy hand-crafted chocolates, artisan-made cheeses, home-roast coffee, organic olive oil and the like.

Leatherwork, such as belts, bags, purses and even saddles, are best sourced in Andalucía. The town of Ubrique (Cádiz) has been a centre of leather production since medieval times, and you can browse and buy from the workshops that line the main street (which also make branded items for the big international fashion names).

Ceramics are widely available, but are especially good in Andalucía (Córdoba region, and around Seville) and in Catalunya (at La Bisbal, northwest of Palafrugell).

In Andalucía you'll also be able to pick up the most authentic **flamenco** accessories such as dresses, fans, shawls and lace.

Smoking laws

Since 2006 smoking in public places in Spain has been regulated by law, and tougher restrictions introduced in 2011 mean that it's now forbidden to smoke in all public buildings and transport facilities, plus bars, restaurants, clubs and cafés. Compared to other countries with smoking restrictions in force, you'll find there's still an awful lot of puffing going on, though the ban is generally observed.

Taxes

Local sales tax, **IVA** (pronounced "eeba"), is eight percent in hotels and restaurants, and eighteen percent in shops. It's usually included in the price though not always, so some hotel or restaurant bills can come as a bit of a surprise – though quoted prices should always make it clear whether or not tax is included. **Non-EU residents** are able to claim back the sales tax on purchases that come to over €90. To do this, make sure the shop you're buying from fills out the correct paperwork, and present this to customs before you check in at the airport for your return flight.

Telephones

Spanish **telephone numbers** have nine digits; mobile numbers begin with a 6 or 7, freephone numbers begin 900, while other 90-plus- and 80-plus-digit numbers are nationwide standard-rate or special-rate services. To **call Spain from abroad**, dial your country's international access code + 34 (Spain's country code) + the nine-digit Spanish number.

Public telephones have instructions in English, and accept coins, credit cards and phonecards. **Phonecards** (*tarjetas*) with discounted rates for calls are available in tobacconists, newsagents and post offices, issued in various denominations either by Telefónica (the dominant operator) or one of its rivals. Credit cards are not recommended for local and national calls, since most have a minimum charge that is far more than a normal call is likely to cost. It's also best to avoid making calls from the

---

SPANISH NATIONAL PUBLIC HOLIDAYS

Jan 1 *Año Nuevo* New Year's Day
Jan 6 *Epifanía* Epiphany
Mar/Apr *Viernes Santo* Good Friday
May 1 *Fiesta del Trabajo* May Day
Aug 15 *La Asunción* Assumption of the Virgin

Oct 12 *Día de la Hispanidad* National Day
Nov 1 *Todos los Santos* All Saints
Dec 6 *Día de la Constitución* Constitution Day
Dec 8 *Inmaculada Concepción*
Dec 25 *Navidad* Christmas Day

phone in your hotel room, as even local calls will be slapped with a heavy surcharge.

You can make international calls from any public pay-phone, but it's cheaper to go to one of the ubiquitous phone centres, or **locutorios**, which specialize in discounted overseas connections. **Calling home from Spain**, you dial ☎00 (Spain's international access code) + your country code + city/area code minus initial zero + number. For **reverse-charge calls**, dial the international operator (☎1008 Europe, ☎1005 rest of the world).

Most European **mobile phones** will work in Spain, though it's worth checking with your provider whether you need to get international access switched on and whether there are any extra charges involved. Even though prices are coming down, it's still expensive to use your own mobile extensively while abroad, and you will pay for receiving incoming calls, for example.

Time

Spain is one hour ahead of the UK, six hours ahead of Eastern Standard Time, nine hours ahead of Pacific Standard Time, eight hours behind Australia, ten hours behind New Zealand, and the same time as South Africa. In Spain, the clocks go forward in the last week in March and back again in the last week in October. It's worth noting, if you're planning to cross the border, that Portugal is an hour behind Spain throughout the year.

Toilets

Public toilets are generally reasonably clean but don't always have any paper. They can very occasionally still be squat-style. They are most commonly referred to and labelled *Los Servicios*, though signs may point you to *baños*, *aseos* or *lavabos*. *Damas* (Ladies) and *Caballeros* (Gentlemen) are the usual distinguishing signs for sex, though you may also see the potentially confusing *Señoras* (Women) and *Señores* (Men).

Tourist information

The Spanish national tourist office, **Turespaña** (Ⓦspain.info), is an excellent source of information when planning your trip. The website is full of ideas, information and searchable databases, and there are links to similar websites of Turespaña offices in your own country.

There are **oficinas de turismo** (tourist offices) in virtually every Spanish town, usually open Monday to Friday 9am to 2pm and 4 to 7pm, Saturday and Sunday 9am to 2pm, but hours vary considerably from place to place. In major cities and coastal resorts the offices tend to remain open all day Saturday and on Sunday morning between April and September.

The information and help available in *oficinas de turismo* also varies: some are very good, and some do little more than hand out a map and ask where you're from. Not all staff speak English, especially in the more rural and out-of-the-way destinations. There's also often more than one information office, especially in bigger towns and cities, where responsibility for local tourism is split between municipal and provincial offices. As a rough rule, the municipal offices are better for specific city information, the provincial offices best for advice about where to go in the region.

Travellers with disabilities

The classic tourist images of Spain – the medieval old towns, winding lanes, the castles and monasteries – don't exactly fill you full of confidence if you're in a wheelchair. However, Spain is changing and facilities are improving rapidly, especially in the more go-ahead, contemporary cities. There are accessible rooms and hotels in all major Spanish cities and resorts and, by law, all new public buildings (including revamped museums and galleries) are required to be fully accessible. Public transport is the main problem, since most local buses and trains are virtually impossible for wheelchairs, though again there are pockets of excellence in Spain. The AVE high-speed train service, for example, is fully accessible, as is every city and sightseeing bus in Barcelona (and large parts of its metro and tram network, too). In many towns and cities, acoustic traffic-light signals and dropped kerbs are common.

Some organizations at home may be able to advise you further about travel to Spain, like the very useful UK-based **Tourism For All** (Ⓦtourismforall .org.uk). Access Travel (Ⓦaccess-travel.co.uk) offers Barcelona city breaks and holidays to five other Spanish resorts, and at the very least, local tourist offices in Spain should also be able to recommend a suitable hotel or taxi company. In Barcelona – the single most clued-up city – there's lots more information on the local tourism website, Ⓦbarcelona turisme.com (click on "Accessible Barcelona").

Madrid

GRAN VÍA AND THE EDIFICIO METRÓPOLIS (P.88)

1

Madrid

Madrid became Spain's capital simply by virtue of its geographical position at the heart of Iberia. When Felipe II moved the seat of government here in 1561, his aim was to create a symbol of the unification and centralization of the country, and a capital from which he could receive the fastest post and communication from every corner of the nation. The site itself had few natural advantages – it is 300km from the sea on a 650-metre-high plateau, freezing in winter, boiling in summer – and it was only the determination of successive rulers to promote a strong central capital that ensured Madrid's survival and development.

Today, Madrid is a vast, predominantly modern city, with a population of some four million and growing. The journey in – through a stream of soulless suburbs and high-rise apartment blocks – isn't pretty, but the streets at the heart of the city are a pleasant surprise, with pockets of medieval buildings and narrow, atmospheric alleys, dotted with the oddest of shops and bars, and interspersed with eighteenth-century Bourbon squares. Compared with the historic cities of Spain – Toledo, Salamanca, Seville, Granada – there may be few sights of great architectural interest, but the monarchs did acquire outstanding picture collections, which formed the basis of the **Prado** museum. This, together with the **Reina Sofía** and the **Thyssen-Bornemisza** museums, state-of-the-art homes to fabulous arrays of modern Spanish painting (including Picasso's *Guernica*) and European and American masters, has made Madrid a top port-of-call on the European art tour.

Aside from these heavyweight cultural attractions, there is a host of smaller museums and palaces which can be almost as rewarding. Sports fans will inevitably be drawn to the Santiago Bernabéu, home to one of the most glamorous and successful clubs in world football, Real Madrid, while a scattering of parks and gardens provide a welcome respite from the hustle and bustle of the city centre.

However, monuments and sights are not really what Madrid is about and as you get to grips with the place, you soon realize that it's the lifestyle of the inhabitants – the **madrileños** – that is the capital's key attraction: hanging out in traditional cafés or summer terrazas, packing the lanes of the Sunday Rastro flea market or playing hard and very late in a thousand **bars**, clubs, discos and *tascas*. Whatever Barcelona or San Sebastián might claim, the Madrid scene, immortalized in the movies of Pedro Almodóvar, remains the most vibrant and fun in the country.

The city centre is also now in better shape than for many years as a result of the impact of a series of urban rehabilitation programmes – funded jointly by the

LA CHATA TAPAS BAR, LA LATINA

Highlights

❶ Monasterio de las Descalzas Reales A fascinating hoard of art treasures hidden away in a convent in the centre of Madrid. **See p.69**

❷ Palacio Real Marvel at the over-the-top opulence in this grandiose former residence of the Spanish monarchs. **See p.71**

❸ El Rastro Take a Sunday stroll from Plaza Mayor through Madrid's shambolic flea market. **See p.72**

❹ A visit to the Prado The Goya, Velázquez and Bosch collections alone make the trip to one of the world's greatest art museums a must. **See p.76**

❺ Guernica See this icon of twentieth-century art set in context at the Reina Sofía. **See p.83**

❻ Real Madrid Watch Real's dazzling roster of big-name players parade their footballing skills at the Santiago Bernabéu stadium. **See p.94**

❼ Tapas Sample the vast array of tasty specialities as you hop from bar to bar in the Huertas or La Latina districts. **See p.105**

❽ A night on the tiles Start late at a bar, then go on to a club and try to make it into the early hours before collapsing over *chocolate con churros*. **See p.113**

HIGHLIGHTS ARE MARKED ON THE MAP ON P.62–63

SHOPS

Adolfo Domínguez	14
Agatha Ruiz de la Prada	3
Alvarez Gómez	11
Cacao Sampaka	4
Caligae	10
Lavinia	1
Mercado Fuencarral	9
Mercado San Antón	13
Pasajes	2
Prénatal	6
Puck	12
Reserva y Cata	7
Sybilla	8
La Tienda Olivarero	5

BARS

Alquímia/Alegoría	32
Aloque	53
La Ardosa	27
Le Cabrera	30
Casa Camacho	21
Castellana 8	16
Finnegans	29
El Jardín Secreto	22
Pepe Botella	18
Teatriz	19
Tupperware	23
El Viajero	48
Vía Lactea	17

CAFÉS, TAPAS BARS & RESTAURANTS

El 26 de Libertad	41		Juana La Loca	50
Al Mounia	37		La Isla del Tesoro	2
Albur	6		El Lateral	13
Alhuzena	1		Melo's	54
Annapurna	15		Momo	43
Baco & Beto	33		La Musa	3
Balear	9		Nina Madrid	4
Bazaar	38		El Pescador	14
El Bocaito	46		Ramón Freixa	
El Buey	44		Madrid	10
Café Barbieri	55		Ribeira do Miño	26
Café Comercial	7		Salvador	40
Café del Espejo	25		Stop Madrid	42
Café Gijón	36		Taberna Angel Sierra	31
Café Oliver	34		Taberna Antonio	
Café del Ruiz	5		Sánchez	51
Los Caracoles			La Tasca Suprema	24
"Casa Amadeo"	52		La Tienda de Vinos	
Casa Mingo	45		(El Comunista)	35
Estay	20		Txirimiri	49
La Giralda	8		El Vegaviana	28
Hevia	11		Viridiana	47
José Luís	12		Zara	39

ACCOMMODATION

Aparto-hotel Rosales	5
Aparto Suites Jardines	
de Sabatini	11
Casón del Tormes	10
Hostal Barrera	16
Hostal Buenos Aires	9
Hostal Residencia	
Don Diego	3
Hostal Santa Bárbara	2
Hostal Sil/Serranos	4
Hostal Zamora	13
Hotel Abalú	8
Hotel Emperador	12
Hotel Galiano	7
Hotel Mora	17
Hotel Orfila	1
Hotel Santo Domingo	14
NH Nacional	18
Petit Palace Ducal	15
Petit Palace Embassy	6

HIGHLIGHTS

1. Monasterio de las Descalzas Reales
2. Palacio Real
3. El Rastro
4. A visit to the Prado
5. Guernica
6. Real Madrid
7. Tapas
8. A night on the tiles

**Map labels:**

PLAZA ALONSO MARTÍNEZ
Alonso Martínez
CALLE GÉNOVA
C. SERRANO ANGUITA
MEJÍA LEQUERICA
C. STA. TERESA
C. ORELLANA
CALLE HERMOSILLA
PASEO CASTELLANA
C. FERNANDO EL SANTO
SERRANO
Museo... ántico
C. FERNANDO VI
C. SAN MATEO
C. REGUERO
Sociedad de Autores
CALLE PELAYO
CALLE FORTUNY
Colón
Museo de Cera
PLAZA LA VILLA DE PARÍS
PLAZA COLÓN
Jardines del Descubrimiento
Serrano
CALLE GOYA
Las Salesas
Palacio de Justicia
Biblioteca Nacional
Museo Arqueológico Nacional
CALLE JORGE JUAN
C. BÁRBARA BRAGANZA
C. CONDE DE XIQUENA
CALLE GRAVINA
PL. CHUECA
AUGUSTO FIGUEROA
Chueca
CALLE PRIM
Teatro Mª Guerrero
CALLE ALMIRANTE
CALLE VILLANUEVA
CALLE RECOLETOS
CALLE CLAUDIO COELLO
CALLE LAGASCA
CALLE VELÁZQUEZ
CHUECA
CALLE SAN MARCOS
C. LIBERTAD
LAS INFANTAS
Casa de las Siete Chimeneas
Cuartel General del Ejército
PASEO RECOLETOS
C. S. OLÓZAGA
SERRANO
C. CONDE ARANDA
SEE "PARQUE DEL RETIRO" MAP for detail
C. COLUMELA
Retiro
Puerta de Alcalá
CALLE ALCALÁ
PL. REY
San José
Edificio Metrópolis
Las travas
CALLE ALCALÁ
Palacio de Linares
Palacio de Cibeles
PLAZA CIBELES
Banco de España
Palacio de Comunicaciones
Parque del Retiro
Círculo de Bellas Artes
CALLE LOS MADRAZO
Banco de España
Museo Naval
CALLE MONTALBÁN
C. JUAN MENA
Museo de Artes Decorativas
Teatro de la Zarzuela
CALLE ZORRILLA
Congreso de los Diputados
PASEO PRADO
Bolsa de Comercio
CALLE MAURA
CALLE ALFONSO XI
Ateneo
Museo Thyssen-Bornemisza
Monumento a los Caídos por España
Salón de Reinos
Cason del Buen Retiro
VENTURA VEGA
PLAZA LAS CORTES
PLAZA CÁNOVAS DEL CASTILLO
PLAZA FELIPE IV
Casa de Lope de Vega
CALLE PRADO
C. FELIPE IV
Real Academia de la Lengua
CALLE CERVANTES
CRUZ ALARCÓN
San Jerónimo el Real
R. Acad. de la Historia
CALLE LOPE VEGA
Las Trinitarias
Museo del Prado
CALLE HUERTAS
C. SANTA MARÍA
CALLE MORATÍN
PLAZA PLATERÍAS MARTÍNEZ
PL. MURILLO
PL. ESPALTER
Antón Martín
CALLE ATOCHA
Cine Doré
C. SAN ILDEFONSO
CALLE SAN PEDRO
La Caixa Forum
Jardines Botánicos
PASEO DUQUE FERNÁN NÚÑEZ
Real Conservatorio de Música
CALLE SANTA ISABEL
Cuesta Moyano
Ministerio de Agricultura
Conv. de Sta. Isabel y agustinas Recoletas
CALLE ARGUMOSA
Centro de Arte Reina Sofía
PLAZA EMPERADOR CARLOS V
Atocha
Estación de Atocha
Estación Sur de Autobuses

1

European Union and local government – in the city's older *barrios* (districts). Improvements have been made to the transport network, with extensions to the metro, the construction of new ring roads, and the excavation of a series of road tunnels designed to bring relief to Madrid's congested streets. The area around the River Manzanares, in particular, has been subject to an ambitious regeneration scheme aimed at turning the river into a focal point for leisure and recreation. The downside to all the

MADRID'S FIESTAS

There are dozens of **fiestas** in Madrid, some of which involve the whole city, others just an individual barrio. The more important dates celebrated in the capital are listed below.

Also well worth checking out are cultural festivals organized by the city council, in particular the **Veranos de la Villa** (July–Sept) and **Festival de Otoño** (Sept–Nov). Many events are free and, in the summer, often open air, taking place in the city's parks and squares. Annual festivals for alternative theatre (Feb), flamenco (Feb), books (end May), dance (April & May), photography (mid-June to mid-July) and jazz (Nov) are also firmly established on the cultural agenda. Full programmes are published in the monthly what's-on magazine *esMadrid*, free from any of the tourist offices (see p.99) and from the city's tourist website (𝕨esmadrid.com).

JANUARY
5: Cabalgata de los Reyes To celebrate the arrival of the gift-bearing Three Kings there is a hugely popular evening procession through the city centre in which children are showered with sweets. It's held on the evening before presents are traditionally exchanged in Spain.

FEBRUARY
Week before Lent: Carnaval An excuse for a lot of partying and fancy-dress parades, especially in the gay zone around Chueca. The end of Carnaval is marked by the bizarre and entertaining parade, El Entierro de la Sardina (The Burial of the Sardine), on the Paseo de la Florida.

MARCH/APRIL
Semana Santa (Holy Week) Celebrated with a series of solemn processions around Madrid, although for a more impressive backdrop head for Toledo (routes and times of processions are available from tourist offices).

MAY
2: Fiesta del Dos de Mayo Held in Malasaña and elsewhere in Madrid. Bands and partying around the Plaza Dos de Mayo, though a bit low-key in recent years.
15: Fiestas de San Isidro Festivities to honour Madrid's patron saint are spread a week either side of this date, and are among the country's biggest festivals. The fiestas also herald the start of the bullfighting season.

JUNE/JULY
End June/beginning July: La Semana del Orgullo Gay (Gay Pride Week) Week-long party throughout Chueca, culminating in a massive carnival-style parade that brings the city centre to a standstill.

AUGUST
6–15: Castizo (Traditional fiestas of San Cayetano, San Lorenzo and La Virgen de la Paloma) in La Latina and Lavapiés *barrios*. Much of the activity – processions, dancing and live music – takes place around Calle Toledo, the Plaza de la Paja and the Jardines de las Vistillas.

DECEMBER
25: Navidad During Christmas, Plaza Mayor is filled with stalls selling festive decorations and displaying a large model of a Nativity scene. El Corte Inglés, at the bottom of c/Preciados, has an all-singing, all-dancing clockwork Christmas scene (Cortylandia), which plays at certain times of the day to the delight of assembled children.
31: Nochevieja (New Year's Eve) is celebrated at bars, restaurants and parties all over the city. Puerta del Sol is the customary place to gather, waiting for the strokes of the clock – it is traditional to swallow a grape on each stroke to bring good luck in the coming year.

redevelopment is that the city still appears to spend much of the time belly-up because of the interminable roadworks and civil-engineering projects.

A brief history

Madrid's history dates back to the ninth century when **Muslims** established a defensive outpost on the escarpment above the River Manzanares which later became known as "Mayrit" – the place of many springs.

It remained a relatively insignificant backwater until 1561 when Felipe II designated the city his **imperial capital** by virtue of its position at the heart of the recently unified Spain. The cramped street plan in the city centre provides a clue as to what the city would have been like at this time and the narrow alleys around the Plaza Mayor are still among Madrid's liveliest and most atmospheric. With the **Bourbons** replacing the Habsburgs at the start of the eighteenth century, a touch of French style, including the sumptuous Palacio Real, was introduced into the capital by Felipe V.

It was the "King-Mayor" **Carlos III**, however, who tried to convert the city into a home worthy of the monarchy after he ascended to the throne in 1759, ordering the streets to be cleaned, sewers and lighting to be installed and work to begin on the Prado museum complex.

The early **nineteenth century** brought invasion and turmoil to Spain as Napoleon established his brother Joseph (or José to Spaniards) on the throne. Madrid, however, continued to flourish, gaining some very attractive buildings and squares, including the Plaza de Oriente and Plaza de Santa Ana. With the onset of the **twentieth century**, the capital became the hotbed of the political and intellectual discussions that divided the country; *tertulias* (political/philosophical discussion circles) sprang up in cafés across the city (some of them are still going) as the country entered the turbulent years of the end of the monarchy and the foundation of the Second Republic.

Madrid was a Republican stronghold during the **Civil War**, with fierce battles raging around the capital as Franco's troops laid siege to the city, eventually taking control in 1939. The Civil War, of course, caused untold damage, and led to forty years of isolation. The city's great spread to **suburbia** began during the Franco era and it has continued unabated ever since, with unbridled property speculation taking its toll on the green spaces that surround the capital. Franco also extended the city northwards along the spinal route of the Paseo de la Castellana, to accommodate his ministers and minions during development extravaganzas of the 1950s and 1960s.

The Spanish capital has changed immeasurably, however, in the three decades since Franco's death, initially guided by a poet-mayor, the late **Tierno Galván**. His efforts

---

ORIENTATION

Madrid's layout is fairly straightforward. At the city's heart is the large oval-shaped plaza **Puerta del Sol** (often referred to as just "Sol"). Around it lie the oldest parts of Madrid, neatly bordered to the west by the **River Manzanares**, to the east by the park of **El Retiro** and to the north by the city's great thoroughfare, the **Gran Vía**.

Madrid's main sights occupy a compact area between the **Palacio Real** and the gardens of **El Retiro**. The great trio of museums – the **Prado**, **Thyssen-Bornemisza** and **Reina Sofía** – lie in a "golden triangle" just west of El Retiro and close to Paseo del Prado. Over towards the river are the oldest parts of the city, centred on the gorgeous, arcaded **Plaza Mayor**, an area known as **Madrid de los Austrias** after the Habsburg monarchs who built it.

To get a feel for the city you should experience the contrasting character and life of the various neighbourhoods (*barrios*). The most central and rewarding of these are the areas around **Plaza de Santa Ana and Calle Huertas**, east of Sol; **La Latina and Lavapiés**, south of Plaza Mayor, where the Sunday market, El Rastro, takes place; and **Malasaña and Chueca**, north of Gran Vía. By happy circumstance, these *barrios* have some of Madrid's finest concentrations of tapas bars and restaurants.

1

– the creation of parks and renovation of public spaces and public life – left an enduring legacy, and were a vital ingredient of the *movida madrileña* "the happening Madrid" with which the city broke through in the 1980s. Since the early 1990s, the centre-right Partido Popular has been in control, bringing with it a more restrictive attitude towards bar and club licensing. Unfortunately, there has also been a simultaneous tendency towards homogenization with the rest of Europe as franchised fast-food joints and coffee bars spring up all over the place. Nevertheless, in making the transition from provincial backwater to major European capital, Madrid has still managed to preserve its own stylish and quirky identity.

Madrid de los Austrias

Madrid de los Austrias (Habsburg Madrid) was a mix of formal planning – at its most impressive in the expansive and theatrical Plaza Mayor – and areas of shanty town development, thrown up as the new capital gained an urban population. The central area of old Madrid still reflects both characteristics, with its twisting grid of streets, alleyways and steps, and its Flemish-inspired architecture of red brick and grey stone, slate-tiled towers and Renaissance doorways.

Puerta del Sol

Ⓜ Sol

The obvious starting point for exploring Madrid de los Austrias (and most other areas of the centre) is the **Puerta del Sol**. This square marks the epicentre of the city – and, indeed, of Spain. It is from this point that all distances are measured, and here that six of Spain's *Rutas Nacionales* officially begin. On the pavement outside the clocktower building on the south side of the square, an inconspicuous stone slab shows **Kilometre Zero**.

The square, which conceals a new subterreanean transport hub, is a popular meeting place, especially by the statue of a bear pawing a *madroño* (strawberry tree)

MADRID'S FREEBIES

Free entrance can be gained to many of Madrid's premier attractions. Sites classed as Patrimonio Nacional, such as the Palacio Real, the Convento de la Encarnación, El Pardo and the Monasterio de las Descalzas, are free to EU citizens at some point on Wednesdays (bring your passport). Museums run by Madrid City Council, including the Museo de los Orígenes, La Ermita de San Antonio, the Templo de Debod and the Museo de Arte Contemporaneo, do not charge admission. Most museums are free for under-18s, and give substantial discounts to retirees and students (bring ID in all cases). In addition, many museums and sights that normally charge entry set aside certain times when entrance is free, and nearly all are free on World Heritage Day (18 April), International Museum Day (May 18), the Día de Hispanidad (Oct 12) and Día de la Constitución (Dec 6). The following are free at these times:

Centro de Arte Reina Sofía Mon–Fri 7–9pm, Sat 2.30–9pm & Sun 10am–2.30pm.
Museo de América Sun 10am–3pm.
Museo Arqueológico Nacional Tues–Sat 9.30am–8pm, Sun 9.30am–3pm (while undergoing refurbishment).
Museo de Artes Decorativas Sun 10am–3pm.
Museo Cerralbo Sat 2–3pm & Sun 10am–3pm.
Museo Lázaro Galdiano Sun 10am–4pm.
Museo del Prado Tues–Sat 6–8pm, Sun 5–8pm, Nov 19 & May 2.
Museo del Romanticismo Sat 2–8.30pm.
Museo Sorolla Sun 10am–3pm.
Museo del Traje Sat 2.30–7pm, Sun 10am–3pm.
Real Academia de Bellas Artes Wed 9am–3pm.

– the city's emblem – at the start of Calle Alcalá and the equestrian bronze of King Carlos III. Statues apart, there's little of note in the square apart from the **Casa de Correos**, built in 1766, originally the city's post office and now home to the main offices of the Madrid regional government. At New Year, the square is packed with people waiting for the clock that crowns the neoclassical facade to chime midnight. Sol's main business, however, is shopping, with giant branches of the **department stores** El Corte Inglés and the French chain FNAC in Calle Preciados, at the top end of the square.

Plaza Mayor
Ⓜ Sol

Follow Calle Mayor (the "Main Street" of the medieval city) west from the Puerta del Sol and you could easily walk right past Madrid's most important landmark: **Plaza Mayor**. Set back from the street and entered by stepped passageways, it appears all the more grand in its continuous sweep of arcaded buildings. It was planned by Felipe II – the monarch who made Madrid the capital – as the public meeting place of the city, and was finished thirty years later in 1619 during the reign of Felipe III, who sits astride the stallion in the central statue. The architect was Juan Gómez de Mora, responsible for many of the civic and royal buildings in this quarter.

The square, with its hundreds of balconies, was designed as a theatre for public events, and it has served this function throughout its history. It was the scene of the Inquisition's *autos-da-fé* (trials of faith) and the executions that followed; kings were crowned here; festivals and demonstrations passed through; plays by Lope de Vega and others received their first performances; bulls were fought; and gossip was spread. The more important of the events would be watched by royalty from their apartments in the central **Casa Panadería**, a palace named after the bakery that it replaced. It was rebuilt after a fire in 1692 and subsequently decorated with frescoes. However, the present delightful, and highly kitsch, array of allegorical figures that adorn the facade was only added in 1992. Today, the palace houses municipal offices and a tourist office (daily 9.30am–8.30pm).

Nowadays, Plaza Mayor is primarily a tourist haunt, full of expensive outdoor cafés and restaurants (best stick to a drink), buskers and caricaturists. However, an air of grandeur clings to the plaza, which still performs public functions. In the summer months and during the major *madrileño* fiestas, it becomes an outdoor **theatre** and **music stage**; and in the winter, just before Christmas, it becomes a **bazaar** for festive decorations and religious regalia. Every Sunday, too, stamp and coin sellers set up their stalls.

Mercado de San Miguel

Set back from the road, near the entrance to the Plaza Mayor, is the splendid decorative ironwork of the **Mercado de San Miguel**. Built in 1916 it was formerly one of the old-style food markets scattered throughout the city, but it has now been refurbished and converted into a stylish tourist-oriented emporium complete with oyster and champagne bar.

The alley taverns

In the alleys just below the square, such as c/Cuchilleros and c/Cava de San Miguel, are some of the city's oldest *mesones*, or **taverns**. Have a drink in these in the early evening and you are likely to be serenaded by passing *tunas* – musicians and singers dressed in traditional costume of knickerbockers and waistcoats who wander around town playing and passing the hat. These men-only troupes are attached to various faculties of the university and are usually students supplementing their grants.

1

A WALKING TOUR OF MADRID DE LOS AUSTRIAS

To get a feel for what the old city might have been like when it was first designated Spanish capital in the sixteenth century take a stroll around the area known as **Madrid de los Austrias**.

Start off at **Plaza de la Villa**, probably the oldest square in the city and home to some of its most ancient buildings, including the fifteenth-century Torre de los Lujanes. Then take the narrow, elbow-shaped Calle del Codo out of the northeastern corner of the plaza, passing the Convento de los Carboneras where the nuns still sell traditional cakes and biscuits, continuing downhill to the tranquil backstreet Calle San Justo. If you bear left past the splendid **Baroque Basílica de San Miguel** you will emerge on to bustling Calle Segovia, one of the ancient entrances into the old city. From here wander down Cava Baja with its succession of traditional *tascas*, former coaching inns and stylish tapas bars. You will end up in **Plaza Humilladeros**, buzzing with people sitting at the terrace bar in the middle of the square and flanked by the elegant Iglesia de San Andrés and the mansion that is now home to the Museo de los Orígenes. Walk past the splendid domed church and turn right into **Plaza de la Paja**, one of the old market squares that once littered the medieval city. Wealthy families would have lived in the mansions that line the square, each with a small garden similar to the peaceful Jardín de Anglona situated at the bottom of the plaza.

Take a left along Calle Príncipe de Anglona and shady Calle Nuncio to rejoin Calle Segovia and bear left up **Calle Cuchilleros**, named after the knife-makers who once plied their trade on the street. Here you will pass the renowned restaurant **Botín**, a *madrileño* institution that lays claim to be the oldest eating establishment in the world, followed by a string of cellar bars offering flamenco and traditional tapas. Don't miss the beautiful wrought-iron work of the **Mercado de San Miguel** before finishing up with a circuit of the arcaded splendour of the **Plaza Mayor**.

Plaza de la Villa and around

West along c/Mayor, towards the Palacio Real, is **Plaza de la Villa**, an example of three centuries of Spanish architectural development. Its oldest surviving building is the eye-catching fifteenth-century **Torre de los Lujanes**, a fine Mudéjar (Moors working under Christian rule) tower, where Francis I of France is said to have been imprisoned in 1525 after his capture at the Battle of Pavia in Italy. Opposite is the old town hall, the **ayuntamiento** (**Casa de la Villa**), begun in the seventeenth century, but remodelled in Baroque style (tours in Spanish only every Mon at 5pm; free; sign up in the tourist office in Plaza Mayor). Finally, fronting the square is the **Casa de Cisneros**, built by a nephew of Cardinal Cisneros in the sixteenth-century Plateresque ("Silversmith") style.

Basílica de San Miguel

C/San Justo 4 • July–Sept 14 Mon–Sat 9.45am–1pm & 6–9pm, Sun 9.40am–1.40pm & 6.30–9pm; Sept 15–June 30 Mon–Sat 9.45am–2pm & 5.30–9pm, Sun 9.40am–2.40pm & 6–9pm • Free • Ⓜ La Latina

Just around the corner from Plaza de la Villa is the flamboyant **Basílica de San Miguel**. Designed by Italian architects at the end of the seventeenth century, the Basílica is one of the few examples of a full-blown Baroque church in Madrid.

Ópera and the Palacio Real

Dominated by the imposing **Palacio Real** and the elegant Plaza de Oriente, **Ópera** is one of the most pleasant and relaxed *barrios* in the city. The area contains the lavishly restored **Teatro Real**, the tranquil gardens of the **Campo del Moro** and the **city cathedral**, while the two unobtrusive monastery complexes of **La Encarnación** and **Las Descalzas Reales** conceal an astounding array of treasures.

San Ginés

C/Arenal 13 • Daily 8.15am–1pm & 6–9pm • Free • ⓜ Sol/Ópera

Situated midway between Sol and Ópera along c/Arenal is the ancient church of **San Ginés**. Of Mozarabic origin (built by Christians under Moorish rule), it was completely reconstructed in the seventeenth century. There is an El Greco canvas of the moneychangers being chased from the temple on show in the **Capilla del Cristo** (on show Mon 12.30pm). Alongside, in somewhat uneasy juxtaposition, stands a cult temple of the twentieth century, the *Joy Madrid* disco, and, behind it, the **Chocolatería San Ginés**, a Madrid institution, which at one time catered for the early-rising worker but now churns out *chocolate con churros* for the late nightclub crowd (see box, p.115).

Descalzas Reales

Pl. de las Descalzas Reales 3 • Guided tours (some in English) Tues–Thurs & Sat 10.30am–12.30pm & 4–5.30pm, Fri 10.30am–12.30pm, Sun & some public hols 11am–1.30pm • €5, joint ticket with Convento de la Encarnación €6, valid for a week, free for EU citizens on Wed • ⓦ patrimonionacional.es • ⓜ Sol/Callao

A couple of blocks north of San Ginés is one of the hidden treasures of Madrid, the **Monasterio de las Descalzas Reales**. It was founded in 1557 by Juana de Austria, daughter of the Emperor Carlos V, sister of Felipe II, and, at the age of 19, already the widow of Prince Don Juan of Portugal. In her wake came a succession of titled ladies (*Descalzas Reales* means "Barefoot Royals"), who brought fame and, above all, fortune to the convent, which is unbelievably rich, though beautiful and tranquil, too. It is still in use, with shoeless nuns tending patches of vegetable garden.

Whistle-stop **guided tours** conduct visitors through the cloisters and up an incredibly elaborate stairway to a series of chambers packed with art and treasures of every kind. The **former dormitories** are perhaps the most outstanding feature, decorated with a series of Flemish tapestries based on designs by Rubens and a striking portrait of St Francis by Zurbarán. These were the sleeping quarters for all the nuns, including St Teresa of Ávila for a time, although the empress María of Germany preferred a little more privacy and endowed the convent with her own luxurious private chambers. The other highlight of the tour is the **Joyería** (Treasury), piled high with jewels and relics of uncertain provenance. The nuns kept no records of their gifts, so no one is quite sure what many of the things are – there is a bizarre cross-sectional model of Christ – nor which bones came from which saint. Whatever the case, it's an exceptional hoard.

Convento de la Encarnación

Pl. de la Encarnación • Guided tours (usually in Spanish only) Tues–Thurs & Sat 10.30am–12.45pm & 4–5.45pm, Fri 10.30am–12.45pm, Sun & some public hols 11am–1.45pm • €3.60, joint ticket with the Monasterio de las Descalzas €6, valid for a week, free for EU citizens on Wed; guided tours only • ⓦ patrimonionacional.es • ⓜ Ópera

Just to the north of Plaza de Oriente is the **Convento de la Encarnación**. This was founded a few years after Juana's convent, by Margarita, wife of Felipe III, though it was substantially rebuilt towards the end of the eighteenth century. It houses an extensive but somewhat disappointing collection of seventeenth-century Spanish art, and a wonderfully bizarre library-like reliquary, reputed to be one of the most important in the Catholic world. The most famous relic housed here is a small glass bulb said to contain the blood of the fourth-century doctor martyr, St Pantaleon, whose blood supposedly liquefies at midnight every July 26 (the eve of his feast day). The tour ends with a visit to the Baroque-style church featuring a beautifully frescoed ceiling.

1

Teatro Real

Pl. de Isabel II • Tours Mon & Wed–Fri 10.30am–1pm, Sat & Sun 11am–1.30pm; closed mid-July to mid-Sept; • €5 (under-7s free); tickets on sale from the box office 10am–1pm • Info and reservations ☎ 915 160 696, ⓦ teatro-real.com • Ⓜ Ópera

West of Sol, c/Arenal leads to the **Teatro Real**, or **Ópera**, which gives this area its name. Built in the mid-nineteenth century, it almost sank a few decades later as a result of subsidence caused by underground canals and was forced to close in 1925; it finally reopened in 1997 after an epic ten-year refurbishment that ended up costing a mind-boggling €150 million. The interior is suitably lavish and merits a visit in its own right, and it makes a truly magnificent setting for opera, ballet and classical concerts (see p.119).

Plaza de Oriente

The opera house is separated from the Palacio Real by the **Plaza de Oriente**, one of the most elegant and agreeable open spaces in Madrid and used in the bad old days by Franco as the venue for his public addresses; small groups of neo-Fascists still gather here on the anniversary of his death on November 21. One of the square's main attractions – and the focus of its life – is the elegant *Café del Oriente*, whose summer terraza is one of the stations of Madrid nightlife. The café (which is also a prestigious restaurant) looks as traditional as any in the city but was in fact opened in the 1980s by a priest, Padre Lezama, who ploughs his profits into various charitable schemes.

The café apart, the dominant features of Plaza de Oriente are **statues**: 44 of them, depicting Spanish kings and queens, which were originally designed to go on the palace facade but found to be too heavy (some say too ugly) for the roof to support. The **statue of Felipe IV** on horseback, in the centre of the square, clearly belongs on a different plane; it was based on designs by Velázquez, and Galileo is said to have helped with the calculations to make it balance.

Catedral Nuestra Señora de la Almudena

C/Bailén 8–10 • Daily: 9am–8.30pm; not open for visits during Mass: Mon–Sat 10am, noon, 6pm & 7pm, Sun & hols 10.30am, noon, 1.30pm, 6 & 7pm • Free • ⓦ museocatedral.archimadrid.es • **Museum** Mon–Sat 10am–2.30pm • €6, €4 for Madrid residents and students • **Crypt** daily 10am–8pm • Ⓜ Ópera

Facing the Palacio Real to the south, across the shadeless Plaza de la Armería, is Madrid's cathedral, **Nuestra Señora de la Almudena**. Planned centuries ago, bombed out in the Civil War, worked upon at intervals since, and plagued by lack of funds, it was eventually opened for business in 1993 by Pope John Paul II. The building's bulky Neoclassical facade was designed to match the Palacio Real opposite, while its cold neo-Gothic interior is largely uninspiring.

To one side of the main facade is a small **museum** containing some of the cathedral's treasures, though the main reason to visit is to gain access to the dome from where you can enjoy some fantastic views over the city and out towards the Sierra. The entrance to the **crypt** with its forest of columns and dimly lit chapels is to be found on c/Mayor.

The Moorish wall and Jardines de las Vistillas

C/Bailén crosses c/Segovia on a high **viaduct** (now lined with panes of reinforced glass to prevent once-common suicide attempts); this was constructed as a royal route from the palace to the church of San Francisco el Grande, avoiding the rabble and river that flowed below. Close by is a patch of **Moorish wall** (*muralla árabe*) from the medieval fortress here, which the original royal palace replaced. Across the aqueduct, the **Jardines de las Vistillas** ("Gardens of the Views") beckon, with their summer terrazas looking out across the river and towards the distant Sierra.

Palacio Real

C/Bailén • April–Sept Mon–Sat 9am–6pm, Sun & hols 9am–3pm; Oct–March Mon–Sat 10am–5pm, Sun & hols 10am–2pm; closed occasionally for state visits • €10; free for EU citizens Oct–March: Wed & Thurs 3–5pm, April–Sept: 4–6pm • ⓦ patrimonionacional.es • ⓜ Ópera

The **Palacio Real**, or Royal Palace, scores high on statistics. It claims more rooms than any other European palace; a library with one of the biggest collections of books, manuscripts, maps and musical scores in the world; and an armoury with an unrivalled assortment of weapons dating back to the fifteenth century. If you're around on the first Wednesday of the month (except July & Aug) between 11am and 2pm, look out for the **changing of the guard** outside the palace, a tradition that has recently been revived.

Guided tours in various languages are available, but a more relaxing option is to hire an audio-guide (€4) and make your own way through the luxurious royal apartments, the Royal Armoury Museum and the Royal Pharmacy. This will give you more time to appreciate the extraordinary opulence: acres of Flemish and Spanish tapestries, endless Rococo decoration, bejewelled clocks, and pompous portraits of the monarchs.

The palace also houses an impressive exhibition space, the **Galería de Pinturas**, which displays work by Velázquez, Caravaggio and Goya, among others, and also hosts temporary **exhibitions**.

The palace

The Habsburgs' original palace burnt down on Christmas Day, 1734. Its replacement, the current building, was based on drawings made by Bernini for the Louvre. It was constructed in the mid-eighteenth century and was the principal royal residence from then until Alfonso XIII went into exile in 1931; both Joseph Bonaparte and the Duke of Wellington also lived here briefly. The present royal family inhabits a considerably more modest residence on the western outskirts of the city, using the Palacio Real on state occasions only.

The **Salón del Trono** (Throne Room) is the highlight for most visitors, containing the thrones installed for Juan Carlos and Sofía, the current monarchs, as well as the splendid ceiling by Tiepolo, a giant fresco representing the glory of Spain – an extraordinary achievement for an artist by then in his seventies. Look out, too, for the marvellous **Sala de Porcelana** (Porcelain Room) and the incredible oriental-style **Salón de Gasparini**.

The outbuildings and annexes

The palace outbuildings and annexes include the recently refurbished **Armería Real**, a huge room full of guns, swords and armour, with such curiosities as the suit of armour worn by Carlos V in his equestrian portrait by Titian in the Prado. Especially fascinating are the complete sets of armour, with all the original spare parts and gadgets for making adjustments. There is also an eighteenth-century **Farmacia**, a curious mixture of alchemist's den and laboratory, whose walls are lined with jars labelled for various remedies. The **Biblioteca Real** (Royal Library) can now only be visited by prior arrangement for research purposes.

The gardens

Jardines de Sabatini April–Sept 9am–10pm; Oct–March 9am–9pm Campo del Moro April–Sept daily 10am–8pm; Oct–March daily 10am–6pm; occasionally closed for state visits

Immediately north of the palace, the **Jardines de Sabatini** provide a shady retreat and venue for summer concerts, while to the rear the larger, and far more beautiful, **Campo del Moro** (access only from the far west side, off the Paseo de la Virgen del Puerto) is an English-style garden with shady paths, monumental fountains and a splendid view of the western facade of the palace.

1

South of Plaza Mayor

The areas south of Plaza Mayor have traditionally been tough, working-class districts, with tenement buildings thrown up to accommodate the expansion of the population in the eighteenth and nineteenth centuries. In many places, these old houses survive, huddled together in narrow streets, but the character of **La Latina** and **Lavapiés** has changed as their inhabitants, and the districts themselves, have become younger, more fashionable and more cosmopolitan. The streets of Cava Baja and Cava Alta in La Latina, for example, include some of the city's most popular bars and restaurants. These are attractive *barrios* to explore, particularly for bar-hopping or during the Sunday-morning flea market, **El Rastro**, which takes place along and around the Ribera de Curtidores (Ⓜ La Latina/Tirso de Molina).

Around La Latina

La Latina is a short walk south from Plaza de la Villa and, if you're exploring Madrid de los Austrias, it's a natural continuation, as some of the squares, streets and churches here date back to the early Habsburg period. One of the most attractive pockets is around **Plaza de la Paja**, a delightful square behind the large church of **San Andrés**, and once home to one of the city's medieval markets. In summer, there are a couple of terrazas here, tucked well away from the traffic.

Iglesia de San Andrés, Capilla del Obispo and Capilla de San Isidro

Pl. de San Andrés & Pl. de la Paja **Iglesia de San Andrés** Mon–Thurs & Sat 8am–1pm & 6–8pm, Fri 6–8pm, Sun 9am–2pm • Free
Capilla del Obispo Tues 9.30am–12.30pm, Thurs 4–4.45pm (reservation only ☎ 915 592 874) • €2 • Ⓦ museocatedral
.archimadrid.es • Ⓜ La Latina

The **Iglesia de San Andrés** and the **Capilla de San Isidro** can be reached from Plaza de San Andrés. Inside is a beautifully sculpted dome depicting angels laden with fruit and a red-marble backdrop fronted by black columns and sculptures of saints. The chapel of San Isidro was built in the mid-seventeenth century to hold the remains of Madrid's patron saint (since moved to the Iglesia de San Isidro). The adjoining Gothic **Capilla del Obispo** (entrance on Plaza de la Paja), with its impressive polychromed altarpiece and alabaster tombs, has only recently been re-opened following a forty-year restoration saga.

EL RASTRO

Madrid's flea market, **El Rastro**, is as much a part of the city's weekend ritual as a Mass or a *paseo*. This gargantuan, thriving shambles of a street market sprawls south from Metro La Latina to the Ronda de Toledo, especially along Ribera de Curtidores. Through it, crowds flood between 10am and 3pm every Sunday – and increasingly on Fridays, Saturdays and public holidays, too. On offer is just about anything you might – or more likely might not – need, from secondhand clothes and military-surplus items to caged birds and antiques.

Some of the goods – broken telephone dials, plastic shampoo bottles half-full of something that may or may not be the original contents – are so far gone that you can't imagine any of them ever selling. Other items may be quite valuable, but on the whole it's the stuff of markets around the world you'll find here: pseudo-designer clothes, bags and T-shirts. Don't expect to find fabulous bargains, or the hidden Old Masters of popular myth: the serious antique trade has mostly moved off the streets and into the surrounding shops, while the real junk is now found only on the fringes. Nonetheless, the atmosphere of El Rastro is always enjoyable, and the bars around these streets are as good as any in the city. One warning: keep a close eye on your bags, pockets, cameras (best left at the hotel) and jewellery. The Rastro rings up a fair percentage of Madrid's tourist thefts.

Museo de los Orígenes

Pl. San Andrés 2 • Aug: Tues–Fri 9.30am–2.30pm, Sat & Sun 10am–2pm; Sept–July: Tues–Fri 9.30am–8pm, Sat & Sun 10am–2pm • Free • ⓦ munimadrid.es/museodelosorigenes • Ⓜ La Latina

Alongside the church of San Andrés is one of the city's newer museums, the **Museo de los Orígenes,** (formerly known as the Museo de San Isidro), housed in a sixteenth-century mansion owned by the counts of Paredes and supposedly once the home of Madrid's patron saint. The city's **archeological collection**, which consists of relics from the earliest settlements along the River Manzanares and nearby Roman villas, is in the basement. The rest of the museum is given over to exhibits on the later history of the city and also **San Isidro** and his miraculous activities, including the well from which he is said to have rescued his own son.

San Francisco el Grande

Pl. de San Francisco 11 • Aug Tues–Sun 11am–12.30pm & 5–7.30pm; rest of year Tues–Fri 11am–12.30pm & 4–6.30pm, Sat & Sun 11am–1.30pm (tickets on sale 10.30am–12.30pm & 5–7pm); €3 with guided tour • Ⓜ La Latina

A couple of minutes' walk southwest of the Museo de los Orígenes down the hill is one of Madrid's grandest, richest and most elaborate churches, **San Francisco el Grande**. Built towards the end of the eighteenth century as part of Carlos III's renovations of the city, it has a dome even larger than that of St Paul's in London. The interior, which you can only visit with a guided tour, contains paintings by, among others, Goya and Zurbarán, and some magnificent frescoes by Bayeu.

Iglesia de San Isidro

C/Toledo 37 • Mon–Sat 7.45am–1pm & 6–8.45pm, Sun & hols 8.30am–2pm & 6–8.30pm • Ⓜ La Latina

The vast **Iglesia de San Isidro** was originally the centre of the Jesuit Order in Spain. After Carlos III fell out with the Order in 1767, he redesigned the interior and dedicated it to the city's patron, whose remains are entombed within. The church acted as the city's cathedral prior to the completion of the Almudena by the Palacio Real, but relics and altarpiece aside, its chief attribute is its size.

Next door is the **Instituto Real**, a school that has been in existence considerably longer than the church and counts among its former pupils such literary notables as Calderón de la Barca, Lope de Vega, Quevedo and Pío Baroja.

Puerta de Toledo

Ⓜ Puerta de Toledo

If you proceed south to the end of Ribera de Curtidores, whose antique shops (some, these days, extremely upmarket) stay open all week, you'll see a large arch, the **Puerta de Toledo**, at one end of the Ronda de Toledo. The only surviving relation to the Puerta de Alcalá in the Plaza de la Independencia, this was built originally as a triumphal arch to honour the conquering Napoleon. After his defeat in the Peninsular Wars, it became a symbol of the city's freedom. Just in front of the arch, the Mercado Puerta de Toledo, once the site of the city's fish market, is set to be converted into a teaching centre for one of the local universities.

Estadio Vicente Calderón

Paseo Virgen del Puerto 67 • ☎ 913 664 707 • ⓦ clubatleticodemadrid.com • Match tickets start at around €30 • Tickets ☎ 902 530 500 and via the website • **Club shop** Mon–Fri 10am–2pm & 5–8pm, Sat & Sun 10am–2pm, match days 11am–45min before kickoff • **Museum** Tues–Sun 11am–7pm • €10 with guided tour, children 4–12 €5 • Ⓜ Pirámides

Alongside the newly regenerated River Manzanares, is the **Estadio Vicente Calderón**, home to Atlético Madrid, arch-rivals of the more glamorous Real (see p.95). The 54,000-capacity stadium houses a decent **club shop** and a **museum** detailing the history and achievements of the club.

1

Lavapiés

A good point to start exploring the *barrio* of **Lavapiés** is the Plaza Tirso de Molina (Ⓜ Tirso de Molina). From here, you can follow c/Mesón de Paredes, stopping for a drink at *Taberna Antonio Sánchez* at no. 13, past rows of wholesale shops to **La Corrala**, on the corner of c/Sombrerete. This is one of many traditional *corrales* – tenement blocks – in the quarter, built with balconied apartments opening onto a central patio. Plays, especially farces and *zarzuelas* (a kind of operetta), used to be performed regularly in Spanish *corrales*, and the open space here usually hosts a few performances in the summer. It has been sympathetically renovated and declared a national monument.

From Metro Lavapiés, you can take **c/Argumosa** towards the Centro de Arte Reina Sofía. Don't miss out on the opportunity to sample some of the excellent local bars on this pleasant tree-lined street while you're here.

Cine Doré

C/Santa Isabel 3 • Closed Mon • Films €2.50 • ☎ 913 691 125 • Ⓜ Antón Martín

To the north of the quarter is the **Cine Doré**, the oldest cinema in Madrid, dating from 1922, with a late Modernist/Art Nouveau facade. It has been converted to house the Filmoteca Nacional, an art-film centre (see p.119) with bargain prices and a pleasant and inexpensive **café/restaurant** (Tues–Sun 5pm–12.45am).

East of Sol: Plaza de Santa Ana to Plaza de la Cibeles

The **Plaza de Santa Ana/Huertas** area lies at the heart of a triangle, bordered to the east by the Paseo del Prado, to the north by c/Alcalá and along the south by c/Atocha, with the Puerta del Sol at the western tip. The city reached this district after expanding beyond the Palacio Real and the Plaza Mayor, so the buildings date predominantly from the nineteenth century. Many of them have literary associations: there are streets named after Cervantes and Lope de Vega (where one lived and the other died), and the *barrio* is host to the Atheneum club, Círculo de Bellas Artes (Fine Arts Institute), Teatro Español and the Congreso de los Diputados (parliament). Just to the north, there is also an important museum, the **Real Academia de Bellas Artes de San Fernando**.

For most visitors, though, the major attraction is that this district holds some of the best and most beautiful **bars** and **tascas** in the city. They are concentrated particularly around Plaza de Santa Ana, which – following a rather seedy period – has been smartened up by the council.

Plaza de Santa Ana and around

Ⓜ Sol/Sevilla

The bars around **Plaza de Santa Ana** really are sights in themselves. On the square itself, the dark-panelled *Cervecería Alemana* was a firm favourite of Hemingway's and has hardly changed since the turn of the twentieth century. Opposite, *La Suiza* café is a great place for a coffee and a cake while watching the world go by. Flanking one side of the plaza is the elegant facade of the emblematic *ME Madrid* hotel, once a favourite of bullfighters and now the designer showpiece for the Sol-Meliá chain.

Viva Madrid, on the northeast corner at c/Manuel Fernández y González 7, should be another port of call, if only to admire the fabulous tilework, original zinc bar and a ceiling supported by wooden caryatids. One block east from here is **c/Echegaray**, home to a string of great bars and restaurants, including the wonderfully delapidated sherry bar, *La Venencia*, at no. 7.

Huertas

The area around pedestrianized **c/Huertas** itself is workaday enough – sleepy by day but buzzing by night – and, again, packed with bars. North of here, and parallel, are two streets named in honour of the greatest figures of Spain's seventeenth-century literary golden age, Cervantes and Lope de Vega. Bitter rivals in life, both are probably spinning in their graves now, since Cervantes is interred in the **Convento de las Trinitarias** on the street named after Lope de Vega, while the latter's house, the **Casa de Lope de Vega**, finds itself on c/Cervantes.

Casa de Lope de Vega

C/Cervantes 11 • Tues–Sun 9.30am–3pm; closed mid-July to mid-Aug • Free • Guided tours: wait for a group to be formed; ring ☎ 914 299 216 to reserve a tour in English • Ⓜ Antón Martín

The charming little **Casa de Lope de Vega** provides a fascinating reconstruction of life in seventeenth-century Madrid; ring the bell and you will be taken on a tour of the golden age dramatist's former home, which includes a delightful little patio garden.

El Congreso

C/de San Jerónimo s/n • Tours Sat every 30min, 10.30am–12.30pm; closed Aug; passport essential • Ⓦ congreso.es • Ⓜ Sevilla

El Congreso de Los Diputados is an unprepossessing nineteenth-century building where the Congress (the lower house) meets. Sessions can be visited by appointment only, though anyone can turn up for the tour on Saturday mornings. You're shown, among other things, the bullet holes left by Colonel Tejero and his Guardia Civil associates in the abortive coup attempt of 1981.

Círculo de Bellas Artes

C/Alcalá 42 • Exhibitions usually Tues–Sat 11am–2pm & 5–9pm, Sun 11am–2pm • Ⓦ circulobellasartes.com • Ⓜ Sevilla

Cut across to c/Alcalá from Plaza de las Cortes and you'll emerge close to the **Círculo de Bellas Artes**, a strange-looking 1920s building crowned by a statue of Pallas Athene. This is Madrid's best arts centre, and includes a theatre, music hall, cinema, exhibition galleries and a very pleasant bar (daily 9.30am–1am) – all marble and leather décor, with a nude statue reclining in the middle of the floor. It attracts the capital's arts and media crowd but is not in the slightest exclusive, nor expensive, and there's an adjoining terraza, too. The Círculo is theoretically a members-only club, but it issues €1 day-membership on the door, for which you get access to all areas.

Plaza de la Cibeles and Real Academia de Bellas Artes

Close to the Círculo and past an imposing array of grandiose buildings on c/Alcalá lies one of Spain's leading art galleries, the **Real Academia de Bellas Artes**, one for art buffs who have some appetite left after the Prado, Thyssen-Bornemisza and Reina Sofía. Half a kilometre to the east is **Plaza de la Cibeles**. Awash in a sea of traffic in the centre of the square are a **fountain** and statue of the goddess Cibeles, which survived the bombardments of the Civil War by being swaddled from helmet to hoof in sandbags. It was designed, as were the two other fountains gushing magnificently along the Paseo del Prado, by Ventura Rodríguez. The fountain is the scene of celebrations for victorious Real Madrid fans (Atlético supporters bathe in the fountain of Neptune just down the road).

Palacio de Cibeles and Casa de América

Ⓜ Banco de España

The monumental wedding-cake building on the far side of Plaza Cibeles was until recently Madrid's main post office. Constructed from 1904 to 1917, **Palacio de Cibeles** is vastly more imposing than the parliament and runs the Palacio Real pretty close. The city council took a shine to it and it now provides a home for the burgeoning

1

municipal offices. There is a huge glass-covered patio to the rear of the building that can be visited between 11am and 9pm on Sundays from May to September and there are plans to turn part of the building into an exhibition space and viewing gallery. Adjacent is a palatial eighteenth-century mansion built by the Marqués de Linares, which is now home to the **Casa de América**, a cultural organization that promotes Latin American art.

Real Academia de Bellas Artes de San Fernando

C/Alcalá 13 • Tues–Sat 9am–3pm, Sun & hols 9am–2.30pm • €5, free Wed • ⓦ rabasf.insde.es • ⓜ Sevilla

The **Real Academia** has traditionally been viewed as one of the most important art galleries in Spain. Admittedly, you have to plough through a fair number of dull academic canvases, but there are some hidden gems. These include a group of small panels by **Goya**, in particular *The Burial of the Sardine* and two revealing self-portraits, and a curious *Family of El Greco*, which may be by the great man or his son. Two other rooms are devoted to foreign artists, in particular Rubens. Upstairs, there is a series of sketches by Picasso, and a brutally graphic set of sculptures depicting the *Massacre of the Innocents* by José Ginés. It is also home to the national chalcography (copper or brass engraving) collection, which includes a number of Goya etchings used for his *Capricho* series on show at the Prado.

The Paseo del Arte

Madrid's three world-class art museums, the Prado, Thyssen-Bornemisza and Centro de Arte Reina Sofía, are all along or close to the Paseo del Prado within a kilometre of each other in what is commonly known as the **Paseo del Arte**. The most famous of the three galleries is the **Prado**, which houses an unequalled display of Spanish art, an outstanding Flemish collection and an impressive assemblage of Italian work. The **Thyssen-Bornemisza** provides an unprecedented excursion through Western art from the fourteenth to the late twentieth centuries. The final member of the trio, the **Centro de Arte Reina Sofía**, is home to the Spanish collection of contemporary art, including the Miró and Picasso legacies and the jewel in the crown – *Guernica*.

Museo del Prado

C/Ruiz de Alarcón 23 • Mon–Sat 9am–8pm, Sun 10am–7pm; Jan 6, Dec 24 & Dec 31 9am–2pm; closed Jan 1, Good Friday, May 1 & Dec 25 • €10 (€11–12 including supplement for temporary exhibitions), free for under-18s; free Mon–Sat 6–7pm, Sun 5–8pm • ⓦ museodelprado.es • ⓜ Banco de España/Atocha

The **Museo del Prado** is Madrid's premier attraction – well over two million visitors enter its doors each year – and one of the oldest and greatest collections of art in the world. Built as a natural science museum in 1775, the Prado opened to the public in 1819, and houses the finest works collected by Spanish royalty – for the most part, avid, discerning and wealthy buyers – as well as Spanish paintings gathered from other sources over the past two centuries. Finding enough space for displaying the works has always been a problem, but after fourteen years of arguments, delays and controversy, the €152 million Rafael Moneo-designed **extension**, which includes a stylish glass-fronted building incorporating the eighteenth-century cloisters of the San Jerónimo church, was finally opened in 2007. The new wing houses the restaurant and café areas, an expanded shop, an auditorium, temporary exhibition spaces, restoration and conservation workshops and a new sculpture gallery.

The museum's highlights are its early Flemish collection – including almost all of **Bosch**'s best work – and, of course, its incomparable display of Spanish art, in particular that of **Velázquez** (including *Las Meninas*), **Goya** (including the *Maja*s and the *Black Paintings*) and **El Greco**. There's also a huge section of Italian painters (**Titian**,

1

PASEO DEL ARTE COMBINED ENTRY TICKET

If you plan to visit all three art museums on the Paseo del Prado during your stay, it's well worth buying the under-advertised **Paseo del Arte ticket** (€17.60), which is valid for a year and allows one visit to each museum at a substantial saving, although it does not include the temporary exhibitions. It's available at any of the three museums.

notably) collected by Carlos V and Felipe II, both great patrons of the Renaissance, and an excellent collection of seventeenth-century Flemish and Dutch pictures gathered by Felipe IV, including **Rubens**' *Three Graces*. The museum has also hosted an increasing number of critically acclaimed temporary displays in recent years. Even in a full day you couldn't hope to do justice to everything here, and it's perhaps best to make a couple of more focused visits.

INFORMATION AND TOURS   **MUSEO DEL PRADO**

Tickets are purchased at the Puerta de Goya opposite the *Hotel Ritz* on c/Felipe IV, and the **entrances** are round the back at the Puerta de los Jerónimos, which leads into the new extension, or at the side at the Puerta de Goya Alta. If you want to avoid the lengthy queues for tickets, a better option is to buy them in advance via the museum website (w museodelprado.es). The Puerta de Murillo entrance, opposite the botanical gardens, is now for school and university groups only.

Organization The museum is broadly arranged according to national schools, but these are still undergoing some minor relocation and the definitive layout is not expected

to be completed until at least 2012; any variations will usually be shown on the free maps available at the desk on your way into the museum.

Tours What follows is, by necessity, only a brief guide to the museum contents. If you want more background on the key paintings pick up an audio-guide (€3.50) or the extensive guide (€19.50) in the bookshop. There are also some useful colour booklets (€1) on Velázquez, Goya, El Greco, Titian and Bosch available at the information desk and in their respective galleries. A lunchtime visit is often a good plan if you want to avoid the worst of the crowds and tour groups.

Exploring the museum

To follow the **route** proposed by the museum, bear right after the Puerta de los Jerónimos entrance and head into the central hallway – the Sala de las Musas. From here you are guided through the early Flemish, Italian and Spanish collections on the ground floor before being directed upstairs. A tour of the sixteenth- and seventeenth-century Italian and French collections in the northern wing gives way to the Flemish and Dutch galleries on the second floor where work from Rubens and Rembrandt is to the fore. Back on the first floor visitors are ushered through the Spanish Golden Age collections with their heavyweight contributions from El Greco, Velázquez and Murillo before enjoying the delights of Goya which stretch up to the second floor once again. From there you return to the ground floor for Goya's *Black Paintings* before concluding the visit with a tour of the grandiose historical epics that make up the remainder of the nineteenth-century Spanish collection.

Spanish painting

The Prado's collections of Spanish painting begin on the ground floor (rooms 12–16) with the cycles of twelfth-century **Romanesque frescoes** reconstructed from a pair of churches from the Mozarabic (Muslim rule) era in Soria and Segovia. **Early panel paintings** – exclusively religious fourteenth- and fifteenth-century works – include a huge *retablo* (altarpiece) by Nicolás Francés; the anonymous *Virgin of the Catholic Monarchs*; Bermejo's *Santo Domingo de Silos*; and Pedro Berruguete's *Auto-da-Fé*.

The Golden Age: Velázquez and El Greco

Upstairs, the collections from Spain's Golden Age – the late sixteenth and seventeenth centuries under Habsburg rule – are prefigured by a fabulous array of paintings by

1

PRADO HIGHLIGHTS

The Prado is much too big for a single visit to do the collection justice; however, if you are pressed for time here is a list of some of the **works you should not miss**.

The Garden of Earthly Delights by Bosch. A surrealistic masterpiece years ahead of its time.

The Triumph of Death by Pieter Brueghel. A disturbing and macabre depiction of hell by the Flemish master.

The Annunciation by Fra Angelico. A ground-breaking early Renaissance work.

Self-portrait by Dürer. Insightful self-portrait by the German genius.

The Descent from the Cross by Van der Weyden. An emotive and colourful depiction of the Deposition.

The Romanesque frescoes. Stunning frescoes from the Romanesque churches in Segovia and Soria.

David and Goliath by Caravaggio. The Italian's theatrical use of chiaroscuro at its best.

The Adoration of the Shepherds by El Greco. One of a series of revolutionary Mannerist works by the Greek-born painter.

Las Meninas by Velázquez. One of the most technically adroit and fascinating paintings in Western art.

Artemisa by Rembrandt. The Dutchman used his wife Saskia as a model for this portrayal of the heroic queen.

Sir Endymion Porter by Van Dyck. A superlative work by the Dutch court painter famous for his portraits of Charles I.

The Three Graces by Rubens. One of the great classically-inspired works by the Flemish genius.

Charles V at Múhlberg by Titian. A magnificent equestrian portrait of the Holy Roman Emperor.

The Lavatorio by Tintoretto. Epic masterpiece depicting Christ washing the feet of the disciples, that once belonged to Charles I.

La Maja Desnuda y La Maja Vestida by Goya. A pair of supremely seductive portraits of a woman reclining on a bed of pillows, one clothed, one naked.

Dos y Tres de Mayo by Goya. Timeless and iconic images on the horror of war.

Goya's Black Paintings. A series of penetrating and haunting images from the latter part of Goya's career.

El Greco (1540–1614), the Cretan-born artist who worked in Toledo from the 1570s. You really need to have taken in the works in Toledo to appreciate fully his extraordinary genius, but the portraits and religious works here (rooms 38–40), ranging from the Italianate *Trinity* to the visionary late *Adoration of the Shepherds*, are a good introduction.

In rooms 41 and 49–52, you confront the greatest painter of Habsburg Spain, **Diego Velázquez** (1599–1660). Born in Portugal, Velázquez became court painter to Felipe IV, whose family is represented in many of the works: "I have found my Titian," Felipe is said to have remarked on his appointment. Velázquez's masterpiece, *Las Meninas* (room 50), is displayed alongside studies for the painting. Manet remarked of it, "After this, I don't know why the rest of us paint," and the French poet Théophile Gautier asked "But where is the picture?" when he saw it, because it seemed to him a continuation of the room. *Las Hilanderas* and *Vulcan's Forge* showing the royal tapestry factory at work, *Christ Crucified* and *Los Borrachos* (*The Drunkards*) are further magnificent paintings. In fact, almost all of the fifty or so works on display (around half of the artist's surviving output) warrant close attention. Don't overlook the two small panels of the *Villa Medici*, painted in Rome in 1650, in virtually Impressionist style. There are several Velázquez canvases, including *The Surrender at Breda*, in the stunning collection of royal portraits and works depicting Spanish military victories.

In the adjacent rooms are examples of just about every significant Spanish painter of the seventeenth century, including many of the best works of **Francisco Zurbarán** (1598–1664), **Bartolomé Esteban Murillo** (1618–82), **Alonso Cano** (1601–67), **Juan de Valdés Leal** (1622–60) and **Juan Carreño** (1614–85). Note, in particular, Carreño's

1

portrait of the last Habsburg monarch, the drastically inbred and mentally retarded Carlos II, rendered with terrible realism. There's also a fine selection of paintings by **José Ribera** (1591–1625), who worked mainly in Naples, and was influenced there by Caravaggio. His masterpieces are considered to be *The Martyrdom of St Philip* and the dark, realist portrait of *St Andrew*, while look out for the bizarre *Bearded Lady*.

Goya

The final suite of Spanish rooms (69–73), which continue up onto the second floor (74–79) and down on to the ground floor (87–89), provides an awesome and fabulously complete overview of the output of **Francisco de Goya** (1746–1828), the largest and most valuable collection of his works in the world, with some 140 paintings and 500 drawings and engravings. Goya was the greatest painter of Bourbon Spain, a chronicler of Spain in his time and an artist whom many see as the inspiration and forerunner of Impressionism and modern art. He was an enormously versatile artist: contrast the voluptuous *Maja Vestida* and *Maja Desnuda* (*The Clothed Belle* and *The Naked Belle*) with the horrors depicted in the *Dos de Mayo* and *Tres de Mayo* (moving, on-the-spot portrayals of the rebellion against Napoleon in the streets of Madrid and the subsequent reprisals). Then there is the series of pastoral cartoons – designs for tapestries – and the extraordinary *Black Paintings* (rooms 87 & 88), a series of disconcerting murals painted on the walls of his home by the deaf and embittered painter in his old age. The many portraits of his patron, Carlos IV, are remarkable for their lack of any attempt at flattery, while those of Queen María Luisa, whom he despised, are downright ugly.

The nineteenth century

The Prado's collection of melodramatic nineteenth-century Spanish art was originally housed in the nearby Casón del Buen Retiro (now the museum's centre for investigation), but has now been relocated to magnificent effect on the ground floor in rooms 90–100. Dramatic works by, Eduardo Rosales and Antonio Gisbert are combined with some fine luminous canvases by Spanish impressionist Joaquin Sorolla.

Italian painting

The Prado's early Italian galleries on the ground floor are distinguished principally by **Fra Angelico**'s *Annunciation* (c.1445) and by a trio of panels by **Botticelli** (1445–1510). The latter illustrate a deeply unpleasant story from the *Decameron* about a woman hunted by hounds; the fourth panel (in a private collection in the US) gives a happier conclusion.

With the sixteenth-century Renaissance, and especially its Venetian exponents on the first floor, the collection really comes into its own. The Prado is said to have the most complete collection of Titians and painters from the Venetian School of any single museum. There are major works by **Raphael** (1483–1520), including a fabulous *Portrait of a Cardinal*, and epic masterpieces from the Venetians **Tintoretto** (1518–94), such as the beautifully composed *Lavatorio*, bought by Felipe IV when Charles I of England was beheaded and his art collection was auctioned off, and **Veronese** (1528–88), as well as **Caravaggio** (1573–1610), with his brutal *David with the Head of Goliath* another highlight. The most important works, however, are by **Titian** (1487–1576) in rooms 19–24. These include portraits of the Spanish emperors *Carlos V* and *Felipe II* (Carlos' suit of armour is preserved in the Palacio Real), and a famous, much-reproduced piece of erotica, *Venus, Cupid and the Organist* (two versions are displayed here), a painting originally owned by a bishop.

Flemish, Dutch and German painting

The biggest name in the **early Flemish collection** (room 3) is **Hieronymus Bosch** (1450–1516), known in Spain as "El Bosco". The Prado has several of his greatest

1

triptychs: the early-period *Hay Wain*, the middle-period *Garden of Earthly Delights*, and the late *Adoration of the Magi* – all familiar from countless reproductions but infinitely more chilling in the original. Bosch's hallucinatory genius for the macabre is at its most extreme in these triptychs, but is reflected here in many more of his works, including three versions of *The Temptations of St Anthony* (though only the smallest of these is definitely an original). Don't miss, either, the amazing table-top of *The Seven Deadly Sins*.

Bosch's visions find an echo in the works of **Pieter Brueghel the Elder** (1525–69), whose *Triumph of Death* must be one of the most frightening canvases ever painted. Another elusive painter, **Joachim Patinir**, is represented by four of his finest works. From an earlier generation, **Rogier van der Weyden**'s *Descent from the Cross* is outstanding; its monumental forms make a fascinating contrast with his miniature-like *Pietà*. There are also important works by Memling, Bouts, Gerard David and Massys.

The collection of **later Flemish and Dutch art** is on the second floor (rooms 30–34) with enough works here to make an excellent comparison between the flamboyant Counter-Reformation propaganda of Flanders and the more austere bourgeois tastes of Holland. **Rubens** (1577–1640) is extensively represented, with the beautifully restored *Three Graces*, *The Judgement of Paris* and a series of eighteen mythological subjects designed for Felipe IV's hunting lodge in El Pardo (though he supervised rather than executed these). There is, too, a fine collection of canvases by his contemporaries, including **Van Dyck**'s dramatic and deeply moving *Piedad*, and his magnificent portrait of himself and Sir Endymion Porter. **Jan Brueghel**'s representations of the five senses and **David Teniers**' scenes of peasant lowlife also merit a closer look. For political reasons, Spanish monarchs collected few works painted from seventeenth-century Protestant Holland; an early **Rembrandt**, *Artemisa*, in which the artist's pregnant wife served as the model, is, however, an important exception (room 34).

The **German room** (9) on the ground floor is dominated by **Dürer** (1471–1528) and **Lucas Cranach the Elder** (1472–1553). Dürer's magnificent *Adam and Eve* was saved from destruction at the hands of the prudish Carlos III only by the intervention of his court painter, Mengs, whose own paintings are on the first floor in room 64. The most interesting of Cranach's works is a pair of paintings depicting Carlos V hunting with Ferdinand I of Austria.

French and British painting

Most of the **French** work held by the Prado is from the seventeenth and eighteenth centuries (rooms 25, 26 and 63 on the first floor). Among the outstanding painters represented is **Nicolas Poussin** (1594–1665), with his Baroque work shown to best effect in *Triumph of David*, *Landscape with St Jerome* and *Mount Parnassus*. The romantic landscapes and sunsets of **Claude Lorraine** (1600–82) are well represented, and look out for **Hyacinthe Rigaud**'s (1659–1743) portrayal of the imperious *Louis XIV*.

British painting is thin on the ground – a product of the hostile relations between the Spanish and English from the sixteenth to nineteenth centuries. There is, however, a small sample of eighteenth-century portraiture from **Joshua Reynolds** (1723–92) and **Thomas Gainsborough** (1727–88) in room 65 on the first floor.

The Tesoro del Dauphin

The museum's basement houses the **Tesoro del Dauphin** (Treasure of the Dauphin), a display of part of the collection of jewels that belonged to the Grand Dauphin Louis, son of Louis XIV and father of Felipe V, Spain's first Bourbon king. The collection includes goblets, cups, trays, glasses and other pieces richly decorated with rubies, emeralds, diamonds, lapis lazuli and other precious stones.

Museo Thyssen-Bornemisza

Paseo del Prado 8 • Tues–Sun 10am–7pm (extended opening in summer months, check website for details); closed Jan 1, May 1 & Dec 25
• €8 for permanent collection, €7–8 for temporary exhibitions, combined ticket €12–13 or Paseo del Arte ticket (see box, p.77); free for
under-12s • ⓦ museothyssen • Ⓜ Banco de España

The **Museo Thyssen-Bornemisza** occupies the old Palacio de Villahermosa, diagonally
opposite the Prado, at the end of Plaza de las Cortes. This prestigious site played a large
part in Spain's acquisition – for a knock-down $350 million in June 1993 – of what
many argue was the world's greatest private art trove after that of the British royals:
seven-hundred-odd paintings accumulated by father-and-son German–Hungarian
industrial magnates. The son, Baron Hans Heinrich Thyssen, died in April 2002 aged
81. Another trump card was the late baron's fifth wife, Carmen Cervera (aka "Tita"
Cervera), a former Miss Spain, who steered the works to Spain against the efforts of
Britain's Prince Charles, the Swiss and German governments, the Getty foundation and
other suitors.

The museum had no expense spared on its design – again in the hands of the
ubiquitous Rafael Moneo, responsible for the remodelling of Estación de Atocha and
the extension at the Prado – with stucco walls (Carmen insisted on salmon pink) and
marble floors. A terribly kitsch portrait of Carmen with a lapdog hangs in the great
hall of the museum, alongside those of her husband and King Juan Carlos and
Queen Sofía. Pass beyond, however, and you are into seriously premier-league art:
medieval to eighteenth–century on the second floor, **seventeenth-century Dutch** and
Rococo and Neoclassicism to Fauves and Expressionists on the first floor, and
Surrealists, **Pop Art** and the **avant-garde** on ground level. Highlights are legion in a
collection that displays an almost stamp-collecting mentality in its examples of nearly
every major artist and movement: how the Thyssens got hold of classic works by
everyone from Duccio and Holbein, through El Greco and Caravaggio, to Schiele
and Rothko, takes your breath away.

Carmen has a substantial collection of her own (over 600 works), which has been
housed in the **new extension**, built on the site of an adjoining mansion and cleverly
integrated into the original format of the museum. It is particularly strong on
nineteenth-century landscape, North American, Impressionist and Post-Impressionist
work. The ground floor is home to a large temporary exhibition space, which has
staged a number of interesting and highly successful shows.

There's a handy cafeteria and restaurant in the new extension; there's also a shop,
where you can buy a wide variety of art books, guides to the museum, postcards and
other souvenirs. In July and August the museum opens a restaurant on the top-floor
terrace: *El Mirador*. Advance tickets for the museum, a good idea in high season, are
available via the website.

The second floor: European old masters and Carmen's collection

Take a lift to the second floor and you will find yourself at the chronological start of
the museum's collections: European painting (and some sculpture) from the fourteenth
to the eighteenth century. The core of these collections was accumulated in the 1920s
and 30s by the late baron's father, Heinrich, who was a friend of the art critics Bernard
Berenson and Max Friedländer. He was clearly well advised. The early paintings include
incredibly good (and rare) devotional panels by the Sienese painter **Duccio di
Buoninsegna**, and the Flemish artists **Jan van Eyck** and **Rogier van der Weyden**. You
then move into a fabulous array of Renaissance portraits (room 5), which include three
of the very greatest of the period: **Ghirlandaio**'s *Portrait of Giovanna Tornabuoni*, **Hans
Holbein**'s *Portrait of Henry VIII* (the only one of many variants in existence that is
definitely genuine) and **Raphael**'s *Portrait of a Young Man. A Spanish Infanta* by **Juan de
Flandes** may represent the first of Henry VIII's wives, Catherine of Aragón, while the
Young Knight by **Carpaccio** is one of the earliest-known full-length portraits. Beyond
these is a collection of **Dürer**s and **Cranach**s to rival that in the Prado, and as you

1

progress through this extraordinary panoply, display cases along the corridor contain scarcely less spectacular works of sculpture, ceramics and gold- and silverwork.

Next in line, in room 11, are **Titian** and **Tintoretto**, and three paintings by **El Greco**, one early, two late, which make an interesting comparison with each other and with those in the Prado. **Caravaggio**'s monumental *St Catherine of Alexandria* (room 12) is the centrepiece of an important display of works by followers of this innovator of chiaroscuro. As you reach the eighteenth century, there is a room containing three flawless **Canaletto** views of Venice (room 17).

Tagged onto this floor are the first galleries (lettered A–H) that make up the initial section of Carmen's collection. **Luca Giordano**'s monumental *Judgement of Solomon* (room A) and a **Van Dyck** *Crucifixion* (room B) are two of the early highlights. Gallery C traces the development of landscapes from early Flemish works through to **Constable**'s marvellous *The Lock*, bought in 1910 for £10.8 million. Beyond are some interesting works by North American and European artists that complement the baron's collection and some soothing Impressionist works by **Degas**, **Renoir**, **Pissarro**, **Monet** and **Sisley**.

The first floor: Americans, Impressionists and Expressionists

The route now takes you downstairs through the remainder of Carmen's collection (rooms I–P), beginning with further Impressionist work, taking in some delightful canvases by **Gauguin** and the Post-Impressionists and ending with some striking Expressionist pieces by **Kandinsky** and **Robert Delaunay**.

From room P, walk along the corridor to rejoin the baron's collection. After a comprehensive round of seventeenth-century Dutch painting of various genres, Rococo and Neoclassicism, you reach some **English portraiture** by Gainsborough, Reynolds and Zoffany (room 28) and **American painting** in rooms 29 and 30. The collection, one of the best outside the US, concentrates on landscapes and includes James Goodwyn Clonney's wonderful *Fishing Party on Long Island Sound*, and works by James Whistler, Winslow Homer and John Singer Sargent.

As with Carmen's collection, **Impressionism** and **Post-Impressionism** are another strong point, with a choice collection of paintings by Vincent van Gogh, including one of his last and most gorgeous works, *Les Vessenots* (room 32). **Expressionism**, meanwhile, is represented by some stunning works by Ernst Ludwig Kirchner, Franz Marc, Wassily Kandinsky and Max Beckmann.

The ground floor: avant-garde

Works on the ground floor run from the beginning of the twentieth century through to around 1970. The good baron didn't, apparently, like contemporary art: "If they can throw colours, I can be free to duck," he explained, following the gallery's opening.

The most interesting work in his "experimental avant-garde" sections is from the **Cubists**. There is an inspired, side-by-side hanging of parallel studies by Picasso (*Man with a Clarinet*) and Braque (*Woman with a Mandolin*). Later choices include a scattering of Joan Miró, Jackson Pollock, Dalí, Rauschenberg and Lichtenstein. In the **Synthesis of Modernity** section, there are some superbly vivid canvases by Max Ernst and Marc Chagall, a brilliant portrait of George Dyer by Francis Bacon, and a fascinating **Lucian Freud**, *Portrait of Baron Thyssen*, posed in front of the Watteau *Pierrot* hanging upstairs.

Centro de Arte Reina Sofía

C/Santa Isabel 52 • Mon & Wed–Sat 10am–9pm, Sun 10am–2.30pm; closed Jan 1 & 6, May 1, Sept 9, Nov 9, Dec 24, 25 & 31 • €6, free Mon–Fri 7–9pm, Sat 2.30–9pm & Sun; free for under-18s and over-65s; or Paseo del Arte ticket (see box, p.77) • ⓦ museoreinasofia.es • ⓜ Atocha

It is fortunate that the **Centro de Arte Reina Sofía**, facing Estación de Atocha at the end of Paseo del Prado, keeps slightly different opening hours and days to its neighbours.

1

For this leading exhibition space and permanent gallery of modern Spanish art – its centrepiece is Picasso's greatest picture, *Guernica* – is another essential stop on the Madrid art circuit, and one that really mustn't be seen after a Prado–Thyssen overdose.

The museum, a vast former hospital, is a kind of Madrid response to the Pompidou Centre in Paris, with transparent lifts shuttling visitors up the outside of the Sabatini building to the permanent collection. Like the other two great art museums, it has also undergone a major **extension** programme – the French architect Jean Nouvel has added a massive state-of-the-art metal-and-glass wing behind the main block. If the queues at the main entrance are too long, try the alternative one in the new extension on the Ronda de Atocha. You can also buy tickets in advance via the website.

The Santini building

It is for **Picasso's Guernica** that most visitors come to the Reina Sofía, and rightly so. Superbly displayed, this icon of twentieth-century Spanish art and politics carries a shock that defies all familiarity. Picasso painted it in response to the bombing of the Basque town of Gernika by the German Luftwaffe, acting in concert with Franco, in the Spanish Civil War. In the fascinating preliminary studies, displayed around the room, you can see how he developed its symbols – the dying horse, the woman mourning her dead, the bull, the sun, the flower, the light bulb – and then return to the painting to marvel at how he made it all work.

The work was first exhibited in Paris in 1937, as part of a Spanish Republican Pavilion in the Expo there, and was then loaned to the Museum of Modern Art in New York, until, as Picasso put it, Spain had rid itself of Fascist rule. The artist never lived to see that time, but in 1981, following the restoration of democracy, the painting was, amid much controversy, moved to Madrid to hang (as Picasso had stipulated) in the Prado. Its transfer to the Reina Sofía in 1992 again prompted much soul-searching and protest, though for anyone who saw it in the old Prado annexe, it looks truly liberated in its present setting. Many Basques believe the painting's rightful home is with them, but studies have revealed cracks and fissures that make the painting too fragile to move once again.

Guernica hangs midway around the permanent collection on the second floor. It is preceded by an intriguing introductory room that examines the ground-breaking Basque and Catalan schools and the representation of landscape and the female figure. Strong sections on **Cubism** and the **Paris School** follow, in the first of which Picasso is again well represented, alongside a fascinating straight-Cubist work by Salvador Dalí (*Cadaqués Countryside*). There are also good collections of other avant-garde Spaniards of the 1920s and 30s, including Juan Gris.

Dalí and **Miró** make heavyweight contributions to the post-*Guernica* halls. The development of Dalí's work and his variety of techniques are clearly displayed here, with works ranging from the classic *Muchacha en la Ventana* to famous surrealist works such as *El Gran Masturbador* and *El Enigma de Hitler*. There is an impressive collection of Spanish sculpture to be found in the final rooms.

The fourth floor covers Spain's postwar years up to the present day and includes Spanish and international examples of **abstract** and **avant-garde** movements. Outstanding pieces from **Francis Bacon** (*Reclining Figure*), **Henry Moore** and **Graham Sutherland** give a British context, while challenging work from **Antoni Tàpies**, **Antonio Saura** and **Eduardo Chillida** provide the Spanish perspective. If the avant-garde work all gets too much, there are also some more accessible offerings from the Spanish realists.

The Area Nouvel

The extension, or **Area Nouvel** as it is now known, consists of three brand-new buildings built around an open courtyard topped by a striking delta-shaped, metallic, crimson-coloured roof. It is home to the temporary exhibition spaces, which have

1

hosted some outstanding shows, including one featuring the Picasso collection from the Musée National in Paris. There is also an auditorium, a library and a bookshop (Mon–Sat 10am–9pm, Sun 10am–2.30pm) selling a wide range of glossy coffee-table volumes, as well as more academic tomes and the informative museum guidebook (€22), which examines eighty key works in detail.

Also housed in the new wing is *Arola Madrid* (Mon 10am–9pm, Wed–Sat 10am–2.30pm), a café-restaurant run under the auspices of leading Catalan chef Sergi Arola. Coffee and cakes are affordable, but lunch or supper will set you back at least €50 a head.

Parque del Retiro and around

When you get tired of sightseeing, Madrid's many parks are great places to escape for a few hours. The most central and most popular of them is **El Retiro**, a delightful mix of formal gardens and wider open spaces. Nearby, in addition to the Prado, Thyssen-Bornemisza and Reina Sofía galleries, are a number of the city's **smaller museums**, plus the startlingly peaceful **Jardines Botánicos**.

Parque del Retiro

Ⓜ Retiro

Originally the grounds of a royal retreat (*retiro*) and designed in the French style, the **Parque del Retiro** has been public property for more than a hundred years. In its 330 acres you can jog, row in the lake (you can rent boats by the Monumento a Alfonso XII), picnic (though officially not on the grass), have your fortune told and – above all – promenade. The busiest day is Sunday, when half of Madrid, replete with spouses, in-laws and kids, turns out for the *paseo*. Dressed for show, the families stroll around, nodding at neighbours and building up an appetite for a long Sunday lunch.

Strolling aside, there's almost always something going on in the park, including a good programme of **concerts** and **fairs** organized by the city council. Concerts tend to be held in the Quiosco de Música in the north of the park. The most popular of the fairs is the Feria del Libro (Book Fair), held in early June, when every publisher and half the country's bookshops set up stalls and offer a 25-percent discount on their wares. At weekends, there are **puppet shows** by the Puerta de Alcalá entrance, and on Sundays you can often watch groups of South American musicians performing by the lake.

A number of **stalls and cafés** along the Paseo Salón del Estanque sell drinks, *bocadillos* and *pipas* (sunflower seeds), and there are terrazas, too, for *horchata* and *granizados*. The park has a safe reputation, at least by day; in the late evening, it's best not to wander alone, and there are plans to close the park completely at night because of an increase in petty vandalism. Note, too, that the area east of La Chopera is known as a cruising ground for gay prostitutes.

Palacio de Velázquez, Palacio de Cristal and the Bosque del Recuerdo

Palacio de Velázquez May–Sept Mon & Wed–Sun11am–9pm; Oct–April Mon & Wed–Sun 10am–6pm • Free **Palacio de Cristal** During exhibitions same hours, but closed when raining • ☎ 915 746 614 for information **Casa de Vacas** • Closed Aug • Free • ⓦ casadevacas.es

Travelling art exhibitions are frequently housed in the beautiful **Palacio de Velázquez**, the nearby **Palacio de Cristal** and **Casa de Vacas**. Look out, too, for **El Ángel Caído** (Fallen Angel), the world's only public statue to Lucifer, in the south of the park. There is also the **Bosque del Recuerdo**, 192 olive trees and cypresses planted in the Paseo de la Chopera in memory of those who died in the train bombings at the nearby Atocha station on March 11, 2004.

Puerta de Alcalá

Ⓜ Retiro/Banco de España

Leaving the park at the northwest corner takes you to the Plaza de la Independencia, in the centre of which is one of the two remaining gates from the old city walls. Built in the late eighteenth century, the **Puerta de Alcalá** was the biggest in Europe at that time and, like the bear and *madroño* tree, has become one of the city's monumental emblems.

Museo de Artes Decorativas

C/Montalbán 12 • Tues–Sat 9.30am–3pm, also open Thurs & Fri 5–8pm in winter and spring, Sun 10am–3pm • €3, free on Sun • Ⓦ mnartesdecorativas.mcu.es • Ⓜ Banco de España/Retiro

1

Just south of Puerta de Alcalá, is the **Museo de Artes Decorativas**, housed in an elegant mansion close to the Retiro. The furniture and decorations here aren't that spectacular, but there are some superb *azulejos* in a magnificent eighteenth-century tiled Valencian kitchen on the top floor.

Museo Naval

Paseo del Prado 5 • Tues–Sun 10am–6pm • closed mid-July to Sept and public hols • Free (bring ID) • Ⓜ Banco de España

A couple of blocks west, in a corner of the Naval Ministry is the **Museo Naval**, strong, as you might expect, on models, charts and navigational aids from or relating to the Spanish voyages of discovery. Exhibits include the first map to show the New World, drawn in 1500, cannon from the Spanish Armada and part of Cortés' standard used in the conquest of Mexico.

San Jerónimo el Real

C/Ruiz de Alarcón 19 • Mon–Fri 8am–1.30pm & 6–8pm, Sat & Sun 9am–1.30pm & 6.30–8pm, Oct–July opens one hour earlier in the afternoon • Ⓜ Banco de España/Atocha

Just behind the Prado is **San Jerónimo el Real**, Madrid's society church, where in 1975 Juan Carlos (like his predecessors) was crowned. Despite significant remodelling and the addition of two Gothic towers, the old form of the church is still clearly visible; but the seventeenth-century cloisters have fallen victim to the Prado extension.

Real Academía Española de la Lengua

C/Felipe IV 4 • Ⓜ Banco de España/Atocha

Opposite to the church is the **Real Academia Española de la Lengua** (Royal Language Academy), whose job it is to make sure that the Spanish language is not corrupted by foreign or otherwise unsuitable words. The results are entrusted to their official dictionary – a work that bears virtually no relation to the Spanish you'll hear spoken on the streets.

Jardín Botánico

Pl. de Murillo 2 • Daily 10am–dusk • €2.50, under-10s free • Ⓦ rjb.csic.es • Ⓜ Atocha

Immediately south of the Prado is the delightful, shaded **Jardín Botánico**. Opened in 1781 by Carlos III (known as *El Alcalde* – "The Mayor" – for his urban-improvement programmes), the garden once contained over 30,000 plants. The numbers are down these days, though the gardens were renovated in the 1980s, after years of neglect, and the worldwide collection of flora is fascinating for any amateur botanist; don't miss the hothouse with its tropical plants and amazing cacti or the bonsai collection of former prime minister Felipe González. Temporary exhibitions take place in the Palacio Villanueva within the grounds.

La Caixa Forum

Paseo del Prado 36 • Daily 10am–8pm • Free • Ⓦ obrasocial.lacaixa.es/nuestroscentros/caixaforummadrid /caixaforummadrid_es.html • Ⓜ Atocha

Opposite the botanical gardens is **La Caixa Forum**, an innovative and stylish exhibition space opened in 2008 by the powerful Catalan bank, that complements the existing attractions on the Paseo del Arte. The centre, which hosts a variety of high-quality temporary art shows, concerts and workshops, is flanked by an eye-catching vertical garden designed by French botanist Patrick Blanc in which some 15,000 plants form an organic carpet extending across the wall. Inside, there's a decent art bookshop and a neat top-floor café that serves a fine €12 lunchtime *menú*.

1

Estación de Atocha

Ⓜ Atocha

On the other side of the botanical gardens is the sloping Cuesta de Moyano, lined with **bookstalls**; although it's at its busiest on Sundays, many of the stalls are open every day. Across the way, the **Estación de Atocha** is worth a look even if you're not travelling out of Madrid. It's actually two stations, old and new, the latter now sadly infamous as the scene of the horrific train bombings that killed 191 people and injured close to 2000 in March 2004. The original station, a glorious 1880s glasshouse, was revamped in the early 1990s with a spectacular tropical-garden centrepiece. It's a wonderful sight from the walkways above, and train buffs and architects will want to take a look at the high-speed AVE trains and the station beyond.

Museo Nacional de Antropología/Etnología

C/Alfonso XII 68 • Tues–Sat 9.30am–8pm, Sun 10am–3pm • €3, under-18s free, free Sat after 2pm & Sun • Ⓦ mnantropologia .mcu.es • Ⓜ Atocha

Also in this area is the **Museo Nacional de Antropología/Etnología** designed to give an overview of different cultures of the world, in particular those intertwined with Spanish history. The most unusual exhibits are to be found in a side room on the ground floor – a macabre collection of deformed skulls, a Guanche (the original inhabitants of the Canary Islands) mummy and the skeleton of a circus giant (2.35m tall).

Real Fábrica de Tapices

C/Fuentarrabia 2 • Mon–Fri 10am–2pm; closed Aug • €4 • Tours evey half-hour (guides usually speak English) • Ⓦ realfabricadetapices .com • Ⓜ Atoche Renfe/Menéndez Pelayo

The **Real Fábrica de Tapices** still turns out handmade tapestries, many of them based on the Goya cartoons in the Prado. They are fabulously expensive, but the entrance fee is a bargain with the tour tracing the fascinating manufacturing process, barely changed in the three hundred years of the factory's existence.

The Gran Vía, Chueca and Malasaña

The **Gran Vía**, Madrid's great thoroughfare, runs from Plaza de Cibeles to Plaza de España, effectively dividing the old city to the south from the newer parts northwards. Permanently jammed with traffic and crowded with shoppers and sightseers, it's the commercial heart of the city, and – if you spare the time to look up – quite a monument in its own right, with its early twentieth-century, palace-like banks, offices and cinemas. Look out for the **Edificio Metrópolis** (1905–11) on the corner of c/Alcalá, complete with cylindrical facade, white stone sculptures, zinc-tiled roof and gold garlands, and the towering **Telefónica** building which was the chief observation post for the Republican artillery during the Civil War, when the Nationalist front line stretched across the Casa de Campo to the west.

North of the Telefónica building, c/Fuencarral heads north to the Glorieta de Bilbao. To either side of this street are two of Madrid's most characterful *barrios*: **Chueca**, to the east, and **Malasaña**, to the west. Their chief appeal lies in an amazing concentration of bars, restaurants and, especially, nightlife. However, there are a few reasons – cafés included – to wander around here by day.

Chueca

Once rather down at heel, Chueca is now one of the city's most vibrant *barrios* and the focal point of Madrid's **gay scene**. At the centre is the lively **Plaza de Chueca**

(ⓜChueca), which is fronted by one of the best old-style *vermut* bars in the city, *Bodega Ángel Sierra*. The whole area has become gentrified in recent years with the rise of a host of stylish bars, cafés and restaurants and the opening of the newly refurbished Mercado de San Antón.

Paseo de Recoletos

From Plaza de Chueca east to **Paseo de Recoletos** (the beginning of the long Paseo de la Castellana) are some of the city's most enticing streets. Offbeat restaurants, small private art galleries, and odd corner shops are in abundance, and the **c/Almirante** has some of the city's most fashionable clothes shops, too. To the north, on Paseo de Recoletos, are a couple of the city's most lavish **traditional cafés**, the *Café Gijón* at no. 21 and *Café del Espejo* at no. 31 (see p.112).

Plaza del Rey

ⓜ Banco de España

The Ministerio de Cultura fronts the **Plaza del Rey**, which is also worth a look for the other odd buildings surrounding it, especially the **Casa de las Siete Chimeneas** (House of Seven Chimneys), which is supposedly haunted by a mistress of Felipe II who disappeared in mysterious circumstances.

Sociedad de Autores

C/Fernando VI 4 • ⓜ Alonso Martínez

On the edge of the Santa Bárbara *barrio*, is the **Sociedad de Autores** (Society of Authors), housed in the only significant *modernista* building in Madrid designed by José Grasés Riera, who was part of the Gaudí school, and featuring an eye-catching facade that resembles a melted candle.

Museo Nacional del Romanticismo

C/San Mateo 13 • May–Oct Tues–Sat 9.30am–8.30pm (closes 6.30pm Nov–April), Sun 10am–3pm • €3, free on Sat after 2pm, Sun • ⓦ museoromanticismo.mcu.es • ⓜ Tribunal

Finally reopened after a nine-year, seven-million-euro restoration, the **Museo Nacional del Romanticismo** has been given a new lease of life with an imaginative and inspiring refurbishment. The museum aims to show the lifestyle and outlook of the late-Romantic era through the re-creation of a typical bourgeois residence in the turbulent reign of Isabel II (1833–68), and this it does brilliantly. Overflowing with a marvellously eclectic and often kitsch hoard of memorabilia, the mansion is decorated with some beautiful period furniture and ceiling frescoes.

Museo de Historia de Madrid

C/Fuencarral 78 • Tues–Fri 9.30am–8pm, Sat & Sun 10am–2pm, Aug Tues–Fri 9.30am–2pm, Sat & Sun 10am–2pm; closed for refurbishment • Free • ⓦ munimadrid.es/museomunicipal • ⓜ Tribunal

Just around the corner from the Museo del Romanticismo, the **Museo de Historia de Madrid** is in the final throes of yet another lengthy restoration. The building itself features a superb churrigueresque facade by Pedro de Ribera, while inside there is a chronological collection of paintings, photos, maps, models, sculptures and porcelain, all relating to the history of the city since it was designated capital in 1561.

Malasaña

The heart, in all senses, of **Malasaña** is the **Plaza Dos de Mayo**, named after the insurrection against Napoleonic forces on May 2, 1808; the rebellion and its aftermath are depicted in Goya's famous paintings at the Prado. The surrounding district bears the name of one of the martyrs of the uprising, 15-year-old Manuela Malasaña, who is also commemorated with a street (as are several other heroes of the time). On the night

1

of May 1, all of Madrid shuts down to honour its heroes, and the plaza is the scene of festivities lasting well into the night.

More recently, the quarter was the focus of the *movida madrileña*, the "happening scene" of the late 1970s and early 80s. As the country relaxed after the death of Franco and the city developed into a thoroughly modern capital under the leadership of the late mayor, Tierno Galván, Malasaña became a focal point for the young. Bars appeared behind every doorway, drugs were sold openly in the streets, and there was an extraordinary atmosphere of new-found freedom. Times have changed and a good deal of renovation has been going on in recent years, but the *barrio* retains a somewhat alternative – nowadays rather grungy – feel, with its bar custom spilling onto the streets, and an ever-lively scene in the Plaza Dos de Mayo terrazas.

The streets have an interest of their own and are home to some fine traditional bars, while on c/Manuela Malasaña you can take your pick from some of the trendiest cafés in town. There are also some wonderful old shop signs and architectural details, best of all the **Antigua Farmacia Juanse** on the corner of c/San Andrés and c/San Vicente Ferrer, with its irresistible 1920s *azulejo* scenes depicting cures for diarrhoea, headaches and suchlike.

San Antonio de los Alemanes
Corredera de San Pablo 16 • Daily 9am–1pm & 6–8pm; closed Aug • €2 • Ⓜ Callao

One of the few specific sights in this quarter is **San Antonio de los Alemanes**, a delightful, elliptical church with dizzying floor-to-ceiling frescoes by Neapolitan artist Luca Giordano depicting the life of St Anthony.

Plaza de España, Moncloa and beyond

Plaza de España provides a breathing space from the densely packed streets to the east. Beyond the square lies a mixture of leafy suburbia, university campus and parkland, including the green swathes of Parque del Oeste and Casa de Campo. Sights include some fascinating minor museums and, further out, the royal palace of El Pardo. The airy terrazas along Paseo del Pintor Rosales provide ample opportunity for refreshment.

Plaza de España
Ⓜ Plaza de España

The **Plaza de España** at the west end of Gran Vía was home, until the flurry of corporate building in the north of Madrid, to two of the city's tallest buildings: the **Torre de Madrid** and the **Edificio de España**. These rather stylish 1950s buildings preside over an elaborate monument to Cervantes in the middle of the square, which in turn overlooks the bewildered-looking bronze figures of Don Quixote and Sancho Panza.

The plaza itself is a little on the seedy side, especially at night. However, to its north, **c/Martín de los Heros** is a lively place, day and night, with a couple of the city's best cinemas, and behind them the **Centro Princesa**, with shops, clubs, bars and a 24-hour branch of the ubiquitous VIPS – just the place to have your film developed at 4am, or a bite to eat before heading on to a small-hours club.

Conde Duque
Ⓜ Plaza de España

Up the steps opposite the Centro Princesa is **c/Conde Duque**, an atmospheric street that contains an intriguing selection of cafés, restaurants and shops, and one that is dominated by the massive former barracks of the royal guard, constructed in the early eighteenth century by Pedro de Ribera. The barracks have been turned into a dynamic cultural centre, **El Centro Cultural de Conde Duque** (ⓦesmadrid.com/condeduque; free), which is home to the city's collection of contemporary art. Just to the east of this, the **Plaza de las Comendadoras** – named after the convent that occupies one side of the square – is a tranquil space bordered by a variety of interesting craft shops, bars and cafés.

Museo Cerralbo

C/Ventura Rodríguez 17 • Tues, Wed, Fri & Sat 9.30am–3pm, Thurs 9.30am–3pm & 5–8pm, Sun & hols 10am–3pm; July & Aug Tues–Sat 9.30am–2pm, Sun & hols 11am–2pm • €3, free Sun • Ⓦ museocerralbo.mcu.es • Ⓜ Plaza de España

A block to the west of Plaza de España an elegant mansion houses the refurbished **Museo Cerralbo**, endowed with the collections of the reactionary politician, poet, traveller and archeologist, the seventeenth Marqués de Cerralbo. The rooms, stuffed with paintings, furniture, armour and artefacts, provide a fascinating insight into the lifestyle of the nineteenth-century aristocracy, though there is little of individual note.

Parque del Oeste

Pl. de España **Teleférico** April–Sept Mon–Fri noon–early eve, Sat & Sun noon–8pm; Oct–March Sat, Sun & public hols noon–dusk • €3.70 single, €5.35 return • Ⓦ teleferico.com • Ⓜ Argüelles/Ventura Rodríguez

The **Parque del Oeste** stretches northwest from the Plaza de España, following the rail tracks of Príncipe Pío up to the suburbs of Moncloa and Ciudad Universitaria. In summer, there are numerous terrazas in the park, while, year-round, a **teleférico** shuttles its passengers high over the river from Paseo del Pintor Rosales to the middle of the Casa de Campo, where there's a bar/restaurant with pleasant views back towards the city. Just below the starting point of the *teleférico* is the beautiful **Rosaleda**, a vast rose garden at its best in May and June.

Templo de Debod

C/Ferraz 1 • April–Sept Tues–Fri 10am–2pm & 6–8pm, Sat & Sun 10am–2pm; Oct–March Tues–Fri 9.45am–1.45pm & 4.15–6.15pm, Sat & Sun 10am–2pm • Free • Ⓦ madrid.es/templodebod • Ⓜ Plaza de España

On the south side of the park, five minutes' walk from Plaza de España, is the **Templo de Debod**, a fourth-century BC Egyptian temple given to Spain in recognition of the work done by Spanish engineers on the Aswan High Dam (which inundated its original site). Reconstructed here stone by stone, it seems comically incongruous, and even more so with a new multimedia exhibition on the culture of Ancient Egypt housed inside.

La Ermita de San Antonio de la Florida

Glorieta de la Florida 5 • Tues–Fri 9.30am–8pm, Sat & Sun 10am–2pm; July 13–23 closed afternoons • Free • Ⓦ madrid.es/ermita • Ⓜ Príncipe Pío

Almost alongside the famous roast chicken and cider restaurant *Casa Mingo* is **La Ermita de San Antonio de la Florida**. This little church on a Greek-cross plan was built by an Italian, Felipe Fontana, between 1792 and 1798, and decorated by **Goya**, whose frescoes are the reason to visit. In the dome is a depiction of a miracle performed by St Anthony of Padua. Around it, heavenly bodies of angels and cherubs hold back curtains to reveal the main scene: the saint resurrecting a dead man to give evidence in favour of a prisoner (the saint's father) falsely accused of murder. Beyond this central group, Goya created a gallery of highly realist characters – their models were court and society figures – while for a lesser fresco of the angels adoring the Trinity in the apse, he took prostitutes as his models. The *ermita* also houses the artist's mausoleum, although his head was stolen by phrenologists for examination in the nineteenth century.

Moncloa

The wealthy suburb of **Moncloa** contains the Spanish prime ministerial home and merits a visit even if you are not using the bus terminal for El Pardo and El Escorial. The metro will bring you out next to the mammoth building housing the Air Ministry and the giant Arco de la Victoria, built by Franco in 1956 to commemorate the

1

Nationalist victory in the Civil War. Beyond this lie the leafy expanses of the Parque del Oeste and the campuses of the **Ciudad Universitaria**. During term time, the area becomes one giant student party on weekend evenings, with huddles of picnickers and singing groups under the trees.

Mirador del Faro
Ⓜ Moncloa; take the Plaza de Moncloa exit

A stone's throw from the Moncloa metro is the **Mirador del Faro**, a futuristic 92-metre-high tower which has been reopened after a six-year 5.6 million-euro refurbishment. The tower provides some great views over the northern part of the city and the mountains beyond. There are plans to open a café/restaurant on the top floor.

Museo de América
Avda. de los Reyes Católicos 6 • May–Oct Tues–Sat 9.30am–8.30pm, Sun 10am–3pm; Nov–April Tues–Sat 9.30am–6.30pm, Sun 10am–3pm • €3, free on Sun • Ⓦ museodeamerica.mcu.es • Ⓜ Moncloa

Just past the Mirador is the **Museo de América**, which contains a fine collection of artefacts, ceramics and silverware from Spain's former colonies in Latin America. The highlight is the fabulous Quimbayas treasure – a breathtaking collection of gold objects and figures from the Quimbaya culture of Colombia.

Museo del Traje
Avda. de Juan de Herrera 2 • Tues–Sat 9.30am–7pm, Sun & hols 10am–3pm (July & Aug open late from 9.30am–10.30pm on Thurs) • €3; free for under-18s, Sat after 2.30pm and all day Sun • Ⓦ museodeltraje.mcu.es • Ⓜ Moncloa

Across the busy road down towards the university is the **Museo del Traje**, a fascinating excursion through the history of clothes and costume. Exhibits include clothes from a royal tomb dating back to the thirteenth century, some stunning eighteenth-century ball gowns and a selection of Spanish regional costumes, as well as shoes, jewellery and underwear. Modern Spanish and international designers are also featured, with a Paco Rabanne miniskirt and elegant dresses from Pedro del Hierro. There is an upmarket restaurant in the grounds with a cool garden terrace in the summer.

Casa de Campo
Swimming pool daily June–Sept 10.30am–8pm • €4 • Ⓜ Batán/Lago, bus (#33) from Príncipe Pío or *teleférico* (see p.91) •

If you want to jog, play tennis, swim, picnic, go to the fairground or see pandas, then the **Casa de Campo** is the place to head for. This enormous expanse of heath and scrub is in parts surprisingly wild for a place so easily accessible from the city; other sections have been tamed for more conventional pastimes.

Picnic tables and café-bars are dotted throughout the park and there's a **jogging track** with exercise posts, a municipal open-air **swimming pool** close to Ⓜ Lago, tennis courts, and rowing boats for rent on the **lake** (again near Ⓜ Lago). Sightseeing attractions include a large and well-organized **zoo** and a popular amusement park, the **Parque de Atracciones** (see p.120), complete with the obligatory selection of heart-stopping, stomach-churning gravity rides. Although some of the remaining **access roads** through the park are frequented by prostitutes, the city council has taken measures to clamp down on the trade, and there are few problems during daylight hours.

El Pardo

Nine kilometres northwest of Madrid in the former royal hunting ground of **El Pardo** is where Franco had his principal residence. A garrison still remains in the town – where most of the Generalísimo's staff were based – but the stigma of the place has lessened over the years, and it is now a popular weekend excursion for *madrileños*, who come here for long lunches in the terraza restaurants, or to play tennis or swim at one of the nearby sports clubs.

1

Palacio del Pardo

C/Manuel Alonso • April–Sept Mon–Sat 10.30am–5.45pm, Sun 9.30am–1.30pm; Oct–March Mon–Sat 10.30am–4.45pm, Sun 10am–1.30pm; closed occasionally for official visits • Guided tours €4, 5–16-year-olds €2.30, free Wed for EU citizens • ⓦ patrimonionacional.es • Buses (#601) from Moncloa (daily 6.30am–midnight, every 10–15 min; 25min **Casita del Príncipe** Fri–Sun Easter to end Sept • ring ☎ 913 761 500 to make the compulsory reservation for a guided tours

Rebuilt by the Bourbons on the site of a hunting lodge of Carlos V, the **Palacio del Pardo** is the tourist focus of the area. The interior is pleasant enough, with its chapel and theatre, a portrait of Isabel la Católica by her court painter Juan de Flandes, and an excellent collection of tapestries, many after the Goya cartoons in the Prado. Guides detail the uses Franco made of the *palacio*, but pass over some of his stranger habits – he kept by his bed, for instance, the mummified hand of St Teresa of Ávila. The country house retreat in the grounds known as the **Casita del Príncipe** was, like the *casitas* (pavilions) at El Escorial, designed by Prado architect Juan de Villanueva, and is highly ornate.

Salamanca and the Paseo de la Castellana

Salamanca, the area north of the Parque del Retiro, is a smart address for apartments and, even more so, for shops. The *barrio* is the haunt of *pijos* – universally denigrated rich kids – and the grid of streets between c/Goya and c/José Ortega y Gasset contains most of the city's designer emporiums. Most of the buildings are modern and undistinguished, though there are some elegant nineteenth-century mansions and apartment blocks. There is a scattering of museums, galleries and exhibition spaces to tempt you up here, too, in particular the **Sorolla** and the **Lázaro Galdiano** museums, two little gems that are often ignored by visitors.

Plaza de Colón and around

Tackling the area from south to north, the first point of interest is **Plaza de Colón** (ⓜColón), endowed at street level with a statue of Columbus (Cristóbal Colón), and some huge stone blocks arranged as a megalithic monument to the discovery of the Americas. Below the plaza and underneath the cascading waterfall facing the city's longest, widest and busiest avenue, the Paseo de la Castellana, is the **Teatro Fernán Gómez** arts centre.

Museo Arqueológico Nacional

C/Serrano 13 • Tues–Sat 9.30am–8pm, Sun 9.30am–3pm • Free while undergoing refurbishment • ⓦ man.mcu.es • ⓜ Colón/Serrano

Adjacent to Plaza de Colón, is the acclaimed **Museo Arqueológico Nacional**. As befitting a national collection, the museum holds some very impressive pieces, among them the celebrated Celto-Iberian busts known as *La Dama de Elche* and *La Dama de Baza*, and a wonderfully rich hoard of Visigothic treasures found at Toledo. The museum also contains some outstanding Roman, Egyptian, Greek and Islamic finds.

Museo de la Biblioteca Nacional

Paseo de Recoletos 20 • Tues–Sat 10am–9pm, Sun & hols 10am–2pm • Free • ⓜ Colón/Serrano

The nearby **Biblioteca Nacional** contains every work published in Spain since 1716, while the **Museo** displays a selection of the library's treasures including Arabic, Hebrew and Greek manuscripts, and has an interesting exhibition on the development of written communication (in Spanish only).

Museo de Arte Público

Paseo de la Castellana 41 • Free • ⓜ Rubén Darío

Further north up the Paseo de la Castellana is the **Museo de Arte Público**, an innovative attempt at using the space underneath the Juan Bravo flyover. However, its haphazard

1

and rather stark collection of sculptures, including the six-tonne suspended block titled *The Meeting* by the late Eduardo Chillada, appears to be more appreciated by the city's skateboard community.

Museo Sorolla

C/Martínez Campos 37 • Tues, Thurs–Sat 9.30am–8pm, July & Aug closes 2.30pm, Sun 10am–3pm • €3, free under-18s, Sun • ⓦ museosorolla.mcu.es • ⓜ Gregorio Marañon/Iglesia

Not far north of here, across the Paseo de la Castellana, is another little jewel of a gallery, the **Museo Sorolla**. There's a large collection of work by the painter **Joaquín Sorolla** (1863–1923), tastefully displayed in his beautifully preserved old home. The best of his paintings, which include beach scenes, portraits and landscapes, are striking, impressionistic plays on light and texture. His old studio is much as he left it, and the house itself, with its cool and shady Andalucian-style courtyard and gardens, is worth the visit alone and makes a wonderful escape from the traffic-choked streets.

Museo Lázaro Galdiano

C/Serrano 122 • Mon & Wed–Sun 10am–4.30pm • €4; free Wed • ⓦ flg.es • ⓜ Gregorio Marañon/Rubén Darío

The **Museo Lázaro Galdiano** is a little farther northeast at the intersection of c/Serrano and c/María Molina. This formerly private collection was given to the state by José Galdiano in 1948 and spreads over the four floors and thirty-seven rooms of his former home. It is a vast jumble of artworks, with some very dodgy attributions, but includes some really exquisite and valuable pieces. Among painters represented are El Greco, Bosch, Gerard David, Dürer and Rembrandt, as well as a host of Spanish artists, including Berruguete, Murillo, Zurbarán, Velázquez and Goya. Other exhibits include a collection of clocks and watches, many of them once owned by Carlos V.

Museo de Ciencias Naturales

C/José Gutiérrez Abascal 2 • Tues–Fri 10am–6pm, Sat 10am–8am (July & Aug 10am–3pm), Sun 10am–2.30pm • €5; free Sun • ⓜ Gregorio Marañon

Back towards the Paseo de la Castellana is the Natural History Museum, whose displays are split between two buildings. One contains a fairly predictable collection of stuffed animals, skeletons and audiovisual displays on the evolution of life on earth, the other is home to some rather dull fossil and geological exhibits.

To the Bernabéu

North along the Paseo de la Castellana, you reach the **Zona Azca** (ⓜNuevos Ministerios/Santiago Bernabéu), a business quarter, once home to the city's tallest skyscraper, the 157-metre Torre Picasso designed by Minori Yamasaki (also the architect of New York's infamous Twin Towers), although now dwarfed by the four new towers erected beyond Plaza Castilla. It is only a short hop across the Castellana to Real Madrid's magnificent **Santiago Bernabéu** stadium, easily the most famous sight in this part of town.

Santiago Bernabéu

C/Concha Espina 1 • Tour Mon–Sat 10am–7pm, Sun 10.30am–6.30pm (closes 5hr before kickoff on match days) • €16, under-14s €11 • ⓦ realmadrid.com • ⓜ Santiago Bernabéu

The **Santiago Bernabéu** stadium provides a suitably imposing home for one of the most famous clubs in world football, Real Madrid. Even if you can't get to see a match, you can take the **stadium tour** which, though very expensive, is understandably popular. It starts with a panoramic view of the massive 80,000-capacity stadium and takes in a visit to the dressing rooms and a walk through the tunnel onto the pitch. Also included is the **trophy exhibition**, complete with endless cabinets of gleaming silverware, with pride of place given to the team's nine European Cups and video footage of their

FÚTBOL IN MADRID

The "Galactico" era may be over following the departure of David Beckham, Zinedine Zidane, Ronaldo and Luís Figo, but **Real Madrid** remains one of the most glamorous teams in club football with an ample quota of superstars including the world's most expensive player, Cristiano Ronaldo. The nine-time winners of the European Cup and thirty-one-time Spanish champions play at the **Bernabéu**, venue of the 1982 World Cup final and a ground that ranks as one of the world's most fabled sporting arenas.

Tickets to games – which have become more difficult to get hold of in recent years – cost from €40 up to €300 for big matches and usually go on sale in the week before a game; Real runs a telephone and online booking service (☎ 902 324 324, ⓦ realmadrid.com – see section titled "proximo partido" for online bookings). They can be purchased by credit card on the ticket line or online for all but the biggest matches. You can also get them through online ticket agency ⓦ servicaixa.com. Pick the tickets up from Servicaixa cashpoints (11am–8pm) or the automatic tills in the shopping centre at the corner of the Bernabéu (Las Esquina del Bernabéu) on the day of the match. If you don't get lucky, you can still catch a glimpse of the hallowed turf by taking the stadium tour.

The capital is also home to another of the country's biggest teams, **Atlético Madrid** (☎ 902 530 500, ⓦ clubatleticodemadrid.com; tickets from around €30, bought via the website or ⓦ servicaixa.com), who play at the **Estadio Vicente Calderón** in the south of the city (ⓜ Pirámides). The more modest Getafe (☎ 916 959 771, ⓦ getafecf.com; tickets from around €30 available via ⓦ entradas.com) and Rayo Vallecano (☎ 914 782 253, ⓦ rayovallecano.es) are both based in working-class suburbs of the city.

greatest triumphs. The tour ends with the obligatory visit to the overpriced club shop – where you soon come to realize why Real is one of the richest football clubs in the world. The stadium also has a surprisingly affordable café (*Realcafé*) and a more expensive **restaurant** (*Puerta 57*), both open to the public and affording views over the pitch (though they are not open during games).

Plaza Castilla
ⓜ Plaza Castilla

The Paseo de la Castellana ends with a flourish at **Plaza Castilla** with four giant skyscrapers constructed on Real Madrid's former training ground, the result of a controversial deal that allowed the club to solve many of its financial problems. The two tallest towers, one of which is designed by Norman Foster, soar some 250 metres into the sky.

ARRIVAL AND DEPARTURE   MADRID

Whatever your point of **arrival** In Madrid, it's an easy business getting into the centre of the Spanish capital. The airport is connected by a speedy metro link, shuttle buses and taxis, while the city's main train and bus stations are all linked to the metro system only a short ride from the centre.

BY PLANE
Aeropuerto de Barajas (general information ☎ 902 404 704, ⓦ aena.es) is 16km east of the city, at the end of Avenida de América (the A2 road). It has four terminals, including the vast new T4 building designed by Richard Rogers and Carlos Lamela, which has helped double the capacity to some seventy million passengers a year. All Iberia's domestic and international flights, as well as airlines that belong to the Oneworld group, such as British Airways and American Airways, use T4 (a 10min shuttle-bus ride from the other terminals); other international flights and budget airlines, including Aer Lingus, EasyJet and Ryanair, go from T1, while Air France, KLM and SAS use T2.

Metro link From the airport, the metro link (Line 8) takes you from T4 and T2 to the city's Nuevos Ministerios station in just 12min (daily 6am–2am; €2.50). From there it's a 15min metro ride to most city-centre locations.

Airport buses The route by road to central Madrid is more variable, depending on rush-hour traffic, and can take anything from twenty minutes to an hour. Airport buses run round the clock from each terminal to Cibeles and Atocha (stops only at Cibeles 11.30pm–6am; €2) with a journey time of around 40min.

Schematic map of the subway network

Metro Lines

1. PINAR DE CHAMARTÍN / VALDECARROS
2. LAS ROSAS / CUATRO CAMINOS
3. VILLAVERDE ALTO / MONCLOA
4. ARGÜELLES / PINAR DE CHAMARTÍN
5. ALAMEDA DE OSUNA / CASA DE CAMPO
6. CIRCULAR
7. HOSPITAL DEL HENARES / PITIS
8. NUEVOS MINISTERIOS / AEROPUERTO
9. MIRASIERRA / ARGANDA DEL REY
10. HOSPITAL INFANTA SOFÍA / PUERTA DEL SUR
11. PLAZA ELÍPTICA / LA FORTUNA
12. METROSUR
R. ÓPERA / PRÍNCIPE PÍO

Light Rail

1. PINAR DE CHAMARTÍN / LAS TABLAS
2. COLONIA JARDÍN / ESTACIÓN DE ARAVACA
3. COLONIA JARDÍN / PUERTA DE BOADILLA

Keys

- Metro Interchange station
- Interchange station with long walking distance
- Station with restricted opening times
- Change of trains
- Madrid-Barajas Airport
- Airport extra charge
- Renfe suburban railway station
- Travel information centre
- Parking
- Suburban bus station
- Interregional bus station
- Railway station
- Transfer Terminal
- Light Rail

B1
B2 Change of fare
B3

Taxis are always available outside, too, and cost around €25 (including a €5.50 airport supplement) to the centre, depending on traffic.

Train A new *cercanías* train line takes you from T4 to Chamartín in the north of the city in around 11min (€2.15)

Car rental Half a dozen or so car rental companies have stands at the airport terminals and can generally supply clients with maps and directions.

Airport facilities Other airport facilities include 24hr currency exchange, ATMs, a post office, left-luggage lockers, a RENFE office for booking train tickets, chemists, tourist offices and hotel reservations desks.

BY TRAIN

Two main stations, Estación de Chamartín and Estación de Atocha, serve destinations throughout Spain and further afield.

Estación de Chamartín Serves trains from France or northern and western Spain (including the high-speed links to Segovia and Valladolid); a modern terminal isolated in the north of the city, connnected by metro with the centre, and by regular commuter trains (*cercanías*) with Estación de Atocha.

Destinations A Coruña (2–3 daily; 7hr 40min–9hr 35min); Ávila (20–25 daily; 1hr 20min–2hr 5min); Bilbao (2 daily; 4hr 47min–4hr 55min); Burgos (6 daily; 2hr 20min–4hr 15min); Ferrol (daily; 9hr 30min); Gijón (4 daily; 5hr 20min–5hr 35min); León (9 daily; 2hr 45min–4hr 30min); Lisbon (daily; 9hr 15min); Lugo (daily; 8hr 50min); Oviedo (4 daily; 4hr 50min–5hr 5min); Pamplona (3 daily; 3hr 5min–3hr 20min); Paris (daily; 13hr 30min); Pontevedra (2 daily; 8hr 5min–9hr 55min); Salamanca (7–10 daily; 2hr 20min–3hr); San Sebastián (2–3 daily; 5hr 20min–6hr 30min); Santander (3–4 daily; 4hr 20min–4hr 30min); Santiago (2–3daily; 7hr 10min–8hr 50min); Segovia (AVE 12–14 daily; 27min; 7 daily 1hr 50min–2hr); Sigüenza (6 daily; 1hr 30min–1hr 40min); Soria (2–3 daily; 2hr 40min–3hr); Valladolid (AVE 19 daily; 56min–1hr 10min; 7 daily–2hr 35min); Vigo (2–3 daily; 7hr 25min–9hr); Vitoria (AVE 2 daily 3hr 40min; 3 daily; 5hr 30min); Zamora (2–3 daily; 2hr 30min–3hr 15min). Plus most other destinations in the northeast and northwest.

Estación de Atocha Centrally located at the end of the southern end of Paseo del Prado, it has two interconnected terminals: one for local services, the other for all points in southern and eastern Spain, including the high-speed AVE trains to Barcelona, Seville, Toledo, Málaga, Valencia and Zaragoza.

Destinations Albacete (14–20 daily; 1hr 40min–2hr 30min); Alcalá de Henares (every 10–15min; 35min); Algeciras (2 daily; 5hr 10min); Alicante (7 daily; 3hr 10min); Almería (2 daily; 6hr 20min); Aranjuez (every 15–20min; 40min); Badajoz (3 daily; 5hr 25min–7hr 45min); Barcelona (16 daily; 2hr 50min–3hr 15min);

Cáceres (5 daily; 3hr 26min–4hr); Cádiz (3 daily; 4hr 15min–4hr 30min); Cartagena (4 daily; 4hr 50min–5hr 15min); Ciudad Real (20–25 daily; 50min–1hr); Córdoba (30 daily; 1hr 40min–2hr); Cuenca (AVE 9–11 daily; 50min; Regional 4 daily; 3hr); El Escorial (every 15–30min; 1hr); Granada (2 daily; 4hr 3min); Guadalajara (AVE 8 daily; 23min; regional every 30min; 40min); Huelva (daily; 3hr 50min); Huesca (1 daily; 2hr 15min); Jaén (4 daily; 4hr 15min); Jerez (3 daily; 3hr 40min); Lleida (8 daily; 2hr 10min); Málaga (11 daily; 2hr 30min–2hr 50min); Mérida (5–9 daily; 4hr 40min–6hr 50min); Seville (17–20 daily; 2hr 20min–2hr 45min); Toledo (12–14 daily; 33min); Valencia (AVE 12 daily; 1hr 38min–2hr 5min; regional 3 daily 6hr–6hr 20min); Zaragoza (18 daily; 1hr 20min). Plus most destinations in the south and west.

Príncipe Pío If you're coming from local towns around Madrid, you may arrive at Príncipe Pío (aka Estación del Norte), fairly close to the centre below the Palacio Real, which is also connected to the metro network.

Information and reservations Call ☎ 902 320 320 or go to ⓦ renfe.com. Tickets can be bought at the individual stations, at Aeropuerto de Barajas arrivals in T1 and T4 (Mon–Fri 8am–3pm) and at registered travel agents. Bear in mind that you'll need to book in advance for most long-distance trains, especially at weekends or holiday time.

BY BUS

Bus terminals are scattered throughout the city. The largest – used by all of the international bus services – is the **Estación Sur de Autobuses** at c/Méndez Álvaro 83 on the corner of c/Retama, 1.5km south of the Atocha station (☎ 914 684 200, ⓦ estaciondeautobuses.com; ⓜ Méndez Álvaro). There are other bus stations at the *intercambiadoras* in Avda. de América (ⓜ Avda. de América), Conde de Casal (ⓜ Conde de Casal), Moncloa (an underground terminal just above ⓜ Moncloa), Príncipe Pío (ⓜ Príncipe Pío) and Pl. Elíptica (ⓜ Plaza Elíptica). Leading bus companies that operate from Madrid include Alsa (ⓦ alsa.es), La Sepulvedana (ⓦ lasepulvedana.es), Arriva (ⓦ arriva.es) and Avanzabus (ⓦ avanzabus.com).

Estación Sur de Autobuses destinations Albacete (10–14 daily; 2hr 45min–3hr 15min); Alicante (5–10 daily; 4hr 50min–5hr); Almería (5 daily; 7hr); Aranjuez (Mon–Fri every 30 min, Sat & Sun hourly; 40min); Arenas de San Pedro (4–10 daily; 2hr); Ávila (5–10 daily; 1hr 35min–1hr 45min); Badajoz (8 daily; 4hr 40min–5hr 45min); Cáceres (7 daily; 3hr 50min–4hr 55min); Ciudad Real (4 daily; 4hr); Córdoba (6 daily; 4hr 45min); Cuenca (9 daily; 2hr–2hr 30min); Gijón (11 daily; 5hr 30min–6hr 30min); Granada (18 daily; 4hr 30min–5hr 30min); Jaén (6 daily; 5hr); León (12 daily; 3hr 30min–4hr 15min); Lisbon (2 daily; 7hr 30min); Málaga (5–12 daily; 6hr); Marbella (2–10 daily; 7hr); Mérida (9 daily; 4–5hr); Oviedo (12–16 daily; 5hr–5hr 15min); Palencia (5 daily; 3hr 15min); Pontevedra

1

(6 daily; 7hr); Salamanca (23 daily; 2hr 30min); Santiago (5 daily; 8–9hr); Seville (8 daily; 6hr); Trujillo (10–15 daily; 2hr 40min–4hr); Valencia (14 daily; 4hr); Valladolid (19 daily; 2hr 15min); Zamora (6 daily; 3hr–3hr 15min); and international services to France.

Intercambiador de Avda. de América destinations Alcalá (every 15min; 45min); Barcelona (12 daily; 7hr 20min–8hr); Bilbao (10–13 daily; 4hr 45min); Guadalajara (every 30min; 55min); Logroño (9 daily; 3hr 45min–4hr); Pamplona (9 daily; 5hr 15min–6hr 30min); San Sebastián (10 daily; 5hr 15min–6hr 20min); Santander (8 daily; 5hr 45min–6hr); Soria (10 daily; 2hr 30min); Vitoria (10 daily; 4hr–4hr 45min); Zaragoza (20 daily; 3hr 45min–4hr).

Intercambiador de Moncloa destinations El Escorial (approx every 15–30min; 55min–1hr). Onward connections to El Valle de los Caídos.

Intercambiador de Plaza Elíptica destinations Toledo (every 30 min; 1hr–1hr 30min).

Intercambiador de Príncipe Pío destinations Segovia (every 30min; 1hr 45min).

Intercambiador Conde de Casal destinations Chinchón (daily every 30min–1hr; 45–55min).

GETTING AROUND

Madrid is a pretty easy city to **get around**. The central areas are walkable; the metro is modern, extensive and efficient; buses are also good and serve some of the more out-of-the-way districts, and taxis are always available.

THE METRO

The clean and highly efficient **metro** (Ⓦ metromadrid .es) is by far the quickest way of getting around Madrid, serving most places you're likely to want to get to. It runs from 6am until 2am, and the flat fare is €1.50 for the central zone (€2 if you want to venture further afield), or €9.30 for a ten-trip ticket (*bono de diez viajes*), which can be used on buses, too. The network has undergone massive expansion in recent years and some of the outlying commuter districts are now connected by light railways, which link with the existing stations (separate tickets are needed for some of these). Lines are numbered and colour-coded, and the direction of travel is indicated by the name of the terminus station. You can

BY CAR

All the main roads into Madrid bring you right into the city centre, although eccentric signposting and even more eccentric driving can be very unnerving. Both ring roads – the M40 and the M30 – and the Paseo de la Castellana are all notorious bottlenecks, although virtually the whole city centre can be close to gridlock during the peak **rush-hour periods** (Mon–Fri 7.30–9.30am & 6–8.30pm). Be prepared for a long trawl around the streets to find **parking**, and even then in most central areas you'll have to buy a ticket at one of the roadside meters (€2.55 for a maximum stay of 2hr in the blue-coloured bays; €1.80 for a maximum stay of 1hr in the green-coloured bays). Charges apply Mon–Fri 9am–8pm, Sat and Aug 9am–3pm. Another option is to put your car in one of the many signposted **parkings** (up to €2/hr and around €29/day). Your own transport is really only of use for out-of-town excursions, so it's advisable to find a hotel with or near a car park and keep your car there during your stay in the city. If you are staying more than a couple of weeks, you can get long-term parking rates at some neighbourhood garages.

Free **maps** of the whole central area of Madrid are available from any of the *turismos* (see p.99).

pick up a free colour map of the system (*plano del metro*) at any station.

BUSES

The comprehensive urban **bus network** (Ⓦ emtmadrid .es) is another good way to get around and see the sights: in the text, where there's no metro stop, we've indicated which bus to take. There are information booths in the Pl. de Cibeles and Puerta del Sol, which dispense a huge route map (*plano de los transportes de Madrid*), and – along with other outlets – sell bus passes. Fares are the same as for the metro, at €1.50 a journey, or €9.30 for a ten-trip ticket (*bono de diez viajes*), which can be used on both forms of transport, but note that you can only buy the

---

THE TOURIST TRAVEL PASS

If you're using public transport extensively, it could be worth getting a **tourist pass (abono túristico)**, covering the metro, train and bus. These are non-transferable, and you'll need to show your passport or identity card at the time of purchase. **Zone A** cards cover central Madrid, **Zone T** cards cover the whole region including buses to Toledo and Guadalajara but not those to the airport. They are available for a duration of one to seven days and range in cost from €6 for a Zone A daily card to €50 for a weekly one for Zone T (under-11s are half-price; under-4s travel free) and can be purchased at all metro stations, the airport and tourist offices. If you're staying longer, passes (*abonos*) covering the metro, train and bus, and available for each calendar month, are worthwhile.

single tickets on the buses themselves (try to have the right money).

Buses run from 6am to midnight. In addition, there are *búho* (owl) night buses that operate on twenty routes around the central area and out to the suburbs: departures are half-hourly from midnight to 5.30am, from Pl. de Cibeles.

TAXIS

One of the best things about getting round Madrid is that there are thousands of **taxis** – white cars with a diagonal red stripe on the side – which are reasonably cheap; €7–8 will get you to most places within the centre and, although it's common to round up the fare, you're not expected to tip. The minimum fare is €2.10 and supplements are charged for the airport, train and bus stations, the IFEMA congress centre, going outside the city limits, and for night trips (10pm–6am). In any area in the centre, day and night, you should be able to wave down a taxi (available ones have a green light on top of the cab) in a short time, although it is more difficult at weekends when half the population is out on the town. To phone for a taxi, call ☎ 915 478 600 (also for wheelchair-friendly cabs), ☎ 914 051 213, ☎ 913 712 131 or ☎ 914 473 232. If you want to make a complaint take the driver's number and ask for the *hoja de reclamaciones* (a claim form). If you leave something in a taxi, ring ☎ 915 279 590.

LOCAL TRAINS

The **local train** network, or *cercanías*, is the most efficient way of connecting between the main train stations and provides the best route out to many of the suburbs and to nearby towns such as Alcalá de Henares. Most trains are air-conditioned, fares are cheap, and there are good connections with the metro. Trains generally run every 15 to 30min from 6am to midnight. For more information, go to the RENFE website at ☎ renfe.com and click on the *cercanías* section for Madrid.

CITY TOURS

The *turismo* in Pl. Mayor (see below) can supply details of a variety of guided English-language **walking tours** around the city on the "Descubre Madrid" programme (tickets from €3.90; ☎ 902 221 424 info at ☎ esmadrid .com/descubremadrid). For a **bus tour** of all the major city sights, wait at the pick-up points outside the Prado, Pl. de España, Pl. de Colón and Pl. de Cibeles. Tickets cost €17.50 (children under 16 €9, under-6s free) and allow you to jump on and off throughout the day at various places throughout the city.

INFORMATION

Oficinas de turismo are at the following locations which are open all-year-round:

Barajas International Airport in T1 (Mon–Fri 8am–8pm, Sat & Sun 9am–2pm; ☎ 913 058 656), T2 and T4 (daily 9.30am–8.30pm; ☎ 913 338 248).
Estación de Atocha (Mon–Fri 9am–8pm, Sat & Sun 9am–1pm; ☎ 913 159 976).
Estación de Chamartín (Mon–Fri 8am–8pm, Sat 9am–2pm; ☎ 913 159 976).
Plaza Mayor 27 (daily 9.30am–8.30pm; ☎ 915 881 636; ⓜ Sol/Ópera).
Plaza de Colón In the underground passageway, accessed at the corner of c/Goya (daily 9.30am–8.30pm; ☎ 915 881 636; ⓜ Colón).

C/Duque de Medinaceli 2 (Mon–Fri 9am–7pm, Sat 9am–3pm; ☎ 914 294 951; ⓜ Banco de España).
Turismo booths are located next to the Reina Sofía, in Pl. de la Cibeles and in Pl. del Callao off Gran Vía (daily 9.30am–8.30pm).
Website and phone numbers The Madrid tourist board's is ☎ esmadrid.com, while the regional authority has one covering the whole of the province (☎ turismomadrid .es). There's tourist information available in English on ☎ 902 100 007, a premium number that links all the regional tourist offices mentioned above, and on ☎ 915 881 636.

THE MADRID CARD

The **Madrid Card** (☎ 902 877 996, ☎ madridcard.com; online purchase at ☎ neoturismo.com) gives the holder the right of admission to over 50 museums and sights, a tour of the Bernabéu, the *teleférico*, an open-top bus tour and a guided walking tour of the old city, as well as discounts at a number of shops and restaurants. It costs €32 for one day (€42 for two, €52 for three) and is on sale via the internet, at T2 at Barajas and at the Plaza Mayor tourist office. There is a variation known as the Madrid Card Cultura directed solely at the museums (from €28/day) and a children's version for under-12s (€32 for three days). Do your sums before you splash out, though, as you would need to cram a lot into a day's sightseeing to get your money's worth. If you just want to concentrate on the big-three art galleries, the Paseo del Arte ticket (see p.77) is far better value, and allows you to take things at a more leisurely pace.

1

ACCOMMODATION

Business hotels apart, most of Madrid's **accommodation** is pretty central. With increasing competition, many *hostales* and hotels have been busy upgrading their facilities and a new breed of stylish, design-conscious, medium-priced hotel has emerged. Many of the expensive hotels do special weekend offers, and prices drop substantially in August when temperatures soar towards 40ºC (air-conditioning is usual and a welcome extra). You'll notice that buildings in the more popular hotel/*hostal* areas often house two or three separate establishments, each on **separate floors**; these are generally independent of each other. One thing to bear in mind is **noise**; bars, clubs, traffic and roadworks all contribute to making Madrid a high-decibel city, so avoid rooms on the lower floors, or choose a place away from the nightlife if you want a bit of peace and quiet. Madrid has just one **campsite**, located well out of the centre, but there are two very handy backpackers' **hostels** right in the heart of the city. There are accommodation services at the airport (Viajes Aira in T1, T2 and T4; ☎ 913 054 224; no fee), the Estación Sur de Autobuses, and Atocha and Chamartín train stations.

If you want to be at the heart of the old town, the areas around **Puerta del Sol**, **Plaza de Santa Ana** and **Plaza Mayor** are the ones to go for; if you're into nightlife, **Malasaña** or **Chueca** may also appeal; for a quieter location and a bit of class, you should opt for the **Paseo del Prado**, **Recoletos** or **Salamanca** areas; if you have children the areas around the parks are good options.

SOL, ÓPERA AND MADRID DE LOS AUSTRIAS

This really is the heart of Madrid, and prices, not surprisingly, are a bit higher than some of the other central areas, though you can still find bargains in the streets around the Pl. Mayor.

Los Amigos Hostal c/Arenal 26, 4º ☎ 915 592 472, ⓦ losamigoshostel.com; ⓜ Ópera/Sol; map p.102. Great backpacking option just a few minutes from Sol. Dormitories cater for 4–6 people, and there are a couple of communal rooms plus free wi-fi. The friendly staff speak English, and bed linen and use of the kitchen are included in the price. Dorm €17, double €45

Casa Madrid c/Arrieta 2, 2º ☎ 915 595 791, ⓦ casademadrid.com; ⓜ Ópera; map p.102. Exclusive boutique-style hotel, offering seven stunning rooms decorated with hand-painted frescoes, classical statues, original paintings and fresh flowers. Ideal for an expensive romantic escape, but not really the place for children. €248

Chic & Basic Mayerling c/Conde de Romanones 6 ☎ 914 201 580, ⓦ chicandbasic.com; ⓜ Tirso de Molina; map p.102. A stylish mid-range hotel with 22 rooms, housed in a former textile warehouse close to c/Atocha. Clean lines and black-and-white decor predominate in the simple, neat rooms. Continental breakfast is included in the price and there's free internet as well as a sun terrace. €80

Hostal La Macarena Cava de San Miguel 8, 2º ☎ 913 659 221, ⓦ silserranos.com; ⓜ Sol; map p.102. A comfortable, family-run *hostal* in a characterful street just off the Pl. Mayor. The well-kept rooms are a little on the small side though they all have satellite TV and a/c. Great location but can be a little noisy. €59

Hostal Tijcal & Hostal Tijcal 2 c/Zaragoza 6, 3º ☎ 913 655 910, ⓦ hostaltijcal.com; ⓜ Sol; map p.102. Situated between Pl. Santa Cruz and Pl. Mayor, this quirky but extremely hospitable *hostal* offers rooms with a/c, bathroom and TV (some also have good views). Continental breakfast available for €3 per person. There is a sister *hostal*, the *Tijcal 2*, at c/Cruz 26 ☎ 913 604 628. €54

★ **Hotel Meninas** c/Campomanes 7 ☎ 915 412 805, ⓦ hotelmeninas.com; ⓜ Ópera; map p.102. A stylish, 37-room hotel owned by the same group as the nearby *Ópera*, and similarly good value. Very helpful staff, excellent attic rooms, flat-screen TVs and free broadband internet access. Breakfast included for internet reservations. Prices vary according to availability but doubles usually start at €100.

Hotel Palacio de San Martín c/Pl. de San Martín 5 ☎ 917 015 000, ⓦ hotel-inturpalaciosanmartin.com; ⓜ Ópera/Sol; map p.102. Situated in a historic building in an attractive square alongside the Monasterio de las Descalzas Reales. Elegant and spacious rooms with period decor, a small gym and sauna, plus an attractive rooftop restaurant. €92

★ **Petit Palace Arenal** c/Arenal 16 ☎ 915 644 355, ⓦ hthoteles.com; ⓜ Sol/Ópera; map p.102. A member of the self-styled High-Tech Hotels chain with 64 sleek, modern rooms. All have a/c and free broadband, and there are some family-friendly rooms too. Two other members of this chain, the *Posada del Peine* and the *Puerta del Sol*, are close at c/Postas 17 and c/Arenal 4. €90

Posada del Leon de Oro c/Cava Baja 12 ☎ 911 191 494, ⓦ posadadelleondeoro.com; ⓜ La Latina; map p.102. This former inn has been converted into a chic, designer hotel with seventeen large, individually decorated rooms complete with walk-in showers, flat-screen TVs and free wi-fi. €100

Posada Real Manuel Pl. de Oriente 2, 3º ☎ 915 598 450, ⓦ posadarealmanuel.com. ⓜ Ópera; map p.102. Formerly known as the Hostal Valencia, this seven-room *posada* has a fabulous location with great views over the plaza towards the Palacio Real. Each room is decorated differently. €72

Room Mate Mario c/Campomanes 4º ☎ 915 488 548, ⓦ room-matehoteles.com; ⓜ Ópera; map p.102. Hip, designer hotel with a perfect spot on a pleasant street close to the Teatro Real. Compact, ultra-cool rooms, neat bathrooms, friendly staff and free internet. Buffet breakfast is included. There is another member of the chain, the *Laura*, at nearby Travesía de Trujillos 3 (☎917 011 670). **€90**

AROUND PLAZA DE SANTA ANA AND HUERTAS

Pl. de Santa Ana and the Huertas area are at the heart of Madrid nightlife, with bars and cafés open until very late at night. The following are all within a few blocks of the square, with the metro stations Antón Martín, Sevilla and Sol close by. Go for rooms on the higher floors if you want to avoid the worst of the noise.

Chic & Basic Colours c/Huertas 14, 2º izda. ☎914 296 935, ⓦchicandbasic.com; ⓜAntón Martín; map p.102. Swish *hostal* in the heart of Huertas with ten design-conscious en-suite rooms, all complete with a/c and plasma TVs. There is a self-service breakfast and a common room where you can read the paper. **€75**

Hostal Alaska c/Espoz y Mina 7, 4º ☎915 211 845, ⓦhostalalaska.com; ⓜSol; map p.102. A selection of brightly decorated rooms all with bathroom, a/c and TV, in this well-run *hostal*. There is also a family apartment available for €100. **€52**

Hostal Barrera c/Atocha 96, 2º ☎915 275 381, ⓦhostalbarrera.com; ⓜAntón Martín; map p.62. A friendly, good-value fourteen-room *hostal* only a short distance from Atocha station and run by an English-speaking owner. Smart a/c rooms are a cut above the rest in this category. Internet access available. **€68**

★ **Hotel Urban** Carrera San Jeronimo 34 ☎917 877 770, ⓦderbyhotels.es; ⓜSevilla/Sol; map p.102. Ultra cool, fashion-conscious, five-star hotel offering a glut of designer rooms, a rooftop pool, summer terrace and "pijo" cocktail bar. It even has its own small museum, consisting of items from owner Jordi Clos' collection of Egyptian and Chinese art. Look out for special deals online. **€180**

International Hostel Posada de Huertas c/Huertas 21 ☎914 295 526, ⓦposadadehuertas.com; ⓜAntón Martín/Sevilla; map p.102. A modern hostel right at the heart of things, close to Pl. de Santa Ana. Dormitories range in size from 4–10 people. There's a common room with TV and internet access, plus laundry facilities and individual lockers. Breakfast is included. **€17**

ME Madrid Pl. de Santa Ana 14 ☎917 016 000, ⓦmemadrid.com; ⓜSol; map p.102. Once a favourite haunt of bullfighters, this giant white wedding-cake of a hotel is now part of Melià's exclusive *ME* chain. Minimalist decor, designer furnishings, high-tech fittings, a super-cool penthouse bar and a chic restaurant serving fusion-style food. Special offers can bring the price down to around €150. **€200**

NH Palacio Tepa c/San Sebastian 2 ☎913 896 490, ⓦnh-hoteles.com; ⓜAntón Martín; map p.102. This luxurious new five-star, 85-room hotel is right in the heart of Huertas, close to Pl. Santa Ana and a stone's throw away from the big museums. It has a range of large, plush rooms including some two-storey suites and wooden-beamed attics. **€150**

★ **Room Mate Alicia** c/Prado 2 ☎913 896 095, ⓦroom-matehotels.com; ⓜSol/Sevilla; map p.102. Perched on the corner of the plaza, the 34-room *Alicia* is in a great location – if a little noisy. Seriously cool decor, stylish rooms and great value. **€90**

AROUND PASEO DEL PRADO

This is a quieter area, though still very central, and it is close to the main art museums, the Parque del Retiro and Estación de Atocha. Some of the city's most expensive hotels are here – as well as a few more modest options.

★ **Hostal Gonzalo** c/Cervantes 34, 3º ☎914 292 714, ⓦhostalgonzalo.com; ⓜAntón Martín; map p.102. This has to be one of the most welcoming *hostales* in the city. It has fifteen bright, en-suite rooms – all of which have a/c and modern bathrooms – and a charming owner. **€55**

Hotel Mora Paseo del Prado 32 ☎914 201 569, ⓦhotelmora.com; ⓜAtocha; map p.62. A good-value, slightly old-fashioned 62-room hotel perfectly positioned for all the galleries on the Paseo del Arte. It's not as smart as the nearby *Nacional*, but it's cheaper, and some of the a/c rooms have pleasant views along the Paseo del Prado. **€84**

Hotel Palace Pl. de los Cortes 7 ☎913 608 000, ⓦwestinpalacemadrid.com; ⓜAtocha/Banco de España; map p.102. A colossal, sumptuous hotel with every imaginable facility, a spectacular, glass-covered central patio, and luxurious rooms – plus none of the snootiness of the *Ritz* across the road. **€245**

NH Nacional Paseo del Prado 48 ☎914 296 629, ⓦnh-hoteles.com; ⓜAtocha; map p.62. A large, plush hotel, part of the NH chain, attractively situated opposite the Jardines Botánicos. Special offers can reduce the price substantially. **€105**

★ **Radisson Blu Madrid Prado** c/Moratín 52 ☎915 242 626, ⓦradissonblu.com/pradohotel-madrid; ⓜAtocha; map p.102. Designer hotel located along the Paseo del Prado featuring sleek rooms in black, brown and white, photos of the Madrid skyline adorning the walls, black slate bathrooms and coffee machines. There is a spa and indoor pool, a whisky bar and a restaurant too. **€130**

Villa Real Pl. de las Cortes 10 ☎914 203 767, ⓦderbyhotels.es; ⓜSevilla; map p.102. Aristocratic hotel with its own art collection owned by Catalan entrepreneur Jordi Clos. Each of the 96 elegant double rooms has a spacious sitting area. The rooftop restaurant, whose walls are decorated with Andy Warhol originals, affords splendid views over the Congresos de Diputados and down towards the Paseo del Prado. **€150**

1

PLAZA DE ESPAÑA, GRAN VÍA AND BEYOND

The huge old buildings along the Gran Vía – which stretches all the way from Pl. de España to c/Alcalá – hide a vast array of hotels and *hostales* at every price, often with a delightfully decayed elegance, though they also suffer from traffic noise. After dark, the area can feel somewhat seedy.

Aparto-hotel Rosales c/Marqués de Urquijo 23 ☎ 915 420 351, ⊛ apartohotel-rosales.com; Ⓜ Argüelles; map p.62. Large, comfortable apartments with separate bedroom, living area and kitchenette. Close to the Parque

◼ ACCOMMODATION			
Los Amigos Hostal	8	Hotel San Lorenzo	1
Casa Madrid	7	Hotel Urban	11
Chic & Basic Colours	22	International Hostel	
Chic & Basic		Posada de Huertas	23
Mayerling	24	ME Madrid	18
Hostal Alaska	13	NH Palacio Tepa	21
Hostal Andorra	2	Petit Palace Arenal	10
Hostal Gonzalo	20	Posada del	
Hostal La Macarena	17	Leon de Oro	25
Hostal Tijcal	15	Posada Real	
Hostal Tijcal 2	16	Manuel	9
Hotel de las Letras	3	Radisson Blu	
Hotel Meninas	4	Madrid Prado	26
Hotel Palace	14	Room Mate Alicia	19
Hotel Palacio		Room Mate Mario	5
de San Martín	6	Villa Real	12

● TAPAS BARS & RESTAURANTS			
El Abuelo	25	Círculo de Belles Artes	8
Almendro 13	51	Corazón Loco	56
Artemisa	20	Domine Cabra	44
El Asador Frontón	58	El Estragón	45
La Barraca	1	La Finca de Susana	11
La Bola	2	La Gloria de Montera	6
El Botín	37	El Lacón	30
Las Bravas	18	Lhardy	14
Café de Oriente	9	La Mallorquina	12
Casa del Abuelo	24	Mercado de San Miguel	27
Casa Labra	10	Mezklum Tech	26
Casa Lastra	61	La Musa Latina	48
Casa Lucio	57	Museo del Jamón	13
Casa Paco	39	Negro Anglona	41
Cervecería Cervantes	36	La Oreja de Oro	21
La Chata	50	Paradis Madrid	15
		Le Petit Bistrot	42

del Oeste and in one of the quieter areas of town, so a good option if you're travelling with children. Prices start at €125 (2-person) and €150 (4-person).

Aparto Suites Jardines de Sabatini Cuesta San Vicente 16 ☎915 419 650, ⓦjardinesdesabatini.com; ⓜPlaza España/Príncipe Pío; map p.62. Convenient

location in between Pl. España and Príncipe Pío station, this upmarket apartment complex offers studios and suites for families and up to four adults with small kitchen areas. Some of the rooms overlook the royal palace. €135

Casón del Tormes c/Río 7 ☎915 419 746, ⓦhotel casondeltormes.com; ⓜPlaza de España; map p.62.

La Platería	49	●BARS		●SHOPS
Posada de la Villa	47	Alhambra	19	El Arco Artesania	15
Prada a Tope	22	Cervecería Alemana	35	Area Real Madrid	6
La Sanabresa	52	Cervecería Santa Ana	33	Camper	3
La Suiza	32	Del Diego	3	Casa de Diego	7
La Taberna de los		Delic	55	Casa Jiménez	1
Cien Vinos	46	La Fidula	43	Casa Mira	9
La Taberna de Dolores	40	The Glass Bar	17	Casa Yustas	10
Tapasentao	60	Gin Club/Mercado		Contreras	12
La Tapería del Prado	54	de la Reina	5	Desnivel	16
El Tempranillo	59	Museo Chicote	4	El Flamenco Vive	8
La Trucha	28	Naturbier	34	FNAC	2
La Vaca Veronica	53	La Venencia	23	Imaginarium	5
Vadebaco	7	Viva Madrid	29	La Librería	11
El Vegetariano	16			Mariano Madrueño	4
Viña P	31			Mercado de San Miguel	13
Viños y Quesos González	38			Seseña	14

1

A neat 63-room hotel in a surprisingly quiet street off Pl. de España, the *Casón del Tormes* is a very good option in this price range. Rooms are comfortable, en suite and a/c, and the English-speaking staff are helpful. Substantial discounts in July & Aug. €103

Hostal Andorra Gran Vía 33, 7º ☎915 323 116, ⊛hostalandorra.com; Ⓜ Callao; map p.102. Simple, clean and homely *hostal*, with bathrooms and a/c in all the compact rooms. €63

Hostal Buenos Aires Gran Vía 61, 2º ☎915 420 102, ⊛hoteleshn.com; Ⓜ Plaza de España; map p.62. Twenty-five pleasantly decorated rooms with a/c, satellite TV and modern bathrooms, plus double-glazing to keep out much of the noise. €65

Hotel Emperador Gran Vía 53 ☎915 472 800, ⊛emperadorhotel.com; Ⓜ Santo Domingo/Plaza de España; map p.62. The main reason to come here is for the stunning rooftop swimming pool with its magnificent views. Otherwise, it is a rather impersonal place, though the recently refurbished rooms are large and well decorated. €110

Hotel de las Letras Gran Vía 11 ☎915 237 980, ⊛hoteldelasletras.com; Ⓜ Gran Vía; map p.62. Design-conscious hotel housed in an elegant, early nineteenth-century building at the smarter end of Gran Vía. The stylish rooms come complete with flat-screen TVs and pillow menus. Downstairs, there's a smooth bar and lounge area and a high-quality restaurant with reasonably priced dishes. €120

★ **Hotel Santo Domingo** c/San Bernardo 1 ☎915 479 800, ⊛hotelsantodomingo.es. Ⓜ Santo Domingo; map p.62. What with the jungle paintings adorning the car park, the private art collection and the rooftop swimming pool with views over the city, this Mercure hotel is full of nice surprises. Rooms have tasteful individual decor, carpeted floors, large beds and walk-in shower rooms. €133

NORTH OF GRAN VÍA AND CHUECA

North of Gran Vía, there are further wedges of *hostales* and hotels on and around c/Fuencarral and c/Hortaleza, near ⓂGran Vía. To the east of c/Fuencarral, Chueca is another nightlife centre and the city's *zona gay*, home to numerous bars, clubs and restaurants.

Hostal Zamora Pl. Vázquez de Mella 1, 4º izqda. ☎915 217 031, ⊛hostalzamora.com; Ⓜ Gran Vía; map p.62. Seventeen well-kept, simple rooms in this pleasant *hostal* overlooking the plaza. All have modern bathrooms, TV, a/c and free wi-fi. There are good-value family rooms, too. €52

Hotel San Lorenzo c/Clavel 8 ☎915 213 057, ⊛hotel-sanlorenzo.com; Ⓜ Gran Vía; map p.102. A former *hostal* that has been upgraded to a neat and tidy three-star hotel offering clean and comfortable rooms with a/c and bathrooms. Quadruples available from €80. €50

Petit Palace Ducal c/Hortaleza 3, 3º ☎915 211 043, ⊛hthoteles.com; Ⓜ Gran Vía; map p.62. Upgraded from an old *hostal* a few years back, this is now one of the self-styled High-Tech chain. Its 58 sleek rooms come complete with all manner of mod cons. €90

MALASAÑA AND SANTA BÁRBARA

Malasaña, west of c/Fuencarral and centred around Pl. Dos de Mayo, is a former working-class district, and now one of the main nightlife areas of Madrid.

Hostal Santa Bárbara Pl. Santa Bárbara 4, 3º ☎914 462 345, ⊛hostalsantabarbaramadrid.com; Ⓜ Alonso Martínez; map p.62. Old-fashioned *hostal* in a good location on this pleasant tree-lined square. Simple, but tidy little rooms, some with a/c and all with bathrooms. €48

Hostal Sil/Serranos c/Fuencarral 95, 2º & 3º ☎914 488 972, ⊛silserranos.com; Ⓜ Tribunal; map p.62. Two well-managed *hostales*, run by a friendly owner, at the quieter end of c/Fuencarral, with a/c, modern bathrooms and TV. €59

★ **Hotel Abalú** c/Pez 19 ☎915 314 744, ⊛hotelabalu .com; Ⓜ Noviciado; map p.62. This boutique hotel, which is a little north of Gran Vía, has some vibrant, individually designed rooms with individual touches such as mini-chandeliers, butterfly prints and patterned mirrors. Suites and a two-person apartment available. Good value. €100

PASEO DE RECOLETOS AND SALAMANCA

This is Madrid at its most chic: the Bond Street/Rue de Rivoli region of smart shops and equally well-heeled apartment blocks. It's a safe, pleasant area, just north of the Parque del Retiro, though a good walk from the main sights.

★ **Hostal Residencia Don Diego** c/Velázquez 45, 5º ☎914 350 760, ⊛hostaldondiego.com; Ⓜ Velázquez; map p.62. Although officially a *hostal*, this is much more like a hotel. All the neat, quiet and comfortable rooms have a/c and satellite TV. Reasonably priced for the area. Some English-speaking staff. €75

Hotel Galiano c/Alcalá Galiano 6 ☎913 192 000, ⊛hotelgaliano.com; Ⓜ Colón; map p.62. Hidden away in a quiet street off the Paseo de la Castellana, this small hotel has an old-world sophisticated air about it and friendly service. Look out for special offers on the website. Car-parking facilities. €130

Hotel Orfila c/Orfila 6 ☎917 027 770, ⊛hotelorfila .com; Ⓜ Colón/Alonso Martínez; map p.62. Exclusive boutique hotel housed in a beautiful nineteenth-century mansion on a quiet street north of Alonso Martínez. Twelve of the exquisite rooms are suites, and there's an elegant terrace for tea and drinks, as well as an upmarket restaurant, too. Of course, none of this comes cheap. €275

Petit Palace Embassy c/Serrano 46 ☎914 313 060, ⊛hthoteles.com; Ⓜ Colón/Goya; map p.62. A four-star member of the sleek High-Tech Hotels chain, close to Pl. de Colón and in the middle of the upmarket Salamanca shopping district. The *Embassy* has 75 rooms, including ten family rooms for up to four people. Free broadband internet access and flat-screen TVs. **€110**

EATING

Madrid's range of **eating** establishments is legion, and includes tapas bars, cafés, *marisquerías* (seafood bars) and *restaurantes*. At almost any of our recommendations you could happily eat your fill – money permitting – though at bars, *madrileños* usually eat just a tapa or share a *ración* of the house speciality, then move on to repeat the procedure down the road. While cafés do serve food, they are much more places to drink coffee, have a *copa* or *caña*, or read the papers. Some also act as a meeting place for the semi-formal *tertulia* – a kind of discussion/drinking group, popular among Madrid intellectuals of the past and revived in the 1980s. Unless stated otherwise, opening hours are typically 1.30–4.30pm and 8pm–midnight.

SOL, PLAZA MAYOR AND ÓPERA

The central area is the most varied in Madrid in terms of price and food. Indeed, there can be few places in the world that rival the streets around **Puerta del Sol** for sheer number of places to eat and drink. Around the smarter **Ópera** district, you need to be more selective, while on **Plaza Mayor** itself, stick to drinks. Unless indicated otherwise, all these places are easily reached from **Metro Sol**.

CAFÉS

Café de Oriente Pl. de Oriente 2; Ⓜ Ópera; map p.102. Elegant, Parisian-style affair with a popular *terraza* looking out towards the Palacio Royal.

La Mallorquina Puerta del Sol 2; Ⓜ Sol; map p.102. Good for breakfast or snacks – try one of their *napolitanas* (cream slices) in the sunny upstairs salon. Daily 9am–9pm.

TAPAS BARS

El Abuelo c/Núñez de Arce 3; map p.102. There's a *comedor* at the back of this down-to-earth bar, where you can order a selection of delicious *raciones* – the *croquetas* are especially good – and a jug of house wine. Closed Mon.

Las Bravas c/Alvarez Gato 3; map p.102. As the name suggests, *patatas bravas* (spicy potatoes) are the tapa to try at this bar, which has patented its own version of the sauce; the *tortilla* is pretty good, too. On the outside of the bar are novelty mirrors, a hangover from the days when this was a barber's and the subject of a story by Valle Inclán. Standing room only and bright lights mean it is not to everyone's liking, though. Other branches nearby at c/Espoz y Mina 13, c/Cruz 15 and Pasaje Mathéu 5.

★ **Casa del Abuelo** c/Victoria 12; map p.102. Tiny, highly atmospheric corner bar serving just its cloyingly sweet red house wine, beer and great cooked prawns – try them *al ajillo* (in garlic) or *a la plancha* (fried). You'll be given a voucher for a free glass of wine at the sister bar round the corner in c/Núñez de Arce.

Casa Labra c/Tetuán 12 ☎ 915 310 081; map p.102. A great, traditional place, where the Spanish Socialist Party was founded in 1879. Order a drink at the bar and a *ración* of *bacalao* (cod fried in batter) or some of the best *croquetas* in town at the counter to the right of the door. There's a

fairly expensive restaurant at the back with classic *madrileño* food on offer. Closed Sun.

Lhardy c/San Jerónimo 8 ☎ 915 213 385, Ⓦ lhardy.com; map p.102. *Lhardy* is one of Madrid's most famous and expensive restaurants. Once the haunt of royalty, it's a beautiful place but greatly overpriced (minimum €60). Downstairs, however, there's a wonderful bar/shop, where you can snack on canapés, *fino* (dry sherry) and *consommé*, without breaking the bank. Closed Sun eve.

★ **Mercado de San Miguel** Pl. de San Miguel Ⓦ mercadodesanmiguel.es; map p.102. Transformed into a traditional neighbourhood market into a hip location for an *aperitivo* and a spot of tapas, this beautiful wrought-iron *mercado* is worth exploring at almost any time of day. There's something for everyone, from vermouth and champagne to saltcod, oysters and sushi.

Museo del Jamón c/San Jerónimo 6; map p.102. The largest branch of this ubiquitous Madrid chain, from whose ceilings are suspended hundreds of *jamones* (hams). The best – and they are not cheap – are the *jabugos* from the Sierra Morena, though a ham croissant is around €5.

La Oreja de Oro c/Victoria 9; map p.102. Standing room only in this spit-and-sawdust bar just opposite *La Casa del Abuelo*. Try the excellent *pulpo a la Gallega* (sliced octopus layered over a bed of potatoes and seasoned with cayenne pepper) washed down with Ribeiro wine served in terracotta bowls. Plenty of other seafood tapas on offer, too. Closed Aug.

RESTAURANTS

El Botín c/Cuchilleros 17 ☎ 913 664 217, Ⓦ botin.es; Ⓜ Sol/Tirso de Molina; map p.102. Established in 1725, the picturesque *El Botín* is cited in the *Guinness Book of Records* as Europe's oldest restaurant. Favoured by Hemingway, inevitably it's become a tourist haunt but not such a bad one, with quality Castilian roasts – especially suckling pig (*cochinillo*) from Segovia and roast lamb (*cordero asado*). There's a €40 *menú* but you could eat for less.

★ **El Buey** Pl. de la Marina Española 1 ☎ 915 413 041, Ⓦ restauranteelbuey.com; Ⓜ Santo Domingo; map p.62. A meat-eaters' paradise specializing in steak – which you fry up yourself on a sizzling hotplate. Very good side

1

dishes, too, including a superb leek and seafood pie, and excellent home-made desserts. All for around €35 a head. Closed Sun.

Casa Paco Pl. Puerta Cerrada 11 ☎913 663 166, ⓦcasapaco1933.com; ⓜLa Latina/Sol; map p.102. This classic, traditional *comedor*, with no-nonsense service, dishes out some of the best-prepared meat dishes in town. Specializes in sirloin steak (*solomillo*), and another delicious cut known as *cebón de buey*. Count on spending about €35. Closed Sun & Aug.

La Finca de Susana c/Arlabán 4 ⓦlafinca-restaurant .com; ⓜSevilla; map p.102. One of two great-value restaurants set up by a group of Catalan friends (the other is *La Gloria de Montera* just off Gran Vía). Tasty *menú* for around €9, consisting of simple dishes served with a little imagination. Tables are close together and you'll need to arrive early to avoid queuing, as you can't book. Opens 1pm for lunch.

Vadebaco c/Campomanes 6 ☎915 417 017, ⓦvadebaco .com; ⓜÓpera; map p.102. Creative tapas and over 350 different wines to choose from in this new arrival on the scene. Cod samosas, mushroom ravioli, risotto and delicious desserts are just some of the offerings served up in chic surroundings. Does a very good value €12 lunchtime *menú*.

PLAZA DE SANTA ANA AND HUERTAS

You should spend at least an evening eating and drinking at the historic, tiled bars in this central area. Restaurants are good, too, and frequented as much by locals as tourists.

CAFÉS

La Suiza Pl. de Santa Ana 2; ⓜSevilla; map p.102. A classic café serving delicious *leche merengada* (a sort of sweet, whipped-milk ice cream), *chocolate con churros* and a massive selection of cakes. Its year-round terraza on the plaza makes a perfect spot for people-watching. Daily 8am–midnight.

TAPAS BARS

Cervecería Cervantes Pl. de Jesús 7; ⓜAntón Martín; map p.102. Prawns are the speciality here – the *tosta de gambas* is delicious – but there's a wide range of other tapas, and the beer is good, too. An excellent place for an *aperitivo*. Closed Sun eve.

El Lacón c/Manuel Fernández y González 8 ⓦmesonellacon.com; ⓜSol; map p.102. A large Galician bar-restaurant with plenty of seats upstairs. Great *pulpo*, *caldo gallego* (meat and vegetable broth) and *empanadas*. They also do boards of cold meats, vegetables, meat and fish. Main courses cost €12–15. Closed Aug.

★ **La Taberna de Dolores** Pl. de Jesús 4; ⓜAntón Martín; map p.102. Splendid *canapés* at this popular and friendly tiled bar at the bottom of Huertas. The beer is really good, and the food specialities include Roquefort and anchovy, and smoked-salmon *canapés*. Get here early if you want a space at the bar.

La Trucha c/Manuel Fernández y González 3 ☎914 295 833; ⓜAntón Martín; map p.102. An ever-popular tapas bar and reasonably priced restaurant sandwiched between Santa Ana and c/Echegaray. Andalucian-style *pescaíto frito*

MADRID'S VEGETARIAN RESTAURANTS

Madrid has a growing number of good-value **vegetarian restaurants**, scattered about the centre. These include:

Artemisa c/Ventura de la Vega 4 ☎914 295 092, ⓦrestaurantartemisa.com; ⓜSevilla; c/Tres Cruces 4 ☎915 218 721; ⓜGran Vía; map p.102. Two branches of this long-standing popular vegetarian (you may have to wait for a table), good for veggie pizzas and paellas, superb vegetable dishes and an imaginative range of salads and soups. Reasonable prices at around €20–25 per head, lunchtime *menú* at €11.25. Daily 1.30–4pm, 9pm–midnight.

El Estragón Pl. de la Paja 10 ☎913 658 982, ⓦelestragonvegetariano.com; ⓜLa Latina; map p.102. Cosy restaurant enjoying a fine setting on the edge of ancient Pl. de Paja, and dishing up big helpings of hearty vegetarian food and decent desserts. A slightly expensive lunchtime *menú* at €14 (dinner *menú* is €19) during the week. Daily 1.30–4.15pm & 8pm–midnight (Fri & Sat open til 12.45am).

★ **La Isla del Tesoro** c/Manuela Malasaña 3 ☎915 931 440, ⓦisladeltesoro.net; ⓜBilbao; map p.62. Cosmopolitan vegetarian food at this great-value place on one of the most interesting streets in Malasaña. Constantly changing, weekly *menú* for €12. Daily 1.30–4pm, 9pm–midnight.

Vegaviana c/Pelayo 35 ☎913 080 381; ⓜChueca; map p.62. A wide range of vegetarian options with an international twist at this small eatery in the heart of Chueca. There's a free-range chicken option for non-veggies, too. Very good value, with big portions meaning you'll struggle to break the €20 mark. Tues–Sat 1.30–4pm & 9–11.30pm.

El Vegetariano c/Santiago 9 (Ópera) ☎917 583 588; ⓜÓpera; map p.102. Simple, but high-quality, home-made vegetarian food with an excellent vegetable lasagne, Asian-inspired dishes, and good desserts including a very tasty apple pie.

1

MADRID CUISINE

Thanks to its status as Spanish capital, Madrid has long provided a home to **almost every regional style of Spanish cooking** from Castilian roasts, Galician seafood and Andalucian fried fish, to Asturian stews, Valencian paellas and Basque *nueva cocina*.

The city also has its own range of home-spun dishes with the famous *cocido madrileño*, a three-course stew of various cuts of meat, chorizo, chickpea and vegetables, topping the list. Other traditional favourites include *callos* (tripe in a spicy tomato sauce), *oreja* (pig's ears), *caracoles* (snails) and a range of offal-based dishes.

But Madrid is becoming increasingly cosmopolitan and dozens of **foreign cuisines** have appeared on the scene in recent years. There are some good Peruvian, Argentinian, Middle Eastern and Italian places and a growing number of oriental-influenced restaurants with some inventive fusion-style cuisine.

(smoked fish) and *pimientos de Padrón* are specialities. Usually very crowded. Closed Sun.

Viña P Pl. de Santa Ana 3; Sol/Sevilla; map p.102. Friendly staff serve a great range of tapas in a bar decked out with bullfighting mementoes and posters. Try the asparagus, stuffed mussels and the mouthwatering *almejas a la marinera* (clams in a garlic and white-wine sauce).

★ **Vinos y Quesos González** c/Leon 12; map p.102. As you'd expect, this great little bar on the busy Calle Leon has an extensive range of wines and cheese on offer, but it also serves up other great tapas including a fantastic *salmorejo*, a range of speciality sausages from around Spain and some imaginative *tostas* covered in a variety of tasty patés.

RESTAURANTS

Domine Cabra c/Huertas 54 914 294 365, restaurantedominecabra.com; Antón Martín; map p.102. An interesting mix of traditional and modern, with *Spanish* standards given the *nueva cocina* treatment. Smallish helpings, tasty sauces – a rarity in Spain. Good-value *menús* at €13.60 and €18.99. Closed Sat lunch, Sun eve in Aug and first half of Sept.

Mezklum Tech c/Príncipe 16 915 218 911, mezklum.com; Sevilla; map p.102. A hyper-cool restaurant decked out in shades of mauve and white and serving a fine array of Mediterranean dishes, with good salads and pastas. It has two good-value lunch time *menús* at under €15, while evening meals cost around €25–30.

★ **Le Petit Bistrot** Pl. Matute 5 914 296 265, lepetitbistrot.net; Sevilla/Antón Martín; map p.102. A genuine French bistro in this quiet plaza just off Huertas. There's a very good €13.20 set lunch (€18.50 on Sat). Classics such as French onion soup, steak in bearnaise sauce, and profiteroles dripping with chocolate sauce. Closed Mon & Sun eve.

Prada a Tope c/Príncipe 11 914 295 221; Sevilla; map p.102. Excellent-quality produce from El Bierzo in León at this branch of the restaurant chain; the *pimientos asados*, *morcilla* and *tortilla* are extremely tasty. Expect to pay €20–25 for a full meal. Closed Mon.

La Sanabresa c/Amor de Diós 12 914 290 338; Antón Martín; map p.102. A real local, with a TV in one corner, and an endless supply of customers who come for its good-quality and reasonably priced dishes. Don't miss the grilled aubergines. *Menú del día* for around €10, otherwise €20. Closed Sun.

★ **La Vaca Verónica** c/Moratín 38 914 297 827; Antón Martín; map p.102. Excellent Argentinian-style meat, really good fresh pasta in imaginative sauces, quality fish dishes and tasty vegetables. Try the *filet Verónica* and the *carabinero con pasta*. The *menú* is a good deal at €15, and the service is friendly. Closed Sat lunch & Sun.

LA LATINA AND LAVAPIÉS

South from Sol and Huertas are the quarters of **La Latina** and **Lavapiés**, whose patchwork of tiny streets retains an appealing neighbourhood feel, and are home to a great selection of bars and restaurants.

CAFÉS

Café Barbieri c/Ave María 45; Lavapiés; map p.62. A relaxed place in the heart of Lavapiés, with unobtrusive music, old-style decor, newspapers and a wide selection of coffees. Open from 3pm.

TAPAS BARS

★ **Almendro 13** c/Almendro 13; La Latina; map p.102. Always packed at weekends, this fashionable wood-panelled bar serves great *fino* from chilled black bottles. Tuck into the house specials of *huevos rotos* (fried eggs on a bed of crisps) and *roscas rellenas* (rings of bread stuffed with various meats).

Los Caracoles "Casa Amadeo" Pl. Cascorro 18 loscaracolesdeamadeo.com; La Latina; map p.62. A favourite since the 1940s, this does a good range of tapas as well as its namesake *caracoles* (snails). The place to come after a trek around the Rastro – although it will be heaving.

La Chata c/Cava Baja 24; La Latina; map p.102. One of the most traditional, and popular, tiled tapas bars in Madrid, with hams hanging from the ceiling, taurine and football mementoes on the walls, and a good selection of *raciones*, including *cebolla rellena* and *pimientos del piquillo rellenos* (stuffed onions and peppers). Closed Sun eve.

Corazón Loco c/Almendro 22 ⊛corazonloco.com; ⓂLa Latina; map p.102. A lively bar just off the Pl. de San Andrés with a good range of tapas and a cosy brick-lined dining area at the back. Two different set lunches are available (Tues–Fri) for €10 and €12.

★ **Juana La Loca** Pl. Puerta de Moros 4; ⓂLa Latina; map p.62. Fashionable hangout serving inventive tapas – tortilla with carmelized onion, tuna carpaccio and ostrich steaks – and a great selection of very tasty, but fairly pricey, *canapés*. Closed Mon & Sun eve.

Melo's c/Avemaría 44; ⓂLavapiés; map p.62. It's standing room only at this very popular Galician bar serving huge *zapatillas* (slippers of Galician country bread filled with *lacón* and *queso*) and great *pimientos de Padrón*. Usually closed Aug.

La Musa Latina c/Costanilla San Andrés 12 ⊛lamusalatina.com; ⓂLa Latina; map p.102. Another style-conscious restaurant on the La Latina scene. Serves a great €11 *menú* and a small selection of modern tapas. It has a cool brick-walled bar downstairs with DJ sessions in the evenings.

Taberna de Antonio Sánchez c/Mesón de Paredes 13 ☎915 397 826; ⓂTirso de Molina; map p.62. Said to be the oldest *taberna* in Madrid, this Lavapiés bar has an appropriately dark, wooden interior complete with stuffed bulls' heads (one of which killed Antonio Sánchez, the son of the founder). Lots of *finos* on offer, plus *jamón* and *queso* tapas or *tortilla de San Isidro* (with salted cod). Closed Sun eve.

★ **La Taberna de los Cien Vinos** c/Nuncio 16; ⓂLa Latina; map p.102. A small, friendly wood-panelled bar with, as the name would suggest, an excellent selection of wines and a constantly changing *menú* of inventive and very tasty *raciones*. Arrive early if you want a seat for the evening. Closed Mon & Sun eve.

Tapasentao c/Almendro 27; ⓂLa Latina; map p.102. On the corner of the Pl. de San Andrés, this is just the place for original, seated tapas. Recommended are the *chorizo*

with wafer-thin chips, the three-cheese salad and the fried mushrooms. There is a less-crowded branch nearby at c/Príncipe Anglona 1.

★ **El Tempranillo** Cava Baja 38; ⓂLa Latina; map p.102. A stylish little bar serving tasty tapas and a vast range of Spanish wines by the glass – a great place to discover a new favourite. Closed two weeks in Aug.

★ **Txirimiri** c/Humilladero 6; ⓂLa Latina; map p.62. Fantastic range of tapas and *pintxos* in this friendly and very popular bar just beside the Mercado de la Cebada. Mouth watering combinations include *tortilla* with caramelized onion, langoustine *croquetas*, mushroom risotto and the house speciality, the Unai hamburger *pintxo*.

RESTAURANTS

El Asador Frontón Pl. Tirso de Molina 7, 1º (entrance just off the square) ☎913 691 617, ⊛asadorfronton.es; ⓂTirso de Molina; map p.102. A limited but high-quality *menú* with a wide range of classic Castilian dishes available – red meats, fish and local vegetables. Good home-made desserts. It will cost around €40 for the works. Closed Aug.

Casa Lastra c/Olivar 3 ☎913 690 837, ⊛casalastra .com; ⓂLavapiés/Antón Martín; map p.102. Very popular local restaurant serving classic Asturian fare, including *entrecot al cabrales* (steak in a strong blue-cheese sauce), *fabada* and, of course, *sidra* (cider). Big portions, and, at around €13, the set lunch is very good value. Closed Wed & Sun eve.

Casa Lucio c/Cava Baja 35 ☎913 653 252, ⊛casalucio .es; ⓂLa Latina; map p.102. A Madrid institution famous for its Castilian specialities such as *cocido*, *callos* (tripe) and roasts, cooked to perfection. Booking is essential. Count on around €50 a head. If you can't stretch to a full meal, try some of the specialities in the front bar. Closed Sat lunch & Aug.

Negro Anglona c/Segovia 13 ☎913 663 753, ⊛negrodeanglona.com; ⓂLa Latina/Ópera; map p.102. All-black decor in this refurbished and romantic pasta and pizza joint, situated in the cellars of an old palace. A handy late-night option, but service can be slow at weekends. Expect to pay around €30 a head.

SUMMER IN MADRID

Although things are beginning to change as Madrid comes into line with the rest of Europe, the Spanish capital experiences a **partial shut-down in the summer**; from the end of July, you'll suddenly find that many of the bars, restaurants and offices are closed, and their inhabitants gone to the coast and countryside. Only in September does the city open fully for business again.

Luckily for visitors, and those *madrileños* who choose to remain, the main sights and museums stay open, and the summer nightlife takes on a momentum of its own in outdoor terrace bars, or *terrazas*. In addition, the city council organizes a major programme of entertainment, Los Veranos de la Villa, and overall it's not a bad time to be in town, so long as you can cope with the soaring temperatures and you're not trying to get anything done.

1

TOP CHEFS IN MADRID

Aside from the burgeoning international cuisine scene in Madrid, further good news for gastronomes is that several of the **country's top chefs** have established flagship restaurants in the capital.

Sergi Arola has set up his *Gastro* at c/Zurbano 31 ☎913 102 169, ⓦsergiarola.es; ⓜAlonso Martínez. This Michelin-starred restaurant offers a constantly changing range of fixed courses on a set menu ranging from €95–160.

Ramón Freixa's exquisite creations are showcased at *Freixa Madrid* in the *Selenza Hotel* (see p.113).

Óscar Velasco runs the Michelin-starred *Santceloni* in the *Hotel Hesperia Paseo de la Castellana* 57 (☎912 108 840, ⓦrestaurantesantceloni.com; ⓜGregorio Marañon), with stunning, but hugely expensive menus at €132 and €165.

Ángel Palacios is head chef at *La Broche* at the *Hotel Miguel Ángel* (c/Miguel Ángel 29 ☎913 993 437, ⓦlabroche.com; ⓜGregorio Marañon), which provides a more accessible set of options ranging from the lunchtime-only Ejecutive *menú* at €28 to the taster menu at €80 and the Gran Festival at €108.

★ **Posada de la Villa** c/Cava Baja 9 ☎913 661 860, ⓦposadadelavilla.es; ⓜLa Latina; map p.102. The most attractive-looking restaurant in La Latina, spread over three floors of a seventeenth-century mansion. Cooking is typically *madrileña*, including superb roast lamb. Reckon on a good €50 per person for the works – though you could get away with less. Closed Sun eve & Aug.

GRAN VÍA, PLAZA DE ESPAÑA AND BEYOND

On the **Gran Vía**, burger bars and fast-food joints tend to fill most of the gaps between shops and cinemas. However, there are a few good restaurants in and around the great avenue.

TAPAS BARS

Alhuzena c/Martín de los Heros 72; ⓜArgüelles; map p.62. Rustic basement bar serving some superb home-made tapas, including two varieties of *croquetas*. For dessert they have some great chocolate crêpes and muffins with ice cream. Closed Sun & Aug.

RESTAURANTS

★ **La Barraca** c/Reina 29 ☎915 327 154, ⓦlabarraca.es; ⓜGran Vía/Banco de España; map p.102. Step off the dingy street into this little slice of Valencia for some of the best paellas in town. Service is attentive but not overfussy, the starters are excellent, and there's a refreshing lemon sorbet for dessert. A three-course meal with wine will set you back around €35 a head.

La Bola c/Bola 5 ☎915 476 930, ⓦlabola.es; ⓜSanto Domingo; map p.102. Established in 1870, this is one of the places to go for *cocido madrileño* (soup followed by chickpeas and other vegetables and then a selection of meats), which is only served at lunchtime (€19). Don't plan on doing anything energetic afterwards, as it is incredibly filling. Service can be a little surly. No cards. Closed Sun eve.

★ **Casa Mingo** Paseo de la Florida 34 ☎915 477 918; ⓜPríncipe Pío; map p.62. Noisy, crowded and fun, *Casa Mingo* is a reasonably priced (around €15 a head) Asturian chicken and cider house just up the road from the Príncipe Pío. Tables are like gold dust, so loiter with your bottle of *sidra* in hand.

La Gloria de Montera c/Caballero de Gracia 10 ⓦlagloriademontera.com; ⓜGran Vía; map p.102. Sister restaurant to *La Finca de Susana* (see p.106), with the same successful formula. Excellent-value *menú* with imaginative, well-presented dishes – but production-line service – in a cool setting on a gloomy street just off the Gran Vía. *Menú* for around €10.

CHUECA AND SANTA BÁRBARA

Chueca – and Santa Bárbara to its north – have a combination of some superb traditional old bars and stylish new restaurants, as well as a vast amount of nightlife.

CAFÉS

Café Comercial Glorieta de Bilbao; ⓜBilbao; map p.62. One of the city's most popular meeting points – a lovely traditional café, well positioned for the Chueca/Santa Bárbara area. Daily 7.30am–1am.

TAPAS BARS

Baco & Beto c/Pelayo 24 ⓦbacoybeto.com; ⓜChueca; map p.62. Exceedingly tasty, creative tapas with great *tostas* and *canapés*. Try the courgette with melted brie and the *croquetas*. An excellent selection of wines, too. Mon–Sat eve & Sat lunch.

★ **El Bocaito** c/Libertad 4–6 ⓦbocaito.com; ⓜChueca; map p.62. Munch away on a variety of delicious *canapés* and tapas, washed down with a cold beer, at this busy bar; their *Luisito*, is the hottest *canapé* your tastebuds are ever likely to encounter. Closed Sat lunch, Sun & two weeks in Aug.

1

Stop Madrid c/Hortaleza 11; Ⓜ Gran Vía; map p.62. An old-time bar specializing in products from Extremadura, revitalized with Belgian, Mexican and German beers, as well as *vermut* on tap. Tapas are largely *jamón* and *chorizo*, with the *Canapé Stop* of ham and tomato doused in olive oil well worth a try.

★ **Taberna Angel Sierra** c/Gravina 11, Pl. Chueca; Ⓜ Chueca; map p.62. One of the classic bars of Madrid, with a traditional zinc counter, constantly washed down. Everyone drinks *vermut*, which is on tap and delicious, and free tapas of the most exquisite *boquerones en vinagre* are despatched; *raciones*, however, are a bit pricey.

RESTAURANTS

El 26 de Libertad c/Libertad 26 ☎915 222 522; Ⓜ Chueca; map p.62. Enjoy creative cuisine at this brightly decorated restaurant popular with the Chueca locals. A good €15 *menú* is available in the week, with more imaginative – and expensive – offerings in the evenings, but service can be slow. Closed Sun eve & Mon eve.

Annapurna c/Zurbano 5 ☎913 198 716, ☻annapurna restaurante.com; Ⓜ Colón; map p.62. One of the best Indian restaurants in Madrid, especially if you go for the tandoori dishes or *thali*. Stylish decor and attentive service. There's a taster *menú* for around €30. Closed Sat lunch & Sun.

Bazaar c/Libertad 21 ☻restaurantbazaar.com; Ⓜ Chueca; map p.62. Fusion-style cuisine with Mediterranean and Asian influences from a relatively new arrival that has already become a big hit on the Chueca scene. Very good value lunchtime *menú* at around €10, though service is impersonal. No reservations, so arrive early to avoid a wait.

Café Oliver c/Almirante 12 ☎915 217 379, ☻cafeoliver .com; Ⓜ Chueca; map p.62. There are strong French and Moroccan influences at this trendy Chueca restaurant with an imaginative set lunch at €14. A filling brunch of pastries, eggs and pancakes is on offer for the popular but overpriced Sunday brunch (€25). Closed Sun eve.

Momo c/Libertad 8 ☎915 327 348; Ⓜ Chueca; map p.62. Relocated a few hundred metres from its former home, this well-established eatery is the place to go for a *menú* with that little bit extra: interesting flavours, sauces and other creative touches. A selection of *menús* available at midday, evening and weekends for €10–15.

Salvador c/Barbieri 12 ☎915 214 524; Ⓜ Chueca; map p.62. A blast from the past with bullfighting decor and specialities such as *rabo de toro* (bull's tail), *gallina en pepitoria*, fried *merluza* (hake) and *arroz con leche* (rice pudding), all of which are excellent. *Menú* at €20 and à la carte around €35. Closed Sun eve & Aug.

★ **La Tasca Suprema** c/Argensola 7 ☎913 080 347; Ⓜ Alonso Martínez; map p.62. This very popular neighbourhood local is worth booking ahead for its Castilian home cooking, done to perfection and including

superb *pimientos de piquillo* (piquant red peppers) and *cocido* (Mon & Thurs). Expect to pay around €25 per person. Open for lunch only; closed Sun & Aug.

La Tienda de Vinos (El Comunista) c/Augusto Figueroa 35; Ⓜ Chueca; map p.62. A long-established, down-to-earth *comedor*; its unofficial (but always used) name dates back to its time as a student haunt under Franco. The garlic soup is recommended. Most dishes are between €5 and €9.

Zara c/Infantas 5 ☎915 322 074; Ⓜ Chueca/Gran Vía; map p.62. Excellent Cuban food at very good prices. *Ropa vieja* (strips of beef), fried yucca, minced beef with fried bananas and other specialities; the *daiquiris* are very good, too. Prices are moderate (under €30). No reservations, so arrive early. Closed weekends and public holidays.

MALASAÑA AND CHAMBERÍ

Malasaña is another characterful area, with a big nightlife scene and dozens of bars. Farther north, in Chamberí, the area around Plaza de Olavide – a real neighbourhood square – offers some good-value places, well off the tourist trail.

CAFÉS

Café del Ruiz c/Ruiz 11; Ⓜ Tribunal/Bilbao; map p.62. A traditional café, serving coffee, cakes and cocktails. A top spot for a late drink or a pep-up coffee before going on to one of the nearby clubs. Daily 11am–2am.

TAPAS BARS

Albur c/Manuela Malasaña 15 ☻restaurantealbur .com; Ⓜ Bilbao; map 62. Wooden tables, rustic decor and excellent food, although the service can be a little slow. The *champiñones en salsa verde* and the *patatas Albur* are both worth sampling; the well-kept wines are the ideal accompaniment.

★ **La Musa** c/Manuel Malasaña 18 ☎914 487 558; Ⓜ Bilbao; map p.62. It's easy to see why *La Musa* – a café, bar and restaurant all rolled into one – has become such a firm favourite on the Malasaña scene. A variety of imaginative – and very tasty – tapas, generous helpings, a strong wine list and chic decor are all part of the recipe for success.

RESTAURANTS

Balear c/Sagunto 18 ☎914 479 115; Ⓜ Iglesia; map p.62.This Levantine restaurant serves only rice-based dishes, but they're superb. There's an inexpensive house cava, and you can turn up any time before midnight. Expect to pay around €30 a head. Closed Sun & Mon eve.

La Giralda c/Hartzenbush 12 ☎914 457 779, ☻restauranteslagiralda.com; Ⓜ Bilbao; map p.62. An *andaluz* fish and seafood restaurant of very high quality: perfectly cooked *chipirones*, *calamares* and all the

1

standards, plus wonderful *mero* (grouper). A second branch, across the road at no. 15, does a similarly accomplished job on *pescados fritos*. Around €30–35 per person. Closed Sun & public holidays.

Nina Madrid c/Manuela Malasaña 10 ☎915 910 046; ⓜBilbao; map p.62. A stylish and modern restaurant serving a very good €12 *menú*, excellent weekend brunches (€23) and a tasty evening sampler *menú* for €28. Imaginative dishes such as duck with cauliflower and sea-urchin sauce, crunchy aubergines in honey, and *croquetas* in satay sauce feature on the main menu.

★ **Ribeira do Miño** c/Santa Brígida 1 ☎915 219 854, ⓦmarisqueriaribeiradomino.com; ⓜTribunal; map p.62. A fabulous-value *marisquería*, serving a seafood platter for two for only €31. Go for the slightly more expensive Galician white wine Albariño to accompany it. Fast, efficient and friendly service.

PASEO DEL PRADO, PASEO DE RECOLETOS AND EL RETIRO

This is a fancier area with few bars of note but some extremely good, if expensive, restaurants, well worth considering, even if you're not staying at the *Ritz*.

CAFÉS

★ **Café del Espejo** Paseo de Recoletos 31; ⓜColón; map p.62. Opened in 1991 but you wouldn't guess it – mirrors, gilt and a wonderful glass pavilion, plus a leafy outside *terraza*. Daily 9am–1am.

Café Gijón Paseo de Recoletos 21; ⓜBanco de España; map p.62. A famous literary café – and a centre of the intellectual/arty *movida* in the 1980s – decked out in Cuban mahogany and mirrors. Has a summer *terraza*. Daily 7.30am–1am.

Círculo de Bellas Artes c/Alcalá 42; ⓜBanco de España; map p.102. A stylish bar, where you can loll on sofas and have drinks at "normal" prices. Outside, in summer, there's a comfortable *terraza*. Daily 9.30am–1am.

TAPAS BARS

La Platería c/Moratín 49; ⓜAtocha/Banco de España; map p.102. Just across the square from *La Tapería* (see below), this touristy but conveniently placed bar has an enormously popular summer *terraza* and a good selection of reasonably priced tapas.

La Tapería del Prado Pl. Platerías de Martínez 1; ⓜAtocha/Banco de España; map p.102. A modern and slightly pricey bar opposite the Prado serving up an inventive range of tapas and *raciones*, plus a decent set lunch at €10.

RESTAURANTS

Al Mounia c/Recoletos 5 ☎914 350 826, ⓦalmounia .es; ⓜColón/Banco de España; map p.62. Moroccan cooking at its best in the most established Arabic restaurant in town, offering a romantic setting with impeccable service. Lunchtime menus available Mon–Thurs at €37 and €40, otherwise expect to pay around €50 a head. Closed Mon & Aug.

Paradis Madrid c/Marqués de Cubas 14 ☎914 297 303, ⓦparadismadrid.es; ⓜBanco España; map p.102. Upmarket Catalan restaurant often frequented by the politicians from the nearby parliament, serving light, high-quality and inventive Mediterranean food on the menu with superb starters, fish and rice dishes. Expect to pay around €45–50. Closed Sat lunch & Sun.

Viridiana c/Juan de Mena 14 ☎915 315 222, ⓦrestauranteviridiana.com; ⓜRetiro/Banco de España; map p.62. A bizarre temple of Madrid *nueva cocina*, offering mouthwatering creations from a constantly changing menu, plus a superb selection of wines. The bill for a three-course meal will come to around €100 a head, but it's an unforgettable experience. Closed Sun, Easter & Aug.

SALAMANCA

Salamanca is Madrid's equivalent of Bond Street or Fifth Avenue, full of designer shops and expensive-looking natives. The recommendations below are correspondingly pricey but high quality.

TAPAS BARS

Hevia c/Serrano 118; ⓜNúñez de Balboa; map p.62. Plush venue and wealthy clientele who come for expensive but excellent tapas and *canapés* – the hot Camembert is a must. Closed Sun & part of Aug.

José Luís c/Serrano 89 ☎915 630 958; ⓜSerrano; map p.62. An upmarket tapas bar with dainty and delicious sandwiches laid out along the bar. You take what you fancy and cough up at the end, in the safe knowledge that the owner will have notched up another few hundred euros to expand his chain of bars in the Americas.

El Lateral Paseo de la Castellana 134; ⓜSantiago Bernabéu; map p.62. A swish place serving a good variety of classic dishes such as *croquetas* and *pimientos rellenos* (stuffed peppers) with a modern twist. Other branches at c/ Velázquez 57 and c/Fuencarral 43.

RESTAURANTS

El Pescador c/José Ortega y Gasset 75 ☎914 021 290; ⓜLista; map p.62. One of the city's best seafood restaurants, run by *gallegos* and with specials flown in from the Atlantic each morning. The clientele can be a bit intimidating, but you'll rarely experience better seafood cooking. Around €60. Closed Sun & Aug.

Estay c/Hermosilla 46 ☎915 780 470, ⓦestayrestaurante .com; ⓜVelázquez; map p.62. Basque-style cuisine in miniature (*canapés* and mini-casseroles) in this pleasant and roomy restaurant. A great range of *pintxos*, including *jamón* with roquefort cheese, langoustine vol-au-vents and a fine wine list too. A meal will cost €25–30. Closed Sun.

Ramón Freixa Madrid c/Claudio Coello 67 ☎917 818 262, ⦿ramonfreixamadrid.com; ⓂSerrano; map p.62. Catalan chef Ramon Freixa's flagship restaurant in Madrid is situated in the luxury surroundings of the *Selenza* hotel and is now the proud owner of two Michelin stars. Creative and impeccably presented dishes from an ever-changing menu featuring superb game and fish options such as hare bathed in quince and ginger essence, crab with oyster and razor shells in a grapefruit and coconut vinaigrette. À la carte dishes range from €25–55, while there is a selection of taster menus available from €70 to €115. Only space for 35 diners so book well in advance. Closed Sun & Mon.

DRINKING AND NIGHTLIFE

Madrid **nightlife** is a pretty serious phenomenon. This is one of the few cities in Europe where you can get caught in traffic jams in the early hours of the morning when the clubbers are either going home or moving on to the dance-past-dawn discos. As with everything *madrileño*, there is a bewildering variety of nightlife venues. Most common are the **discobares** – bars of all musical and sexual persuasions, whose unifying feature is background (occasionally live) pop, rock, dance or salsa music. These get going from around 11pm and stay open routinely until 2am, as will the few quieter **cocktail bars** and **pubs**.

For *discotecas*, entry charges are quite common (€5–18), but tend to cover you for a first drink. Free passes can often be picked up from public relations personnel who hang around in the streets outside, in tourist offices or bars. Be aware that many *discotecas* are fairly ephemeral institutions and frequently only last a season before opening up somewhere else under a different name, so it's a good idea to consult listing magazines *La Guía del Ocio, Metrópoli, esMadrid* or the website ⦿ clubbingspain.com for the very latest information.

BARS

Madrid's **bar scene** caters to every conceivable taste in terms of drinks, music and atmosphere, though in recent years, the notoriously late opening hours have been somewhat curtailed by the local authorities, who are attempting to get bars to close by 2am.

SOL, PLAZA DE SANTA ANA AND HUERTAS

Alhambra c/Victoria 5; ⓂSol; map p.102. A friendly tapas bar by day, *Alhambra* transforms itself into a fun *discobar* by night with the crowds spilling over into the *El Buscón* bar next door. Mon–Wed 11am–1.30am, Thurs 11am–2am, Fri & Sat 11am–3.30am.

Cervecería Alemana Pl. de Santa Ana 6; ⓂSol; map p.102. Refurbished but still stylish old beer house, once frequented by Hemingway. Order a *caña* and go easy on the tapas, as the bill can mount up fast. Daily except Tues 10am–12.30am, Fri & Sat until 2am.

Cervecería Santa Ana Pl. de Santa Ana 10; ⓂSol; map p.102. Cheaper than the *Alemana*, with tables outside, friendly service and a good selection of tapas. Daily 11am–1.30am.

La Fidula c/Huertas 57 ⦿myspace.com/lafidula; ⓂAntón Martín; map p.102. A fine bar where you can sip *fino* to the accompaniment of live music – classical, jazz, tango and acoustic – performed on the tiny stage (€6 when there's a live act). See website for details. Daily 8pm–3am.

The Glass Bar c/San Jeronimo 34; ⓂSevilla; map p.102. Housed in the ultra-chic five-star *Hotel Urban*, this glamorous, glass-fronted cocktail bar has become a compulsory stop for the well-heeled crowd. In summer, there's a terrace bar on the sixth floor. Mon–Sat 11am–3am.

Naturbier Pl. de Santa Ana 9; ⓂSol; map p.102. Next door to the *cervecerías Alemana* and *Santa Ana*, the *Naturbier* brews its own tasty, cloudy beer and serves a variety of German sausages to accompany it. Daily 8pm–3am.

★ **La Venencia** c/Echegaray 7; ⓂSol; map p.102. For a real taste of old Madrid, this is a must: a rather delapidated wood-panelled bar, serving just sherry – try the extra-dry *fino* or *manzanilla* – cured tuna (*mojama*) and delicious olives. Decoration has remained unchanged for decades, with ancient barrels and posters. Daily 7.30pm–1.30am; closed Aug.

Viva Madrid c/Manuel Fernández y González 7; ⓂAntón Martín; map p.102. Another fabulous tiled bar – both outside and in – with quite pricey wines and sherry, plus basic tapas. Nearly always packed. Daily 1pm–2.30am.

GRAN VÍA

★ **Del Diego** c/Reina 12; ⓂGran Vía; map p.102. An elegant New York-style cocktail bar set up by a former *Museo Chicote* waiter and now better than the original place. There's a friendly, unhurried atmosphere, and it's open until the early hours. The house special is the vodka-based Del Diego, but the mojitos and margaritas are great, too. Mon–Sat 9pm–3am; closed Aug.

Gin Club/Mercado de la Reina Gran Vía 12; ⓂGran Vía; map p.102. Multipurpose tapas bar, restaurant and *bar de copas*. At the back, with its mirror ceilings, black leather chairs, is the chill-out cocktail bar, the *Gin Club*, offering over 20 different brands at between €7–12, although you can also get a decent mojito here if you prefer something different.

El Jardín Secreto c/Conde Duque 2; ⓂPlaza de España; map p.62. Cosy, dimly lit bar on the corner of a tiny square close to Pl. de España, serving reasonably priced drinks and cocktails. Service is friendly and the atmosphere unhurried. Mon–Thurs & Sun 5.30pm–12.30am, Fri & Sat 6.30pm–2.30am.

1

Museo Chicote Gran Vía 12 🖥museo-chicote.com; 🚇Gran Vía; map p.102. Opened back in 1931, *Chicote* was once a haunt of Buñuel and Hemingway. It's lost some of its charm but is still a very fashionable place, with evening music sessions. Mon–Sat 5pm–1.30am.

LA LATINA AND LAVAPIÉS

★**Aloque** c/Torrecilla del Leal 20; 🚇Antón Martín; map p.62. A relaxed wine bar where you can try top-quality *vino* by the glass; the innovative tapas served up in the tiny kitchen at the back are excellent. Daily 7.30pm–1am; closed Aug.

Delic Pl. de la Paja 8; 🚇Antón Martín; map p.102. Serving home-made cakes, fruit juices and coffee, this is a pleasant café by day, transforming into a crowded but friendly cocktail bar by night. Mon 8pm–2am, Tues–Sun 11am–2am. Closed first half of Aug.

El Viajero Pl. de la Cebada; 🚇La Latina; map p.62. Bar, disco, restaurant and summer *terraza* on different floors of this fashionable La Latina nightspot. Great views of San Francisco el Grande from the *terraza* at the top. The food

(meat, pizzas and pastas) is good, but pricey. Tues–Sat 1.30–2.30am, Sun noon–8pm. Closed first half Jan, second half Aug.

CHUECA, MALASAÑA AND SANTA BÁRBARA

★**La Ardosa** c/Colón 13; 🚇Tribunal; map p.62. One of the city's classic *tabernas*, serving limited but very tasty tapas including great *croquetas*, *salmorejo* and an excellent home-made *tortilla*. Prides itself on its draught beer and Guinness. Daily 8.30am–2am.

★**Le Cabrera** c/Bárbara de Braganza 2 🖥lecabrera .com; 🚇Colón; map p.62. A chic new arrival on the Madrid scene serving drinks and creative tapas in the dazzling gastro bar on the ground floor and expertly mixed cocktails in the cosier basement area. There's another branch in the Casa de América at Paseo de Recoletas 2. Daily 4pm–2am.

Casa Camacho c/San Andrés 2 (just off Pl. Dos de Mayo); 🚇Tribunal; map p.62. An irresistible old neighbourhood *bodega*, with a traditional bar counter, *vermut* on tap and basic tapas. An ideal place to start the evening. Packed out at weekends. Daily noon–1.30am.

TERRAZAS

With the introduction of a new law banning smoking inside bars and restaurants, **terrazas** have become more popular than ever in Madrid and many places now have at least a few tables set up on the city pavements year-round.

In summer many more bars migrate on to the streets, especially the trendy designer ones that lie along **Paseo de Recoletos** and its continuation, **Paseo de la Castellana**. Beyond **Plaza de Colón** and up to the **Bernabéu** more fashionable terrazas with music, a posey clientele and higher prices often appear in the summer. Be aware, however, that many of the terrazas run by clubs vary their sites year by year as they fall foul of the increasingly strict licensing and noise regulations.

Atenas Parque de Atenas (just off c/Segovia); 🚇Ópera. Lively summer terraza set in the park down by the river and not far from the bars and clubs of La Latina.

Jardines Las Vistillas c/Bailén (on the south side of the viaduct); 🚇Ópera. This popular terraza is good for a relaxing drink while enjoying the *vistillas* ("little vistas") over towards the Almudena cathedral and the Guadarrama mountains to the northwest.

Paseo del Pintor Rosales 🚇Argüelles. There is a clutch of terrazas catering for all tastes and popular with families along this avenue on the edge of the Parque del Oeste.

Paseo de Recoletos and, Paseo de la Castellana On the nearer reaches of Paseo de Recoletos is the refined garden terraza at the *Casa de América* (no. 2) and those of the old-style cafés *Gijón* (no. 21) and *Espejo* (no. 31), popular meeting points for *madrileños* of all kinds.

Plaza de Comendadoras 🚇Ventura Rodríguez. One of the city's few traffic-free squares, this has a couple of very popular terrazas – attached to the *Café*

Moderno and to the Mexican restaurant next door.

Plaza Dos de Mayo 🚇Tribunal. The terraza on Malasaña's main square is always a lively affair, favoured by a grungy teenage crowd.

Plaza de Oriente 🚇Ópera. The *Café de Oriente* terraza is a station of Madrid nightlife and enjoys a marvellous location next to the opera house, gazing across the plaza to the Palacio Real.

Plaza de la Paja 🚇La Latina. One of the most pleasant terrazas in the heart of old Madrid in this former market square in La Latina.

Plaza San Andrés 🚇La Latina. Just the other side of the church of San Andrés a host of bars spills out onto this atmospheric plaza. The place is buzzing in the summer, and makes a great meeting place before a bar crawl around the area.

Plaza de Santa Ana 🚇Sol. Several of the *cervecerías* here have outside seating, and there's a *chiringuito* (a makeshift bar) in the middle of the square throughout the summer.

CHOCOLATE BEFORE BED

If you stay up through a Madrid night, then you must try one of the city's great institutions – the **Chocolatería San Ginés** (daily 9.30am–7am) on Pasadizo de San Ginés, off c/Arenal between the Puerta del Sol and Teatro Real. Established in 1894, this serves *chocolate con churros* to perfection – just the thing after a night's excess. There's an almost mythical madrileño custom of winding up at San Ginés after the clubs close (not that they do any longer), before heading home for a shower and then off to work. And why not?

Finnegans Pl. de las Salesas 9 w finnegansmadrid .com; m Colón/Alonso Martínez; map p.62. A large Irish bar with several rooms, complete with bar fittings and wooden floors brought over from the Emerald Isle. English-speaking staff, and TV sports and a pub quiz on Mon nights. Daily 1pm–2am.

Pepe Botella c/San Andrés 12 (on Pl. Dos de Mayo); m Tribunal; map p.62. An old-style elegance still clings to this little bar with friendly staff, marble-topped tables, low-volume music and no fruit machines. Daily 11am–3am; Aug from 3pm.

Tupperware c/Corredera Alta de San Pablo 26; m Tribunal; map p.62. You'll find a refreshingly cosmopolitan musical diet at this classic Malasaña nightspot. Daily 9pm–3.30am.

Vía Lactea c/Velarde 18; m Tribunal; map p.62. Call in here to see where the *movida* began. *Vía Lactea* was a key meeting place for Spain's designers, directors, pop stars and painters in the 1980s, and it retains its original decor from the time, billiard tables included. There's a stage downstairs. It attracts a young, studenty clientele and is packed at weekends. Daily 8pm–3am.

SALAMANCA

Alquimia/Alegoría c/Villanueva 2 (entrance on c/Cid) w alegoria-madrid.es; m Retiro; map p.62. A restaurant-bar-club modelled on an English gentlemen's club, with over-the-top Baroque decor. It's a popular backdrop for media presentations and pop videos. Daily 9pm–5am; entrance €9.

Castellana 8 Paseo de la Castellana 8; m Colón; map p.62. A designer cocktail bar and restaurant with a summer terrace on the first section of the Paseo de la Castellana after the Pl. de Colón. Relaxed music, a fairly *pijo* clientele and decent food served in the restaurant. Daily 1.30–4pm & 9pm–3am.

★ **Teatriz** c/Hermosilla 15; m Serrano; map p.62. This former theatre was refurbished by Catalan designer Javier Mariscal and Frenchman Philippe Starck, and is as stylish a place as they come. There is a tapas bar at the entrance, a bar on the stage and a restaurant in the stalls. Best stick to a drink and appreciate the elegant makeover. Bar 9pm–3am; restaurant 1.30–4.30pm & 9pm–1am; closed Sat lunch, Sun & Aug.

DISCOTECAS

Discotecas – or clubs – aren't always that different from *discobares*, though they tend to be bigger and flashier, with a lot of attention to the lighting, sound system and decor. They start late and stay open until around 4am, some till 6am and a couple till noon. In summer, some of the trendier clubs suspend operations and set up outdoor *terrazas* (see box opposite).

SOL, ÓPERA AND PLAZA DE SANTA ANA

Joy Madrid c/Arenal 11 w joy-eslava.com; m Sol/Ópera; map p.102. *Joy* may not be at the cutting edge of the club scene, but judging by the queues, it remains one of the city's most popular and successful clubs. If you can't get in, console yourself with the *Chocolatería San Ginés* on the street behind (see box, above). Daily 11.30pm–6am; €10–15, including first drink.

Stella c/Arlabán 7 w web-mondo.com; m Sevilla; map p.102. With its varied and danceable funk and electronica in the *Mondo* (Thurs & Sat) and *Room* (Fri) sessions, this sleek club is a big favourite with the city's serious partygoers. Thurs–Sat 1–6am; €12–15 including first drink.

Torero c/Cruz 26; m Sol/Sevilla; map p.102. A very popular and enjoyable two-storey disco right in the heart of the Santa Ana area, but the door policy is pretty strict and it can become rather overcrowded at weekends. Closed Sun & Mon; €10.

PASEO DEL PRADO/ATOCHA

Kapital c/Atocha 125 w grupo-kapital.com/kapital; m Atocha; map p.62. A seven-storey macro-disco, complete with three dancefloors, lasers, go-go dancers, a cocktail bar and a top-floor terrace. House, funk and R&B. Thurs–Sat midnight–6am, plus Sun-night session from 8pm; entry can be free but usually €10–15.

GRAN VÍA AND PLAZA DE ESPAÑA

Bash Pl. de Callao 4 w tripfamily.com; m Callao; map p.62. *Bash* is one of the major venues on the Madrid club scene. There's funk and hip-hop on Wed, electro and techno on Thurs and the *OHM* techno-house session on Fri & Sat, which is popular with a gay crowd. For those with real stamina, there's also a Sun-night session. Sessions usually begin around midnight; €12–15 including first drink.

1

GAY AND LESBIAN MADRID

Much of Madrid's nightlife has a big gay input and **gay men** especially will feel at home in most of the listings in our "Discotecas" section. However, Plaza Chueca and the surrounding streets, especially c/Pelayo, harbour at least a dozen exclusively gay bars and clubs, as well as a café that's traditionally gay – the *Café Figueroa* at c/Augusto Figueroa 17. Wandering about, be aware that the area just north of Gran Vía is a red-light and drug centre, so taxis are best late at night. The **lesbian scene** is more disparate.

The main gay organization in Madrid is **Coordinadora Gay de Madrid**, c/Puebla 9 (Mon–Fri 10am–2pm & 5–8pm; Aug from 7pm; ☎915 230 070, ⓦcogam.org; ⓜGran Vía), which can give information on health, leisure and gay rights. Feminist and lesbian groups are based at the Centro de la Mujer, c/Barquillo 44, 1º izda. ☎913 193 689. For a good one-stop shop with lots of info on the gay scene, try Berkana Bookshop, c/Hortaleza 64 (Mon–Sat 10.30am–9pm, Sun noon–2pm & 5–9pm; ⓦlibreriaberkana.com; ⓜChueca).

BARS AND DISCOTECAS

Café Acuarela c/Gravina 10; ⓜChueca. Comfortable café, with kitsch Baroque-style decor. The perfect place for a quiet drink, and popular with a mixed crowd. Daily from about 11am–2am.

Cool c/Isabel la Católica 6; ⓜSanto Domingo. Futuristic, style-conscious mixed club with a large gay following. Expect to pay €10–15 entry fee, and don't arrive until late. Thurs–Sat midnight–6am, Sun 9pm–2am.

La Lupe c/Torrecilla del Leal 12; ⓜAntón Martín. A mixed gay, lesbian and alternative bar. Good music, cheap drinks and occasional cabaret.

Medea c/Cabeza 33; ⓜTirso de Molina/Antón Martín. A women-only disco with a huge dancefloor and wide-ranging selection of music. Gets going from about 1am.

El Mojito c/Olmo 6; ⓜTirso de Molina. Friendly Lavapiés cocktail bar with a mixed gay and lesbian clientele. Daily 9pm–2.30am.

Ricks c/Clavel 8; ⓜGran Vía. A varied-clientele *discobar* that gets packed at weekends when every available space is used for dancing. Open and light, with a friendly atmosphere – but drinks are pricey. Daily 11.30pm–5.30am.

Stars Dance Café c/Marqués de Valdeiglesias 5; ⓜGran Vía. Quiet and low-key during the day, gradually livening up as the night goes on. It's a popular meeting point for the gay community but the clientele is mixed. Daily 10am–2am.

Truco c/Gravina 10; ⓜChueca. A long-established women's bar with a popular summer terraza that spills out onto Chueca's main plaza. Mon–Thurs 5pm–3am, Fri & Sat noon–3am.

Morocco c/Marqués de Leganés 7 ⓦmoroccoclub.es; ⓜSanto Domingo; map p.62. Fun, unpretentious disco with a slightly older clientele and a varied diet of Spanish pop. Fri & Sat midnight–6am; €10 entry with drink.

Tropical House Gran Vía 54; ⓜSanto Domingo; map p.62. One of the biggest and best salsa venues in the city. Dance the night away or simply enjoy the spectacle as you watch the experts. Thurs for Salsa, Sun & Tues for ballroom; €7 with drink.

CHUECA/SANTA BÁRBARA

Pachá c/Barceló 11 ⓦpacha-madrid.com; ⓜTribunal; map p.62. An eternal and very popular survivor on the Madrid disco scene. House and techno on Saturdays, with more varied music on other nights. Wed–Sat midnight–5am; €12–15 including first drink.

SALAMANCA AND THE NORTH

Macumba Clubbing Estación de Chamartín s/n ⓦspaceofsound.net; ⓜChamartín; map p.62. The nearest Madrid gets to Ibiza, *Macumba* holds very popular Fri- and Sat-night sessions on top of the Estación Chamartín. If you've still got energy left, the *Space of Sound* "after hours" club will allow you to strut your stuff from 9am on Sun. Sessions normally begin at midnight; €15.

Moma 56 c/José Abascal 56 ⓦmoma56.com; ⓜGregorio Marañon; map p.62. An exclusive, New York-style club, popular with *pijos* and the upmarket glamour crowd. Also inside are the *Kashira Japanese and Italian* restaurant and a bar serving cocktails and light Mediterranean and fusion food. Club open Thurs–Sat midnight–6am; €10.

MUSIC, FILM AND THEATRE

Most nights in Madrid, you can take in performances of **flamenco**, **salsa**, **rock** (local and imported), **jazz**, **classical music** and **opera** at one or other of the city's venues. Often, it's the smaller, offbeat clubs that are the more enjoyable, though there are plenty of large auditoria for big-name concerts. In summer, events are supplemented by the council's

Veranos de la Villa cultural programme, and in autumn by the **Festival de Otoño**. These also encompass **theatre** and **film**, both of which have healthy year-round scenes.

FLAMENCO

Flamenco underwent something of a revival in Madrid in the 1990s, in large part owing to the "new flamenco" artists, like Ketama and Joaquín Cortés, who were unafraid to mix it with a bit of blues, jazz, even rock. A new generation of younger but more traditional artists such as Niña Pastori and Estrella Morente is now more popular. Madrid has its own flamenco festival in May, when you stand a chance of catching some of the bigger names. For up-to-date and authoritative information on the flamenco scene, try ⓦ flamenco-world.com. The club listings below span the range from purist flamenco to crossover experiments, and most artists – even major stars – appear in them. Although the following may open earlier, be aware that in many cases performances won't really get going until around midnight.

Almonte c/Juan Bravo 35 ☎ 915 632 504, ⓦ almontesalarociera.com; ⓜ Diego de León. A little slice of Andalucía in this *sala rociera* where it's easy to imagine you've been transported to Seville as you watch the locals strut their stuff. A few more *finos* and you'll pluck up the courage to have a go yourself.

Café de Chinitas c/Torija 7 ☎ 915 595 135, ⓦ chinitas .com; ⓜ Santo Domingo. One of the oldest flamenco clubs in Madrid, with a dinner-dance spectacular. It's expensive, but the music is authentic. Reservations are essential, though you may get in late when people start to leave (at this time, you don't have to eat, and the steep entrance fee of €32 does at least include your first drink). Mon–Sat 8pm–midnight.

Candela c/Olmo 2 ☎ 914 673 382; ⓜ Antón Martín. A legendary bar frequented by musicians – the late, great Camarón de la Isla is reputed to have sung here until 11am on one occasion. Tues–Sun 10.30pm–2am.

Las Carboneras Pl. Conde de Miranda ☎ 915 428 677, ⓦ tablaolascarboneras.com; ⓜ Sol. A relative newcomer to the restaurant/*tablao* scene, geared to the tourist market but a good alternative if you want to get a taste of flamenco; around €60 including dinner. Shows: Mon–Thurs 10.30pm, Fri & Sat 8.30pm & 11pm.

Cardamomo c/Echegaray 15 ⓦ cardamomo.net; ⓜ Sevilla/Sol. This flamenco bar has evolved into a well-respected fully blown *tablao* in recent years. The show with a drink will cost you €32, while dinner will set you back an extra €32. Check the website for the schedule.

★ **Casa Patas** c/Cañizares 10 ☎ 913 690 496, ⓦ casapatas.com; ⓜ Antón Martín. A small but very popular flamenco *tablao* that gets its share of big names. The best nights are Thurs and Fri. €27–30. Mon–Sat 9pm–2am

Corral de la Morería c/Morería 17 ☎ 913 658 446, ⓦ corraldelamoreria.com; ⓜ La Latina. A renowned and atmospheric venue for some serious flamenco acts but again expensive at about €40 for show plus a drink and double that if you want to dine in the restaurant. Daily 8pm–2am, shows at 10pm & midnight

POP, ROCK AND BLUES

Madrid is very much on the international rock tour circuit and you can catch big (and small) American and British acts in front of enthusiastic audiences. Sports arenas such as Atlético Madrid's Vicente Calderón football stadium and Las Ventas bullring are used for some of the biggest acts, while in the smaller clubs, you have a chance of seeing a very wide range of local bands.

CLUBS AND BARS

La Coquette c/Hileras 14; ⓜ Ópera. A small, crowded basement bar, where people sit around in the near-dark watching the band perform on a tiny stage. Live music most nights with blues on Wed & Thurs. Daily 8pm–2.30am.

Honky Tonk c/Covarrubias 24 ☎ 914 456 886; ⓜ Alonso Martínez. Nightly blues and rock sets in this late-opening bar just north of Alonso Martínez. Daily 10pm–5am.

Libertad 8 c/Libertad 8 ☎ 915 321 150, ⓦ libertad8cafe .es; ⓜ Chueca. *Libertad 8* made its name during the *movida*, but this friendly little bar in Chueca still acts as a venue for up-and-coming singer-songwriters and even has its own record label. Tues–Sun 1pm–2am.

MADRID LISTINGS

Listings information is in plentiful supply in Madrid. The newspapers *El País* (ⓦ elpais.es) and *El Mundo* (ⓦ elmundo.es) have excellent daily listings, and on Fridays both publish magazine sections devoted to events, bars and restaurants in the capital.

If your time in Madrid doesn't coincide with the Friday supplements, or you want maximum info, pick up the weekly listings magazine *La Guía del Ocio* (ⓦ guiadelocio.com; €1) at any kiosk. The *ayuntamiento* publishes a monthly pamphlet *esMadrid* (in English and Spanish), which is free from any of the tourist offices and lists forthcoming events in the city (also see ⓦ esmadrid .com). *In Madrid* (ⓦ in-madrid.com), meanwhile, is a free English-language monthly paper – available in many bars and tourist offices – that features useful reviews of clubs and bars.

1

Siroco c/San Dimás 3 ☎915 933 070, ⓦsiroco.es; ⓜSan Bernardo. Live bands play most nights at this popular little soul club, not far north of the Gran Vía; €5–10. Closed Sun.

El Sol c/Jardines 3 ☎913 611 184, ⓦelsolmad.com; ⓜSol/Gran Vía. Celebrating thirty years on the scene, this down-to-earth club hosts around twenty live concerts a month, but continues afterwards (usually from about 1.30am) as a disco playing house, soul and acid jazz. €10. Tues–Sat midnight–5.30am.

MAJOR CONCERT VENUES

Madrid Arena Avda. Portugal s/n ⓦmadridarena.org; ⓜLago. Large arena in the Casa de Campo used for concerts and sports events with a capacity of over 10,000.

Palacio de Deportes Avda. Felipe II s/n ☎912 586 016, ⓦpalaciodedeportes.com; ⓜGoya. The city's sports arena that replaced the old one that burned down in 2001. It's used for big shows of the Lady Gaga, Ricky Martin, Rihanna variety.

Palacio de Vistalegre Avda. Plaza de Toros ☎915 639 493, ⓦpalaciovistalegre.com; ⓜOporto/Vista Alegre. This covered bullring in the south of the city has become one of the favoured venues of touring groups.

La Riviera Paseo Bajo Virgen del Puerto s/n, Puente de Segovia ☎913 652 415, ⓦsalariviera.net; ⓜPuerta del Ángel. A fun disco (weekends only) and concert venue right next to the river, which has hosted its fair share of big groups including Coldplay and the Black Eyed Peas.

LATIN MUSIC

Madrid attracts big-name **Latin artists**, who tend to play at the venues below. The local scene is a good deal more low-key, but there's enjoyable salsa, nonetheless, in a handful of clubs.

Galileo Galilei c/Galileo 100 ⓦsalagalileogalilei.com; ⓜIslas Filipinas. A bar, concert venue and disco all rolled into one. Latin music is regularly on offer, but you'll need to check the website to find out which night, as it also hosts cabaret, flamenco and singer-songwriters. Mon–Sat 9pm–3am.

Oba-Oba c/Jacometrezo 4; ⓜCallao. Samba and lambada, with lethal *caipirinhas* from the bar. Daily 11pm–5.30am.

El Son c/Victoria 6; ⓜSol. Live Cuban music (Mon–Thurs) at this small Latin club, which has picked up where its predecessor *Massai* left off. There's no space to stand and watch, so make sure you bring your dancing shoes. Daily from 7pm.

JAZZ

Madrid doesn't rank up there with London, Paris or New York on the **jazz** front, but the clubs are friendly, unpretentious places. Look out for the annual **jazz festival** staged at a variety of venues in November.

Bogui Jazz c/Barquillo 29 ☎915 211 568, ⓦboguijazz.com; ⓜChueca. Back In action after a two-year licensing wrangle with the local council, *Bogui* has jazz sets every evening from Thurs–Sat followed by a disco; €10 entry for concerts. Thurs–Sat 10.30pm–5am.

★ **Café Berlin** c/Jacometrezo 4 ☎915 215 753, ⓦnuevocafeberlinmadrid.webgarden.es; ⓜCallao/Santo Domingo. Jazz and blues sessions often take place in this elegant Art Nouveau café just off the Gran Via. It also stages soul, flamenco and tango concerts too. Mon–Sat 11pm–5am, Fri & Sat till 6am.

Café Central Pl. del Ángel 10 ☎913 694 143, ⓦcafecentralmadrid.com; ⓜSol. A small and relaxed jazz club that gets the odd big name, plus strong local talent. The Art Deco café is worth a visit in its own right. €12–14 for gigs, otherwise free. Daily 1.30pm–2.30am.

Café Jazz Populart c/Huertas 22 ☎914 298 407, ⓦpopulart.es; ⓜAntón Martín. Nightly sets from jazz and blues bands. €6 for gigs, otherwise free. Daily from 6pm, sets start 11pm & 12.30am.

Clamores c/Albuquerque 14 ☎914 457 938, ⓦsalaclamores.com; ⓜBilbao. A large, low-key and enjoyable jazz bar with accomplished (if not very famous) artists, not too exorbitant drinks and a nice range of snacks. €5–12 for gigs, otherwise free. Sets start around 10.30pm; bar is open until 4am.

CLASSICAL MUSIC AND OPERA

The **Teatro Real** is the city's prestigious opera house and the **Auditorio Nacional de Musica** is home to the

---

TICKETS

Tickets for most big rock concerts are sold by Fnac, c/Preciados 28 ☎915 956 190 (ⓜCallao), and El Corte Inglés, c/Preciados 1–4 ⓦelcorteingles.es (ⓜSol). For theatre and concert tickets try Entradas.com ☎902 221 622, ⓦentradas.com; Caixa Catalunya/Tele Entrada ☎902 101 212, ⓦtelentrada.com; Ticketmaster ☎902 150 025, ⓦticketmaster.es; and Servi-Caixa ☎902 332 211, ⓦservicaixa.com. For last-minute discount tickets to shows and events, try the Taquilla Último Minuto booth at Plaza del Carmen 1 (Wed, Thurs, Sun 5–8pm, Fri & Sat 5–10pm); ⓦwww.taquillaultimominuto.com; ⓜSol). The website ⓦatrapalo.com also sells discount tickets for the theatre and musicals.

1

Orquesta Nacional de España. Equally enjoyable are the salons and small auditoria for chamber orchestras and groups.

Auditorio Nacional de Música c/Príncipe de Vergara 146 ☎913 370 140, ⊛auditorionacional.mcu.es; ⓜCruz del Rayo. Home of the Spanish National Orchestra and host to most international visiting orchestras.

Teatro Monumental c/Atocha 65 ☎914 291 281; ⓜAntón Martín. A large theatre, that is home to the Spanish state TV orchestra, offering orchestral concerts, opera, *zarzuela* and flamenco recitals.

Teatro Real Pl. Isabel II; info ☎915 160 660, box office ☎915 160 606, ticket line ☎902 244 848, ⊛teatro-real.com; ⓜÓpera. Madrid's opulent opera house, and a fantastic setting for some prestigious productions. Tickets range from €12 to €150, but you'll need to book well in advance for the best seats.

Teatro Zarzuela c/Jovellanos 4 ☎915 245 400, ⊛teatrodelazarzuela.mcu.es; ⓜSevilla. The main venue for Spanish operetta.

Teatros Canal c/Cea Bermúdez 1 ☎915 802 070, ⊛teatroscanal.com; ⓜRíos Rosas. New theatre complex which stages regular classical concerts at reasonable prices.

FILM

Cines – cinemas – can be found all over the central area, and there's a handful of grand old picture houses strung out along the length of the Gran Vía. These offer major releases dubbed into Spanish, though a number of cinemas have regular **original language** screenings, with subtitles; these are listed in a separate *versión original/subtitulada* (*v.o.*) section in the newspapers. **Tickets** for films cost around €7.50, but most cinemas have a *día del espectador* (usually Mon or Wed) when they cost around €5.50. Be warned that on Sunday night half of Madrid goes to the movies, and queues can be long.

Filmoteca/Cine Doré c/Santa Isabel 3; ⓜAntón Martín. A beautiful old cinema, now home to an art-film centre, with imaginative programmes of classic and contemporary films, all shown in *v.o.* at an admission price of just €2.50 (closed Mon). In summer, there are open-air screenings on a little *terraza* – they're very popular, so buy tickets in advance.

Golem, Renoir and **Princesa** c/Martín de los Heros 12 & 14 and c/Princesa 5 ⊛golem.es, ⊛cinesrenoir.com; ⓜPlaza de España. This trio of multiscreen cinemas, within 200m of each other, show regular *v.o.* films.

Ideal Yelmo Cineplex c/Doctor Cortezo 6 ⊛yelmocineplex.es; ⓜSol/Tirso de Molina. A centrally located, nine-screen complex that shows a good selection of *v.o.* films.

Pequeño Cine Estudio c/Magallanes 1–2 ⊛pcinee studio.es; ⓜQuevedo/San Bernardo. A small independent cinema specializing in classic films in *v.o.*

Verdi c/Bravo Murillo 28 ⊛cines-verdi.com; ⓜCanal/Quevedo. A newcomer on the scene, which shows an interesting range of *v.o.* films.

THEATRE AND CABARET

Madrid is enjoying a renaissance in theatre; you can catch anything from Lope de Vega to contemporary and experimental productions, and there's also a new wave of cabaret and comedy acts. Look out, too, for the annual **Festival de Otoño** running from September to November, and the alternative **theatre festival** in the month of February.

Teatro de la Abadía c/Fernández de los Ríos 42 ☎914 481 181, ⊛teatroabadia.com; ⓜQuevedo/Argüelles. A beautifully decorated theatre set in pleasant grounds just off the main street. It has staged some very successful productions and is especially popular during the Festival de Otoño.

Teatro de Bellas Artes and Círculo de Bellas Artes c/Marqués de Riera 2 ☎915 324 437, ⊛teatrobellasartes.es; Círculo ☎913 605 400 or 902 422 442, ⊛circulobellasartes.com; ⓜBanco de España. The *teatro* is a beautiful old theatre with a reputation for quality, while the *círculo* has a theatre staging more adventurous productions.

Teatro Español c/Príncipe 25 ☎913 601 484, ⊛teatroespanol.es; ⓜSol/Sevilla. A classic Spanish theatre on the site of one of the city's old *corrales*.

Teatro Fernán Gómez Pl. de Colón ☎914 800 300, ⊛teatrofernangomez.esmadrid.com; ⓜColón. A range of dramas, dance and musical productions at this arts centre named after the late Spanish actor.

Teatro de Madrid Avda. de la Ilustracion s/n ☎917 301 750, ⊛teatromadrid.com; ⓜBarrio del Pilar. A large, modern theatre next to the large La Vaguada shopping centre in the north of the city, presenting some excellent ballet, drama and touring cultural shows.

Teatro María Guerrero c/Tamayo y Baus 4 ☎913 102 949 or 913 101 500, ⊛cdn.mcu.es; ⓜColón. This is the headquarters of the Centro Dramático Nacional, which stages high-quality Spanish and international productions in a beautiful neo-Mudéjar interior.

Teatro Nuevo Apolo Pl. Tirso de Molina 1 ☎913 690 637; ⓜTirso de Molina. Madrid's principal venue for major musicals.

Teatro Valle-Inclán c/Pl. de Lavapiés ☎915 058 800, ⊛cdn.mcu.es; ⓜLavapiés. Opened in 2006, the state-of-the-art Valle-Inclán provides a second home for the Centro Dramático Nacional.

Teatros Canal c/Cea Bermúdez 1 ☎915 802 070, ⊛teatroscanal.com; ⓜRíos Rosas. Two large theatres in this complex hosting music, dance and drama. One of the spaces used for the regional theatre festival in the spring and acclaimed touring productions.

1

PEDRO ALMODÓVAR

Arguably Spain's most influential filmmaker, **Pedro Almodóvar** emerged as part of the **movida madrileña**, the thriving alternative cultural scene in Madrid that developed following the death of Franco. He made his feature-film debut in 1980 with the cheap and transgressive *Pepi, Lucy, Bom and a Whole Load of Other Girls*. His prodigious output during the 1980s included *Matador* (1986), a dark thriller linking sexual excitement with the violence of the bullfight; *The Law of Desire* (1987), a story involving a gay film director, his transsexual brother/sister, murder and incest; as well as the internationally successful *Women on the Edge of a Nervous Breakdown* (1988). Madrid was used as the backdrop to many of his films, which reflected the spirit of liberation that reigned in the Spanish capital in the 1980s.

His productions have benefited from the performances of actors such as Carmen Maura, Victoria Abril, Rossy de Palma and Antonio Banderas, and over time they have gained in narrative coherence and production values while retaining the capacity to offend – notably with *Tie Me Up, Tie Me Down* (1990). One of the very few directors able to attract audiences across the globe with films in a language other than English, Almodóvar's 1995 *Flower of My Secret* pushed him more into the mainstream, while *All About My Mother* (1999), which marked a return to his trademark obsession with transsexuals, won him an Oscar for Best Foreign Film. *Talk to Her* (2002) was if anything even more successful, and won Almodóvar another Oscar, this time for Best Screenplay – perhaps marking Spanish cinema's escape from the "foreign films" ghetto. In *Bad Education* (2004), he explored Franco-era religious schooling and the issue of sexual abuse by the Catholic clergy, while in the well-received *Volver* (Returning) (2006), which starred Penélope Cruz, he looked to his own childhood in La Mancha and to his sisters and late mother for inspiration. He revisited many of his favourite themes in the romantic thriller *Los Abrazos Rotos* (2009), which also starred Cruz, and although the film did not reach the heights of some of his previous work, it still served to strengthen his reputation as Spain's leading director.

CHILDREN

Many of the big sights may lack children-specific services or activities, but there's plenty to keep kids occupied for a short stay. There are various **parks** (El Retiro being a particular favourite), a host of well-attended public **swimming pools** and an increasing number of **child-oriented attractions**. Children are welcome in nearly all cafés and restaurants. See ⓦ saposyprincesas.com for more ideas.

IN THE CITY

Imax Madrid Parque Tierno Galván ☎ 914 674 800, ⓦ imaxmadrid.com; ⓜ Méndez Alvaro. Futuristic cinema with three different types of screen showing natural history-style features in Spanish. €8.50.

Museo de Cera (Wax Museum) Paseo de Recoletos 41 ☎ 913 192 649, ⓦ museoceramadrid.com; ⓜ Colón. Expensive, tacky, and the figures bear little resemblance to the originals, but nevertheless popular with children. There's also a train of horrors and a film history of Spain. €16, under-10s & over-65s €12, under-4s free. Mon–Fri 10am–2.30pm & 4.30–8.30pm, Sat, Sun & public hols 10am–8.30pm.

Museo del Ferrocarril Paseo de las Delicias 61 ☎ 902 228 822, ⓦ museodelferrocarril.org; ⓜ Delicias. An impressive collection of engines, carriages and wagons that once graced the railway lines of Spain. Of more interest to the younger ones is the fascinating collection of model railways and the mini-railway (Sat 11.30am–2pm; 1€). There's an atmospheric little cafeteria housed in one of the more elegant carriages. The station was used as a backdrop in the film classic

Doctor Zhivago. €5, 4–12-year-olds €3.50, under-4s free. Tues–Sun 10am–3pm.

Parque de Atracciones Casa de Campo ☎ 902 345 009, ⓦ parquedeatracciones.es; ⓜ Batán/bus #33 & #65. A theme park packed full of rides, whose attractions include the 100km/hr Abismo rollercoaster, the swirling Tarantula ride, the 63-metre vertical drop La Lanzadera and the whitewater-rafting ride Los Rápidos. Access-only €10.60, €29.90 for a day-ticket which includes most rides for anyone over 1.20m tall, €23.90 for children between 90cm and 1.20m tall (reductions for purchases via the website), children under 90cm tall go free. Oct–March Sat, Sun & public hols noon–7pm; April–Sept most days noon–midnight (consult website).

Parque Secreto Pl. Conde del Valle de Suchel 3 ☎ 915 931 480, ⓦ parquesecreto.com; ⓜ San Bernardo. One of the most central and best-equipped children's playcentres, with a café, too. €2.50–3 for 30min.

Planetario Parque Tierno Galván ☎ 914 673 461, ⓦ planetmad.es; ⓜ Méndez Álvaro. Exhibition halls, audiovisual displays and projections on a variety of astronomical themes (all in Spanish). €3.55, under-14s €1.55.

SWIMMING POOLS AND AQUAPARKS

Outdoor swimming pools are open between June and September. The Piscina Canal Isabel II, Avda. de Filipinas 54 (daily 10am–8.30pm; Ⓜ Ríos Rosas), is a large and well-maintained pool, and the best central option. Alternatively, try the open-air *piscina* in the Casa de Campo (daily 10am–8.30pm; Ⓜ Lago). There are also two aquaparks around the city, the closest being Aquópolis de San Fernando (Ⓦ san-fernando.aquopolis.es), 16km out on the N-II Barcelona road (buses #221, #224A and #226 from the *intercambiador* at Avda. de América).

Zoo–Aquarium Casa de Campo ☎ 917 119 950, Ⓦ zoomadrid.com; Ⓜ Casa de Campo/Batán/bus #33. Over 2000 different species, including big cats, gorillas, koalas and venomous snakes, plus an impressive aquarium with sharks, a children's zoo, a parrot show and a dolphinarium. €19.40, under-7s €15.70, under-3s free. Daily 11am–dusk.

OUT OF THE CITY

Cosmo Caixa Pintor Velázquez s/n, Alcobendas ☎ 914 845 200, Ⓦ fundacio.lacaixa.es; bus #151–154, 156 & 157 from Pl. Castilla, train from Estación de Atocha to Valdelasfuentes, then a 15min walk. A fun, interactive science museum located in the suburb of Alcobendas. Tues–Sun 10am–8pm; €3, under-16s €2. Supplements for the planetarium and special activities.

Faunia Avda. de las Comunidades 28 ☎ 913 016 210, Ⓦ faunia.es; Ⓜ Valdebernardo, bus #71 from Pl. Manuel Becerra (Ⓜ Manuel Becerra). An innovative nature park re-creating a series of ecosystems that provide a home to 720 different animal species. Highlights are the Arctic dome with its penguins, and the storms in the indoor tropical rainforest. An entertaining and educational experience for children of all ages. €25.50, under-12s €19.50, under-3s free (discounts via website). Daily 10am–dusk.

SHOPPING

Shopping districts in Madrid are pretty defined. The biggest range of stores is along the Gran Vía and the streets running north out of Puerta del Sol, which is where the **department stores** – such as El Corte Inglés – have their main branches. For **fashion** (*moda*), the smartest addresses are calles Serrano, Goya, Ortega y Gasset and Velázquez in the Salamanca *barrio*, while more alternative designers are in Malasaña and Chueca (c/Almirante, especially). For street fashion, there's plenty on offer around c/Fuencarral. The **antiques** trade is centred towards the Rastro, on and around c/Ribera de Curtidores, while for **general weirdness**, it's hard to beat the shops just off Pl. Mayor, where luminous saints rub shoulders with surgical supports and Fascist memorabilia. If you want international shops or chain stores, head for Madrid 2, a large shopping centre next to Ⓜ Barrio de Pilar. There is a smaller, more upmarket mall at ABC Serrano, with entrances at c/Serrano 61 and Paseo de la Castellana 34 (Ⓜ Rubén Darío).

Most areas of the city have their own **mercados del barrio** – indoor markets, devoted mainly to food. Among the best are the refurbished **Mercado de San Miguel** (just west of Pl. Mayor) and **Mercado de San Antón** in Chueca (Ⓜ Chueca), while there are more traditional markets in the Pl. de la Cebada (Ⓜ La Latina) and c/Santa Isabel (Ⓜ Antón Martín). The city's biggest market is, of course, **El Rastro** – the flea market – which takes place on Sundays in La Latina, south of Plaza (see box, p.77). Other specialized markets include the secondhand book stalls on Cuesta del Moyano, near Estación de Atocha, and the stamp and coin markets in Pl. Mayor on Sundays.

CRAFTS AND MISCELLANEOUS

Alvarez Gómez c/Serrano 14 Ⓦ alvarezgomez.com; Ⓜ Serrano; map p.62. Gómez has been making the same perfumes in the same bottles for the past century. The scents – carnations, roses, violets – are as simple and straight as they come. Mon–Sat 10am–2pm & 5–8.30pm.

El Arco Artesanía Pl. Mayor 9; Ⓜ Sol; map p.102. This shop is at the heart of tourist Madrid, but the goods are a far cry from the swords, lace and castanets that fill most stores in the area. Crafts include ceramics, leather, wood, jewellery and textiles. There's a gallery space for exhibitions, too. Mon–Sat 11am–9pm, Sun 11am–2.30pm.

Area Real Madrid c/Carmen 3; Ⓜ Sol; map p.102. Club store just off Sol where you can pick up replica shirts and all manner of – expensive – souvenirs related to the club's history. Mon–Sat 10am–9pm, Sun 11am–8pm. There is another branch in the shopping centre at Real's Bernabéu

stadium at c/Padre Damián gate 55. (ⒶSantiago Bernabéu). Mon–Sun 10.30am–8.30pm.

★ **Casa de Diego** Puerta del Sol 12 Ⓦ casadediego .com; Ⓜ Sol; map p.102. An old-fashioned shop with helpful staff selling a fantastic array of Spanish fans (*abanicos*) ranging from cheap offerings at under €10 to beautifully hand-crafted works of art costing up to €200. Mon–Sat 9.30am–8pm.

Casa Jiménez c/Preciados 42; Ⓜ Callao; map p.102. Elaborately embroidered *mantones* (shawls) made in Seville, with prices ranging from €100 to €600, as well as gorgeous fans starting at around €40. Mon–Sat 10am–1.30pm & 5–8pm, closed Sat pm in July and all day Sat in Aug.

Casa Yustas Pl. Mayor 30 Ⓦ casayustas.com; Ⓜ Sol; map p.102. Madrid's oldest hat shop, established in 1894. Pick from traditional designs for men's and women's hats (*sombreros*), caps (*gorras*) and berets (*boinas*). There's also a large range of souvenir-style goods including Lladró porcelain figurines. Mon–Sat 9.30am–9.30pm, Sun & public hols 11am–9.30pm.

Contreras c/Mayor 80 w manuelcontreras.com; m Sol/Ópera; map p.102. An award-winning guitar workshop run on this site for over forty years by the Contreras family. The perfect place for budding flamenco artists to buy the genuine article. Mon–Fri 10am–1.30pm & 5–8pm, Sat 10am–1.30pm.

El Flamenco Vive c/Condé de Lemos 7 w elflamencovive.com; m Ópera; map p.102. A fascinating little piece of Andalucía in Madrid, specializing in all things flamenco, from guitars and CDs to polkadot dresses and books. Mon–Sat 10.30am–2pm & 5–9pm.

Seseña c/Cruz 23; m Sol; map p.102. A tailor specializing in traditional *madrileño* capes for royalty and celebrities. Clients have included Luis Buñuel, Gary Cooper and Hillary Clinton. Mon–Sat 10am–1.30pm & 4.30–8pm.

BOOKS AND MAPS

Desnivel Pl. Matute 6 w libreriadesnivel.com; m Antón Martín; map p.102. This centrally located bookshop stocks a good range of guides and maps covering mountaineering and hiking in all parts of Spain. Mon–Sat 10am–2pm & 4.30–8.30pm.

FNAC c/Preciados 28 w fnac.es; m Callao; map p.102. The book department of this huge store is a good place to sit and peruse books and magazines in all languages. Also sells CDs, computer equipment and electronic goods. Mon–Sat 10am–9.30pm, Sun & hols noon–9.30pm.

La Librería c/Mayor 80 w edicioneslalibreria.com; m Sol; map p.102. A tiny place full of books just about Madrid. Most are in Spanish, but many would serve as coffee-table souvenirs. It's also a good place to pick up old prints and photos of the city. Mon–Fri 10am–2pm & 4.30–7.30pm, Sat 11am–2pm.

Pasajes c/Genova 3 w pasajeslibros.com; m Alonso Martínez/Colón; map p.62. Specializes in English and foreign-language books. Also has a useful noticeboard service for flat-sharing and Spanish classes. Mon–Sat 9.30am–9.30pm.

CLOTHES AND SHOES

Adolfo Domínguez c/Serrano 5 w adolfodomínguez.com; m Retiro; map p.62. Domínguez has opened a massive new five-storey flagship store for his classic modern Spanish designs – a wide range of colours and free lines for both men and women. Mon–Sat 10am–8.30pm.

Agatha Ruiz de la Prada c/Serrano 27 w agatharuizdelaprada.com; m Colón/Goya; map p.62. Outlet for the brightly coloured clothes and accessories of this *movida* designer. There's a children's line, stationery and household goods, too. Mon–Sat 10am–8.30pm.

Caligae c/Augusto Figueroa 27; m Chueca; map p.62. One of a string of shoe shops located on this busy Chueca

street, selling discounted designer footwear. Mon–Fri 10am–2pm & 5–8pm, Sat 10.30am–2pm & 5–8pm.

Camper c/Preciados 23 w camper.es; m Callao; map p.102. Spain's best shoe-shop chain, with covetable designs at modest prices. There are lots of other branches around the city. Mon–Sat 10am–2pm & 5–8.30pm.

Mercado Fuencarral c/Fuencarral 45 w mdf.es; m Tribunal/Gran Vía; map p.62. Funky shopping mall catering for the young fashion-conscious crowd, filled with clubwear shops, record stores, jewellers, a café and tattoo parlour. Mon–Sat 10am–10pm.

Sybilla Callejón Jorge Juan 12 w sybilla.es; m Retiro; map p.62. Sybilla was Spain's top designer of the 1980s and she remains at the forefront of the scene, with prices to match. Women only. Mon–Sat 10am–2pm & 4.30–8.30pm.

FOOD AND DRINK

★ **Cacao Sampaka** c/Orellana 4 w cacaosampaka.com; m Alonso Martínez/Colón; map p.62. Every conceivable colour, shape and flavour of chocolate is available in this chocoholics' paradise. The only surprise is that the restaurant has some non-chocolate snacks on the menu. Daily 10am–9pm; closed Aug 8–21.

Casa Mira c/San Jerónimo 30; m Sol; map p.102. An old, established *pastelería*, setting up 150 years ago and selling delicious *turrón*, *mazapán*, *frutas glaseadas* and the like. Daily 10am–2pm & 5–9pm.

Lavinia c/José y Gasset 16 w lavinia.es; m Núñez de Balboa; map p.62. Massive wine shop in the upmarket *barrio* of Salamanca, with a great selection from Spain and the rest of the world. Mon–Sat 10am–9pm.

Mariano Madrueño c/Postigo San Martín 3; m Callao; map p.102. The place to get wines and liqueurs such as *Pacharán* sloe gin. Mon–Fri 9.30am–2pm & 5–8pm, Sat 9.30am–2pm.

★ **Mercado San Antón** c/Augusto Figueroa 24; w mercadosananton.com; m Chueca; map p.62. Like the Mercado San Miguel near Pl. Mayor, this local market has been transformed into a trendy meeting place on the Chueca scene with gourmet foodstands, a wine bar, a café, a sushi stall and a stylish terrace restaurant. Market open Mon–Sat 10am–10pm; terrace and restaurant Mon–Thurs & Sun 10am–midnight, Fri & Sat 10am–1.30pm.

★ **Reserva y Cata** c/Conde de Xiquena 13 w reservaycata.com; m Colón/Chueca; map p.62. Well-informed staff at this friendly specialist shop will help you select from some of the best new wines in the Iberian Peninsula. Mon 5–9pm, Tues–Fri 11am–3pm & 5–9pm, Sat 11am–3pm.

★ **Tienda Olivarero** c/Mejia Lequerica 1 w pco.es; m Alonso Martínez; map p.62. Outlet for olive growers' co-operative boasting around ninety different varieties of olive oil. Mon–Fri 10am–2pm & 5–8pm, Sat 10am–2pm.

CHILDREN

Imaginarium c/Carmen ⓦimaginarium.es; Ⓜ Sol; map p.102. Toys, games and activities with an educational twist for children of all ages.

Prénatal c/Goya 99; Ⓜ Goya; map p.62; Madrid 2, La Vaguada, Avda. Monforte de Lemos; Ⓜ Barrio del Pilar Spanish equivalent of Mothercare, with more branches around the city – and often a little cheaper. Mon–Sat 10am–9pm.

Puck c/Duque de Sesto 30 ⓦjugeteriapuck.com; ⓂGoya; map p.62. An old-fashioned toy shop selling high-quality wooden toys, dolls' houses and puzzles. Mon–Sat 10am–2pm & 5–8pm.

DIRECTORY

Banks and exchange Branches of El Corte Inglés have exchange offices with long hours and reasonably competitive rates; the most central is on c/Preciados, close to Puerta del Sol.

Bicycles Madrid is a bike-unfriendly city. For tours outside the city, get in touch with Bravo Bike at Juan Mendizábal 19 bajo izda (☎917 582 945/607 448 440, ⓦbravobike.com; ⓂVentura Rodríguez) or Bike Spain at Pl. de la Villa 1 (☎915 590 653/677 356 586, ⓦbikespain.info; ⓂÓpera).

Bullfights Madrid's main Pl. de Toros, the monumental Las Ventas (c/Alcalá 237, ⓦlas-ventas.com; ⓂVentas), hosts some of the year's most prestigious events, especially during the May *San Isidro* festivities, though the main season runs from March to October. Tickets (€5–120) are available at the box office at Ventas (March–Oct Thurs–Sun 10am–2pm & 5–8pm, from 10am on day of fight; ☎902 150 025, ⓦtaquillatoros.com; and from the authorized booths along c/Victoria near Sol).

Car rental Offices include: Atesa Atocha ☎915 061 846, ⓦatesa.com (ⓂAtocha Renfe); Avis, Gran Vía 60 ☎915 484 204, reservations ☎902 180 854, ⓦavisworld.com (ⓂSanto Domingo); Europcar c/San Leonardo 8 ☎915 418 892, ⓦeuropcar.com (ⓂPlaza de España); Hertz, Atocha Station ☎902 023 932, ⓦhertz.com (ⓂAtocha Renfe); EasyCar ⓦeasycar.com; Pepecar at Atocha and Chamartín stations ☎807 414 243, ⓦpepecar.com.

Disabled access Madrid is not particularly well geared up for disabled visitors (*minusválidos*), although the situation is gradually improving. The Organización Nacional de Ciegos de España (ONCE; National Organization for the Blind, c/Prim 3 ☎915 325 000, ⓦonce.es) provides specialist advice, as does the Federación de Asociaciones de Minusválidos Físicos de la Comunidad de Madrid (FAMMA; c/Galileo 69 ☎915 933 550, ⓦfamma.org). ⓦdiscapnet .es is also a useful source of information (Spanish only). Wheelchair-friendly taxis can be ordered from Eurotaxi (☎630 026 478/687 924 027) and Radio Taxi (☎915 478 200/915 478 600).

Embassies Australia, Torre Espacio, Paseo de la Castellana 259D (☎913 536 600, ⓦembaustralia.es; Ⓜ Begoña); Britain, Torre Espacio, Paseo de la Castellana 259D (☎917 146 300, out of hours emergency ☎917 146 400, ⓦukinspain.com; Ⓜ Begoña); Canada, Torre Espacio, Paseo de la Castellana 259D (☎913 828 400, ⓦcanadainternational. gc.ca/spain-espagne/index.aspx; Ⓜ Begoña); Ireland, Paseo de la Castellana 46 (☎914 364 093, ⓦdfa.ie/home/index .aspx?id=5520; ⓂRubén Darío); New Zealand, c/Pinar 7, 3º (☎915 230 226, ⓦnzembassy.com/spain; ⒼGregorio Marañon); USA, c/Serrano 75 (☎915 872 200, ⓦembusa.es; ⓂRubén Darío); South Africa, c/Claudio Coello 91 (☎914 363 780, ⓦsudafrica.com; ⓂRubén Darío).

Health First-aid stations are scattered throughout the city and open 24hr, including c/Navas de Tolosa 10, just south of Pl. Callao (☎915 210 025; ⓂCallao). Central hospitals include El Clínico San Carlos, c/Profesor Martín Lagos s/n (☎913 303 747; ⓂIslas Filipinas); Hospital Gregorio Marañon, c/Dr Esquerdo 46 (☎915 868 000, ⓂO'Donnell); Ciudad Sanitaria La Paz, Paseo de la Castellana 261 (☎917 277 000; ⓂBegoña). English-speaking doctors are available at the Anglo-American Medical Unit, c/Conde de Aranda 1 (☎914 351 823; Mon–Fri 9am–8pm, Sat 10am–3pm; ⓂRetiro). The Clinica Dental Pl. Prosperidad at Pl. Prosperidad 3, 2ºB (☎914 158 197; ⓂProsperidad), has some English-speaking dentists as does the Clinica Dental Cisne at c/Magallanes 18 (☎914 463 221; ⓂQuevedo).

Internet access There's free wi-fi at many newspaper stands and on buses, while the city centre is peppered with *locutorios* that provide internet. Workcenter on Pza. Canalejas (☎913 601 395 (ⓂSevilla/Sol; daily 8am–11pm) and La Casa de Internet, c/Luchana 20 (ⓂBilbao), are well-equipped, central internet cafés. *Café Comercial* on the Glorieta de Bilbao (ⓂBilbao) has an internet café upstairs. Prices are €1–€3.50/hr.

Left luggage Facilities (*consignas*) at Barajas Airport in terminals 1, 2 & 4 (24hr; €4.22–5.42 per day); the Estación Sur bus station; and lockers at Atocha (5.45am–10.15pm; €2.40–4.50/day) and Chamartín (7am–11pm; €2.40–4.50/day).

Pharmacies Open 24hr: c/Mayor 59 (☎915 480 014; ⓂSol); c/Toledo 46 (☎913 653 458; ⓂLa Latina; c/Atocha 46 (☎913 692 000; ⓂAntón Martín); c/Goya 12 (☎915 754 924; ⓂSerrano).

Police Stations (*comisarías*) at c/Leganitos 19 (☎915 487 945; ⓂPlaza de España/Santo Domingo), c/Huertas 76 (☎9 13 221 027; ⓂAntón Martín) and c/Luna 29 (☎915 211 236; ⓂCallao).

Post offices In El Corte Inglés, c/Preciados 1 (ⓂSol), and another with extended hours at c/Mejía Lequerica 7 (ⓂAlonso Martínez).

Telephones The main *telefónica* office at Gran Vía 30 (ⓂGran Vía) has ranks of phones and is open until midnight.

Around Madrid

THE AQUEDUCT AT SEGOVIA (P.159)

Around Madrid

The lack of historic monuments in Madrid is more than compensated for by the region around the capital. Within a radius of 100km – and within an hour's travel by bus and train – are some of Spain's greatest cities. Not least of these is **TOLEDO**, which preceded Madrid as the country's capital. Immortalized by El Greco, who lived and worked there for most of his later career, the city is a living museum to the many cultures – Visigothic, Moorish, Jewish and Christian – which have shaped the destiny of Spain. If you have time for just one trip from Madrid, there is really no other choice.

That said, **Segovia**, with its stunning Roman aqueduct and irresistible Disney-prototype castle, puts up strong competition, while Felipe II's vast palace-cum-mausoleum of **El Escorial** is a monument to out-monument all others. And there are smaller places, too, less known to foreign tourists: **Aranjuez**, an oasis in the parched Castilian plain, famed for its asparagus, strawberries and lavish Baroque palace and gardens; the beautiful walled city of **Ávila**, birthplace of St Teresa; and Cervantes' home town, **Alcalá de Henares**, with its sixteenth-century university. For walkers, too, trails amid the sierras of **Gredos and Guadarrama** provide enticing escapes from the midsummer heat.

All of the towns in this chapter can be visited as easy day-trips from Madrid, but they also offer interesting jumping-off points into Castile and beyond.

Toledo

TOLEDO remains one of Spain's great cities. Redolent of past glories, it is packed with memorable sights – hence the whole city's status as a National Monument and UNESCO Patrimony of Mankind – and enjoys an incomparable setting. Be aware, however, that the extraordinary number of day-trippers can take the edge off what was once the most extravagant of Spanish experiences.

Set in a landscape of abrasive desolation, Toledo sits on a rocky mound where every available inch has been built upon: churches, synagogues, mosques and houses are heaped upon one another in a haphazard, cobblestoned spiral.

To see the city at its best, it is advisable to avoid peak holiday periods and stay at least a night: a day-trip will leave you hard pressed to see everything. More importantly, in the evening with the crowds gone and the city lit up by floodlights – resembling one of **El Greco**'s moonlit paintings – Toledo is a different place entirely.

There are two main entrances to the old city of Toledo: via the mechanical staircase that scales the hill from the Puerta de Bisagra opposite the tourist office and leaves you close to the Convento de Santo Domingo Antiguo, or up Calle Real del Arrabal to the Plaza Zocódover. Once there, the street **layout** can appear confusing, but the old core is so

A VIEW OF TOLEDO

Highlights

❶ **A view of El Greco's Toledo** The terrace bar of the parador provides the perfect viewing point of the ancient city. **See p.139**

❷ **Toledo's Catedral** An awesome construction featuring a stunning mixture of opulent decorations and styles befitting a former capital. **See p.133**

❸ **Savour strawberries and cream at Aranjuez** Indulge in the town's famous sweet treat at the street cafés by the royal palace. **See p.140**

❹ **El Escorial** Marvel at Felipe II's massive monastery complex perched spectacularly in the foothills of the Sierra de Guadarrama. **See p.143**

❺ **Hiking in the sierra** Head for the hills of Guadarrama or Gredos for a break from the city heat. **See p.148** & **p.157**

❻ **A walk along the walls at Ávila** Superb views of the town and the harsh Castilian landscape. **See p.154**

❼ **The aqueduct at Segovia** A marvel of Roman engineering situated at the entrance to the historic mountain city. **See p.159**

❽ **The fountains at La Granja** A beautiful display at the royal retreat near Segovia. **See p.166**

HIGHLIGHTS ARE MARKED ON THE MAP ON P.128

small that it should never take too long to get back on track; part of the city's charm is that it's a place to wander in and absorb. Don't leave without seeing at least the El Grecos, the cathedral, the synagogues and Alcázar, but give it all time and you may stumble upon things not listed in this or any other guidebook. Enter any inviting doorway and you'll find stunning patios, rooms and ceilings, often of Mudéjar workmanship.

Brief history

Toledo was known to the Romans, who captured it in 192 BC, as Toletum, a small but well-defended town. Taken by the Visigoths, who made it their capital, it was already an important cultural and trading centre by the time the **Moors** arrived in 712. The period that followed, with Moors, Jews and Mozárabes (Christians subject to Moorish rule) living together in relative equality, was one of rapid growth and prosperity and

AROUND MADRID

N

CASTILLA Y
LEÓN

Valladolid
Coca
Sepúlveda
Turégano
Pedraza

SIERRA DE GUADARRAMA

Segovia
7 La Granja
8 5 Rascafría
Buitrago del Lozoya
Pto. de Los Cotos
Patones
Pto. de Navacerada
Cercedilla
Manzanares el Real
Ávila 6
El Escorial
4
El Pardo
Guadalajara
Alcalá de Henares
San Martin de Valdeiglesias
MADRID
Navalcarnero
Chinchón
A5-E90
Aranjuez 3
Tarancón
Torrijos
Talavera de la Reina
Ocaña
Toledo 1 2
CASTILLA-
LA MANCHA
Orgaz
Ciudad Real
Jaén & Córdoba

HIGHLIGHTS
1 A view of El Greco's Toledo
2 Toledo's Catedral
3 Savour strawberries and cream at Aranjuez
4 El Escorial
5 Hiking in the sierra
6 A walk along the walls at Ávila
7 The aqueduct at Segovia
8 The fountains at La Granja

0   25
kilometres

FIESTAS

FEBRUARY–APRIL

First Sunday in February: Santa Agueda Women's Festival Married women take over city administration, and parade and celebrate in traditional costume.

Semana Santa (Holy Week): Formal processions in Toledo and a Passion play on Saturday in the Plaza Mayor at Chinchón.

Mid-April: Fiesta del Anís y del Vino, Chinchón Ample tastings of these two local products.

MAY–AUGUST

Thursday after Trinity, possibly in June: Corpus Christi Solemn, costumed religious procession in Toledo when the Catedral's magnificent sixteenth-century *custodia* is paraded around.

24–29 June: San Juan y San Pedro Lively procession with floats and music in Segovia.

15 August: Virgen de la Asunción Chinchón's celebrations include an *encierro*, with bulls running through the street.

15 August: Virgen del Sagrario Amazing fireworks display in Toledo.

17–25 August: Entertaining fiestas in La Granja, (near Segovia) Parades, bullfighting, fireworks and the fountains in full flow, and in Orgaz (near Toledo) which honours its patron saint with further celebrations.

Last week in August: Spectacular parades of giant puppets, and theatre, music and dance in Alcalá de Henares.

SEPTEMBER & OCTOBER

First weekend in September: Motín de Aranjuez Re-enactment of the Mutiny of Aranjuez in Aranjuez.

27 September: La Virgen de la Fuencisla The image of Segovia's patron saint is carried from the sanctuary in the Eresma valley to the cathedral.

25 October: San Frutos Fiestas, Segovia Concerts, celebrations and parades in honour of the city's patron saint.

Toledo became the most important northern outpost of the Muslim emirates. Though there are few physical remains of this period, apart from the enchanting miniature mosque of **Cristo de la Luz**, the long domination has left a clear mark on the atmosphere and shape of the city.

When the Christian king Alfonso VI "reconquered" the town in 1085, with the assistance of El Cid, Moorish influence scarcely weakened. Although Toledo became the capital of Castile and the base for campaigns against the Moors in the south, the city itself was a haven of cultural tolerance. Not only was there a school of translators revealing the scientific and philosophical achievements of the East, but Arab craftsmen and techniques remained responsible for many of the finest buildings of the period: look, for example, at the churches of **San Román** or **Santiago del Arrabal** or at any of the old **city gates**.

At the same time Jewish culture remained powerful. There were, at one time, at least seven **synagogues** – of which two, **Santa María la Blanca** and **El Tránsito**, survive – and Jews occupied many positions of power. The most famous was Samuel Levi, treasurer and right-hand man of Pedro the Cruel until the king lived up to his name by murdering him and stealing his fortune. From this period, too, dates the most important purely Christian monument, Toledo's awesome **Catedral**.

This golden age ended abruptly in the sixteenth century with the transfer of the capital to Madrid, following hard on the heels of the Inquisition's mass expulsion of Muslims and Jews; some of the latter responded by taking refuge in Catholicism, becoming known as *conversos*. The city played little part in subsequent Spanish history until the Civil War with the siege of the Alcázar (see box, p.133) and it remains, despite the droves of tourists, essentially the medieval city so often painted by El Greco.

2

La Puebla de Montalbán & ◀

TOLEDO

2

Ávila
Madrid
Aranjuez

Hospital de Tavera
CARRETEROS
DUQUES DE LERMA
PASEO DE MERCHAN
CARDENAL TAVERA
RONDA
LOS
PZA. HONDA
TINTOREROS
COV. ACHUELAS
Bus Station
ESPINO
PERALA
Hospedería de los Reyes
RÍO LLANO
AVENIDA DE CASTILLA

Puente de Azarquiel
N400

PASEO DE LA ROSA
Train Station
Aranjuez

LA CARRERA
PLAZA SOLAR DE LA ANTEQUERUELA
PZA. DE LA VIRGEN
Puerta Nueva de Bisagra
RONDA DEL GRANADAL
PZA. DE LA ANTEQUERUELA
PZA. DE LOS ALFARES
LA ANTEQUERUELA
AZACANES
RFA. EL URABAL

GERARDO LOBO

Puerta del Sol
②
CARRETAS
Puerta de Valmardón
PASEO DEL MIRADERO
CUESTA DE ARMAS
CRISTO DE LA LUZ
Mezquita del Cristo de la Luz
NÚÑEZ DE ARCE
P
Convento de Santa Fe

DEL CONDE
PZA. ARMELITAS
CARMELITAS
LOS ALFILERITOS
③
LA SILLERÍA
ⓘ
SANTA FE
CERVANTES
Hospital y Museo de Santa Cruz
PLAZA DE ZOCODOVER
①
NUEV.A
CIÓN. DE MENORES
④
LA PLATA
COBENJ
⑤
Puerta Rey Wamba
PL. DE LA CONCEPCIÓN
Palacios de Galiana y Huerta del Rey
Puente & Puerta de Alcántara
PASEO DE LA ROSA
③

San Vicente
S. SAN ENTE
Convento de las Agustinas Calzadas
SAN GINÉS
TOMECO
SERPE
⑥
ALFÉRECES PROVISIONALES
PZA. DE LA MAGDALENA
BARRIO
③
CERVANTES
PASEO DEL CARMEN
Acueducto Romano

Mezquita de Tornerías
NUNCIO VIEJO
CAMBADO
SINAGOGA
HOMBRE DE PALO
⑦
⑧
Corral de San Diego
CARMELITAS
HORNO DE LOS BIZCOCHOS
CUESTA DE CARLOS V
El Alcázar
QUINTI
CERVANTES
Puerta de Doce Cantos

ARCO DEL PALACIO
⑨
JUAN LABRADOR
PLAZA MAYOR
GENERAL MOSCARDO
Pte. Nuevo de Alcántara

Palacio arzobispal
Posada de la Hermandad
⑩
PL. DEL SECO
PASEO

ⓘ
PL. DEL AYUNTAMIENTO
CARDENAL CISNEROS
⑪
⑦
SIXTO RAMÓN PARRO
PL. DE S. JUSTO
La Catedral

Ayuntamiento
⑧
POZO AMARGO
VICARIO
BARCO
LA CANDELARIA
CTA. S. JUSTO
CUESTA DEL CAN

STA. ISABEL
JOSÉ BONO
AVE MARÍA
POZO
CAPEDA
③
San Justo
CUESTA DEL CAN

Convento de Santa Isabel
Convento de San Juan de la Penitencia
RÍO TAJO
CARRETERA DE CIRCUNVALACIÓN

San Andrés
PABLO
BDA. DEL BARCO
PASEO DE CABESTREROS
AMARGO
SOS
PLEGUETRO

STA. NA
San Lucas

SAN SEBASTIÁN

Casa del Diamantista

Ferry

0 ——— 150
metres

▼ **⑬**

2

The Alcázar

C/Unión s/n • June–Sept Mon–Sat 10am–9pm, Sun 10am–3pm; Oct–May Mon–Sat 10am–7pm, Sun 10am–3pm • €5, under-18 free, free Sun • ⓦ museo.ejercito.es

If one building dominates Toledo, it's the bluff, imposing fortress of the **Alcázar**. Originally the site of a Roman palace, Emperor Carlos V ordered the construction of the current fortress in the sixteenth century, though it has been burned and bombarded so often that little remains of the original building. The monument enjoyed iconic status during the Franco era after the Nationalist forces inside, under siege by the Republican town, were eventually relieved by an army heading for Madrid which took severe retribution on the local inhabitants. After the war, Franco's regime completely rebuilt the fortress as a monument to the glorification of its defenders.

Following a tortuous relocation and refurbishment programme lasting the best part of the last decade, the Alcázar is now home to an impressive state-of-the-art **army museum**. Encompassing a new building constructed over the archeological remains of the original fortress, the museum offers two fascinating routes which navigate visitors through its extensive collections – one historic and one thematic. Spain's military history, the organization of its armed forces and the art of war are all dealt with in exhaustive detail, while exhibits include everything from medieval swords and suits of armour to toy soldiers and Civil War memorabilia.

Mezquita de las Tornerías

Pl. Solarejo 7 • Mon–Fri 10am–2pm • Free

A couple of blocks to the west of the Alcázar is the **Mezquita de las Tornerías**, a renovated eleventh-century mosque, deconsecrated by the Reyes Católicos around 1500, and notable for the fact that it has two storey. The mosque now houses a centre for the promotion of local handicrafts with occasional exhibitions of beautifully made local products.

Hospital y Museo de Santa Cruz

C/Cervantes 3 • Mon–Sat 10am–6.30pm, Sun 10am–2pm • Free

Just north of the Alcázar, off Plaza de Zocódover, is the **Hospital y Museo de Santa Cruz**, a superlative Renaissance building with a fine Plateresque facade, housing some of the greatest El Grecos in Toledo, including *The Assumption*, a daringly unorthodox work of feverish spiritual intensity, and a *Crucifixion* with the town as a backdrop. As well as outstanding works by Goya and Ribera, the **museum** also contains a huge collection of ancient carpets and faded tapestries (including a magnificent fifteenth-century Flemish tapestry called *The Astrolabe*), a military display (note the flags borne by Don Juan of Austria at the Battle of Lepanto), sculpture and a small archeological collection. Don't miss the patio with its ornate staircase – the entrance is beside the ticket office.

The Catedral

C/Cardenal Cisneros • Areas that need tickets: Mon–Sat 10am–6pm & Sun 2– 6pm, main body closed noon–3.30pm, choir closed Sun morning; New Museums closed Mon • €7, free Sun pm for Spanish citizens; audio-guides €3 • ⓦ catedralprimada.es

In a country overflowing with massive religious institutions, the metropolitan **Catedral** has to be something special – and it is. A robust Gothic construction that took over 250 years (1227–1493) to complete, it has a richness of internal decoration in almost every conceivable style, with masterpieces of the Gothic, Renaissance and Baroque periods. The exterior is best appreciated from outside the city, where the hundred-metre spire and the weighty buttressing can be seen to greatest advantage. From the street it's less impressive, so hemmed in by surrounding houses that you can't really sense the scale or grandeur of the whole.

The Coro

Inside the cathedral, the central nave is divided from four aisles by a series of clustered pillars supporting the vaults, 88 in all, the aisles continuing around behind the main altar to form an apse. There is magnificent **stained glass** throughout, mostly dating from the fifteenth and sixteenth centuries, particularly beautiful in two rose windows above the north and south doors. Beside the south door (Puerto de los Leones) is a huge, ancient **fresco of St Christopher**.

At the physical heart of the church, blocking the nave, is the **Coro**, itself a panoply of sculpture. The wooden stalls are in two tiers. The lower level, carved in 1489–95 by Rodrigo Alemán, depicts the conquest of Granada, with each seat showing a different village being taken by the Christians. The portraits of Old Testament characters on the stalls above were executed in the following century, on the north side by Philippe Vigarni and on the south by Alonso Berruguete, whose superior technique is evident. He also carved the large **Transfiguration** here from a single block of alabaster. The *reja* (grille) that encloses the Coro is said to be plated with gold, but it was covered in iron to disguise its value from Napoleon's troops and has since proved impossible to renovate.

The Capilla Mayor and Transparente

The **Capilla Mayor** stands directly opposite the Coro. Its gargantuan altarpiece, stretching clear to the roof, is one of the triumphs of Gothic art, overflowing with intricate detail and fanciful embellishments. It contains a synopsis of the entire New Testament, culminating in a Calvary at the summit.

THE SIEGE OF THE ALCÁZAR

At the outset of the **Spanish Civil War**, on July 20, 1936, Colonel José Moscardó – a leading Nationalist rebel – and the cadets of the military academy under his command were **driven into the Alcázar**. They barricaded themselves in with a large group that included six hundred women and children, and up to a hundred left-wing hostages (who were never seen again).

After many phone calls from Madrid to persuade them to surrender, a Toledo attorney phoned Moscardó with an ultimatum: within ten minutes the Republicans would shoot his son, captured that morning. Moscardó declared that he would never surrender and told his son, "If it be true, commend your soul to God, shout Viva España, and die like a hero." (His son was actually shot with others a month later in reprisal for an air raid.) Inside, though not short of ammunition, the defenders had so little food they had to eat their horses.

The number of Republican attackers varied from 1000 to 5000. Two of the three mines they planted under the towers exploded but nothing could disturb the solid rock foundations, while spraying petrol all over the walls and setting fire to it had no effect. Finally, General Franco decided to relieve Moscardó and diverted an army that was heading for Madrid. On September 27, General José Varela commanded the successful attack on the town, which was followed by the usual bloodbath. The day after Franco entered Toledo to consolidate his victory, he was declared head of state.

Directly behind the main altar is an extraordinary piece of fantasy – the Baroque **Transparente**. Wonderfully and wildly extravagant, with its marble cherubs sitting on fluffy marble clouds, it's especially magnificent when the sun reaches through the hole punched in the roof for just that purpose. You'll notice a red cardinal's hat hanging from the vaulting just in front of this. Spanish primates are buried where they choose, with the epitaph they choose and with their hat hanging above them, where it stays until it rots. One of them chose to be buried here, and there are other pieces of headgear dotted around the cathedral.

The Capillas

There are well over twenty **chapels** embedded into the walls of the cathedral, all of which are of some interest. Many of them house fine tombs, particularly the **Capilla de Santiago**, the octagonal **Capilla de San Ildefonso** and the gilded **Capilla de Reyes Nuevos**.

In the **Capilla Mozárabe**, Mass is still celebrated daily according to the ancient Visigothic rites. When the Church tried to ban the old ritual in 1086 the people of Toledo were outraged. The dispute was put to a combat, which the Mozárabe champion won, but the Church demanded further proof: trial by fire. The Roman prayer book was blown to safety, while the Mozárabe version remained, unburnt, in the flames. Both sides claimed victory, and in the end the two rituals were allowed to coexist. If you want to attend Mass, be there at 9.30am and look out for the priest – you may well be the only congregation.

The Tesoro, Sacristía and Sala Capitular

The **Capilla de San Juan** houses the riches of the cathedral **Tesoro** (Treasury), most notably a solid silver *custodia* (repository for Eucharist wafers), ten foot high and weighing over two hundred kilos.

An even more impressive accumulation of wealth is displayed in the **Sacristía** (Sacristy), where paintings include a *Disrobing of Christ* and portraits of the Apostles by El Greco, Velázquez's portrait of *Cardinal Borja* and Goya's *Christ Taken by the Soldiers*. The adjoining rooms house works of art that were previously locked away or poorly displayed. Among them are paintings by Caravaggio, Gerard David and Morales, and El Greco's most important piece of sculpture, a polychromed wooden group of *San Ildefonso and the Virgin*.

The **Sala Capitular** (Chapter House) has a magnificent sixteenth-century *artesonado* (wooden sculptured) ceiling and portraits of all Spain's archbishops to the present day.

Santo Tomé and the Burial of the Count of Orgaz

C/Santo Tomé • Mid-March–mid-Oct 10am–6.45pm; mid-Oct–mid-March 10am–5.45pm • €2.30, free Wed after 4pm for EU citizens • W santotome.org

A little way to the west of the Catedral is one of Toledo's outstanding attractions: El Greco's masterpiece, **The Burial of the Count of Orgaz**. It's housed, alone, in a small annexe to the church of **Santo Tomé** and depicts the count's funeral, at which SS Stephen and Augustine appeared in order to lower him into the tomb. It combines El Greco's genius for the mystic, exemplified in the upper half of the picture where the count's soul is being received into heaven, with his great powers as a portrait painter and master of colour. The identity of the sombre-faced figures watching the burial has been a source of endless speculation. On two identities, however, there is universal agreement; El Greco painted himself seventh from the left looking out at the viewer and his son in the foreground. Less certain are the identities of the rest of the mourners, but the odds are on for Felipe II's presence among the heavenly onlookers, even though he was still alive when it was painted. A search for the count's bones came to an end in early 2001 when they were unearthed from a tomb located, appropriately enough, directly below the painting.

Palacio de Fuensalida and the Taller del Moro

Palacio de Fuensalida Undergoing refurbishment; closed to the public **Taller del Moro** Also closed for restoration

Next to Santo Tomé is the **Palacio de Fuensalida**, a beautiful fifteenth-century mansion where Carlos V's Portuguese wife Isabel died. A garden separates it from the **Taller del Moro**, three fourteenth-century rooms of a Mudéjar palace with magnificent decoration and doorways intact. It is approached through its own entrance in the c/Taller del Moro.

Museo del Greco

Paseo del Tránsito • April–Sept Tues–Sat 9.30am–8pm, Sun 10am–3pm; Oct–March Tues–Sat 9.30am–6.30pm, Sun 10am–3pm • €3, €5 combined entry with Museo Sefardí • ⓦ museodelgreco.mcu.es

From Santo Tomé, the c/Alamillo leads down to the old **Judería** (Jewish quarter) and the **Museo del Greco** devoted to the life and work of the Greek-born artist so closely associated with the city. This refurbished exhibition space, given a new lease of life after a €6 million renovation, houses his famous *View and Map of Toledo*, a full series of the *Twelve Apostles*, completed later than the set in the cathedral and subtly different in style, and other work by the Greek-born painter and his disciples. Several of the rooms also re-create the atmosphere of the artist's original living quarters in the city.

Sinagoga del Tránsito and the Museo Sefardí

C/Samuel • Museo Sefardí Tues–Sat 9.30am–6pm, Sun 10am–2pm • €3, €5 combined entry with Museo del Greco, free Sat pm & Sun

Almost next door to the Museo del Greco is the **Sinagoga del Tránsito**. Built along Moorish lines by Samuel Levi in 1366, it became a church after the expulsion of the Jews. The interior is a simple galleried hall, brilliantly decorated with polychromed stuccowork and superb filigree windows. Hebrew inscriptions praising God, King Pedro and Samuel Levi adorn the walls. It houses a small **Museo Sefardí** (Sephardic Museum) tracing the distinct traditions and development of Jewish culture in Spain.

Museo de Victorio Macho

Pl. de Victorio 2 Macho • Mon–Sat 10am–7pm, Sun 10am–3pm • €3 • ⓦ realfundaciontoledo.es

Opposite the Sinagoga del Tránsito, splendidly situated on a spur overlooking the Río Tajo, is the **Museo de Victorio Macho**, which contains the sculptures, paintings and

---

EL GRECO AND TOLEDO

Even if you've never seen **Toledo** – and even if you've no idea what to expect – there's an uncanny familiarity about your first view of it, with the Alcázar and the cathedral spire towering above the tawny mass of the town. This is due to **El Greco**, whose constant depiction of the city (as background, even, for the Crucifixion) seems to have stuck, albeit unwittingly, somewhere in everyone's consciousness.

Domenikos Theotokopoulos, "the Greek", was born in Crete in 1541 and worked in Venice and Rome before going to Spain. He had originally hoped to get work on the decoration of El Escorial, but after being rejected by Felipe II, he arrived in Toledo in about 1577. His first major commission was to produce a series of paintings for the church of Santo Domingo el Antiguo and many others followed, including his most famous work: *The Burial of the Count of Orgaz*. El Greco remained in the city until his death in 1614 which came while he was working on a commission for the Hospital de Tavera. He was buried in Santo Domingo el Antiguo.

Many of El Greco's extraordinary paintings – some of the most individual, most intensely spiritual visions of all Spanish art – remain scattered throughout the city. Years ahead of his time, his work went on to influence artists for centuries to come, including Manet, Cezanne and Picasso.

Hortension Félix Paravicino, a Spanish preacher and poet who was a subject of one of El Greco's paintings, commented "Crete gave him life and the painter's craft, Toledo a better homeland, where through death he began to achieve eternal life."

sketches of the Spanish artist Victorio Macho (1887–1966), set in a delightfully tranquil garden with great views across the river valley. The auditorium on the ground floor shows a documentary (available in English) about the city and its history.

Sinagoga de Santa María la Blanca

C/Reyes Católicos 4 • Daily 10am–6pm, summer closes 7pm • €2.30, free Wed pm for EU citizens

The only other surviving synagogue, **Santa María la Blanca**, is a short way further down c/Reyes Católicos. Like El Tránsito, which it pre dates by over a century, it has been both church and synagogue, though, as it was built by Mudéjar craftsmen, it actually looks more like a mosque. Four rows of octagonal pillars each support seven horseshoe arches, all of them with elaborate and individual designs moulded in plaster, while a fine sixteenth-century retablo has been preserved from the building's time as a church. The whole effect is quite stunning, accentuated by a deep-red floor tiled with decorative *azulejos*.

Monasterio de San Juan de los Reyes

C/San Juan de los Reyes 2 • Daily 10am–6.45pm, winter closes 5.45pm • €2.30, free Wed after 4pm for EU citizens

Down c/Reyes Católicos from Santa María la Blanca you come to the superb church of **San Juan de los Reyes**, its exterior bizarrely festooned with the chains worn by Christian prisoners from Granada released on the reconquest of their city. It was originally a Franciscan convent founded by the "Catholic Kings", Fernando and Isabel, to celebrate their victory at the Battle of Toro. Designed in the decorative Late Gothic style known as Isabelline (after the queen), its double-storeyed cloister is quite outstanding: the upper storey has an elaborate Mudéjar ceiling, and the crests of Castile and Aragón – seven arrows and a yoke – are carved everywhere in assertion of the new unity brought by the royal marriage.

Convento de Santo Domingo el Antiguo

Pl. Santo Dominguo el Antiguo • Mon–Sat 11am–1.30pm & 4–7pm, Sun 4–7pm • €2

A little way to the north of San Juan de los Reyes and close to the mechanical staircase leading out of the old city is the **Convento de Santo Domingo el Antiguo**. The church's chief claim to fame is that it contains El Greco's remains, which can be glimpsed through a peephole in the floor. The nuns display their art treasures in the old choir, but more interesting is the high altarpiece of the church, El Greco's first major commission in Toledo. Unfortunately, most of the canvases have gone to museums and are here replaced by copies, leaving only two *St John*s and a *Resurrection*.

Museo de los Concilios y Cultura Visigoda

Pl. San Román • Tues–Sat 10am–2pm & 4–6.30pm, Sun 10am–2pm • Free

Southeast of Convento de Santo Domingo el Antiguo back towards the cathedral is the **Museo de Cultura Visigodo** which can be found in the church of **San Román**. Moorish and Christian elements – horseshoe arches, early murals and a splendid Renaissance dome – combine to make it one of the most interesting churches in Toledo. Visigothic jewellery, documents and archeological fragments make up the bulk of the collection.

The Puerta del Sol and Mezquita del Cristo de la Luz

Cuesta de los Carmelitos Descalzos 10 • March–Sept Mon–Fri 10am–2pm & 3.30-6.40pm; Oct–Feb Mon–Fri 10am–2pm & 3.30–5.45pm, Sat & Sun 10am–5.45pm • €2.30, free on Wed after 4pm for EU citizens

If you leave the old city by the Cuesta de Armas, which runs out of the Plaza de Zocódover and down the hill, you will come across the battlements of the **Puerta**

del Sol, a great fourteenth-century Mudéjar gateway. Tucked behind the gateway on the Cuesta de los Carmelitas Descalzos is the tiny mosque of **Mezquita del Cristo de la Luz**. Although this is one of the oldest Moorish monuments in Spain (it was built by Musa Ibn Ali in the tenth century on the foundations of a Visigothic church), only the nave, with its nine different cupolas, is the original Arab construction. The apse was added when the building was converted into a church, and is claimed to be the first product of the Mudéjar style. According to legend, as King Alfonso rode into the town in triumph, his horse stopped and knelt before the mosque. Excavations revealed a figure of Christ, still illuminated by a lamp, which had burned throughout three and a half centuries of Muslim rule – hence the name Cristo de la Luz. The outstandingly elegant mosque, set in a small park and open on all sides to the elements, is so small that it seems more like a miniature summer pavilion, but it has an elegant simplicity of design that few of the town's great monuments can match.

Santiago del Arrabal and the Puerta Bisagra

Pl. Santiago del Arrabal 4

Below the Puerta del Sol on the way out of the old city is the intriguing brickwork exterior of the Mudéjar church of **Santiago del Arrabal**, while at the foot of the hill and marooned in a constant swirl of traffic is Toledo's main gate, the sixteenth-century **Puerta Nueva de Bisagra**. Its patterned-tile roofs bear the coat of arms of Carlos V. Alongside is the gateway that it replaced, the ninth-century Moorish portal through which Alfonso VI and El Cid led their triumphant armies in 1085.

Hospital de Tavera

C/Duque de Lerma 2 • Mon–Sat 10am–1.30pm & 3–6.30pm, Sun 10am–2.30pm • €4.50

Beyond the city walls along the Paseo de Merchán is the **Hospital de Tavera**. This Renaissance palace with beautiful twin patios houses the private collection of the Duke of Lerma. The gloomy interior is a reconstruction of a sixteenth-century mansion dotted with fine paintings, including a *Day of Judgement* by Bassano; the portrait of Carlos V by Titian is a copy of the original in the Prado. The hospital's archives are kept here, too: thousands of densely handwritten pages chronicling the illnesses treated. The museum contains several works by El Greco, and Ribera's gruesome portrait of a freak "bearded woman". Also here is the death mask of Cardinal Tavera, the hospital's founder, and in the church of the hospital is his ornate marble tomb – the last work of Alonso de Berruguete.

ARRIVAL AND DEPARTURE   TOLEDO

By train There's a high-speed train service from Atocha station in Madrid (12–14 daily; 33min; €18 return; it's essential to book in advance at the station or from most travel agents in the city). Toledo's train station is some way out on the Paseo de la Rosa, a 20min walk – take the left-hand fork off the dual carriageway and cross the Puente de Alcántara – or a bus ride (#5 or #6 or the tourist shuttle) to the heart of town.

Destinations Albacete (3 daily; 2hr 5min); Cuenca (3 daily; 1hr 27min).

By bus Every 30min from the Pl. Elíptica terminal in Madrid (1hr–1hr 30min; €8.68 return). The bus station is on Avda. de Castilla la Mancha in the modern, lower part of the city; bus #5 runs to Pl. Zocódover, though if you take

shortcuts through the *barrio* at the bottom of the hill just inside the walls, it's a mere 10min walk to the Puerta Nueva de Bisagra.

Destinations Ciudad Real, for the south (daily; 2hr); Cuenca (Mon–Fri 1 daily; 2hr 30min); Guadamur (7 daily; 20min); Orgaz (3–10 daily; 30min); La Puebla de Montalbán (5 daily Mon–Fri, daily Sat; 40min); Talavera de la Reina, for Extremadura (10 daily; 1hr).

By car The best places to park are in the streets beyond the Circo Romano in the new town (Mon–Fri 10am–2pm & 5–8pm, Sat 10am–2pm; 0.78€/hr) or in the underground car park close to the mechanical staircase (Mon–Fri 7am–10pm, Sat, Sun & hols 8am–10pm) that leads up into the old city.

2

2

GETTING AROUND

On foot Walking is the only way to see the city itself, but be aware that resident cars have a tendency to roar along even the tiniest alleyways in the centre. Information on an array of walking tours is available at the *oficinas de turismo* (see below), while the local office next to the Catedral offers free guided visits to some of the lesser known parts of the city. You can also check ⓦ toledopaisajes.com, ⓦ conocetoledo.com and ⓦ odelotoledo.com.

INFORMATION

Regional tourist office Opposite Puerta Nueva de Bisagra outside the city walls (summer Mon–Sat 9am–7pm, winter Mon–Fri 9am–6pm, Sun & hols 9am–3pm; ☎ 925 220 843, ⓦ turismocastillalamancha.com).

Local tourist offices In the train station (daily 9.30am–5.30pm; ☎ 925 239 121, ⓦ toledo-turismo.com); at the top of the mechanical staircase leading into the city from the Puerta de Bisagra (Cuesta de la Granja s/n; Mon–Fri 10am–5pm, Sat & Sun 10am–3.50pm); and in the plaza next to the Catedral (daily 10am–6pm; ☎ 925 254 030).

Tickets You can save on the entry fees to a number of the sights such as the synagogues, San Juan de los Reyes and Santo Tomé if you invest in the €8 Bono Turístico.

Information point In the Zococentro shop, c/Sillería 14 in the centre (daily 10.30am–6pm, till 7pm in the summer, opens at 11am on Sat & Sun; ☎ 925 220 300).

Internet access *There are* several *locutorios* with internet access in and around Pl. de la Magdalena and at c/Santo Tomé 1 (€2/hr).

ACCOMMODATION

Booking a room in advance is important in Toledo, especially at weekends, or during the summer. The tourist offices have lists of all the **accommodation** available in town, while there is also a central booking agency (ⓦ loshotelesdetoledo .com, ☎ 902 513 223). Be aware that prices in many places almost double at Easter, bank holidays and at Corpus Christi, but that outside these times and mid week, hotels often offer substantially reduced rates.

Casona de la Reyna c/San Sebastián 26 ☎ 925 282 052, ⓦ casonadelareyna.com. Situated in the quiet San Cipriano area of the old town close to the Judería, this functional mid-range hotel has 25 spacious, classically decorated rooms with a/c and private parking. €60

Castillo San Servando Across the Puente de Alcántara and just off Paseo de la Rosa on Cuesta de San Servando ☎ 925 224 554, ☎ 925 224 558, ⓔ alberguesclm@jccm. es. Toledo's youth hostel is across the river from the Alcázar in a wing of the fourteenth-century Mudéjar-style Castillo San Servando, a 15min walk (signposted) from the train station. It has a fine view of the city, a pool and communal areas. Booking is advised and a YH card required. Closed mid-Aug to mid-Sept. Two- or four-room dormitories: under-30s €13.58, over-30s €16.30

★ **Hostal del Cardenal** Paseo de Recaredo 24 ☎ 925 224 900, ⓦ hostaldelcardenal.com. A splendid old mansion with a famous restaurant and delightful patio gardens, located outside the city wall, near Puerta Nueva de Bisagra. €125

Hostal Casa de Cisneros c/Cardenal Cisneros ☎ 925 228 828, ⓦ hostal-casa-de-cisneros.com. Upmarket boutique-style *hostal* in a refurbished sixteenth-century townhouse with ten en-suite, wood-beamed a/c rooms situated opposite the Puerta de Leones entrance of the cathedral. €70

Hostal Descalzos c/Descalzos 30 ☎ 925 222 888, ⓦ hostaldescalzos.com. Very good-value, centrally located *hostal*, handy for the main sights. Some of the modern a/c en-suite rooms have lovely views, plus there's a small open-air pool. €50

★ **Hostal La Posada de Manolo** c/Sixto Ramón Parro 8 ☎ 925 282 250, ⓦ laposadademanolo.com. An atmospheric *hostal* in a carefully refurbished period house close to the cathedral with small brick-lined and beamed rooms, all with a/c and free wi-fi. €66

Hostal Santo Tomé c/Santo Tomé 13 ☎ 925 221 712, ⓦ hostalsantotome.com. New *hostal* next door to the church of the same name with a range of simple, comfortable a/c rooms including a four-bed attic family room. €52

Hotel Abad c/Real del Arrabal 1 ☎ 925 283 500, ⓦ hotelabadtoledo.com. A smart hotel situated in a former ironworks close to the Mezquita de la Luz. The 22 rooms have brick-lined walls and warm colours, and those in the loft are particularly nice. There are family apartments available for €135–160. €70

Hotel Pintor el Greco c/Alamillos de Tránsito 13 ☎ 925 285 191, ⓦ hotelpintorelgreco.com. A well-equipped and nicely furnished hotel in a refurbished seventeenth-century bakery situated in the old Jewish quarter. It has 60 comfortable rooms, many with fine views across the Tajo, and private parking. Special offers available. €75

★ **Hotel Santa Isabel** c/Santa Isabel 24 ☎ 925 253 120, ⓦ hotelsantaisabel.net. The best of the mid-range hotels occupies a converted nobleman's house right in the centre of town. Airy rooms (some with views), wood-panelled floors and safe parking (€10 per night). €65

Palacio Eugenia de Montijo Pl. del Juego de la Pelota 7 ☎ 925 274 690, ⓦ palacioeugeniademontijo.com. Five-star luxury hotel in the heart of the old town close to the cathedral with its own spa and a high-class restaurant run by the Adolfo chain. **€100**

Parador Conde de Orgaz Cerro del Emperador s/n ☎ 925 221 850, ⓦ paradores.com. Superb views of the city from the terrace of Toledo's top hotel, but the drawback is that it's a fair walk from the centre. Light and airy rooms and a splendid outdoor pool if the heat gets to much in summer. **€130**

CAMPSITE

Camping El Greco Carretera de Toledo–Puebla de Montalbán ☎ 925 220 090, ⓦ campingelgreco.es. There are great views of the city from this riverside campsite – and a bar to enjoy them from – plus a swimming pool to cool off in after a hard day's sightseeing. A 30min walk from the Puerta de Bisagra: cross the Puente de la Cava towards Puebla de Montalbán, then follow the signs. Two adults plus car **€25.40**

EATING AND DRINKING

Toledo is a major tourist centre and inevitably many of its **cafés**, **bars** and **restaurants** are geared to passing trade. However, the city is also popular with Spanish visitors, so decent, authentic places do exist – and there's a bit of nightlife, too.

La Abadía Pl. San Nicolás 3 ☎ 925 251 140, ⓦ abadiatoledo.com. There's a constantly changing €11 lunchtime menu in this popular restaurant which also serves some good specialities such as partridge and wild boar steak. Daily around 1.30–4pm & 8.30pm–midnight.

Adolfo c/Granada 6 ☎ 925 227 321, ⓦ adolforestaurante .com. One of the most prestigious restaurants in town, tucked behind a marzipan café, in an old Jewish townhouse (ask to see the painted ceiling in the eleventh-century cellar downstairs), and serving imaginative, high-quality, but over-priced food, using local ingredients such as partridge, with a meal costing in the region of €70–90. Closed Sun eve, Mon & two weeks in July.

Adolfo Colección c/Nuncio Viejo 1. If you can't afford to eat at the *Adolfo* restaurant (above), have a glass of wine and some designer tapas at this elegant little bar run by the same people. Closed Sun eve, Mon & two weeks in July.

★ **Alfileritos 24** c/Alfileritos 24 ☎ 925 239 625, ⓦ alfileritos24.com. A cool, relaxed, brick-lined bar-restaurant serving an imaginative and tasty €10 lunchtime bar menu and a more elaborate and expensive €17.95 restaurant version. À la carte options include a squid and vegetable rice dish and venison steak with roast apple. A

good place for a drink, too. Daily around 1.30–4pm and 8.30pm–midnight.

As de Espadas Paseo de la Rosa 64 ☎ 925 212 707. An excellent restaurant close to the railway station serving imaginative dishes such as chickpeas with spinach and squid and high-quality meat and fish. It also does good home-made desserts and has an extensive wine list. Allow between €55–60 a head. Daily around 1.30–4pm & 8.30pm –midnight.

Casa Aurelio c/Sinagoga 1 & 6 ☎ 925 224 105, ⓦ casa-aurelio.com. Two branches of a popular Toledano group of restaurants (there's another one next to the cathedral in the Pl. del Ayuntamiento) serving up good, standard Castilian food. Mains range from €18–25.

Casa Ludeña Pl. Magdalena 13. One of many places around this square, but this is the most authentic. It offers a good-value €10 *menú* and some of the best *carcamusa* in town.

Los Cuatro Tiempos c/Sixto Ramón Parro 5 (close to the cathedral) ☎ 925 223 782, ⓦ restauranteloscuatro tiempos.com. An excellent restaurant with local specialities such as *cochinillo*, *perdiz* and *cordero* given a modern twist. The *menú* is around €20, main courses are €18–20. Closed Sun eve.

CUISINE AROUND MADRID

The **food** to be found in most of the areas **around Madrid** owes much to **Castilian tradition** with roast meats such as *cochinillo* (suckling pig) and *cordero* (roast lamb) providing the signature dishes in many restaurants. Cooked to perfection so the meat is deliciously tender and falling off the bone (in some restaurants they even cut the *cochinillo* with plates), meals are served with almost no side dishes, bar the odd chip or potato.

But one of the chief pleasures of eating in the areas around the Spanish capital is that **local specialities** still remain. In Toledo, for example, many of the more traditional restaurants offer *carcamusa* – a meat in a spicy tomato sauce, and game such as partridge (*perdiz*), pheasant (*faisán*) and quail (*cordoniz*). In Segovia Castilian roasts are to the fore, while in nearby La Granja the rather healthier *judiones* (large white beans) are on offer. Like La Granja, Ávila is also renowned for its beans, this time haricot beans with sausage (*judías del barco*), as well as its delicious, and massive, T-bone steaks (*chuletón de Ávila*), and for the most sickly sweet of desserts, the *yemas de Santa Teresa* (candied egg yolks). If all that proves too much, head for the oasis of Aranjuez where vegetables (in particular asparagus) and fresh strawberries are the local speciality.

2

Mille Grazie c/Cadenas 2 ☎ 925 254 270 . A busy, down-to-earth Italian restaurant with a wide variety of pasta and pizza dishes. The Panzotti Mille Grazie with its spinach stuffing and walnut and cream sauce is particularly good. Closed Mon & Sun eve.

★ **El Palacete** c/Soledad 2 ☎ 925 225 375, ⓦ restauranteelpalacete.com. Located in a beautifully restored building dating back to the eleventh century, this high-quality restaurant serves well-presented meat and fish dishes and offers great lunchtime menus at €25 (€30 weekends). Closed Sun & Mon eve.

La Perdiz c/Reyes Católicos 7 ☎ 925 252 919. A popular place which does a good *menú de degustación* for around €30 and has a fine selection of local wines. Owned by the same people as *Adolfo* (see above). Closed Sun eve, Mon & two weeks in July.

Venta de Aires c/Circo Romano 35 ☎ 925 220 545. A popular restaurant housed in a famous old inn, a little way out of the centre, with outdoor eating in the summer and specializing in grilled meat, fish and rice dishes. Allow €35 a head. Closed Sun eve.

NIGHTLIFE

By Spanish standards, Toledo's **nightlife** is rather tame. You'll find most late-night bars running along c/Sillería and its extension c/Alfileritos, west of Pl. de Zocódover. In the old core, there are several discobars close to Pl. de Zocódover, while in the new town the area around Pl. de Cuba is packed with bars and clubs. Out of the tourist season, between September and March, classical concerts are held in the cathedral and other churches; details can be obtained from the *oficinas de turismo*.

Broadway Jazz Club c/Alfonso XII, 12. This centrally located club offers frequent jazz concerts.

Círculo de Arte Pl. de San Vicente ⓦ circuloartetoledo .org. A converted chapel now used as a venue for live music, exhibitions, poetry reading and the like. Also makes a classy location for a coffee or drink. Daily from 10am to late (depends on live acts).

Enebro Pl. Santiago Caballeros 1. A wine bar that makes a good early evening stop, serving free tapas with each drink. There's another branch at Pl. San Justo 9. Daily from 10am.

El Trébol c/Santa Fé 15. Very popular bar between Pl. Zocódover and the Museo de Santa Cruz serving some great tapas and the house speciality *bombas* (potatoes stuffed with meat and fried). A tasty range of *bocadillos* and some good tortilla too. Daily 10am–3.30pm & 7pm–midnight.

El Último Pl. Colegio Infantes 4. This small bar/club frequently offers live music, but specializes in jazz and blues. It also organizes photography and painting exhibitions. Daily from 7.30pm.

Aranjuez

A short train journey from Madrid is **Aranjuez**, a little oasis at the confluence of the Tajo and Jarama rivers on the southern edge of the province of Madrid, where the eighteenth-century Bourbon rulers set up a spring and autumn retreat. The beauty of Aranjuez is its greenery – it's easy to forget just how dry and dusty most of central Spain is until you come upon this town, with its lavish palaces and luxuriant gardens, which inspired the composer Joaquín Rodrigo to write the famous *Concierto de Aranjuez*. Famed for its summer strawberries (served with cream – *fresas con nata* – at roadside stalls) and asparagus, Aranjuez functions principally as a weekend escape from Madrid and most people come out for the day, or stop en route to or from Toledo.

Palacio Real

Palace Tues–Sun: April–Sept 10am–6.15pm; Oct–March 10am–5.15pm • €4.50 without a guide, €5 with a guide, free Wed for EU citizens **Gardens** Daily 8am–dusk • Free • ⓦ patrimonionacional.es

The showpiece eighteenth-century **Palacio Real** and its **gardens** were an attempt by the Spanish Bourbon monarchs to create a Versailles in Spain; Aranjuez clearly isn't in the same league, but it's a very pleasant place to while away a few hours.

The palace, which is situated alongside the river, is more remarkable for the ornamental fantasies inside than for any virtues of architecture. There seem to be hundreds of rooms, all exotically furnished, most amazingly so the **Porcelain Room**, entirely covered in decorative ware from the factory that used to stand in Madrid's

Retiro park. Most of the palace dates from the reign of the "nymphomaniac" Queen Isabel II, and many of the sexual scandals and intrigues that led to her eventual removal from the throne in 1868 were played out here.

Outside, on a small island, are the fountains and neatly tended gardens of the **Jardín de la Isla**. The **Jardín del Príncipe**, on the other side of the main road, is more attractive, with shaded walks along the river and plenty of spots for a siesta.

Real Casa del Labrador

June–Sept Tues–Sun 10am–6.15pm; Oct–March Tues–Sun 10am–5.15pm • €5, free Wed for EU citizens • Visits by appointment only • ☎ 918 910 305

At the far end of the **Jardín del Príncipe** is the **Casa del Labrador**, an opulent house containing more silk, marble, crystal and gold than would seem possible in so small a place, as well as a huge collection of fancy clocks. The guided tour goes into great detail about the weight and value of every item.

Museo de Faluas Reales

Tues–Sun: April–Sept 10am–6.15pm; Oct–March 10am–5.15pm • €3 unguided, €5 with guide, free Wed for EU citizens

Also in the gardens, by the river, is the small **Casa de los Marinos** or **Museo de Faluas Reales**, which houses the brightly coloured launches in which royalty would take to the river. You can do the modern equivalent and take a boat trip through the royal parks from the jetty by the bridge next to the palace (Tues–Sun 11am–sunset; €7).

ARRIVAL AND DEPARTURE   ARANJUEZ

By train An old wooden steam train (May–July & Sept to mid-Oct Sat & Sun; €28, under-10s €20; ☎ 902 228 822), the *Tren de la Fresa*, also runs between Madrid and Aranjuez; it leaves Atocha station at 10.05am and returns from Aranjuez at 6pm, arriving back at Atocha at 7pm. The price includes a guided bus tour in Aranjuez, entry to the main monuments and *fresas con nata* on the train. The less romantic, but highly efficient, standard trains leave every fifteen to thirty minutes from Atocha, with the last train returning from Aranjuez at about 11.30pm (€3.20).

By bus Buses run every half-hour during the week and every hour at weekends from Estación Sur (€3.50 each way; 40min).

INFORMATION AND GETTING AROUND

Oficina de Turismo Casa de Infantes, facing the Pl. de San Antonio (daily 10am–6pm; ☎ 918 910 427, ⓦ aranjuez .es).

Getting around A bus service occasionally connects the various sights and if you have children the *chiquitren*, a motorized mini-train (March–Sept: Tues–Sun 10am–8pm; €5, children €3) is a good option, but everything is within easy walking distance, and the town's a very pleasant place to stroll around.

ACCOMMODATION

It's essential to reserve a room in advance, as **accommodation** is not plentiful.

Hostal Castilla c/Andalucía 98 ☎ 918 912 627, ⓦ hostalcastillaaranjuez.com. A straightforward and neat *hostal* with a/c rooms surrounding an Andalucian-style courtyard close to the main sights. Breakfast included. €60

★ **Hotel El Cocherón 1919** c/Montesinos 22 ☎ 918 754 350, ⓦ elcocheron1919.com. Boutique-style hotel close to the Palacio and gardens with 18 individually decorated rooms, a large and tranquil central patio area and a small bar/cafetaria. €78

Hotel Don Manuel c/Príncipe 71 ☎ 918 754 086, ⓦ egidohoteles.com. A comfortable hotel, close to the royal palace and across the road from the Jardín del Príncipe, with functional rooms and free wi-fi. €60

NH Príncipe de la Paz c/San Antonio 22 ☎ 918 099 222, ⓦ nh-hoteles.com. A smart NH hotel complete with all the usual business facilities, bar and restaurant, and conveniently located next to the palace. €94

CAMPSITE

Camping Internacional Aranjuez On a far bend of the Río Tajo ☎ 918 911 395, ⓦ campingaranjuez .com. This large campsite with 162 pitches is equipped with a swimming pool, a supermarket and a children's club, and rents out bicycles and canoes. Two adults plus car €28.

2

EATING AND DRINKING

The splendid nineteenth-century **Mercado de Abastos** on c/Stuart is a good place to buy your own food for a picnic (including, in season, the famous strawberries and asparagus).

La Alegria de la Huerta Carretera de Madrid 4 ☎918 912 938. Near to the bridge across the Tajo on the main road in from Madrid offers a speciality *arroz con bogavante*, pheasant and *cochinillo*. Lunchtime menu with dishes such as stuffed aubergines and the obligatory strawberries and cream for €15. Closed weekday evenings & Tues.

Casa José c/Abastos 32 ☎918 911 488. Renowned restaurant serving high-quality *nouvelle cuisine*. Offers an excellent seasonal taster menu at €75 and a standard menu at around €60 which includes offerings such as glacéed artichokes and suckling pig in orange and parsley. Closed Sun eve & Mon.

Casa Pablete c/Stuart 108. A traditional bar good for tapas and *raciones*. Closed Tues & Aug.

Casa Pablo c/Almíbar 42 ☎ 918 911 451, ⓦcasapablo .net. Castilian food at a reasonable price served in traditional surroundings in this long-standing Aranjuez favourite, whose walls are covered with pictures of local dignitaries and bullfighters. Closed Aug.

El Rana Verde Pl. Santiago Rusiñol s/n ☎918 019 171. Probably the best-known restaurant in the area, the pleasant riverside eatery dates back to the late nineteenth century and serves up a range of decent, if unspectacular menus for €17, €18 and €30. Daily around 1.30–4pm & 8.30pm–midnight.

Chinchón

CHINCHÓN, 45km southeast of Madrid, is an enchanting little place, with a fifteenth-century castle and a picture-postcard **Plaza Mayor**, encircled by whitewashed buildings festooned with wooden balconies. Providing the backdrop to the Plaza Mayor is the Neo classical **Iglesia de la Asunción** which houses Goya's depiction of the Assumption. The town is best-known for being the home of *anís* – a mainstay of breakfast drinkers across Spain. Your best bet for a sample of the spirit is one of the local bars or the Alcoholera de Chinchón, a shop on the Plaza Mayor. The **Museo Etnológico** (Tues–Fri 11am–2pm & 4–8pm, Sat & Sun 11am–3pm & 4–8pm; free; ⓦmuseolaposada.es), at c/Morata 5, off the Plaza Mayor; has some of the traditional *anís*-making machines on display.

ARRIVAL AND INFORMATION
CHINCHÓN

By bus From Aranjuez #430 from Avda. de las Infantas (Mon–Fri hourly, Sat & Sun 8 daily; 55 min); from Madrid #337 every 30min from the bus station at Avda. Mediterraneo 49 (Ⓜ Conde Casal); 45–55min.

Turismo Pl. Mayor (Mon–Fri 10am–6pm, Sat & Sun 11am–3pm & 4–6pm; ☎918 935 323, ⓦciudad-chinchon .com).

ACCOMMODATION

Hostal Chinchón c/Grande 16 ☎918 935 398, ⓦhostalchinchon.com. Situated close to the Pl. Mayor this is a modest but very pleasant option with 10 decent-sized a/c doubles and triples. There is a terrace pool, restaurant/bar and free wi-fi too. **€50**

★ **Parador de Chinchón** c/Los Huertos 1 ☎918 940

836, ⓦparadores.com. Situated in a sixteenth-century former Augustinian monastery close to the Pl. Mayor, this historic parador has an outdoor pool, tranquil patio gardens, large rooms and a very good restaurant. Look out for offers on the website. **€168**

EATING AND DRINKING

★ **Casa de Pregonero** Pl. Mayor ☎918 940 696, ⓦlacasadelpregonero.com. Adds modern touches to traditional dishes and has some mouthwatering starters and desserts such as strawberry and asparagus gazpacho and mandarin sorbet with rum; reckon on at least €40 a head. Closed Tues.

★ **Mesón La Balconada** Pl. Mayor ☎918 941 303, ⓦrestaurantelabalconada.com. Excellent restaurant in one of the balconied buildings overlooking the plaza,

serving top-quality Castilian specialities such as *cochinillo* and *cordero* as well as some quality fish dishes. An extensive wine list too. Expect to pay around €45 per person. Daily around 1.30–4pm & 8.30pm –midnight.

Mesón del Comendador Pl. Mayor ☎918 940 420. One of a cluster of good restaurants serving classic Castilian fare at modest prices. Closed Wed.

Mesón Cuevas del Vino c/Benito Hortelano 13 ☎918 940 206, ⓦcuevasdelvino.com. Situated in an old olive

CHINCHÓN FIESTAS

If you're visiting over Easter, you'll be treated to the townsfolk's own enactment of the **Passion of Christ**, though be aware that the small town becomes packed with visitors at this time. Every year in mid-April, the town holds the **Fiesta del Anís y del Vino**, an orgy of anís- and wine-tasting. An older annual tradition takes place on July 25, when the **feast of St James** (Santiago in Spanish) is celebrated with a bullfight in the Plaza Mayor, with further *corridas* in the August fiestas (usually Aug 13–18).

2

oil mill, with its own *bodega*, this restaurant first opened its doors back in 1964, with luminaries such as Orson Welles and Yul Brynner passing through its doors in the early years. There is a taster menu, which includes *cordero* or *cochinillo*, available at €37.50. Closed Tues & Aug.

Mesón del Duende c/Grande 36 ☎918 940 807, ⓦmesonelduende.com. One of the more reasonably priced restaurants in town in a little courtyard not far from the Pl. Mayor, serving classic Castilian food. Daily around 1.30–4pm & 8.30pm–midnight.

San Lorenzo del Escorial and Valle de los Caídos

Northwest of Madrid, in the foothills of the Sierra de Guadarrama, is one of Spain's best-known and most visited sights – Felipe II's vast monastery-palace complex of **El Escorial**. The vast granite building, which contains a royal palace, a monastery, a mausoleum, four thousand rooms, fifteen cloisters and one of the finest libraries of the Renaissance, embodies all that was important to one of the most powerful rulers in European history. The town around the monastery, **San Lorenzo del Escorial**, is an easy day-trip from Madrid; if you plan to travel on, rail and road routes continue to Ávila and Segovia. The heart of the **Sierra de Guadarrama** lies just to the north, and is Madrid's easiest mountain escape.

Tours from Madrid to El Escorial often take in the grim Francoist monument **El Valle de los Caídos** where the dictator and many Civil War dead are buried.

El Escorial

Tues–Sun: April–Sept 10am–6pm; Oct–March 10am–5pm • €10 (entry covers monastery, Palacio de los Borbones, outlying lodges and gardens); extra €7 for a guided tour, €4 for audio-guide; free Wed Oct–March after 3pm, April–Sept after 4pm for EU citizens • ⓦ patrimonionacional.es

The monastery of **El Escorial** was the largest Spanish building of the Renaissance: rectangular, overbearing and austere, from the outside it resembles a prison more than a palace. Built between 1563 and 1584 to commemorate the victory over the French at the battle of San Quentin on August 10, 1557 (San Lorenzo's Day), it was originally the creation of Juan Bautista de Toledo, though his one-time assistant, **Juan de Herrera**, took over and is normally given credit for the design. **Felipe II** planned the complex as both monastery and mausoleum, where he would live the life of a monk and "rule the world with two inches of paper". Later monarchs had less ascetic lifestyles, enlarging and richly decorating the palace quarters, but Felipe's simple rooms remain the most fascinating.

Visits to the **Real Monasterio del Escorial** have become more relaxed in recent years, and you can use your ticket (purchased in the **visitors' entrance**) to enter, in whatever sequence you like, the basilica, sacristy, chapter houses, library and royal apartments. To escape the worst of the crowds avoid Wednesday afternoons and try visiting just before lunch.

The Biblioteca and Patio de los Reyes

A good starting point is the west gateway, the traditional **main entrance**, facing the mountains. Above it is a gargantuan statue of San Lorenzo holding the gridiron on which he was martyred. Within is the splendid **Biblioteca** (Library), adorned with shelves designed by Herrera to harmonize with the architecture, and frescoes by Tibaldi and his assistants, showing the seven Liberal Arts. Its collections include the tenth-century Codex Albeldensis, St Teresa's personal diary, some gorgeously executed Arabic manuscripts and a Florentine planetarium of 1572 demonstrating the movement of the planets according to the Ptolemaic and Copernican systems. Beyond is the **Patio de los Reyes**, named after the six statues of the kings of Israel on the facade of the basilica straight ahead. Off to the left is a school, to the right the monastery, both of them still in use.

Basílica

In the **Basílica**, notice the flat vault of the Coro above your head as you enter, which is apparently entirely without support, and the white marble Christ carved by Benvenuto Cellini and carried here from Barcelona on workmen's shoulders. The east end is decorated by Italian artists: the sculptures are by the father-and-son team of Leone and Pompeo Leoni, who also carved the two facing groups of Carlos V with his family and Felipe II with three of his wives; Mary Tudor is excluded. The reliquaries near the altar are said to hold the entire bodies of ten saints, plus 144 heads and 306 arms and legs.

Sacristía, Salas Capitulares and the Panteón Real

The **Sacristía** and **Salas Capitulares** (Chapter Houses) contain many of the monastery's religious treasures, including paintings by Titian, Velázquez and José Ribera. Beside the sacristy a staircase leads down to the **Panteón Real**, the final resting place of all Spanish monarchs since Carlos V, with the exception of Felipe V and Fernando VI. The deceased monarchs lie in exquisite gilded marble tombs: kings (and Isabel II) on one side, their spouses on the other.

Just above the entry is the Pudridero Real, a separate room in which the bodies (which are covered in lime) rot for twenty years or so before the cleaned-up skeletons are moved to the final resting place. The royal children are laid in the **Panteón de los Infantes**; the tomb of Don Juan, Felipe II's bastard half-brother, is grander than any of the kings', while the wedding-cake babies' tomb with room for sixty infants is more than half full.

Museos Nuevos, Salones Reales and Claustro Grande

What remains of the Escorial's art collection – works by Bosch, Gerard David, Dürer, Titian, Zurbarán and many others, which escaped transfer to the Prado – is kept in the elegant suite of rooms known as the **Museos Nuevos** (New Museums). Don't miss the **Sala de las Batallas**, a magnificent gallery lined with an epic series of paintings depicting the most notable imperial battles. The surprisingly modest **Salones Reales** (Royal Apartments) contain the austere **quarters of Felipe II**, with the chair that supported his gouty leg and the deathbed from which he was able to contemplate the high altar of the basilica. However, Felipe's successors occupied the more lavish **Palacio de los Borbones**, that takes up the northeastern corner of the complex.

Claustro Grande and Patio de los Evangelistas

You can wander at will in some of the Escorial's courtyards; most notable is the **Claustro Grande**, with frescoes of the *Life of the Virgin* by Tibaldi, and the secluded gardens of the **Patio de los Evangelistas** which lie within, while on the southern flank lies a series of parterre gardens known as the Jardín de los Frailes.

Outlying lodges

Casita del Príncipe & Casita del Infante April–Sept Tues–Sun 10am–7pm, Oct–March 10am–5pm • Guided visits

The **Casita del Príncipe** (aka Casita de Abajo) and the **Casita del Infante** (aka Casita de Arriba) are two eighteenth-century royal lodges located within the grounds of El Escorial, both full of decorative riches, and built by Juan de Villanueva, Spain's most accomplished Neoclassical architect – so worth seeing in themselves as well as for their formal gardens.

2

COMING TO TERMS WITH THE PAST

El Valle de los Caídos is probably the most controversial and emotive physical expression of the Francoist dictatorship that still remains in present-day Spain. Partly built by Popular Front prisoners in the 1940s and 50s, this pharaonic memorial to the fascist triumph in the Civil War towers over a valley that conceals tens of thousands of corpses moved there under Franco's orders. After the burial of the founder of the Falange Party José Antonio Primo de Rivera and Franco himself, the mausoleum became a place of homage for neo-fascists who continued to commemorate the dictator's death every November 20 by parading their fascist paraphernalia at the site. But the future of the monument has finally been exposed to official scrutiny following the decision of the socialist government to set up a committee to decide how to turn the site into a monument to reconciliation.

The removal of Franco's remains is one option, but the destruction of the giant cross appears to have been dismissed as has the possibility of evicting the Benedictine monks who inhabit the site. The most likely outcome is the establishment of a museum or interpretation centre which will put the monument in its context and use it as a reminder of the horrors that resulted from the Civil War. But the debate has shown how raw feelings remain in Spain and how problematic the country has found the experience of coming to terms with its traumatic past.

It was not until 2007, over thirty years after the death of the dictator, that the socialist government introduced what became known as the "historical memory" law, which recognised victims of the Franco regime, prohibited political events at the Valle de los Caídos and provided some state help for the identification and eventual exhumation of the victims of Francoist repression whose corpses still lie in over two thousand mass graves scattered across Spain. Even that step was resisted by government opponents who preferred to turn a blind eye to the deep wounds left by the Civil War and its aftermath. But grassroots campaigns, often led by relatives of the victims, to dig up the mass graves forced the government to break its silence and confront the issue.

At last there is the prospect that Spain may finally try to come to terms with matters that have been swept under the carpet for so many years. As Catalan photographer Francesc Torres, one of the leading lights in the movement to shed light on Spain's obscure past, has said: "History is resilient. You can cover it, but it's not going away."

The Casita del Infante, which served as the present King Juan Carlos' student digs, is a short way up into the hills and affords a good view of the Escorial complex; follow the road to the left from the main entrance and then stick to the contours of the mountain around to the right – it's well signposted.

The Casita del Príncipe, in the Jardines del Príncipe below the monastery, is larger and more worthwhile, with an important collection of Giordano paintings and four pictures made from rice paste.

Silla de Felipe

Around 3km out of town is the **Silla de Felipe** – "Felipe's Seat" – a chair carved into a rocky outcrop with a great view out towards the palace. His majesty is supposed to have sat here to watch the construction going on. You can reach it on foot by following the path through the arches beyond the main entrance to the monastery by the Biblioteca; keep to the left as you go down the hill and then cross the main road and follow the signs. If you have a car, take the M 505 Ávila road and turn off at the sign after about 3km.

El Valle de los Caídos

Currently closed, though typically April–Sept Tues–Sun 10am–6pm, Oct–March 10am–5pm • €5, Wed free for EU citizens • Ⓦ patrimonionacional.es

Nine kilometres north of El Escorial nestled among the mountains is **El Valle de los Caídos** (The Valley of the Fallen). This is an equally megalomaniac yet far more chilling monument: an underground basilica hewn under Franco's orders, allegedly as a memorial to the Civil War dead of both sides, though in reality as a shrine to the *generalísimo* and his regime.

It remains a controversial place to this day. The Socialist government of José Luis Rodríguez Zapatero tried to depoliticize the site and passed a law that prevents its use by Falangist supporters keen to glorify the Franco era, while it has also set up a commission to decide how to turn it into a monument symbolizing reconciliation rather than Nationalist victory and oppression. The monument has been closed since late 2009, provoking protests from right-wing and Catholic religious groups.

To get to the monument itself you have to travel some 6km along a road which winds its way up from the main entrance gate. Above is a vast 150-metre-high cross, reputedly the largest in the world, and visible for miles along the A6 motorway towards Segovia.

The **basilica complex** denies its claims of memorial "to the Civil War dead of both sides" almost at a glance. The debased and grandiose fascist-style architectural forms employed, the grim martial statuary, the constant inscriptions "Fallen for God and for Spain" and the proximity to El Escorial intimate the complex's true function: the glorification of General Franco and his regime. The dictator himself lies buried behind the high altar, while the only other named tomb, marked simply "José Antonio", is that of his guru, the Falangist leader José Antonio Primo de Rivera, who was shot dead by Republicans at the beginning of the war. The "other side" is present only in the fact that the complex was built by the Republican army's survivors – political prisoners on quarrying duty.

ARRIVAL AND INFORMATION   SAN LORENZO DEL ESCORIAL

By train There are trains every 15–30min from Madrid (5.45am–11.30pm; 1hr) from Atocha, calling at Chamartín. If you arrive by train, get straight on the local bus that shuttles you up to the centre of town – they leave promptly and it's a long uphill walk.

Destinations Ávila (7 daily; 1hr); Madrid (29 daily; 1hr). If you want to go on to Segovia you will have to backtrack down the train line to Villalba and then take one of the trains from Madrid.

By bus Buses (#661 & #664 from the *intercambiador* at Moncloa) run every 15min on weekdays and hourly at weekends and take around an hour to arrive. Stay on the bus and it will take you right up to the monastery. To get to

El Valle de los Caídos from El Escorial, you can get a local bus #660 run by Herranz, which starts from the office in Pl. de la Virgen de Gracía, just north of the visitors' entrance to the monastery (departs 3.15pm, returns 5.30pm) though this is not operational while the monument is closed.

Destinations Guadarrama (every 30min–1hr; 15min); Madrid (every 15–30min; 1hr); Valle de los Caídos (daily; 15min).

Turismo c/Grimaldi 4 (Tues–Sat 10am–2pm & 3–6pm, Sun 10am–2pm; ☎ 918 905 313, ⓦ sanlorenzoturismo.org), on the small street to the north of the visitors' entrance to the monastery, running into c/Floridablanca.

ACCOMMODATION

Most **hotels** are close to the monastery, but in summer it's a favourite retreat from the heat of Madrid, so it's wise to book in advance.

HOTELS AND HOSTALES

Hostal Cristina c/Juan de Toledo 6 ☎ 918 901 961. Sixteen small, clean, en-suite rooms in this friendly family-run *hostal* next door to the plush *Hotel Victoria Palace*. A good-value option. €45

Hotel Botánico c/Timoteo Padrós 16 ☎ 918 907 879, ⓦ botanicohotel.com. Twenty individually decorated rooms in this plush hotel set in the verdant grounds of a former palace. €100

Hotel Florida c/Floridablanca 12–14 ☎ 918 901 520, ⓦ hflorida.com. A well-appointed mid-range place, now part of the Best Western chain. There are fifty rooms with a/c and for an extra €16 you get a superior room with views of the monastery. €85

Hotel Miranda & Suizo c/Floridablanca 18–20 ☎ 918 904 711, ⓦ hotelmirandasuizo.com. A few doors up from the *Florida*, this is a traditional but very comfortable option with 52 smart rooms (some with views of the monastery) and a lively bar and café. €55

Hotel Parrilla Príncipe c/Mariano Benavente 12 ☎ 918 901 611, ⓦ parrillaprincipe.com. An unflashy, but friendly hotel located in an eighteenth-century mansion. Simple rooms and a good restaurant. €80

NH Hotel Victoria Palace c/Juan de Toledo 4 ☎ 918 969 890, ⓦ nh-hoteles.es. Now part of the NH chain, El Escorial's top hotel has its own pool, views of the monastery, sleek rooms and all the facilities you would expect in this category. €75

2

HOSTEL

El Escorial c/Residencia 14 ☎918 905 924, ⓦreaj .com. A large 58-berth youth hostel situated up on the hill above the monastery. There is another, smaller, hostel down in the park beside the monastery, the *Santa María del Buen Aire* (☎918 903 640), which has a pool and camping space, but it is usually packed with school groups (YH cards needed for both hostels). Over-26s **€12.50**, under-26s **€8.50**

CAMPSITE

Caravaning El Escorial Carretera de Guadarrama a El Escorial km 3.5 ☎902 014 900, ☎918 902 412, ⓦcampingelescorial.com. A very well-equipped campsite with several swimming pools and three tennis courts situated 6km out on the road back towards Guadarrama. A little noisy during summer weekends. Two adults plus car **€27.40**.

EATING AND ENTERTAINMENT

Scattered about town are plenty of small **bars**, which offer snacks and tapas. For evening **entertainment** the eighteenth-century Teatro Coliseo at c/Floridablanca 20 offers jazz and classical concerts and theatrical productions year-round. Details of shows can be picked up from the *oficina de turismo*, or check out the free weekly *La Semana del Escorial.*

El Charolés c/Floridablanca 24 ☎918 905 975. Renowned for its fish and stews, this restaurant is at the top end of the scale. It does a €35 *menú* on weekdays with an excellent *cocido* on Wed & Fri, otherwise expect to pay around €50 a head.

La Cueva c/San Antón 4 ☎918 901 516, ⓦmesonlacueva.com. An atmospheric wooden-beamed *mesón* that is a good bet for both tapas and a larger meal. *Menús* available at €18 or €31 with standards such as trout and suckling pig.

★ **La Fonda Genara** Pl. de San Lorenzo 2 ☎918 901 636, ⓦrestaurantegenara.com. Popular, but slightly overpriced, place on this lively plaza and inside the *centro coliseo*, which is filled with theatrical mementos and has a wide-ranging menu of good-quality Castilian fare. The extensive lunchtime menu is €15 (€20 weekends) without

drinks, while if you eat à la carte expect to pay around €35 per person.

Hotel Parilla Príncipe c/Floridablanca 6 ☎918 901 548, ⓦparrillaprincipe.com. A well-regarded restaurant situated in this small hotel, serving specialities such as roast partridge and goat. Around €35–40. Closed Tues.

Los Pilares c/Juan de Toledo 58 ☎918 961 972, ⓦrestaurantelospilares.com. Near the bus station, *Los Pilares* provides a wide range of Castilian food, rice dishes and some very good tapas at the bar too. Mains range between €12–19. Daily around 1.30–4pm & 8.30pm –midnight.

Restaurante Alaska Pl. San Lorenzo 4 ☎918 904 365. Offering Castilian meat specialities and fish dishes with a very good value weekday lunchtime €12 *menú* and a more sophisticated one with lobster and *cochinillo* available for both lunch and dinner at €36.

The Sierra de Guadarrama

The routes from Madrid and El Escorial to Segovia strike through the heart of the **Sierra de Guadarrama** (ⓦsierranorte.com), and it is a beautiful journey. The road is occasionally marred by suburban development, especially around **Navacerrada**, Madrid's main ski station, but from the train it's almost entirely unspoilt. There are plenty of opportunities for walking, but make sure you buy the appropriate maps in Madrid.

If you want to base yourself in the mountains for a while you'd do best to head for **Cercedilla**. Alternatively, over to the east, there is **Manzanares el Real**, with its odd medieval castle and reservoir-side setting.

In the shadow of the mountains to the north lies the Valle de Lozoya. At the western end are the village of **Rascafría** and the nearby Benedictine monastery of El Paular, and to the east the old fortified town of **Buitrago** with a medieval core and small Picasso museum.

Cercedilla

CERCEDILLA is an alpine-looking village perched at the foot of the valley leading up to the Puerto de la Fuenfría and makes an excellent base for summer walking. It is much frequented by *madrileños* at weekends, as it has the advantage of being accessible.

The village is the starting point for a very pleasant five-hour round-trip **walk** along the pine-fringed Calzada Romana (old Roman road) up to the Puerto de la Fuenfría (1796m), with its striking views down into Segovia province. Follow the signs up to Las Dehesas where there is an **information centre** (see below) which provides maps and advice on walks in the area, then head past the meadows and follow the clearly indicated path up to the Puerto.

ARRIVAL AND INFORMATION
CERCEDILLA

By bus Every half-hour (50min–1hr 10min) from the *intercambiador* in Moncloa.
By train Madrid–Segovia line, over 20 daily 6am–11pm from Atocha calling at Chamartín, 9 daily going on to

Segovia; 40–50min; Cotos (6 daily; 40 min); Puerto de Navacerrada (6 daily; 25min).
Turismo Las Dehesas (daily 9am–6pm; ☎918 522 213, ⓦ cercedilla.es).

ACCOMMODATION AND EATING

Las Dehesas Carretera de Las Dehesas, s/n ☎918 520 135, ⓦ reaj.com. Another youth hostel, 2km up the road in the meadows leading up to Fuenfría. YH card essential. Over-26s **€12.50**, under-26s **€8.50**
Los Frutales Carretera de las Dehesas 41 ☎918 520 244, ⓦ los-frutales.com. Serves good *croquetas*, *trucha* (trout) and meat dishes with a cool terrace in summer and a pleasant rural setting.
Hostal Longinos – El Aribel c/Emilio Serrano 71 ☎918 521 511, ⓦ hostalaribel.com. Convenient location close to the railway station, but otherwise nothing special, this alpine-style *hostal* has 23 en-suite rooms and a café-bar. **€45**

Luces del Poniente c/Lina de Ávila 4 ☎918 525 587, ⓦ lucesdelponiente.com. A tranquil rural hotel with thirteen spacious, individually decorated rooms, a covered pool and spa area (April–Oct) and a relaxing garden terrace area. Rooms are only €68 from Sunday to Thursday outside the summer months. **€113**
Villa Castora Carretera de Las Dehesas 29 ☎918 520 334, ⓦ reaj.com. Youth hostel with double, quadruple and five-bed dormitories, conveniently located close to the town. YH card essential. Over-26s **€12.50**, under-26s **€8.50**

Puerto de Navacerrada and Cotos

From Cercedilla, you can embark on a wonderful little train ride to the **Puerto de Navacerrada**, the most important pass in the mountains and the heart of the ski area, or a little farther on to **Cotos** where a number of well-maintained walks around the **Parque Natural de Peñalara** (ⓦ parquenaturalpenalara.org) begin. The train runs hourly over weekends and holidays (€11.80 return) and passes through the *parque natural*, an extension of the upper Manzanares basin: watch out for roe deer and wild boar. In winter it is possible to ski in both Navacerrada and Cotos, but be prepared for long queues and traffic jams at weekends.

Hiking in the high peaks

Navacerrada is also the starting point for a number of impressive walks along the **high peaks**, while Cotos is the gateway to the highest peak in the Sierra, Peñalara (2430m). It can be reached in about four hours, but is a reasonably tough ascent. Less challenging but very enjoyable is the easy, well-indicated hike to the glacial lake, the Laguna Grande.

INFORMATION
COTOS

Information There is a small information booth just above the small café close to the Cotos train station that will give advice on all routes (summer Mon–Fri

10am–6pm, Sat, Sun & hols 10am–8pm; winter daily 10am–6pm; ☎918 520 857).

Monasterio del Paular and Rascafría

Guided tours Mon–Wed, Fri & Sat noon, 1pm & 5pm, Thurs noon & 1pm, Sun 1pm, 5pm & 6pm • In Spanish only • Free • ⓦ monasterioelpaular.com. • Buses link with Madrid (*intercambiador* Pl. Castilla) 2–3 times a day; 2hr 15min.

Some 10km below Cotos in the beautiful Valle de Lozoya just outside the pleasant mountain village of **Rascafría** stands the **Monasterio de Santa María de El Paular**, originally a Carthusian monastery founded at the end of the fourteenth century, and now home to a handful of Benedictine monks who provide guided tours of the silent cloisters and the main church. The remainder of the building is given over to a low-key hotel run by the Sheraton chain with a tranquil patio area.

2

ACCOMMODATION   RASCAFRÍA

Los Calizos On the road to Miraflores ☎918 691 112, ⓦloscalizos.com. A tranquil, twelve-room hotel, a little way out of Rascafría, with a fine restaurant and extensive grounds. Price includes breakfast and an evening meal for two. **€130**

Hostal Rural El Valle Avda. del Valle 39 ☎918 691 213, ⓦhotelruralelvalle.com. A cheaper, but cosy option

closer to the village. Thirty rooms, some of which have cooking facilities. **€50**

Sheraton Santa María de El Paular Carretera M 604 km 26.5 ☎918 691 011, ⓦsheratonelpaular.com. Part of the monastery now turned into a parador-style hotel with a delightful courtyard bar, ideal for cool summer refreshments, a pool and 44 large, pleasant. **€100**

Manzanares el Real

Castle Tues–Fri 10am–4pm, Sat & Sun 10am–6pm • €3 • Dramatized visits at 12.30pm and 1.30pm at weekends Feb–Dec; €6

Some 50km north of Madrid, on the shores of the Santillana *embalse* (reservoir), lies **Manzanares el Real**, a town which in former times was disputed between the capital and Segovia. Nowadays it's geared to Madrid weekenders, whose villas dot the landscape for miles around. The town's one attraction is the **castle**, which despite its eccentric appearance is a perfectly genuine fifteenth-century construction, built around an earlier chapel. It was soon modified into a palace by the architect Juan Guas, who built an elegant gallery on the south side and false machicolations on the other, and studded the tower with stones resembling cannonballs. The interior has been heavily restored, but it makes for an interesting visit.

ARRIVAL AND INFORMATION   MANZANARES EL REAL

By bus From the *intercambiador* in Pl. de Castilla (ⓦPlaza de Castilla) hourly; 45min.

Oficina de turismo (Mon–Fri noon–3pm, Sat & Sun

10am–2pm; ⓦmanzanareselreal.org). For information about the region as a whole consult the website ⓦsierranorte.com.

ACCOMMODATION

Hotel Parque Real c/Padre Damián 4 ☎918 539 912, ⓦhotelparquereal.com. Old-fashioned, but serviceable 24-room hotel in the centre of town with its own bar and restaurant. **€61**

La Fresneda Carretera M608, km19.5 ☎918 477 213, ⓦcampingfresneda.com. Recently updated campsite

on the road towards Soto del Real, with pool bar area, small playground and shady pitches. Two adults plus car **€21.60**.

El Ortigal c/Montañero 19 ☎918 530 120. Campsite at the foot of La Pedriza, with great views and its own pool, situated on the northern side of the town.

EATING

Restaurante Parra c/Panaderos 15 ☎918 539 577. Better value than many of the Sierra restaurants, this one

serves up similar fare with Castilian meat dishes and paellas topping the bill. A decent wine list too.

La Pedriza

Access limited to 350 cars a day at weekends • Free • Information centre daily 10am–6pm • ☎918 539 978 • Buses from the *intercambiador* in Pl. de Castilla in Madrid (daily every 30min 7.30am–9.30pm; 45min–1hr).

Nearby is the ruggedly beautiful **La Pedriza**, a spur of the Sierra de Guadarrama that has been declared a regional park. There are some enjoyable walks by the river and around the granite dome El Yelmo, as well as some much-revered technical climbs, notably the ascent to the jagged Peña del Diezmo. The park is also home to a very large colony of **griffon vultures**.

Buitrago de Lozoya

Farther east, beyond the road to Burgos, lies the attractive little town of **Buitrago de Lozoya**, a fortified settlement with defensive walls that date from the twelfth century, a fine Mudéjar church (daily 9am–2pm & 4–8pm) and, more surprisingly, a small **Picasso museum** (Tues, Thurs & Fri 11am–1.45pm & 4–6pm, Wed 11am–1.45pm, Sat 10am–2pm & 4–7pm, Sun 10am–2pm; free). The collection, based on work donated by the artist to his friend and local barber Eugenio Arias, features an interesting selection of sixty minor pieces dating from between 1948 and 1972.

ARRIVAL AND INFORMATION **BUITRAGO DE LOZOYA**

By bus Hourly buses from the *intercambiador* in Pl. de Castilla; 1hr 20min.

Oficina de turismo c/Tahona 19 (Wed–Sat 10am–2pm & 4–6pm, Sun 10am–2pm; ⟐ buitrago.org).

Patones de Arriba

On the southern edge of the so-called Sierra Pobre is the picturesque mountain village of **PATONES DE ARRIBA**, abandoned in the 1930s but since restored and now a fashionable weekend destination for many *madrileños*. The black slate architecture of the village is undeniably beautiful, the views are good, and you can be assured of a fine meal, but there is little else to detain the casual visitor. The village is closed to cars, so you will need to leave vehicles in the car park in nearby **Patones de Abajo** and walk the 2.5km up the sign posted path.

ARRIVAL AND INFORMATION **PATONES DE ARRIBA**

By bus Two or three buses (#197) daily from the *intercambiador* in the Pl. de Castilla in Patones Abajo.

Oficina de turismo ⟐ portal.patones.net.

ACCOMMODATION

★ **El Tiempo Perdido** Travesía del Ayuntamiento 5 y 7 ☎ 918 432 152, ⟐ eltiempoperdido.com. Luxury boutique hotel with seven individually decorated rooms (some with small balconies) housed in one of the beautiful slate cottages in this tranquil village. The owner Paco Bello is also the chef at the excellent *El Poleo* restaurant which is contained within the hotel. Open only at weekends and the eve of holidays. **€110**

EATING

El Abuelo Manolo c/Buenavista 29 ☎ 918 432 947. Traditional restaurant with excellent views and a great summer terrace serving red-meat staples and some delicious home-made *croquetas*. Also houses a café serving a range of teas and some very tasty cakes. Daily around 1.30–4pm & 8.30pm–midnight.

El Poleo Travesía del Arroyo 3 ☎ 91 843 21 01, ⟐ eltiempoperdido.com. Attached to the hotel *El Tiempo Perdido* and owned by Cordobés chef Paco Bello, this restaurant takes a creative angle on the local cuisine with dishes such as roast lamb with honey and couscous. You can eat outside on the picturesque patio in summer. Daily around 1.30–4pm & 8.30pm–midnight.

Ávila

Two things distinguish **Ávila**: its eleventh-century **walls**, two perfectly preserved kilometres of which surround the old town, and the mystic writer **Santa Teresa**, who was born here and whose shrines are a major focus of religious pilgrimage. Set on a high plain, with the peaks of the Sierra de Gredos as a backdrop, the town is quite a sight, especially if you approach with the evening sun highlighting the golden tone of the walls and the details of the 88 towers. The walls make orientation straightforward, with the **cathedral** and most other sights contained within. Just outside the southeast corner is the city's main square, **Plaza Santa Teresa**, and the most imposing of the old gates, the **Puerta del Alcázar**.

Convento de Santa Teresa

Pl. de la Santa 2 • Daily 9am–1pm & 3.30–7.30pm • **Free Reliquary** Daily 9.30am–1.30pm & 3.30–7pm • **Free Museum** Daily: summer 10am–2pm & 4–7pm; winter 10am–1.30pm & 3.30–5.30pm • €2

The obvious place to start a tour of Teresa's Ávila is the **Convento de Santa Teresa**, built over the saint's birthplace just inside the south gate of the old town and entered off the Paseo del Rastro. Most of the convent remains *de clausura*, but you can see the very

2

ÁVILA

■ ACCOMMODATION

Las Canceras	8
Hospedería La Sinagoga	6
Hostal Bellas	7
Hostal Don Diego	2
Hostal San Juan	4
Hotel Las Leyendas	9
Palacio de Valderrábanos	5
Palacio de los Velada	3
Parador Raimundo de Borgoña	1

■ EATING AND DRINKING

El Almacén	2
Bar El Rincon	4
La Bodeguita de San Segundo	3
Las Canceras	7
Casa Patas	8
La Casona	6
El Molino de la Losa	1
La Posada de la Fruta	5

spot where she was born, now a fabulously ornate chapel in the Baroque church, which is decorated with scenes of the saint demonstrating her powers of levitation to various august bodies. A small reliquary, beside the gift shop, contains memorials of Teresa's life, including not only her rosary beads, but also one of the fingers she used to count them with. In the crypt of the monastery is a **museum** dedicated to the saint's life and work. Packed full of memorabilia, accounts of her miraculous deeds and numerous translations of her work, it provides a truly hagiographic vision of Teresa's life.

Monasterio de la Encarnación

Paseo de la Encarnación s/n • Summer: Mon–Fri 9.30am–1pm & 4–6pm, Sat & Sun 10am–1pm & 4–6pm; winter Mon–Fri 9.30am–1pm & 3.30–6pm, Sat & Sun 10am–1.30pm & 4–6pm • €2

Heading through the old town, and leaving by the Puerta del Carmen, you can follow a lane, c/Encarnación, to the **Monasterio de la Encarnacíon**. The entrance to the museum is in the patio – ring the bell and wait if it appears to be unattended and you will eventually be ushered in. Teresa lived here for much of the time between 1535 and 1574, the last three years as the prioress. Each room is labelled with a miraculous act she performed or vision that she witnessed, while everything she might have touched or looked at is also on display. A small museum section also provides a reasonable introduction to the saint's life, with maps showing the convents, papal bulls, and a selection of her sayings – the pithiest, perhaps, "Life is a night in a bad hotel."

Convento de San José

Pl. de las Madres 4 • Daily: summer 10am–1.30pm & 4–7pm; winter 10am–1.30pm & 3–6pm • €1.20

A third Teresan sight lies five minutes east of the cathedral outside the city walls. This is the **Convento de San José**, the first monastery that the saint founded, in 1562. Its museum contains relics and memorabilia, including the coffin in which Teresa once slept and a signed handkerchief stained with her blood. The tomb of her brother Lorenzo is in the larger of the two churches, which was the work of one of the El Escorial architects, Francisco de Mora.

Los Cuatro Postes

Lastly, you might want to make your way up to **Los Cuatro Postes**, a little four-posted shrine, 1.5km along the Salamanca road west of town and a fine vantage point from which to admire the walls of the town. It was here, aged 7, that the infant Teresa was recaptured by her uncle, running away with her brother to seek Christian martyrdom fighting the Moors.

The Catedral

Pl. de la Catedral • Summer Mon–Fri 10am–7.30pm, Sat 10am–8pm, Sun noon–6.30pm; winter Mon–Fri 10am–5pm, Sat 10am–6pm, Sun noon–5pm; last tickets given out 45min before closing • €4

Ávila's **Catedral** was started in the twelfth century but has never been finished, as evidenced by the missing tower above the main entrance. The earliest Romanesque parts were as much fortress as church, and the apse actually forms an integral part of the city walls.

Inside, the succeeding changes of style are immediately apparent; the **Romanesque** parts are made of a strange red-and-white mottled stone, then there's an abrupt break and the rest of the main structure is pure white stone with **Gothic** forms. Although the proportions are exactly the same, this newer half of the cathedral seems infinitely more spacious. The *coro*, whose elaborate carved back you see as you come in, and two chapels in the left aisle, are **Renaissance** additions. Here you can admire the elaborate

2

SANTA TERESA DE ÁVILA

Santa Teresa (1515–82) was born to a noble family in Ávila and from childhood began to experience visions and religious raptures. Her religious career began at the Carmelite convent of La Encarnación, where she was a nun for 27 years. From this base, she went on to reform the movement and found convents throughout Spain. She was an ascetic, but her appeal lay in the mystic sensuality of her experience of Christ, as revealed in her autobiography, for centuries a bestseller in Spain. As joint patron saint of Spain (together with Santiago), she remains a central pillar in Spanish Catholicism and schoolgirls are brought into Ávila by the busload to experience first-hand the life of the woman they are supposed to emulate. She died in Alba de Torres just outside Salamanca, and the Carmelite convent, which contains the remains of her body and a dubious reconstruction of the cell in which she passed away, is another major target of pilgrimage. On a more bizarre note, one of Santa Teresa's mummified hands has now been returned to Ávila after spending the Franco years by the bedside of the dictator.

marble tomb of a fifteenth-century bishop known as El Tostado (the "toasted" or "swarthy"), while the thirteenth-century *sacristía* with its star-shaped cupola and gold inlay decor, and the treasury-museum with its monstrous silver *custodia* and ancient religious images are also worth a visit.

Basilíca de San Vicente

Pl. de San Vicente 1 • Mon–Sat: summer 10am–6.30pm; winter 10am–1pm & 4–6.30pm (no visits during Mass) • €1.60

The **Basilíca de San Vicente** marks the site where San Vicente was martyred, and his tomb narrates the gruesome story of torture and execution by the Romans. Legend has it that following the martyrdom a rich Jew, who had been poking fun at the martyrs, was enveloped and suffocated by a great serpent that miraculously emerged from the rocks. On the verge of asphyxiation he repented and converted to Christianity, later building the church on the very same site, and he, too, is said to be buried here. In the crypt you can see part of the rocky crag where San Vicente and his sisters were executed and from which the serpent later supposedly appeared. Like the cathedral, the building is a mixture of architectural styles. The warm pink glow of the sandstone of the church is a characteristic feature of Ávila, also notable in the **church of San Pedro** (daily 10.30am–noon & 7–8pm) in Plaza de Santa Teresa.

Capilla de Mosén Rubí

Pl. de Mosén Rubí 9 • Tues–Sun: summer 5–7pm; winter 4–6pm • Free

One of the most eye-catching of the city's monuments, the polygonal **Capilla de Mosén Rubí** was started in the fifteenth century, but owing to a lengthy legal dispute and a lack of funds it was not completed until the following century. The delay explains the chapel's two distinct architectural styles – Gothic and Renaissance – which are evident in the interior design. The magnificent marble tombs of the benefactors take pride of place in the centre of the chapel.

City walls

Summer daily 10am–8pm; winter Tues–Sat 10am–6pm • €4; children €2.50

The **city walls**, a mixture of red limestone, granite and brick, were built under Alfonso VI, following his capture of the city from the Moors in 1090; they took his Muslim prisoners nine years to construct. At closer quarters, they prove a bit of a facade, as the old city within is sparsely populated, most of modern life having moved into the new developments outside the fortifications. It's possible to walk along two sections of the walls from Puerta de Carnicerías to Puerta del Carmen and from Puerta del Alcázar to

Puerta del Rastro; the former being the best with some stunning views of the town. There have been some experiments with night-time opening in the summer (usually 10pm–12.30am Sun–Wed), but check with the tourist office. Tickets are available from the green kiosk by the Puerta del Alcázar and the tourist office at Puerta de Carnicerías.

Museo Provincial

Pl. del Navaillos 3 • Tues–Sat: summer 10am–2pm & 5–8pm; winter 10am–2pm & 4–7pm; Sun 10am–2pm • €1.20, free Sat & Sun

Just outside the city walls, through the Puerta de Carnicerías, is the small **Museo Provincial**, housed in the sixteenth-century Palacio de los Deanes where the cathedral's deans once lived. Today, its eclectic exhibits include collections of archeological remains, ceramics, agricultural implements and traditional costumes, as well as some fine Romanesque statues and a wonderful fifteenth-century triptych depicting the *Life of Christ*. The ticket also allows you entry to the museum storeroom in the church of Santo Tomé El Viejo just opposite.

Monasterio de Santo Tomás

Pl. de Granada 1 • Daily 10am–1pm & 4–8pm • €3; closed Feb 1–6, 15 Oct & Dec 25; Museo Oriental same hours as monastery except closed on Mon & Tues mornings in summer; guided tours Sat, Sun & hols at 6pm • €3 • ⓦ monasteriosantotomas.com

The **Monasterio de Santo Tomás** is a fifteen-minute walk south of the old city. Established by the Reyes Católicos Fernando and Isabel in the later fifteenth century, the monastery is set around three cloisters and contains a fine, carved Gothic choir in the main church. Within are the tombs of Don Juan, the only son of the Reyes Católicos, and Isabel's confessor and later head of the Inquistion Torquemada. Alongside is the **Museo Oriental**, which contains memorabilia brought back from the Far East by Dominican missionaries.

ARRIVAL AND DEPARTURE
ÁVILA

By train From Madrid (Chamartín station) there are around 20 trains a day to Ávila (1hr 20min–2hr 5min). The train station is a 15min walk to the east of the old town, and a local bus connects it with Pl. Victoria, a little west of the cathedral. On foot, follow the broad Paseo de la Estación to its end, by the large church of Santa Ana, and head straight on to reach Pl. Santa Teresa.

Destinations El Escorial (9 daily; 1hr); Madrid (20–25 daily; 1hr 20min–2hr 5min); Medina del Campo (15 daily; 20–40min); Salamanca (6 daily; 1hr 30min).

By bus Buses are less frequent (Estación del Sur; 8 on weekdays, 4 at weekends; 1hr 35min–1hr 45min) and use a terminal on the Avda. de Madrid, a little closer in: walking from here, cross the small park opposite, then up c/Duque de Alba, or take a local bus to Pl. Victoria.

Destinations Arenas de San Pedro (daily Mon–Fri; 1hr 30min); Madrid (8 daily; 1hr 35min); Salamanca (2–3 daily; 1hr 30min); Segovia (2–7 daily; 1hr).

By car Follow signs for the walls (*murallas*) or the parador and you should be able to park just outside the old town.

INFORMATION

Turismo Casa de las Carnicerías, c/San Segundo 17 (daily: July–mid-Sept daily 9.30am–8pm; mid-Sept–June Mon–Sat 9.30am–2pm & 4–7pm, Sun 9.30am–5pm; ☎ 920 211 387, ⓦ turismocastillayleon.com).

Visitors' centre Avda. de Madrid 39, just beyond the Basílica de San Vicente (daily 9am–5.30pm; ☎ 920 225 969, ⓦ avilaturismo.com).

ACCOMMODATION

There are numerous cheap **hostales** around the train station and along Avda. José Antonio, but you should be able to find something nearer the walled centre of town.

Las Cancelas c/Cruz Vieja 6 ☎ 920 212 249, ⓦ lascancelas.com. Fourteen a/c rooms in this converted fifteenth-century building, some of which have good views of the cathedral and walls. There's a decent bar and a pleasant patio restaurant, too. **€86**

★ **Hospedería La Sinagoga** c/Reyes Católicos 22 ☎ 920 352 321. As the name suggests, this marvellous little 21-room hotel was a synagogue in the fifteenth century. Modern, comfortable and good-value rooms in a tastefully restored and atmospheric building. **€95**

2

Hostal Bellas c/Caballeros 19 ☎920 212 910, ⊕hostalbellas.com. Eager-to-please owners run this centrally located *hostal*. Most rooms have showers and there are discounts out of season. €47

Hostal Don Diego c/Marqués de Canales y Chozas 5 ☎920 255 475, ⊕hostaldondiego.net. A friendly, family-run and good-value *hostal* just opposite the parador. All thirteen rooms have bath or shower. €50

Hostal San Juan c/Comuneros de Castilla 3 ☎920 251 475, ⊕hostalsanjuan.es. There are thirteen comfortable, pine-furnished double rooms with bathrooms in this recently refurbished *hostal* in the centre of the old town. €48

★ **Hotel Las Leyendas** c/Francisco Gallego 3 ☎920 352 042, ⊕lasleyendas.es. A new arrival on the Ávila hotel scene, this sixteenth-century mansion has nineteen tastefully refurbished rooms, with exposed brick and stone work on some of the walls, wooden beams and minimalist decor. Some rooms have views of the Sierra. There is free

wi-fi and a restaurant, *La Bruja*, serving up a refreshing mix of creative tapas and Castilian classics. €90

Palacio de Valderrábanos Pl. de la Catedral 9 ☎920 211 023, ⊕palaciovalderrabanoshotel.com. This former bishop's palace next to the cathedral has large, slightly old-fashioned but comfortable rooms and frequently offers great cut-price deals. €80

Palacio de los Velada Pl. de la Catedral 10 ☎920 255 100, ⊕veladahoteles.com. A beautifully converted sixteenth-century palace with a stunning cloistered bar and the priciest hotel in town, but look out for the website deals that can bring the price down to as low as €60. €355

Parador Raimundo de Borgoña c/Marqués de Canales y Chozas 2 ☎920 211 340, ⊕paradores.com. A converted fifteenth-century mansion close to the city walls. While not the most exciting parador in Spain, it is pleasant enough and has all the usual comforts. €144

EATING AND DRINKING

Ávila has a decent if unexceptional array of **bars** and **restaurants**, some of them sited just outside the walls. Local specialities include the Castilian *cordero asado* (roast lamb), *judias del barco con chorizo* (haricot beans with sausage), *mollejas* (cow's stomach) and *yemas de Santa Teresa* (candied egg-yolk) – the last of these sold in confectioners all over town. For nightlife head outside the city walls to c/Capitán Peña where the strip of four *bares de copas* next to each other keeps the walking to a minimum.

★ **El Almacén** Carretera Salamanca 6 ☎920 254 455. One of the best restaurants in the province situated in a former storehouse across the river, close to Los Cuatro Postes, with great views of the city walls. It serves quality meat and fish dishes with a creative touch and excellent desserts, and boasts a lengthy wine list. Somewhat overpriced, however, at around €50 a head. Closed Sun eve & Mon.

Bar El Rincón Pl. Zurraquín 6. To the north of Pl. de la Victoria, this down-to-earth bar attached to a *hostal* serves up a generous three-course *menú* for around €10. Excellent *calamares* and seafood dishes on offer too. Daily around 1.30–4pm and 8.30pm to midnight.

★ **La Bodeguita de San Segundo** c/San Segundo 19 ⊕vinoavila.com. Buried into the wall by the Puerta de Carnicerías, this critically acclaimed wine bar has a fantastic selection from Rioja, Ribera de Duero, Rueda, Penedes, Somantano and Galicia, and serves up a tasty range of accompanying tapas too. Daily around 1.30–4pm & 8.30pm–midnight.

Las Cancelas c/Cruz Vieja 6 ☎920 212 249. Next to the cathedral and in the hotel of the same name, this friendly restaurant with a great interior patio is popular with locals and serves some excellent *cordero asado* (roast lamb). À la

carte will cost around €35. Daily around 1.30–4pm & 8.30pm–midnight.

Casa Patas c/San Millán 4. A well-established bar, with a good range of classic tapas, such as *albóndigas* (meatballs) and *callos* (tripe in a spicy sauce) and a little *comedor* (evenings only), near the church of San Pedro. Closed Wed & Sept.

La Casona Pl. de Pedro Dávila 6 ☎920 256 139. Popular two-storey restaurant in this plaza by the Puerta del Rastro specializing in Castilian meat dishes and fish with *menús* starting at around €10.

El Molino de la Losa c/Bajada de la Losa 12 ☎920 211 101, ⊕elmolinodelalosa.com. A converted fifteenth-century mill out by Los Cuatro Postes, with a deserved reputation for quality cuisine. However, it is on the expensive side with mains costing between €16 and €23. Closed Mon & mid-Oct to mid-March.

La Posada de la Fruta Pl. de Pedro Dávila 8 ☎920 254 702, ⊕posadadelafruta.com. With an attractive, sunny, covered courtyard, this is a nice place for a drink, and also serves some good standard Castilian fare with a good-value €12 *menú*.

The Sierra de Gredos

The **Sierra de Gredos** continues the line of the Sierra de Guadarrama, enclosing Madrid to the north and west. A major mountain range, with peaks in excess of 2500m,

Gredos offers the best trekking in central Spain, including high-level routes across the passes, as well as more casual walks around the villages.

By bus, the easiest access to this spectacular region is from Madrid to Arenas de San Pedro, from where you can explore the range, and then move on west into the valley of La Vera in Extremadura. If you have your own transport, you could head into the range south from Ávila along the N502. Stop at any one of the villages on the north side of the range, along the Tormes valley, such as Hoyos del Espino or Navarredonda and explore the spectacular circular walks from there.

Arenas de San Pedro and around

ARENAS DE SAN PEDRO is a sizeable town with a somewhat prettified fifteenth-century castle, the Castillo de la Triste Condesa, a Gothic church and the half-built eighteenth century palace, the Palacio del Infante Don Luis de Borbón.

Grutas del Águila

Daily 10.30am–1pm & 3–6pm, closes an hour later in summer • €7; under-5s free

Some 9km away close to the village of Ramacastañas are the **caves** known as the Grutas del Águila, lined with an impressive array of bizarre limestone formations stained with orange, yellow and brown from the trace elements in the rocks.

Walks to the Gredos watershed

The main reason to stop at Arenas is to make your way up to the villages of **EL HORNILLO** and **El ARENAL**, respectively 6km and 9km to the north, the trailheads for **walks up to the Gredos watershed**. There are no buses but it's a pleasant walk up from Arenas to El Arenal

---

WALKS IN GREDOS

The **two classic walks** in the Gredos mountains are best approached from the so-called Plataforma, at the end of a twelve-kilometre stretch of paved road running from the village of Hoyos del Espino (see p.158), where you can purchase detailed maps of the area. You could also reach this point by walking up from El Hornillo or El Arenal on the southern side of the range, although it makes for a tougher challenge. A functional pamphlet of the area can be obtained from the tourist office on the Plaza de San Pedro, in Arenas de San Pedro (Mon–Fri 10am–1pm & 4–7pm, Sat 10am–1pm; ☎ 920 372 368, ⓦ arenasdesanpedro.es).

CIRCO DE LAGUNA GRANDE

The **Circo de Laguna Grande** is the centrepiece of the Gredos range, with its highest peak, Almanzor (2593m) surrounded by pinnacles sculpted into utterly improbable shapes. The path begins at the car park at the end of the road coming from Hoyos and climbs towards the high Pozas meadow. From there you can reach the large glacial lake at the end of the valley, a spectacular two-hour walk that winds its way down the slopes on a well-defined path. The route is best done in late spring, summer or early autumn, as snow makes it a treacherous walk in winter.

CIRCO DE LAS CINCO LAGUNAS

For a tougher and much longer route – the **Circo de las Cinco Lagunas** – you can continue on from the Laguna Grande, where there is a *refugio* and camping area, to the Cinco Lagunas (allow 8hr from the Plataforma). Take the signposted path to the right just before the lake, which follows an old hunting route used by Alfonso XIII, up to the Portilla del Rey pass. From there you will be able to look down on the lakes – which are reached along a sharp, scree-laden descent. The drop is amply rewarded by virtual solitude, even in midsummer, and sightings of *Capra pyrenaica victoriae*, the graceful (and almost tame) Gredos mountain goat. There are also species of salamander and toad found only in the area. It is another four to five hours on to the village of Navalperal de Tormes, which is 14km west of Hoyos del Espino.

on a track running between the road and the river – start out past the sports centre and swimming pool in Arenas.

Mombeltrán

MOMBELTRÁN, 12km north (an enjoyable, mainly downhill, walk from Arenas), is an attractive alternative stop, with its fifteenth-century **castle** of the dukes of Albuquerque set against a stunning mountain backdrop.

2

Valle del Tormes

On the north side of Gredos is the beautiful **Valle del Tormes**, which enjoys spectacular views across to the highest peaks in the range. The village of **HOYOS DEL ESPINO**, 20km west along the AV941, makes a good base, as there are several places to stay, a few decent bars, and shops where you can stock up on supplies. A few kilometres to the east is **Navarredonda**, another good base from which to explore the area, while the nearby picturesque village of San Martín del Pimpollar is the base of the excellent ★ **Gredos Guides** (☎ 920 348 817, 626 066 223, ⊛ gredosguides.es), a small business run by local expert and fluent English-speaker Juanfran Redondo who organizes a fantastic range of personally tailored ecological and adventure activities throughout the local area, from hiking and mountain biking to mushroom hunting and nature walks.

ARRIVAL AND DEPARTURE — SIERRA DE GREDOS

By bus Buses run from the Estación Sur in Madrid to Arenas de San Pedro (4–10 daily; 2hr) and to Hoyos del Espino (1 bus daily; 4hr). There are daily buses from Ávila that call at Hoyos on their way to Barco de Ávila and a twice-daily service to Arenas.

ACCOMMODATION

The *casas rurales* that are scattered throughout the villages often make a good base, especially if you are travelling in a group (information line ☎ 902 424 141, ⊛ casasgredos.com and ⊛ gredos.com).

ARENAS AND GUISANDO

Hostal Castillo c/Ctra. Candeleda 2 ☎ 920 370 091. Clean, simple and neat rooms, some of which overlook the castle, in this friendly and good-value *hostal*. **€38**

Hostal El Fogón de Gredos c/Linarejo 6 ☎ 920 374 018. If you want a mountain location, then this is your best bet. Situated a couple of kilometres outside Guisando on the flanks of the mountains, this two-star *hostal* has simple, comfortable rooms and a decent restaurant. **€52**

Hostería Los Galayos Pl. Condestable Dávalos 2 ☎ 920 371 379, ☎ 920 371 379. Pleasant three-star hotel with old-style rooms perched on the corner of this central square which also has a reliable restaurant. **€64**

Posada de la Triste Condesa c/Dr Juan Torres 9 ☎ 920 372 567. Rustic accommodation with three cosy double rooms around a delightful flower-strewn interior patio. Breakfast included. **€65**

VALLE DEL TORMES

Camping Gredos On the road from Hoyos del Espino towards the Plataforma ☎ 920 207 585. A riverside campsite by the Puente del Duque with plenty of shady pitches and wooden bungalows for rent. Easter to mid-Oct. Two adults plus car **€13.50**.

★ **Hotel Milano Real** Hoyos del Espino ☎ 920 349 108, ⊛ elmilanoreal.com. Wonderful hotel on the outskirts of the village with a high-quality restaurant serving an excellent gourmet *menú* at €40 and a cheaper seasonal one at €24. Eight suites (€212), each decorated according to a theme from Arabic to Japanese, Colonial to Manhattan, thirteen comfortable doubles and a delightful garden area. **€116**

★ **Hotel Rural las 4 Calles** c/Mayor 57, San Martín del Pimpollar ☎ 920 348 817, ☎ 626 066 223. Very friendly local hotel in this picturesque village with five en-suite rooms and a cosy little seating area. The owner Juanfran can organize a range of outdoor activities for visitors from nature walks to hikes and mountain biking. Price includes breakfast. **€50**

Youth hostel Navarredonda ☎ 920 348 005. Well-situated youth hostel not far from the parador on the outskirts of the village with a large summer pool, good communal areas and some great views of the mountains. Two- and four-bed rooms. YH card needed. **€11.60**, under-30s **€8.60**

Camping Navagredos Navarredonda ☎ 920 207 476. Large, pine-forested campsite with 300 pitches on the fringes of the Sierra and close to the Río Tormes. Wooden bungalows on offer. Open May–Sept. Two adults plus car **€16.40**.

★ **Casa de Arriba** c/Cruz 19, Navarredonda ☎920 348 024, ⓦcasadearriba.com. Cosy and comfortable *casa rural* at the top of the hill in Navarredonda, serving breakfasts and meals too. A pleasant garden area for relaxing when the sun is out. €79

Parador Navarredonda, km 10 on the AV941 ☎920 348 048, ⓦparadores.com. Spain's first-ever parador, which has undergone a major refurbishment programme in recent years and enjoys some great views across the mountains. The traditional-style rooms are large and comfortable while the restaurant serves up some high-quality local produce. €133

Segovia

2

After Toledo, **SEGOVIA** is the standout trip from Madrid. A relatively small city, strategically sited on a rocky ridge, it is deeply and haughtily Castilian, with a panoply of squares and mansions from its days of Golden Age grandeur, when it was a royal resort and a base for the Cortes (parliament). It was in Segovia that Isabel la Católica was proclaimed queen of Castile in 1474.

For a city of its size, there are a stunning number of architectural monuments. Most celebrated are the breathtaking **Roman aqueduct**, the Gothic **cathedral** and the fairy-tale **Alcázar**, but the less obvious attractions – the cluster of ancient churches and the many mansions found in the lanes of the old town, all in a warm, honey-coloured stone – are what really make it worth a visit. If you have time, take a walk out of the city alongside the river and out to the fascinating church of **Vera Cruz**.

The aqueduct

The most photographed sight in Segovia is the magnificent **aqueduct**. Over 800m of granite, supported by 166 arches and 120 pillars and at its highest point towering some 30m above the Plaza de Azoguejo, it stands up without a drop of mortar or cement. No one knows exactly when it was built, but it was probably around the end of the first century AD under either Emperor Domitian or Trajan. It no longer carries water from the Río Acebeda to the city, and in recent years traffic vibration and pollution have been threatening to undermine the entire structure, but the completion of a meticulous restoration programme should ensure it remains standing for some time to come. If you climb the stairs beside the aqueduct you can get a view looking down over it from a surviving fragment of the city walls.

Museo Zuloaga

Pl. de Colmenares s/n • July–Sept Tues–Sat 5–8pm, Sun 10am–2pm; rest of year Mon–Sat 10am–2pm & 4–7pm, Sun 10am–2pm • €1.20, Sat & Sun free

Some 200m up the hill to the right of the aqueduct and nestled against the walls is the **Museo Zuloaga**, a museum dedicated to the ceramicist Daniel Zuloaga and housed in the Romanesque Iglesia San Juan de los Caballeros, where the noble families of the city used to meet. Inside is a striking display of the artist's work, including some marvellous painted tiles and a scene of the Apostles with Christ that was designed to surround the family fireplace and which were modelled on those at the Monasterio de Santo Domingo de Silos in Burgos.

Casa de los Picos and the Alhóndiga

Passing under the aqueduct and up the hill along c/Cervantes and c/Juan Bravo, you will be directed towards the old city past the curious fifteenth-century **Casa de los Picos** (House of Spikes), with its waffle-like facade made up of pyramid-shaped stones to your right and the former corn exchange, the **Alhóndiga**, down a few steps on your left.

2

SEGOVIA

Convento de
los Carmelitas

Iglesia de
las Vera Cruz

Monasterio de
El Parral

CARRETERA DE ZAMARRAMALA

MARQUES DE VILLENA

San
Marcos

CALLE SAN MARCOS

SAN
MARCOS

Río Eresma

Casa de
la Moneda

Río Eresma

PASEO DE SANTO

Río Clamores

CUESTA DE LOS HOYOS

Muralla

POZO DE LA NIEVE

Puerta de
Santiago

SAN PEDRO DE LOS PICOS

Alcázar

Plaza de la
Reina Eugenia

CALLE DE VELARDE

Jardín de
Fromkes

PASEO DE DON JUAN II

CALLE DE DAOIZ

LAS
CAÑONGIAS

Casa Museo
de Antonio
Machado

San
Esteban

PLAZA
DE SAN
ESTEBAN

Museo de
Brujería

San
Andrés

S.
ESTEBAN

DECAN PARDOS

Pal. de los
Marqueses
del Arco

PLAZA DE
LA MERCED

Ayuntamiento

ESCUDERO

Muralla

C. MARQUES DEL ARCO

Casa del Sol
(Museo de Segovia)

Catedral

Puerta de
San Andrés

LA JUDERÍA

PASEO DE LOS HOYOS

SAN VALENTÍN

N

Convento del
Sancti Spiritu

0   100
metres

CARRETERA DE ÁVILA

NIGHTLIFE

Geographic Chic	**2**
La Tasquina	**1**

ACCOMMODATION

Camping Acueducto	**9**
La Casa Mudéjar	**6**
Emperador Teodosio	**12**
Hostal Don Jaime	**10**
Hostal Hidalgo	**7**
Hostal Plaza	**3**
Hotel Alcázar	**1**
Hotel Infanta Isabel	**5**
Hotel Los Linajes	**2**
Hotel Palacio	
San Facundo	**4**
Hotel San	
Antonio El Real	**11**
Las Sirenas	**8**

EATING & DRINKING

Bar José María	**3**
El Bernardino	**5**
Casa Amado	**8**
La Codorniz	**9**
La Cueva de	
San Esteban	**1**
Vino	**2**
Judería	**4**
Mesón de Candido	**7**
Mesón del Duque	**6**

L PARRAL

Monasterio de
San Vicente

SAN VICENTE

Río Eresma

2

ALAMEDA DEL PARRAL

Monasterio de
Santa Cruz

San
Lorenzo

CALLE DEL DOCTOR VELASCO

Convento
de las Oblatas

PASEO DEL OBISPO

CALLE DEL CARDENAL ZÚÑIGA

APUCHINOS

DOMINGO DE GUZMÁN

San Nicolás

Torre de
Hércules

LA TRINIDAD

La Trinidad

ALDEAGUILA

Palacio de los
Condes de Mansilla

1

PLAZA DE
GUEVARA

San Juan de los
Caballeros
(Museo Zuloaga)

ZA DE
OR

3

CRONISTA
LECEA

EL SAN
FACUNDO CALLE SAN AGUSTÍN

LOS CABALLEROS

PLAZA DE
COLMENARES

i

3

Muralla

San
Miguel

HERRERÍA

Torre de los
Arias Dávila

PLAZA
HUERTOS

4

INFANTA ISABEL

6

2

Casa del
Hidalgo

CEPRUOSA

PL. DEL
CORPUS

SAN

MARTÍN

E. MARTÍN HIGUERA

PLAZA
DEL CONDE
DE CHESTE

Convento del
Corpus Christi

JOSÉ CANALEJAS

7

Museo de Arte
Contemporáneo

LA RÁVILA

San Martín

San
Sebastián

PASEO DEL SALÓN

C DE

PZA. DE SAN
MARTÍN

Torreón de
Lozoya

PLAZA DE
AVENDAÑO

JUAN BRAVO

8

CV23

VÍA DE ROMA

Alhóndiga

Casa de
los Picos

i

PLAZA
DE LA
ARTILLERÍA

AVDA. PADRE CLARET

DE SAN MILLÁN

CALLE DE CERVANTES

5

6

PLAZA DEL
AZOGUEJO

San Justo

ZA DEL
CTU
RITU

Palacio del
Conde
Alpuente

DEL CARMEN

Acueducto

C. OCHOA ONDATEGUI

PLAZA DE
SAN JUSTO

10

TEODOSIO GARCÍA

El
Salvador

TENIENTE OCHOA

CALLE DE SAN FRANCISCO

C. S. ALFONSO RODRÍGUEZ

PLAZA
DEL
SALVADOR

PASEO EZEQUIEL GONZÁLEZ

AVDA. DE FERNÁNDEZ LADREDA

8

San
Clemente

E. MONTALVO

PLAZA DE
DÍAZ SANZ

CALLE LASMORENAS

SAN MILLÁN

9

Colegio de
Artillería

San
Millán

Soria, Cuéllar & Valladolid ▲

La Granja, Madrid, Train Station & ▲ 9

Convento de San Antonio Real & ▶ 11

Plaza de San Martín

A little farther on is the **Plaza de San Martín**, one of the city's grandest squares, whose ensemble of buildings includes the fourteenth-century **Torreón de Lozoya** (open for art exhibitions Mon–Fri 6–9pm, Sat & Sun noon–2pm & 6–9pm) and the twelfth-century **church of San Martín**, which demonstrates all the local stylistic peculiarities. It has the characteristic covered portico, a fine arched tower and a typically Romanesque aspect; like most of Segovia's churches, it can be visited only when it's open for business, during early morning or evening services. In the middle of the plaza is a **statue of Juan Bravo**, a local folk hero who led the *comuneros* rebellion against Carlos V in protest against tax increases, the undermining of local power and the influence of foreign advisers.

La Trinidad and Plaza San Esteban
Daily 10am–2pm & 4–7pm

North of here, the church of **La Trinidad** preserves the purest Romanesque style in Segovia: each span of its double-arched apse has intricately carved capitals, every one of them unique. Nearby – and making a good loop to or from the Alcázar – is the **Plaza San Esteban**, worth seeing for its superb, five-storeyed, twelfth-century church tower.

The Catedral
Pl. Mayor • Daily spring/summer: 9.30am–6.30pm, autumn/winter: 9.30am–5.30pm, except during Mass • €3, free Sun 9.30am–1.15pm • Guided tours at 11am & 4.30pm

Calle Juan Bravo eventually leads on to the bar-filled **Plaza Mayor**. Dominating one corner of the plaza are the exuberant lines of the **Catedral**. Construction began in 1525, on the orders of Carlos V, to make amends for the damage done to the city during the *comuneros* revolt. However, it was not completed for another two hundred years, making it the last major Gothic building in Spain. Accordingly it takes the style to its logical – or perhaps illogical – extreme, with pinnacles and flying buttresses tacked on at every conceivable point. Though impressive for its size alone, the interior is surprisingly bare for so florid a construction and its space is cramped by a great green marble *coro* at its very centre. The treasures, which include a splendid series of tapestries, are almost all confined to the **museums** which open off the cloisters. Look out for the marvellous golden *artesonado* ceiling in the sala capitular. On the opposite side of the plaza is the **Iglesia San Miguel**, the church where Isabel la Católica was crowned queen of Castile in 1474.

Casa-Museo de Antonio Machado
C/Desamparados 5 • Wed–Sun 11am–2pm & 4–7pm (guided tours in Spanish) • €1.50, free Wed

Down beside the cathedral, c/Daoiz leads past a line of souvenir shops to the twelfth-century Romanesque church of San Andrés. Off to the right is the **Casa-Museo de Antonio Machado**. This little house displays the spartan accommodation and furnishings of one of Spain's greatest poets of the early twentieth century; Machado is generally more associated with Soria, but spent the last years of his life teaching here.

The Judería

Segovia was once home to one of Spain's biggest Jewish communities and there are several interesting remnants from that period tucked away in the streets of the old **Judería** to the south of the Plaza Mayor.

Corpus Christi

Tues 4–7pm, Wed–Sun 10am–2pm & 4–7pm • Donation

The **synagogue**, which now serves as the convent church of **Corpus Christi**, is in a little courtyard at the end of c/Juan Bravo near the east end of the cathedral. You can see part of its exterior from the Paseo del Salón. During the nineteenth century it was badly damaged by fire, so what you see now is a reconstruction.

Centro Didáctico de la Judería

Wed–Sun 11am–2pm & 4–7pm • €1.50; free Thurs

Close by is the **Centro Didáctico de la Judería**, which houses a limited exhibition about Jewish culture and is located in the former house of Abraham Senneor, a rabbi who lived in Segovia in the fifteenth century.

Puerta de San Andrés and the Museo de Segovia

Puerta de San Andrés Sat & Sun 11am–2pm & 4–7pm • €1.50 **Provincial museum** July–Sept Tues–Sat 10am–2pm & 5–8pm, Sun 10am–2pm; Oct–June Tues–Sat 10am–2pm & 4–7pm, Sun 10am–2pm • €1.20, free Sat & Sun

Just south of here is the **Puerta de San Andrés**, one of the old gates into the Judería and back towards the Alcázar in the old Jewish slaughterhouse (Casa del Sol) is the **city museum**, which contains an interesting and comprehensive range of exhibits detailing the history of Segovia from prehistoric times to the present day. There is an informative explanatory video on the construction of the aqueduct and some fascinating Visigoth and Medieval exhibits. Across the other side of the valley is the old **Jewish cemetery**.

The Alcázar

Daily: April–Sept 10am–7pm; Oct–March 10am–6pm • €4.50, access to the tower an additional €2, free third Tues in the month for EU citizens • ⓦ alcazardesegovia.com

Beyond the Plaza Mayor and the Judería, perched on the northwestern tip of the city walls, is the **Alcázar**. An extraordinary fantasy of a castle, with its narrow towers and flurry of turrets, it will seem eerily familiar to just about every visitor, having apparently served as the model for the Disneyland castle in Orlando. It is itself a bit of a sham; although it dates from the fourteenth and fifteenth centuries, it was almost completely destroyed by a fire in 1862 and rebuilt as a deliberately hyperbolic version of the original. Still, it should be visited if only for the beautiful *artesonado* ceilings and the magnificent panoramas from the tower.

WALKS AROUND SEGOVIA

Segovia is an excellent city for **walks**. Drop down onto the path that winds its way down into the valley from the Alcázar on the north side of the city wall and you'll reach the Río Eresma. Head west and you'll pass close to Vera Cruz and the Convento de los Carmelitas, with some great views of the Alcázar, before turning back towards the city; head east and you can follow the beautiful tree-lined path alongside the river and wend your way back up the hill to the old town in a round trip of a little over an hour. On your way round you can visit the **Monasterio de El Parral** (July & Aug Tues 4–7pm, Wed–Sun 10am–2pm & 4–7pm; rest of year Tues–Sat 10am–12.30pm & 4.15–6.30pm, Sun 10–11.30am & 4.15–6.30pm; donation); or better still, follow the track that circles behind Vera Cruz to the monastery. El Parral is a sizeable and partly ruined complex occupied by Hieronymites, an order found only in Spain. Ring the bell for admission and you will be shown the cloister and church; the latter is a Late Gothic building with rich sculpture at the east end. Gregorian Masses can be heard during the week at 1pm in spring and summer and on Sundays at noon.

For the best view of all of Segovia, take the main road north for 2km or so towards **Cuéllar**. A panorama of the whole city, including the aqueduct, gradually unfolds.

Vera Cruz and the Convento de las Carmelitas

Tues 4–7pm, Wed–Sun 10.30am–1.30pm & 4–7pm, winter closes 6pm; closed Nov • €2

The best of Segovia's ancient churches is undoubtedly **Vera Cruz**, a remarkable twelve-sided building outside town in the valley facing the Alcázar, which can be reached by taking the path down to Paseo San Juan de La Cruz. It is traditionally thought to have been built by the Knights Templar in the early thirteenth century on the pattern of the church of the Holy Sepulchre in Jerusalem, and once housed part of the True Cross (hence its name; the sliver of wood itself was moved to the nearby village church of La Magdalena at Zamarramala). Inside, the nave is circular with ghostly vestiges of beautiful murals still visible on the walls, and its heart is occupied by a strange two-storeyed chamber – again twelve-sided – in which the knights, as part of their initiation, stood vigil over the cross. Climb the tower for a highly photogenic vista of the city.

While you're over here you could take in the prodigiously walled **Convento de las Carmelitas** (summer Tues–Sun 10am–1.30pm & 4–8pm; winter same times, but closes an hour earlier in the eve; free/voluntary donation), which is also referred to as the monastery of San Juan de la Cruz, and contains the gaudy mausoleum of its founder saint.

Convento de San Antonio Real

Tues–Sat 10am–2pm & 4–6.30pm, till 7pm in summer • €2

If you follow the line of the aqueduct away from the old city you will come to the **Convento de San Antonio Real**, a little gem of a palace, and now also serving as a luxury hotel (see p.165). Originally founded by Enrique IV in 1455 contain an intriguing collection of Mudéjar and Hispano-Flemish art, some outstanding *artesonado* ceilings and a wonderful fifteenth-century wooden calvary.

San Millán and San Justo

San Millán Daily 10am–2pm & 4.30–7.30pm, but subject to changes **San Justo** Nov–Feb Mon–Sat 10.30am–12.45pm & 4–6pm, rest of year closes an hour later in the evening

Back towards the city, but still outside the old walls, stand two fine Romanesque churches. Between the bus station and the aqueduct is the church of **San Millán**, with a fine Mozárabe tower and open porticoes. Its interior has been restored to its original form. Facing the aqueduct is **San Justo**, which has a wonderful Romanesque wall-painting in the apse and a twelfth-century sculpture of Christ complete with hinged arms.

ARRIVAL AND DEPARTURE

By train The high-speed train from Chamartín (12–14 daily; return tickets from €10.60) take just 27min, though the train station is quite a way out of town (take the #11 bus, which goes to the aqueduct every 15min). If you take a regional train it will take you a lot longer (7 daily; 1hr 50min–2hr), but it goes to the old station nearer to the centre (then take bus #8). Destinations Cercedilla (9 daily; 40min); Madrid (27 daily; 27 min–1hr 48min).

By bus There are regular buses from Madrid (operated by La Sepulvedana, Intercambiador de Príncipe Pío; ⓂPríncipe Pío; every 30 min, 1hr 45min; €6.85) that drop you at the bus station to the west of the aqueduct. Destinations Ávila (2 daily; 1hr); La Granja (20 daily; 25min); Madrid (every 30min; 1hr 45min); Salamanca (2 daily; 2hr 45min); Valladolid (hourly; 2hr 10min–2hr 30min).

INFORMATION

Turismo Offices at: Pl. Mayor 10 (July–mid-Sept daily 9am–8pm; rest of year Mon–Sat 9.30am–2pm & 4–7pm, Sun 9.30am–5pm, ☎921 460 334, ⓦturismocastillayleon. com); the high-speed train station Camino de la Ermita de Juarrillos (Wed–Fri 9am–5pm, Sat & Sun 10.30am–6.30pm); the bus station on Paseo Ezequiel González (Wed–Sun 10am–6pm); and the main road in from Madrid at Avda. de la

Constitución (Wed–Sun 10am–4pm).
Local council visitors' reception office Pl. de Azoguejo, just beneath the aqueduct (☎921 466 720, ⓦturism odesegovia.com; Mon–Fri & Sun 10am–7pm, Sat 10am–8pm). You can pick up an audio-guide for the city (€10) here or sign up for a guided tour (Mon–Fri 11.15am, Sat 11.45am & 4.30pm, Sun 11.45am; €12.50, €9.20 children).

ACCOMMODATION

Most of the **accommodation** is to be found in the streets around the Pl. Mayor and Pl. de Azoguejo, but rooms can be hard to come by even out of season, so it's worth booking ahead. Be warned that in winter, at over 1000m, the nights can be very cold and sometimes snowy.

La Casa Mudéjar c/Isabel Católica 8 ☎921 466 250, ⓦ lacasamudejar.com. Characterful hotel located in a restored mansion sandwiched between the Pl. Mayor and the Judería. Well-appointed rooms with historic touches such as beautiful carved *artesonado* ceilings, a patio restaurant that serves some traditional *sefardí* dishes with fruit sauces, and a small spa area (€17.50/hr). €90

Emperador Teodosio Paseo Conde de Sepúlveda 4 ☎921 441 111, ☏921 441 047. Located between the train and bus stations, this pleasant, spacious student residence becomes a youth hostel between July and mid-Sept. Free internet connection. YHA card needed. €11.60, under-30s €8.60

Hostal Don Jaime c/Ochoa Ondátegui 8 ☎921 444 787, ⓦ viasegovia.com/hostaldonjaime. An excellent budget option, this comfortable sixteen-room *hostal* is close to the aqueduct. All doubles have their own bathroom. €50

Hostal Hidalgo c/José Canalejas 5 ☎921 463 529, ⓦ el-hidalgo.com. Functional *hostal* with decent a/c rooms and a good patio restaurant in a small, beautiful old building overlooking the church of San Martín. €50

Hostal Plaza c/Cronista Lecea 11 ☎921 460 303, ⓦ hostal-plaza.com. A smart *hostal*, centrally located just off the Pl. Mayor, with 20 a/c doubles and four triples, all with simple but stylish decor. It also has its own garage. €51

★ **Hotel Alcázar** c/San Marcos 5 ☎921 438 568, ⓦ alcazar-hotel.com. A tranquil, upmarket boutique hotel with luxurious rooms situated next to the Río Eresma with a tranquil garden affording views of the Alcázar. €120

Hotel Infanta Isabel Pl. Mayor 12 ☎921 461 300, ⓦ hotelinfantaisabel.com. A very comfortable hotel with 37 rooms done out with nineteenth-century-style furnishings and ideally positioned right on the Pl. Mayor. €110

Hotel Los Linajes c/Dr Velasco 9 ☎921 460 475, ⓦ loslinajes.com. A decent-value cosy hotel set in part of an old palace in a quiet corner of the walled city. It has a fine garden overlooking the river valley, and all rooms have a/c. €60

Hotel Palacio San Facundo Pl. San Facundo 4 ☎921 463 061, ⓦ hotelpalaciosanfacundo.com. An old Segovian mansion not far from the Pl. Mayor converted into a swish business-style hotel with slickly decorated rooms and a stylish, covered patio bar. €110

★ **Hotel San Antonio El Real** San Antonio El Real s/n ☎921 413 455, ⓦ sanantonioelreal.es. Luxury hotel located inside a splendid old convent just up from the aqueduct. The 51 rooms are large, sumptuously decorated and with all the facilities you could want. €95

Las Sirenas c/Juan Bravo 30 ☎921 462 663, ⓦ hotelsirenas.com. Chintz decor, big rooms, a neat garden and terrace all at a very reasonable price. €66

CAMPSITE

Camping Acueducto Avda. Don Juan de Borbón 49 ☎921 425 000, ⓦ campingacueducto.com. The nearest campsite, 3km out on the road to La Granja; take a #6 "Nueva Segovia" bus from the Pl. Mayor. A quiet site with a swimming pool and plenty of shade. Open Easter–Sept. Two adults plus car €41.

EATING AND DRINKING

Segovia takes its cooking seriously, with restaurants of Madrid quality – and prices to match. Culinary specialities include *cochinillo asado* (roast suckling pig) and *judiones*, large white beans from La Granja.

Bar José María c/Cronista Lecea 11, just off Pl. Mayor ⓦ rtejosemaria.com. Bar-annexe to one of Segovia's best restaurants, *Di Viror*, serving delicious and modestly priced tapas.

★ **El Bernardino** c/Cervantes 2 ☎921 462 477, ⓦ elbernardino.com. A friendly place serving the Castilian classics of *cochinillo* and *cordero*, but better value than some of the city's more famous restaurants. The *menú segoviano* with *cochinillo* is under €30, while they also do a decent-value kids' menu. Daily around 1.30–4pm & 8.30pm–midnight.

Casa Amado Avda. Fernández Ladreda 9 ☎921 432 077, ⓦ restauranteamado.com. A small but popular local restaurant serving traditional dishes, near the Pl. Azoguejo.

Allow €35 per head, although there are also *menús* at around half this price. Closed Wed & the second half of Oct.

La Codorniz c/Hermanos Barral 3 ☎921 463 897, ⓦ restaurantelacodorniz.com. Inexpensive *menús*, some great *tortilla* and lots of *combinados* involving *codorniz* (quail) at this unpretentious place opposite San Millán church.

La Cueva de San Esteban c/Valdeáguila 15, off the top end of Pl. San Esteban ☎921 460 982, ⓦ lacuevadesanesteban.com. A cavern-restaurant and bar serving draught beer and an extensive range of tapas, popular with locals and excellent value. There are *menús* at €10 and €15.

★ **Di Vino** c/Valdeáguila 7 ☎921 460 789, ⓦ restaurant edivino.com. A high-class restaurant housed in an old

2

convent owned by the same people as *La Cueva de San Estebán* (see above). Expect excellent food, good service and imaginative touches to Castilian classics. There's a lunchtime *menú for* €18 and a *menú de degustación* for around €40 depending on what's in season. Closed Tues.

La Judería c/Judería Vieja 5 ☎921 461 402. Close to the *catedral*, this restaurant offers a mixture of Sephardic-style dishes such as hummus and falafel, together with traditional Castilian cuisine. Helpings are pretty small, but offers a range of *menús* from between €20 to €30. Closed Wed.

Mesón de Cándido Pl. Azoguejo 5 ☎921 428 103, ⓦmesondecandido.es. In the shadow of the aqueduct you will find the city's most celebrated restaurant: the place for *cochinillo* and other roasts. Allow around €40 per person. Daily around 1.30–4pm & 8.30pm–midnight.

Mesón del Duque c/Cervantes 12 ☎921 462 487,

ⓦrestauranteduque.es. Rival to the nearby *Cándido*, and also specializing in Castilian roasts, though it claims to be the oldest restaurant in the city. Offers a range of different *menús* including the obligatory *cochinillo* and *cordero* in the €30 to €40 bracket. Daily around 1.30–4pm & 8.30pm–midnight.

OUT OF TOWN

La Posada de Javier In the village of Torrecaballeros, 8km northeast on the N110 ☎921 401 136, ⓦlaposadadejavier.es. Serious *madrileño* – and *segoviano* – gourmands eat out in the neighbouring villages, and this lovely old farmhouse is one of the most popular choices. It isn't cheap, however, with a *menú* costing at least €30. Booking is essential at weekends. Closed eves Mon–Thurs & Sun, Mon & July.

NIGHTLIFE

Pl. Mayor, with its cathedral backdrop, makes a great place for a drink and a snack, but the biggest clusters of **bars** can be found in the narrow streets that lead off the plaza and back down by the aqueduct along Avda. Fernández Ladreda.

Geographic Chic c/Infanta Isabel 20. Bar-club modelled on an English-style pub with dark wood furnishings, comfy sofas and a varied diet of music. Daily 8pm–3am.

La Tasquina c/Valdeláguila 3. Popular wine bar close to the Pl. Mayor serving some tasty tapas to accompany a wide selection of wines and cavas. Daily 1.30–4pm & 8.30–11pm.

Around Segovia

Segovia has a major outlying attraction in the elegant Bourbon summer palace and gardens of **La Granja**, 10km southeast of the town on the CL601 Madrid road, and connected by regular bus services. True Bourbon aficionados, with time and transport, might also want to visit a second palace and hunting museum 12km west of La Granja at **Riofrío**.

La Granja

Pl. de España 17 • April–Sept Tues–Sun 10am–7pm; Oct–March Tues–Sat 10am–2.30pm & 3–6pm, Sun 10am–3pm (last entry an hour before closing); gardens daily 10am–dusk • Guided tour €5, unguided €4.50 (combined ticket with Riofrío €8 & €7.50), free Wed for EU citizens • ⓦ patrimonionacional.es

The **Palacio Real de la Granja de San Ildefonso** was built by the reluctant first Bourbon king of Spain, Felipe V, no doubt homesick for the luxuries of Versailles. Its glories are the mountain setting and the extravagant wooded grounds and gardens, but it's also worth casting an eye over the **palace**. Though destroyed in parts and damaged throughout by a fire in 1918, much has been well restored and is home to a superlative collection of sixteenth-century tapestries, one of the most valuable in the world. Everything is furnished in plush French imperial style, but it's almost all of Spanish origin; the majority of the huge chandeliers, for example, were made in the **glass factory** in the village of San Ildefonso (Tues–Fri 10am–3pm, Sat 10am–6pm, Sun & hols 10am–3pm; €4; ⓦfcnv.es). Here you can visit an exhibition on the history of the craft and still see the glass being blown and decorated in the traditional manner.

The highlight of the **gardens** is its series of **fountains**, which culminates in the fifteen-metre-high jet of La Fama. They're fantastic and really not to be missed, which means timing your visit for 5.30pm on Wednesdays, weekends and holidays (€3.40) when some are switched on (they may not be switched on during periods of water shortage, so it's best to check on ☎921 470 019 or the website beforehand). Only on three saints' days in the year – normally May 30 (San Fernando), July 25 (Santiago) and August 25 (San Luís) – are all of the fountains set to work, with accompanying crowds to watch. The enormous monumental fountain known as the Baños de Diana operates on Saturday nights in summer (10.30–11.30pm July 17–Sept 4; 1€) and is illuminated together with the palace facade.

Riofrío

April–Sept Tues–Sun 10am–7pm; Oct–March Tues–Sat 10am–2.30pm & 3–6pm, Sun 10am–3pm (last entry an hour before closing) • €4, combined ticket with La Granja €8 & €7.50; free Wed for EU citizens • ⓦ patrimonionacional.es

The palace at **Riofrío** was built by Isabel, the widow of Felipe V, in the fear that she would be banished from La Granja by her stepson Fernando VI. He died, however, leaving the throne for Isabel's own son, Carlos III, and Riofrío was not occupied until the nineteenth century, when Alfonso XII moved in to mourn the death of his young queen Mercedes. He, too, died pretty soon after, which is perhaps why the palace has a spartan and slightly tatty feel.

The complex, painted in dusty pink with green shutters, is surrounded not by manicured gardens but by a **deer park**, into which you can drive but not wander. Inside the palace, you have to join a guided tour, which winds through an endless sequence of rooms, none stunningly furnished. About half the tour is devoted to a **museum of**

NORTH FROM SEGOVIA: A CASTLE TOUR

It is said there were once ten thousand **castles** in Spain. Of those that are left, some five hundred are in a reasonable state of repair, and Segovia province has an especially rich selection. Drivers en route to Valladolid and the Río Duero (see Chapter 5) can construct an enjoyable route to see the best of them; there are buses (from Segovia or Valladolid), but you may end up spending the night in places that really only warrant a quick stop and a cup of coffee.

Fifty kilometres northwest of Segovia, the fortress (Mon–Fri 10.30am–1pm & 4.30–6/7pm, Sat & Sun 11am–1pm & 4/4.30–6/7pm, closed first Tues of each month; €2.50) at the small town of **Coca** is the prettiest imaginable, less a piece of military architecture than a country house masquerading as one. Built in about 1453, as the base of the powerful Fonseca family, it's constructed from pinkish bricks, encircled by a deep moat and fantastically decorated with octagonal turrets and elaborate castellation – an extraordinary design strongly influenced by Moorish architecture. There are five **buses** a day here from Segovia, though Coca itself is fairly unremarkable; drivers should push on to **Medina del Campo** for lunch (in Castilla y León; see p.398), itself the site of another fabulous castle.

The castle at **Turégano** (Wed–Sun 11am–2pm & 4–6pm; summer 5–8pm; €2), 28km north of Segovia, is essentially a fifteenth-century structure enclosing an early thirteenth-century church. However, it's east of here, off the main Segovia–Soria road (N110), that the most rewarding diversions are to be made. Eight kilometres east of Turégano, **PEDRAZA** in particular is almost perfectly preserved from the sixteenth century. The village is protected on three sides by a steep valley; the only entrance is the single original gateway (which used to be the town prison), from where the narrow lanes spiral up towards a large Plaza Mayor, still used for a bullfighting festival in the first week in September. The **Castillo de Pedraza** (erratic hours) is where the 8-year-old dauphin of France and his younger brother were believed to be imprisoned in 1526, given up by their father François I who swapped his freedom for theirs after he was captured at the battle of Pavia. **Sepúlveda**, a little further north (and off the highway between Madrid and Burgos), is less of a harmonious whole, but has an even more dramatic setting, strung out high on a narrow spit of land between the Castilla and Duratón river valleys. Its physical and architectural high point is the distinctive Romanesque church of **El Salvador**, perched high above its ruined castle. Ask at the tourist office (Pl. del Trigo 6 Sepúlveda; Wed 10.30am–2.30pm, Thurs 10.30am–2.30pm & 3.30–6.30pm, Fri, Sat & Sun 10.30am–2pm & 4–7pm; ☎921 540 237, ⓦ sepulveda.es) for details of routes down into the spectacular gorge that is home to one of the country's biggest colonies of griffon vultures.

2

hunting; the most interesting items here are reconstructions of cave paintings, including the famous Altamira drawings.

ARRIVAL AND INFORMATION

By bus There are up to 20 buses a day (10 at weekends) to La Granja from the bus station in Segovia (25min; €1.15).

By train There are eight local trains a day from Segovia to Navas de Riofrío (8min; €1.30). From there it is a 1km walk to Riofrío. Regional line trains from Chamartín station in

AROUND SEGOVIA

Madrid to Segovia also stop at Navas de Riofrío (7 daily; 1hr 39min; €6.40).

Turismo La Granja Pl. de los Dolores 1 (Jan–March, Nov & Dec Mon 10am–3pm, Tues–Sat 10am–1.30pm & 3–7pm, Sun 10am–3pm; April–Oct daily 10am–1.30pm & 3–7pm; ☎921 473 953, ⓦ realsitiodesanildefonso.com).

ACCOMMODATION

Hotel Roma c/Guardas 2 ☎921 470 752, ⓦ hotelroma .org. Friendly two-star hotel right outside the palace gates with comfortable rooms and a restaurant serving local specialities. €65

★ **Isabel de Farnesio** Travesia de La Reina 4 ☎921 471 078, ⓦ isabeldefarnesio.es. A new arrival, this chic, design-conscious hotel has 23 immaculately decorated doubles and a handful of luxurious suites. There is a spa

area too, providing a selection of beauty treatments. €90

Parador Casa de los Infantes, c/Fuentes 3, San Ildefonso de la Granja ☎921 010 750, ⓦ paradores .com. A plush parador with pool and spa area housed in the eighteenth-century Casa de los Infantes built by Carlos III for two of his sons. Large, modern rooms and an excellent restaurant specializing in local dishes such as *judiones*, lamb and suckling pig. €172

EATING AND DRINKING

Casa Zaca c/Embajadores 6 ☎921 470 087, ⓦ casazaca .com. Great place in La Granja to stop off for lunch, this former post-house has been serving up quality home-style local cuisine since 1940 and remains a family business. Good value too with a meal and wine costing in the region of €35.

Martinho c/Valenciana 5 ☎921 470 198, ⓦ restaurant emartinho.es. Close to the Palacio Real, this little

ochre-fronted restaurant is a delight, especially if you want something that goes beyond the standard Castilian dishes: delicately cooked fish, creative meat dishes and some great desserts. Worth taking the chef's advice on the specials which can range from chickpeas and langoustines to steak burgers stuffed with paté. Good value given the quality ingredients.

Alcalá de Henares

ALCALÁ DE HENARES, a little over 30km east from Madrid, is one of Europe's most ancient university towns, and renowned as the birthplace of **Miguel de Cervantes**. In the sixteenth century the university was a rival to Salamanca's, but in 1836 the faculties moved to Madrid and the town went into decline. Almost all the artistic heritage was lost in the Civil War and nowadays it's virtually a suburb of Madrid. It is not somewhere you'd want to stay longer than it takes to see the sights.

Universidad Antigua

Pl. San Diego • Regular 45min guided tours usually in Spanish Mon–Fri 10am–1pm & 4–7pm, Sat, Sun & hols 11am–2pm & 4.30–7.30pm • €4

The **Universidad Antigua** stands at the heart of the old town; endowed by Cardinal Cisneros (also known as Cardinal Jiménez) at the beginning of the sixteenth century, it features a fabulous Plateresque facade and a Great Hall, the **Paraninfo**, with a gloriously decorated Mudéjar *artesonado* ceiling. Next door, the **Capilla de San Ildefonso** has another superb ceiling, intricately stuccoed walls and the Italian marble tomb of Cardinal Cisneros, although his actual remains are buried in the cathedral in Plaza de los Santos Niños.

Museo Casa Natal de Cervantes

C/Mayor 48 • Tues–Sun 10am–6pm • Free • ⓦ museo-casa-natal-cervantes.org

The **Museo Casa Natal de Cervantes** on the porticoed c/Mayor claims to have been the birthplace of Cervantes in 1547: though the house itself is hardly thirty years old, it's authentic in style, furnished with genuine sixteenth-century objects, and contains a small museum with a few early editions of *Don Quixote* and other curiosities related to the author.

Monasterio de San Bernardo

Pl. de las Bernardas • Sat, Sun & hols guided tours at 11.30am, 12.30pm, 1.30pm, 5pm, 6pm & 7pm • €2.50

To the west of the university, the **Monasterio de San Bernardo** was founded by the Cistercians in 1617 with the building designed by Juan Gómez de Mora, architect of the Plaza Mayor and Casa de la Villa in Madrid. From the interior you can appreciate the church's splendid elliptical cupola with its balconied walkway. The monastery is also home to a museum of religious art which re-creates the atmosphere of a monastery of that era, complete with cells and kitchen.

Corral de Comedias

Pl. de Cervantes 15 • Guided tours 11.30am, 12.30pm, 1.30pm, 5pm, 6pm, Sat, Sun & hols 11am, 11.45am, 12.30pm, 1.15pm, 4pm (Sun only), 4.45pm, 5.30pm (Sat only) • €2.50

Just off the central Plaza Cervantes is the oldest surviving public theatre in Europe, the **Corral de Comedias**, which has been brought to life once more after a twenty-year restoration programme. Originally dating from 1601, the theatre was discovered beneath a crumbling old cinema by three drama students in 1980. Like Shakespeare's Globe, it was a hub of rowdy heckling and lively dramatics throughout the first half of the seventeenth century.

Museo Arqueológico and the Casa de Hippolytus

Museo Arqueológico Tues–Sat 11am–7pm, Sun 11am–3pm • Free Casa de Hippolytus May–Oct Tues–Fri 10am–2pm, Sat & Sun 10am–2pm & 5–8pm; Nov–April Tues–Fri 10am–2pm, Sat & Sun 10am–2pm & 4–7pm • Free

Other sights include the regional **Museo Arqueológico**, near to the Monasterio de San Bernardo which houses an interesting array of Roman finds. On the outskirts of town on Avenida de Madrid are the foundations of a Roman villa, the **Casa de Hippolytus**, which was originally a school for the children of wealthy Romans, complete with a temple, baths, and a garden containing exotic animals. The centrepiece is a magnificent mosaic signed by Hippolytus, depicting fishermen at sea and a vast array of aquatic life.

ARRIVAL AND INFORMATION
ALCALÁ DE HENARES

By train Chamartín or Atocha; daily every 15–30min from 5.30am–11.45pm from Madrid. If you like everything organized for you, Renfe issue a train ticket and guided tour package for €9 and €11.20. For a more atmospheric trip you could catch the *Tren de Cervantes*, which leaves Atocha at 11am on Saturday and Sunday (mid-Sept to early Dec; €20, €15 for children aged 4–11; ☎918 892 694), complete with staff in period costume, and including a guided tour of the main sights, before returning to Madrid at 7pm.

By bus Daily every 15min, from the *intercambiador* at Avda. de América in Madrid.
Turismo Just off the central Pl. de Cervantes (daily: summer 10am–8pm; winter 10am–2pm & 4–7pm; ☎918 892 694, ⓦturismoalcala.com); also at Pl. de los Santos Niños (same hours; ☎918 810 634). Arranges guided tours (Sat, Sun & hols at noon and 5pm; €6) and has maps and other handy information.

EATING AND DRINKING

★ **Hostería del Estudiante** c/Los Colegios 3 ☎918 880 330. Run by the Parador chain and situated in part of the old university this is probably the best restaurant in town, serving up local cuisine such as *migas* (breadcrumbs, garlic, chorizo and pepper) and roast meats. Expect to pay €35–40 per person. Closed Aug.

Castilla-La Mancha and Extremadura

HANGING HOUSE, CUENCA (P.179)

Castilla-La Mancha and Extremadura

The vast area covered by this chapter is some of the most travelled, yet least visited, country in Spain. Once south of Toledo, most tourists thunder nonstop across the plains of Castilla-La Mancha to Valencia and Andalucía, or follow the great rivers through Extremadura into Portugal. At first sight this is understandable. Castilla-La Mancha, in particular, is Spain at its least welcoming: a huge, bare plain – the name La Mancha comes from the Arab *manxa*, meaning steppe – burning hot in summer, chillingly exposed in winter. But this impression is not an entirely fair one – away from the main highways the villages are as friendly as any in the country, and in the northeast, where the mountains start, are the extraordinary cliff-hanging city of Cuenca and the historic cathedral town of Sigüenza. Castilla-La Mancha is also the agricultural and wine-growing heartland of Spain and the country through which Don Quixote cut his despairing swathe.

It is in **Extremadura**, though, that there is most to be missed by just passing through. This harsh environment was the cradle of the *conquistadores*, men who opened up a new world for the Spanish empire. Remote before and forgotten since, Extremadura enjoyed a brief golden age when its heroes returned with their gold to live in splendour. **Trujillo**, the birthplace of Pizarro, and **Cáceres** were built with *conquistador* wealth, the streets crowded with an array of perfectly preserved and very ornate mansions of returning empire builders. Then there is **Mérida**, the most completely preserved Roman city in Spain, and the monasteries of **Guadalupe** and **Yuste**, the one fabulously wealthy, the other rich in imperial memories. Finally, for some wild scenery and superb fauna, northern Extremadura has the **Parque Natural de Monfragüe**, where even the most casual birdwatcher can look up to see eagles and vultures circling the cliffs.

Castilla-La Mancha

The region that was for so long called **New Castile** – and that until the 1980s held Madrid in its domain – is now officially known as **Castilla-La Mancha**. The main points of interest are widely spaced on an arc drawn from Madrid, with little between. If you are travelling east on **trains and buses** towards Aragón, the only worthwhile stops are Sigüenza (en route to Zaragoza) or Cuenca (en route to Teruel). To the south, Toledo has bus links within its own province, but heading for Andalucía or Extremadura you'd do better returning to Madrid and starting out again; the Toledo rail line stops at the town.

If you have a **car**, and are **heading south**, the Toledo–Ciudad Real road, the Montes de Toledo and the wetland Parque Nacional de las Tablas de Daimiel all provide good

CHERRY BLOSSOMS, VALLE DE JERTE

Highlights

❶ Museo de Arte Abstracto, Cuenca
One of the famous hanging houses is the
wonderful setting for this gem of a museum.
See p.181

❷ La Ciudad Encantada Explore the weird
and wonderful limestone formations near
Cuenca. **See p.183**

❸ Cherry blossoms, Valle de Jerte Take in
the spectacular display in this picturesque valley
when the trees burst into bloom for ten days in
spring. **See p.195**

**❹ Vulture spotting, Parque Natural de
Monfragüe** You don't have to be a dedicated

ornithologist to be impressed by these
prehistoric-looking creatures. **See p.200**

❺ Trujillo A visit to the birthplace of Pizarro is
worthwhile for the view of the town from the
Cáceres road alone. **See p.201**

❻ Evening in Cáceres Wander around the
atmospheric historic core at night. **See p.206**

❼ Jamón Treat yourself to a *ración* of the cured
dried ham washed down with *pitarra* wine.
See p.194

❽ The Roman ruins in Mérida Marvel at the
stunning array of Roman buildings and artefacts.
See p.211

HIGHLIGHTS ARE MARKED ON THE MAP ON P.174

CASTILLA-LA MANCHA & EXTREMADURA

N

PORTUGAL

Valladolid

Medina del Campo

Salamanca

Guarda

Ciudad Rodrigo

La Alberca

El Barco de Ávila

Ávila

N110

EX109

SIERRA DE GATA

Pinofranqueado

Béjar

LAS HURDES

Gata

EX204

EX370

Hervás

3

LA VERA

Arenas de San Pedro

Candeleda

Coria

Cuacos de Yuste

Plasencia

Jarandilla de la Vera

Talavera de la Reina

Castelo Branco

Convento del Palancar

Villareal de San Carlos

Navalmoral de la Mata

Oropesa

CM 4000

To

PARQUE NATURAL DE MONTFRAGÜE

4

EX208

EX118

La Puebla de Montalbán

CM401

Alcántara

E1307

MONTES DE TOLEDO

Valencia de Alcántara

Arroyo de la Luz

Cáceres

6

Trujillo

5

Guadalupe

PARQUE NACION DE CABAÑEROS

Montánchez

7

N5

EXTREMADURA

Villanueva de la Serena

Évora & Setúbal

Elvas

Badajoz

Mérida

8

Castuera

Olivenza

Mourão

Villanueva del Fresno

Jerez de los Caballeros

Zafra

Córdoba

Seville

CASTILLA Y
LEÓN

Atienza

Sigüenza

Medinaceli

ARAGÓN

egovia

Molina de Aragón

Guadalajara

PARQUE NEAR
ALTO TAJO

MADRID

Teruel

② LA CIUDAD
ENCANTADA

① Cuenca

Tarancón

SEGÓBRIA

Motilla del
Palancar

VALENCIA

Aranjuez

edo

CASTILLA-
LA MANCHA

Belmonte

Alarcón

Valencia

Consuegra

PARQUE
NACIONAL
TABLAS DE
DAIMIEL

Alcázar de
San Juan

Alcalá de Júcar

Daimiel

Chinchilla de
Monte-Aragón

Real

Calatrava La Vieja

Manzanares

Albacete

Almagro

PARQUE NATURAL
LAGUNAS DE RUIDERA

Calatrava La
Nueva

Valdepeñas

Hellín

ANDALUCÍA

MURCIA

Murcia

Jaén

Granada

HIGHLIGHTS
① Museo de Arte Abstracto, Cuenca
② La Ciudad Encantada
③ Cherry blossoms, Valle de Jerte
④ Vulture spotting,
   Parque Natural de Monfragüe
⑤ Trujillo
⑥ Evening in Cáceres
⑦ Jamón in Extremadura
⑧ The Roman ruins in Mérida

•••••••• AVE High-speed Line

0   25

kilometres

FIESTAS

FEBRUARY
First weekend: La Endiablada ancient festival in Almonacid Marquesado (near Cuenca) All the boys dress up as devils and parade through the streets.
Week before Lent Carnaval everywhere.

MARCH/APRIL
Easter: Semana Santa (Holy Week) major fiestas in Cáceres and Trujillo Valverde de la Vera has the tradition of Los Empalaos, men who re-enact Jesus' journey to the Cross by roping their outstretched arms to huge wooden bars as they walk the streets of town at night. Magnificent celebrations (floats, penitents) in Cuenca.
April 23: San Jorge Enthusiastic celebrations continue for several days in Cáceres.

MAY
First half of May: WOMAD At Cáceres. Renowned world music festival set against the wonderful backdrop of the historic core.

JUNE
23–27: San Juan Manic in Coria A bull is let loose for a few hours a day, with people dancing and drinking in the streets and running for their lives when it appears.

JULY/AUGUST
Throughout July: Spanish Classical Drama Festival at Almagro Golden-age drama takes the stage at this prestigious festival.
Throughout July and August: Drama Festival in Mérida Classical works performed in the atmospheric setting of the original Roman theatre.

SEPTEMBER
First week: Vendimia celebrations at Valdepeñas
Week leading up to third Sunday Festivals in Jarandilla and Madrigal de la Vera with bulls running in front of cows – which are served up on the final day's feast.

alternatives to the sweltering A4 *autopista*. **Heading east**, through Cuenca to Teruel, the best route is to follow the Río Júcar out of the province, by way of the weird rock formations in the Ciudad Encantada and the source of the Río Tajo. **Heading west**, into Extremadura, the A5 is one of the dullest and hottest roads in Spain and can be avoided by following the M501/CL501 through the Sierra de Gredos or by cutting onto it from Talavera de la Reina; this would bring you to the Monastery of Yuste by way of the lush valley of La Vera.

The following sections cover the main sights and routes of Castilla-La Mancha in a clockwise direction, from northeast to southwest of Madrid.

Sigüenza

SIGÜENZA, 120km northeast of Madrid, is a sleepy little town with a beautiful cathedral. At first glance it seems quite untouched by contemporary life, though appearances are deceptive. Its origins date back to Celtiberian times and it was used by both the Romans and Visigoths as a military outpost. Following the Reconquest it became an important medieval settlement, though its influence gradually declined in successive centuries. Taken by Franco's troops in 1936, the town was on the Nationalist front line for most of the Civil War, and its people and buildings paid a heavy toll. However, the postwar years saw the cathedral restored, the Plaza Mayor recobbled and the bishop's castle rebuilt, so that the only evidence of its troubled history is in the facades of a few buildings, including the pencil-thin cathedral bell tower, pockmarked by bullets and shrapnel.

Catedral

C/Serrano Sanz • Daily 9.30am–2pm & 4.30–8pm; frequent guided tours of chapels Tues–Sun • €4

Sigüenza's main streets lead you towards the hilltop **Catedral**, built in the pinkish yellow stone that characterizes the town. Begun in 1150 by the town's first bishop, Bernardo of Agen, it is essentially Gothic, with three rose windows, though it has been much altered over the years. Facing the main entrance is a huge marble *coro* with an altar to a thirteenth-century figure of the Virgin. To the right of the *coro* is the cathedral's principal treasure, the alabaster tomb of Martín Vázquez de Arce, known as El Doncel (the page boy); a favourite of Isabel la Católica, he was killed fighting the Moors in Granada. On the other side of the building is an extraordinary doorway: Plateresque at the bottom, Mudéjar in the middle and Gothic at the top – an amazing amalgam, built by a confused sixteenth-century architect. Take a look, too, at the sacristy, whose superb Renaissance ceiling has 304 heads carved by Covarrubias. In a chapel opening off this (with an unusual cupola, best seen in the mirror provided) is an El Greco *Annunciation*. More treasures are displayed in the rooms off the **cloister**.

3

Museo Diocesano del Arte Antiguo

Pl. Obispo Don Bernardo • Daily Tues–Sat 11am–2pm & 4–7pm (5–8pm in summer), Sun 11am–2pm • €3

Housed in a refurbished sixteenth-century mansion close to the cathedral, the **Museo Diocesano del Arte Antiguo** displays artworks from the Stone Age to the twentieth century, including Greek and Roman sculptures, textiles, manuscripts and a vast array of sacred paintings including work by Morales, Madrazo and a particularly saccharine *Mary as a Child* by Zurbarán.

El Castillo

Pl. del Castillo

From **Plaza Mayor**, c/Mayor leads up to the castle passing close by the **church of San Vicente**. The **castle** started life as a Roman fortress, was adapted by the Visigoths and further improved by the Moors as their Alcazaba. Reconquered in 1124, it became the official residence of the warlike Bishop Bernardo and his successors. The Civil War virtually reduced the castle to rubble, but it was almost completely rebuilt in the 1970s and converted into a parador. You can still visit the central patio even if you are not staying at the hotel.

Casa del Doncel

Summer Tues–Thurs 11am–2pm & 5–7pm (winter 4–6pm), Fri & Sat 11am–2pm & 5pm–8pm, Sun & hols 11am–2pm

Opposite the church of San Vicente is the striking Gothic construction known as the **Casa del Doncel**, dating back to the thirteenth century and one of the most emblematic buildings in Sigüenza. The Mudéjar-style interior, which has undergone recent refurbishment, is worth a peek.

ARRIVAL AND DEPARTURE   SIGÜENZA

By train Around six trains a day run from Madrid to Sigüenza (1hr 30–1hr 40min). *Renfe* operates a special "tren medieval" excursion which leaves Chamartín station in Madrid (most Sat March–July & Sept–Nov; departs Chamartín 10am, arrives Sigüenza 11.25am or 11.45am, returns 6.30pm or 7.40pm arriving at Chamartín 8pm or 9.15pm; €27, children 4–13 €16; price includes a guided tour of the town and entry to the main sights. The train station is five minutes from the centre of this compact town. **Destinations** Madrid (7 daily; 1hr 40min); Medinaceli (2 daily; 17min); Zaragoza (2hr–2hr 30min).

INFORMATION

Turismo To the west of the cathedral at c/Serrano Sanz 9 (Mon–Thurs 10am–2pm & 4–6pm, Fri 10am–2pm & 4–8pm, Sat 10am–2.30pm & 4–7pm, Sun 10am–2pm; summer opens and closes an hour later Mon–Sat pm; ☎ 949 347 007, ⓦ siguenza.es); another office in La Ermita del Humilladero (same hours). Between May and September the offices run guided tours of the town for groups of six or more people (Mon–Sat 11.30am & 6.30pm, Sun 11.30am; €6).

CASTILLA-LA MANCHA CUISINE

La Mancha is renowned for its simple, down-to-earth **cuisine** based on local ingredients and traditional recipes made famous in Cervantes' classic *Don Quixote*. Dishes such as *gazpacho manchego* (a stew usually made from rabbit mixed with pieces of unleavened bread), *atascaburras* (puréed potato with salted cod and garlic) and *pisto manchego* (a selection of fried vegetables in a tomato sauce and often topped with a fried egg) are among the staples. The region is famed for its garlic and saffron, but perhaps the most celebrated of all foods from the region is **Manchego cheese** of which there is a bewildering array, though it can be divided into two main types: *semi-curado* (semi-cured) and *curado* (cured) – both must come from the local Manchegan breed of sheep, though the latter is stronger and more expensive. To accompany the cheese, there is nothing better than a glass of wine: the Valdepeñas vineyards which have traditionally been known more for the quantity than the quality of their product have improved significantly in recent years.

ACCOMMODATION

The town makes for a relaxing stopover en route to Soria and the north or as a base for exploring the rest of the region.

Hostal Posta Real c/San Vicente 1 ☎ 949 390 490, ⓦ postareal.com. Modern *hostal* with 23 simple, but comfortable and quite stylish en-suite rooms. **€65**

Hotel El Doncel Paseo de la Alameda 1 ☎ 949 390 001, ⓦ eldoncel.com. A recently refurbished eighteen-room hotel, with smart rooms mixing the traditional and the modern. The *Doncel* is also home to a very good restaurant serving some high-quality regional cuisine. **€78**

El Motor Avda. Juan Carlos I 2 ☎ 949 390 827, ⓦ hostalelmotor.com. A neat and simple, a/c two-star *hostal*, with its own bar and restaurant, on the road coming into town from Madrid. **€43**

★ **Parador de Sigüenza** Pl. del Castillo s/n ☎ 949 390 100, ⓦ paradores.com. Located in the town's twelfth-century castle, this atmospheric parador enjoys a stunning hilltop location, with fine views from the rooms on the upper floors. High-quality local specialities and seasonal produce are served up in the imposing dining room. **€156**

EATING

For **meals**, as well as the options below, try the hotel restaurants at *El Motor*, *El Doncel* and the *Parador*.

Asador Sigüenza Paseo de la Alameda ☎ 949 393 073, ⓦ asadordesiguenza.es. Specializes in roast lamb and goat, but also serves game dishes and an excellent selection of grilled vegetables. Daily around 1.30–4pm & 8.30pm–midnight.

Cafetería Atrio Pl. Obispo Don Bernardo 6. In the shadow of the cathedral, this relaxed bar serves excellent tapas and has a great summer terraza. Daily around 1.30–4pm & 8.30pm–midnight.

★ **Gurugu de la Plazuela** Travesaña Alt, 17, next to the Plazuela de la Cárcel ☎ 949 390 134, ⓦ gurugudela plazuela.com. Dating back to the seventeenth century, this tavern specializes in wild mushrooms with some sixteen different varieties on the menu. Very reasonable prices too. Thurs–Sat 12.30–4pm & 8pm–midnight, Sun 12.30–4pm & open in eve June–Sept.

Mesón Los Soportales Pl. Mayor 3. A great location opposite the cathedral, this bar makes a good base for a drink and a spot of tapas. Daily around 1.30–4pm & 8.30pm–midnight.

Medinaceli

Northeast from Sigüenza, just over the border in the Soria province of Castilla y León, is the picturesque town of **MEDINACELI**, perched in an exhilarating, breezy position above the Río Jalón. Highly evocative of its former glory as a Roman and Moorish stronghold, the original old town is sited 3km above the dull modern village, which lies on the main Madrid–Barcelona rail and road routes. Straight up the hill from the new village is the distinctive **Arco Romano** – a triple arch, in fact – that's unique in Spain. Its presence is something of a mystery: such monuments were usually built to commemorate military triumphs, but the cause of celebration at Medinaceli is unknown. A bit further along the road stands the dilapidated Moorish **castle**, now a mere facade sheltering a Christian cemetery. The quiet streets are full of ancient mansions with proud coats of arms, the grandest of which is the Palacio del Duque de Medinaceli on the Plaza Mayor, which not that long ago featured in a David Beckham Pepsi commercial set in the Middle Ages. It's an easy day-trip from Sigüenza, around a twenty-kilometre drive.

Atienza

Northwest of Medinaceli, **ATIENZA** is a characterful former fortress town with five Romanesque churches and an almost impregnable castle perched high on the hill above. A good route for drivers heading south is to make for **Cuenca**, past great reservoirs watered by the Tajo and Guadiela rivers, and skirting around the **Alcarria** region.

Cuenca and around

The mountainous, craggy countryside around **CUENCA** is as dramatic as any in Spain. The city, the capital of a sparsely populated province, is an extraordinary looking place, enclosed on three sides by the deep gorges of the Huécar and Júcar

CUENCA

EATING & DRINKING
Bar Clásicos	2
La Bodeguilla de Basilio	4
El Figón del Huécar	1
Manolo de la Osa	7
Mesón Casas Colgadas	3
La Ponderosa	6
Posada Tintes	5

ACCOMMODATION
Hospedería de Cuenca	2
Hostal Posada de San José	4
Hostal San Pedro	3
Hotel Alfonso VIII	9
Hotel Cueva del Fraile	6
Hotel Leonor de Aquitania	1
Parador de Cuenca	5
Posada Huécar	8
Rincón del Júcar (Hostal Calderón)	7

rivers, with balconied houses hanging over the cliff top – the finest of them tastefully converted into a wonderful museum of abstract art. No surprise, then, that this is a popular weekend outing from Madrid; to get the most from a visit, try to come on a weekday, and stay overnight; with this much time, you can make the short trip to see the bizarre limestone formations of the **Ciudad Encantada** and visit the picturesque source of the Río Cuervo.

The Ciudad Antigua

At the centre of the rambling **Ciudad Antigua** is the Plaza Mayor, a fine space, entered through the arches of the Baroque *ayuntamiento* and ringed by cafés and ceramic shops. Follow the road out of the Plaza and up the hill and you get some fantastic views of the surrounding countryside.

The Catedral and Tesoro Catedralicio

Pl. Mayor • Both daily 10am–1.30pm & 4–6pm, July–Sept closes 6.30pm and open all day on Sat & Sun, closed some feast days • €2.80, free first Mon of the month

Occupying most of the east side of the Plaza Mayor is the **Catedral**, whose incongruous, unfinished facade betrays a misguided attempt to beautify a simple Gothic building after the tower collapsed. The interior is much more attractive, especially the carved Plateresque arch at the end of the north aisle and the chapel next to it, with distinctly un-Christian carvings round its entrance.

Alongside is a small **Tesoro Catedralicio**, which contains some beautiful gold and silver work, as well as wooden doors by Alonso Berruguete.

Museo Diocesano

C/Obispo Valero 3 • Tues–Sat 10am–2pm & 4–6pm, Sun 11am–2pm, July & Aug Tues–Sat 10am–2pm & 5–8pm • €2

Further religious treasures are to be found in the adjacent **Museo Diocesano**, including two canvases by El Greco, a magnificent *Crucifixion* by Gerard David and a Byzantine diptych unique in Spain. The museum also houses a marvellous collection of tapestries and carpets.

Museo de Cuenca

C/Obispo Valero 12 • Summer Tues–Sat 10am–2pm & 5–7pm, Sun 11am–2pm; winter Tues–Sat 10am–2pm & 4–7pm, Sun 11am–2pm • €1.20, free Sat & Sun

Right opposite the Museo Diocesano is the excellent **Museo de Cuenca**, which traces the city's history from prehistoric times and showcases a good Roman collection from local finds.

Museo de Arte Abstracto

Casas Colgadas • Tues–Fri 11am–2pm & 4–6pm, Sat 11am–2pm & 4–8pm, Sun 11am–2.30pm • €3, under 10 free • ⓦ march.es/arte /cuenca

The artistic highlight of Cuenca has to be the nearby **Museo de Arte Abstracto**, a gallery established in the 1960s by Fernando Zóbel, one of the leading artists in Spain's "abstract generation". It is now run by the prestigious Fundación Juan March, which displays works from a core collection of abstract painting and sculpture by, among many others, Eduardo Chillida, José Guerrero, Lucio Muñoz, Antonio Saura, Antonio Tàpies and Fernando Zóbel, and hosts some of the best exhibitions to be found in provincial Spain. The museum itself is a stunning conversion of one of the extraordinary Casas Colgadas ("Hanging Houses"), a pair of fifteenth-century houses, with cantilevered balconies, literally hanging from the cliff face.

For the best views of the houses cross the Puente de San Pablo **footbridge** that heads across the gorge to the parador.

Fundación Antonio Saura

Pl. San Nicolás • winter Mon & Wed–Sat 11am–2pm & 4–7pm, Sun 11am–2pm; summer Mon & Wed–Sat 11am–2pm & 5–8pm, Sun 11am–2pm • €2 • ⓦ fundacionantoniosaura.es

Housed in the eighteenth-century mansion known as the Casa Zavala is the **Fundación Antonio Saura**, which contains some important and striking work by the renowned Spanish surrealist who died in Cuenca in 1998. The foundation also hosts regular exhibitions of paintings, photographs and sculpture.

3

Museo del las Ciencias

Pl. de la Merced 1 • Tues–Sat 10am–2pm & 4–7pm, Sun 10am–2pm • €1.20 for museum, €1.20 for the planetarium • ⓦ pagina.jccm .es/museociencias

Housed in an old convent and an adjoining modern extension, the **Museo del las Ciencias** is an ambitious, and largely successful, attempt to explain the origins of the universe and the history of the earth in the context of the local region. It has recently been remodelled and now contains more interactive exhibits and is very child-friendly.

Ars Natura

C/Río Gritos 5, Cerro Molina • Tues–Sat 10am–2pm & 4–7pm (closes an hour later in summer), Sun 10am–2pm • €3, under 18 free • ⓦ centroarsnatura.es

The **Ars Natura** is a brand-new state-of-the-art interpretation centre focusing on the flora, fauna, geology and climate of the Castilla-La Mancha region and man's interaction with it. It features plenty of child-friendly interactive exhibits, a garden area that displays local plant species and an upmarket restaurant (see p.183).

3

ARRIVAL AND DEPARTURE

CUENCA AND AROUND

By train Cuenca has recently been connected to the AVE high-speed train network and is now just a 50min trip from Madrid on the line to Valencia. The Fernando Zóbel AVE station is some 3km out of town and has regular bus connections to the city centre (line #12). The slower but considerably cheaper regional trains stop at the more central station at c/Mariano Catalina 10, which has a regular bus link to the old town.

Destinations Madrid (AVE 11 daily, 50min; €38.70; regional 4 daily, 2hr 30min–2hr 55min; €11.60); Valencia (AVE 5 daily, 58min; regional 4 daily, 3hr).

By bus The bus station is on the southern edge of the modern part of town close to the old train station at c/Fermin Caballero 20.

Destinations Albacete (2 daily; 1hr 45min); Madrid (9 daily; 2hr–2hr 30min); Valencia (1–3 daily; 2hr 45min–3hr 30min).

By car The old town of Cuenca – the Ciudad Antigua – stands on a high ridge, looped to the south by the Río Huécar and the modern town and its suburbs. If you're driving in, follow signs for the *catedral* and try one of the car parks beyond that up at the top of the old town.

INFORMATION

Oficina de turismo Pl. Mayor (daily 9am–2pm & 4–6.30pm, summer same hours except Sat & Sun 9am–9pm; ☎ 969 241 051, ⓦ cuenca.es and ⓦ turismocuenca.com). There is another office in the new town at Pl. Hispanidad

(Mon–Thurs 10am–2pm & 5–8pm, Fri & Sat 10am–8pm, Sun 10am–2pm). The Pl. Mayor office runs guided tours of the old town (€5, under 12 free; ☎ 969 241 051).

ACCOMMODATION

You'll find many **places to stay** in the new town, with a concentration of *hostales* along c/Ramón y Cajal, but there are several reasonably priced options in the old town.

Hospedería de Cuenca c/San Pedro 27 ☎ 969 239 117, ⓦ hospederiadecuenca.com. Stylish boutique hotel in the old town just up the hill from the Pl. Mayor. Fourteen individually decorated rooms with sleek wooden furnishings and swish bathrooms scattered over the six floors of this old mansion. **€70**

★ **Hostal Posada de San José** c/Julián Romero 4 ☎ 969 211 300, ⓦ posadasanjose.com. A lovely old building with a tranquil garden in the old town near the cathedral. It has only 22 stylishly decorated rooms, so be sure to book ahead. There's a good-quality restaurant, too, and an extra €15 will get you a room with a view over the gorge. **€75**

Hostal San Pedro c/San Pedro 34 ☎ 969 234 543, ⓦ hostalsanpedro.es. A great position up in the old town close to the cathedral, this comfortable little *hostal* has

eight neat rooms, some with views and seating areas, and all with smart bathrooms. **€60**

Hotel Alfonso VIII c/Parque de San Julián 3 ☎ 969 212 512, ⓦ hotel-alfonsoviii.com. A nicely located modern three-star hotel in the new town, facing the park. They also offer two-room apartments from €99 depending on the time of year. **€59**

Hotel Cueva del Fraile Ctra. Cuenca-Buenache km 7 ☎ 969 211 571, ⓦ hotelcuevadelfraile.com. A sixteenth-century former monastery 5km out from Cuenca. The rooms are pleasantly furnished in antique style and the extensive grounds include a pool. It also has its own restaurant serving local specialities. **€50**

★ **Hotel Leonor de Aquitania** c/San Pedro 58–60 ☎ 969 231 000, ⓦ hotelleonordeaquitania.com. Cuenca's prime hotel, beautifully situated in an eighteenth-century nobleman's house in the old town. Tastefully decorated rooms with superb views and prices to match. A great spot for a meal, too. **€60**

Parador de Cuenca Convento de San Pablo ☎ 969 232 320, ⓦ paradores.com. Expensive, but not that special, although it does have a pool and great views across the gorge to the Casas Colgadas. **€168**

Posada Huécar c/Paseo del Huécar 3 ☎ 969 214 201, ⓦ posadahuecar.com. A characterful inn on the banks of the Río Huécar with pleasant rustic furnishings in the rooms, all of which have en-suite bathrooms. Provides free cots for babies. **€50**

Rincón del Júcar (Hostal Calderón) Avda.Virgen de la Luz 3 ☎ 969 238 365, ⓦ hostalcalderon.net. A neat well-appointed *hostal* with ten simply furnished en-suite rooms and its own cafetería located close to a park down by the rivers in the new town. **€60**

CAMPSITE

Carvanning Cuenca 6km north of the city on the CM 2105 (no bus) ☎ 969 231 656, ⓦ campingcuenca.com. A riverside location for this extremely well appointed campsite with a great pool, surrounded by shady pines. Closed mid-Oct to mid–March. Two adults plus car **€20.80**.

EATING, DRINKING AND NIGHTLIFE

The Pl. Mayor is the place to head for evening *copas*, with its vibrant and diverse range of **bars**. The liveliest joints are on c/ Severo Catalina and in the little alleyways overlooking the Río Júcar. Another popular area is on and around c/Parque del Huécar by the Júcar, while there are a host of *barses de copas* around the stations and c/Fermin Caballero.

Bar Clásicos c/Severo Catalina 5. A cosy little place in the street below the Pl. Mayor. It does a good-value *menú* and has a small terrace that overlooks the Río Júcar.

La Bodeguilla de Basilio c/Fray Luis de León 3. Head for the crowded bar and order a drink rather than the *comedor* at the back and you will get the chance to sample a decent range of *raciones*, frequently accompanied by a free *tapa* while you wait. Good value and enjoyable, as long as you don't mind standing. Noon–4pm & 7pm–12.30am.

★ **El Figón del Huécar** c/Julián Romero 6 ☎ 969 240 062, ⓦ figondelhuecar.es. Inventive cuisine in this place up in the old town. Dishes range from puff pastry stuffed with vegetables and crayfish to lamb chops fried in brandy. Mains €16–22. Tues–Sat 1.30–4pm & 9–11pm, Sun 1.30–4pm.

★ **Manolo de la Osa at Ars Natura** c/Río Gritos 5, Cerro Molina ☎ 969 219 512, ⓦ manueldelaosa.com. Opened up by renowned chef Manolo de la Osa at the Ars Natura interpretation centre on the edge of town, this is an exceptional restaurant serving up a range of original and creative takes on traditional dishes. The €50 taster menu

includes some fantastic salads, tuna with peaches and figs and suckling pig. Closed Sun eve and Mon. Daily around 1.30–4pm & 8.30pm–midnight.

★ **Mesón Casas Colgadas** c/Canónigos 3 ☎ 969 223 509, ⓦ mesoncasascolgadas.com. A classy restaurant in the old town housed in one of the Hanging Houses. There are two set-menu options, one at €38 which features suckling pig, roast lamb and Manchego specialities and the other at €27 which includes a fish dish and lamb stew. 1.30–4pm & 9–11pm; closed Mon eve & Tues.

La Ponderosa c/San Francisco 20. Standing-room-only in this popular and long-established bar in the new town near to the Parque San Julián. Serves up quality *raciones* including *mollejas* (sweet meats), local tomatoes and a range of local specialities. Daily around 1.30–4pm & 8.30pm–midnight.

Posada Tintes c/Tintes 7. This popular and atmospheric local serves up a wide range of moderately priced dishes. Nothing too elaborate, but big helpings and very good value. Tues–Sun 2–4.30pm & 9pm–midnight.

La Ciudad Encantada

Daily: summer 10am–8.30pm; winter 10am–6pm • €3

The classic excursion from Cuenca is to the **Ciudad Encantada**, a twenty-square-kilometre "park" of karst limestone outcrops, sculpted by erosion into a bizarre series of abstract, natural and animal-like forms. A few of the names – "fight between an elephant and a crocodile", for example – stretch the imagination a little, but the rocks are certainly amazing, and many of the creations really do look knocked into shape by human hands. The fantasy landscape was used as a backdrop for Arnold Schwarzenegger's first major film, *Conan the Barbarian*.

The most interesting area of sculptures is enclosed and the extensive car park and restaurants outside testify to its popularity with weekending *madrileños*. However, off season, or during the week, you can have the place almost to yourself. Just outside the entrance there are signs to the **Mirador de Uña**, providing excellent views over the valley. You will need your own transport to get to the park, which is around 20km northeast of

Cuenca, on signed backroads towards Albarracín. If you get stuck, there is a quiet and comfortable **hostal**, the *Ciudad Encantada* (☎969 288 194, ⓦhotelciudadencantada .com; €52–68), opposite the entrance gate.

Another 30km farther north on the CM2106 past Tragacete is the **source of the Río Cuervo**, a moss-covered crag peppered with waterfalls.

East into Teruel

If you have transport, the route east from the Ciudad Encantada towards Albarracín is a delight, edging through the verdant **Júcar Gorge** and across the wild, scarcely populated Serranía de Cuenca. En route, still in Cuenca province, you might stop at **UÑA**, a village sited between a lagoon and a barrage. Just over the provincial border, in Teruel province, the road between Uña and Frías de Albarracín runs past a point known as García, close to the **source of the Río Tajo** where the great river begins its journey across Iberia to the Atlantic.

Hotel Castillo de Uña c/Egido 23 ☎969 282 917, ⓦcastillodeuna.es. This lakeside hotel has decent rooms, a panoramic restaurant and a garden bar. **€50**

Segóbriga

April–Sept Tues–Sun 9am–9pm; Oct–March 10am–6pm • €4, under-11s free

Just south of the A3 motorway that runs between Madrid and Valencia, near the village of Saelices, **SEGÓBRIGA** makes a worthy detour for anyone interested in Roman ruins. References to the town date back to the second century BC and it developed into a prosperous settlement largely thanks to the presence of nearby gypsum mines. The town reached its peak about four hundred years later, but declined under the Visigoths and was effectively abandoned during the Arab occupation. The best-preserved structures are the theatre and amphitheatre – which had a capacity for 5500 people – but there are also some interesting additions made by the Visigoths. There is an informative interpretation centre on the site that recounts the history of what was a fairly important settlement.

Alarcón

Just off the old NIII road between Honrubbia and Motilla del Palancar is the lively little town of **ALARCÓN**, occupying an imposing defensive site sculpted by the burrowing of the Río Júcar. Almost completely encircled and walled, the village is accessible by a spit of land just wide enough to take a road that passes through a succession of **fortified gateways**.

At the top of the village is an exquisite **castle**, eighth century in origin and captured from the Moors in 1184 after a nine-month siege.

Hostal Don Juan c/ Marqués de Villena 4 ☎969 330 429, ⓦhostaldonjuan.es. An affordable option, this newly built *hostal* has five neat doubles, some with seating areas. You'll need to book ahead in summer or at weekends. **€60**

★ **Parador Marqués de Villena** ☎969 330 315, ⓦparadores.com. The Arabic fortress has now been converted into one of the country's smallest and most atmospheric paradores with just fourteen, brick-lined doubles. Book ahead in summer or at weekends. **€235**

EATING

The parador, with its atmospheric dining hall, is probably the best **place to eat**, and there is cheaper fare served at the bars on the main Pl. de Don Juan Manuel.

La Cabaña de Alarcón c/Alvaro de Lara 21 ☎969 330 373, ⓦrestaurantelacabanadealarcon.es A good-value restaurant with a cool library-like interior and a terrace overlooking the valley, serving up a range of well-presented locally inspired dishes. Mains cost between €10–16. Daily noon–4pm & 8pm–midnight.

Albacete province

Travelling between Madrid or Cuenca and Alicante or Murcia, you'll pass through **Albacete province**, one of Spain's more forgettable corners. Hot, arid plains for the most part, the province shelters the lovely **Alcalá del Júcar** and the humdrum provincial capital, **Albacete**. Scenically, the only relief is in the hyperactive **Río Júcar**, which, in the north of the province, sinks almost without warning into the plain.

Alcalá del Júcar

If you are driving, it's certainly worth making a detour off the main roads east to take the scenic route along the banks of the Río Júcar, between Valdeganga and the stunning village of **ALCALÁ DEL JÚCAR**. Almost encircled by the river, the village is an amazing sight, with its houses built one on top of the other and burrowed into the white cliff-face. Several of these **cuevas** (caves) have been converted into bars and restaurants and make a great place for a drink, with rooms carved up to 170m through the cliff and windows overlooking the river on each side of the loop. They're open daily in summer but otherwise only at weekends.

Alcalá also boasts a **castle** (summer 11am–2pm & 5–8pm; winter 11am–2pm & 3–6pm; €2) – adapted at intervals over the past 1500 years, though today just a shell – with great views.

ACCOMMODATION	ALCALÁ DEL JÚCAR

Hostal Pelayo Avda. Constitución 4 ☎ 967 473 099, ⓦ hotelpelayo.net. Decent rooms (some with balconies) and its own restaurant and terrace next to the river. **€55**

Hostal Rambla Paseo de los Robles 2 ☎ 967 474 064, ⓦ hostalrambla.es. Another good option in a shady spot by the river. Simple, comfortable rooms, some with small balconies and its own restaurant. **€50**

EATING AND DRINKING

La Asomada c/La Asomada 107 ☎ 652 182 440. Restaurant/*bodega* by the castle and serving quality tapas based on ecological ingredients which the owner produces herself. Fri 8pm–midnight, Sat, Sun & hols 11am–4pm & 8pm–midnight.

Las Cuevas del Diablo c/Tal y Cual 12 ☎ 637 418 297, ⓦ cuevasdeldiablo.com. A series of bars, a disco and even a small museum have been carved out into this 70-metre-long tunnel that ends in a fantastic *mirador* across the valley. The "diablo" is eccentric owner Juan José Martínez, a self-confessed Don Juan character with a comedy Dalí-esque moustache. Entry fee €3, drink included. Daily 10am–9pm, but disco hours vary.

Albacete

ALBACETE was named Al-Basit – "the plain" – by the Moors, but save for a few old backstreets, it is basically a modern city. The **Catedral** is noteworthy for the presence of Ionic columns instead of normal pillars astride its nave. The **Pasaje Lodares** is also worth seeking out. A stunning iron-and-glass gallery constructed in 1925, it is adorned with neo-Baroque and modernist decoration and lined with shops.

Museo de Albacete

Parque de Abelardo Sánchez • Tues–Sat 10am–2pm & 4.30–7pm, Sun 10am–2pm, open mornings-only in summer • €1.20, free Sat & Sun

The **Museo de Albacete**, whose prize exhibits are five small Roman dolls, perfectly sculpted and jointed, and an array of local Roman mosaics, has a more than respectable archeological and ethnographical collection. Local-born painter Benjamin Palencia donated 120 works that form the basis of the art collection.

Museo de la Cuchillería

Pl. de la Catedral • Tues–Sat 10am–2pm & 5.30–8pm, Sun 10am–2pm • €3, under 18 free • ⓦ museo-mca.com

For Spaniards, Albacete is synonymous with high-quality knives and the **Museo de la Cuchillería**, housed in the intriguing green-tiled mock-Gothic Casa Hortelano by the cathedral, will tell you all you want to know about this speciality that, as with Toledo, can be traced back to the Moors.

Museo del Niño

C/Méjico • Mon–Fri 9.30am–1.30pm • Free • ⓦ museodelnino.es

The family-oriented **Museo del Niño** has exhibits on the history of childhood with sections covering school life, recreation and home. Exhibits include dolls, toys, puppets and comics. The museum will move into a new base in another former school in the course of the next few years.

ARRIVAL AND DEPARTURE   ALBACETE

By train Albacete is connected to the high-speed train network on the route between Madrid and Valencia (19 trains daily; 1hr 30min–2hr 30min). The new train station is on c/Federico García Lorca on the northeastern edge of the city.
Destinations Alicante (9 daily; 1hr 30min); Madrid (19 daily; 1hr 30min–2hr 30min); Valencia (7 daily; 1hr 30min).

By bus The bus from Madrid takes around 3hr and drops you at the terminus by the high-speed train station on c/ Federico García Lorca.
Destinations Alicante (7 daily; 1hr 50min–2hr 25min); Cuenca (2–3 daily; 2hr 45min); Madrid (25 daily; 2hr 45min–3hr).

INFORMATION

Turismo c/Tinte (Mon–Thurs 9.30am–7pm, Fri 10am–2pm & 4–8pm, Sat 10am–6pm, Sun 10am–2pm; ☎ 967 580 522, ⓦ albaceteturistico.es).

ACCOMMODATION

Hotel San José c/San José de Calasanz 12 ☎ 967 507 402, ⓦ hotelsanjose-albacete.es. This three-star hotel offers modern comfort with large rooms close to the pleasant city-centre park. **€70**

EATING AND DRINKING

The city is full of **tapas bars** and **restaurants** serving high-quality local produce with several good options to be found in the streets around the cathedral.

Casa Paco c/La Roda 26 ☎ 967 220 041. Well-known and popular restaurant serving up a mixture of regional specialities such as partridge and *gazpacho manchego* together with more creative offerings. Closed Sun eve.

Nuestro Bar c/Alcalde Conangla 102 ☎ 967 243 373, ⓦ nuestrobar.es. Renowned local bar serving great tapas and a vast range of regional cuisine, all at reasonable prices. Closed Sun eve.

Ciudad Real and the heartland of La Mancha

There is a huge gap in the middle of the tourist map of Spain between Toledo and the borders of Andalucía, and from Extremadura almost to the east coast. This, the province of **Ciudad Real**, comprises the heartland of **La Mancha**. The tourist authorities try hard to push their Ruta de Don Quixote across the plains, highlighting the windmills and other Quixotic sights: the signposted central part of the route, which starts at Belmonte and finishes at Consuegra, can be done in a day, but much of it is fanciful and, unless you're enamoured with the book, it's only of passing interest.

Nonetheless, there are a few places that merit a visit if you've got time to spare, most notably **Consuegra**, for the best windmills, **Almagro**, for its arcaded square and medieval theatre, and **Calatrava**, for the castle ruins of its order of knights. It is also the heart of wine-producing country, and many of the *bodegas* in **Valdepeñas** offer free tastings. The **websites** ⓦ quijote.es and ⓦ castillalamancha.es both give more information about the area.

Consuegra

CONSUEGRA lies just to the west of the A4 *autovía*, roughly midway from Madrid to Andalucía, and has the most picturesque and typical of Manchegan settings, below a

DON QUIXOTE

Not a novel in the modern sense, **Miguel de Cervantes'** *Don Quixote de La Mancha* (published in 1604) is a sequence of episodes following the adventures of a country gentleman in his fifties, whose mind has been addled by romantic tales of chivalry. In a noble gesture, he changes his name to Don Quixote de La Mancha, and sets out on horseback, in rusty armour, to right the wrongs of the world. At his side throughout is Sancho Panza, a shrewd, pot-bellied rustic given to quoting proverbs at every opportunity. During the course of the book, Quixote, an instantly sympathetic hero, charges at windmills and sheep (mistaking them for giants and armies), makes ill-judged attempts to help others and is mocked by all for his efforts. Broken-hearted but wiser, he returns home and, on his deathbed, pronounces: "Let everyone learn from my example … look at the world with common sense and learn to see what is really there."

Cervantes' life was almost as colourful as his hero's. The son of a poor doctor, he fought as a soldier in the sea battle of Lepanto, where he permanently maimed his left hand and was captured by pirates and put to work as a slave in Algiers. Ransomed and sent back to Spain, he spent the rest of his days writing novels and plays in relative poverty, dying ten years after the publication of *Don Quixote*, "old, a soldier, a gentleman and poor".

Spanish academics have spent as much time dissecting the work of Cervantes as their English counterparts have Shakespeare's. Most see *Don Quixote* as a satire on the popular romances of the day, with the central characters representing two forces in Spain: Quixote the dreaming, impractical nobility, and Sancho the wise and down-to-earth peasantry. There are also those who read in it an ironic tale of a visionary or martyr frustrated in a materialistic world, while others see it as an attack on the Church and establishment. Debates aside, this highly entertaining adventure story is certainly one of the most influential works to have emerged from Spain.

3

ridge of eleven restored (and highly photogenic) windmills. The first of these is occupied by the town's **oficina de turismo** while others house shops and workshops. They share their plateau with a ruined **castle** (summer daily 9.15am–1.45pm & 4.45–6.45pm; winter Mon–Fri 9.15am–1.45pm & 4.45–6.45pm, Sat, Sun & hols 10.45am–1.45pm, 3.45–5.45pm; €3, €2 on Mon & Wed) which was once the headquarters of the Order of St John in the twelfth century and offers splendid views of the plain from its windswept ridge. The town below is also attractive, with a lively Plaza Mayor and many Mudéjar churches.

INFORMATION
CONSUEGRA

Turismo Occupies the first windmill (usually open June–Sept Mon–Fri 9am–2pm & 4.30–7pm, Sat & Sun 10.30am–2pm & 4.30–7pm; Oct–May Mon–Fri 9am–2pm & 3.30–6pm, Sat & Sun 10.30am–2pm & 4.30–7pm; ⓦ consuegra.es). Good for information on the Ruta de Don Quixote.

ACCOMMODATION

Vida de Antes c/Colón 2 ☎925 480 609, ⓦ lavidadeantes.com. A cosy little hotel with nine individually designed rooms laid out around an interior patio. Breakfast is an extra €4–6. **€70**

Hotel Las Provincias Ctra. Toledo-Alcázar ☎925 482 000, ⓦ restaurantelasprovincias.com. Busy and comfortable hotel with ten en-suite rooms and a good restaurant. Located on the northern edge of town. **€50**

Ciudad Real

The city of **CIUDAD REAL**, capital of the province at the heart of this flat country, makes a good base for excursions and has connections by bus with most villages in the area. It has a few sights of its own, too, including a Mudéjar gateway, the **Puerta de Toledo**, which fronts the only surviving fragment of its medieval walls, at the northern edge of the city on the Toledo road. Further in, take a look at the fourteenth-century **church of San Pedro**, an airy, Gothic edifice, housing some exquisite chapels and an elaborate fifteenth-century alabaster *retablo*.

3

Museo Provincial

C/Prado 4 • Closed for refurbishment, but typically Sept–mid-July Tues–Sat 10am–2pm & 5–8pm, Sun 10am–2pm, mid-July & Aug
Tues–Sat 9am–2pm, Sun 10am–2pm • Free

The **Museo Provincial** is a modern building opposite the cathedral, with two floors of local archeology (the second also has some stuffed local wildlife) and a third devoted to artists of the region.

Museo de Don Quijote

Ronda de Alarcos 1 • Tues–Sat 10am–2pm & 5–8pm, July & Aug Tues–Sat 10am–2pm • Free

In the entertaining **Museo de Don Quijote** personalities from the story guide you round the exhibits that include some smart audiovisuals bringing the tale to life.

ARRIVAL AND DEPARTURE   CIUDAD REAL

By train Ciudad Real's train station, with high-speed AVE connections to Madrid and south to Seville and Córdoba, lies out of town at the end of Avenida de Europa; bus #5 connects with the central Pl. de Pilar.
Destinations Almagro (5 daily; 1hr 15min); Madrid (25 daily; 50min–1hr).

By bus The bus station is located on the Ronda de Ciruela.
Destinations Almagro (6 daily; 1hr); Córdoba (daily; 4hr 30min); Jaén (2 daily; 4hr); Madrid (4 daily; 4hr); Toledo (daily; 3hr); Valdepeñas (3 daily; 2hr).

NATIONAL PARKS AND RESERVES IN LA MANCHA

A respite from the arid monotony of the Castilian landscape, and a treat for bird watchers, is provided by the oasis of **La Mancha Húmeda** ("Wet La Mancha"). This is an area of lagoons and marshes, both brackish and fresh, along the high-level basin of the Río Cigüela and Río Guadiana. Drainage for agriculture has severely reduced the amount of water in recent years, so that the lakes effectively dry up in the summer, but there is still a good variety of interesting plant and bird life. You're best off visiting from April to July when the water birds are breeding, or from September to midwinter when migrating birds pass through.

PARQUE NACIONAL DE LAS TABLAS DE DAIMIEL

Major parks between Ciudad Real and Albacete include the **Parque Nacional de las Tablas de Daimiel**, 11km north of Daimiel itself, which is renowned for its bird life (over 200 species visit the park over the course of the year). There's an information centre (daily: summer 8.30am–8pm; winter 8am–6.30pm; ☎ 926 693 118) alongside the marshes. The park is accessible only by car or taxi, and Daimiel has little accommodation on offer:

Hostal Las Brujas Paseo del Carmen, Daimiel ☎ 926 852 289, ⓦ restaurantelasbrujas.es. Excellent-value place on the outskirts of town with simply furnished rooms and a popular restaurant. **€33**

Hotel Las Tablas c/Virgen de la Cruces 5, Daimiel ☎ 926 852 108, ⓦ hotellastablas.com. Hotel in the centre of town. Price includes breakfast. **€77**

PARQUE NATURAL DE LAS LAGUNAS DE RUIDERA

More traveller-friendly, but crowded in the summer months, is the **Parque Natural de las Lagunas de Ruidera**, northeast of Valdepeñas (frequent buses from Albacete). You'll find an information centre (July & Aug daily 10am–9pm; Sept–June Wed–Sun 10am–2pm & 4–6pm; ☎ 926 528 116) on the roadside, as you enter Ruidera from Manzanares, and several nature trails inside the park, as well as swimming and boating opportunities. Accommodation includes:

Los Batanes Ctra. Las Lagunas km 8, Ruidera ☎ 926 699 076, ⓦ losbatanes.com. Campsite with a large pool and grassy sunbathing area close to the Laguna Redondilla. Two adults plus car **€23**.

Doña Ruidera Pedazo de lo Alto, Ruidera ☎ 926 525 064, ⓦ hotelruidera.es. Good-value apartahotel large rooms and a couple of two-bedroom apartments with views of the lake at €150 each. **€59**

Hostal La Noria Avda. Castilla-La Mancha 61, Ruidera ☎ 926 528 032. Down-to-earth and friendly nineteen-room *hostal* in the village of Ruidera. **€38**

Hotel Entrelagos Ctra. Las Lagunas ☎ 926 528 022, ⓦ entrelagos.com. Two-star hotel with simple en-suite rooms and its own little beach on the edge of one of the lakes. **€58**

INFORMATION

Oficinas de Turismo The main tourist office is on the Pl. Mayor (Tues–Sat 10am–2pm & 5–9pm, Sat & Sun 10am–2pm; summer Tues–Sun 10am–2pm; ☎ 926 210 044, ⓦ ciudadrealturismo.com, ⓦ tierradecaballeros .com). There is also an information booth at the train station.

ACCOMMODATION

Keep in mind that finding a **place to stay** is not always easy, so it's worth booking ahead.

Hostal Plaza Pl. de Agustín Salido 2 ☎ 926 954 335. A modern, comfortable well-equipped *hostal* with neat rooms, wi-fi and an adjoining bar-restaurant. **€40**
Hotel Santa Cecilia c/Tinte 3 ☎ 926 228 545, ⓦ santacecilia.com. A reasonably priced four-star in the centre of town. Rooms are slightly old fashioned, but it has its own pool. **€70**

EATING AND DRINKING

Ciudad Real has an impressive range of **tapas bars**. The town's **nightlife** at the weekend generally starts off with tapas on c/Palma, carrying on to the bars along Avenida Torreón del Alcázar and around.

La Casuca c/Palma 10. Home-made cooking at reasonable prices and a decent range of local wines in this popular bar-restaurant close to the centre of town.
Mesón El Ventero Pl. Mayor 9 ☎ 926 216 588. Look out for local specialities like *migas* (breadcrumbs, garlic, *chorizo* and pepper) and *atascaburras* (puréed potato, garlic and cod). 1.30–4pm & 9pm–midnight.
Miami Park Ronda Ciruela 34 ☎ 926 222 043, ⓦ miami-park.es. A wide range of stylish tapas and *raciones* on offer at this up market restaurant. Seasonal taster menus also on offer from around €39. Mon–Sat 10am–1am.

Almagro

Twenty kilometres east of Ciudad Real is **ALMAGRO**, an elegant little town, which for a period in the fifteenth and sixteenth centuries was quite a metropolis in southern Castile, partly thanks to the influence of the Fuggers, bankers to the Habsburg king and Holy Roman Emperor Carlos I (Charles V).

Corral de las Comedias

Pl. Mayor 18 • Jan–March & Oct–Dec daily 10am–2pm & 4–7pm; April–June & Aug–Oct daily 10am–2pm & 5–8pm; July 10am–2pm & 6–9pm (dramatized visits on Fri, Sat & Sun eve) • €3–4

Today, Almagro's main claim to fame is the **Corral de las Comedias**, a perfectly preserved sixteenth-century open-air theatre, unique in Spain. Plays from its sixteenth- and seventeenth-century heyday – the golden age of Spanish theatre – are performed regularly in the tiny auditorium, and throughout July it hosts a fully fledged theatre festival (ⓦ festivaldealmagro.com).

Museo Nacional del Teatro

C/Gran Maestre 2 • Tues–Fri 10am–2pm & 4–7pm, Sat 11am–2pm & 4–6pm, Sun 11am–2pm, July Tues–Fri 11am–2pm & 6–9pm, Sat 11am–2pm & 6–9pm, Sun 11am–2pm • €3

Across the square from the Corral de las Comedias, the **Museo del Teatro** houses costumes, photos, posters, model theatres and other paraphernalia documenting the history of drama from Greek and Roman times to the present, but is probably only of passing interest to anyone other than theatre buffs.

Museo de Encaje

Callejón del Villar • Jan–March & Oct–Dec Tues–Fri 10am–2pm & 4–7pm, Sat 10am–2pm & 4–6pm, Sun 10am–2pm; April–June, Aug & Sept Tues–Fri 10am–2pm & 5–8pm, Sat 10am–2pm & 5–7pm, Sun 10am–2pm; July Mon–Fri 10am–2pm & 6–9pm, Sat 10am–2pm & 6–8pm, Sun 10am–2pm • €1.50

As well as its theatre festival, Almagro is renowned for its lace and embroidery work showcased in the **Museo de Encaje**, which also looks at the techniques, origins and history of the craft.

3

Plaza Mayor

The **Plaza Mayor** is magnificent: more of a wide street than a square, it is arcaded along its length, and lined with rows of green-framed windows – a north-European influence brought by the Fugger family, Carlos V's bankers, who settled here. Also resident in Almagro for a while were the Knights of Calatrava (see below), though their power was on the wane by the time the **Convento de la Asunción de Calatrava** was built in the early sixteenth century. Further traces of Almagro's former importance are dotted throughout the town in the grandeur of numerous **Renaissance mansions**.

Back in the Plaza Mayor, you can have an open-air snack or browse among the shops in the arcades, where **lacemakers** at work with bobbins and needles are the main attraction. On Wednesday mornings there's a lively **market** in c/Ejido de San Juan.

ARRIVAL AND INFORMATION ALMAGRO

By train Almagro is connected to Madrid with one train a day (2hr 40min) and to Ciudad Real with six trains (13min); the train station is a short distance from the centre of town along the Paseo de la Estación.

By bus Buses, connecting the city to Ciudad Real, stop near the *Hotel Don Diego* on the Ronda de Calatrava.

Turismo South of Pl. Mayor on c/Bernadas 2 (Jan–March &

Oct–Dec Tues–Fri 10am–2pm & 4–7pm, Sat 10am–2pm & 4–6pm, Sun 11am–2pm; March–June, Aug & Sept Tues–Fri 10am–2pm & 5–8pm, Sat 10am–2pm & 5–7pm, Sun 11am–2pm; July Tues–Fri 10am–2pm & 6–9pm, Sat 10am–2pm & 6–8pm, Sun 11am–2pm; ☏ 926 860 717, ⊛ ciudad-almagro.com).

ACCOMMODATION

Almagro is a great **place to stay**, although accommodation can be fairly limited during the theatre festival and at holiday weekends, so make sure you book ahead.

★ **Casa del Rector** c/Pedro Oviedo 8 ☏ 926 261 259, ⊛ lacasadelrector.com. Some delightful and well-appointed rooms, each with their own individual decor, set in three distinct areas of this classy hotel; for atmosphere go for the ones around a beautiful interior patio. The hotel also has a spa. **€126**

Hospedería Almagro Ejido de Calatrava s/n ☏ 926 882 087, ☏ 926 882 122. Over forty simple and functional rooms in this neat hotel located next to the convent. Also

has a pleasant patio bar and restaurant. **€45**

Hostal Los Escudos c/Bolaños 55 ☏ 926 861 574, ⊛ hostallosescudos.es. Thirteen individually decorated, a/c rooms in this upmarket little *hostal* well located for all the main sights. **€55**

Parador de Almagro c/Gran Maestre ☏ 926 860 100, ⊛ paradores.com. Housed in a sixteenth-century Franciscan convent, this historic parador features some peaceful interior courtyards and a great swimming pool. **€156**

EATING AND DRINKING

Tapas **bars** cluster around the Pl. Mayor; and the *bodega* at the parador is worth a stop for a drink, too.

La Cuerda Pl. del General Jorreto 6 ☏ 926 882 805. Just in front of the train station, this is a friendly place specializing in rice and fish dishes. Eating à la carte will cost around €30 a head, while the lunchtime *menú del día* at closer to €10 is very good value. Closed Mon eve and first 2 weeks in Sept.

★ **Mesón El Corregidor** c/Jerónimo Ceballos 2 ☏ 926 860 648, ⊛ elcorregidor.com. The best restaurant in

town, serving up a range of different menus starting at €22 a head and going up to €55. Specialities include game and locally grown vegetables. There is a very pleasant patio bar in the same builiding. Closed Mon & first week in Aug.

La Posada de Almagro c/Gran Maestre 5 ☏ 926 261 201. There are two beautiful interior patios in this restaurant that specializes in local delicacies and roast lamb. A meal costs in the region of €35 a head. Closed Tues.

El Campo de Calatrava

The area known as **El Campo de Calatrava**, in between Almagro and Ciudad Real, was the domain of the **Knights of Calatrava**, a Cistercian order of soldier-monks created in the twelfth century which was at the forefront of the reconquest of Spain from the Moors.

So influential were they in these parts that Alfonso X created Ciudad Real as a royal check on their power. Even today, dozens of villages for many kilometres around are suffixed with their name.

Calatrava La Vieja

Carrión de Calatrava • Tues–Sun: April–Sept 10am–9pm; Oct–March 10am–6pm • €4

Founded by the Moors back in the eighth century, the fortified settlement of Qal'at Rabah acted as the powerbase of the Caliphate of Córdoba in this strategically important region. It was recaptured by the Christians in the mid-twelfth century and subsequently became the first headquarters of the Knights of Calatrava. The medieval walled fortress with its towers and remains of buildings such as the *mezquita* can be clearly seen during the visit.

Calatrava La Nueva

Aldea del Rey • April–Sept Tues–Fri 11am–2pm & 5.30–8.30pm, Sat 10am–2pm & 5.30–8.30pm, Sun 10am–2pm & 5–9pm; Oct–March Tues–Fri 11am–2pm & 4–6pm, Sat 10am–2pm & 4–6pm, Sun 10am–6pm • Free

In the opening decades of the thirteenth century, the knights pushed their headquarters south to a commanding hilltop 25km south of Almagro, protecting an important pass – the Puerto de Calatrava – into Andalucía. Here, in 1216, they founded **Calatrava La Nueva**, a settlement that was part monastery and part castle, and whose main glory was a great Cistercian church. Here you get a good idea of what must have been an enormously rich and well-protected fortress. The church itself is now completely bare but preserves the outline of a striking rose window and has an amazing stone-vaulted entrance hall. On the hill opposite is a further castle ruin, known as **Salvatierra**, which the knights took over from the Moors.

Valdepeñas and beyond

The road from Ciudad Real through Almagro continues to **VALDEPEÑAS**, centre of the most prolific wine region in Spain just off the main Madrid–Andalucía motorway. You pass many of the largest **bodegas** on the slip road into town coming from the north and Madrid; most of them offer free tastings. Another option is the high-tech **Museo del Vino** at c/Princesa 39, close to Plaza de España (Tues–Sat 10am–2pm & 5–7pm, Sun 11am–2pm; summer Tues–Sat 10am–2pm & 6–9pm, Sun 11am–2pm; €3). The town holds a popular wine **festival** at the beginning of September. There is also a **windmill**, on c/Francisco Mejía, which the tourist office says "could be the biggest in Europe", and opposite a museum dedicated to the abstract drawings of local artist Gregorio Prieto (Tues–Sat 10am–2pm & 5–8pm, Sun 11.30am–2pm; free).

Gorge of Despeñaperros

Heading south beyond Valdepeñas, you enter Andalucía through the **Gorge of Despeñaperros** (literally, "Throwing Over of the Dogs"), a narrow mountain gorge once notorious for bandits and still a dramatic natural gateway that signals a change in both climate and vegetation, or as Richard Ford put it (travelling south to north), "exchanges an Eden for a desert".

INFORMATION   VALDEPEÑAS

Oficina de Turismo Pl. España (June–Sept Mon–Sun 9am–2pm & 5–8pm; Oct–May Tues–Sat 10am–2pm & 4–6pm, Sun 11.30am–1.30pm; ☎926 312 552, ⓦvaldepenas.es).

ACCOMMODATION

Hotel & Spa Veracruz Pl. Veracruz ☎926 313 000, ⓦhotelveracruzplaza.com. A modern well-equipped hotel with large rooms and its own spa. Offers trips of the local *bodegas* and wine-therapy beauty treatments. **€80**

Hotel Central c/Capitán Fillol 4 ☎926 313 388, ⓦhotelcentralval.com. Some 25 straightforward en-suite rooms in this decent-value hotel with its own parking in the centre of town. **€58**

The Montes de Toledo

The **Montes de Toledo** cut a swathe through the upper reaches of La Mancha, between Toledo, Ciudad Real and Guadalupe. If you're heading into Extremadura, and have time and transport, the deserted little roads across these hills (they rise to just over 1400m) provide an interesting and atmospheric alternative to the main routes. This is an amazingly remote region to find so close to the centre of Spain: its people are so unused to visitors that in the smaller villages you'll certainly get a few odd looks.

Toledo to Navalmoral de la Mata

The CM4000, west of Toledo, provides a direct approach into **Extremadura**, linking with the A5 from Madrid to Trujillo, and with roads north into the valley of **La Vera** (see opposite). It follows the course of the Río Tajo virtually all the way to uninspiring **TALAVERA DE LA REINA**, known for its manufacture of ceramics.

Oropesa and around

OROPESA is best known for its **castle**, a warm, stone building on a Roman site, rebuilt from Moorish foundations in the fifteenth century by Don García Álvarez de Toledo. Below it, stretches of the old town walls survive, along with a few noble mansions and a pair of Renaissance churches. There are great views from the neatly manicured gardens across to the hulking silhouettes of the Gredos mountains on the horizon, beyond which an attractive minor road, from **Oropesa**, with its castle parador, runs to **El Puente del Arzobispo** and south of the river to the Roman site of **Los Vascos**.

ACCOMMODATION OROPESA

Parador Virrey de Toledo Oropesa ☎ 925 430 000, ⓦ paradores.com. Installed in part of the splendid village castle, this is the best place to stay in the area. A great terrace pool, large communal areas and a good restaurant serving a range of local specialities. **€138**

Navalmoral de la Mata

West from Oropesa, **NAVALMORAL DE LA MATA** has nothing to offer other than its road, rail and bus connections to more engrossing places such as the **Monasterio de Yuste** across the rich tobacco-growing area to the north, **Plasencia** to the west, and **Trujillo** and **Guadalupe** to the south.

Into the hills

The most accessible route into the Montes de Toledo from Talavera is via the CM4000 and then the CM4009 and CM403 south of La Puebla de Montalbán, which runs through the backwater village of **Las Ventas Con Peña Aguilera**, overlooked by rock-studded hills, including a curious outcrop shaped like three fat fingers – the name Peña Aguilera means "Crag of Eagles". Southwest of Las Ventas, a tiny road leads to **San Pablo de los Montes**, a delightful village of fine stone houses nestling against the mountains.

If you keep to the CM403 south of Las Ventas, you will come to the main pass over the Montes de Toledo, the **Puerto del Milagro**, with great views of the hills dipping down on either side to meet the plain. Past the Puerto del Milagro, you can drive through lovely scenery towards Ciudad Real, or turn right along the CM4017 at the El Molinillo junction to follow a road through the hills via Retuerta del Bullaque to **Navas de Estena**. Here the road curves round to the north, passing a large crag with caves 5km beyond Navas, allowing you to loop round to Navahermosa and on to the CM401 to Guadalupe.

Extremadura

Once neglected and overlooked by many visitors, **Extremadura** has established itself on the tourist trail – and deservedly so. The grand old *conquistador* towns of **Trujillo** and **Cáceres** are excellent staging posts en route south from Madrid or Salamanca; **Mérida** has numerous Roman remains and an exemplary museum of local finds; and there is superb bird life in the **Parque Natural de Monfragüe**. Almost inaccessible by public transport, but well worth visiting, is the great **monastery of Guadalupe**, whose revered icon of the Virgin has attracted pilgrims for the past five hundred years. The lush hills and valley of **La Vera** are the first real patch of green you'll come to if you've driven along the A5 west from Madrid.

La Vera

Characterized by its lovely *gargantas* – streams – **La Vera** lies just south of the Sierra de Gredos, a range of hills tucked above the **Río Tiétar** valley. In spring and summer, the area attracts bands of weekenders from Madrid to the picturesque villages of **Candeleda** and **Jarandilla**. At the heart of the region is the **Monasterio de Yuste**, the retreat chosen by Carlos V to cast off the cares of empire.

Jarandilla and around

The main village in these parts is **JARANDILLA DE LA VERA**, which has good **walking** around it. A track into the hills leads to the village of **El Guijo de Santa Bárbara** (4.5km) and then ends, leaving the ascent of the rocky valley beyond to walkers. An hour's trek away up the Garganta de Jaranda is a pool known as El Trabuquete and a high meadow with shepherds' huts known as Pimesaíllo. On the other side of the valley – a serious trek needing a night's camping and good area maps – is the **Garganta de Infierno** (Stream of Hell) and natural swimming pools known as **Los Pilones**.

The village of **Villanueva de la Vera** to the east of Jarandilla along the EX203 has gained a certain amount of notoriety for its **Pero Palo** fiesta, in which donkeys are horribly mistreated. It seems strange to imagine any cruelty, given the rural idyll hereabouts and the incredibly house-proud appearance of the villages, especially **Losar**, which has an almost surreal display of topiary.

The Monasterio de Yuste

April–Sept Tues–Sun 10am–7pm, Oct–March 10.30am–2pm & 3–6pm, Sat, Sun & hols 10.30am–6pm • Compulsory guided tour in Spanish €2.50, free Wed • ⓦ patrimonionacional.es

There is nothing especially dramatic about the **Monasterio de Yuste**, the retreat created by Carlos V after renouncing his empire: just a simple beauty and the rather stark accoutrements of the emperor's last years. The monastery, which is signposted from Cuacos de Yuste on the Jarandilla–Plasencia road, had existed here for over a century before Carlos' retirement and he had earmarked the site for some years, planning his modest additions – which included a pleasure garden – while still ruling his empire from Flanders. He retired here with a retinue that included an Italian clockmaker, Juanuelo Turriano, whose inventions were his last passion.

The imperial apartments are draped throughout in black, and exhibits include the little sedan chair in which Carlos was brought here, and another designed to support the old man's gouty legs. If you believe the guide, the bed and even the sheets are the very ones in which the emperor died, though since the place was sacked during the Peninsular Wars and deserted for years after the suppression of the monasteries, this seems unlikely. A door by the emperor's bed opens out over the church and altar so that even in his final illness he never missed a service. Outside, there's a snack bar and picnic spots, and you'll find a track signposted through the woods to Garganta La Olla (see p.194).

Cuacos de Yuste

The Monasterio de Yuste is 2km into the wooded hills from **CUACOS DE YUSTE**, an attractive village with a couple of squares, including the tiny Plaza de Don Juan de Austria, named after the house (its upper storey reconstructed) where Carlos' illegitimate son Don Juan lived when visiting his father. The surrounding houses, their overhanging upper storeys supported on gnarled wooden pillars, are sixteenth-century originals, and from the beams underneath the overhang, tobacco is hung out to dry after the harvest.

3

Garganta La Olla

Just beyond Jaraíz de la Vera, a left turning leads for around 5km to **GARGANTA LA OLLA**, a beautiful, ramshackle mountain village set among cherry orchards. There is a signposted short-cut track to the Monasterio de Yuste, and several other things to look out for: the **Casa de Putas** (a brothel for the soldiers of Carlos V's army, now a butcher's but still painted the traditional blue) and the **Casa de la Piedra** (House of Stone), a house whose balcony is secured by a three-pronged wooden support resting on a rock. The latter is hard to find; begin by taking the left-hand street up from the square and then ask.

ARRIVAL
LA VERA

By bus Buses run through the village of Jarandilla, en route between Madrid and Plasencia; the stop is outside *Bar Charly* on the main road (daily; 3hr 30min).

ACCOMMODATION

JARANDILLA AND AROUND

Don Juan de Austria spa hotel Avda. Soledad Vega Ortiz 101 ☎ 927 560 206, ⓦ donjuandeaustria.com. Recently refurbished rooms, some with views of the Sierra and the castle, and a small spa in this good mid-range option in the village. **€70**

★ **Parador Carlos V** Avda. García Prieto 1 ☎ 927 560 117, ⓦ paradores.com. A magnificent parador in the fifteenth-century castle where the emperor stayed during the construction of Yuste. A splendid palm-fringed courtyard, period furnishings and a very good restaurant serving Extremeño cuisine. **€163**

Posada de Pizarro Cuesta de Carros 1 ☎ 927 560 727, ⓦ laposadadepizarro.com. A comfortable option containing ten en-suite rooms, each decorated with frescoes on the bedroom walls. Breakfast included. **€40**

★ **Ruta Imperial** c/Machoteral ☎ 927 561 330, ⓦ hotelruralrutaimperial.com. Grass lawns (a rarity in central Spain), a terrace restaurant overlooking the Garganta coming down from the mountains, an outdoor pool and comfortable rooms at an affordable price. **€70**

CAMPSITES

Jaranda Ctra. EX203, km 47 ☎ 927 560 454, ⓦ camping jaranda.es. Attractive campsite by the river with plenty of shady pitches, cabins for rent, a pool and a supermarket. Open mid-March to Sept. Two adults plus car **€18.10**.

Minchones Just outside Villanueva de la Vera east of Jarandilla along the EX203 ☎ 927 565 403. Superb campsite flanking one of the gargantas. Easter & June to mid-Sept.

CUACOS DE YUSTE

★ **La Vera** Avda. Constitución 5 ☎ 927 172 178, ⓦ verahotel.com. A good family-run hotel, with 27 simple but comfortable en-suite rooms, a restaurant and a swimming pool. Breakfast included. **€75–97**

GARGANTA LA OLLA

Hotel Rural Carlos I Avda. Libertad ☎ 927 179 678, ⓦ hotelcarlosprimero.com. A good-value option in this village. Individually decorated rooms, a couple of larger suites with sitting areas and a bar-restaurant serving up local dishes. **€65**

EXTREMEÑO CUISINE

Given that **Extremadura** remains a largely agricultural region, it is hardly surprising its **cuisine** is renowned for high-quality local ingredients, whether it be the trout from the streams in the Gredos mountains, the *pimentón* (paprika) from the Vera, the goats' cheese from Cáceres or the succulent cherries from the Valle de Jerte. Signature dishes include the humble *migas* (bread crumbs, paprika, ham, garlic and olive oil) and *patatas revolconas* (delicious paprika-flavoured potatoes), but to most Spaniards ham is the gastronomic product they most associate with Extremadura.

Together with the Sierra Morena in Andalucía, the Extremaduran sierra is the only place in the country that supports the pure-bred Iberian pig, source of the best **jamón**. For its ham to be as flavoursome as possible, the pig, a subspecies of the European wild boar exclusive to the Iberian Peninsula, is allowed to roam wild and eat acorns for several months of the year. The undisputed kings of hams in this area, praised at length by Richard Ford in his *Handbook for Travellers*, are those that come from Montánchez, in the south of the region. The village is midway between Cáceres and Mérida, so if you're in the area try some in a bar, washed down with local red wine – but be warned that the authentic product is extremely expensive, a few thinly cut slices often costing as much as an entire meal. The local wine, *pitarra*, is an ideal accompaniment.

El Valle de Jerte

Immediately north of La Vera, the main Plasencia–Ávila road follows the valley of the **Río Jerte** (from the Greek *Xerte*, meaning "joyful") to the pass of Puerto de Tornavacas, the boundary with Ávila province. The villages here are more developed than those of La Vera but the valley itself is stunning and renowned for its orchards of cherry trees, which for a ten-day period in spring cover the slopes with white blossom. If you're anywhere in the area at this time, it's a beautiful spectacle.

If you have transport, you can follow a minor route across the sierra to the north of the valley from **Cabezuela del Valle** to **Hervás**, following the highest road in Extremadura, which rises to 1430m.

On the **southern side** of the valley, the main point of interest is the **Puerto del Piornal** pass, just behind the village of the same name. The best approach is via the villages of **Casas del Castañar** and **Cabrero**. Once at the pass you can continue over to Garganta La Olla in La Vera.

Plasencia

Set in the shadow of the Sierra de Gredos, and surrounded on three sides by the Río Jerte, **PLASENCIA** looks more impressive from afar than it actually is. Once you get up into the old city the walls are hard to find – for the most part they're propping up the backs of houses – and the cathedral is barely half-built, but it still merits a visit. Opposite the cathedral is the **Casa del Deán** (Dean's House), with an intriguing balcony like the prow of a ship. Continuing away from the cathedral along c/Blanca you come out at the **Plaza de San Nicolás**, where, according to local tradition, the church was built to prevent two local families from shooting arrows at each other from adjacent houses.

Plasencia has some lively bars, delightful cafés and a fine, arcaded **Plaza Mayor**, the scene of a farmers' **market** every Tuesday morning, held here since the twelfth century.

Parque de la Isla

At the entrance to the city on the main road in from Ávila is the very pleasant **Parque de la Isla** on the banks of the Río Jerte; head here for a relaxing walk or picnic. A little north of here are the remaining 55 arches of the sixteenth-century **aqueduct**, designed by Juan de Flandes, that used to bring in the city's water supply.

La Catedral

Pl. de la Catedral **La Catedral Nueva** Summer Mon–Sat 9am–1pm & 5–7pm, Sun 9am–1pm; winter Mon–Sat 9am–1pm & 4–6pm, Sun 9am–1pm · Free **La Catedral Vieja** Summer Mon–Sat 9am–12.30pm & 5–6.30pm, Sun 9–11.30am; winter Mon–Sat 9am–12.30pm & 4–5.30pm, Sun 9–11.30am · €1.50

Plasencia's **Catedral** is in fact two churches – old and new – built back-to-back. Work began on the second church, **La Nueva,** at the end of the fifteenth century, but after numerous technical hitches it was eventually abandoned in 1760 when the open end was simply bricked up. It does have some redeeming features, however, most notably the Renaissance choirstalls intricately carved by Rodrigo Alemán and described with some justice by the National Tourist Board as "the most Rabelaisian in Christendom".

The older, Romanesque part of the cathedral, known as **La Vieja**, was built between the thirteenth and fourteenth centuries and now houses the obligatory **museum**, and the entrance fee includes access to the similarly aged **cloisters**.

Museo Etnográfico Textil Provincial

Plazuela Marqués de la Puebla · July to mid-Sept Mon–Sat 9.30am–2.30pm; mid-Sept to June Wed–Sat 11am–2pm & 5–8pm, Sun 11am–2pm · Free · ⓦ brocense.com/textil

The **Museo Etnográfico Textil Provincial** contains some colourful costumes and local crafts reflecting local traditions. Many of the exhibits are still much in evidence in the more remote villages in the north of Plasencia province.

3

ARRIVAL AND DEPARTURE

By train The train station is some distance away from the centre – take a taxi (around €5) unless you fancy the hike. Destinations Badajoz (2 daily; 3hr); Cáceres (4 daily; 1hr 10min); Madrid (up to 5 daily; 2hr 50min); Mérida (4 daily; 2hr 15min).

By bus The bus station is about 15min walk from the centre, along the gently inclining Avenida del Valle to the west. Destinations Cáceres (4–5 daily; 1hr 20min); Jarandilla (2 daily; 2hr); Madrid (2 daily; 4hr); Salamanca (4 daily; 2hr).

By car If you're driving, be warned the town is a warren of narrow one-way streets and poor signing and therefore notoriously difficult to navigate.

INFORMATION

Turismo c/Santa Clara 2, just off the Pl. de la Catedral (Mon–Fri 9am–2pm & 4–9pm, Sat & Sun 10am–2pm & 4–8pm; ☎ 927 423 843, ⊛ plasencia.es). There is also a provincial office in the Pl. Torre Lucia next to the city walls (Mon–Fri 9am–2pm & 4–6pm, Sat & Sun 9.45am–2pm; ☎ 927 017 840, ⊛ turismoextremadura.com).

ACCOMMODATION

La Chopera 2.5km out on the Ávila road ☎ 927 416 660, ⊛ campinglachopera.com. A large riverside campsite with decent facilities and a swimming pool. Closed Oct–April. Two adults plus car €18.

Hostal La Muralla c/Berrozana 6 ☎ 927 413 874, ⊛ hostallamuralla.es. A professionally run thirteen-room *hostal* with a/c rooms and a central location. €39

Hotel Alfonso VIII c/Alfonso VIII 32 ☎ 927 410 250, ⊛ hotelalfonsoviii.com. A smart four-star hotel with classically decorated rooms, located on the main road near the post office. All the facilities you'd expect. €76

Parador Pl. de San Vicente Ferrer s/n ☎ 927 425 870, ⊛ paradores.com. Housed in a beautiful restored fifteenth-century Gothic convent with large rooms, a cloister, stone staircases and a huge dining room, this parador also has a convenient central location. €172

EATING AND DRINKING

This is the land of the **pincho**, a little sample of food provided free with your beer or wine – among which is the local *pitarra* wine. Finding good restaurants is not as easy as finding bars in Plasencia (try the area between the cathedral and the Pl. Mayor): there are over fifty bars in the old town alone, mostly found on c/Patalón (go down c/Talavera from the main square and it's the second turning on the left).

RESTAURANTS

Casa Juan c/Arenillas 2 ☎ 927 42 40 42, ⊛ restaurantecasajuan.com. Good-quality regional dishes with some refined touches in this critically acclaimed restaurant in the old part of town. A good-value €20 *menú* available weekday lunchtimes. Closed Thurs.

Los Monges c/Sor Valentina Mirón 24, just up from Puerta Berronzana ☎ 927 420 808, ⊛ losmonges.com. A good-quality family restaurant serving up some fine local produce with a creative twist. Expect to pay around €40 a head.

Restaurante Succo Vidrieras 7 ☎ 927 412 932, ⊛ restaurantesucco.es. Minimalist decor and excellent creative food at decent prices in this restaurant close to the Pl. Mayor. The beautifully presented dishes include warm salad with baby squid and langoustines, and goat casserole with mushrooms. Closed Sun eve and all day Sun in July & Aug.

BAR

La Herradura c/Patalón 28. A busy bar that is a good bet for *pinchos*, hot and cold tapas and a glass of *pitarra* wine. Their speciality dish is *torreznos a la plancha* (deliciously unhealthy bits of fried fatty pork).

Valle del Ambroz

A little further to the west of the Valle de Jerte and almost as pleasing to the eye is the **Valle del Ambroz**. Dotted with picturesque villages set against a backdrop of some magnificent mountain scenery, the valley, which follows the Roman Vía de la Plata, heads up towards the picturesque town of **Hervás** and on towards Bejar in the region of Castilla y León.

Hervás

Pleasant little **HERVÁS**, perched on the flanks of the valley, makes a good base from which to explore the area. It also has attractions of its own including a fascinating, former Jewish quarter and a couple of small museums.

Museo de la Moto Clásica

Carretera de la Garganta • July–Sept Mon–Fri 10.30am–1.30pm & 5–9pm, Sat & Sun 10.30am–9pm; Oct–June Tues–Fri 10.30am–
1.30pm & 4–7pm, Sat & Sun 10.30am–1.30pm & 4–8pm • €10, under 12 free • ⓦ museomotoclasica.com

The overpriced **Museo de la Moto Clásica**, housed in a series of conical pavilions on the
edge of town, contains an impressive though eccentrically displayed private collection
of classic motorbikes, cars, bicycles and carriages, including giant Cadillacs, World War
II sidecars and horse-drawn carts.

Museo Pérez Comendador-Leroux

C/Asensio Neila 5 • Tues 4–8pm, Wed–Fri 11am–2pm & 4–8pm, Sat & Sun 10.30am–2pm • €1.20 • ⓦ mpcl.net

The **Museo Pérez Comendador-Leroux**, which is situated in a splendid eighteenth-
century mansion, is home to works of local sculptor Enrique Pérez Comendador, his
French artist wife Magdalena Leroux and some of their friends and associates.

ARRIVAL AND INFORMATION

HERVÁS

By bus Twice daily from Cáceres via Plasencia (2hr 5min),
three times a day from Salamanca (1hr 35min) and from
Madrid (3hr 20min).

By car From Plasencia take the N630 north towards
Salamanca and then the EX205 to Hervás.
Turismo c/Braulio Navas 6 (Tues–Fri 10am–2pm & 5–7pm,
Sat & Sun 10am–2pm; ☎ 927 473 618, ⓦ hervas.es).

ACCOMMODATION AND EATING

★ **Jardín del Convento** Pl. del Convento ☎ 927 481
161. A beautiful and tranquil little hotel in a refurbished
former nineteenth-century convent with six rooms and a
small cottage apartment with space for four people set in
the delightful gardens. €70

★ **Restaurante Mesón Nardi** c/Braulio Navas 19B
☎ 927 481 323. Imaginative and well-presented dishes
based on local ingredients and specialities in this friendly
place on a pedestrian street in the centre of town. Expect to
pay around €20–30 a head. Closed Tues.

Las Hurdes

Las Hurdes, the abrupt rocky lands north of Plasencia, have always been a rich source of
mysterious tales. According to legend, the region was unknown to the outside world
until the time of Columbus, when two lovers fleeing from the court of the Duke of
Alba chanced upon it. The people who welcomed them were supposedly unaware of
the existence of other people or other lands. Shields and other remnants belonging to
the Goth Rodrigo and his court of seven centuries earlier were discovered by the
couple, giving rise to the saying that the Hurdanos are descendants of kings.

Fifty years ago, the inhabitants of the remoter areas were still so unused to outsiders
that they hid in their houses if anyone appeared. In 1932, **Luis Buñuel** filmed an
unflatteringly grotesque documentary, *Las Hurdes: Tierra Sin Pan* ("Land Without
Bread"), here, in which it was hard to discern any royal descent in his subjects.
Modernity has crept up on the villages these days, though they can still feel wild and
very remote, and the soil is so barren that tiny terraces have been constructed on the
riverbeds as the only way of getting the stubborn land to produce anything.

Las Hurdes villages

You could approach Las Hurdes from Plasencia, Salamanca or Ciudad Rodrigo, the
region borders the Sierra de Francia – (see p.386). Coming from Plasencia the village of
PINOFRANQUEADO marks the start of the region. It has a campsite, *hostales* and a
natural swimming pool. Fifteen kilometres farther along on the road at Vegas de Coria
you can turn off to reach **NUÑOMORAL**, the village best connected to the outside world.
A good base for excursions, it also has a bank alongside its **hostal** – not a common sight
in these parts.

A few kilometres to the north of Nuñomoral, the tiny village of **LA HUETRE** is worth a
visit; take a left fork just before the village of Casares de las Hurdes. The typical
slate-roofed houses are in decent condition and have an impressive setting, surrounded

by steep rocky hills. Walkers might also head for the remote and disarmingly primitive settlement of **EL GASCO**, at the top of Valle de Malvellido, the next valley to the south, where there is a huge waterfall beneath the Meancera Gorge.

ARRIVAL AND INFORMATION	LAS HURDES
By bus Early morning buses connect Nuñomoral to both Ciudad Rodrigo and Plasencia. **By car** From Plasencia take the EX370 and then the EX204. **Turismo** Avda. de Las Hurdes, Caminomorisco (Wed–Sun	10am–2pm & 4.30–7.30pm; ☏ 927 435 329, ⌨ todohurdes .com). The website ⌨ mancomunidadhurdes.org also has plenty of useful information on the region.

ACCOMMODATION AND EATING

Hotel Hospedería Hurdes Reales c/Factoría, Las Mestas ☏ 927 434 139, ⌨ hospederiasdeextremadura. es. Large rooms, a decent restaurant and a small outdoor pool in this modern hotel set in beautiful surroundings in the	village of Las Mestas in the northern part of Las Hurdes. **€70** **Pensión El Hurdano** Avda. Padre Rizabala, Nuñomoral ☏ 927 433 012. An excellent and inexpensive *hostal* which also does big dinners. **€35**

The Sierra de Gata

The **Sierra de Gata** creates a westerly border to Las Hurdes, in a series of wooded hills and odd outcrops of higher ground, in parts stunningly beautiful. To explore the whole region, you need your own transport and certainly a detailed local **map** – regular Spanish road maps tend to be pretty sketchy.

The Sierra de Gata is almost as equally isolated as Las Hurdes – in some of the villages the old people still speak *maniego*, a mix of Castilian Spanish and Portuguese. For a trip into the heart of the region, take the EX204 south from Las Hurdes to **Villanueva de la Sierra** and follow the EX205 west. A couple of kilometres past the Río Arrago, a very minor road veers north towards **Robledillo de Gata**, a village of old houses packed tightly together. A shorter, easier detour, south of the EX205, around 5km on, goes to the hilltop village of **Santibáñez el Alto**, whose oldest houses are built entirely of stone, without windows. At the top of town, look out for a tiny bullring, castle remains and the old cemetery – there's a wonderful view over the Borbollón reservoir from here. Another 3km along the EX205, a turn-off to the north takes you on a winding road up to the pretty village of **Gata**. Farther west on the EX205 is the largest village of the region, **Hoyos**, which has some impressive mansions. Lastly, farther along the EX205, another turning leads north to **San Martín de Trevejo**, one of the prettiest of the many lonely villages around.

ARRIVAL	SIERRA DE GATA
By car Take the EX370 from Plasencia and then the EX204 northwards before bearing west onto the EX205.	

ACCOMMODATION

Campsite Sierra de Gata ☏ 927 672 168, ⌨ camping-extremadura.com. Four km from the village of Gata on the banks of a stream, this campsite has a large outdoor pool, a small bar and plenty of shade. Two adults plus car **€18**. **Finca El Cabezo** Villamiel ☏ 927 672 903, ⌨ elcabezo .com. Characterful and cosy *casa rural* with six large, rustic	rooms. Breakfast included in the price. **€85** **Hotel Rural El Redoble** Pl. de la Paz 23, Hoyos ☏ 927 514 665, ⌨ el-redoble.com. Simply furnished hotel with nine air-conditioned en-suite rooms and a restaurant/ bar. **€40**

Coria

South of the Sierra de Gata, **CORIA** makes an interesting stop. It looks nothing much from the main road, but it's actually a cool, quiet old town with lots of stately whitewashed houses. The fifteenth-century **convent** (Mon–Fri & Sun 9.30am–12.45pm & 4.15–6.45pm, Sat 4.15–6.45pm; €1.50) with its Gothic-Renaissance cloister is enclosed within third- and fourth-century **Roman walls**. For the most part these are built into and around the houses, but a good stretch is visible between the deserted tower of the fifteenth-century castle, built by the dukes of Alba, and the cathedral.

Catedral

Pl. de la Catedral • Daily 10am–1pm & 4–6pm; summer opens and closes an hour later in the afternoons; museum closed Mon • museum €2

The **Catedral** has beautifully carved west and north portals in the Plateresque style of Salamanca and, inside, the choirstalls and *retablo* are worth seeing. The building overlooks a striking medieval bridge across fields, the river having changed course three hundred years ago.

Museo Carcel Real

C/Monjas 2 • Wed–Sun 10.30am–2pm & 4.30–7.30pm (opens and closes an hour later in the afternoons in summer) • Free

The former town prison now houses the local archeological museum, **Museo Carcel Real**, with exhibits dating from the time the Celto-Iberians first settled in the area.

Convento del Palancar

Tues–Sun 10am–1pm & 4.30–6.45pm; ring the doorbell • Voluntary donation

A detour off the EX109, south of Coria, will take you to the **Convento del Palancar**, a monastery founded by San Pedro de Alcántara in the sixteenth century and said to be the smallest in the world at only seventy square metres. It's hard to imagine how a community of ten monks could have lived in these cubbyholes, though San Pedro himself set the example, sleeping upright in his cubicle. A small monastic community today occupies a more modern monastery alongside; ring the bell and a monk will come and show you around.

To reach Palancar, turn left off the EX109 just after Torrejoncillo and follow the road towards **Pedroso de Acim**; a left turn just before the village leads to the monastery.

ARRIVAL AND INFORMATION   CORIA

By car South from the Sierra de Gata along the EX109 towards Cáceres or take the EX08 from Plasencia.
Oficina de Turismo Inside the *ayuntamiento* on Avda. de

Extremadura (usually Mon–Fri 9.30am–2pm & 5–7.30pm, Sat & Sun 10am–2pm, winter opens and closes an hour earlier in the afternoons; ☎927 501 351, ⍟coria.org).

ACCOMMODATION

Hotel Los Kekes Avda. Sierra de Gata 49 ☎927 504 080, ⍟hotelkekes.com. A modest hotel which has 20 recently refurbished air-conditioned doubles and an adjoining restaurant. €40

Palacio Coria Pl. de la Catedral ☎927 506 449, ⍟hotelpalaciocoria.es. Housed in the seventeenth-century former bishop's palace, this good-value hotel has 30 smart rooms with modern facilities and a decent restaurant. €70

Parque Natural de Monfragüe

South of Plasencia a pair of dams, built in the 1960s, has turned the **ríos Tajo and Tiétar** into a sequence of vast reservoirs. It's an impressive sight and a tremendous area for wildlife: almost at random here, you can look up to see storks, vultures and even eagles circling the skies. The best area for concerted wildlife viewing – and some very enjoyable walks – is the **PARQUE NATURAL DE MONFRAGÜE**, Extremadura's only protected area, which extends over 44,000 acres to either side of the Plasencia–Trujillo road. Transport of your own is an advantage unless you are prepared to do some walking.

Walking in the park

If you're **walking** in Monfragüe, it's best to stick to the colour-coded paths leading from the park's headquarters at **Villarreal de San Carlos**. Each of them is well paint-blobbed and leads to rewarding birdwatching locations. Elsewhere, it is not easy to tell where you are permitted to wander – it's very easy to find yourself out of the park area in a private hunting reserve.

MONFRAGÜE'S WILDLIFE

There are **over two hundred species of animals in Monfragüe**, including reptiles, deer, wild boar and the ultra-rare Spanish lynx. Most important is the bird population, especially the black stork – this is the only breeding population in western Europe – and birds of prey such as the black vulture (not averse to eating tortoises), the griffon vulture (partial to carrion intestine), the Egyptian vulture (not above eating human excrement), the rare Spanish imperial eagle (identifiable by its very obvious white shoulder patches), the golden eagle and the eagle owl (the largest owl in Europe). Ornithologists should visit Monfragüe in May and June, botanists in March and April, and everybody should avoid July to September, when the heat is stifling.

The Green Route

The **Green Route**, to the Cerro Gimio, is especially good – a two-and-a-half-hour stroll looping through woods and across streams, in a landscape unimaginable from Villarreal, to a dramatic cliff-top viewing station.

The Red Route

The longer **Red Route** heads south of Villarreal, over a bridge across the Río Tajo, and past a fountain known as the Fuente del Francés after a young Frenchman who died there trying to save an eagle. Two kilometres farther is a great crag known as the Peñafalcón, which houses a large colony of griffon vultures, and the Castillo de Monfragüe, a castle ruin high up on a rock, with a chapel next to it; there is an observation post nearby. All these places are accessible from the EX208 and if you're coming in on the bus, you could ask to get off here. There are also two routes of 8km and 12km respectively that have been designed for **cars** and include a number of viewing points.

The dehesas

On the south side of the park, towards Trujillo, you pass through the **dehesas**, strange Africa-like plains, among the oldest woodlands in Europe. The economy of the *dehesas* is based on grazing, and the casualties among the domestic animals provide the vultures of Monfragüe with their daily bread. The information centre in Villarreal also provides details of routes that can be done on horseback or bicycle.

ARRIVAL AND DEPARTURE   PARQUE NATURAL DE MONFRAGÜE

By train The nearest train station is Monfragüe, 18km from Villarreal de San Carlos and a stop for slow trains on the Madrid–Cáceres line.

By bus There is just one bus along the road, which runs between Plasencia and Torrejón El Rubio (Mon–Fri; departs from Plasencia bus station 8.30am).

By car The easiest approach to the park is along the EX208 from Plasencia to Trujillo, which runs past the park headquarters at Villarreal de San Carlos.

INFORMATION

Information centre At the park's headquarters at Villarreal de San Carlos (daily: summer 9am–7.30pm; winter 9am–6pm; ☎927 199 134, ⓦmonfrague.com). Pick up a leaflet with a map detailing three colour-coded walks from the village and details about activities such as horseriding and walking in the park. There is also a seasonal shop, selling wildlife T-shirts and the like, and a useful guide to the park (in Spanish).

ACCOMMODATION AND EATING

VILLARREAL DE SAN CARLOS

Casa Rural El Cabrerin ☎927 199 002, ⓦelcabrerin .com. Four straightforward a/c rooms in this little *casa rural* which can also be rented out as a whole for larger groups. **€55**

Casa Rural Al Mofrag ☎927 199 205, ☎686 454 393, ⓦcasaruralalmofrag.com. Right in the centre of the park, close to the information centre, this *casa rural* has six simple, a/c, comfortable rooms and an outdoor pool open in summer. **€55**

Casa Rural Monfragüe ☎927 199 003, ⓦmonfrague rural.com. Owned by the same people as the *Cabrerin*, this *casa rural* has six large, airy a/c rooms with an option in some of them to add an extra bed. **€55**

TORREJÓN EL RUBIO
Hospedería Parque de Monfragüe ☎927 455 278, ⓦhospederiasdeextremadura.es. A more upmarket hotel with a pool and a good restaurant offering a range of local specialities and barbecues on the terrace in summer. Clean lines and simple decor in the 60 rooms. **€70**
Hotel Carvajal Pl. de Pizarro 54 ☎927 455 260, ⓦhotelcarvajal.es. Just to the south of the park, this thirteen-room hotel-restaurant is friendly and good value

for money. Breakfast included. **€60**

CAMPSITE
Camping Monfragüe 12km north of Villarreal on the Plasencia road ☎927 459 233, ⓦcampingmonfrague.com. A well-equipped, year-round site near the turning to the Monfragüe train station with a swimming pool and restaurant. It also has bikes for rent to get to Monfragüe. Two adults plus car **€28.40**.

Trujillo

TRUJILLO is the most attractive town in Extremadura: a classic **conquistador** stage set of escutcheoned mansions, stork-topped towers and castle walls. A very small place, still only a little larger than its extent in *conquistador* times. Much of it looks virtually untouched since the sixteenth century, and it is redolent above all of the exploits of the conquerors of the Americas; Francisco Pizarro, the conqueror of Peru, was born here, as were many of the tiny band who with such extraordinary cruelty aided him in defeating the Incas.

Plaza Mayor

At the centre of a dense web of streets is the **Plaza Mayor**, a grand square overlooked by a trio of palaces and churches, and ringed by a half-dozen cafés and restaurants, around which life for most visitors revolves. In the centre is a bronze statue of Pizarro – oddly, the gift of an American sculptor, one Carlos Rumsey, in 1929.

Palacio de la Conquista
In the square's southwest corner is the **Palacio de la Conquista**, the grandest of Trujillo's mansions with its roof adorned by statues representing the twelve months. Just one of

many built by the Pizarro clan, it was originally inhabited by Pizarro's half-brother and son-in-law Hernando, who returned from the conquests to live here with his half-Inca bride (Pizarro's daughter).

Iglesia de San Martín

Mon–Sat 10am–2pm & 4.30–7.30pm, Sun 10am–noon & 4.30–6.30pm • €1.40

Diagonally opposite the Palacio de la Conquista, and with a skyline of storks, is the bulky church of **San Martín**. Its tombs include, among others, that of the family of Francisco de Orellana, the first explorer of the Amazon.

Palacio de los Duques de San Carlos

Currently closed for renovation, though typically Mon–Sat 10am–1pm & 4.30–6.30pm, Sun 10am–12.30pm • €1.40

The **Palacio de los Duques de San Carlos** is home to a group of nuns who moved out of their dilapidated convent up the hill and restored this palace in return for the lodgings. The chimneys on the roof boast aggressively of cultures conquered by Catholicism in the New World – they are shaped like the pyramids of Aztecs, Incas and others subjected to Spanish rule.

Palacio de Juan Pizarro de Orellana

Closed for restoration, though typically Mon–Fri 10am–1pm & 4–6pm, Sat & Sun 11am–2pm & 4.30–6.30pm • Free

Of the many other town mansions, or **solares**, the most interesting is the **Palacio de Orellana-Pizarro**, just west of the main square. Go in through the superb Renaissance arched doorway to admire the courtyard, an elegant patio decorated with the alternating coats of arms of the Pizarros – two bears with a pine tree – and the Orellanas.

North of Plaza Mayor

From the plaza, c/Ballesteros leads up to the walled upper town, past the domed **Torre del Alfiler** with its coats of arms and storks' nests, and through the fifteenth-century gateway known as the **Arco de Santiago**.

Iglesia de Santiago

Daily: summer 10.30am–2pm & 4–7pm; winter 10.30am–2pm & 5–8pm • €1.50

Built up against the walls of the Arco de Santiago is the **Iglesia de Santiago**, which dates from the thirteenth century and was sometimes used as a venue for council meetings in the Middle Ages, while opposite it is the **Palacio de los Chaves**, which was where the Reyes Católicos, Fernando and Isabel, stayed when they were in town.

Iglesia de Santa María Mayor

Daily 10am–2pm & 4–7pm, summer closes 7.30pm • €1.40

The most interesting and important of the town's many churches, **Santa María Mayor** is located a short way up the hill beyond the gateway. The building is basically Gothic but contains a beautiful raised Renaissance *coro* noted for the technical mastery of its almost flat vaults. There is a fine Hispano-Flemish reredos by Fernando Gallego, and tombs including those of the Pizarros – Francisco was baptized here – and Diego García de Paredes, a man known as the "Sansón Extremeño" (Extremaduran Samson). Among other exploits, this giant of a man, armed only with his gargantuan sword, is said to have defended a bridge against an entire French army and to have picked up the font, now underneath the *coro*, to carry holy water to his mother. You are allowed to clamber up the **tower**, which provides magnificent views of the town, the parched plains over towards Cáceres, and the Sierra de Gredos.

Casa Museo Pizarro and Museo de la Coria

Casa Museo Pizarro Daily 10am–2pm & 4–7pm, summer opens and closes an hour later in the afternoons • €1.40 **Museo de la Coria** Sat, Sun & public hols 11.30am–2pm • Free

Located in the Pizarros' former residence, the **Casa Museo Pizarro** is a small, relatively dull affair, with little beyond period furniture and a few panels on the conquest of Peru.

For those who want to delve deeper, the **Museo de la Coria**, housed in an old Franciscan convent nearby, has more detailed exhibits on the Conquest.

The Castle

Daily 10am–2pm & 4–7pm, summer opens and closes an hour later in the afternoons • €1.40

The **castle** is now virtually in open countryside; for the last hundred metres of the climb you see nothing but the occasional broken-down remnant of a wall clambered over by sheep and dogs. The **fortress** itself, Moorish in origin but much reinforced by later defenders, has been restored, and its main attraction is the panoramic view of the town and its environs from the battlements. As you look out over the barren heath that rings Trujillo, the extent to which the old quarter has fallen into disrepair is abundantly evident, as is the castle's superb defensive position.

Museo de Queso y Vino

C/Francisco Pizarro • Daily 11am–3pm & 6–8pm • €2.30 • Ⓦ quesovino.com

Down towards the main road to Cáceres and housed in a former convent is the **Museo de Queso y Vino**, showcasing two of the region's star products with displays on how they are made, taster sessions and a shop selling a range of local delicacies.

ARRIVAL AND DEPARTURE | TRUJILLO

By bus The town is well served by buses, with up to ten a day to and from Madrid (4–5hr) and eight from Cáceres (45min). Coming in by bus, you'll arrive in the lower town, just 5min walk from the Pl. Mayor.

By car If you're driving, follow the signs to the Pl. Mayor, and with luck you should be able to park beyond the square and farther along c/García de Paredes.

INFORMATION

Turismo Pl. Mayor (daily 11am–2pm & 4.30–7.30pm; ☎ 927 322 677, Ⓦ trujillo.es). Sells discount tickets for combined visits to some of the main sites (€4.70–5.30) and provides guided tours (in Spanish) of the town at 11am and 5pm (€7.95).

ACCOMMODATION

Trujillo could be visited easily enough as a day-trip from Cáceres, but it's definitely worth staying the night. **Places to stay** are in high demand – so book ahead if you can. The *turismo* can provide accommodation lists. The best rooms are in the old town close to the Pl. Mayor.

★ **Casa de Orellana** c/Palomas 5–7 ☎ 927 659 265, Ⓦ casadeorellana.com. Just four doubles and a single in this delightful and exclusive little hotel located in a fabulous refurbished fifteenth-century mansion close to the Pl. Mayor. Price includes breakfast. **€140**

Hostal La Cadena Pl. Mayor 8 ☎ 927 321 463. A homely *hostal*, with simple a/c rooms overlooking all the action, and a decent restaurant. **€40**

Hostal Trujillo c/Francisco Pizarro 4–6 ☎ 927 322 274, Ⓦ hostaltrujillo.com. A pleasant *pensión* situated in a fifteenth-century building between the Pl. Mayor and the bus station. Twenty a/c rooms and a good restaurant. **€50**

Hotel Victoria Pl. de Campillo 22 ☎ 927 321 819, Ⓦ hotelvictoriatrujillo.es. A friendly hotel in an elegant old nineteenth-century mansion, with a pool, restaurant and comfortable en-suite rooms. **€75**

Izan Trujillo Pl. del Campillo 1 ☎ 927 458 900, Ⓦ izanhoteles.es. Situated in the converted Convento de San Antonio, this swish four-star hotel has 72 classically decorated double rooms and a swimming pool. **€150**

★ **El Mirador de las Monjas** Pl. de Santiago 2 ☎ 927 659 223, Ⓦ elmiradordelasmonjas.com. Up in the old part of town by the castle, this homely *hostería* has five comfy rooms with modern bathrooms and a good restaurant serving some excellent local produce. **€50**

Palacio Santa María c/Ballesteros 6 ☎ 927 659 190, Ⓦ nh-hotels.com. A chain hotel, but more atmospheric than its brethren, set in a beautiful refurbished sixteenth-century mansion and tucked down a small street behind the Pl. Mayor. Slick, modern facilities, including a rooftop pool. **€90**

Parador de Trujillo Pl. Santa Beatriz de Silva ☎ 927 321 350, Ⓦ paradores.com. Top-end accommodation in a

sixteenth-century former *convento* north of the Pl. Mayor. Two beautiful cloistered patio areas and large rooms. **€163**
Pensión Emilia c/Pl. Campillo 28 ☎927 320 083, ⓦlaemilia.com. A clean and comfortable *pensión* located down by the main road into town with warm, classical decor and a restaurant and bar downstairs. **€50**

★ **Posada dos Orillas** c/Cambrones 6 ☎927 659 079 ⓦdosorillas.com. Thirteen individually designed rooms in this converted inn in the heart of the old quarter. It has a delightful patio area where you can have breakfast and a restaurant serving up some imaginative, well-presented salads and local specialities. **€70**

EATING AND DRINKING

There are plenty of **bar-restaurants** on the Pl. Mayor, and for budget eating, all the *pensiones* around Pl. Campillo have reasonably priced *menús* on offer. At the weekend, **nightlife** revolves around the streets splaying out of Pl. Mayor and down in the newer parts of town.

Bizcocho Pl. Mayor 11 ☎927 322 017, ⓦrestaurante bizcochotrujillo.com. A reliable restaurant serving regional specialities and good meat dishes. It has two separate dining areas and a summer terrace looking out on to the plaza. Around €40 a head.
El Burladero Pl. Mayor 7. A good bar to start the night, serving imaginative tapas and a decent selection of wine.
Emilia c/Pl. Campillo 28 ☎927 321 216, ⓦlaemilia. com. A *pensión* located down towards the main road, which offers one of the most competitive *menús* in town.
La Majada ☎927 320 349. Situated some 4km south of town on the road to Mérida in a pleasant garden with a play area for children. Good fish, local sausages and partridge. Around €35–40 a head. Closed Mon.

Mesón La Troya Pl. Mayor 10 ☎927 321 364. Trujillo's best-known restaurant. Offers a huge *menú* for €15 although it is a case of quantity over quality and they'll probably serve you a giant *tortilla* as a starter before you have even ordered.
★ **Pizarro** Pl. Mayor 13 ☎927 310 925. Rather better quality food than *La Troya* and more manageable quantities, costing around €30 à la carte, and about half that for the *menú*. Closed Tues.
La Sonata c/Ballesteros 10 ☎927 322 884, ⓦlasonata .es. Tucked away in a street just north of the Pl. Mayor, this serves some well-presented Extremeño specialities. It does a tasty *menú* for €14 and a more sophisticated version featuring mains such as wild boar, lamb and salmon for €23.

Guadalupe

The small town of **GUADALUPE**, perched up in the sierra to the west of Trujillo, is dominated in every way by the great **Monasterio de Nuestra Señora de Guadalupe**, which for five centuries has brought fame and pilgrims to the area. It was established in 1340, on the spot where an ancient image of the Virgin, said to have been carved by St Luke, was discovered by a shepherd fifty or so years earlier. The delay was simply a question of waiting for the Reconquest to arrive in this remote sierra, with its lush countryside of forests and streams.

In the fifteenth and sixteenth centuries, Guadalupe was among the most important pilgrimage centres in Spain: Columbus named the Caribbean island in honour of the Virgin here, and a local version was adopted as the patron saint of Mexico. Much of the monastic wealth, in fact, came from returning **conquistadores**, whose successive endowments led to a fascinating mix of styles. The **monastery** was abandoned in the nineteenth-century Dissolution, but was later reoccupied by Franciscans, who continue to maintain it.

The town itself is a fitting complement to the monastery and countryside: a net of narrow cobbled streets and overhanging houses constructed around the Plaza Mayor, the whole overshadowed by the monastery's bluff ramparts. There's a timeless feel, only slightly diminished by modern development on the outskirts, and a brisk trade in plastic copies of religious treasures.

The church and monastery

Church Daily 8.30am–9pm • Free **Monastery** Daily 9.30am–1pm & 3.30–6.30pm • Guided tour €4, 6–14-year-olds €1.50 • ⓦmonasterioguadalupe.com

The **monastery church** opens onto the Plaza Mayor (aka Plaza de Santa María). Its gloomy Gothic interior is, like the rest of the monastery, packed with treasures from generations of wealthy patrons.

The entrance to the **monastery** proper is to the left of the church. The (compulsory) guided tour begins with a Mudéjar **cloister** – two brick storeys of horseshoe arches with a strange pavilion or tabernacle in the middle – and moves on to the **museums**, with an apparently endless collection of rich vestments, early illuminated manuscripts and religious paraphernalia, along with some fine artworks including a triptych by Isenbrandt and a small Goya. The **Sacristía**, beyond, is the finest room in the monastery. Unaltered since it was built in the seventeenth century, it contains eight paintings by Zurbarán, which, uniquely, can be seen in their original context – the frames match the window frames and the pictures themselves are a planned part of the decoration of the room.

Climbing higher into the heart of the monastery, you pass through various rooms filled with jewels and relics before the final ascent to the Holy of Holies – the Camarín. From this tiny room high above the main altar you can look down over the church while a panel is spun away to reveal the highlight of the tour – the bejewelled and richly dressed **image of the Virgin**. The Virgin is one of the few black icons ever made – originally carved out of dark cedarwood, its colour has further deepened over the centuries under innumerable coats of varnish. The story goes that the image was originally carved by St Luke, made its way to Spain and was then hidden during the Arab occupation for over five hundred years. It was eventually rediscovered by a local cowherd on the banks of the Río Guadalupe at the beginning of the thirteenth century.

On the way out, drop in at the **Hospedería del Real Monasterio**, around to the right. The bar, in its Gothic cloister, with lovely gardens outside, is one of the world's more unusual places to enjoy a *Cuba libre*.

3

ARRIVAL AND DEPARTURE

GUADALUPE

By bus Buses leave from either side of Avenida de Barcelona, uphill from the *ayuntamiento*, 200m from the Pl. Mayor: Mirat operates services to Trujillo and Cáceres, Avanzabus runs buses to Madrid (some change at Talavera de a Reina).

Destinations Cáceres (2 daily; 2hr 30min); Madrid (3 daily; 3hr 15min); Mérida (4 daily; 2hr); Trujillo (2 daily; 2hr–2hr 30min).

INFORMATION

Turismo Pl. Mayor (summer Tues–Fri 10am–2pm & 5–7pm, Sat & Sun 10am–2pm; winter Tues–Fri 10am–2pm & 4–6pm, Sat & Sun 10am–2pm; ☎927 154 128, ⓦ puebladeguadalupe.net).

ACCOMMODATION

There are plenty of **places to stay** in Guadalupe and the only times you're likely to have difficulty finding a room are during Easter Week or around September 8, the Virgin's festival day.

★ **Hospedaría del Real Monasterio** Pl. Juan Carlos s/n ☎927 367 000, ⓦmonasterioguadalupe.com. Housed in a wing of the monastery and popular with Spanish pilgrims, it's much better value than the parador, very atmospheric and serves excellent food in the giant dining room, too. **€65**

Hostal Alba Taruta c/Alfonso Onceno 16 ☎927 254 144, ⓦhostalalbataruta.com. Friendly, family-run *hostal* close to the main plaza with simple old-style rooms. The *comedor* downstairs serves an inexpensive range of *platos*. **€55**

Hostal Isabel Pl. Santa María 13 ☎927 367 126, ⓦhostalisabelguadalupe.es. A modern *hostal* offering neat, comfortable rooms with bath, and a bar downstairs.

They have another branch with the same name next to the parador with antique furnished rooms and a/c for the same price. **€40**

Parador de Guadalupe c/Marqués de la Romana 12 ☎927 367 075, ⓦparadores.com. A beautiful parador, housed in a fifteenth-century hospital and a former school, with a swimming pool and immaculate patio gardens. **€144**

CAMPSITE

Las Villuercas ☎927 367 139. Some 2km out of town towards Trujillo, close to the main road. A quiet campsite with a pool and bar-restaurant. Open all year. Two adults plus car **€12**.

EATING AND DRINKING

You can **eat** at most *hostales* and *pensiones*, with just about everywhere – including the restaurants on Pl. Mayor – serving *menús* for around €10.

Hospedaría del Real Monasterio Pl. Juan Carlos s/n 927 367 000, monasterioguadalupe.com. A great setting for a meal with a choice of the grand dining room or the outdoor courtyard. Meals will cost between €25–35, but they also do a set menu for under €20.

Mesón del Cordero c/Alfonso Onceno 27 927 367 131. Serves good home-cooking with grand views from the dining room thrown in. Roast lamb and local vegetable produce are the specialities. Good value at around €25–30 a head. Closed Mon.

The Sierra de Guadalupe

A truly superb view of Guadalupe set in its sierra can also be enjoyed from the road (EX118) north to Navalmoral. Five kilometres out of town, the **Ermita del Humilladero** marks the spot where pilgrims to the shrine traditionally caught their first glimpse of the monastery.

The surrounding **Sierra de Guadalupe** is a wild and beautiful region, with steep, rocky crags abutting the valley sides. If you have your own transport, you could strike northwest of the EX102 at Cañamero, up to the village of **Cabañas del Castillo**, nestling against a massive crag and ruined castle; the handful of houses are mostly empty, as only twelve inhabitants remain. Beyond here, you can reach the main **Navalmoral–Trujillo road** close to the **Puerto de Miravete**, a fabulous viewpoint, with vistas of Trujillo in the far distance. Another great driving route, again leaving the EX102 at Cañamero, is to follow the narrow road **through Berzocana** to Trujillo.

Cáceres

CÁCERES is in many ways remarkably like Trujillo. It features an almost perfectly preserved walled town, the Ciudad Monumental, packed with *solares* built on the proceeds of American exploration, while every available tower and spire is crowned by a clutch of storks' nests. As a provincial capital, however, Cáceres is a much larger and livelier place, especially in term time, when the students of the University of Extremadura are in residence. With its Roman, Moorish and *conquistador* sights, and a number of great bars and restaurants, it is an absorbing and highly enjoyable city. It also provides a dramatic backdrop for an annual **WOMAD** festival, held over the second weekend in May and attracting up to 70,000 spectators.

The walled **Old Town** stands at the heart of Cáceres, with a picturesque **Plaza Mayor** just outside its walls. These are basically Moorish in construction, though parts date back to the Romans – notably the **Arco del Cristo** – and they have been added to, refortified and built against throughout the centuries. The most intact section, with several original adobe Moorish towers, runs in a clockwise direction, facing the walls from the Plaza Mayor. Almost everything of interest is contained within – or a short walk from – this area; try and base yourself as close to it as possible.

The Old Town

Entering the Old Town – the **Parte Vieja**, as it's also known – from the Plaza Mayor, you pass through the low **Arco de la Estrella**, an entrance built by Manuel Churriguera in the eighteenth century. To your left, at the corner of the walls, is one of the most imposing *conquistador solares*, the **Casa de Toledo-Moctezuma** with its domed tower. It was to this house that a follower of Cortés brought back one of the New World's more exotic prizes, a daughter of the Aztec emperor, as his bride. The building houses the provincial historical archives, and also stages occasional exhibitions.

Walking straight ahead through the Arco de la Estrella brings you into the **Plaza de Santa María**, flanked by another major *solar*, the Casa de los Golfines de Abajo and the Palacio Episcopal.

Concatedral de Santa María and Palacio de los Carvajal

Pl. de Santa María **Concatedral de Santa María** Mon–Fri 10am–2pm & 4.30–8pm, Sat 9.30am–12.50 & 4–6.15pm, Sun 9.30–11.50am & 5–6.15pm, opens and closes an hour later in the afternoons in summer • €1 for museum **Palacio de los Carvajal** Daily 8am–9pm • Free

3

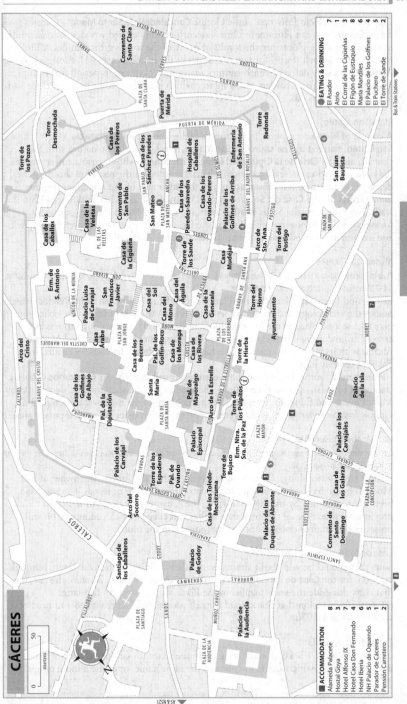

CÁCERES

0 — 50 metres

● EATING & DRINKING
El Asador	7
Atrio	1
El Corral de las Cigüeñas	3
El Figón de Eustaquio	8
María Mandiles	6
El Palacio de los Golfines	4
El Puchero	5
El Torre de Sande	2

Bus & Train Stations ▶

■ ACCOMMODATION
Alameda Palacete	8
Hostal Goya	3
Hotel Alfonso IX	7
Hotel Casa Don Fernando	4
Hotel Iberia	6
NH Palacio de Oquendo	5
Parador de Cáceres	1
Pensión Carretero	2

▼ N521 & A-5

Opposite the Palacio Episcopal is the Gothic **Concatedral de Santa María** – Cáceres' finest. Inside, you can illuminate a fine sixteenth-century carved wooden *retablo*, while in the surrounding gloom are the tombs of many of the town's great families. Climb the *campanario* (bell tower) for fantastic views of the historic core (€1). Alongside is the **Palacio de los Carvajal**, a fifteenth-century mansion decked out in period furnishings and concealing a patio garden with a fig tree which is believed to be between three and four hundred years old.

Plaza San Mateo

A couple of blocks southwest, at the town's highest point, is the **Plaza de San Mateo**, flanked by the **church of San Mateo**, another Gothic structure with fine chapels, and the **Casa de la Cigüeña** (House of the Stork), whose narrow tower was the only one allowed to preserve its original battlements when the rest were shorn by royal decree. It is now a military installation. On the other side of the square, notice the **family crests** on the **Casa del Sol**, and indeed on many of the other buildings within the walls. Near the Casa del Sol is another *solar*, the **Casa del Mono** (House of the Monkey), which is now a public library; the facade is adorned with grotesque gargoyles and a stone monkey is chained to the staircase in the courtyard.

Museo de Cáceres

Pl. de las Veletas • Mid-April to Sept Tues–Sat 9am–2.30pm & 5–8.15pm, Sun 10.15am–2.30pm; Oct to mid-April Tues–Sat 9am–2.30pm & 4–7.15pm, Sun 10.15–2.30pm • €1.20, EU citizens free

Just behind Plaza San Mateo, in the Plaza de las Veletas, is the **Casa de las Veletas**, which houses the archeology and ethnology sections of the **Museo de Cáceres**. The collections here take second place to the building itself: its beautifully proportioned rooms are arrayed around a small patio and preserve the *aljibe* (cistern) of the original Moorish Alcázar with its horseshoe arches. It also has an extraordinary balustrade, created from Talavera ceramic jugs.

From here, a footbridge leads to the museum's art collection in the **Casa de los Caballos** (House of Horses), open mornings only. The modern art and sculpture includes works by Miró, Picasso and Eduardo Arroyo, while the highlight of the medieval section is El Greco's *Jesús Salvador*. There is also a temporary exhibition space for contemporary artists.

Casa Árabe/Museo Yusuf Al Burch

Cuesta del Marqués 4 • Variable hours but generally daily summer 10.30am–2pm & 5–8pm, winter Mon & Tues 10.30am–2pm, Wed–Sun 10.30am–2pm & 4.30–7pm • €1.50

A short stroll away along c/Rincón de la Monja is the **Casa Árabe**. The owner of this Moorish house has had the bright idea of decorating it more or less as it would have been when occupied by its original owner. The Alhambra it's not, but it at least provides a context for all the horseshoe arches and curving brick ceilings and it still possesses the original cistern supplied by water from the roof.

Casa de los Golfines de Arriba

Something could be said about almost every other building in the Old Town, but look out, too, for the **Casa de los Golfines de Arriba** on c/Adarve Padre Rosalío, the alleyway that runs alongside the walls parallel to the Plaza Mayor. It was in this latter *conquistador* mansion that Franco had himself proclaimed Generalísimo and head of state in October 1936.

Outside the walls

Outside the walls, it's worth wandering up to the sixteenth-century **church of Santiago de los Caballeros**, which fronts the plaza of the same name, opposite a more or less contemporary mansion, **Palacio de Godoy**, with its corner balcony. The church, open only for Masses, has a fine *retablo* by Alonso Berruguete.

For a good view of the Old Town, exit the walls through the Arco del Cristo down to the main road and turn right onto c/Fuente Concejo, following the signs for about five minutes or so.

ARRIVAL AND DEPARTURE   CÁCERES

By train or bus Both the train and bus stations are around 3km out from the old town, at the far end of Avda. de Alemania. It's not a particularly enjoyable walk, so it's best to take bus #1, which runs down the *avenida* to Pl. de San Juan, a square adjoining the Pl. Mayor; an irregular shuttle bus from the train station (free if you show a rail ticket) also runs into town, to the Pl. de América, a major traffic junction west of the Old Town.

Train destinations Badajoz (3 daily; 2hr); Lisbon (daily; 5hr 50min); Madrid (5 daily; 4hr); Mérida (5 daily; 1hr).

Bus destinations Alcántara (2 daily; 1hr 30min); Badajoz (3 daily; 1hr 15min–1hr 45min); Coria (3 daily; 1hr 15min); Madrid (8 daily; 3hr 40min–4hr 45min); Mérida (4 daily; 1hr); Plasencia (4–5 daily; 1hr 20min); Salamanca (4 daily; 3hr 30min); Seville (8 daily; 4hr); Trujillo (6 daily; 40min–1hr).

By car If you're driving, be warned that increasing pedestrianization is making access to some streets impossible by car; your best bet is to park on Avda. de España, on the main road in from Madrid, or outside the Old Town.

INFORMATION

Turismo Pl. Mayor (Mon–Fri 9am–2pm & 4–6pm, summer 8am–3pm, Sat & Sun 10am–2pm; ☎927 010 834, ⓦturismoextremadura.com & ⓦturismo.caceres.es). In addition to this regional *turismo* there is a municipal office

(summer Tues–Sun 10am–2pm & 5.30–8.30pm; winter Tues–Sun 10am–2pm & 4.30–7.30pm, ☎927 247 172) opposite the parador in the Old Town at c/Olmo 11.

ACCOMMODATION

It's worth noting that **accommodation** right on the Pl. Mayor can get rather noisy at night.

★ **Alameda Palacete** c/Margallo 45 ☎927 211 674, ⓦalamedapalacete.com. Nine fascinatingly decorated rooms, each with its own individual ambience in this delightful little hotel not far from the Pl. Mayor. Suites are available from €85–100. Breakfast included. **€70**

Hostal Goya Pl. Mayor 11 ☎927 249 950. A good-value *hostal* on the Pl. Mayor, with simple, old-fashioned en-suite rooms. Those with views over the plaza are an extra €10. **€50**

Hotel Alfonso IX c/Moret 20 ☎927 246 400, ⓦhotelalfonsoix.com. Well located on a pedestrianized street off c/Pintores, this hotel offers smart en-suite rooms with a/c, satellite TV and free wi-fi. **€75**

★ **Hotel Casa Don Fernando** Pl. Mayor 30 ☎927 214 279, ⓦcasadonfernando.com. Perfectly situated on the main plaza, this slick, designer-style hotel has 36 stylishly furnished doubles and a decent café-bar. **€100**

Hotel Iberia c/Pintores 2 ☎927 247 634, ⓦiberiahotel

.com. A tastefully restored 38-room hotel with classically decorated rooms in a corner of the Pl. Mayor. Breakfast included. **€75**

NH Palacio de Oquendo Pl. de San Juan 11 ☎927 215 800, ⓦnh-hotels.com. Now part of the NH chain, this smart, well-appointed hotel is in a sixteenth-century palace, just outside the walls of the Old Town, and is in many ways a nicer and certainly better value place than the parador. **€85**

Parador de Cáceres c/Ancha 6 ☎927 211 759, ⓦparadores.com. The parador occupies an elegant and atmospheric *conquistador* mansion in the Ciudad Monumental – the only hotel within the walls. **€168**

Pensión Carretero Pl. Mayor 22–23 ☎927 247 482, ⓦcaceresjoven.com. Best value in town – very basic, large rooms, spotless bathrooms and a TV lounge – though some rooms can be noisy at the weekend. **€30**

EATING, DRINKING AND NIGHTLIFE

There is a good range of **bars**, **restaurants** and **bodegas** in and around the Pl. Mayor, while the Old Town offers a bit more style at modest prices. Cáceres has the best nightlife in the region – especially during term time – with the night starting off in the bars along c/Pizarro, south of Pl. de San Juan, moving on to c/Dr Fleming and the discos in the nearby Pl. de Albatros. There are several late-night bars around Pl. Mayor and a string of interesting watering holes in and around c/Donoso Cortés, while live music can be heard in many places along the nearby c/General Ezponda.

3

RESTAURANTS

El Asador c/Moret 34 ☎ 927 223 837. A reasonably priced restaurant, off c/Pintores, serving great-tasting local dishes and fronted by a popular tapas bar. Daily around 1.30–4pm & 8.30pm–midnight.

Atrio Pl. de San Mateo 1 ☎ 927 242 928, ⓦ restauranteatrio.com. An exclusive Michelin-starred restaurant, now relocated in the Old Town, with an extensive menu and sophisticated food. Allow at least €60 per head and the *menú de degustación* is double that; keep an eye on the price of the wine too. Closed Sun eve.

★ **El Figón de Eustaquio** Pl. de San Juan 12 ☎ 927 244 362, ⓦ elfigondeeustaquio.com. This long-established and popular restaurant features an extensive list of regional dishes, cooked with care. Allow €25–30 a head, although there are a range of lunchtime *menús* from €17–22. Daily around 1.30–4pm & 8.30pm–midnight.

El Palacio de los Golfines c/Adarve Padre Rosalío 2 ☎ 927 242 414, ⓦ palaciogolfines.es. Stylishly presented food in a magnificent setting in an old palace just inside the city walls. There's an extensive wine list, too. Expect to pay around €35. Closed Sun eve.

El Puchero Pl. Mayor 10 ☎ 927 232 241, ⓦ restaurant eelpuchero.com. The cheapest restaurant on the plaza, with an ever-popular terraza; home-style cooking but as you would expect, the food is not outstanding. Closed Mon.

★ **El Torre de Sande** c/Los Condes 3 ☎ 927 211 147, ⓦ torredesande.com. Another top-class restaurant in the middle of the Old Town, it has refined food and attentive service for around €45 a head or a set menu for €35. There is a delightful summer terrace serving tapas and *raciones* too. Closed Sun eve & Mon.

BARS

★ **El Corral de las Cigüeñas** Cuesta de Aldana 6. A beautiful spot in the Old Town with tables in a large, palm-shaded courtyard. A great place to enjoy a breakfast snack, a lunchtime *aperitivo* or a night-time cocktail. Live music and other acts.

María Mandiles c/Sergio Sanchéz 7. This popular bar a few minutes' walk to the northwest of the Old Town is hard to miss with its pink exterior and dark wooden decor. A good music selection at night with 80s and 90s classics at weekends.

Northwest of Cáceres

Northwest of Cáceres is the vast **Embalse de Alcántara**, one of a series of reservoirs harnessing the power of the Río Tajo in the last few kilometres before it enters Portugal. The scheme swallowed up large tracts of land and you can see the old road and railway to Plasencia disappearing into the depths of the reservoir (their replacements cross the many inlets on double-decker bridges), along with the tower of a castle.

The EX207 loops away to the south of the reservoir, through **Arroyo de la Luz** and **Brozas**, each with fine churches, before reaching **Alcántara**, with its superb Roman bridge across the Tajo. The Portuguese border – and the road to Costelo Branco and Coimbra – is just a dozen kilometres beyond.

Alcántara

The name **ALCÁNTARA** comes from the Arabic for "bridge" – in this case a beautiful six-arched **Puente Romano** spanning a gorge of the Río Tajo. Completed in 105 AD, and held together without mortar, it was reputed to be the loftiest bridge ever built in the Roman Empire, although it's far from certain which bits, if any, remain genuinely Roman.

The bridge is quite a distance from the town itself, which is built high above the river; if you're on foot, don't follow the signs via the road – instead, head to the far side of the town and down the steep cobbled path.

Further Roman remains include a **triumphal arch** dedicated to Trajan and a tiny **classical temple**. The dominating landmark, however, is the restored **Convento San Benito**, erstwhile headquarters of the Knights of Alcántara, one of the great orders of the Reconquest. For all its enormous bulk, the convent and its church are only a fragment; the nave of the church was never built. Outside, the main feature is the double-arcaded Renaissance gallery at the back; it serves as the backdrop for a season of classical plays in August. Entry to the convent (frequent guided tours all day Tues–Sat & Sun morning; free) is through the adjacent Fundación de San Benito, which has been making attempts to restore the cloister and the Plateresque east end with its elaborate wall-tombs.

Alcántara also contains the scanty remains of a **castle**, numerous **mansions** and street after street of humble whitewashed houses. The place is marvellous for scenic walks, whether in the town, along the banks of the Tajo or – best of all – in the hills on the opposite bank.

ARRIVAL AND INFORMATION   ALCÁNTARA

By bus Buses, which run twice a day to and from Cáceres, stop at a little square ringed by cafés at the entrance to the historic part of the town.

Turismo Avda. de Mérida 21 (May–Sept Tues–Fri 10am–

2pm & 5–7pm, Sat & Sun 10.30am–2.30pm; Oct–April Tues–Fri 10am–2pm & 4–6pm, Sat & Sun 10.30am–12.30pm; ☎ 927 390 863, ⓦ alcantara.es). Very helpful and can provide a town map.

ACCOMMODATION

Hospedería Conventual Carretera Poblado de Iberdrola s/n ☎ 927 390 367, ⓦ hospederiasdeextremadura.es. A little way to the north of the town this good-value 28-room hotel is housed in a beautifully restored fifteenth-century convent. Large rooms, modern bathrooms, a pool and a good restaurant. **€70**

Puente de Alcántara Crta. EX117, Finca Los Cabezos de Alcántara ☎ 927 390 934, ⓦ campingalcantara .com. Shady, grass pitches in this campsite which also has bungalows for hire, a pool and good views. They can help organize birdwatching trips, hikes and excursions on bikes and horseback. Two adults plus car **€18**.

Mérida

Some 70km to the south of Cáceres on the N630, the former capital of the Roman province of Lusitania, **MÉRIDA** (the name is a corruption of *Augusta Emerita*), contains more **Roman remains** than any other city in Spain. Even for the most casually interested, the extent and variety of the remains here are compelling, with everything from engineering works to domestic villas, by way of cemeteries and places of worship, entertainment and culture. With a little imagination, and a trip to the wonderful modern museum, the Roman city is not difficult to evoke – which is just as well, for the modern city, in which the sites are scattered, is no great shakes.

Each July and August, the Roman theatre in Mérida hosts a **theatre festival** (ⓦ festivaldemerida.es), including performances of classical Greek plays and Shakespeare's Roman tragedies.

The Roman sites

Built on the site of a Celto-Iberian settlement and founded by Emperor Augustus in 25 BC as a home for retired legionaries, Mérida became the tenth city of the Roman Empire and the final stop on the Vía de la Plata, the Roman road that began in Astorga in northern Castile. The old city stretched as far as the modern bullring and Roman circus, covering only marginally less than the triangular area occupied by the modern town.

The Puente Romano and Alcazaba

Alcazaba combined ticket or €4

The obvious point to begin your tour is the magnificent **Puente Romano**, the bridge across the islet-strewn Río Guadiana. It is sixty arches long (the seven in the middle are fifteenth-century replacements) and was still in use until the early 1990s, when the nearby **Puente de Lusitania** – itself a structure to admire – was constructed by Spanish architect Santiago Calatrava.

Defence of the old bridge was provided by a vast **Alcazaba**, built by the Moors to replace a Roman construction. The interior is a rather barren archeological site, although in the middle there's an *aljibe* to which you can descend by either of a pair of staircases.

Templo de Diana to the Arco Trajano

Museo de Arte Visigodo Tues–Sun: summer 10am–2pm & 5–7pm; winter 10am–2pm & 4–6pm • Free

Northeast of the Alcazaba, past the airy sixteenth-century Plaza de España, the heart of the modern town, is the so-called **Templo de Diana**, adapted into a Renaissance

3

MÉRIDA

EATING & DRINKING		ACCOMMODATION	
Bar-Restaurante Briz	1	La Flor de al-Andalus	1
Casa Benito	4	Hostal El Alfarero	5
Casa Nano	6	Hostal Bueno	2
Restaurante Nicolás	2	Hostal Senero	4
Restaurante Rufino	5	Hotel Adealba	7
La Tahona Nueva	3	Hotel Mérida Palace	6
		Parador Vía de la Plata	3

mansion, and farther along are remains of the **Foro**, the heart of the Roman city. To the west of the plaza in c/Santa Julia, the Convento de Santa Clara houses the **Museo de Arte Visigodo**, with a collection of about a hundred lapidary items. It will eventually be housed alongside the Museo Nacional de Arte Romano. Just behind here is the great **Arco Trajano**, once wrongly believed to be a triumphal arch; it was, in fact, a marble-clad granite monumental gate to the forum.

Morerías archeological site
Combined ticket or €4

Heading to the river from the Arco Trajano you'll also discover the **Morerías archeological site** along c/Morerías, where you can watch the digging and preservation of houses and factories from Roman through Visigoth to Moorish times – particularly of interest are the well-preserved Roman mosaics.

Teatro Romano, Anfiteatro and Casa Romana del Anfiteatro
Teatro Romano and Anfiteatro Combined ticket or €8 **Casa Romana del Anfiteatro** Combined ticket or €4

A ten-minute walk east of the Plaza de España will take you to Mérida's main archeological site containing the theatre and amphitheatre. The elaborate and beautiful **Teatro Romano** is one of the best preserved anywhere in the Roman Empire. Constructed around 15 BC, it was a present to the city from Agrippa, as indicated by the large inscription above the passageway to the left of the stage. The stage itself, a two-tier colonnaded affair, is in particularly good shape, and many of the seats have been entirely rebuilt to offer more comfort to the audiences of the annual July and August season of classical plays (ⓦfestivaldemerida.es).

Adjoining the theatre is the **Anfiteatro**, a slightly later and very much plainer construction. As many as 15,000 people – almost half the current population of Mérida – could be seated to watch gladiatorial combats and fights with wild animals. The **Casa Romana del Anfiteatro** lies immediately below the museum, and offers an approach to it from the site. It has wonderful mosaics, including a vigorous depiction of grape-treading.

The Museo Nacional de Arte Romano
March–Nov Tues–Sat 10am–2pm & 4–9pm, Sun 10am–2pm; Dec–Feb Tues–Sat 10am–2pm & 4–6pm, Sun 10am–2pm • €3, free Sat pm & Sun am

The **Museo Nacional de Arte Romano**, constructed in 1986 above the Roman walls, is a wonderfully light, accessible building, using a free interpretation of classical forms to present the mosaics and sculpture as if emerging from the ruins. The exhibits, displayed on three levels of the basilica-like hall, include statues from the theatre, the Roman villa of **Mithraeus** (Mitreo; see p.214) and the vanished forum, and a number of mosaics – the largest being hung on the walls so that they can be examined at each level. Individually, the finest exhibits are probably the three statues, displayed together, depicting Augustus, the first Roman emperor; his son Tiberius, the second emperor; and Drusus, Augustus' heir apparent until (it is alleged) he was murdered by Livia, Tiberius' mother.

COMBINED TICKET

The best way to see the Roman sights is to buy the excellent-value **combined ticket**, costing €12 (9–16-year-olds, pensioners and holders of student cards €6 if EU citizens) and valid over a number of days. It covers the Teatro Romano and Anfiteatro, the Roman villas Casa del Anfiteatro and Casa del Mitreo, the Columbarios burial ground, the Circo Romano, the archeological site at Morerías, the Alcazaba and the Basílica de Santa Eulalia (all daily: summer 9.30am–1.45pm & 5–7.15pm; winter 4–6.15pm) though not the Museo de Arte Romano, and is available at any of the sites.

The ruins outside the centre

Santa Eulalia, Mitreo and Columbarios burial ground all combined ticket or €4 each

The remaining monuments are on the other side of the train tracks. From the museum, it's a fifteen-minute walk if you cut down the streets towards Avenida de Extremadura and then head east out of the city to the **Circo Romano**, essentially an outline, where up to 30,000 spectators could watch horse and chariot races. Across the road from here, a stretch of the **Acueducto de San Lázaro** leads off towards the Río Albarregas.

The more impressive aqueduct, however, is the **Acueducto de los Milagros**, of which a satisfying portion survives in the midst of vegetable gardens, west of the train station. Its tall arches of granite, with brick courses, brought water to the city in its earliest days from the reservoir at Proserpina, 5km away. The best view of the aqueduct is from a low and inconspicuous **Puente Romano** across the Río Albarregas; it was over this span that the Vía de la Plata entered the city.

Two further sights are the church of **Santa Eulalia**, by the train station, which has a porch made from fragments of a former temple of Mars, and a second Roman villa, the **Mitreo**, in the shadow of the Plaza de Toros, south of the museum and theatres. The villa has a magnificent but damaged mosaic depicting the cosmos. A short walk away is the **Columbarios burial ground** with two family sepulchres and an interesting series of exhibits on Roman death rites.

Proserpina and Cornalvo reservoirs

You can swim in the **Embalse de Proserpina**, a Roman-constructed reservoir 5km north of town (special buses from Paseo de Roma, May–Aug; €1), and a popular escape to cool off in summer; it's lined with holiday homes, has a campsite and a small beach area but is best avoided at weekends. Alternatively, if you have transport, head to the **Embalse de Cornalvo**, 18km east of Mérida (turn left after the village of Trujillanos). There's a Roman dyke here, and a small national park has been created in the area with walking trails in the surrounding forest.

ARRIVAL AND DEPARTURE   MÉRIDA

By train The train station is pretty central, with the theatre site and Pl. de España no more than 10min walk away.
Destinations Badajoz (7 daily; 45min); Cáceres (4 daily; 1hr); Madrid (4 daily; 4hr 30min–5hr 50min); Plasencia (2 daily; 2hr 25min); Seville (daily; 4hr 35min).
By bus The bus station is on the other side of the river and is a grittier 20min walk from the town centre, along

Avda. de Libertad, which extends from the new single-arch bridge.
Destinations Badajoz (8 daily; 45min); Cáceres (7 daily; 1hr); Jerez de los Caballeros (1–3 daily; 2hr); Madrid (8–9 daily; 4hr 20min); Murcia (daily; 9hr); Salamanca (5 daily; 4hr); Seville (6–8 daily; 3hr 15min, some stopping in Zafra); Trujillo (4 daily; 2hr); Zafra (1–3 daily; 1hr 10min).

INFORMATION

Oficina de Turismo Just outside the gates to the theatre and amphitheatre site (summer daily 9.30am–2pm & 5–8pm; winter daily 9.30am–2pm & 4.30–7pm; ☎924 330 722). There are other offices (daily 9.30am–2pm &

5–9pm; ☎924 009 730, ⓦturismomerida.org) on Calle José Sáenz de Buruaga and on Pl. de España (Mon–Fri 9.30am–2pm & 4.30–7pm, summer opens and closes 30min later in the afternoons).

ACCOMMODATION

There is no shortage of **places to stay**, though prices tend to be on the high side.

★ **La Flor de al-Andalus** Avda. Extremadura 6 ☎924 313 356, ⓦlaflordeal-andalus.es. A new self-styled boutique *hostal* close to the train station and with eighteen rooms decorated in Andalucian style, each named after a flower and with a/c and free wi-fi. **€50**
Hostal El Alfarero c/Sagasta 40 ☎924 303 183,

ⓦhostalalfarero.com. A very cosy *hostal* with twelve a/c doubles and two triples. Pastel colours, stylish bathrooms and a neat little patio area. **€50**
Hostal Bueno c/Calvario 9 ☎924 302 977, ⓦhostalbuenomerida.com. A basic but clean *hostal* – all the rooms have tiny bathrooms. There is a sister *hostal, La*

Salud, about 200m away at c/Vespasiano 41, if this one is full. **€40**

Hostal Senero c/Holguín 12 ☎924 317 207, ⓦhostalsenero.com. A long-established, friendly *hostal* with neat rooms situated around a quiet courtyard close to the main plaza. **€42**

Hotel Adealba c/Ramiro Leal 18 ☎924 388 308, ⓦhoteladealba.com. Another new arrival on the scene, this design-conscious hotel close to the Alcazaba has large rooms with wooden floors and clean lines and a spa. Look out for offers on the website. **€165**

★ **Hotel Mérida Palace** Pl. de España 19 ☎924 383 800, ⓦhotelmeridapalace.com. An upmarket five-star hotel located in a former palace on the city's main plaza with

a great interior patio area. It's part of the MCA chain. **€119**

Parador Vía de la Plata Pl. Constitución 3 ☎924 313 800, ⓦparadores.com. Well-run and friendly parador in an eighteenth-century Baroque convent, near the Arco de Trajano. **€156**

CAMPSITE

Camping Lago de Proserpina ☎924 123 055. Signposted off the A5 and the road to Cáceres, this is a pleasant site by the Embalse de Prosperina 5km north of town, offering swimming, fishing and windsurfing. There are plans to upgrade the facilities and convert it into a luxury campsite in the near future. Closed mid-Sept to March. Two adults plus car **€14**.

EATING AND DRINKING

The whole area between the train station and the Pl. de España is full of **bars** and cheap **restaurants**.

Bar-Restaurante Briz c/Félix Valverde Lillo 7, just off Pl. de España. A reliable and popular restaurant offering the local speciality *raciones* and a good-value €11 *menú*. Closed Sun eve.

Casa Benito c/San Francisco 3. Bullfighters' ephemera line the walls of this bar, which serves the local speciality tapas, *pitarra* wine and good breakfasts. Closed Sun.

Casa Nano c/Castelar 3. Pleasant restaurant, offering good fish dishes and two *menús* at €12 and €23, the latter a very good option with lamb casserole or local speciality lamb with plums on offer. Daily around 1.30–4pm & 8.30pm–midnight.

Restaurante Nicolás c/Félix Valverde Lillo 13. A good range of Extremaduran dishes such as *migas* and gazpacho stew with a *menú* at €13, otherwise allow €25 a head. Located close to the Mercado Municipal. Closed Sun eve.

Restaurante Rufino Pl. de Santa Clara 2. Traditional dishes in lovely surroundings at this centrally located restaurant, opposite the Museo Visigodo. Allow €15–20 a head or try the substantial €14 *menú*. Closed Sun.

La Tahona Nueva c/Alvarado 5. Refurbished local which stages regular gigs, exhibitions and other cultural events. Friendly and fun. Mon–Fri 9pm–2am, Sat & Sun 1pm–2am.

Badajoz

The valley of the Río Guadiana, followed by road and rail, waters rich farmland between Mérida and **BADAJOZ**. The main reason for visiting this provincial capital, traditional gateway to Portugal and the scene of innumerable sieges, is still to get across the border. It's not somewhere you'd want to stay very long – crude modern development has largely overrun what must once have been an attractive old centre, and few of the monuments have survived – but food and lodging are cheap, and it does serve as a useful stopover. The city's troubled history, springing from its strategically important position on the Río Guadiana, is its main claim to fame. Founded by the Moors in 1009, the city was taken by the Christian armies of Alfonso IX in 1230, used as a base by Felipe II against the Portuguese in 1580, stormed by British forces under the Duke of Wellington in 1812 and taken by Franco's Nationalist troops in 1936.

Catedral and the museo

Pl. de España • Museo Tues–Sat: summer 11am–1pm & 6–8pm; winter 11am–1pm & 5–7pm • €3

At the heart of old Badajoz is the **Plaza de España** and the squat thirteenth-century **Catedral**, a fortress-like building, prettified a little during the Renaissance by the addition of a portal and embellishment of the tower. The **museo** contains work by local-born artist Luís de Morales (1520–86).

Alcazaba

Museo Arqueológico Tues–Sun 10am–3pm • Free

Northeast of Plaza de España, c/San Juan leads to **Plaza Alta**, once an elegant arcaded

▲ Cáceres

EATING & DRINKING
Cocina Portugesa	4
Dosca II	5
Los Monjes	2
La Toja	1
El Tronco	3

ACCOMMODATION
Gran Hotel Zurbarán	2
Hostal Niza I	4
Hostal Niza II	3
Hotel Río	1

0 ⸻ 250
metres

3

BADAJOZ

▼ Museo de Arte Contemporáneo & Bus Station

concourse, whose facades are decorated with a dazzling Mudéjar-style design, and what remains of the town's fortress, the **Alcazaba**. This is largely in ruins but preserves Moorish entrance gates and fragments of a Renaissance palace inside. Part of it houses a **Museo Arqueológico**, with local Roman and Visigothic finds. Defending the townward side is the octagonal Moorish **Torre del Aprendiz**, or Torre Espantaperros ("dog-scarer" – the dogs in question being Christians).

Museo de la Ciudad

Pl. de Santa María • April–Sept Tues–Sat 10am–2pm & 5–8pm, Sun 10am–2pm • Free

Nearby the Alcazaba is the **Museo de la Ciudad**, which presents an interesting and well-thought-out survey of the city's chequered history from prehistoric times to the present day, as well as containing works by one of the city's most famous sons, the artist Luís de Morales.

Puente de Palmas

The city's other main distinguishing feature is the Río Guadiana, spanned by the graceful **Puente de Palmas**, or Puente Viejo. The bridge was designed by Herrera (architect of El Escorial) as a fitting first impression of Spain, and leads into the city through the **Puerta de Palmas**, once a gate in the walls, now standing alone as a sort of triumphal arch.

TO THE PORTUGUESE BORDER AND BEYOND

The **Portuguese frontier** is 4km west of Badajoz. You can get to Elvas, the first sizeable town on the Portuguese side of the border, by local bus (Mon–Fri 5 daily 6.30am–8.30pm). From here there are eleven long-distance buses (2hr 45min) and two trains per day to **Lisbon** (4hr 30min).

Museo de Bellas Artes

C/Duque de San Germán • Sept–May Tues–Fri 10am–2pm & 4–6pm, Sat & Sun 10am–2pm; June–Aug Tues–Sat 10am–2pm & 6–8pm, Sun 10am–2pm • Free

From Plaza de España behind the Puerta de Palmas, c/Santa Lucía will take you towards the **Museo de Bellas Artes**, which includes works by Morales and a couple of good panels by Zurbarán.

Museo Extremeño e Iberoamericano de Arte Contemporáneo

C/Virgen de Guadalupe • Tues–Sat 10am–1.30pm & 5–8pm, Sun 10am–1.30pm • Free • ⓦ meiac.es

Near Plaza de la Constitución and off Avenida Calzadillas Maestre is the **Museo de Arte Contemporáneo**. This striking circular, rust-coloured building houses a wealth of modern paintings, installations and sculpture, by artists from Spain, Portugal and Latin America.

ARRIVAL AND DEPARTURE
BADAJOZ

By train The train station is on the far side of the river, up the road that crosses the Puente de Palmas and on c/Carolina Coronado. Buses #1 and #2 go to the Pl. de la Libertad, or it's around €4 in a taxi.
Destinations Cáceres (3 daily; 1hr 40min); Madrid (2 daily; 5hr 30min); Mérida (6 daily; 35–50min).
By bus If you're arriving by bus, you'll have a 15min-plus walk to the centre, as the station is located on c/José

Rebollo López towards the southern edge of the city. Your best bet is to hop on city bus #3 or #4 to Avda. de Europa.
Destinations Cáceres (7 daily; 2hr); Córdoba (3 daily; 5hr); Madrid (7 daily; 4hr 30min–5hr); Mérida (8 daily; 45min); Murcia (daily; 9hr 20min); Olivenza (12 daily; 30min); Seville (2–5 daily; 4hr 30min); Zafra (8 daily; 1hr 30min).
By car For parking follow the signs to Pl. de Minayo where you'll find an attended underground car park.

INFORMATION

Oficina de Turismo Pasaje San Juan, just off Pl. de España (June–Sept Mon–Fri 10am–2pm & 6–8pm, Sat 10am–2pm; Oct–May Mon–Fri 10am–2pm & 5–7pm, Sat 10am–2pm; ☎924 224 981, ⓦturismobadajoz.com).

There is another one down the hill on Pl. de la Libertad (Mon–Fri 10am–2pm & 5–7pm, Sat & Sun 10am–2pm; ⓦturismoextremadura.com), which is good for information on the whole region.

ACCOMMODATION

There's plenty of **accommodation** available in Badajoz, much of it inexpensive, making it a good stopover on the way into Portugal.

Gran Hotel Zurbarán Gómez de Solís 1 ☎924 001 400, ⓦhotelhusazurbaran.com. A sleek, business-style hotel, with swimming pool and renowned restaurant. Look out for weekend deals that can bring the price down to as low as €50. €70
Hostal Niza I and II c/Arco Agüero 34 & 45 ☎924 223

881, ⓦhostal-niza.com. Simple, clean rooms with en-suite bathroom in these two *hostales*. €43
Hotel Río Avda. Adolfo Díaz Ambrona s/n ☎924 272 600, ⓦgruporiodehoteles.com. At the far end of Puente de la Universidad, this upmarket 101-room hotel has a swimming pool, parking and a good restaurant. €65

EATING, DRINKING AND NIGHTLIFE

The area around c/Muñoz Torrero, a couple of blocks below the Pl. de España, is the most promising for reasonably priced **food** and **tapas**.

Cocina Portuguesa c/Muñoz Torrero 7 ☎924 224 150, ⓦcocinaportuguesa.com. The best budget bet in Badajoz, with tasty, reasonably priced Portuguese cooking

(mains cost between €7 and €12) and a selection of good-value *menús*. Daily around 1.30–4pm & 8.30pm –midnight.

Dosca II Avda. de Colón 3, just off Pl. Santo Domingo. This place is very popular with locals, serving a wide range of generous, well-cooked specialities in the nautically themed restaurant. Does a generous €11 *menú*. Daily around 1.30–4pm & 8.30pm–midnight.

Los Monjes Gran Hotel Zurbarán, Paseo Castelar ☎ 924 223 741. Probably the best food in town, with a pricey range of Spanish dishes. À la carte will set you back over €40, though there's also a lunchtime buffet at half the price. Reservation recommended. Daily around 1.30–4pm & 8.30pm–midnight.

La Toja c/Sanchez de la Rocha 22 – the Portugal road ☎ 924 273 477, ⊛ restaurantelatoja.com. A good-quality restaurant, run by a *gallego*, so serving food from Extremadura and Galicia. A bit of a trek from the centre, though it has its own parking. Allow around €35 a head. Closed Sun eve & 15 days in Feb.

El Tronco c/Muñoz Torrero 16 ☎ 924 236 253. Perhaps the best reason to stay in town, *El Tronco* has a vast range of superb-value bar snacks and excellent regional food and wine in the restaurant. Closed Sun eve.

Southern Extremadura

The routes **south from Mérida** or **Badajoz** cross territory that is mostly harsh and unrewarding, fit only for sheep and the odd cork or olive tree, until you come upon the foothills of the Sierra Morena, on the borders of Andalucía. En route, **Olivenza**, a town that has spent more time in Portugal than Spain, is perhaps the most attractive stop, and offers a road approach to Évora, the most interesting city of southern Portugal.

Olivenza

Twenty-five kilometres southwest of Badajoz, whitewashed **OLIVENZA** seems to have landed in the wrong country; long disputed between Spain and Portugal, it has been Spanish since 1801. Yet not only are the buildings and the town's character clearly Portuguese, the oldest inhabitants still cling to this language. There's a local saying here: "The women from Olivenza are not like the rest, for they are the daughters of Spain and the granddaughters of Portugal."

The walls, castle and the Museo Etnográfico

Museo winter Tues–Fri 11am–2pm & 4–7pm, Sat 10am–2pm & 4–7pm, Sun 10am–2pm; summer Tues–Fri 11am–2pm & 5–8pm, Sat 10am–2pm & 5–8pm, Sun 10am–2pm • €1

The town has long been strongly fortified, and traces of the **walls and gates** can still be seen, even though houses have been built up against them. They extend up to the **castle**, which has three surviving towers and holds the **Museo Etnográfico**, displaying an interesting and comprehensive range of exhibits detailing all aspects of life in the region.

Iglesias Santa María del Castillo and Santa María Magdalena

Tues–Sat 11am–2pm & 4–7pm, both open and close an hour later in the afternoon in summer, Sun 11am–2pm

Right beside the castle is the seventeenth-century church of **Santa María del Castillo** and around the corner, **Santa María Magdalena**, built a century later. The latter is in the distinctive Portuguese Manueline style, with arcades of twisted columns; the former is a more sober Renaissance affair with three aisles of equal height and a notable work of art in the huge "Tree of Jesse" *retablo*. Just across the street from Santa María Magdalena is a former **palace**, now the public library, with a spectacular Manueline doorway.

INFORMATION   **OLIVENZA**

Turismo Pl. de España (summer Tues–Fri 10am–2pm & 5–8pm, Sat & Sun 10am–2pm; winter Tues–Fri 10am–2pm & 4–7pm, Sat & Sun 10am–2pm; ☎ 924 490 151).

ACCOMMODATION AND EATING

★ **Hotel Palacio Arteaga** c/Moreno Nieto 5 ☎ 924 491 129, ⊛ palacioarteaga.com. Situated in the centre of town in an elegant mansion, this boutique-style hotel has 19 individually decorated rooms with a/c and free wi-fi and a beautiful interior patio area. It also has a good restaurant serving a range of Portuguese and Extremeño dishes. **€90**

3

LAND OF THE CONQUISTADORES

Extremadura is a tough country that bred tough people, if we are to believe the names of places like Valle de Matamoros (Valley of the Moorslayers), and one can easily understand the attraction that the New World and the promise of the lush Indies must have held for its inhabitants.

Francisco Pizarro, the conqueror of Peru, and **Francisco de Orellano**, the explorer of the Amazon, both came from Trujillo, while the ruthless **Hernán Cortés**, who led the destruction of the Aztec empire, hailed from Medellín in Badajoz. Jerez de los Caballeros also produced its crop of *conquistadores*. The two most celebrated are **Vasco Núñez de Balboa**, discoverer of the Pacific, and **Hernando de Soto** (also known as the Conqueror of Florida), who in exploring the Mississippi became one of the first Europeans to set foot in North America.

Jerez de los Caballeros

The road from Badajoz to **JEREZ DE LOS CABALLEROS** is typical of southern Extremadura, striking across a parched landscape whose hamlets – low huts and a whitewashed church strung out along the road – look as if they have been dumped from some low-budget Western set of a Mexican frontier town.

Churches

San Miguel Daily noon–2pm & 5–6.30pm **San Bartolomé** Daily 10am–noon & 4–5pm

Jerez de los Caballeros is a quiet, friendly place, through which many tourists pass but few stay. The church towers dominate the walled old town: a passion for building spires gripped the place in the eighteenth century, when three churches had new ones erected; the first is **San Miguel**, in the central Plaza de España, made of carved brick; the second is the unmistakeable red-, blue- and ochre-glazed tower of **San Bartolomé**, on the hill above it, with a striking tiled facade; and the third, rather dilapidated, belongs to **Santa Catalina**, outside the walls.

The Castle and the Iglesia de Santa María de Encarnación

Above the Plaza de España the streets climb up to the restored remains of a **castle** of the Knights Templar (this was once an embattled frontier town), mostly late thirteenth century but with obvious Moorish influences. Adjoining the castle, and pre dating it by over a century (as do the town walls), is the church of **Santa María**. Built on a Visigothic site, it's more interesting seen from the battlements above than from the inside. In the small park below the castle walls, a café commands fine views of the surrounding countryside and the magnificent sunsets.

INFORMATION   **JEREZ DE LOS CABALLEROS**

Turismo Ayuntamiento, Pl. de San Agustín (Mon–Fri 9.30am–2.30pm & 4.30–6.30pm, Sat 10am–2pm & 4–6.30pm, Sun 10am–2pm; ☏ 924 730 372, ⊛ turismo .jerezcaballeros.es).

ACCOMMODATION AND EATING

La Ermita c/Dr Benitez 9 ☏ 924 731 476. Authentic bar-restaurant housed in an old chapel in the centre of town, serving tasty Extremeño and Andalucian tapas and *pitarra* wine. Closed Wed eve.

Posada de las Cigüeñas c/Santiago 7–9 ☏ 924 731 446,

⊛ laposadadelasciguenas.com. A seven-room *posada* with a pool, bar area and a sun terrace. Some of the individually decorated rooms have balconies with great views over the town. €75

Zafra

If you plan to stick to the main routes or are heading south from Mérida, **ZAFRA** is rather less of a detour, though it's also much more frequented by tourists. Two beautiful arcaded plazas, the Plaza Grande and the Plaza Chica, adjoin each other in the town centre. But the town is famed mainly for its **castle** – now converted into a parador – which is remarkable for the white marble Renaissance patio. The region is also renowned for its wines, and you can visit the **Bodega Medina**, c/Cestria (Mon–Fri 10.30am–2pm & 5–8pm, Sat 10am–2pm; ☎924 575 060, ⓦbodegasmedina.net; by appointment).

Nuestra Señora de la Candelaria
C/Tetuán • Summer Mon, Tues, Thurs, Fri 10.30am–1pm & 6.30–8.30pm, Sat & Sun 11am–1pm; winter opens and closes an hour earlier in the afternoons

The most attractive of several interesting churches is **Nuestra Señora de la Candelaria**, with nine panels by Zurbarán in the *retablo* and a chapel by Churriguera; the entrance is on c/José through a small gateway, around the side of the church.

Convento de Santa Clara
C/Sevilla • Mon–Fri 5–7pm, Sun & hols 10.30am–1pm & 4–6pm

Also worth a look are the tombs of the Figueroa family (the original inhabitants of the castle) in the **Convento de Santa Clara**, just off the main shopping street; ring the bell to get in. Like many convents it also sells home-made cakes and biscuits.

INFORMATION ZAFRA

Turismo Pl. de España (Mon–Fri 9.30am–2pm & 5–8pm, Sat & Sun 10am–1.30pm & 6–8pm, winter opens and closes an hour earlier in the afternoons; ☎924 551 036, ⓦzafra.es, ⓦrutadelaplata.com). You can make an appointment to visit the Bodega Medina here.

ACCOMMODATION

★ **Casa Palacio Conde de la Corte** c/Pilar Redondo 2 ☎924 563 3811, ⓦcondedelacorte.com. A beautiful, luxurious boutique-style hotel with bull fighting-themed rooms, a great Andalucian patio area and pool. Price includes breakfast. **€110–160**

Hostal Carmen Avda. Estación 9 ☎924 551 439, ⓦhostalcarmen.com. A very tidy *hostal* with facilities closer to that of a hotel. Also boasts an excellent medium-priced restaurant. **€46**

Hotel Las Palmeras Pl. Grande 14 ☎924 552 208, ⓦhotellaspalmeras.net. Well-appointed, good-value *hostal* with standard rooms, an elegant patio and bar-restaurant with a summer terraza. **€40**

Parador Pl. Corazón de María 7 ☎924 554 540, ⓦparadores.com. Housed in a fifteenth-century castle in the centre, and the rooms in this parador are suitably palatial. A splendid courtyard, a tranquil pool and an excellent restaurant are all part of the attraction. **€156**

EATING

★ **La Rebotica** c/Boticas 12 ☎924 554 289, ⓦlareboticadezafra.com. A small and very popular restaurant in the centre of town (make a reservation first) with a wide selection of high-quality local dishes such as ox-tail or steak with figs in brandy sauce. Expect to pay around €35 a head. Closed Sun eve & Mon.

Andalucía

MEZQUITA, CÓRDOBA (P.312)

Andalucía

The popular image of Spain as a land of bullfights, flamenco, sherry and ruined castles derives from Andalucía, the southernmost territory and the most quintessentially Spanish part of the Iberian Peninsula. Above all, it's the great Moorish monuments that compete for your attention here. The Moors, a mixed race of Berbers and Arabs who crossed into Spain from Morocco and North Africa, occupied al-Andalus for over seven centuries. Their first forces landed at Tarifa in 710 AD, and within four years they had conquered virtually the entire country; their last kingdom, Granada, fell to the Christian Reconquest in 1492. Between these dates, they developed the most sophisticated civilization of the Middle Ages, centred in turn on the three major cities of Córdoba, Seville and Granada.

Each one preserves extraordinarily brilliant and beautiful monuments, of which the most perfect is **Granada**'s Alhambra palace, arguably the most sensual building in all of Europe. **Seville**, not to be outdone, has a fabulously ornamented Alcázar and the grandest of all Gothic cathedrals. Today, Andalucía's capital and seat of the region's autonomous parliament is a vibrant contemporary metropolis that's impossible to resist. **Córdoba**'s exquisite Mezquita, the grandest and most beautiful mosque constructed by the Moors, is a landmark building in world architecture and not to be missed.

These three cities have, of course, become major tourist destinations, but it's also worth leaving the tourist trail and visiting some of the smaller **inland towns** of Andalucía. Renaissance towns such as **Úbeda**, **Baeza** and **Osuna**, Moorish **Carmona** and the stark white hill-towns around **Ronda** are all easily accessible by local buses. Travelling for some time here, you'll get a feel for the landscape of Andalucía: occasionally spectacularly beautiful but more often impressive on a huge, unyielding scale.

The region also takes in mountains – including the **Sierra Nevada**, Spain's highest range. You can often ski here in March, and then drive down to the coast to swim the same day. Perhaps more compelling, though, are the opportunities for walking in the lower slopes, **Las Alpujarras**. Alternatively, there's good trekking among the gentler (and much less known) hills of the **Sierra Morena**, north of Seville.

On the **coast**, it's easy to despair. Extending to either side of **Málaga** is the **Costa del Sol**, Europe's most heavily developed resort area, with its poor beaches hidden behind a

THE VILLAGE OF BUBIÓN

Highlights

❶ Semana Santa Andalucía's major Holy Week festival is memorably celebrated in Seville, Málaga, Córdoba and Granada. **See p.228**

❷ Seville Andalucía's pulsating capital city is a treasure house of churches, palaces and museums. **See p.263**

❸ Flamenco The passionate dance, song and music of the Spanish south. **See p.275**

❹ Siping sherry in Jerez Andalucía's classic wine is made in Jerez and makes the perfect partner for tapas. **See p.302**

❺ Coto de Doñana Explore Europe's largest and most important wildlife sanctuary. **See p.304**

❻ Mezquita, Córdoba This 1200-year-old Moorish mosque is one of the most beautiful ever built. **See p.312**

❼ Alhambra Granada's Moorish palace is the pinnacle of Moorish architectural splendour in Spain. **See p.330**

❽ Las Alpujarras A wildly picturesque region dotted with traditional mountain villages. **See p.350**

HIGHLIGHTS ARE MARKED ON THE MAP ON P.226

remorseless density of concrete hotels and apartment complexes. However, the region offers two alternatives, much less developed and with some of the best beaches in all Spain. These are the villages **between Tarifa and Cádiz** on the Atlantic, and those **around Almería** on the southeast corner of the Mediterranean. The latter allow warm swimming in all but the winter months; those near Cádiz, more easily accessible, are fine from about June to September. Near Cádiz, too, is **Parque Nacional Coto de**

ANDALUCÍA

EXTREMADURA

PORTUGAL

Zafra

Encinasola

Aroche
Sta. Barbara de Casas
Jabugo
Almonaster la Real
Aracena
Zufre
El Real de la Jara

S I E R R A

Belalcázar
Santa Eufemia
Hinojosa del Duque
Pozot
Peñarroya Pueblonuevo
Belmez
M
Fuente-Obejuna
Espiel

CÓRDOBA

Córdoba

Alanis
Cazalla de la Sierra

Nerva
Minas de Riotinto
Tharsis

Guadalquivir

HUELVA

Valverde del Camino
La Palma del Condado
Niebla

Lora del Rio
Écija
Me

Carmona
SEVILLA
Osuna
Estepa

Ayamonte
Huelva
Almonte
Punta-Umbria
Mazagon
El Rocío

② ③
Seville (Sevilla)

Utrera
Morón de la Frontera

Vila Reat de Santo Antonio

Costa de la Luz

PARQUE NACIONAL COTO DE DOÑANA ⑤

Guadalquivir

El Chor
MÁLAGA

Sanlúcar de Barrameda
Chipiona

Arcos de la Frontera
Zahara
Ronda

④ Jerez
CÁDIZ

El Puerto de Sta. Maria
Cádiz
Chiclana
Medina Sidonia
Alcalá de los Gazules

Gaucín
Casares
AUTOPISTA DEL SOL
Mar
Estepona

ATLANTIC OCEAN

Conil
Vejer de la Frontera
Jimena de la Frontera
San Roque
Algeciras
Gibraltar

Costa del Sol

Baelo Claudia
Tarifa

Ceuta

Tangier
MOROCCO

Canary Islands

HIGHLIGHTS
① Semana Santa
② Seville
③ Flemenco
④ Sipping sherry in Jerez
⑤ Coto de Doñana
⑥ Mezquita
⑦ Alhambra
⑧ Las Alpujarras

Doñana, Spain's largest and most important nature reserve, which is home to a spectacular range of flora and fauna.

The realities of life in contemporary Andalucía can be stark. **Unemployment** in the region is the highest in Spain – over twenty percent in some areas – and a large proportion of the population still scrapes a living from seasonal agricultural work. The *andaluz* villages, bastions of anarchist and socialist groups before and during

ANDALUCIA'S FIESTAS

FEBRUARY

1: San Cecilio Fiesta in Granada's traditionally gypsy quarter of Sacromonte.
Week before Lent: Carnaval An extravagant week-long event in all the Andalucian cities. Cádiz, above all, celebrates, with uproarious street parades, fancy dress and satirical music competitions.

MARCH/APRIL

Easter: Semana Santa (Holy Week) You'll find memorable processions of floats and penitents at Seville, Málaga, Granada and Córdoba, and to a lesser extent in smaller towns such as Jerez, Arcos, Baeza and Úbeda. All culminate with dramatic candlelight processions at dawn on Good Friday, with Easter Day itself more of a family occasion.
Last week of April: Feria de Abril Week-long fair at Seville: the largest fair in Spain.

MAY

First week: Cruces de Mayo Celebrated in Córdoba and includes a "prettiest patio" competition in a town full of prize examples.
Early May (week after Feria de Abril): Feria del Caballo A somewhat aristocratic horse fair is held at Jerez de la Frontera.
Pentecost: Romería del Rocío Horse-drawn carriages and processions converge from all over the south on El Rocío (Huelva).
Last week: Feria de la Manzanilla Prolonged binge in Sanlúcar de Barrameda to celebrate the town's major product, with flamenco and sporting events on the river beach.

JUNE

13: San Antonio Fiesta at Trevélez (Las Alpujarras) with mock battles between Moors and Christians.
Third week The Algeciras Feria Real is another major event of the south.
End June/early July: International Festival of Music and Dance Major dance/flamenco groups and chamber orchestras perform in Granada's Alhambra palace, Generalife and Carlos V palace.

JULY

Early July: International Guitar Festival Brings together top international acts from classical, flamenco and Latin American music in Córdoba.
End of month: Virgen del Mar Almería's major annual shindig, with parades, horseriding events, concerts and lots of drinking.

AUGUST

First week The first cycle of horse races along Sanlúcar de Barrameda's beach, with heavy official and unofficial betting; the second tournament takes place two weeks later.
5: Trevélez observes a midnight *romería* to Mulhacén.
13–21: Feria de Málaga One of Andalucía's most enjoyable fiestas for visitors, who are heartily welcomed by the ebullient *malagueños*.
15: Ascension of the Virgin Fair With *casetas* (dance tents) at Vejer and elsewhere.
Noche del Vino Riotous wine festival at Competa (Málaga).
23–25: Guadalquivir festival Bullfights and an important flamenco competition, at Sanlúcar de Barrameda.

SEPTEMBER & OCTOBER

First two weeks Sept: Feria de Ronda Ronda's annual *feria*, with flamenco contests and Corrida Goyesca – bullfights in eighteenth-century dress.
First/second week Sept: Vendimia Celebrating the vintage at Jerez.
27–Oct 1: Feria de San Miguel In Órgiva (Las Alpujarras) featuring traditional dancing and a huge paella cook-up.

ANDALUCÍA'S CUISINE

The most striking feature of Andalucía's cuisine is its **debt to the Moors**. In their long period of hegemony over the region the North Africans introduced oranges and lemons as well as spices such as cumin and saffron and refined techniques for growing olives and almonds. Their chilled soups such as *ajo blanco* (made with ground almonds) and gazpacho are still a welcome refresher in high summer temperatures. Of course, gazpacho is today made with tomatoes and green peppers, both brought back from the Americas by Columbus, who sailed from Andalucía.

The region is also the birthplace of **tapas**, the classic tidbits that Spaniards love to tuck into as they drink. Between 6 and 9pm most evenings city bars are humming with conversations of *tapeadores* (as aficionados are termed). One of Andalucía's favourite tapas is **jamón serrano**, mountain-cured ham from prime producing zones in the Sierra de Aracena and the Alpujarras. The most prized ham of all is *jamón ibérico* from black Iberian pigs, and in the curing village of Jabugo this is graded into five levels of quality with the very best accorded five *jotas* or "j"s (for Jabugo). If you can afford it, the taste is mouthwateringly delicious and far superior to the standard white-pig *jamón* sold in supermarkets.

Andalucía is also known in Spain as the *zona de los fritos* (fried food zone) and **fried fish** is a regional speciality. *Chanquetes* (whitebait), sardines, *calamares* and *boquerones* (anchovies) are all *andaluz* favourites and the seafood *chiringuitos* (beach restaurants) of Málaga are famous for their **fritura malagueña** (assorted fried fish).

Inland, Andalucía is a mountainous region and the specialities here are **carnes de caza** (game). *Jabalí* (wild boar), *venado* (venison), *cabrito* (kid) and *perdiz* (partridge) all make memorable meals in the hands of a competent chef.

The wine par excellence of Andalucía – particularly to accompany tapas – is **fino** (dry sherry) from Jerez de la Frontera, although nearby Sanlúcar de Barrameda's *manzanilla* and *montilla* (produced in Córdoba) are similar and display their own prized characteristics.

the Civil War, saw little economic aid or change during the Franco years, and although much government spending has been channelled into improving infrastructure such as hospitals and road and rail links, the lack of employment opportunities away from the coastal tourist zones persists. For all its poverty, however, Andalucía is also Spain at its most exuberant – those wild and extravagant clichés of the Spanish south really do exist and can be absorbed at one of the hundreds of annual **fiestas**, **ferias** and **romerías**.

Málaga

MÁLAGA seems at first an uninviting place. It's the second city of the south (after Seville), with a population of half a million, and is also one of the poorest: an estimated one in four of the workforce are jobless. Though the clusters of high-rises look pretty grim as you approach, the city does have some compelling attractions. The elegant central zone is now largely pedestrianized with the focal and marble-paved **Calle Marqués de Larios** – lined with fashionable stores – its most elegant thoroughfare. This leads into the **Plaza de la Constitución**, the city's main square, with a monumental fountain flanked by slender palms, and the terraces of numerous cafés and restaurants. The centre has a number of interesting churches and museums, not to mention the **birthplace of Picasso** and the **Museo Picasso Málaga**, housing an important collection of works by Málaga's most famous son. Perched on the hill above the town are the formidable citadels of the **Alcazaba** and **Gibralfaro**, magnificent vestiges of the seven centuries that the Moors held sway here. The city authorities hope that a revamped **seafront** and cleaned-up coastline will make the city attractive as a beach resort and has encouraged new hotels, restaurants and bars along the promenades east and west of the centre.

4

TAPAS BARS & RESTAURANTS	
Al-Yamal	25
Antigua Casa Guardia	23
Antonio	17
Bar Lo Güeno	19
Bar Los Pueblos	22
Bar-Restaurante Palacios	26
Bodegas Quitapeñas	20
Cañadu	7
El Tapeo de Cervantes	1
Il Laboratorio	4
La Moraga	24
Orellana	18
Parador Gilbralfaro	6
Sal Gorda	21
Tapadaki	3
El Tintero	14
Uvedoble	16
El Vegetariano	13

BARS	
Anden	9
Asucar	8
La Botellita	10
Calle Bruselas	5
Cruces de Caminos	11
El Pimpi	12
Puerta Oscura	15
Vino Mío	2

MÁLAGA

Málaga is also renowned for its **fish** and **seafood**, which can be sampled at tapas bars and restaurants throughout the city, as well as at the old fishing villages of **El Palo** and **Pedregalejo**, now absorbed into the suburbs, where there's a seafront *paseo* lined with some of the best **marisquerías** and **chiringuitos** (beachside fish restaurants) in the province.

The Alcazaba

Tues–Sun: April–Sept 9.30am–8pm; Oct–March 8.30am–5.45pm • €2.10, €3.40 combined ticket with Gibralfaro; Free entry Sun pm

The impressive **Alcazaba** is the place to make for if you're killing time between connections. It's just fifteen minutes' walk (or 5min bus ride) from the train or bus stations, and can be clearly seen from most central points. To the left of its entrance on c/Acazabilla stands the **Teatro Romano** (Roman Theatre) accidentally discovered in 1951, and – following excavation and restoration – now a venue for various outdoor

ACCOMMODATION	
Albergue Juvenil Málaga	13
Hostal El Cenachero	14
Hostal La Hispanidad	16
Hostal La Palma	12
Hostal Victoria	10
Hotel California	3
Hotel Don Curro	9
Hotel Ibis	5
Hotel Larios	6
Hotel Lola	15
Hotel Los Naranjos	4
Hotel Málaga Palacio	8
Hotel Montevictoria	1
Hotel Trebol	7
Parador Gibralfaro	2
Pensión Juanita	11

entertainments. The citadel, too, is Roman in origin, with blocks and columns of marble interspersed among the Moorish brick of the double- and triple-arched gateways.

The main structures, reopened in 2002 following a three-year restoration, were begun by the Moors in the eighth century, probably soon after their conquest, but the palace higher up the hill dates from the early decades of the eleventh. This was the residence of the Arab emirs of Málaga, who carved out an independent kingdom for themselves upon the break-up of the Western Caliphate. Their independence lasted a mere thirty years, but for a while their kingdom included Granada, Carmona and Jaén. The complex's **palace** was heavily restored in the 1930s, but some fine stuccowork, the ceilings and elegant patios give a flavour of the sumptuous edifice it must once have been. The interior displays Moorish ceramics found during the archeological excavations. You can avoid the climb up to the palace by taking a **lift** built into the hill and accessed on c/Guillen Sotelo, directly behind the *ayuntamiento*.

The Gibralfaro

Tues–Sun: April–Sept 9.30am–8pm; Oct–March 8.30am–5.45pm • Combined ticket with Alcazaba €3.40

Above the Alcazaba, and connected to it by a long double wall (the *coracha*), is the **Gibralfaro castle**. It's reached by climbing a twisting path that skirts the southern walls, passing bougainvillea-draped ramparts and sentry-box-shaped Moorish wells. You can also approach from the town side, as the urban buses and tourist coaches do, but this is a rather unattractive walk and not one to be done alone after sundown. If you want to avoid the climb altogether, you can take bus #35 heading east from the Paseo del Parque, which stops just outside the entrance.

Last used in 1936 during the Civil War, the castle, like the Alcazaba, has been wonderfully restored and now houses an interesting **museum** devoted to its history – a scale model lets you see how the city would have looked in Moorish times. A walk around the battlements affords terrific **views** over the city, while the nearby parador (reached by following the road leading out of the castle's car park for 100m and turning right into the parador's grounds) has a pleasant terrace café and restaurant with more fine views.

The Catedral

Mon–Fri 10am–6pm, Sat 10am–5pm; closed Sun except for services • €5

The city's most conspicuous edifice seen from the heights of the Gibralfaro is the peculiar, unfinished **Catedral**. Constructed between the sixteenth and eighteenth centuries, it still lacks a tower on the west front because a radical *malagueño* bishop donated the earmarked money to the American War of Independence against the British. Unfortunately – and despite its huge scale – it also lacks any real inspiration and is distinguished only by an intricately carved seventeenth-century *sillería* (choir stall) by noted sculptor Pedro de Mena. However, **Iglesia del Sagrario** (same ticket and hours), on the cathedral's northern flank, is worth a look, if only for its fine Gothic portal, dating from an earlier, uncompleted Isabelline church. Inside, a restored and magnificent gilded Plateresque **retablo**, which is brilliantly illuminated during services, is the work of Juan de Balmaseda.

Museo Picasso Málaga

C/San Agustín • Tues–Sun 10am–8pm • Permanent collection €6, temporary collection €4.50, combined ticket €8; free entry on the last Sunday of the month • ⓦ museopicassomalaga.org

Just around the corner from the cathedral is the **Museo Picasso Málaga**, housed in the elegant sixteenth-century mansion of the counts of Buenavista. It was opened by the king and queen in 2003, 112 years after Picasso left Málaga at the age of 10 and to where he returned only once for an unhappy, fleeting visit in his late teens. In later life, he toyed with the idea of "sending two lorries full of paintings" to set up a museum in Málaga but vowed never to set foot in Spain while the ruling General Franco – who described the artist's work as "degenerate" – was still alive. Picasso died in 1973 and was outlived by the dictator by two years.

The **permanent collection** consists of 285 works donated by Christine and Bernard Ruiz-Picasso, the artist's daughter-in-law and grandson, while the **temporary collection** comprises loaned works and special exhibitions (not necessarily connected with Picasso). Though not on a par with the Picasso museums in Paris and Barcelona, the museum does allow you to see some of the lesser-known works that Picasso kept for himself or gave away to his lovers, family and friends – rather harshly described as the "less saleable stuff" by one critic.

The museum also has a good, if cramped, **bookshop** and an equally cramped **café**, although this spills out onto a pleasant garden terrace in fine weather. The museum opens on certain Saturday evenings throughout the summer (€2; details from museum), with live music in the garden and other events.

The collection

Among the highlights of the collection are, in Room 2, *Olga Koklova con Mantilla* (a portrait of his first wife, draped in a hotel tablecloth) and a moving portrait of his son Paul, painted in 1923. Other rooms have canvases from the breadth of Picasso's career including his Blue, Pink and Cubist periods, as well as sculptures in wood, metal and stone and a few ceramics. Two other influential women who figured prominently in the artist's long and turbulent love life are also the subject of powerful images: in Room 5, *Cabeza de Mujer 1939* is a portrait of the beguiling yet tragic Dora Maar, and in Room 8, *Jacqueline Sentada* is a seated representation of his second wife, Jacqueline Roque. An interesting, newly acquired work in the same room is *Desnudo acostado* (Reclining nude), where Picasso explores a whole range of body positions in a single image.

It's worth pointing out that the collection is rotated and thus not all the works mentioned above may be on show at any one time.

The archeological remains and the Palacio de Buenavista

An unexpected surprise lies in the museum's basement – **archeological remains** revealed during the building's refurbishment. These include substantial chunks of a Phoenician city wall and tower dating from the seventh century BC which would have protected these early colonists from attacks by the Iberian tribes. From later periods there are parts of a Roman *salazones* factory used to produce the famous *garum*, a fish-based sauce and Roman delicacy, and also vestiges of the cellar of the sixteenth-century **Palacio de Buenavista**. A case nearby displays some of the finds unearthed in the excavations, including Phoenician, Greek and Roman pottery fragments and a sixth-century-BC Egyptian scarab.

Museo de las Bellas Artes

The **Museo de las Bellas Artes** that was formerly housed in the Museo Picasso is due to be relocated to the Aduana (the old customs building on the Paseo del Parque). The refurbishment of this elegant eighteenth-century palace is nearing completion at the time of writing and the new museum (also housing the city's important archeological collection) is expected to open some time in 2012. Either of the tourist offices should have the latest news on this. The collection includes significant works by Murillo and Zurbarán, among others.

Casa Natal de Picasso

Pl. de la Merced • Daily 9.30am–8pm • €1

Picasso was born a couple of hundred metres away from the museum that houses his works in the Plaza de la Merced, where the **Casa Natal de Picasso** is home to the Fundación Picasso, a centre for scholars researching the painter's life and work. A recently revamped exhibition space now displays lithographs, etchings and washes by Picasso – mainly with women as the subject matter – while on the stairs are photos of the artist at various stages in his long life. The stairs lead to a reconstructed reception room, furnished as it might have looked when Picasso was growing up here at the end of the late nineteenth century. Among the items on display are some embroidered bed linen by the artist's mother, a canvas by his art-teacher father, and the infant Picasso's christening robe used in the ceremony at the nearby Iglesia de Santiago.

Centro de Arte Contemporaneo

C/Alemania • July & Aug Tues–Sun 10am–2pm & 5–9pm; Sept–June Tues–Sun 10am–8pm • Free • ⓦ cacmalaga.org

Building on the success of the Picasso museum, the city is now turning itself into an art lover's hotspot with this superb modern art museum and the Museo Carmen Thyssen.

Sited on the east bank of the Río Guadalmedina, the **Centro de Arte Contemporaneo** is an impressive modern art museum housed in a former market building. The permanent collection displays works by international artists Louise Bourgeois, Cindy Sherman and Damien Hirst, while Spain is represented by Juan Muñoz, Miquel Barceló and Juan Uslé among others. Check out the centre's website for information on frequent temporary exhibitions. A **cafetería** has a pleasant riverview terrace.

Museo Carmen Thyssen

C/Compañia • Tues–Sun 10am–8pm • €6 • ⓦ carmenthyssenmalaga.org

Just off the west side of Plaza de la Constitución and housed in the refurbished sixteenth-century Palacio de Villalón is the **Museo Carmen Thyssen**, named after the spouse of the late baron whose collection forms the core of the Thyssen-Bornemisza museum in Madrid. Opened in 2011, the museum comprises 230 loaned works from Thyssen's personal collection of Spanish nineteenth-century art. Displayed on three floors (the fourth floor houses temporary exhibitions which have featured Monet, Picasso, Matisse and Miró) and divided into sections titled "Romantic", "Naturalist Landscape", and "Fin-de-siècle", most of the works are perhaps more interesting for the glimpses they give of Spanish and *andaluz* life and times than intrinsic artistic merit or originality.

The exceptions to this are mainly in the third floor's "Fin-de-siècle" collection where five paintings by nineteenth-century Valencian Impressionist Joaquín Sorolla y Bastida are fine examples of his hallmark high-keyed colouring and vigorous brushwork. The evocative *Lavanderas de Galicia* is perhaps the best of the bunch and demonstrates a deft understanding of light and colour. Other interesting works here include *Julia* by Ramón Casas i Carbó, a rather arrogantly-posed image of the lottery seller who was to become his wife, Gustavo Bacarisas' *Feria*, and paintings by *córdobes* artist Julio Romero de Torres (see p.319).

The first floor has a somewhat incongruously titled "Old Masters" room displaying a handful of older works including an image of *San Marina* by Zurbarán and a moving polychromed wood sculpture, *The Dead Christ*, an anonymous Italian work from the thirteenth century. The museum also has a *cafetería* as well as a shop selling books on, and reproductions of, the artworks.

Jardín Botánico La Concepción

Guided tours Tues–Sat: April–Sept 9.30am–8.30pm; Oct–March 9.30am–5.30pm; last visit 90min before closing • €4.20; Tues free after 4.30pm in summer and 1.30pm in winter

A pleasant trip out of town is to the **Jardín Botánico La Concepción**, 5km north of the city and signposted off the N331 *autovía*. A spectacular tropical garden, much of which was planted in the nineteenth century, this formerly private estate was founded in the 1850s by Amelia Loring, granddaughter of the British consul, and purchased in 1990 by the Málaga city council, since when it has been open to the public. Specimens on view include exotic blooms, thirty species of palm, and other trees of all shapes and continents, such as the Australian banyan with its serpentine aerial roots.

Bus #61 from the north side of the Alameda Principal will drop you at the gates (Sat & Sun), or at its terminus 700m short (Mon–Fri). Another way of visiting the garden by bus is to use the Málagatour sightseeing bus (see p.235), which has a stop here. A **taxi** costs about €12 one way from the centre.

ARRIVAL AND DEPARTURE   **MÁLAGA**

BY AIR

From the airport (☎ 902 404 704), the **electric train** (*ferrocarril*) provides the easiest approach to Málaga (every 30min; 20min June–Sept 7am–11.45pm; €1.40). Follow the signs from the Llegadas (Arrivals) hall, crossing the car park, to the station. The Málaga platform is the one farthest away and reached by an underpass; stay on the train right to the end of the line – the **Centro-Alameda** stop (12min).

Alternatively, city **bus** Linea A leaves from outside the Terminal 3 Arrivals hall (every 30min 7am–midnight; €1.20), stopping at the train and bus stations en route to the centre and the Paseo del Parque near the port, from where you can also pick it up in the opposite direction when you're returning to the airport. A **taxi** into town from the rank outside the Arrivals hall will cost around €20 depending on traffic and time of day, and takes roughly fifteen minutes.

BY TRAIN

The city's impressive new RENFE train station is southwest of the heart of town; bus #3 runs from here to the centre every 10min or so. For current timetables and ticket information, consult RENFE ☎ 902 240 202, ⓦ renfe.es.
Destinations Algeciras (3 daily, change at Bobadilla; 3hr); Córdoba (4 daily; 2hr 20min, AVE 1hr); Fuengirola (every 30min from airport; 35min); Granada (2 daily, change at Antequera; 3hr 30min); Madrid (11 AVE daily; 2hr 40min); Ronda (1 daily, change at Bobadilla; 3hr); Seville (6 daily; 2hr 30min).

BY BUS

The bus station is just behind the RENFE station, from where all buses (run by a number of different companies) operate. In summer, it's best to arrive an hour or so early for the bus to Granada, since tickets can sell out.
Destinations Algeciras (8 daily; 2–3hr); Almería (7 daily; 3hr 30min); Almuñécar (9 daily; 2hr); Cádiz (7 daily; 3hr 45min); Córdoba (5 daily; 3hr 30min); Fuengirola (8 daily; 45min); Gibraltar (stops at La Linea border; 5 daily; 3hr);

Granada (20 daily; 2hr); Huelva (daily; 4hr 30min); Jaén (4 daily; 3hr); Jerez de la Frontera (3 daily; 4hr 30min); Madrid (11 daily; 6hr); Marbella (25 daily; 45min); Motril (6 daily; 2hr); Nerja (24 daily; 1hr); Ronda (18 daily; 2hr); Salobreña (6 daily; 1hr 45min); Seville (11 daily; 2hr 30min); Úbeda/Baeza (3 daily; 4hr).

BY CAR

Arriving in Málaga **by car** you face the serious problem of parking and will have little choice but to use one of the many signed car parks around the centre or use a garage connected to your accommodation (for which you will still need to pay but many hotels offer a variety of discounts). Note that **theft** from cars is rampant in Málaga and you should never leave anything valuable on view in a street-parked vehicle, especially overnight.

BY FERRY

Málaga has the remnants of a **passenger ferry port**, the Estación Marítima, though these days there's a service only to the Spanish enclave of Melilla in Morocco, with Trasmediterranea (7hr; ☎ 902 454 645, ⓦ trasmediterranea .es). If you're heading for Fes and eastern Morocco, this is a useful connection – particularly so for taking a car over – though most people go for the quicker services at Algeciras and Tarifa to the west. A useful site for checking the latest ferry schedules is ⓦ directferries.co.uk.
Destinations Melilla (2 daily in summer; see website for winter timetables; 3hr 45min–8hr).

INFORMATION AND TOURS

Turismo Pasaje de Chinitas 4 (Mon–Fri 9am–7.30pm, Sat & Sun 9.30am–3pm; ☎ 952 308 911); can provide information on cultural events and accommodation, and sells a detailed map of the city.
Turismo municipal On Pl. de la Marina (daily 9am–6pm, April–Sept closes 8pm; ☎ 951 926 020), with other branches at the bus station and in the airport Arrivals hall.
Bus tours One way to get to grips quickly with the city is on

an open-topped bus tour. This hop-on, hop-off service is operated by Málagatour (☎ 902 101 081, ⓦ city-ss.com; €17, kids €8.50, tickets valid 24hr); buses leave the bus station every half-hour (9.15am–7pm) with about a dozen stops around the centre (see website for route map), including the cathedral, Pl. de la Merced, the Alameda and the Gibralfaro.

ACCOMMODATION

Málaga boasts dozens of hotels and *hostales* in all budget categories. The best places to start looking for budget **accommodation** are the area just south of the Alameda Principal and the streets east and west of c/Marques de Larios, which cuts between the Alameda and Pl. de la Constitución. Prices quoted are the highest rates but many hotels and *hostales* do website and seasonal special offers which often slash prices significantly.

BUDGET

Albergue Juvenil Málaga Pl. de Pio XII ☎ 952 308 500. Modern youth hostel on the western outskirts of town, with double and single rooms, dormitories, disabled facilities and its own sun terrace. Tends to fill up in season, so book ahead. Bus #18 heading west across the river from the Alameda will drop you nearby. Dorms

under-26 €21, over-26 €27; Double under-26 €42, over-26 €54
Hostal El Cenachero c/Barroso 5 ☎ 952 224 088. Clean, quiet, friendly and reasonably priced *hostal*; left off the seafront end of c/Córdoba. Most rooms en suite (four with terrace) and does frequent special offers outside high season. €58

4

Hostal La Hispanidad Explanada de la Estación 5 ☎ 952 311 135, �🖥 www.hostalhispanidad.com. Facing the train station, this is a useful sleepover if you've got an early train (or bus) to catch. The labyrinthine interior has refurbished en-suite rooms named after different countries of the Americas, with a/c and TV, and there are plenty of eating places nearby. Free wi-fi zone. **€40**

Hostal La Palma c/Martínez 7 ☎ 952 226 772, �🖥 www .hostallapalma.es. One of the best budget places in town with a/c en-suite doubles in addition to simpler rooms sharing bath; frequently offers discounts. Free wi-fi. **€40**

Hostal Victoria c/Sancha de Lara 3 ☎ 952 224 223, �🖥 www.hostalvictoriamalaga.com. Pleasant *hostal* with good-value double and single rooms, just north of the Alameda. Free wi-fi. **€50**

Pensión Juanita c/Alarcón Luján 8 ☎ 952 213 586, �🖥 www.pensionjuanita.es. Central and friendly *pensión* offering rooms with or without bath on the fourth floor (with a lift). Large family rooms also available. **€49**

MODERATE AND EXPENSIVE

Hotel California Paseo de Sancha 17, 500m east of the bullring ☎ 952 215 164, ⁣🖥 www.hotelcalifornianet .com. Charming small hotel near the beach with flower-bedecked entrance. The well-appointed rooms come with a/c, wi-fi and safes, the hotel has its own garage. Five-night minimum stay in Aug. Buses #11, #34 and #35 from the Alameda will drop you outside. **€105**

Hotel Don Curro c/Sancha de Lara 7 ☎ 952 227 200, ⁣🖥 www.hoteldoncurro.com. Central and comfortable, if rather featureless, hotel with a/c rooms and its own car park. Some views from top-floor rooms. **€121**

Hotel Ibis Paseo Guimbarda 5 ☎ 952 070 741, ⁣🖥 www .ibishotel.com. On the west bank of the Guadalmedina, this is part of the international chain, offering functional rooms at attractive prices with frequent website special offers. Can arrange parking. Free wi-fi. **€69**

Hotel Larios c/Marqués de Larios 2 ☎ 952 222 200, ⁣🖥 www.hotel-larios.com. Modern, upmarket and central hotel inside the shell of an original Art Deco edifice; satellite TV, room safes, wi-fi and a panoramic rooftop bar are among the features. Does frequent special offers. B&B **€125**

Hotel Lola c/Casas de Campos 17 ☎ 952 579 300, ⁣🖥 www.room-matehotels.com. New designer-chic

boutique hotel where rooms come with plasma TV, free internet, DVD player, minibar and room safe. Also has own bar-restaurant and garage. **€107**

Hotel Málaga Palacio Cortina del Muelle 1 ☎ 952 215 185, ⁣🖥 www.espanol.marriot.com. This central four-star hotel with harbour-view rooms pampers its guests with free minibar and bathrobes. Facilities include rooftop pool and restaurant with spectacular views and a gym. Online special offers. **€140**

★ **Hotel Montevictoria** c/Conde de Ureña 58 ☎ 952 656 525, ⁣🖥 www.hotelmontevictoria.com. Sweet little hotel with friendly proprietors in an elegant garden villa in the hills above Málaga, with great views over the city. Slightly pricier rooms 104 & 105 have their own private terrace. Bus #36 from the Alameda (ask for the c/Conde de Ureña stop) stops almost outside. **€84**

Hotel Los Naranjos Paseo de Sancha 35. ☎ 952 22 43 16, ⁣🖥 www.hotel-losnaranjos.com. Very pleasant small hotel east of the bullring near the beach. Rooms come with terrace and there are spectacular sea views from front-facing rooms on highest floors; features include a/c, strongbox and garage. Free wi-fi. Buses #11, #34 and #35 from the Alameda will drop you outside. **€160**

Hotel Trebol c/Moreno Carbonero 3 ☎ 952 608 702, ⁣🖥 www.hoteltrebol.com. Pleasant new small hotel in the atmospheric market area with modern a/c rooms. Features include flat-screen TV, internet connections and a wi-fi zone. **€55**

★ **Parador Gibralfaro** Monte de Gibralfaro ☎ 952 221 902, ⁣🖥 www.paradores.es. You won't get a better panoramic view of the coast than from this eagle's nest on top of the Gibralfaro hill. It's quite small as paradores go, which adds to its charm, plus there's a pretty good restaurant (see p.237) and it also squeezes in a pool and has its own garage. **€180**

CAMPING

Camping Torremolinos Loma del Paraíso 2 ☎ 952 382 602, ⁣🖥 campingtorremolinos.com. Torremolinos' campsite, 10km west of Málaga along the coast, has plenty of shade and good facilities. It's 3km east of the centre of the resort on the main N340 Málaga–Cádiz highway, 500m from the sea. **€6.50**, **€7.20** per tent, **€6.10** per vehicle

EATING AND DRINKING

Málaga has no shortage of **places to eat and drink,** and, though it's hardly a gourmet paradise, the city has a justified reputation for seafood. Its greatest claim to fame is undoubtedly its **fried fish**, acknowledged as the best in Spain. You'll find many fish restaurants grouped around the Alameda, although for some of the very best you need to head out to the suburbs of Pedregalejo and El Palo, served by bus #11 (from Paseo del Parque). On the seafront *paseo* at **Pedregalejo**, almost any of the cafés and restaurants will serve up terrific seafood. Farther on, after the *paseo* disappears, you find yourself amid fishing shacks and smaller, sometimes quite ramshackle, cafés in **El Palo**, an earthier sort of area for the most part, with a beach and huts, and – in summer or at weekends – an even better place to eat.

TAPAS BARS

Bar Lo Güeno c/Marín García 9, off c/Larios. Excellent and atmospheric tapas place; *pincho* (spicy shrimp) and *habas* (broad beans with black sausage) are specials. They also have a very good small restaurant sited immediately opposite. Daily 12.30pm–midnight.

Bodegas Quitapeñas (aka La Manchega) c/Marín García 4. Another fine old drinking den with its own off-site bodega (which can be visited). Many tapas for under €2 – *jibias guisadas* (stewed cuttlefish) is a speciality – and you can wash them down with Málaga's traditional Moscatel and Sierras de Málaga wines. Daily 12.30–4pm & 7.30pm–midnight.

★ **Orellana** c/Moreno Monroy 5. The diminutive size of the bustling *Orellana*, near to Pl. de la Constitución, is in inverse proportion to its reputation as one of the best in town. Daily 8am–11pm; closed Wed.

Tapadaki c/Carretería 69. A stylish new tapas and *raciones* bar serving a fusion of Asian and Spanish tapas; try their *solomillo de cerdo y shitake* (pork loin with mushrooms). Does special offers on bottled wines. Daily 1–4pm & 8pm–midnight.

★ **El Tapeo de Cervantes** c/Carcer 8. This Lilliputian but outstanding bar near the Teatro Cervantes, merits at least one visit. Here you'll find a cosy *ambiente* and some creative tapas priced between €3–5 –be sure to sample their atun rojo en salsa coliflor (tuna in a cauliflower sauce). Tues–Sat 1–4pm & 7.30–11.30pm; Sun 7:30–11.30pm; closed Mon.

Uvedoble c/Cister 15. Modernistic bar offering "designer" tapas in a minimalist setting with a small but interesting tapas and *raciones* menu. Try their *croquetas caseras ibéricos* (croquettes with jamón) or *ensalada de membrillo* (quince salad). Also does tasty desserts. Mon–Sat noon–4pm & 8pm–midnight.

RESTAURANTS

Al-Yamal c/Blasco de Garay 3, near Hostal El Cenachero. Good Arabic restaurant serving up pricey but authentic meat in spicy sauces, couscous – *cordero* (lamb) couscous is a house special – and other typical dishes. Good selection of Moroccan wines. Daily 7.30pm–midnight; closed Sun.

Antigua Casa Guardia c/Pastora at the junction with the Alameda. This is one of Málaga's oldest bars dating from the nineteenth century and one of the few still serving the traditional sweet Málaga wine (Falstaff's "sack"), made from muscatel grapes and dispensed from huge barrels. Try washing it down with shellfish sold from a stall at the rear of the bar. The new-season wine, *Pedriot*, is incredibly sweet; much more palatable is *Seco Añejo*, which has matured for a year. Daily 9am–10pm; closed Sun.

Antonio Fernando Lesseps 7. Popular small and central restaurant serving well-prepared *malagueño* dishes with an outdoor terrace in an atmospheric cul-de-sac off the

north end of c/Nueva; *menú* for around €12. Daily 1.30–4pm & 9–11pm.

Bar Los Pueblos c/Ataranzas, almost opposite the market. This busy diner serves satisfying, inexpensive food all day – bean soups and *estofados* are its specialities; gazpacho is served in half-pint glasses. Daily 8am–10pm.

Bar-Restaurante Palacios c/Eslava 4, near the train station. Plain, honest food in a vibrant *comedor popular* with friendly waiters; has a *menú* for €9, and specialities include *jamón iberico*, fish *surtido* and a mean paella. Daily 1.30–4pm & 8.30–11.30pm.

Cañadu Pl. de la Merced 21. Relaxed vegetarian restaurant serving a good selection of salad- and pasta-based dishes as well as couscous and *ajo blanco* (cold garlic soup) accompanied by organic wines and beers. Daily 9am–midnight.

Il Laboratorio Pl. San Pedro de Alcántara, off c/Carretería. Italian-style pizzeria-trattoria serving (besides pizzas) salads and daily specials. They also do breakfasts – try their *revueltos* (scrambled eggs) – and there's a small outdoor terrace under the trees on this charming *plazuela*. Daily 10am–midnight.

La Moraga Paseo Marítimo ☎ 952 224 153. Michelin-starred top chef Dani García has instituted a chain of stylish tapas and *raciones* bars. This one replaced one of the city's oldest seafront restaurants – although it has retained the sea-view terrace. The interior styling is "Seventies boutique" and the portions are small, if creatively edged. You could try the mini "bull burgers" – a new take on the US's national dish – or a whole fried *lubina* (sea bass) for €25 per person. The staff are young and enthusiastic, but although Sr García designed the menu he is rarely around. Daily 1.30–4pm & 8–11.30pm.

★ **Parador Gilbralfaro** Monte Gilbralfaro ☎ 952 221 902. Superior dining on the terrace with spectacular views over the coast and town. The house specialities are *malagueño* fish and meat dishes, and the *menú* is excellent value at around €23.50 (lunch) or €33 (dinner) with reasonable wine prices. Ring to book a frontline table. Main dishes €10–20. If you can't face the climb, take a taxi or bus #35 east along Paseo del Parque. Daily 1–4pm & 7.30–10.30pm.

★ **Sal Gorda** Avda. Canovas de Castillo 12. Excellent little *raciones* (and *media raciones*) bar-restaurant serving up a mouthwatering range of seafood and shellfish. Their *arroz marinero* at around €26 (for two – and sometimes even cheaper as one of their special offers) is recommended. Also has outstanding Asturian *sidra* (cider) on draught. Daily 1–4.30pm & 8–11.30pm.

El Tintero El Palo. Right at the far eastern end of the seafront, just before the *Club Náutico* (bus #11; ask for "*Tintero*"), this is a huge beach restaurant where the waiters charge round with plates of fish (around €7.50 each) and you shout for, or grab, anything you like. Beware of the platters or *bandejas* which can cost significantly

4

more. The fish to go for are, above all, *mero* (a kind of gastronomically evolved cod) and *rosada* (dogfish and catfish), along with Andalucian regulars such as *boquerones* (fresh anchovies), *gambas* (prawns) and *sepia* (cuttlefish). *Haute cuisine* it certainly isn't, but for sheer entertainment it's a must. Daily 1.30–4.30pm & 8.30–11.30pm.

El Vegetariano Pozo del Rey 5, just north of the Teatro Romano. Atmospheric little veggie place offering a variety of imaginative pasta-, cheese- and salad-based dishes. Daily 1–4pm & 9–11.30pm; closed Sun.

NIGHTLIFE

Most of Málaga's **nightlife** is northeast of the cathedral along and around **calles Granada and Beatas** and the streets circling the nearby **Plaza de Uncibay**. In the summer months, there's also a scene nearer the sea at **Malagueta**, south of the bullring. At weekends and holidays, dozens of youth-oriented disco bars fill the crowded streets in these areas, and over the summer – though it's dead out of season – the scene spreads out along the seafront to the suburb of **Pedregalejo**. Here the streets just behind the beach host most of the action, and dozens of *discotecas* and smaller music bars lie along and off the main street, Juan Sebastián Elcano. Málaga's daily paper, *Sur*, is good for local entertainment **listings**; there's also an English edition (*Sur in English*) on Fridays, available from *turismos* and hotels.

Anden Pl. de Uncibay. Disco bar with a wild crowd and a playlist featuring Spanish pop, house and reggae. Two big dance rooms are serviced by four bars, and there are often queues to get in. Fri & Sat only; 11pm–late.

Asúcar Junction of c/Juan de Padilla & c/Lazcano west of Pl. de Uncibay. The place to come for salsa in Málaga. Daily 8pm–late.

La Botellita Pasaje Mitjana, slightly west of Pl. Uncibay. Wild place packed to the rafters with young local revellers dancing to the tunes of the Spanish Top 40. At the end of this alley, the tiny Pl. Marqués Vado del Maestre is filled with drinking bars and plenty of night-time action. 9pm–late.

Calle de Bruselas Pl. de la Merced 16. A laid back, mainly gay, Belgian-style bar serving breakfasts (until 1pm), bar food during the day and *copas* after dark. Stages frequent live music and events and has a lively terrace that stays open into the small hours. Daily 9am–2am (weekends 3am).

Cruces de Caminos c/Convalecientes, north of Pl.

Uncibay. A late-opening bar specializing in Spanish rock and techno. Thurs–Sat 11pm–3.30am.

★ **El Pimpi** c/Granada 62. Cavernous and hugely popular *bodega*-style bar serving up, among other concoctions, tasty *vino dulce* by the glass or bottle. There are tapas to go with the drinks and you can do a bit of celebrity-spotting on their wall of photos (including a young Antonio Banderas). Don't miss a superb terrace (with Alcazaba view) out the back. A great place to kick-start the evening. Daily noon–4pm & 7pm–1am.

Puerta Oscura c/Molina Lario 5 near the cathedral. Slightly incongruous classical-music bar – sometimes with live performers – which also mounts art exhibitions; serves cocktails, ices and baguettes. T-shirts are definitely a no-no here. Daily 7pm till 2am; closed Sun.

Vino Mío c/Alamos 11. Friendly lunchtime-onwards bar-restaurant serving creative tapas and fusion food (Morrocan/Asian/Spanish) with some veggie options and a free flamenco show (Mon–Sat) at 8.30pm. Daily 1.30pm–1am.

DIRECTORY

Banks Numerous banks all over town have ATMs, especially along c/Marqués de Larios and on Pl. de la Constitución. El Corte Inglés will also change currency free of charge.

Books Málaga's best travel bookshop is Mapas y Compañía, c/Compañía 33, west of Pl. de la Constitución – they sell IGN walking maps, as well as 1:50,000 Mapas Cartografía Militar (military maps). The most central general bookshop is Librería Luces, Alameda Principal 16 (north side), which stocks a selection of titles in English.

Consulates UK, Edificio Eurocom, c/Mauricio Moro Pareto 2 ☎952 352 300; US, Avda. Juan Gómez 8, Fuengirola ☎952 474 891; Republic of Ireland, Avda. de los Boliches 15, Fuengirola; ☎952 475 108.

Football After spending a few seasons in Division 2, in 2008 C.F. Málaga were promoted back into the top flight and appear to have consolidated their status under former Real Madrid coach Manuel Pellegrini. Games are at La

Rosaleda stadium, Paseo de Martiricos s/n, at the northern end of the Río Guadalmedina. Tickets can be purchased from the stadium (☎952 614 210, ⊛www.malagacf.es).

Hospital Hospital Carlos Haya, Avda. Carlos Haya, 2km west of the city centre ☎951 290 000.

Internet Free wi-fi connection is available in the vicinity of the Teatro Cervantes and along the central c/Marqués de Larios. Conventional cybercafés near the centre include Locutorio Telsat, c/Gómez Pallete 7, near the Teatro Cervantes (daily 10am–midnight).

Left luggage There are lockers and a *consigna* at the train station (daily 6.15am–12.45am), and lockers at the bus station (daily 6.30am–11pm).

Pharmacy Farmacia Caffarena (24hr) on the Alameda at no. 2, near the junction with c/Marqués de Larios ☎952 212 858.

Police The Policía Local are at Avda. La Rosaleda 19 (☎952

126 500); in emergencies, dial ☎092 (local police) or ☎091 (national).

Post office c/Santa Lucía 7, slightly north of Pl. Constitución (Mon–Fri 8.30am–8.30pm, Sat 8.30am–1pm).

Shopping El Corte Inglés, Avda. de Andalucía 4, is a great department store and its basement supermarket has a terrific selection of the nation's wines and spirits. La Mallorquina, Pl. Felix Saenz (near the market), is a good place to pick up *malagueño* cheeses, wines, almonds and dried fruit. Flamenca, c/Calderería 6, north of the cathedral (ⓦwww.flamenka.com), stocks a range of *trajes de flamenco* (costumes), as well as shoes, instruments and flamenco CDs, DVDs and books.

Garganta del Chorro

Fifty kilometres northwest of Málaga lies the deep, rugged canyon of the Río Guadalhorce, known as the **Garganta del Chorro**. It's an amazing place – an immense five-kilometre-long cleft in a vast limestone massif, which has become Andalucía's major centre for rock-climbers. The gorge's most stunning feature, however, is a concrete catwalk, El Camino del Rey, which threads the length of the gorge, hanging precipitously halfway up its side. Built in the 1920s as part of a hydroelectric scheme, it was one of the wonders of Spain, but it has fallen into disrepair, and access to the catwalk has finally been cut at each end of the gorge, making it impossible to reach without a guide and climbing gear. It's still possible to explore the rest of the gorge, however, and get a view of the *camino* by doing the walk described below. A glimpse of both gorge and *camino* can also be had from any of the trains going north from Málaga – the line, slipping in and out of tunnels, follows the river for a considerable distance along the gorge, before plunging into a last long tunnel just before its head.

The walk from El Chorro

One of the best ways of viewing the gorge is to follow a twelve-kilometre **walk** (vehicles should follow the same route) from the village of **EL CHORRO**. Take the road from the train station, signposted "Pantano de Guadalhorce", reached by crossing over the dam and turning right, then following the road north along the lake towards the hydroelectric plant. After 8km turn right at a junction to reach – after 2km – the bar-restaurant *El Mirador*, poised above a road tunnel and overlooking the various lakes and reservoirs of the Guadalhorce scheme. From the bar (where you should leave any transport) a dirt track on the right heads towards the gorge. Follow this and take the first track on the right after about 700m. This climbs for some 2km to where it splits into two small trails. The trail to the left leads after 300m to a magnificent **viewpoint** over the gorge from where you can see the Camino del Rey clinging to the rock face. The right-hand track climbs swiftly to an obvious peak, the **Pico de Almochon**, with more spectacular views, this time over the lakes of the Embalse de Guadalhorce.

ARRIVAL AND DEPARTURE	GARGANTA DEL CHORRO
By train and bus El Chorro is served by a single daily direct train (55min; currently running at 6.19pm), but no buses, from Málaga. There is a bus to El Chorro from nearby Alora (at 12.30pm Mon–Fri) which is served by ten daily trains.	**By car** To get there with your own transport, take the MA402 heading west from Málaga towards Alora (where the road is titled the A343) and turn west at Valle de Abdalajís along the minor MA226, a journey of around 65km.

ACCOMMODATION

Bar-Restaurante Garganta del Chorro ☎952 497 219, ⓦwww.lagarganta.com. Near the station, this restaurant and rooms complex has pleasant rooms inside a converted mill and overlooking a pool. **€81**

Camping El Chorro ☎952 495 244, ⓦwww.albergue campingelchorro.com. In the village, this is an excellent campsite with a pool and restaurant, reached by heading downhill to your right for 400m after getting off the train. They also rent out wood cabins sleeping up to six. Cabins €55

★ **Finca La Campana** ☎ 626 963 942, ⓦwww .el-chorro.com. Signs from the station will direct you 2km to this farmhouse set in rural surroundings with a bunkhouse, double rooms sharing bath and a cluster of

pleasant cottages sharing a pool. Run by Swiss climber Jean Hofer, the place also offers courses in rock climbing and caving, rents out mountain bikes, kayaks on the nearby lake/reservoir, and can arrange hiking excursions, as well as guided trips along the Camino del Rey using ropes to gain access. Bunks €12, double €29, cottages €42

EATING AND DRINKING

For **food**, besides the campsite's economical bar-*cafetería* and the pricier *Garganta*'s more upmarket restaurant, there are few other options.

Bar Isabel Train station. Actually on the station platform, this bar-cum-grocery-store offers a few basic tapas and *raciones* and – if Isabel is in the mood – sometimes *platos combinados*. Daily 9am–10pm.

Antequera and around

ANTEQUERA, some 55km north of Málaga on the main rail line to Granada, is an undistinguished, modern town, but it does have peripheral attractions in a number of fine churches, a group of prehistoric dolmen caves among the most important on the Spanish peninsula, and a fine old Plaza de Toros.

Nuestra Señora del Carmen

Pl. del Carmen • Tues–Fri 10.30am–1.30pm & 4.30–5.45pm, Sat & Sun 11am–2pm • €2

The finest of Antequera's collection of Baroque churches (the *turismo* can provide a full list) is **Nuestra Señora del Carmen** on Plaza del Carmen. The church's rather plain facade little prepares you for the eighteenth-century interior, now painstakingly restored to its former glory. The main altar's sensational thirteen-metre-high *retablo* – one of the finest in Andalucía – is a masterly late-Baroque extravaganza of carved wood by Antonio Primo and Diego Márquez, its centrepiece a Virgin in a *camarín* (shrine) flanked by a bevy of polychromed saints and soaring angels.

The dolmen caves

Tues–Sat 9am–6pm, Sun 9.30am–2.30pm • Free

Antequera's most visited monuments are the group of prehistoric dolmen caves on the town's northern edge. Now enclosed in a futuristic new "dolmen park" with visitor centre, car park and a Centro de Interpretación. The grandest and most famous of these megalithic monuments is the **Cueva de Menga**, its roof formed by an immense 180-tonne monolith. Dating from around 2500 BC a columned gallery leads to an oval burial chamber, probably the final resting place of an important chieftain. The nearby **Cueva de Viera** dating from a century or two later has cut stones but a smaller burial chamber. To reach the dolmens, take the Granada road out of town – an easy ten-minute walk – to the turning, rather insignificantly signposted, after about 1km on the left.

Two kilometres away, a third cave, **El Romeral** (same hours), is different (and later) in structure, with a domed ceiling of flat stones; get instructions (and a map) of how to reach it from the visitor centre.

The Plaza de Toros

Museum Tues–Fri 10.30am–2pm & 4–6pm, Sat & Sun 10.30am–2pm • Free

The **Plaza de Toros** in the newer part of town on the Alameda de Andalucía is also worth a look, and staged its first *corrida* in August 1848. Whatever your view on bullfighting, it's difficult not to pick up the atmosphere the old place generates, especially when you survey the amphitheatre from the matador's position in the centre of the burning sand. The ring also has a small museum filled with the usual bullfighting photos, *trajes de luces* (bullfighters' suits) and other taurino paraphernalia.

INFORMATION	ANTEQUERA

Turismo Town maps and information on El Torcal are available from a helpful tourist office on the central Pl. San Sebastián (June–Sept Mon–Sat 11am–2pm & 5–8pm, Sun 11am–2pm; Oct–May Mon–Sat 10.30am– 1.30pm & 4–7pm, Sun 11am–2pm; ☎952 702 505, ⓦturismoantequera.com), alongside the church of the same name.

ACCOMMODATION

A good base for visits to nearby El Torcal, Antequera has plenty of **accommodation** options and prices are reasonable. The Antequera *turismo* can provide information regarding some attractive *casas rurales* to rent near El Torcal.

Camping Torcal ☎952 111 608, ⓦwww.comple joruraltorcal.com. Camping is no longer allowed inside the *parque natural*, but this campsite lies on the park's edge just off the C3310, 6km south of Antequera. Closed Oct– March. €6; €5 per tent; €5 per vehicle

★ **Hospedería Coso San Francisco** c/Calzada 25 ☎952 840 014, ⓦcososanfrancisco.com. Comfortable and good-value a/c en-suite rooms with TV plus a friendly welcome make this a winner. Also has a very good restaurant. €40

Hotel Plaza San Sebastián Pl. San Sebastián 4 ☎952 844 239, ⓦhotelplazasansebastian.com. Attractive two-star hotel facing the church of San Sebastián offering well-equipped a/c rooms with satellite TV. Exterior rooms €75, interior €55

Número Uno c/Lucena 40 ☎952 843 134, ⓦhotel numerouno.com. A relatively new hotel with pleasant a/c en-suite rooms with TV, plus a roof terrace above a popular bar-restaurant. €35

Parque Natural de El Torcal

Centro de Visitantes daily 10am–5pm • ☎952 702 505 or ☎617 444 772

Approaching Antequera along the old road from Málaga (MA424) via Almogía and Villenueva de la Concepción, you pass the entrance to the popular natural park famed for its haunting rock sculptures. **Parque Natural de El Torcal**, 13km south of Antequera, is one of the most geologically arresting of Spain's natural parks. A massive high plateau of glaciated limestone tempered by a lush growth of hawthorn, ivy and wild rose, it can be painlessly explored using the three walking routes that radiate from the centre of the park, outlined in a leaflet available from the **Centro de Visitantes**.

Trails

The best-designed and most exciting **trails** are the yellow and red routes, the former climaxing with suitable drama on a cliff edge with magnificent views over a valley. The latter gives fantastic vantage points of the looming limestone outcrops, eroded into vast, surreal sculptures. Because of the need to protect flora and fauna, the red route is in a restricted zone and can only be visited with a **guide** (ask at the *centro*). The **green** and **yellow routes** (waymarked) can be walked without a guide, the former taking about forty minutes if you don't dawdle, the latter about two hours. In early summer on the popular green route you may find yourself competing with gangs of schoolkids, who arrive en masse on vaguely educational trips, excitedly trying to spot La Copa (the wine glass), El Lagarto (the lizard) and La Loba (the she-wolf), as well as other celebrated **rock sculptures**. Keep an eye on the skies while you're here, for griffon vultures are frequent visitors and, with their huge wingspans, make a spectacular sight as they glide overhead.

ARRIVAL AND DEPARTURE

EL TORCAL

By bus Buses run from Málaga (Mon–Fri 5 daily, Sat & Sun daily); ask the driver to drop you at the road for El Torcal from where it's a four-kilometre uphill slog to the visitor centre.

By taxi turístico The most convenient way to visit the park without your own transport is the *taxi turístico*, which can be arranged through the *turismo* in Antequera; for €42, a taxi will drop up to four passengers off at the Centro de Recepción and wait (roughly an hour) until you have completed the green route before returning you to Antequera.

Nerja

The eastern section of the Costa del Sol ribbons east of the city of Málaga as far as Almería, and is generally uninspiring. Inland there are plenty of attractive sierras to explore but, though far less developed than its twin coastal strip to the west of Málaga, there's little to tempt you to stop before you reach the twin resorts of Nerja and Almuñécar – which are its saving feature. First, some 40km out of Málaga, comes **NERJA**, nestling in the foothills of the Almijara range. This was a village before it was a resort, so it has some intrinsic character, and villa development has been shaped around it.

The focus of the whitewashed old quarter is the **Bálcon de Europa**, a striking palm-fringed belvedere overlooking the sea. The beaches flanking this are also reasonably attractive, with a series of quieter coves within walking distance. There are plenty of other great **walks** around Nerja, too, well documented in the *turismo*'s own leaflets; or, at Smiffs Bookshop, c/Almirante Ferrandiz 10, you can buy individual leaflets detailing walks in the area by local resident and hiker Elma Thompson.

The Cuevas de Nerja

Daily July & Aug 10am–7.30pm; rest of year 10am–2pm & 4–6.30pm; • €8.50 • ⓦ www.cuevadenerja.es

Nerja's chief tourist attraction, the **Cuevas de Nerja**, 3km east from the town, are a heavily commercialized series of caverns, impressive in size – and home to the world's longest-known **stalactite** at 63m – though otherwise not tremendously interesting. They also contain a number of prehistoric paintings, but these are not currently on public view.

ARRIVAL AND INFORMATION

NERJA

By bus The main bus station (actually a stand) is on c/San Miguel at the north end of town close to Pl. Cantarero; from here hourly buses leave for the *cuevas*. It's a 5min walk south from the bus station to the beach and centre.

Turismo c/Carmen 1 (July–Sept daily 10am–2pm & 6–10pm; Oct–June Mon–Fri 10am–2pm & 5–8pm, Sat 10am–1pm; ☎ 952 521 531, ⓦ www.nerja.org), next to the *ayuntamiento* and just west of the Bálcon de Europa.

ACCOMMODATION

Hostal Marissal Paseo Bálcon de Europa 3 ☎ 952 520 199, ⓦ www.hostalmarissal.com. Excellent *hostal* in the town's prime location – actually on the belvedere. En-suite balcony rooms come with a/c, TV and strongbox and many (try for rooms 102–5 or 204–5) have sea view; it also rents apartments (€115) in the same location. **€70**

Hostal Mena c/El Barrio 15 ☎ 952 520 541, ✉ info@hostalmena.es. Central rooms come with bath, sea views and a/c or fans plus a delightful garden at the rear in this very friendly *hostal*. **€43**

Hotel Paraiso del Mar c/Carabeo 22 ☎ 952 521 621, ⓦ www.hotelparaisodelmar.es. With similar views to the parador, this is a very pleasant hotel where all rooms come with jacuzzi and many have sea-view balconies.

There's also a pool, gardens and sauna dug out of the cliff face. Sea view **€154**, inland view **€135**

Parador Nacional c/Almuñécar 8 ☎ 952 520 050, ⓦ www.parador.es. Overlooking one of Nerja's most popular beaches, Playa de Burriana, to which you descend with a private lift, this is a modern parador with comfortable rooms and a pool set in attractive gardens. **€180**

CAMPING

Camping Nerja ☎ 952 529 714, ⓦ www.nerjacamping.com. Located 4km east of town along the N340 this is a decent campsite with shade, pool, bar and restaurant. **€5.75**; **€5.75** per tent; **€4.50** per vehicle

Almuñécar

The lively resort of **ALMUÑÉCAR** is marred by a number of towering holiday apartments, and the rocky grey-sand beaches are rather cramped, but the esplanade behind them, with palm-roofed bars (many serving free tapas with each drink) and restaurants, is fun, and the old quarter – clustered around a sixteenth-century castle – attractive. The two main beaches, the **Playa San Cristóbal** and the **Playa Puerta del Mar** are separated by the towering headland of the Peñon del Santo.

ARRIVAL AND INFORMATION
ALMUÑÉCAR

By bus The bus station, which has frequent connections to Málaga and Granada, is at the junction of avenidas Juan Carlos I and Fenicia, northeast of the centre.

Turismo In an imposing neo-Moorish mansion on Avda.

de Europa (daily 10am–2pm & 5–8pm, July & Aug 6–9pm; ☎ 958 631 125, ⓦ www.almunecar.info), behind the Playa San Cristóbal beach at the west end of the town.

ACCOMMODATION

The pressure on **accommodation** in Almuñécar is not quite as acute as at Nerja. There are more than enough hotels to cope with the summer crush, while good-value *hostales* encircle the central Pl. de la Rosa in the old town.

Hostal Plaza Damasco c/Cerrajos 16, ☎ 958 630 165. Cosy and recently renovated *hostal* just off the plaza it's named after, offering a/c en-suite rooms with TV. **€50**

Hostal Rocamar c/Córdoba 3, near the bus station ☎ 958 630 023. Good-value small hostal offering en-suite rooms equipped with fans and TV. **€40**

★ **Hotel Casablanca** Pl. San Cristóbal 4 (aka Pl. Abderramán) ☎ 958 635 575, ⓦ www.hotelcasablanca almunecar.com. The wonderful *Casablanca* has just had a refit making it one of the most charming hotels on the

coast. Fifty metres from the beach with a splendid neo-Moorish facade, the hotel boasts comfortable a/c terrace balcony rooms with great sea views (on the front). The friendly family proprietors make this an all-round winner. Free wi-fi and garage parking. **€70**

Hotel La Najarra c/Guadix 12 ☎ 958 630 873, ⓦ www.hotelnajarra.com. Well-equipped hotel with a/c rooms plus garden pool, tennis courts and easy parking a couple of minutes' walk from the Playa de San Cristóbal. **€78**

EATING AND DRINKING

There are numerous **places to eat** along the seafront, many of them offering cheap, if unspectacular fare. Many of the town's more interesting possibilities are set further back in the *casco antiguo* or old quarter.

Bar-Taberna El Cortijillo Pl. Kelibia 4. Lively *freiduría* and *raciones* bar popular with young locals and one of many in an attractive square with a lively scene on summer nights. Daily 1–4pm & 7pm–midnight.

Bodega Francisco c/Real 15, north of Pl. Rosa. Wonderful old bar with barrels stacked up to the ceiling and walls covered with ageing *corrida* posters and mounted

boars' heads. The *fino* and *montilla* are both excellent, and the bar offers a wide range of tapas and *platos combinados*. A dining area has recently been added and impromptu flamenco sometimes adds to the fun. Daily 1–4pm & 8–11.30pm; closed Sun.

Horno de Candida c/Orovia 3 ☎ 958 883 284. The restaurant of Almuñécar's hotel school is located in an

4

GETTING AROUND THE COSTA DEL SOL

One of the major selling points of the **Costa del Sol** is its ease of access. Hundreds of flights arrive here every week, and **Málaga airport** is positioned midway between **Málaga**, the main city on the coast, and **Torremolinos**, its most grotesque resort. You can easily reach either town by taking the electric train (*cercanía*) that runs every thirty minutes (daily 7am–11.45pm) along the coast between Málaga and **Fuengirola**, 20km to the southwest. Frequent bus connections also link all the major coastal resorts, while a toll *autopista* (motorway) between Málaga and Sotogrande has taken the strain off the often-overloaded coastal highways. Inland, Granada, Córdoba and Seville are all within easy reach of Málaga; so, too, are **Ronda** and the beautiful "White Towns" to the west, and a handful of relatively restrained coastal resorts, such as **Nerja**, to the east.

elegant mansion which itself incorporates a remarkable Moorish brick oven (*horno*), now a dining room. The food is excellent and there's a wonderful roof terrace as well. It's in the mid-price zone with a *menú de degustación* for around €30. 1–4.30pm & 7.30pm–midnight; closed Wed.

La Última Ola Paseo Puerto del Mar 4. This excellent seafront fish restaurant also serves tapas and, pandering to carnivores, squeezes a few meat dishes onto its menu as well. One of its noted offerings is *dorada a la gaditana* (sea bream). Main dishes €8–15. Daily noon–5pm & 8pm–midnight.

The Costa del Sol resorts

West of Málaga – or more correctly, west of Málaga airport – the real **Costa del Sol** gets going, and if you've never seen this level of tourist development, it's quite a shock. These are certainly not the kind of resorts you could envisage anywhere else in Europe. The 1960s and 1970s hotel and apartment tower-blocks were followed by a second wave of property development in the 1980s and 1990s, this time villa homes and leisure complexes, funded by massive international investment. It's estimated that 300,000 foreigners now live on and around the Costa del Sol, the majority of them British and other Northern Europeans, though marina developments such as Puerto Banús have also attracted Arab and Russian money.

Approached in the right kind of spirit, it is possible to have fun in resorts like **Torremolinos**, **Fuengirola** and, at a price, in **Marbella**. But if you've come to Spain to be in Spain, put on the shades and keep going at least until you reach Estepona.

Fuengirola

Twenty kilometres southwest of Málaga, beyond the vast, bizarre resort of Torremolinos, lies **FUENGIROLA**, very slightly less developed and infinitely more staid than its neighbour. It's not so conspicuously ugly, but it is distinctly middle-aged and family-oriented. The huge, long beach has been divided up into restaurant-beach strips, each renting out lounge chairs and pedal-boats.

INFORMATION FUENGIROLA

Turismo Located at Avda. Jesús S. Rein 6 (Mon–Fri 9.30am–2pm & 5–7pm, Sat 9.30am–1.30pm; ☎952 467 457, ⓦwww.visitafuengirola.com), close to the train (☎952 128 080) and bus (☎952 475 066) stations.

ACCOMMODATION

Camping Fuengirola Carretera Nacional 340, km 207 ☎952 474 108, ⓦwww.campingfuengirola.net. The nearest campsite lies 2km to the east of the centre and is reached via a turn-off near the junction of the N340 and the road to Mijas; bus "Línea Roja" from Avda. Ramón y Cajal on the main Marbella road will take you there.

Hostal Cuevas c/Capitan 7 ☎952 460 606. Near to the Pl. de la Constitución, this is a good option for pleasant a/c en-suite rooms with TV. Free wi-fi zone. **€60**

Hostal Italia c/de La Cruz 1, off the east side of Pl. de la Constitución ☎952 474 193, ⓔhostal-italia@gmail .com. This friendly *hostal* is the nicest option around the town's focal plaza for a/c en-suite rooms with TV and balcony. Free wi-fi zone. **€75**

Hotel Las Piramides Paseo Marítimo s/n ☎952 583 297, ⓦhotellaspiramides.com. Fuengirola's upmarket option, this four-star giant at the western end of the seafront has sea-view rooms, its own pool and lots of luxury frills. Free wi-fi. **€200**

EATING

The warren of streets to the south of the pedestrianized main square (Pl. Constitución) are lined with **restaurants** of a rather depressing similarity while many of Fuengirola's very best restaurants and tapas bars are slightly outside the normal tourist beat.

★ **Bar La Paz Garrido** Avda. de Mijas. Just north of the Pl. de la Constitución, this hugely popular bar-restaurant serves up some of the best-value seafood in town – the gazpacho, *boquerones a la plancha* (fried anchovies) and *patatas bravas* (spicy sautéed potatoes) are highly recommended. Daily 12.30–11pm.

Mesón Don Pé c/de la Cruz s/n. One of the few restaurants worth recommending in the zone south of the Pl. de la Constitución, this specializes in mid-price meat dishes and *cochinillo asado* (suckling pig). Daily 7.30–11.30pm.

Monopol c/Palangreros 7. *Monopol* is a good little French-style bistro with a very reasonable *menú gourmet* for €19.80 (excluding wine). Besides meat and fish dishes, it also serves up salads and pasta. Daily 7.30–10.30pm; closed Sun.

Old Swiss House c/Marina 28. This small mid-priced restaurant has Swiss-influenced cooking with a dash of panache – including the *crêpes suzette* dessert. Daily 1–3.30pm & 6–11pm; closed Tues.

La Plaza Pl. de la Constitución. This pleasant bar with a popular terrace on the square opens for breakfast and does snacks and salads throughout the day. In the evening it serves *copas* (late-night drinks). Daily 9am–11pm.

Marbella and around

Sheltered by the hills of the Sierra Blanca, **MARBELLA** stands in considerable contrast to most of what's come before. Since it attracted the attentions of the smart set in the 1960s the town has zealously polished its reputation as the Costa del Sol's most stylish resort. Glitz comes at a price, of course: many of the chic restaurants, bars and cafés cash in on the hype, and in the old town – where most visitors spend their time – everything costs considerably more. Until the recent financial crash Marbella had the highest per capita income in Europe and more Rolls-Royces than any European city apart from London. In recent years, the Spanish government and authorities have been exercised by the arrival in Marbella of Russian and Italian mafia bosses who have been buying up property and using the town as a base to control their criminal empires, activities that led to the discovery by police in 2005 of Europe's biggest-ever money-laundering operation, channelling billions of dollars from worldwide crime syndicates into Marbella-registered companies. In an ironic twist of history, there's been a massive return of Arabs to the area, especially since the late King Fahd of Saudi Arabia built a White House lookalike, complete with adjacent mosque, on the town's outskirts, where the Saudi royal family and a veritable army of courtiers and servants spend the summer months.

The old town

To be fair, Marbella has been spared the worst excesses of concrete architecture and also retains the greater part of its **old town** – set back a little from the sea and the new development. Centred on the attractive Plaza de los Naranjos and still partially walled, the old town is hidden from the main road and easy to miss. Slowly, this original quarter is being bought up and turned into clothes and jewellery boutiques and restaurants, but the process isn't that far advanced. You can still sit in an ordinary bar in a small old square and look up beyond the whitewashed alleyways to the mountains of Ronda.

The beaches

South of the centre, there are three excellent **beaches** stretching east from Playa de la Badajilla and Playa de Venus to Playa de la Fontanilla to the west, which gets progressively less crowded the farther west you go.

Puerto Banús

The seriously rich don't stay in Marbella itself. They secrete themselves away in villas in the surrounding hills or laze around on phenomenally large and luxurious yachts at the marina and casino complex of **Puerto Banús**, 6km west of town. As you'd expect, Puerto Banús has more than its complement of big-name designer boutiques, cocktail bars and restaurants, most of them very pricey.

ARRIVAL AND INFORMATION **MARBELLA**

By bus From the bus station (☎ 952 764 401) in the north of the town, buses #2 or #7 will drop you close by the old town; otherwise, it's a 20min walk south along c/Trapiche.

Turismo Pl. de los Naranjos (Mon–Fri 9am–9pm, Sat 10am–2pm; ☎ 952 823 550). It can help with accommodation, and provides a street-indexed town map and list of addresses.

ACCOMMODATION

All Marbella's budget **accommodation** is in the old town, or on or around c/Luna just east of here. Pressure on rooms is tight in July and extremely so in August, when you'll need to book ahead.

Albergue Juvenil c/Trapiche 2 ☎ 952 771 491. To the north of the old town, the *Albergue Juvenil* has economical beds in smart double and four-person en-suite rooms, and there's also a pool. Under-26 **€21**, over-26 **€27**

Hostal Berlin c/San Ramón 21 ☎ 95 282 13 10, ⊕ www.hostalberlin.com. Sparkling and very friendly *hostal*; all rooms come with bath, a/c and satellite TV, and free internet access is available to guests (also wi-fi throughout). Bargain rates outside July & Aug. **€60**

Hostal El Gallo c/Lobatos 44 ☎ 95 282 79 98, ⊕ www .hostalelgallo.es. Good-value en-suite a/c rooms with TV above a great little restaurant. Free wi-fi. **€60**

Hostal Guerra Llanos de San Ramón 2 ☎ 95 277 42 20. Clean, simple and economical rooms with bath, some with balcony, on the eastern flank of the old town near the beach. Free wi-fi. **€40**

Hostal Juan c/Luna 18 ☎ 952 779 475, ⊜ pensionjuan@ hotmail.com. This *hostal* has a friendly proprietor and good-value en-suite rooms with TV and fridge on a tranquil street. Free wi-fi. **€45**

Hotel El Fuerte Avda. Severo Ochoa 10 ☎ 952 861 500, ⊕ www.fuertehotels.com. The older and more charming of two four-star hotels with the same name fronting the Playa de Venus. Amenities include beach access, gardens, pool, gym, tennis courts and sauna. **€200**

★ **Hotel La Morada Mas Hermosa** c/Montenebros 16, ☎ 952 924 467, ⊕ www.lamoradamashermosa .com. Sited to the north of Pl. de los Naranjos, this is an enchanting small hotel in a refurbished eighteenth-century townhouse with elegant, individually styled a/c rooms (most with terraces). **€108**

EATING AND DRINKING

Although it now has a Michelin double-rosetted restaurant (*Calima* in the *Hotel Gran Meliá Don Pepe*) Marbella's best-value eating and drinking places aren't always the most obvious. Avoid the touristy and overpriced **restaurants** on the Pl. de los Naranjos, which turn the whole square into their dining terrace after dark – you're better off seeking out some of Marbella's excellent **tapas bars** and less brassy restaurants. And despite it's high-roller reputation, it's possible to dine well in Marbella at normal *andaluz* prices.

TAPAS

Bar Altamirano Pl. de Altamirano 4, southeast of Pl. Naranjos. Great place for some of the freshest seafood tapas and *raciones* in town; has a terrace with tables spread across a small square. Daily 11am–4pm & 6.30–midnight.

Cervecería Simon c/Pablo Casals 1, near the seafront at the western end of the central zone. Fine tapas at low prices and a pleasant terrace on which to enjoy them. Specials include *chopitos fritas* (cuttlefish) and *rabo de toro* (stewed bull's tail). Daily 1–4pm & 6–11pm.

El Estrecho c/San Lázaro 12. Founded in 1954, this is an excellent and atmospheric little tapas bar with a wide range of possibilities. There's a small dining room off to the side if you want to make a meal of it and cool jazz sounds often float in the background. Try their *carne mechada* (larded meat) or *mejillones tigres* (tiger mussels). In the same alley, *Tierr Aranda* (opposite) and the nearby *Casa Bar Bartolo* (with a roof terrace) are also worth a visit. Daily noon–midnight.

Marisquería La Pesquera Pl. de la Victoria s/n, west of Pl. de los Naranjos. More restaurant than *raciones* bar these days, this remains a town favourite, with first-class *fino*, too. House specials include *cigalitas cocidas* (Dublin Bay prawns) and *almejas marinera* (clams in wine). Daily 12.30pm–1am.

★ **Taberna de Santiago** Paseo Marítimo 5. Actually on the Avda. del Mar leading to the sea, this is the tapas and *raciones* bar of the famous nearby *restaurante* (see below). Everything is top quality and the prices are very reasonable: an *ensalada mixta*, *ración* of *bacalao con tomate* (cod in tomato sauce) and half-litre *jarra* of house wine is easily enough for two and weighs in at under €30; or try a paella at €18 for two. Has a pleasant sea-view terrace. Should you feel like pushing the boat out you could also try *Santiago's* oyster bar next door. Daily noon–11pm.

RESTAURANTS

El Gallo c/Lobatas 44. Good, popular and economical little neighbourhood restaurant serving up traditional *andaluz* dishes such as *langostino pil pil* (prawns with chilli) and *conejo al ajillo* (rabbit in garlic). There's a great-value *menú* for €10. Daily 12.30–4pm & 8–11pm; closed Thurs.

★ **Santiago** Avda. Duque de Ahumada s/n ☎ 952 770 078, ⊕ restaurantesantiago.com. For a splurge, head for *Santiago*, near the Puerto Deportivo, one of Marbella's swankiest and oldest restaurants, founded in the 1950s by Santiago Domínguez – who started out with a *chiringuito* on the beach opposite. Over fifty years later Santiago is still overseeing his restaurant and bars and is famous throughout Spain as one of the great restaurateurs. The restaurant serves excellent traditional food (both fish and meat) with a creative touch. The "value for money" philosophy is typified by a recommended *menú de degustación* (€50 including wine). The restaurant has an attractive seafront terrace. Daily 1–4.30pm & 8–11pm.

Sociedad de Pesca Deportiva Puerto Deportivo, Local 5, to the left as you enter the port. The Marbella fishermen's club should know a thing or two about seafood and they serve up reasonably-priced delicious fish and *mariscos* at their restaurant with a terrace in the port. Try their *almejas a la marinera* (clams in wine) or *boquerones fritos* (fried anchovies). Noon–4pm & 7.30–11pm; closed Mon.

NIGHTLIFE

Marbella has one of the liveliest **nightlife** scenes on the *costa*, with action centred around Pl. Puente de Ronda, Pl. de Africa in the old town and Pl. de Olivos to the west of here. The once riotious Puerto Deportivo, the seafront yacht harbour, also has a scene, although this has cooled down in recent years due to complaints about noise. It now boasts many laid back *copas* bars with terraces filled with sofas and easy chairs.

Buddha Avda. del Mar 3. Central retro *discoteca* and club with themed nights (such as *música Cubana*, salsa, and 60s sounds). Daily 10pm–late.

Club Premiere Pl. de Olivos 2. Lively music venue often staging live gigs ranging from pop to electronica and acid-jazz. One of a clutch of clubs around this square. Daily 10pm–early hours.

Dreamer's Carretera de Cádiz 175, Río Verde. One of the bigger and better clubs on the outskirts of Puerto Banús playing a range of garage, house and techno sounds. Only hits its stride in the small hours. Daily 10pm–late.

Town House c/Alamo 1. Long-established *bar de copas* with rock and electronica sounds. Open all year, they light a roaring fire in winter. Daily 10pm–late.

Estepona and around

The coast continues to be upmarket (or "money-raddled", as Laurie Lee put it) until you reach **ESTEPONA**, about 30km west, which is about as Spanish as the resorts round here get. It lacks the enclosed hills that give Marbella character, but the hotel and apartment blocks that sprawl along the front are restrained in size, and there's space to breathe. The fine sand beach has been enlivened a little by a promenade studded with flowers and palms, and, away from the seafront, the old town is very pretty, with cobbled alleyways and two delightful plazas. At the beginning of July, the Fiesta y Feria week transforms the place, bringing out whole families in flamenco-style garb.

Plaza de Toros museum complex

All Mon–Fri 9am–3pm, Sat 10am–2pm • Free

From May onward, Estepona's **bullfighting** season gets under way in a modern bullring reminiscent of a Henry Moore sculpture. This building has now taken on an additional role as the location for no fewer than four museums: the **Museo Etnográfico** (folk museum), the **Museo Arqueológico**, the **Museo Paleontológico** (paleontology) and, perhaps the most interesting, the **Museo Taurino** (bullfighting), with fascinating exhibits and photos underlining the importance of *taurinismo* in Andalucian culture.

Selwo Adventure Park

July & Aug daily 10am–8pm (see website rest of year opening times) • €24.50, children (up to age 9) €17; discount tickets with a reduction of €6 are available from the Estepona *turismo* • ⓦ www.selwo.es

The **Selwo Adventure Park** is a landscaped zoo 6km to the east of town where the two-thousand-plus resident animals are allowed to roam in "semi-liberty" and there are re-creations of African Zulu and Masai villages. To reach the park, there are signed exits indicated from the N340 and the A7-E15 Autopista del Sol, plus regular buses from all the major Costa del Sol resorts.

Casares

Beyond Estepona, 8km along the coast, a minor road (the MA546) climbs a farther 13km into the hills to **CASARES**, one of the classic *andaluz* White Towns. In keeping with the genre, it clings tenaciously to a steep hillside below a castle, and has attracted

4

its fair share of arty types and expats. But it remains comparatively little known; bus connections are just about feasible for a day-trip (leaving 1pm, returning 4pm; further details from the *turismo*).

ARRIVAL AND INFORMATION ESTEPONA

By bus The station is on Avenida de España, to the west of the centre behind the seafront.

Turismo The efficient and centrally located *turismo* at Avda. San Lorenzo 1, west of the centre near the seafront (Mon–Fri 9am–8pm, Sat 10am–1.30pm; ☎ 952 802 002), will supply town maps and can help you find a room.

ACCOMMODATION

Outside August you should have no problem finding a **room** in Estepona.

Camping Parque Tropical 6km east of town on the N340, km162 ☎952 793 618. Estepona's nearest campsite is set back a few hundred metres from the beach in a former tropical garden with plenty of shade plus a spectacular conservatory-pool and restaurant. €4; €5 per tent; €5 per vehicle

Hostal El Pilar Pl. Las Flores ☎952 800 018, ✉ hostalpilar@telefonica.net. Friendly *hostal* on a charming plaza offering en-suite balcony rooms with a/c and TV. Free wi-fi zone. €55

Hotel Mediterráneo Avda. de España 68, on the seafront to the east of the focal c/Terraza ☎95 279 33 93, 🌐 www.mediterraneo-estepona.com. Functional but good-value seafront hotel, where rooms have bath, TV and (mostly) sea views. €65

Pensión San Miguel c/Terraza 16 ☎95 280 26 16. Friendly establishment with its own bar, a little west of Pl. Las Flores. All rooms are en suite and come with a/c and TV. Free wi-fi zone. €50

EATING AND DRINKING

Among Estepona's many **places to eat** is a bunch of excellent *freidurías* and *marisquerías* among which *Aguilar* behind the seafront at c/Real 54, and *La Palma* at c/Terraza 57, the town's main street, are both worth a try.

★ **La Escollera** Puerto Pesquero. At the foot of the lighthouse in the fishing harbour, adjoining the Puerto Deportivo, this is a vibrant, reasonably priced restaurant for excellent fish and *mariscos*. In addition to a great tapas bar there's a wonderful sea-view terrace restaurant. Daily 1–4pm & 7–10.30pm; closed Mon.

Restaurante El Gavilán del Mar Pl. Arce. A decent place for seafood (meat dishes are also on offer), specializing in paella, and with a terrace on this charming square. Try their *sardinas asadas* (grilled sardines). Daily 11am–midnight.

Gibraltar

GIBRALTAR's interest is essentially its novelty: the genuine appeal of the strange, looming physical presence of its rock, and the dubious one of its preservation as one of Britain's last remaining colonies. For most of its history it has existed in a limbo between two worlds without being fully part of either. It's a curious place to visit, not least to witness the bizarre process of its opening to mass tourism from the Costa del Sol. Ironically, this threatens both to destroy Gibraltar's highly individual hybrid society and at the same time to make it much more British, after the fashion of the expat communities and huge resorts of the Costa. In recent years, the economic boom Gibraltar enjoyed throughout the 1980s, following the reopening of the border with Spain, has started to wane, and the future of the colony – whether its population agrees to it or not – is almost certain to involve closer ties with Spain.

The town has a necessarily simple layout, as it's shoehorned into the narrow stretch of land on the peninsula's western edge in the shadow of the towering Rock. **Main Street** (La Calle Real) runs for most of the town's length, a couple of blocks back from the port. On and around Main Street are most of the shops, together with many of the British-style pubs and hotels.

BRITISH SOVEREIGNTY IN GIBRALTAR

Sovereignty of the Rock (a land area smaller than the city of Algeciras across the water) will doubtless eventually return to Spain, but at present a **stalemate** exists regarding the colony's future. For Britain, it's a question of divesting itself of the colony without incurring the wrath of Gibraltar's citizens who are implacably opposed to any further involvement with Spain. For Spain, there are unsettling parallels with the *presidios* (Spanish enclaves) on the Moroccan coast at Ceuta and Melilla – both at present part of Andalucía. Nonetheless, the British presence is in practice waning and the British Foreign Office clearly wants to steer Gibraltar towards a new, harmonious relationship with Spain. To this end, they are running down the significance of the military base, and now only a token force of under a hundred British troops remains – most of these working in a top-secret high-tech bunker buried deep inside the Rock from where the Royal Navy monitors sea traffic through the Strait (accounting for a quarter of the world's movement of all shipping).

In 1967, just before Franco closed the border in the hope of forcing a quick agreement, the colony voted on the return to Spanish control of the Rock – rejecting it by 12,138 votes to 44. Most people would probably sympathize with that vote – against a Spain that was then still a dictatorship – but more than forty years have gone by, and Spanish democracy is now secure, and the arguments are becoming increasingly tenuous. May 1996 saw a change in the trend of internal politics, with the defeat of the colony's pugnaciously anti-Spanish Labour government (following two previous landslide victories) and the election of a new **Social Democratic administration** led by Peter Caruana. Caruana won further victories in 2000, 2004 and 2007.

The ruling PSOE socialist **Spanish administration** elected in 2004 has repeated the claims over Gibraltar voiced by all its predecessors, and the political stalemate seems set to continue for as long as Britain uses the wishes of the Gibraltarians as a pretext for blocking any change in the colony's status – a policy that infuriates the Spanish government, whose former foreign minister, Abel Matutes, stated that the wishes of the residents "did not apply in the case of Hong Kong".

Yet Gibraltarians stubbornly cling to British status, and all their institutions are modelled on British lines. Contrary to popular belief, however, they are of neither mainly Spanish nor British blood, but an ethnic mix descended from Genoese, Portuguese, Spanish, Menorcan, Jewish, Maltese and British forebears. **English** is the official language, but more commonly spoken is what sounds to an outsider like perfect Andalucian Spanish. It is, in fact, *llanito*, an Andalucian dialect with the odd borrowed English and foreign words reflecting its diverse origins – only a Spaniard from the south can tell a Gibraltarian from an Andalucian.

4

Around the Rock

Cable car Daily: 9.30am–6pm, last trip down 5.45pm • £9 return, £7.50 one way **All sites** Daily: summer 9am–7pm; winter 9am–6.15pm • Nature reserve £0.50, inclusive ticket for cave, tower and exhibition €10, under-12s half price

From near the southern end of Main Street you can hop on a **cable car**, which will carry you up to the summit – **The Top of the Rock** as it's logically known – via **Apes' Den** halfway up, a fairly reliable viewing point to see the tailless monkeys. Although the cable car's fare structure militates against it, after riding to the top it's possible to walk back down, a pleasant twenty- to thirty-minute stroll. From The Top of the Rock you can look over the Strait of Gibraltar to the Atlas Mountains of Morocco and down to the town, the elaborate water-catchment system cut into the side of the rock, and ponder whether it's worth heading for one of the beaches such as Catalan Bay (see p.252). The area at the top of the Rock, containing the Apes' Den, St Michael's Cave and other sights, is called the **Upper Rock Nature Reserve**; the attractions in this zone cost extra and may only be accessed with an **inclusive ticket,** available from tourist offices or at each attraction. A grand tour of the Rock takes a half- to a full day.

St Michael's Cave

From the cable-car stop at The Top of the Rock, it's an easy walk south along St Michael's Road through the Nature Reserve, home to six-hundred-plus plant and tree species, to **St Michael's Cave**, an immense natural cavern that led ancient people to

LA LINEA
DE LA
CONCEPCIÓN

Catalan
Bay

CATALAN BAY RD

Water
Catchments

ROYAL TOWER ROAD

Upper
Galleries

SIGNAL STATION ROAD

Top of the Rock

CHARLES V WA

QUEEN'S ROAD

OLD QUEEN'S ARG

Airport

The Moorish
Castle
(Tower of Homage)

Gibraltor: A City
Under Siege
Exhibition

WILLIS'S ROAD SEE INSET

GREEN LANE

WINSTON CHURCHILL AVE

Police &
Customs

FLAT BASTION ROAD

PRINCE ED WARD'S ROAD

ENGINEER LANE

Cab
Ca

MAIN STREET

ⓘ

QUEENSWAY

QUEENSWAY

Bahía
de Gibraltar

Marina
Bay

Queensway
Quay

Tangier Ferry
& Hydrofoil

Puerto
de Gibraltar

North
Mole

Detached
Mole

● EATING & DRINKING	
Buddies Pasta Casa	2
Cannon Bar	7
The Clipper	10
Corks Wine Bar	8
Gibraltar Arms	11
The Horseshoe	4
Marrakech	1
Piccadilly Garden Bar	5
Royal Calpe	9
Saccarello's Coffee House	6
Smiths Fish & Chips	3

0   100
metres

believe the Rock was hollow and gave rise to its old name of Mons Calpe (Hollow Mountain). The cave was used during the last war as a bomb-proof military hospital and nowadays hosts occasional concerts. If you're adventurous, you can arrange at the tourist office for a guided visit to Lower St Michael's Cave, a series of chambers going deeper down and ending in an underground lake.

The Tower of Homage
If you walk rather than take the cable car to the top, you could visit the **Tower of Homage**, reached via Willis' Road. Dating from the fourteenth century, this is the most visible surviving remnant of the old **Moorish Castle**.

Gibraltar: A City Under Siege
Near to the Tower of Homage on Willis' Road itself, and housed in a former ammunition store – with some eighteenth-century graffiti etched into its walls – is the **Gibraltar: A City Under Siege** exhibition, which uses tableax to explain the various sieges the Rock has endured during its three hundred years as a British colony.

The Upper Galleries
Farther up you'll find the **Upper Galleries** (aka the Great Siege Tunnels), blasted out of the rock during the Great Siege of 1779–82, in order to point guns down at the Spanish lines.

Walking down the Rock

To **walk down** from The Top of the Rock (20min), follow Signal Station Road and St Michael's Road to O'Hara's Road and the **Mediterranean Steps** – a very steep descent most of the way down the east side, turning the southern corner of the Rock. You'll pass through the **Jews' Gate** and into Engineer Road, from where the return to town is through the Alameda Gardens and past the evocative **Trafalgar Cemetery**, with a good line in imperial epitaphs and where some of those who perished at the Battle of Trafalgar are buried.

The Gibraltar Museum

Mon–Fri 10am–6pm, Sat 10am–2pm • £2

The **Gibraltar Museum**, in Bomb House Lane, is mainly concerned with gilding the imperial story, although the building also holds two well-preserved and beautiful fourteenth-century **Moorish baths** as well as a rather incongruous Egyptian mummy washed up in the bay.

Nelson's Anchorage

Mon–Sat 9.30am–6.15pm • £1, free with inclusive Rock ticket

The only other sight of possible interest is **Nelson's Anchorage**, on Rosia Road, where a monstrous **100-tonne Victorian gun** marks the site where Nelson's body was brought ashore – preserved in a barrel of rum – from HMS *Victory* after the Battle of Trafalgar in 1805.

Offshore excursions

Offshore excursions include daily dolphin-spotting **boat trips**, run by companies operating from Marina Bay, including Dolphin Safari (£22.50, children £13.50; ☎20071914) and Dolphin World (£25, children £12.50; mobile ☎54481000), which offers a money-back guarantee should you not see dolphins. You should ring first to book places or ask the tourist office to do it for you.

Catalan Bay

Gibraltar has plans to reclaim an area equivalent to that of the present town from the sea, and is currently doing feasibility surveys on pumping up sand from the sea bed. But at present, there's just the one tiny fishing village at **Catalan Bay**, which is where you'll find the Rock's best **beach** backed by a characterless stretch of seafront reminiscent of a hum-drum British holiday resort. The inhabitants of the village like to think of themselves as very distinct from the townies on the other side of the Rock. It's easily reached by following Devil's Tower Road from near the airport (20min walk) or on bus #4 from the centre.

ARRIVAL AND DEPARTURE   GIBRALTAR

By air Bland Travel (Cloister Building, Irish Town ☎20079478, ⓦwww.blands.gi; closed Sat & Sun), the leading travel agent in Gibraltar can assist with booking easyJet (2 daily), British Airways (daily) and Monarch Airlines (daily) flights to London and the latter's (4 weekly) flights to Manchester.

By bus Owing to the relatively scarce and pricey accommodation, you're far better off visiting the Rock on a day-trip from La Línea or Algeciras. The border with Gibraltar is a 5min walk from the centre of La Línea. Just over the border buses (#9; every 15min) make the short journey to Main Street and the town centre. This is also an easy 10min walk across part of the airport runway.
Destinations Buses from Algeciras go to La Línea on the hour and half-hour (30min).

By car If you have a car, don't attempt to bring it to Gibraltar – the queues at the border are always atrocious

and parking is a nightmare owing to lack of space. Use the underground car parks in La Línea – there's one beneath the central Pl. de la Constitución – and either take the bus or walk into Gibraltar.

By ferry (to Morocco) One decidedly functional attraction of Gibraltar is its role as a port for Morocco. A catamaran service, the *Tanger Jet*, sails to Tangier (Fri 6.30pm; 1hr) and back (Sun 4pm local time); check with the agent for the current timetable. Tickets – available from the agent Turner, 65/67 Irish Town (☎20078305, ⓔturner@gibtelecom.net) – cost £39 one way and £70 return for a foot passenger (email the agent for vehicle charges). Bland Travel (see above) runs twice-weekly day-trips to Tangier in Morocco on Monday, Wednesday and Friday (Tetouan & Tangier; £75), which includes a guided tour and lunch. A useful site for checking the latest ferry schedules is ⓦdirectferries.co.uk.

INFORMATION

Turismo In the focal Casemates Square (Mon–Fri 9am–5.30pm, Sat 10am–3pm, Sun 10am–1pm; ☎20045000, ⓦvisitgibraltar.gi), and there's a sub-office in the customs and immigration building at the border (Mon–Fri 9am–4.30pm, Sat 10am–3pm; ☎50762). Much of Gibraltar – with the exception of the cut-price booze

shops – closes down at the weekend, but the tourist sights remain open, and this can be a quiet time to visit.
Internet access and free wi-fi are available at the public library in the John Mackintosh Hall (Mon–Fri 9.30am–7.30pm), at the south end of Main Street; it's also a cultural centre and mounts frequent exhibitions.
Currency The Gibraltar pound is used (the same value as the British pound, but different notes and coins); if you pay in euros, you generally fork out about five percent more. It's best to change your money once you arrive in Gibraltar, since the exchange rate is slightly higher than in Spain and there's no commission charged. Gibraltar pounds can be hard to change in Spain.

PHONING GIBRALTAR
From Spain, the UK and Europe dial 00 + 350 + number
From North America dial 011 + 350 + number

ACCOMMODATION

Shortage of space on the Rock means that **places to stay** are at a premium and there's little in the budget category. No **camping** is allowed on the peninsula, and if you're caught sleeping rough or inhabiting abandoned bunkers, you're likely to be arrested and fined.

Bristol Hotel Cathedral Square ☎ 20076800, ⓦ www .bristolhotel.gi. Long-established place with refurbished rooms and a pool (supplement for sea view). **£81**.

Cannon Hotel 9 Cannon Lane ☎ 20051711, ⓦ www .cannonhotel.gi. Small, pleasant hotel close to Main St with a/c rooms, some sharing bath. B&B **£42**

Emile Youth Hostel Montagu Bastion, Line Wall Rd ☎ 20051106, ⓦ www.emilehostel.net. Gibraltar's privately run youth hostel has the cheapest beds in town, but it's not the most attractive location. Dorms **£17**, basic shared-bathroom doubles **£40**

Queen's Hotel Boyd St ☎ 20074000, ⓦ www.queens hotel.gi. Decent, traditional hotel offering comfortable rooms, many with terrace balconies. Charges **£70** for the cheapest non-sea-view double (supplement for sea view).

Rock Hotel 3 Europa Rd ☎ 20073000, ⓦ www.rock hotelgibraltar.com. Flagship hotel immediately below the Apes' Den, trading on its imperial connections – rooms are decorated in "colonial style" and come with ceiling fans and a trouser press. Doubles with sea view **£160**

EATING AND DRINKING

Restaurants are far more plentiful than places to stay, though by Spanish standards are still relatively expensive: pub snacks or fish and chips are reliable stand-bys. Main Street is crowded with touristy places, among which *Smiths Fish and Chip Shop*, at no. 295 near the Convent, is a long-established institution. Gibraltarian **pubs** mimic traditional English styles (and prices), but are often rowdy, full of soldiers and visiting sailors.

RESTAURANTS

Buddies Pasta Casa 15 Cannon Lane, off the east side of Main Street by the cathedral. Decent pasta in all its varieties is served up here – as well as the ubiquitous fish and chips. Daily noon–10pm.

The Clipper 78 Irish Town. *The Clipper* serves British-style pub grub – a house special is steak-and-ale pie – along with a variety of beers. Daily 10am–11pm.

Corks Wine Bar 79 Irish Town. *Corks Wine Bar* is a tranquil venue and offers a variety of salads and pasta dishes as well as pub-style favourites such as steak-and-Guinness pie. Daily 10am–10pm; closed Sun.

Marrakech Restaurant 9 Governor's Parade. An interesting Moroccan option in the centre of town, with a pleasant terrace. A wide-ranging menu offers couscous (chicken, lamb and vegetarian), tagines and other Magrebí dishes and a set *menú* for around £10. Daily 1–10.30pm.

Saccarello's Coffee House 57 Irish Town. *Saccarello's Coffee House* is a local institution and a great place for tea and home-made confectionery. It also does lunch dishes such as pies and lasagna and there's free wi-fi throughout. Daily 10am–7.30pm; closed Sun.

PUBS

Cannon Bar Cannon Lane, behind the cathedral. One of Gibraltar's few (relatively) quiet pubs with friendly staff, decent food and a small terrace. Daily 11am–late.

Gibraltar Arms 186 Main St. British-style boozer in the heart of the action with the usual all-day pub food (including their all-day British breakfast). Tends to stay open longer than its neighbours. Daily 11am–late.

The Horseshoe 193 Main St. Decent and hearty pub grub with an outdoor terrace. Serves a range of British and international beers. Daily 11am–late.

Piccadilly Garden Bar 3 Rosia Rd, just beyond the Referendum Gates (aka South Port). A garden bar serving breakfasts (British and Spanish) as well as meat and fish dishes. Daily 11am–late.

Royal Calpe 176 Main St. Pub with outdoor terrace and pub grub – the house special is chicken-and-mushroom pie although they also do quiches and salads. Wide selection of beers. Both kitchen and pub are known to close early when trade is slack. Daily 11am–late.

4

Algeciras

ALGECIRAS occupies the far side of the bay from Gibraltar, spewing out smoke and pollution in the direction of the Rock. The last town of the Spanish Mediterranean, it must once have been an elegant resort; today, it's unabashedly a port and industrial centre, its suburbs extending on all sides. When Franco closed the border with Gibraltar at La Línea it was Algeciras that he decided to develop to absorb the Spanish workers formerly employed in the British naval dockyards, thus breaking the area's dependence on the Rock.

Most travellers are scathing about the city's ugliness, and unless you're waiting for a bus or train, or heading **for Morocco**, there's admittedly little reason to stop. Yet some touch of colour is added by the groups of Moroccans in transit, dressed in flowing *jallabahs* and slippers, and lugging unbelievable amounts of possessions. Algeciras has a real port atmosphere, and even passing through it's hard to resist the urge to get on a boat south, if only for a couple of days in Tangier. Once you start to explore, you'll also discover that the **old town** has some very attractive corners that seem barely to have changed in fifty years, especially around Plaza Alta.

ARRIVAL AND DEPARTURE ALGECIRAS

By train At Algeciras, the train line begins again, heading north to Ronda, Córdoba and Madrid. The route to Ronda is one of the best rail journeys in Andalucía; there are four departures a day.

Destinations Córdoba: (1 daily; 3hr 15min); Granada (3 daily; 4hr 20min); Madrid (2 daily; AVE 5hr 20min); all Algeciras northbound trains go via Ronda (1hr 40min) and Bobadilla.

By bus The main bus station (☎ 956 653 456) is in c/San Bernardo, behind the port, next to the *Hotel Octavio* and just short of the train station.

Destinations Cádiz (hourly 7am–10pm; 2hr 15min); La Línea (for Gibraltar: every 30min; 30min); Madrid (4 daily; 8hr); Seville (7 daily; 2hr 30min); Tarifa (every 30min).

By ferry Morocco is easily visited from Algeciras: in summer, there are crossings to Tangier and to the Spanish *presidio* of Ceuta, little more than a Spanish Gibraltar with a brisk business in duty-free goods, but a relatively painless

way to enter Morocco. Tickets cost €30 (normal ferry) or €36 (fast) one-way to Tangier or Ceuta, and are sold at scores of travel agents along the waterfront and on most approach roads. For up-to-date information on hydrofoils and fast-ferries, check with the *turismo* or with the ferry companies: Trasmediterránea, on the harbourfront (☎ 956 583 400, ⓦ trasmediterranea.es), or Viajes Transafric at Avda. Marina 4 (☎ 956 654 311, ⓦ transafric.com), fronting the port. Viajes Transafric also do a daily all-inclusive day-trip to Tangier by fast-ferry, which includes a guided tour, lunch and time for shopping (€59). Wait till Tangier – or if you're going via Ceuta, Tetouan – before buying any Moroccan currency; rates in the embarkation building kiosks are very poor. A useful site for checking the latest ferry schedules is ⓦ directferries.co.uk.

Destinations Ceuta (up to 25 daily; 35min); Tangier (up to 30 daily; 1hr–2hr 30min).

INFORMATION

Turismo On c/Juan de la Cierva (Mon–Fri 9am–7.30pm, Sat & Sun 9.30am–3pm; ☎ 956 784 131, ⓦ www.ayto -algeciras.es), the pedestrianized avenue running east–west between the harbour and the train and bus stations.

They can provide a town map, help with finding a room and have up-to-date ferry schedules.

Internet A ccess at Locutorio Central, c/Teniente Maroto 2 (daily 10am–10pm), southeast of the market.

The White Towns towards Ronda

Andalucía is dotted with small, brilliantly whitewashed settlements – the **Pueblos Blancos** or "**White Towns**" – most often straggling up hillsides towards a castle or towered church. Places such as **Mijas**, up behind Fuengirola, are solidly on the tourist trail, but even here the natural beauty is undeniable. All of them look great from a distance, though many are rather less interesting on arrival. Arguably the best lie in a roughly triangular area between Málaga, Algeciras and Seville; at its centre, in a region of wild, mountainous beauty, is the spectacular town of **Ronda**.

Castellar de la Frontera

The first White Town on the route proper is **CASTELLAR DE LA FRONTERA**, 27km north of Algeciras, a bizarre village enclosed within the walls of a striking thirteenth-century Moorish castle, whose population, in accord with some

TOWARDS RONDA FROM THE COAST

Of several possible approaches to Ronda from the coast the stunningly scenic route up **from Algeciras**, via Gaucín, is the most rewarding – and worth going out of your way to experience. It's possible by either bus or train (a spectacularly scenic option), or, if you've time and energy, can be walked in four or five days. En route, you're always within reach of a river and there's a series of hill towns, each one visible from the next, to provide targets for the day. Casares is almost on the route, but more easily reached from Estepona.

From Málaga, most buses to Ronda follow the coastal highway to San Pedro before turning into the mountains via the modern A376 *autovía*, dramatic enough, but rather a bleak route, with no villages and only limited views of the sombre rock face of the Serranía; an alternative route, via Álora and Ardales, is far more attractive and is taken by a couple of daily buses. The two-hour train ride up from Málaga is another scenic option with three connecting services daily, including a convenient early-evening departure.

grandiose scheme, was moved downriver in 1971 to the "new" town of Nuevo Castellar, turning the castle settlement into a ghost village. Although remote and isolated much of the village inside the castle has been restored and now has a couple of bars as well as accommodation.

ACCOMMODATION CASTELLAR DE LA FRONTERA

Casas Rurales de Castellar The same company that runs *Hotel Castellar* also runs *Casas Rurales de Castellar* which consists of a number of restored village houses with a decent restaurant attached. **€50**

Hotel Castellar ☎ 956 693 150, ⟐ www.tugasa.com. Of the two places to stay inside the castle walls, *Hotel Castellar* occupies part of the castle and has well-equipped rooms with fine views. B&B **€100**

Jimena de la Frontera and around

JIMENA DE LA FRONTERA, 20km north of Castellar de la Frontera along the A369, is a far larger and more open hill-town, rising to a grand Moorish castle with a triple-gateway entrance and round keep. In recent years it has become home to a considerable number of British expats who probably feel the need to be within working and shopping distance of Gibraltar.

Parque Natural de los Alcornocales

Jimena is also a gateway to the **Parque Natural de los Alcornocales**, a vast expanse of verdant hill country stretching south to the sea and north to El Bosque and covered with *alcornocales* (cork oaks). A haven for large numbers of birds and insects, the park is also a paradise for walkers. *Walking in Andalucía* by Guy Hunter-Watts also describes half a dozen walks in the park, two starting in Jimena.

ACCOMMODATION JIMENA DE LA FRONTERA

Camping Los Alcornocales ☎ 956 640 060, ⟐ www .campingalcornocales.com. Jimena's campsite occupies a suberb location with great views on the north side of town (reached by following c/Sevilla to the end), and has its own restaurant. **€4.50**, **€5.40** per tent, **€3.75** per vehicle

Hostal El Anon c/Consuelo 34 ☎ 956 640 113, ⟐ www .hostalanon.com. The charming and friendly *Hostal El Anon* is perhaps the best place to stay, comprising a series of tastefully renovated houses and stables with bar, restaurant and rooftop pool. **€67**

EATING AND DRINKING

Bar Ventorrillero Pl. de la Constitución 2. At the foot of c/Sevilla, the town's main artery, this is a friendly bar-restaurant with a lunchtime *menú* for around €8. Daily 9am–midnight.

Restaurante Bar Cuenca Avda. de los Deportes, on the way into town. This is perhaps the town's best place to eat, serving tapas and meals in its main room and with a pretty terrace patio at the rear. Main dishes €7–15. Daily 10am–4pm & 8–11pm.

Gaucín

Beyond Jimena, it's 23km farther along the A369 passing through woods of cork oak and olive groves to reach **GAUCÍN**. Almost a mountain village, Gaucín commands tremendous views (to Gibraltar and the Moroccan coast on a very clear day), and makes a great place to stop over.

ARRIVAL AND DEPARTURE

By bus and train You can reach Gaucín by bus or by train, but the train station (at El Colmenar on the fringes of the Cortés nature reserve) is 13km away. From here it's a bracing and mostly uphill hike to the village; a taxi (around €20 one way) can be arranged at *Bar-Restaurante Flores* fronting the station (☎ 952 153 026). They also do decent meals (€8 *menú*), and there are several other bars here. The train line between Gaucín and Ronda passes through a handful of tiny villages. En route, you can stop off at the station of Benaoján-Montejaque, from where it's an hour's trek to the prehistoric Cueva de la Pileta (see p.260). From Benaoján, Ronda is just three stops (30min) down the line.

ACCOMMODATION

Hostal Moncada c/Luís Armiñan ☎ 952 151 324. En-suite a/c rooms above a restaurant and next to the *gasolinera* (where you should enquire; get a room at the back for a view) as you come into the village from Jimena. **€40**

Hotel Rural Fructuosa c/Covento 67 ☎ 952 151 072, ⌨ www.lafructuosa.com. A more upmarket option in the village proper is the charming *Hotel Rural Fructuosa*, with its own restaurant nearby. **€98**

Ronda

The full natural drama of **RONDA**, rising amid a ring of dark, angular mountains, is best appreciated as you enter the town. Built on an isolated ridge of the *sierra*, it's split in half by a gaping river gorge, **El Tajo**, which drops sheer for 130m on three sides. Still more spectacular, the gorge is spanned by a stupendous eighteenth-century arched bridge, the **Puente Nuevo**, while tall, whitewashed houses lean from its precipitous edges.

Much of the attraction of Ronda lies in this extraordinary view, or in walking down by the Río Guadalvín, following one of the donkey tracks through the rich green valley. Birdwatchers should look out for the lesser kestrels nesting in the cliffs beneath the Alameda; lower down you can spot crag martins. The town has a number of **museums** and, surprisingly, has sacrificed little of its character to the flow of day-trippers from the Costa del Sol.

Ronda divides into three parts: on the south side of the bridge is the old Moorish town, **La Ciudad**, and farther south still, its **San Francisco** suburb. On the near north side of the gorge, and where you'll arrive by public transport, is the largely modern **Mercadillo** quarter.

La Ciudad

La Ciudad retains intact its Moorish plan and a great many of its houses, interspersed with a number of fine Renaissance mansions. It is so intricate a maze that you can do little else but wander at random. However, at some stage, make your way across the eighteenth-century **Puente Nuevo** bridge, peering down the walls of limestone rock into the yawning Tajo and the Río Guadalvín, far below.

Puente Nuevo

Mon–Fri 10am–7pm, until 6pm Nov–March, Sat & Sun10am–3pm • €2

The spectacular eighteenth-century **Puente Nuevo** bridge spanning the gorge between the Mercadillo and La Ciudad quarter was originally the town prison, and last saw use during the Civil War, when Ronda was the site of some of the south's most vicious massacres. Hemingway, in *For Whom the Bell Tolls*, recorded how prisoners were thrown alive into the gorge. The bridge itself is a remarkable construction and has its own **Centro de Información**, housed in the former prison above the central arch with exhibits documenting its construction and history; entry is to the side of the parador in Plaza de España.

Casa del Rey Moro gardens

C/Santo Domingo 17 • Daily 10am–7pm • €4 • ☎ 678 428 407

Once you're across the bridge, veering left along c/Santo Domingo (aka c/Marqués de Parada), will bring you to the somewhat arbitrarily named **Casa del Rey Moro** (House of the Moorish King), an early eighteenth-century mansion built on Moorish foundations. The gardens (but not the house itself) have recently been opened to the public, and from here a remarkable underground stairway, the Mina, descends to the river; these 365 steps (which can be slippery after rain), guaranteeing a water supply in times of siege, were cut by Christian slaves in the fourteenth century. There's a viewing balcony at the bottom where you can admire El Tajo's towering walls of rock and its bird life, although the long climb back up will make you wonder whether it was worth it.

Palacio del Marqués de Salvatierra

C/Santo Domingo

The **Palacio del Marqués de Salvatierra** is a splendid Renaissance mansion with an oddly primitive, half-grotesque frieze of Adam and Eve on its portal together with the colonial images of four Peruvian Indians. The house is still used by the family.

Baños Árabes

Mon–Fri 10am–7pm, Sat & Sun 10am–3pm • €3, free on Mon

At the foot of c/Santo Domingo you reach the two old town bridges – the **Puente Viejo** of 1616 and the single-span Moorish **Puente de San Miguel**; nearby, on c/San Miguel on the southeast bank of the river, are the distinctive hump-shaped cupolas and glass roof-windows of the old **Baños Árabes**. Dating from the thirteenth century and recently restored, the complex is based on the Roman system of cold, tepid and hot baths and is wonderfully preserved; note the sophisticated barrel-vaulted ceiling and brickwork octagonal pillars supporting horseshoe arches.

Santa María La Mayor

Pl. Duquesa de Parcent • Daily 10am–7pm • €3

At the centre of La Ciudad, on Ronda's most picturesque square, the Plaza Duquesa de Parcent, stands the cathedral church of **Santa María La Mayor**, originally the Moorish town's Friday mosque. Externally, it's a graceful combination of Moorish, Gothic and Renaissance styles with the belfry built on top of the old minaret. The interior is decidedly less interesting, but you can see an arch covered with Arabic calligraphy, and just in front of the street door, a part of the old Arab *mihrab*, or prayer niche, has been exposed.

Casa de Mondragón

C/Montero • Mon–Fri 10am–7pm, Oct–March until 6pm, Sat & Sun 10am–3pm • €3

Slightly west of Plaza Duquesa lies the fourteenth-century **Casa de Mondragón**, probably the real palace of the Moorish kings. Inside, three of the patios preserve original stuccowork and there's a magnificent carved ceiling, as well as a small museum covering local archeology and aspects of Moorish Ronda.

Museo Lara

C/Armiñán 29 • Daily 11am–8pm, Oct–March until 7pm • €4

To the northeast of the Plaza Duquesa de Parcent, on c/Armiñán, which bisects La Ciudad, you'll find the **Museo Lara**, containing the collection of *rondeño* Juan Antonio Lara, a member of the family that owns and runs the local bus company of the same name. An avid collector since childhood, Señor Lara has filled the spacious museum with a fascinating collection of antique clocks, pistols and armaments, musical instruments and archeological finds, as well as early cameras and cinematographic equipment.

Museo del Bandolero
C/Armiñan 65 • Daily 10.45am–7.30pm • €3.50

The **Museo del Bandolero** is largely devoted to celebrating the Serranía's illustrious, mainly nineteenth-century bandits and includes displays of their weapons, as well as tableaux and audiovisual presentations.

The southern end of La Ciudad

Near the southern end of La Ciudad, to the right, are the ruins of the **Alcázar**, once impregnable until razed by the French ("from sheer love of destruction", according to the nineteenth-century hispanist Richard Ford) in 1809. Beyond here the principal gates of the town, the magnificent Moorish **Puerto de Almocabar**, through which passed the Christian conquerors (led personally by Fernando), and the triumphal **Puerta de Carlos V**, erected later during the reign of the Habsburg emperor, stand side by side at the entrance to the suburb of San Francisco.

Mercadillo and Plaza de Toros
Bullring and museum open daily 10am–8pm, Oct–March until 6pm • €6

The **Mercadillo** quarter, which grew up in the wake of the Reconquest, is of comparatively little interest, although it is now the town's commercial centre. There is only one genuine monument here, the eighteenth-century **Plaza de Toros** sited on Plaza Teniente Arce, close to the beautiful cliff-top *paseo*, Paseo de Orson Welles, offering spectacular views towards the Sierra de Ronda. Ronda played a leading part in the development of bullfighting and was the birthplace of the modern *corrida* (bullfight). The ring, built in 1781, is one of the earliest in Spain and the fight season here is one of the country's most important. At its September *feria*, the *corrida goyesca*, honouring Spain's great artist Goya, who made a number of paintings of the fights at Ronda, takes place in eighteenth-century costume. You can wander around the arena, and there's a **museum** inside stuffed with memorabilia such as famous bullfighters' *trajes de luces* (suits) and photos of the ubiquitous Ernest Hemingway and Orson Welles – both avid aficionados – visiting the ring.

ARRIVAL AND DEPARTURE   RONDA

By bus Ronda's bus station – used by all bus companies – is on Pl. Redondo in the Mercadillo quarter, to the northeast of the bullring.

Destinations Arcos de la Frontera (2 daily; 2hr 30min); Cádiz (2 daily; 3hr 15min); Grazalema (2 daily; 35min); Jerez de la Frontera (2 daily; 2hr 30min); Málaga (12 daily; 2hr); Marbella (4 daily; 1hr); San Pedro de Alcantara (2 daily; 45min); Seville (5 daily; 2hr 30min); Ubrique (2 daily; 1hr 30min); Zahara de la Sierra (1 daily; 55min).

By train Ronda's train station lies a 5min walk east of the bus station on Avda. Andalucía, in the Mercadillo quarter to the northeast of the bullring. The station is 10min walk or easy bus or taxi ride from the centre.

By car Arriving by car, your best bet for street parking is to park as far out as possible (near the train station is usually feasible where there's also a pay car park), or head straight for one of the central pay car parks (clearly signed).

INFORMATION

Turismo At the northern end of the focal Pl. de España (Mon–Fri 9am–7.30pm, Sat & Sun 9.30am–3pm; ☎ 952 871 272), and can help with accommodation and provide a map.

Municipal tourist office Opposite the south side of the bullring (Mon–Fri 10am–7pm, 6pm Oct–March, Sat 10am–2pm & 3–5pm, Sun 10am–2.30pm; ☎ 952 187 119).

Website ◍ turismoderonda.es is also a good source of information on all aspects of the town.

Internet access is available at Mundial, c/Cruz Verde 21, a little southeast of the bus station.

ACCOMMODATION

Most of the **places to stay** are in the **Mercadillo** quarter, although some more-upmarket hotels have recently opened up in the old Moorish quarter, **La Ciudad**, on the south side of El Tajo. Both zones are within easy walking distance of Pl. de España.

Alavera de los Baños c/San Miguel s/n, next door to the Baños Árabes ☎952 879 143, ⓦwww.alaveradelosbanos.com. Enchanting small hotel with stylish rooms, garden, pool and views from rear rooms of grazing sheep on the hill across the river. Free wi-fi. **€95**

Hostal Andalucía c/Martínez Astein 19 ☎952 875 450, ⓦwww.andalucia.net. Pleasant en-suite rooms in leafy surroundings opposite the train station. **€42**

Hostal Ronda Sol c/Cristo 11, near the intersection with c/Seville ☎952 874 497. Good-value budget *hostal* for rooms with shared bath, but check what you're offered as two interior rooms (lacking windows) are a bit claustrophobic. **€25**

Hotel Colón c/Pozo 1, on the Pl. de la Merced ☎952 870 218, ⓦwww.hotelcolon.es. Charming small hotel with a/c en-suite facilities and – in rooms 301 & 302 – your own spacious roof terrace. Free wi-fi zone. **€48**

★ **Hotel San Gabriel** c/José Holgado 19, La Ciudad ☎952 190 392, ⓦwww.hotelsangabriel.com. One of the recently arrived hotels in La Ciudad, this is a stunning restoration of an eighteenth-century mansion, with beautifully furnished a/c rooms, an amusing five-seater cinema for guests (library of classic DVDs) and welcoming proprietors. Free wi-fi. **€90**

Parador de Ronda Pl. de España ☎952 877 500, ⓦwww.parador.es. Ronda's imposing parador has spectacular views overlooking El Tajo, plus a pool, terrace bar and very good restaurant. **€180**

CAMPING

Camping El Sur Carretera Ronda–Algeciras km 2.8 ☎952 875 939. Ronda's campsite with pool, bar and restaurant, lies some 2km out of town along the road to Algeciras. **€4.80**, **€2.30** per tent, **€4.80** per vehicle

EATING AND DRINKING

Most of Ronda's bargain **restaurants** are grouped round Pl. del Socorro and nearby Pl. Carmen Abela, though there are also some to be found near Pl. de España.

★ **Bar Faustino** c/Santa Cecilia 4, off Pl. Carmen Abela. Lively place for economical tapas, *raciones* and *platos combinados* with friendly service and an upstairs dining area. Stays open until well beyond midnight and has an open-air patio. Daily noon–late; closed Mon.

★ **Bar Maestro** c/Espinel 7, near Pl. de Toros. Great hole-in-the-wall (and one of Ronda's oldest tapas venues) with a tempting menu recited verbally by the proprietor. It's also a bar *taurino*, so the photos of past *torero* greats plus Hemingway and Welles (all one-time customers) gaze down from the walls. Try their *costillas* (pork ribs). Daily 8.30am–midnight; closed Mon.

Café Alba c/Espinel 44, the main pedestrianized shopping street. Piping-hot *churros* and delicious breakfast coffee. If this popular place is too packed, the nearby *Cafetería La Ibense* is a good alternative. Daily 8am–10pm.

Parador de Ronda Pl. de España ☎952 877 500. The parador's upmarket restaurant has an excellent choice of local and regional dishes such as *rabo de toro* (bull's tail), many of them appearing on a *menú* for €23 (lunch) or €33 (dinner). Daily 1–4pm & 8–11pm.

Patatín Patatán c/Borrego 7, off the east side of Pl. del Socorro. Popular tapas bar with a buzzing *ambiente* and a wide range of specials, including *patatas all-i-oli* (potatoes in garlic sauce) and *habas a la rondeña* (broad beans). *La Viña*, next door at no. 9, is also good. Daily 11am–4pm & 7–11pm; closed Wed.

Restaurante del Escudero Paseo de Blas Infante 1, near the Pl. de Toros ☎952 871 367. Superb, stylish restaurant housed in an elegant mansion with Ronda's best garden terrace, offering views towards the Serranía de Ronda. There's a *menú* for around €12. Daily 1–4pm & 7.30–11pm; closed Sun eve.

Tragabuches c/José Aparicio 1 ☎952 190 291. Ronda's most acclaimed restaurant is named after a celebrated eighteenth-century *rondeño* bullfighter-turned-bandit, and, with an adventurous menu (devised by top chef Benito Gómez) and minimalist decor, is worth a splurge. They offer a tasting *menú* for around €60. Booking advised. Daily 1–4pm & 8.30pm–midnight; closed Sun eve & Mon.

Around Ronda

Ronda makes an excellent base for exploring the superb countryside of the Serranía de Ronda to the south or for visiting the remarkable **Cueva de la Pileta**, with prehistoric cave paintings, and the Roman ruins of **Ronda la Vieja**.

Ronda la Vieja

Wed–Sun 10am–2pm; hours could be changed; confirm with either tourist office • Free

Some 12km northwest of Ronda are the ruins of a town and **Roman theatre** at a site known as **Ronda la Vieja**, reached by turning right 6km down the main A376 road to Arcos/Seville. At the site a friendly farmer, who is also the guardian, will present you with a plan (in Spanish). Based on Neolithic foundations – note the recently discovered prehistoric stone huts beside the entrance – it was as a Roman town in the first century AD that Acinipo (the town's Roman name) reached its zenith. Immediately west of the theatre, the site's most imposing ruin, the ground falls away in a startlingly steep escarpment offering fine views all around, taking in the picturesque hill-village of Olvera to the north.

Cueva de la Pileta

Daily guided visits on the hour 10am–1pm & 4–6pm • €8; limit of 25 persons per tour, booking essential at peak times • ☎ 952 167 343

West from Ronda is the prehistoric **Cueva de la Pileta**, a fabulous series of caverns with some remarkable paintings of animals (mainly bison), fish and what are apparently magic symbols. These etchings and the occupation of the cave date from about 25,000 BC – hence predating the more famous caves at Altamira in northern Spain – to the end of the Bronze Age. The tour lasts an hour on average, but can be longer, and is in Spanish – though the guide does speak a little English. There are hundreds of bats in the cave, and no artificial lighting, so visitors carry lanterns; you may also want to take a jumper, as the caves can be extremely chilly. Be aware if you leave a car in the car park that thieves are active here.

ARRIVAL AND DEPARTURE CUEVA DE LA PILETA

By train and bus To reach the caves from Ronda, take either an Algeciras-bound local train to Estación Benaoján-Montejaque (4 daily; 25min), or a bus, which drops you a little closer in Benaoján. There's a bar and restaurant at the train station if you want a bite to eat before the 6km walk (1hr) to the caves. Follow the farm track from the right bank of the river until you reach the farmhouse (30min). From here, a track goes straight uphill to the main road just before the signposted turning for the caves.

By car If you're driving, follow the road to Benaoján and take the signed turn-off, from where it's about 4km.

Towards Cádiz and Seville

Ronda has good transport connections in most directions. Almost any route to the north or west is rewarding, taking you past a whole series of White Towns, many of them fortified since the days of the Reconquest from the Moors – hence the mass of "de la Frontera" suffixes.

Perhaps the best of all the routes, though a roundabout one, and tricky without your own transport, is to **Cádiz** via Grazalema, Ubrique and Medina Sidonia. This passes through the spectacular **Parque Natural Sierra de Grazalema** before skirting the nature reserve of **Cortes de la Frontera** (which you can drive through by following the road beyond Benaoján) and, towards Alcalá de los Gazules, running through the northern fringe of **Parque Natural de los Alcornocales**, which derives its name from the forests of cork oaks, one of its main attractions and the largest of its kind in Europe.

Grazalema

Twenty-three kilometres from Ronda, **GRAZALEMA** is a striking white village at the centre of the magnificent Parque Natural Sierra de Grazalema, a paradise for hikers and naturalists. The **Puerto de las Palomas** (Pass of the Doves – at 1350m the second-highest pass in Andalucía) rears up behind the village. Cross this (a superb walk or drive), and you descend to Zahara de la Sierra and the main road west (see below).

INFORMATION GRAZALEMA

Turismo Located on Pl. Asomaderos, off the main square, Pl. de España (daily 10am–2pm & 3.30–7pm; ☎ 956 132 052), can provide information about the park,

accommodation in the village and activities such as horseriding, and also sells good walking maps.

ACCOMMODATION

Camping Tajo Rodillo ☎ 956 132 418. Grazalema's campsite is located above the village at the end of c/Las Piedras. €5.50; tent €5.50; parking free

Casa Las Piedras c/Las Piedras 6 ☎ 956 132 014, ⓦ casadelaspiedras.org. The only budget option, this is located above the main square. It has en-suite rooms and there's a wi-fi zone. It also rents out some apartments

nearby. Rooms €48, apartments €55

★ **La Mejorana** c/Santa Clara 6 ☎ 956 132 327, ⓦ lamejorana.net. One of the most attractive places to stay in the village, this welcoming *hostal* offers comfortably furnished rooms in an elegant *casa señorial* complete with pool. B&B €58

EATING AND DRINKING

The **bars and restaurants** on and around Pl. de España are generally reasonably priced, if not outstanding.

Cádiz El Chico Pl. de España 8. Located on the main square, this is one of the town's better restaurants and specializes in dishes of the *sierra – cordero al horno de leña* (lamb in a wood-fired oven) is a signature dish. There's a *menú* for €14. Daily noon–5pm & 8pm–midnight.

Casa de las Piedras c/Las Piedras 32. The *hostal*'s kitchen is also worth a try and serves game and rabbit dishes in addition to *trucha de El Bosque* (trout). It also offers a good-

value *menú* for €12. Daily 1.30–3.30pm & 8–10pm.

Torreón c/Agua 44. Reliable, traditional restaurant for dishes of the *sierra* including game and venison. The *sopa de Grazalema* is the region's hearty mountain soup, and there are also fish dishes and salads. The wine list is fairly priced and you can eat in the cosy dining room upstairs or, in better weather, on a street terrace below. Main dishes €8–15. Daily 12.30–4pm & 8–10.30pm.

Ubrique

From Grazalema, following the scenic A374 towards Ubrique takes you through the southern sector of the natural park, a landscape of dramatic vistas and lofty peaks. The road snakes through the charming ancient villages of Villaluenga del Rosario and Benaocaz with plenty of opportunities for hikes – perhaps down Benaocaz's six-kilometre-long paved Roman road – along the way. **UBRIQUE**, 20km southwest of Grazalema, is a natural mountain fortress and was a Republican stronghold in the Civil War. Today, it's a prosperous and bustling town, owing its wealth to the medieval guild craft of **leather working**. Shops selling the output of numerous workshops (footwear and bags, often at bargain prices) line the main street, Avenida Dr Solis Pascual.

Zahara de la Sierra

Heading directly to Jerez or Seville from Ronda, a scenic rural drive along the Grazalema park's eastern fringes, you pass below **ZAHARA DE LA SIERRA** (or *de los Membrillos* – "of the Quinces"), perhaps the most perfect example of these fortified hill towns. Set above a lake (in reality, the man-made *embalse*, or reservoir, which has dramatically changed the landscape to the north and east of town), Zahara is a landmark for many kilometres around, its red-tiled houses huddling round a church and castle perched on a stark outcrop of rock. Once an important Moorish citadel, the town was captured by the Christians in 1483, opening the way for the conquest of Ronda – and ultimately Granada.

Hostal Marqués de Zahara c/San Juan 3, the main street ☎956 123 061. A pleasant and central *hostal* with en-suite balcony rooms, a shady patio and its own restaurant nearby. **€50**

Hostal Los Tadeos Paseo de la Fuente s/n ☎956 123 086. Near the swimming pool on the eastern edge of the village, this is a decent option for rooms with bath and views. **€35**

Hotel Arco de la Villa Camino Nazarí s/n ☎956 12 32 30, ⓦwww.tugasa.com. On the road leading up to the castle, this is a good value and recently constructed hotel with spectacular views over the nearby *embalse*. **€60**

Arcos de la Frontera

Of more substantial interest, and another place to break the journey, is **ARCOS DE LA FRONTERA**, taken from the Moors in 1264, over two centuries before Zahara fell – an impressive feat, for it stands high above the Río Guadalete on a double crag and must have been a wretchedly impregnable fortress. This dramatic location, enhanced by low, white houses and fine sandstone churches, gives the town a similar feel and appearance to Ronda – only Arcos is poorer and, quite unjustifiably, far less visited. The streets of the town are if anything more interesting, with their mix of Moorish and Renaissance buildings. At its heart is the Plaza del Cabildo, easily reached by following the signs for the parador, which occupies one side of it. Flanking another two sides are the castle walls and the large Gothic-Mudéjar church of **Santa María de la Asunción**; the last side is left open, offering plunging views to the river valley. Below the town to the north lies **Lago de Arcos** (actually a reservoir) where locals go to cool off in summer.

Turismo Located on the hill leading up from the new to the old town at Cuesta de Belén 5 (April–Sept Mon–Sat 9.30am–2pm & 3–7.30pm, Oct–March Mon–Sat 9.30am–6.30pm; ⓦwww.ayuntamientoarcos.org). It can provide a town map and also does guided tours of the old town (Mon–Fri 11am & 6pm; €4).

ACCOMMODATION

A number of **hostales** providing budget accommodation have recently opened up in the old town, formerly the exclusive preserve of a clutch of upmarket hotels. Staying a little out of town, at the **Lago de Arcos**, where there are two hotels, is another possibility – though you'll need insect repellent in summer. There's a bus service to the lake.

IN TOWN

★ **La Casa Grande** c/Maldonado 10 ☎956 703 930, ⓦwww.lacasagrande.net. Perched along the same cliff-top as the parador, this elegant hotel has beautiful rooms inside a restored *casa señorial* with a columned inner patio and a sensational view from the terrace of their bar across the river valley. They also offer more expensive suites. Free wi-fi. **€85**

Hostal-Bar San Marcos c/Marqués de Torresoto 6 ☎956 700 721. Excellent *hostal* in the old town, offering pleasant rooms with bath. The friendly proprietors run a cosy bar-restaurant downstairs with a *menú* for €7. **€35**

★ **Parador de Arcos de la Frontera** Pl. del Cabildo ☎956 700 500, ⓦparador.es. Perched on a rock pedestal – with reassuringly reinforced foundations to prevent it from sliding over the cliff – this is one of the smaller paradores with elegant balcony rooms to enjoy the view. There's a delightful patio (open to the public for drinks and afternoon tea) and the "crow's nest" terrace has the best views in town. Also has a restaurant with a recommended *menú* for €32. **€163**

Pensión Callejón de las Monjas c/Dean Espinosa 4 ☎&ⓕ956 70 23 02. Decent if cramped *pensión* in the heart of the old town; all rooms are en suite and some slightly pricier ones come with a/c and terrace. **€30**

ON LAGO DE ARCOS

Hacienda El Santiscal 3km out of town on the lakeside ☎956 70 83 13, ⓦsantiscal.com. Small country hotel in a beautiful converted *hacienda* with very pleasant a/c rooms, restaurant and a pool in the grounds. Horseriding available. **€107**

Hotel Mesón de la Molinera Lago de Arcos ☎956 70 80 02, ⓦmesondelamolinera.com. Tranquil location on the waterfront with stunning views towards Arcos on its hill top. The hotel offers well-equipped balcony rooms with wi-fi and strongbox, while cheaper accommodation is on offer in chalet-style bungalows. Also has its own bar and restaurant. Easy parking. Rooms **€80**, bungalows **€60**

EATING AND DRINKING

There are plenty of places to **eat and drink** in Arcos in both the upper old town and the modern lower town. In addition to the places below a number of the accommodation options mentioned above have their own restaurants.

Alcaraván c/Nueva 1, close to the castle walls. Atmospheric cave restaurant serving tapas and *platos asados* (roasted meats) as well as a variety of salads. Daily 11am–4pm & 7.30pm–midnight; closed Mon.

Bar-Restaurante Terraza c/Múñoz Vásquez. Below the old town, in the gardens of the Paseo de Andalucía, this is a pleasant place to sit out, and serves a wide variety of inexpensive *platos combinados* and offers a *menú* for €8. Daily 9am–11pm.

Mesón Los Murales Pl. de Boticas 1. One of the best low-priced options in the old town, close to the church of San Pedro, and serving an economical *menú* for €9. Has a pleasant street terrace. Daily 11am–4pm & 7.30–11pm.

Seville (Sevilla)

"Seville," wrote Byron, "is a pleasant city, famous for oranges and women." And for its heat, he might perhaps have added, since **SEVILLE**'s summers are intense and start early, in May. Seville has three important monuments and an illustrious history, but what it's essentially famous for is its own living self – the greatest city of the Spanish south, of Carmen, Don Juan and Figaro, and the archetype of Andalucian promise. This reputation for gaiety and brilliance, for theatricality and intensity of life does seem deserved. It's expressed on a phenomenally grand scale at the city's two great festivals – **Semana Santa** (Holy Week at Easter) and the **Feria de Abril** (which starts two weeks after Easter Sunday and lasts a week). Either is worth considerable effort to get to. Seville is also Spain's second most important centre for **bullfighting**, after Madrid.

Despite its elegance and charm, and its wealth, based on food processing, shipbuilding, aircraft construction and a thriving tourist industry, Seville lies at the centre of a depressed agricultural area and has an unemployment rate of nearly twenty percent – one of the highest in Spain. The total refurbishment of the infrastructure boosted by the 1992 Expo – including impressive new roads, seven bridges, a high-speed rail link and a

4

MOORISH SEVILLE

Seville was one of the earliest Moorish conquests (in 712) and, as part of the **Caliphate of Córdoba**, became the second city of al-Andalus. When the caliphate broke up in the early eleventh century it was by far the most powerful of the independent states (or *taifas*) to emerge, extending its power over the Algarve and eventually over Jaén, Murcia and Córdoba itself. This period, under a series of three Arabic rulers from the **Abbadid dynasty** (1023–91), was something of a golden age. The city's court was unrivalled in wealth and luxury and was sophisticated, too, developing a strong chivalric element and a flair for poetry – one of the most skilled exponents being the last ruler, al-Mu'tamid, the "poet-king". But with sophistication came decadence, and in 1091 Abbadid rule was overthrown by a new force, the **Almoravids**, a tribe of fanatical Berber Muslims from North Africa, to whom the Andalucians had appealed for help against the rising threat from the northern Christian kingdoms.

Despite initial military successes, the Almoravids failed to consolidate their gains in al-Andalus and attempted to rule through military governors from Marrakesh. In the middle of the twelfth century, they were in turn supplanted by a new Berber incursion, the **Almohads**, who by about 1170 had recaptured virtually all the former territories. Seville had accepted Almohad rule in 1147 and became the capital of this last real empire of the Moors in Spain. Almohad power was sustained until their disastrous defeat in 1212 by the combined Christian armies of the north, at Las Navas de Tolosa. In this brief and precarious period, Seville underwent a renaissance of public building, characterized by a new vigour and fluidity of style. The Almohads rebuilt the Alcázar, enlarged the principal mosque – later demolished to make room for the Christian cathedral – and erected a new and brilliant minaret, a tower over 100m tall, topped with four copper spheres that could be seen for miles around: the Giralda.

SEVILLE (SEVILLA)

0   250
metres

Estación FF.CC.
Santa Justa

ACCOMMODATION

Albergue Juvenil Sevilla	7
Las Casas del Rey de Baeza	4
Hostal Alameda	10
Hostal Doña Feli	11
Hostal Pérez Montilla	2
Hostal Puerta Carmona	1
Hotel Amadeus	6
Hotel Murillo	5
Hotel Simón	8
Patio de la Cartuja	12
Pensión Doña Trinidad	3
Sacristía de Santa Ana	9

LIVE MUSIC & CLUBS

Abril	1
Antique	11
Bar Garlochi	7
Boss	8
Fun Club	9
Kudeta	10
Urbano Comix	4

FLAMENCO VENUES

Bar Quita Pesares	6
La Carbonería	2
Casa de la Memoria	
de Al-Andalus	5
Los Gallos	3

TAPAS BARS

Bar Anselma	32
Bar Bistec	27
Bar Caracoles	11
Bar Eslava	28
Bar Europa	13
Bar Giralda	8
Bulebar	20
Casa Morales	14
El Rinconcillo	7
Sopa de Ganso	12
Taberna Coloniales II	16
Las Teresas	5

RESTAURANTS & CAFÉS

La Albahaca	4
As-Sawirah	26
Bar Modesto	1
Bar-Restaurante	
Casa Manolo	30
Contenedor	10
Café Rayuela	9
El Faro de Triana	29
La Judería	3
Kaede	2
Kiosko de las Flores	18

Mesón del Pulpo	15
Mesón Serranito	24
Nueva Victoria	31
Pando	25
Pizzeria San Marco	6
La Primera del Puente	19
Restaurante Los	
Gallegos	21
Río Grande	17
Taberna El	
Alabardero	22
Zarabanda	23

4

revamped airport – was intended to regenerate the city's (and the region's) economic fortunes, but has hardly turned out to be the catalyst for growth and prosperity promised at the time. Indeed, some of the colossal debts are still unpaid two decades later.

Seville's **old city** – where you'll want to spend most of your time – is sited along the east bank of the Guadalquivir. At its heart, side by side, stand the three great monuments: the **Giralda tower**, the **Catedral** and the **Alcázar**, with the cramped alleyways of the **Barrio Santa Cruz**, the medieval Jewish quarter and now the heart of tourist life, extending east of them.

North of here is the main shopping and commercial district, its most obvious landmarks **Plaza Nueva**, **Plaza Duque de la Victoria** and the smart, pedestrianized **c/Sierpes**, which runs roughly between them. From **La Campana**, the small square at the northern end of c/Sierpes, c/Alfonso XII runs down towards the river by way of the **Museo de Bellas Artes**, second in importance in Spain only to the Prado in Madrid. Across the river is the earthier, traditionally working-class district of **Triana**, flanked to the south by the **Los Remedios** *barrio*, the city's wealthier residential zone where the great April *feria* takes place.

The Catedral

July & Aug Mon–Sat 9.30am–4pm, Sun 2.30–6pm; Sept–June Mon–Sat 11am–5pm, Sun 2.30–6pm; ticket valid for Catedral and the Giralda • €8, under-16s free • ⓦ www.catedraldesevilla.es

Seville's **Catedral** was conceived in 1402 as an unrivalled monument to Christian glory – "a building on so magnificent a scale that posterity will believe we were mad". To make way for this new monument, the Almohad mosque that stood on the proposed site was almost entirely demolished. Meanwhile, the canons, inspired by their vision of future repute, renounced all but a subsistence level of their incomes to further the building.

The cathedral was completed in just over a century (1402–1506), an extraordinary achievement, as it's the largest Gothic church in the world. As Norman Lewis says, "It expresses conquest and domination in architectural terms of sheer mass." Though it is built upon the huge, rectangular base-plan of the old mosque, the Christian architects (probably under the direction of the French master architect of Rouen cathedral) added the extra dimension of height. Its central nave rises to 42m, and even the side chapels seem tall enough to contain an ordinary church. The total area covers 11,520 square metres, and new calculations, based on cubic measurement, have now pushed it in front of St Paul's in London and St Peter's in Rome as the largest church in the world, a claim upheld by the *Guinness Book of Records*, a copy of whose certificate is proudly displayed in the church.

The monument to Christopher Columbus

Entry to the cathedral is via the Puerta de San Cristóbal on the building's south side; you are guided through a reception area and bookshop that brings you into the church to the west of the portal itself. Turn right once inside to head east, where you will soon be confronted by the **Tomb of Christopher Columbus** (Cristóbal Colón in Spanish). Columbus' remains were originally interred in the cathedral of Havana, on the island that he had discovered on his first voyage in 1492. But during the upheavals surrounding the declaration of Cuban independence in 1902, Spain transferred the remains to Seville, and the monumental tomb – in the late Romantic style by Arturo Mélida – was created to house them. However, doubts have always been voiced concerning the authenticity of the remains, and in 2002 scientists from the University of Granada carried out DNA tests in an attempt to confirm that they are those of Columbus – but these proved inconclusive. The mariner's coffin is held aloft by four huge allegorical figures, representing the kingdoms of León, Castile, Aragón and

Navarra; the lance of León should be piercing a pomegranate (now inexplicably missing), symbol of Granada (and the word for the fruit in Spanish), the last Moorish kingdom to be reconquered.

The nave

As you move into the **nave**, sheer size and grandeur are, inevitably, the chief characteristics of the cathedral. But once you've grown accustomed to the gloom, two other qualities stand out with equal force: the rhythmic balance and interplay between the parts, and an impressive overall simplicity and restraint in decoration. All successive ages have left monuments of their own wealth and style, but these have been limited to the two rows of side chapels. In the main body of the cathedral only the great box-like structure of the **coro** stands out, filling the central portion of the nave.

The Capilla Mayor

The *coro* extends and opens onto the **Capilla Mayor**, dominated by a vast **Gothic retablo** composed of 45 carved scenes from the Life of Christ. The lifetime's work of a single craftsman, Fleming Pieter Dancart, this is the supreme masterpiece of the cathedral – the largest and richest altarpiece in the world and one of the finest examples of Gothic woodcarving. The guides provide staggering statistics on the amount of gold involved.

The Sacristía de los Cálices

Before proceeding around the edge of the nave in a clockwise direction it's best to backtrack to the church's southeast corner to take in the **Sacristía de los Cálices** where many of the cathedral's main art treasures are displayed, including a masterly image of *Santas Justa y Rufina* by Goya, depicting Seville's patron saints, who were executed by the Romans in 287. Should you be interested in studying the many canvases here or the abundance of major artworks placed in the various chapels, it's worth calling at the bookshop near the entrance to purchase a copy of the official *Guide to the Cathedral of Seville*, which deals with them in detail.

The Sacristía Mayor

Alongside this room is the grandiose **Sacristía Mayor**, housing the treasury. Embellished in the Plateresque style, it was designed in 1528 by Diego de Riaño, one of the foremost exponents of this predominantly decorative architecture of the late Spanish Renaissance. Amid a confused collection of silver reliquaries and monstrances – dull and prodigious wealth – are displayed the **keys** presented to Fernando by the Jewish and Moorish communities on the surrender of the city; sculpted into the metal in stylized Arabic script are the words "May Allah render eternal the dominion of Islam in this city". Through a small antechamber here you enter the oval-shaped **Sala Capitular** (chapterhouse), with paintings by Murillo and an outstanding **marble floor** with geometric design.

Puerta del Nacimiento

Continuing to the southwest corner and the **Puerta del Nacimiento** – the door through which pass all the *pasos* and penitents who take part in the Semana Santa processions – you then turn right (north) along the west wall, passing the Puerta Principal.

The Capilla de San Antonio

In the northwest corner, the **Capilla de San Antonio** has Murillo's *Vision of St Anthony* depicting the saint in ecstatic pose before an infant Christ. A magnificent work: try to spot where the restorers joined San Antonio back into place after he had been crudely hacked out of the picture by thieves in the nineteenth century. He was eventually discovered in New York – where art dealers recognized the work they were being asked to buy – and returned to the cathedral. *The Baptism of Jesus* above this is another fine work by the same artist.

The Capilla Real

The nave's north side leads to the Puerta de la Concepción, through which you will exit – but before doing so, continue to the northeast corner to view the domed Renaissance **Capilla Real**, built on the site of the original royal burial chapel and containing the body of Fernando III (El Santo) in a suitably rich, silver shrine in front of the altar. The large tombs on either side of the chapel are those of Fernando's wife, Beatrice of Swabia, and his son, Alfonso the Wise. The chapel is reserved for services and private prayer and may only be viewed via the entrance in Plaza Virgen de los Reyes (Mon–Sat 8am–2pm & 4–7pm; free). You are now close to the entry to the Giralda tower.

La Giralda

Same ticket as cathedral

The **entrance to the Giralda** lies to the left of the Capilla Real in the cathedral's northeast corner. Unquestionably the most beautiful building in Seville, the **Giralda**, named after the sixteenth-century *giraldillo*, or weather vane, on its summit, dominates the city skyline. From the entrance you can ascend to the **bell chamber** for a remarkable **view** of the city – and, equally remarkable, a glimpse of the Gothic details of the cathedral's buttresses and statuary. But most impressive of all is the tower's inner construction, a series of 35 gently inclined ramps wide enough to allow two mounted guards to pass.

The minaret

The Giralda tower, before it was embellished with Christian additions (see below), was the mosque's **minaret** and the artistic pinnacle of Almohad architecture. Such was its fame that it served as a model for other minarets at the imperial capitals of Rabat and Marrakesh. It was used by the Moors both for calling the faithful to prayer (the traditional function of a minaret) and as an observatory, and was so venerated that they wanted to destroy it before the Christian conquest of the city. This they were prevented from doing by the threat of Alfonso (later King Alfonso X) that "if they removed a single stone, they would all be put to the sword". Instead, it became the bell tower of the Christian cathedral.

The Giralda's construction

The Moorish structure took twelve years to build (1184–96) and derives its firm, simple beauty from the shadows formed by blocks of brick trelliswork (a style known as *sebka*), different on each side, and relieved by a succession of arched niches and windows. The original harmony has been somewhat spoiled by the Renaissance-era addition of balconies and, to a still greater extent, by the four diminishing storeys of the belfry – added, along with the Italian-sculpted bronze figure of "Faith" which surmounts them, in 1560–68, following the demolition by an earthquake of the original copper spheres. Even so, it remains in its perfect synthesis of form and decoration one of the most important and beautiful monuments of the Islamic world.

The Patio de los Naranjos

To reach the cathedral's exit, move east along the nave's north side to reach the Puerta de la Concepción, passing through this to enter the Patio de los Naranjos. Along with the Giralda tower, this was the only feature to be spared from the original mosque. In Moorish times the mosque would have been entered via the Puerta del Pardon, now the visitor exit. Taking its modern name from the orange trees that now shade the patio, this was the former mosque's entrance courtyard. Although somewhat marred by Renaissance additions, the patio still incorporates a **Moorish fountain** where worshippers carried out at ritual ablutions prior to worship. Interestingly, it incorporates a sixth-century font from an earlier Visigothic cathedral, which was in its turn levelled to make way for the mosque.

Archivo de las Indias

Mon–Sat 9.30am–4.45pm, Sun 10am–1.45pm; guided visits daily at noon and 1pm • Free

If the Columbus tomb has inspired you, or you have a keen interest in the navigator's travels, visit the sixteenth-century **Archivo de las Indias**, between the cathedral and the Alcázar. Originally called La Casa Lonja, it served as the city's old stock exchange (*lonja*). Built in the severe and uncompromising style of El Escorial near Madrid, and designed

SEVILLE: THE OLD CITY

by the same architect, Juan de Herrera, in the eighteenth century it was turned into a storehouse for the archive of the Spanish empire – a purpose it served for almost three hundred years. In 2006, this mountain of documentation (of vital importance to scholars) was moved to another building around the corner and the Archivo was renovated, enabling visitors to enjoy Herrera's masterpiece in all its splendour once again. The exterior is defined by four identical facades, while corner pyramids supporting weather vanes are the main decorative feature. Inside, the sumptuous marble floors, bookcases in Cuban wood, arcaded central patio, and grand staircase in pink and black marble are a visual feast. The upper floor houses temporary **exhibitions** of interesting documents from the archive; these frequently include items such as Columbus' log and a letter from Cervantes (pre-*Don Quixote*) petitioning the king for a position in the Americas – fortunately for world literature, he was turned down.

The Ayuntamiento

Pl. de San Francisco • Guided visits Tues, Wed & Thurs 5.30pm, Sat noon; closed Aug • Free

Another building worth a look and sited slightly to the north of the cathedral is the sixteenth-century **Ayuntamiento**, with a richly ornamented Plateresque facade by Diego de Riaño. The equally impressive interior – with Riaño's star-vaulted entrance hall and council chamber with gilded coffered ceiling – is open for guided visits.

The Alcázar

April–Sept Tues–Sat 9.30am–7pm; Oct–March Tues–Sat 9.30am–5pm • €7.50 • ⊕ www.patronato-alcazarsevilla.es

Rulers of Seville have occupied the site of the **Alcázar** from the time of the Romans. Here was built the great court of the **Abbadids**, which reached a peak of sophistication and exaggerated sensuality under the cruel and ruthless al-Mu'tadid – a ruler who enlarged the palace in order to house a harem of eight hundred women, and who decorated the terraces with flowers planted in the skulls of his decapitated enemies. Later, under the **Almohads**, the complex was turned into a citadel, forming the heart of the town's fortifications. Its extent was enormous, stretching to the Torre del Oro on the bank of the Guadalquivir.

Parts of the Almohad walls survive, but the present structure of the palace dates almost entirely from the Christian period. Seville was a favoured residence of the Spanish kings for some four centuries after the Reconquest – most particularly of **Pedro the Cruel** (Pedro I; 1350–69) who, with his mistress María de Padilla, lived in and ruled from the Alcázar. Pedro embarked upon a complete rebuilding of the palace, employing workmen from Granada and utilizing fragments of earlier Moorish buildings in Seville, Córdoba and Valencia. Pedro's works form the nucleus of the Alcázar as it is today and, despite numerous restorations necessitated by fires and earth tremors, it offers some of the best surviving examples of **Mudéjar architecture** – the style developed by Moors working under Christian rule. Later monarchs, however, have left all too many traces and additions. Isabel built a new wing in which to organize expeditions to the Americas and control the new territories; Carlos V married a Portuguese princess in the palace, adding huge apartments for the occasion; and under Felipe IV (c.1624) extensive renovations were carried out to the existing rooms. On a more mundane level, kitchens were installed to provide for General Franco, who stayed in the royal apartments whenever he visited Seville.

Entry and the Salón del Almirante

The Alcázar is entered from the Plaza del Triunfo, adjacent to the cathedral. The gateway, flanked by original Almohad walls, opens onto a courtyard where Pedro I (who was known as "the Just" as well as "the Cruel", depending on one's fortunes) used to give judgement; to the left is his **Sala de Justicia** and beyond this the **Patio del Yeso**, the only surviving remnant of the Almohads' Alcázar. The main facade of the palace stands at the end of an inner court, the **Patio de la Montería**; on either side are galleried buildings erected by Isabel. This principal facade is pure fourteenth-century Mudéjar and, with its delicate, marble-columned windows, stalactite frieze and overhanging roof, is one of the finest things in the whole Alcázar.

The Salón del Almirante

As you will exit on the other side of the complex, it's probably better to look round the **Salón del Almirante** (or Casa de Contración de Indias), the sixteenth-century building on the right, before entering the main palace. Founded by Isabel in 1503, this gives you a standard against which to assess the Moorish forms. Here most of the rooms seem too heavy, their decoration ceasing to be an integral part of the design. The only notable exception is the **Sala de Audiencias** (or Capilla de los Navigantes, Chapel of the Navigators) with its magnificent *artesonado* ceiling inlaid with golden rosettes; within is a fine sixteenth-century *retablo* by Alejo Fernández depicting Columbus (in gold) and Carlos V (in a red cloak) sheltering beneath the Virgin. In the rear, to the left, are portrayed the kneeling figures of the Indians to whom the dubious blessings of Christianity had been brought by the Spanish conquest.

The royal apartments

Daily 10am–1.30pm

The **royal apartments**, known as the **Palacio Real Alto**, have now been opened for visits when not in use, and a temporary desk located in front of the Salón del Almirante sells tickets (€4) for a guided tour lasting about thirty minutes. This takes in the **royal chapel** with a fine early sixteenth-century *retablo* by Nicola Pisano; the so-called **bedroom of Pedro I**, with fine early Mudéjar plasterwork; and the equally splendid **Sala de Audiencias** – with more stunning plaster and tile decoration – which is still used by the royal family when receiving visitors in Seville.

Palacio de Pedro I

As you enter the main palace, the **Palacio de Pedro I**, the "domestic" nature of Moorish and Mudéjar architecture is immediately striking. This involves no loss of grandeur but simply a shift in scale: the apartments are remarkably small, shaped to human needs, and take their beauty from the exuberance of the decoration and the imaginative use of space and light. There is, too, a deliberate disorientation in the layout of the rooms, which makes the palace seem infinitely larger and more open than it really is. From the entrance court a narrow passage leads straight into the central courtyard, the **Patio de las Doncellas** (Patio of the Maidens), its name recalling the Christians' tribute of one hundred virgins presented annually to the Moorish kings. The heart of the patio has recently been restored to its fourteenth-century original state after having been buried under a tiled pavement for four centuries. Archeologists have replanted the six orange trees that once grew in sunken gardens to either side of a central pool. The pool is now filled with goldfish – as it was in the time of Pedro I – a medieval way of eliminating mosquitoes in summer. The court's stuccowork, *azulejos* and doors are all of the finest Granada craftsmanship. Interestingly, it's also the only part of the palace where Renaissance restorations are successfully fused – the double columns and upper storey were built by Carlos V, whose *Plus Ultra* ("yet still farther") motto recurs in the decorations here and elsewhere.

Salons de Carlos V and Embajadores

Past the **Salón de Carlos V**, distinguished by a superb ceiling, are three rooms from the original fourteenth-century design built for María de Padilla (who was popularly thought to use magic in order to maintain her hold over Pedro – and perhaps over other gallants at court, too, who used to drink her bath water). These open onto the

Salón de Embajadores (Salon of the Ambassadors), the most brilliant room of the Alcázar, with a stupendous *media naranja* (half-orange) wooden dome of red, green and gold cells, and horseshoe arcades inspired by the great palace of Medina Azahara outside Córdoba. Although restored, for the worse, by Carlos V – who added balconies and an incongruous frieze of royal portraits to commemorate his marriage to Isabel of Portugal here – the salon stands comparison with the great rooms of Granada's Alhambra. Adjoining are a long dining hall (*comedor*) and a small apartment installed in the late sixteenth century for Felipe II.

Patio de las Muñecas

The last great room of the palace – the **Patio de las Muñecas** (Patio of the Dolls), takes its curious name from two tiny faces decorating the inner side of one of the smaller arches. It's thought to be the site of the harem in the original palace. In this room, Pedro is reputed to have murdered his brother Don Fadrique in 1358; another of his royal guests, Abu Said of Granada, was murdered here for his jewels (one of which, an immense ruby that Pedro later gave to Edward, the "Black Prince", now figures in the British crown jewels). The upper storey of the court is a much later, nineteenth-century restoration. On the other sides of the patio are the **bedrooms** of Isabel and of her son Don Juan, and the arbitrarily named **Dormitorio del los Reyes Moros** (Bedroom of the Moorish Kings).

Palacio de Carlos V

To the left of the main palace loom the large and soulless apartments of the **Palacio de Carlos V** – something of an endurance test, with endless tapestries (eighteenth-century copies of the sixteenth-century originals now in Madrid) and pink, orange or yellow paintwork. Their classical style asserts a different and inferior mood.

The gardens

It's best to hurry through to the beautiful and rambling **Jardines de los Reales Alcázares** (gardens), the confused but enticing product of several eras, where you can take a well-earned rest from your exertions. Here you'll find the vaulted baths in which María de Padilla is supposed to have bathed (in reality, an auxiliary water supply for the palace), and the **Estanque de Mercurio** with a bronze figure of the messenger of the gods at its centre. This pool was specially constructed for Felipe V in 1733, who whiled away two solitary years at the Alcázar fishing here and preparing himself for death through religious flagellation. Just to the left of the pool a path beyond the Puerta de Marchena leads to a pleasant **cafetería** with a terrace overlooking the gardens. South of here towards the centre of the gardens there's an unusual and entertaining **maze** of myrtle bushes and, nearby, the **pavilion** (*pabellón*) **of Carlos V**, the only survivor of several he built for relaxation.

Antigua Fábrica de Tabacos

Free entry in term time

Immediately south of the Alcázar and fronting Avda. San Fernando lies the old tobacco factory and the setting for Bizet's *Carmen*. Now part of the university, the massive **Antigua Fábrica de Tabacos** was built in the 1750s and retains its position as the largest building in Spain after El Escorial. At its peak in the following century, it was also the country's largest single employer, with a workforce of some four thousand women, *cigarreras* – "a class in themselves", according to Richard Ford, who were forced to undergo "an ingeniously minute search on leaving their work, for they sometimes carry off the filthy weed in a manner her most Catholic majesty never dreamt of." Open when the university is in session, you are free to wander through the public areas and use the *cafetería*.

Parque María Luisa and Plaza de España

Ten minutes' walk to the south of the Alcázar, lies the **Parque de María Luisa** and the adjoining **Plaza de España**. These are wonderfully relaxing places to get away from the city bustle and are among the most pleasant – and impressive – public spaces in Spain.

The Parque de María Luisa formerly formed part of the vast grounds of the Palacio de San Telmo. The palace's nineteenth-century owner, the dowager duchess María Luisa, donated the park to the city in 1893 which then named it after her. Amid the ornamental pools and tree-shaded avenues lie various pavilions from the ill-fated Spanish Americas Fair. The Plaza de España was designed as the centrepiece of the fair, which was somewhat scuppered by the 1929 Wall Street crash. A vast semicircular complex, with its fountains, monumental stairways and mass of tile work, it would seem strange in most Spanish cities, but here it looks entirely natural, carrying on the tradition of civic display. At the fair, the plaza was used for the Spanish exhibit of industry and crafts, and around the crescent are *azulejo* scenes representing each of the provinces – an interesting record of the country at the tail end of a moneyed era. The buildings here fell into a terrible state in the latter part of the twentieth century, but have now been superbly restored and refurbished. The tiny strip of canal fronting the plaza has been refilled with water and *sevillanos* can be seen once again pottering about in the little rented boats.

Museo Arqueológico and Museo de Costumbres Populares

Tues–Sat 9am–8.30pm, Sun 9am–2.30pm (same hours for both) • €1.50; free with EU passport

Scattered about and around the edges of the Parque de María Luisa are more buildings from the 1929 Spanish Americas Fair, some of them amazingly opulent. Two of the grandest mansions – facing each other across an ornamental garden – are sited at the park's southern end and have been pressed into service to house the city's archeological and folk museums.

The farthest south is the city's **Museo Arqueológico**, the most important archeology collection in Andalucía. The main exhibits include a hoard of prehistoric treasure found in the Seville suburb of Camas in 1958, as well as Roman mosaics and artefacts from nearby Itálica and a unique Phoenician statuette of Astarte-Tanit, the virgin goddess once worshipped throughout the Mediterranean.

Opposite is the fabulous-looking **Museo de Costumbres Populares** (Popular Arts Museum) with an equally fine patio. The museum has displays of costumes, implements, furniture, photos and posters from times past, with interesting displays relating to traditional arts and crafts and the April *feria*. The basement ceramic display – illustrating the regional developments of this craft inherited from the Moors – is a highlight.

Barrio Santa Cruz

The **Barrio Santa Cruz** is very much in character with the city's romantic image, its streets narrow and tortuous to keep out the sun, the houses brilliantly whitewashed and festooned with flowering plants. Many of the windows are barricaded with *rejas* (iron grilles), behind which girls once kept chaste evening rendezvous with their *novios* who were forced to *comer hierro* ("eat iron") as passion mounted.

Casa de Pilatos

Daily 9am–7pm, Oct–Feb until 6pm • €6 ground floor only, both floors €8 (including audio-guide); Wed 3–7pm free for EU citizens with passport or ID card

Of the numerous mansions, by far the finest is the so-called **Casa de Pilatos**, built by the Marqués de Tarifa on his return from a pilgrimage to Jerusalem in 1519 and popularly thought to have been in imitation of the house of Pontius Pilate. In fact, it's an interesting and harmonious mixture of Mudéjar, Gothic and Renaissance styles, featuring brilliant *azulejos*, a tremendous sixteenth-century stairway and one of the most elegant domestic patios in the city.

Hospicio de los Venerables Sacerdotes

Daily 10am–2pm & 4–8pm; guided visits every 30min • €4.75; Sun 4–8pm free

Patios are a feature of almost all the houses in Santa Cruz: they are often surprisingly large and in summer they become the principal family living room. One of the most beautiful is within the Baroque **Hospicio de los Venerables Sacerdotes**, near the centre in a plaza of the same name – one of the few buildings in the *barrio* worth actively seeking out. The former hospice also displays some outstanding artworks including **sculptures** by Martínez Montañés and a painting of the *Last Supper* by Roelas, plus some wonderfully restored **frescoes** by Lucás Valdés and Valdés Leal in addition to a *Fray Pedro de Oña* by Zurbarán displaying the artist's special gift for portraying white draperies. The museum has recently added a Centro Velázquez which – in addition to other works by the Spanish master – displays a fine *Santa Rufina* and a spectacular *Inmaculada Concepción*.

Museo del Baile Flamenco

C/Manuel Rojas Marcos 3 • Daily 9.30am–7pm • €10 • ☎ 954 340 311, ⓦ www.museoflamenco.com

A few minutes' walk north of here lies the **Museo del Baile Flamenco**, an innovative and entertaining museum dedicated to the history and evolution of this emblematic *andaluz* art form. Set up in collaboration with celebrated flamenco dancer Cristina Hoyos, the museum is interactive (and multilingual), employing the latest sound and image technology to familiarize visitors with the origins of flamenco and the range of dance styles or "*palos*", which can all be seen at the touch of a button. The museum also stages concerts of flamenco.

The river and around

Down by the **Río Guadalquivir** are pedal-boats for idling away the afternoons, and at night a surprising density of local couples. The main riverside landmark here is the twelve-sided **Torre del Oro**, built by the Almohads in 1220 as part of the Alcázar fortifications. It was connected to another small fort across the river by a chain that had to be broken by the Castilian fleet before their conquest of the city in 1248. The tower was later used as a repository for the gold brought back from the Americas – hence its name.

Hospital de la Caridad

Entry on c/Temprado • Mon–Sat 9am–1pm & 3.30–7pm, Sun 9am–12.30pm • €5 including audio-guide • ⓦ www.santa-caridad.org

The **Hospital de la Caridad** was founded in 1676 by Don Miguel de Mañara, the inspiration for Byron's *Don Juan*. According to the testimony of one of Don Miguel's friends, "There was no folly which he did not commit, no youthful indulgence into which he did not plunge … (until) what occurred to him in the street of the coffin." What occurred was that Don Miguel, returning from a reckless orgy, had a vision in which he was confronted by a funeral procession carrying his own corpse. He repented his past life, joined the Brotherhood of Charity (whose task was to bury the bodies of vagrants and criminals), and later set up this hospital for the relief of the dying and destitute, for which purpose it is still used. Don Miguel commissioned a series of eleven paintings by Murillo for the chapel; seven remain (the French stole the others during the Napoleonic occupation), including a superlative image of *San Juan de Dios* for which Mañara himself posed as the model. Alongside them hang two *Triumph of Death* pictures by Valdés Leal. One, depicting a decomposing bishop being eaten by worms (beneath the scales of justice labelled *Ni más, Ni menos* – No More, No Less), is so powerfully repulsive that Murillo declared that "you have to hold your nose to look at it". The mood of both works may owe a lot to the vivid memory of the 1649 plague that killed almost half the population of the city.

Museo de Bellas Artes

Tues 2.30–8.30pm, Wed–Sat 9am–8.30pm, Sun 9am–2.30pm • €1.50; free with EU passport

Near the Plaza de Armas bus station is one of Spain's most impressive art galleries, the **Museo de Bellas Artes**, housed in recently modernized premises in a beautiful former convent. The collection is frequently rotated, so not all the works mentioned here may be on show.

Room 1

Among the highlights is a wonderful late fifteenth-century sculpture in painted terracotta in Room 1, *Lamentation over the Dead Christ*, by the Andalucian **Pedro Millán**, the founding father of the Seville school of sculpture. A marriage of Gothic and expressive naturalism, this style was the starting point for the outstanding seventeenth-century period of religious iconography in Seville.

Rooms 2 to 4

A later example, in Room 2, is a magnificent *San Jerónimo* by the Italian **Pietro Torrigiano**, who spent the latter years of his life in the city. Room 3 has a *retablo* of the *Redemption* (c.1562), with fine woodcarving by Juan Giralte, while a monumental *Last Supper* by Alonso Vázquez covers an end wall of Room 4.

Room 5

Beyond a serene patio and cloister, Room 5 is located in the monastery's former church, where the recently restored paintings on the vault and dome by the eighteenth-century *sevillano*, Domingo Martínez, are spectacular. Here also is the nucleus of the collection: **Zurbarán**'s *Apotheosis of St Thomas Aquinas*, as well as a clutch of works by **Murillo** in the apse, crowned by the great *Immaculate Conception* – known as "*La Colosal*" to distinguish it from the other work here with the same name. In an alcove nearby you'll see the same artist's *Virgin and Child*; popularly known as *La Servilleta* because it was said to have been painted on a dinner napkin, the work is one of Murillo's greatest.

Rooms 6 to 10

Upstairs, Room 6 (quadrated around the patio) displays works from the Baroque period, among which a moving *Santa Teresa* by **Ribera** – Spain's master of *tenebrismo* (darkness penetrated by light) – and a stark *Crucifixion* by Zurbarán stand out. Room 10 contains more imposing canvases by Zurbarán, including *St Hugo visiting the Carthusian Monks at Supper* and another almost sculptural *Crucifixion* to compare with the one in Room 6. Here also are sculptures by **Martínez Montañés**, the sixteenth-century "Andalucian Lysippus", whose early *St Dominic in Penitence* and *San Bruno* from his mature period display mastery of technique.

Rooms 11 to 14

The collection ends with works from the Romantic and Modern eras. In Room 11, an austere late canvas by **Goya** of the octogenarian *Don José Duaso* compensates for some not terribly inspiring works accompanying it. In Room 12, Gonzalo Bilbao's *Las Cigarreras* is a vivid portrayal of the wretched life of women in the tobacco factory during the early years of the last century. Room 13 has an evocative image of *Sevilla en Fiestas* dated 1915 by Gustavo Bacarisas and the monumental canvas by José Villegas Cordero, *La Muerte del Maestro*, depicting the death of a *torero*, which was purchased by the Junta de Andalucía in 1996. Finally, in Room 14 there's *Juan Centeño y su cuadrilla* by Huelvan artist Daniel Vásquez Díaz, who worked in Paris and was a friend of Picasso. This stirring image of the *torero* and his team provides an appropriately *andaluz* conclusion to a memorable museum.

Triana

Over the Río Guadalquivir is the **Triana** *barrio*, scruffy, lively and well away from the tourist trails. This was once the heart of the city's *gitano* community and, more specifically, home of the great flamenco dynasties of Seville who were kicked out by developers early last century and are now scattered throughout the city. The *gitanos* lived in extended families in tiny, immaculate communal houses called *corrales* around courtyards glutted with flowers; today, only a handful remain intact. Triana is still, however, the starting point for the annual pilgrimage to El Rocío (end of May), when a myriad painted wagons leave town, drawn by oxen. It houses, too, the city's oldest working **ceramics factory**, Santa Ana, where the tiles, many still in the traditional, geometric Arabic designs, are hand-painted in the adjoining shop.

La Cartuja

Tues–Sat 11am–9pm, Sun 11am–3pm • €3; free Tues–Fri 7–9pm & Sat 11am–9pm with EU passport • ⓦ caac.es

At Triana's northern edge lies **La Cartuja**, a fourteenth-century former Carthusian monastery expensively restored as part of the Expo '92 World's Fair. Part of the complex is now given over to the **Centro Andaluz de Arte Contemporáneo** (same hours and ticket) which stages rotating exhibitions from a large and interesting collection of contemporary work by *andaluz* artists, including canvases by Antonio Rodríguez Luna, Joaquín Peinado, Guillermo Pérez Villalta, José Guerrero and Daniel Vásquez Díaz. Two other galleries stage temporary exhibitions by international artists and photographers (see website for details).

Isla Mágica

April–Nov daily 11am–7.30pm, closes 11pm July & Aug • €29; evening-only tickets €27; reductions for kids • ⓦ islamagica.es

The remnants of much of the **Expo '92 site** itself have been incorporated into the **Isla Mágica**, an amusement park based on the theme of sixteenth-century Spain, with water and roller-coaster rides, shows and period street animations (included in ticket price).

Outside the city: Itálica and around

The Roman ruins and remarkable mosaics of **Itálica** and the exceptional Gothic **Monasterio San Isidoro del Campo** lie some 9km to the north of Seville, just outside the village of **Santiponce**.

To get here by public transport, take a **bus** from the Plaza de Armas station (bus #M172; every 30min, Sun every hour), a journey of about twenty minutes. The easiest way to see both monuments (noting the opening hours) is to ask the bus to drop you at the monastery stop ("Parada Monasterio") on the outward journey. You can then cover the 1.5km (15min walk or take a later bus) through Santiponce to the Itálica site entrance (from where buses return to the city).

Itálica

April–Sept Tues–Sat 8.30am–9pm, Sun 9am–3pm; Oct–March Tues–Sat 9am–5.30pm, Sun 9am–3pm • €1.50; free with EU passport

Itálica was the birthplace of two emperors (Trajan and Hadrian) and one of the earliest Roman settlements in Spain, founded in 206 BC by Scipio Africanus as a home for his veterans. It rose to considerable military importance in the second and third centuries AD, was richly endowed during the reign of Hadrian (117–138) and declined as an urban centre only under the Visigoths, who preferred Seville, then known as *Hispalis*. Eventually, the city was deserted by the Moors after the river changed its course, disrupting the surrounding terrain.

Throughout the Middle Ages, the ruins were used as a source of stone for Seville, but somehow the shell of its enormous **amphitheatre** – the third largest in the Roman world – has survived. Today, it's crumbling perilously, but you can clearly detect the rows of seats, the corridors and the dens for wild beasts. Beyond, within a rambling and unkempt grid of **streets** and **villas**, about twenty **mosaics** have been uncovered. Most are complete, including excellent coloured floors depicting birds, Neptune and the seasons, and several fine black-and-white geometric patterns.

Santiponce

There's a well-preserved **Roman theatre** in **SANTIPONCE** itself, signposted from the main road. Santiponce is not well endowed with facilities, but the *Ventarillo Canario* **restaurant** almost opposite the Itálica site entrance does good *platos combinados* and is famous for its grilled steaks served on wooden slabs with *papas arrugadas* – small baked potatoes in *mojo* spicy sauce.

Monasterio San Isidoro del Campo

Wed & Thurs 10am–2pm, Fri & Sat 10am–2pm & 5.30–8.30pm (Oct–March 4–7pm), Sun 10am–3pm • €2; Wed free

A little over 1km to the south of Santiponce on the road back to Seville lies the former Cistercian **Monasterio San Isidoro del Campo**. Closed for many years, it has now been painstakingly and gloriously restored and shouldn't be missed.

Founded by the thirteenth-century monarch Guzmán El Bueno of Tarifa, the monastery is a masterpiece of Gothic architecture, which, prior to its confiscation during the nineteenth-century Disentailment, was occupied by a number of religious orders. Among these were the *ermitaños jerónimos* (Hieronymites) who, in the fifteenth century, decorated the central cloister and the Patio de los Evangelistas with a remarkable series of **mural paintings** depicting images of the saints – including scenes from the life of San Jerónimo – as well as astonishingly beautiful floral and Mudéjar-influenced geometric designs. In the seventeenth century, the monastery employed the great *sevillano* sculptor Martínez Montañés to create the magnificent **retablo mayor** in the larger of the complex's twin churches.

ARRIVAL AND DEPARTURE
SEVILLE

BY PLANE

The **airport** bus, operated by Amarillos (every 30min; €2.40), takes thirty minutes to the centre and terminates at the Puerta de Jerez, near the Alcázar, stopping at the train station en route. A taxi from the airport into the centre costs €21.27 (officially regulated fare for up to 4 people) plus €1 per bag (slightly more Sun and after 10pm). The current fare can be obtained from the taxi authority ☎ 954 505 840 or any *turismo*.

BY TRAIN

Points of arrival are straightforward, though the **train station**, Santa Justa, is a fair way out on Avenida Kansas City, the airport road. Bus #32 will take you from here to Pl. de la Encarnación, from where all sights are within easy walking distance; alternatively, buses #70 and #C1 will take you to the Prado de San Sebastián bus station. A bus map detailing all routes is available from the *turismo*. For timetables and ticket information, consult RENFE ☎ 902 240 202, ⊛ renfe.es.

Destinations Algeciras (5 daily, change at Córdoba/ Bobadilla; 5hr); Badajoz (3 daily, change at Puertollano; 5hr 15min); Cádiz (14 daily; 2hr); Córdoba (AVE 19 daily, 45min; 5 *cercanías* daily, 1hr 20min); Granada (4 daily; 3hr); Huelva (3 daily; 1hr 35min); Madrid (AVE 14 daily; 3hr 20min); Málaga (10 daily; 2hr 30min); Mérida (daily; 4hr 20min).

BY BUS

The **main bus station** is at Prado de San Sebastián (☎ 954 417 111), from where most destinations are served; exceptions include buses for Badajoz, Extremadura (the provinces of Cáceres and Badajoz), Huelva, Madrid and international destinations, which arrive at and depart from the station at Pl. de Armas (☎ 954 908 040) by the Puente del Cachorro on the river.

Destinations Albufeira, Portuguese Algarve (via Ayamonte and Faro; 4 daily; 2hr 30min); Algeciras (4 daily; 3hr 30min); Almería (3 daily; 5hr 45min); Aracena (2 daily; 1hr 20min); Badajoz (4 daily; 3hr 30min); Cádiz (10 daily; 1hr 45min); Carmona (16 daily; 30min); Córdoba (8 daily; 1hr 45min); Écija (9 daily; 1hr 15min); El Rocío (3 daily; 1hr 30min); Granada (8 daily; 3hr); Huelva (20 daily; 1hr 15min); Jerez de la Frontera (7 daily; 1hr 15min); Madrid (8 daily; 6hr); Málaga (6 daily; 2hr 30min); Matalascañas (4 daily; 2hr); Mérida (5 daily; 1hr 15min); Ronda (6 daily; 2hr).

BY CAR

Driving in Seville is an ordeal, especially in the narrow streets of *barrios* such as Santa Cruz and on-street parking spaces are almost impossible to find. Your best bet for parking is to find a pay **car park** (they are signed all around the central zone), or to choose accommodation with a garage (for which you will be charged extra).

GETTING AROUND

Metro The city is engaged in constructing a metro system that will crisscross Seville. The first sections linking the southern suburbs to the Puerto de Jerez and Triana opened in 2009.

Tram A new tram system will also be expanded in the years to come but presently runs only from Pl. Nueva to the

Prado de San Sebastián bus station.

Open-top bus tour Good if you're pressed for time, this hop-on, hop-off service is operated by Sevirama (☎ 954 560 693); buses leave half-hourly from the riverside Torre del Oro, stopping at or near the main sites (all-day ticket €16).

INFORMATION

Turismo is at Avda. de la Constitución 21 (Mon–Fri 9am–7.30pm, Sat 10am–3.30pm; ☎ 954 787 578); they have accommodation lists and can give you a copy of the very useful free listings magazine *El Giraldillo*.

Municipal tourist office Less chaotic, at Pl. San Francisco 19, near the *ayuntamiento* (Mon–Fri 9am–7.30pm, Sat & Sun 10am–2pm; ☎ 955 471 232, ⊛ www.turismosevilla .org), with a sub-office at Santa Justa train station.

ACCOMMODATION

Seville has some of the finest **hotels** in Andalucía. The most attractive area to stay is undoubtedly the **Barrio Santa Cruz**, though this is reflected in the prices, particularly during high season (April–June), though there are a few reasonably priced places in the *barrio* and on its periphery (especially immediately north, and south towards the bus station) and they're at least worth a try before heading elsewhere. Slightly farther out, another promising area is to the north of the Pl. Nueva, and especially over towards the river and the Pl. de Armas bus station. The once-drab **Alameda de Hércules** is now one of the city's foremost up-and-coming zones.

If you're arriving during any of the major **festivals**, particularly Semana Santa or the Feria de Abril (April fair), you're strongly advised to book ahead – be aware also that this is when hotel rates are at their highest. The rates quoted below are for high season which is the price point below "*temporada extra*" (extra high season) charged during Semana Santa and the Feria de Abril. If you are interested in these dates, contact the hotels or check their websites.

BARRIO SANTA CRUZ AND CATHEDRAL AREA

★ **Las Casas del Rey de Baeza** Pl. Jesús de la Redención 2 ☎ 954 561 496, ⊛ hospes.com. Wonderful hotel with rooms arranged around an eighteenth-century *sevillano corral*. The plant-bedecked interior patio is a picture, and stylishly furnished pastel-shaded rooms come with traditional exterior *esparto* blinds, a neat finishing touch – and there's a rooftop pool to cool off in. **€226**

Hostal Pérez Montilla Pl. Curtidores 13 ☎ 954 421 854, ⊕ info@pensionperezmontilla.com. Spotless *hostal* on a tranquil square. Cheaper rooms come without bath; those with have a/c. Prices can drop when business is slack. **€35**

Hostal Puerta Carmona Pl. de San Agustín 5 ☎ 954 988 310, ⊛ hostalpuertacarmona.es. Very pleasant *hostal* with good-value modern en-suite rooms with a/c and TV; they will advise on where to park nearby. Free wi-fi. **€55**

★ **Hotel Amadeus** c/Farnesio 6, near the Iglesia de Santa Cruz ☎ 954 501 443, ⊛ hotelamadeussevilla.com. Welcoming hotel housed in an eighteenth-century *casa señorial* and owned by an aficionada of the great composer. There's a *sala de música*, and the soundproofed and stylish rooms come with a/c, satellite TV, wi-fi and free internet access. There's a grand piano in the patio and they even loan guests musical instruments. The house is topped off with a

stunning roof terrace (with telescope) for breakfasting. **€95**

Hotel Murillo c/Lope de Rueda 7 ☎ 954 216 095, ⊛ hotelmurillo.com. Traditional hotel in a restored mansion close to Pl. Santa Cruz with all facilities plus amusingly kitsch features, including suits of armour and paint-palette key rings. Wi-fi zone. **€70**

Hotel Simón c/García de Vinuesa 19 ☎ 954 226 660, ⊛ hotelsimonsevilla.com. Well-restored mansion in an excellent position across from the cathedral. All rooms are en suite and a/c, and this can be a bargain out of high season. Wi-fi zone. **€75**

Pensión Doña Trinidad c/Archeros 7 ☎ 954 541 906, ⊛ donatrinidad.com. Sparkling Santa Cruz *hostal* with tastefully decorated en-suite rooms (some single) around a central patio. **€40**

SANTA CATALINA, SAN PEDRO, ALAMEDA DE HÉRCULES

Hostal Alameda Alameda de Hércules 31 ☎ 954 900 191, ⊛ hostalalameda.es. Modern, pleasant and very friendly *hostal* overlooking the tree-lined Alameda. En-suite rooms come with a/c and TV; also has simpler rooms sharing bath. En suite **€45**, sharing bath **€25**.

★ **Hostal Doña Feli** c/Jesus del Gran Poder 130 ☎ 954 901 048, ⊛ www.hostaldfeli.com. At the northern end of the atmospheric Alameda de Hércules this is a very pleasant (and economically priced) small *hostal* with cosy en-suite rooms equipped with a/c and TV. Own garage with low rates. **€50**

Hotel Sacristía de Santa Ana Alameda de Hércules 22 ☎ 954 915 722, ⊛ hotelsacristia.com. Beautiful hotel with delightful rooms – the preferable external ones have Alameda views – inside a seventeenth-century *casa señorial* with many original features. Features include wi-fi and DVD players for rent. **€99**

Patio de la Cartuja c/Lumbreras 8, off west side of Alameda's northern end ☎ 954 900 200, ⊛.patiosdes evilla.com. Stylish and excellent-value apartment-hotel created from an old *sevillano corral*; en-suite apartments with balconies, kitchen and lounge are set around a tiled patio. Free wi-fi and own garage. **€112**

YOUTH HOSTEL AND CAMPING

Albergue Juvenil Sevilla c/Isaac Peral 2 ☎ 954 613 150 (they tend not to answer). Leafy, if often crowded, youth hostel some way out in the university district; take bus #34 from the Prado de San Sebastián bus station to get there. Dorm beds: under-26 **€17.50**, over-26 **€23.50**; double rooms (two persons): under-26 **€35**, over-26 **€47**.

Camping Villsom 10km out of town on the main Cádiz road ☎ &₣ 954 720 828. Recently overhauled campsite with a pool. Half-hourly buses from Avenida de Portugal (near the Prado de San Sebastián bus station) take 20min – the M-132 signed "Dos Hermanas por Barriadas" will drop you outside. **€4.65**, **€4.65** per tent, **€5** per vehicle

EATING AND DRINKING

Seville is packed with lively and enjoyable **bars and restaurants**, and you'll find somewhere to eat and drink at just about any hour. With few exceptions, anywhere around the major sights and the **Barrio Santa Cruz** will be expensive. The two most promising central areas are down **towards the bullring** and north of here towards the Pl. de Armas bus station. The **Plaza de Armas** area is slightly seedier but has the cheapest *comidas* this side of the river. Wander down c/Marqués de Paradas, and up c/Canalejas and c/San Eloy, and find out what's available. Across the river in **Triana**, c/Betis and c/Pureza are also good hunting grounds.

RESTAURANTS AND CAFÉS

BARRIO SANTA CRUZ AND AROUND THE CATEDRAL

La Albahaca Pl. Santa Cruz 29 ☎ 954 220 714. Charming traditional restaurant housed in a converted mansion where three intimate period rooms hung with paintings provide the ambience. Fairly expensive, but there's a *menú* for around €20. Mon–Sat noon–4pm & 8pm–midnight; closed Sun.

Bar Modesto c/Cano y Cueto. At the north end of Santa Cruz, this mid-priced bar-restaurant offers a tempting *menú* (€20) and great tapas. House specials include *punta de solomillo* (pork tenderloin) and *coquinas* (clams). Daily 8am–2am.

Café Rayuela c/Miguel de Mañara 9. Pleasant lunchtime venue serving value-for-money *raciones* and salads at outdoor tables in a pedestrianized street behind the *turismo. Menú* for €9.50. Daily 9am–10pm.

La Judería c/Cano y Cueto 13 ☎ 954 412 052. Solid mid-priced restaurant with a good-value daily *menú* for €20. *Revueltos* are a speciality here. Daily 1.30–3.30pm & 8–11pm.

Kaede c/Sta. María la Blanca 32. Authentic and entertaining Japanese restaurant at a new address. Sushi, sashimi or tempura are included on a good-value *menú* for €15. If you opt for Sapporo beer rather than *té japonés* (free with the *menú*) you'll substantially increase the bill. Daily 1–4pm & 8pm–midnight.

Mesón del Pulpo c/Tomás Ibarra 10. Excellent little Galician restaurant popular with locals. Specializes (as its name implies) in *pulpo a la gallega* (octopus), and there's a decent *menú* for €10. Daily 9am–4pm & 8–midnight.

Pizzeria San Marco c/Mesón del Moro 4. Good and economical Italian pasta and pizzas served inside a remarkable twelfth-century Moorish bathhouse. Daily 1.30–4.30pm & 8.30pm–12.30am; closed Mon.

TRIANA AND THE RÍO GUADALQUIVIR

As-Sawïrah c/Galera 5. Superb Moroccan restaurant offering a variety of North African dishes including a delicate couscous and their house special *tajin de cordero con membrillos* (lamb with quinces). Lunch *menú* €12. Tues–Sat 2–3.30pm & 9–11.30pm; Sun 2–3.30pm; closed Mon.

Bar-Restaurante Casa Manolo c/San Jorge 16. Buzzing Triana bar-restaurant with tapas and *raciones* (or breakfast) in the bar or economical *platos combinados* in a dining room just off it. Daily 9am–6pm & 8pm–1am.

El Faro de Triana Puente de Triana ☎ 954 331 251. Sitting atop the western end of the Puente de Triana (aka Puente de Isabel II), the dining room and roof terrace here give amazing river views. Tapas at the bar and *raciones* at the tables consist of fish, meat and seafood. Tues–Sun 11am–4.30pm & 7.30pm–12.30am; closed Mon.

Kiosko de las Flores c/Betis near to the Río Grande. Wonderful riverside location for this former *freiduría*, now a mid-priced restaurant specializing in fish and seafood. Their terrace has great views over the river to the Torre del Oro. Tapas are served at the bar and there's a *menú* for €20. Tues–Sat 11am–4pm & 5pm–midnight, Sun 11am–4pm; closed Mon.

★ **Nueva Victoria** c/Torneo 85. Superb new place comprising a bright and airy bar with terrace and more serious starched table linen and flowers-on-the-table restaurant further in. Both serve up excellent food at moderate prices. Tapas in the bar are in fact *media-raciones* (a bit bigger than a *tapa*) and priced at around €5–7 a plate. Here you could try the *queso gratinado con pimientos* (goat's cheese with peppers) or, in the restaurant, the *venao* (venison), *solomillo* (pork loin) and *carrillada* (pork cheek) are all equally succulent. There's also a choice of *menús* ranging between €14–20. Main dishes in the restaurant €6–18. Daily noon–midnight.

La Primera del Puente c/Betis 66. The riverside terrace of the restaurant over the road has one of the city's best vistas; soft-talk a waiter to get a frontline table. You can enjoy low-priced, generous *raciones* or *media raciones* of fish, meat and seafood. Reasonably priced wine list. Thurs–Tues 11.30am–4.30pm & 8pm–1am; closed Wed.

Río Grande c/Betis 70 ☎954 273 956. This mid-priced Triana restaurant has the best view in town from its terrace on the river's west bank facing the Torre del Oro, and is the ideal venue for a lunchtime feast of traditional meat and fish dishes. Their next-door tapas bar – with its own terrace – is also worth a visit. Daily 1–4pm & 8pm–midnight.

★ **Taberna El Alabardero** c/Zaragoza 20 ☎954 502 721. Elegant nineteenth-century *casa-palacio sevillana* with attractive decor and an upmarket clientele. Pricey – and outstanding – restaurant upstairs where the *menú de degustación* costs €55 or €70 with wine; however, a daily bargain €12.90 lunchtime *menú* (€17.50 eves, €19.90 Sat & Sun) in the patio bar below comes from the same kitchen. Daily 1.30–4.30pm & 8–midnight; closed Aug.

CENTRO, LA MACARENA, ALAMEDA AND SANTA JUSTA

Contenedor c/San Luís 50, opposite the church of San Luís. Relaxed and friendly diner with daily specials such as *arroz con setas y pato* (duck and mushroom rice) as well as curries and fish and meat dishes. There's a piano for any customers inclined to tinkle the ivories and they stage art exhibitions on the walls. Daily 9–11pm; Fri, Sat & Sun also 1.30–4pm.

Mesón Serranito Alfonso XII 9, behind the El Corte Inglés department store. Cosy little restaurant beyond a lively tapas bar out front, with excellent fish and meat dishes and a *menú* for around €9. Daily 8am–midnight.

Pando c/San Eloy 47. Lively, stylish tapas and *raciones* restaurant, which also does salads. Wide range of meat and fish dishes: try their *merluza en sidre* (hake in cider). An ideal lunch stop. Mon–Sat 8am–5pm & 8–11.30pm.

Restaurante Los Gallegos c/Capataz Franco. Friendly and inexpensive Galician restaurant in a tiny alley off c/Martín Villa, serving *gallego* specialities (try their *tarta de Santiago* dessert). *Menú* for €14. Daily 11am–11pm; closed Sun eve.

Zarabanda c/Padre Tarín 6. Economical and friendly little family restaurant cooking pizzas and traditional dishes to a high standard. Also does salads and is just the place for a lunch stop. Noon–5pm & 8pm–12.30am; closed Mon eve.

TAPAS BARS

For casual eating and drinking and taking **tapas** – Seville's great speciality – there are **bars** all over town. The tapas venues all serve barrelled sherries from nearby Jerez and Sanlúcar (the locals drink the cold, dry *fino* with their tapas, especially *camarones*, or shrimps); a *tinto de verano* is the local version of *sangría* – wine with lemonade, a great summer drink. Outside the centre, you'll find lively bars in the **Plaza Alfalfa** area, and across the river in **Triana** – particularly in and around c/Castilla and c/Betis. Over recent years, a zone that has emerged as a focus for artistic, student and gay barhoppers is the **Alameda** (de Hércules).

BARRIO SANTA CRUZ AND AROUND THE CATEDRAL

Bar Europa Junction of c/Alcaicería de Loza and c/Siete Revueltas. Fine old watering-hole with lots of cool tiled walls, plus excellent *manzanilla* and a variety of tapas served on marble-topped tables. Daily 9am–midnight.

★ **Bar Giralda** c/Mateus Gagos 1. Excellent and popular bar in a converted ancient Moorish bathhouse, with a wide selection of tapas. House specials include *calabacín al horno* (baked courgette). Mon–Sat 9.30am–12.30am; closed Mon.

Casa Morales c/García de Vinuesa 11. Atmospheric traditional bar (founded 1850) with barrelled wine and a few *tablas* (tapas served on wooden boards). Mon–Sat noon–4pm & 8pm–midnight; closed Sun.

★ **Las Teresas** c/Santa Teresa 2. Good beer and sherry served in this atmospheric bar with hanging cured hams and tiled walls lined with faded *corrida* photos. It's also worth stopping here for breakfast the morning after. Try the *pulpo al la gallega* (Galician octopus). Daily 9am–midnight.

★ **Taberna Coloniales II** c/Fernández y González 36. Offspring of the similarly named establishment in Pl. Cristo de Burgos, this is up to the same high standard. Tapas are served at the bar, but cornering a table will allow you to feast on a wide (and fair-priced) range including *solomillo al whisky* (pork loin); and they also let you round it off with coffee and *desserts de la casa*. Daily 12.30pm–midnight.

TRIANA AND THE RÍO GUADALQUIVIR

Bar Anselma c/Pagés del Corro 49. Fine old place with a neo-Moorish facade owned by a *dueña* with many Rocío connections (every night at midnight the lights are dimmed and the Rocío hymn is sung). If you're lucky, you

4

may just catch some of the best impromptu flamenco in town. House specials include *caldereta* (lamb stewed in *fino*), and *pisto* (stewed vegetables). Mon–Sat 10pm–late; closed Sun.

Bar Bistec c/Pelay y Correa 34. Ancient and hearty Triana hostelry, with outdoor tables in summer. Specials include *cabrillas* (spicy snails), *codorniz en salsa* (quail) and *pan de mi pueblo* (cod gazpacho). Daily 11.30am–4.30pm & 8pm–1am; closed Wed.

CENTRO, LA MACARENA, ALMEDA AND SANTA JUSTA

Bar Caracoles c/Pérez Galdos. Classic tapas bar in the vibrant Alfalfa *barrio* just off its focal square. There's a spacious bar for winter dining but in summer everyone sits out on their terrace. House specials include (you've guessed it) *caracoles* as well as *solomillo al whisky* (pork loin in grog) and *bacalao a la Bilbaina* (cod in chilli sauce). Daily 12.30pm–4.30 & 8pm–midnight.

Bar Eslava c/Eslava 3–5. Very good and extremely popular – which often means you can't get through the door – tapas

bar with an outstanding, equally excellent restaurant attached. Also has a very good restaurant next door. Daily 1–4.30pm & 9–11.30pm; closed Sun eve & Mon.

Bulebar Alameda de Hércules 83. Lively *copas* bar that does good tapas and stays open late, with an outdoor plant-filled terrace looking onto the Alameda. They often stage theatre or other music shows. Daily 4pm–2am.

★ **El Rinconcillo** c/Gerona 32. Seville's oldest bar (founded in 1670) does a fair tapas selection as well as providing a hang-out for the city's literati. Renowned for its *espinacas con garbanzos* (spinach with chickpeas), one of the city's most popular tapas. Daily 1pm–midnight.

Sopa de Ganso ("Duck Soup") c/Pérez Galdos 8. Young, lively bar in one of the city's main nightlife zones. On offer are *tagarninas* (a pastie) and *pudín de verduras* (vegetable bake). Until midnight it operates as a tapas bar and – on the stroke of twelve – the illumination changes from orange to blue, the food stops and it becomes a late-night *copas* bar with cool sounds. Daily 1pm–3am.

NIGHTLIFE

Seville is a wonderfully late-night city, and in summer and during fiestas, the streets around the central areas – particularly the Pl. de Alfalfa, Alameda de Hércules and Triana riverfront zones – are often packed out until the small hours. Throughout the summer, the Alcázar, the Prado de San Sebastián gardens and other squares host occasional **free concerts**. Information on these should be available from the *turismo*, the local press and the *El Giraldillo* listings magazine.

FLAMENCO

Flamenco music and dance is on offer at dozens of places in the city, some of them extremely tacky and expensive. Unless you've heard otherwise, avoid the fixed "shows", or *tablaos* (many of which are a travesty, even using recorded music) – the spontaneous nature of flamenco makes it almost impossible to timetable into the two-shows-a-night cabaret demanded by impresarios.

Bar Quita Pesares Pl. Jerónimo de Córdoba. Owned and run by a flamenco singer, this is a chaotic place where there's often impromptu music, especially at weekends, when things get lively around midnight. Mon–Sat noon–4pm & 8pm–2am; closed Sun.

La Carbonería c/Levies 18. An excellent bar that often has spontaneous flamenco (try Thurs after 10pm). It used to be the coal merchants' building (hence the name) and is a rambling, simple and welcoming place. They also do tapas and *raciones*. Daily 8pm–late.

Casa de la Memoria de al-Andalus c/Jiménez de Enciso 28 ☎954 560 670, ✉memorias@terra.es. This cultural centre is dedicated to promoting the art of flamenco and features up-and-coming talent – many flamenco luminaries made their first appearances here. It stages nightly flamenco performances at 9pm with occasional extra concerts at 7.30pm and 10.30pm (ring or

stop by for details). Space is limited and tickets must be booked in advance – in person or by phone or email. €15 or €13 for students with ID.

Los Gallos Pl. Santa Cruz ⊛tablaolosgallos.com. Along with the *Casa de la Memoria* (see below) this is the nearest you'll get to the real thing in a commercial setting. Professional *cantantes* do their best to create some *duende* (magic) and sometimes succeed. However, it's pricey (€30 incl. one drink). Daily shows at 8pm and 10pm.

Museo del Baile Flamenco Regular concerts are also staged at the Museo del Baile Flamenco (see p.275). Visit their website for details.

LIVE MUSIC AND CLUBS

Earlier on in the evening, Seville's *discotecas* attract a very young crowd; the serious action starts after midnight and often lasts till well beyond dawn. For rock and pop music the bars around Pl. Alfalfa and Alameda de Hércules have the best of the action.

Abril c/Luís Montoto 118. The ultimate in chic, trendy *sevillano* nightlife and known for hosting well-known international DJs. If you're in the mood to dance, this is the place. Thurs–Sun midnight until 3–7am.

Antique Avda. Matemáticos Rey Pastor y Castro s/n, near southern edge of Isla Mágica theme park. Popular with Seville's fancier dancers, this place comes with a transparent dancefloor and music that goes from Latin pop to heavier stuff. Open Fri, Sat & Sun only Oct–March; midnight to late.

Bar Garlochí c/Boteros 26, one block northeast of Pl. Alfafa. Claims the title as the city's most eccentric bar, a wonderfully kitsch "religious shrine" complete with incense, candles and flying angels. Their sacrilegious Sangre de Cristo crimson cocktail is a must. Mon–Sat 9pm–late; closed Mon.

Boss c/Betis 67. Cavernous Triana *discoteca* which takes off after midnight; has a penchant for house. Thurs–Sat 11pm–late.

Bulebar Alameda de Hércules 83. Late-opening bar with a plant-filled terrace facing the Alameda. Often stages theatre, music or other events and serves tapas and pasteles (cakes). Daily 7pm–3am.

Fun Club Alameda de Hércules 86. Popular weekends-only music and dance bar – favouring rock, reggae, hip-hop and salsa – with live bands. Thurs–Sat from 11.30pm–late.

Kudeta Pl. Legión 8 inside the Pl. de Armas shopping mall. Three-storey Asian-fusion resto-lounge-*discoteca* where you can follow a meal by smoking a hookah on terrace loungers or take a drink in the *discoteca*. Club daily 11pm–7am; bar from 3pm daily.

Urbano Comix c/Matahacas 5, near the Convento de Santa Paula in Macarena. Popular student bar with zany urban decor for rock, punk and R&B sounds plus live bands, staying open till dawn. Daily 9.30am–late.

DIRECTORY

Airport For flight information, call ☎ 954 449 000.

Banks and currency exchange ATMs are located throughout the centre of town, including around Avda. de la Constitución and Pl. Duque de la Victoria. Bureaux de change can be found here also, as well as on Pl. Nueva.

Books and newspapers A wide range of books in English (and other languages) is stocked by Casa del Libro, c/Velázquez 8, just east of c/Sierpes. Vértice, c/San Fernando 33, near the Alcázar, is also good. El Corte Inglés, Pl. Duque de la Victoria, also stocks English titles as well as international press. A more comprehensive range of international newspapers is stocked by a kiosk in front of the *pastelería La Campana* at the northern end of c/Sierpes.

Bullfights The main *corridas* are staged during the April *feria*, but not regularly outside this month. Details and tickets – costing between €25–150 depending on seat – from the Pl. de Toros (☎ 902 223 506) on fight days from 4.30pm or in advance (with commission) from the Impresa Pagés ticket office at c/Adriano 37.

Football Seville has two major Primera Division teams: Sevilla CF plays at the Sánchez Pizjuán stadium (☎ 954 535 353, ⓦ sevillafc.es) and Real Betis – newly promoted back to the first division in 2011 – uses the Manuel Ruiz de Lopera stadium (☎ 902 191 907, ⓦ realbetisbalompie.es), in the southern suburbs. Match schedules are in the local or national press, and tickets are surprisingly easy to get hold of for many matches (check the stadium or *turismos*).

Hiking maps The excellent LTC, Avda. Menéndez Pelayo 42 in Santa Cruz (☎ 954 425 964), and Risko, Avda. Kansas City 26, close to Santa Justa train station (☎ 954 570 849), stock maps, and the latter has a wide range of outdoor equipment.

Hospital English-speaking doctors are available at Hospital Universitario Virgen Macarena, c/Dr Marañon s/n (☎ 955 008 000), behind the Andalucía parliament building to the north of the centre. For emergencies, dial ☎ 061.

Internet access There are numerous internet cafés in the city centre. One near El Corte Inglés is Planeta Verde, c/Trajano 10 (daily 10am–10pm), and the Municipal Tourist Office, in Pl. San Francisco, also has screens.

Left luggage There are coin-operated lockers (ask for the *consigna*) at the Santa Justa train station in a basement (to the right as you enter). There are left luggage offices at the Prado de San Sebastián (daily 9am–9pm), and Pl. de Armas (9.30am–1.30pm & 3–6pm) bus stations; note that the latter one is not inside the bus station but around the right side of the building where there are taxis.

Lost property Oficina de Objetos Perdidos, c/Manuel V. Sagastizabál 3, next to the Prado de San Sebastián bus station (Mon–Fri 9.30am–1.30pm; ☎ 954 420 403).

Markets Entertaining Sunday *mercadillos* (roughly 10am–2pm depending on weather) take place on Pl. del Cabildo opposite the cathedral (stamps, coins, pins, ancient artefacts), and on Pl. del Museo in front of the Museo de las Bellas Artes (various art, tiles and woodcarvings). Calle Feria's long-standing El Jueves (Thursday market) with secondhand articles and antiques, east of the Alameda de Hércules, is another good one.

Police Central local police stations are at c/Arenal 1 (☎ 954 275 509) and c/Credito 11 (☎ 954 289 555), off the north end of the Alameda de Hércules. Dial ☎ 092 (local police) or ☎ 091 (national) in an emergency.

Post office Avda. de la Constitución 32, by the cathedral; *Lista de Correos* (poste restante) Mon–Fri 8.30am–8.30pm, Sat 9.30am–2pm.

Taxis The main central ranks are in Pl. Nueva, the Alameda de Hércules and the Pl. de Armas and Prado de San Sebastián bus stations. The basic charge for a short journey is around €5. A reliable taxi service, Radio Taxi, will come and collect you if you ring them on ☎ 954 580 000.

4

The Sierra Morena

The longest of Spain's mountain ranges, the **Sierra Morena** extends almost the whole way across Andalucía – from Rosal on the Portuguese frontier to the dramatic pass of Despeñaperros, north of Linares. Its hill towns marked the northern boundary of the old Moorish Caliphate of Córdoba, and in many ways the region still signals a break, with a shift from the climate and mentality of the south to the bleak plains and villages of Extremadura and Castilla-La Mancha. The range is not widely known – with its highest point a mere 1110m, it's not a dramatic *sierra* – and even Andalucians can have trouble placing it.

Aracena and around

Some 90km northwest of Seville, **ARACENA** is the highest town in the Sierra Morena with sharp, clear air, all the more noticeable after the heat of the city. A substantial but pretty place, it rambles partly up the side of a hill topped by the **Iglesia del Castillo**, a Gothic-Mudéjar church built by the Knights Templar around the remains of a Moorish castle. The town is flanked to the south and west by a small offshoot of the Sierra Morena – the **Sierra de Aracena** – a wonderfully verdant corner of Andalucía with wooded hills and villages with cobbled streets.

Gruta de las Maravillas

Daily 10.30am–1.30pm & 3–6.30pm; guided hourly visits, half-hourly at weekends • €8.50

Although the church is certainly worth the climb, Aracena's principal attraction is the **Gruta de las Maravillas**, the largest and arguably the most impressive cave in Spain. Supposedly discovered by a local boy in search of a lost pig, the cave is now illuminated and there are guided tours as soon as a couple of dozen or so people have assembled; to protect the cave there's now a strict limit of 35 persons per visit. At weekends and holiday periods, try to visit before noon – coach parties with advance bookings tend to fill up the afternoon allocation. On Sunday, there's a constant procession, but usually plenty of time to gaze and wonder. The cave is astonishingly beautiful, and funny, too – the last chamber of the tour is known as the Sala de los Culos (Room of the Buttocks), its walls and ceiling an outrageous, naturally sculpted exhibition, tinged in a pinkish-orange light.

ARRIVAL AND INFORMATION
ARACENA

By bus The station, Avda. de Sevilla s/n, lies on the southeast side of town close to the Parque Municipal.
Turismo At the Gruta (daily 10am–2pm & 4–6pm; ☎663 937 877, ⓦ www.sierradearacena.net).

Internet At Servicio Informatica, on c/Constitución, near the main Pl. Marqués de Aracena (Mon–Fri 10.30am–2pm & 5.30–8.30pm, Sat 10.30am–2pm).

ACCOMMODATION

Campsite ☎959 501 005. Campsite with pool about 3km out along the Seville road, then left for 500m on the road towards Corteconcepción. Closed Oct–March.
Casa Manolo c/Barberos 6 ☎959 128 014. The best of a limited choice of places to stay, and at the bottom end of the scale with rooms sharing bathrooms. €22
Hotel Sierra de Aracena Gran Vía 21 ☎959 126 175, ⓦ www.hsierradearacena.es. Offers relative luxury. €60

EATING AND DRINKING

Aracena is at the heart of a prestigious *jamón*-producing area, so try to sample some, and, when they're available, the delicious wild asparagus and local snails – in the fields in spring and summer, respectively.

Café-Bar Manzano Pl. del Marqués de Aracena. One of the town's most popular bars has now added a restaurant just around the corner. The bar serves a range of well-prepared tapas and *raciones* and has a terrace on the square. The restaurant serves up economical *sierra* cuisine and has a *menú* for €15. 8am–midnight; closed Tues.
Casas Pozo La Nieve 39. One of the town's top three restaurants, this is sited near the Gruta de las Maravillas

SIERRA MORENA PRACTICALITIES

The Morena's **climate** is mild – sunny in spring, hot but fresh in summer – but it can be very cold in the evenings and mornings. A good **time to visit** is between March and June, when the flowers, perhaps the most varied in the country, are at their best. You may get caught in the odd thunderstorm, but it's usually bright and hot enough to swim in the reservoirs or splash about in the clear springs and streams, all of which are good to drink. If your way takes you along a river, you'll be entertained by armies of frogs and turtles plopping into the water as you approach, by lizards, dragonflies, bees, hares and foxes peering discreetly from their holes – and, usually, no humans for miles around.

GETTING AROUND

East–west **transport** in the *sierra* is very limited. Most of the bus services are radial and north–south, with Seville as the hub, and this leads to ridiculous situations where, for instance, to travel from Aracena to Cazalla de la Sierra, a distance of some 80km, you must take a bus to Seville, 70km away, and then another up to Cazalla – a full day's journey of nearly 150km.

   Buses from Seville to the *sierra* leave from the Plaza de Armas station. If you just want to make a quick foray into the hills, **Aracena** is probably the best target (and the most regularly served town). If you're planning on some walking, it's also a good starting point: before you leave Seville, however, be sure to get yourself a decent **map** (see below) which, though it will probably be crammed with misleading information, should point you in the right direction to get lost somewhere interesting.

and only open lunchtimes. All the pork-based dishes are excellent, as is the *jamón* and *salchichón* (salami), plus there's a *menú* for around €20. Main dishes €8–16. Daily 12.30–4.30pm.

★ **Restaurante José Vicente** Avda. Andalucía 51 ☎ 959 128 455. For a memorable splurge this is the place to come. Arguably the town's best restaurant, patrons gather to savour the five grades of Jabugo *jamón ibérico* (black-pig ham) under the approving gaze of owner/chef Vicente

Sousa. The €20 *menú*, which often includes a mouthwatering *solomillo ibérico* (black-pig loin), is recommended. Daily 1.30–5pm & 8.30pm–12.30am; closed Tues.

La Serrana Pozo de la Nieve s/n ☎ 959 127 613. The third of the triumvirate of Aracena's best restaurants, and located opposite *Casas* (above), this is another place where *sierra* cooking is at its best. All the pork dishes are recommended and there's a *menú* for around €20. Main dishes €8–20. Daily 1–5pm.

Walking in the Sierra de Aracena

If you intend to do some **walking in the sierra**, you can get useful information (including maps and leaflets on flora and fauna) on the surrounding Parque Natural Sierra de Aracena y Picos de Aroche from an **information centre** in the ancient *cabildo* (town hall), Plaza Alta 5 (Sept–June Tues–Sun 10am–2pm & 4–6pm; July & Aug 10am–2pm & 6–8pm). You should also ask at the Aracena *turismo* for the free *Senderos de la Sierra de Aracena y Picos de Aroche* map listing 23 waymarked routes, and they also sell a more detailed *Mapa Guía de la Sierra de Aracena y Picos de Aroche*. A good **hiking guide**, *Sierra de Aracena* by David & Ros Brawn (Discovery Walking Guides), details 27 clearly described walks in the *sierra* ranging between four and fourteen kilometres. An accompanying map for the book is sold separately, and all walks have GPS waypoints identifying key locations en route.

Almonaster La Real

The **sierra villages** – Jabugo, Aguafría, Almonaster La Real – all make rewarding bases for walks, though all are equally ill-served by public transport (details from the Aracena *turismo*). The most interesting is **ALMONASTER LA REAL**, whose castle encloses a tiny ninth-century mosque, **La Mezquita** (daily 9am–7pm; free), with what is said to be the oldest *mihrab* in Spain. Tacked onto the mosque is the village bullring, which sees action once a year in August during the annual *feria*.

THE KING OF HAMS

Surrounding Aracena is a scattering of attractive but economically depressed villages, most of them dependent on the **jamón industry** and its curing factory at Jabugo. Jamón serrano (mountain ham) is a tapa or *bocadillo* standard throughout Spain, and some of the best, jamón de bellota (acorn-fed ham), comes from the Sierra de Aracena, where herds of sleek black pigs grazing beneath oak trees are a constant feature. In October, the acorns drop and the pigs, waiting patiently below, gorge themselves, become fat and are promptly whisked off to be slaughtered then cured in the dry mountain air. The meat of these black pigs is exceptionally fatty when eaten as pork but the same fat that marbles the meat adds to the tenderness during the curing process. This entails first of all covering the hams in coarse rock or sea salt to "sweat", after which they are removed to cool cellars to mature for up to two years. *Jamón serrano* from mass-produced white pigs is matured for only a few weeks, hence the incomparable difference in taste. At Jabugo the best of the best is then further graded from one to five *jotas* (the letter "J" for Jabugo) depending on its quality. A whole leg of *cinco jotas jamón* will set you back anything from €250 to €350. The *turismo* can provide details of where to sample and buy.

ACCOMMODATION AND EATING

ALMONASTER LA REAL

Hotel Casa García ☎ 955 143 109. At the entrance to the village, the *Hotel Casa García* is a comfortable place to stay. It also has a good restaurant, with tasty *jamón* and *sierra* specialities. **€53**

★ **Las Palmeras** c/Carretera s/n. Perhaps the village's best place for food is the plant-bedecked *Las Palmeras* on the road into the village before *Casa García*. Voluble proprietor Alejandro produces everything on the economical (and ecological) menu himself, from the tasty *caña de lomo* (cured ham from his own black pigs) to the salads (which shouldn't be missed) from his *huerta* (vegetable garden). **Daily noon–5pm & 8–11pm.**

The Costa de la Luz

Stumbling on the villages along the **Costa de la Luz**, between Algeciras and Cádiz, is like entering a new land after the dreadfulness of the Costa del Sol. The journey west from Algeciras seems in itself a relief, the road climbing almost immediately into rolling green hills, offering fantastic views down to Gibraltar and across the Strait to the just-discernible white houses and tapering minarets of Moroccan villages. Beyond, the Rif mountains hover mysteriously in the background, and on a clear day, as you approach **Tarifa**, you can distinguish Tangier on the edge of its crescent-shaped bay. Beyond Tarifa lies a string of excellent golden-sand beaches washed by Atlantic breakers and backed by a clutch of low-key resorts such as **Conil**. Inland, the haunting Moorish hill town of **Vejer de la Frontera** beckons, while set back from the sea at Bolonia is the ancient Roman settlement of **Baelo Claudia**.

Tarifa

TARIFA, spreading out beyond its Moorish walls, was until the mid-1980s a quiet village, known in Spain, if at all, for its abnormally high suicide rate – a result, it is said, of the unremitting winds that blow across the town and its environs. Today, it's a prosperous, popular and, at times, very crowded resort, following its discovery as Europe's prime **windsurfing** and **kitesurfing** spot. There are equipment-rental shops along the length of the main street, and regular competitions are held year-round. Development is moving ahead fast as a result of this new-found popularity, but for the time being it remains an attractive place for a stopover.

San Mateo

Daily 8.30am–1pm & 5.30–9pm • Free

If windsurfing is not your motive for visiting, there can still be an appeal in wandering the crumbling ramparts, gazing out to sea or down into the network of lanes that surround the fifteenth-century, Baroque-fronted church of **San Mateo**, which has a beautiful late-Gothic interior.

Castillo de Guzman
Tues–Sun 11am–2pm & 4–6pm • €2

Worth a look is the **Castillo de Guzman**, the site of many a struggle for this strategic foothold into Spain. It's named after Guzmán el Bueno (the Good), Tarifa's infamous commander during the Moorish siege of 1292, who earned his tag for a superlative piece of tragic drama. Guzmán's 9-year-old son had been taken hostage by a Spanish traitor, and surrender of the garrison was demanded as the price of the boy's life. Choosing "honour without a son, to a son with dishonour", Guzmán threw down his own dagger for the execution. The story – a famous piece of heroic resistance in Spain – had echoes in the Civil War siege of the Alcázar at Toledo, when the Nationalist commander defied similar threats, an echo much exploited for propaganda purposes.

ARRIVAL AND DEPARTURE   TARIFA

By bus Frequent services to Seville, Málaga, Cádiz and points in between. The station's at the northern end of town near the *gasolinera* (petrol station) from where the main Algeciras–Cádiz road (c/Batalla del Salado) leads to the walled old town, a 5- to 10min walk. Along here there's a supermarket, fried-fish and *churro* stalls, and windsurfing-equipment shops.

By ferry Tarifa offers the tempting opportunity for a trip to Morocco – a day-trip by catamaran to Tangier is feasible. Information on schedules and fares is available from the *turismo* or the friendly travel agency Viajes Baelo Tour, Avda. Constitución 5 (☎ 956 681 242), near the *turismo*. A useful site for checking the latest ferry schedules is ⓦ directferries.co.uk.

INFORMATION

Turismo The welcoming *turismo*, on the central Paseo la Alameda (Mon–Fri 10am–2pm & 4–6pm, Oct–March 9.30am–1.30pm & 4–6pm, Sat & Sun all year 10am–2pm; ☎ 956 680 993, ⓦ aytotarifa.com), can help with maps and accommodation.

Internet access is available at Ciber Pandor@, c/Sancho IV El Bravo 13a, opposite the Hotel Misiana (Mon–Sat 10am–2pm & 5–9pm).

ACCOMMODATION

Tarifa has plenty of **places to stay**, though finding a bed in summer (or when there's a surfing tournament) can often be a struggle, with crowds of windsurfers cornering every available room. A little way out of town to the west, there are six **campsites** and the *turismo* can provide a list of these or visit ⓦ campingsandalucia.es. You should be aware that we quote the high-season price which in Tarifa can fall by up to sixty-percent outside July and August.

Casa Facundo c/Batalla del Salado 47 ☎ 956 684 298, ⓦ www.hostalfacundo.com. Reliable and friendly family *hostal* on the main road into town just outside the walls, offering dorm beds, rooms sharing bath and en-suite

rooms with TV. Despite the crisis they are going ahead with the construction of a grand new hotel across the road opening in 2012. Dorm beds €25, rooms sharing bath €71, en-suite €86

WHALE- AND DOLPHIN-WATCHING TRIPS

Tarifa is home to **whale- and dolphin-watching** excursions in the Strait of Gibraltar, which leave daily from the harbour. The trip is a fairly steep €30 (reductions for under-14s), but this includes another trip free of charge if there are no sightings. Places must be booked in advance from either of two non-profit-making organizations: **Whale Watch**, Avda. de la Constitución 6, close to the *turismo* (☎ 956 682 247, reservations ☎ 639 476 544, ⓦ whalewatchtarifa.net), and **FIRMM** (Foundation for Information and Research on Marine Mammals), c/Pedro Cortés 3, slightly west of the church of San Mateo (☎ 956 627 008, ⓦ firmm .org). A more commercial operation, **Turmares**, with an office on the beach road near the foot of the Paseo de la Alameda (☎ 956 680 741, ⓦ turmares.com), also runs whale-spotting trips (€30, kids €20) with a glass-bottomed boat.

★ **Hostal Africa** c/María Antonia Toledo 12 ☎ 956 680 220, ✉ hostal_africa@hotmail.com. Charming, small *hostal* with clean and simple rooms with and without bath and spectacular sea views from a communal terrace. Sharing bath €65, en-suite €50

Hostal La Calzada c/Justina Pertíñez 7 ☎ 956 680 366. Popular and friendly *hostal* in the centre of the old town, close by the church of San Mateo, offering a/c en-suite rooms with TV. Wi-fi zone. €90

Hostal-Restaurante Villanueva Avda. Andalucía 11 ☎ 956 684 149. Welcoming and good-value *hostal*, with en-suite rooms with TV above a good restaurant (see below). €65

Hotel Misiana c/Sancho IV El Bravo 18 ☎ 956 627 083, ⓦ www.misiana.com. Central, stylish place with arty decor whose rooms are decorated with modern art and Moroccan furnishings. €135

EATING AND DRINKING

Tarifa has a wide range of **places to eat**, divided between the old town inside the walls and the new town beyond this. This is another place to try Cádiz's tasty *urta* (sea bream), available all over town.

★ **Bar El Francés** Paseo c/Sancho IV El Bravo 21. A highly popular French tapas and *raciones* bar adding a subtly Gallic touch to such staples as *calamares*, *rabo de toro* and *tortilla de camarones*. Has a small street terrace. Daily 12.30–4.30pm & 8pm–12.30am.

Bar Morilla c/Sancho IV El Bravo 2. Central bar where *tarifeños* gather to breakfast or munch early-evening tapas while contemplating the ancient stones of nearby San Mateo. Later, cloths are thrown over the tables as the restaurant hits its stride. Daily 10am–1am.

★ **Mandragora** c/Independencia 3 ☎ 956 681 291. One of a number of restaurants and tapas bars in town offering dishes from both sides of the straits. But this is a cut above the rest and in addition to Moroccan couscous and *berenjenas bereber* (aubergine), it does excellent

raciones, including *boquerones rellenos* (stuffed anchovies) and tasty dishes like *rape con crema de erizos y setas* (monkfish with wild mushrooms in a sea-urchin sauce). 1.30–4.30pm & 8–11pm; closed Sun.

Restaurante Villanueva Avda. Andalucía 11. Fine restaurant of the *hostal* of the same name; their *urta* is prepared in five different ways and there's a good-value *menú* for €8. Daily 1.30–4.30pm & 8.30–11pm.

Tarifa Eco Center c/San Sebastián 4, outside the walls ☎ 956 627 220, ⓦ tarifaecocenter.com. This interesting complex has an organic vegetarian restaurant (pasta, pizzas, quiches, *tabouli* etc) out front, eco-shop at the rear and a chill-out zone serving herbal and other teas to the side. Off a courtyard terrace are rooms offering yoga pilates and other courses. Daily 10am–midnight.

NIGHTLIFE

Apart from bars staging live music to keep the windsurfers happy, there's little in the way of entertainment beyond style **bars** such as that attached to the hotel *Misiana* and *Bamboo*, Paseo de la Alameda 2, plus a couple of *discotecas*. Tarifa's main summer **nightlife** scene happens when the town council erects *carpas* (disco tents) on the Playa de los Lances beach at the eastern end of town. It's also worth finding out what's happening at the *Tarifa Eco Center*, as they stage frequent concerts and show films.

Tarifa Beach

Heading northwest from Tarifa, you find the most spectacular **beaches** of the whole of the Costa de la Luz – wide stretches of yellow or silvery-white sand, washed by some magical rollers. The same winds that have created such perfect conditions for windsurfing can, however, sometimes be a problem for more casual enjoyment, sandblasting those attempting to relax on towels or mats and whipping the water into whitecaps.

The beaches lie immediately west of town. They get better as you move past the tidal flats and the mosquito-ridden estuary – until the dunes start and the first campervans lurk among the bushes. At **TARIFA BEACH**, a little bay 9km from town, there are restaurants, a windsurfing school, campsites and a string of pricey hotels, including the *Hurricane Hotel*.

ACCOMMODATION   TARIFA BEACH

Camping Paloma Los Algarbes, 10km northwest of town ☎ 956 684 203, ⓦ www.campingpaloma.com. Not quite as close to the beach as some others, but the

magnificent Playa de Valdevaqueros is only 500m distant. There's plenty of shade plus a restaurant, pool and supermarket on site.

Camping Río Jara On the N340 road 4km northwest of town ☎956 680 570, ⓦwww.campingsdetarifa.com. The nearest campsite to the town with plenty of shade and access for disabled campers.

Camping Torre de la Peña On the N340 7km northwest of town ☎56 684 903, ⓦwww.campingtp .com. A decent campsite close to the sea with plenty of

shade, pool and a decent restaurant.

Hurricane Hotel Carretera Cádiz s/n ☎956 68 49 19, ⓦwww.hotelhurricane.com. Set in dense gardens 7km west of Tarifa at the ocean's edge, this luxurious California-style hotel has tastefully decorated a/c rooms, fully equipped gym, two pools, stables, windsurfing school and its own restaurant. B&B €168

Bolonia

Tues–Sun 10am–7pm, June–Sept until 8pm, Nov–Feb until 6pm • €1.50; free with EU passport

At the Roman town of **BOLONIA**, or *Baelo Claudia* as the Romans knew it, beyond a new visitor centre and museum you can make out the remains of three temples and a theatre, as well as a forum, numerous houses, and a fascinating factory for making *garum* fish sauce, a Roman culinary passion. The site can be reached down a small side road that turns off the main Cádiz road 15km after Tarifa.

ACCOMMODATION   BOLONIA

There's a fine **beach** here with bars and eating places and a few **places to stay**.

★ **Hostal La Hormiga Voladora** c/El Lentiscal 15 ☎956 688 562. The excellent *Hostal La Hormiga Voladora*, with garden rooms (some en suite) close to the beach is the

best choice around. It's located at the eastern end of the village next to the *Panadería Beatriz*. €65

EATING AND DRINKING

There are a couple of *chiringuitos* actually on the beach serving grilled fish where you could try the *Bahía de Bolonia* – otherwise most of the places to eat are in the small village of Bolonia itself.

Las Rejas Close to the Hostal La Hormiga Voladora. *Las Rejas* is perhaps Bolonia's best restaurant. All the fish and *mariscos* are fresh – as is of course the tuna in season – and

they can rustle up a decent lunchtime paella if you're looking for a beach snack.

Vejer de la Frontera

While you're on the Costa de la Luz, be sure to take time to visit **VEJER DE LA FRONTERA**, a classically white, Moorish-looking hill town set in a cleft between great protective hills that rear high above the road from Tarifa to Cádiz. The drama of Vejer is in its isolation and elevated position, both easily appreciated from an approach road that winds upwards for a dizzying 4km. This eventually arrives at the Parque de los Remedios and a **car park**, which, given Vejer's tortuously narrow streets, one-way system and traffic congestion, you'd be strongly advised to make use of if you've arrived by car; this is also where the **bus** drops you. From here you'll need to ascend a further 300m along c/Los Remedios to reach La Plazuela, the effective centre of town.

Until the end of the twentieth century, the women of Vejer wore long, dark cloaks that veiled their faces like nuns' habits; despite being adopted as the town's tourist icon, this custom seems now to be virtually extinct outside the town *feria*, but the place has a remoteness and Moorish feel as explicit as anywhere in Spain. There's a castle and a church of curiously mixed styles (mainly Gothic and Mudéjar), but the main fascination lies in exploring the brilliant white and labyrinthine alleyways, wandering past iron-grilled windows, balconies and patios, and slipping into a succession of bars.

INFORMATION

Turismo In the Parque de los Remedios, Avda. de los Remedios 2 (April–Sept Mon–Fri 10am–2pm & 6–8pm, Sat 10am–2pm & 6–8pm, Sun 11am–1pm; Oct–March Mon–Fri 10am–2pm & 4–6pm, Sat 10am–2pm; ☎956 451 736, ⓦwww.turismovejer.es), which can provide a useful town map, accommodation list and information on budget *casas particulares* nearby.

ACCOMMODATION

★ **La Casa del Califa** Pl. de España 16 ☎956 447 730, ⓦwww.lacasadelcalifa.com. One of Vejer's most striking hotels is *La Casa del Califa*, occupying a refurbished, rambling house, parts of which date back to Moorish times; the stylish rooms are decorated with Moroccan fittings and guests have use of two patios with fine views and a library. Free wi-fi. Also has a charming *casa rural* next door with rooms around a pool. *Rough Guide* readers with this guide can claim (at check-in) a ten-percent reduction. Both B&B. Hotel **€94–104**, *casa rural* **€110**

Casa Rural Leonor c/Rosario 25, near the Castillo ☎956 451 085, ⓦwww.casaleonor.com. A charming *casa rural* in a converted Moorish dwelling with comfortable en-suite rooms, friendly proprietors, and fabulous views towards Morocco from a roof terrace. They also have apartments nearby sleeping up to four. Rooms **€50**, apartments **€80**

★ **El Cobijo de Vejer** c/ San Filmo 7 ☎956 45 50 23,

ⓦwww.elcobijo.com. Excellent *hostal* inside a traditional house with delightful flower-filled patio and individual rooms on various levels. The higher-priced *Zahara* and *Xauen* (the latter has two fabulous terraces) with their own kitchens are the ones to go for. All rooms are a/c, internet-connected with wi-fi, and have fridges and satellite TV. B&B **€80–103**

Hotel Convento de San Francisco La Plazuela ☎956 451 001, ⓦwww.tugasa.com. A good place to start looking for accommodation is at the delightful *Hotel Convento de San Francisco*, where you can also get town maps if the *turismo* is closed; it's rather hidden away, so ask for directions. **€67**

CAMPING

Campsite ☎956 450 988. Vejer's campsite lies below town on the main N340 Málaga-to-Cádiz road. Closed Oct–May.

EATING AND DRINKING

Vejer has plenty of places for **eating and drinking** scattered all around the old town. Besides tapas bars and budget restaurants there are a couple of places worth paying a bit extra for.

Bar Peneque Pl. de España 27. Traditional and entertaining local bar built into a cave with tables at the back for munching *raciones* should you not feel like joining in the domino games favoured by regulars. Daily 9am–11pm.

El Jardín del Califa Pl. de España 16. The mid-priced restaurant attached to the hotel of the same name has a Moroccan chef and serves up a variety of Moroccan and Middle-Eastern inspired dishes on a tree-shaded courtyard terrace. Specialities include tagines and spicy fish dishes. A

recently added, stylish bar offers stunning views from its roof terrace. Daily 1–3.30pm & 8–11pm.

Mesón Pepe Julián c/Juan Relinque 7, just off La Plazuela. Popular local bar with *azulejo*-lined walls serving up decent tapas – specials include *chorizo ibérico* and *calamares* (squid). Daily noon–5pm & 8–11pm.

El Refectorio La Plazuela. The upmarket restaurant of the *Hotel Convento de San Francisco* is a very good mid-priced restaurant offering many local specialities and also has a *menú turístico* for €16. Daily 1–4pm & 8–11pm.

Conil

Back on the coast, a dozen or so kilometres on, lies the increasingly popular resort of **CONIL**. Outside July and August, though, it's still a good place to relax, and in mid-season the only real drawback is trying to find a room. Conil Town, once a poor fishing village, now seems entirely modern as you look back from the beach, though when you're actually in the streets you find many older buildings, too. The majority of the tourists are Spanish (with a lesser number of Germans), so there's an enjoyable atmosphere, and, if you are here in mid-season, a very lively nightlife.

The beach

The **beach**, Conil's *raison d'être*, is a wide bay of brilliant yellow sand stretching for many kilometres to either side of town and lapped by an amazingly, not to say disarmingly, gentle Atlantic – you have to walk a long way before it reaches waist height. The area immediately in front of town is the family beach; up to the northwest you can walk to some more sheltered coves, while across the river to the southeast is a topless and nudist area. Walking along the coast in this direction, the beach is virtually unbroken until it reaches the cape, the familiar-sounding **Cabo de Trafalgar**, off which Lord Nelson achieved victory and met his death on October 21, 1805. If the winds are blowing, this is one of the most sheltered beaches in the area. It can be reached by road, save for the last 400m across the sands to the rock.

ARRIVAL AND INFORMATION CONIL

By bus Most buses use the Transportes Comes station on c/Carretera; walk towards the sea and you'll find yourself in the centre of town.

Turismo Along the way at the junction of c/Carretera and c/Menéndez Pidal (daily: May–Oct 8am–2pm &

5.30–8.30pm; Nov–April 8.30am–2.30pm; ☎956 440 501, ⓦconil.org); it's worth picking up a copy of their useful free booklet *Conil en su Bolsillo*, which details all the town's tapas bars, restaurants and much more.

ACCOMMODATION

Accommodation needs are served by numerous hotels and *hostales,* augmented in high season by a multitude of private rooms for rent; full details on all of these are available from the *turismo*.

Hostal La Posada c/Quevedo s/n, just northeast of Pl. de España ☎956 44 41 71, ⓦwww.laposadadeconil.com. Dapper *hostal* with clean and tidy en-suite a/c rooms with TV – many with sea views – above a good restaurant with terrace. Also has a pool and wi-fi zone. B&B €80

Hostal La Villa Pl. de España 6 ☎956 44 10 53. Economical en-suite rooms above a bar-restaurant on a central square. Open May–Oct. €45–55

Hotel Flamenco Playa Fuente de Gallos ☎956 44 07 11, ⓦwww.hipotels.com. Fronting the Fuente del Gallo beach this elegant and newly refurbished 100-roomer is

one of the resort's older luxury places set in a tranquil location. Well-appointed rooms have balcony terraces and sea views and there's a bar-restaurant, two garden pools and steps down to a fine strand. B&B €152

CAMPING

Camping Fuente del Gallo Urbanización Fuente de Gallo s/n ☎956 440 137, ⓦwww.campingfuentedegallo.com. The nearest campsite to the town lies a stiff 3km walk (or easy taxi ride) north of the centre and is sited 400m inland from the superb Playa la Fontanilla with good facilities, bar-restaurant and pool. €6.50, €6.50 per tent, €4 per vehicle

EATING AND DRINKING

Seafood is king here and Conil has lots of good **restaurants** along the front; try the *ortiguillas* – deep-fried sea anemones – which you see only in the Cádiz area. Two of the best restaurants, *Francisco* and *La Fontanilla*, are side by side on the Playa de la Fontanilla, the town's northernmost beach.

Cádiz

CÁDIZ is among the oldest settlements in Spain, founded about 1100 BC by the Phoenicians and one of the country's principal ports ever since. Its greatest period, however, and the era from which the central part of town takes most of its present appearance, was the eighteenth century. Then, with the silting up of the river to Seville, the port enjoyed a virtual monopoly on the Spanish-American trade in gold and silver, and on its proceeds were built the cathedral – itself golden-domed (in colour at least) and almost Oriental when seen from the sea – grand mansions, public buildings, dockyards, warehouses and the smaller churches.

Inner Cádiz, built on a peninsula-island, remains much as it must have looked in those days, with its grand, open squares, sailors' alleyways and high, turreted houses. Literally crumbling from the effect of the sea air on its soft limestone, it has a tremendous atmosphere – slightly seedy, definitely in decline, but still full of mystique.

ACCOMMODATION

Casa Caracol	2
Las Cuatro Naciones	5
Hospedería Las Cortes	3
Hostal Bahía	1
Hostal Canalejas	4
Hostal España	7
Hostal Fantoni	6
Hotel Parador Atlántico	8

EATING & DRINKING

El Aljibe	1
Cervecería Marisquería Aurelio	2
El Faro & Bar El Faro	8
Freiduría Europa	6
Freiduría Las Flores	5
Mesón El Candil	7
Restaurante Atxuri	3
Restaurante El Sardinero	4

4

CÁDIZ

Castillo de San Sebastián ▼

Unlike most other ports of its size, Cádiz seems immediately relaxed, easy-going and not at all threatening, even at night. Perhaps this is due to its reassuring shape and compactness, the presence of the sea, and the striking **sea fortifications** and waterside **alamedas** making it impossible to get lost for more than a few blocks. But it probably owes this tone as much to the town's tradition of liberalism and tolerance – one maintained through the years of Franco's dictatorship even though this was one of the

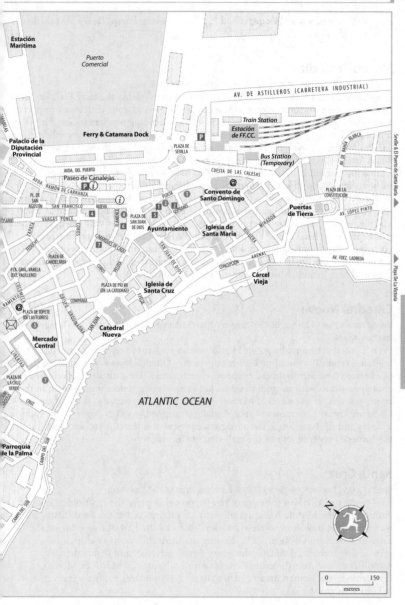

first towns to fall to his forces, and was the port through which the Nationalist armies launched their invasion. In particular, Cádiz has always accepted its substantial gay community, who are much in evidence at the city's brilliant **Carnaval** celebrations. The city is making elaborate preparations to celebrate the bicentenary of the 1812 Constitution (Spain's first, called "La Pepa") and setting up of the Cortes (parliament), in opposition to the Napoleonic blockade. The major monument commemorating this event will be a **new road bridge** named "La Pepa" linking Puerto Real across the bay with the old town.

Museo de Cádiz

Tues 2.30–8.30pm, Wed–Sat 9am–8.30pm, Sun 9.30am–2.30pm • €1.50; free with EU passport

The **Museo de Cádiz**, the province's most important, overlooks the leafy Plaza de Mina and incorporates the **archeological museum** on the ground floor with many important finds and artefacts from the city's lengthy history, including two remarkable fifth-century-BC Phoenician carved sarcophagi in white marble (one male, the other female), unique to the western Mediterranean. The upper floor houses the **Museo de Bellas Artes**. This contains a quite exceptional series of saints painted by Francisco Zurbarán, brought here from the Carthusian monastery at Jerez and one of only three such sets in the country (the others are at Seville and Guadalupe) preserved intact, or nearly so. With their sharply defined shadows and intense, introspective air, Zurbarán's saints are at once powerful and very Spanish – even the English figures such as Hugh of Lincoln, or the Carthusian John Houghton, martyred by Henry VIII when he refused to accept him as head of the English Church. Perhaps this is not surprising, for the artist spent much of his life travelling round the Carthusian monasteries of Spain and many of his saints are in fact portraits of the monks he met. Other important artists displayed here include Murillo, Rubens and Alonso Cano.

Catedral Nueva

Mon–Sat 10am–6.30pm & 4.30–7pm, Sat 10am–7pm, Sun 1–7pm • €5 including museum, free Sun 11am–1pm • **Torre de Poniente** Daily 10am–6pm €4

Even if you don't normally go for High Baroque, it's hard to resist the attraction of the huge and seriously crumbling eighteenth-century **Catedral Nueva**, now nearing the end of a belated (and astronomically expensive) restoration. The cathedral is decorated entirely in stone, with no gold in sight, and in absolutely perfect proportions. In the crypt, you can see the tomb of Manuel de Falla, the great *gaditano* (as inhabitants of Cádiz are known) composer of such Andalucía-inspired works as *Nights in the Gardens of Spain* and *El Amor Brujo*. For a magnificent view over the city, you can also climb the **Torre de Poniente**, one of the cathedral's twin towers.

Santa Cruz

Mon 5.30–7.45pm, Tues–Sat 10am–1pm & 5.30–7.45pm, Sun 10am–12pm & 6.15–7.30pm • Free

East of the cathedral on the edge of the Barrio del Populo, the city's oldest quarter dating from the Middle Ages, lies the "old" or original cathedral, **Santa Cruz**. This was one of the buildings severely knocked about by the Earl of Essex during the English assault on Cádiz in 1596, causing the thirteenth-century church to be substantially rebuilt. A fine Gothic entry portal survived, and inside there's a magnificent seventeenth-century *retablo* with sculptures by Martínez Montañés. A first-century-BC **Roman theatre** (daily 10am–2.30pm; free) has been excavated behind, close to the sea.

Torre Tavira

C/Marqués del Real Tesoro 10• Daily: June–Sept 10am–8pm; Oct–May 10am–6pm • €5

North of the cathedral along c/Sacramento, the **Torre Tavira** is an eighteenth-century mansion with the tallest tower in the city, from where there are great **views** over the rooftops to the sea beyond; it also houses an entertaining **camera obscura**.

Hospital de las Mujeres

Mon–Thurs 10am–1.30pm & 5.30–8pm, Fri & Sat 10am–3.30pm • €1.50; ask the porter for admission

One of the most impressive Baroque buildings in the city, the chapel of the **Hospital de las Mujeres**, houses a brilliant **El Greco**, *St Francis in Ecstasy*. It's one of the Cretan artist's finest portrayals of the saint, although it's a rather sombre study using copious shades of grey.

Santa Cueva

C/Rosario • Tues–Fri 10am–1pm & 4.30–7.30pm, Sat & Sun 10am–1pm • €3

A short walk southeast from the Museo de Cádiz, the eighteenth-century **Oratorio de Santa Cueva** houses three fine Goya frescoes. The church is divided into two dramatically contrasting parts; in the elliptical **upper oratory** beneath an elegant dome are three frescoes representing the *Miracle of the Loaves and Fishes*, the *Bridal Feast* (either side of the main altar) and the *Last Supper* (above the entrance), an unexpected depiction of Christ and the disciples dining sprawled on the floor, Roman style. The other works here are depictions of biblical scenes by minor artists.

The beaches

Cádiz has two main **beaches** – the excellent **Playa de la Victoria** (and its less commercial continuation the Playa de la Cortadura), to the left of the promontory approaching town (reached from the centre on bus #1 from Plaza de España), and the often overcrowded **Playa de la Caleta** on the peninsula's western tip.

ARRIVAL AND DEPARTURE   CÁDIZ

By train The station is on the periphery of the old town, close to Pl. de San Juan de Dios, busiest of the city's many squares. For current timetables and ticket information, consult RENFE ☎ 902 240 202, ⌨ renfe.es.

Destinations Córdoba (3 daily; 3hr); Granada (5 daily, change at Seville; 5hr); Madrid (2 daily; 5hr); Seville (9 daily; 2hr).

By bus Currently all buses arrive and depart from a temporary bus station to the side of the train station. The nearby port area of the Puerto Comercial is being redeveloped and the city's plan at the time of writing is to relocate a new bus station here. Either *turismo* will be able to provide information on this.

Destinations Algeciras (10 daily; 2hr 15min); Arcos de la Frontera (5 daily; 1hr 30min); Chipiona (9 daily; 1hr 15min); Conil (13 daily; 1hr); El Puerto de Santa María (23 daily; 30min); Granada (5 daily; 5hr); Jerez de la Frontera (13 daily; 45min); Málaga (4 daily; 3hr 45min); Sanlúcar de Barrameda (5–9 daily; 1hr); Seville (9 daily; 1hr 45min); Tarifa (6 daily; 2hr); Vejer de la Frontera (6 daily; 1hr).

By car Coming by car, you'll soon discover sea-locked Cádiz's acute lack of parking space, and if you don't want to spend an age searching you'd be best off taking accommodation with a garage (all the hotels will assist with parking) or heading for a car park – two of the most central inside the city walls are by the train station and along Paseo de Canalejas near the port.

By ferry Today the only long-distance ferry services from Cádiz are to the Canary Islands. Trasmediterranea, Estación Marítima (☎ 956 227 421, ⌨ trasmediterranea.es), currently operates a weekly sailing (Tues 5pm) to Las Palmas and Tenerife. Local ferries sail across the bay to El Puerto de Santa María and the beach resort of Rota. The service to El Puerto has a normal boat named *El Vapor* (5 daily; 40min; €5 return) and a catamaran service (every 30min between 7.45am–9.25pm; €4.30 return). All three services including the boat to Rota (7 daily; 50min; €8.40 return) sail from the same dock on the south side of the Puerto Comercial. A useful site for checking the latest ferry schedules is ⌨ directferries.co.uk.

Destinations Las Palmas (1 weekly; 39hr); El Puerto (boat: 5 daily; 40min; €5 return; catamaran: every 30min between 7.45am–9.25pm; €4.30 return); Rota (7 daily; 50min; €8.40 return); Tenerife (1 weekly; 48hr).

INFORMATION AND TOURS

Turismo Avda. Ramón de Carranza (Mon–Fri 9am–7.30pm, Sat & Sun 9am–5pm; ☎ 956 203 191) near to Pl. San Juan de Dios; there's also a useful *turismo municipal* on the Paseo de Canalejas (April–Sept Mon–Fri 9am–7pm, Sat–Sun 9am–5pm; Oct–March Mon–Fri 8.30am–6.30pm, Sat & Sun 9am–5pm; ☎ 956 241 001).

Internet access is available at Novap Computers, Cuesta de las Calesas 45 (daily 10am–11pm), near the train station, and Ciber Columela, c/Columela 2 (daily 9am–10.30pm) off Pl. de las Flores.

Open-top bus tour Two competing companies do the same hop-on, hop-off clockwise route around the peninsula. Tour por Cádiz (10am–11pm; €10.99) and Cádiz Tour (10am–9pm; €12 with a slightly longer route) both have stops at or near Pl. San Juan de Dios, the cathedral, Parque Genoves, Playa de la Victoria and places in between. With Cádiz Tour, your ticket is valid for 24 hours from the time you board; Tour por Cádiz tickets are valid only on the day of purchase.

ACCOMMODATION

In tune with the city itself, much of Cádiz's budget **accommodation** has seen better days. Although things are slowly improving, there's still a shortage of good-quality accommodation in all categories. Radiating out from the Pl. San Juan de Dios is a dense network of alleyways crammed with **hostales** and **fondas** and a few less inviting options. More salubrious places to stay are to be found a couple of blocks away, towards the cathedral or Pl. de Candelaria.

★ **Casa Caracol** c/Suárez de Salazar 4 ☎ 956 261 166, ⓦ hostel–casacaracol.com. Friendly backpackers' place with dorm beds in a large house near Pl. San Juan de Dios. Also has some double rooms sharing bath and pricier en-suite rooms in a new *hostal* nearby. Price includes breakfast, free wi-fi and internet access and use of kitchen. Dorm €18, double €40

Las Cuatro Naciones c/Plocia 3 ☎ 956 255 539. Clean, unpretentious place with low-priced rooms sharing bath, close to Pl. San Juan de Dios. €41

★ **Hospedería Las Cortes** c/San Francisco 9 ☎ 956 212 668, ⓦ www.hotellascortes.com. Splendid newish hotel in a stylishly restored *casa señorial*. Elegant rooms have a/c and minibar and come internet and wi-fi connected. Facilities include sauna and gym, and there's a *cafetería* and restaurant. Can advise on parking. High-season price Aug only. €150

Hostal Bahía c/Plocia 5 ☎ 956 259 061, ⓦ www.hostalbahiacadiz.com. Reasonable-value and conveniently located *hostal*, offering a/c rooms with bath. Request their more attractive balcony rooms. €78

Hostal Canalejas c/Cristóbal Colón 5 ☎ 956 264 113, ⓦ www.hostalcanalejas.com. Pleasant two-star *hostal* in completely restored townhouse. En-suite rooms come with a/c and TV, and there's a wi-fi zone plus car park nearby. Avoid the windowless interior rooms though. €80

Hostal España Marqués de Cádiz 9 ☎ 956 285 500, ⓦ www.pensionespana.com. Pleasant *hostal* inside a restored *casa palacio* with reasonable rooms (with and without bath) with fans ranged around a patio. Sharing bath €45, en suite €60

Hostal Fantoni c/Flamenco 5 ☎ 956 282 704 ⓦ www.hostalfantoni.es. Good-value *hostal* in renovated town-house with lots of *azulejos* and cool marble, offering simple and en-suite rooms, the latter with a/c and TV. Wi-fi zone. €70

Hotel Parador Atlántico Parque Genovés 9 ☎ 956 226 905, ⓦ parador.es. The unloved old parador has been razed and replaced by a spanking-new state-of-the-art rectilinear construction fronting the sea. Opening its doors in early 2012 it will hold 124 rooms and suites, all with terrace balcony and sea view. Features include full-size pool, solarium, bars, restaurant and gardens. €180

EATING AND DRINKING

There are great **places to eat** all over town and the streets around Pl. San Juan de Dios, Pl. de las Flores and Pl. de la Libertad (containing the market) are all places where you'll find good bars and restaurants. In sea-girthed Cádiz, of course, fish is king and nowhere more so than in the old fishermans' quarter, the Barrio de la Viña. Here in the streets surrounding a tiny square named Pl. Tío de la Tiza – particularly along c/Virgen de la Palma – *gaditanos* gather to scoff themselves at economical *marisquerías*.

A FEAST MADE IN HEAVEN

Takeaway **fried fish** was invented in Cádiz (despite English claims to the contrary), and there are numerous *freidurías* (fried-fish shops) around the town, as well as stands along the beach in season. Few eating experiences here can beat strolling the city streets while dipping into a *cartucho* (paper funnel) of *pescado frito*. In the bars, *tortilla de camarones* (shrimp fritter) is another superb local speciality. Worth seeking out are:

Freiduría Europa c/Hospital de Mujeres 21. Fried-fish shop, similar and nearby to *Las Flores*.

★ **Freiduría Las Flores** On the square of the same name. Outstanding If you buy a take-away from here you can carry your *cartucho* to the terrace tables of the nearby bar *La Marina*, fronting the post office. Order a glass (or bottle) of chilled white wine to wash it down with, and you've got a feast made in heaven.

El Aljibe c/Plocia 25 ☎956 26 66 56. A good substitute when the nearby *Atxuri* is closed and a very good restaurant in its own right serving up a range of traditional dishes on a menu that changes four times a year. Also serves very good tapas in its bar. *Menú de degustación* €32 including wine. Daily 1–5pm & 8pm–midnight.

★ **Bar El Faro** c/San Félix 15. Tapas bar of the renowned restaurant (see below), and probably the best in town. A stand-up place where the *finos* are first rate, the service is slick and the seafood tapas are mouthwateringly delicious. House specials include *tortillitas de camarones* (shrimp fritters) and *tostaditas de pan con bacalao* (cod). Daily 1–4pm & 8pm–midnight.

★ **Cervecería-Marisquería Aurelio** c/Zorilla 1, near Pl. Mina. Vibrant, tiled seafood tapas bar with excellent *manzanilla*. Founded by the legendary and late Aurelio, who sold shellfish outside the entrance for many years, specials include *merluza rebozada* (hake) and *ortiguillas* (fried sea anemones). They'll also serve you a great fish supper at tables in a side room. Daily 12.30–5pm & 8.30pm–1am.

★ **El Faro** c/San Félix 15 ☎956 21 10 68. In the heart of the Barrio de la Viña, this is one of the best fish restaurants in Andalucía. House specialities include *pulpo* (octopus),

merluza (hake), *urta* (sea bream), and a delicious *arroz marinero* (Andalucian paella). There's a *menú de degustación* for €45 (excluding wine) and a *menú* for around €20 (Mon–Fri) which you may need to ask for. Their excellent tapas bar is also well worth a visit. Daily 12.30–3.30pm & 5.30–11.30pm.

Mesón El Candil c/Abreu 7. Very pleasant restaurant whose popularity has led to it occupying premises on both sides of this small *plazuela* with a charming terrace between. The chef has been fronting the *fogón* (stove) here for four decades so he should know by now how to prepare the house special *pescado plancha a la Pepe*. Meat is also on offer and there's a *menú* for €8. Daily 1–4pm & 8–11.30pm.

Restaurante Atxuri (former Achuri) c/Plocia 7 ☎956 253 613. This is an outstanding and highly popular Basque fish restaurant offering excellent Basque- and *andaluz*-inspired fish dishes at reasonable prices. Also has an excellent tapas bar. Booking advisable. 1.30–5.30pm & 9–11.30pm; closed eves Sun–Wed.

Restaurante El Sardinero Pl. San Juan de Dios 4. Traditional *gaditano* fish restaurant offering good-quality fish dishes served on a pleasant terrace. Daily 8am–2am.

El Puerto de Santa María

Just 10km across the bay, **EL PUERTO DE SANTA MARÍA** is the obvious choice for a day-trip from Cádiz, a traditional family resort for both *gaditanos* and *sevillanos* – many of whom have built villas and chalets along the fine **Playa Puntillo**. This strand is a little way out from town (10–15min walk or local bus ride), a pleasant place to while away an afternoon; there are friendly beach bars where for ridiculously little you can nurse a litre of *sangría* while munching *mariscos*.

The sherry bodegas

In the town itself, the principal attraction is a series of **sherry bodegas** – long, whitewashed warehouses flanking the streets and the banks of the river. Until the train was extended to Cádiz, all shipments of sherry from Jerez came through Santa María, and its port is still used to some extent. Many of the firms offer tours and tastings to visitors – the most worthwhile tours are offered by two of the town's major producers, Osborne, c/Los Moros 7 (visits: in English Mon–Fri 10.30am; in Spanish Mon–Fri midday; ☎956 869 100; €7.50; booking required), and Fernando de Terry, c/Santísima Trinidad 2 (Mon–Thurs 10.30am &12.30pm; €8; ☎956 151 500), situated in a beautiful, converted, seventeenth-century convent. The *turismo* can provide details of visits to smaller *bodegas*.

ARRIVAL AND DEPARTURE

EL PUERTO DE SANTA MARÍA

By ferry The ferry from Cádiz (known locally as *El Vapor*, alluding to the earlier steamboats) is quicker and cheaper than the bus at €3 one way, €5 return; the forty-minute trip across the bay departs from the Muelle Reina Victoria jetty (near the train station) at 10am, noon, 2pm, 4.30pm, 6.30pm and 8.30pm (summer only), returning to Cádiz at

9am, 11am, 1pm, 3.30pm, 5.30pm and 7.30pm (summer only), with extra sailings in season according to demand (especially in the evening).

By catamaran A faster catamaran service (roughly hourly; last return sailing 9.25pm; ☎902 450 550; €1.95 one way) also leaves from the Muelle Reina Victoria jetty.

INFORMATION

Turismo Housed in the splendid Baroque Palacio de Aranibar, Pl. del Castillo facing the Castillo de San Marcos (daily: May–Sept 10am–2pm & 6–8pm; Oct–April 10am–2pm & 5.30–7.30pm; ☎ 956 483 715, ⊛ turismoelpuerto.com). Here you can pick up a detailed street map as well as a Ruta del Tapeo leaflet to help find the best tapas bars.

Internet Locutorio Santa María, c/Santa María 2 near the focal Pl. de España (daily 10am–3pm & 6–10pm).

ACCOMMODATION

Camping Playa Las Dunas Paseo Marítimo Playa de la Puntilla ☎ 956 872 210, ⊛ www.lasdunascamping.com. Large campsite near the beach with plenty of shade plus pool, restaurant and supermarket. Bus #2 from the Pl. de las Galeras Reales (ferry quay) will take you there. €5.17, €5 per tent, €4.42 per vehicle

Hostal Loreto c/Ganado 17 ☎ 956 542 410, ⊛ www.pensionloreto.com. Pleasant *hostal* with a delightful patio. Rooms come with or without bath; en suites have ceiling fans, fridge and TV. €42

Hotel Santa María Avda. Bajamar s/n ☎ 956 873 211, ⊛ www.hotelsantamaria.es. Good-value three-star river front hotel in a converted eighteenth-century *palacio* with a/c rooms, restaurant, garage (or there's easy parking by the river) and rooftop pool. €123

★ **Pensión Santa María** c/Pedro Múñoz Seco 38 ☎ 956 853 631. Very welcoming family *pensión*, for spotless rooms with and without bath (with a negligible difference in price), run by an ebullient *dueña andaluza* (female proprietor). She'll even do a bit of washing for you. If you want to practice your Spanish, here's the place to stay. €30

EATING AND DRINKING

The best areas in town for **places to eat** are the Ribera del Marisco, a street upstream from the ferry dock lined with a variety of seafood restaurants and bars serving tapas and *raciones*, and the nearby Pl. de la Herrería.

★ **Romerijo** Ribera del Marisco. This enormous, economical and justifiably popular seafood bar dominates the strip here. You can get a takeaway of *mariscos* in a *cartucho* (paper funnel) from their shop and eat it at outdoor tables where buckets are provided for debris and waiters serve beer; the *cóctel de mariscos* (seafood cocktail) or any of the six types of *langostinos* (prawns) are delicious. The same firm's *freiduría* restaurant over the road is equally excellent, and a generous *frito variado* (assorted fried fish) easily serves two. Daily noon–midnight.

Sol y Sombra Pl. de Ahuja, facing the bullring. Taking its name from the nearby bullring's seating arrangements, this is often a lively venue – especially on fight days – and prepares good and cheap tapas. House specials include *fideos con almejas* (vermicelli with clams) and paella. Its restaurant is also recommended and does a lunchtime *menú* for €10. Daily 8am–midnight; closed Wed.

Sanlúcar de Barrameda

Like its neighbour El Puerto, **SANLÚCAR DE BARRAMEDA**, 15km to the northwest, also has its sherry connections. Nine kilometres east of Chipiona and set at the mouth of the Guadalquivir, it's the main depot for **manzanilla** wine, a pale, dry variety much in evidence in the bars, which you can also sample during visits to the town's **bodegas**. Sanlúcar is also the setting for some exciting **horse races** along the beach in the first and third weeks of August (check with the *turismo* for exact dates), a great time to be here.

Bodega Antonio Barbadillo

C/Sevilla 25 • Visits in English Tues–Sat 11am • €3 • ☎ 956 385 500, ⊛ www.barbadillo.com

The town's major producer, **Bodega Antonio Barbadillo**, near the castle, is one of the most interesting *bodegas* to visit with a stop at their shop and museum thrown in at the end. A list of Sanlúcar's seven other *bodegas* offering visits is available from the *turismo* (see below).

Barrio Alto

There's not a great deal to see here, although the attractive old quarter in the upper town, or **Barrio Alto**, is worth taking time to explore. The town's port was the scene of a number of important maritime exploits: Magellan set out from here to circumnavigate the globe; Pizarro embarked to conquer Peru; and 4km upriver, from the fishing harbour of Bonanza, Columbus sailed on his third voyage to the Americas. The few buildings of interest are all located in the Barrio Alto, reached by following the Cuesta de Belén uphill from the lower town.

Palacio de los Duques de Medina Sidonia

Visits Sun 11am & noon • €4; book in advance • ☎ 956 360 161, ⓦ www.fcmedinasidonia.com

The most significant of the upper *barrio*'s buildings, this is the magnificent sixteenth- to eighteenth-century ducal palace of **Medina Sidonia**, stuffed with paintings by Spanish masters, including Goya. Until her death in 2008 the duchess of Medina Sidonia (last in a family line going back to the Middle Ages) lived here and earlier had been an inveterate opponent of the Franco regime. The palace and family estate is now in the care of the foundation she founded. The guided tour of the house and its beautiful gardens takes an hour. Part of the palace now houses a *hospedería* (hotel) and very pleasant *cafetería*.

Nuestro Señora de la O

Tues–Sat open at service times: Mon–Sat 7–9pm & Sun 10am–1pm & 7–9pm

The thirteenth-century church of **Nuestro Señora de la O** with a fine Gothic-Mudéjar portal depicting lions bearing coats of arms and an impressive *artesonado* ceiling within, is connected to the Palace of Medina Sidonia.

Castillo de Santiago

Tues–Sat free entry to the Pl. de Armas courtyard and restaurant; guided visits to the castle at 11am & 12.30pm • €7, kids €3

Just along c/Eguilaz east from here, lies the **Castillo de Santiago**, constructed by the second duke of Medina Sidonia in the fifteenth century. Fernando and Isabel once put up here when visiting the dukes, and it served as a barracks for the invading French army in the early nineteenth century and later as a prison. A ruin for most of the last century, it has recently been renovated and the guided visits enable you to see the castle's barbicans and hexagonal tower as well as the Plaza de Armas and towers with stunning views over the town and the river towards the Parque Nacional Coto de Doñana.

A CRUISE INTO PARQUE NACIONAL COTO DE DOÑANA

One of the best things about Sanlúcar is its shell-encrusted **river beach** and warm waters, a couple of kilometres' walk from the town centre and usually quite deserted. This is flanked, on the opposite shore, by the beginnings of the **Parque Nacional Coto de Doñana** (see p.304), whose vast marshy expanses (strictly regulated access) signal the end of the coast road to the west. Visits to the park from Sanlúcar are possible with a boat cruise, which, while it doesn't allow for serious exploration, is nevertheless a wonderful introduction to this remarkable area. The trip lasts approximately four hours and allows two short, guided walks inside the park to spot wildlife. The **Real Fernando** – which has a cafetería on board – leaves daily from the Bajo de Guía quay (Mon–Sat June–Sept 10am & 5pm; March, April, May & Oct daily 10am & 4pm; Nov–Feb daily 10am; €16.35, under-12s half-price; booking essential on ☎ 956 363 813, ⓦ www.visitasdonana.com). Tickets should be collected (at least 30min before sailing) from the Fábrica de Hielo, Bajo de Guía s/n, the national park's **exhibition centre** (daily 9am–8pm) opposite the *Real Fernando*'s jetty. Also note that binoculars are pretty essential, and, while they can be hired on board, having your own is a distinct advantage.

INFORMATION

Turismo Calzada del Ejército (July & Aug Mon–Fri 10am–2pm & 6–8pm; rest of year Mon–Fri 10am–2pm &

SANLÚCAR

4–6pm; ☎ 956 366 110, ⓦ sanlucardebarrameda.es), on the avenue leading to the river estuary.

ACCOMMODATION

There's a shortage of budget accommodation in Sanlúcar, and in August you'll be pushed to find anything at all. This is when a number of *casas particulares* open to mop up the overflow. Enquire at the *turismo* for information about these.

★ **Hostal Gadir** c/Caballeros 19 ☎ 956 360 078, ⓔ info@hostalgadir.com. Wonderful new and friendly, family-run *hostal* with sparkling a/c rooms, some with terrace others with jacuzzi. Rooms 3, 4, 5 & 10 (with jacuzzi) have a superb view of the gardens of the Palacio de Orleáns y Borbón opposite. All rooms come with TV and free wi-fi. A bargain in high season, it's a steal at other times of the year. Also offers single rooms. **€50**, singles **€35**

Hotel Barrameda c/Ancha 10 ☎ 956 385 878, ⓦ www .hotelbarrameda.com. A newish, central and welcome addition to the town's accommodation options offering light and airy a/c rooms with plasma TV, some with balcony. Also has a pleasant patio, solarium roof terrace and wi-fi throughout. **€80**

Pensión Blanca Paloma Pl. de San Roque ☎ 956 363 644, ⓔ hostal_blanca_paloma@yahoo.es. Good-value and friendly *pensión* with simple rooms sharing bath in a central position on this small plaza. **€30**

Pensión Bohemia c/Don Claudio 5 ☎ 956 369 599. Comfortable en-suite a/c rooms with TV – albeit slightly dark due to windows facing an internal corridor – in a quiet street near the church of Santo Domingo. **€47**

★ **Posada de Palacio** c/Caballeros 11 ☎ 956 36 48 40, ⓦ www.posadadepalacio.com. An elegant converted eighteenth-century *casa palacio* in the Barrio Alto with a delightful patio and tastefully furnished rooms with character. Roof-top terraces, bar and an intimate atmosphere together make this rather special. **€109**

EATING AND DRINKING

For **eating and drinking**, you shouldn't miss *Casa Balbino* (below). For more elaborate fare, head to the Bajo de Guía – a river beach backed by a line of great seafood restaurants. You can take a taxi or walk there by continuing past the *turismo* to the end of the Calzada del Ejército and turning right (or east) when you hit the river, about 1km from the town centre.

★ **Bar-Restaurante El Bigote** Bajo de Guía 10 ☎ 956 362 696. Celebrated establishment and one of the "big two" on the waterfront which has recently edged in front of its neighbour. You can eat outstanding tapas in their lively bar next door or more formally in the restaurant, where the fish and the house *arroz de marisco* (seafood paella) are outstanding. An upstairs dining room offers panoramic views across the river towards the Doñana national park. Main dishes €10–20; reservation advised. Daily 1–4pm & 8.30–11.30pm; closed Sun.

★ **Casa Balbino** Pl. del Cabildo 11. Behind an unassuming facade lies one of the best tapas bars in

Andalucía. Long established, its walls are hung with faded photos and the obligatory bulls' heads, and the smoothly efficient bar staff will guide you through a daunting tapas menu. There is a (self-service) terrace on the square. Daily noon–5pm & 8pm–1am.

Mirador de Doñana Bajo de Guía s/n ☎ 956 364 205. The second of the Bajo de Guía's "big two" occasionally rests on its laurels, but is nevertheless an outstanding restaurant with a summer terrace overlooking the river. Try their *mi barca de Doñana*, white fish in a tomato sauce served in an edible "boat". Main dishes €9–20. Daily 1–4pm & 8–11.30pm; closed Mon.

Jerez de la Frontera

JEREZ DE LA FRONTERA, 30km inland towards Seville, is the home and heartland of sherry (itself an English corruption of the town's Moorish name – *Xerez*) and also, less known but equally important, of Spanish brandy. An elegant and prosperous town, it's a tempting place to stop, arrayed as it is round the scores of wine *bodegas*, with plenty of sights to visit in between.

Life is lived at a fairly sedate pace for most of the year here, although things liven up considerably when Jerez launches into one or other of its two big **festivals** – the May Horse Fair (perhaps the most snooty of the Andalucian *ferias*), or the celebration of the vintage towards the end of September.

Centro Andaluz de Flamenco

Pl. de San Juan • Mon–Fri 9am–2pm • Free • W www.centroandaluzdeflamenco.es

Jerez is famous throughout Spain for a long and distinguished **flamenco** tradition, and if you're interested in finding out more about Andalucía's great folk art, then a visit to the **Centro Andaluz de Flamenco** in the atmospheric *gitano* quarter, the Barrio de Santiago, is a must. There's an audiovisual introduction to *El Arte Flamenco* (hourly on the half-hour), plus videos of past greats and information on flamenco venues in the town.

Visiting the bodegas

The **tours of the sherry and brandy processes** can be interesting – almost as much as the sampling that follows – and, provided you don't arrive in August when much of the industry closes down, there are a great many firms to choose from. The visits are conducted either in English (very much the second language of the sherry world) or a combination of English and Spanish and last for about an hour. Many of these *bodegas* were founded by British Catholic refugees, barred from careers at home by the sixteenth-century Supremacy Act, and even now they form a kind of Anglo-Andalucian tweed-wearing, polo-playing aristocracy (on display, most conspicuously, at the Horse Fair). The González cellars – the *soleras* – are perhaps the oldest in Jerez and, though it's no longer used, preserve an old circular chamber designed by Eiffel (of the tower fame). If you feel you need comparisons, you can pick up a list of locations and opening times of the other *bodegas* from the *turismo*.

The González Byass and Pedro Domecq bodegas

González Byass c/María González • 12 visits daily except Sun afternoon noon, 1pm, 2pm, 5pm, 6.30pm • €11 with wine tasting • ☎ 956 357 016, W www.bodegastiopepe.com **Pedro Domecq** c/San Ildefonso 3 • Reservation required; Mon–Fri 4 visits on the hour 10am–1pm, Sat noon• €8 with wine tasting • ☎ 956 151 500, W www.bodegasfundadorpedrodomecq.com

Jerez's "big two" are **González Byass**, makers of the famous Tio Pepe brand, and the neighbouring **Pedro Domecq**, producers of the equally well known La Ina brand. Besides manufacturing sherry, both *bodegas* are also major brandy producers.

The Alcázar

July–Sept Mon–Fri 10am–7.30pm, Sat & Sun 10am–2.30pm; Oct & Feb–June Mon–Fri 9.30am–6pm, Sat & Sun 9.30am–3pm; Nov–Jan daily 10am–2.30pm • €3 or €5.40 including camera obscura

The substantial **Alcázar** lies just to the south of the focal Plaza del Arenal. To reach the entrance, take a right off the southern end of Plaza del Arenal into Plaza Monti, at the end of which you turn left into c/M. María González. The entrance lies uphill on the left. Constructed in the twelfth century by the Almohads, though much altered since, the Alcázar has been extensively excavated and restored in recent years. The **gardens** have received particular attention: the plants and arrangements have been modelled as closely as possible – using historical research – on the original. The interior contains a well-preserved mosque complete with *mihrab* from the original structure, now sensitively restored to its original state after having been used as a church for many centuries. The eighteenth-century **Palacio de Villavicencio** constructed on the west side of the Alcázar's Patio de las Armas (parade ground) houses a **camera obscura** (same hours) offering views of the major landmarks of the town as well as the sherry vineyards and the sea beyond.

Catedral de San Salvador

Mon open for service at 8pm, Tues–Sat 11am–1pm & 6–8pm, Sun service at 12.30pm • Free

West of Plaza del Arenal, the eighteenth-century **Catedral de San Salvador** was rather harshly dismissed by British hispanist Richard Ford as "vile Churrigueresque" because of its mixture of Gothic and Renaissance styles, but an elegant facade – largely the work of Vincente Acero – is not without merit. Inside, over-obvious pointing gives the building an unfinished, breeze-block aspect, while, in the sacristy, there's a fine, little-known painting by Zurbarán – *The Sleeping Girl*. The most exciting time to be here is September, when on the broad steps of the cathedral, below the free-standing bell tower – actually part of an earlier, fifteenth-century Mudéjar castle – the wine harvest celebrations begin with the crushing of grapes.

Archeological museum

Pl. del Mercado • June–Aug Tues–Sun 10am–2.30pm; Sept–May Tues–Fri 10am–2pm & 4–7pm, Sat & Sun 10am–2.30pm • €3

An excellent **archeological museum** lies five minutes north of the centre on the edge of the Barrio de Santiago; star exhibits include a seventh-century-BC Greek military helmet, a Visigothic sarcophagus and a fine caliphal bottle vase from the Moorish period.

Real Escuela Andaluz del Arte Ecuestre

Avda. Duque de Abrantes s/n **Performances** Tues & Thurs noon, plus Fri noon in August • €19–25 **Visits** non-performance days 10am–1.15pm • €10 • Information & reservations ☎ 956 319 635, ⓦ www.realescuela.org

Evidence of Jerez's great enthusiasm for horses can be seen at the **Real Escuela Andaluz del Arte Ecuestre** (Royal Andalucian School of Equestrian Art), which offers the chance to watch them performing to music. Training, rehearsals (without music) and visits to the stables take place on other weekdays.

4

ARRIVAL AND DEPARTURE
JEREZ DE LA FRONTERA

By plane From Jerez airport (7km out of town on the NIV; ☎ 956 150 083), there are daily buses to the centre between 6.30am and 9.45pm (€1.10) with a less frequent service from the bus station in the reverse direction. A taxi from the airport costs approximately €16–20.

By train The train and bus stations are located eight blocks (10min walk) east of the town's central square, Pl. del Arenal. The train station, Estación de Ferrocarril, Pl. de Estación s/n (☎ 902 240 202), is next to the bus station. Frequent trains link Jerez with Cádiz, Seville and Córdoba. To reach the centre, take #10 urban bus from outside the station.

By bus The bus station, Estación de Autobuses, Pl. Estación s/n (☎ 956 149 990), is next to the train station. To reach the centre, take #10 urban bus from outside the station.

Destinations Algeciras (7 daily; 1hr 30min); Arcos de la Frontera (17 daily; 35min); Cádiz (17 daily; 45min); Chipiona (10 daily; 40min); Córdoba (3 daily; 3hr 30min); El Puerto de Santa María (15 daily; 30min); Málaga (3 daily; 5hr); Ronda (7 daily; 2hr 30min); Sanlúcar de Barrameda (12 daily; 30min); Seville (7 daily; 1hr 30min); Vejer de la Frontera (1 daily; 1hr 30min).

By car Coming by car, you'll meet the familiar problem of finding a place to park; to avoid being clamped or towed, use the pay car parks signed in the centre or park farther out and walk in. There is a huge underground car park beneath the Pl. del Arenal.

INFORMATION

Turismo Attached to the Convento de Santo Domingo (June–Sept Mon–Fri 10am–3pm & 5–7pm, Sat & Sun 10am–2.30pm; Oct–May Mon–Fri 10am–3pm & 4.30–6.30pm, Sat & Sun 9.30am–2.30pm; ☎ 956 341 711, ⓦ www.turismojerez.com) and reached by following the pedestrianized main street, c/Larga, north from the centre;

it's well stocked with information about the town and the area and can supply a detailed town map.

Internet access is available a little to the northwest of Pl. del Arenal at Ciber Jerez, c/Santa María 3, near the market (Mon–Sat 10am–10.30pm, Sun 5–10.30pm).

ACCOMMODATION

There's usually no problem finding **rooms** in Jerez except during April and May, when Semana Santa, the Festival de Jerez, the World Motorcycle Championship (held at the town's Formula 1 racing circuit) and the Feria del Caballo (May Horse Fair) come one after the other and fill the town to bursting point. During these events (*"temporada extra"*) prices can double or even treble; we have quoted the normal high-season price.

Albergue Juvenil Avda. Blas Infante 30 ☎856 814 001. Good-value hostel, with a pool, but out in the suburbs; take bus #9 from outside the bus station. Under-26 €21, over-26 €27

Hostal Las Palomas c/Higueras 17 ☎956 343 773, ⓦwww.hostal-las-palomas.com. The most central budget option, with clean and simple rooms, some en suite. €33

Hotel Al Andalus c/Arcos 29 ☎956 323 400, ⓦwww.alandalusjerez.com. Comfortable hotel with two pretty patios. Recently refurbished rooms – the better ones lie off the inner patio – are equipped with a/c and TV. Free wi-fi. €50

Hotel El Ancla c/Mamelón 15 ☎956 321 297, ⓦwww.helancla.com. Welcoming and good-value place, fronting the upper end of the Alameda Cristina on the north side of the centre. Some rooms overlooking the noisy street (not so at night) are compensated for by views of square and fountains. Free wi-fi. €54

★ **Hotel Chancilleria** c/Chancilleria 21 in the Barrio de Santiago ☎956 301 038, ⓦwww.hotelchancilleria.com. Delightful new hotel with excellent rooms equipped with CD and DVD players, plus there's a very good restaurant and a fine roof terrace with bar and views. B&B €70

Hotel Doña Blanca c/Bodegas 11 ☎956 34 87 61, ⓦwww.hoteldonablanca.com. One of the most central and intimate of the upper-range places with well-equipped a/c balcony rooms with minibar and satellite TV, in a quiet street. Free wi-fi and own garage. €49

★ **Hotel-Hostal San Andrés** c/Morenos 12 ☎956 340 983, ⓦwww.hotel-sanandres.com. Excellent and friendly hotel-*hostal* offering both en-suite and rooms sharing bath, with a charming patio below. Free wi-fi. Sharing bath €40, with bath €45

EATING AND DRINKING

Jerez's booming sherry trade ensures that the town's **restaurants** are kept busy, and a few of these are very good indeed. Befitting the capital of sherry production Jerez also has a range of great bars where *fino* – the perfect partner for tapas – can be sampled on its own turf.

★ **Bar Juanito** c/Pescadería Vieja 4. In a small passage off the west side of Pl. del Arenal, this is the best tapas bar in town, with a menu as endless as the number of excellent *finos* on offer. Specials include *berza a jerezano* (chickpea stew). Mon–Sat noon–5pm & 8.30pm–midnight; closed Sun.

Bodegón El Patio c/San Francisco de Paula 2 ☎956 34 07 36. Housed in a former *bodega*, this mid-priced *ambiente jerezano* restaurant offers well-prepared meat and fish dishes. *Cochinillo asado* (suckling pig) is a house special. The *menú* is around €18. Daily 11.30am–4pm & 8pm–midnight.

La Carboná c/San Francisco de Paula 2. Cavernous but wonderfully atmospheric mid-priced place inside an old bodega, specializing in charcoal-grilled fish and meat and – in season – fresh tuna. Daily 12.30–4pm & 8–11.30pm.

Restaurante Gaitán c/Gaitán 3 ☎956 16 80 21. Small, attractive upmarket restaurant very popular with *jerezanos* specializing in Basque and *andaluz* dishes. Among a range of fish and meat dishes *cordero al brandy* (lamb in a brandy sauce) is a house special. Main dishes €12–16. Daily 1–4.30pm & 8–11.30pm; closed Sun eve.

Sabores c/Chancilleria 21. The excellent mid-priced restaurant of the *Hotel Chancillería* gives *andaluz* traditional cooking a creative twist. Try the *carrillada de ternera con cremoso de calabaza* (cow's cheek in pumpkin sauce). There's also a very pleasant garden terrace. Mon–Sat 12.30–4pm & 8pm–midnight; closed Sun.

Huelva province

The **province of Huelva** stretches between Seville and Portugal, but aside from its scenic section of the Sierra Morena to the north and a chain of fine **beaches** to the west of the provincial capital, it's a pretty dull part of Andalucía, laced with large areas of swamp – the *marismas* – and notorious for mosquitoes. This distinctive habitat is, however, particularly suited to a great variety of wildlife, especially birds, and over 60,000 acres of the delta of the Río Guadalquivir (the largest roadless area in western Europe) have been fenced off to form the **Parque Nacional Coto de Doñana**. Here, amid sand dunes, pine woods, marshes and freshwater lagoons, live scores of flamingos, along with rare birds of prey, thirty pairs of the endangered Spanish lynx, mongooses and a startling variety of migratory birds.

Parque Nacional Coto de Doñana

The seasonal pattern of its delta waters, which flood in winter and then drop in the spring, leaving rich deposits of silt, raised sandbanks and islands, gives **Coto de Doñana**

VISITING PARQUE NACIONAL COTO DE DOÑANA

Visiting Doñana involves (perhaps understandably) a certain amount of frustration. At present, it's open only to a **boat cruise** from Sanlúcar (see p.300) and to brief, organized **tours** (March–Sept daily 8.30am & 5pm; Oct–Feb Tues–Sun 8.30am & 3pm; €27) by all-terrain 24-seater buses – four hours at a time along one of five charted, eighty-kilometre routes. The starting point for the tours (run by the Cooperativa Marismas del Rocío, Ⓦ www.donanavisitas.es) and the place to book them (essential, and as far ahead as possible in high season), is at the Centro de Recepción de Acebuche, 4km north of Matalascañas towards El Rocío and Almonte (daily 8am–8pm, closes 7pm Oct–March). The number for phone bookings is ☎ 959 430 432 (English spoken) or at the Cooperativa's office, Plaza del Acebuchal 16, El Rocío. The tours are quite tourist-oriented and point out only spectacular species such as flamingos, imperial eagles, deer and wild boar (binoculars are pretty essential). If you're a serious ornithologist, enquire instead at the *centro* about organizing a private group tour.

There are excellent birdwatching **hides** (daily 8am–8pm) at the El Acebuche, La Rocina and El Acebrón reception centres, as well as a 1.5-kilometre footpath from El Acebuche, which creates a mini-trek through typical *cotos*, or terrains, to be found in the reserve. Although binoculars are on hire, they sometimes run out, and you're advised to bring your own. All three centres have exhibitions and displays covering the species to be seen in the park and the history of human activity within its boundaries.

---

its uniqueness. Conditions are perfect in winter for ducks and geese, but spring is more exciting; the exposed mud draws hundreds of flocks of breeding birds. In the marshes and amid the cork-oak forests behind, you've a good chance of seeing squacco herons, black-winged stilts, whiskered terns, pratincoles and sand grouse, as well as flamingos, egrets and vultures. There are, too, occasional sightings of the Spanish imperial eagle, now reduced to a score of breeding pairs. Conditions are not so good in late summer and early autumn, when the *marismas* dry out and support far less bird life.

It is no Iberian Arcadia, however, and given the region's parlous economic state the park is under constant threat from development. Even at current levels the drain on the water supply is severe, and made worse by **pollution** of the Guadalquivir by farming pesticides, Seville's industry and Huelva's mines. The seemingly inevitable disaster finally occurred in 1998 when an upriver mining dam used for storing toxic waste burst, unleashing millions of litres of pollutants into the Guadiamar, which flows through the park. The noxious tide was stopped just 2km from the park's boundary, but catastrophic damage was done to surrounding farmland, with nesting birds decimated and fish poisoned. What is even more worrying is that the mining dams have not been removed (the mines are a major local employer) but merely repaired.

Equally disturbing are the proposals for a huge new tourist centre to be known as the Costa Doñana, on the very fringes of the park. Campaigning by national and international environmental bodies resulted in this project being shelved, but the threat remains, much of the pressure stemming from local people who see much-needed jobs in this or similar proposals.

El Rocío

Set on the northwestern tip of the *marismas*, **EL ROCÍO** is a tiny village of white cottages and a church stockade where perhaps the most famous pilgrimage-fair of the south takes place annually at Pentecost. This, the **Romería del Rocío**, is an extraordinary spectacle, with whole village communities and local "brotherhoods" from Huelva, Seville and even Málaga converging in lavishly decorated ox carts and on horseback. Throughout the procession, which climaxes on the Saturday evening, there is dancing and partying, while by the time the carts arrive at El Rocío they've been joined by busloads of pilgrims swelling numbers in recent years to close on half a million. The fair commemorates the miracle of Nuestra Señora del Rocío (Our Lady of the Dew), a statue found in the thirteenth century – so it is said – on this spot and resistant to all attempts to move it elsewhere. The image, credited with all kinds of magic and fertility powers, is paraded before the faithful early on the Sunday morning.

In spring, as far as **birdwatching** goes, the town is probably the best base in the area. The adjacent *marismas* and pine woods are teeming with birds, and following tracks east and southeast of El Rocío, along the edge of the reserve itself, you'll see many species (up to a hundred if you're lucky).

ACCOMMODATION   EL ROCÍO

The village makes a nice **place to stay**, with wide, sandy streets, cowboy-hatted horseriding farmers and a frontier-like feeling, and prices for most of the year are reasonable. That said, don't even think about getting a room during the *romería* as they not only cost over ten times normal prices, but are booked up years ahead. All the accommodation options listed below (except the *Hospedería*) have their own decent restaurants.

Hospedería Puente del Rey, Avda. Canaliega 1 ☎959 442 575. A ringer for the hotel in the film *The Shining*, this huge and rather incongruous hotel has gone through a series of owners, name changes and makeovers. Rooms come with a/c, fridge and TV. €70

Hostal Cristina c/Real 32 ☎959 406 513. One of El Rocío's oldest budget establishments, this welcoming place has en-suite rooms and its own restaurant. €50

Hostal Isidro Avda. Los Ansares 59 ☎959 44 22 42. On the village's east side, this is a pleasant place for a/c en-suite rooms above a restaurant. €48

★ **Hotel Toruño** Pl. Acebuchal 22 ☎959 442 323, ⓦwww.toruno.es. The best of the more expensive places is *Hotel Toruño*, with comfortable rooms overlooking the *marismas*. The best view is from Room 225 but some of the ground-floor rooms (109, 111 & 115) also allow you to spot flamingos, herons, avocets and lots more while lying in bed. B&B €80

The Columbus Trail

It has to be said that the city of Huelva is perhaps the least attractive and least interesting of Andalucía's provincial capitals. However, nearby – and easily reached by buses from Huelva or with your own transport – is the Columbus Trail: a clutch of locations associated with the fifteenth-century **voyages of Christopher Columbus**.

Across the Río Tinto estuary from Huelva, the monastery of **La Rábida** and the villages of **Palos** and **Moguer** are all places connected with the voyages of Columbus (Cristóbal Colón in Spanish) to the New World.

La Rábida

April–Sept Tues–Sat guided tours hourly 10am–1pm & 4–7pm, Sun 10.45am–1pm & 4–7pm; Oct–March Tues–Sat 10am–1pm & 4–6.15pm, Sun 10.45am–1pm & 4–6.15pm • €3 • ⓦwww.monasteriodelarabida.com

La Rábida, 8km from Huelva and easily reached by bus, is a charming and tranquil fourteenth-century Franciscan monastery whose fifteenth-century abbot was instrumental in securing funds for the voyage from the monarchs Fernando and Isabel. The guided tour includes the Sala Capitular (chapterhouse) where the final plans for the voyage were made and the monastery's fourteenth-century church where Columbus and his crew prayed before setting sail.

Muelle de la Carabelas

June–Sept Tues–Fri 10am–2pm & 5–9pm, Sat & Sun 11am–8pm; Oct–May Tues–Sun 10am–7pm • €3.55

Nearby, on the estuary, the **Muelle de la Carabelas** (Harbour of the Caravels) has impressive full-size replicas of the three caravels that made the epic voyage to the New World, while an adjoining museum features among its displays facsimiles of Columbus' geography books annotated in his surprisingly delicate hand.

San Jorge

Mon–Fri 10am–noon & 6–7.30pm

The church of **San Jorge** in **Palos** is where, in August 1492, Columbus and his crew heard Mass before setting sail from the now silted-up harbour. The church's southern

Mudéjar portal through which Columbus – flanked by his captains – left the church, can be seen as well as the nearby La Fontanilla, a medieval well from which the ships took on water for the voyage.

Convent of Santa Clara
Hourly guided tours Tues–Sat 10.30am–6.30pm, Sun 10.30am–12.30pm • €3

At the whitewashed town of **MOGUER** is the fourteenth-century **Convent of Santa Clara**, in whose church Columbus spent a whole night in prayer as thanksgiving for his safe return. The tour also takes in some notable artworks and the ancient monastery's cloister and refectory.

Nuestra Señora de la Granada
The compact and beautiful whitewashed town of Moguer is the birthplace of the Nobel Prize-winning poet Juan Ramón Jiménez (1881–1958), and boasts a scaled-down, whiter version of Seville's Giralda attached to the church of **Nuestra Señora de la Granada**.

GETTING AROUND   THE COLUMBUS TRAIL

Frequent buses from **Huelva's main bus station** at Avda. Dr Rubio s/n (☎ 902 114 492) link La Rábida, Palos and Moguer, and both Palos and Moguer have accommodation.

ACCOMMODATION

Hostal Platero c/Aceña 4 Niño, Moguer 13 ☎ 959 372 159. If you want to stay overnight, head for *Hostal Platero*, with good-value en-suite rooms. **€30**

Hotel La Pinta c/Rábida 79, Palos ☎ 959 530 164. The pleasant *Hotel La Pinta* is a good bet for a/c en-suite rooms with its own decent restaurant a few doors away. **€65**

West to Portugal

From Huelva it's best either to press on inland to the Sierra de Aracena (see p.284) or straight **along the coast to Portugal**. There are a number of good beaches and some low-key resorts noted for their seafood, such as **Isla Cristina**, along the stretch of coastline between Huelva and the frontier town of **Ayamonte**, but not much more to detain you. A good bus service along this route and a new road suspension bridge across the Río Guadiana estuary and border, linking Ayamonte and **Vila Real de Santo Antonio** in Portugal, make for a relatively painless crossing of the country border. From this approach, a good first night's target in Portugal is **Tavira**, on the Algarve train line. Note that Portugal is an hour behind Spain throughout the year.

Seville to Córdoba

The direct route from **Seville to Córdoba**, 135km along the valley of Guadalquivir, followed by the train and some of the buses, is a flat and rather unexciting journey. There's far more to see following the route just to the south of this, via **Carmona** and **Écija**, both interesting towns, and more still if you detour further south to take in **Osuna** as well. There are plenty of buses along these roads, making travel between the villages easy. Overnighting, too, is possible, with plenty of places to stay – although Carmona is an easy day-trip from Seville.

Carmona

Set on a low hill overlooking a fertile plain, **CARMONA** is a small, picturesque town made recognizable by the fifteenth-century tower of the Iglesia de San Pedro, built in imitation of the Giralda. The tower is the first thing you catch sight of and it sets the tone for the place – an appropriate one, since the town shares a similar history to

Seville, less than 30km distant. It was an important Roman city (from which era it preserves a fascinating subterranean necropolis), and under the Moors was often governed by a brother of the Sevillan ruler. Later, Pedro the Cruel built a palace within its castle, which he used as a "provincial" royal residence.

Iglesia de San Pedro
Mon & Thurs–Sun 11am–2pm plus Wed–Mon service at 8.30pm • €1.20

The **Iglesia de San Pedro** is a good place to start exploring the town; it dominates Carmona's main thoroughfare, c/San Pedro, and has a splendid Baroque *sagrario* (sacristy) by Figueroa within.

Puerta de Sevilla
Guided tours April–Sept Mon–Fri 10.15am–3pm & 4.30–6pm, Sat & Sun 10am–3pm; Oct–March Mon–Fri 10am–6pm, Sat & Sun 10am–3pm, • €2; Mon free

From the nearby Paseo del Estatuto, looking east, you get a view of the magnificent Moorish **Puerta de Sevilla**, a grand, fortified Roman gateway (with substantial Carthaginian and Moorish elements) to the old town; it now houses the *turismo*, which organizes guided tours of the gate's upper ramparts. The **old town** is circled by 4km of ancient walls, inside which narrow streets wind up past Mudéjar churches and Renaissance mansions.

Plaza San Fernando
Follow c/Prim uphill to **Plaza San Fernando** (or Plaza Mayor), modest in size but dominated by splendid Moorish-style buildings. Behind it, and just to the south, there's a bustling fruit and vegetable **market** most mornings in the porticoed Plaza del Mercado.

Santa María la Mayor
Mon–Sat 9am–2pm & 5.30–7.30pm, Sat 9–11.30am, closed second half Aug, first half Sept • €3

To the east of Plaza San Fernando, is **Santa María la Mayor**, a fine Gothic church built over the former Almohad Friday (main) mosque, whose elegant patio it retains, complete with orange trees and horseshoe arches. Like many of Carmona's churches, it is capped by a Mudéjar tower, possibly utilizing part of the old minaret.

Museo de la Ciudad
Mon 10am–2pm, Tues–Fri 10am–2pm & 6.30–8.30pm, Sun 9.30am–2pm • €2, Tues free

To the east of Plaza San Fernando again, and housed in the graceful eighteenth-century Casa del Marqués de las Torres, is the **Museo de la Ciudad**, documenting the history of the town with mildly interesting displays of artefacts from the prehistoric, Iberian, Carthaginian, Roman, Moorish and Christian epochs. The museum has a *cafetería*, open to all.

Pedro's Alcázar
Parador bars, restaurants and public areas open to nonguests

Dominating the ridge of the town are the massive ruins of **Pedro's Alcázar**, an Almohad fortress transformed into a lavish residence by the fourteenth-century king. He employed the same Mudéjar craftsmen who worked on the Alcázar in Seville. It was destroyed by an earthquake in 1504 and partly rebuilt by Fernando (after Isabel's death) but then fell into ruin. What remains has now been incorporated into a remarkably tasteful parador, and various bars and restaurants.

Puerta de Córdoba
Following c/Martín López and its continuations east from Plaza de San Fernando for 500m will bring you to an imposing Roman gateway, the **Puerta de Córdoba** where the town comes to an abrupt and romantic halt. This was the start of the ancient

Córdoba road (once the mighty Via Augusta heading north to Zaragoza and Gaul, now a dirt track) which dropped down from here to cross the vast plain below. Following the road for a few kilometres will lead you to a five-arched Roman bridge, just visible on the plain below.

Roman necropolis

Guided tours only, English spoken: Tues–Fri 9am–6pm, Sat & Sun 9am–3.30pm • €2, free with EU passport

The extraordinary **Roman necropolis** lies on a low hill at the opposite end of Carmona; walking out of town from San Pedro, take c/Enmedio, the middle street (parallel to the main Seville road) of three that leave the western end of Paseo del Estatuto and follow this for about 450m. Here, amid the cypress trees, more than nine hundred family tombs dating from the second century BC to the fourth century AD can be found. Enclosed in subterranean chambers hewn from the rock, the tombs are often frescoed and contain a series of niches in which many of the funeral urns remain intact. Some of the larger tombs have vestibules with stone benches for funeral banquets, and several retain carved family emblems (one is of an elephant, perhaps symbolic of long life). Most spectacular is the **Tumba de Servilia** – a huge colonnaded temple with vaulted side-chambers. Opposite the site is a partly excavated **amphitheatre**.

ARRIVAL AND INFORMATION CARMONA

By bus Buses from Seville stop on the central Paseo del Estatuto in sight of the landmark ancient gateway, the Puerta de Sevilla.
By car Your best bet is to use the reasonably priced car park beneath the Paseo de Estatuto.

Turismo The Puerta de Sevilla also houses an efficient *turismo* (Mon–Sat 10am–6pm, Sun 10am–3pm; ☎954 190 955, ⓦwww.turismo.carmona.org), which is well stocked with information and can provide a town map and guide to Carmona's tapas bars.

ACCOMMODATION

Carmona has a shortage of **places to stay**, especially in the budget category; particularly in spring and high summer, it's worth ringing ahead. The cheaper places lie outside the walls, while a clutch of more upmarket options all occupy scenic locations in the old town.

★ **Hospedería Palacio Marqués de las Torres** c/Fermín Molpeceres 2 ☎954 196 248, A delightful eighteenth-century palace converted into a welcoming option in the old town. In addition to comfortable en-suite a/c double rooms there are intriguing dormitories divided into two-bed and four-bed partitioned cubicles sharing bath. Free internet access and wi-fi. Cubicle beds €23, rooms €65
Hostal Comercio c/Torre del Oro 56 ☎954 140 018. Built into the Puerta de Sevilla gateway, this is a charming small *hostal* with compact a/c en-suite rooms (without TV) around a pretty patio. €55
Hotel San Pedro c/San Pedro 3 ☎95 419 00 87. This is

a central and pleasant budget option for a/c en-suite rooms with TV. €59
★ **Parador Nacional** Alcázar Rey Don Pedro ☎95 414 10 10, ⓦparador.es. Despite more recent competition at this end of the market, a superb location, patios and swimming pool ensure that this is still the nicest – and best value – of the luxury places in town. Pay a few euros extra for a room with a balcony. It's worth calling in for a drink at the bar, to enjoy the fabulous views from the terrace. €180
Posada San Fernando Pl. San Fernando 8 ☎954 141 408, ⓦposadasanfernando.com. New and attractive small hotel on the town's focal square offering individually styled rooms with a/c, minibar and plasma TV. €65

EATING AND DRINKING

There are plenty of places to eat both in the old and new towns, and you don't need to spend a fortune to eat well.

Bar Goya c/Prim 42. This lively tapas bar is housed in a fifteenth-century edifice off the west side of Pl. de San Fernando, with a nice terrace. House specials include *alboronía* (ratatouille) and *chipirón plancha en salsa verde* (fried squid in green sauce). Daily 9am–midnight; closed Wed.
Mingalario Pl. Cristo del Rey 1, facing the church of El

Salvador. In the old town this is another fine old bar with excellent tapas. House specials include *gambas al ajillo* (shrimps in garlic). Daily 10am–midnight.
★ **Molino de la Romera** c/Pedro s/n, close to the Alcázar ☎954 142 0 00. With a great terrace view across the *campiña* and housed in a sixteenth-century Moorish oil

mill, this pleasant restaurant serves up regional dishes, has a good-value *menú* for around €12 and also does *raciones*. Its *dulces* are prepared by the nuns of the nearby Convento de Santa Clara. 1–4pm & 8–11pm. Closed Sun.

Parador Nacional Alcázar Rey Don Pedro ☏ 95 414 10 10. The restaurant of the parador is a model of baronial splendour which can be experienced on a *menú del día* for €33 that includes many local dishes; they also offer vegetarian and diabetic *menús*, a laudable initiative. Daily 1–4pm & 8–11pm.

El Tapeo c/Prim 9. Tapas bar-restaurant offering a decent tapas selection – try the *espinacas con garbanzos* or *berenjenas fritas* (aubergine). Aside from a range of meat and fish dishes, the restaurant also offers a good-value *menú* for €10. Daily 8am–4pm & 7–11pm.

Écija

Lying midway between Seville and Córdoba in a basin of low sandy hills, **ÉCIJA** is known, with no hint of exaggeration, as *la sartenilla de Andalucía* ("the frying pan of Andalucía"). In mid-August, it's so hot that the only possible strategy is to slink from one tiny shaded plaza to another, or with a burst of energy to make for the riverbank.

The heat is worth enduring, since this is one of the most distinctive and individual towns of the south, with eleven superb, decaying church towers, each glistening with brilliantly coloured tiles. It has a unique domestic architecture, too – a flamboyant style of twisted and florid forms, best displayed on c/Castellar, where the magnificent painted and curved frontage of the huge **Palacio de Peñaflor** (interior currently closed; enquire at the *turismo*) runs along the length of the street; the building has a fine patio and until recently housed Écija's public library. Other sights not to be missed are the beautiful polychromatic tower of the church of **Santa María**, overshadowing the main Plaza de España, and the **Palacio de Benamejí**, a stunning eighteenth-century palace on c/Castillo, south of Plaza de España, with a beautiful interior patio, now declared a national monument.

Museo Histórico Municipal

June–Sept Tues–Sat 10am–2pm, Sun 10am–3pm; Oct–May Tues–Sat 10am–1.30pm & 4.30–6.30pm, Sun 10am–3pm • Free

The magnificent eighteenth-century Palacio de Benamejí, a short walk southwest of Plaza de España, is now home to the **Museo Histórico Municipal**, the town museum displaying archeological finds from all periods. There is a particularly interesting section on Astigi's (the town's Roman name) role in the olive-oil trade – Spanish oil was prized in Imperial Rome. One sensational recent addition is the **Amazona de Écija**, a stunning, two-metre high, almost totally intact first-century-AD Roman statue accidentally discovered in the 2002 excavations to build a car park beneath the Plaza de España. Two metres tall and depicting an Amazon resting against a pillar, it is of the highest craftsmanship and still bears traces of ochre paint. The statue has now become the town's civic icon and at the time of writing the museum is being expanded within the palace to house the town's wonderful collection of Roman mosaics.

Plaza Mayor

The town's focal **Plaza Mayor** (Plaza de España) was a building site for seven years during the construction of a subterranean car park. Following this upheaval, the revamped square has been turned into a rather desolate and controversial modern architectural eyesore jarring with the Baroque splendours surrounding it. A **Roman bath** discovered in the course of these works – just one of many archeological discoveries – can now be viewed under a canopy in the plaza's southeast corner.

INFORMATION	**ÉCIJA**

Turismo Located at the Museo Histórico Municipal (see above) inside the Palacio de Benamejí (daily 10am–2pm, closed Sat & Sun July & Aug; ☏955 902 933, ⬡www.turismoecija.com).

Internet The Biblioteca Municipal (public library; Mon–Fri 9.30am–1.30pm & 4–8.30pm, Sat 9.30am–1.30pm) off the western end of the Pl. Mayor in an elegant mansion has free internet and wi-fi access.

ACCOMMODATION

Hotel Palacio de los Granados c/Emilio Castelar 42 ☎ 955 905 344, ⓦ www.palaciogranados.com. To the east of the Pl. de España this is a beautifully restored eighteenth-century mansion with delightful patios, small pool, and rooms are decorated with original contemporary artworks. **€130**

Hotel Platería c/Garcilópez 1 ☎ 955 90 27 54, ⓦ www

.hotelplateria.net. Off the east side of the Pl. Mayor, this comfortable hotel has modern a/c rooms and its own restaurant. **€62**

Hotel Sol Pirula c/Miguel de Cervantes 50 ☎ 954 830 300, ⓦ www.hotelpirula.com. South of the centre, this modern hotel has decent air-conditioned rooms above its own restaurant. Free wi-fi. **€71**

EATING AND DRINKING

Bar La Reja c/Garcilopez 1. Next door to the *Hotel Platería*, this bar has a wider choice of tapas and *raciones*. Specialities include fish and *mariscos*. Daily noon–midnight.

Casa Emilio On the south side of the Pl. Mayor. A decent stop for tapas and *raciones*; try their local cheeses and

charcutería (cured pork). Daily 10am–11pm.

Hotel Platería c/Garcilópez 1 ☎ 955 90 27 54. The restaurant of this hotel is reliable and serves a bargain weekday *menú* for €7. Main dishes include *solomillo ibérico* (pork loin). Daily noon–4pm & 7.30–10.30pm.

Osuna

OSUNA (like Carmona and Écija) is one of those small Andalucian towns that are great to explore in the early evening: slow in pace and quietly enjoyable, with elegant streets of tiled, whitewashed houses interspersed with fine **Renaissance mansions**. The best of these are off the main street, c/Carrera, which runs down from the central Plaza Mayor, and in particular on c/San Pedro, which intersects it; at no. 16, the **Cilla del Cabildo** has a superb geometric relief round a carving of the Giralda, and, farther along, the eighteenth-century **Palacio de El Marqués de la Gomera** – now a hotel and restaurant (see p.312) – is a stunning Baroque extravaganza. There's also a marvellous **casino** on Plaza Mayor, with 1920s Mudéjar-style decor and a grandly bizarre ceiling, which is open to all visitors and makes an ideal place for a cool drink.

The old university and Colegiata

May–Sept Tues–Fri 10am–1.30pm & 4–7pm, July & Aug closed Sun pm; Oct–April Tues–Fri 10am–1.30pm & 3.30–6.30pm. Colegiata with guided tour €3, La Encarnación €2, old university patio open during term time except July & Aug (free)

Two huge stone buildings stand on the hill top: the **old university** (suppressed by reactionary Fernando VII in 1820 and the lavish sixteenth-century **Colegiata**, which contains the gloomy but impressive pantheon and chapel of the dukes of Osuna, descendants of the kings of León and once "the lords of Andalucía", as well as a museum displaying some fine artworks, including imposing canvases by Ribera. Opposite the entrance to the Colegiata is the Baroque convent of La Encarnación (same hours as Colegiata), which has a fine plinth of Sevillan *azulejos* round its cloister and gallery.

INFORMATION   OSUNA

Turismo 300m northwest of the Pl. Mayor at c/Carrera 83 (Tues–Sat 9.30am–1.30pm & 4–6pm, Sun 9.30am–

1.30pm; ☎ 954 815 732, ⓦ ayto-osuna.es), can provide a town map.

ACCOMMODATION

Accommodation in Osuna is not plentiful, but outside of national holiday periods and the local *feria* (third or fourth week in May) there's usually no great problem finding a place to stay. All the same, it's worth ringing ahead.

Hostal Caballo Blanco c/Granada 1 ☎ 95 481 01 84. Welcoming and comfortable *hostal* with en-suite a/c rooms with TV in a remodelled old coaching inn. It has an equally good restaurant and large car park at the back. **€55**

Hostal Granadino Pl. Salitre 1 ☎ 954 810 000. Slightly

further away from the centre and southwest of the Pl. Mayor, this is a friendly place offering a/c en-suite rooms above a restaurant. **€42**

Hotel Esmeralda c/Tesorero 7 ☎ 955 821 073, ⓦ www .hotelesmeralda.es. After a complete refit this is a

4

transformed hotel with elegant a/c en-suite rooms with minibar, TV, safe and wi-fi. Stunning rooftop terrace with plunge pool. Has own restaurant and (free) parking. €65

★ **Hotel Palacio Marqués de la Gomera** c/San Pedro 20, ☎ 954 81 22 23, ⌨ www.hotelpalaciodelmarques .es. The town's four-star option, set inside one of the most beautiful *casa palacios* in the country, is a dream. A national monument in its own right, this eighteenth-century mansion has a breathtakingly beautiful patio with a Baroque chapel just off it and all rooms are tastefully and individually furnished. Room 7 was used by Franco Zeffirelli when here making a film about the life of María Callas and has a spectacular exterior balcony, while the irresistibly romantic Room 10 is situated in the palace's tower. There's a restaurant on-site too. Sun–Thurs €78, Fri & Sat €89

EATING AND DRINKING

There are **food and drink** possibilities all over town and many of the accommodation options (see above) also have restaurants of their own.

Bar San Agustín c/San Agustín 15. Good little neighbourhood bar-restaurant offering economical *platos combinados*. 9am–11pm; closed Thurs.

★ **Casa Curro** Plaza Salitre 5. The town's best (and liveliest) tapas and *raciones* bar cooks up a tasty range of seafood and meat dishes. There's a superb restaurant in the back, too. 1–4pm & 8–11pm; closed Mon.

Hostal Caballo Blanco c/Granada 1. The *hostal's* restaurant is very good for *comida casera* serving up dishes such as *redondillo guisado* (beef stew) and *gachas de osuna* (local gruel) as well as the usual standards. Daily 1.30–4pm & 8–10.30pm.

Mesón del Duque Pl. de la Duquesa 2, uphill from the Pl. Mayor. Excellent little mid-priced bar-restaurant, with the best terrace in town. Wide range of meat and fish dishes including *lomo a la almendra* (pork loin with almonds) and a weekday *menú* for around €10. Daily 9am–midnight.

4

Córdoba

CÓRDOBA lies upstream from Seville beside a loop of the Guadalquivir, which was once navigable as far as here. It is today a minor provincial capital, prosperous in a modest sort of way. Once, however, it was the largest city of Roman Spain, and for three centuries it formed the heart of the western Islamic empire, the great medieval caliphate of the Moors.

It is from this era that the city's major monument dates: the **Mezquita**, the grandest and most beautiful mosque ever constructed by the Moors in Spain. It stands right in the centre of the city, surrounded by the old Jewish and Moorish quarters, and is a building of extraordinary mystical and aesthetic power. Make for it on arrival and keep returning as long as you stay; you'll find its beauty increases with each visit, as, of course, is proper, since the mosque was intended for daily attendance.

The Mezquita apart, Córdoba itself is a place of considerable charm. It has few grand squares or mansions, tending instead to introverted architecture, calling your attention to the tremendous and often wildly extravagant **patios**. These have long been acclaimed, and they are actively encouraged and maintained by the local council, which runs a "Festival of the Patios" in May. Away from the Mezquita, Córdoba's other remnants of Moorish – and indeed Christian – rule are not individually very striking. The river, though, with its great **Arab waterwheels** and recently restored and pedestrianized **Roman bridge** (the Puente Romano), is an attractive area in which to wander.

Just 7km outside the town, more Moorish splendours are to be seen among the ruins of the extravagant palace complex of **Medina Azahara**, undergoing fascinating reconstruction.

La Mezquita

Mon–Sat 10am–7pm, Sun 8.30–10am & 2–7pm; Oct–March until 5pm • Free entrance at side doors Mon–Sat 8.30am–10am for services but without lighting • €8, kids €4

The development of the **Mezquita** paralleled the new heights of confidence and splendour of ninth- and tenth-century Córdoba. Abd ar-Rahman III provided it with a new minaret (which has not survived but which provided the core for the later belfry),

MOORISH CÓRDOBA

Córdoba's **domination of Moorish Spain** began thirty years after its conquest – in 756, when the city was placed under the control of **Abd ar-Rahman I**, the sole survivor of the Umayyad dynasty, which had been bloodily expelled from the eastern caliphate of Damascus. He proved a firm but moderate ruler, and a remarkable military campaigner, establishing control over all but the north of Spain and proclaiming himself *emir*, a title meaning both "king" and "son of the caliph". It was Abd ar-Rahman who commenced the building of the Great Mosque (*La Mezquita*, in Spanish), purchasing from the Christians the site of the cathedral of St Vincent (which, divided by a partition wall, had previously served both communities). This original mosque was completed by his son **Hisham** in 796 and comprises about one-fifth of the present building, the first dozen aisles adjacent to the Patio de los Naranjos.

The **Cordoban emirate**, maintaining independence from the eastern caliphate, soon began to rival Damascus both in power and in the brilliance of its civilization. **Abd ar-Rahman II** (822–52) initiated sophisticated irrigation programmes, minted his own coinage and received embassies from Byzantium. He in turn substantially enlarged the mosque. A focal point within the culture of al-Andalus, this was by now being consciously directed and enriched as an alternative to Mecca; it possessed an original script of the Koran and a bone from the arm of Mohammed and, for the Spanish Muslim who could not get to Mecca, it became the most sacred place of **pilgrimage**. In the broader Islamic world, it ranked third in sanctity after the Kaaba of Mecca and the al-Alqsa mosque of Jerusalem.

In the tenth century, Córdoba reached its zenith under a new *emir*, **Abd ar-Rahman III** (912–61), one of the great rulers of Islamic history. He assumed power after a period of internal strife and, according to a contemporary historian, "subdued rebels, built palaces, gave impetus to agriculture, immortalized ancient deeds and monuments, and inflicted great damage on infidels to a point where no opponent or contender remained in al-Andalus. People obeyed en masse and wished to live with him in peace." In 929, with Muslim Spain and part of North Africa firmly under his control, Abd ar-Rahman III adopted the title of "caliph". It was a supremely confident move and was reflected in the growing splendour of Córdoba, which had become the largest, most prosperous city of Europe, outshining Byzantium and Baghdad (the new capital of the eastern caliphate) in science, culture and scholarship. At the turn of the tenth century, Moorish sources boast of the city's 27 schools, 50 hospitals (with the first separate clinics for the leprous and insane), 900 public baths, 60,300 noble mansions, 80,455 shops and 213,077 houses.

4

80m high, topped by three pomegranate-shaped spheres, two of silver and one of gold and each weighing a tonne. But it was his son, **al-Hakam II** (961–76), to whom he passed on a peaceful and stable empire, who was responsible for the most brilliant expansion. He virtually doubled its extent, demolishing the south wall to add fourteen extra rows of columns, and employed Byzantine craftsmen to construct a new *mihrab*, or prayer niche; this remains complete and is perhaps the most beautiful example of all Moorish religious architecture.

Al-Hakam had extended the mosque as far to the south as was possible. The final enlargement of the building, under the chamberlain-usurper **al-Mansur** (977–1002), involved adding seven rows of columns to the whole east side. This spoiled the symmetry of the mosque, depriving the *mihrab* of its central position, but Arab historians observed that it meant there were now "as many bays as there are days of the year". They also delighted in describing the rich interior, with its 1293 marble columns, 280 chandeliers and 1445 lamps. Hanging inverted among the lamps were the bells of the pilgrimage cathedral of Santiago de Compostela. Al-Mansur made his Christian captives carry them on their shoulders from Galicia – a process that was to be observed in reverse after Córdoba was captured by Fernando el Santo (the Saint) in 1236.

Entering the Mezquita

As in Moorish times, the **Mezquita** is approached through the **Patio de los Naranjos**, a classic Islamic ablutions court that preserves its orange trees, although the fountains for

Train & Bus Station

ALHAKEN II

FRAY L. DE GRANADA

AVENIDA DE CERVANTES

AVDA. DE LOS MOZÁRABES

AGR

DOCE DE OCTUBRE

Medina Azahara

0   200
metres

N

AVENIDA DE MEDINA AZAHARA

ALBÉNIZ

Ciudad
Jardín

ANTONIO   MAURA

A. DE LA CRUZ CEBALLOS

CAMINO DE LOS SASTRES

GLORIETA CRUZ ROJA

ALCALDE V.ELASCO NAVARRO

Airport

AVENIDA DE LA REPÚBLICA ARGENTINA

PASEO DE LA VICTORIA

Jardines de
la Victoria

Jardines de
la Agricultura

AVENIDA DEL GRAN CAPITÁN

ALONSO DE BURGOS

DOCE - DE

PLAZA
A. GRILLO

DATO

DUQUE DE FERNÁN NÚÑEZ

EDUARDO

LOPE DE HOCES

CASTRO

JOSÉ ZORRILLA

GÓNGORA

CONDE DE GONDOMAR

Colegiata de
San Hipólito

E. LUCENA

CABRERA

CRUZ CONDE

Iglesia de
San Miguel

S. ÁLVARO

S. ZOILO

Iglesia de
San Nicolás
de la Villa

SEVILLA

SAN FELIPE

MÁLAGA

R. RIVERA

DUEÑAS

ALFONSO

PLAZA DE
LAS TENDILLAS

CLAUDIO

GLORIA

MORETRA

PLAZA
R Y CAJAL

PLAZA
DR. EMILIO
LUQUE

ARGOTE

JESÚS MARÍA

R. SÁNCHEZ

San
Juan

CÁRDENAS

RELO

MUÑDA

DE CÓRDOBA

PLAZA DE
LA COMPAÑÍA

JUAN DE MENA

VALERA

JUAN

CANTÁVERA

PERO

MORALES

FERIA

S. DE TELMO

HORNO FERNANDO

TEJÓN

L. DE AUSTRIA

VILLADARES

BARROSO

ANGL

AUX S. ANA

LEIVA AGUILAR

LA
JUDERÍA

BLANCO. BELMONTE

Museo
Arqueológico

AMBROSIO

DIARIO

HERNE

PUERTA DE
ALMODÓVAR

FERNÁNDEZ

RUANO

ALMANZOR

Casa Andalusí

Sinagoga

JUDÍOS

Museo
Taurino

CAIRUÁN

CÁZAR

ROMERO

CÁRDENAL

PLAZA
MAIMÓNIDES

CONDE Y LUQUE

Convento de
la Encarnación

PLAZA. DE
JERÓNIMO
PÁEZ

CALLEJA DE
LAS FLORES

HORNO DEL
CRISTO

J. ROMERO
DE TORRES

Iglesia
de San
Francisco

CAREZAS

JAN

Plaza de
Potro

E. R. TORRES

AVDA. DOCTOR FLEMING

BARROQUER

DR. MARAÑÓN

DOCTOR

LUNA

ALBUCASIS

PL. JUDA
LEVI

DEANES

CÁRDENAL

HERRERO

ENCARNACIÓN

MAGISTRAL GLEZ. FRANCÉS

ORSO

S. CLARA

CARDEREROS

PIMENTERA

LUCANO

M. ROJA

TOMÁS CONDE

MANRIQUE

Hospital
de San
Sebastián

PLAZA
CAMPO DE
LOS MÁRTIRES

TORRIJOS

La Mezquita

Museo
Diocesano

LUIS DE LA CERDA

PLAZA
ALMÓNDIGA

CRUZ
DEL RASTRO

PASEO DE LA RIBERA

SAN BASILIO

ENMEDIO

CABALLERIZAS   REALES

AMADOR DE LOS RÍOS

CORREGIDOR

Alcázar
de los Reyes
Cristianos

Triunfo de
San Rafael

DE

RONDA

Puerta del
Puente

ISASA

Jardín Botánico, Seville & Granada

AVENIDA DEL ALCÁZAR

Puente
Romano

Río Guadalquivir

Torre de la Calahorra & 18

CÓRDOBA

4

ACCOMMODATION

Albergue Juvenil	7
Campamento Municipal	1
Casa de los Azulejos	3
Fonda Agustina	16
Hospedería Churrasco	5
Hostal Alcázar	15
Hostal Almanzor	17
Hostal & Hotel Maestre	13
Hostal Plaza Corredera	4
Hostal El Portillo	10
Hostal Séneca	8
Hotel Amistad Córdoba	6
Hotel Hespería Córdoba	18
Hotel Las Casas de la Judería	11
Hotel Marisa	9
Hotel Mezquita	12
Parador La Arruzafa	2
Pensión Los Arcos	14

EATING & DRINKING

Albergue Juvenil	8
Amaltea	12
Bar Plateros	10
Casa Paco Acedo	1
El Choto	6
El Churrasco	7
El Gallo	3
Mesón San Basilio	13
Los Mochuelos	11
La Pataíta	4
El Rincón del Carmen	9
Taberna Salinas	5
Taberna San Miguel (El Pisto)	2

ritual purification before prayer are now purely decorative. Originally, when in use for the Friday prayers, all nineteen naves of the mosque were open to this court, allowing the rows of interior columns to appear an extension of the trees with brilliant shafts of sunlight filtering through. Today, all but one of the entrance gates is locked and sealed, and the mood of the building has been distorted from the open and vigorous simplicity of the mosque to the mysterious half-light of a cathedral.

Nonetheless, a first glimpse inside the Mezquita is immensely exciting. "So near the desert in its tentlike forest of supporting pillars," Jan Morris found it, "so faithful to Mahomet's tenets of cleanliness, abstinence and regularity." The mass of supporting pillars was, in fact, an early and sophisticated innovation to gain height. The original architect had at his disposal columns from the old Visigothic cathedral and from numerous Roman buildings; they could bear great weight but were not tall enough, even when arched, to reach the intended height of the ceiling. His solution (which may have been inspired by Roman aqueduct designs) was to place a second row of square columns on the apex of the lower ones, serving as a base for the semicircular arches that support the roof. For extra strength and stability (and perhaps also deliberately to echo the shape of a date palm, much revered by the early Spanish Arabs), the architect introduced another, horseshoe-shaped arch above the lower pillars. A second and purely aesthetic innovation was to alternate brick and stone in the arches, creating the red-and-white-striped pattern that gives a unity and distinctive character to the whole design.

The mihrab

The uniformity was broken only at the culminating point of the mosque – the domed cluster of pillars surrounding the sacred *mihrab*, erected under al-Hakam II. The *mihrab* has two functions in Islamic worship: it indicates the direction of Mecca (and hence of prayer) and it amplifies the words of the imam, or prayer leader. At Córdoba, it is also of supreme beauty.

The inner vestibule of the niche (frustratingly fenced off) is quite simple in comparison, with a shell-shaped ceiling carved from a single block of marble. The chambers to either side – decorated with exquisite Byzantine mosaics of gold, rust red, turquoise and green – constitute the *maksura*, where the caliph and his retinue would pray.

The cathedral

Originally, the whole design of the mosque would have directed worshippers naturally towards the *mihrab*. Today, though, you almost stumble upon it, for in the centre of the mosque squats a Renaissance **cathedral coro**. This was built in 1523 – nearly three centuries of enlightened restraint after the Reconquest – and in spite of fierce opposition from the town council. The erection of a *coro* and *capilla mayor*, however, had long been the "Christianizing" dream of the cathedral chapter and at last they had found a monarch – predictably Carlos V – who was willing to sanction the work. Carlos, to his credit, realized the mistake (though it did not stop him from destroying parts of the Alhambra and Seville's Alcázar); on seeing the work completed, he told the chapter, "You have built what you or others might have built anywhere, but you have destroyed something that was unique in the world." To the left of the *coro* stands an earlier and happier Christian addition – the Mudéjar **Capilla de Villaviciosa**, built by Moorish craftsmen in 1371 (and now partly sealed up). Beside it are the dome and pillars of the **earlier mihrab**, constructed under Abd ar-Rahman II.

The belfry and outer walls

The belfry, the **Torre del Alminar** (currently closed), at the corner of the Patio de los Naranjos, is contemporary with the cathedral addition. Close by, the **Puerta del Perdón**, the main entrance to the patio, was rebuilt in Moorish style in 1377. It's worth making a tour of the Mezquita's **outer walls** before leaving; parts of the original "caliphal" decoration surrounding the portals (in particular, some exquisite lattice work) are stunning.

Torre de la Calahorra

Daily: May–Sept 10am–2pm & 4.30–8.30pm; Oct–April 10am–6pm • €4.50

At the eastern end of the Roman bridge over the Guadalquivir, the medieval **Torre de la Calahorra** houses a gimmicky, high-tech museum containing models of the pre-cathedral Mezquita, weird talking tableaux and a rather incongruous multimedia presentation on the history of man; there's a great panoramic **view**, though, from the top of the tower towards the city. As you cross the bridge you can see near the western riverbank, the wheels and the ruined mills that were in use for several centuries after the fall of the Muslim city, grinding flour and pumping water up to the fountains of the Alcázar.

Museo Diocesano

July & Aug Mon–Sat 9.30am–3pm; Sept–June 9.30am–1.30pm & 4–6pm • €1.50, free with Mezquita ticket

The site of the original Alcázar, or caliph's palace, is now occupied by the palace of the bishopric, inside which is housed the **Museo Diocesano**, a museum of religious art with some fine examples of medieval wood sculpture.

Alcázar de los Reyes Cristianos

July–Sept Tues–Sat 8.30am–2.30pm, Sun 9.30am–2.30pm ; Oct–June Tues–Sat 8.30am–7.30pm, Sun 9.30am–2.30pm; gardens only Tues–Sun 8pm–midnight • €4

After the Christian conquest, the Alcázar was rebuilt a little to the west by Fernando and Isabel, hence its name, **Alcázar de los Reyes Cristianos**. The buildings are a bit dreary, having served as the residence of the Inquisition from 1428 to 1821, and later as a prison until 1951. However, they display some fine mosaics and other relics from Roman Córdoba, among which is one of the largest complete Roman mosaics in existence, and the wonderful **gardens** are a great place to get your breath back.

Jardín Botánico

April–June Tues–Sat 10am–8pm, Sun 10am –3pm; July & Aug Tues–Sat 10am–3pm & 7pm–midnight, Sun 10am–3pm; Sept–March Tues–Sat 10am–6pm, Sun 10am–3pm • €2 • ⓦ www.jardinbotanicodecordoba.com

Three hundred metres downriver from the Alcázar on the opposite bank lies the university's **Jardín Botánico**, displaying exotic trees, shrubs and plants from all over the world, including Andalucía's very own arboreal rarity, the **pinsapo Spanish fir**, a pre-Ice Age survivor transplanted from its only European habitat in the Sierra de Grazalema. The garden has a pleasant **cafetería**.

Plaza de la Corredera

To the northeast of the Mezquita, near the Museo Arqueológico and in an area that was once the *plateros* or silversmiths' quarter, you'll find **Plaza de la Corredera**, a once ramshackle but now wonderfully refurbished colonnaded square, much resembling Madrid's or Salamanca's Plaza Mayor. Unique in Andalucía, the square's complete enclosure occurred in the seventeenth century and presented the city with a suitable space for all kinds of spectacles. These have included burnings by the Inquisition as well as bullfights, from which event the tiny Callejón Toril (Bull Pen) on the square's eastern side takes its name. Now bars and restaurants line the square, and their terraces are popular places to sit out on summer evenings.

La Judería

Between the Mezquita and the beginning of Avda. del Gran Capitán lies **La Judería**, Córdoba's old Jewish quarter, and a fascinating network of lanes – more atmospheric and less commercialized than Seville's Barrio Santa Cruz, though tacky souvenir shops are beginning to gain ground.

Sinagoga

C/Judíos 20 • Tues–Sat 9.30am–2pm & 3.30–5.30pm, Sun 9.30am–2pm • €0.30, free with EU passport

Near the heart of the quarter is a **sinagoga**, one of only three synagogues in Spain – the other two are in Toledo – that survived the Jewish expulsion of 1492. This one, built in 1316, is minute, particularly in comparison with the great Santa María in Toledo, but it has some fine stuccowork elaborating on a Solomon's-seal motif and retains its women's gallery. Outside is a statue of Maimónides, the Jewish philosopher, physician and Talmudic jurist, born in Córdoba in 1135.

La Casa Andalusí

C/Judíos 12• Daily 10.30am–7.30pm • €2.50

Just along from the synagogue there's a restored twelfth-century mansion, **La Casa Andalusí**, which attempts to re-create the atmosphere of the Moorish period with furniture and a variety of exhibits.

Museo Taurino

Bullfighting museum Tues–Sat 10am–2pm & 5.30–7.30pm, Sun 9.30am–2.30pm • €3, free on Fri

Near La Casa Andalusí is the small **Museo Taurino**. It warrants a look, if only for the kitschy nature of its exhibits: row upon row of bulls' heads, two of them given this "honour" for having killed matadors. Beside a copy of the tomb of Manolete – most famous of the city's *toreros* – is exhibited the hide of his taurine nemesis, Islero.

Museo Arqueológico

Tues 2.30–8.30pm, Wed–Sat 9am–8.30pm, Sun 9am–2.30pm • €1.50, free with EU passport

The **Museo Arqueológico**, now in a completely new building adjoining its former home, the beautiful sixteenth-century mansion of Casa Páez, has a basement viewing area that incorporates the *grados* (seats) of the Roman theatre both it and the mansion are built on top of. The museum is a work in progress; when funds are available it is intended to refurbish the Casa Páez to house an extensive Moorish collection, currently in storage. For the time being items on view include well-presented Iberian and Roman sculptures as well as Caliphal ceramics and *azulejos*.

Plaza del Potro

A couple of blocks below the archeological museum, back towards the river, you'll come upon **Plaza del Potro**, a fine old square named after the colt (*potro*) that adorns its recently restored fountain. This, as a wall plaque proudly points out, is mentioned in *Don Quixote*, and indeed Cervantes himself is reputed to have stayed at the inn opposite, the **Posada del Potro**, which has an atmospheric cattle yard within. Recently restored, it is currently used as a centre for the study of flamenco and stages exhibitions and sporadic concerts (details from the *turismo*).

Museo de Bellas Artes

Pl. del Potro • Tues 2.30–8.30pm, Wed–Sat 9am–8.30pm, Sun 9am–2.30pm • €1.50, free with EU passport

The **Museo de Bellas Artes** is a fairly unremarkable collection of paintings alleviated by a few minor works by Murillo and Valdés Leal. Among the modern stuff there is an interesting and recently purchased Dalí-esque work, *Mujeres Vela* (Women Sailing), by Montero artist Antonio Rodríguez Luna (1910–85).

Museo Julio Romero de Torres

Pl. del Potro • May–Sept Tues–Sat 10am–2pm & 5.30–7.30pm, Sun 9.30am–2.30pm; Oct–April Tues–Sat 8.30am–2.30pm, Sun 9.30am–2.30pm • €4, free on Fri

Across the courtyard from the Museo de Bellas Artes, the small **Museo Julio Romero de Torres** is devoted to the Córdoban artist Romero de Torres (1874–1930), a painter of some sublimely dreadful canvases, many of which depict reclining female nudes with furtive male guitar-players. Should you wish to decide for yourself, the nightmarish *Cante Jondo* or the raunchy *Oranges and Lemons* should be enough to give the measure of Romero's oeuvre; alternatively, just flick through a catalogue in the foyer.

Palacio del Marqués de Viana

Guided tours April–Sept Tues–Sun 9am–3pm; Oct–April 10am–7pm, Sun 9.30am–2.30pm • €6, patios only €3; last entry 15min before closing

In the north of town, towards the train station, are numerous Renaissance churches – some converted from mosques, others showing obvious influence in their minarets – and a handful of convents and palaces. The best of these, still privately owned although not by the family, is the **Palacio del Marqués de Viana**, whose main attraction for many visitors is its twelve flower-filled patios. The house itself – an ongoing work started in the fourteenth century – is mildly interesting and the guided tour leads you through drawing rooms, gaudy bedrooms (one with a telling Franco portrait), kitchens and galleries while pointing out furniture, paintings, weapons and top-drawer junk the family amassed over the centuries.

ARRIVAL AND DEPARTURE — CÓRDOBA 4

By train From the splendid combined train and bus station on Pl. de las Tres Culturas, on Avda. de América at the northern end of town, head east to the junction with broad Avda. del Gran Capitán; this leads down to the old quarters and the Mezquita (15min walk or bus #3 from outside the station).

Destinations Algeciras (2 daily; 3hr 15min); Cádiz (2 daily; 3hr); Granada (2 daily; 2hr 30min); Jaén (4 daily; 1hr 45min); Madrid (19 AVE daily; 1hr 50min); Málaga (11 AVE daily; 50min); Ronda (2 daily; 2hr); Seville (22 AVE daily; 45min).

By bus Buses arrive at the combined train and bus station on Pl. de las Tres Culturas. See train information above for details on getting to the centre.

Destinations Badajoz (2 daily; 4hr 25min); Écija (6 daily; 55min); Granada (8 daily; 2hr 30min); Jaén (8 daily; 1hr 30min); Madrid (7 daily; 4hr 50min); Málaga (4 daily; 2hr); Seville (7 daily; 1hr 45min).

By car Arriving by car can be a pain, especially during rush hour in the narrow streets around the Mezquita. Parking in the centre is also a major headache, and it's worth considering staying somewhere that doesn't require traversing the old quarter. Better still is if you park up for the duration of your stay – Avda. de la República Argentina bordering the Jardines de la Victoria on the western edge of the old quarter, and across the river in the streets either side of the *Hotel Hespería Cordoba* are possible places – and get around the city on foot, which is both easy and enjoyable.

INFORMATION

Turismo At the Palacio de Congresos y Exposiciones at c/Torrijos 10 (Mon–Fri 9am–7.30pm, Sat & Sun 9.30am–3pm; ☎ 957 355 179), alongside the Mezquita.

Municipal tourist office Córdoba's municipal tourist office (🖳 turismodecordoba.org) has joined forces with a private company to provide tourist information from three central kiosks: at Pl. Campo de los Martires, almost facing the Alcázar (daily 9am–2pm & 5–7.30pm); in Pl. de las Tendillas in the centre of the modern town (daily 10am–1.30pm & 5.30–8pm); and on the main concourse of the train station (daily 9am–2pm & 5–7.30pm).

Guided walks The municipal tourist office also offers guided walks around the old city (Paseos por Córdoba; English spoken; €16); the walks start from the Pl. de Tendillas office at 9.30am, last an hour and a half, and end up at a typical *cordobés* taverna.

Opening hours Córdoba changes its monument timetables more than any other town in Andalucía – it's wise to check with one of the tourist offices for the latest information.

Internet Ch@t, c/Claudio Marcelo 15, near the focal Pl. de las Tendillas (Mon–Sat 10am–2pm & 5–9.30pm) in the new town, and, in the old quarter, *Hostal El Pilar del Potro* at c/Lucano 12 (daily 10am–1pm & 5–10pm).

ACCOMMODATION

The majority of **places to stay** are concentrated in the narrow maze of streets to the north and east of the Mezquita. Finding a room at any time of the year – except during Semana Santa and the May festivals (the city's busiest month) – isn't usually a problem. It's also worth bearing in mind that Córdoba's high season (the price we quote) is April–June, while July and August are the hotel trade's low-season months when the more upmarket places often drop their prices dramatically.

Albergue Juvenil Pl. Judá Levi ☎957 355 040, reservations ☎902 510 000, ⓦwww.inturjoven.com. Excellent and superbly located modern youth hostel (with twin, triple and four-person en-suite rooms), which also serves meals and has wi-fi throughout. It's a prime destination for budget travellers, so you may need to book ahead at busy periods. Under-26 €17.50, over-26 €23.50.

Casa de los Azulejos c/Fernando Colón 5 ☎957 470 000, ⓦwww.casadelosazulejos.com. Stylish, small boutique hotel with distinctively furnished rooms, featuring iron bedsteads and artworks, ranged around a leafy patio, itself used for art shows. Car park. Free wi-fi. €150

Fonda Agustina c/Zapatería Vieja 5 ☎957 470 872. Charming and spotlessly clean little *fonda*, with basic rooms in a tranquil location. €40

Hospedería de Churrasco c/Romero 38 ☎957 294 808, ⓦwww.elchurrasco.com. Elegant and welcoming nine-room hotel in the Judería belonging to the restaurant of the same name. Entry is through a double patio, and rooms are classically furnished with chintz drapes and bedcovers, and some have terraces. Facilities include minibar, in-room internet and wi-fi and rooftop terrace/solarium. €140

★ **Hostal Alcázar** c/San Basilio 2 ☎957 202 561, ⓦwww.hostalalcazar.com. Comfortable and welcoming family-run *hostal* with a nice patio and a range of rooms (most en suite)with a/c and TV. Also has some good-value apartments opposite (€80 for up to four; two-night minimum stay). Wi-fi zone. B&B €45

Hostal Almanzor Corregidor Luís de la Cerda 10 ☎957 485 400, ⓦwww.hostal-almanzor.es. East of the Mezquita, a pleasant and recently refurbished *hostal* for a/c, en-suite rooms with TV. Free use of car park. €60

★ **Hostal & Hotel Maestre** c/Romero Barros 4 & 16 ☎957 475 395 for the hostal, ☎957 472 410 for the hotel, ⓦwww.hotelmaestre.com. Excellent *hostal* between c/San Fernando and the Pl. del Potro and neighbouring hotel with attractive a/c en-suite rooms with TV. Also has some good-value two-person apartments. *Rough Guide* readers with this guide get free underground parking (excluding April & May). *Hostal* €45, hotel €55, apartments €66

Hostal Plaza Corredera c/Rodríguez Marín 15 ☎957 470 581, ⓦwww.hostallacorredera.com. Clean, friendly and recently refurbished place with rooms sharing bath, and great views over the plaza from some. Wi-fi zone. €40

Hostal El Portillo c/Cabezas 2 ☎957 472 091, ⓦwww.hostalelportillo.com. Beautiful, refurbished and friendly old *hostal* with elegant patio, offering en-suite a/c singles and doubles. €45

★ **Hostal Séneca** c/Conde y Luque 7 ☎957 473 234, ⓦwww.sensesandcolours.com. Wonderful place to stay, with simple and en-suite rooms around a stunning patio with Moorish pavement where you can take breakfast. Very popular, so book ahead. €80

Hotel Amistad Córdoba Pl. de Maimónides 3 ☎957 420 335, ⓦwww.nh-hoteles.com. Stylish upmarket hotel with comfortable rooms incorporating two eighteenth-century mansions, near the old wall in the Judería. Car park available. Frequently offers specials (see website). €139

Hotel Las Casas de la Judería c/Tomás Conde 10 ☎957 202 095, ⓦwww.casasypalacios.com. Córdoba's first five-star hotel is under the same proprietors as the similarly named hotel in Seville. This also is an exquisitely charming restoration of an ancient *casa palacio* and rooms are arranged around patios with tinkling fountains and scented flowers. The elegant rooms are decorated with period furnishings and artworks and come with satellite TV and all the five-star frills. Also has a spa, restaurant and garage. €315

Hotel Hespería Córdoba Avda. de la Confederación s/n ☎957 421 042, ⓦwww.hoteles-hesperia.es. Luxurious four-star hotel with great views across the river towards the Mezquita and city from rooms at the front. Features include restaurant, *cafetería*, pool and rooftop bar (with the same view) and easy access to the town across the pedestrianized Puente Romano. Own car park or easy parking nearby. Does frequent special offers (see website). €169

Hotel Marisa c/Cardenal Herrero 6 ☎957 473 142, ⓦwww.hotelmarisacordoba.com. Two-star hotel with a superb position immediately outside the Mezquita. Rooms come with a/c but not TV. Own garage. €85

Hotel Mezquita Pl. Santa Catalina 1 ☎957 475 585, ⓦwww.hotelmezquita.com. Atmospheric and central hotel in a converted sixteenth-century mansion with excellent a/c rooms. Wi-fi zone. €105

Parador La Arruzafa Avda. de la Arruzafa s/n, off Avda. El Brillante ☎957 275 900, ⓦwww.parador.es. Córdoba's modern parador is located on the outskirts of the city 5km to the north of the Mezquita, but compensates with pleasant gardens, a pool and every other amenity (including a shooting range). **€156**

Pensión Los Arcos c/Romero Barros 14 ☎ 957 485 643, ⓦ www.pensionlosarcos.com. Excellent *hostal* with simple rooms (some en suite) around a delightful patio. **€39–45**

CAMPING

Campamento Municipal El Brillante Avda. El Brillante 50 ☎ 957 403 836. Córdoba's local campsite (with restaurant and pool) is 2km north of the centre in the El Brillante *barrio*, and served by bus #10 or #11 from the bus station. Tents and equipment for hire. **€7**, **€5** per tent, **€5** per vehicle

EATING AND DRINKING

Bars and **restaurants** are on the whole reasonably priced – you need only to avoid the touristy places round the Mezquita. There are lots of good places to eat in La Judería and in the old quarters off to the east, above Paseo de la Ribera. Two celebrated specialities worth trying here are *rabo de toro* (slow-stewed bull's tail) and *salmorejo*, the deliciously hunky *cordobés* variant of gazpacho, made with bread, tomatoes, oil and chopped *jamón* often topped up with sliced hard-boiled eggs.

Albergue Juvenil Pl. Judá Levi s/n. The youth hostel's *cafetería* (open to all) has some of the cheapest food in town, with hearty three-course lunch and dinner *menús* a bargain €8. Daily 2–3pm & 8.30–9.30pm.

★ **Amaltea** c/Ronda de Isasa 10 ☎ 957 491 968. Excellent organic restaurant with lots of veggie options, run by a charming Wolverhampton-educated *cordobésa*. Specialities of the house include *couscous con verduras* (vegetables*)*. Plenty of organic wines and a few special beers, too – try the Alhambra 1925. Some dishes are pricier, but it's possible to eat here for under €15. 12.30–4pm & 20.30–midnight; closed Mon.

★ **Bar Plateros** c/San Francisco 6. Headquarters of the Plateros chain of tapas bars in a converted former convent. What started in 1868 as a mutual benefit society for the workers in Córdoba's silversmith trade eventually branched out into the *bodega* business, presently owning three excellent bars around the city. Now over a century old and serving a wide range of tapas – house specials include *arroz con bacalao* (cod paella) and *perdiz en escabeche* (marinated partridge). The bar is light and airy with a glass-covered patio complemented by hanging plants and *azulejos*. Mon–Sat 8am–4pm & 8pm–midnight; closed Sun.

Casa Paco Acedo Beneath the Torre de la Malmuerta. The house specialities at this celebrated, good-value *cordobés* institution include *salmorejo* and a memorable *rabo de toro*. Mon–Sat noon–4pm & 8.30–midnight; closed Sun.

El Choto c/Almanzor 10 ☎ 957 760 115. Attractive, small and serious restaurant with a small outdoor terrace offering a range of well-prepared fish and meat dishes including its signature dish *choto asado* (roast kid). There's a four-course *menú de degustación* for €35 (including wine) and a *menú de la casa* for around €22 (both Tues–Fri). 1–5pm & 7.30–midnight; closed Sun eve & Mon.

★ **El Churrasco** c/Romero 16 (not c/Romero Barros) ☎ 957 290 819. This renowned restaurant with attractive rooms and patio is famous for its *churrasco* (a grilled pork dish, served with pepper sauces) and *salmorejo* (a thick Cordoban version of gazpacho with hunks of ham and egg).

Expensive but offers an interesting *menú de degustación* for around €32. Daily 1–4pm & 8–midnight; closed Aug.

★ **El Gallo** c/María Cristina 6. Another classic old *cordobés* drinking hole, which has changed little since it opened at the turn of the twentieth century; try their *gambas rebozadas* (fried prawns) washed down with outstanding *amargoso montilla* from their own *bodega*. Daily 1–5pm & 7pm–1am.

Mesón San Basilio c/San Basilio 19. Good, unpretentious and busy local restaurant offering well-prepared fish and meat *raciones* and *platos combinados*, plus weekday *menús* for €8 (lunch) and €18 (dinner). Wed–Mon noon–4pm & 8pm–midnight; closed Tues.

Los Mochuelos c/Agustín Moreno 51. Traditional tapas and *raciones* restaurant with large variety of dishes including *revuelto de setas con salmón* (scrambled eggs with wild mushrooms and salmon) and *mochuelitos* (spicy meat); plenty of atmosphere, stacked sherry butts, bullfight posters and a pleasant patio. Daily 8.30am–4.30pm & 7pm–midnight.

La Pataita c/Barroso 3. Decent tapas bar in the Judería with song and dance flamenco performances on Fri & Sat at 10pm (€12). On Fri & Sat at 4pm and 6pm you get a free flamenco show (singing only) for the price of a drink in the bar. Daily 8am–11pm.

El Rincón del Carmen c/Romero 4. Small, pleasant café-restaurant with a charming patio terrace below and restaurant upstairs, serving reasonably priced *raciones* and *media raciones*. *Menú* for €15. Daily 9am–midnight.

★ **Taberna Salinas** c/Tundidores 3. Century-old, reasonably priced *taberna* with dining rooms around a charming patio. Good *raciones* place – try their *naranjas con bacalao* (cod with oranges) – and serves a great *salmorejo*. 12.30–4pm & 8–11.30pm. Closed Sun & Aug.

Taberna San Miguel (El Pisto) Pl. San Miguel 1. Known to all as *El Pisto* (The Barrel), this is one of the city's legendary bars – over a century old – and not to be missed. Wonderful *montilla* and tapas; *rabo de toro* and *callos en salsa picante* (tripe in spicy sauce) are house specials. Mon–Sat noon–4pm & 8.30pm–12.30am; closed Sun & Aug.

4

THE RISE AND FALL OF MEDINA AZAHARA

Medina Azahara was a perfect symbol of the western caliphate's extent and greatness, but it was to last for less than a century. Al-Hakam II, who succeeded Abd ar-Rahman, lived in the palace, continued to endow it, and enjoyed a stable reign. However, distanced from the city, he delegated more and more authority, particularly to his vizier Ibn Abi Amir, later known as **al-Mansur** (the Victor). In 976, al-Hakam was succeeded by his 11-year-old son Hisham II and, after a series of sharp moves, al-Mansur assumed the full powers of government, keeping Hisham virtually imprisoned at Medina Azahara, to the extent of blocking up connecting passageways between the palace buildings.

Al-Mansur was equally skilful and manipulative in his wider dealings as a dictator, retaking large tracts of central Spain and raiding as far afield as Galicia and Catalunya; consequently, Córdoba rose to new heights of prosperity. But with his death in 1002 came swift decline, as his role and function were assumed in turn by his two sons. The first died in 1008; the second, Sanchol, showed open disrespect for the caliphate by forcing Hisham to appoint him as his successor. At this, a popular revolt broke out and the caliphate disintegrated into civil war and a series of feudal kingdoms. Medina Azahara was looted by a mob at the outset, and in 1010 was plundered and burned by retreating Berber mercenaries.

Medina Azahara

April–Sept Tues–Sat 10am–8.30pm, Sun 10am–2pm; Oct–March Tues–Sat 10am–2pm & 5–6.30pm, Sun 10am–2pm; confirm winter hours with site ☎ 957 355 506 • €1.50, free with EU passport but a ticket still needs to be collected

Seven kilometres to the northwest of Córdoba lie the vast and rambling ruins of **Medina Azahara**, a palace complex built on a dream scale by **Caliph Abd ar-Rahman III**. Naming it after a favourite, az-Zahra (the Radiant), he spent one-third of the annual state budget on its construction each year from 936 until his death in 961. Ten thousand workers and 1500 mules and camels were employed on the project, and the site, almost 2km long by 900m wide, stretched over three descending terraces. In addition to the palace buildings, it had a zoo, an aviary, four fishponds, three hundred baths, four hundred houses, weapons factories and two barracks for the royal guard. Visitors, so the chronicles record, were stunned by its wealth and brilliance: one conference room was provided with pure crystals, creating a rainbow when lit by the sun; another was built round a huge pool of mercury.

The Royal House

For centuries following its downfall the site continued to be looted for building materials; parts, for instance, were used in the Seville Alcázar. But in 1944 excavations unearthed the remains of a crucial part of the palace – the **Royal House**, where guests were received and meetings of ministers held. This has been meticulously reconstructed and, though still fragmentary, its main hall must rank among the greatest of all Moorish rooms. It has a different kind of stuccowork from that at Granada or Seville – closer to natural and animal forms in its intricate Syrian *Hom* (Tree of Life) motifs. Unlike the later Spanish Arab dynasties, the Berber Almoravids and the Almohads of Seville, the caliphal Andalucians were little worried by Islamic strictures on the portrayal of nature, animals or even men – the beautiful hind in the Córdoba museum is a good example – and it may well have been this aspect of the palace that led to such zealous destruction during the civil war.

The reconstruction of the palace gives a scale and focus to the site. Elsewhere, you have little more than foundations to fuel your imaginings, amid an awesome area of ruins, hidden beneath bougainvillea and rustling with cicadas. Perhaps the most obvious of the outbuildings yet excavated is the Aljama mosque, just beyond the Royal House, which sits at an angle to the rest of the buildings in order to face Mecca.

The gardens

A decade ago, biologists from Córdoba University carried out a study of soil samples from the site to gain an understanding of exactly which plants and flowers the Moors had cultivated in the extensive **gardens**. When the study was completed, reconstructive planting began, and the trees, shrubs and herbs are now maturing into a delightful and aromatic garden the caliphs would recognize.

ARRIVAL AND DEPARTURE MEDINA AZAHARA

By car To reach the Centro de Interpretación, follow Avda. de Medina Azahara west out of town, onto the road to Villarubia and Posadas. About 4km down this road, make a right turn (signed for the site), after which it's another 1km to the Centro de Interpretación. Note that you are now obliged to park your car here and take the dedicated bus service to the site. If you continue up the road to the site car park (now for staff only) you will arrive at a locked gate forcing you to turn around and go back.

By bus City bus #01 from a stop on the Avda. de la República Argentina (at the northern end, near a petrol station) will drop you off at the intersection from where it's a 1km walk to the Centro de Interpretación. Ask the driver for "El Cruce de Medina Azahara". A dedicated bus service also links the city with the site (April–Sept Tues–Sat 10.15am & 5pm, Sun 9.30am & 10.15am; Oct–March Tue–Sun 9.30am & 10.15am; €7 return which includes the bus to the site). The bus departs from a signed stop on the Glorieta (roundabout) Cruz Roja at the southern end of Paseo de la Victoria (confirm

this at the tourist office), but tickets must be purchased in advance from any municipal tourist office kiosk (see p.319). Tickets cannot be purchased on the bus.

By taxi A taxi will cost you about €25 one way for up to five people, or there's a special round-trip deal ("Taxi-Tour Córdoba") for €45, which includes a one-hour wait at the site while you visit. A convenient taxi rank is located outside the *turismo* on the west side of the Mezquita.

Guided trips Córdoba Vision runs guided trips to the site (Tues–Sun 11am; €20; ☎ 957 299 777, English spoken); buses leave from the same stop on Avda. del Alcázar as the bus service. The tour bus will park at the Centro de Interpretación and both you and the guide will use the bus service to the site.

Visiting the site Visitors must arrive at the Centro de Interpretación, a complex incorporating a museum, shop and *cafetería*; from here take a bus (every 10–20min; €2.10 return) from the car park for the 2km journey to the site; once you have your ticket you can walk to the site but it is all uphill.

Jaén province

There are said to be over 150 million olive trees in the province of Jaén. They dominate the landscape as infinite rows of green against the orange-red earth, occasionally interspersed with stark white farm buildings. It's beautiful on a grand, sweeping scale, though concealing a bitter and entrenched economic reality. The majority of the olive groves are owned by a mere handful of families, and for most residents this is a very poor area.

Sights may not be as plentiful here as in other parts of Andalucía, but there are a few gems worth going out of your way to take in. Fairly dull in itself, the provincial capital of **Jaén** merits a visit for its fine cathedral and Moorish baths, while farther to the northwest **Baeza** and **Úbeda** are two remarkable Renaissance towns filled with architectural gems. Extending northeast from the town of Cazorla, **Parque Natural de Cazorla**, Andalucía's biggest natural park, is a vast expanse of dense woodlands, lakes and spectacular crags.

Jaén

JAÉN, the provincial capital and by far the largest town, is an uneventful sort of place with traces of its Moorish past in the winding, narrow streets of the old quarter and in the largest surviving Moorish baths in Spain. Activity is centred on Plaza de la Constitución and its two arterial streets, Paseo de la Estación and Avda. de Madrid. The town is overlooked by the Cerro de Santa Catalina, a wooded hill topped by a recently restored Moorish fort, now partly transformed into a spectacular parador.

Catedral

Mon–Sat 10am–2pm & 4–7pm, Sun 10am–noon & 4–7pm; museum daily 10.30am–1pm & 5–8pm • Church free, museum €5

West of the focal Plaza de la Constitución is the imposing seventeenth-century Renaissance **Catedral**, by the great local architect Andrés de Vandelvira, whose design had the most influence over the building as it looks today. The spectacular **west facade**, flanked by twin sixty-metre-high towers framing Corinthian pillars and statuary by the seventeenth-century master Pedro Roldán, is one of the masterpieces of Andalucian Renaissance architecture.

Baños Árabes

Tues–Sat 9am–9.30pm, Sun 9.15am–2.45pm • Free

To the north of the cathedral, between the churches of San Andrés and Santo Domingo, you'll find the painstakingly restored Moorish *hammam* in the **Baños Árabes**. Among the finest of their kind in Spain, the baths were originally part of an eleventh-century Moorish palace, and are now located inside the sixteenth-century Palacio de Villardompardo, which was constructed over it. On view are the various rooms (containing hot, tepid and cold baths), with pillars supporting elegant horseshoe arches and brickwork ceilings pierced with distinctive star-shaped windows.

Museo Provincial

Tues 2.30–8.30pm, Wed–Sat 9am–8.30pm, Sun 9am–2.30pm • Free

Jaén's **Museo Provincial**, Paseo de la Estación 29, has a large archeological collection including some remarkable fifth-century-BC Iberian sculptures, now set to become the centrepiece of a major new museum of Iberian art.

ARRIVAL AND INFORMATION	JAÉN

By train The train station (☎ 953 270 202) lies to the left a further 1km or so beyond, along Paseo de la Estación (bus #19 from the centre).

Destinations Cádiz (3 daily, change at Córdoba; 4hr 30min); Córdoba (4 daily; 1hr 30min); Madrid (3 daily Mon–Sat, daily Sun); Seville (3 daily; 2hr 50min).

By bus The bus station (☎ 953 250 106) is at Pl. Coca de la Pinera, 300m northeast of Pl. de la Constitución.

Destinations Almería (4 daily; 4hr); Baeza/Úbeda (15 daily; 1hr 25min); Cazorla (2 daily; 2hr 30min); Córdoba (8 daily; 2hr); Granada (14 daily; 1hr 10min); Madrid (5 daily; 4hr 20min); Málaga (4 daily; 3hr 15min); Seville (daily; 4hr).

Turismo To the rear of the cathedral on c/Ramón y Cajal (Mon–Fri 9am–7.30pm, Sat & Sun 9.30am–3pm; ☎ 953 190 455, ⊛ www.aytojaen.es).

Internet access is available at the central Almadena Telecom, c/Hurtado 18 (daily 11am–3pm & 5–11pm).

ACCOMMODATION

Places to stay in town are limited and – with the exception of a youth hostel – relatively expensive. There's usually no problem in finding accommodation at any time of the year and there are no seasonal rate changes. Mosquitoes can be a real problem in the town during the high summer season when places with air-conditioning come into their own.

★ **Albergue Inturjoven** c/Borja s/n ☎ 953 313 540, ⊛ www.inturjoven.com. Behind the imposing facade of a former eighteenth-century hospital lies the new youth hostel's excellent modern, if minimalist in style, en-suite a/c rooms and "apartments" (which add a *salón* but no kitchen). There's also a pool. Somewhat incongruously the *albergue* also houses a full-blown spa with a variety of detox and anti-*edad* (ageing) cures costing much more than the rooms. Under-25 **€21**, over-25 **€27**

Hostal Estación RENFE Estación de Tren ☎ 953 27 46 14, ⊛ www.hostalestacionferrocarriljaen.com. RENFE's own *hostal* at the front of the station is a rather swish affair

with comfortable a/c rooms with TV, wi-fi throughout and a car park. **€56**

Hotel Europa Pl. de Belén 1 ☎ 953 22 27 00, ⊛ www. gremiodehospedaje.com. Perhaps the best of the more upmarket places in the centre, where attractive a/c rooms come with safe and satellite TV. Garage. B&B **€85**

★ **Parador Castillo de Santa Catalina** Castillo, sited on a hill 3km from town ☎ 953 23 00 00, ⊛ parador.es. For a truly memorable experience you could stay at this most spectacularly sited hotel. The comfortable rooms have fine balcony views with a sheer drop to the valley below; facilities include a pool, restaurant, bar and ample parking. **€161**

EATING AND DRINKING

C/Nueva, off the east side of Pl. Constitución, has a clutch of **places to eat** and there is a bunch of tapas bars in the streets to the north of the cathedral.

Bar del Posito Pl. Deán Mazas s/n. Above the west side of the focal Pl. de la Constitución, you'll find this busy café-bar which serves tapas and *raciones* until late; also has a terrace with outdoor tables. Daily noon–midnight.

La Gamba de Oro c/Nueva 5. A solid choice for seafood tapas and *raciones*. Serves a wide tapas range and also has a menú for €10. Daily 11am–5pm & 8pm–midnight.

Mesón Río Chico c/Nueva 12. Popular tapas bar and *marisquería*. House specials include *almejas al ajillo* (clams in garlic) and a signature dish *pastel de verduras* (vegetable tart). Daily noon–4.30pm & 8pm–midnight.

Tasca Los Amigos c/Bernardo López 10, slightly north of the cathedral. Atmospheric neighbourhood tapas bar specializing in *jamón* and *morcilla* (blood pudding); there's a cluster of similar bars in the surrounding streets and alleys. Daily 10am–4pm & 7.30pm–1am.

La Viña c/Maestra 8. This is a stylish *cervecería*, restaurant and *raciones* bar with a pleasant street terrace. Serves a range of salads – try the *ensalada de naranja* – as well as full meals. Daily 9am–5pm & 8–11pm.

Baeza

Less than an hour from Jaén are the elegant twin towns of Baeza and Úbeda. Each has an extraordinary density of exuberant Renaissance palaces and richly endowed churches, plus fine public squares. Both towns were captured from the Moors by Fernando el Santo and, repopulated with his knights, stood for two centuries at the frontiers of the reconquered lands facing the Moorish kingdom of Granada.

   BAEZA is tiny, compact and provincial, with a perpetual Sunday air about it. At its heart is the Plaza Mayor – comprised of two linked plazas, Plaza de la Constitucíon at the southern end with a garden, and smaller Plaza de España to the north – flanked by cafés and very much the hub of the town's limited animation.

   There are no charges to enter any of Baeza's monuments (except the cathedral), but you may offer the guardian a small *propina* (tip).

4

Plaza de Leones

The **Plaza de Leones**, an appealing cobbled square enclosed by Renaissance buildings, stands slightly back at the southern end of Plaza de la Constitución. Enclosed by Renaissance buildings with an ancient central fountain, its eastern flank has the former Audiencia (court house), now housing the *turismo*. Here, on a rounded balcony, the first Mass of the Reconquest is reputed to have been celebrated. The adjoining gate, the Puerta de Jaén, was a memento (or rebuke) left by Carlos V to the town that had opposed him and commemorates the Germanic ruler's procession through here in 1526, en route to marry Isabel of Portugal.

Palacio de Jabalquinto

Patio open Mon–Fri 9am–2pm

Finest of the town's mansions is the **Palacio de Jabalquinto**, now a seminary, with an elaborate "Isabelline" front (showing marked Moorish influence in its stalactite decoration). Built in the fifteenth century by the Benavides family, the tranquil interior patio has a double tier of arcades around a central fountain and a superb Baroque **staircase** with fine carving.

Catedral de Santa María

Mon–Fri 10am–2pm & 4–7pm, Sat & Sun 10am–7pm • Church free; museum with audio-guide €4

Close by, the rather squat sixteenth-century **Catedral de Santa María**, is another design by Vandelvira. Like many of Baeza and Úbeda's churches, it has brilliant painted *rejas* (iron screens) created in the sixteenth century by Maestro Bartolomé, the Spanish master of this craft. His work enclosing the choir, with depictions of a Virgin and Child accompanied by angels and cherubs, is stunning. In the cloister, part of the old mosque (which the church replaced) has been uncovered, but the cathedral's real novelty is a huge silver *custodia* – cunningly hidden behind a painting of St Peter, which whirls aside for a €1 coin.

Walks

There are some good **walks** around town; wandering up through the Puerta de Jaén on Plaza de los Leones and along the Paseo de las Muralla (aka Paseo de Don Antonio Machado) takes you round the edge of Baeza with fine views over the surrounding plains. You can cut back to Plaza Mayor via the network of narrow stone-walled alleys – with the occasional arch – that lies behind the cathedral.

ARRIVAL AND INFORMATION   BAEZA

By bus The bus station (☎953 742 453) is at the end of c/San Pablo and along Paseo Arca del Agua.

By train The nearest train station is Linares-Baeza, 14km from Baeza and served by frequent trains from Seville, Córdoba and Granada (there's a connecting bus for most trains, except Sat & Sun; €20 taxi ride). Most bus connections are via Úbeda.

Turismo On Pl. de Leones, in the former Audiencia or court building (Mon–Fri 9am–7.30pm, Sat & Sun 9.30am–3pm; ☎953 779 982), where you can pick up a map; they can also provide details of daily guided tours of the town.

Internet access is available at the central Micro Ware, c/Portales Tundidores 13, facing Paseo de la Constitución (Mon–Thurs 10.30am–2pm & 5–9.30pm, Fri–Sun 11am–2pm & 5–10pm).

ACCOMMODATION

The town has a decent range of **places to stay**, some of which are architectural gems. There's usually no problem finding rooms in Baeza except during the summer *feria* in mid-August and even then you should have no trouble if you ring ahead. It's worth noting that many hotels have a weekend surcharge policy so if you can avoid a Friday-to-Saturday stay prices often fall considerably.

★ **Aznaitin** c/Cabreros 2, to the southeast of Pl. de los Leones ☎953 740 788, ⓦwww.hostalaznaitin .com. Splendid new *hostal* in the old quarter with stylishly decorated en-suite rooms. Friendly service, attractive pool, wi-fi zone and breakfast included adds up to an outstanding deal. Easy parking nearby or use their garage. Reduced rates Sun–Thurs. €53

Hotel Baeza c/Concepción 3 ☎953 748 130, ⓦwww .trhhoteles.com. Well-equipped a/c rooms partly housed in a stylishly converted Renaissance monastery with a glassed-in patio. They do frequent cut-price deals so it's worth giving them a ring or checking the website. B&B €50–70

Hotel Baeza Monumental c//Cuesta de Prieto 6 ☎953 73 72 82, ⓦwww.hotelbaezamonumental.com. Very pleasant small hotel with attractive rooms equipped with plasma satellite TV, minibar, strongbox; and there's internet access plus a car park. B&B €70 (reduced rates Sun–Thurs).

★ **Hotel Puerta de la Luna** c/Pintada Alta s/n ☎953 74 70 19, ⓦwww.hotelpuertadelaluna.com. Beautiful four-star hotel situated in a refurbished seventeenth-century *casa palacio*. Facilities include two delightful patios, restaurant, gym, library, spa and a small pool. The comfortably furnished tiled-floor rooms are airy and well equipped, and it has its own car park. €90

EATING AND DRINKING

La Almazara c/Benavides 15, slightly east of the Pl. de España. A good place for dining alfresco is the pleasant terrace of this mid-priced restaurant. The bonus of a terrace table is also being able to feast your eyes on Baeza's magnificent sixteenth-century *ayuntamiento* opposite. Serves well-prepared meat, fish and game dishes and there's a weekday *menú* for €11 or €18 weekends. Daily noon–4pm & 8–11pm.

Cafetería Mercantil Pl. de España s/n. This century-old bar is a great place to kick off your day with a lazy breakfast on the town's best terrace. Late in the day it serves good tapas and *raciones* and there's a winter dining room upstairs. Tapas include *tortilla española* (Spanish omelette) and *boquerones en vinagre* (anchovies). Daily 8.30am–11pm.

El Sarmiento Pl. del Ardeciano 10, behind the cathedral. Specializing in *carnes asados* (roasted meat dishes) this is an excellent restaurant with a pleasant terrace on this attractive square; there's a weekday *menú* for €17. Daily 1.30–5pm & 8.30–midnight; closed Sun eve & Mon.

Úbeda

ÚBEDA, 9km east of Baeza and built on the same escarpment overlooking the valley of the Guadalquivir, looks less promising when you reach it. Don't be put off by the modern suburbs, though, for hidden away in the old quarter is one of the finest architectural jewels in the whole of Spain, and perhaps even Europe. Follow the signs to the Zona Monumental and you'll eventually reach the **Plaza de Vázquez de Molina**, a tremendous Renaissance square and one of the most impressive of its kind on the peninsula. Most of the buildings round the square are the late sixteenth-century work of Andrés de Vandelvira, the architect of Baeza's cathedral and numerous churches in both towns. One of these buildings, the **Palacio de las Cadenas**, originally a palace for Felipe II's secretary, houses Úbeda's *ayuntamiento* and features a magnificent facade fronted by monumental lions.

Capilla del Salvador
Mon–Sat 10am–2pm & 4.30–7pm, Sun 11.15am–2pm & 4.30–7.30pm • €3

At the eastern end of the square, the **Capilla del Salvador**, erected by Vandelvira, though actually designed by Diego de Siloé, architect of the Málaga and Granada cathedrals, is the finest church in Úbeda. It's a masterpiece of Spanish Renaissance architecture with a dazzling Plateresque facade, its highlight a carving of the Transfiguration of Christ flanked by statues of San Pedro and San Andrés. Inside, the Transfiguration theme is repeated in a brilliantly animated *retablo* by Alonso de Berruguete, who studied under Michelangelo. Entry to the church is via a doorway on the south side.

San Pablo
Mon–Wed 11am–noon, Tues–Fri 11am–1pm & 5–7.30pm, Sat 11am–1pm, Sun 12.15–1.30pm

Following calles Contador and Horno north out of Plaza de Vázquez de Molina leads to yet another delightful square, Plaza del Primero de Mayo, with a bandstand and superb arcaded sixteenth-century **Ayuntamiento Viejo** (Old Town Hall) from where councillors once watched heretics – denounced by the Inquisition – burn in fires located on the site of the modern bandstand. Here also is the idiosyncratic church of **San Pablo**, incorporating various Romanesque, Gothic and Renaissance additions and crowned by a Plateresque tower. It also boasts a thirteenth-century exterior and a superb portal.

INFORMATION   ÚBEDA

Turismo Housed in its own Renaissance mansion, the Palacio del Marqués de Contadero, c/Baja Marqués 4, just to the west of the Pl. de Vázquez de Molina (Mon–Fri 9am–7.30pm, Sat & Sun 9.30am–3pm; ☎ 953 779 204), can provide a town map.

ACCOMMODATION

You'll find the only budget **places to stay** within walking distance of the bus station, in the modern part of town. The *casco antiguo* (old quarter) now has a choice of more upmarket places, some in stunning ancient palaces and mansions. Úbeda's high season is in April and May and thus hotel (but not *hostal*) rooms tend to be significantly cheaper in July and August. As in Baeza, many hotels apply a Friday-to-Saturday surcharge.

Hostal Victoria c/Alaminos 5 ☎ 953 79 17 18. A five-minute walk east of the bus station, this is a comfortable, welcoming *hostal* offering pleasant, a/c en-suite rooms with TV. It has its own car park, too. €38

Hotel María de Molina Pl. del Ayuntamiento s/n ☎ 953 795 356, ◍ www.hotelmariademolina.es. In the heart of the old quarter, this hotel is housed in a magnificent sixteenth-century *casa palacio* with a superb patio. Rooms come with a/c, strongbox and satellite TV, and some have balconies. Also has a pool, solarium and free wi-fi. €80

★ **Parador Condestable Dávalos** Pl. de Vázquez de Molina 1 ☎ 953 750 345, ◍ parador.es. On arguably the most beautiful *plaza* in Andalucía, Úbeda's parador is housed in a fabulous sixteenth-century Renaissance mansion, with some of the well-appointed rooms overlooking the square. Call in for a drink if you're not staying. €180

Rosaleda de Don Pedro c/Obispo Toral 2, in the old quarter ☎ 953 796 111, ◍ www.rosaledadedonpedro .com. Efficient three-star hotel offering well-equipped rooms with satellite TV and a small pool in their terrace garden at the rear. Has own restaurant, library and garage. €54

EATING AND DRINKING

There are plenty of **places to eat** around Avda. Ramón y Cajal in the new town.

El Gallo Rojo c/Torrenueva 3, north of the old quarter. Set back from the road, this is one of the town's better and more reasonably priced restaurants, offering local specialities such as *jabalí al horno* (oven-baked wild boar) and a *menú* for €12 and outdoor tables in the evening. Daily noon–midnight.

Parador Condestable Dávalos Pl. de Vázquez de Molina 1. If you want to dine in style in the old quarter, the parador's expensive restaurant serves superbly prepared regional dishes that are available on a tasting *menú* (€38); there are also equally good-value lunchtime and evening *menús* for €33. Daily 1–4pm & 8–11pm.

Pintor Orbaneja c/Virgen de Guadalupe 5. Just north of *El Gallo Rojo*, this place serves up tapas in its bar and more elaborate fish and meat dishes in its adjoining restaurant.

There's a weekday *menú* for €13. Main dishes €8–15. Daily 11am–5pm & 8–11pm.

Restaurante Marqués Pl. Marqués de la Rambla 2. Serves a good-value *menú* for €15 often featuring *merluza con almejas y esparragos* (hake with clams and asparagus). Also has a terrace on this picturesque square. Daily 1–4pm & 8–11pm.

El Seco c/Corazón de Jesús 8. Close to the Pl. del Ayuntamiento, this mid-priced restaurant is a cut above the norm; it is noted for its tasty *potaje carmelitano* (chickpea, leek and cod soup) but also does excellent meat and game dishes and there's a weekday *menú*. Main dishes €12–20. Daily 1–4pm & 8–11pm; closed evenings Sun–Thurs.

Cazorla

During the Reconquest of Andalucía, **CAZORLA** acted as an outpost for Christian troops, and the two castles that still dominate the town testify to its turbulent past – both were originally Moorish but later altered and restored by their Christian conquerors. Today, it's the main base for visits to the **Parque Natural de las Sierras de Segura y Cazorla**, a vast protected area of magnificent river gorges and forests. Cazorla also hosts the **Fiesta de Cristo del Consuelo**, with fairgrounds, fireworks and religious processions on September 16–21.

Cazorla itself is constructed around three main squares. Buses arrive in the busy, commercial **Plaza de la Constitución**, linked by the main c/de Muñoz to the second square, **Plaza de la Corredera** (or *del Huevo*, "of the Egg", because of its shape). The *ayuntamiento* is here, a fine Moorish-style palace at the far end of the plaza. Beyond, a labyrinth of narrow, twisting streets descends to Cazorla's liveliest square, **Plaza de Santa María**, which takes its name from the old cathedral that, damaged by floods in the seventeenth century, was later torched by Napoleonic troops. Its ruins, now preserved, and the fine open square form a natural amphitheatre for concerts and local events as well as being a popular meeting place.

Museo de Artes y Costumbres

Pl. de Santa María • Tues 3–8pm, Wed–Sat 9am–8pm, Sun 9am–2pm • Free

The lower square, Plaza de Santa María, is dominated by **La Yedra**, an austere, reconstructed castle tower, which houses the **Museo de Artes y Costumbres**, an interesting folklore museum displaying domestic utensils, clothing, textiles and furniture from bygone times.

INFORMATION   CAZORLA

Turismo is at Paseo del Santo Cristo 17, 100m north of Pl. de la Constitución (daily: April–Sept 10am–2pm & 5.30–8pm; Oct–March 10am–2pm & 5–7.30pm; ☎953 710 102, ⓦwww.cazorla.es), and can provide a useful town map. There's also a privately run office inside a shop called La Despensa del Parque in Pl. de la Constitución (daily 10am–1pm & 5.30–9pm; ☎953 721 351, ⓦwww.turisnat.org); this also acts as an agent for Turisnat, one of the major providers of activities in the park, and ostensibly exists to promote Land Rover excursions, photo safaris and the like. However, they do sell the reliable Editorial Alpina hiking maps for the *parque natural*.

PARQUE NATURAL DE LAS SIERRAS DE SEGURA Y CAZORLA

Even casual visitors to **Parque Natural de las Sierras de Segura y Cazorla** are likely to see a good variety of wildlife, including *Capra hispanica* (Spanish mountain goat), deer, wild pig, birds and butterflies. Ironically, though, much of the best viewing will be at the periphery, or even outside the park, since the wildlife is most successfully stalked on foot and walking opportunities within the park itself are surprisingly limited.

The main **information centre** inside the park is the Torre del Vinagre Centro de Interpretación (Tues–Sun 10am–2pm & 5–8pm, Oct–March 4–6pm; ☎953 713 017). It's worth getting hold of a good **map** from here (also available from Despensa del Parque in Cazorla): the 1:100,000 map, *Parque Natural de las Sierras de Cazorla y Segura*, and the 1:50,000 version, *Cazorla*, are recommended, but best of all is the 1:40,000 set of map and guide packs to the Sierras de Cazorla and Segura (divided into three zones), published by Editorial Alpina, which are the most accurate maps available, detailing *senderos* (footpaths), mountain-bike routes, refuges, campsites and hotels. In addition to the hiking routes marked on the maps above, Guy Hunter-Watts' *Walking in Andalucía* details five clearly described walks in the park of between 5km and 19km.

Two daily **buses** link Cazorla with **Coto Ríos** (Mon–Fri only depart 7.15am & 2.30pm, return 9am & 4.15pm; 1hr 15min) in the middle of the park (confirm these with the bus company Carcesa on ☎953 721 142). Distances between points are enormous, so to explore the park well you'll need a car or to be prepared for long treks.

There are ten official **campsites** throughout the park, which are accurately marked on the Editorial Alpina map. There's more accommodation at Coto Ríos, with three privately run campsites and a succession of *hostales*. Before setting out, you can also get the latest update on transport, campsites and accommodation from the *turismo* in Cazorla.

4

ACCOMMODATION

Outside August, finding a **place to stay** is usually no problem, as most visitors are either en route to, or leaving, the park. It's worth noting that outside the high summer months it can get quite chilly here in the evenings and while all the hotel rooms have heating, not all the *hostales* do, so enquire if you think this may be a problem.

Albergue Juvenil Pl. Mauricio Martínez 6 ☎953 711 301, ⊛www.inturjoven.com. Cazorla's tidy youth hostel, housed in a former convent, has some double rooms and a pool, and is reached by following c/Juan Domingo (reached via steps) from Pl. de la Constitución. B&B.Under 26 **€16.50**, over 26 **€27**

Camping Cortijo ☎953 72 12 80. Cazorla's campsite is located beyond the Castillo de la Yedra, 1km from the centre; to get there, follow the Camino San Isicio from Pl. de Santa María.

Hostal Betis Pl. Corredera 19 ☎953 72 05 40. Friendly proprietor, central location and good-value accommodation for rooms sharing bath; rooms at the rear (nos. 101–104) have great views. **€26**

Hotel Guadalquivir c/Nueva 6 ☎953 720 268, ⊛www.hguadalquivir.com. Central, charming and friendly small hotel offering en-suite a/c rooms with fridge and TV. Free internet access and wi-fi. **€45**

Hotel Sierra de Cazorla 2km outside Cazorla, in the village of La Iruela ☎953 72 00 15, ⊛www.hotel sierradecazorla.com. Modern complex comprising three- and four-star hotels plus a spa. The three-star option is particularly good-value with balcony rooms (best views from A10–A17) and scenic surroundings; there's also a restaurant, bar and great pool. Produces its own walks guide for guests. Surcharge in Aug. **€68**

Parador El Adelantado 25km away in the park ☎953 72 70 75, ⊛parador.es. Somewhat featureless modern building made attractive by its wonderful woodland setting and a swimming pool. Make sure to get a room with a view (rooms 4–11 and 18–22 are the ones to go for). Also has its own bar and restaurant. **€133**

Pensión Taxi Travesía de San Antón 7 ☎953 720 525. Up steps opposite the bus stop in Pl. de la Constitución, this is a friendly budget option with a good-value *comedor* (dining room). En-suite rooms have a/c, heating and TV. **€40**

EATING AND DRINKING

★ **Bar La Montería** Pl. de la Corredera 20. One of the most popular of Cazorla's tapas bars this has a short – but top-quality – *menú*. Patatas a lo pobre (sautéed potatoes with garlic) is a house special or you could try their noted "*plato olímpico*" for €5 which gets you a selection of tapas

to share. Daily 11am–5pm & 8–11pm.

Bar Rincón Serrano Pl. de la Corredera 12, on the same square as the above. Another good bar which is usually packed due to its custom of giving a free *tapa* (which is chosen for you) with every drink. Daily 11am–5pm & 8–11pm.

Mesón la Cueva Pl. Santa María 10. Atmospheric and rustic bar-restaurant offering tapas and *raciones* including *ensalada de pimientos* (grilled peppers). The restaurant serves up mountain fare such as wild boar and venison cooked on a wood-fired range; the *conejo* (rabbit) is recommended. Daily 11am–5pm & 8–11pm.

Mesón Don Chema Escaleras del Mercado 2. Down steps off focal c/Muñoz, this is an economical restaurant specializing in *carnes de monte* (mountain game). Other specialities

include *jamón ibérico* and *queso curado* (cured cheese). Also has a *menú* for €12. Daily noon–4pm & 8–11pm.

★ **La Sarga** Pl. del Mercado 13 ☎953 721 507. Cazorla's top **restaurant** with a very pleasant room; *lomo de jabalí en salsa de castañas* (wild boar with chestnut sauce) is one of a number of game options prepared here, and there's a daily *menú* for €18 or a *menú de degustación* for €27. Alternatively, they offer a five-creative-tapas selection for €9.50. Daily 1.30–4pm & 8.30–11pm.

Granada

If you see only one town in Spain, it should be **GRANADA**. For here, extraordinarily well preserved and in a tremendous natural setting, stands the **Alhambra** – the most exciting, sensual and romantic of all European monuments. It was the palace fortress of the Nasrid sultans, rulers of the last Spanish Moorish kingdom, and in its construction Moorish art reached a spectacular and serene climax. But the building seems to go further than this, revealing something of the whole brilliance and spirit of Moorish life and culture. There's a haunting passage in Jan Morris' book, *Spain*, which the palace embodies:

"Life itself, which was seen elsewhere in Europe as a kind of probationary preparation for death, was interpreted [by the Moors] as something glorious in itself, to be ennobled by learning and enlivened by every kind of pleasure."

Built on the slopes of three hills, the rest of the city basks in the Alhambra's reflected glory. Because the Moorish influence here was so ruthlessly extinguished following capitulation to the Catholic monarchs Fernando and Isabel, Granada tends to be more sober in character and austere in its architecture than Andalucía's other provincial capitals. Many visitors, once they've viewed the Alhambra, are too jaded or can't be fussed to take in the city's other sights, which is a pity, for Granada has much to offer. The hill-top **Albaicín**, the former Moorish town, is a fascinating quarter full of narrow alleyways and small squares, and a great place for an hour's stroll. Not far away, too, is the cathedral with the gem of the **Capilla Real** attached to it, the final resting place of the Catholic monarchs who ended Moorish rule in Spain. Add in an **archeological museum**, **Moorish baths** and some fine churches, including a spectacular **La Cartuja** monastery, and you have more than enough to start you thinking about extending your stay.

The Alhambra

Daily 8.30am–8pm, Nov–March until 6pm; last admission 1hr before closing time • €13

There are three distinct groups of buildings on the Alhambra hill: the **Palacios Nazaríes** (Royal Palace, or Nasrid Palaces), the palace gardens of the **Generalife** and the **Alcazaba**. This last, the fortress of the eleventh-century Ziridian rulers, was all that existed when the Nasrid ruler Ibn al-Ahmar made Granada his capital, but from its reddish walls the hill top had already taken its name: *Al Qal'a al-Hamra* in Arabic means literally "the red fort". Ibn al-Ahmar rebuilt the Alcazaba and added to it the huge circuit of walls and towers that forms your first view of the castle. Within the walls he began a palace, which he supplied with running water by diverting the River Darro nearly 8km to the foot of the hill; water is an integral part of the Alhambra and this engineering feat was Ibn al-Ahmar's greatest contribution. The Palacios Nazaríes was essentially the product of his fourteenth-century successors, particularly Yusuf I and Mohammed V, who built and redecorated many of its rooms in celebration of his accession to the throne (in 1354) and the taking of Algeciras (in 1369).

THE ALHAMBRA >

ACCOMMODATION

Albergue Juvenil	19
Casa del Aljarife	7
Casa del Capitel Nazari	8
Casa Morisca	3
Hostal Britz	10
Hostal Costa Azul	14
Hostal Landázuri	11
Hostal San Joaquin	15
Hostal Viena	9
Hostal Zurita	18
Hotel América	5
Hotel Albero	17
Hotel Guadalupe	2
Hotel Los Angeles	13
Hotel Macía Plaza	12
Hotel Palacio Santa Inés	6
Hotel Los Tilos	16
Parador de San Francisco	4
Posada Doña Lupe	1

RESTAURANTS & TAPAS BARS

Al Sur de Granada	9
Bar-Restaurante Sevilla	14
Bodegas Castañeda	11
Bodegas La Mancha	13
El Carmen de San Miguel	5
Casa Cepillo	16
Casa López Correa	8
Mesón La Alegría	15
Mesón casa Blas	7
Mesón El Trillo del Reca	4
La Mimbre	1
La Ninfa	6
Parador de San Francisco	2
Restaurante-Bar Las Tomasas	3
Restaurante León	10
Restaurante-Marisquería Cunini	17
Seis Peniques	12

Casa del Chapiz

SAN LUIS

ALBAICÍN

CARRIL DE SAN AGUSTÍN

FRAILES DE S. AGUSTÍN

SAN GREGORIO ALTO

PAGES

Iglesia del Salvador

S. Juan de los Reyes

PANADEROS

Mirador de San Nicolás

Arco de las Pesas

PL. DE S. NICOLÁS

NUEVA DE SAN NICOLÁS

San Bartolomé

ALJIBE DE TRILLO

Cvto. de la Concepción

LARGA SAN CRISTÓBAL

MIRADOR DE ROLANDO

CENICEROS

San Cristóbal

PILAR SECO

Cvto. de Sta. Inés

Cvto. de Sta. Isabel la Real

CARRETERA DE MURCIA

CUESTA DE LA ALHACABA

Palacio de Daralhórra

SANTA ISABEL

MOLDERAR

Casa de Porras

YEGUAS

PL. SAN MIGUEL BAJO

San José

SAN JOSÉ

San Gregorio Bético

Iglesia de San Ildefonso

PL. DE LA MERCED

ZENETE

CRUZ DE QUIRÓS

CALDERERÍA NUEVA

Hospital Real

AVENIDA DE CAPUCHINOS

HOSPICIO

PLAZA DEL TRIUNFO

Puerta de Elvira

PL. DE LOS NARANJOS

ELVIRA

Jardines del Triunfo

GRAN VÍA DE COLÓN

C. BAZÁN

SAN AGUSTÍN

CÁRCEL

AVDA. DE LA CONSTITUCIÓN

ACERA DEL TRIUNFO

SAN JUAN DE DIOS

MANO DE HIERRO

TENDILLAS

PL. DE S. AGUSTÍN

Free Memory

Colegio de Niñas Nobles

SANTA BÁRBARA

Hospital e Iglesia de San Juan de Dios

ARRIOLA

Igl. de los Santos Justo y Pastor

SAN JERÓNIMO

S. Felipe Neri

DR. SEVERO OCHOA

RECTOR LÓPEZ ARGUETA

Colegio de San Bartolomé y Santiago

Universidad

TRINIDAD

DUQUESA

PLAZA DE LA TRINIDAD

CONDE INFANTES

MÁLAGA

FÁBRICA VIEJA

TABLAS

BUENSUCESO

Convento De San Jerónimo

PLAZA DE LOS LOBOS

0   200
metres

Murcia

La Cartuja

Jaén & Madrid

Bus Station

Train Station

4

Antequera & Málaga

GRANADA

NIGHTLIFE

Camborio	2
La Estrella	8
Fondo Reservado	5
Granada 10	12
Jazz Café Bohemia	15
Makeba	10
Peatón Pub	16
Planta Baja	17
Potemkin	9
Quilombo	4
La Sal	13
Seis Colores	14
Son	11

FLAMENCO VENUES

Los Faroles	1
El Niño de los Almendras	7
Peña Plateria	3
Sala Vimaambi	6

The Alhambra after the Moors

Following their conquest of the city in 1492, **Fernando and Isabel** lived for a while in the Alhambra. They restored some rooms and converted the mosque but left the palace structure unaltered. As at Córdoba and Seville, it was **Emperor Carlos V**, their grandson, who wreaked the most insensitive destruction, demolishing a whole wing of rooms in order to build a Renaissance palace. This and the Alhambra itself were simply ignored by his successors, and by the eighteenth century the Palacios Nazaríes was in use as a prison. In 1812, it was taken and occupied by **Napoleon's forces**, who looted and damaged whole sections of the palace, and on their retreat from the city tried to blow up the entire complex. Their attempt was thwarted only by the action of a crippled soldier (José García) who remained behind and removed the fuses; a plaque honouring his valour has been placed in the Plaza de los Aljibes.

Two decades later, the Alhambra's "rediscovery" began, given impetus by the American writer **Washington Irving**, who set up his study in the empty palace rooms and began to write his marvellously romantic *Tales of the Alhambra* (on sale all over Granada – and good reading amid the gardens and courts). Shortly after its publication, the Spaniards made the Alhambra a **national monument** and set aside funds for its restoration. This continues to the present day and is now a highly sophisticated project, scientifically removing the accretions of later ages in order to expose and meticulously restore the Moorish creations.

INFORMATION AND TICKETS   THE ALHAMBRA

Information To check any changes to opening times, admission charges or booking procedures, visit the Alhambra's website ⓦ alhambra-patronato.es.

TICKETS

Buying tickets in person To protect the Alhambra, only 6600 daily admissions are allowed. If you're buying tickets in person, you have two options: you can buy them at the entrance (ticket office opens at 8am), where queues can be long, or by credit card from a number of ServiCaixa machines in a small building signed off the car park nearby; insert your card into the machine and request a day and time. All tickets will state whether they are for morning (8.30am–2pm) or afternoon (2–8pm, Oct–March until 6pm) sessions, and you must enter between the stated times (once inside, you may stay as long as you wish). However, you should bear in mind that tickets put on sale in the manners above are only what remain after pre-booked ticket sales (see below), which could well mean in high season that no tickets are on sale at the entrance.

Buying tickets in advance Alternatively, and this is the method strongly recommended by the Alhambra to guarantee entry on a specific day, you can book in advance, either online (ⓦ alhambra-tickets.es and ⓦ servicaixa.com; €1 booking fee) or by phone on (from Spain) ☏ 902 888 001 or (from abroad) ☏ 934 923 750 (24hr service). Tickets should then be collected (at least 1hr before your time slot for the Palacios Nazaríes, allocated when booking; see below) from the Alhambra ticket office. You will need your credit card and passport for identification.

VISITING THE ALHAMBRA

The tickets have **sections** for each part of the complex – Alcazaba, Palacios Nazaríes, Generalife – which must be used on the same day. Note that you will not be allowed to enter the complex (even with pre-booked tickets) less than an hour before closing time. To alleviate the severe overcrowding that used to occur, tickets are stamped with a half-hour **time slot** during which you must enter the Palacios Nazaríes. You will not be allowed to enter before or after this time, but once inside the palace you can stay as long as you like: any waiting time can be spent in the Alcazaba, museums or at one of the numerous cafés dotted around the complex. Note, too, that the Museo de la Alhambra and the Museo de las Bellas Artes, both in the Palacio de Carlos V, have different hours and admission fees to those of the Alhambra. It's also worth pointing out that only the palaces, museums and Generalife gardens require a ticket to gain entry – the rest you are allowed to wander around freely.

SPECIAL EVENTS

The Alhambra is also open for **floodlit visits**, limited to the Palacios Nazaríes (March–Oct Tues–Sat 10–11.30pm, ticket office open 9.45–10.15pm only; Nov–Feb Fri & Sat 8–9.30pm, ticket office open 7.45–8.15pm only; €13), and occasional **concerts** are held in its courts (details from the *turismo*). Availability of tickets (which can be pre-booked) is subject to the same terms as for daytime visits.

Approaches

The standard **approach** to the Alhambra is along the Cuesta de Gomérez, the semi-pedestrianized road that climbs uphill from Granada's central Plaza Nueva. The only vehicles allowed to use this road now are taxis and those belonging to residents. Alternatively, a dedicated minibus service, the **Alhambrabus** (lines #30 or #32; daily 7am–10pm, every 10min; €1.20), departs from Plaza Isabel La Católica near the cathedral. This will drop you outside the Alhambra's entrance and ticket office.

To get there **by car**, you'll need to use the route that is signed from the Puerta Real, to the south of the cathedral; this guides you along *paseos* del Salón and de la Bomba, eventually bringing you to the Alhambra's car park, close to the entrance and ticket office on the eastern edge of the complex.

Should you decide to **walk** up the hill along the Cuesta de Gomérez (a pleasant 20min stroll from Plaza Nueva), after a few hundred metres you reach the **Puerta de las Granadas**, a massive Renaissance gateway erected by Carlos V. Here two paths diverge to either side of the road: the one on the right climbs up towards a group of fortified towers, the **Torres Bermejas**, which may date from as early as the eighth century. The left-hand path leads through the woods past a huge terrace-fountain (again courtesy of Carlos V) to the main gateway – and former entrance – of the Alhambra. This is the **Puerta de la Justicia**, a magnificent tower that forced three changes of direction, making intruders hopelessly vulnerable. It was built by Yusuf I in 1340 and preserves above its outer arch the Koranic symbol of a key (for Allah the Opener) and an outstretched hand, whose five fingers represent the five Islamic precepts: prayer, fasting, alms-giving, pilgrimage to Mecca and the oneness of God. The **entrance and ticket office** to the Alhambra – at the eastern end, near to the Generalife – lies a further five-minute walk uphill, reached by following the wall to your left.

The citadel

Within the citadel stood a complete "government city" of mansions, smaller houses, baths, schools, mosques, barracks and gardens. Of this only the **Alcazaba** and the **Palacios Nazaríes** remain; they face each other across a broad terrace (constructed in the sixteenth century over a dividing gully), flanked by the majestic though incongruous **Palacio de Carlos V**.

Within the walls of the citadel, too, are the beautiful *Parador de San Francisco* (a converted monastery, where Isabel was originally buried – terrace bar open to non guests), and the *Hotel América*. There are a handful of **drinks stalls** around as well, including one, very welcome, in the Plaza de los Aljibes, just beyond the Puerta del Vino, and another in the Portal gardens (towards the Palacio de Carlos V after you leave the Palacios Nazaríes).

The Alcazaba

The entrance to the Alhambra brings you into the complex at the eastern end, near to the Generalife gardens. However, as you will have a time slot for entering the Palacios Nazaríes (usually up to an hour ahead), it makes sense chronologically and practically to start your visit with the **Alcazaba** at the Alhambra's opposite, or western, end, entered through the **Puerta del Vino** – named from its use in the sixteenth century as a wine cellar.

The Alcazaba is the earliest and most ruined part of the fortress. At its summit is the **Torre de la Vela**, named after a huge bell on its turret, which until recent years was rung to mark the irrigation hours for workers in the *vega*, Granada's vast and fertile plain. It was here, at 3pm on January 2, 1492, that the Cross was first displayed above the city, alongside the royal standards of Aragón and Castile and the banner of St James. Boabdil, leaving Granada for exile in the Alpujarras, turned and wept at the sight, earning from his mother Aisha the famous rebuke: "Do not weep like a woman for what you could not defend like a man." To gain access to the Palacios Nazaríes you

THE ALHAMBRA

0 — 50
metres

1 Torre de la Vela	11 Baños Reales
2 Torre del Homenaje	12 Cripta del Palacio de Carlos V
3 Torre Quebrada	13 Sala de los Abencerrajes
4 Patio de Machuca	14 Puerta de la Rawda
5 Mexuar	15 Sala de los Reyes
6 Patio del Cuarto Dorado	16 Patio de los Leones
7 Cuarto Dorado	17 Sala de las Dos Hermanas
8 Salón de Embajadores	18 Jardín de la Daraxa
9 Sala de la Barca	19 Patio de la Azequia
10 Patio de los Arrayanes	20 Patio de la Sultana

need to recross the **Plaza de los Aljibes**. In Nasrid times, this area was a ravine dividing the hill between the Royal Palace on one side, and the Alcazaba on the other. Following la *reconquista*, the ravine was filled in to hold two rainwater cisterns (*aljibes*) and the surface above laid out with fortifications. During the construction of Carlos V's palace in the sixteenth century, the area was cleared to create a parade ground, the rather desolate form it retains today.

Entering the Palacios Nazaríes

It is amazing that the **Palacios Nazaríes** has survived, for it stands in utter contrast to the strength of the Alcazaba and the encircling walls and towers. It was built lightly and often crudely from wood, brick and adobe, and was designed not to last but to be renewed and redecorated by succeeding rulers. Its buildings show a brilliant use of light and space, but they are principally a vehicle for ornamental stucco decoration.

Arabic inscriptions feature prominently in the ornamentation. Some are poetic eulogies to the buildings and builders, others to various sultans (notably Mohammed V). Most, however, are taken from the Koran, and among them the phrase *Wa-la ghaliba illa-Llah* (There is no Conqueror but God) is tirelessly repeated. This became the battle cry (and family motto) of the Nasrids upon Ibn al-Ahmar's return in 1248 from aiding the Castilian war of Fernando III against Muslim Seville; it was his reply to the customary, though bitterly ironic, greetings of Mansur (Victor), ridiculing his role as a feudal puppet of the Christian enemy.

The palace is structured in three parts, each arrayed round an interior court and with a specific function. The sultans used the **Mexuar**, the first series of rooms, for business and judicial purposes. In the **Serallo**, beyond, they received embassies and distinguished guests. The last section, the **Harem**, formed their private living quarters and would have been entered by no one but their family or servants.

The Mexuar

The council chamber, the main **reception hall** of the Mexuar, is the first room you enter. It was completed in 1365 and hailed (perhaps formulaically) by the court poet and vizier Ibn Zamrak as a "haven of counsel, mercy, and favour". Here the sultan heard the pleas and petitions of the people and held meetings with his ministers. At the room's far end is a small oratory, one of a number of prayer niches scattered round the palace and immediately identifiable by their distinctive alignment (to face Mecca). This "public" section of the palace, beyond which few would have penetrated, is completed by the Mudéjar **Cuarto Dorado** (Golden Room), decorated under Carlos V, whose *Plus Ultra* motif appears throughout the palace, and the **Patio del Cuarto Dorado**. This has perhaps the grandest facade of the whole palace, for it admits you to the formal splendour of the Serallo.

The Serallo

The Serallo – the part of the complex where important guests were received – was built largely to the design of Yusuf I, a romantic and enlightened sultan who was stabbed to death by a madman while worshipping in the Alhambra mosque. Its rooms open out from delicate marble-columned arcades at each end of the long **Patio de los Arrayanes** (Patio of the Myrtles).

At the court's north end, occupying two floors of a fortified tower, is the royal throne room, known as the **Salón de Embajadores** (Hall of the Ambassadors). As the sultan could be approached only indirectly, it stands at an angle to the entrance from the Mexuar. It is the largest room of the palace, perfectly square and completely covered in tile and stucco decoration. Among the web of inscriptions is one that states simply "I am the Heart of the Palace." Here Boabdil signed the terms of his city's surrender to the Catholic kings, whose motifs (the arms of Aragón and Castile) were later worked into the room's stunning wooden dome, a superb example of *lacería*, the rigidly geometric "carpentry of knots". Here, too, so it is said, Fernando met Columbus to discuss his plans for finding a new sea route to India – which led to the discovery of the Americas. The dome itself, in line with the mystical-mathematical pursuit of medieval Moorish architecture, has a complex symbolism representing the seven heavens. Carlos V tore down the rooms at the southern end of the court; from the arcade there is access (frequently closed) to the gloomy **Chapel Crypt** (*cripta*) of his palace, which has a curious "whispering gallery" effect.

The Harem

The **Patio de los Leones** (Court of the Lions), which has become the archetypal image of Granada, constitutes the heart of the harem. The stylized and archaic-looking lions beneath its fountain (due to be returned to their place in 2012 after a lengthy restoration) probably date, like the patio itself, from the reign of Mohammed V, Yusuf's successor; a poem inscribed on the bowl tells how much fiercer they would look if they weren't so restrained by respect for the sultan. The court was designed as an interior garden and planted with shrubs and aromatic herbs; it opens onto three of the palace's finest rooms, each of which looks onto the fountain.

The most sophisticated rooms in this part of the complex, apparently designed to give a sense of the rotary movement of the stars, are the two facing each other across the court. The largest of these, the **Sala de los Abencerrajes**, has the most startlingly beautiful ceiling in the Alhambra: sixteen-sided, supported by niches of stalactite vaulting, lit by windows in the dome and reflected in a fountain on the floor. This light

MOORISH GRANADA

Granada's glory was always precarious. It was established as an independent kingdom in 1238 by **Ibn al-Ahmar**, a prince of the Arab Nasrid tribe that had been driven south from Zaragoza. He proved a just and capable ruler, but all over Spain the Christian kingdoms were in the ascendant. The Moors of Granada survived only through paying tribute and allegiance to Fernando III of Castile – whom they were forced to assist in the conquest of Muslim Seville – and by the time of Ibn Ahmar's death in 1275 theirs was the only surviving Spanish Muslim kingdom. It had, however, consolidated its territory (stretching from just north of the city down to a coastal strip between Tarifa and Almería) and, stimulated by refugees, developed a flourishing commerce, industry and culture.

By a series of shrewd manoeuvres Granada maintained its autonomy for two and a half centuries, its rulers turning for protection, in turn as it suited them, to the Christian kingdoms of Aragón and Castile and to the Merinid Muslims of Morocco. The city-state enjoyed a particularly confident and prosperous period under **Yusuf I** (1334–54) and **Mohammed V** (1354–91), the sultans responsible for much of the existing Alhambra palace. But by the mid-fifteenth century, a pattern of coups and internal strife became established and a rapid succession of rulers did little to stem Christian inroads. In 1479, the kingdoms of Aragón and Castile were united by the marriage of Fernando and Isabel, and within ten years they had conquered Ronda, Málaga and Almería. The city of Granada now stood completely alone, tragically preoccupied in a civil war between supporters of the sultan's two favourite wives. The Reyes Católicos made escalating and finally untenable demands upon it, and in 1490 war broke out. **Boabdil**, the last Moorish king, appealed in vain for help from his fellow Muslims in Morocco, Egypt and Ottoman Turkey, and in the following year **Fernando and Isabel** marched on Granada with an army said to total 150,000 troops. For seven months, through the winter of 1491, they laid siege to the city, and on January 2, 1492, Boabdil formally surrendered its keys. The Christian Reconquest of Spain was complete.

and airy quality stands at odds with its name and history, for here Abu'l-Hasan (Boabdil's father) murdered sixteen princes of the Abencerraje family, whose chief had fallen in love with his favourite, Zoraya; the crimson stains in the fountain are popularly supposed to be the indelible traces of their blood, but are more likely to be from rust.

At the far end is the **Sala de los Reyes** (Hall of the Kings), whose dormitory alcoves preserve a series of unique paintings on leather. These, in defiance of Koranic law, represent human scenes; it's believed that they were painted by a Christian artist in the last decades of Moorish rule. The second of the two facing chambers on the court's north side, the **Sala de las Dos Hermanas** (Hall of the Two Sisters), is more mundanely named – from two huge slabs of marble in its floor – but just as spectacularly decorated, with a dome of over five thousand "honeycomb cells". It was the principal room of the sultan's favourite, opening onto an inner apartment and balcony, the **Mirador de Daraxa** (known in English as the "Eyes of the Sultana"); the romantic garden patio below was added after the Reconquest.

The Peinador de la Reina

Beyond, you are directed along a circuitous route through **apartments** redecorated by Carlos V (as at Seville, the northern-reared emperor installed fireplaces) and later used by Washington Irving. Eventually you emerge at the **Peinador de la Reina**, or Queen's Tower, a pavilion that served as an oratory for the sultanas and as a dressing room for the wife of Carlos V; perfumes were burned beneath its floor and wafted up through a marble slab in one corner.

The Baños Reales

From here, passing the **Patio de la Lindaraja** (added in the sixteenth century – though the basin of its marble fountain was taken from outside the Mexuar), you reach the

Baños Reales (Royal Baths). These are tremendous, decorated in rich tile mosaics and lit by pierced stars and rosettes once covered by coloured glass. The central chamber was used for reclining and retains the balconies where singers and musicians – reputedly blind to keep the royal women from being seen – would entertain the bathers. At present, entry is not permitted to the baths, though you can make out most of the features through the doorways. The visit route exits via the exquisite **Pórtico del Partal**, with the **Torre de las Damas** (Ladies' Tower) and elegant portico overlooking a serene pool. What appears no more than a garden pavilion today is in fact the surviving remnant of the early fourteenth-century Palace of the Partal, a four-winged structure originally surrounding the pool, the Alhambra's largest expanse of water. The **Jardines del Partal** lie beyond this, and the nearby gate brings you out close to the entrance to the Palacio de Carlos V.

Palacio de Carlos V

The grandiose **Palacio de Carlos V** seems totally out of place here, its austere stone-built architecture jarring with the delicate Oriental style and materials of the Moorish palace. Begun in 1526 it was never finished – the coffered ceilings of the colonnade were added only in the 1960s before which the Ionic columns had projected into open sky – as shortly after commissioning it, Carlos V left Granada never to return. Despite its incongruity the edifice is, however, a distinguished piece of Renaissance design in its own right – the only surviving work of Pedro Machucha, a former pupil of Michelangelo.

Museo de Bellas Artes

Tues 2.30–8pm, Wed–Sat 9am–8pm, Sun 9am–2.30pm; Nov–March Tues–Sat until 6pm • €1.50, free with EU passport

On the palace's upper floor – reached by steps from a circular central courtyard where bullfights were once held – is a mildly interesting **Museo de Bellas Artes**. Here are displayed some notable examples of *andaluz* wood sculpture by seventeenth-century *granadino* Alonso Cano among others, as well as some vibrantly coloured abstract works by twentieth-century artist José Guerrero, who spent part of his life in New York and was influenced by American Expressionism.

Museo de la Alhambra

Tues–Sun 9am–2.30pm • €1.50, free with EU passport

The lower floor holds the **Museo de la Alhambra** (aka Museo Hispano-Musulman), a small but fascinating collection of Hispano-Moorish art, displaying many items discovered during the Alhambra restoration including fine woodcarving and tilework. The star exhibit is a beautiful fifteenth-century metre-and-a-half-high **Alhambra vase** (Jarrón de las Gacelas), made from local red clay enamelled in blue and gold and decorated with leaping gazelles.

The Generalife

Paradise is described in the Koran as a shaded, leafy garden refreshed by running water where the "fortunate ones" may take their rest. It is an image that perfectly describes the **Generalife**, the gardens and summer palace of the sultans. Its name means literally "Garden of the Architect", and the grounds consist of a luxuriantly imaginative series of patios, enclosed gardens and walkways.

By chance, an account of the gardens during Moorish times, written rather poetically by the fourteenth-century court vizier and historian Ibn Zamrak, survives. The descriptions that he gives aren't all entirely believable, but they are a wonderful basis for musing as you lie around by the patios and fountains. There were, he wrote, celebrations with horses darting about in the dusk at speeds that made the spectators rub their eyes (a form of festival still indulged in at Moroccan *fantasías*); rockets shot into the air to be attacked by the stars for their audacity; tightrope walkers flying through the air like birds; and men bowled along in a great wooden hoop, shaped like an astronomical sphere.

Today, devoid of such amusements, the gardens are still evocative – above all, perhaps, the **Patio de los Cipreses** (aka Patio de la Sultana), a dark and secretive walled garden of sculpted junipers where the Sultana Zoraya was suspected of meeting her lover Hamet, chief of the unfortunate Abencerrajes. Nearby, too, is the inspired flight of fantasy of the **Escalera del Agua**, a staircase with water flowing down its stone balustrades. From here you can look down on the wonderful old Arab quarter of the Albaicín.

The Albaicín

Declared a UNESCO World Heritage Site in 1994, the **Albaicín** stretches across a fist-shaped area bordered by the river, the Sacromonte hill, the old town walls and the winding Calle de Elvira (parallel to the Gran Vía de Colón). The best approach is along Carrera del Darro, beside the river. Coming from the Alhambra, you can make your way down the Cuesta de los Chinos – a beautiful path and a short cut.

Baños Árabes

Carrera del Darro 31 Tues–Sat 10am–2.30pm • Free

On Carrera del Darro are the remains of the **Baños Árabes**, a marvellous and little-visited Moorish public bath complex. Built in the eleventh century, the sensitively restored building consists of a series of brick-vaulted rooms with typical star-shaped skylights (originally glazed) and columns incorporating Visigothic and Roman capitals.

Baños Árabes Al Andalus

C/Santa Ana 16 • Daily 10am–midnight, reservation required • Bath only €22 • ☎ 958 229 978

Just to the east of Plaza Nueva behind the church of Santa Ana, the Baños Árabes Al Andalus gives you some idea of what a **Moorish bathhouse** would have been like when functioning. Here you can wallow in the graded temperatures of the re-created traditional baths – decorated with mosaics and plaster arabesques – or take tea in the peaceful *tetería* (tea room) upstairs.

Casa de Castril

Carrera del Darro 43 • Tues 2.30–8.30pm, Wed–Sat 9.30am–8.30pm, Sun 9.30am–2.30pm • €1.50, free with EU passport

On Carrera del Darro, the **Casa de Castril**, a Renaissance mansion, houses the town's **archeological museum**. Of particular note here are some remarkable finds from the Neolithic Cueva de los Murciélagos (Cave of the Bats) in the Alpujarras; there are also exhibits from Granada's Phoenician, Roman, Visigothic and Moorish periods. Beside the museum, c/Zafra ascends to the church of **San Juan** (with an intact thirteenth-century minaret) and then, following a series of convoluted turnings the church of **San Nicolás**, whose square offers a stunning **view of the Alhambra**, considered the best in town.

SECURITY IN THE ALBAICÍN

Although you certainly shouldn't let it put you off visiting the atmospheric Albaicín quarter, it's worth bearing in mind that the area has been the scene of repeated **thefts** from tourists. To ensure your visit is a happy one, take all the usual precautions: avoid carrying around large amounts of money or valuables (including airline tickets and passports – a photocopy of the latter will satisfy museums), and keep what you have in safe pockets instead of shoulder bags. If you do get something snatched, don't offer resistance; crime in these streets rarely involves attacks to the person, but thieves will be firm in getting what they want. Finally, try not to look like an obvious tourist (map/guidebook in hand is a dead giveaway) or flaunt expensive-looking photographic equipment or mobile phones, and keep to the streets where there are other people about, particularly at night.

Sacromonte

Centro Interpretación del Sacromonte (aka Museo Cuevas de Sacromonte) Tues–Sun 10am–2pm & 5–8.30pm, Nov–Feb 4–7pm • €5

From the church of San Nicolás, continuing east parallel with the river takes you up into the gypsy cave-quarter of **Sacromonte**. Like many cities in Andalucía, Granada has an ancient and still considerable *gitano* population, from whose clans many of Spain's best flamenco guitarists, dancers and singers have emerged. They have traditionally lived in caves in this area, although these days the *barrio* is better known for its nightlife. If you wander up here in the daytime, take a look at the old **caves** on the far side of the old Moorish wall – most of them deserted after severe floods in 1962. There are fantastic views from the top. Sacromonte now has its own museum, the **Centro Interpretación del Sacromonte**, Barranco de los Negros s/n, depicting the life and times of the *barrio*.

The Capilla Real

Daily 10.30am–1.30pm & 4–7.30pm, Nov–Feb 11am–1.30pm & 3.30–6.30pm • €3.50

In addition to the city's Moorish legacy, it's worth the distinct readjustment and effort of will to appreciate the city's later Christian monuments, notably the **Capilla Real** (Royal Chapel), in the centre of town adjoining the cathedral at the southern end of Gran Vía de Colón. It's an impressive building, flamboyant Late Gothic in style and built ad hoc in the first decades of Christian rule as a mausoleum for Los Reyes Católicos, the city's "liberators".

The tombs

The actual **tombs** are as simple as could be imagined: Fernando (marked with a not-easily-spotted "F" on the left of the central pair) and Isabel, flanked by their daughter Joana ("the Mad") and her husband Felipe ("the Handsome"), resting in lead coffins placed in a plain crypt. But above them – the response of their grandson Carlos V to what he found "too small a room for so great a glory" – is a fabulously elaborate **monument** carved in Carrara marble by Florentine Domenico Fancelli in 1517, with sculpted Renaissance effigies of the two monarchs; the tomb of Joana and Felipe alongside is a much inferior work by Ordóñez. In front of the monument is an equally magnificent **reja**, the work of Maestro Bartolomé of Jaén, and a splendid **retablo** behind depicts Boabdil surrendering the keys of Granada.

Isabel, in accordance with her will, was originally buried on the Alhambra hill (in the church of San Francisco, now part of the parador), but her wealth and power proved no safeguard of her wishes. The queen's final indignity occurred during the 1980s when the candle that she asked should perpetually illuminate her tomb was replaced by an electric bulb – it was restored in 1999 following numerous protests.

The Sacristy

In the Capilla's **Sacristy** is displayed the sword of Fernando, the crown of Isabel and her outstanding personal collection of **medieval Flemish paintings** – including important works by Memling, Bouts and van der Weyden – and various Italian and Spanish paintings, including panels by Botticelli, Perugino and Pedro Berruguete.

The Catedral

Mon–Sat 10.45am–1.30pm & 4–8pm, Sun 4–8pm, Nov–Feb until 7pm • €3.50

For all its stark Renaissance bulk, Granada's **Catedral**, adjoining the Capilla Real and entered from the door beside it, is a disappointment. It was begun in 1521, just as the chapel was finished, but was then left incomplete well into the eighteenth century. At least it's light and airy inside, though, and it's fun to go round putting coins in the slots to light up the chapels, where an El Greco *St Francis* and sculptures by Pedro de Mena and Martínez Montañés will be revealed.

San Juan de Dios

Northwest of the cathedral, ten minutes' walk along c/San Jerónimo, the Hospital of
San Juan de Dios, with a pair of spectacular Renaissance patios, lies beyond a majestic
portal. The inner patio has wonderful but sadly deteriorating frescoes depicting the San
Juan's miracles. The hospital is still in use, but the porter will allow you a brief look.
Next door, the hospital's church, a Baroque addition, has a Churrigueresque *retablo* – a
glittering, gold extravaganza by Guerrero.

Convento de San Jerónimo

Daily 10am–2.30pm & 4–7.30pm, Nov–Feb until 6.30pm • €3.50

The elegant Renaissance **Convento de San Jerónimo** was founded by the Catholic
Monarchs, though built after their death, with two imposing patios and a wonderful
frescoed church. The largest of the patios (or cloisters in this context) is an elegant work by
Diego de Siloé with two tiers of 36 arches. The church, also by Siloé has been wonderfully
restored after use as a cavalry barracks and has fabulous eighteenth-century frescoes.

La Cartuja

Daily 10am–1pm & 4–8pm, Nov–March until 6pm • €3.50

On the northern outskirts of town, **La Cartuja** is perhaps the grandest and most
outrageously decorated of all the country's lavish Carthusian monasteries. It was
constructed at the height of Baroque extravagance – some say to rival the Alhambra
– and has a chapel of staggering wealth, surmounted by an altar of twisted and
coloured marble. It lies a further ten- to fifteen-minute walk beyond the Hospital of
San Juan de Dios; bus line #8, going north along the Gran Vía, also passes by.

4

Lorca's Granada

One of the ghosts that walks Granada's streets and plazas is that of Andalucía's greatest poet
and dramatist **Federico García Lorca** who was born in 1898 in Fuente Vaqueros, a village in
the *vega*, the fertile plain to the west of the city. In the summer months the family – Lorca's
father was a wealthy landowner – moved to the Huerta de San Vicente, now in the city
suburbs but then a tranquil rural plot on the city's edge. Both sites can be visited.

Huerta de San Vicente

Tues–Sun 10am–12.30pm & 5–7.30pm. Nov–March closes 6.30pm • €3 • Southbound bus #4 from Gran Via or Pl. del Carmen (direction
Palacio de Deportes) or a taxi

West of the centre, the **Huerta de San Vicente** comprises the house – with Lorca's
bedroom – where he composed many of his best-known poems. The visit enables you
to see the light and airy rooms and – in the poet's room – some original furniture
including his work desk, bed and a poster of the Barraca theatre company which he
helped to set up. When the Lorcas had it the house was surrounded by five acres of
fruit trees and vegetable plots. Today it sits in the centre of what is claimed to be
Europe's largest rose garden, Parque Federico García Lorca, the city's belated tribute.

Casa Museo Federico García Lorca

April, May, June & Sept Tues–Sat 10am–1pm & 5–6pm, Sun 10am–1pm; July & Aug Tues–Sun 10am–2pm; Oct–March Tues–Sat
10am–1pm & 4–5pm, Sun 10am–1pm; guided visits on the hour • €1.80 • ☎ 958 516 453, ⓦ www.museogarcialorca.org • Buses (hourly
from 9am, last bus returns 8pm; 20min) leave from Avda. de Andaluces, fronting the train station

To the west of the city, in pleasant **Fuente Vaqueros**, Lorca's birthplace, has been
transformed into a museum, the **Casa Museo Federico García Lorca**, and contains an
evocative collection of Lorca memorabilia. The village makes a pleasant overnight stop,
and **accommodation** is available at *Hostal-Restaurante Moli-Lorc*, c/Ancha Escuelas 11

(☎958 516 532; €36), next to the church, which incidentally holds the font where Lorca was baptized.

ARRIVAL AND DEPARTURE

BY PLANE

The **airport** is 17km west of the city on the A92 *autovía*; buses connect with Pl. Isabel La Católica in the centre of town (14 daily; 30min; €3 one way). Buses run out to the airport from a stop on the east side of Gran Vía opposite the cathedral. Check with the operator (Gonzalez S.L.; ☎958 490 164, ⌨autocaresjosegonzalez.com) for the latest timetable. Alternatively, a taxi costs about €20–25.

BY TRAIN

The **train station** (☎902 240 202) is 1km or so out on Avda. de Andaluces, off Avda. de la Constitución; to get into town, take bus #3, #4, #6 or #9, which run direct to Gran Vía de Colón and the centre, or bus #11, which takes a circular route – inbound on the Gran Vía and back out via the Puerta Real and Camino de Ronda. The most central stop is by the cathedral on the Gran Vía.

Destinations Algeciras (3 daily, 4hr 15min); Almería (4 daily; 2hr 20min); Antequera (daily; 2hr 20min); Córdoba (2 daily; 2hr 30min); Linares-Baeza (2 daily; 2hr 20min); Madrid (daily; 4hr 50min); Málaga (8 daily, change at Antequera; 2hr 40min); Ronda (3 daily; 2hr 30min); Seville (4 daily; 3hr).

BY BUS

The city's main **bus station** is on Carretera de Jaén (☎958 185 480), some way out of the centre in the northern suburbs – bus #3 or #33 from outside will drop you near the cathedral (15min) – and handles all services except those to the Lorca museum at Fuente Vaqueros (see p.343). For departure information, check with the individual companies: Alsina Graells (serving Madrid, Jaén, Úbeda, Córdoba, Seville, Málaga, Las Alpujarras, Motril, Guadix, Almería & the coast; ☎958 185 480); Empresa Bonal (the north side of the Sierra Nevada; ☎958 465 022); Empresa Autedía (Guadix Mojácar; ☎958 185 480); and Empresa Bacoma (Valencia/Alicante & Barcelona; ☎902 422 242). All terminals are on bus routes #3, #4 and #11.

Destinations Alicante (4 daily; 4hr 15min); Almería (8 daily; 3hr 45min); Cádiz (4 daily; 5hr); Cazorla (2 daily; 4hr); Córdoba (8 daily; 2hr 45min); Jaén (12 daily; 1hr 15min); Madrid (13 daily; 5hr); Málaga (21 daily; 2hr); Mojácar (2 daily; 4hr); Motril (11 daily; 1hr 45min); Ronda (2 daily; 3hr 45min); Seville (6 daily; 3hr 40min); Sierra Nevada (daily; 45min); Lanjarón & Órgiva (6 daily; 1hr 30min; 2 daily to other villages in the Alpujarras); Solynieve (Pradollana) (3–4 daily in winter, daily in summer; 25min); Valencia (5 daily; 9hr 20min); Úbeda/Baeza (9 daily; 2hr 20min).

BY CAR

Arriving **by car** you'll face the usual snarl-ups in the centre of town (try to time your arrival with the *siesta*) and the near-impossibility of finding on-street parking. You must also be careful not to enter the **restricted-access central streets** such as the Gran Vía and Reyes Católicos. If you ignore warning signs and enter these streets your numberplate will be photographed and you will be fined €80 (unless your hotel is actually in one of these streets – no exceptions are allowed).

Car parks (*parking subterráneo*) are located at Puerta Real (down the right-hand side of the post office); La Caleta, near the train station; and on c/San Agustín, beneath the municipal market off the west side of Gran Vía near the cathedral. Long-term free street parking places are often to be found along Carrera del Genil and the Paseo del Salón, slightly southwest of the centre or across the bridges over the Genil to the southeast.

INFORMATION AND TOURS

Turismo The city's best and most efficient tourist office is the municipal tourist office at Pl. Mariana Pineda 10 (Mon–Fri 9am–8pm, Sat 10am–7pm, Sun 10am–3pm; ☎958 247 128, ⌨granadatur.com). The city's rather lethargic Junta de Andalucía *turismo*, c/Santa Ana 2 (Mon–Fri 9am–7.30pm, Sat 9.30am–3pm & 4–7pm, Sun 9.30am–3pm; ☎958 575 202), is up steps to the right of the church of Santa Ana off Pl. Nueva. They often run out of maps and other printed information. They also have a sub-office in the Alhambra's ticket office (open same hours as the monument).

Guided walks Cicerone Granada's tour (daily 10.30am, 11am Nov–Feb; 2hr; English & Spanish; €12, under-14 free; book in high season; ☎600 412 051, ⌨ciceronegranada .com) starts at the green and white "Meeting Point" kiosk in the northeast corner of Pl. Bib Rambla and takes in the city's major sights (but not the Alhambra).

Listings The monthly *Guía del Ocio* (available from newspaper kiosks) details most of what's happening on the cultural and entertainment front, though it tends to be less up to date than the city's daily paper, *Ideal*, which is particularly good in its weekend editions.

ACCOMMODATION

Granada has some of the most beautiful **hotels** in Spain, most noticeably in the atmospheric Albaicín but also along the Gran Vía, c/Reyes Católicos, in and around Pl. Nueva and Puerta Real and off Pl. del Carmen. In the university zone, Pl. de la

Trinidad (and east of here) is another good place to look, along with the semi-pedestrianized (taxis and residents only) Cuesta de Gomérez, which leads up from Pl. Nueva towards the Alhambra. In high season (April–June & Sept) and especially during Semana Santa (Easter Week), you should book as far ahead as possible.

All hotels have either their own **car park** or garage (€10–20 per vehicle per day) or can advise on finding a parking place for your vehicle. The main problem, almost anywhere, is **noise**, though the recently built road to the Alhambra, diverting traffic away from the centre, has made a big difference.

Albergue Juvenil Camino de Ronda 171, at the junction with Avda. Ramón y Cajal ☎958 002 900, ⓦwww.inturjoven.com. Granada's youth hostel is conveniently close to the train station: turn left onto Avda. de la Constitución and left again onto Camino de Ronda. From the bus station, take bus #3 to the cathedral and then the circular #11, which will drop you outside. It's efficiently run with lots of facilities, and all rooms are en-suite doubles; the staff are friendly but the food is institutional; it can also be booked up for days ahead in summer. Under-26 €17.50, over-26 €23.50

★**Casa del Aljarife** Placeta de la Cruz Verde 2 ☎958 222 425, ⓦwww.casadelaljarife.com. This welcoming upmarket Albaicín *hostal* occupies a restored sixteenth-century mansion near the heart of the *barrio*, has three attractive en-suite a/c rooms (two with Alhambra views) around a patio, and there's free internet access and wi-fi. €95

★**Casa del Capitel Nazari** Cuesta de Aceituneros 6 ☎958 215 260, ⓦwww.hotelcasacapitel.com. Another beautiful sixteenth-century *palacio* transformed into an enchanting small hotel with elegant rooms overlooking a triple-tiered patio; room 22 has an Alhambra view. Special offers in July, Aug, Jan & Feb can cut prices significantly. Parking nearby. €110

★**Casa Morisca** Cuesta de la Victoria 9 ☎958 215 796, ⓦwww.hotelcasamorisca.com. Stunningly romantic small Albaicín hotel inside an immaculately renovated fifteenth-century Moorish mansion with exquisite patio; there are re-created Moorish furnishings throughout, and room 15 (with Alhambra views) is the one to go for. Exterior rooms cost more. Wi-fi and free street parking. €125

Hostal Britz Cuesta de Gomérez 1 ☎958 223 652, ⓔreservabritz@hotmail.com. Very comfortable, welcoming and well-placed *hostal*, en route to the Alhambra. Some rooms en suite, and some singles. Sharing bath €36, en suite €48

★**Hostal Costa Azul** c/Rosario 5 ☎958 222 298, ⓦwww.hostalcostaazul.com. Friendly, central, small *hostal* for pleasant a/c en-suite rooms. Has own restaurant and free internet and wi-fi. Also rents out some luxurious apartments nearby. *Rough Guide* readers with this guide can claim a fifteen-percent discount on apartments. Rooms €55, apartments €65

Hostal Landázuri Cuesta de Gomérez 24 ☎958 221 406, ⓦwww.hostallandazuri.com. Pleasant, good-value rooms, some en suite, plus its own restaurant, bar and a roof terrace with a view of the Alhambra. Own parking and free wi-fi. Some singles. Sharing bath €34, en suite €45

Hostal San Joaquin c/Mano de Hierro 14 ☎958 282 879, ⓦwww.pensionsanjoaquin.com. Great, rambling old *hostal*, with simple rooms (some en suite with TV) and charming patios. €40

Hostal Viena c/Hospital de Santa Ana 2 ☎958 221 859, ⓔpensionviena@pensionviena.es. In a quiet street, this is a pleasant, efficient, Austrian-run *hostal* offering a/c rooms with and without bath. Own garage. Sharing bath €40, en suite €48

Hostal Zurita Pl. de la Trinidad 7 ☎958 275 020, ⓦwww.pensionzurita.com. Friendly place where immaculate rooms come with and without bath, and all have TV and a/c. Wi-fi zone and own garage. Sharing bath €34, en suite €42

Hotel Albero Avda. Santa María de la Alhambra 6 ☎958 226 725, ⓦwww.hotelalbero.com. Excellent-value and friendly small hotel on the access road to the Alhambra to the south of the centre. Sparkling a/c balcony rooms come with TV, and there's easy street parking. Ring if you have problems finding them (English spoken). Free wi-fi. €45

Hotel América Real de la Alhambra 53 ☎958 227 471, ⓦhotelamericagranada.com. Charming one-star hotel in the Alhambra grounds; however, the welcome isn't the warmest and you're paying for location rather than creature comforts (a/c but no TV) and prices have risen steeply (and unjustifiably) here. Booking essential. €120

Hotel Guadalupe Paseo de la Sabica s/n ☎958 225 730, ⓦwww.hotelguadalupe.es. Comfortable and well-appointed hotel a stone's throw from the Alhambra's entrance – some of the a/c rooms have partial Alhambra views. Clients get reduced-rate parking in Alhambra car park, or the Alhambra bus from Pl. Nueva drops you nearby. Does frequent offers, and in July and Aug, rates are cut by thirty percent. €75

Hotel Los Angeles Cuesta Escoriaza 17 ☎958 221 423, ⓦwww.hotellosangeles.net. Pleasant and good-value four-star hotel on a leafy, quiet avenue within easy walking distance of the Alhambra. All rooms come with minibar and terrace balcony, and there's a garden, pool and car park. €85

Hotel Macía Plaza Pl. Nueva 4 ☎958 227 536, ⓦwww.maciahoteles.com. Centrally located hotel, with pleasant rooms overlooking this atmospheric square. Does frequent discounts and special offers. If full, they have a

4

couple of other same-standard hotels nearby. Exterior rooms cost more. Ten percent discount for *Rough Guide* readers with this guide. €120

★ **Hotel Palacio Santa Inés** Cuesta de Santa Inés 9 ☎ 958 222 362, ⊚ www.lugaresdivinos.com. Sumptuous six-room hotel in a restored sixteenth-century Mudéjar mansion on the edge of the Albaicín, with views of the Alhambra. The nearby, slightly cheaper but equally attractive *Carmen de Santa Inés* (same phone no.) is owned by the same proprietors and occupies a restored Moorish *carmen* (garden villa). €120

Hotel Los Tilos Pl. de Bib-Rambla 4 ☎ 958 266 712, ⊚ www.hotellostilos.com. Pleasant, two-star hotel well located near the cathedral on an atmospheric square; make sure you request an exterior room if you don't want to overlook a gloomy light-well. All rooms a/c, and some higher ones (try 301 & 302 or 401 & 402) have great Alhambra views. B&B €80

Parador de San Francisco Real de la Alhambra ☎ 958 221 440, ⊚ paradores.es. Without question the most desirable – and most expensive – place to stay in Granada; a fifteenth-century converted monastery in the Alhambra grounds. We quote the cheapest standard room but suites (costing double this) have the best views. Booking (at least three months ahead) is essential. If you aren't staying, call in for a drink at the attractive terrace bar. €320

Posada Doña Lupe Avda. del Generalife s/n ☎ 958 221 473, ☎ 958 221 474. A stone's throw from the Alhambra, this rambling and potentially inviting place is blighted by a rule-ridden student-hostel atmosphere (toilet paper and towels are doled out at check-in); numerous price permutations for rooms with and without bath, some exceptionally cheap. Has a small rooftop pool. €30

CAMPING

Camping Reina Isabel 4km along the Zubia road to the southwest of the city ☎ 958 590 041. With a pool, this is a less noisy and shadier site than the *Sierra Nevada*, making a pleasant rural alternative; can be reached by the Zubia-bound bus from the bus station, but with your own transport the city is still in easy reach. €6, €4.50 per tent, €4.50 per vehicle

Camping Sierra Nevada Avda. de Madrid 107 ☎ 958 150 062. Closest site to the centre (bus #3 from the centre or 3min walk south from the bus station), and with a welcome pool. Closed Nov–Feb. €6, tent plus car €14

EATING

When it comes to **restaurants**, Granada certainly isn't one of the gastronomic centres of Spain, possibly due in part to the *granadino* **tapas bars** that tempt away potential diners by giving out some of the most generous tapas in Andalucía – one comes "free" with every drink (more cynical *granadinos* will tell you that drinks prices are hiked to cover the *tapa*). A flavour of North Africa is to be found along **c/Calderería Nueva** and its surrounds in "Little Morocco", where you'll find health-food stores, as well as numerous Moroccan tearooms and eating places. This street is useful for assembling picnics for Alhambra visits, as is the revamped ultramodern **Mercado Municipal** in Pl. San Agustín just north of the cathedral (Mon–Sat early until 1.30pm). The warren of streets between **Plaza Nueva** and the **Gran Vía** has plenty of good-value places, particularly tapas bars, as does the area around **Plaza del Carmen** (near the *ayuntamiento*) and along c/Navas. Another good location is the **Campo del Príncipe**, a pleasant square below the south side of the Alhambra hill, with a line of open-air restaurant terraces, highly popular on summer nights.

RESTAURANTS

CITY CENTRE AND ALBAICÍN

Bar-Restaurante Sevilla c/Oficios 12 ☎ 958 221 223. One of the few surviving prewar restaurants, and once a haunt of Lorca, this is a pleasant restaurant with a *menú de degustación* for around €40 and a tourist *menú* for €17, plus an outdoor terrace – beneath the walls of the Capilla Real – in the evenings. 12.30–4.30pm & 8pm–midnight; closed Sun eve.

Casa Cepillo c/Pescadería 8, off c/Príncipe. Cheap and cheerful *comedor* with an excellent-value *menú* for around €10; the soups are especially good. 9am–11.30pm; closed Sun.

Mesón La Alegría c/Moras 4. This economical *mesón* is a favourite of *granadinos* working nearby and specializes in *carnes a la brasa* (charcoal grilled meats). Daily 1–5pm & 8.30pm–midnight.

Mesón Casa Blas Pl. San Miguel Bajo 15. This very popular bar-restaurant is probably the best of the bunch on this atmospheric square. House specials include *rabo de toro* and *pastel de berenjena* (aubergine terrine) and there's a *menú* for €16. Tues–Sat noon–5pm & 8pm–midnight, Sun 8pm–midnight; closed Mon.

Mesón El Trillo del Reca Callejón del Aljibe del Trillo 3 ☎ 958 225 182. Enchanting little mid-priced restaurant in an Albaicín *carmen* offering Basque-influenced cuisine: *bacalao al pil-pil* (salted cod with garlic) is a signature dish. Has outdoor tables on a delightful garden patio shaded by pear and quince trees. 1.30–3.30pm & 7.30–11.30pm; closed Tues.

★ **Restaurante-Bar Las Tomasas** Carril de San Agustín 4 ☎ 958 224 108. Mid-priced restaurant serving *cocina andaluz* in a huge and beautiful *carmen* with a stunning terrace view of the floodlit Alhambra at night. *Ajo* *blanco* (white gazpacho) is a speciality. You can also nurse a *tinto de verano* here if you don't want to eat. 2–4pm & 8–11pm; closed Sun, also lunch in July & Aug.

Restaurante León c/Pan 3. Long-established *cordobés* restaurant and serving many *carne de monte* (game) dishes, with a good-value *menú* for €10. Daily 1–4pm & 8–11.30pm.

★ **Restaurante-Marisquería Cunini** c/Pescadería 9 ☎958 250 777. One of Granada's most established and outstanding upmarket restaurants serving mainly fish. Also has a superb tapas bar attached. Despite having recently expanded its dining area, booking is still advised. Tues–Sat 12–4pm & 8–midnight, Sun noon–4pm.

AROUND TOWN

El Carmen de San Miguel Pl. Torres Bermejas 3 ☎958 226 723. One of Granada's noted places to eat, with a fabulous terrace looking out over the city (book a frontline table). One of the restaurant's signature dishes, *cochinillo confitado a la vainilla* (suckling pig with vanilla), typifies its innovative approach (occasionally overdone) to *andaluz* cuisine. *Menús de degustación* for €32 and €55. Mon–Sat 1.30–4pm & 8.30–11.30pm; closed Sun.

★ **Casa López Correa** c/de los Molinos 5, in the Realejo barrio. Wonderfully cosy and atmospheric English-run neighbourhood café. An eclectic menu includes excellent salads and pastas and lots more – try their chilli con carne or tandoori chicken. There's a *menú* for €10 and Friday-night jam sessions (post-10pm) feature locals who bring along instruments to play jazz, rock, blues, flamenco or whatever. Cocktails are on offer nightly after 10pm. Mon–Fri noon–4pm & 8pm–1am, Sat 8pm–1am, closed Sun.

La Mimbre Paseo del Generalife s/n. With a delightful terrace shaded by willows (*mimbres*), this is one of the best of the restaurants on the Alhambra hill. The food is good, but they are sometimes overwhelmed in high season.

There's a decent *menú* for around €17.50, which you may need to ask for. Daily 9am–4.30pm & 8–11.30pm.

La Ninfa Campo del Príncipe. Popular Italian restaurant for pizzas, pasta and salads that puts out tables on this pleasant plaza, and is often full to bursting at weekends. Daily 1–4.30pm & 7.30pm–12.30am.

Parador de San Francisco Alhambra ☎958 221 440. The parador's restaurant is one of the best in an upmarket chain often noted for its blandness. There's a pleasant dining room plus a terrace with fine views, and regional specialities appear on a varied and not-too-bank-breaking *menú* (€34). Daily 1–4pm & 8–11.30pm.

Seis Peniques Pl. de Padre Suárez. A very good little bar-restaurant with a small terrace facing the Casa de los Tiros. Offers great tapas in the bar and serves a decent *menú* in the restaurant for €8.50. Daily 8am–midnight.

TAPAS BARS

Al Sur de Granada c/Elvira 150. A thoroughly modern and very friendly bar-shop serving delicious cheese, *jamón* and *salchichón* tapas; they often stage tastings of local *granadino* wines (which are gaining a reputation) plus exhibitions of work by local artists. All these stay open until around midnight. Daily 10am–midnight.

Bodegas Castañeda c/Almericeros 1. Enjoyable – if slightly touristy these days – century-old tapas institution. Has some outdoor tables. Recommended tapas include paté and cheese *tablas* ("boards" – on which they're served), *montaditos* (tapas on bread) and baked potatoes. Daily 11am–4pm & 7pm–1am.

Bodegas La Mancha c/Joaquín Costa 10. A monumental spit-and-sawdust establishment (slightly more refined after refurbishment) hung with hams and with great wine vats stationed behind the bar. Tasty tapas include *jamón ibérico* and they also sell hot and cold *bocadillos* to eat in or take away. Daily 11am–4pm & 7pm–1am.

DRINKING AND NIGHTLIFE

Camborio Camino del Sacromonte s/n. Fashionable *discobar* housed in a cave, which is especially lively at weekends and lifts off about 4am. Be alert for bag-snatchers in this area. Tues–Sat 10pm–late.

La Estrella c/Cuchilleros. Congested, steamy *discobar* with great sounds. 10pm–4am.

Fondo Reservado c/Santa Ines 4. Funky gay and straight bar with a hilarious drag show every weekend. 11pm–4am.

Granada 10 c/Carcél Baja 10, off Gran Vía near the cathedral. Small and popular central *discoteca* inside a beautifully restored old retro cinema. 10pm–late.

Jazz Café Bohemia Pl. Lobos 11, northwest of Pl. Trinidad. Relaxed jazz bar with cool sounds, and walls lined with photos and memorabilia. 3pm–late.

Makeba Placeta de Silleria, east of the cathedral. Lively

and popular African-and-Russian-run reggae/African sounds bar with a special Reggae Night Wednesdays with free tapas. 10pm–late.

Peatón Pub c/Socrates 25, off c/Pedro Antonio de Alarcón. Rock bar popular with a student crowd. Other places nearby include *Babel*, *Van Gogh* and *Genesis*. 10pm–late.

Planta Baja Horno de Abad, off Carril del Picón. Long-established *discobar* – garage and lounge are big here – now in a new home with plenty of live gigs. 10pm–late.

★ **Potemkin** Pl. Hospicio Viejo s/n. Great pint-sized *copas* bar with cool sounds (mainly first half of twentieth-century jazz) which also stages art exhibitions on its walls. A great feature here is Japanese chef Hide's tapas which are excellent. He also does sushi nights (Tues–Thurs) when even more mouthwatering tapas from his homeland are on

4

offer. There's also a midday lunch special (with a veggie option) for €8. Mon–Sat 1.30–4.30pm & 8.30pm–1am, Sun 8.30pm–2am; closed Aug.

Quilombo c/Carril de San Cecilio 21. With a pool table and big dancefloor that starts humming around 3am. Sometimes stages live music. Wed–Thurs midnight–6am, Fri & Sat midnight–7am.

La Sal c/Santa Paula 11. Originally a lipstick lesbian dance bar, but now attracting male gays, too. Tues–Sun 11pm–4am.

Seis Colores c/Tendillas de Santa Paula, west of Gran Vía. With lots of action this is now the hottest gay venue in town. Younger crowd than many of the other gay bars. 10pm–late.

Son c/Joaquín Costas 3. Ultra-cool bi-level bar with older salsa upstairs and younger heavy-metal scene downstairs. 11pm–late.

FLAMENCO

When it comes to **flamenco**, finding anything near the real thing in Granada is not as easy as you might think. Shows in Sacromonte, traditionally the home of the city's flamenco performers, are generally shameless rip-offs and – unless you've heard otherwise – to be avoided.

El Niño de los Almendras c/Muladar de Doña Sancha, at the junction with c/La Tiña and southeast of Pl. San Miguel Bajo, Albaicín. This tiny, unsigned bar – done up inside to resemble a cave – is owned by the flamenco singer of the same name. Only open Fri nights (starts around midnight), but there's unforgettable flamenco when it happens.

Los Faroles Sacromonte. An exception to our warning posted in the introduction, this is sited almost at the very end of the line of "caves" – ask anyone for directions as it's well known. This is also a good place for a lunch time or evening drink, with a view of the Alhambra from its terrace. The genial owner is a fount of information on flamenco and the impromptu real thing often happens here after dark. Daily 11am–late.

Peña Platería Plazoleta de Toqueros 7, Albaicín ☎ 958 210 650, ⓦ www.laplateria.org.es. Private club devoted to the celebration of Andalucía's great folk art. There are frequent flamenco performances (Thurs or Sat are your best chances; entry €8), and visitors are generally welcomed so long as they show a genuine interest and aren't in too large a group. You'll need to arrive between 9–10pm, speak some Spanish and use a bit of charm. Closed Aug.

Sala Vimaambi Cuesta de San Gregorio 30, Albaicín ☎ 958 227 334, ⓦ www.vimaambi.com. A cultural and craft centre with frequent presentations of flamenco and *raíces* (roots) music from North Africa and South America. Concerts usually take place on Fri & Sat at 9pm & 10.30pm (€15 including a drink) but ring or check their website for the current programme.

DIRECTORY

Books, newspapers and maps Metro, c/Gracia 31, off c/Alhóndiga, to the southwest of Pl. de la Trinidad, is the best international bookshop, with a wide selection of books on Granada, Lorca, etc, plus walking maps. For maps, try also the Librería Dauro at c/Zacatín 3 (a pedestrian street between the cathedral and c/Reyes Católicos), or for a more specialist selection Cartografica del Sur, c/Valle Inclán 2, southwest of the train station.

Hospital Cruz Roja (Red Cross), c/Escoriaza 8 ☎ 958 222 222; Hospital Clinico San Cecilio, Avda. del Doctor Olóriz, near the Pl. de Toros ☎ 958 023 000. For advice on emergency treatment, phone ☎ 061.

Internet access There are cafés with free wi-fi all over town and wi-fi access should be possible near the news kiosk on Pl. María Pineda. Two central places are Free Memory, c/San Jerónimo 14 (daily 10am–2.30pm & 4.30–10pm), and Locutorio Azahara c/Colcha s/n (daily 9am–midnight), southwest of Pl. Nueva.

Police For emergencies, dial ☎ 091 (national) or ☎ 092 (local). The Policía Local station is at Pl. de Campos 3 ☎ 958 808 502. There's also a property lost-and-found section in the *ayuntamiento* building on Pl. del Carmen (☎ 958 248 103).

Post office Puerta Real (Mon–Fri 9am–8pm, Sat 9am–2pm).

Parque Nacional Sierra Nevada

The mountains of the **Sierra Nevada**, designated Andalucía's second national park in 1999, rise to the south of Granada, a startling backdrop to the city, snowcapped for much of the year and offering good trekking and also skiing from late November until late May. The ski slopes are at **Solynieve**, an unimaginative, developed resort just 28km away from the city centre. From here, you can make the two- to three-hour trek up to **Veleta** (3400m), the second-highest peak of the range (and of the Iberian Peninsula); this is a perfectly feasible day-trip from Granada by bus.

SIERRA NEVADA PRACTICALITIES

FLORA AND FAUNA

The Sierra Nevada is particularly rich in **wild flowers**, with fifty varieties unique to these mountains. **Wildlife** abounds away from the roads; one of the most exciting sights is the *Cabra hispanica*, a wild horned goat that (with luck) you'll see standing on pinnacles, silhouetted against the sky. Birdwatching is also superb, with the colourful hoopoe – a bird with a stark, haunting cry – a common sight.

INFORMATION AND TRANSPORT

The best **map** of the Sierra Nevada including the lower slopes of the Alpujarras is the one co-produced by the Instituto Geográfico Nacional and the Federación Española de Montañismo (1:50,000), generally available in Granada. A 1:40,000 **map and guide set**, *Sierra Nevada and La Alpujarra*, published in English by Editorial Alpina, is also good and comes with a booklet describing walks in the park and information on flora and fauna.

To reach the *parque nacional* with your **own transport**, take the Acera del Darro and follow signs for the Sierra Nevada. The park's **visitor centre**, "El Dornajo", is signposted just off the road, at the 22km mark (daily 10am–2pm & 5–7pm, Oct–March 4–6pm; ☎ 958 340 625, ⓦ www.mma.es). It sells guidebooks, maps and hats (sun protection is vital at this altitude), and has a permanent exhibition on the park's flora and fauna. They can provide hiking information (English spoken) and rent out horses and mountain bikes. The centre also has a **cafetería** with a stunning terrace view. Beyond the visitor centre, the route into the park continues for a further 10km to pass the Solynieve ski resort, and 2km farther on lies the *Albergue Universitario*, where the bus terminates.

Buses from Granada are operated by Autocares Bonal (☎ 958 465 022) with a daily service to Solynieve (€9 return) and, just above this, the *Albergue Universitario* (departs 9am, returns from *Albergue Universitario* 5pm, Solynieve 5.10pm). Tickets should be bought in advance at the bus station, although you can pay on board if the bus isn't full. For the winter service (Oct–March), ring the bus company or check with the *turismo*.

The Veleta ascent

From the *Albergue Universitario*, the Capileira road (closed to vehicles) runs past the **Pico Veleta**; now asphalted, it is perfectly – and tediously – walkable. With your own transport, it's possible to shave a couple of kilometres off the walk to the summit by ignoring the no-entry signs at the car park near the *Albergue* and continuing on to a second car park farther up the mountain, from which point the road is then barred. Although the peak of the mountain looks deceptively close from here, you should allow two to three hours up to the summit and two hours down. There is no water en route so you'd be advised to take some along; the summit makes a great place for a picnic. Weather permitting, the **views** beyond the depressing trappings of the ski resort are fabulous: the Sierra Subbética of Córdoba and the Sierra de Guadix to the north, the Mediterranean and Rif mountains of Morocco to the south, and nearby to the southeast, the towering mass of **Mulhacén** (3483m), the Spanish peninsula's highest peak.

Solynieve

SOLYNIEVE ("Sun and Snow" aka Pradollano), which lies outside the boundaries of the national park, is a hideous-looking ski resort regarded by serious alpine skiers as something of a joke, but with snow lingering so late in the year, it does have obvious attractions.

ACCOMMODATION

PARQUE NACIONAL SIERRA NEVADA

Albergue Juvenil c/Peñones 22 ☎ 958 575 116, ⓦ www.inturjoven.com. For budget accommodation, try the modern and comfortable *Albergue Juvenil*, on the edge of the ski resort, where you can get great-value (outside the Nov–March ski season) double and four-bed rooms, all en suite. They also rent out skis and equipment. Summer/winter under-26 **€21**, over-26 **€27**

Albergue Universitario ☎ 958 481 003, ⊚ www .nevadensis.com. Three kilometres away in isolated Peñones de San Francisco lies one more option: the *Albergue Universitario* with bunk rooms, doubles sharing bath, and a restaurant. B&B €22

CAMPING

Campsite ☎ 958 340 407. The only one in the area is at the Ruta del Purche, 15km out of Granada and halfway to Solynieve, with a supermarket and restaurant. The bus will drop you at the road leading to the site, from where it's a good 1km walk. Car & tent €8.50, per person €4.50

Las Alpujarras

Beyond the mountains, farther south from Granada, lie the great **valleys of the Alpujarras**, first settled in the twelfth century by Berber refugees from Seville, and later the Moors' last stronghold in Spain.

The valleys are bounded to the north by the Sierra Nevada, and to the south by the lesser *sierras* of Lujar, La Contraviesa and Gador. The eternal snows of the high *sierras* keep the valleys and their seventy or so villages well watered all summer long. Rivers have cut deep gorges in the soft mica and shale of the upper mountains, and over the centuries have deposited silt and fertile soil on the lower hills and in the valleys; here the villages have grown, for the soil is rich and easily worked. The intricate terracing that today preserves these deposits was begun as long as two thousand years ago by Visigoths or Ibero-Celts, whose remains have been found at Capileira.

Lanjarón

The road **south from Granada to Motril** climbs steeply after leaving the city, until at 860m above sea level it reaches the **Puerto del Suspiro del Moro** – the Pass of the Sigh of the Moor. Boabdil, last Moorish king of Granada, came this way, having just handed

THE MOORS AND AFTER

When they came to occupy the Alpujarras, the **Moors** set about improving agricultural techniques and modified the terracing and irrigation in their inimitable way. They transformed the Alpujarras into an earthly paradise, and here they retired to bewail the loss of their beloved lands in **al-Andalus**, resisting a series of royal edicts demanding their forced conversion to Christianity. In 1568, they rose up in a final, short-lived revolt, which led to the expulsion of all Spanish Moors. Even then, however, two Moorish families were required to stay in each village to show the new Christian peasants, who had been marched down from Galicia and Asturias to repopulate the valleys, how to operate the intricate irrigation systems.

Through the following centuries, the land fell into the hands of a few wealthy families, and the general population became impoverished labourers. The Civil War passed lightly over the Alpujarras: the occasional truckload of Nationalist youth trundled in from Granada, rounded up a few bewildered locals and shot them for "crimes" of which they were wholly ignorant; Republican youths came up in their trucks from Almería and did the same thing. Under Franco, the stranglehold of the landlords increased and there was real hardship and suffering. Today, the population has one of the lowest per capita incomes in Andalucía, with – as a recent report put it – "a level of literacy bordering on that of the Third World, alarming problems of desertification, poor communications and a high degree of underemployment".

Ironically, the land itself is still very fertile – oranges, chestnuts, bananas, apples and avocados grow here – while the recent influx of **tourism** is bringing limited wealth to the region. The so-called "High" Alpujarras have become popular with Spanish tourists and also with migrants from northern Europe who have purchased property here; Pampaneira, Bubión and Capileira, all within half an hour's drive from Lanjarón, have been scrubbed and whitewashed. Though a little over-prettified, they're far from spoilt, and have acquired shops, lively bars, good, unpretentious restaurants and small, family-run **pensiones**. Other villages, less picturesque or less accessible, have little employment, and are sustained only by farming.

LAS ALPUJARRAS

PUBLIC TRANSPORT IN THE ALPUJARRAS

There are several **buses** a day from both Granada and Motril to **Lanjarón** and **Órgiva**, and one a day from Almería in the east. There are also buses from Granada (daily 8.30am & 6pm) to Ugíjar (4hr), in the **"Low" Alpujarras**, via a less scenic route through Lanjarón, Órgiva, Torvizcón, Cadiar, Yegen and Valor.

A direct **bus** from Granada to the more spectacular **"High" Alpujarras** (noon & 4.30pm) runs via Trevélez to Bérchules (returns 5.50am & 5.05pm, passing Trevélez 6.15am & 5.30pm). The return buses arrive in Granada at 9.25am and 8.50pm respectively (with another service from Trevélez to Granada at 4pm). Further information is available from the bus operator Alsina Graells (☎ 902 422 242).

over the keys of his city to the Reyes Católicos. From the pass you catch your last glimpse of the city and the Alhambra. Just beyond Béznar is the turning to **Lanjarón** and **Órgiva**, the market town of the region. **LANJARÓN** has been subject to tourism and the influence of the outside world for longer than anywhere else in the Alpujarras owing to the curative powers of its **spa waters**, sold in bottled form throughout Spain.

Balneario

March–Dec; ☎ 958 770 137, ⓦ www.balneariodelanjaron.com

Between March and December, the spa baths are open, and the town fills with the aged and infirm – should you wish to try a cure at the **Balneario** at the village's western end, a basic soak will cost €15, with add-ons for massage, mud baths and all kinds of other alarming-sounding *tracciónes* and *inyecciónes*.

The Moorish castle

Details from the *turismo*

Lanjarón itself is little more than a ribbon of buildings, mostly modern, flanking the road through the village, the Avda. Alpujarra, and its continuation, the Avda. Andalucía. Below this thoroughfare, marking Lanjarón's medieval status as the gateway to the Alpujarras, is a **Moorish castle**, newly refurbished and due to open in 2009. A ten-minute stroll reveals its dramatic setting – follow the signs down the hill from the main street and out onto the terraces and meadows below the town.

Walks around Lanjarón

The countryside and mountains within a day's walk of Lanjarón, however, are beyond compare. A track off the backstreets behind town takes you steeply up to the vast spaces of the **Reserva Nacional de la Sierra Nevada**. For a somewhat easier day's walk out of Lanjarón, go to the bridge just east of town and take the sharply climbing, cobbled track that parallels the **river**. After two to two and a half hours through small farms, with magnificent views and scenery, a downturn to a small stone bridge permits return to Lanjarón on the opposite bank. Allow a minimum of six hours and it would be wise to confirm with the *turismo* that the route is open before setting out.

ARRIVAL AND INFORMATION   LANJARÓN

By bus Midway along the same street as the municipal tourist office (now c/Real) is the bus stand with a ticket office at no. 123 (☎ 958 770 003) near the Caja Rural bank.

Turismo Opposite the Balneario, Avda. Andalucía s/n

(Mon–Sat 10am–2pm & 4.30–8.30pm, Sun 10–2pm; ☎ 958 770 462).

Internet access is available at Cyberplay Lanjarón, Avda. de Andalucía 30, at the eastern end of the main street to the side of the La Caixa bank (daily except Wed 6pm–midnight).

ACCOMMODATION

Hotel Alcadima c/Francisco Tarrega 3 ☎ 958 770 809, ⓦ www.alcadima.com. Farther along the road, a signed

turn-off leads downhill to the excellent *Hotel Alcadima*, with the best pool and restaurant terrace in town, and many of the comfortable rooms have stunning balcony views towards the castle. Free wi-fi. **€85**

Hotel España Avda. Alpujarra 42 ☎ 958 770 187, ⓦ www.lanjaron.biz. The grand-looking *Hotel España*, next door to the Balneario, has played host to Lorca and Manuel de Falla in its time. Slightly past its prime, it is nevertheless good value, very friendly and has a pool. B&B **€45**

Hotel Paris Avda. Alpujarra 23 ☎ 958 770 556, ⓦ www.hotelparislanjaron.com. A charming and very good value hotel on the main street. Rooms come with TV and there's a decent restaurant and large pool. **€44**

EATING AND DRINKING

Lanjarón has plenty of **restaurants** and tapas bars, too, many attached to the hotels (the *España*'s is worth trying), which often offer good-value *menús*.

Bar Galvez c/Real 95, at the eastern end of the main street. Popular and economical bar-restaurant serving up tapas and *raciones* as well as *platos combinados*. A good choice if you're on a tighter budget with a *menú* for around €11. Daily 1–4pm & 8–11pm.

Hotel Castillo Alcadima c/Francisco Tarrega 3 ☎ 958 770 809. Perhaps the best choice for dining out is the terrace restaurant of the hotel of the same name which is a pretty well perfect place to while away a summer evening with a superb terrace view of the castle. Specialities include meat dishes of the *sierra* but also fish and some vegetarian possibilities including an *ensalada alpujarreña* and a menú for €15. Daily 1– 4pm & 8–11pm.

Órgiva

Heading east out of Lanjarón brings you after 11km to **ÓRGIVA** (also spelled Órjiva), the "capital" and market centre of the western Alpujarras. It is closer to the heart of the valley but is still really only a starting point; if the bus goes on to Capileira, you may want to stay on it. If you're **driving**, it's worth noting that petrol stations become scarcer from this point on.

Órgiva is a lively enough town, though, with plenty of bars and hotels and an animated **Thursday market** that draws in shoppers from far and wide. On the main street is an over-restored Mudéjar palace, now housing the *ayuntamiento*, and the sixteenth-century church of **Nuestra Señora de la Expectación**, whose towers add a touch of fancy to the townscape.

ACCOMMODATION

ÓRGIVA

Alma Alpujarreña c/González Robles 49 ☎ 958 784 085. For budget accommodation, one of the nicest places is the pretty *Alma Alpujarreña*, a little beyond the traffic lights at the town's main (and solitary) intersection, with simple and en-suite rooms plus a leafy terrace restaurant. **€50**

Camping Órgiva Ctra. A348 km 18.9 ☎ 958 784 307. Órgiva's campsite, with ample shade plus a pool, bar and restaurant, lies 2km south of town reached by continuing along the road where the bus drops you. It also rents out cabins and bungalows, has its own restaurant and pool and can advise on walking routes and renting horses in the nearby Sierra de Lújar. **€5**, **€5** per tent, **€4** per vehicle

Hotel-Hostal Mirasol Avda. González Robles 3 ☎ 958 785 159. Good-value rooms with TV and free wi-fi on the way in from Lanjarón. **€45**

EATING AND DRINKING

Alma Alpujarreña c/González Robles 49 ☎ 958 784 085. The *hostal* has a decent and economical restaurant with a good-value *menú* for €8.50. House specials include a tasty *sopa de ajo* (garlic soup) and a *paella vegetal* (vegetarian). Daily 1–4pm & 8–11pm.

La Almazara c/González Robles 53, almost next door to the pensión Alma Alpujarreña. Offers a range of hearty mountain dishes as well as excellent freshly made pizzas. Also has a pleasant garden terrace. Main dishes €7–15. 12.30–4pm & 8–11pm; closed Wed.

Baraka c/Estación 12. An economical place worth seeking out in the upper town near the market, this is a pleasant small Moroccan-style café and *tetería* offering felafel, couscous, tagines and a variety of teas. 8am– midnight; closed Fri.

El Limonero in c/Yanez 27, off the main road downhill from La Almazara. Órgiva's most creative restaurant has a very pleasant rustic-modern dining room plus a small terrace. Signature dishes include *paletilla de cordero* (oven baked lamb) and *lubina con salsa* (sea bass). Main dishes €10–20. Daily 7–11pm.

The High (western) Alpujarras

The best way to experience the **High Alpujarras** is to walk, and there are a number of paths between Órgiva and Cadiar, at the farthest reaches of the western valleys. Equip yourself with a compass and the Instituto Geográfico Nacional/Federación Española de Montañismo 1:50,000 map or the Editorial Alpina map, which cover all the territory from Órgiva up to Bérchules (Alpina) and Berja (IGN/FEM) respectively. Alternatively, a bus from Lanjarón (daily 1pm) winds through all the upper Alpujarran villages. **Walkers' guides** to the Alpujarras are now beginning to mushroom (see p.921).

Cañar, Soportújar and Carataunas

From Órgiva, the first settlements you reach, almost directly above the town, are **CAÑAR** and **SOPORTÚJAR**, the latter a maze of sinuous white-walled alleys. Like many of the High Alpujarran villages, they congregate on the neatly terraced mountainside, planted with poplars and laced with irrigation channels. Both villages are perched precariously on the steep hillside with a rather sombre view of Órgiva in the valley below, and the mountains of Africa over the ranges to the south.

Just below the two villages, the tiny hamlet of **CARATAUNAS** is particularly pretty and puts on a lively start to its Semana Santa on Palm Sunday, when an effigy of Judas is tossed on a bonfire. Two kilometres out of Carataunas a turn-off on the left (signed "Camino Forestal") beyond the *Los Llanos* restaurant ascends 6km (the last three a rugged unpaved track) to the Buddhist monastery of Osel Ling.

4

ACCOMMODATION AND EATING · CAÑAR AND SOPORTÚJAR

Bar Correillo c/Real, behind the church in Soportújar ☎ 958 787 578. Bar which can provide excellent-value en-suite rooms. **€40**

Poqueira Gorge

Shortly after Carataunas the road swings to the north, and you have your first view of the **Poqueira Gorge**, a huge, sheer gash into the heights of the Sierra Nevada. Trickling deep in the bed of the cleft is the Río Poqueira, which has its source near the peak of Mulhacén. The steep walls of the gorge are terraced and wooded from top to bottom, and dotted with little stone farmhouses. Much of the surrounding country looks barren from a distance, but close up you'll find it's rich with flowers, woods, springs and streams.

Pampaneira

A trio of villages – three of the most spectacular and popular in the Alpujarras – teeters on the steep edge of the gorge. The first is neat, prosperous and pretty **PAMPANEIRA**.

Above Pampaneira, on the very peak of the western flank of the Poqueira gorge, is the **Tibetan Buddhist Monastery of Osel Ling** ("Place of Clear Light"), founded in 1982 by a Tibetan monk on land donated by the communities of Pampaneira and Bubión. The simple, stone-built monastery, complete with stupas and stunning **views** across the Alpujarras, welcomes visitors between 3pm and 6pm daily; lectures on Buddhism are held regularly and facilities exist for those who want to visit for periods of retreat in cabins dotted around the site (☎958 343 134 for details).

INFORMATION · PAMPANEIRA

Information centre On its leafy main square, Pl. de la Libertad, is Nevadensis, an information centre for the Natural and National Parks of the Sierra Nevada (Sun & Mon 10am–3pm, Tues–Sat 10am–2pm & 4–6pm; ☎958 763 127, ⓦnevadensis.com); they also sell large-scale topographical maps of the zone, and offer horseriding tours and guided treks, including an ascent of Mulhacén. Other activities on offer include mountain biking, climbing, canyoning and cross-country skiing. If you're thinking of a longer stay, this is also where you can pick up a list of hostels, village houses and farmhouses for rent throughout the Alpujarras.

ACCOMMODATION

Hostal Pampaneira c/José Antonio 1, at the entrance to the village ☎958 763 002, ⓦhostalpampaneira .com. Homely *hostal* above a bar-restaurant with functional en-suite rooms with TV and heating. €42

Hotel Estrella c/Huertos 21, 200m along the road climbing above the village ☎958 763 981, ⓦestrella delasnieves.com. This plush new hotel has well-equipped en-suite rooms, many with their own terrace balcony and spectacular views. Facilities include a garden pool, free wi-fi and garage. €70

EATING AND DRINKING

Bar Belezmín Pl. Libertad 11. On the village's main square, this is one of the village's best places to eat with a menu filled with hearty *alpujarreña* dishes such as *jabalí* (wild boar) and *perdiz* (partridge). Daily 1–4pm & 8–10.30pm.

Casa Julio Avda. de la Alpujarra 9, up some steps near the Hostal Pampaneira. Another place offering solid mountain fare accompanied with vegetables from its own *huerta* (vegetable garden). House specials include *gitanilla de habichuelas* (mountain stew) and there's an €8 *menú*. Daily 10am–4pm & 8–11pm.

Hostal Pampaneira c/José Antonio 1. The *hostal*'s restaurant is also worth a try and cooks up many local dishes with style. Try the *potaje de garbanzos* (a warming chickpea soup). There's a *menú* for €9. Daily 1–4pm & 8–11pm.

Bubión

BUBIÓN is backed for much of the year by snowcapped peaks. The village has a private **museum**, the Casa Alpujarreña (Sun–Fri 11am–2pm, Fri & Sat also 5–7pm; €1.80), just off Plaza de la Iglesia, the main square, displaying aspects of the folklore, daily life and architecture of the Alpujarras in a traditional house.

INFORMATION AND ACTIVITIES

Information Rustic Blue (☎958 763 381, ⓦrusticblue .com), a privately run information office on the main road to the right as you enter the village, can also book horseriding and walking tours and help with accommodation in fully equipped houses across the Alpujarras.

Horseriding trips For trips of one to five days, contact the friendly Rancho Rafael Belmonte (☎958 763 135, ⓦwww .ridingandalucia.com), at the bottom of the village near Rustic Blue, or the long-established Dallas Love (☎958 763 038, ⓦspain-horse-riding.com).

ACCOMMODATION

Las Terrazas Pl. del Sol 7 ☎958 763 034, ⓦwww. terrazasalpujarra.com. This is a comfortable and welcoming hostal with rustic tile-floored en-suite rooms with heating, many with views. It also rents out some apartments and does a good-value breakfast for €2.50. €34

Los Tinaos c/Parras s/n, downhill from the above ☎958 763 217, ⓦwww.lostinaos.com. This option offers some excellent heated apartments that come with garden terrace, kitchen, satellite TV and fine views. €60

EATING AND DRINKING

The two **best places to eat** in the village feature *alpujarreño* specialities such as *migas* (breadcrumbs fried in garlic) and *plato alpujarreño* (a hefty fry-up) on their menus.

La Artesa c/Carretera s/n Just over the road from *La Teide* this is another good place for solid mountain cooking with a *menú* for €8.50. Daily 1–4pm & 8–11pm; closed Sun eve & Mon.

La Teide c/Carretera s/n, on the road running through the village. This is the better of the two restaurants on opposite sides of the road here and has a leafy terrace and a good-value weekday *menú* for €9. Daily noon–4pm & 8–11pm.

Capileira

Two kilometres north of Bubión, CAPILEIRA is the highest of the three villages and the terminus of the road – Europe's highest, but now closed to traffic – across the heart of the Sierra Nevada from Granada.

Just downhill from the information kiosk lies the village's interesting **museum** (Tues–Sun 11.30am–2.30pm; €1), containing displays of regional dress and handicrafts, as well as various bits and pieces belonging to, or produced by, Pedro

Alarcón, the nineteenth-century Spanish writer who made a trip through the Alpujarras and wrote a (not very good) book about it.

ARRIVAL AND INFORMATION
CAPILEIRA

By bus In addition to the direct daily afternoon **bus** from Granada, anything going to Ugíjar and Berja will come very close to Capileira; buses to Granada and Órgiva pass by in the early morning with two in the late afternoon. If you're thinking of doing any walking in this zone, this is probably the best village in which to base yourself.

Information A kiosk for the national park is at the centre of the village (daily 10am–2pm & 5–8pm), near where the

bus drops you, which hands out a village map and acts as an information office.

Maps In addition to the information in the various villages, more fine walking routes are detailed in *34 Alpujarras Walks* by Charles Davis, *Landscapes of Andalucía* by John and Christine Oldfield, *Walking in Andalucía* by Guy Hunter-Watts and *Holiday Walks in the Alpujarra* by Jeremy Rabjohns.

ACCOMMODATION

El Cascapeñas Carretera de la Sierra 5 ☎ 958 763 011, ⓦ elcascapeñas.com. Near the bus stop, this has good-value en-suite rooms with TV, split between a *hostal* and hotel. **€45**

Finca Los Llanos Carretera Sierra Nevada s/n ☎ 958 763 071, ⓦ hotelfincalosllanos.com. This is a relatively luxurious option with apartment-style rooms with kitchenettes and terraces; facilities include a pool and good restaurant. B&B **€75**

Hostal Atalaya c/Perchel 3 ☎ 958 763 025, ⓦ hostalatalaya.com. To the right as you enter the village, this is a

pleasant little place with en-suite rooms with TV and terrific views from those at the front. **€30**

Mesón-Hostal Poqueira c/Dr Castilla 11 ☎ 958 763 048, ⓦ hotelpoqueira.com. Near the bus stop, this is a welcoming option for en-suite heated rooms, some with terraces and views, and there's also a pool and good restaurant with a *menú* for around €10. It also has some attractive apartments sleeping up to four (€50–80) for longer stays. They are building a new hotel in the centre of the village to be completed in 2012. Rooms: *hostal* **€40**, hotel **€60**

EATING AND DRINKING

Bar–Restaurante El Tilo c/Calvario 1. On the focal Pl. Calvario in the lower village, this is a decent place for *platos combinados* or *chacinería* (cured pork products) or simply watching-the-world-go-by drinks on its tranquil terrace shaded by a lime tree. Daily 10am–11pm.

Bodega La Alacena c/Trocadero 1. Downhill from *El Tilo*, this is a popular option for *jamón* and cheese tapas and its shop also sells local products such as honey, wine, cheese and hams. Daily 10am–2pm & 6–10pm.

Casa Ibero c/Parra 1, near the museum. The tangerine-tinted dining room of *Casa Ibero* (open evenings only) is a popular place for vegetarian dishes such as couscous,

Indian and other adventurous concoctions. Daily 7.30–11pm; closed Sun eve & Wed.

La Casa de Paco y Pilar Carretera Sierra Nevada 16, uphill near the hotel Finca Los Llanos. Cosy restaurant with well-prepared *alpurrajeño* specialities (with some vegetarian options). Has a pleasant garden terrace and a €10 *menú*. Daily 11am–4pm & 8pm–midnight.

Mesón Rural Panjuila c/Carretera 24, a little way uphill from the bus stop. This is a pleasant and economical rustic place for *alpujarreña* specialities with a €9.50 *menú*. Daily 11am–4pm & 8–11pm.

The High Route to Trevélez

PITRES and **PÓRTUGOS**, 6km east of Pampaneira and the next two villages on the High Route, are perhaps more "authentic" and less polished. Down below the main road (GR421) linking Pitres and Pórtugos are the three villages of Mecina Fondales (and its offshoot, Mecinilla), Ferreirola and Busquistar; along with Pitres, these formed a league of villages known as the *Taha* under the Moors. **FERREIROLA** and **BUSQUISTAR** are especially attractive, as is the path between the two, clinging to the north side of the valley of the Río Trevélez. You're out of tourist country here and the villages display their genuine characteristics to better effect, while all around you is some of the best Alpujarran walking country. **TREVÉLEZ**, at the end of an austere ravine carved by the Río Trevélez, is purportedly Spain's highest permanent settlement, with cooler temperatures year-round than its neighbours. In traditional Alpujarran style, it has lower, middle and upper quarters (*barrios bajo, medio* and *alto*) overlooking a grassy, poplar-lined valley where the river starts its long descent.

ACCOMMODATION   THE HIGH ROUTE TO TREVÉLEZ

There are plenty of places to stay along the route but outside high summer make sure that the room heating is adequate as nights can be chilly.

Casa Sonia c/San Francisco 5, Busquístar ☎958 857 503, ⊛www.casasoniaenbusquistar.com. This is a charming *casa rural* in the heart of the village near the church, with elegant en-suite a/c rooms, some with great views. B&B **€58**

Hostal Fernando c/del Pista del Barrio Medio s/n, Trevélez ☎958 858 565. Located in the *barrio medio* this is a friendly place with good-value heated (useful outside July & Aug) en-suite rooms. **€30**

★ **Hotel La Fragua I** c/Antonio 4, barrio alto ☎958 858 626, ⊛hotellafragua.com. This is probably the most pleasant place to stay in the village which is why it's popular with hiking groups; thus you may be better off ringing ahead to be sure of a room. They've recently added *Hotel La Fragua II* nearby (with pool), but space can still be tight. Offers pine-furnished en-suite heated rooms with TV and wi-fi, many with fine views. The proprietors can provide information on walking and other mountain pursuits such as horseriding and mountain biking. Also has a superb and justly popular restaurant (with veggie options) between the two hotels which shouldn't be missed. **€48**

Hotel de Mecina Fondales c/La Fuente s/n Mecina Fondales ☎958 766 241, ⊛www.hoteldemecina.com. A delightful and comfortable hideaway, where many rooms come with terrace balcony and fine views. Also has an excellent garden pool and can provide information on

renting horses and mountain bikes. B&B **€88** (*Rough Guide* readers with this guide get 10 percent off).

Hotel San Roque c/Cruz 1, Pitres, on the east side of the village ☎958 857 528. For accommodation in Pitres, you could try the *Hotel San Roque*, which has decent rooms with (on the south side) views. B&B **€58**

Refugio de los Albergues Pitres ☎958 343 176. On the village's eastern edge, the *Refugio de los Albergues* is an old Civil War hostel with dormitory beds and a single double room sharing bath. Also has a communal kitchen. Dorm **€10**, double **€30**

★ **Sierra y Mar** c/Albaycin 3, Ferreirola ☎958 766 171, ⊛www.sierraymar.com. A delightful Scandinavian-run guesthouse in a traditional mountain dwelling, with fine views and where the owners – enthusiastic walkers – will advise on routes in the area. B&B **€62**

CAMPING

Balcón de Pitres Carretera Órgiva–Ugíjar km 51 ☎958 766 111. Pitres' campsite with restaurant and pool, is located in a stunning position 1km west of the village with fine views. **€5**, **€5** per tent, **€4.50** per vehicle

Camping Trevélez ☎958 858 735. Trevélez's campsite lies 1km out along the Órgiva road; conditions are arctic in midwinter, but it also rents out some heated cabins (€30–70). **€4.65**, **€4.16** per tent, **€3.90** per vehicle

EATING AND DRINKING

MECINILLA

Hotel de Mecina Fondales c/La Fuente s/n. The hotel has its own decent restaurant offering well-prepared Alpujarran cuisine. Its bar is also open for breakfast. Daily 1–4pm & 8–11pm.

L'Atelier c/Alberca s/n, in the adjoining hamlet of Mecinilla ☎958 857 501. Arguably the best place for food here is this French-run restaurant specializing in vegetarian/vegan cuisine, and located in the old village bakery. Booking is advised at weekends. It also lets a few rooms (B&B €50) and has singles. Daily 1–4pm & 8–11pm; closed Tues.

TREVÉLEZ

Besides *La Fragua*'s excellent restaurant (see above), other places to eat here are spread between the three *barrios*.

Mesón Haraicel c/Real s/n just above the barrio bajo's main square, Pl. Francisco Abellán. Economical restaurant serving meat and fish dishes as well as salads; also offers tapas and *raciones* in its bar. Small outdoor terrace. Daily 9.30am–9pm.

Mesón del Jamón c/Carcel s/n. Trevélez's *jamón serrano* is a prized speciality and an obsession throughout eastern Andalucía and this is a good place to try it. Also serves *platos combinados*. Daily 9am–10pm.

Mesón Joaquín c/Puente s/n. In the lower *barrio*, this is another good place to try the local *jamón* which you can also purchase in larger quantities from its *jamón* store opposite. The restaurant also does *platos combinados* and *solomillo de cerdo* (pork loin) is a house special. There's also a *menú* for €9. Daily 10am–4pm & 7–10pm.

Bérchules

Heading east from Trevélez, you come to **Juviles**, an attractive village straddling the road, followed, 5km further on, by **BÉRCHULES**, a high village of grassy streams and chestnut woods, also famous for its *jamón*. It is a large, abruptly demarcated settlement, three streets wide, on a sharp slope overlooking yet another canyon.

ACCOMMODATION
BÉRCHULES

Alojamiento Rural La Tahoma c/Baja de la Iglesia s/n ☎ 958 769 051. This place (as the street name implies) is just below the church and offers excellent-value apartments with kitchen, *salón* and TV, and one-night stays are possible. **€30**

Hotel Los Bérchules ☎ 958 852 530, ⓦ hotelberchules .com. On the main road into the village, this two-star hotel

has comfortable rooms above its own restaurant and there's also a pool. **€52**

El Mirador de Berchules Pl. de Zapata 1 ☎ 958 769 090, ⓦ miradordeberchules.com. In the upper village (ask for directions), this is an attractive option for studios and apartments with terraces and views. Also has its own good tapas bar, restaurant and pool. **€55–60**

EATING AND DRINKING

Bar Vaqueras Pl. Victoria s/n. This earthy bar on the village's main square is a good place to stop for breakfast or,

later in the day, tapas and *raciones*. Daily 9am–11pm.

Cádiar

Just below Bérchules, **CÁDIAR**, is the central town – or "navel" as Gerald Brenan termed it – of the Alpujarras, more attractive than it seems from a distance, and springs into life when a colourful **produce market** is held on the 3rd and 18th of every month, sometimes including livestock. The annual **Fuente del Vino** wine and cattle fair (Oct 5–9) turns the waters of the fountain literally to wine.

ACCOMMODATION
CÁDIAR

★ **Alquería de Morayma** ☎ 958 343 303, ⓦ alqueria morayma.com. The most tempting place to stay here is an out-of-town option, 2km away along the A348 towards Torvizcón, where this excellent-value apart-hotel is housed in a converted *alpujarran cortijo* sited in 86 acres of farmland. There are charmingly rustic rooms and apartments (almost same price) many with patio terraces,

and it has its own good restaurant (open to nonguests). Guests can go mountain biking and horseriding, and there are also plenty of hiking trails. The *Morayma's* own organic farm and vineyard on the estate, the *bodega* of which is open to visitors, also supplies the restaurant and provides its virgin olive oil and bottled wine. **€58**

Eastern Alpujarras

Cádiar and Bérchules mark the end of the western Alpujarras, and a striking change in the landscape; the dramatic, severe but relatively green terrain of the Guadalfeo and Cádiar valleys gives way to open rolling and much more arid land. The villages of the eastern Alpujarras display many of the characteristics of those to the west, but as a rule they are poorer and much less visited by tourists. There are attractive places to visit nonetheless though, among them **Yegen**, which Brenan wrote about, and the market centre of **Ugíjar**.

Yegen

In **YEGEN**, made famous by **Gerald Brenan**, some 7km northeast of Cádiar, there's a plaque on the house (just along from the central fountain) where the author lived during his ten or so years of Alpujarran residence. His autobiography of these times, *South from Granada*, is the best account of rural life in Spain between the wars, and describes the visits made here by Virginia Woolf, Bertrand Russell and the arch-complainer Lytton Strachey. Disillusioned with the strictures of middle-class life in England after World War I, Brenan rented a house in Yegen and shipped out a library of two thousand books, from which he was to spend the next eight years educating himself. He later moved to the hills behind Torremolinos, where he died in 1987, a writer better known and respected in Spain (he made an important study of St John of the Cross) than in his native England.

Brenan connections aside, Yegen is one of the most characteristic Alpujarran villages, with its two distinct quarters, cobbled paths and cold-water springs.

ACCOMMODATION

YEGEN

Bar La Fuente Pl. de Fuente s/n ☎958 851 067, ⓦwww.pensionlafuente.com. Opposite the fountain in the square, this is a small *hostal* offering rooms with and without bath and whose bar is decorated with some old photos of Brenan. **€40**

El Rincón de Yegen Camino de Gerald Brenan s/n ☎620 446 872, ⓦwww.aldearural.com/rincondeyegen. Heading east out of Yegen, you'll find more upmarket accommodation at this pleasant country hotel where

heated rooms come with TV. There are also apartments for longer stays, as well as a pool and a good, inexpensive restaurant. **€43**

El Tinao c/Carretera s/n ☎958 851 212, ⓔltinaoyegen @hotmail.com. Bright and airy en-suite rooms at this *hostal* located on the main road through, which also rents a couple of fully equipped houses in the village (3 nights minimum). **€30**

EATING AND DRINKING

Bar La Fuente Pl. Fuente s/n. A good breakfast option and later in the day also serves tapas and *raciones* as well as *platos combinados*. Daily 9am–10pm.

Bar Muñoz c/La Iglesia s/n, in the barrio bajo. An

atmospheric old bar frequented by Brenan in the old village serving simple tapas (mainly *jamón* and cheese) and where, on cooler nights, locals gather around the *chimenea* (fireplace) to keep warm. Daily 9am–11pm.

Towards Almería

If you don't enter Almería province via the Alpujarras following the winding A348 that eventually arrives at Almería city, the most straightforward route from Granada – and that followed by buses – is along the **A92 autovía**.

La Calahorra
Wed 10am–1pm & 4–6pm • €3

The main landmark, 16km beyond the town of Guadix, famous for its cave dwellings, is a magnificent sixteenth-century castle on a hill (15min hike) above the village of **La Calahorra**, one of the finest in Spain, with a remarkable Renaissance patio within. If it's closed, visit the guardian's house – avoiding *siesta* time – at c/de los Claveles 2 (☎958 677 098; Spanish only), and he will open it up for a consideration.

ACCOMMODATION

LA CALAHORRA

Hostal-Restaurante La Bella Carretera de Aldeire 1 ☎958 677 000. For rooms, try the central *Hostal-Restaurante*

La Bella, which, in addition to en-suite rooms, also has a decent restaurant with a decent weekday €9 *menú*. **€40**

Puerto de la Ragua and beyond

From La Calahorra a minor mountain road, the A337, climbs dizzily and scenically to the **Puerto de la Ragua**, at 1993m Andalucía's highest all-weather pass. It's another route into the Alpujarras, and once through the pass the road descends to Yegen. If you're driving, you might want to keep going straight on the *autovía*, meeting the Almería–Sorbas road at what has become known as **Mini Hollywood** (see p.363), the preserved film set of *A Fistful of Dollars*.

Almería province

The **province of Almería** is a strange corner of Spain. Inland, it has an almost **lunar landscape** of desert, sandstone cones and dried-up riverbeds. The coast to the east of the provincial **capital** is still largely unspoilt; lack of water and roads frustrated development in the 1960s and 70s and it is only now beginning to take off. Limited development allowed the creation in the 1980s of the **Parque Natural de Cabo de Gata**, a haven for flora and fauna. To the west of Almería is another story, though, with a sea of plastic greenhouses spreading in a broad swathe for a good 30km across the Campo de Dalías, the source of much of Almería's new-found wealth.

4

A number of **good beaches** are accessible by bus, and in this hottest province of Spain they're worth considering during what would be the off-season elsewhere, since Almería's summers start well before Easter and last into November. In midsummer, it's incredibly hot (frequently touching 38°c/100°F in the shade and often well above), while all year round there's an intense, almost luminous, sunlight. This and the weird scenery have made Almería one of the most popular **film locations** in Europe – much of *Lawrence of Arabia* was shot here, along with scores of spaghetti Westerns.

Almería

ALMERÍA is a pleasant, modern city, spread at the foot of a stark grey mountain in the heart of Almería province. Once you've seen the stunning Moorish Alcazaba, an austere cathedral and a wonderfully presented archeological museum there's not a lot left to do. Any time left over is probably best devoted to sampling the cafés, tapas bars and terrazas in the streets circling the Puerta de Purchena, the focal junction of the modern town, or strolling along the main Paseo de Almería down towards the harbour and taking day-trips out to the beaches along the coast. The city's own **beach**, southeast of the centre beyond the train lines, is long but dismal.

The Alcazaba

Tues–Sun 9am–8.30pm, Nov–March until 6.30pm • €1.50, free with EU passport

At the summit of the stark, grey hill overlooking the city is a tremendous **Alcazaba**, probably the best surviving example of Moorish military fortification, with three huge walled enclosures, in the second of which are the remains of a mosque, converted to a chapel by the Reyes Católicos. In the eleventh century, when Almería was an independent kingdom and the wealthiest, most commercially active city of Spain, this citadel contained immense gardens and palaces and some twenty thousand people. Its grandeur was reputed to rival the court of Granada, but comparisons are impossible since little beyond the walls and towers remains, the last remnants of its stuccowork having been sold off by the locals in the eighteenth century.

The Catedral

Mon–Fri 10am–2pm & 4–5pm, Sat 10am–2pm • €3

From the Alcazaba, however, you do get a good view of the coast, of Almería's **cave quarter** – the Barrio de la Chanca on a low hill to the left – and of the city's strange, fortified **Catedral**, built in the sixteenth century at a time when the southern Mediterranean was terrorized by the raids of Barbarossa and other Turkish and North African pirate forces; its corner towers once held cannon.

Museo Arqueológico

Tues 2.30–8.30pm, Wed–Sat 9am–8.30pm, Sun 9am–2.30pm • €1.50, free with EU passport

Almería's splendid and recently constructed **Museo Arqueológico**, Carretera de Ronda 91, off the east side of Avda. Federico García Lorca, is also worth a visit and has an impressive collection of important artefacts from the prehistoric site of Los Millares, as well as interesting Roman and Moorish collections, including some fine Moorish ceramics.

ARRIVAL AND DEPARTURE
ALMERÍA

By air Almería's international airport is 8km out of town with a connecting bus service (#20, labelled "El Alquián") every half-hour (between 7am–9pm) from the junction of Avda. Federico García Lorca and c/Gregorio Marañon.

By train Almería's bus and train stations (☎ 902 240 202) have been combined into a striking Estación Intermodal, on Carretera de Ronda, a couple of blocks east of Avda. de

Federico García Lorca, with the bus terminals and train platforms side by side.

Destinations Granada (4 daily; 2hr 20min); Seville (4 daily; 5hr 30min).

By bus Almería's bus station (☎ 950 262 098) has frequent connections with provincial and regional destinations.

Destinations Agua Amarga (6 daily; 1hr 30min); Cabo de

ALMERÍA

N

ACCOMMODATION

Albergue Juvenil	5
Camping La Garrofa	6
Hostal Estación	3
Hotel La Perla	2
Hotel Sevilla	1
Hotel Torreluz	4

EATING

Bodega Aranda	1
Bodega Las Botas	2
Casa Puga	4
El Quinto Toro	3
Teteria Restaurante Almedina	5

Muralla de San Cristóbal

Catedral

Alcazaba

Hospital Provincial

Gobierno Militar

Gobierno Civil

Palacio de Justicia

Teatro Cervantes

Basílica de Nuestra Señora del Mar

Diputación

Gata/San José (6 daily; 55min); Carboneras (6 daily; 1hr 15min); Córdoba (1 daily; 4hr); Granada (7 daily; 4hr); Jaén (4 daily; 4hr); Madrid (5 daily; 7hr); Málaga (7 daily; 3hr 30min); Mini Hollywood, now Oasis (4 daily; 40min); Mojácar (7 daily; 1hr 40min); Níjar (2 daily Mon–Fri; 35min); Seville (3 daily; 5hr 45min); Tabernas (7 daily; 40min); Ugíjar (2 daily; 2hr 45min).

By ferry There are boats to Melilla on the Moroccan coast throughout summer (fewer out of season), a journey that can pay dividends in both time and money over Algeciras if you're driving (daily; 6hr; June–Sept high-speed ferry 4hr). For information and tickets, contact Compañía Trasmediterránea, Parque Nicolás Salmerón 19, near the port (☎ 950 236 956, ⊛ trasmediterranea.es). The boat to Nador in Morocco (daily April–Sept; 6hr) is run by Ferrimaroc, which has an office at the port (☎ 950 274 800, ⊛ ferrimaroc.com).A useful site for checking the latest ferry schedules is ⊛ directferries.co.uk.

Destinations Melilla (11 weekly; 3hr); Nador (12 weekly; 6hr).

INFORMATION

Turismo On c/Parque de Nicolás Salmerón (Mon–Fri 9am–7.30pm, Oct–May 8.30am–2pm, Sat & Sun 9.30am–3pm; ☎ 950 175 220). They have a list of most buses out of Almería, as well as train and boat schedules.

Internet Ciber el Puerto, c/Alvárez de Castro 24, near the turismo (daily 10am–10pm).

ACCOMMODATION

Albergue Juvenil Almería c/Isla de Fuerteventura s/n ☎ 950 269 788. A swish 150-double-room affair on the east side of town next to the Estadio Juventud sports arena; take bus #1 from the junction of Avda. Federico García Lorca and c/Gregorio Marañon. Under-26 €21, over-26 €27

Hostal Estación c/Calzada de Castro 37 ☎ 950 267 239. Sited close to the train and bus stations with decently furnished en-suite rooms and garage parking. €38–45

Hotel La Perla Pl. del Carmen 7 ☎ 950 238 877, ⊛ githoteles.com. The city's oldest hotel once played host to big-name stars making Westerns at Mini Hollywood. Offers pleasant a/c rooms with satellite TV; some at the rear can be rather cramped, so check what you're offered. €60

Hotel Sevilla c/Granada 25 ☎ 950 230 009. Welcoming, modern, small hotel with en-suite rooms equipped with a/c and TV. Wi-fi zone. €63

Hotel Torreluz Pl. Flores 2 ☎ 950 234 399, ⊛ torreluz .es. One of the town's leading hotels contains good-value three- and four-star options in the same complex. Aimed at the corporate sector, the rather staidly furnished rooms underline this. €40

CAMPING

La Garrofa Carretera Nacional 340 km435 ☎ 950 235 770. The city's nearest campsite is sited on the coast at La Garrofa, some 5km west, easily reached by the buses to Aguadulce and Roquetas de Mar. €5.10, €5.60 per tent, €5.60 per vehicle

EATING AND DRINKING

Almería has a surprising number of interesting and good-value places to **eat and drink**. Most of the best are around the Puerta de Purchena and in the web of narrow streets lying between the Paseo de Almería and the cathedral.

Bodega Aranda Rambla del Obispo Orbera 8, near the Puerta de Purchena. Great tapas bar which fairly hums at lunch times when local professionals come to grab a bite. In former days this was the "sordid" pensión where a penurious Gerald Brenan put up in 1921 (sleeping 6 to a room) while waiting for a letter with money from England – which never came. Daily noon–4pm & 7–10pm.

Bodega Las Botas c/Fructuoso Pérez 3, just south of the Puerta de Purchena. Great tapas place with hanging jamón serrano shanks and upturned sherry-butt tables; the excellent fino and manzanilla (served with a free tapa) goes well with the house special, merluza en escabeche (marinated hake). Daily noon–4pm & 7.30–midnight.

★ **Casa Puga** Corner of c/Lope de Vega and c/Jovellanos. With hams hanging from the ceiling, marble-topped tables and walls covered with azulejos, this is an outstanding tapas bar – founded in 1870 – with a great atmosphere and loyal clientele; try the atún en escabeche (marinated tuna) or boquerones en vinagre (fresh anchovies in vinegar). Mon–Sat noon–4pm & 8pm–midnight; closed Sun.

★ **El Quinto Toro** c/Reyes Católicos 6. Top-notch atmospheric tapas bar taking its name from the fifth bull in the corrida (reputed to always be the best). Friendly service and mouthwatering patatas a lo pobre (potatoes baked with garlic; lunch times only). The same proprietor also runs El Quinto Toro II slightly southeast of here at the junction of c/Javier Sanz with c/Padre Santaella which is also worth a visit. 9.30am–4pm & 7pm–midnight; closed Sun.

★ **Tetería-Restaurante Almedína** c/Paz 2. Very friendly little Moroccan-run tetería which serves full meals later in the day including couscous and chicken and lamb tagines. Often stages live concerts of flamenco and North African music at weekends. Daily 1–11pm.

Mini Hollywood

Daily 10am–9pm, Nov–May until 7pm • €19, under-12s €9

The N-340a northwest from Almería towards Tabernas follows the Andarax riverbed before forking right into the badlands, an area resembling Arizona, which looks as if it should be the backdrop for a Hollywood Western. Just beyond the fork, at **Mini Hollywood** (aka Oasys Parque Temático), you discover that someone else had the same idea first. This is a full-blown Western movie set, and a visit here is hard to resist – especially if you're travelling with kids – although it's probably better value if you time your arrival to coincide with one of the shows. Once inside you can walk around the set of *A Fistful of Dollars* and various other spaghetti Westerns that were filmed here, and wander down Main Street into the *Tombstone Gulch* saloon for a drink. The fantasy is carried a step further with acted-out "shows" (noon & 5pm, June–Sept also 8pm), when actors in full cowboy rig blast off six-guns during a mock bank raid or re-enact the "capture, escape and final shooting of Jesse James". The complex has also added a somewhat incongruous **zoo**, featuring birds and reptiles, as well as rhinos, lions and other big cats prowling depressingly small cages. Further along the same road is another movie location, Fort Bravo (aka Texas Hollywood), with similar features (plus an Indian tepee village and Mexican town), opening hours and prices. Mini Hollywood is served by regular buses from Almería's Intermodal bus–train station.

Níjar

Following the A7-E15 east from Almería brings you, after 24km, to the turn-off for **NÍJAR**, famed throughout Andalucía for its pottery. A neat, white and typically Almerian town, with – in the upper *barrio* – narrow streets designed to give maximum shade, it makes for an interesting visit inland from the coast and Parque Natural de Cabo de Gata to the south.

Níjar is firmly on the tourist trail owing to the inexpensive **handmade pottery** manufactured in workshops and sold in the shops along the broad main street – Avda. García Lorca – and c/Real to the west, where many of the potters have their workshops. The more authentic potters, however, are located in the **barrio alfarero**, along c/Real running parallel to the main street, where the workshops of Gongora, Granados, El Oficio and the friendly and cheaper Angel y Loli (at no. 54) are located; also, in a tiny street off the southern end of c/Real, is the studio-shop (named "La Tienda de los Milagros") of talented English ceramic artist Matthew Weir. Níjar is known, too, for its *jarapas*: quilts, curtains and rugs made from rags, and widely on sale around the town.

INFORMATION   NÍJAR

Turismo At the junction of c/Real with Avda. García Lorca (Mon 10am–2pm, Tues–Sat also 4–8pm; ☎ 950 612 243, ⓦ www.nijar.es), and can provide literature on the town and region.

ACCOMMODATION AND EATING

Bar La Untá On the main street at no. 6. *Bar La Untá* is a very good bar-restaurant with a street terrace.

Montes On the main street at no. 26 ☎ 950 360 157. Montes has good-value en-suite rooms. **€30**

El Pipa Pl. La Glorieta. The best of the bunch of the tapas and *raciones* bars in the upper square, Pl. La Glorieta, beyond the church.

El Cabo de Gata and the Costa de Almería

Almería's best **beaches** lie along its eastern coast, the Costa de Almería. Those to the west of the city, particularly surrounding the "ugly sisters" resorts of Aguadulce and Roquetas de Mar, have already been exploited, and what remains is rapidly being covered with *invernaderos*, or plastic tents, for fruit and vegetable production. In stark contrast, the eastern stretch of the Almerian coastline offers some of the most relaxing beaches left in Spain: half-abandoned fishing communities that have only begun to be promoted for tourists relatively recently. Outside the centres of **Mojácar** and **San José** development is low-key, and with a short walk along the coast you should be able to find plenty of relatively secluded spots to lay your towel.

El Cabo de Gata

The closest resort with any appeal is the modest **EL CABO DE GATA**, now inside the **Parque Natural de Cabo de Gata**, where there is a long expanse of coarse sand. Five buses a day run between here and Almería. Arriving at El Cabo, you pass a lake, the **Laguna de Rosa**, protected by a conservation society and home to flamingos and other waders throughout the summer. Around the resort are plentiful bars, cafés and shops, plus a fish market. The beach gets windy in the afternoons, and it's a deceptively long walk eastwards to **Las Salinas** (The Salt Pans) for a couple of bar-restaurants and a café.

A few kilometres south of here, the **Faro de Cabo de Gata** (lighthouse) marks the cape's southern tip. There's also a **mirador** here from where you can get a great view of the rock cliffs and – on clear days – Morocco's Rif mountains.

INFORMATION   EL CABO DE GATA

Information In the lighthouse car park an information cabin (June–Oct daily 11am–3pm & 6–8pm) has maps and information on the natural park.

ACCOMMODATION

Camping Cabo de Gata Carretera Cabo de Gata s/n, on the coast 2km northwest of the village ☎950 160 443. Decent campsite with reasonable, if not plentiful, *shade* and where facilities include a pool and restaurant. **€6**, **€5.50** per tent, **€5.50** per vehicle

Hostal Las Dunas c/Barrio Nuevo 58 ☎950 370 072. Some 100m inland from the seafront, this friendly but slightly pricey option has functional a/c en-suite rooms with TV. **€55**

EATING AND DRINKING

At Las Salinas there's a good tapas and *mariscos* bar, *La Almadraba*, while just before you reach the Cabo de Gata lighthouse there's another good tapas bar, *El Faro*, serving up tasty, locally caught fried fish.

San José

SAN JOSÉ is an established and popular family resort, set back from a sandy beach in a small cove, with shallow water. More fine **beaches** lie within easy walking distance and one of the best – Playa de los Genoveses – a kilometre-long golden strand, can be reached by a track to the southwest.

ARRIVAL AND INFORMATION   SAN JOSÉ

By bus San José is served by two daily buses to and from Almería, with a journey time of 50min.

By road Although it's possible to hike to the resort along a coastal track from the Faro de Cabo de Gata (lighthouse), this is now closed to vehicles. Going by road entails retracing your route to the resort of El Cabo de Gata and following the inland road via the village of El Pozo de los Frailes.

Information On the main street, Avda. de San José, near the centre of the village, you'll find a Centro de Información for the natural park (daily 10am–2pm & 5.30–8.30pm; ☎950 380 299), which has lots of information on guided walks and horse treks, plus a complete list of accommodation.

Internet At the Centro de Información and the nearby *Bla Bla Bla*, Pasaje Curry s/n (daily 9am–midnight).

ACCOMMODATION

Accommodation can be hard to come by in summer, but outside high season (July & Aug only and the rate we quote) rates fall sharply.

Albergue Juvenil c/Montemar s/n ☎950 380 353, ⓦalberguesanjose.com. Reached by the same road leading to the campsite this privately run youth hostel has

86 places divided between rooms sleeping from two to eight persons. It is usually booked solid at Easter and in Aug. **€14**

Cortijo El Sotillo Carretera San José s/n ☎ 950 61 11 00, ⓦ cortijoelsotillo.es. To the left on the main road in and a kilometre from the centre, this is a refurbished eighteenth-century ranch-house converted into a four-star country hotel with elegant rustically furnished rooms, excellent mid-priced restaurant, bar, pool, tennis courts, and stables with horses for hire. **€150**

Hostal Aloha c/Cala Higuera s/n ☎ 950 380 461, ⓦ hostalaloha.com. Recently refurbished *hostal* with excellent a/c en-suite balcony rooms and the bonus of a fine palm-fringed pool at the rear; they also have a very good tapas bar below. B&B **€80**

Hostal Brisa Mar c/Ancla s/n ☎ 950 380 431, ⓦ brisamar.com. To the left of the main road as you come in, this is a recent arrival with bright and airy a/c en-suite balcony rooms with TV and a pretty garden. **€70**

Hostal Sol Bahía c/Correos 5 ☎ 950 380 114, ⓦ solbahiasanjose.es. Near the main junction in the centre of the village, this is one of the better-value central places, offering spacious a/c en-suite balcony rooms with TV. **€70**

Hotel Agades Agidir c/Córdoba s/n ☎ 950 380 390, ⓦ hotelagades.com. Very pleasant option with a/c en-suite balcony rooms with satellite TV, plus garden pool, bar and restaurant. Sited on the right-hand side of the main road as you come in (a 5min walk from the village). **€95**

EATING AND DRINKING

There are numerous **places to eat** around the beach and harbour zones, plus a couple of well-stocked supermarkets. For fresh fish, try the restaurants overlooking the harbour.

Bar-Restaurante El Emigrante c/Correo s/n. Near the village's main junction, this is a friendly and good-value place facing the *Hostal Sol Bahía*; it offers a variety of fish and meat *platos combinados*, also does tapas and has a *menú* for €12. Daily 9am–midnight.

La Cueva Paseo Marítimo 36. This is a harbourside restaurant noted for its *salmonetes* (red mullet fried with garlic) and *ensalada de salmón* (salmon salad). It also does meat and pasta dishes and has a pleasant terrace. Main dishes €7–18. Daily 1–4pm & 8–11pm; closed Tues.

El Tempranillo Paseo Marítimo s/n. Sited next door to La Cueva, this is another reliable fish restaurant which also does tasty paellas. Has a terrace overlooking the harbour. Main dishes €8–15. Daily noon–5pm & 7–11pm.

Los Escullos, La Isleta and Las Negras

The isolated and peaceful resort of **LOS ESCULLOS**, has a reasonable sandy beach fronted by a formidable eighteenth-century fort, the recently refurbished **Castillo de San Felipe**.

Two kilometres farther east, **LA ISLETA** is another fishing hamlet, and although development is happening it's still a place with a sleepy atmosphere and lots of charm. There's a rather scruffy village beach but a much better one a few minutes' walk away in the next bay to the east – the Playa la Ola.

LAS NEGRAS, 5km farther on, is another place with a decidedly Spanish feel, where there's a cove with a pebbly beach and a few bars and restaurants.

ACCOMMODATION   LOS ESCULLOS, LA ISLETA AND LAS NEGRAS

If the *hostal* in Las Negras is full, you can enquire in the village shop, Estanco Piedra García (☎ 950 388 075, ⓦ www.lasnegras.com, English spoken), about a room in a private house or renting an apartment nearby.

Arrecife c/Bahía 6, close to the village shop in Las Negras ☎ 950 388 140. This is an attractive and good-value *hostal* with a/c en-suite sea-view rooms with terrace balconies. **€49**

Casa Emilio Los Escullos ☎ 950 389 761, ⓦ www.hostalcasaemilio.com. Close to the beach, this is a pleasant *hostal-restaurante* offering a/c en-suite rooms with terrace balcony above a decent restaurant. **€60**

Hostal Isleta de Moro La Isleta ☎ 951 389 713. A *hostal* overlooking the harbour, *Hostal Isleta de Moro* has reasonably priced en-suite balcony rooms with sea view, plus a popular bar-restaurant for tapas and good fish meals below. **€55**

CAMPING

La Caleta Las Negras ☎ 950 525 237. A campsite set in a tranquil location with its own bay, reached via a signed one-kilometre road just outside the village on the way in. Facilities include minimarket, pool and bar-restaurant. **€6.30**, **€7.45** per tent, **€6.30** per vehicle

Camping Los Escullos Los Escullos ☎ 950 389 811. Campsite set back from the sea with limited shade; facilities include bar-restaurant, pool and games courts. **€7.25**, **€4.70** per tent, **€4.70** per vehicle

Agua Amarga

There's no road from Las Negras to Agua Amarga (10km north as the crow flies); to reach it by road you'll need to head 5km inland to the village of Fernan Pérez from where a new road heads east for 11km to reach the small resort. Agua Amarga is served by frequent direct **buses** from Almería.

AGUA AMARGA is a one-time fishing hamlet that has transformed itself into a pleasant and easy-going resort. A fine sand EU-blue-flagged beach is the main attraction, and this is backed by a tasteful crop of villas.

ACCOMMODATION   AGUA AMARGA

Apartamentos Playa c/Aguada s/n ☎ 950 138 246, ⓦ www.costamarga2002.es. This proprietor has a variety of fully-equipped apartments sleeping up to four around the resort, most only a few metres from the beach. **€90**

Hotel Family c/La Lomilla 6 ☎ 950 138 014, ⓦ .hotel family.es. The best-value place to stay is this welcoming French-run *hostal*, set back from the south end of the beach

with comfortable tile-floored rooms, pool and very good French–Spanish restaurant with an excellent-value *menú* for €23. B&B **€85**

Hotel El Tío Kiko c/Embarque 12, on a rise behind Hotel Family ☎ 950 138 080, ⓦ eltiokiko.com. One of a clutch of new luxury places here, this is a boutique hotel with terrace sea-view rooms arranged around a pool. B&B **€125**

EATING AND DRINKING

Hotel las Calas c/Desagüe 1a, near Hotel Family. The restaurant of this hotel offers a selection of reasonably priced fish and rice-based dishes such as *arroz con bogovante* (lobster). Main dishes €9–20. Daily 1–4pm & 7–11pm.

Restaurante Palmera c/Aguada 4. With a terrace fronting the beach this is another popular seafood

restaurant although prices tend to be a little higher here. Daily 1–4pm & 7–11pm.

Los Tarahis c/Desagüe s/n. With a sea-view terrace, this is a decent place serving fish and *arrozes* (such as paellas) as well as seafood salads. Daily 1–4pm & 8–10.30pm.

Mojácar

MOJÁCAR is eastern Almería's main resort, hugely popular with Spaniards and foreign visitors throughout summer. The coastal strip takes its name from the ancient hill village that lies a couple of kilometres back from the sea – Mojácar Pueblo – a striking agglomeration of white cubist houses wrapped round a harsh outcrop of rock. In the 1960s, when the main Spanish *costas* were being developed, this was virtually a ghost town, its inhabitants having long since taken the only logical step and emigrated. The town's fortunes suddenly revived, however, when the local mayor, using the popularity of other equally barren spots in Spain as an example, offered free land to anyone willing to build within a year. The scheme was a modest success, attracting one of the decade's multifarious "artist colonies", now long supplanted by package-holiday companies and second-homers. The long and sandy **beach**, down at the development known as Mojácar Playa, is excellent and the waters (like all in Almería) are warm and brilliantly clear.

Mojácar Pueblo

MOJÁCAR PUEBLO is linked to the coastal resort 2km below by a road that climbs from a prominent seafront junction called "El Cruce"; hourly **buses** also make the climb from here until 11.30pm, after which it's a punishing hike or a taxi. The village is more about atmosphere than sights, and once you've cast an eye over the heavily restored fifteenth-century church of **Santa María**, the main diversion is to wander the narrow streets with their flower-decked balconies and cascading bougainvillea, and call in at the numerous boutiques and bars.

INFORMATION   MOJÁCAR

Turismo Pl. Fronton, opposite the church of Santa María (Mon–Fri 10am–2pm & 5–7pm, Sat 10am–1.30pm;

☎ 950 615 025, ⓦ www.mojacar.es). You'll need their free map to negotiate the maze of narrow streets.

ACCOMMODATION

Hostal Arco Plaza Edificio Pl., just off the main square ☎950 472 777, ✉arcoplazam@yahoo.es. Pleasant small *hostal* and a reasonable deal for air-conditioned en-suite rooms with TV. **€35**

★ **Mamabel's** c/Embajadores 3 ☎950 472 448, ⊛www.mamabels.com. Easily the best of Mojácar Pueblo's upmarket options, this offers beautiful individually styled en-suite rooms (No. 1 is a dream), some with stunning views. **€75**

EATING AND DRINKING

Casa Minguito Pl. del Ayuntamiento s/n. With a pleasant terrace, this longstanding restaurant serves meat and fish dishes as well as a tasty paella for two €26 or a *menú* for €15. Daily noon–4pm & 7pm–midnight.

Mamabel's c/Embajadores 3. The excellent mid-priced restaurant of the hotel of the same name is one of the village's best dining-out options, not least because of its spectacular terrace with vertiginous coastal views. It is noted for its excellent paellas and couscous and has a good-value *menú* for €20. Main dishes €8–20. Daily 1–4pm & 8–10.30pm. Closed Sun eve.

Rincón de Embrujo c/La Iglesia s/n. With a terrace on the *plazuela* fronting the church, this is a handy and economical place for *platos combinados* and *raciones* of seafood like *boquerones fritos* (fried anchovies) or *chipirones* (baby squid). Daily 10am–2pm & 7–midnight.

Mojácar Playa

The beach resort of **MOJÁCAR PLAYA** is a refreshingly brash alternative to the upper village and caters to a mix of mainly Spanish tourists who fill its four-kilometre-long beach all summer. The busy road behind the strand is lined with hotels, restaurants and bars stretching north and south of the main junction, El Cruce, marked by a large *centro comercial*.

INFORMATION

Just south of the *centro comercial* **internet** access is available at Indal-futur, Paseo del Mediterráneo 293 (Mon–Fri 9am–2pm & 5–10pm, Sat & Sun 11am–2pm & 6–11pm). The *turismo's* **map** also covers the coastal strip and is a useful aid to getting your bearings.

ACCOMMODATION

There are plenty of *hostales* and hotels lining the seafront of Mojácar Playa and outside July and August (the resort's only high season months) prices fall by up to forty percent.

El Cantal de Mojácar Paseo Mediterráneo s/n ☎950 478 204. A kilometre or so south of El Cruce, this is a good campsite and not too far from the beach.

Hotel El Puntazo ☎951 478 229, ⊛hotelelpuntazo .com. One of the more established upmarket places for air-conditioned sea-view terrace rooms with minibar and strongbox. **€139**

Hotel Río Abajo ☎950 478 928, ⊛rioabajomojacar.com. Some 2km north of El Cruce where the Río de Aguas meets the sea, this is a pleasant, leafy complex with en-suite rooms actually on the beach. Has own pool and diving school and breakfast is available. **€60**

Hotel Sal Marina Avda. del Mediterráneo s/n ☎950 472 404. South of El Cruce, this is a seafront hotel with very pleasant air-conditioned balcony rooms with sea views; drops prices by thirty percent outside July & Aug. **€65**

EATING AND DRINKING

Albatros Avda. del Mediterráneo s/n, a kilometre south of the El Cruce junction. A beachfront *chiringuito* close to the *Hotel El Puntazo*, this is a reliable place for fresh fish and *mariscos*. Daily noon–4pm & 8–10.30pm.

Casa Egea c/Las Ventanicas 127, 2km south of El Cruce. On the seafront, this is a long-established and reliable seafood restaurant where you can choose, weigh and price your fish before it's cooked (thus avoiding nasty shocks). Its neighbour *Omega* is similar and also good and serves salads and pasta-based dishes. Main dishes €10–20. Daily 10.30am–5pm & 7.30pm–midnight.

Restaurante Sal Marina Avda. del Mediterráneo s/n. On the landward side of the road, and attached to the hotel of the same name, this is a decent restaurant specializing in fish and seafood cuisine. Has a pleasant sea-view terrace. Main dishes €8–15. Daily 1–4pm & 7–10.30pm; closed Oct–April.

4

Castilla y León and La Rioja

VINEYARDS NEAR SAN VICENTE, LA RIOJA (P.414)

5

Castilla y León and La Rioja

The foundations of modern Spain were laid in the kingdom of Castile. Stretching north from Madrid, and incorporated within the modern *comunidad* of Castilla y León (ⓦturismocastillayleon.com), it's a land of frontier fortresses – the *castillos* from which it takes its name – and a vast, fertile central plateau, the 700- to 1000-metre-high *meseta* that is given over almost entirely to grain. Beyond the historic cities, huge areas stretch to the horizon without a single landmark, not even a tree, though each spring a vivid red carpet of poppies decorates fields and verges. The Río Duero runs right across the province and into Portugal, with the river at the heart of one of Spain's great wine-producing regions, Ribera del Duero; another, more famous wine region lies to the north in the autonomous *comunidad* of La Rioja, whose vineyards line the banks of the Río Ebro.

It was Castile that became the most powerful force of the Reconquest, extending its domination through military gains and marriage alliances. By the eleventh century, Castile had merged with and swallowed León; through Isabel's marriage to Fernando in 1469 it encompassed Aragón, Catalunya and eventually the entire peninsula. The monarchs of this triumphant age were enthusiastic patrons of the arts, endowing their cities with superlative monuments, above which, quite literally, tower the great Gothic cathedrals of **Salamanca**, **León** and **Burgos**. These three cities are the major draws of the region, though in **Valladolid**, **Zamora** and even unsung **Palencia** and **Soria** are outstanding reminders of the glory days of Old Castile. But equally in many lesser towns – notably **Ciudad Rodrigo**, **El Burgo de Osma** and **Covarrubias** – you'll be struck by a wealth of art and architecture that's completely at odds with their current status.

Outside the main population centres, the sporadic and depopulated villages, bitterly cold in winter, burning hot in summer, are rarely of interest. That said, there are a few enclaves of mountain scenery, from the **Sierra de Francia** in the deep southwest to the lakeland of the **Sierra de Urbión** in the east. Moreover, the wine region of La Rioja has charms that go way beyond its famous product – the likeable provincial capital of **Logroño** is known for its lively tapas bars, while high in the Riojan hills are unsung mountain villages and monasteries that reward the intrepid driver.

The final feature of the region is the host of Romanesque churches, monasteries and hermitages, a legacy of the **Camino de Santiago**, the great pilgrim route from the Pyrenees to Santiago de Compostela. It cuts through La Rioja and then heads west across the upper half of Castilla y León, taking in the great cathedral cities of Burgos and León, but also many minor places of great interest, from **Frómista** in the central plains to **Astorga** and **Villafranca del Bierzo**.

LAS MÉDULAS

Highlights

❶ **Universidad de Salamanca** The graceful university buildings of Salamanca are an essential first stop in this most captivating of cities. **See p.378**

❷ **Museo Nacional Colegio de San Gregorio, Valladolid** The finest collection of Renaissance sculpture in Spain – housed in a magnificently restored monastic church. **See p.395**

❸ **La Rioja's monasteries** Take a fantastic mountain drive to the wine region's peerless monasteries. **See p.415**

❹ **Dinosaur-hunting, Enciso** Set out on the trail of La Rioja's 120-million-year-old dinosaurs. **See p.417**

❺ **Burgos cathedral** The tourist crowds can't dull the appeal of this extraordinary masterpiece of Gothic art. **See p.418**

❻ **Covarrubias** Possible winner of the "most charming small town in Castile" award? **See p.424**

❼ **Hostal de San Marcos, León** A sumptuous monastery on the Santiago pilgrim route is now one of Spain's finest paradores. **See p.437**

❽ **Las Médulas** The devastation wreaked by Roman gold mining created an eerily captivating landscape. **See p.443**

HIGHLIGHTS ARE MARKED ON THE MAP ON P.372

CASTILLA Y LEÓN & LA RIOJA

CANTA

GALICIA

Santiago de Compostela

Riaño

Cerve
de Pisue

Rioscuro

La Robla

Cistierna

CASTILLA

EL BIERZO

Villafranca
del Bierzo

León

O Barco

Ponferrada

Astorga

Saldaña

Villa Rom
La Olmed

Orellán

A6

Sahagún

Carrión de
los Condes

8
LAS MÉDULAS

La Bañeza

Quintanilla

Vill
de

Villa Romana La Tejada

A6

Puebla
de Sanabria

N601

Villalón
de Campos

Paredes
de Nava

A52

Benavente

N610

N610

Palencia

Moreruela

Medina de
Rioseco

Bragança

Villalpando

Ampudia

N630

PORTUGAL

LEÓN

Valladolid

A11-E82

Toro

Zamora

Río Duero

Tordesillas

N122

Medina del
Campo

2

Embalse de
Almerdra

Olmedo

A6

Ledesma

Río Douro

Arévalo

Vitigudino

Salamanca

1

N501

Peñaranda
de Bracamonte

Porto

Alba de
Tormes

Ávila

Ciudad
Rodrigo

A62-E80

SIERRA DE FRANCIA

Peña
de Francia
(1723m)

Miranda
del Castañar

Guijuelo

SIERRA DE GATA

La Alberca

Piedrahita

LAS
HURDES

Béjar

PARQUE NATURAL
LAS BATUECAS-
SIERRA DE FRANCIA

0   50

kilometres

HIGHLIGHTS
1. Universidad de Salamanca
2. Museo Nacional Colegio de San Gregorio
3. La Rioja's monasteries
4. Dinosaur-hunting, Enciso
5. Burgos Cathedral
6. Covarrubias
7. Parador Hostal de San Marcos, León
8. Las Médulas

5

FIESTAS

FEBRUARY–APRIL

Week before Lent: Carnaval Particularly lively in Ciudad Rodrigo, when the Carnaval del Toro (Ⓦcarnavaldeltoro.es) sees bull-running and bullfights in the streets and squares.
Semana Santa (Holy Week) Easter is even more fanatically observed here than in most areas – celebrations take place in all the big cities, particularly Valladolid, León, Salamanca and Zamora, including hooded penitents and processions of holy statues.

MAY/JUNE

Pentecost (7th Sun after Easter) Week-long Feria Chica in Palencia.
Corpus Christi (2nd Thurs after Pentecost) Celebrations in Palencia and Valladolid; the following day, the festival of El Curpillos is celebrated in Burgos.
First two weeks of June: FIACyL Salamanca's International Arts Festival features street concerts, urban art, DJ sets and neighbourhood events.
June 11: Fiestas de San Bernabé Logroño's festivities run for a week around this date.
24: Día de San Juan Fiesta with bullfights and dance in León and more religious observances in Palencia. The following week there's a big fiesta in Soria.
29: Día de San Pedro Burgos starts a vibrant two-week fiesta, when *gigantillos* parade in the streets, and there are concerts, bullfights and all-night parties. Also big celebrations in León, while in Haro (where festivities started on the 24th) there's the drunken Batalla del Vino.

AUGUST–SEPTEMBER

Aug 15: Fiesta de la Assumption Colourful festivals in La Alberca and Peñafiel.
Aug 16: Día de San Roque Fiesta in El Burgo de Osma; also bullfights in the wooden plaza in Peñafiel.
Last week Aug: Fiesta de San Agustín In Toro, with the "fountain of wine" and *encierros*.
Sept 8: Fiesta Virgen de la Vega First day of the fiesta in Salamanca, beginning the evening before and lasting two weeks, as well as the famous bull-running in Tordesillas.
Sept 21: Día de San Mateo Major *ferias* in Valladolid and especially Logroño, where the Rioja harvest is celebrated with a week's worth of hijinks.

Salamanca

SALAMANCA is the most graceful city in Spain. For four centuries it was the seat of one of the most prestigious universities in the world and at the intellectual heart of the burgeoning Spanish crown's enterprise – the *conquistador* Hernán Cortés and St Ignatius of Loyola were students while Columbus came here in 1486 in an initially unsuccessful attempt to persuade a university commission of enquiry to back his exploration plans. City and university declined in later centuries, and there was much damage done during the Napoleonic Wars, but the Salamanca of today presents a uniformly gorgeous ensemble from Spain's Golden Age, given a perfect harmony by the warm golden sandstone with which its finest buildings were constructed. It's still a relatively small place with a population of 160,000 but an awful lot of those are students, both Spanish and foreign, which adds to the general level of gaiety.

You'll need to set aside the best part of two full days to see everything in Salamanca, and even then you might struggle – time has a habit of flashing by in a city so easy on the eye that simply strolling around often seems like the best thing to do. Highlights are many, starting with the most elegant Plaza Mayor in Spain before moving on to the two cathedrals, one Gothic and the other Romanesque, and the beautiful surviving university buildings. After this, it's down to individual taste when it comes to deciding exactly how many stately Renaissance palaces, embellished churches, sculpted cloisters, curio-filled museums and religious art galleries you'd like to see.

Plaza Mayor

The grand **Plaza Mayor** is the hub of Salamantine life. Its vast central expanse is enclosed by a continuous four-storey building, broken only by the grand *ayuntamiento* (city hall) on its northern side. The building was the work of Andrea García Quiñones and of Alberto Churriguera, younger brother of José, and nowhere is the Churrigueras' inspired variation of Baroque (see box, p.380) so refined as here. Cafés, restaurants and small shops ring the arcades, and some *pensiones* and hotels occupy parts of the upper storeys, but signs, advertising, lights and other modern clutter are not allowed to intrude upon the harmonious facades. Right around the arcades, facing out into the square, are medallion portraits of Spain's nobility and royalty through the ages, including the current king and queen and, a more surprising survivor, that of "Franco, Caudillo de España" (northeast corner, above *Confitería Madrileña*).

Mercado Central

Pl. del Mercado • Mon–Thurs 9am–2.30pm, Fri & Sat 9am–3.30pm

Arches from Plaza Mayor lead out into the surrounding shopping streets, including, on the east side, to Plaza del Mercado and the red-brick-and-iron **Mercado Central**. The city's small two-tier market is a good place for picnic provisions, and it's surrounded on all sides by lively restaurants and tapas bars.

Convento y Museo de las Úrsulas

C/Las Úrsulas, entrance near Campo de San Francisco • Tues–Sun 11am–1pm & 4.30–6pm; closed last Sun of month • €2 • ☎ 923 219 877

The unusual open-topped tower of the **Convento y Museo de las Úrsulas** rises above a charming quarter west of Plaza Mayor. Inside, sitting in the dark, cheery Franciscan nuns scrabble for change for the rare visitor and then turn on the lights so that you can inspect the primitive artworks, including the portrait of Úrsula herself – a Romano-British princess of the fourth century AD, martyred by the Huns while on pilgrimage to Rome. Look up for the greater treasure – the impressive, decorated, coffered ceiling – and on the way out examine the superb marble **tomb of Archbishop Alonso Fonseca**, founder of the convent.

Casa de las Muertes

C/Bordadores • No public access

Facing the east wall of the Convento de las Úrsulas is the impressive Plateresque facade of the **Casa de las Muertes** (House of the Dead), the mansion of leading Salamantine architect Juan de Álava, named for the four small skulls at the base of the upper windows.

CASTILIAN CUISINE

It often seems like there's part of a pig, sheep or a cow on every plate in **Castile** – steaks can be gargantuan, the traditional roast meats, found everywhere, are *cochinillo* (suckling pig), *lechazo* (lamb) and *cabrito* (kid), while hearty Castilian appetites think nothing of limbering up first with a thick *sopa castellano*, usually containing chickpeas or white haricot beans, both staple crops from the *meseta*. In **Salamanca province**, *jamones* (hams) and *embutidos* (sausages) are at their best; in **Burgos** it's *morcilla* (black pudding) that's king. If you're feeling faint at the thought of so much meat – and Castilian menus can, truth be told, get a little monotonous – then the legendary tapas bars of **León** and **Logroño** ride to the rescue, where bite-sized morsels, from cuttlefish to mushrooms, offer a change of pace and diet. Only really in **La Rioja** does the traditional, heavy Castilian diet give way to something lighter and more varied. The rivers that irrigate the vines also mean freshwater fish, particularly trout, while La Rioja is the one part of the region where the contemporary Spanish foodie buzz has scored a real foothold.

5

SALAMANCA

N

Train Station ▲

Van Dyck Tapas Bars ▲

BARS
Clavel Ocho	3
Irish Rover	10
Posada de las Ánimas	1

CAFÉS, TAPAS & RESTAURANTS
El Ave	12
El Corrillo	9
Dulcinea	4
El Grillo Azul	5
Mesón Cervantes	6
El Pecado	7
Río de la Plata	11
Victor Gutiérrez	8

ACCOMMODATION
Hostal Catedral	9
Hostal Sara	7
Hotel Abba Fonseca	11
Hotel Emperatriz 1	6
Hotel Estrella Albatros	8
Hotel Palacio de Castellanos	10
Hotel San Polo	5
Meliá Las Claras	12
Parador de Salamanca	4
Pensión Los Ángeles	3
Petit Palace Las Torres	2
Room Mate Vega	1

CLUB
Camelot	1

5

Universidad Pontifícia de Salamanca

C/La Compañía • Tues–Fri 10.30am–12.45pm & 5–6.30pm, Sat 10am–1pm & 5–7.15pm, Sun 10am–1pm • Spanish-only guided tours set off every 45 minutes • €3 • ☎ 923 277 100, ⓦ www.upsa.es

Salamanca actually has two universities, the minor one being the **Universidad Pontifícia de Salamanca**, a short walk south of Plaza Mayor. It was originally linked to the university proper, but the faculties of theology and canon law were excluded from the main institution in 1852, and Pontifícia was later formally established as a separate religious university in 1940 by Pope Pius XII. Guided tours around the grand central building, a former Jesuit college first founded in 1617, start at a magnificent stone staircase, *la escalera noble*, that seems to hang suspended in the air. They then take in the richly decorated main hall and the grandiose Baroque cloister, around the upper level of which Jesuit priests once walked meditational circuits, believing themselves to be closer to heaven at such a height. The tour ends in the vast Baroque church of **La Clerecía**, next door to the university.

Casa de las Conchas

C/La Compañía 2 • Mon–Fri 9am–9pm, Sat 9am–2pm & 4–7pm, Sun 10am–2pm & 4–7pm • Free • ☎ 923 269 317

The early sixteenth-century mansion called the **Casa de las Conchas** (House of Shells) is named after the rows of carved scallop shells that decorate its facade, symbol of the pilgrimage to Santiago. The building is now partly a public library and exhibition space, but you can look into the courtyard and enjoy a good view of the towers of La Clerecía church from the upper storey.

Universidad de Salamanca

C/Libreros • Mon–Sat 9.30am–1.30pm & 4–7pm, Sun 10am–1.30pm; last entry 30min before closing • €4, free Mon morning, and free for under-12s • ☎ 923 294 400, ⓦ www.usal.es

You'll know when you've arrived at Salamanca's central honey-trap, the **Universidad de Salamanca**, also known as the Universidad Civil, by the milling tour groups, all straining their necks to examine the magnificent facade. It's the ultimate expression of the Plateresque style, covered with medallions, heraldic emblems and floral decorations, amid which lurks a hidden frog said to bring good luck and marriage within the year to anyone who spots it unaided. The centre of the facade is occupied by a portrait of Isabel and Fernando, surrounded by a Greek inscription

---

LA UNIVERSIDAD DE SALAMANCA

The **Universidad de Salamanca** was founded by Alfonso IX in 1218, and, after the union of Castile and León, became the most important in Spain. Its rise to international stature was phenomenal, and within thirty years Pope Alexander IV proclaimed it equal to the greatest universities of the day. As at Oxford, Paris and Bologna, theories formulated here were later accepted as fact throughout Europe. The university continued to flourish under the Reyes Católicos, and in the sixteenth century it was powerful enough to resist the orthodoxy of Felipe II's Inquisition, but eventually, freedom of thought was stifled by the extreme clericalism of the seventeenth and eighteenth centuries. Books were banned for being a threat to the Catholic faith, and mathematics and medicine disappeared from the curriculum. During the Peninsular War, the French demolished 20 of the 25 colleges, and by the end of the nineteenth century there were no more than three hundred students (compared to 6500 in the late sixteenth century). The university saw a revival in the early part of the twentieth century, particularly under the rectorship of celebrated philosopher and man of letters Miguel de Unamuno. Today, numbers are higher than ever (around 30,000 students) and Salamanca Uni has a certain social cachet, though academically it ranks well behind Madrid, Barcelona and Seville. It does, however, run a highly successful **language school** – nowhere else in Spain will you find so many young foreigners.

commemorating their devotion to the university. There are several sections to visit, though the fee paid at the main entrance covers just the tour of the main building's lecture rooms and library.

Aula Fray Luís de León and library

The university's old lecture rooms are arranged around a courtyard. The **Aula Fray Luís de León** preserves the rugged original benches and the pulpit where this celebrated professor lectured. In 1573, the Inquisition muscled its way into the room and arrested Fray Luís for alleged subversion of the faith; five years of torture and imprisonment followed, but upon his release he calmly resumed his lecture with the words, "As we were saying yesterday..."

An elegant Plateresque stairway leads to the upper storey, where you'll find the old university **library**, stuffed with thousands of antiquated books on wooden shelves and huge globes of the world. There's a faded magnificence here, which gives some idea of Renaissance Salamanca's academic splendour.

Museo de Salamanca

Patio de las Escuelas 2 • Tues–Sat 10am–2pm & 4–7pm, plus July–Sept afternoons till 8pm, Sun 10am–2pm • €1.20, free weekends

Across from the university entrance is a small, enclosed square housing the **Museo de Salamanca**. This occupies an exquisite fifteenth-century mansion – originally the home of Isabel's personal physician – which is at least as interesting as the collection of Spanish religious paintings and sculpture contained within.

Museo de la Universidad

Patio de Escuelas Menores • Tues–Sun 9.30am–1.15pm • Free

At the back of the Patio de Escuelas, a beautifully sculpted double arch leads through to the cloistered Renaissance courtyard of the **Escuelas Menores**, which served as a kind of preparatory school for the university proper. A succession of weekend newlyweds poses here for photographs while, on the far side of the courtyard, the building marked "Museo de la Universidad" features a remarkable zodiacal ceiling, the so-called **Cielo de Salamanca**, once housed in the university chapel. As your eyes adjust to the light, centaurs, serpents and the Grim Reaper all come into focus amid the twinkling stars.

Catedral Nueva

Entrances on Pl. de Anaya and c/Cardenal Pla y Deniel • Daily 9am–8pm, closes 1–4pm Nov–April • Free • ☎ 923 217 476, ⓦ catedralsalamanca.org

Salamanca's **Catedral Nueva**, begun in 1512, was a glorious last-minute assertion of Gothic architecture. However, for financial reasons, construction eventually spanned two centuries and thus the building incorporates a range of styles. The main entrance on c/Cardenal Pla y Deniel is contemporary with that of the university and equally dazzling in its wealth of ornamental detail. Inside, when you stand under the dome, you can clearly see the transition from plain Gothic at the bottom to colourful, exuberant late Baroque at the top. Alberto Churriguera and his brother José both worked here – the former on the choir stalls (fenced off, but lit by enough natural light to appreciate their beauty), the latter on the majestic dome.

Outside, **Plaza Anaya** is one of *the* great meeting-places for Salamanca students, who lounge in the grass beds of the rose gardens; while from the slightly raised cathedral terrace you get a classic city view of domes, spires and honey-coloured facades.

5

SALAMANCA STYLE

Two great architectural styles were developed, and see their finest expression, in Salamanca. **Plateresque** is a decorative technique of shallow relief and intricate detail, named for its resemblance to the art of the silversmith (*platero*); Salamanca's native sandstone, soft and easy to carve, played a significant role in its development. Plateresque art cuts across Gothic and Renaissance frontiers – the decorative motifs of the university, for example, are taken from the Italian Renaissance but the facade of the Catedral Nueva is Gothic in inspiration. The later **Churrigueresque** style, an especially ornate form of Baroque, takes its name from **José Churriguera** (1665–1725), the dominant member of a prodigiously creative family, best known for their huge, flamboyant altarpieces.

Catedral Vieja

Pl. de Anaya • Entrance and ticket kiosk inside Catedral Nueva • May–Oct daily 10am–7.30pm; Nov–April daily 10am–12.30pm & 4–5.30pm • €4.75 • ☎ 923 217 476, ⓦ catedralsalamanca.org

You can't really tell from the outside, but Salamanca has two cathedrals – the earlier, Romanesque **Catedral Vieja**, or "old cathedral", is dwarfed by its Catedral Nueva ("new cathedral") neighbour, through which it's entered. The chapels opening off the cloisters were used as university lecture rooms until the sixteenth century and one, the **Capilla de Obispo Diego de Anaya**, contains the oldest organ in Europe (mid-fourteenth century). Otherwise, the old cathedral's most distinctive feature is its dome, known as the **Torre de Gallo** (Cock Tower) on account of its rooster-shaped weather vane. Fashioned like the segments of an orange, the dome derives from Byzantine models and is similar to those at Zamora and Toro; there's a good view of it from Patio Chico, the courtyard at the back of the cathedrals.

Exposición Ieronimus

Pl. Juan XXIII • Daily 10am–7.30pm • €3.75, free Tues 10am–noon

At the rear of the Catedral Vieja is the entrance to the **Exposición Ieronimus**, primarily a collection of rare documents relating to the cathedral and named after the first bishop of Salamanca. This may not tempt you in, though the exhibition occupies the medieval **Torre Mocha**, through which you get to clamber, and which has outstanding views over the city.

Museo Art Nouveau y Art Deco

C/El Expolio 14 • April to mid-Oct Tues–Fri 11am–2pm & 5–9pm, Sat & Sun 11am–9pm; mid-Oct to March Tues–Fri 11am–2pm & 4–7pm, Sat & Sun 11am–8pm • €4, free Thurs 11am–2pm • ☎ 923 121 425, ⓦ museocasalis.org

Explore the alleys behind the Catedral Vieja and you'll stumble upon Salamanca's quirkiest museum, the **Museo Art Nouveau y Art Deco**, contained within the Casa Lis. The mansion was built for an Art Nouveau enthusiast at the turn of the twentieth century and is partly constructed from vibrantly painted glass (the best views of the house are actually from the ring road below). There's a terrific miscellany of objects inside, from bronze statues and porcelain figures to jewellery and furniture, with notable exhibits including the famous scent bottles René Lalique designed for Guerlain and Worth.

Convento de San Esteban

Pl. del Concilio de Trento • Daily 10am–1.30pm & 4–7.15pm • €3 • ☎ 923 215 000

On the eastern edge of the historic quarter stands the vast **Convento de San Esteban**, whose facade portrays yet another faultless example of Plateresque art – the graphic

5

central panel depicts the stoning of its patron saint, St Stephen. Paying for entry also allows you to see the lavish Baroque *retablo* by José Churriguera – a mighty 27m high, and one of the artist's first commissioned works in Salamanca – as well as the choir, the handsome cloister and the museum of sacred art.

Convento de las Dueñas

Pl. del Concilio de Trento • Mon–Sat 10.30am–12.45pm & 4.30–6.45pm • €2 • ☎ 923 215 442

The most beautiful cloisters in the city are at the **Convento de las Dueñas**, across the road from the Convento de San Esteban. Built in the sixteenth century on an irregular pentagonal plan, the imaginative upper-storey capitals are wildly carved with rams' heads, scallop shells, winged cherubs, mythical beasts and an extraordinary range of human faces. The nuns here sell boxes of delicious crumbly almond pastries (known as *amarguillos*) from a booth next to the entrance.

Convento de Santa Clara

C/Santa Clara 2 • Mon–Fri 9.35am–1.10pm & 4.20–6.10pm, Sat & Sun 9.30am–2.10pm; entry is by 50min guided tour only and departures are not always reliable, though the first tour of the morning, 9.35am, and first tour of the afternoon, 4.20pm, generally take place • €3 • ☎ 923 269 623

The thirteenth-century **Convento de Santa Clara** was found to be concealing unsuspected treasure when the whitewash was taken off the chapel walls in 1976. Underneath was an important series of frescoes from the thirteenth to the eighteenth century, while Romanesque and Gothic columns and a stunning sixteenth-century polychrome ceiling were also uncovered in the cloister. But the most incredible discovery was made in the church, where the Baroque ceiling was found to be false; rising above this, you can see the original fourteenth-century beams, decorated with heraldic motifs of the kingdoms of Castile and León.

The Puente Romano

For a terrific city view up to the walls and spires of Salamanca, walk down below the cathedrals to the **Río Tormes** and cross the arched **Puente Romano**, built in the first century AD – try not to look back until you're most of the way across.

Museo de Historia de la Automoción

Pl. del Mercado Viejo • Tues–Sun 10am–2pm & 5–8pm • €3.50 • ⓦ museoautomocion.com

On the city side of the Río Tormes, a riverside promenade runs east past Salamanca's other main bridges. It starts behind the **Museo de Historia de la Automoción**, which provides a brief overview of the history of automobiles before presenting ninety gleaming vintage vehicles on three floors.

ARRIVAL AND DEPARTURE
SALAMANCA

The compact *casco histórico*, with the Pl. Mayor at its heart, spreads back from the Río Tormes, bounded by a loop of avenues. Bus and train stations are on opposite sides of the city, each about a 15min walk or a €5 taxi ride from the centre.

By train From the train station on Paseo de la Estación, go left to Pl. de España, from where c/Azafranal or c/Toro lead directly to the Pl. Mayor. For current timetables and ticket information, consult RENFE ☎ 902 320 320, ⓦ renfe.com. Destinations Ávila (9 daily; 1hr); Burgos (4 daily; 2hr 30min); Madrid (8 daily; 2hr 30min); Valladolid (10 daily; 1hr 15min–1hr 30min).

By bus The bus station is on Avda. de Filiberto Villalobos (☎ 923 236 717, ⓦ estacionautobusessalamanca.es). From here turn right and keep straight until you reach Pl. Mayor. Companies with ticket offices at the bus station include Vivas (for Zamora/León and Astorga/Ponferrada; ☎ 923 223 587, ⓦ autocaresvivas.es); El Pilar (Ciudad Rodrigo; ☎ 923 222 608, ⓦ elpilar-arribesbus.com); Auto-Res/Avanza (Valladolid/

Madrid; ☎ 923 232 266, ⓦ avanzabus.com); and Alsa (Ávila/ Madrid, Valladolid/Burgos and Portugal; ☎ 902 422 242, ⓦ alsa.es).

Destinations Astorga/Ponferrada (1–2 daily; 2hr 40min/3hr 30min); Ávila (8 daily; 1hr 30min); Burgos (3 daily; 3hr 30min); Cáceres (8 daily; 3hr 45min); Ciudad Rodrigo (Mon–Fri hourly, Sat 6 daily, Sun 4 daily; 1hr); León (4–5 daily; 3hr–3hr 30min); Madrid (hourly; 2hr 30min);

Palencia (up to 7 daily; 2hr 15min); Porto/Lisbon, Portugal (1–2 daily; 6hr/9hr); Valladolid (up to 8 daily; 1hr 15min–1hr 40min); Zamora (hourly; 1hr 10min).

By car Driving into the centre, all the main hotels and car parks are clearly signposted. You'll be able to unload outside most hotels (though not on every street in the old centre), but street **parking** is usually restricted to two hours, so it's best to use one of the garages or car parks (€16–20 per day).

INFORMATION

Turismo Pl. Mayor 32 (Mon–Fri 9am–2pm & 4.30–8pm, Sat 10am–8pm, Sun 10am–2pm; winter Mon–Sat closes 6.30pm; ☎ 923 218 342, ⓦ salamanca.es). There are also

seasonal offices (July–Sept, variable hours) inside the train and bus stations.

ACCOMMODATION

With the exception of the parador, all the places reviewed below are in the *casco histórico*, and you'll be able to walk to everything in five minutes or so. There are some splendid boutique and classy lodgings, but many budget *pensiones* are more or less permanently occupied by students during the academic year. You may be approached at the train or bus station and offered private rooms, which will usually be the lowest-priced options available. Otherwise, c/Meléndez and c/Jesús (both just south of Pl. Mayor) are good places to look for cheap rooms.

Hostal Catedral Rúa Mayor 46, 1° ☎ 923 270 614, ⓦ hostalcatedralsalamanca.com. Clean, bright, budget *hostal* with pretty, traditionally furnished rooms and a charming welcome. It's in a great location, and most rooms have cathedral views. **€50**

★ **Hostal Sara** c/Meléndez 11 ☎ 923 281 140, ⓦ hostalsara.org. The best – and friendliest – budget option on this busy street, 100m from Pl. Mayor. Its fifteen rooms are comfortably furnished, and feature wood floors and tiled bathrooms. Internal rooms are nice and quiet. **€60**

Hotel Abba Fonseca Pl. San Blas 2 ☎ 923 011 010, ⓦ abbafonsecahotel.com. A contemporary four-star hotel on a tranquil square a 10min walk from Pl. Mayor. Many rooms have lovely views across the city (though there are cheaper rooms without the views). **€100**

Hotel Emperatriz I c/La Compañía 44 ☎ 923 219 200, ⓦ emperatrizhotel.com. A two-star hotel in an old mansion, part of a chain of three in the city. Rooms are comfortable and good value, even if they don't quite live up to the historic setting. **€55**

★ **Hotel Estrella Albatros** c/Grillo 18 ☎ 923 266 033, ⓦ estrellaalbatros.com. The secret at this terrific four-star boutique hotel, a few minutes' walk from the old centre, is the sweeping city-view from the roof. Spacious, contemporary rooms are in soft colours and blonde wood, while classy bathrooms have smoked-glass sinks and jacuzzi-baths. There's garage parking, and you can usually score better room rates online. **€120**

Hotel Palacio de Castellanos c/San Pablo 58–64 ☎ 923 261 818, ⓦ nh-hotels.com. The glassed-in Renaissance cloister converted into a lobby-lounge sets the

tone in this lovely, marbled four-star hotel on the site of a former palace. Rooms are smart, rather than luxurious, but there's a fine restaurant, *Trento*. Book online in advance for some very good rates. **€90**

Hotel San Polo c/Arroyo de Santo Domingo 2 ☎ 923 211 177, ⓦ hotelsanpolo.com. A charming three-star hotel arranged around the ruins of a sixth-century Roman church – there are terrace tables in the ruined nave. The only downside is the traffic noise from the front-facing rooms. **€65**

★ **Meliá Las Claras** c/Marquesa Almarza 31 ☎ 923 128 500, ⓦ solmelia.com. Very comfortable, contemporary four-star hotel in a quiet corner of town – it's easy to find by car and has garage parking. Spacious rooms in muted colours provide a tranquil base, the buffet breakfast is excellent, and there's a good restaurant. Online rates available for around €80. **€110**

Parador de Salamanca c/Teso de la Feria 2, 2km from city centre ☎ 923 192 082, ⓦ parador.es. The best thing about Salamanca's modern parador is the magnificent view of the city across the river. There's also a very welcome swimming pool with the same views, and parking for guests, but the location does mean a trip into the centre each day for sightseeing. Advance rates go as low as €80. **€160**

Pensión Los Angeles Pl. Mayor 10, 2 & 3° ☎ 923 218 166, ⓦ pensionlosangeles.com. The city's best-sited *pensión*, with four en-suite rooms boasting stunning views over the Pl. Mayor, plus another five shared-bath doubles with rooftop views. It's distinctly no-frills, and room prices vary according to aspect and season – down to as low as €25 in some rooms at some times of the year. **€60**

5

Petit Palace Las Torres c/Concejo 4 ☎ 923 212 100, ⓦ hthoteles.com. For a touch of class on the main square, this three-star budget-boutique hotel has stylish, if small, rooms that overlook the Pl. Mayor, as does the breakfast room. **€70**

Room Mate Vega Pl. del Mercado 16 ☎ 923 272 250, ⓦ room-matehotels.com. Part of a young and funky boutique chain, *Vega* is a classy restoration of an old building, opposite the market and just a stone's throw from Pl. Mayor. Rooms are all nice, bright and chic, but "executive" rooms are more spacious. **€55**

EATING AND DRINKING

Salamanca is a great place for hanging out in bars and cafés, but not so great for eating, at least at the budget end of the scale. Lunchtime *menús* aside, at night you can easily spend €50 a head in the better **restaurants**, while sitting outside to eat in the Pl. Mayor or anywhere nearby attracts a hefty mark-up. Just south of Pl. Mayor, the adjacent c/Meléndez and Rúa Mayor are packed with bars and restaurants, with enticing tables set out in the pedestrianized streets. There's another bunch of popular restaurants and tapas places near the market (around Pl. del Mercado and up c/Pozo Amarillo), but the best **tapas bars** in the city are a fifteen-minute walk north of the old centre, along c/Van Dyck (follow Paseo Doctor Torres Villaroel, cross Avda. Portugal, and Van Dyck is two streets up, on the right). A score of bars and restaurants along this street serve tapas and *raciones*, specializing in sausages, grills and Castilian meats, at considerably better prices than down in the tourist zone.

CAFÉS AND RESTAURANTS

El Ave c/Libreros 24 ☎ 923 264 511. A favourite spot right by the university. Breakfast, tapas, sandwiches and *platos* are standard items (most things cost €3–8, *menú del día* €10), but you can also get shakes, juices and a choice of teas, and it's another euro to sit outside under the shady parasols. Daily 8am–midnight; closed last week Dec & first week Jan.

★ **El Corrillo** c/de Meléndez 18 ☎ 923 271 917, ⓦ cafecorrillo.com. This arty café-bar and restaurant is great for a long lunch (from 1.30pm) or lazy dinner (from 9pm) in the pretty square out back, with a big menu (mains €5–15) that mixes traditional dishes (lamb chops, chicken in cider) with flashier, so-called *vanguardista* cooking (say, pigeon with onion confit or tuna tartare with wild berries). The *menú del día* (€12, plus €2 terrace surcharge) falls somewhere between the two, otherwise there's breakfast for €5. Every Thursday night it morphs into a hip jazz club, with live acts from 10pm. Daily 8.30am–3am.

Dulcinea c/Pozo Amarillo 5 ☎ 923 217 843. Probably the best-value restaurant in the centre, this reliable, old-fashioned place near the market has two straightforward *menús* at €11 and €20, and an à la carte menu of regional meat and fish dishes that won't break the bank (mains €9–14). Daily 1–4pm & 8.30pm–midnight.

El Grillo Azul c/Grillo 1 ☎ 923 219 233. The only place in town where strict vegetarians can be confident of getting a decent meal. There's an €11 *menú del día* served day and night (otherwise dishes €6–9), while alongside all the usual veggie rice, pasta bakes and tofu dishes are more sophisticated things like asparagus risotto or scrambled eggs with mushrooms and almonds. Tues–Sat 1–4pm & 8–11pm, Sun 1–4pm.

Mesón Cervantes Pl. Mayor 15 ☎ 923 217 213, ⓦ mesoncervantes.com. There are two selling points here: a prime position overlooking Pl. Mayor (arrive early at meal times for a window seat) and all-day food service. The filling, all-in-one *platos combinados* are €10–16, or there's

drinks, tapas, *raciones*, salads and sandwiches. Daily 8.30am–midnight.

★ **El Pecado** Pl. Poeta Iglesias 12 ☎ 923 266 558, ⓦ elpecadorestaurante.es. The funky townhouse interior of leopardskin banquettes and deep pink walls is the backdrop for some equally adventurous regional cuisine – the spicy *patatas bravas* are given their kick with wasabi oil, or you can try things like *chipirones* stuffed with olives and cinnamon rice. Dishes cost €10–20, though there's an excellent-value €15 *menú*, served day and night, of simpler food like pasta, homemade burgers or grilled tuna. Daily 1–4pm & 9pm–midnight.

Río de la Plata Pl. Peso 1 ☎ 923 219 005. The well-regarded regional Castilian cuisine here is a real step up in quality from most places in the area – as are the prices. Hearty rustic dishes (mostly €14–25) range from rabbit stew to hake casserole; fish is a speciality, as are seasonal *horta* (countryside) dishes using ingredients like asparagus, beans and mushrooms. Tues–Sun 1–3.30pm & 9pm–midnight; closed 2 weeks in July & 2 weeks in Feb.

Victor Gutierrez c/San Pablo 66 ☎ 923 262 973, ⓦ restaurantevictorgutierrez.com. Michelin-star seekers make a beeline for Victor Gutierrez's place, where tasting menus at €55 and €80 showcase the chef's innovative style – his seasonal menus lean heavily on his Peruvian origins, while good old Castilian produce is also given an Asian twist or two. You'll need a reservation. Daily 1.30–3.30pm & 8.30–11pm.

★ **Vinodiario** Pl. de los Basilios 1 ☎ 923 614 925. Terrific contemporary wine bar with food, just off the main tourist track in a nice square with outdoor tables. There are some great wines by the glass, plus superior meals and *raciones*, including brochette of mozzarella with cherry tomatoes, smoked salmon, grilled peppers, and a ground-beef-and-herb hamburger (most dishes €5–15). Daily 10am–1am.

NIGHTLIFE

There's a whole host of student-oriented **bars and clubs** on the southeast edge of the *casco histórico*, particularly in the arcades of the Gran Vía, in Pl. de San Justo and near the market (near c/Varillas). Another area for bars and clubs is around the Convento de las Úrsulas, while if you're looking for quantity over quality try the infamous **bars de litros** just to the north of here, which sell drinks in litre "buckets" – you'll find several around Pl. de San Juan de Bautista.

BARS

★ **Clavel Ocho** c/Clavel 8 ☎923 265 183, ⓦclavelocho.com. One of several amenable bars that put out tables in two interlinked squares just below the market, underneath the San Julian church walls. A good place to start the evening, while DJ sessions kick off after midnight most nights of the week. Mon–Sat 4pm–3am.

Irish Rover Rúa Antigua 11 ☎923 210 035, ⓦtheirishroversalamanca.com. This Irish pub opposite La Clerecía is known as "The Rov", by its expat and student fans. It's a full-on wet-T-shirt and toga-party kind of place – converting into a raucous late-night *discoteca* at weekends – but also puts on up-and-coming Spanish bands. Sun–Thurs 5pm–3am, Fri & Sat 5pm–5am.

Posada de las Ánimas Pl. San Boal 7; no phone, ⓦposadadelasanimas.com. The terraza is a bit hidden away from the main drag (and shared with the equally likeable bar *Juanita*), and don't miss the weird interior of cherubs, chandeliers and dolls' houses. Daily 6pm–3am.

CLUBS

Camelot c/Bordadores 3 ☎923 219 091, ⓦcamelot salamanca.com. Everyone in town knows this fun bar and *discoteca*, housed in part of the Convento de las Úrsulas. The interior, an ex-church, is a mix of medieval and industrial decor, with a bar on the first floor, above the dancefloor, and there are terraza seats outside. Daily 6pm–2am, weekends until 5am.

DIRECTORY

Bookshop Librería Portonaris, Rúa Mayor 35, has a reasonable selection of English-language books.

Hospitals Hospital Clínico, Paseo San Vicente 182 ☎923 291 100; Hospital Virgen de la Vega, Paseo San Vicente 58–182 ☎923 291 200.

Internet access At Pl. Mayor 10, underneath *Pensión Los Angeles* (daily noon–midnight).

Language courses Spanish-language courses offered by

the Universidad de Salamanca (ⓦusal.es/curespus) are heavily subscribed, but there are loads of other schools.

Laundry At Pasaje Azafranal 19, off c/Azafranal (daily: summer 10am–8pm; winter 9.30am–2pm & 4–8pm).

Police Policía Nacional, Ronda Sancti Spiritus 8–12 ☎923 127 700. In an emergency, call ☎091.

Post office Gran Vía 25 (Mon–Fri 8.30am–8.30pm, Sat 9.30am–2pm).

Ciudad Rodrigo

The unspoiled frontier town of **CIUDAD RODRIGO** – 90km southwest of Salamanca, astride the road to Portugal – is worth a detour even if you don't plan to cross the border. It's an endearingly sleepy place which, despite an orgy of destruction during the Peninsular War, preserves a rather austere castle (now a parador), a handsome Plaza Mayor and quiet old-town streets full of Renaissance mansions. It's also still completely encircled by impressive walls and ramparts, and the thirty-minute walk around (and on top of) them is the best way to get an overview of the whole town. Given its history, it's perhaps surprising that there's much left to see at all. Ciudad Rodrigo was a crucial border point in the **Peninsular War**, guarding the route between Spain and Portugal. The town fell to the French after a fierce fight in 1810, but was later re-taken by the British in 1812 following a devastatingly rapid siege (cannonball dents are still visible above the doorway on one side of the cathedral). A triumphant rampage of looting followed, and when order was restored, the troops paraded out dressed in a ragbag of stolen French finery – a bemused Wellington muttering to his staff, "Who the devil are those fellows?"

ARRIVAL AND DEPARTURE

CIUDAD RODRIGO

By train There is a train station, a fair walk north of the centre, though there's only one train a day to Lisbon (currently at 6.07am), and another to Hendaye in France

(11.32pm; via Salamanca, Valladolid and Burgos, all in the dead of night).

By bus From Salamanca, the bus is easily the most

5

convenient way to get to Ciudad Rodrigo; the bus station is a five-minute walk north of the old town.

By car Salamanca is under an hour's drive away. You can easily park outside the town walls, or try your luck with the limited spaces on Pl. Mayor.

INFORMATION

Turismo Pl. de Amayuelas (Mon–Fri 9am–2pm & 5–7pm, Sat & Sun 10am–2pm & 5–8pm; ☎923 460 561, ⓦciudadrodrigo.net), just through the rampart tunnel.

There's also useful tourist information on ⓦturismociudadrodrigo.com.

ACCOMMODATION

Hostal Puerta del Sol c/Rúa del Sol 33 ☎923 460 671, ⓦhostalesenciudadrodrigo.com. Trim little en-suite rooms by the Puerta del Sol gate, and a cosy feel throughout. Public parking 1min away through the gate. **€60**

★ **Hotel Conde Rodrigo I** Pl. de San Salvador 7 ☎923 461 404, ⓦconderodrigo.com. An old mansion loaded with character – check out the period-piece panelled bar. The rooms are nothing flashy, but perfectly decent and with good bathrooms, and it's very quiet at the

rear. There's also private garage parking nearby (you can unload outside). **€60**

Parador de Ciudad Rodrigo Pl. Castillo 1 ☎923 460 150, ⓦparador.es. The main historic hotel has an unrivalled location in the old castle, which has been beautifully restored. There are views to all sides, and some very grand rooms and public spaces, as well as a restaurant and a car park. Advance online bookings can shave around €40 off the room rate. **€160**

EATING AND DRINKING

★ **Estoril** c/General Pando 11 ☎923 460 550, ⓦrestaurante-estoril.com. The best place in town for modern interpretations of regional cuisine – marinated quail salad, milk-fed lamb, duck with blackberry sauce, etc. Meals are served in the formal, but unstuffy, restaurant to the rear (mains €13–20); otherwise there's a café at the front for tapas and *raciones*. Daily: café from 9am–11pm; restaurant: 1–4pm & 8–11pm.

El Rodeo c/Gigantes 10 ☎923 482 017. Simple,

old-fashioned restaurant offering hearty local specialities, such as scrambled eggs with *farinato* (pork and bread sausage). There's a *menú* for €10, or you can eat in the evening for around €20. Daily 1–4pm & 8.30–11pm.

El Sanatorio Pl. Mayor 13–15 ☎923 460 024. Atmospheric little bar-restaurant whose walls are covered in bullfighting photos from decades of *corridas* and fiestas. Dishes €5–10. Daily 9am–midnight.

Sierra de Francia

The protected mountain region of the **Sierra de Francia** marks the southern region of Salamanca province, with the most obvious target the captivating "national monument" village of **La Alberca**. It makes a good walking base for the surrounding hills and valleys, notably the stunning **Valle de Las Batuecas**, with its isolated monastery and ancient rock art. There are daily buses to La Alberca from Salamanca, but the area is otherwise best explored by car, in which case you'll also be able to make a half-day's circuit via the equally venerable hill-town of **Miranda del Castañar**.

La Alberca

Although ringed by the trappings of mass tourism these days, the centre of **LA ALBERCA** still maintains an extraordinary collection of late medieval, half-timbered houses. It's very pretty, and an obvious honeytrap for weekenders and coach parties who trawl the rather-too-clean cobbled lanes shopping for basketware and other souvenirs. The smell and dirt of the farmyard may be long gone, but La Alberca is still known for its *embutidos* and *jamones*, and every second shop displays the rich, nutty hams, smoked pork and cured sausages. A granite porker stands outside the church, while the most elegant houses are found in the arcaded **Plaza Mayor**, which is ringed by cafés and restaurants and dominated by a stone cross.

ARRIVAL AND INFORMATION   **LA ALBERCA**

By bus La Alberca is 45km southeast of Ciudad Rodrigo, and 73km southwest of Salamanca. Cosme buses (ⓦ autocarescosme.com) run here once or twice daily from Salamanca, stopping on the edge of the old quarter, though departure times don't suit a day-trip.

By car You should eventually find somewhere to park on the main through-roads, though there's also a large car park a few hundred metres out on the Batuecas road, just

past the *Hotel Antiguas Eras* and right next to the Casa del Parque information office.

Turismo Casa del Parque, Carretera Las Batuecas (Tues, Wed & Thurs 10am–2pm, Sat, Sun & hols 10am–2pm & 4–6pm, mid-July to mid-Sept till 8pm; ☎ 923 415 213). The local town hall has a useful tourist website, ⓦ laalberca.com.

ACCOMMODATION AND EATING

Accommodation is expensive for what you get, and the best deals are found further up the Batuecas road, a few minutes' walk from the centre. There are a few cheaper *pensiones* in town (though some are a little bleak), while there's one terrific boutique hotel in a nearby village. Half a dozen **bars and restaurants** ring Pl. Mayor, and there are a few more down neighbouring streets serving tapas and meals: none particularly cheap, all agreeably rustic.

Hostal La Alberca Pl. Padre Arsenio, off Pl. Mayor ☎ 923 415 116, ⓦ hostallaalberca.com. These simple en-suite rooms offer the town's best value at the budget end of the scale. There's also central heating – essential on a winter visit in these parts. **€40**

Hotel Antiguas Eras Batuecas road ☎ 923 415 113, ⓦ antiguaseras.com. Agreeable three-star hotel with spacious, pleasant rooms, distant hill views and a family-friendly welcome. **€70**

Hotel Las Batuecas Batuecas road ☎ 923 415 188, ⓦ hotelasbatuecas.com. Three-star hotel and restaurant with a rustic *ambiente clásico* and old-fashioned rooms. Summer deals on the website offer the best deals. Restaurant 1–4pm & 9–11pm. **€80**

Hotel Doña Teresa Mogarraz road ☎ 923 415 308, ⓦ hoteldeteresa.com. The smartest choice in town, this four-star hotel has an on-site spa and restaurant, and landscaped pool and gardens nearby. Restaurant 1–4pm & 9–11pm. **€100**

★ **Villa de Mogarraz** c/Miguel Angel Maillo 54, Mogarraz, 7km east of La Alberca ☎ 923 418 080, ⓦ hotelspamogarraz.com. For the finest lodgings in the area, drive the short distance east to the equally ancient village of Mogarraz, where this restored mansion offers wonderfully stylish bedrooms featuring plenty of exposed stone, reclaimed wood and antique colonial furniture. There are hip spa facilities and a good restaurant too, known for its grilled meats (meals around €35). Room rates increase by €10 at weekends. Restaurant 1–4pm & 9–11pm. **€90**

CAMPING

Al-Bereka 2km out on the Salamanca road ☎ 923 415 195, ⓦ albereka.com. The local campsite is more of a holiday complex, with rustic cabins and apartments to rent (from €75), as well as separate pools for adults and children, plus café and restaurant. Closed Nov–April. **€4.20** per person plus **€3.50–4.50** per tent.

Parque Natural Las Batuecas-Sierra de Francia

La Alberca sits in the middle of the **PARQUE NATURAL LAS BATUECAS-SIERRA DE FRANCIA**, and at the centre of an excellent network of hiking trails. These are well signposted and easily followed, especially if you've already stopped for maps at the Casa del Parque information office in La Alberca.

Peña de Francia

The most obvious route on a clear day is up to the summit of **Peña de Francia** (1723m), not quite the highest point in the range but the most panoramic. The trail is signposted a couple of hundred metres outside La Alberca on the Batuecas road, by the Cooperativa Chacinera (across from the *Hotel Antiguas Eras*); it's a very specific 8.3km on foot (6hr round trip) or 17km by road. There's the church and sanctuary of Our Lady of the Peña de Francia at the windswept summit, along with a welcome *cafetería* and even lodgings at the *Hospedería del Santuario Peña de Francia*.

Valle de Las Batuecas

The Batuecas road out of La Alberca climbs in 3.5km to the pass of **El Portillo** (1247m), surrounded by rugged hills. From here, the road drops sharply for another 9km, via a

5

series of hairpin bends, into the **Valle de Las Batuecas**, where a signpost points you up a short track to a parking area outside the **Monasterio San José de Las Batuecas**. There's also a more direct seven-kilometre path (3hr 30min each way) from La Alberca, over the pass and down to the monastery. This sylvan retreat in a hidden valley was founded at the beginning of the seventeenth century, and is a closed Carmelite order (no public access). However, a signposted path around the side of the monastery leads along the babbling river to a series of three **rock-art** sites dating from between 5000 and 2500 BC, depicting hunting and pastoral scenes of goats and deer, and even human figures. The closest site, Cabras Pintadas, is an enjoyable half-hour's walk and scramble from the monastery gate.

Miranda del Castañar

By car it's a good half-day's excursion to continue on to **Miranda del Castañar** from the Monasterio San José de Las Batuecas, first heading south for 5km to the junction at **Las Mestas**, just across the border in Extremadura. Following signs for Cepeda and Salamanca then takes you around the eastern edge of the *parque natural*, eventually arriving (after 27km) at Miranda, a similarly ancient town to La Alberca, though this time set within the walls of a honey-coloured castle. There are sweeping views to all sides, a couple of rather nice *casas rurales* and upmarket restaurants, and a café or two.

Zamora and around

ZAMORA, 62km north of Salamanca and only 50km from the Portuguese border, is the quietest of the great Castilian cities, with a population of just 65,000. In medieval romances, it was known as *la bien cercada* (the well-enclosed) on account of its strong fortifications; one siege here lasted seven months. Its old quarters, still walled and medieval in appearance, are spread out along the top of a ridge that slopes down to the banks of the Río Duero, crossed at it widest point by a lovely sixteen-arched bridge. The city's surviving Romanesque churches are its most distinctive feature, while the beguiling streets and squares of the old town make for an attractive overnight stay. When it's time to move on, the obvious routes are east to Valladolid, with a stop in the small town of **Toro**, or north to León, via **Benavente** and its parador; Bragança, the first main town over the border in Portugal, is just over 100km away on a good, fast road.

Romanesque churches

All March–Sept 10am–1pm & 5–8pm, Oct–Dec 10am–2pm & 4.30–6.30pm • Free

The joy of Zamora lies in its quiet, western old-town quarter – looking decidedly spruce and scrubbed these days – and, above all, in its dozen pale-stone **Romanesque churches**, with their unassumingly beautiful architecture, and towers populated by colonies of storks. The majority date from the twelfth century and reflect Castile's sense of security following the victorious campaigns against the Moors by Alfonso VI and El Cid. All are worthy of a closer look, though **San Juan de Puerta Nueva** (Plaza Mayor; closed Tues), **La Magdalena** (Rúa de los Francos; closed Tues) and **Santiago del Burgo** (c/Santa Clara; closed Mon) are considered the highlights.

Museo de la Semana Santa

Pl. de Santa María La Nueva • Tues–Sat 10am–2pm & 5–8pm, Sun 10am–2pm • €3

Opposite the church of Santa María La Nueva, the **Museo de la Semana Santa** contains the *pasos* – statues depicting the Passion of Christ – which are paraded through the streets during Zamora's famous Holy Week processions (ⓦssantazamora.es).

5

ZAMORA

ACCOMMODATION

Hostal La Reina	1
Hostería Real de Zamora	4
Hotel Horus Zamora	2
Parador Condes de Alba y Aliste	3

CAFÉS & RESTAURANTS

El Rincón de Antonio	2
Zamora	1

5

Catedral

Pl. de la Catedral • Daily: April–Sept 10am–2pm & 5–8pm; Oct–March 10am–2pm & 4.30–6.30pm • €4, free Mon pm

The **Catedral**, enclosed within the ruined citadel at the far end of town, is now shining very brightly after restoration. Begun in 1151, its mainly Romanesque body is largely hidden behind an overbearing Renaissance facade, above which the building's most striking feature – a Byzantine-inspired dome similar to that of the Catedral Vieja at Salamanca – perches in incongruous splendour. However, it springs a surprise inside, with its famous carved **choir stalls**, which depict devout scenes and mystical animals as well as lusty carryings-on between monks and nuns. Access to the cathedral is through the associated **Museo Catedralicio**, on the other side of the cloisters, which houses the city's celebrated "Black Tapestries", a series of fifteenth-century Flemish masterpieces woven in stunning detail.

Castillo

Parque del Castillo • Always open • Free

Next to the cathedral are the impressive moated remains of the **Castillo**, now laid out as a shady park; wander round the back for majestic views over the surrounding countryside and Río Duero, along with Zamora's burgeoning suburbs.

ARRIVAL AND DEPARTURE ZAMORA

The **train and bus stations** are close to each other, but a fair way from the centre, thirty minutes' walk north of Pl. Mayor. Alternatively, it's a ten-minute ride on bus #4 (every 20min), which leaves from outside the bus station and runs down Avenida Tres Cruces, dropping you at Pl. Sagasta by Pl. Mayor; note the return bus departs from outside the market.

By train From the train station on Ctra. de la Estación, walk straight out over the roundabout in front to join the Avda. Tres Cruces.
Destinations Madrid (3 daily; 3hr 30min–4hr); Santiago de Compostela (3 daily; 4hr 30min); Valladolid (daily; 1hr 40min); Vigo (3 daily; 5hr).
By bus The bus station is on Avda. Alfonso Peña (☏980 521 282); turn right out of the main entrance, then right again around the side of the terminal to reach the main

road; turn left here and follow Avda. Tres Cruces into town.
Destinations León via Benavente (4–6 daily; 2hr); Madrid (6 daily; 2hr 45min–3hr 15min); Palencia (2 daily; 2hr 15min); Salamanca (hourly; 1hr 10min); Toro (Mon–Sat roughly hourly, Sun 3 daily; 30min); Valladolid (Mon–Fri hourly, Sat & Sun 4–6 daily; 1hr 30min).
By car Car parks in the centre are well signposted, but some of the old town is residents-only access and parking.

INFORMATION

Zamora Turismo Pl. de Arias Gonzalo 6, near the cathedral (daily: April–Sept 10am–2pm & 5–8pm; Oct–March 10am–2pm & 4–7pm; ☏980 533 694, ⓦzamora .es). The regional office is on the edge of the old town at

Avda. Príncipe de Asturias 1 (daily: July to mid-Sept 9am–8pm, Fri & Sat until 9pm; mid-Sept to June 9am–2pm & 5–8pm; ☏980 531 845 or 902 203 030).

ACCOMMODATION

Zamora has a reasonable spread of **accommodation**, most of it within a short walk of the old quarter. The only time you will have difficulty finding a room is over Easter week, during the famous processions, when prices double and accommodation is booked solid.

★ **Hostal La Reina** c/La Reina 1, 1º ☏980 533 939. The best budget accommodation, with mostly bright, spacious rooms in an unbeatable location right by Pl. Mayor. Some rooms overlook the square, some are en suite, and some a bit dowdier than others, so it pays to specify or look at a couple. **€40**
Hostería Real de Zamora c/Cuesta del Pizarro 7 ☏980 534 545, ⓦhosteriasreales.com. The poor man's

parador is set in the 400-year-old Palacio de Inquisidores, complete with tiled staircases, a cobbled Renaissance patio and goldfish pond. Pretty rooms are ranged around the patio gallery, and some have river views, while simple meals are served around the patio or in the beamed dining room. **€80**
Hotel Horus Zamora Pl. del Mercado 20 ☏980 508 282, ⓦhotelhorus.com. Handsome boutique lodgings in

a restored mansion right opposite the market. Most of the rooms are nice and quiet, with some set in the eaves, and there's a good contemporary restaurant and garage parking – though there's also restricted street parking outside in the market square. **€70**

★ **Parador Condes de Alba y Aliste** Pl. de Viriato 5 ☎ 980 514 497, ⓦ parador.es. Zamora's classy parador is a stunning conversion of a fifteenth-century palace in the heart of town, mixing lovely rooms with princely trappings throughout, from the heroic medallions surmounting the internal courtyard to the idly positioned suits of armour. An elevated garden-terrace and open-air summer pool have city views, while a fine restaurant serves updated regional cuisine (mains around €20). Special room rates go as low as €100. **€160**

EATING AND DRINKING

Zamora's most celebrated dishes are hearty affairs like *sopas de ajo* (garlic soup), *arroz de la Zamorana* (rice flavoured with pigs' trotters), and *habones Sanabreses* (broad beans cooked in a meaty paprika broth). Most **restaurants** and **cafés** are found around the Pl. Mayor and in the side streets and squares off c/Santa Clara. There's also a cluster of no-nonsense **tapas bars** in the alleys around Pl. del Maestro (east end of c/Santa Clara, by the church of San Torcuato), while a lively run of twenty or so music and drinking **bars** down the narrow c/de los Herreros, just off Pl. Mayor, is where the weekend starts.

★ **El Rincón de Antonio** Rúa de los Francos 6 ☎ 980 535 370, ⓦ elrincondeantonio.com. The town's most inventive restaurant takes creative Castilian cuisine to a different level. With classy mains at €25 or so, and the *menú degustación* at €55, it's a special-occasion place, but you can always just drop in for fancy tapas at the bar (what they call *cocina en miniatura*) at €2–3 a pop. Daily 1–3.30pm & 8.30–11pm.

Zamora Pl. Mayor ☎ 980 521 064. For a budget meal on the main square, right by the lovely medieval church, the *Zamora* caters to most tastes. There are various *menús*, ranging from €10 to €23, available day and night, providing anything from a simple salad and grilled trout to stewed Zamoran broad beans and a steak. Daily 10am–midnight.

North of Zamora

Heading north from Zamora, it's 140km to León (or a two-hour bus ride) on a fast road (N630 then A66) through the baking wheat fields of the *meseta*. Drivers can at least break the journey at a couple of interesting places.

Monasterio de Moreruela

Around 40km north of Zamora, look for a marked turn-off from the N630 (on the left) at the dusty roadside village of Granja de Moreruela. "Granja" means farm, meaning the village was originally an outlying property of the medieval **Monasterio de Moreruela**, which lies 3.7km from the highway down a paved country lane. It's now in ruins, and home to a large colony of storks, but is an evocative sight nonetheless, under a carpet of daisies and poppies, with rolling farmland to all sides.

Benavente

Thirty kilometres further north, the small town of **BENAVENTE** is rather charming once you penetrate the outskirts, with busy pedestrianized shopping streets set around a honey-coloured stone church or two. A broad landscaped *paseo* on a bluff offers extensive views over the surrounding countryside, while at the end of the gardens, the *Parador de Benavente* occupies the remains of the town's impressive castle.

Toro

TORO, 30km east of Zamora, looks dramatic seen from below: "an ancient, eroded, red-walled town spread along the top of a huge flat boulder", as Laurie Lee described it in *As I Walked Out One Midsummer Morning*. At closer quarters it turns out to be a rather ordinary provincial town, though embellished with one outstanding Romanesque reminder of past glory. Toro is also increasingly well known for its gutsy red **wines**, and the local tourist office can point you in the direction of local wineries open to the public.

5

> ## THE BATTLE OF TORO
>
> Toro – a historic military stronghold – played a role of vital significance in both Spanish and Portuguese history. The **Battle of Toro** in 1476 effectively ended Portugal's interest in Spanish affairs and laid the basis for the unification of Spain. On the death of Enrique IV in 1474, the Castilian throne was disputed: almost certainly his daughter Juana la Beltraneja was the rightful heiress, but rumours of illegitimacy were stirred up and Enrique's sister Isabel seized the throne. Alfonso V of Portugal saw his opportunity and supported Juana. At Toro, the armies clashed in 1476 and the Reyes Católicos – Isabel and her husband Fernando – defeated their rivals to embark upon one of the most glorious periods in Spanish history.

Colegiata de Santa María la Mayor

Off Pl. Mayor • March–Sept Tues–Sun 10.30am–2pm & 5–7.30pm; Oct–Dec Tues–Sun 10am–2pm & 4.30–6.30pm • Church free, cloisters €1

Toro's pride and joy is the **Colegiata de Santa María la Mayor**, whose west portal (c.1240), inside the church, is one of the most beautiful examples of Romanesque art in the region. Its seven recessed arches carved with royal and biblical themes still retain much of their colourful original paint. Also inspect *The Virgin of the Fly*, a notable fifteenth-century painting hanging in the sacristy – the eponymous insect perches on the Virgin's robes. Around the back of the church is a wide terrace with a famous view over the *meseta*, with the Río Duero far below.

ARRIVAL AND INFORMATION   TORO

By bus and car Buses to Toro are reasonably frequent (Zamora–Valladolid route; hourly service, fewer at weekends) and stop on the main road that skirts the north side of town – it's best to park outside town here, too. Walk through the big arch and straight on for about five minutes, through the clock tower, to reach Pl. Mayor, with the Colegiata immediately behind.

Turismo Pl. Mayor 6 (Tues–Sun 10am–1pm & 4–7pm; ☎ 980 694 747, ⓦ toroayto.es).

ACCOMMODATION AND EATING

You're unlikely to want to stay the night, given the superior charms of nearby Zamora or Valladolid. Toro's a more realistic coffee or lunch stop – its Pl. Mayor is lined with characteristic red-brick houses and stone arcades, with many enticing **tapas bars** and **restaurants**.

Valladolid and around

VALLADOLID, at the centre of the *meseta* and capital of the Castilla y León region, ought to be dramatic and exciting. Many of the greatest figures of Spain's Golden Age – Fernando and Isabel, Columbus, Cervantes, Torquemada, Felipe II – lived in the city at various times, and for five years at the turn of the seventeenth century it vied with Madrid as the royal capital. It had wealth and prestige, yet modern Valladolid – a busy, working city of 400,000 – lost much that was irreplaceable, as many of its finest palaces and grandest streets were swept away during subsequent centuries. Nonetheless, much that remains is appealing in a city centre of restored squares and gleaming churches, including a series of excellent art museums, one of which holds the finest collection of religious sculpture anywhere in Spain. While it doesn't have the overriding beauty of Salamanca, or the stand out monumental presence of Burgos or León, Valladolid is an easy city to like – whether it's the pretty shaded gardens of the Campo Grande, or the student bars lined up under the shadow of a majestic Gothic church. The best time to get a sense of the city's historic traditions is **Semana Santa** (Holy Week), when Valladolid is host to some of the most extravagant and solemn processions in Spain.

Outside the city, there are easy side-trips to the handsome small towns of **Tordesillas** and **Medina del Campo**, both now on the quiet and sleepy side but, like Valladolid, also boasting significant histories.

VALLADOLID

BARS
Café España	7
Café Herminios	2
El Penicilino	1

TAPAS BARS AND RESTAURANTS
Bar Jamoneria Sarmiento	4
El Caballo de Troya	8
Covadonga	3
Jero	5
La Mejillonera	10
Milvinos	9
Otras Luces	6

ACCOMMODATION
Hostal París	5
Hotel Imperial	4
Hotel El Nogal	3
Hotel Roma	1
Meliá Recoletos	2
Pensión La Cueva	6

5

Plaza Mayor

The heart of Valladolid is the spacious **Plaza Mayor**, a broad expanse surrounded by arcaded buildings painted a striking, uniform red. Originally laid out in the sixteenth century after a fire had devastated the city, it was the first plaza of its kind in the country, becoming the model for countless similar civic centrepieces in both Spain and its South American colonies. Though much rebuilt since, it's still one of the grandest urban spaces in Spain, scene of festival celebrations and concerts throughout the year. Its arcade cafés make a pleasant place to watch the world go by, while many of Valladolid's best tapas bars and restaurants can be found in the narrow streets just off its western edge.

Mercado del Val

C/de Francisco Zarandona • Mon–Sat 7am–3pm

The main city market lies just north of Plaza Mayor, and clocks in at a rather impressive 112m long. Inside the nineteenth-century cast-iron shed you can debate the pros and cons of buying an entire suckling pig or a bag of snails, while along the street outside are half a dozen popular tapas bars and restaurants.

Museo Patio Herreriano

C/Jorge Guillén 6 • Tues–Fri 11am–2pm & 5–8pm, Sat 11am–8pm, Sun 11am–3pm • €3, Wed €1 • ☎ 983 362 771, ⓦ museopatioherreriano.org

The annexe around the back of the brilliant-white, restored Monasterio de San Benito y Santa Isabel houses the **Museo Patio Herreriano**. It's a beautiful space dedicated to contemporary Spanish art (from 1918 to the present day), with galleries on several floors wrapped around a Renaissance courtyard of luminous pale gold stone. There's a permanent display of works by artists at the forefront of Spanish Cubism, Surrealism and abstract art, including Rafael Barradas, Joaquin Torres-García, Julio González and Ángel Ferrant, but also temporary exhibitions by young contemporary artists and sculptors, sometimes of the light-flashing-pointlessly-in-a-room variety but often with bouts of real quality, too. A stylish café-bar sits on the modern patio outside.

Museo de Valladolid

Pl. de Fabio Nelli • Tues–Sat 10am–2pm & 4–7pm, July–Sept till 8pm, Sun 10am–2pm • €1.20, free weekends • ☎ 983 351 389

A classic piece of architecture from Valladolid's golden age, the city's finest Renaissance mansion holds the galleries of the **Museo de Valladolid**, containing the municipal archeological and art collections. The building – notably the impressive main staircase and internal courtyard – is magnificent; the old-fashioned displays less so, being the usual run of prehistoric bones, Bronze Age tools, Roman grave goods and medieval art.

Catedral

Visitors' entrance on Pl. de la Universidad • Tues–Fri 10am–1.30pm & 4.30–7pm, Sat & Sun 10am–2pm • €2.50 • ⓦ catedral-valladolid.com

The city's seventeenth-century **Catedral** is built right on top of the remains of its medieval predecessor (part of whose structure can still be seen at the back), and its construction employed the not inconsiderable talents of Juan de Herrera (architect of El Escorial) and Alberto Churriguera. However, only half of it was ever built and what stands is something of a disappointment – rather plain, rather severe and rather hard to view as a whole. Inside, the highlight is the *retablo mayor* by Juan de Juni (and even this was actually made for the Gothic Santa María la Antigua in the plaza behind). You may decide to give the whole thing a miss, since unless you attend Mass you're officially supposed to stump up for a tour of both cathedral and the treasures of the diocesan museum, the **Museo Diocesano y Catedralicio**.

FOOTSTEPS OF THE FAMOUS

Felipe II was born (1527) in Valladolid, and in other circumstances perhaps his home city might have become the permanent Spanish capital, and not Madrid. As it was, Valladolid was only briefly the capital (1601–06), but Felipe's birthplace, the Palacio de los Pimentel (c/ Angustias), has a memorial plaque, and his statue is over the way in Plaza San Pablo. Another surviving palace, Palacio de los Viveros (c/Ramon y Cajal), is where the royal teenagers **Fernando and Isabel** married in 1469, later to be the "Catholic Monarchs" of a new, triumphant Spain; while the widely travelled **Miguel Cervantes** spent a few years in the city, too – what's thought to have been his house (Casa Cervantes, just off c/Miguel Iscar) is now a small museum. However, the city is perhaps proudest of **Christopher Columbus** (Cristóbal Colón), who died here in 1506 – Valladolid devoted an entire year in 2006, and spruced up the old town, to celebrate the five-hundredth anniversary of the old mercenary's demise, and there's a replica of the house he died in, known as Casa Colón, on c/Colón.

Iglesia de San Pablo

Pl. de San Pablo • No public access

If the city's cathedral is no looker, you don't have to walk far to find a church that delivers. Protected by fourteen lions on pedestals brandishing heraldic plaques, the exuberant **Iglesia de San Pablo** – the sole surviving part of a Dominican convent destroyed in the nineteenth century – has an imaginal facade that combines a wild mixture of styles in a froth of sculpted columns, expressive figures, and star and floral motifs. Added to by various regal and noble sponsors over a century or so, it's actually in two different styles, the lower part a lavish form of late Gothic known as Isabelline, the upper a Plateresque confection, similar to the Catedral Nueva and Convento de San Esteban at Salamanca.

Museo Nacional Colegio de San Gregorio

C/Cadenas de San Gregorio 1–3 • Tues–Sat 10am–2pm & 4–7.30pm, Sun 10am–2pm • €3, free Sat afternoon & Sun • ☎ 983 250 375, Ⓦ museosangregorio.mcu.es

The most extraordinary sculpted facade of all in Valladolid is that of the **Colegio de San Gregorio**, adorned not just with coats of arms and crowned lions, but sculpted twigs, naked children clambering in the branches of a pomegranate tree and long-haired men carrying maces. Considered to be from the workshop of master sculptor Gil de Siloé, it's very much like icing on a cake – Jan Morris, for one, was convinced that the flamboyant facade must be edible. The collegiate church was built by the Bishop of Burgos – Chancellor of Castile and confessor to Queen Isabel – as a theological college, and was richly endowed, most obviously with a gleaming two-tier courtyard of twisted stone columns, and an upper gallery that's a sculpted Plateresque flight of fancy of heraldic, mythic and regal symbols. Inside, too, the building has been majestically restored and now contains the unmissable religious art and sculpture collection of the **Museo Nacional**.

The stunningly presented collection from the sixteenth to eighteenth centuries includes some of the most brilliant works of the Spanish Renaissance. Set in majestic galleries on two floors, ranged around the San Gregorio courtyard, the hugely expressive statues, sculptures, *retablos* and other artworks were often commissioned directly for churches and monasteries, and it's rare to see such vibrant pieces at these close quarters – while if you look up, almost every gallery has its own antique coffered ceiling of gilt and painted wood, transplanted here from other religious foundations.

Sixteenth-century artists such as **Alonso Berruguete** (1490–1561), **Diego de Siloé** (1495–1565) and the Frenchman **Juan de Juni** (1507–77) adapted the classical revival to the religious intensity of the Spanish temperament, and the results are often magnificent and sometimes quite beautifully brutal: weeping crucifixion wounds, severed heads, cadaverous bodies, agonized faces and rapt expressions fill the galleries. The dissolved

5

Valladolid monastery of San Bento el Real provides two pieces that are typical of the richness and power on display: its *retablo mayor* has a life-sized St Benedict almost striding out from the surrounding scenes of his miracles, while in an upper gallery sit the intricately carved and painted choir stalls, preserved in their jaw-dropping entirety.

Palacio de Villena

C/Cadenas de San Gregorio • Tues–Sat 10am–2pm & 4–7.30pm, Sun 10am–2pm • Free

Across the street from the San Gregorio facade stands the Renaissance **Palacio de Villena**, used as the museum's centre for temporary exhibitions and public events. It also contains one final, and extraordinary, flourish, namely the so-called **Belén Napolitano** or Nativity tableau – in an eighteenth-century Neapolitan street, between the hanging laundry, itinerant musicians and fruit sellers, the three Wise Men troop towards the manger on camels.

ARRIVAL AND DEPARTURE   VALLADOLID

Arrival points are centred on the large triangular park that is the Campo Grande: the **train station** is at the foot of the park, and the **bus station** a few minutes' walk west. It's a fifteen-minute walk up to town from the train station, or there are taxis outside – it's a €5 ride to Pl. Mayor.

By plane There's a small airport (information on ☎983 415 500, ⓦaena.es) 10km outside the city, served by domestic flights and Ryanair services from London Stansted. Buses (€3) run to the centre, while a taxi should cost €20–25.

By train The train station is on c/del Norte Recondo, below Campo Grande, and the AVE high-speed train service (reservations recommended) makes Valladolid just over an hour's jump from Madrid. It's also more convenient by train from Valladolid to Palencia, Burgos, León and Medina del Campo. For current timetables and ticket information, consult RENFE ☎902 320 320, ⓦrenfe.com.

Destinations Burgos (up to 13 daily; 1hr–1hr 20min); León (up to 10 daily; 1hr 30min–2hr); Madrid (AVE 6 daily, 1hr; other services at least hourly, 1hr 30min–2hr 45min); Medina del Campo (hourly; 20–30min); Palencia (hourly; 30min); Salamanca (10 daily; 1hr 15min–1hr 30min); Zamora (daily; 1hr 40min).

By bus The Estación de Autobuses is at c/Puente Colgante 2 (☎938 236 308). Bus companies include Auto Res/ Avanza to Tordesillas/Salamanca (☎983 220 274, ⓦavanzabus.com) and La Regional to Tordesillas, Toro, Zamora, Palencia, Peñafiel and the Duero (☎983 308 088, ⓦlaregionalvsa.com).

Destinations El Burgo de Osma (3 daily; 2hr); Burgos (5 daily; 2hr 30min); León (8 daily; 2hr); Madrid (hourly; 2hr 15min); Palencia (Mon–Fri hourly, Sat 6 daily, Sun 3 daily; 1hr); Peñafiel (Mon–Sat 7 daily, Sun 4 daily; 1hr); Salamanca (up to 8 daily; 1hr 15min–1hr 40min); Segovia (hourly; 2hr); Soria (3 daily; 3hr); Zamora (Mon–Fri hourly, Sat & Sun 4–6 daily; 1hr 30min).

By car It's easiest to use one of the signposted car parks for overnight stays. There's one right under Pl. Mayor, for example, and the town's hotels round here all offer overnight parking for around €15.

INFORMATION

Turismo Acera de Recoletos, near the top of the Campo Grande (Easter week & July to mid-Sept daily 9am–8pm; rest of the year Mon–Sat 9am–2pm & 4–7pm, Sun 9.30am–5pm; ☎983 219 310, ⓦvalladolidturismo.com).

ACCOMMODATION

The main concentration of **accommodation** – in all price ranges – is in the pleasant area around Pl. Mayor, though there are also some nicely sited places down the east side of Campo Grande.

★ **Hostal París** c/Especería 2 ☎983 370 625, ⓦhostalparis.com. The best mid-range place, with very agreeable rooms for the price. Some of the front ones have glassed-in street-facing balconies, though it's quieter at the back. Two cafés downstairs have good breakfast deals. **€60**

Hotel Imperial c/del Peso 4 ☎983 330 300, ⓦhimperial.com. Old-fashioned hotel in a beautiful Renaissance mansion right by Pl. Mayor. Everything is a bit

on the fussy side, and the columned bar is certainly a talking point. **€70**

Hotel El Nogal c/Conde Ansúrez 10 ☎983 340 333, ⓦhotelelnogal.com. A smart three-star, offering tasteful rooms with crimson drapes and wood floors, and up-to-date – if rather small – bathrooms (the single rooms are a bit on the pokey side, too). There's a bar and restaurant too, with tables on Pl. del Val around the back. **€70**

Hotel Roma c/Héroes del Alcázar de Toledo 8 ☎ 983 351 833, ⓦ hotelromavalladolid.com. Rather charming hotel in a great location (some rooms throw their French windows open onto a little square opposite a church), plus there's a restaurant and its own parking. Advance web rates go as low as €50. **€80**

Meliá Recoletos c/Acera de Recoletos 13 ☎ 983 216 200, ⓦ solmelia.com. The city's finest boutique lodgings, opposite Campo Grande and not far from the train station, in a handsomely restored mansion. Upper-storey "loft" rooms have particularly good views. The same chain also has a cheaper city-centre hotel. **€110**

Pensión La Cueva c/Correos 4 ☎ 983 330 072. Simple *pensión* with en-suite doubles and cheaper singles, above a lively tapas bar and restaurant. Expect noise. **€40**

EATING AND DRINKING

Pl. Mayor has the best outdoor **cafés** for a drink with views, while c/Correos, just to the west, is lined with largely upscale **tapas bars and restaurants** (though you'll still get a *menú del día* here for €15). There are two good areas for late-opening **bars**: either around the small modern square of Pl. Marti y Monso, just off Pl. Mayor, or anywhere around the cathedral and the nearby Santa María de la Antigua church.

TAPAS BARS

Bar Jamonería Sarmiento c/Conde Ansúrez 11 ☎ 983 355 514. A cross between a deli and a bar, this great little place presents a choice of cold cuts and simple tapas, *morcilla* or *jamón* to *ventresca* tuna salad, accompanied by some fine regional wines from €2 a glass. Daily 11.30am–3pm & 7.30pm–midnight.

★ **Jero** c/Correos 11 ☎ 983 353 508. Valladolid has an annual creative tapas competition and *Jero* often comes out on top, with its remarkable sculpted canapés called things like "Matrix", "Galactico" or "Mission Impossible" (this last, for example, a *bacalo*-and-mushroom *montadito* topped with tomato confit, prawn and almond crunch), sold at a couple of euros a pop. Bar noon–midnight, restaurant 1–4pm & 9pm–midnight; closed Tues.

La Mejillonera c/de la Pasión 5 ☎ 983 373 527. The city's seafood specialist – a no-nonsense beer-and wooden-table joint for mussels in *marinara* sauce or bread rolls filled with *calamari* for around €3 each. Daily 11.30am–3pm & 6.30–11.30pm.

RESTAURANTS

El Caballo de Troya c/Correos 1 ☎ 983 339 355. An enticing blend of historic *palacio* and contemporary design, set around a gem of a Renaissance courtyard, with meals either in the fancy restaurant or slightly cheaper taverna, both with *menús* (€25 in the restaurant; €14 in the taverna) and pricier à la carte dishes. Mon–Sat 1.30–4pm & 9pm–midnight.

★ **Covadonga** c/Zapico 1 ☎ 983 330 798. For a straightforward meal try this family-run place near the market, dishing up home-cooked food at bargain prices, with nothing much over €7 or €8 and lots for considerably less (only a huge *chuletón* at €14 might break the budget). You can hardly go wrong – only the television, broadcasting to Mars, spoils the experience. Mon–Sat 1–4pm & 8.30–11pm.

Milvinos Pl. Marti y Monso ☎ 983 344 336, ⓦ milvinos. com. Slick, contemporary grill-house with a terrific wine list. Anything from a house burger to tuna steak or a *chuletón* is available, plus carpaccios and salads, but veer away from the €18 *menú* and you'll easily spend €50. Mon 1.30–4pm, Tues–Sat 1.30–4pm & 9–11pm.

Otras Luces Pl. Mayor 22 ☎ 983 380 705. The grandstand location is enough for many (it's open all day, from breakfast onwards), but the four-corners-of-the-world cuisine also pulls in punters eager for a change. Expect *patatas bravas* to *pad Thai*, by way of *teriyaki* chicken and gourmet burgers (dishes €11–19), plus it's hot on organic meat, regional cheeses, free-range eggs, estate-bottled olive oils and the like, which also sets it apart from its neighbours. Daily 8am–1am.

BARS

Café España Pl. Fuente Dorada 8 ☎ 983 371 764. A nice, straight-up café-bar with a small stage at the back, serving as a regular venue for live music (mostly free), from singer-songwriters to tango and flamenco. Daily 9am–midnight.

Café Herminios Pl. de la Universidad ☎ 983 306 209. Opens late-afternoon for *terraza* drinks and cocktails, but becomes more of a thumping jazz bar as the night wears on, with DJs and live acts pumping out acid jazz, blues, Latin, Cuban and Brazilian sounds. Daily 5pm–3am.

★ **El Penicilino** Pl. de la Libertad; no phone. Studenty, yes, but a fine bar, with a bit more about it than many around the cathedral area. You'll be lucky to score an outdoor table, but it's nice and pub-like inside. Daily 5pm–2am.

Tordesillas

The quiet riverside town of **TORDESILLAS**, 30km southwest of Valladolid, boasts an important place in Spain's (indeed, the world's) history. It was here, with papal

5

authority, that the **Treaty of Tordesillas** (1494) divided "All Lands Discovered, or Hereafter to be Discovered in the West, towards the Indies or the Ocean Seas" between Spain and Portugal, along a line 370 leagues west of the Cape Verde Islands. Brazil, allegedly discovered six years later, went to Portugal – though it was claimed that the Portuguese already knew of its existence but had kept silent to gain better terms. The rest of the New World, including Mexico and Peru, became Spanish, with the consequences to play out across the generations.

Today's town is a low-key delight of faded red-brick buildings set around a charming, arcaded Plaza Mayor. There's a museum or two, though nothing essential, and several timeworn churches, while a long medieval bridge extends across the wide Río Duero. There's swimming from a small beach on the other side, and a bar that's handily sited for an evening breeze off the river.

Real Convento de Santa Clara

Paseo Juana de Castilla • Tues–Sat 10am–1.30pm & 4–5.45pm, April–Sept till 6.30pm, Sun 10.30am–1.30pm & 3.30–5.30pm; Arab baths also closed Wed year-round • €3.60, €4.60 including Arab baths • ☎ 983 770 463, ⓦ clarisastordesillas.es

The town's only significant monument is the **Real Convento de Santa Clara**, which overlooks the Duero and is known as "The Alhambra of Castile" for its delightful Mudéjar architecture. Originally built as a royal palace, it has a story to tell as the place of confinement of the unfortunate **Juana la Loca** (Joanna the Mad), daughter of Fernando and Isabel, who spent 46 years here in a windowless cell. After Isabel's death, she ruled Castile jointly with her husband Felipe I from 1504–06 but was devastated by his early death, and for three years afterwards toured the monasteries of Spain, keeping the coffin perpetually by her side and stopping from time to time to inspect the corpse. In 1509, she reached Tordesillas, where first Fernando and, later, her son, Carlos V, declared her insane, imprisoning her for half a century and assuming the throne of Castile for themselves.

Several of the Convento's rooms and spaces are open to the public, including the pretty patio, with its horseshoe arches and Moorish decoration, while the former palace's fourteenth-century **Baños Árabes** (Arab baths) can also be visited – though they're closed during wet weather to protect the Mudéjar wall paintings from humidity damage.

ARRIVAL AND DEPARTURE	**TORDESILLAS**

By bus Tordesillas is on the Valladolid–Zamora/Salamanca routes (hourly service, slightly fewer at weekends; 30min) and the bus station is just outside the old centre – you can see the old town walls from the terminal.

By car Parking is easy near the bridge, beneath the old town.

INFORMATION

Turismo Casas del Tratado, overlooking the river and signposted from the Pl. Mayor (Tues–Sat 10am–1.30pm & 4–6.30, April–Sept till 7.30pm, Sun 10am–2pm; ☎ 983 771 067, ⓦ tordesillas.net).

ACOMMODATION AND EATING

Hostal San Antolín c/San Antolín 8 ☎ 983 796 771, ⓦ hostalsanantolin.com. The best of the town's modest accommodation options, on a quiet old street in the centre. Rooms are nicely furnished, in vibrant colours, and non-guests are welcome at the decent grill-restaurant (*menú del día* €12 weekdays, weekends €18, otherwise meals around €30), where you can eat lunch or dinner. Restaurant 1–4pm & 9–11pm. **€45**

Parador de Tordesillas Carretera Salamanca, 1km out on the Salamanca road ☎ 983 770 051, ⓦ parador.es. The very tranquil parador is almost country club in feel, with shaded grounds, a sizeable outdoor pool and comfortable, rustic-style rooms. The regional Castilian restaurant is a treat, too (*menú del día* €27, mains around €20), while if you book online in advance room rates come down as low as €80. Restaurant 1–4pm & 9–11pm. **€150**

Medina del Campo

MEDINA DEL CAMPO, 23km south of Tordesillas and around 55km from Valladolid, stands below one of the region's great castles, the Moorish, brick-built Castillo de la

Mota. The castle sits on one side of the train line, the town on the other, and it's also worth walking into the centre to see what's left of Renaissance Medina del Campo (Market of the Field), which in the fifteenth and sixteenth centuries was one of the most important market towns in Europe. Merchants came from as far afield as Italy and Germany to attend its *ferias* (fairs), and the handsome **Plaza Mayor de la Hispanidad** – ringed by cafés and restaurants – is still evocative of the days when the town's bankers determined the value of European currencies.

Castillo de la Mota

Avda. del Castillo • Mon–Sat 10am–2pm & 3.45–6pm, April–Sept till 7pm, Sun 10am–2.30pm • €4 • ☎ 983 812 724, ⓦ castillodelamota.es

A classic child's design if there ever was one – four square towers, battlements and a deep moat – the **Castillo de la Mota** often hosted the court of Queen Isabel, and later served as both prison and girls' boarding school. A visitor centre throws light on the castle's history, while areas open to the public include the main courtyard and lower rooms, including the impressive brick-vaulted chapel.

Museo de las Ferias

C/San Martín 26, near Pl. Mayor • Tues–Sat 10am–1.30pm & 4–7pm, Sun 11am–2pm • €2 • ☎ 983 837 527, ⓦ museoferias.net

For the story of Medina's fifteenth- and sixteenth-century fairs, visit the **Museo de las Ferias**, which traces the history from their origins as simple trade gatherings to their later role as essential European money markets. Exhibits – from Flemish textiles to Italian silver – demonstrate the wealth that once poured into this now small town.

ARRIVAL AND DEPARTURE	MEDINA DEL CAMPO
By train The quickest way here is by train from Valladolid; there's an hourly service and the journey takes 20–30min.	Turn right out of the station and keep walking for the castle and underpass to town.

Palencia and around

PALENCIA, 47km north of Valladolid, is Castile's least-known city, and capital of a small and equally unheralded province of the same name. That it has a rich past goes without saying, especially in Roman and medieval times – Spain's oldest university was founded here in 1208, though it was later swallowed up by that of Salamanca. But today's modest city of 80,000 has no great sights, though the authorities are working hard to promote what little is left: there are pretty riverside gardens, famous Semana Santa processions and numerous restored plazas, most dominated by churches built in a rather gaunt white stone, but while all are diverting, none – save the cathedral – is outstanding. It's actually in the wider province that Palencia reveals its charms, especially in the north in the so-called Montaña Palentina – a region of peaks, lakes and Romanesque churches – but also along the Palencian section of the Santiago pilgrimage route (see p.426).

Catedral San Pantolín

Pl. de la Inmaculada • May–Oct Mon–Fri 10am–1.30pm & 4.30–7.30pm, Sat 10am–2pm & 4–5.30pm, Sun 4.30–8pm; Nov–April Mon–Fri 10am–1.30pm & 4–7pm, Sat 10am–1.30pm & 4–5.30pm, Sun 4–7pm • €2, including museum €3 • ⓦ diocesispalencia.org/catedral

The older part of the city centre is at its most attractive near the Gothic **Catedral San Pantolín**, which faces a large open square surrounded by restored buildings. The exterior is plain by Spanish standards; and as Palencia fell into decline soon after the cathedral's completion, there's an almost complete absence of Baroque trappings inside. However, this simply focuses attention on the highlights within, notably the stunning *retablo mayor*, which contains twelve beautiful little panels, ten of them painted by Juan de Flandes, court painter to Isabel – it's the best collection of his work anywhere. A staircase leads down into the atmospheric crypt, containing the worn, carved

5

columns of the earlier Visigothic and Romanesque churches on this site, and an ancient well. The ticket also includes entry to the enclosed cloisters, but to see the treasures of the on-site **Museo Catedralicio** (including an early El Greco and some Flemish tapestries), you'll have to pay another euro.

There are charming **riverside gardens** behind the cathedral, with two old stone bridges, while following the river further up, at the top of town, leads to more extensive parkland.

Plaza Mayor and around

Halfway along the main pedestrianized street of c/Mayor lies Palencia's principal square, **Plaza Mayor**, arcaded against the fierce Castilian summer sun and the biting winter winds. It's modest but attractive, like Palencia itself, with the old cast-iron market hall just visible off one side of the square and the thirteenth-century church of **San Francisco** off the other. If the church pricks your interest, with a map from the *turismo* you can then track down the other Romanesque and Gothic churches worth a second glance, all signposted on a walking route through town.

ARRIVAL AND DEPARTURE   PALENCIA

Palencia's adjacent **bus and train stations** are located at the north end of the city centre. The roundabout of Pl. León is over on the far side of the gardens to your left as you leave either terminal; from here the long, pedestrianized c/Mayor – the main shopping street – runs up to the Pl. Mayor (10min walk).

By train The train station is on Pl. de los Jardinillos. Destinations Burgos (9 daily; 45min–1hr); León (up to 12 daily; 1hr–1hr 30min); Valladolid (hourly; 30min).
By bus The Estación de Autobuses is on c/Pedro Berruguete (☎ 979 743 222, ⊛ autobuses-palencia.es).
Destinations Burgos (up to 3 daily; 1hr 15min); Carrión de los Condes (3 daily; 45min); Frómista (Mon–Sat 3–4 daily;

30min); Madrid (6 daily; 3hr); Salamanca (up to 7 daily; 2hr 15min); Valladolid (hourly; 1hr); Zamora (2 daily; 2hr 15min).
By car Short-term street parking is easy, or head for one of the signposted car parks, like that at Pl. Pío XII (c/Mayor), by the river at the southern end of town, where overnight parking costs around €13.

INFORMATION

Turismo c/Mayor 31 (Mon–Fri 9am–2pm & 5–8pm, Sat 10.30am–2.30pm; ☎ 979 706 523, ⊛ palenciaturismo.com).

ACCOMMODATION

It's hard to come up with convincing reasons to stay the night, given that Palencia is only half an hour from Valladolid and an hour from Burgos. **Accommodation** is at least reasonably priced and rarely full. If you prefer to see Palencia by day and stay outside the city, look no further than *Casa del Abad* in nearby Ampudia (see p.401).

Diana Palace Avda. de Santander 12 ☎ 979 018 050, ⊛ eurostarshotels.com. For a comfortable night in a four-star business hotel, try the *Diana Palace*, opposite the train station – there are really good web deals often available. **€65**
Hotel Plaza Jardinillos c/Eduardo Dato 2 ☎ 979 750

022. This is convenient – right by Pl. León and across from the stations – and if not quite the "máximo confort" promised, the stylish lobby and glass reception table suggest they might get around to upgrading the functional rooms at some point. **€40**

EATING AND DRINKING

Pl. Mayor comes into its own in the early evening, as families come out for a stroll and a drink. Later on, head for the small, modern bar-lined courtyard known as **Plaza Seminario**, a short walk west of Pl. Mayor, off c/Cardenal Almaraz.

Taberna Plaza Mayor Pl. Mayor 1 ☎ 979 740 410. You'll be able to eat a €12 *menú del día* at several places around the main square, including this more upmarket-than-most

tapas bar and restaurant, which has a straightforward lunch spread and a wider à la carte menú (dishes €5–18). Daily 10am–midnight.

Basílica de San Juan de Baños

5

Baños de Cerrato, near Venta de Baños, 7km south of Palencia • April–Oct Tues–Sun 10am–1.30pm & 5–8pm; Nov–March Tues–Sun 10am–1.30pm & 4–6pm • €1, free Wed • Roughly hourly buses from Palencia bus station (only 3 or 4 at weekends) run out to Baños in around 15min

A tucked-away village just outside Palencia contains the oldest church in the entire peninsula – *Monumento Nacional 1* in the catalogue. The seventh-century **Basílica de San Juan de Baños**, established by the Visigoth King Recesvinto in 661, has tiny lattice windows and horseshoe arches, and incorporates materials from Roman buildings.

Ampudia

20km southwest of Palencia, along the P 901

For a complete change of pace from the Castilian cities to all sides, make the quick drive from Palencia up onto the high farming plain, where the industrial suburbs soon give way to shimmering meadows, rippling cornfields and scores of wind turbines. The tiny town of **Ampudia**, with a population of well under a thousand, is a quiet gem, boasting two long porticoed streets whose seventeenth-century houses are supported by tree-trunk columns, some of which are several hundred years old. Once a serious feudal stronghold, Ampudia has a huge castle set on higher, grassy ground, with sweeping views, and an equally majestic Gothic church, though the somnolent streets, shuttered houses and dung-spattered farms at the town's edge are a more reliable indicator of its current status. That said, there is one magnificent place to stay here, ideal for a luxurious night out in the sticks.

ACCOMMODATION AND EATING

AMPUDIA

★ **Posada Real la Casa del Abad de Ampudia** 📞 979 768 008, 🌐 rusticae.es. The former abbot's house is now a remarkable rustic-chic hotel. A bright sun mural shines down from the entrance cupola, while gorgeous rooms feature bold colour washes on rough plaster walls, reclaimed-wood furniture and designer bathrooms.

Exposed stone and ancient beams abound, there's a retractable roof over the lounge-bar patio, while the classy restaurant – serving grilled hake to *chuletón* (mains €20–24) – occupies the old wine press. There's also a pool and some very elegant spa facilities. Restaurant 1–4pm & 9–11pm. **€120**

Along the Río Duero to Soria

The **Río Duero** long marked the frontier between Christian and Arab territory. It meanders right across central Castile, between Zamora and Soria, with the eastern section in particular, from Valladolid, marked by a series of spectacular castles and old market towns, some restored as tourist attractions, others crumbling to dust. This part of the river is also at the heart of one of Spain's greatest wine-producing areas, the **Ribera del Duero** (see box, p.402). It's a fine route to follow by car (N122), stopping off for lunch in rustic *posadas* and for walks in the beautiful surroundings. You can make the trip by bus, but if you do, realistically, you'll only be able to see the major towns of Peñafiel and El Burgo de Osma.

Peñafiel

First stop beyond Valladolid is **PEÑAFIEL**, 60km to the east, whose fabulous castle is visible long before you reach the town. Standing on a narrow ridge, and at 210m long but only 23m across, it bears an astonishing resemblance to a huge ship run aground. At the edge of town and entirely surrounded by balconied wooden buildings, the other extraordinary sight is Plaza del Coso, which doubles as perhaps the most spectacular bullring in Spain during Peñafiel's Día de San Roque festival every August.

5

THE WINES OF THE RIBERA DEL DUERO

Some of Spain's most celebrated red wine comes from the demarcated region of **Ribera del Duero** (w riberadelduero.es), including the country's best-known and most expensive wine, Vega Sicilia. Around 170 wineries are found along the Duero, with many of the *bogedas* concentrated between Peñafiel and Aranda del Duero, 40km to the east. If you'd like to make winery visits (not all are open for tours, including Vega Sicilia), the comprehensive website is a good place to start – some wineries require advance reservations, though many have shops that are open to casual buyers mornings and afternoons. **Bodegas Alejandro Fernandez** (w pesqueraafernandez.com) makes its fabulous Tinto Pesquera at Pesquera de Duero, 4km north of Peñafiel, while the acclaimed **Señorio de Nava** (w senoriodenava.es) is based at Nava de Roa, 13km to the east.

Castillo de Peñafiel

April–Sept Tues–Sun 11am–2.30pm & 4.30–8.30pm; Oct–March Tues–Sun 11.30am–2pm & 4–7pm • Castle €3, combined ticket with Museo Provincial del Vino €6, or €15 with wine tasting • ☎ 938 881 199, w museodelvinodevalladolid.com

It's quite a hike up to the **Castillo de Peñafiel** – it's far easier to drive – which was built in the mid-fifteenth century out of the region's distinctive white stone. Guided visits around the castle take around forty minutes or so, after which you're encouraged to explore the **Museo Provincial del Vino**, where you can learn all about the Ribera del Duero wines – and even taste a few if you wish.

ARRIVAL AND DEPARTURE   PEÑAFIEL

By bus From Valladolid, buses drop you on the west side of the Río Duratón – walk down to the river and cross the bridge, then turn right and walk up to the central Pl. de España. The street off the top of this square leads in five minutes to Pl. del Coso.

By car Parking's not usually a problem, but if the town centre proves tricky, use the massive free car park a little way out on the road up to the castle.

ACCOMMODATION AND EATING

There are a couple of cheapish places to stay in the centre, but Peñafiel probably only warrants a night if you can run to one of the grander choices.

Hotel Convento Las Claras Pl. Adolfo Muñoz Alonso ☎ 938 878 168, w hotelconventolasclaras.com. This restored seventeenth-century convent by the bridge, now a four-star riverside hotel, retains its erstwhile elegance, with its cloister-lobby, tree-shaded terrace and garden-pool. There's a good restaurant as well as a terrace café with a lunchtime *menú del día*. Restaurant 1–4pm & 9–11pm. **€130**

Hotel Ribera del Duero Avda. Escalona 17 ☎ 983 873 111, w hotelriberadelduero.com. A contemporary three-star hotel set in a rather fine old flour mill on the edge of town (Soria road), whose stylish rooms almost all have castle views. Deals on the website offer a room with dinner at the restaurant, from around €90 per person. Restaurant 1–4pm & 9–11pm. **€100**

Peñaranda del Duero

Past Aranda del Duero, a short eight-kilometre detour from the highway at La Vid leads through rolling vineyards to the gorgeous, honey-toned town of **PEÑARANDA DEL DUERO**, whose restored historic kernel sits beneath another battlemented castle. It's a popular weekend getaway, hence the rather upmarket accommodation and pristine houses, but nothing detracts from the first view of the picture-perfect Plaza Mayor – Renaissance palace on one side, bulky church on the other and flower-decked wooden houses in the lanes beyond.

With a day to spare, there's a signposted local **walk** (21km) that leads up hill and down dale from Peñaranda, through the pine woods. Back at La Vid, by the highway, marvel how such a small village with such a small name has quite such a large monastery.

El Burgo de Osma and around

There's more of the almost absurdly picturesque Río Duero scenery at **EL BURGO DE OSMA**, once a very grand place boasting both cathedral and university. Today, there are gleaming town walls, a lovely riverside promenade and ancient colonnaded streets overhung by houses supported on precarious wooden props. It's quaint and gorgeous in equal measure, and while the dominant cathedral is the only actual sight, the town rewards a leisurely stroll up the arcaded main street to Plaza Mayor. On summer nights, as the temperature drops, the families of El Burgo use the main square, with its cafés and tree-shaded benches, as playground, exercise yard and social club. Out of town, there are easy drives to all sorts of fascinating destinations, from canyon park to mighty fortress, which makes El Burgo well worth a night's stay.

ARRIVAL AND INFORMATION
EL BURGO DE OSMA

By bus and car El Burgo is 63km east of Aranda del Duero, and around 160km from Valladolid. The **bus station** is on the main Valladolid–Soria road through town, with free street parking along the road here, and Pl. Mayor just a

minute or two's walk away.
Turismo Pl. Mayor, inside the former Hospital de San Agustín (Mon & Thurs–Sun 10am–2pm & 4–7pm, July & Aug daily, same hours; ☎ 975 360 116, ⊛ burgosma.es).

ACCOMMODATION

There's lots of **accommodation** and – given the attraction of town and surroundings – much incentive to stay the night. At all three hotels below, you can park virtually outside.

Hospedería El Fielato Avda. Juan Carlos I, 1º, at c/Mayor ☎ 975 368 236, ⊛ hospederiaelfielato.es. Decent rooms, if nothing glam, at a very reasonable place right next door to the *Hotel II Virrey*. **€65**
Hotel II Virrey c/Mayor 2 ☎ 975 341 311, ⊛ virrey palafox.com. The town's best hotel comes complete with baronial fittings that are virtually tourist attractions in their own right. The rooms are rather more modern, with contemporary fabrics and furnishings. There's a café at the hotel (which is entered from either the main road

through town or Pl. Mayor); the restaurant (see below) is further up the main road, and website deals often include dinner. **€90**
Posada del Canónigo c/San Pedro de Osma 19 ☎ 975 360 362, ⊛ posadadelcanonigo.es. At the bottom of the cathedral square, one of the former canons' houses – built right next to the town wall – is now atmospheric *Posada del Canónigo*, with a pretty courtyard and rustic rooms with carved wooden headboards. Stay midweek or outside summer and rates drop €10 a night. **€80**

EATING AND DRINKING

El Burgo is a pork and steak town, and you can eat big, meaty **meals** at a number of *asadores*, including a couple of places along c/Mayor. The *Hotel II Virrey* is the local pig specialist – it even has a "pork museum" and an annual spring pig slaughter (*matanza*).

Casa Engracia c/Ruiz Zorrilla 3, off c/Mayor ☎ 975 340 155. Good for a meal at modest prices – there's tapas and drinks in the bar or meals in the small *comedor* at the back, where straightforward meat and fish grills go for €8–14, accompanied by decent local wine from ceramic jugs. Daily 10am–midnight, meals 1–4pm & 9–11pm.

Restaurante Virrey c/Universidad 7 ☎ 975 340 222. In an undistinguished building on the main road, this is the best restaurant in town, renowned for its regional cuisine (mains €12–20). Pork in all guises is the *raison d'être* – especially at *matanza* weekends, when 24-dish tasting menus celebrate every cut of pork imaginable. Tues–Sat 1.30–4pm & 9–11pm, Sun 1.30–4pm.

Parque Natural del Cañón del Río Lobos

Visitor centre April–Sept daily 10am–8pm; Oct–March Mon–Fri 10am–2pm & 5–8pm, Sat & Sun 10am–8pm • ☎ 975 363 564

Don't miss the excursion north of El Burgo de Osma to the impressive **Parque Natural del Cañón del Río Lobos**. It's a quick fourteen-kilometre drive on a ruler-straight road to the small village of Ucero, just outside which (under the ruined castle) is the Casa del Parque **visitor centre**. From the visitor centre, the main road runs another kilometre or so up to the stone bridge over the source of the Río Ucero, where you've a choice. The signposted left turn here runs along the valley floor towards the Romanesque **Ermita de**

5

San Bartolomé. There's a bar-restaurant near the turn, and plenty of parking and picnic places further in among the trees, from where paths run into the spectacular gorge – one of the walks from the visitor centre runs to the hermitage and back. The main road, meanwhile, twists up for 3km to the top of the canyon and the **Mirador de la Galiana** (1122m), affording mesmerizing views of the canyon walls and the circling eagles and vultures. It's worth noting that everything in the park is very busy in August, at Easter and on bank holidays, when it's not particularly *tranquilo* anywhere – the size of the car parks gives the game away.

Calatañazor

Halfway between El Burgo de Osma and Soria, just off the N122, lies tiny **CALATAÑAZOR**, a sleepy medieval village overseen by skimpy castle ruins and some remarkable old houses, with their distinctive conical chimneys, decorative coats of arms and wooden balconies. It often seems deserted, though there's enough weekend and holiday trade to warrant several shops selling local honey, dried wild mushrooms and cheese.

ACCOMMODATION AND EATING

Casa del Cura ☎ 975 183 642, ⓦ posadarealcasadelcura .com. If you fancied a very quiet night, these rustic-chic lodgings make for a comfortable stay. There's also a rather fancy restaurant (meals around €30), with an outdoor terrace overlooking the gorge. Restaurant open 1–4pm & 9–11pm. **€80**

Fortaleza de Gormaz

15km southeast of El Burgo de Osma, near Gormaz • Always open • Free

The stupendous **Fortaleza de Gormaz** lies on the back route to Berlanga de Duero (Recuerda road). You'll see the fortress long before you climb to it, passing the nondescript village of Gormaz. It was originally built by the Moors in the tenth century, and two of their keyhole doorways survive, as well as a later medieval tower dating from after the castle was captured and modified by the Christians. The fortress was once one of the largest fortified buildings in Spain – the inside is now a shell, albeit an enormous one, hundreds of metres across, and there are 28 towers in all, ruined but still mightily impressive. There are magnificent panoramas from here, down to the snaking Río Duero and the giant patchwork of fields in the cultivated plains below.

Berlanga de Duero

BERLANGA DE DUERO lies south of the N122 (Soria road), and a fair way south of the Río Duero as well, although it still takes the river's name. It's another quiet backwater that was rather more important in times past – once again, the main sight is a **castle**, whose massive cylindrical towers and older double curtain-wall, reminiscent of Ávila, loom above the town. The way up is through a doorway in a ruined Renaissance palace, just a few minutes' walk from the centre. The **Plaza Mayor** is arcaded by precarious wooden posts sitting on stone pillars, while the other dominant monument is the **Colegiata de Nuestra Señora del Mercado**, one of the last flowerings of the Gothic style. Its unusually uniform design is a consequence of rapid construction – it was built in just four years. Berlanga also has several fine mansions, some pretty arcaded streets and **La Picota**, a "pillar of justice" to which offenders were tied (it's just outside the old town, on the El Burgo road).

ARRIVAL AND DEPARTURE

BERLANGA DE DUERO

By bus and car There's a daily bus service here from Soria, which stops just out of the old centre, on the El Burgo road. The town stands just off the CL116 between El Burgo de Osma and Almazán (27km from the former); coming from Gormaz (14km), follow the signs for Recuerda and then Morales.

ACCOMMODATION AND EATING

Though there are a couple of inexpensive, small hotels, both with reasonably priced restaurants attached, only students of (very) small town life will be sufficiently taken with Berlanga to want to stay. If you're just looking for a quick coffee, try the nice old bar on the main square.

Ermita de San Baudelio de Berlanga

Casillas de Berlanga, 8km south of Berlanga de Duero; follow the pink signs from town • April–Sept Wed–Sat 10am–2pm & 4–8pm, Oct–March closes 6pm, Sun & hols 10am–2pm • €0.60, free Sat & Sun

The thousand-year-old **Ermita de San Baudelio de Berlanga** is the best-preserved and most important example of Mozarabic style in Spain. Five years after being declared a national monument, in the 1920s, its marvellous cycle of frescoes was acquired by an international art dealer and exported to the US. After much fuss, the Spanish government got some of them back on indefinite loan, but they are now kept in the Prado. In spite of this loss, the simple hillside hermitage remains a beauty. Its eight-ribbed interior vault springs from a central pillar, while much of the space is taken up by the tribune gallery of horseshoe arches. Some original frescoes do remain, including two bulls from the great sequence of animals and hunting scenes.

Soria and around

SORIA is a modest provincial capital of around 40,000 – an attractive place, despite encroaching suburbs, and the inspiration behind much of Antonio Machado's best-loved verse (the Seville-born poet lived here from 1907 to 1912). It stands between a ridgeback of hills on the banks of the Duero, with a castle ruin above and a medieval centre dotted with mansions and Romanesque churches. You can see all the sights easily in a day, but a quiet night or two has its attractions, especially if you use the city as a base to explore some of Castile's loveliest countryside. The Roman site of **Numancia**, in particular, is an easy side-trip, while to the northwest rises the **Sierra de Urbión**, the weekend getaway of choice for Soria's inhabitants.

Parque Alameda de Cervantes

Always open • Free

For once, it isn't the Plaza Mayor – quiet and handsome though that is – that's the focal point of town; instead Soria's best feature is its central botanical gardens, the **Parque Alameda de Cervantes**. In early evening, the whole of Soria seems to decamp here for strolls, games and chats, and there are occasional concerts in the extremely curious bandstand, the so-called "Tree of Music" – as it's wrapped entirely around a large tree, and far above head height, the musicians have to wind their way up a metal staircase to perform.

Museo Numantino

Paseo del Espolón 8 • Tues–Sat 10am–2pm & 4–7pm, July–Sept till 8pm, Sun & hols 10am–2pm • €1.20, free Sat & Sun • ☎ 975 221 397

Just back from the central gardens you'll find the excellent **Museo Numantino**, which gathers together the region's major archeological finds, from Neolithic bones to medieval ceramics. The Celtic-Iberian and Roman displays do much to illuminate a visit to the nearby site of Numancia.

5

SORIA

CAFÉS, TAPAS & RESTAURANTS
Fogón del Salvador	1
Mesón Castellano	3
Nueva York	2
Taberna La Niña	4

ACCOMMODATION
Hostal Alvi	3
Hostería Solar de Tejada	1
Hotel Soria Plaza Mayor	2
Parador Antonio Machado	4

Zaragoza (N122)

San Polo

CARRETERA DE AGREDA

Río Duero

Alameda del Soto

S. PRUDENCIO

metres

0   150

CAMINO MONTE DE LAS ANIMAS

PASEO DEL POSTIGUILLO

Monasterio de San Juan de Duero

PUENTE MEDIEVAL

NTRA. SRA. DE CALATAÑAZOR

Ermita de la Virgen del Mirón

SAN AGUSTÍN

PASEO S. JUAN DE NARROS

Concatedral de San Pedro

Ruinas de San Nicolás

Cerro del Castillo

FERNÁN GONZÁLEZ

PRÍNCIPE CAUTIVO

MARTÍN DE S. CLEMENTE

PASEO DEL MIRÓN

SSMA. TRINIDAD

SANTA APOLONIA

Convento de Monjas Carmelitas

PLAZA CINCO VILLAS

REAL

PLAZA SANTA CATALINA

LAS ROSAS

LOS POSTIGOS

CORDÓN LÓPEZ

Logroño (N111) & Numancia

CARRETERA DE

LOGROÑO

SANTO TOMÉ

Iglesia de Santo Domingo

PLAZA BERNARDO ROBLES

Palacio de los Condes de Gómara

PLAZA TIRSO DE MOLINA

PLAZA AYLLON

Sta. María la Mayor

AGUIRRE

PLAZA MAYOR

Centro Cultural

Ntra. Sra. del Espino

TOVASOMA

SANTA CLARA

PLAZA DEL VERGEL

Palacio de los Ríos y Salcedo

PLAZA DE SAN CLEMENTE

COLLADO

ZAPATERÍA

Palacio de Alcántara

Ayuntamiento

Diputación Provincial

CABALLEROS

ALFÉREZ PROVISIONAL

CLEMENTE SÁENZ

PLAZA SANTA MARÍA

CASAS

CASAS

PUERTAS DE PRO

NUMANCIA

PLAZA RAMÓN BENITO ACEÑA

PLAZA DE SAN ESTEBAN

S. Juan de Rabanera

ALBERCA

JUAN ANTONIO GIMÓN

VERGUILLA

PASEO DE SANTA BÁRBARA

STO. ÁNGEL DE LA GUARDA

GARCÍA SOLIER

AVDA. DE VALLADOLID

SAN BENITO

SAN BENITO

ROTA DE CALATAÑAZOR

MANUEL V. TUDÓ

EL ESPÓN

PLAZA DE TOROS

PLAZA DEL SALVADOR

PLAZA MARIANO GRANADOS

CAMPO

SANTA MARÍA

MEDINACELI

AVENIDA NAVARRA

LAS CORTES

AVENIDA DE MARIANO VICEN

AVENIDA DE LA VICTORIA

Museo Numantino

PASEO DEL ESPOLÓN

San Francisco

NICOLÁS RABAL

SAN PEDRO

STA. TERESA DE JESÚS

SAN SATURIO

SAN MILLÁN

Parque Alameda de Cervantes

Bus Station, Valladolid (N122) & Burgos/Sierra Urbión (N234)

Iglesia de Santo Domingo

5

C/Santo Tomé, main entrance on Pl. del Vergell • Open only for services

Of all the central churches, the highlight is the rose-coloured facade of the twelfth-century convent church of **Santo Domingo**, a few minutes' walk north of the main pedestrianized street. The recessed arches of the main portal are magnificently sculpted with scenes from the Life of Christ, surrounded by a wonderful gallery of heavily bearded musicians who resemble the lost medieval ancestors of ZZ Top – look out, in particular, for the fetching three-in-a-bed scene.

Concatedral de San Pedro

Pl. de San Pedro • July–Sept Tues–Sun 11am–2pm & 5–7pm; rest of the year, weekdays open for services, Sat 11am–2pm & 4–6pm, Sun 11am–2pm • Church free, cloisters €2

Down towards the river is Soria's now rather isolated cathedral, the **Concatedral de San Pedro**, whose interior takes the Spanish penchant for darkness to a ridiculous extreme. However, light and harmony are restored in the three bays of a superb Romanesque cloister, which belonged to the cathedral's predecessor. The fourth side of the cloister is glassed in and contains the cathedral's best-preserved sculpture, a magnificent late twelfth-century work showing Christ's entry into Jerusalem.

Monasterio de San Juan de Duero

Paseo de las Ánimas • July–Sept Tues–Sat 10am–2pm & 5–8pm, Sun & hols 10am–2pm; Oct–June Tues–Sat 10am–2pm & 4–7pm, Sun & hols 10am–2pm • €0.60, free Sat & Sun • ☎ 975 230 218

Standing on the old bridge over the Duero, at the foot of town, you suddenly realize that you're out of Soria and in the country. Just over the bridge stands the **Monasterio de San Juan de Duero**, whose ruined cloister is one of the most striking medieval monuments you'll ever see. Built in the thirteenth century by Mudéjar masons, each of the four sides of the cloister is in a different style, mixing Moorish, Romanesque and Gothic elements, with keyhole doorways and beautifully interlinked arches. The bare church, meanwhile, is now a museum, with two unusual freestanding temples inside boasting vivid, carved capitals.

ARRIVAL AND DEPARTURE

SORIA

By train The train station is at the extreme southwest of the city, but limited services mean you're far more likely to arrive by bus.

By bus The bus station is on Avda. de Valladolid (☎ 975 225 160) at the western side of the city, a fifteen-minute walk from the centre.

Destinations Burgos (1–3 daily; 2hr–2hr 30min); El Burgo de Osma (Mon–Sat 2 daily, Sun daily; 1hr); Logroño (up to 5

daily; 1hr 30min); Madrid (8 daily; 2hr 30min); Medinaceli (2 daily; 1hr); Pamplona (5 daily; 2hr); Valladolid via Peñafiel (3 daily; 3hr); Vinuesa (2–3 daily; 35min); Zaragoza (9 daily; 2hr).

By car Street parking is easy to find, but is limited to the usual two hours in metered zones, so follow the signs to central car parks for overnight parking.

INFORMATION

Turismo c/Medinaceli 2, near Parque Alameda de Cervantes (July to mid-Sept daily 9am–8pm; mid-Sept to

June Mon–Sat 9.30am–2pm & 4–7pm, Sun 9.30am–5pm; ☎ 975 212 052, ⚲ sorianitelaimaginas.com).

ACCOMMODATION

Soria's tourists are rarely great in number, so finding a place to **stay** shouldn't be a problem. There are plenty of centrally located budget options, and a reasonable choice of mid-range and four-star hotels.

Hostal Alvi c/Alberca 2 ☎ 975 228 112, ⚲ hostalalvi.com. Nice en-suite *hostal* rooms on a quiet side-street in a good central location, and with garage parking available. **€55**

Hostería Solar de Tejada c/Claustrilla 1 ☎ 975 230

054, ⚲ hosteriasolardetejada.es. With its exposed wood and old stone walls, and charmingly decorated rooms all painted in different colours with coordinated fabrics, this is the best mid-range option in the city. **€60**

5

Hotel Soria Plaza Mayor Pl. Mayor 10 ☏ 975 240 864, ⓦ hotelsoriaplazamayor.com. This small boutique townhouse two-star has pride of place in Soria's prettiest old-town square. Some rooms in the eaves retain their old beams, while decor, fabrics, bathrooms and public areas are all in the best contemporary style. **€80**

★ **Parador Antonio Machado** Parque del Castillo ☏ 975 240 800, ⓦ parador.es. Soria's modern red-brick and glass parador has a beautiful hill-top location in the grounds of the ruined castle – there are steps down the hillside into the town centre (15min). Rooms are very spacious, with wooden floors and glassed-in balconies with stunning countryside views. Breakfast comes with the same glorious outlook, and the restaurant is a good choice for regional dishes (*menú* €33). You'll get a room much of the time for €90–110; check online for the best rates. **€160**

EATING AND DRINKING

Good **tapas** is the norm in Soria, while **restaurant** menus – here on the edge of Castile – show welcome Basque and Riojan influences, with fish and vegetables suddenly much more in evidence. The best selection of tapas bars is in **Plaza Ramón Benito Aceña**, at the end of the main drag, where the locals stand around outside at high circular tables and big wooden barrels. There's a grungier set of bars in nearby **Plaza de San Clemente** (just behind Citibank, off c/El Collado), while **c/Manuel Vicente Tutot**, behind the Museo Numantino, has a line of old-fashioned bars for Soria's cheapest eats. There are kiosk cafés in the **Parque Alameda de Cervantes**, nice for an early evening drink.

★ **Fogón del Salvador** Pl. del Salvador 1 ☏ 975 230 194, ⓦ fogonsalvador.com. An excellent *asador*, with tapas bar at the front and a more formal restaurant at the back, dominated by a huge wood-fired beehive oven and two mounted bulls' heads. The cuisine is typically meat-oriented – the steaks and chops are *buey* (ox) rather than *vaca* (beef), thus are hung longer, are darker in colour and richer tasting, or there are things like roast *cabrito*, a leg of lamb big enough for two, plus platters of smoked meats. Mains cost €15–20, with a weekday *menú* for around €15. Daily 1–4pm & 9pm–midnight.

Mesón Castellano Pl. Mayor 2 ☏ 975 213 045. Located in a cosy building of warm brick, with hams hanging from the wooden beams. You can hang out at the front with a cold beer, eat tapas at the bar or settle down for big meals in the *comedor*, where meat and fish dishes (including trout from the Río Ucero) run between €11 and €26. Daily 9am–midnight.

Nueva York c/Collado 18, at Pl. San Blas y el Rosel ☏ 975 212 784. The city's best pastry and cake place, also nice for breakfast, with tables outside on an old-town square. Daily 8am–10pm.

Taberna La Niña Pl. Mayor 11 ☏ 686 938 179. The "Little Girl Tavern" is rather more old-school than the name suggests, a nice tiled place that's good for an early evening drink on Soria's most handsome square. Specialities are sandwiches (from €4) and cheese and meat platters to share (€14–18), and there's good regional wine by the glass. Daily 11am–midnight.

Numancia

Off the N111 to Logroño, just outside the village of Garray • Tues–Sat 10am–2pm & 4–8pm, Oct–March closes 6pm, Sun 10am–2pm • €0.60, free weekends

Around 7km north of Soria lie the evocative ruins of **Numancia**, a hill-top Celtic-Iberian (third to second century BC) and later Roman settlement. Numancia was one of the last towns to hold out against the Romans, falling to Scipio in 133 BC; its long and fierce resistance was turned into a tragic play by Cervantes and dubbed "a sort of Vietnam for Rome" by novelist Carlos Fuentes. It's a stunningly sited spot, with extensive remains of streets, drains, courtyards and public baths, some reconstructed houses and a stretch of wall, and a good English-language interpretive leaflet available.

Sierra de Urbión

Summer weekends and holidays see locals flock to the tranquil slopes of the **Sierra de Urbión**, northwest of Soria, with its network of hiking and cycling trails, and even skiing at Santa Inés. Nearest Soria, the lower section of what is a protected "reserva nacional" is focused on the shores of an enormous reservoir, the Embalse de la Cuerda del Pozo, which has pine-wood and beachside picnic areas and plenty of watersports facilities. Just to the north is the main village of Vinuesa, while the real highlight of the range lies further north still – the lovely alpine glacial lake of Laguna Negara.

Vinuesa

VINUESA makes the most obvious base for the Sierra de Urbión. It's a pleasant village, attuned to tourists, with many restored old houses, a church adopted by nesting storks, a suspicious number of banks and ATMs, and even a late-night bar or two.

ARRIVAL AND DEPARTURE   VINUSEA

By bus The village is 33km from Soria (N234), and there are daily buses from Soria or Burgos.

ACCOMMODATION AND EATING

Half a dozen moderate **accommodation** options (mostly two-star-*hostal* standard) line the main road that leads down to the Laguna Negara turn-off. Nearly all the *hostales* have their own restaurants.

Camping Cobijo 2km along the Laguna Negara road ☎ 975 378 331, ⓦ www.campingcobijo.com. The local campsite is a large pine-shaded resort-style affair, with swimming pool, bikes for rent, a restaurant and a little supermarket. It also has basic rooms (sleeping 2) and bungalows (sleeping 3–6). Closed Nov–Easter. Rooms **€50**, bungalows **€90–125**, camping **€4.80** per person, plus **€4.80** per tent.

Virginia c/Castillo de Vinuesa 21 ☎ 975 378 555, ⓦ virginiarh.net. Easily the pick of the local hotels, close to the bridge near the turn-off, with handsome rooms and a good-value restaurant of the same name just across the road (lunch around €12, dinner €20). Restaurant 1–4pm & 9–11pm. **€60**

Laguna Negara

Having come this far, it's definitely worth the drive up to the **Laguna Negara**, a shining body of water hemmed in by a dramatic amphitheatre of granite cliffs. There's a lakeside boardwalk and several hiking trails, including the serious ascent from the lake to the summit of **Pico Urbión** (2229m), just over the border in La Rioja. To reach the lake follow the signs (18km) from Vinuesa until you reach a small upper car park just 300m from the *laguna*; at busy times, or if the barrier is closed, you'll have to park at the much larger car park, 1km back down the road (20min walk), near the seasonal café-restaurant.

Logroño and La Rioja province

One of Spain's most famous wine regions, La Rioja takes its name from the Río Oja, which flows from the mountains down to the Río Ebro, the latter marking the northern border of **La Rioja province** (ⓦ lariojaturismo.com). Confusingly, the demarcated wine region and province are not quite the same thing, since many of the best vineyards are on the north bank of the Ebro, in the Basque province of Araba – Alava in Castilian, the so-called Rioja Alavesa (see p.482). Nevertheless, the main wine towns are all in La Rioja proper, starting with the enjoyable provincial capital, **Logroño**, which is a great place to spend a couple of days eating and drinking. The province is traditionally divided further into two parts, with the busy little wine town of **Haro** being the mainstay of the **Rioja Alta**. This makes the best base for any serious wine touring, though there are *casas rurales* in many of the surrounding villages, too. It's also here, west of Logroño, that the Camino de Santiago winds on towards Burgos. East of Logroño is the **Rioja Baja**, the southeastern part of La Rioja province, which has quite a different feel – there are vineyards, but the main attraction is following in the footsteps of La Rioja's ancient dinosaurs.

Logroño is the hub for all local bus and train services, but if you want to do any more than see the towns of Nájera, Haro and Calahorra, it's far better to have your own transport, as connections to the smaller villages are rarely convenient for day-trips.

5

Logroño

LOGROÑO, lying on the Río Ebro, is a prosperous city of around 150,000 – a pleasant place of elegant streets, open squares and riverside parkland. The wine trade is not as immediately apparent here as in, say, Haro, and there are few cultural attractions that demand attention – the principal museum, the Museo de la Rioja, has been under restoration for many years. But the big draw is the city's lively old quarter, the so-called Casco Antiguo, with an unparalleled selection of excellent tapas bars, for which it's worth making a considerable detour. The two main annual events – each fuelled by copious wine-drinking – are the **Fiestas San Bernabé** (June), a week's worth of enjoyably rowdy local festivities, from street fairs and *pelota* tournaments to folk concerts and costumed processions, and the even more exuberant **Fiesta de San Mateo** (September), which coincides with the annual *vendimia* (grape harvest).

Sala Amos Salvador

C/Once de Junio • Tues–Sat 11am–1pm & 6–9pm, Sun & hols noon–2pm & 6–9pm • Exhibitions usually free • ☎ 941 259 202, ⓦ culturaderioja.org

Located in a former medieval convent on c/Marques de San Nicolas, the seat of the regional government – the **Parlamento de la Rioja** – faces a cobbled square with several late-night cafés. There's no public access to the government offices, but part of the building also once served as a nineteenth-century tobacco factory, the **Fabrica de Tabacos**,

● TAPAS BARS & RESTAURANTS	
Café Moderno	1
Casa Pali	9
Las Cubanas	4
La Cueva	3
Mesón del Abuelo	6
Paganos	7
Pata Negra	8
La Taberna de Baco	2
La Taberna del Laurel	10
Vinissimo	5

■ ACCOMMODATION	
Hostal Niza	3
Hotel Marqués de Vallejo	4
Hotel Portales	2
Pensión La Bilbaina	1

and is now used as a contemporary art and exhibition centre, the **Sala Amos Salvador**; the tall red-brick factory chimney still stands around the back on c/de Portales.

Iglesia de Santiago el Real

C/Barriocepo 6 • Daily 8.15am–1.15pm & 6.30–7pm • Free

Before the wine trade brought prosperity to Logroño, the town owed its importance for some six centuries to the Camino de Santiago, hence the church dedicated to the saint, which stands close to the iron bridge over the Río Ebro. High on the south side (ie not the side facing the river) of the lofty sixteenth-century church of **Santiago el Real**, above the main entrance, is a magnificent eighteenth-century Baroque equestrian statue of St James, mounted on a stallion that Edwin Mullins (in *The Pilgrimage to Santiago*) describes as "equipped with the most heroic genitals in all Spain, a sight to make any surviving Moor feel inadequate and run for cover". On the other side of the church, the landscaped Parque del Ebro gardens are good for a stroll.

Concatedral Santa María de la Redonda

C/de Portales 14 • Mon–Sat 8am–1pm & 6–8.45pm, Sun 9am–2pm & 6.30–8.45pm • Free

Logroño has many fine churches, principal among which is the mouthful of a cathedral, the **Concatedral Santa María de la Redonda**, which faces the old market square. The cathedral was originally a late Gothic hall church with a lovely, sweeping elevation that was extended at both ends in the eighteenth century – the twin-towered facade is a beautiful example of the Churrigueresque style. The evening *paseo*, meanwhile, fills the adjacent main street, c/Portales, packing out the bars and cafés under the arcades.

Mercado de Abastos and around

C/de Sagasta 1 • Mon–Fri 7.30am–2pm & 4–8pm, Sat 7.30am–2pm

The daily market, the **Mercado de Abastos**, is definitely worth a visit (it's right by many of the best tapas bars), and on the corner here you'll also find Vinos El Peso (c/Peso 1), a wine shop with a decent selection of regional wines. For traditional *botas de vino* (leather flagons filled with wine), stroll down and have a look at Felix Barbero Botas Rioja (c/Sagasta 8).

ARRIVAL AND DEPARTURE   **LOGROÑO**

Logroño is some 100km north of Soria, and 115km east of Burgos. The bus and train stations lie in the modern part of town, south of the central gardens of the **Paseo del Espolón**.

By train The train station is 400m south of the bus station, down Avda. de España.

Destinations Burgos (4 daily; 2hr 15min); Haro (2 daily; 40min); Madrid (daily; 3hr 15min); Palencia (daily; 3hr); Valladolid (daily; 3hr 45min); Vitoria (daily; 1hr 30min); Zaragoza (6 daily; 2hr).

By bus Logroño bus station, Avda. España 1 (☎941 235 983), is a five-hundred-metre (10min) walk from the centre along c/General Vara de Rey.

Destinations Bilbao (4–6 daily; 2hr 30min); Burgos

(Mon–Fri 7 daily, Sat & Sun 3–4 daily; 2hr); Calahorra (Mon–Sat 6–7 daily, Sun 3 daily; 1hr); Haro (Mon–Fri 7 daily, Sat & Sun 3–4 daily; 1hr); Nájera (Mon–Fri every 30–60min, Sat & Sun roughly hourly; 30min); Pamplona (up to 6 daily; 2hr); Soria (up to 5 daily; 1hr 30min); Vitoria (6–7 daily; 1hr).

By car Metered street parking and signposted garages are easy to find, though there's a large, free car park just opposite the surviving bit of medieval wall known as Murallas del Revellín, on the edge of the old town.

WHAT'S YOURS?

Cosecha (which literally means "harvest"), when used on its own, refers to young wines in their first or second year, which tend to have a fresh and fruity flavour – you'll also see these wines advertised as the *vino de año*. **Crianzas** are wines that are at least in their third year, having spent at least one year in an oak cask and several months in the bottle. **Reservas** are vintages that have been aged for three years with at least one year in oak; and **gran reservas** have spent at least two years in oak casks and three years in the bottle.

5

INFORMATION

Fundación Logroño Turismo c/Portales 50 (Oct–June Mon–Sat 10am–2pm & 4.30–7.30pm, Sun 10am–2pm; July–Sept Mon–Sat 9am–2pm & 5–8pm, Sun 10am–2pm; ☎ 941 273 353, ⊛ logroturismo.org), provides a free map of town. Turismo de la Rioja (Mon–Fri 10am–2pm &

4–7pm, Sat & Sun 10am–2pm & 5–7pm; ☎ 902 277 000, ⊛ lariojaturismo.com), stocked with useful information on the whole Rioja region, is in a modern building on the edge of the Paseo del Espolón. Cultural news and events are covered on ⊛ culturalrioja.org.

ACCOMMODATION

You shouldn't have trouble finding **accommodation**, except during the week-long Fiesta de San Mateo, which starts on September 21, for which rooms are booked months in advance. The lowest-priced accommodation is in the old town; business-class three- and four-star places line the avenues in the more modern parts of town.

Hostal Niza c/Capitán Gallarza 13 ☎ 941 206 044, ⊛ hostalniza.com. A reasonable mid-range *hostal* in the heart of the old town, by the market and tapas bars, with decent en-suite rooms that do the job. **€60**

Hotel Marqués de Vallejo c/Marqués de Vallejo 8 ☎ 941 248 333, ⊛ hotelmarquesdevallejo.com. This old-town hotel has been treated to a thorough makeover, giving it something of a boutique feel. Soundproofed rooms have polished wood floors and contemporary furnishings, and bathrooms are very swish. There's also adjacent private parking. Outside peak periods, rooms

often go for a lot less. **€100**

Hotel Portales c/Portales 85 ☎ 941 502 794, ⊛ hotelportales.es. Smart three-star hotel in contemporary style, right on the edge of the old town, with garage parking. The website usually has some good deals. **€75**

★ **Pensión La Bilbaina** c/Capitán Gallarza 10 ☎ 941 254 226. Very smart en-suite rooms (including singles) at excellent prices. Everything is freshly painted and squeaky clean, though furnishings are a bit ascetic (bed, wardrobe, chair). Street-facing rooms are apt to be noisy at weekends. **€50**

EATING AND DRINKING

Logroño's old town is thick with bars and restaurants, and the local **cuisine** is celebrated for its potato and bean dishes, seasonal vegetables (particularly peppers, asparagus and mushrooms) and thick steaks. But Logroño's mini-masterpieces are its **tapas bars**, clustered in the bar-run alleys of **c/Laurel** and **Travesía de Laurel**, and the similar **c/San Juan**. In these two locales alone are around fifty different bars, each with their own advertised speciality, from grilled mushrooms to octopus. Punters spill out in the alleys at the drop of a hat, washing it all down with a glass of the superb local Rioja wine. There are useful detailed bar guides on ⊛ logropincho.com.

Café Moderno c/Francisco Martínez Zaporta 9 ☎ 941 220 042, ⊛ cafemoderno.com. A gloriously ornate café, established in 1916, with an antique bar full of old photographs, and locals playing board games inside. It's a good spot for breakfast, or a glass of *tinto* in the evening; there are reasonably priced meals, too. Daily 9am–midnight.

Casa Pali c/Laurel 11 ☎ 941 256 795. An old-town classic, knocking out tapas treats such as fried asparagus or *berenjena con queso* (aubergine with melted cheese). Daily 12.30–3pm & 8.30pm–midnight; closed Tues.

Las Cubanas c/San Agustín 17 ☎ 941 220 050, ⊛ lascubanas.net. Best choice for a more refined night out, this classy restaurant dates from the 1920s, but the interior is sleek and contemporary. There's a choice of dishes from a modish Riojan menu (mains €13–21), say ravioli of shrimp and *bacalao* followed by hake and clams served with a *salsa verde*. Mon–Sat 1–4pm & 9pm–midnight.

La Cueva c/San Juan 13 ☎ 675 671 388. A few tapas bars claim the mantle of mushroom king (the *Ángel* on c/Laurel has its admirers), but this is the place for grilled mushroom *pinchos* par excellence. Daily 12.30–3pm & 8.30pm–midnight.

★ **Mesón del Abuelo** c/Laurel 12 ☎ 941 224 663. At bright, bustling "Grandad's House", the tapas specialities are *chipirones* (baby squid), *sepia* (cuttlefish strips) and thin pork steaks, plonked on the grill and then doused in garlic sauce, for a couple of euros at a time. In the dining room, split by a low glass partition so you can still see the action, there's bigger portions of grilled dishes like langoustine, stuffed peppers and lamb chops (dishes €6–15), and a good wine list that has plenty of decent Riojas at value-for-money prices. Daily 12.30–3pm & 8pm–midnight.

Paganos c/Laurel 22 ☎ 941 220 074. A no-nonsense, stand-up place specializing in *pinchos morunos* (mini pork kebabs), which come on a long skewer handed across the bar or out of the serving hatch by the grill-maestro. Their other star dish is creamy tortilla, stuffed with potato or *chorizo*, cut into wedges and served on a slice of bread. Daily 12.30–3pm & 8pm–midnight.

Pata Negra c/Laurel 24 ☎ 941 213 645. The mural of acorn-rooting pigs on the wall is the clue, and this renowned *jamonera* (ham specialist) serves big cured meat platters at a price (up to €18) – or you can snack on mini-sandwiches (all under €3) mixing things like *jamón* and blue cheese or tuna and hot peppers, washed down with various grades of Rioja wine, all absurdly cheap. Daily 12.30–3pm & 8.30pm–midnight.

★ **La Taberna de Baco** c/San Agustín 10 ☎941 213 544. A truly excellent tapas bar, with a range of delicious specialities: try the *bombita* (potato-and-mushroom ball) or the *migas* (garlic and breadcrumb mixture with a fried egg) and brilliant fried green tomatoes. There are a few tables if you want to make a meal of it. Daily 1–4pm & 8pm–midnight.

La Taberna del Laurel c/Laurel 9 ☎941 220 143. Often

bursting at the seams with patrons eagerly stuffing themselves with the house speciality, *patatas bravas*. Daily 12.30–3pm & 8.30pm–midnight.

★ **Vinissimo** c/San Juan 23 ☎941 258 828. Fantastically creative tapas (*brochetas* of chicken, prawn or even wild boar are a speciality), plus a carefully selected wine list add up to a more refined tapas bar than usual. A small dining room offers a good-value *menú* (€10, weekends €12) and various à la carte options. Daily 1–4pm & 9pm–midnight; closed Wed, & Thurs lunch.

Haro and around

The capital of Rioja Alta is **HARO**, a modern, working town 44km northwest of Logroño. It's entirely devoted to the wine trade, but has some lovely reminders of a grand past in an old centre that's worth at least a short stop – perhaps even overnight if the winery visits take their toll. Apart from harvest time (Sept), when everything shifts up a gear, the best time to be in Haro is in June, starting with the **Semana del Vino** (Wine Week, usually second week), when the bars and restaurants come together to offer *crianza* and *reserva* wine-tastings at bargain prices. There's more of the same during the continuous **fiestas** of San Juan, San Felices (the town's patron saint) and San Pedro (June 24–29), when there are outdoor concerts, street parades and the climactic **Batalla del Vino** (June 29), when thousands of people climb the Riscos de Bilibio (a small mountain near the town) to be drenched from head to foot in wine.

Plaza de la Paz and around

At the centre of town is **Plaza de la Paz**, a sloping square whose glass-balconied mansions overlook an archaic bandstand. An antique sign on the arcade at the top of the square is entirely in keeping with the prevailing sepia tone, prohibiting carriages from entering the narrow streets beyond and threatening a one-peseta fine for transgressors. The very small old quarter off the square is attractive in a faded kind of way, with parallel lanes leading up to the landmark Renaissance church of **Santo Tomás**, with its 68-metre-high wedding-cake tower and richly carved portal.

Centro de Interpretación del Vino de la Rioja

C/Breton de los Herreros 4 • Fri & Sat 10am–2.30pm & 3.30–6pm, Sun 10am–2pm • €3 • ☎ 941 305 719, ⓦ vinodelarioja.org

The **Centro de Interpretación del Vino de la Rioja**, behind Haro's bus station, is the regional government's formal showcase for its wine production – hugely informative (there's an English audio-guide available) but unfortunately closed for most of the week. They also offer weekend wine-tasting courses, though visitors with a more casual interest, who just want to taste a wine or two, are better served by visiting one of the local *bodegas* (see box, p.414).

Museo de la Cultura del Vino

Bodega Dinastía Vivanco, Briones, 6km southeast of Haro on the N232 • June–Sept Tues–Sun 10am–8pm; Oct–May Tues–Thurs & Sun 10am–6pm, Fri & Sat 10am–8pm; last entry 1hr 30min before closing • Museum €7.50, *bodega* tour €6.50 (reservations required), combination ticket €12 • ☎ 941 322 323 or 902 320 001, ⓦ www.dinastiavivanco.com

The best single visit for anyone interested in Rioja wine is the impressive museum at the Dinastía Vivanco family *bodega*, just outside Haro (you'll pass by on the drive from Logroño). It's a slick operation all round, with a comprehensive museum that covers every aspect of wine production, and guided tours of the associated winery that set off several times daily, taking you out into the vineyard and then down into the underground bowels of the operation. Add in a "tasting bar", with its automatic

5

TOURING BODEGAS IN LA RIOJA

Wine is at the very heart of La Rioja's identity (⟨w⟩riojawine.com), and few people will pass through without wanting to visit a *bodega* and taste a few *vinos*. In **Haro**, there are a dozen *bodegas* within walking distance of town, most clustered around the train station – they offer daily tours (usually in English in the mornings), but you have to make a reservation (Haro *turismo* can advise about current tour times). Some are free, some charge €3–5 for tours and tastings lasting from ninety minutes to two hours. Scores of other wineries lie within half an hour's drive of Haro or Logroño, and tend to be open for drop-in visits without appointment. They've all got wine shops attached, and some have excellent restaurants. A good target is the striking village of **San Vicente de la Sonsierra** – you'll see its hill-top church and castle on the drive across to Haro – which has no fewer than sixteen wineries in the vicinity, while some of the most celebrated vineyards lie close to the town of **Laguardia** (see p.482), 19km northwest of Logroño or 26km east of Haro, in the Basque **Rioja Alavesa** region.

Bodegas Bilbaínas ⟨t⟩941 310 147, ⟨w⟩bodegas bilbainas.com. One of the oldest *bodegas* in Haro, established in 1901, home of the classic Viña Pomal wines and their flagship contemporary label, La Vicalanda.
Bodegas Muga ⟨t⟩941 311 825, ⟨w⟩bodegasmuga .com. Muga has a good visitor centre in Haro where you can learn about its painstaking traditional methods, such as using egg whites to clean the wine of impurities.

La Encina, Bodegas y Viñedos ⟨t⟩941 305 630, ⟨w⟩laencinabodegas.com. Just to the north of Haro, overlooking the river at the pretty village of Briñas, is this classy, minimalist winery making wines under the Tobelos name.
López de Heredia ⟨t⟩941 310 244, ⟨w⟩www .lopezdeheredia.com. Stand out attraction at this Haro winery is the eye-catching Modernist wine shop designed by Zaha Hadid.

wine-dispensers, a well-stocked shop, café with vineyard views, fancy restaurant and vine-planted gardens, and you could easily spend half a day here.

ARRIVAL AND DEPARTURE   HARO

By train The train station is a fifteen-minute walk from the centre, down over the bridge on the other side of the river.
By bus Services from Logroño by bus are far more frequent and the **bus station** is slightly closer in: from the traffic circle,

follow the sign for "Centro Ciudad", straight up c/La Ventilla, bearing left for Pl. de la Paz at the *Casa Terete* restaurant.
By car Haro is only small, and finding free on-street parking isn't usually a problem.

INFORMATION

Turismo Pl. Monseñor Florentino Rodríguez, opposite *Hotel Los Agustinos* (Mon–Fri 10am–2pm, Sat 10am–2pm &

4–7pm; July–Sept Mon–Sat 10am–2pm & 4.30–7.30pm; Sun 10am–2pm; ⟨t⟩941 303 366, ⟨w⟩haroturismo.org).

ACCOMMODATION

★ **Hospedería Señorío de Briñas** c/Travesía de la c/Real 3, Briñas, 6km north of Haro ⟨t⟩941 304 224, ⟨w⟩hotelesconencantodelarioja.com. For a real country treat, make the short drive out to this magnificent baronial mansion in a charming gem of a riverside village. Rooms use the exposed stone and archaic features to rather ravishing effect, and there's a spa in the old wine cellars. €120
Hotel Los Agustinos c/San Agustín 2 ⟨t⟩941 311 308, ⟨w⟩hotellosagustinos.com. This converted Augustinian convent founded in 1373, whose centrepiece is a

magnificent glass-covered cloister, is now a four-star hotel, with rooms that are a mix of traditional furnishings and up-to-date comforts. If you're staying here, you're unlikely to eat anywhere other than the fine restaurant, *Las Duelas* (closed Jan), which is a contemporary Spanish place (mains from around €23) with dining in the hotel cloister. €130
Pensión La Peña c/La Vega 1, just off Pl. de la Paz ⟨t⟩941 310 022. The best budget accommodation in town, with cosy, well-kept rooms, some of them en suite and many with a balcony overlooking the main plaza. €45

EATING AND DRINKING

Even the humblest *tapa* is transformed by a glass of Rioja, and you'll get plenty – and very cheaply – in the dozen or so **bars and restaurants** that lie the short distance between Pl. de la Paz and Santo Tomás church.

El Portillo Pl. San Martín 3 ☎ 941 305 025, ⓦ elportillorestaurante.com. In a cute little square below the church, this is less rustic and more contemporary than most, with fancy tapas (including a carpaccio of artichoke and *bacalao*), a good lunchtime *menú* for €13 and à la carte meals for around €30. Tues–Sun 1–4pm & 9pm–midnight.

Meson Los Berones c/Santo Tomás 23 ☎ 941 310 707. There's traditional Riojan tapas and good-value meals, day and night, in this rustic bar with a few wooden tables at the back. The €14 *menú* runs from grilled lamb chops to salt cod drenched in a spicy tomato sauce. Daily noon–midnight.

Nájera

The Camino de Santiago sweeps through Logroño and on towards Burgos, passing to the south of Haro. At the small riverside town of **NÁJERA**, 15km south of Haro, dramatically sited below a pink, cave-riddled rock formation, you're ostentatiously welcomed to the "Capital of Furniture" (Nájera is known for its fixtures and fittings). Old and modern Nájera are separated by the grassy riverbanks of rippling Río Najerilla – there's plenty of free parking on either side – while just across the footbridge from the charming old town, there's a riverside **market** every Thursday.

Monasterio Santa María la Real

Pl. de Santa María • Tues–Sat 10am–1pm & 4–7pm, Oct–April till 5.30pm, Sun 10am–12.30pm & 4–6pm • €3 • ☎ 941 361 083, ⓦ santamarialareal.net

Dominating the old town is the stork-topped Gothic **Monasterio Santa María la Real**. This contains a royal pantheon of ancient monarchs of Castile, León and Navarra, though best of all is the attractive sixteenth-century cloister of rose-coloured stone and elaborate tracery.

ACCOMMODATION	NÁJERA

Hotel San Fernando Paseo San Julián 1 ☎ 941 363 700, ⓦ sanmillan.com. Reasonable rooms – nothing striking, but good for a comfortable night – plus a rather unexpected traditional red English phone box in the lobby. **€80**

Santo Domingo de la Calzada

Next stop for pilgrims, the last in La Rioja, is **SANTO DOMINGO DE LA CALZADA**, a small town 20km west of Nájera that owes its history and much of its living to the Santiago pilgrim route. The cathedral, with its fourteenth-century Mudéjar cloister, is dedicated to town founder Domingo de la Calzada, and since the earliest days of the pilgrimage there has been a welcome here for wayfarers – a steady stream still picks its way though town, with plenty of inexpensive *menús del día* on offer at local restaurants to raise strength and spirits. The former medieval pilgrims' hospital is now a fine parador, with the current *Albergue de Peregrinos* sited nearby, facing the pretty, arcaded Plaza de la Alameda. For all this, though, only the very centre of town around the cathedral is particularly attractive and, unless you're a foot-weary pilgrim or staying at the parador, there's no pressing need to stay long in town – Ezcaray to the south (see p.416) is a far better overnight stop.

ACCOMMODATION	SANTO DOMINGO DE LA CALZADA

Parador Santo Domingo de la Calzada Pl. del Santo 3 ☎ 941 340 300, ⓦ parador.es. Only the wealthier sort of pilgrim gets the luxurious comforts of the parador these days, in light rooms that occupy a modern annexe, grafted on to the old pilgrims' hospital. It's all nicely – if traditionally – done; book in advance and you'll be able to beat the official rates quite easily. **€170**

The mountain monasteries of Suso, Yuso and Valvanera

Around 18km from Nájera (a little further from Santo Domingo), the stone village of **San Millán de la Cogolla** serves as gateway to the magnificent twin mountain monasteries

5

known as **Yuso** and **Suso**. You can see these easily as a half-day diversion from the main Rioja route, while a third monastery, **Valvanera**, lies further south, off the **LR-113**, the trans-mountain road that provides a dramatic journey south and west between Nájera and Salas de los Infantes (90km; 2hr drive). This twists ever higher up the glorious, lush valley of the Rio Najerilla, hugging the sides of the huge hydroelectric Mansilla dam, before careering across the bare uplands of the **Sierra de la Demanda** to cross into Castilla y León. The route makes a great roundabout approach to Burgos, and you'll emerge close to the equally magnificent monastery of Santo Domingo de Silos (see p.425).

Monasterio de Yuso

Easter–Sept Tues–Sun 10am–1.30pm & 4–6.30pm, plus Mon in Aug; Oct–Easter Tues–Sat 10am–1pm & 3.30–5.30pm • Guided 50min visits €5 • ☎ 941 373 049, ⓦ monasteriodeyuso.org

The immense lower **Monasterio de Yuso** dominates the valley, built in the sixteenth and seventeenth centuries to house the relics of the crowd-pulling sixth-century saint, San Millán. It's at the centre of some fairly big tourist business, with one wing of the monastery housing a four-star hotel, a couple of big restaurants and enough parking to accommodate the entire Spanish nation, should it choose to all come at once.

Monasterio de Suso

Tues–Sun 9.30am–1.30pm & 3.30–6.30pm • Half-hourly tours from 9.55am and 3.55pm; reservations required at the lower ticket office at Yuso (access from the hotel courtyard) • €3 • ☎ 941 373 049, ⓦ monasteriodeyuso.org

The much older **Monasterio de Suso** lies a few hundred metres up in the hills, hidden from public view. You're taken up by shuttle bus to see the beautiful, haunting building, the original site of Millán's burial before he was sanctified in 1030 and later transferred down the hill into surroundings more in keeping with a patron saint.

ACCOMMODATION	SAN MILLÁN DE LA COGOLLA

Hostería del Monasterio Monasterio de Yuso ☎ 941 373 277, ⓦ sanmillan.com. Situated in one wing of the monastery, this is rather a grand place to spend the night – especially if you splash out on the Royal Suite, once the abbot's quarters. **€135**

Posada de San Millán ☎ 941 373 161, ⓦ lapoasa dadesanmillan.es. In front of the Yuso complex, this simpler, rustic residence has just half a dozen inexpensive rooms. **€50**

Monasterio de Valvanera

No public access to monastery buildings • ☎ 941 377 044, ⓦ valvanera.com

There's another wonderfully sited monastery, the **Monasterio de Valvanera**, 35km further south of San Millán de la Cogolla (and a 5km detour off the LR113 mountain road). If anything, the location is even more dramatic than Yuso and Suso – sited 1000m above a steep-sided valley, with the tidy terraces of the Benedictine monks' vegetable gardens below. It's worth stopping briefly for the views – there's a bar and restaurant and some simple accommodation here – and to experience a monastic retreat with none of the crowds of more renowned counterparts.

Ezcaray

For summer and winter escapes – hiking in the wooded valley of the Rio Oja, skiing on the heights above – locals make a beeline up the LR 111 to the pretty resort of **EZCARAY**, 15km south of Santo Domingo de la Calzada. It was a thriving textile centre in earlier centuries, which explains the mammoth former "royal factory" and dye shop you pass on the way into town (now partly converted into lodgings), while the ruined sixteenth-century bridge (destroyed by a flash flood in 1881) and the fortified medieval church in the centre also speak of former grandeur. Tourism has led to a smartening-up of Ezcaray's landscaped riverside gardens, porticoed streets and ancient squares – its big, solid stone houses, many supported on gnarled wooden pillars, have small, deep-set windows to help keep out the winter chill. Ezcaray is an attractive place to spend the night, particularly as it has acquired a reputation as a foodie destination, with some excellent local restaurants, including one of Spain's finest regional gastro-hotels.

ACCOMMODATION AND EATING EZCARAY

★ **Echaurren** c/Padre José García 19, opposite the main church ☎ 941 354 047, ⓦ rusticae.es. This family-run place, now in its fifth generation, features some very comfortable (and recently revamped) guest rooms above two restaurants – *Echaurren* (mains €17–23, *menú del día* €22), with a menu based on traditional Riojan recipes from the current chef's mother; and the contemporary, creative, Michelin-starred *El Portal* (tasting menus at €65 and €80). Expect the finest seasonally-led cuisine in either, from a traditional *potaje* of chickpeas and monkfish to modish long-and-low-temperature-cooked white asparagus. Meanwhile, the associated *Bistro Comilón*, ten metres away, serves moderately priced dishes (€10–17) from steak to *bacalao*. Restaurants Mon–Sat 1.30–3.30pm & 9.15–11pm, Sun 1.30–3.30pm; Echaurren also opens Sun 9.15–11pm in July & Aug; El Portal is closed Mon July–Dec, & Mon–Tues Jan–June. **€120**

La Rioja Baja

Forty kilometres from Logroño, Calahorra is the main town of **La Rioja Baja**, the southeastern part of the province. After the wine towns of the Rioja Alta it's a disappointment, and there's no pressing need to stop, though its parador brings some out this way. However, Calahorra does offer an attractive back-country route to Soria, via Arnedo, 12km southwest of town, where the scenery suddenly changes from cultivated flatland to vivid red rock, punctured by hundreds of caves, both natural and man-made, used in the past as houses and hermitages. From here – past attractive riverside **Arnedillo**, until reaching the tiny valley-bottom village of Yanguas, 30km southwest – the LR115 makes a twisting journey through the narrow Río Cidacos gorge, before climbing up over the bare tops for the sweeping run into Soria, another 50km to the south. It takes a couple of hours all told from Calahorra to Soria, though it's much the best idea to break in the middle at **Enciso** for a spot of dinosaur-hunting. A hundred and twenty million years ago (in the early Cretaceous period), the southeastern part of La Rioja was a steamy marshland where dinosaurs roamed, leaving their footprints in mud that later fossilized, and you can spend an enjoyable day in the area tracking the tracks.

Arnedillo

ARNEDILLO, 24km southwest of Calahorra, is the one place in Rioja Baja where you might be tempted to stay the night. It's a pretty spot, a minor spa set in a deep river valley beneath spiky crags, with the church at the very bottom by the river. From here it's an easy matter to stroll off into the lovely surroundings, along the river and up the side valleys, past ruined watermills, restored hermitages and waterside allotments.

ACCOMMODATION AND EATING ARNEDILLO

★ **Casa Cañas** Avda. del Cidacos 23 ☎ 941 394 022, ⓦ restaurantecasacanas.com. At *Casa Cañas* they are very proud of their "century at your service", and so they should be – the food is excellent, with succulent grills the speciality, alongside Riojan staples like *pochas* (stewed white beans) and vegetable *minestra*. The *menú* is €12, or eat à la carte for around €20. Mon, Tues & Thurs–Sat 1–4pm & 9–11pm.

Hospederia Las Pedrolas ☎ 941 394 401. Although there's a *hostal* or two up on the main through-road, above the village, the best place to rest your head is this charming rustic house right outside the village church. **€85**

Enciso

The village of **ENCISO**, 11km from Arnedillo and 35km southwest of Calahorra, is the main dinosaur centre and the easiest place to see some preserved footprints. You can either drive out to the main sites, or there's a well-signposted six-kilometre circular

5

walk from Enciso's Centre Paleontológico. There are lots of other signposted dinosaur sites in the vicinity, at Munilla or Préjano, for example, though many are on 4WD dirt tracks. A mountain bike would be ideal, or pack your hiking boots.

Centre Paleontológico

June to mid-Sept daily 11am–2pm & 5–8pm; rest of the year Mon–Sat 11am–2pm & 3–6pm, Sun 11am–2pm • €3 • ☎ 941 396 093, ⓦ dinosaurios-larioja.org

A jumble of houses on the hillside shelters the **Centre Paleontológico**, where there's information about all of the region's dinosaur sites. Parking is just over the old bridge (on the Soria side of the village), where it's planned to build an even larger *paleoaventura* centre. Brown signposts here point you to the nearby sites of **Virgen del Campo** and **Valdecevillo**, both featuring lots of visible tracks in the stone as well as huge replica dinos to thrill the kids.

Burgos

BURGOS was the capital of Old Castile for almost five hundred years, the home of El Cid in the eleventh century, and the base, two centuries later, of Fernando III, the reconqueror of Murcia, Córdoba and Seville. It was Fernando who began the city's famous Gothic cathedral, one of the greatest in all Spain, and Burgos is a firm station on the pilgrim route. During the Civil War, Franco temporarily installed his Fascist government in the city and Burgos owes much of its modern expansion to Franco's "Industrial Development Plan", a strategy to shift the country's wealth away from Catalunya and the Basque Country and into Castile. Even now, such connotations linger – the Capitanía General building still displays a 1936 plaque (admittedly, under protective glass) honouring Franco, the "supreme authority of the nation".

But Burgos is also a changed city, much scrubbed and restored over the last few years due to its candidature for **European City of Culture** for 2016 (ⓦburgos2016.es). Every paving stone in the centre looks to have been relaid, and while it's no longer a clearly medieval city, the handsome buildings, squares and riverfront of the old town are an attractive prospect for a night's stay. Despite the encroaching suburban sprawl and a population of almost 200,000, when it comes down to it, Burgos really isn't that big. You can easily see everything in the centre in a day, and while its lesser churches inevitably tend to be eclipsed by the cathedral, the two wonderful monasteries on the outskirts are by no means overshadowed.

Catedral

Pl. del Rey San Fernando • Daily 9.30am–7.30pm, last entrance at 6.30pm, closed Tues between 4pm and 4.30pm • €5, free Tues after 4.30pm • ☎ 947 204 712

The *casco histórico* is totally dominated by the **Catedral**, one of the most extra-ordinary achievements of Gothic art. Its spires can be seen above the rooftops from

---

IT'S A MIRACLE

The most highly venerated place of worship inside the cathedral is the **Capilla del Santísimo Cristo de Burgos**, which contains a cloyingly realistic image of Christ (c.1300), endowed with real human hair and nails and covered with the withered hide of a water buffalo, still popularly believed to be human skin. Legend has it that the icon was modelled directly from the scene at the Crucifixion and that – miracle of miracles – it requires a shave and a manicure every eighth day. The chapel, however, is closed to anyone clutching a cathedral visitor's ticket – worshippers enter instead via the Puerta de Santa María outside.

BURGOS

0 — 150
metres

Plaza de
España

Castillo
de Burgos CAB

Seminario
Mayor
San Jerónimo

San Esteban

ALV. YÁÑEZ
HOSPITAL CIEGOS
FERNÁN GONZÁLEZ ARCO PILAR
AVELLANOS
C. PUERTO DEL REY
C. CARDENAL SEGURA
CALLE SAN CALVO
S. Lorenzo

ALMIRANTE BONIFAZ
C. DE LA MONEDA
SANTANDER
CALLE DE SAN JUAN

Casa del
Cordón
PUEBLA

CALLE SAN LESMES

Arco de
Fernán
González

POZO
SECO
LLANA DE
AFUERA
DOÑA JIMENA

CALLE DE LA PALOMA
CALLE DE SOMBRERERÍA

PLAZA DE
LA LIBERTAD
PL. DE STO.
DOMINGO
PLAZA DE STO.
DOMINGO DE GUZMÁN

S. Nicolás

Catedral

PLAZA
MAYOR

Diputación
Palacio
Provincial

CALLE VITORIA

Gobierno
Civil

GRAN TEATRO

Santa
Águeda
PLAZA DE
STA. MARÍA
PL. REY
SAN FERNANDO

Ayuntamiento

PLAZA
DEL CID

Teatro
Principal AVENIDA DEL ARLANZÓN
Río Arlanzón

CALLE DE SANTA ÁGUEDA
EDUARDO MARTÍNEZ DEL CAMPO
NTRA. SRA. DE LA ASUNCIÓN

PASEO DEL ESPOLÓN
Arco de
Santa María
PUENTE DE
STA. MARÍA

PUENTE DE
SAN PABLO
PLAZA
CONDE DE
CASTRO

PASEO SIERRA DE ATAPUERCA

Cartuja de Miraflores & Camposte

Palacio
Arzobispal

BARRANTES
APARICIO Y RUIZ
AVENIDA DEL GENERALÍSIMO

PASEO DE ANDRÉS MANJÓN
VALLADOLID
C. CALERA
TRINAS
SAN PABLO

Museo de
la Evolución
Humana

CALLE BURGUENSE

CALLE DE SANTA CRUZ
C. HÉROES
PASEO SIERRA DE ATAPUERCA

PLAZA DE
CASTILLA

Casa de Angulo

PLAZA
DE VEGA

La Merced

PLAZA DEL
DR. ALBIÑANA
CALLE CONCEPCIÓN

SAN COSME

Museo de
Burgos

Bus
Station
ARANDA DE DUERO

Market

C. MIRANDA
CALLE DEL TINTE
CALLE DE SANTA CRUZ

N

Río Arlanzón
CALLE DE LA MERCED
PASEO DEL EMPECINADO
C. C. GUADALHORCE

S. Cosme &
S. Damián

CALLE DEL CEMEN
CALLE BEBRID GIMENO

CALLE DE MADRID
SAN PABLO

Iglesia
del
Carmen

AVENIDA VALENCIA DEL CID

C. DE LA ESTACIÓN
C. SANTA DOROTEA

■ **ACCOMMODATION**
Hotel Conde de Miranda	6
Hotel Jacobeo	2
Hotel Mesón del Cid	5
Hotel Norte y Londres	1
Hotel La Puebla	3
Pensión Peña	4

● **CAFÉS, TAPAS & RESTAURANTS**
Bar Gaona Jardín	8
La Cantina del Tenorio	2
Casa Ojeda	6
Cervecería Morito	7
La Esencia	3
La Favorita	1
Juarreño	5
Mesón Los Herreros	4

all over town, and it's an essential first stop in Burgos. The cathedral has emerged
from a lengthy period of restoration, looking cleaner than it has for centuries,
though visiting it has been reduced to something of a production line, with a
separate visitor centre, well-stocked gift-shop and one-way flow inside to keep
tourists from worshippers.

The interior
Moorish influences can be seen in the cathedral's central **dome** (1568), supported on
four thick piers that fan out into remarkably delicate buttresses – a worthy setting for
the **tomb of El Cid** and his wife Jimena, marked by a simple slab of pink veined marble
in the floor below. Otherwise, perhaps the most striking thing about the vast interior is
the size and number of its side chapels, with the octagonal **Capilla del Condestable**,
behind the high altar, possibly the most splendid of all, featuring a ceiling designed to
form two concentric eight-pointed stars. In the **Capilla de Santa Ana**, the magnificent
retablo is by Gil de Siloé, a Flanders-born craftsman whose son Diego crafted the
adjacent double stairway, the glorious **Escalera Dorada**.

Cloisters and Museo Catedralicio
The tourist route through the church leads out of the main body of the cathedral and
into the spacious two-storey **cloisters**, and beyond this to a series of chapels that house

5

the **Museo Catedralicio,** with its collection of religious treasures and two El Cid mementoes, namely his marriage contract and a wooden trunk. The light-filled lower cloister also has an audio-visual history of the church and its architecture, including a look at the various restoration projects.

Arco de Santa María

Tues–Sat 11am–2pm & 5–9pm, Sun 11am–2pm • Free • ☎ 947 288 868

The main approach to the old town and cathedral is across the **Puenta de Santa María**, where you're confronted by the **Arco de Santa María**, a gateway that originally formed part of the town walls. There are temporary art exhibitions held inside, and you can also view its exquisite Mudéjar ceiling, but it's the exterior that really catches the eye. It was embellished with statues in 1534–36 in order to appease Carlos V after Burgos' involvement in a revolt by Spanish noblemen against their new Flemish-born king. Carlos' statue is glorified here in the context of the greatest Burgalese heroes: Diego Porcelos, founder of the city in the late ninth century; Nuño Rasura and Laín Calvo, two early magistrates; Fernán González, founder of the Countship of Castile in 932; and, above all, **El Cid Campeador**, who is surpassed in popular sentiment only by St James in his legendary exploits against the Moors.

Museo de la Evolución Humana

Paseo Sierra de Atapuerca • Tues–Fri 10am–2.30pm & 4.30–8pm, Sat, Sun & daily in July & Aug 10am–8pm • €6, free Wed afternoons; €11 including bus tour to archeological site • ☎ 902 024 246, ⓦ museoevolucionhumana.com

With Burgos smartening itself up for its City of Culture bid, the main new cultural addition is the Modernist riverfront cube housing the **Museo de la Evolución Humana**. This takes the important fossil finds and early human archeological sites at the local Atapuerca mountains as the starting-point for an entertaining and informative tour through the history of human evolution. Wide-ranging displays cover subjects from the first use of fire to Darwin's expeditions aboard the *Beagle*, with the whole museum – and indeed human evolution itself – rooted in the idea of the connective eco systems that have allowed *Homo sapiens* and their ancestors to develop over millions of years. The museum also runs daily bus tours out to the Atapuerca archeological sites, where fossils and tools have been found dating back well over a million years – some of the earliest such finds in Europe.

EL CID CAMPEADOR

Principal landmark along the leafy Burgos riverfront – right on the Puente de San Pablo – is the magnificent equestrian **statue of El Cid**, complete with flying cloak, flowing beard and raised sword. The city lays full claim to the Castilian nobleman, soldier and mercenary, born Rodrigo Díaz in the nearby village of Vivar in 1040 or thereabouts. Actually, his most significant military exploits took place around Valencia, the city he took back briefly from the Moors after a long siege in 1094, but no matter – El Cid (from the Arabic *sidi* or lord) is a local boy, whose heroic feats (not all strictly historically accurate) have been celebrated in Spain since the twelfth century. His honorific title, **Campeador** ("Supreme in Valour"), is some indication of the esteem in which he's always been held, though there's generally a veil drawn over his avarice and political ambition, not to mention the fact that, as an exiled sword-for-hire in the 1080s, El Cid turned out for Moorish princes as easily as for Christian kings. He died in Valencia in 1099, and the city fell again to the Moors in 1102, after which his wife Jimena took El Cid's body to the monastery of San Pedro de Cardeña, south of Burgos, where it rested for centuries. The body disappeared to France after the ravages of the Peninsular War, but husband and wife were reburied together in Burgos cathedral in 1921.

Centro de Arte Caja de Burgos (CAB)

C/de Saldaña • Tues–Fri noon–2pm & 5.30–8pm, Sat 11.30am–2.30pm & 5.30–9pm, Sun 11.30am–2.30pm • Free • ☎ 947 256 550, ⓦ cabdeburgos.com

The city's newest arts centre sits in a striking modern building right at the top of the steps by the church of San Esteban – it's a convenient stop on the way up to the castle. There are usually a couple of free exhibitions on at any one time – contemporary Spanish art and installations are its bread and butter – while CAB also puts on all sorts of other shows, events and workshops.

Castillo de Burgos

April–June Sat & Sun 11am–2pm & 4–7pm; July–Sept daily 11am–2pm & 5–8.30pm; Oct–March Sat & Sun 11am–2pm • €3.70 • ☎ 947 203 857

The highest point of town is marked by the **Castillo de Burgos**, a huge fortress that was largely destroyed by the French in 1813 – there are steps from opposite the church of San Esteban, which you can reach up c/Pozo Seco, behind the cathedral. The walls, battlements and staircases have been restored, and there's also a museum covering the history of the town, but even if you don't plan to go inside it's worth the short climb up the hill anyway, for the views from a *mirador* over the cathedral and town. Beyond stretch the shaded green spaces of the town's parkland.

Monasterio de las Huelgas

Tues–Sat 10am–1pm & 3.45–5.30pm, Sun 10.30am–2pm • €5, free Wed • ☎ 947 201 630 • Around 1.5km west of the city centre (20min walk), cross Puente de Santa María, turn right and follow the signs along the river bank

The Cistercian **Monasterio de las Huelgas** is remarkable for its wealth of Mudéjar craftsmanship. Founded in 1187 as the future mausoleum of Alfonso VIII (who died in 1214) and his wife Eleanor, daughter of Henry II of England, it became one of the most powerful convents in Spain. It was popularly observed that "If the pope were to marry, only the abbess of Las Huelgas would be eligible!" A community of nuns still lives here (making pottery that's for sale), and though you can enter through the gatehouse into the impressive courtyard, you have to pay to go any further.

It's very definitely worth it. The main **church**, with its typically excessive Churrigueresque *retablo*, contains the tombs of no fewer than sixteen Castilian monarchs and nobles, including Eleanor and Alfonso. Napoleon's troops paid their usual violent courtesy visit, and robbed the convent of its valuables, but remarkably, when the surviving tombs were later opened, many were found to contain regal clothes, embroidery and jewellery, now on display in a small **museum**. Other highlights include a set of delicate Romanesque cloisters, **Las Claustrillas**, and the ceiling of the main Gothic cloisters, which is adorned with patches of Mudéjar decoration. The **Capilla de Santiago** also has a fine Mudéjar ceiling and pointed horseshoe archway. Its cult statue of St James has an articulated right arm, which enabled him to dub knights of the Order of Santiago (motto: "The Sword is Red with the Blood of Islam") and on occasion even to crown kings.

Cartuja de Miraflores

Tues–Sat 10.15am–3pm & 4–6pm, Sun 11am–3pm & 4–6pm • €1 • Around 4km east of the centre – follow the path along the south bank of the river (towards *Camping Fuentes Blancas*), bear right up the hill at the Fuente del Prior park (45min) and cross the road for the monastery, or it's well signposted by road all the way from town

The second of the town's two notable monasteries, the **Cartuja de Miraflores**, famous for its three dazzling masterpieces by sculptor Gil de Siloé, lies in a secluded spot, a very pleasant hour's walk from the centre. The monastery buildings are still in use and you can only visit the **church** (1454–1488), which is divided, in accordance with

5

Carthusian practice, into three sections: for the public, the lay brothers and the monks. In front of the high altar lies the star-shaped carved alabaster tomb of Juan II of Castile (1405–1454) and Isabel of Portugal, of such perfection that it forced Felipe II and Juan de Herrera to admit "We did not achieve very much with our Escorial". Isabel la Católica, a great patron of the arts, commissioned it from Gil de Siloé in 1489 as a memorial to her parents. The same sculptor carved the magnificent altarpiece, plated with the first gold shipped back from the Americas and featuring scores of figures with expressive faces, so delicately carved that even the open pages of a Bible and parchment rolls are depicted. Finally comes the smaller but no less intricate tomb of the Infante (Crown Prince) Alfonso, brother of Queen Isabel, through whose untimely death in 1468 she was later able to claim the throne of Castile.

ARRIVAL AND DEPARTURE   BURGOS

The Río Arlanzón bisects the city and neatly delimits the *casco histórico*, or old quarter, on the north bank.

By train Burgos Rosa de Lima station is on Avda. Príncipe de Asturias, 5km northeast of the centre, but bus #25 runs from right outside the entrance every thirty minutes to Pl. España, a 20min journey. For current timetables and ticket information, consult RENFE ☎ 902 320 320, ⊛ renfe.com.
Destinations Bilbao (5 daily; 2hr 30min–4hr 30min); León (4 daily; 2hr); Logroño (2hr 15min); Madrid (7 daily; 2hr 30min–4hr 15min); Palencia (9 daily; 45min–1hr); Salamanca (4 daily; 2hr 30min); Valladolid (up to 13 daily; 1hr–1hr 20min); Vitoria (10 daily; 1hr 15min–1hr 30min); Zaragoza (4 daily; 4hr).
By bus The bus station is on c/de Miranda (☎ 947 288 855) on the south side of the river – it's a short walk up to cross the bridges into town.
Destinations Bilbao (8 daily; 2hr); Carrión de los Condes (daily; 1hr 20min); Covarrubias (Mon–Fri 2 daily, Sat

daily; 1hr); Frómista (daily; 1hr); León (4–5 daily; 2hr direct, otherwise up to 3hr); Logroño via Nájera (Mon–Fri 7 daily, Sat & Sun 3–4 daily; 2hr); Madrid (10 daily; 2hr 45min); Palencia (up to 3 daily; 1hr 15min); Pamplona (4 daily; 3hr 30min); Salamanca (3 daily; 3hr 30min); San Sebastián (7 daily; 3hr 30min); Santander (4 daily; 3hr); Soria (up to 3 daily; 2hr–2hr 30min); Santo Domingo de Silos (Mon–Sat daily; 1hr 30min); Valladolid (5 daily; 2hr 30min); Vinuesa (2–3 daily; 2hr 15min); Zaragoza (4 daily; 4hr).
By car Short-term parking is available out of the centre along the river, though there are large central signposted car parks, including under Pl. Mayor, at Pl. de Vega (near the bus station), and at Pl. de España. Overnight parking costs around €15.

INFORMATION AND TOURS

Turismo c/Nuño Rasura 7, down an alley in a new building off Pl. del Rey San Fernando, near the cathedral (daily: June–Sept 10am–8pm; Oct–May 10am–2pm & 4.30–7.30pm; ☎ 947 288 874, ⊛ www.aytoburgos.es). Another office at Pl. de Alonso Martínez 7 (daily: July–Sept 9am–8pm, Fri & Sat until 9pm; Oct–June 9am–2pm & 5–8pm; ☎ 947 203 125, ⊛ turismoburgos.org), a

five-minute walk northeast of the cathedral, also has information on Burgos province.
Trén Turístico A trolley-train rumbles around town (hourly departures 3–7pm, weekends and holidays 11am–7pm), departing from outside the cathedral – it's €4, though the evening, floodlit tours (Fri–Sun plus hols departs 9.15pm, €5) might be the better choice.

ACCOMMODATION

It's generally nicest to stay over the river, closer to the old town, though many of the new three- and four-star hotels are on the outskirts or even further out.

Hotel Conde de Miranda c/de Miranda 4 ☎ 947 265 267. Right on top (literally) of the bus station might not be your first choice of location, but this smart little two-star has bright rooms with squeaky laminate floors and cute marble bathrooms. There's street parking right outside, or a garage nearby. **€60**
Hotel Jacobeo c/San Juan 24 ☎ 947 260 102, ⊛ hoteljacobeo.com. Snazzy one-star outfit that offers small, trim rooms in muted, contemporary colours. There's

a breakfast bar downstairs, though you're very close to all the cafés and restaurants. **€75**
Hotel Mesón del Cid Pl. de Santa María 8 ☎ 947 208 715, ⊛ mesondelcid.es. The best rooms to get here have balconies with great cathedral views. Other than that, it's the most traditional hotel in the old town, a three-star in a handsome building, with its own parking and a restaurant that's set apart from the main building. **€85**
Hotel Norte y Londres Pl. Alonzo Martínez 10 ☎ 947

264 125, ⓦ hotelnorteylondres.com. A two-star hotel in a very attractive *belle époque* house, right in the centre. There's a traditional feel throughout, and rooms reflect the period but are cosy and comfortable; a fair few triples offer a bit more space and flexibility. Book online for better rates. **€65**

★ **Hotel La Puebla** c/Puebla 20 ⓣ 947 200 011, ⓦ rusticae.es. This elegant townhouse sporting elegant, contemporary design is the best boutique choice in the city. Huge beds and striking wall-coverings dominate the 19 rooms, and while space is tight you can't fault black-marble designer bathrooms featuring his-and-her sinks and rain-showers. Helpful staff can organize bike rental, and advise about parking; web offers go as low as €55 on certain days. **€95**

Pensión Peña c/Puebla 18 ⓣ 947 206 323. The top budget option in Burgos, this is a welcoming and immaculate *pensión*. It's right in the old town and popular with *camino* hikers, so advance reservations are essential. **€40**

CAMPSITE

Camping Fuentes Blancas Parque de Fuentes Blancas ⓣ 947 486 016, ⓦ campingburgos.com. Out along the river, a 45min walk or a bus ride from the centre (catch it from Avda. del Arlanzón, along the river by the Cid statue). Facilities are excellent, including a pool and restaurant, bikes for rent, and bungalows (from €40 per night). Closed Oct–March. **€4.65** per person, plus **€3.70** per tent

EATING, DRINKING AND NIGHTLIFE

You'll find plenty of **restaurants** in Burgos serving traditional Castilian dishes, including the local speciality, *morcilla* (a kind of black pudding or blood sausage, mixed with rice). Good **tapas bars** are legion, especially down the narrow bar-run of c/San Lorenzo (off Pl. Mayor), but also along c/Avellanos, and near the cathedral around c/de la Paloma. Burgos **nightlife**, meanwhile, is mainly generated by the local students, who hang out in the lively "pubs" and music bars in the open spaces of c/Huerto del Rey and c/Llana de Afuera, behind the cathedral – just follow the crowds. There's a more stylish scene over on c/Puebla and c/San Juan, where some fancier *copas* places hide behind smoked glass. After 3am, check out the late-night bars and **clubs** around the modern courtyard known as Pl. de Las Bernardas, just off c/Las Calzadas, east of the *casco histórico*, which are usually open till 7am.

CAFÉ

Juarreño Pl. Mayor 25 ⓣ 947 213 490, ⓦ juarreño .com. The best address in town for cakes, sweets and pastries – beautifully concocted, artisan-made chocs, bombóns, croissants and cakes from a masterful *pastelería*. There are seats on the main square too. Mon–Thurs 9.30am–9.30pm, Fri 9.30am–10.30pm, Sat 10am–10.30pm, Sun 10am–9.30pm.

TAPAS BARS AND RESTAURANTS

Bar Gaona Jardín c/Sombrerería 29 ⓣ 947 206 191. Pick your way into the interior, modelled on an *andaluz* garden, where beautifully sculpted bite-sized *pinchos* (from €2) line the bar (specialities include the signature foie gras with apple purée). It can be hard to find the first time – it's tucked down a dead-end alley, around the block from c/de la Paloma (and is not to be mistaken for the *Gaonas* more mainstream tapas bar and restaurant on that street). Tues–Sun 11am–3.30pm & 7pm–midnight.

La Cantina del Tenorio c/Arco del Pilar 10 ⓣ 947 269 781, ⓦ lacantinadeltenorio.es. Atmospheric stone tavern with a nice line in creative fish *pinchos*, including anchovy and pickled peppers, smoked salmon and cherry tomatoes, and razor clams and olives. Tapas and *raciones* €2–12. Mon–Sat 1pm–midnight, Sun 1–4pm.

Casa Ojeda c/Vitoria 5 ⓣ 947 209 052, ⓦ restaurant eojeda.com. One of the oldest and grandest places in town, dividing its efforts between deli, café, beer-house and

restaurant. It's an ornately decorated space, with a smart Castilian restaurant upstairs and cheaper eats in the *comedor* or at the bar, though you're looking at *platos combinados* from €12.50 and à la carte dishes in the restaurant from around €20. Daily noon–midnight; restaurant 1–4pm & 8–11pm, closed Sun eve.

★ **Cervecería Morito** c/Diego Porcelos 1, cnr c/Sombrerería ⓣ 947 267 555. The best budget dining spot in town, permanently rammed with locals at meal times. It's a no-nonsense bar serving huge freshly cooked, meal-in-one platters for around €8 (tuna *tortilla*, *calamari* and salad, say), or big stuffed sandwiches, *raciones*, salads and egg dishes (all €4–8), plus cheap-as-chips drinks. Daily noon–midnight.

★ **La Esencia** c/Peubla 18 ⓣ 947 263 296, ⓦ restaurant elaesencia.es. Much more of a refined experience than most in town, for fine dining with a contemporary edge – think seasonal vegetable tempura or red-pepper confit, followed by seared tuna with shiitake mushrooms or baked hake with a leek and carrot salsa. It's all beautifully presented, and fairly reasonably priced, with dishes at €14–22 and a good-value €25 tasting menu (Tues–Thurs nights only) of perfectly judged little dishes. Tues–Sat 1.30–4pm & 9–11.30pm, Sun 1.30–4pm.

La Favorita c/Avellanos 8 ⓣ 947 205 949, ⓦ lafavoritaburgos.com. The self-professed "urban tavern" reboots the genre, offering classic tapas and *pinchos* – croquetas to grilled foie gras, egg scrambles to tuna and chilli

5

brochettes – but in a rustic-chic city bar setting. *Pinchos* start at €2, but dishes run up as high as €18 for a plate of bellota ham. Daily noon–midnight.

★ **Mesón los Herreros** c/San Lorenzo 20 ☎ 947 202 448, ⓦ mesonlosherreros.es. At busy times, you have to perch around the barrel table-tops outside on the street at

this classic old-town tapas bar. There's a famously wide range of tapas and *raciones* (snails to stuffed mussels, €1.50–8) and, like the other places along here, there's also an upstairs *comedor* for meals – the *menú del día* is €12, €15 at weekends. Daily noon–midnight; restaurant 1–4pm & 8–11pm.

South and east of Burgos

South and east of Burgos lies a quartet of renowned sights – ancient hermitage, lavish abbey cloister and two very different restored towns – that are all easy excursions by car. They would make a fine, if busy, day's tour from Burgos, or can be seen en route to Soria, down the N234, though for an alternative overnight stop it's a hard choice between the dramatic parador at Lerma and the small-town charms of Covarrubias.

Ermita de Santa María de Lara

Quintanilla de las Viñas • May–Sept Wed–Sun 10am–2pm & 4–8pm; Oct–April Wed–Sun 10am–5pm; closed last weekend in each month • Free

Down the N234 towards Soria, past the first signposted turn-off for Covarrubias, there's a detour after 34km to the dusty village of Quintanilla de las Viñas, which retains a rare Visigothic church and hermitage, the **Ermita de Santa María de Lara**. It's a remarkable survivor, a simple stone building on a bare hillock outside the village, dating back to around 700 AD. Only a third of its original size (the ground plan is still shown in the stone foundations outside), it nonetheless packs an emotive punch, not least in the delicately carved exterior friezes depicting grapes, animals, birds and a scallop shell over the door – centuries of pilgrims have left cruder scratched crosses on the walls. Inside, there's a stone arch with capitals representing the sun and moon, and a block that is believed to be the earliest representation of Christ in Spanish art. There's a custodian on site during opening hours, but outside official visiting times you'll only be able to see the exterior.

Covarrubias

The small town – village really – of **COVARRUBIAS**, 40km south of Burgos, is superbly preserved, with many white half-timbered houses and an air of sleepy gentility throughout. Set by an old bridge overlooking the Río Arlanza, the *casco histórico* is arranged around three adjacent plazas of ever increasing prettiness. The late Gothic **Colegiata de San Cosme y San Damián** is the main church, crammed with tombs that give an idea of the grandeur of the town in earlier times. The whole ensemble is studiously quaint, and attracts weekend tourists in numbers, but it's not yet overwhelmed – there's an antiques shop and a classy butcher-deli or two, but there are also locals tending to brimming flower boxes and children playing around the worn stone crosses.

ARRIVAL AND DEPARTURE   COVARRUBIAS

By bus and car It's easiest to come by car, since the limited bus service from Burgos means you'll probably have to stay the night. There's plenty of parking outside the

village – you're not supposed to drive inside – and everything is within two or three minutes' walk, and easy to find.

ACCOMMODATION AND EATING

Hotel Nuevo Arlanza Pl. Mayor ☎ 947 400 511, ⓦ hotelnuevoarlanza.com. For views over the main square, ask for a front-facing room at the three-star *Nuevo Arlanza*; it

also has its own restaurant, serving classic country Castilian cuisine, from *morcilla* to grilled trout. You'll usually get a better deal on rooms if you avoid July, August and weekends. **€85**

★ **Hotel Rey Chindasvinto** Pl. del Rey Chindasvinto 5 ☎ 947 406 560. Right next to the main church, this is the town's best-value hotel, with charming owners and rustic wood-trimmed rooms. **€60**

Pension Casa Galín Pl. Mayor ☎ 947 406 552, ⓦ casagalin.com. Brightly furnished budget rooms in the main square, above a rustic tapas bar and restaurant where you'll get a straightforward meal at a reasonable price. The *menú del día* (€12) is usually available at night, too. Restaurant Mon & Wed–Sat 1–4pm & 9–11pm, Sun 1–4pm. **€45**

Santo Domingo de Silos

The Benedictine abbey of **Santo Domingo de Silos**, 18km southeast of Covarrubias, is one of Spain's greatest Christian monuments. It's surrounded by the fawn stone buildings of a small village of the same name, which has half a dozen small hotels and a few cafés and restaurants, all rather overpriced – indeed, having seen the abbey, there's no great reason to stay, as nearby Covarrubias is a far better overnight option.

Abadía de Santo Domingo de Silos

C/Santo Domingo • **Abbey** Tues–Sat 10am–1pm & 4.30–6pm, Sun & hols 4.30–6pm • €3.50 • **Services** Mon–Sat 9am, Sun noon, plus daily 7pm, and others • ☎ 947 390 049, ⓦ www.abadiadesilos.es

The defining feature of the **Abadía de Santo Domingo de Silos** is a double-storey, eleventh-century **Romanesque cloister**, with eight graphic sculpted reliefs on the corner pillars. They include *Christ on the Road to Emmaus*, dressed as a pilgrim to Santiago (complete with scallop shell), in solidarity with pilgrims who make a hefty detour from the main route to see the tomb of Santo Domingo, the eleventh-century abbot after whom the monastery is named. The same sculptor was responsible for about half of the **capitals**, which besides a famous bestiary include many Moorish motifs, giving rise to speculation that he may have been a Moor. Whatever the case, it is an early example of the effective mix of Arab and Christian cultures, which was continued in the fourteenth century with the vivid, painted Mudéjar wood-beamed ceiling. A quite different sculptor carved many of the remaining capitals, including the two that ingeniously tell the stories of the Nativity and the Passion in a very restricted space. Visits to the monastery also usually include entry to the eighteenth-century **pharmacy**, which has been reconstructed in a room off the cloister. Meanwhile, the monks who sing at the abbey are considered one of the top three **Gregorian choirs** in the world – you may remember their 1994 platinum-selling CD *Chant* – and many visitors make a point to attend a service to hear the singing.

Lerma

The upper town of **LERMA**, high above the Río Arlanza, takes some beating as a piece of vanity building, constructed almost entirely between 1606 and 1617 at the behest of the Duke of Lerma, court favourite of the weak Felipe III. A pious man, Lerma established no fewer than six monasteries and convents in town, while on the site of the former castle he erected an enormous ducal palace, fronted by a sweeping, arcaded plaza. This is now a magnificent parador – well worth planning an itinerary around – while the restored town lends itself to a half-day visit in any case, particularly if you coincide with the weekly Wednesday market that takes up the entire main square.

ARRIVAL AND DEPARTURE   **LERMA**

By bus and car There are daily buses from Burgos, 37km to the north, but realistically Lerma is a stop for drivers, overnight or otherwise, in combination with Covarrubias, 23km to the east, and Santo Domingo de Silos beyond. You can park right outside in the vast square, except during the day on Wednesdays (market day).

5

ACCOMMODATION

Parador de Lerma Pl. Mayor ☎ 947 177 110, ⓦ parador.es. Everything is quite lovely in the beautifully restored ducal palace, with the tone set by the stunning central courtyard around which are found the public areas and restaurant (open to non guests). Meanwhile, palatial terracotta-tiled rooms look directly out on to the burned countryside far below. Rates drop to €120 if you book far enough in advance. **€180**

EATING AND DRINKING

The pricey **restaurants** around the plaza all specialize in *lechazo asado* (roast suckling lamb), cooked in wood-fired ovens – around €35 or so for a serving for two people. For cheaper meals, walk straight down the steep hill from the main plaza and out through the town gate to the main road, where there's a handful of less rarefied restaurants and *hostales*.

The Camino de Santiago: Burgos to León

The central section of the great pilgrim route, the **Camino de Santiago**, cuts across the northern plains of Castilla y León, with the stretch from Burgos to León seen as one of the most rewarding – not for the walking, which can be flat and dull, but in terms of the art and architecture encountered along the way. From Burgos the *camino* runs south of the main road, via Castrojeriz and, more importantly, **Frómista**, before running up to **Carrión de los Condes** and **Sahagún**, the latter two towns both on the A231 Burgos–León road. With a car, rather than a rucksack and boots, there are also a couple of possible short detours off the main road to see the **Roman remains** on either side of Carrión de los Condes.

Frómista

FRÓMISTA still trades on the *camino*, but today's small crossroads of a town has only a fraction of the population of medieval times. Its undisputed highlight is the **church of San Martín**, which was originally part of an abbey that no longer exists. Carved representations of monsters, human figures and animals run right around the roof of the eleventh-century church, which was built in a Romanesque style unusually pure for Spain, with no traces of later additions. A couple of other churches in Frómista are also associated with the *camino*, and there's usually a steady trail of walkers and cyclists passing through, taking advantage of the simple accommodation here.

THE CAMINO DE SANTIAGO IN CASTILLA Y LEÓN

With the vineyards and well-watered countryside of La Rioja behind you, the **Camino de Santiago** arrives at Burgos and the start of the plains of Castile. Pilgrims are sharply divided about the *meseta*. Fans praise the big skies and the contemplative nature of the unchanging views, while detractors bemoan the bone-chilling wind that blows for nine months of the year, and the depressing way that you can see your destination hours before you reach it. It's certainly the flattest, driest part of the path and, if it's cold in winter, the lack of shade makes it uncomfortably hot in summer. The route often shadows the main road along a purpose-built gravel track, but there are many well-marked detours along isolated tracks crunchy with wild thyme.

Highlights are, of course, the glorious Gothic cathedrals of Burgos and León, after which the *meseta* ends at the town of Astorga, 50km west of León. From here you'll climb to the highest pass of the *camino* (1517m), where mist and fog can descend year-round and snow makes winter travel difficult. Traditionally, pilgrims bring a stone from home to leave on a massive pile at Cruz de Hierro, just before the pass. Things warm up considerably as you descend through gorgeous scenery to the Bierzo valley, 50km from Astorga, where the charming riverside town of Villafranca del Bierzo is an ideal place to rest before heading uphill into Galicia. For practicalities on the *camino*, see p.556.

Villalcázar de Sirga

Thirteen kilometres along the *camino* from Frómista (the route shadows the road), **VILLALCÁZAR DE SIRGA** has another notable church, Santa María la Blanca, built by the Knights Templar in the heart of the village. The Gothic style here begins to assert itself over the Romanesque, as witnessed by the figure sculpture on the two portals and the elegant pointed arches inside. Meanwhile, as pilgrims strike onwards past the village they are confronted by surely one of the most depressing signposts along the whole route – "Carrión de los Condes, 6km" (oh good), "Santiago de Compostela, 463km" (oh heck).

Carrión de los Condes and around

If the myths are to be believed, quiet, conservative **CARRIÓN DE LOS CONDES**, 80km west of Burgos and 40km north of Palencia, has a sensational past. In typically inflammatory fashion, it was reputed to be the place where, before the Reconquest, Christians had to surrender one hundred virgins annually to the Moorish overlords – a scene depicted on the badly worn portal of the church of Santa María del Camino, situated at the edge of the old town (where the *camino* comes into Carrión). Its pilgrim days have bestowed another dozen churches and monasteries upon Carrión, including the vast bulk of the Monasterio de San Zoilo – across the sixteenth-century bridge on the far side of town – whose cloister contains the tombs of the counts (*condes*) of Carrión, from whom the town's name comes. The pilgrim route picks its way through the centre, crossing the main square, Plaza del Generalísimo, still named for Franco after all these years. On hot days, it's the riverside park that is most tempting, especially if you've just walked here, while quick onward car journeys take you away from town to the region's remarkable Roman treasures. Come on a Thursday (market day) and Carrión's generally somnolent pulse is raised a little.

ARRIVAL AND DEPARTURE

CARRIÓN DE LOS CONDES

By bus and car Buses from Burgos, León and, more frequently, Palencia, stop outside the *Bar España*, on the main road at the edge of town, opposite the church of Santa María del Camino. There's plenty of free parking nearby.

INFORMATION

Punto de Información Callejón de Santiago (Mon 10am–2pm, Tues–Fri 10am–2pm & 4–6pm, Sat 10am–2pm & 4–7pm, Sun 10am–2pm; ☎ 979 880 932, ⊛ carriondeloscondes.es), is inside the Museu Contemporaneo – it's up the passage by the church of Santiago, facing the main square.

ACCOMMODATION AND EATING

There are several simple *pensiones* and pilgrim *albergues* in town, and some lovely rural accommodation in the nearby countryside. Most cafés and restaurants – including one or two overlooking the main square – are aimed firmly at the passing pilgrim trade, so prices everywhere are reasonable.

★ **Estrella del Bajo Carrión** c/Mayor 32, Villoldo, CL615, 11km south of Carrión ☎ 979 827 005, ⊛ rusticae .es. The glam choice hereabouts is this delightful gastro-retreat in a nearby village, which combines sweeping spaces, clean lines and huge floor-to-ceiling windows throughout. Spacious, all-in-white rooms are heavy with designer flair (larger studios cost €130), and there's a sun deck outside under a spreading tree. Breakfast is really good, while the handsome restaurant (open to non guests; mains €20–30) serves creative regional cuisine using seasonal ingredients, from grilled veg with a slug of estate-bottled olive oil to wood-grilled venison. Restaurant 1–4pm & 9–11pm. **€90**

Hostal La Corte c/Santa María 34 ☎ 979 880 138, ⊛ hostalacorte.com. On a budget, try these straightforward rooms right opposite Santa María del Camino church. The restaurant below is the place for good-value meals, from a €3 pilgrim's breakfast to a €10 *menú*, or there are mains from €9–16, trout to *chuletón*. Restaurant open for breakfast, plus 1–4pm & 9–11pm. **€45**

Hotel Real Monasterio San Zoilo c/San Zoilo ☎ 979 880 049, ⊛ sanzoilo.com. By far the most historic accommodation in town is this resolutely traditional three-star hotel converted from part of the monastery – follow the signs, over the bridge, to find it. It also has Carrión's most notable restaurant (*menú del día* €19, otherwise mains €13–20), serving fancied-up regional cuisine, from lamb to fish. Restaurant 1–4pm & 9–11pm. **€90**

5

Villa Romana La Olmeda

Pedrosa de la Vega, signposted 3km south of Saldaña, off CL615 • Tues–Sun 10.30am–6.30pm, last entry 6.15pm • €5, joint ticket with Villa Romana La Tejada €6, free Tues after 3pm • ☎ 979 119 997, ⓦ villaromanalaolmeda.com

It's a quick 19km drive northwest of Carrión on a ruler-straight road to the well-signposted **Villa Romana La Olmeda**, which is considered one of the most important domestic Roman sites in Spain, boasting more than 1000 square metres of well-preserved mosaics. Founded as a country estate in the first century AD, but extensively remodelled on palatial lines in the fourth century AD, La Olmeda was more than a mere villa – rather a thriving centre of local agriculture and industry. But faced with the slow collapse of the Roman Empire, the estate gradually fell into disrepair, its buildings demolished, the villa's mosaic floors buried under farmland and its very existence forgotten. It was rediscovered in 1968 and has since been fully excavated, with the entire complex of buildings and the surviving mosaics now sheltered under a dramatic, modernist steel hangar standing in open countryside. Raised walkways lead you around the complex, past reception and dining rooms, bedrooms, offices, storerooms, kitchens and baths, all radiating out from a central patio-garden. Touch-screen monitors with computer-generated graphics show how the rooms might have looked, while the mosaics themselves are an impressive tour-de-force of polychromatic geometric designs, hunting scenes and more elaborate mythological sequences. There's also a café at the site.

Saldaña and the Museo de La Olmeda

Iglesia de San Pedro • Tues–Sun 10am–1.30pm & 4.30–7pm • Free entrance with ticket for Villa Romana La Olmeda, otherwise €2.50

For the archeological finds from the Olmeda villa site, you have to continue 3km further north up the CL615 to the small town of **SALDAÑA**, whose medieval church of San Pedro has been pressed into service as the **Museo de La Olmeda**; follow the "Museo Archeológico" signs from the central Plaza Mayor. Glass cases in the church nave present a snapshot of Roman country life 1600 years ago, with displays of coins, lamps, belt buckles, rings, necklaces, hunting weapons and cooking utensils, recovered from the site excavations. Saldaña itself has a charming *casco histórico* of timber and brick houses ranged around its central square, near which you'll be able to park, and there are several cafés.

Villa Romana La Tejada

Quintanilla de la Cueza, 17km southwest of Carrión, off the N120 • April–Sept Tues–Sun 10am–2pm & 5–8pm; Oct & March Tues–Sun 10.30am–1.30pm & 4–6pm; closed Nov–Feb • €3, joint ticket with La Olmeda €6 • ☎ 979 715 100

The other Roman villa site near Carrión is a bit harder to find, and nowhere near as impressive, though it is just as rewarding in its own way. The **Villa Romana La Tejada** is just past the dead-end hamlet of Quintanilla de la Cueza; there's an easy-to-miss sign off the highway (on the left, coming from Carrión), from where a narrow 1km road leads to a parking area surrounded by a high green hedge. The villa itself is hidden within a vast, unsightly shed, and is much less visited than La Olmeda, with which it is contemporary. But the surviving mosaics are another extraordinary reminder of the wealth that once characterized this now rather remote rural area, while La Tejada also shows off the hypocaust heating system that was de rigueur for any self-respecting Roman villa of the period.

Sahagún

From Carrión de los Condes the direct *camino* route west continues 35km to the small town of **SAHAGÚN**, once the seat of the most powerful monastery in all Spain. Although this is now little more than a ruined shell, several other churches in Sahagún repay the trip into town, particularly as the most interesting are built of red brick in characteristic Mudéjar (ie, Moorish-influenced) style. A steady stream of pilgrims trudges into and out of Sahagún most days, but otherwise it really only warrants a quick stop for coffee and a tour of the churches before heading on to León.

Iglesia de San Tirso

C/San Tirso, by Parque San Benito, signposted through town • April–Sept Wed–Sat 10.15am–2pm & 4.30–8pm, Sun 10.15am–2pm; Oct–March Wed–Sat 10.15am–2pm & 3–5.55pm, Sun 10.15am–2pm • Free

The most delicate of Sahagún's churches is the beautifully restored twelfth-century **San Tirso**, a Mudéjar brick construction of great grace. If the beauty is all on the outside, it's still worth coinciding with the opening times, because inside the simple interior is a fascinating series of scale wooden models of all the town's famous churches – complete with doors that open and roofs that lift off to display minutely constructed interiors, complete with altars and pews.

Ruins of San Benito

Parque San Benito

Adjacent to San Tirso church is all that's left of the mighty twelfth-century monastery of **San Benito**, once without compare in Spain (there's a model of the original inside San Tirso). Originally dedicated to San Facundo and San Primitivo, only one ruined, fenced-off chapel remains of the medieval complex – the more prominent bell-tower and the free-standing arched gateway across the road, the so-called **Arco de San Benito**, both also in ruins, were much later additions.

Iglesia de San Lorenzo

Pl. San Lorenzo, signposted off Pl. Mayor • **Church** currently under restoration • **Museo de Semana Santa** Wed–Sat 11.30am–1.30pm & 5–6.30pm • Free

Most imposing of the Mudéjar brick churches is thirteenth-century **San Lorenzo**, with its squat, square campanile – the church is currently propped up as the intricate brickwork has sagged over the centuries. In the adjacent building the small **Museo de Semana Santa** presents a fairly gory collection of life-sized, blood-spattered Christs either being led to the cross or crucified upon it. The museum is run by volunteers, so the hours are not always reliable.

ARRIVAL AND DEPARTURE   SAHAGÚN

By train Sahagún is an easy side trip from either Palencia or León; it's on the train route between the two (around 40min from either) and the station is a ten-minute walk from Pl. Mayor, down Avenida Constitución.

By car Signs through town lead you to San Tirso and San Benito, and there's convenient parking near the San Benito ruins.

EATING AND DRINKING

Restaurante Luís Pl. Mayor 4 ☎ 987 782 058. The most appealing of the cafés and taverns that ring the small central square, with a carved wooden ceiling, old-fashioned interior and arcade seating. There's a pilgrim *menú* for just €8, plus tapas and sandwiches, while the restaurant dishes (€10–20) include Sahagún's famous leeks (*puerros*) served in a variety of ways – with carpaccio of *bacalao*, for example, or mixed with mushrooms and clams. Daily 9am–midnight; restaurant 1–4pm & 9–11pm.

León

Even if they stood alone, the stained glass in the cathedral of **LEÓN** and the Romanesque wall paintings in its Panteón Real would merit a very considerable journey, but there's much more to the city than this. An attractive provincial capital that welcomes *camino* pilgrims by the thousand, it also presents itself as a lively university town with one of the best tapas bar scenes in Spain. Handsome old- and new-town areas complement each other, set back from extensive riverside gardens, and, while the city's major monuments are renowned, León is a fine place simply to spend a relaxed day or two. Large parts of the encircling medieval walls are still intact, and the tangle of narrow streets within is shabby in part, though the ramshackle buildings in faded ochre and rose pink give the

LEÓN

CAFÉS, TAPAS & RESTAURANTS	
El Besugo	7
Degustaciones	9
Tradicionales	2
La Despensa de	
Puerta Moneda	14
Latino	6
Palacio Jabalquinto	8
El Rincón del Gaucho	5
Taberna La Piconera	12
Las Termas	3
La Trebede	11
Zuloaga	4

BARS	
Barry's Irish Pub	1
Cervecería Céltica	9
El Gran Café	10
León Antiguo	13

ACCOMMODATION
Hostal Albany	2
Hostal Bayón	6
Hostal Boccalino	4
Hostal San Martín	3
Hotel Residencia Londres	7
Hotel Residencia Reina	5
Parador Hostal San Marcos	8
Plaza Mayor	1

5

casco antiguo a charm all of its own. By day, apart from the crowds around the cathedral and San Isidoro, it's much quieter in the pretty lanes and squares, though always with the accompanying footfall of arriving *camino* hikers making their way into town. At night, the old town bursts into life, with the streets thronged with people and the bars packed out. Things really take off during **Semana Santa**, and for the **fiestas** of San Juan and San Pedro in the last week of June. The celebrations, concentrated around the Plaza Mayor, get pretty riotous, with an enjoyable blend of medieval pageantry and buffoonery.

Brief history

Aside from an early Roman presence, León's history is that of the Reconquest. In 914, as the Christians edged their way south from Asturias, Asturian king Ordoño II transferred his capital from Oviedo to León. Despite being sacked by the dreaded al-Mansur in 996, the new capital rapidly eclipsed the old, and as more and more territory came under the control of León it was divided into new administrative groupings: in 1035, the county of Castile matured into a fully fledged kingdom with its capital at Burgos. For the next two centuries, León and Castile jointly spearheaded the war against the Moors until, by the thirteenth century, Castile had come finally to dominate her mother kingdom. These two centuries were nevertheless the period of León's greatest power, from which date most of her finest buildings.

Catedral

Pl. Regia • July–Sept Mon–Fri 8.30am–1.30pm & 4–8pm, Sat 8.30am–1.30pm & 4–6pm, Sun 8.30–11am, 1.45–2.30pm & 5–8pm; Oct–June Mon–Sat 8.30am–1.30pm & 4–7pm, Sun 8.30am–2.30pm & 5–7pm • Free • ☎ 987 875 770, ⓦ catedraldeleon.org

All eyes are drawn to León's mighty Gothic **Catedral**, which dates from the final years of the city's period of greatness. Its stained-glass **windows** in particular (thirteenth century and onwards) are equal to the masterpieces in any European cathedral – there are 2000 square metres of them (second in size only to Chartres), providing a stunning kaleidoscope of light streaming in through soaring walls of multicoloured glass. While such extensive use of glass is purely French in inspiration, the colours used here – reds, golds and yellows – are essentially Spanish. The glass screen added to the otherwise obscuring *coro* gives a clear view up to the altar, and only enhances the sensation of all-pervasive light with its bewildering refractions.

The west facade

Take a moment outside before entering to appreciate the magnificent triple-arched **west facade** (on Plaza Regia), dominated by a massive rose window and comprising two towers and a detached nave supported by flying buttresses – a pattern repeated at the south angle. Above the central doorway, the Last Judgement is in full swing, with the cooking pots of Hell doing a roaring trade in boiled sinners.

Museo Catedralicio Diocesano

July–Sept Mon–Fri 9.30am–2pm & 4–7.30pm, Sat 9.30am–2pm & 4–7pm; Oct–June Mon–Fri 9.30am–1.30pm & 4–7pm, Sat 9.30am–1.30pm; last entry 1hr before closing • Full visit €5, partial visit €3, cloisters only €2

You can walk around the main body of the cathedral and enjoy the stained glass for free, but to see the cloisters, carved choir stalls, rich side-chapels and museum treasures you have to pay to visit what's known as the **Museo Catedralicio Diocesano**; there's a separate ticket desk inside the cathedral. The full visit also includes a guided tour of the whole complex (in Spanish), though this does tend to go on a bit. You can bypass the tour by opting for a partial visit, which includes the cloister and a selection of chapels and rooms of religious art, or simply visit the **cloister** alone. This is definitely worth doing: it's magnificently carved, and there's just enough left of the faded wall frescoes and coloured detail between the delicate ribbed arches to indicate how expressively rich and vibrant the cloisters once were.

FROM TOP LEÓN CATEDRAL; TAPAS IN CASTILLA Y LEÓN PROVINCE

5

Plataforma

C/Cardenal Landazuri, to the left of the main facade • **Daytime tours** every 30min: July–Sept Tues–Fri 10am–1.30pm & 4–7.30pm, Sat 10am–1.30pm; Oct–May Tues–Fri 10am–1pm & 4–6.30pm, Sat 10am–1pm; June Tues–Sat 10am–1pm & 4–6.30pm • €3 • **Night visits** April–Sept Fri & Sat 11.30pm & 12.15am • €6 • ⓦ catedraldeleon.org/proyectocultural

The masterful stained glass and stonework of the cathedral is undergoing a long-term restoration (set to continue for around another decade) which, for once, works to visitors' advantage because a platform (the entrance is signposted "Plataforma") has been erected above the central nave to allow the craftsmen to work safely. Small-group tours are allowed up during the day to get extraordinarily close to the stained glass – it really is a quite magnificent, and very different, viewpoint to that from the main body of the church below. Summer-season night visits offer yet another perspective, as the lack of daylight brings out the natural colour of the stonework while the stained glass (now lit by artificial lighting) shines out of the dark shadows of the cathedral. Note that the ascent to the platform involves climbing a springy metal staircase up 16-metre-high scaffolding – not to everyone's taste.

Plaza Mayor and around

A couple of minutes' walk south of the cathedral lies the elegant, arcaded **Plaza Mayor**, for once not the absolute focus of attention in town and all the quieter for it, during the day at least. It's on the edge of the nightlife zone, which spills out from nearby **Plaza de San Martín**, also rather charming, though every building here is a bar or restaurant. Come the evening, and out come the pan-handlers, cigarette bums and dodgy DVD merchants, mingling with the crowds.

Plaza de Santa María del Camino

Hands-down plaza winner in León is **Plaza de Santa María del Camino**, a gorgeous cobbled square with two big shady trees, a surviving wooden arcade and the pretty Romanesque church of Nuestra Señora del Mercado – the name a reminder that the square was once the site of the city's grain market (it's still known as Plaza del Grano). The squat church tower (facing c/Herreros) is flanked by two dinky, if regal, stone lions.

Plaza del Conde Luna and around

The daily **Mercado del Conde Luna** sits in the middle of **Plaza del Conde Luna**, and offers a crash-course in Leonese cuisine, especially the meats which you'll see on every menu – not just the familiar *chorizo*, lamb and steak, but tripe and trotters, *morcilla* (blood sausage) and *costilla de cerdo* (smoked pork ribs). The market is surrounded by the old town's most characteristic shopping streets, such as c/de la Rúa and c/Azabachería – on the latter, at no. 20, for example, is the beautiful **Don Queso** cheese shop.

Palacio de los Condes de Luna

Pl. del Conde Luna • Tues–Sun 10am–8pm • Free • ☎ 987 216 794

Facing the market, the square's most historic building is the sixteenth-century **Palacio de los Condes de Luna**, former home of the counts (*condes*) of Luna, with its elegant facade and blind window arcade. It's now owned by the regional government, who in 2010 installed an exhibition celebrating the 1100-year anniversary of the kingdom of León (which lasted from 910 to 1230), a period much vaunted in these parts. It wasn't clear at the time of writing if the exhibition would continue indefinitely, but it's worth passing by to check, since the palace has been beautifully restored and may be open for other exhibitions and events.

Iglesia de San Salvador del Palat del Rey

C/Conde Luna, just off Pl. del Conde Luna • Hours vary according to exhibitions • Free

Possibly the oldest church in the city, **San Salvador** was founded by Ramiro II in the tenth century and served as an early pantheon for the Asturian kings (hence the "Palat del Rey" tag), until superseded by that of San Isidoro. There's virtually noting left of the original church, or its Mozarabic successor, but this is another building that has been lovingly restored to serve as an exhibition hall, focusing on art, architecture and photography.

Plaza de Santo Domingo

The foot of the old town is marked by a series of striking buildings ranged around the traffic circle of **Plaza de Santo Domingo**. The modest **Ayuntamiento** sits back in its own square, across the road from the Renaissance **Palacio de los Guzmanes**. But it's the mock-Gothic, exuberantly turreted **Casa de Botines** that steals the show, an early (1892–93) work of *modernista* architect Antoni Gaudí, now an exhibition space and Caja España bank building. Saint George (the Catalan patron saint) is doing his best to subdue a dragon above the entrance, while sitting on a bench opposite is a bronze statue of Gaudí himself, examining his plans for the building.

Basílica de San Isidoro

Pl. de San Isidoro • Daily 7.30am–9pm • Free

Founded by Fernando I, who united the two kingdoms of León and Castile in 1037, the mighty **Basílica de San Isidoro** was commissioned both as a shrine for the bones of San Isidoro and as a mausoleum for Fernando and his successors. Backing into the very walls of the city, it's a beautiful construction, dating mainly from the mid-twelfth century and thus one of the earliest Romanesque buildings in Spain. Two adjacent doorways show fine sculpted reliefs, of the Descent from the Cross (right) and the Sacrifice of Abraham (left), the latter surmounted by a later Renaissance pediment topped by the horse-riding San Isidoro himself. Inside, the saint's bones lie in a reliquary on the high altar.

Panteón Real

Basílica de San Isidoro, entrance on Pl. de San Isidoro • July & Aug Mon–Sat 9am–8pm, Sun 9am–2pm; Sept–June Mon–Sat 10am–1.30pm & 4–6.30pm, Sun 10am–1.30pm • €4, free Thurs pm • ☎ 987 876 171, ⊚ sanisidoroleon.net

The royal bones (of eleven kings and twelve queens) were laid to rest in tombs in the adjacent **Panteón Real** (signposted "Museo"), essentially two crypt-like chambers constructed between 1054 and 1063 as a portico of the church. It's a deeply atmospheric space, with two squat columns in the middle of the Panteón carved with thick foliage, rooted in Visigothic tradition. Moreover, towards the end of the twelfth century, these extraordinarily well preserved vaults were then covered in some of the most significant **frescoes** in Spanish Romanesque art. These present a vivid splash of colour, depicting not just biblical scenes and stories but also an agricultural calendar, for example (on the underside of one entire arch). The central dome is occupied by Christ Pantocrator surrounded by the four Evangelists depicted with animal heads – allegorical portraits that stem from the apocalyptic visions in the Bible's Book of Revelation. Your ticket also allows you to visit the cloister, as well as the small museum of glittering church treasures and the impressive library.

Museo Bíblico y Oriental

Basílica de San Isidoro, entrance at Pl. de San Martino • Tues–Sat 10am–2pm & 5–9pm, Sun 10am–2pm • €3 • ☎ 987 213 200, ⊚ biblicoyoriental.es

To the side of San Isidoro in the collegiate church buildings, the **Museo Bíblico y Oriental** is an unsung gem of a museum, home to some fascinating early manuscripts

5

and objects relating to the history, archeology and languages of the Bible and the Orient. In essence, this means an exceptional – and ravishingly displayed – collection of pages from ancient Bibles and liturgical works (with texts in Hebrew, Aramaic, Greek and Coptic), finely worked carvings and crosses from the first few centuries after Christ, and an entire series of Mesopotamian writing tablets dating back to 3500 BC. There's also a rather splendid eighteenth-century Neapolitan Nativity panorama, alive with expressive, rustic figurines.

Convento de San Marcos and around

Pl. de San Marcos • 15min walk from the old town

The pilgrim route on to Astorga lies across the old bridge on the west side of town. Here, at the opulent **Convento de San Marcos**, and on presentation of the relevant documents, pilgrims were allowed to regain their strength before the gruelling Bierzo mountains west of León. The original pilgrims' hospital and hostel was built in 1168 for the Knights of Santiago, one of several chivalric orders founded in the twelfth century to protect pilgrims and lead the Reconquest. In the sixteenth century, it was rebuilt as a kind of palatial headquarters, its massive one-hundred-metre-long facade lavishly embellished with Plateresque appliqué designs: over the main entrance, Santiago is depicted swatting Moors with ease. The monastery is now a parador, and is strictly off-limits to non guests beyond its foyer, bar and restaurant, but there are fine views of the building from the square and the nearby riverside gardens.

Iglesia San Marcos and Museo de León

Pl. de San Marcos • Tues–Sat 10am–2pm & 4–7pm, July–Sept till 5–8pm, Sun 10am–2pm • €0.60, free Sat & Sun • Guided visits (included in entry fee) Tues, Wed & Fri at 1pm, Thurs at 5.30pm

There's unimpeded access to the adjacent monastery church, the **Iglesia San Marcos**, which is vigorously speckled with the scallop-shell motif of the pilgrimage. Follow the signs through the side chapels to the **Museo de León**, housed in the sacristy. This is a collection of monumental statuary and paintings, as well as some appealing church treasures including a thirteenth-century processional cross made of rock crystal. There are also guided visits from here to see the celebrated *coro alto* of the church, which has a fine set of carved stalls by Renaissance sculptor Juan de Juni.

Museo de Arte Contemporáneo

Avda. de los Reyes Leoneses 24 • Tues–Fri 10am–3pm & 5–8pm, Sat & Sun 11am–3pm & 5–9pm • Free • ☎ 987 090 000, ⓦ musac.es • 15min walk north of San Marcos

The city's main centre for contemporary art and culture is the dazzling **Museo de Arte Contemporáneo**. The multicoloured glass facade was inspired by the stained-glass windows in the cathedral, and regularly changing exhibitions feature works and installations by Spanish and international artists.

ARRIVAL AND DEPARTURE   LEÓN

León's *casco antiguo*, with most of the historic sights and best bars and restaurants, lies east of the Río Bernesga, with the modern part of the city laid out in between. The main **train and bus stations** are on the river's west bank, from where it's a twenty-minute walk up to the cathedral. There's also a minibus shuttle (#14) that runs on the hour between 8am and 10pm (Mon–Fri only) between the bus station and Pl. de Santo Domingo, c/Ancha and Pl. Mayor.

BY TRAIN

RENFE train station Mainline train services are from the RENFE station, Avda. de Astorga on the west bank of the river (RENFE ☎ 902 320 320, ⓦ renfe.com).

FEVE train station León also has a second station, at Avda. de Padre Isla on the north side of town, from where FEVE trains (FEVE ☎ 987 271 210, ⓦ feve.es) run a long daily route to and from Bilbao.

Destinations Astorga (9 daily; 40min); Bilbao (daily; 5hr); Burgos (4 daily; 2hr); Logroño (2 daily; 4hr); Madrid (up to

11 daily; 3hr–4hr 30min); Oviedo (9 daily; 2hr); Palencia via Sahagún (up to 12 daily; 1hr–1hr 30min); Ponferrada (8 daily; 1hr 30min–2hr); Valladolid (up to 10 daily; 1hr 30min–2hr); Vigo (3 daily; 6hr 30min).

BY BUS

Estación de Autobuses Paseo del Ingenero Saenz de Miera (☎987 211 000). Alsa (ⓦalsa.es) has services to Burgos and Astorga; Abel (ⓦautocaresabel.com) to Sahagún and Palencia; Vivas (ⓦautocaresvivas.es) to Zamora/Salamanca.

Destinations Astorga/Ponferrada (hourly; 50min/2hr); Burgos (4–5 daily; 2hr direct, otherwise up to 3hr); Carrión de los Condes (daily; 2hr); Madrid (12 daily; 3hr 30min); Oviedo (9 daily; 1hr 30min); Salamanca (4–5 daily; 2hr); Valladolid (8 daily; 2hr); Zamora (4–6 daily; 2hr).

BY CAR

Parking is much easier in the modern district than the old town. Car parks are signposted as you drive in, or there's plenty of short-term street parking.

INFORMATION

Turismo Pl. Regia, opposite the cathedral (July, Aug & Easter week daily 9am–8pm; Sept–June Mon–Sat 9am–2pm & 4–7pm, Sun 9.30am–5pm; ☎987 237 082, ⓦaytoleon.com).

ACCOMMODATION

In the **casco antiguo**, there's a cluster of budget places around the atmospheric Pl. Mayor, though anything without double-glazing close to the bars and restaurants can be very noisy at night. If you're on a bigger budget, you might prefer one of the decent mid-range options nearby. The **new town** offers a greater choice of cheaper places, as well as the luxurious parador, and you're only ever a fifteen-minute walk or less from all the action.

CASCO ANTIGUO

★ **Hostal Albany** c/la Paloma 13 ☎987 264 600, ⓦalbanyleon.com. One of the best mid-range places in town, right opposite the cathedral, a spiffy, modern two-star *hostal* with compact en-suite rooms. It's a firm favourite with footsore pilgrims, and also has a great café on the square and a fine attached restaurant (see p.438). **€60**

Hostal Boccalino Pl. de San Isidoro 1 ☎987 223 060, ⓦhostalboccalino.com. Sits on a lovely square overlooking San Isidoro church. The rooms are above a café-bar, and have parquet floors, good bathrooms with decent showers, double-glazing and church views; across the square is the associated restaurant, a good-value pizza and pasta place. **€60**

★ **Hostal San Martín** Pl. Torres de Omaña 1, 2° ☎987 875 187, ⓦsanmartinhostales.com. An excellent *hostal* with simple but stylish rooms painted in pastel shades – though you can expect some noise from nearby bars if you're at the front. There's a fair choice of rooms, and you can pay as little as €25 single or €35 double if you're prepared to share bathroom facilities. **€45**

Plaza Mayor Pl. Mayor 15–17 ☎987 344 357, ⓦnh-hotels.com. Chic boutique style in a classy refit of one of the square's handsome arcaded buildings. Facilities and services are four-star standard, and include one of super-chef Ferran Adrià's *Nhube* contemporary bistro-style restaurants. Best rates are online. **€95**

NEW TOWN

Hostal Bayón c/Alcázar de Toledo 6, 2° ☎987 231 446. Handsome budget *hostal* with stripped-pine floors, high ceilings, large windows, quiet rooms and firm beds throughout. There are only five rooms, so it's essential to book ahead. **€40**

Hotel Residencia Londres Avda. de Roma 1, 1° ☎987 222 274, ⓦhostallondres.com. Large, spotless singles and doubles with cork-tile floors, some with particularly spacious bathrooms, and big windows onto the street. For breakfast, you can pop over the road to the fabulously retro *Cantabrico* café. **€45**

★ **Hotel Residencia Reina** c/Puerto de la Reina 2 ☎987 205 212, ⓦhotelreina.com. A surprisingly funky one-star hotel, quite centrally located, with excellent-value rooms (singles/doubles just with washbasin as low as €17/30), the better ones en suite. The cheery, English-speaking hosts have taken some care with the decor and furnishings, and there's a really laidback feel. **€40**

★ **Parador Hostal San Marcos** Pl. San Marcos 7 ☎987 237 300, ⓦparador.es. The sensational parador occupies one of León's most dramatic buildings. Bedrooms are of the antiques, four-poster and chandelier kind, though with all mod cons, and the best throw open windows right onto the vast square below. There's a sense of calm and majesty throughout – an enormous two-tier cloister sits at the centre of the building, and long, hushed corridors are lined with imperial rugs, ancient chests, iron tables and oil paintings. There's a good restaurant (mains from €23), and some sheltered garden seating in a quiet spot above the river. Web offers go as low as €120. **€225**

EATING, DRINKING AND NIGHTLIFE

The liveliest **tapas bars and restaurants** are found around Pl. de San Martín – an area known as the **Barrio Húmedo** (the Wet Quarter) for the amount of liquid sloshing around. Bars here will give you a free *pincho* with every drink, so you can eat pretty well if you hop from bar to bar ordering *cortos* – small tumblers of beer for around a euro or so a pop. The other good area for bars is along c/Cervantes and in the surrounding little squares, where there's a mix of traditional tapas places and more contemporary *copas* and music bars. Music **bars and clubs** tend to open Thursday to Saturday, between 11pm and 5am.

TAPAS BARS

Degustaciones Tradicionales c/Mariano Domínguez Berrueta 6 ☎987 214 732, ⓦdegustacionestradicionales .com. The "traditional tastes" in this fancily refurbished antique bar near Pl. Mayor are mainly regional cured meats and cheese, and the wine selection is excellent. Tues 8pm–midnight, Wed–Sun 1–4pm & 8pm–midnight.

La Despensa de Puerta Moneda c/Puerta Moneda 1 ☎987 170 317. A lovely little upscale grocery store that doubles as a cosy bar – *pinchos* of ham or *chorizo* are carved right off the counter, you pick a bargain glass of regional Bierzo wine and then find a place to perch amid the boxes of tomatoes, preserved vegetables and tins of peas. Mon–Fri 10am–3pm & 5–9pm, Sat 10am–3pm.

Latino Pl. San Martín 10 ☎987 262 109, ⓦrestaurantelatino.es. Right on the liveliest bar-zone square, the *Latino* is serious about its food and wine, and usually offers a choice of two free snacks with a drink. There's also a separate restaurant menu with a wide variety of Leonese dishes (€8–16), from grilled oyster mushrooms to hake casserole. Daily 1–4pm & 8pm–midnight.

★ **El Rincón del Gaucho** c/Azabachería 1, no phone. Tucked in a back alley off San Martín, this classic old-town tapas bar is best known for its delicious, garlicky *patatas gauchos*, served with every drink. Daily 1pm–midnight.

★ **La Trebede** Pl. Torres de Omaña, no phone. An intimate bar that's a bit of an Old Curiosity Shop, once you start to examine the shelves and ornaments. There's always a good *tapa* served with your drink, plus more than thirty wines by the glass. Daily 1–4pm & 8pm–midnight.

RESTAURANTS

El Besugo c/Azabachería 10 ☎987 256 995. A good choice for a well-priced meal in the bar zone – look beyond the spit-and-sawdust bar and head upstairs to the old-fashioned *comedor*, where hoary old waiters dispense a large range of *raciones* and simple meat and fish grills, with plenty of choice for under €10 (otherwise dishes up to €14, *menú del día* €12). Daily 1–4pm & 8.30pm–11pm; closed Tues.

Palacio Jabalquinto c/Juan de Arfe 2 ☎987 215 322, ⓦpalaciojabalquinto.com. Set on the first floor around the courtyard of an impressive seventeenth-century palace, with an innovative menu of *nouveau* Leonese cuisine including lots of fresh fish. Mains are €15–20, though lunch is a better deal at €20 (€30 on Sundays). Daily 1–4pm & 9–11pm.

Taberna La Piconera Pl. Santa María del Camino 2 ☎987 263 456. Lunch here on the pretty cobbled square is a treat, enjoying a simple but tasty €10 *menú* that pulls in the passing pilgrims. It's a contemporary place inside, with *raciones* to share – prawns to carpaccio – and a good line in Leonese grilled meats (dishes €8–18). Daily 1–4pm & 9–11.30pm.

★ **Las Termas** c/Paloma 13 ☎987 264 600, ⓦrestaurantelastermas.es. Connected to the *Hostal Albany*, but a sleek little number in its own right, serving creative regional cuisine at good prices (*menú del día* €13, or €20 at night Mon–Thurs, otherwise dishes €10–22). Menus change regularly, but seasonal salads (say smoked fish with balsamic vinegar) and gutsy mains (like fresh anchovies with caramelised garlic and *pimientos*) are typical. Their separate café, just around the corner facing the main square, also has the best cathedral views, and good cakes and home-made ice cream. Daily 1–3.30pm & 8.30–11.30pm.

★ **Zuloaga** c/Sierra Pambley 3 ☎987 237 814, ⓦrestaurantezuloaga.com. There's no better-looking restaurant in town, from the cobblestone bar and grand open spaces of the dining room to the romantic candlelit garden terrace. The food keeps pace too, a seasonal menu of Leonese cuisine with an unusual amount of flair and imagination. Main courses like monkfish with clams, steak in a local blue-cheese sauce or venison with wild berries start at €16, though there's a weekday lunchtime *menú* for the same price. Daily 1–4pm & 9pm–midnight.

BARS

Barry's Irish Pub Pl. Mayor 23 ☎987 000 000, ⓦbarrys.es. The main Irish pub in town, part bar and part *discoteca* at the weekends, with grandstand seats on the central plaza. Daily 6pm–3am.

Cervecería Céltica c/Cervantes 10 ☎987 230 774. Noisy beer-house that's all the rage for foreign and Spanish beers on tap, including the knock-your-socks-off Belgian brews. Daily 6pm–3am.

El Gran Café c/Cervantes 9 ☎987 272 301, ⓦelgrancafeleon.com. Rock-and-roll bar with a regular diet of indie and rock gigs, plus a free Tuesday night jam session (from 9pm) that's a city stalwart. Daily 5pm–3am.

León Antiguo Pl. Ordoño IV, no phone. A rather more civilised place than many to start the night, with an outdoor terrace overlooking the El Cid gardens and the Gaudí towers. Daily 6pm–2am.

5

NO ONE SHALL PASS

En route to Astorga, romantics will want to make the slight diversion off the highway to the small town of **Hospital de Órbigo**, 36km southwest of León. It was here, legend has it, that in 1434 Don Suero de Quiñones, a jilted knight, defeated three hundred men in a jousting tournament at the town's famous twenty-arched medieval bridge. Standing on the beautifully restored bridge today, it's easily imagined – astride a horse, furious at the world, picking off all-comers with a whacking great lance. And as only foot traffic is allowed, the long, cobbled bridge is still one of those places where the Camino de Santiago really reaches back into history, with knots of hiking pilgrims crossing all day, falling gratefully into one of the small cafés at the Astorga end of the bridge.

DIRECTORY

Concerts Main city concert hall is the Auditorio Ciudad de León, Avda. Reyes Leonese 4 (☎987 244 663, ⓦauditoriociudaddeleon.net), for everything from symphony orchestras to Gregorian choirs.
Hospital Hospital San Juan de Dios, Avda. San Ignacio de Loyola 73 ☎987 232 500.
Laundry Lavandería La Paloma, c/Paloma 6 (closed Sat pm).
Police Policía Municipal, Paseo del Parque (☎987 255 500, emergency ☎092); Policía Nacional, Villa Benavente 6 (☎987 218 900, emergency ☎091).
Post office Main branch at the southern end of Avda. de Independencia, by Pl. de San Francisco (Mon–Fri 10am–2pm & 4.30–8.30pm, Sat 10am–2pm).
Taxis Radio Taxi León ☎987 261 415; Taxi Villaquilambe ☎987 285 355.

Astorga

For the very fittest of the pilgrims, it was one day's walk (50km) southwest of León to the next major stop at **ASTORGA**. The town has a long history – originally settled by the Romans (of whom many traces remain), sacked by the Moors in the eleventh century, then rebuilt and endowed with the usual hospices and monasteries, but as the pilgrimage lost popularity in the late Middle Ages, Astorga fell into decline. These days it's a bustling, if small, provincial capital that once again places much emphasis on the pilgrimage, full of footsore hikers and Santiago souvenir shops, not to mention an incongruously grand cathedral and an even more out-of-place *modernista* bishop's palace, the latter now used as a museum dedicated to the *camino*.

Catedral de Santa María

Pl. Catedral • **Catedral** Mon–Sat 9–11.30am, Sun 11am–1pm • Free **Museo Catedralicio** May–Sept Tues–Sat 10am–2pm & 4–8pm, Sun 11am–2pm; Oct–April Tues–Sat 11am–2pm & 4–6pm, Sun 11am–2pm • €2.50, joint ticket with Museo de los Caminos €4 • ☎987 615 820

Astorga's **Catedral de Santa María** looks better than it has in centuries after a thorough restoration. Built between 1471 and 1693 (though on the site of a much older church), it has notable twin towers either side of the majestically carved main door, one in pink-tinged stone, one in green, colours that are repeated inside the nave on the soaring fluted columns. You can join worshippers and see the cathedral for free in the morning, but sightseers are encouraged to buy a ticket for the **Museo Catedralicio**, which in any case includes a visit to the church. Even if you're not normally interested in ecclesiastical treasures, the beautifully presented series of museum rooms is worth seeing. As well as the usual cases of robes, capes, mitres, crosses and chalices, there are some remarkable pieces here, from a beautiful painted twelfth-century wooden tomb to a pair of carved lions on hind legs holding candles in their paws.

5

Museo de los Caminos

Pl. Eduardo del Castro • May–Sept Tues–Sat 10am–2pm & 4–8pm, Sun 11am–2pm; Oct–April Tues–Sat 11am–2pm & 4–6pm, Sun 11am–2pm • €2.50, joint ticket with Museo Catedralicio €4

Standing across from the cathedral – and to many minds, upstaging it – the **Palacio Episcopal**, or Bishop's Palace, was commissioned by a Catalan bishop from his architect countryman Antoni Gaudí in 1887. It's a quite extraordinary building, more so inside than out, though even the exterior resembles some kind of horror-movie castle. Gaudí took the Gothic style as his inspiration and ran with it, resulting in a building of soaring brick and tile arches, intricate decorative work and luminous stained glass, culminating in an exquisite chapel that beats anything in the next-door cathedral hands down. The spectacular palace rooms now house the **Museo de los Caminos**, which traces the story of the pilgrimage through statues and artworks dating from its medieval origins, as well as examples of the documents issued at Santiago to certify that pilgrims had "travelled, confessed and obtained absolution". There's also a basement full of Roman altars and funerary statues and an attic devoted to contemporary regional art – together with a bird's-eye view down into the shining chapel.

Museo Romano

Pl. de San Bartolomé • May–Sept Tues–Sat 10.30am–2.30pm & 5–7.30pm, Sun 10.30am–2.30pm; Oct–April Tues–Sat 10am–1.30pm & 4–6pm, Sun 10am–1.30pm • €2.50 • ☎ 987 616 937

Astorga's Roman past is covered in the fascinating **Museo Romano**, which displays local archeological finds alongside changing exhibitions on various themes. However, the town also preserves a rich set of excavated remains, including a surviving "Bear and Birds" mosaic in a wealthy private Roman house, the **Casa Romana** – located just a few steps along the road from the museum.

Jardín de la Sinagoga

P. San Francisco • Always open • Free

Astorga is ringed by an almost complete circuit of **walls**, late Roman in origin though much added to over the centuries. It's only a short walk from the Roman museum to the **Jardín de la Sinagoga**, which retains a section of the old Roman sewer system and is also the best place for a view from the walls out over the plains beyond.

ARRIVAL AND DEPARTURE   **ASTORGA**

By train The train station is a long way from the town centre, and it makes far more sense to arrive and depart by bus.

By bus The bus station on Avda. de la Murallas (☎ 987 619 100) is centrally located, right opposite the Palacio Episcopal; there are frequent services from León and Ponferrada.

Destinations León (hourly; 50min); Ponferrada (hourly; 1hr); Villafranca del Bierzo (4–6 daily; 1hr 40min).

By car Free parking is easy outside of the old town, either in the bays along the bus station road opposite the Palacio Episcopal, or in the large car park a little further down under the town walls.

THE MARAGATOS

Astorga is the traditional market town of the **Maragatos**, a distinct ethnic group of unknown origin, possibly descended from the Berbers of North Africa, who crossed into Spain with the first Moorish incursions of the early eighth century. For several centuries, they dominated the Spanish carrying trade with their mule trains. Marrying only among themselves, they maintained their traditions and individuality well into recent decades. However, apart from the locally famous Maragato *cocido* – a typically hearty stew made with up to seven types of meat and sausage, plus chickpeas and cabbage – their only obvious legacy to Astorga is the pair of colourful clockwork figures dressed in traditional costume who jerk into action to strike the hour on the town-hall clock in Plaza Mayor.

INFORMATION

Turismo Pl. Eduardo de Castro 5, across from the Palacio Episcopal (Tues–Sat 10am–1.30pm & 4–6.30pm, Sun 10am–1.30pm; ☎987 618 222, ⓦ ayuntamientodeastorga .com).

ACCOMMODATION AND EATING

Astorga is an easy day-trip from León, but there's plenty of agreeable central accommodation if you fancied staying the night. Local **restaurants**, meanwhile, all advertise the delights of the *cocido maragato* (see box, p.440) for around €18 per head – you eat the meats first, then the veg, then drink the broth, and good luck in finishing what tend to be gigantic portions. Astorga also has a reputation for its chocolate, production of which flourished here in the eighteenth and nineteenth centuries; there's even a chocolate museum in town and plenty of shops to buy the stuff in. Nicest places for a drink and a bite of tapas are the **cafés** and **bars** around Astorga's finest square, Pl. Mayor.

★ **Casa de Tepa** c/Santiago 2 ☎987 603 299, ⓦ rusticae.es. Most atmospheric lodging in town is this handsome eighteenth-century townhouse with ten quiet, refined rooms (traditionally furnished, though with marble rain-shower bathrooms), and a sunny terrace-garden where you can eat breakfast in summer. It's run with a personal, charming touch, with the tone set by the displayed greetings cards from the Spanish royal family. In August prices are €10 higher, for a bit more space in a suite add €25, while private parking costs €10. **€90**

La Pesesta Pl. de San Bartolomé 3, just off Pl. Mayor ☎987 617 275, ⓦ restaurantelapeseta.com. There's no quibbling among the locals when it comes to the town's best regional restaurant, in the hands of the same family for five generations (founded 1871). Specialities, apart from the ubiquitous *cocido maragato*, are *alubias con almejas* (beans with clams), or anything from lamb to spicy *bacalao*, with mains in the entirely-reasonable-for-the-quality €11–15 range. There are also fifteen straightforward *hostal* rooms upstairs. Restaurant Mon 1–4pm & 9–11pm, Tues 1–4pm, Wed–Sat 1–4pm & 9–11pm. **€60**

Castrillo de los Polvazares

A fascinating side-trip from Astorga takes in the improbably pretty village of **Castrillo de los Polvazares**, considered to be an archetypal Maragato settlement (see box, above), and now zealously preserved as a local heritage showpiece. There's basically one long main cobbled street, and a small, stork-topped church, with the rest being a charming collection of eighteenth-century, russet-coloured stone cottages flaunting window boxes and signs advertising honey (*miel*) for sale. Only residents can drive in (there's a car park by the bridge at the entrance to the village), so catch Castrillo at the right time – traffic free, and only the cobbled footfall of pilgrims to disturb the timeless scene – and it resembles nothing so much as a Hardyesque Wessex village. There are several cafés and restaurants, and three or four places to stay if you fancied a quiet night out of town instead.

ARRIVAL AND DEPARTURE

By car Castrillo de los Polvazares is 5km west of Astorga on road LE142; by car, follow the "todos direcciones" and "Benavente" signs out of the centre to the roundabout and

CASTRILLO DE LOS POLVAZARES

look for the sign, or on foot follow any backpacking pilgrim, as the *camino* runs from Astorga straight to the village.

ACCOMMODATION AND EATING

Hostería Casa Coscolo ☎987 691 984, ⓦ casacoscolo .com. Not just hiking pilgrims will fall gratefully into this little hotel in the lovely village of Castrillo de los Polvazares. The restored stone and wood house has four simple rooms, brightly furnished in different seasonal colours, and a restaurant on hand to introduce you to the *cocido maragato* and other regional dishes. It's right by the church – the charming street address, which you don't need, is El Rincón (ie, the corner). Restaurant 1–4pm & 9–11pm, winter hours can vary. **€60**

5

Ponferrada

At first sight, the heavily industrialized, bowl-shaped valley centred on the large town of **PONFERRADA** seems to have little to offer, but the mountainous terrain of the Bierzo has scenery as picturesque as any in Spain. The town itself sums up this dichotomy, dominated by its outlying industrial concerns and spreading suburbs, yet with a charming, unspoiled old quarter, through which trudge weary pilgrims girding their loins for the mountains to come. Old and new towns are separated by the Río Sil, spanned by the iron bridge that gave Ponferrada its name, above which loom the high walls of the impressive castle.

Plaza del Ayuntamiento and around

The old town at least is worth a slow stroll and a cup of coffee in one of the restored squares. From the main square, **Plaza del Ayuntamiento**, the obvious route passes through the quaint **Puerta del Reloj** (Clock Gateway), heading down to pretty **Plaza Virgen de la Encina**, which is overlooked by the town's finest Renaissance church and the curtain wall of the castle.

Castillo de los Templarios

Avda. del Castillo • May–Sept Tues–Sat 4.30–8.30pm, Sun 11am–2pm; Oct–April Tues–Sat 11am–2pm & 4–6pm, Sun 11am–2pm • €6 • ☎ 987 402 244

There are a couple of local museums in Ponferrada, but the only essential sight is the one you can hardly miss – the **Castillo de los Templarios**, which stands high above the river. Established by the Knights Templars in the thirteenth century, it's a textbook castle with fancy turrets and battlements, all gleaming after a handsome restoration.

ARRIVAL AND DEPARTURE   PONFERRADA

By train and bus The train station is centrally located, on the edge of the town centre. From the bus station, head across the open space outside to the far left-hand corner to pick up c/General Gómez Nuñez (subsequently Avda. Pérez Colino) and walk straight down it for 10min to reach the river, from where you'll see the castle up on your left.

By car If you're driving from Astorga, you'll hit the old town first, on the east side of the Río Sil, and can avoid the new section altogether. There's parking on the edge of the old town, as well as under Pl. del Ayuntamiento, or free street parking on the bridge, below the castle.

INFORMATION

Turismo c/Gil y Carrasco 4, by the castle (Sept–May Mon–Sat 10am–2pm & 4–7pm, Sun 10am–2pm; June–Aug Mon–Sat 10am–2pm & 4–8.30pm, Sun 10am–2pm; ☎ 987 424 236, ⓦ ponferrada.org/turismo).

ACCOMMODATION, EATING AND DRINKING

There are plenty of **hotels** and *hostales* in the new town, all signposted as you drive in (and detailed on the tourist office website). But it's nicest to stay in the old quarter, where there's a simple choice.

Hotel Aroi Bierzo Plaza Pl. del Ayuntamiento 4 ☎ 987 409 001, ⓦ aroihoteles.com. Charming warm-toned rooms in a converted townhouse on the main square, with nice views from the windows. You can also grab an outdoor table for tapas and drinks from *La Taberna* (the former wine cellar), and there's contemporary regional cuisine in the hotel's *La Violeta* restaurant (mains €16–24). Restaurant 1–4pm & 9–11pm. **€80**

La Capricciosa c/Paraisín 1, at Pl. Virgen de la Encina ☎ 987 111 603, ⓦ lacapricciosa.es. Prime position, with views over the pretty square, church and castle walls. It's an Italian place, with pizzas (€7–9) from the wood-fired oven – though they also use the traditional oven for pricier roast lamb and suckling pig dishes. Daily noon–4pm & 7pm–midnight; closed Tues.

Hotel Los Templarios c/Flórez Osorio 3 ☎ 987 411 484, ⓦ hotellostemplarios.info. Straightforward budget rooms in a small hotel with its own restaurant (*menú del día* €12). You'll find it just through the Clock Gateway from the main square. Restaurant 1–4pm & 9–11pm. **€50**

Las Médulas

Twenty kilometres southwest of Ponferrada lie **Las Médulas**, the jagged remains of hills ravaged by Roman strip-mining. Nine hundred thousand tonnes of gold were ripped from the hillsides using specially constructed canals, leaving an eerie, mesmerizing landscape reminiscent of Arizona, peppered with caves and needles of red rock. Just outside Carucedo (on the N536), the road splits, with the right fork leading 3km up to the village of Las Médulas. This is a pretty place of restored stone houses, climbing roses and spreading chestnut trees set behind the largest rock outcrops, with a gaggle of studiously rustic cafés and bars that caters for day-trippers.

Aula Arqueológica and local walks

Las Médulas · April–Sept daily 10am–1.30pm & 4–8pm; Oct–March Sat 10am–1.30pm & 3.30–6pm, Sun 10am–2pm · €1.50

There's information on the region in the visitor centre, the **Aula Arqueológica**, outside which you'll have to park as cars aren't allowed into the village. Various signposted **trails** lead into the dramatic mine workings, the shortest being the hike to Somido lake (3km return; 45min), for great views of the outcrops, and the Las Valiños trail (4km; 1hr 15min), which takes you partly inside the old mines themselves.

Mirador de Orellán

The **Mirador de Orellán** offers the most spectacular panorama over the whole area of crumbling peaks. A detour of the Las Valiños trail leads up here, or you can drive directly by taking the left fork out of Carucedo and winding up for 4.5km, through the village of Orellán. It's a steep six-hundred-metre walk from the car park to the viewing platforms.

Villafranca del Bierzo

The last halt before the climb into Galicia, **VILLAFRANCA DEL BIERZO**, 22km from Ponferrada, was where pilgrims on their last legs could chicken out of the final trudge. Those who arrived at the Puerta del Perdón (Door of Forgiveness) at the simple Romanesque **church of Santiago** could receive the same benefits of exemption of years in Purgatory as in Santiago de Compostela itself. The town itself is quietly enchanting, with a jumble of old-town streets, slate-roofed houses, encircling hills, cool mountain air and the clear Río Burbia providing a setting vaguely reminiscent of the English Lake District. The historic pilgrim connection makes it a great place to stop for the night, with plenty of reasonably priced accommodation and a multitude of restaurants offering good-value pilgrim *menús*.

ARRIVAL AND DEPARTURE

VILLAFRANCA DEL BIERZO

By bus and car Hourly buses from Ponferrada stop near the parador, on the edge of town as you drive in. For parking, keep straight on right through Pl. Mayor to reach the parking spaces by the town gardens.

ACCOMMODATION AND EATING

Hotel San Francisco ☎987 540 465, ⊛hotelsanfrancisco.org. If you want a step up from simple pilgrim lodgings, but don't want to break the bank, the small one-star hotel on the central plaza is a decent bet. **€55**

Parador de Villafranca del Bierzo Avda. Calvo Sotelo ☎987 540 175, ⊛parador.es. Local standards are set by the recently refurbished parador, just three minutes' walk from Pl. Mayor. It's clad in local stone and slate, with comfortable rooms looking out over the local hills, a small vine-shaded terrace and both indoor and outdoor swimming pools. There are good room offers on the website, while the restaurant is the best place to eat in town. Restaurant 1–4pm & 9–11pm. **€135**

Euskal Herria: the País Vasco and Navarra

PLAYA DE LA CONCHA, SAN SEBASTIÁN (P.453)

Euskal Herria: the País Vasco and Navarra

The name the Basque people give to their own land, Euskal Herria, covers the three Basque provinces that today form the *Comunidad Autónoma del País Vasco* (in Basque, "Euskadi") – Gipuzkoa, Bizkaia and Araba – as well as Navarra (Nafarroa) and part of southwestern France. Much of this region is immensely beautiful, and especially so along the coast, where green and thickly forested mountains, interspersed with stark individual hills, seem in places to emerge from the sea itself. Yes, it often rains, and much of the time the countryside is shrouded in a fine mist, but so long as you don't mind the occasional shower, summer here offers a glorious escape from the unrelenting heat of the south.

Despite the heavy industrialization that has helped to make this one of the wealthiest areas in Spain, **Euskal Herria** is remarkably unspoiled – neat and quiet inland, rugged and wild along the coast. **San Sebastián** is a major resort city, with superb if crowded beaches and magnificent food, but lesser-known, similarly attractive villages line the coast all the way to **Bilbao**, home to the magnificent Museo Guggenheim. Inland, **Pamplona** boasts its exuberant Fiestas de San Fermín, while many other destinations have charms of their own, from the drama of the **Pyrenees** to the laidback elegance of **Vitoria-Gasteiz**.

Look out especially for quiet rural **accommodation** options, here in abundance thanks to the Basque government's **nekazalturismoa** (*agroturismo*) programme, which offers the opportunity to stay in traditional Basque farmhouses and private homes, usually in areas of outstanding beauty, at very reasonable cost (€45–75). In Navarra, as in much of the country, these are known as **casas rurales**, or *landa exteak*. You can get details from the region's many excellent local **tourist offices** (which also handle bookings), or online at ⓦnekatur.net, and, for Navarra, ⓦcasasruralesnavarra.com.

While a reasonable network of **buses** connects all the sizeable towns, the easiest way to get around the Basque Country is by car. In particular, if you want to follow the coast, the dramatic hills and cliffs mean there isn't always a shoreline road; with public transport especially you have to keep returning to the main roads way inland. **Train** services are relatively poor. San Sebastián lies on a major route to and from France, which also passes through Vitoria-Gasteiz, but Bilbao is off the main line on a minor spur, and direct trains between Bilbao and San Sebastián are much slower than the equivalent buses. Bilbao is, however, the eastern terminus of the entirely separate **FEVE** narrow-gauge railway (ⓦfeve.es), which follows the Atlantic coast west to Santander, Oviedo and beyond.

Brief history

When the **Romans** invaded, they defeated a group called the Aquitani, who inhabited large areas of southwestern Gaul and northern Iberia, and spoke an ancestral version of Basque. However, they allowed the wild tribes known as the Vascones, who lived in the

Highlights

❶ **Playa de La Concha, San Sebastián** This graceful crescent strand, curving away from the delightful old town, has to count as one of the greatest urban beaches in the world. **See p.453**

❷ **Pintxos** The Basques prepare their tapas with a real gourmet flair, so snacking is an irresistible treat – especially in San Sebastián. **See p.459**

❸ **Mundaka estuary** Sublime scenery; world-class surfing; the beautiful seaside village of Mundaka; and Gernika, the Basque spiritual capital. **See p.467**

❹ **Museo Guggenheim, Bilbao** This swirling titanium edifice has become the symbol of the regenerated city. **See p.469**

❺ **Bodegas Ysios** An architectural extravaganza, designed to celebrate the rich red wines of Rioja. **See p.483**

❻ **Fiestas de San Fermín** Pamplona's famous fiesta is rowdy, dirty and lunatic, but for once the bulls get a fair shot. **See p.486**

❼ **Olite** Delightful village of ochre-coloured stone mansions on the edge of the Navarran plains. **See p.493**

❽ **Bardenas Reales** This eerie Wild-West desertscape is perhaps the last thing you'd expect to find in the Basque Country. **See p.495**

HIGHLIGHTS ARE MARKED ON THE MAP ON PP.448–449

EUSKAL HERRIA: THE PAÍS VASCO & NAVARRA

N

Bordeaux

Hondarribia
Hendaye
Larrun
(900m)
Urdazubi-
Urdax

2 Errenteria
Irún
Bera de
Bidasoa
Amaiur-
Maia
Erratzu

San Sebastían-
Donostia

Hernani

FRANCE

Pau

Elizondo

Oronoz-
Mugairi

P Y R E N E E S

Auritz-
Burguete
Orreaga-
Roncesvalles

Santuario
de San Miguel

Arakil

Ochagavía
Isaba

Roncal

6 Pamplona

NAVARRA

Fecho

Ansó

Lumbier

Monasterio de
San Salvador de Leyre

Puente
La Reina

Yesa

Javier

Pantano de
Yesa

Jaca

Estella

Monasterio
de Irache

Sangüesa

San Martín
de Unx
Ujué

Tafalla

7 Olite

Sos del Rey
Católico

ARAGÓN

Calahorra

Olmedo

Alfaro

PARQUE
NATURAL
BARDENAS
REALES

8

Arguedas

Ejea de los
Caballeros

Huesca

Tudela

Cervera del
Río Alhama

Rio Ebro

Tarazona

Zaragoza

HIGHLIGHTS

1 Playa de la Concha
2 Pintxos
3 Mundaka estuary
4 Museo Guggenheim
5 Bodegas Ysios
6 Fiestas de San Fermín
7 Olite
8 Bardenas Reales

0 — 25
kilometres

THE BASQUES

The origins of **the Basques** remain mysterious. They are a distinct people, generally with a different build from the French and Spanish and a different blood group distribution from the rest of Europe. Their language, the complex **Euskara**, is unrelated to any other, and was already spoken in Spain when Indo-European languages such as Celtic and Latin began to arrive from the East three thousand years ago. Written records were scarce until the first books in Euskara were published in the mid-sixteenth century; language and culture were maintained instead through oral traditions, including that of the *bertsolariak* – popular poets specializing in improvised verse, a tradition still alive today.

Archeological and genetic evidence suggests that the Basque people may be the last surviving representatives of Europe's first modern human population, commonly known as **Cro-Magnon man**. Skull fragments, believed to date from around 9000 BC, have been shown to be identical to present-day Basque cranial formation. Much anthropological work, above all by the revered José Miguel de Barandiarán (who died in 1991, aged 101), lends itself to the view that the Basques have continuously inhabited the western Pyrenees for thousands of years.

mountains of Euskal Herria, to keep their language and independence in return for allowing free passage and trading rights.

Later rulers were not so accommodating. Successive **Visigoth** kings tried and failed to eradicate the Basques. The **Moors** conquered the lowlands of Araba (Alava in Castilian) and Navarra as far north as Pamplona, but never gained a grip on the mountainous north. This new enemy, however, forced the Basques, hitherto a collection of more or less allied tribes, to unite. In 818, a Basque leader, Iñigo Iñiguez, was proclaimed the first ruler of the **Kingdom of Navarre**. In due course, the Basques embraced Christianity, while retaining ancestral customs including the ancient laws by which they governed themselves. First written down (in Castilian) during the twelfth century, these laws and privileges, maintained as oral traditions, were known as **fueros**.

Once the Reconquest was complete and Spain was being welded into a single kingdom, Navarre (by now ruled by French monarchs) was a missing piece. The Reyes Católicos persuaded the Bizkaians, Gipuzkoans and Arabans to split away from Navarre and join Castile. In return the *fueros* would be respected, including exemption from customs duty, conscription and central taxation. Under duress, the Navarrese agreed to the same deal, and by 1512 all four territories were subject to rule from Madrid. The Basques have jealously defended their right to self-government ever since.

Basque nationalism

Basque determination for self-rule increased when the Liberals, victors in the Carlist War, abolished the *fueros* in 1876. The late nineteenth and early twentieth centuries saw the emergence of Basque nationalism as an ideology. The conservative **Basque Nationalist Party** (PNV) was founded in 1895 by Sabino Arana, the son of a Carlist shipbuilder.

At the start of the Civil War, the Nationalists seized control of predominantly conservative Navarra and Araba, while Bizkaia and Gipuzkoa, dominated by left-leaning industrial cities, supported the Republic. After Navarrese troops captured Irun in 1936 and cut off the northern Republican zone from France, San Sebastián rapidly surrendered. An autonomous Basque government, in practice limited to Bizkaia, lasted just nine months. Franco finally conquered the Basques in June 1937, after a vicious campaign that included the infamous German bombing of **Gernika**.

After the war, Franco's boot went in hard. Public use of the Basque language was forbidden and central control was asserted with the gun. But state violence succeeded only in nurturing a new resistance, **ETA** (Euskadi ta Askatasuna – "Basque Homeland and Freedom"), founded in 1959. Its most spectacular success was the assassination in Madrid of Franco's right-hand man and probable successor, Admiral Carrero Blanco in 1973.

Separatism today

Things started to change following the **transition to democracy**. The new constitution granted the Basques limited autonomy, with their own parliament and tax collection. Today, there's a regional police force, the red-bereted *ertzaintza*, and the Basque language is taught in schools and universities. The Basque flag (*ikurriña*) flies everywhere. Basque demands for independence have not ended, however, and the violence has continued. Since 1968, ETA is estimated to have killed around 850 people, with targets ranging from members of the Spanish police and armed forces to Basque businessmen and politicians, academics, journalists, the tourist industry and random civilians. At the time of writing, however, the latest in a long succession of ceasefires was appearing to hold, while Basque separatists were achieving electoral success as part of the Bildu coalition, raising hopes of a new era of peace.

FIESTAS

JANUARY

19–20: Festividad de San Sebastián Twenty-four hours of festivities, including a *tamborrada*, a march with pipes and drums.

FEBRUARY

Weekend before Ash Wednesday: Carnaval Throughout the region, but especially in Bilbao, San Sebastián and Tolosa.

MARCH/APRIL

March 4–12 A series of pilgrimages to the castle at Javier, birthplace of San Francisco Javier.
Semana Santa (Holy Week) Extensive Easter celebrations in Vitoria; also in Segura.
Easter Sunday: Aberri Eguna The Basque National Day celebrated, particularly in Bilbao.
April 28: Fiesta de San Prudencio Celebrated with *tamborradas* in Vitoria.

JUNE

24: Fiestas de San Juan In Lekeitio, Laguardia and Tolosa.
Last week: Fiesta de San Pedro In Mundaka, with Basque dancing.

JULY

First week: Fiesta at Zumaia with dancing, Basque sports and an *encierro* on the beach.
7–14: Fiestas de San Fermín In Pamplona, featuring the famous Running of the Bulls.
22: Fiesta de la Magdalena In Bermeo, with torch-lit processions of fishing boats and the usual races and Basque sports.
24–28: *Encierro* in Tudela.

AUGUST

First weekend: Patron saint's celebration in Estella.
4–9: Fiesta de la Virgen Blanca In Vitoria, with bullfights, fireworks and *gigantones*.
14–17: Fiestas de Andra Mari In Ondarroa.
15: Semana Grande An explosion of celebration: notably in Bilbao, with Basque games and races; Gernika with an *encierro*; and San Sebastián, where the highlight is an International Fireworks Competition.

SEPTEMBER

First week: Euskal Jaiak Basque games in San Sebastián.
4: Fiesta de San Antolín In Lekeitio, where the local youth attempt to knock the head off a goose.
9: Día del Pescador In Bermeo.
12: *Encierro* in Sangüesa.
14: Patron saint's day in Olite, with yet more bulls.
Last two weeks: International Film Festival In San Sebastián.

San Sebastián

Making the most of its glorious location, curving languidly around a magnificent semicircular bay that's lined with golden sand, **SAN SEBASTIÁN** ranks among the great resort cities of Europe. Although it's the capital of its region, Gipuzkoa, and has a reputation as a hotbed of Basque nationalism, it has never been a major port, or much of an industrial centre. Instead its primary identity, ever since the Spanish royal family first decamped here for the summer in 1845, has been as a summer playground. In July and August especially, it tends to be packed out, and its hotels are among the most expensive in Spain.

While the superb sheltered **beach** on its very doorstep is the biggest attraction of all, San Sebastián also boasts a charming old-town core, the **Casco Viejo**, squeezed up against the foot of verdant Monte Urgull. The new town to the south, known as **Centro** and the commercial hub of the city, holds a fine crop of century-old *belle époque* edifices, though they're interspersed between rather too many dreary newer buildings for this to be an area where you're likely to spend much time.

The official name of the city, **Donostia-San Sebastián**, is a tautology, in that Donostia is a Basque name for Saint Sebastian. Some say Sebastian was martyred in the Roman port of Ostia, and is thus the Don (saint) of Ostia; others that Ostia (or Osti) is simply an abbrevation of Sebastian.

Casco Viejo

Although San Sebastián's old town, or **Casco Viejo**, does indeed stand on the site where the city first developed, almost nothing you see predates the disastrous fire, set by British troops, which devastated the town in 1813. As a result, with little trace of its original walls surviving either, it's a formal grid far removed from the typical old quarters of other Spanish cities. Nonetheless, it's as much of a delight as any, its narrow streets and occasional pretty squares thronged in the daytime with shoppers and sightseers, and at night with revellers eager to sample its legendary crop of *pintxos* bars and restaurants.

At the heart of the Casco Viejo, the **Plaza de la Constitución** makes a great arena for the city's many festivals. It even served as a bullring in the past; hence the numbers painted on the balconies to all sides. Amazingly, each window originally belonged to a separate apartment, each barely wider than a corridor; many of the dividing walls have now been removed, however, to make larger living spaces.

Museo San Telmo

Pl. Zuloaga • Tues–Sun 10am–8pm • €5 • ⓦ santelmomuseoa.com

Reopened in spectacular new premises in 2011, the **Museo San Telmo** ambitiously sets out to trace the cultural and spiritual evolution of human beings from their very earliest origins. The focus soon narrows, however, towards simply accounting for the state of Basque society today. Displays use everyday artefacts from every period to illustrate both continuity and change. In addition, the museum also holds a wide-ranging collection of paintings from the fifteenth century onwards, again with a focus on Basque artists.

SAN SEBASTIÁN'S FESTIVALS

San Sebastián's busy annual calendar of fiestas and festivals kicks off on the stroke of midnight at the start of January 20, the feast day of its namesake saint. Carnival too is celebrated in style, but the two biggest events of the year are the five-day **Jazz Festival** in late July (☎943 481 900, ⓦjazzaldia.com), which attracts some of the world's best-known performers and DJs, and the week-long **Film Festival** in the second half of September (ⓦsansebastianfestival.com).

Basílica de Santa María

C/Mayor • Mon–Sat 8am–2pm & 4–8pm • Free

Visible all the way from the unremarkable cathedral in the new town, the Baroque facade of the **Basílica de Santa María** dominates the far end of the slender c/Mayor, the main artery of the old town. Although it dates from the eighteenth century, it only became a basilica following a Papal visit in 1966; the pope's coat of arms can be seen along with a caravel of the kind used by Columbus, and an image of San Sebastián himself. You enter the main door to find that thanks to the church's squashed-up position below Monte Urgull, the nave unexpectedly stretches not straight ahead of you but from side to side, with a huge altarpiece to your right and an alabaster Greek cross by Eduardo Chillida above the font to your left.

Monte Urgell

San Sebastián was originally founded as a fishing settlement at the foot of the wooded **Monte Urgell**, a steep headland that until the slender connecting spit was built over was virtually an island in its own right. It takes barely twenty minutes to walk around the base of the hill, along a level path that offers tremendous sunset views, or a little longer to climb up to its summit via one of the many trails and stairways that lead up from the Casco Viejo. Topped by a massive statue of Christ, which towers over the Castillo de la Mota, the hillside intersperses formal gardens and wilder stretches, one of which, on the far side, cradles a small **cemetery** devoted to English soldiers who died during the First Carlist War, in the 1830s.

Castillo de la Mota

Monte Urgell • May–Sept daily 11am–8pm; Oct–April Tues–Fri 10am–2pm & 3–5.30pm, Sat & Sun 10am–5.30pm • €1

The **castle** atop Monte Urgell would be worth entering simply to enjoy the magnificent views across the city and bay, but it also holds an enjoyable **museum**. Its entertaining romp through the city's history begins with the eleventh century, but focuses especially on the growth of tourism, with some great photos and film footage from the 1920s and 1930s.

Aquarium

April–June & Sept Mon–Fri 10am–8pm, Sat & Sun 10am–9pm; July & Aug daily 10am–9pm; Oct–March Mon–Fri 10am–7pm, Sat & Sun 10am–8pm • €12, under-13s €6 • ⓦ aquariumss.com

San Sebastián's modern **aquarium** occupies a large concrete building on the harbourfront outside the old town below Monte Urgull. To some visitors' disappointment, it's as much museum as aquarium, recounting the history of the Basque relationship with the sea, and exhibiting an entire whale skeleton. Nonetheless, it does hold tanks filled with live fish, the largest of which enables visitors to walk through a glass tunnel while fearsome sharks swim overhead.

Playa de La Concha

Ferries to Santa Clara: every 30min in summer, daily 10am–8pm • €3

The glorious crescent of sand that curves all the way west from the old town to the pleasant but unremarkable suburb of Ondarreta, the **Playa de La Concha**, has to rank among the very finest city beaches in the world. Even in the depths of winter it's usually busy with walkers and playing children, while on summer days every inch tends to be covered in roasting flesh. Swimmers keen to escape the crowds can head out to floating platforms moored offshore. Slightly further out, a little pyramidal island, the **Isla de Santa Clara**, is accessible via regular ferries that set off from near the aquarium, just outside the old town. Also at the old-town end of the beach, the strange-looking building that resembles a boat seen side-on is the **Real Club Náutico** (Royal Sailing Club), built in the Rationalist style in 1928.

6

SAN SEBASTIÁN: CASCO VIEJO

Castillo de la Mota
Museo San Telmo
PZA. DE ZULOAGA
Iglesia de San Vicente
Kursaal
Basílica de Santa María
MONTE URGELL
Aquarium

MONTE IGELDO
Parque de Atracciones
El Peine de los Vientos
Isla de Santa Clara

Funicular Railway

Real Club de Tennis
Bahía de la Concha

Playa de Ondarreta

Palacio de Miramar

Playa de La Concha

ONDARRETA
Parque del Palacio Real de Miramar
MIRAKONTXA

ANTIGUO

ACCOMMODATION			
Albergue La Sirena Ondarreta	13	Pensión Aida	9
Hotel de Londres y de Inglaterra	10	Pensión Amaiur	2
		Pensión Anne	6
Hotel Ezeiza	12	Pensión Basic Confort	4
Hotel María Cristina	7	Pensión Bellas Artes	14
Hotel Parma	1	Pensión Edorta	5
Hotel Record	8	Pensión Izar Bat	3
		Pensión La Perla	11

CLUBS	
Bar Be Bop	1
Bataplán	2

SAN SEBASTIÁN

MAR CANTÁBRICO

Punta del Castillo

Cementario de
los Ingleses

Castillo de
la Mota

Iglesia
de San
Vicente

Basílica de
Santa María

CASCO
VIEJO

Real Club
Náutico

Ayuntamiento

Parque de
Aldérdi Eder

CENTRO

Catedral del
Buen Pastor

Parque
Basoerdi

EuskoTren
(Estación
de Amara)

Parque
Araba

ORLANS

Playa de la Zurriola

Kursaal

GROS

Mercado
Central

RENFE
Station
(Estación
del Norte)

Río Urumea

Parque de
Cristina Enea

Río Urumea

● RESTAURANTS

Aralar	11
Arzak	21
Bokado	19
Branka	24
Casa Gandarias	3
Casa Vergara	6
La Fabrica	13
Itxaropena	14
Mugaritz	20
Restaurante Martín Berasategui	26

● CAFÉS

Café de la Concha	25
Gozotegia Oiartzun	16

● BARS

Akerbeltz	10
Garagar	15
Zurriola Marítimo	17

● PINTXOS BARS

Bar Astalena	4
Bar Goiz Argi	8
Bideluze	22
Borda Berri	9
La Cepa	2
La Cuchara de San Telmo	1
Etxaniz	12
A Fuego Negro	5
Hikamika	23
Mil Catas	18
Tximista	7

SEE "SAN SEBASTIÁN:
CASCO VIEJO" MAP
FOR DETAILS

6

Palacio de Miramar

Marking an end to the seafront boulevard of the new town – most of the buildings along which, thanks to poor planning, are sadly dreary – is the stony headland that's topped by a former royal retreat, the **Palacio de Miramar**. The mansion itself is closed to the public, but its rolling gardens are now an attractive park.

Playa de Ondarreta and El Peine de los Vientos

At high tide, an outcrop splits the beach in two; its smaller western portion therefore technically has its own name, the **Playa de Ondarreta**. At its far western end, just past the small suburb of Ondarreta, the seafront promenade finally stops amid the rocks. The paved plaza here forms part of Eduardo Chillida's remarkable, and unmissable, 1977 sculpture, **The Comb of the Winds** (*El Peine de los Vientos*). Two mighty iron arms claw at the waves immediately offshore, while blowholes in the plaza itself emit an eerie breathing sound most of the time, interspersed with occasional towering jets of spray.

Monte Igeldo

Funicular railway daily: summer 10am–8pm; winter 11am–7pm; every 15min • €1.50, or €2.70 return

Forming a matching pair with Monte Urgull above the old town, the wooded hill of **Monte Igeldo** rises above the west end of the Playa de Ondarreta. Its summit can be reached via a **funicular railway**, which sets off from behind Ondarreta's beachfront tennis club. Up at the top, as well as tremendous views of the bay, you can enjoy a splendidly fading pay-per-ride amusement park.

Gros

The district of **Gros** lies just across the mouth of the Río Urumea from the old town. San Sebastián's "other" beach, the **Playa de la Zurriola**, stretches in front. Much less sheltered than the Playa de La Concha, its counterpart to the west, and thus prone to stronger waves, it's very popular with surfers.

Kursaal

ⓦ kursaal.com.es

Gros is dominated by the huge, glass **Kursaal**, arrayed along its own seafront promenade, which consists of two starkly angular blocks referred to by architect Rafael Mono as "two beached rocks". Its main feature is a concert hall that's home to September's film festival, and it also holds substantial exhibition space.

ARRIVAL AND DEPARTURE   **SAN SEBASTIÁN**

By train RENFE (ⓦ renfe.es) trains using the Estación del Norte in Gros, just across the river from the new town, include services to Burgos (5 daily; 3hr); Irún (9 daily; 25min); Madrid (2 daily; 5hr 20min); Pamplona (2 daily; 1hr 45min); Salamanca (2 daily; 6hr); Vitoria (8 daily; 1hr 40min); and Zaragoza (2 daily; 3hr 40min). EuskoTren (ⓦ euskotren.es) trains run east and west from the Estación de Amara – at the south end of Centro, roughly 20min walk from the Casco Viejo – to destinations including Bilbao (hourly; 2hr 40min) and Irún (8 daily; 35min).

By bus The main bus station, on Paseo de Francia, close to

the RENFE train station in Gros, is used by services to and from Bilbao (every 30min; 1hr 10min); Hondarribia (every 20min; 30min); Irún (constantly; 30min); Lekeitio (4 daily; 1hr 20min); Bera (Vera) de Bidasoa (2 daily; 50min); and Vitoria (6 daily; 2hr 30min).

By car You can't drive into San Sebastián's Casco Viejo. Parking can be extremely problematic. If your hotel doesn't have its own car park – and very few do – head straight for the underground garages below Alameda del Boulevard (for the old town) or Pl. de Cervantes (for the beach).

INFORMATION

Turismo Boulevard 8, on the edge of the Casco Viejo (Mon–Thurs 9am–1.30pm & 3.30–7pm, Fri & Sat 10am–7pm, Sun 10am–2pm; ☎ 983 481 166, ⓦ sansebastianturismo.com).

ACCOMMODATION

San Sebastián offers a fine crop of hotels, from *belle époque* beachfront palaces to charming old-town houses, but be warned that it's renowned for some of the highest rates in Spain. For a summer stay, or the film festival in September, you can expect to pay over €100 even for a run-of-the-mill room, and you'll need to book as far in advance as possible.

CASCO VIEJO

Hotel Parma Paseo de Salamanca 10 ☎ 943 428 893, ⓦ hotelparma.com. It would be hard to pick a better location, poised at the edge of the old town, and handy for the beach; the one snag is it can be noisy at night. There's nothing special about the building itself, and the rooms too are rather bland and fading, though those on the upper level enjoy great sea views. Friendly and helpful staff make a big difference. **€140**

Pensión Amaiur c/31 de Agosto 44, 2º ☎ 943 429 654, ⓦ pensionamaiur.com. Classic old-style budget hotel, in a venerable old house deep in the warren-like streets of the old town. All the rooms differ in size – some sleep four – and are decorated in widely varying styles. None is en suite, but each shares a bathroom with one other. You can get a double without a window for €50, but it's not recommended. **€60**

Pensión Anne c/Esterlines 15, 2º ☎ 943 421 438, ⓦ pensionanne.com. Welcoming old-town hotel, with smallish but reasonably pleasant rooms, furnished much like a private home. Generally two rooms share each bathroom, but it's possible to get a bathroom to yourself. **€64**

Pensión Basic Confort c/Puerto 17, 2º ☎ 943 422 581, ⓦ basicconfort.com. With its modern en-suite bathrooms and spotless decor this old-town hotel is not as basic as the name might suggest, but despite being in one of San Sebastián's older houses it could be almost anywhere. Its ten guest rooms are named after world cities and decorated in widely varying (but generally uninspiring) styles; for functional comfort in a central location, it's not bad value. **€119**

★ **Pensión Edorta** c/Puerto 15, 1º ☎ 943 423 773, ⓦ pensionedorta.com. Welcoming family-run hotel, upstairs in a historic house in the heart of the old town, just up from the harbour. Bright, attractive rooms abound in period charm, with exposed stonework and ancient beams. The cheapest rates are for those without en-suite facilities; pay €20 extra to get your own top-quality bathroom. **€70**

Pensión Izar Bat c/Fermin Calbetón 6, 1º ☎ 943 431 573, ⓦ pensionizarbat.com. Small, clean rooms, with comfortable beds and tiny en-suite bathrooms, but little else; you can also expect little help from the management. Considering its location in the prime nightlife district, it's reasonably quiet. **€70**

CENTRO

Hotel de Londres y de Inglaterra c/Zubieta 2 ☎ 943 440 770, ⓦ hlondres.com. The very welcoming *grande dame* of San Sebastián hotels, this impressive white nineteenth-century edifice commands a superb position overlooking the beach, just a short walk from the old town. Live it up in style in a spacious, very comfortable room with huge seafront windows and all modern amenities. Look for good low-season offers. **€225**

Hotel María Cristina Paseo Republica Argentina 4 ☎ 943 437 600, ⓦ hotel-mariacristina.com. Landmark hotel, dominating the rivermouth near the edge of the old town, that's the epicentre of September's film festival. Entirely refurbished to mark its centenary in 2012, its sumptuous *belle époque* rooms are the last word in old-style luxury, boasting huge beds and opulent bathrooms. **€295**

Pensión Bellas Artes c/Urbieta 64, 1ºB ☎ 943 474 905, ⓦ pension-bellasartes.com. Welcoming upscale *pensión*, run by an exceptionally hospitable, English-speaking mother-and-daughter team. Large comfortable rooms with exposed brickwork, glassed-in balconies, and good en-suite facilities. **€107**

★ **Pensión La Perla** c/Loiola 10, 1º ☎ 943 428 123, ⓦ pensionlaperla.com. Great-value *pensión* in the middle of the new town, handy for bus and train stations as well as the old town and beach. Friendly service and simple but spacious rooms, all en suite and some equipped with balconies. **€65**

GROS

Hotel Record Calzada Vieja 35 ☎ 943 285 768, ⓦ hotelrecord.com. Somewhat incongruous little stand-alone hotel in a quiet residential corner of Gros a short walk from the beach, within easy reach of the old town. The rooms are far from fancy, but there's on-site parking, decent breakfasts, and scope to accommodate family groups. **€106**

Pensión Aida Iztueta 9, 1º ☎ 943 327 800, ⓦ pensionesconencanto.com. Part of a small group of central hotels, all similar, this welcoming nine-room *pensión* stands in a relatively quiet location close to the main train station, Zurriola beach, and old town. All rooms are newly and brightly decorated, with exposed stone and en-suite facilities. For maximum peace, opt for an "interior" room, though those facing out are equipped with balconies (and cost a few euros more). **€82**

ONDARRETA

Albergue La Sirena Ondarreta Paseo de Igeldo 25 ☎ 943 310 268, ⓦ reaj.com. The city's busy youth hostel is about as far as it could be from the old town, in a large pink mansion up the hill above the very far end of Ondarreta beach (bus #5, #16 or #25). There's a 2am curfew and 11pm "quiet" rule, while rates depend on the number of beds in your dorm, and your age. For an under-30 in a two- or four-bunk room, **€16.50**

Hotel Ezeiza Avda. Satrústegui 13, Playa de Ondarreta ☎ 943 214 311, ⊛ hotelezeiza.com. This friendly hotel, facing the smaller of the bay's beaches, a long walk from the city centre, makes a good-value base for families looking for lower-key pleasures than the full-on city experience. All rooms are en suite and well maintained, with bright modern furnishings; most have lovely sea views. **€108**

EATING, DRINKING AND NIGHTLIFE

As the epicentre of the culinary revolution that has seen contemporary Basque cuisine acclaimed as being little short of the future of food, San Sebastián is a paradise for anyone who loves to eat. What's more, in addition to its world-famous gourmet restaurants it also holds an astonishing profusion of bars that serve the latest concoctions in the form of **pintxos**. While it's very easy to sniff out your own favourites as you explore the Casco Viejo, to get you started it's worth joining one of the tourist board's guided tours, **Sabores de San Sebastián** (July & Aug Tues & Thurs 11.30am, otherwise irregular days throughout the year), which for €18 buys you drinks and *pintxos* in three old-town bars.

CAFÉS

Café de la Concha Paseo de La Concha 12 ☎ 943 473 600, ⊛ cafedelaconcha.com. Don't come to this café-restaurant for the food, which is indifferent at best, and even the coffee's pretty poor, but come nevertheless, for the unmissable panorama of La Concha beach, stretching away below the promenade-level terrace, and the entire bay beyond. Daily 9am–11pm.

Gozotegia Oiartzun c/Igentia 2 ☎ 943 426 209, ⊛ pasteleriaoiartzun.com. Most customers drop in at this *pastelería*, facing from the edge of the Casco Viejo across to the ornate town hall, just to pick up one of the superb array of cakes, but it also serves the city's best coffee, and has a few pavement tables for those who prefer to linger. Daily 8am–9pm.

PINTXOS BARS

Bar Astalena c/Iñigo 1 ☎ 943 425 245. Tapas bar in a great location, at the edge of the main old-town square. It serves a mouthwatering selection of *pintxos*, cold at one end of the bar and hot at the other, with all sorts of ham and shellfish delights, and delicious pistachio croquettes for vegetarians. Daily noon–4pm & 7pm–midnight.

Bar Goiz Argi c/Fermín Calbetón 4 ☎ 943 425 204. Hugely popular Casco Viejo *pintxos* bar with a contemporary edge and no seating whatsoever. It's deservedly renowned for its prawn brochettes, but everything's good, with a fine mixture of hot and cold snacks. The restaurant in the basement is good too, but entirely separate. Mon 10am–3.15pm, Wed–Sun 10am–3.15pm & 6.15–11.15pm.

Bideluze Pl. de Gipuzkoa 14 ☎ 943 422 880. Funky café-bar, in the new town facing an open garden square, attracting an arty crowd with its mismatched tables and chairs and general feel of an old grocery store. Highly creative *pintxos*, with plenty of eggy treats at breakfast time, and abundant sandwiches; in the evening it attracts a mixed crowd of drinkers. Daily 9am–11pm.

⭐ **Borda Berri** c/Fermín Calbetón 12 ☎ 943 430 342. Rustic, inviting old-town *pintxo* place, with yellow walls, little seating and usually eager crowds. There's no food on display; everything on the changing blackboard menu is cooked to order, in substantial starter-size portions that cost around €3.50. Fabulously tasty treats include a black-ink risotto with baby squid, though you'll need a strong stomach to sample the cod tripe in lurid green sauce. Daily noon–3.30pm & 7–11pm.

La Cepa c/31 de Agosto 7 ☎ 943 426 394, ⊛ barlacepa.com. Bustling, old-fashioned tapas bar in the heart of the old town, with hams festooning the ceiling and glass-topped tables holding tiny trinkets such as casino chips and candies. Inexpensive *pintxos* are listed on the blackboard, along with more substantial *raciones*, like the succulent ham, *jamón jabugo*, costing €10.50 for a half *ración*. Mon & Wed–Sun 11am–midnight.

La Cuchara de San Telmo c/31 de Agosto 28 ☎ 943 422 899, ⊛ lacucharadesantelmo.com. Long, narrow bar, squeezed into the far edge of the old town at the foot of Monte Urgull. Decorated in splashy colours, it attracts an alternative crowd, who usually spill out into the square outside. The *pintxos* are superb, with chunky meat and fish options and irresistible *tortilla*. Tues 8.30–11pm, Wed–Sun 1–3.30pm & 8.30–11pm.

Etxaniz c/Fermín Calbetón 24 ☎ 943 430 342. Tiny little hole-in-the-wall bar in the Casco Viejo, with bright green walls and no seats – there's not even a shelf to put down your food or drink – but a buzzy atmosphere. The counter is spread with a great selection of pungent (lots of garlic), delicious snacks, generally priced at just €1.50, and served much later than elsewhere. Daily 1–4pm & 9pm–3am.

⭐ **A Fuego Negro** c/31 de Agosto 31 ☎ 650 135 373, ⊛ afuegonegro.com. Hip, ultramodern old-town bar, decked out in crisp red and white, with an extensive menu of cocktails, wines and shots, and a staggering array of beautiful and succulent *pintxos*, many with a distinct molecular edge. A €35 tasting menu allows you to sample several, but it's simplest to try whatever catches your eye – like the trio of crab, avocado and licorice balls, a tiny meal in itself. Daily except Mon 12.30–4pm & 8–11pm.

BASQUE CUISINE

Basque cuisine has become renowned in the last twenty years not just as the finest in Spain, but as ranking among the best in the world. Cutting-edge chefs such as Martín Berasetegui, Juan Mari Arzak, and Andoni Aduriz, the stars of the **nueva cocina vasca** (new Basque cuisine), delight in creating inventive new combinations and preparations, and restaurants throughout the region are crowded with eager diners happy to pay premium prices for superb food.

That said, Basque food doesn't have to be expensive. For visitors, the perfect way to sample it is in the form of **pintxos**, the Basque equivalent of tapas. Bar counters throughout the region, and above all in San Sebastián, are piled high with fabulously enticing and utterly delectable goodies, freshly cooked and almost invariably excellent. Usually priced at around €2, they're so irresisistible that you may find you never quite make it to a restaurant for a sit-down meal – but you'll still come away raving about the Basque Country as one of the greatest foodie destinations on earth.

Seafood is a major ingredient of many Basque signature dishes. Look out especially for *bacalao* (cod) *a la vizcaina* or *al pil-pil*, *merluza* (hake) *a la vasca*, *txipirones en su tinta* (squid cooked in its ink) or *txangurro* (spider crab).

6

Hikamika c/Echaide 4 ☎943 431 335. The new town's best *pintxos* make *Hikamika* a popular lunch spot for workers in nearby businesses. With its minimalist white walls and black lacquer tables, it looks more like a modern wine bar, but the food is great; try the *ropa vieja*, Cuban-style shredded pork, or the cod with onions. They also serve good coffee. Mon–Sat 9am–6pm.

Mil Catas c/Zabaleta 55 ☎943 321 656. This pared-down bar, a block back from Zurriola beach, is a great place to try out the latest molecular concoctions without paying restaurant prices. A well-heeled, older crowd flocks to sample such exquisite morsels as scallops with cockle foam or octopus with orange, costing around €3.50 and washed down with fine wines. Shame about the muzak soundtrack though. Daily 1–3.30pm & 8–11pm.

Tximista c/Pescadería 1 ☎943 422 370. Tiny little turquoise-and-red bar on the corner of the main square in the old town. Excellent *pintxos* laid out along the counter and friendly service, while the outside tables make the perfect venue for a coffee or drink on the square itself. Daily 10am–11pm.

RESTAURANTS

Aralar c/Puerto 10 ☎943 423 086, ⊕bararalar.com. The pleasant little dining room of this unpretentious old-town place, behind a tapas bar that offers the usual array of *pintxos*, is a good place to come when you simply feel like eating a substantial plate of good food – such as prawns with garlic, or clams – for around €10. Daily 10.30am–midnight.

★ **Arzak** Avda. Alcalde Elosegui 273 ☎943 285 593, ⊕arzak.es. What might look like a typical family-owned *taberna*, on the lower slopes of Monte Ulia 3km east of the centre beyond Gros, is in fact the crucible of Basque *nueva cocina*, triple-starred by Michelin. Father-and-daughter

team Juan Mari and Elena Arzak prepare a different selection of stunningly creative dishes each day, with the set menu priced at €189 – look out especially for pigeon or lamb. Behind the scenes, a fully-fledged research lab is hard at work developing new concoctions. Tues–Sat 1–3.15pm & 5.45–11pm; closed mid-June to early July and last 3 weeks in Nov.

Bokado Pl. Jacques Cousteau 1 ☎943 431 842, ⊕www.bokadogrupo.com. Stylish contemporary restaurant in an unbeatable setting – on the concrete roof of the aquarium, below Monte Urgell at the mouth of the bay – with tables both indoors and outside. Besides serving two set menus, at €45 and €53, they also offer *pintxos*, such as spider crab and leek ravioli, at €1.70–3, and *raciones* for around €10. Tues–Sat 1–4pm & 9–11pm, Sun 1–4pm.

Branka Paseo de Eduardo Chillida 13 ☎943 317 096, ⊕branka-tenis.com. In a magnificent spot at the far west end of the bay, just short of Chillida's *Peine de los Vientos* sculpture – and appended to an exclusive tennis club – this modern structure holds an expensive restaurant upstairs and a less formal café downstairs. The latter makes an ideal lunchtime break in a day's stroll, offering ham, seafood or vegetable *raciones* at around €14 for a full portion, €8 for half. Café Mon–Thurs 9am–midnight, Fri & Sat 9am–2.30am; restaurant Mon–Sat 1.30–4pm & 8.30–11pm.

Casa Gandarias c/31 de Agosto 23 ☎943 426 362, ⊕restaurantegandarias.com. Very popular old-town restaurant, for once with as much of an emphasis on meat – from cured hams to chunky steaks – as fish. As usual, there's a big selection of *pintxos*, but head for a table at the back and settle down for a solid, well-cooked meal. Daily 11am–midnight.

Casa Vergara c/Mayor 21 ☎943 431 073 ⊕casavergara .com. Tucked away below the church at far end of c/Mayor in the old town, this fine old bar-restaurant makes a dependable option whatever your appetite, with an excellent spread of interesting *pintxos*, but also good-value *raciones* and full meals. Daily except Wed 1–4pm & 7pm–midnight.

La Fabrica c/Puerto 17 ☎ 943 432 110, ☷ restaurant elafabrica.es. One of the best-value modern restaurants in the city, housed in a bare-bones former brewery in the Casco Viejo. Chef Inigo Bozai specializes above all in delicious fish dishes, available on a wide selection of set menus, ranging from €23 for a weekday lunch up to €35 and €38 for dinner on Fri & Sat. Mon–Sat 1–3.30pm & 8.30–11pm.

Itxaropena c/Embeltrán 16 ☎ 943 424 576, ☷ restauranteitxaropena.com. Charming, cosy old-town cider-house restaurant that serves hearty, high-quality traditional cuisine on menus ranging from €20 – which can get you paella, squid and dessert, plus cider to drink – up to €75 for two people. Tues–Sat 1.30–3.30pm & 8–11pm, Sun 1–3.30pm.

Mugaritz Aldura Aldea 2, Errenteria ☎ 943 522 455, ☷ mugaritz.com. Regularly hailed as one of the top ten restaurants in the world and helmed by Andoni Aduriz, one of the great masters of molecular cuisine, *Mugaritz* represents contemporary Basque cuisine at its most outré. Inevitably, some ordinary diners find it pretentious, but visit with an open mind and you may well be blown away. The two main drawbacks are the location, in a rural hillside cottage 12km southeast of the centre, and the price – the only option is the changing daily menu of fifteen dishes, costing €135. Mid-April to mid-Dec only: Wed–Sat 1–6.30pm & 8pm–1.30am, Sun 1–6.30pm; May–Sept also open Tues 8pm–1.30am.

Restaurante Martín Berasategui c/Loidi 4, Lasarte-Oria ☎ 943 366 471 ☷ martinberasategui.com. Contemporary rather than molecular, this three-star Michelin restaurant is housed in a bright modern structure in the hills 10km southwest of the city. Its eponymous chef remains rooted in traditional Spanish cuisine, while adding his own subtle twists. À la carte prices are in the region of €50 and up for a main course, while the full tasting menu is €165. Wed–Sat 1–3.30pm & 8.30–11pm, Sun 1–3.30pm.

BARS

Akerbeltz c/de Mari 19 ☎ 943 451 452. Tiny little bar overlooking the harbour from the western side of the Casco Viejo, with a kitsch Stone Age theme. Crowds of drinkers tumble out onto the steps outside; stay indoors for pounding music and a gay-friendly vibe. Daily 4pm–2.30am.

Garagar Boulevard 22 ☎ 943 422 840. Big old pub on the inland edge of the Casco Viejo, with an authentic wood-panelled interior and plenty of draught beers, plus extensive café seating on the pavement outside. Mon–Thurs & Sun 10am–3am, Fri & Sat 10am–4am.

Zurriola Marítimo Avda. de Zurriola 41 ☎ 943 297 853, ☷ zurriolamaritimo.com. This hip modern bar, also known as *ZM*, in prime position directly above Zurriola beach, comes into its own around sunset, when its huge plate-glass windows offer spectacular views out to sea. Attracting a mixed but generally youthful crowd, it serves cocktails, drinks, *pintxos* and *raciones*, plus breakfast goodies, sandwiches and fuller meals, and also has lots of outdoor seating. Live theatre or music performances most evenings. Tues–Thurs & Sun 10am–5.30am, Fri & Sat 10am–6.30am.

CLUBS

Bar Be Bop Paseo de Salamanca 3 ☎ 943 429 869, ☷ barbebop.com. Despite the name, this long-established club, facing the river at the east end of the Casco Viejo, treats punters not only to live cool jazz, but also has frequent DJ nights, with funk, soul and Latin on the playlist too. Late at night, when it's often the last old-town bar still open, it can get very full. Mon–Fri 3.30pm–4.30am, Sat & Sun 3.30pm–3.30am.

Bataplán Paseo de La Concha 12 ☎ 943 473 601, ☷ bataplandisco.com. Very glitzy dance club overlooking the main beach, with a fabulous outdoor terrace for hot nights. Daily 11pm–6am.

Hondarribia

The frontier town of **HONDARRIBIA**, immediately across the mouth of the Bidasoa river from Hendaye in France, makes an appealing stopover just under 40km east of San Sebastián. Down at water level, where the broad boulevards just back from the pretty harbour are lined with pavement cafés, it feels like a resort, but its fortified **Casco Antiguo**, a delightful little enclave just higher up, offers a real sense of history. Filled with sturdily attractive medieval mansions, it centres on the **Plaza de Armas**, where the pick of the crop, the **Castille de Carlos V**, dates all the way back to the tenth century, and now houses an irresistible parador. The town beach, **Playa Hondartza**, lies a short walk north of the newer part of town.

ARRIVAL AND INFORMATION

HONDARRIBIA

By bus Hondarribia is served by regular buses from San Sebastián (every 20min; 30min), via the nearest train station at Irún.

Turismo Pl. de Armas 9 (July–Sept Mon–Fri 10am–7.30pm,

Sat & Sun 10am–2pm & 4–8pm; Oct–June Mon–Fri 9.30am–1.30pm & 4–6.30pm, Sat & Sun 10am–2pm; ☎ 943 643 677, ⓦ bidasoaturismo.com).

ACCOMMODATION

Hotel Palacete Pl. de Gipuzkoa 5 ☎ 943 640 813, ⓦ hotelpalacete.net. Pleasant little medieval mansion in the heart of the old town, with a nice little courtyard and tasteful modern rooms. Good rates in low season. **€104**

Hotel Obispo Pl. del Obispo ☎ 943 645 400, ⓦ hotel obispo.com. Fourteenth-century palace with long-range sea views from the edge of the old town, converted into a hotel that offers a blend of modern furnishings and traditional rooms with balconies, plus free use of bicycles. **€168**

Hotel San Nikolas Pl. de Armas 6 ☎ 943 644 278, ⓦ hotelsannikolas.com. Pretty townhouse in the Casco Antiguo, with pastel-blue balconies. Its sixteen en-suite rooms are relatively plain, but have comfortable beds. **€105**

Parador de Hondarribia Pl. de Armas 14 ☎ 943 645 500, ⓦ parador.es. While the entrance to the magnificent Castille de Carlos V is on the Casco Antiguo's main square, the lavishly appointed rooms of the so-called *Emperador* offer tremendous hilltop views across to France, and there's also an excellent restaurant. **€250**

EATING AND DRINKING

While the Casco Antiguo is very short of restaurants and bars, the streets parallel to the waterfront down in the harbour are packed with so many *pintxos* bars and restaurants that you can simply browse in search of whatever meets your fancy.

Hermandad de Pescadores c/Zuloaga 12 ☎ 943 642 738, ⓦ hermandadpescadores.com. Hondarribia's finest seafood restaurant is in a 750-year-old building set just back from the harbour in the lower part of town. Crowds of eager

diners squeeze onto wooden benches in its no-nonsense dining room to enjoy fresh fish at very reasonable prices. July–Sept daily except Mon noon–11pm; Oct–June Wed noon–4pm, Thurs–Sun noon–11pm.

Inland from San Sebastián: Gipuzkoa

Gipuzkoa, the smallest province in Spain, is in many ways the heartland of Basque language and culture. Medieval towns such as **Tolosa**, with its traditional *carnaval*, and **Oñati**, famous for its ancient university, are set in spectacular mountain scenery. In the nearby Sierra de Urkilla, the **Santuario de Arantzazu** is a prime pilgrimage destination for Basques.

Tolosa

TOLOSA, 24km south of San Sebastián, is famous for its **carnival**, celebrated with fervour over six days in February. Considered by Basques as superior to the carnival in San Sebastián, it was the only one whose tradition was maintained throughout the Franco era. Although fairly industrialized, Tolosa has an extensive **Casco Histórico** with an impressive town square, Plaza Euskal Herria, and is also well known for its *pintxos*: sample the *guindillas de Ibarra* (pickled green chilli peppers), and the *alubias de Tolosa* (kidney beans, usually served with blood sausage, cabbage and pork), considered the best in the region.

Tolosa has the largest **market** in the Basque Country, held on Saturday; activity centres on the distinctive, partly covered, Plaza Berdura in the heart of the old town. Nearby, at Pl. Zaharra 3, not far from the *turismo*, Gorrotxategi ranks among the most famous **chocolate** and sweet shops in Spain.

ARRIVAL AND INFORMATION

TOLOSA

By bus Tolosa is served by direct buses from San Sebastián (10 daily; 30min) and Vitoria (2 daily; 2hr 30min).

Turismo Pl. Santa María 1, near the river in the old town

(Mon–Sat 10am–1.30pm & 3–7pm, Sun 10am–2pm; ☎ 943 697 413, ⓦ tolosaldea.net).

6

ACCOMMODATION

Hotel Oria c/Oria 2 ☎ 943 654 688, ⓦ hoteloria.com. Plush, business-oriented modern hotel, 500m south of the old town, with smart and very comfortable rooms, plus its own restaurant and *asador*, offering a €27 cider-house *menú* (closed Sun). **€90**

EATING AND DRINKING

Astelena Pl. Euskal Herria 4 ☎ 943 650 996, ⓦ astelena .com. Good-value restaurant on the main arcaded square in Tolosa's old town. There's some outdoor seating, but it's cosier inside. The changing €11.50 lunch menu, featuring for example lentils and anchovies, is recommended. Daily noon–4pm & 7.30–10.30pm.

★ **Beti Alai** c/Arrostegieta ☎ 943 673 381, ⓦ astelena .com. The pick of the crop on the narrow alleyway that is old Tolosa's main nightlife area. Very good *pintxos* in the bar downstairs, including delicious *pastel de bacalao*, and full meals in the dining room upstairs, with lunch from €11.50. Daily except Wed 12.30–3.30pm & 8–11pm.

Oñati and around

Without doubt the most interesting inland town in Gipuzkoa, **OÑATI**, 65km southwest of San Sebastián, was decribed by the Basque painter Zuloaga as the "Basque Toledo". Its many historic buildings include some fine examples of Baroque architecture, including, at opposite ends of the arcaded Foruen Enparantz, the Baroque town hall and the parish church of **San Miguel**. All the counts of Oñati from 988 until 1890 lie buried in the latter's crypt, while its cloister is unusual in that it is actually built over the river.

Look out for various Navarran-style *casas torres*, as well as private family mansions, and the Plateresque-style sixteenth-century monastery of **Bidaurreta**.

University of Sancti Spiritus

Mon–Fri 9am–5pm, Sat & Sun 11am–2pm • Free

The **University of Sancti Spiritus**, which dominates Oñati, was for many centuries the only functioning university in Euskal Herria. Open from 1548 until 1901, it remains intact. Visitors are free to wander around the complex; the main facade, with its four pilasters adorned with figures, and the serene courtyard, are particularly impressive.

Santuario de Arantzazu

Daily 9.30am–9.30pm • Free • Hourly buses from Oñati

Clinging spectacularly to the mountainside above a gorge 9km south of Oñati, the **Santuario de Arantzazu** is a prime pilgrimage site for Basques, venerating **Our Lady of Arantzazu** (Santa María), the patron saint of Gipuzkoa. Although a monastery on this site dates back to the fifteenth century, the present spiky building was built in 1950 and features contemporary work by the sculptors Chillida (the doors) and Sáenz de Oteiza (part of the facade). The severe, Modernist architecture might not be to everyone's taste, but it's worth looking inside for the soaring stained-glass windows.

ARRIVAL AND INFORMATION
OÑATI AND AROUND

By bus There are direct buses from the region's major cities.

Turismo c/San Juan 14, opposite Sancti Spiritus (April–Sept Mon–Fri 10am–2pm & 3.30–7.30pm, Sat 10am–2pm & 4.30–6.30pm, Sun 10am–2pm; Oct–March Mon–Fri 10am–1pm & 4–7pm, Sat & Sun 11am–2pm; ☎ 943 783 453, ⓦ www.oinati.org). Oñati's helpful *turismo* can arrange guided visits to the university and church.

ACCOMMODATION AND EATING

Arregi c/Garagaltza 21 ☎ 943 783 657, ⓦ casaruralarregi .es. Rural *agriturismo*, run by a friendly family, 2km northwest of town, with chunkily furnished, good-value rooms and its own restaurant (closed Sat). **€45**

Etxe-Aundi Torre Auzu ☎ 943 781 956, ⓦ etxeaundi .com. Stately hotel, housed in a sixteenth-century tower in Torre Auzu, 2km northwest of town. Comfortable rooms, and a good on-site restaurant. **€70**

Hotel Ongi Ostatua c/Zaharra 19 ☎ 943 718 285, ⓦ hotelongi.com. Simple but perfectly adequate lodging, just behind the university. Rates for the eighteen en-suite rooms drop considerably at weekends. **€54**

The Costa Vasca

West from San Sebastián, both road and rail run inland, following the Río Oria, then towards the coast at the sprawling overdeveloped town of Zarautz, some 20km from San Sebastián. From here on, the **Costa Vasca** is glorious – a rocky and wild coastline, with long stretches of road hugging the edge of the cliffs – all the way to Bilbao. The hillsides, particularly around Getaria, are famous for the production of *txakoli*, a fizzy wine popular in the summer. The farther you go, the less developed the resorts become.

6

Getaria

The tiny fishing port of **GETARIA**, 25km west of San Sebastián, lies not far beyond Zarautz. Founded in 1209, and sheltered by the humpbacked islet of **El Ratón** (The Mouse), it later became a major whaling centre. These days its crescent beach is usually thronged with surfers and other holiday-makers. The village itself preserves the magnificent fourteenth-century church of **San Salvador**, whose altar is raised theatrically above the heads of the congregation.

The first man to sail around the world, **Juan Sebastián Elcano**, was born in Getaria around 1487 – his ship was the only one of Magellan's fleet to make it back home. Every four years on August 6, during the village's **fiestas**, Elcano's landing is re-enacted on the beach; the next will be in 2015.

Museo Cristóbal Balenciaga

Aldemar Parkea 6 • June–Sept Tues–Sun 10am–8pm; Oct–May Tues–Thurs 10am–5pm, Fri–Sun 10am–7pm • €8 • ☎ 943 008 840, ⓦ cristobalbalenciagamuseoa.com

After many years of languishing incomplete on the hillside above Getaria, a lavish new museum dedicated to the life and work of the locally born fashion designer **Cristóbal Balenciaga** (1895–1972) finally opened in 2011. Housed in a spectacular modern addition to the Palacio Aldemar, its thematic galleries display around 1400 individual garments, with separate areas devoted to daywear, cocktail dresses, wedding dresses, and so on.

ARRIVAL AND INFORMATION   GETARIA

By bus Getaria is served by direct buses from San Sebastián (12 daily; 40min) and Zumaia (12 daily; 15min).

Turismo Aldamar Parkea 2, close to the Balenciaga museum (Easter to mid-Sept Tues–Sun 10am–1.30pm & 4.30–7.30pm; ☎ 943 140 957, ⓦ getaria.net).

ACCOMMODATION

Casa Rural Itsas-Lore c/Aitzaga Auzoa 14 ☎ 943 140 619, ⓦ itsaslore.com. Very charming, newly built rural house, 2km up the hillside from Getaria on the way towards Santa Bárbara, with great views of the sea and the mountains. Each bathroom is shared by two of the comfortable guest-rooms. One-night stays incur a hefty surcharge; rates are for multi-day stays. **€75**

★ **Saiaz Getaria** c/Roke Deuna 25 ☎ 943 140 143, ⓦ saiazgetaria.com. Magnificent fifteenth-century mansion, topped by formidable stone towers, now stylishly converted to hold seventeen exceptionally comfortable bedrooms; pay around €20 extra to secure a full-on sea view. **€109**

EATING AND DRINKING

Elkano c/Herrerieta 2 ☎ 943 140 024, ⓦ restaurant eelkano.com. At his attractive restaurants in the heart of the old town, veteran chef Pedro Arregui does truly excellent fresh fish and seafood meals for around €60 a head. July to mid-Sept daily 1–3pm & 8–11pm; mid-Sept to June Tues & Sun 1–3pm, Wed–Sat 1–3pm & 8–11pm.

Mayflower Katrapuna 4 ☎ 943 140 658. Traditional grill overlooking the harbour, offering such delights as superb sardines, barbecued chicken, and *chipirones a lo Pelayo* (tiny cuttlefish with onion). You can eat well for around €20 a head; the daily *menú* is a real bargain. Daily 12.30–3.30pm & 8–11pm.

Ondarroa

ONDARROA, the easternmost coastal town in Bizkaia, looks very different to the small resorts farther east towards San Sebastián. Squeezed in on either side of the mouth of a narrow, steep-sided river, it's quite a workaday town, with its seaward end dominated by a no-nonsense **fishing port** filled with an eclectic set of trawlers. However, it does make an interesting place to stop over, redeemed by the presence of an attractive **beach** within very easy walking distance east of the harbour, and the more substantial beach of **Saturrarán** around the headland beyond that.

Church of Santa María

Founded in 1327, Ondarroa was razed to the ground by French troops in 1794, but the Late Gothic **church of Santa María**, in the centre, survived. Its extremely ornate facade includes flower and animal motifs and a "court" of twelve figures including a king, queen, pilgrims, crossbowmen, a minstrel and a wet nurse.

ARRIVAL AND INFORMATION   ONDARROA

By bus Ondarroa is served by direct buses from the nearest station at Deba, 8km east (5 daily; 10min).

Turismo On the port at Kofradi Zaharra-Erribera 9

(July–Sept daily 10am–2pm & 4–8pm; Oct–June Mon–Sat 10.30am–1.30pm & 4–7pm, Sun 10.30am–2.30pm; ☏ 946 831 951, ⓦ ondarroa.eu).

ACCOMMODATION

Camping Saturraran Saturraran ☏ 943 603 847, ⓦ www.campingseuskadi.com/saturraran. Summer-only campsite, 1km east of Ondarroa and set a short walk back from the glorious sheltered beach at Saturraran. Closed Oct–May. Two adults with a car **€13.50**

Pensión Patxi c/Artabide 2 ☏ 609 986 446. Ondarroa's only accommodation option, a simple but good-value *pensión* a couple of streets back from the fray near the harbour. **€45**

Lekeitio

As one of the nicest seafront towns in the Basque Country, the fine old port of **LEKEITIO**, on the west side of a broad river-mouth 10km west from Ondarroa, now welcomes plenty of pleasure boats to complement its active fishing fleet. Worth visiting either for a day or overnight, it's blessed with two fine **beaches** – one beside the harbour, and the other, better, across the river to the east. The little wooded island that stands in the middle of the bay can be reached on foot when the tide drops low enough.

Church of Santa María

Mon–Sat 8am–noon & 5–7.30pm • ⓦ www.basilicadelekeitio.com

Stop in at the **church of Santa María**, dominating the town from a high perch above the harbour, to see its magnificent sixteenth-century Flemish Gothic altarpiece, the third largest on the peninsula after those of the cathedrals of Seville and Toledo.

ARRIVAL AND INFORMATION   LEKEITIO

By bus Lekeitio is served by direct buses from the nearest station at Deba, 25km east (5 daily; 45min).

Turismo On the main waterfront square, Independentziaren

Enparantza (daily 10am–2pm & 4–8pm; ☏ 946 844 017, ⓦ www.lekeitio.com).

ACCOMMODATION

Aisia Lekeitio Santa Elena s/n ☏ 946 842 655, ⓦ aisiahoteles.com/ing_zita.asp. This somewhat faded grand hotel occupies a great position facing the harbourfront beach, a short walk east of the town centre. Half of its 42 en-suite rooms enjoy superb sea views, for just a few euros extra, and there's also a restaurant and

seawater therapy centre. **€96**

★ **Hotel Palacio Oxangoiti** c/Gamarra 2 ☏ 944 650 555, ⓦ oxangoiti.net. Very central hotel, in a fine townhouse a few steps from the harbour, with seven comfortable en-suite rooms. **€110**

Hotel Zubieta Portal de Atea s/n ☏ 946 843 030,

ⓦhotelzubieta.com. Charming, very elegant hotel, set in the gardens of an old palace on the inland side of town, not far from the harbour. Bright, well-furnished en-suite rooms and excellent breakfasts. **€103**

EATING AND DRINKING

Bar Marina Muelle Txatxo Kaia 1 ☎946 840 658. Lekeitio is literally teeming with places to eat and drink, with a long line of harbourfront restaurants and *pintxos* bars. This large, bare-bones bar on the corner of the quayside nearest the church has a few harbourfront tables and a good selection of inexpensive tapas. Daily noon–11pm.

Kaia Muelle Txatxo Kaia 5 ☎946 840 284. This old fishermen's tavern serves good-value meals on a large quayside terrace, with a wide range of fixed-price *menús*. Be sure to try the baby squid. Tues–Sat 12.30–3.30pm & 7–10.30pm, Sun noon–4pm.

Elantxobe

The well-preserved fishing village of **ELANTXOBE**, 10km west of Lekeitio, merits a detour back to the coast from the main road west. When the access road forks just before town, head left for the main village, or right to drop down to the harbour. From the tiny central square (so small that buses have to park on a turntable and be manually spun around before they can leave), an incredibly steep cobbled street lined with attractive fishermen's houses, c/Nagusia, connects the village to the harbour below. In the other direction, it continues 2km up to the cemetery from where a signposted track leads to **Mount Ogoño**, at 280m the highest cliff on the Basque coast.

ARRIVAL AND DEPARTURE   ELANTXOBE

By bus Buses stop in the main square.

By car You can park just before the harbour, but spaces are limited.

ACCOMMODATION

Caserio Arboliz c/Arboliz 12 ☎946 276 283, ⓦarboliz .com. This conspicuous white-painted house, perched on the clifftop in Ibarrangelu, 1km southeast of Elantxobe, has been converted into a comfortable rural *agroturismo*, with kitchen facilities available, and a lovely sea-view garden. **€63**

Itsasmin Ostatua c/Nagusia 32 ☎946 276 174, ⓦitsasmin.com. Simple *pensión* in the heart of Elantxobe. All its twelve rooms are en suite; half have little street-side balconies with harbour views. **€65**

EATING AND DRINKING

Makues c/Bide 1 ☎946 276 127. The best of Elantxobe's small crop of restaurants, just below the main square, and offering good dinner *menús* at €18 and €25. Daily except Tues 1–3pm & 8–10.30pm.

Gernika

GERNIKA, beside the Río Oka 25km northeast of Bilbao, is the traditional heart of Basque nationalism. It was here that the Basque parliament met until 1876, and here, under the **Tree of Gernika**, that their rights were reconfirmed by successive rulers. Gernika is best known now, however, for **Picasso**'s nightmare painting, which commemorates its saturation bombing during the Spanish Civil War, one of the first such raids ever perpetrated on a civilian centre. In just four hours on April 27, 1937, planes from the Condor Legion, which had been lent to Franco by Hitler and taken off from Vitoria-Gasteiz, destroyed the centre of Gernika, which had been chosen as the target largely for its symbolic importance. Around 250 people died, many of whom were attending the weekly market that's still held every Monday in the Plaza de Gernika. The nearby town of Durango had been bombed a few days earlier, but because there were no foreign observers, the reports were simply not believed. While the German government acknowledged its involvement in the bombing in 1997, to this day the Spanish government has never admitted its role.

For the Basques, a visit to Gernika is more of a pilgrimage than a tourist trip. The parliament, church and tree remained miraculously unscathed by the bombing, but the rest of the town was destroyed and has been rebuilt. It's now rather nondescript, and not really a place to spend much time on a holiday, though the arcaded main street, **Artekalea**, has a certain appeal. As for Picasso's picture, which he started to paint the day news of the bombing reached him in Paris, it was finally brought "home" to Spain after the death of Franco, and is now exhibited in the Centro de Arte Reina Sofía in Madrid.

6

Gernika Peace Museum

Foru Pl., c/Artekalea • July & Aug Tues–Sat 10am–8pm, Sun 10am–3pm; Sept–June Tues–Sat 10am–2pm & 4–7pm, Sun 10am–2pm • €4 • ☎ 946 270 213, ⓦ peacemuseumguernica.org

On the small open plaza across from the *turismo*, the **Gernika Peace Museum** sets out to commemorate the town's own tragedy and explore the very concept of peace. A reconstructed living room of a typical local house enables visitors to live through the bombing raid, complete with sound effects, while an extended section honours all the victims of the ongoing Basque conflict, listed according to whether they were killed by ETA, the security forces, or other groups.

Museo Euskal Herria

C/Allendesalazar 5 • July & Aug Tues–Sat 10am–2pm & 4–7pm, Sun 10.30am–2.30pm & 4–7.30pm, Sept–June closed Sun afternoon • €3, free on Sat • ☎ 946 255 451, ⓦ bizkaia.net/euskalherriamuseoa

Housed in an eighteenth-century mansion near the Basque parliament building, the **Museo Euskal Herria** traces the history of the Basque Country from its earliest prehistoric inhabitants. Each of its component regions, including the Kingdom of Navarre and the areas now belonging to France, is examined in systematic detail. There's some interesting material, but with captions in Basque and Spanish only, it's liable to fall rather flat for English-speaking visitors.

The Batzarretxea and the Tree of Gernika

C/Allendesalazar • Daily: summer 10am–2pm & 4–7pm; winter 10am–2pm & 4–6pm • Free • ⓦ jjggbizkaia.net

Although the government of the Basque Country as a whole is in Vitoria-Gasteiz, the **Batzarretxea**, or Casa de las Juntas, a short walk from the centre of Gernika, is home to the parliament of Bizkaia, which was reactivated in 1979. Visitors can enter the building itself, but the real attraction is what's left of the **Tree of Gernika** (Gernikako Arbola), the traditional meeting place of the Basque people. Now just a stump, protected in a little columned pavilion, it stands in the adjacent grounds, close to a replacement oak planted in 2005.

Europa Park and around

Stretching behind both the Batzarretxea and the Museo Euskal Herria, **Europa Park** contains ornamental gardens, a fast-flowing stream, and peace sculptures by Henry Moore and Eduardo Chillida. The Gothic church of **Santa María la Antigua** alongside is adorned with portraits of the various nobles of Bizkaia who pledged allegiance to the *fueros*.

ARRIVAL AND INFORMATION
GERNIKA

By bus Frequent buses from Bilbao stop at Pl. Saraspe in the town centre.

By train Gernika's central station is a stop on the EuskoTren line between Bilbao (every 30min; 50min) and Bermeo (every 30min; 20min).

Turismo c/Artekalea 8 (mid-June to mid-Sept Mon–Sat 10am–7pm, Sun 10am–2pm; mid-Sept to mid-June Mon–Sat 10am–2pm & 4–7pm, Sun 10am–2pm; ☎ 946 255 892, ⓦ www.gernika-lumo.net).

ACCOMMODATION

Hotel Gernika c/Carlos Gangoiti 17 ☎ 946 250 350, ⓦ hotel-gernika.com. Gernika's largest and most comfortable hotel is north of the centre, 500m on the road towards Bermeo. There's nothing remarkable about its

forty en-suite rooms, but they're reasonably well kept and quiet, and there's a decent tapas bar next door. €90
Pensión Akelarre Ostatua c/Barrenkale 5 ☎656 762 217, ⓦhotelakelarre.com. Cheap central *pensión*, right

behind the *turismo*, with seventeen plain but brightly painted rooms equipped with showers. The front desk is closed 1–6pm, and after 9pm, but you can check in by inserting a credit card next to the door. €55

EATING

★ **Baserri Maitea** c/Atzondoa, Forua ☎946 253 408, ⓦbaserrimaitea.com. The spacious dining room within this beautiful 300-year-old Basque farmhouse, a couple of kilometres north of Gernika, makes a great spot to enjoy traditional dishes roasted in a wood-fired oven. Typical meat and fish main courses cost around €22, while set menus range from €38 to €70. May–Oct Mon–Sat 1–3.30pm & 9–11pm, Sun 1–3.30pm; Nov–April Mon–Thurs 1–3.30pm, Fri & Sat 1–3.30pm & 9–11pm.
Boliña c/Barrenkale 3 ☎946 250 300, ⓦhotelbolina .net. Behind the tourist office, this is the best-value

restaurant in the centre of Gernika, and also holds a handful of cheap rooms. There's a €10 lunch menu, while the full evening tasting menu, with a good range of meat and fish, costs €32. Daily 12.30–3pm & 7.30–10.30pm.
Zallo Barri c/Juan Kaltzada 79 ☎946 251 800, ⓦzallobarri.com. Smart restaurant, 500m south of the centre, that's home to highly acclaimed chef Iñigo Ordorica. Individual dishes for around €20, tasting menus at €43 and €54. Mon–Sat 1–3.30pm & 8–11pm, Sun 1–3.30pm.

Mundaka

Flowing north from Gernika, the Río Oka broadens into an estuary that's fringed by hilly pinewoods and dotted with islets. A succession of sandy coves offer great swimming, but the best spots are at Sukarrieta and especially **MUNDAKA**. This lovely little village remains amazingly unspoiled, despite having achieved legendary status for its magnificent **surfing**, which includes what's claimed to be the longest left break in the world. Although Mundaka has frequently hosted world championship events, conditions tend to vary considerably from year to year. In good years, during the peak winter season, it's often possible to watch the surfers battle its trademark "Wave" from the *plaza* next to the church.

Playa de Laída

Passenger ferry: June–Sept 10am–8pm; every 20min • €1.20
From the inlet slightly south of the port, a passenger ferry plies across the river. In summer, swimmers leap into the water from all along the shoreline and quayside in Mundaka. The nearest proper beach, however, lies across the river. From the inlet slightly south of the port, a passenger ferry makes frequent trips to **Playa de Laída**, an enormous area of white sand, which at low tide stretches across the mouth of the bay in an unbroken crescent.

ARRIVAL, INFORMATION AND ACTIVITIES   MUNDAKA

By train Mundaka is on the EuskoTren line between Bilbao (every 30min; 50min), Gernika (every 30min; 15min), and Bermeo (every 30min; 5min).
Turismo Next to the harbour on c/Kepa Deuna (daily

10.30am–2pm & 4.30–7.30pm; ☎946 177 201, ⓦmundaka.org).
Surfing The Mundaka Surf Shop, close to the port (☎946 876 721, ⓦmundakasurfshop.com), sells and rents equipment and offers surf lessons.

ACCOMMODATION

Hotel Mundaka c/Florentino Larriñaga 9 ☎946 876 700, ⓦhotelmundaka.com. Attractive, surfer-friendly hotel, just off Mundaka's main square. Clean, comfortable rooms and a friendly welcome. €82
★ **Hotel El Puerto** c/Portu 1 ☎946 876 625, ⓦhotelelpuerto.com. This delightful hotel faces out to sea from right beside the fishing port, and has a lovely shaded terrace. Several of its en-suite rooms have great

sea views. Be warned it's liable to be noisy at night in summer. €90
Portuondo ☎946 877 701, ⓦcampingportuondo .com. This appealing campsite, popular with surfers, is perched high above the water a short walk south of town, and has steps leading down to a rocky beach. There's a decent restaurant on site (closed Mon), and rental cabins also available. Two adults with car €21.60

Bermeo

BERMEO, 3km north of Mundaka, is a venerable old port that boasts the largest remaining fishing fleet in these waters. Apart from the riot of red, green and blue boats in the harbour, there's very little to see in the town itself – and surprisingly enough, neither are there any tapas bars or restaurants worth recommending. However, it makes a good base for visiting the estuary beaches nearby, and it's also worth driving 8km west to visit the remarkable little island shrine of **San Juan de Gaztelugatxe**, reached by crossing a little causeway and climbing two hundred steep steps.

ARRIVAL AND INFORMATION   BERMEO

By train Bermeo lies at the end of the EuskoTren line from Bilbao (every 30min; 55min), Gernika (every 30min; 20min) and Mundaka (every 30min; 5min).
Turismo Parque de Lamera, on the waterfront (summer Mon–Sat 10am–8pm, Sun 10am–2pm & 4–7pm; winter Mon–Fri 10am–2pm & 4–7pm, Sat 10am–1pm & 4–7pm, Sun 10am–2pm; ☏ 946 179 154, ⓦ bermeo.org).

ACCOMMODATION

★ **Hostal Torre Ercilla** Talaranzko 14, 1º ☏ 946 187 598, ⓔ torrercilla@euskalnet.net. Top-notch inexpensive accommodation a few streets up from the port behind Santa María church. Ask for the spacious corner room, with a balcony and glassed-in gallery as well as en-suite bathroom. **€60**

★ **Lurdeia** Artike auzoa, s/n ☏ 946 477 001, ⓦ lurdeia .com. Lovely rural *agriturismo*, attached to a hilltop organic farm, with large, tastefully decorated and very comfortable rooms with magnificent long-distance ocean views. It's reached by a convoluted but clearly signposted 9km drive south from the centre of Bermeo. **€65**

Bilbao

Stretching for some 14km beside the Río Nervión, **BILBAO** (Bilbo) is a large city that seldom feels like one. Even though its urban sprawl now fills the narrow valley, you can always see the green slopes of the mountains to either side beyond the high-rise buildings of the city centre. Bilbao's great achievement has been to reinvent itself since the collapse of its traditional industrial base at the end of the last century. The dramatic success since 1997 of the **Museo Guggenheim**, which transformed a postindustrial wasteland right in the city centre into a major tourist attraction, triggered further visionary redevelopments that continue to this day, including the construction of a new metro and airport.

Holding around 350,000 people in its urban core, and a further 500,000 in the metropolitan district, modern Bilbao is much the biggest city in the Basque Country, and serves as the capital of Bizkaia province. While it can't match San Sebastián for beaches, or sheer prettiness, Bilbao still has plenty to offer, from its exuberant cutting-edge architecture and stimulating museums, to the lively alleyways of its old town, the **Casco Viejo**, and its friendly inhabitants.

From the compact old town, at the eastern edge of the city centre on the river's right bank, an easy and pleasant stroll leads all the way to the Guggenheim, crossed by way of the showpiece **Zubizuri** footbridge. Only when Bilbao industrialized, in the nineteenth century, did it expand back onto the left bank, to create the much larger new town, or **Ensanche**. All but encircled by a huge loop in the river, this remains the commercial heart of the city, with its broad avenues radiating from the central Plaza Moyúa.

The Casco Viejo

What's now known as the "old town", the **Casco Viejo**, is not in fact the oldest part of Bilbao. The city started out as a cluster of small fishing villages on the left bank of the river, whereas the Casco Viejo grew up across the river between the fourteenth and nineteenth centuries. All the oldest buildings that still survive, however, are now concentrated here, and it's the most enjoyable area to explore on foot. A tight-knit labyrinth of old stone lanes, filled with bars and restaurants and cradling the delightful arcaded main square, the Plaza Nueva, it also holds some interesting museums.

Euskal Museoa Bilbao

Pl. Unamuno 4 • Tues–Sat 11am–5pm, Sun 11am–2pm • €3, free Thurs • ⓦ euskal-museoa.org

Devoted to Basque ethnology and history, the somewhat dour, old-school **Euskal Museoa Bilbao** is housed in the former Colegio de San Andrés. The cloister at its heart is a lovely retreat from the city bustle, and holds a stylized Iron Age statue known as the *Mikeldi*, depicting a hog with a disc in its belly that's thought to have been used in ancient rituals. Displays in the museum itself trace Basque fishing traditions back over ten thousand years, follow local shepherds as far as the western US, and explain the growth of Bilbao. There's also a huge relief model of the whole of Bizkaia. None of the captions are in English.

Arkeologi Museoa

Calzadas de Mallona 2, Pl. Unamuno • Tues–Sat 10am–2pm & 4–7.30pm, Sun 10.30am–2pm • €3 • ⓦ euskal-museoa.org

Bilbao's small **archeology museum** has recently been hived off from the Euskal Museoa, and rehoused across the same old-town square in a converted former train station – not that you'd ever recognize it as such. Successive galleries on its three floors cover specific eras of human history in Bizkaia, from the Neanderthals onwards, with eye-catching displays but little detail. Exhibits include a surprising number of actual skeletons, plus a small shipwrecked fishing vessel from the fifteenth century.

Mercado de la Ribera

C/de la Ribera • Mon & Sat 8am–3pm, Tues–Fri 8am–2.30pm & 5–8pm

Seven centuries after a daily food market was first established on the right bank of the Río Nervión, the **Mercado de la Ribera** remains the epicentre of life in Bilbao's old town. In its current form, it's an amalgam of a superbly elegant Art Nouveau building from 1929 with a modern revamp that has given it huge new windows, more space, and greater ease of access. Be sure to venture in to relish its vast array of fresh produce and seafood.

Museo Guggenheim

July & Aug daily 10am–8pm; Sept–June Tues–Sun daily 10am–8pm • €13, under-12s free • Free guided tours 11am, 12.30pm, 4.30pm & 6pm; book 2 weeks in advance • ☎ 944 359 090, ⓦ guggenheim.org/bilbao

Frank Gehry's astounding **Museo Guggenheim** looms over the left bank of the Río Nervión, ten minutes' walk west of the Casco Viejo. Completed in 1997, it was hailed by architect Philip Johnson as "the greatest building of our time". The construction of such a showpiece project on a derelict industrial site represented a colossal gamble by the Basque government, which hoped to stimulate the revitalization of Bilbao. Amazingly enough, it worked. A gargantuan sculpture, whose sensual titanium curves glimmer like running water in the sun, it has inevitably overshadowed the artworks it contains.

The best way to approach the museum is along the river, either along the quayside, or by crossing the high Puente de la Salve road bridge from Deusto on the north bank. One of Louise Bourgeois' fearsome spindle-legged spiders, *Maman*, patrols the water's edge, while Anish Kapoor's column of glittering silver bubbles, *Tall Tree and the Eye*, stands in a reflecting pool alongside the building. The actual entrance, however, is via a walkway that descends from the structure's city side. Jeff Koons' enormous *Puppy* here, clad in colourful living flowers, was originally installed as a temporary exhibit for the opening ceremony, but became a permanent fixture after *bilbainos* clamoured for it to stay.

Inside the museum

Once inside, visitors flow seamlessly through the various galleries in no fixed order, crisscrossing the vast, light-filled atrium on walkways. Gehry called the largest room

6

BILBAO

ACCOMMODATION

Arriaga Suites	10
Bilbao Akelarre Hostel	5
Gran Hotel Domine	2
Hesperia Bilbao	1
Hostal Begoña	8
Hostal-Residencia Ría de Bilbao	7
Hotel Carlton	9
Hotel Itturrienea Ostatua	13
Hotel López de Haro	6
Meliá Bilbao	3
Miró	4
Pensión Ladero	11
Pensión Mardones	12
Pensión Mendez I & II	14

on the ground floor his "fish gallery"; stretching away beneath the road bridge, it's permanently given over to Richard Serra's disorienting sculpture series, *The Matter of Time*, consisting of eight enormous shapes of weathered steel, coiled and labyrinthine.

The rest of the museum hosts top-flight temporary exhibitions, and also displays a rotating selection from the Guggenheim Foundation's unparalleled collection of twentieth-century art, which features works by all the major modern and contemporary

● CAFÉS	
Café La Granja	9
Café Iruña	7

● PINTXOS BARS	
Berton	16
Café Bar Bilbao	15
Gatz	17
El Globo	10
Gure Toki	13
Irrintzi	18
Los Fueros	12
Taurino Taberna	8
Xukela	19

● RESTAURANTS	
Bascook	5
Bistro Guggenheim	1
Casa Rufo	20
Etxanobe	3
Restaurante Atea	2
Río Oja	19
Serantes	11
Victor Montes	14
Zortziko	4

● BARS	
Dubliners	6
Lamiak	21
Taberna Txomin Barullo	22

■ CLUBS & LIVE MUSIC VENUES	
Azkena	2
BilboRock-La Merced	7
Bullitt Groove Club	6
Conjunto Vacío	7
Cotton Club	4
Image Club	3
Kafe Antzokia	1
New High Club	5

figures, including Kandinsky, Klee, Mondrian, Picasso, Cézanne, Chagall, Warhol, Calder and Rauschenberg, to name a few.

Zubizuri

Resembling a vast white sail filled by a fresh wind, Santiago Calatrava's spectacular pedestrian-only **Zubizuri** – the name simply means "white bridge" – curves majestically across the Río Nervión a few minutes' walk west of the old town. It makes the ideal midpoint of a stroll to or from the Guggenheim; just be careful on its glass floor in wet weather. When it first opened, the bridge only provided access on the left bank to the Muelle de Uribitarte, down along the quayside. The extended walkway that now connects with the higher Alameda Mazarredo was only added in 2006; Calatrava was so incensed by this corruption of his vision that he sued the local council and won €30,000 compensation.

Funicular de Artxanda

Daily every 10min: Mon–Fri 7.15am–11pm, Sat & Sun 8.15am–11pm; Oct–May until 10pm • €0.90

Three blocks north of the river, not far from the Zubizuri, the Plaza Funicular marks the foot of the **Funicular de Artxanda**, an inclined railway built to serve commuters to the newer residential suburbs in 1931. It sweeps passengers 770m up the mountainside in less than five minutes. There are no views along the way, but once at the top you emerge into a circular park that offers fabulous panoramas not only over the city but across into the verdant neighbouring valley.

Museo de Bellas Artes

Parque de Doña Casilda de Iturriza • Tues–Sun 10am–8pm • €6, free on Wed • ⓦ museobilbao.com

Inevitably doomed to play second fiddle to the Guggenheim, Bilbao's **Museo de Bellas Artes**, a short walk southwest in a very pleasant green park, is a high-quality art museum in its own right. Its sizeable permanent collection, housed in a bright, spacious modern annexe to its original core, ranges from anonymous pieces of medieval religious art up to the present day. Highlights include El Greco's stark *St Francis*, Gauguin's *Washerwomen in Arles*, and Anish Kapoor's *Pool*, an impenetrable dish of reflective black lacquered steel. Basque artists are much better represented than in the Guggenheim; look out for Anselmo Guinea's 1899 Art Nouveau panel *Back From the Pilgrimage*, and José Arrue's slightly later depictions of idyllic village life.

Alhóndiga

Pl. Arriquabar 4 • No fixed hours • Free • ⓦ alhondigabilbao.com

A long-abandoned former wine warehouse, a short walk south of Plaza Moyúa in the centre of the new town, has recently been converted under the supervision of Philippe Starck to become the **Alhóndiga**. Entering at street level, visitors encounter a rather baffling space, its low ceiling supported by 43 squat Starck-designed pillars in wildly differing styles and materials. A fiery red sun hangs in the centre. Exploring further, you'll find various elements include a number of cafés and restaurants, a cinema down in the basement, assorted performance and exhibition spaces, and a gym.

Museo Marítimo Ría de Bilbao

Muelle Ramón de la Sota • June–Sept Tues–Sun 10am–8pm; Oct–May Tues–Fri 10am–6pm, Sat & Sun 10am–8pm • €5 •
ⓦ museomaritimobilbao.org

The fancy **Museo Marítimo Ría de Bilbao** is located at quayside level, just west of the Euskalduna, an impressive edifice of rusty iron, glass, steel and concrete that hosts conferences and classical performances. The museum itself explains in intricate detail exactly how the *ría* between the city and the sea has been cleared over the centuries to deal with ever larger marine traffic. It's all very worthy, and you can clamber aboard assorted vessels in the old docks of the Euskalduna Shipyard outside. Sadly, however, hardly anyone seems to bother to visit.

MUSEO GUGGENHEIM (SEE P.469); BODEGAS YSIOS (SEE P.483) >

Sopelana and Plentzia

For Sopelana, use Ⓜ Larrabasterra; for Plentzia use Ⓜ Plentzia

Bilbao is well provided with **beaches** along the mouth of the estuary and around both headlands. Metro Line 1 makes it easier to reach those on the east bank, for example at **Sopelana**, home to the nudist Playa de Arrietara. The beach at **Plentzia**, at the far end of the line, 15km out, is generally cleaner and not quite so crowded.

6 Getxo

For Getxo use Ⓜ Algorta; for Portugalete use Ⓜ Aleeta

Getxo, 10km downstream at the head of the port and consisting of several distinct communities, makes a particularly nice excursion. Its ancient fishing-port core, set on a hilltop not far east of the rivermouth, remains pretty and lively, and stands just above two nice beaches, Ereaga and Arrigunaga. Just before the river widens into the port, Getxo is connected with **Portugalete** on the west bank via the remarkable Vizcaya Bridge. The little gondola that dangles from this preposterous late nineteenth-century "**transporter bridge**" carries passengers (€0.30), and even half a dozen cars at a time (€1.25), across the river every few minutes.

ARRIVAL AND DEPARTURE — BILBAO

BY AIR

Aeropuerto de Bilbao Bilbao's airport is 12km north of town. A taxi into town costs around €28, while Bizkaiabus services (every 20min in summer, 30min in winter; €1.30) takes 20min to reach Pl. Moyúa in the centre of the new town (Ensanche), and continues to the Termibús station (Ⓜ San Mamés).

BY TRAIN

Estación de Abando The main RENFE train station is on Pl. Circular, across the river from the Casco Viejo, and sees services to Barcelona (2 daily; 6hr 30min); Logroño (2 daily; 2hr 30min); Madrid (2 daily; 5hr); and Salamanca (daily; 5hr 30min).

Estación de Atxuri South of the Casco Viejo on the right bank of the river, the Estación de Atxuri is used by frequent EuskoTren (Ⓦ euskotren.es) trains to San Sebastián (2hr 40min), Gernika (45min) and Bermeo (1hr 15min).

Estación de Santander FEVE services (Ⓦ feve.es) from this highly decorative station, on the riverbank right below the Estación de Abando, head west along the coast to Santander (3 daily; 3hr) and beyond.

BY BUS

Termibús station Most long-distance and international bus companies use the Termibús station, which fills an entire block between Luis Briñas and Gurtubay. To reach the town centre, change onto a local bus, head a block north to the San Mamés metro station or simply walk.
Destinations Barcelona (4 daily; 7hr 30min); Bermeo, via Gernika and Mundaka (30 daily; 1hr 10min); Burgos (11 daily; 3hr); Castro Urdiales (5 daily; 1hr); Elantxobe (3 daily; 1hr 30min); Lekeitio (5 daily; 1hr 30min); León (1 daily; 5hr 30min); Madrid (14 daily; 4hr 45min); Oñati (2 daily; 1hr 10min); Ondarroa (20 daily; 1hr 20min); Pamplona (6 daily; 2hr 15min); San Sebastián (every 30min; 1hr 10min); Santander (every 30min; 1hr 30min); Santiago (3 daily; 10hr); Vitoria (every 30min; 1hr 15min); Zaragoza (7 daily; 4hr).

BY CAR

Driving If you're driving into Bilbao, the motorways are very efficient at delivering you to the centre, but once there traffic is consistently dreadful; you're better off parking straight away in the car park nearest your accommodation, and walking from there.

BY FERRY

Zierbena Ferries from Portsmouth to Bilbao dock at Zierbena, across the river from Getxo, 14km north of the city centre; regular buses and trains run from the docks to the centre of town.

INFORMATION

Turismo Bilbao has tourist offices (☏ 944 795 760, Ⓦ bilbao .net) outside the Teatro Arriaga at the edge of the old town (Mon–Fri 11am–2pm & 5–7.30pm, Sat 9.30am–2pm & 5–7.30pm, Sun 9.30am–2pm); next to the Museo Guggenheim (July & Aug Mon–Sat 10am–7pm, Sun 10am–3pm; Sept–June Tues–Fri 11am–6pm, Sat 11am–7pm, Sun 11am–3pm); at Pl. Ensanche 11 (Mon–Fri 9am–2pm & 4–7.30pm); and at the airport (Mon–Fri 7.30am–11pm, Sat & Sun 8.30am–11pm).

GETTING AROUND

By foot Central Bilbao is small enough to walk around comfortably; indeed, the riverside stroll between the Casco Viejo and the Guggenheim is a highlight for many visitors.

By taxi TeleTaxi ☎ 944 102 121, Radio Taxi Bilbao ☎ 944 448 888.

By metro The city boasts the modern Metro Bilbao (ⓦ metrobilbao.net) designed by Norman Foster. An easy, efficient service runs every 4min from Plentzia (northeast of Getxo) to Extebarri, south of the city centre; a second line runs out to Santurtzi on the western side of the rivermouth. While the network is divided into three zones, all journeys in the city centre (including the Casco Viejo) lie within the same zone (€1.45).

By bus For parts the metro doesn't reach, there are red municipal buses (€1.30) with route maps at the green bus shelters, or for longer journeys (including to the airport) the blue-and-yellow Bizkiabuses.

By tram The green EuskoTran trams (€1.30) run along a single line, linking the Casco Viejo and the Museo Guggenheim with San Mamés and the bus station.

Tickets If you plan to use the transport system frequently, buy a BilbaoCard from any *turismo* (€6/10/12 for 1/2/3 days), which provides unlimited travel on all Bilbao's various modes of transport in the Creditrans network – the metro, tram, municipal and provincial buses and Artxanda funicular – and offers discounts of ten to fifty percent at various museums and shops.

ACCOMMODATION

The nicest area to stay has to be the **Casco Viejo**, though that's dominated by budget hotels and *pensiones*, and everywhere is liable to be very noisy at night. Bilbao's luxury hotels tend to be scattered across **Ensanche**; many feature hip, contemporary architecture and award-winning restaurants, and can offer amazingly good value. Staying in **Deusto** or **Castaños**, on the north bank of the river, makes a good alternative. For help with bookings, try the *turismo*'s central **reservation** service (☎ 902 877 298, ⓦ bilbaoreservas.com).

CASCO VIEJO

★ **Arriaga Suites** c/Bidebarrieta 3 ☎ 635 707 247, ⓦ arriagasuites.com. Six large, pleasantly furnished, and great-value suites, in prime position at the main approach to the Casco Viejo. Each is named after a Basque musician associated with the nearby theatre, and offers a fridge and wi-fi. €72

Hotel Iturrienea Ostatua c/Santa María 14 ☎ 944 161 500, ⓦ iturrieneaostatua.com. Clean, very friendly hotel, tucked away near the river in the Casco Viejo, with the feel of a B&B (breakfast is served until 12.30pm daily). There's exposed stonework and antique furniture throughout, while the walls are hung with original art and moody photographs of Bilbao's industrial past. All rooms are en suite with wi-fi; many have plants trailing over balconies, and double-glazing to cut down noise from the many nearby bars. €66

Pensión Ladero c/Lotería 1, 4º ☎ 944 150 932, ⓦ pensionladero.es. Unbeatable rates for eighteen clean, bare-bones rooms, sleeping from one to three guests, and sharing use of four spotless shared bathrooms. No lift. There is also a fifth-floor annexe reached by a narrow spiral staircase. No reservations: first-come, first-served. €35

Pensión Mardones c/Jardines 4, 2º & 4º ☎ 944 153 105, ⓦ hostalmardones.com. Clean, functional rooms, not all of them en suite, with uninspiring but decent furnishings and dark wood floors; the fourth floor is preferable to the second-floor annexe. The *Amboto* restaurant alongside is recommended. €50

Pensión Mendez I & II c/Santa María 13, 1º & 4º ☎ 944 160 364, ⓦ pensionmendez.com. Comfortable and clean rooms, simply but adequately furnished; they're hardly luxurious, but good value for anyone simply looking for a place to sleep. Those in *Mendez II* are slightly better, with en-suite bathrooms. Cash only, reservations by phone only. *Mendez I* €35, *Mendez II* €50

ENSANCHE

★ **Gran Hotel Domine** Alameda de Mazarredo 61 ☎ 944 253 300, ⓦ granhoteldominebilbao.com. The work of designer Javier Mariscal, this is a wonderfully inspiring five-star hotel, appropriately close to the Guggenheim and sporting one of the most creative lobbies you'll ever see. Each floor has a unique design, while the luxurious rooms have bathrooms with transparent glass, and tubs designed by Philippe Starck. Reserve ahead for the best rates. €136

Hostal Begoña c/Amistad 2, 1º ☎ 944 230 134, ⓦ hostalbegona.com. Solid mid-range option, near the FEVE station and just a couple of minutes' walk over the bridge from the Casco Viejo. The colourful rooms have lino floors, good en-suite facilities, comfortable beds and wi-fi, but no views. €58

Hotel Carlton Pl. Moyúa 2 ☎ 944 162 200, ⓦ hotelcarlton.es. The *grande dame* of Bilbao's hotels, built in 1919 and still an atmospheric place to stay, with its abundant marble and dramatic stained-glass cupola. The rooms are tasteful and extremely comfortable, and several boast huge arched windows. Look for bargain rates online. €75

Hotel López de Haro Obispo Orueta 2–4 ☎ 944 235 500, ⓦ hotellopezdeharo.com. Luxury five-star hotel built in 1890, with comfortable, modern rooms and bathrooms, but retaining nineteenth-century touches. Great location, and extremely tranquil. €76

★ **Meliá Bilbao** c/Lehendakari Leizaola 29 ☎ 944 280 000, ⓦ solmelia.com. One of Bilbao's most distinctive buildings, a bold, creative design inspired by Eduardo Chillida, utilizing Iranian pink marble and rusty garnet tones for the exterior, and green and white marble in the bathrooms. The stylish rooms are luxuriously comfortable, with huge, incredibly comfy beds; there's also a pool. €96

Miró Alameda de Mazarredo 77 ☎ 946 611 880, ⓦ www.mirohotelbilbao.com. Attractive fifty-room hotel, with minimalist decor, bathrooms finished in black marble (separated from the chic, white-coloured rooms by a curtain), and a decent spa. €108

CASTAÑOS AND DEUSTO

Bilbao Akelarre Hostel c/Morgan 4–6 ☎ 944 057 713, ⓦ bilbaoakelarrehostel.com. Modern, well-run and well-equipped hostel near the university, a short walk from the Guggenheim. Some double rooms, plus dorms sleeping from four to twelve. Rates include free breakfast, coffee, tea and wi-fi. Twelve-bed dorm (per person) €17.50, doubles €42

Hesperia Bilbao Paseo Campo de Volantín 28 ☎ 944 051 100, ⓦ hesperia-bilbao.com. Smart, modern riverfront hotel, in a funky, contemporary building lined with pastel-coloured glassed-in balconies, near the Zubizuri bridge. Rooms come with sleek, minimalist furnishings and plasma-screen TVs. Bike rental, free wi-fi and parking. €89

Hostal-Residencia Ría de Bilbao Ribera de Deusto 32 ☎ 944 765 060, ⓦ riabilbao.com. A quiet place overlooking the river, 10min walk from the Euskalduna. Garden and cooking facilities; apartments for longer stays. Highly recommended if you don't mind staying well away from the action. €50

EATING AND DRINKING

While not quite on a par with San Sebastián, Bilbao ranks among the culinary capitals of Spain. **Innovative restaurants** and Michelin-star winners knock out everything from traditional Basque fare to high-class *nueva cocina vasca* meals that can cost as much as a five-star hotel room, while the **pintxos bars** are equally mouthwatering. Taking a high-speed *txikiteo* (*pintxos* crawl) through the Casco Viejo is an essential part of any visit – the best targets tend to be clustered in the *siete calles* (seven streets), bordered by c/de la Ronda and c/Pelota, but there are also some good options on c/Diputación in Ensanche. Bilbao's most famous dish is undoubtedly **cod** (*bacalao*), traditionally served with *salsa vizcaina* (a sauce of red onions and peppers) or *al pil-pil* (a garlic-based sauce). **Bars** (most serving *pintxos*) can be found all through the Casco Viejo; c/Barrenkale is the heart of the madness, but the outdoor tables in the beautiful Pl. Nueva make a great place for a more relaxed drink in the early evening. Ensanche too holds plenty of pubs and bars.

CAFÉS

Café La Granja Pl. Circular ☎ 944 230 813, ⓦ cafesdebilbao.net. This spacious and slightly faded Art Nouveau café features iron columns and beautiful lamps. Drinks and *pintxos* are served all day, and there's live traditional music some evenings. A popular rendezvous for commuters at either end of the working day, it also offers wi-fi. Mon–Sat 5.30am–2am.

★ **Café Iruña** Colón de Larreategui ☎ 944 237 021, ⓦ cafesdebilbao.net. Historic café and bar, facing the little Jardines de Albia park, and established in 1903. Elaborate murals and ornate Mudéjar decor and tiling make it marvellously atmospheric. Equipped with wi-fi, it's busy around breakfast time; later on it's a great spot for a drink or a few *pintxos* – the €2.20 *pinchos morunos*, or mini-kebabs, are especially worth trying. Mon–Sat 8.30am–4pm & 8pm–midnight, Sun 1–4pm.

PINTXOS BARS

Berton c/Jardines 11 ☎ 944 167 035, ⓦ xixili.com/berton. Friendly Casco Viejo bar, a warm inviting space with some outside tables and lots of drinking space inside. Fresh modern *pintxos* for around €2.70, including quails'

eggs with prawns and mushrooms, and lots of ham options, plus *raciones* of ham, anchovies and the like. Tues–Sun 11am until late.

★ **Café Bar Bilbao** Pl. Nueva 6 ☎ 944 151 671, ⓦ bilbao-cafebar.com. Exceptional anchovy, ham and *bacalao al pil-pil pintxos*, served by *simpático* staff, with everything labelled on the counter in the stylish old blue-tiled café, and some tables on the Casco Viejo's lovely main square. Daily 9am–11pm.

Los Fueros c/Fueros 6 ☎ 944 150 614. If you fancy getting away from the old-town crowds, nip behind the back of Pl. Nueva and try this small bar, specializing in grilled prawns (*gambas*) and barnacles (*percebes*). Mon, Tues & Thurs–Sat 11am–3pm & 6.30–10pm, Sun 10.30am–3pm.

Gatz c/Santa María 10 ☎ 944 154 861, ⓦ bargatz.com. Cosy late-night tapas bar in the old town, serving exquisite *pintxos* such as delicious cod, or the Basque equivalent of ratatouille in a tiny tart, to a mixed younger crowd. Good selection of wines and beers. Mon–Fri 1–3pm & 7–11pm, Sat 1pm–midnight, Sun 1–3pm.

El Globo c/Diputación 8 ☎ 944 150 614, ⓦ barelglobo.com. Creative, high-quality *pintxos* near Pl. Moyúa in the central Abando district. The interior decor is part wine bar, part upscale sandwich bar, and there's also outdoor seating – order through the hatch in the wall. Plentiful seafood options include baby squid with caramelized onions, or you can opt for goats' cheese. Mon–Fri 8am until late, Sat 11am–midnight.

Gure Toki Pl. Nueva 12 ☎944 158 037. Tiny tapas bar, tucked in the corner of the Casco Viejo's main square. Irresistible, eye-catching "*pintxos ornamentales*" include lovely langoustine and squid concoctions, or you can buy a more substantial salad to eat at the barrels in the square itself. Mon, Tues & Thurs 9am–10.30pm, Fri & Sat 9am–11pm, Sun 9am–3.30pm.

Irrintzi c/Santa María 8 ☎944 167 616, ⓦirrintzi.es. Hip, buzzing old-town tapas bar, with groovy murals and an indie soundtrack, plus some of Bilbao's most creative *pintxos*, such as a *crema* of *bacalao* (cod) served in a glass. Mon–Thurs 9am–11pm, Fri & Sat 10am–midnight, Sun noon–10pm.

Taurino Taberna c/Ledesma 5 ☎944 013 452. This hole-in-the-wall place, on the appealing, bar-filled, pedestrianized c/Ledesma in the new town, stands out from the crowd for its wall-to-ceiling bullfighting-themed decor. Besides its sheer atmosphere, however, it also serves a great range of snacks, from *tortilla* to grilled-vegetable sandwiches. Mon–Fri 10am–10pm, Sat 10am–11pm.

Xukela c/El Perro 2 ☎944 159 772, ⓦxukela.com. With its red panelling and check tablecloths, this perennially popular Casco Viejo tapas bar is oddly reminiscent of a French bistro, and serves substantial enough *raciones* to make a hearty meal; but it's best known for its wide range of snacks and top-class wine list. It has a lot of open space for drinkers who prefer to stand. Daily 1.30–11.30pm.

RESTAURANTS

Bascook c/Barroeta Aldamar 8 ☎944 009 977, ⓦbascook.com. Swiftly established as Bilbao's most popular new restaurant, *Bascook* is the brainchild of chef Aitor Elizegi. His playful ideas include having a menu that's also a magazine, and offering three separate cuisines – world, vegetarian and, for those with time to linger, slow food. Take your pick from all three, with mains at €12–15 and a set lunch menu for €20. Daily 1–3pm & 8.30–11.30pm.

Bistro Guggenheim Guggenheim Museum ☎944 239 333, ⓦbistroguggenheimbilbao.com. Revamped in 2011, the Guggenheim's in-house café serves a great-value lunch *menú* (€18.40) of zestful modern Basque cuisine; it's the perfect complement to a morning in the museum itself. Tues–Sun 9.30am–8.30pm.

Casa Rufo c/Hurtado de Amézaga 5 ☎944 432 172. Deservedly popular *cocina* in the Abando district, with three cosy, themed dining rooms specializing in three main

items: cod and two types of unbelievably succulent steak (*chuleton*), the main reason you'll need a reservation – it's priced by the kilo. Count on spending close to €50 per person. Mon–Sat 1.30–3.30pm & 8.45–11.30pm.

Etxanobe Euskalduna, Avda. Abandoibarra 4 ☎944 421 071, ⓦen.etxanobe.com. Enjoying tremendous views of the city from its open-air terrace, the Michelin-starred Euskalduna restaurant is run by celebrated Basque chef Fernando Canales. His innovative contemporary cuisine is available on seven set menus, ranging from €59 for the tasting menu up to €125. Mon–Sat 1–3.30pm & 8.30–11pm; closed first 3 weeks of Aug.

Restaurante Atea Paseo de Uribitarte 4 ☎944 005 869, ⓦatearestaurante.com. Good-value, central restaurant south of the river near the Zubizuri bridge, where the modern dining room lurks behind the facade of a former customs warehouse, and there are also outdoor tables. With the emphasis on a quick turnaround, the €16.75 set lunch is a tray holding three *pintxos* plus main course, salad and dessert. Daily 1.30–4pm & 8.30–11pm.

Río Oja c/El Perro 6 ☎944 150 871. Old-fashioned, much-loved and exceptionally inexpensive Casco Viejo restaurant with an unusual emphasis on hearty stews (*cazuelas*) and sauces, displayed on the bar for diners' inspection. With clams in green sauce for €12, or quail stew for just €8, this is a place to experiment a little. Tues–Sun 9am–11pm.

Serantes c/Licenciado Poza 16 ☎944 212 129, ⓦmarisqueriaserantes.com. Full meals at this top-notch *marisquería* come to about €50 per head; watch for specials on *langostino* and other crustacean delights. They also have an excellent tapas bar, serving pricey but top-quality bar food. Daily 10am–1am.

Victor Montes Pl. Nueva 8 ☎944 157 067, ⓦvictormontes.com. Atmospheric bar and dining room, lined with a collection of over 1600 wines, on the attractive main square of the old town. Traditional grills, special hams and fresh fish are served in the main, very popular dining room, or sumptuous *pintxos* in the bar; there are tables on the square in summer. Mon–Sat 1.30–4pm & 8–11pm, Sun 1.30–4pm.

Zortziko c/Alameda de Manzarredo 17 ☎944 239 743, ⓦzortziko.es. Effortlessly classy, highly acclaimed restaurant, with classic French decor and an array of fine *nueva cocina* dishes. Chef Daniel García's creations are best sampled on the set tasting menus, and especially the eleven-course €85 option. Tues–Sat 1–3.30pm & 9–11.30pm.

BARS

Dubliners Pl. Moyúa 6 ☎944 236 214. Bilbao is full of Irish pubs and this is one of the best, with pints of Guinness and Murphy's going for €5 and hearty *menús* for €17.50. Mon–Thurs & Sun 8.30am–11pm, Fri & Sat 8.30am–3am.

6

Lamiak c/Pelota 8 ☎ 944 159 642. A large café-bar with a cool gallery packed with tables upstairs, and a fashionable crowd at the weekends. Mon–Thurs & Sun 4pm–midnight, Fri & Sat 4pm–2am.

Taberna Txomin Barullo c/Barrencalle 40 ☎ 944 152 788. A great, laidback café-bar in the old town, with nationalist murals and a friendly alternative crowd. Daily noon–midnight.

NIGHTLIFE AND ENTERTAINMENT

The city has a vibrant **nightlife**, especially at the weekends – and goes totally wild during the August **fiesta**, with scores of open-air bars, live music and impromptu dancing everywhere and a truly festive atmosphere. Bilbao also has a reasonably vibrant **club** scene, with the edgier San Francisco district south of the Casco Viejo, across the river and home to Bilbao's West African and Moroccan population, a hot area for dancing till dawn. Hard rock and punk fans tend to congregate in the grungy bars along c/Iturribide, northeast of the Casco Viejo. For **live music** listings, check the local newspaper *El Correo* (☯ elcorreo.com).

CLUBS AND LIVE MUSIC VENUES

Azkena c/Ibañez de Bilbao 26 ☎ 944 240 890, ☯ azkena.com. Popular live-music space and bar, with simple, minimalist decor and a dancefloor that tends to get busy late in the evenings. Mon–Thurs 5pm–2am, Fri & Sat 5pm–5am.

BilboRock-La Merced Muelle de la Merced 1 ☯ www .bilbao.net/bilborock. Large, retro-styled converted church, just across the Puente La Merced from the Casco Viejo, that's among the city's best live venues for rock and alternative music. Irregular hours; depends on schedules.

Bullitt Groove Club c/Dos de Mayo 3 ☎ 944 163 036, ☯ bullittgrooveclub.com. Hip bar-cum-club, with an eclectic clientele and mix of music, from the latest dance sounds to indie and rock. Thurs 8pm–1am, Fri 8pm–2am, Sat 6am–noon & 8pm–2am, Sun 6am–noon.

Conjunto Vacio Muelle de la Merced 3 ☎ 607 432 083, ☯ conjuntovacio.net. Much-loved, gay-friendly nightclub, just across the river from the old town, with a Sunday morning session for hardcore clubbers. Fri & Sat midnight–4am, Sun 9am–1pm.

Cotton Club c/Gregorio de la Revilla 25 ☎ 944 104 951, ☯ cottonclubbilbao.es. Popular live-music and disco venue, entered on c/Simón Bolívar, featuring everything from jazz and blues to rock and house. Beer starts at €3, and there's no cover. Mon–Thurs 4.30pm–3am, Fri & Sat 6.30pm–6.30am, Sun 6.30pm–3am.

Image Club c/Sabino Arana, Berango ☎ 944 682 866, ☯ theimageclub.com. The largest warehouse-type dance club in the region is several kilometres northwest of the centre, 15min walk from ⓜ Berango, with two floors, balconies, and big-name DJs flown in to compete with the local stars. Fri midnight–6am, Sat midnight–7am.

Kafe Antzokia c/San Vicente 2 ☎ 944 246 107, ☯ kafeantzokia.com. This cinema-turned-nightclub has an emphasis on live shows, and attracts big names, from world music and reggae to folk- and punk-influenced groups and Basque musicians. Resident DJs spin an eclectic mix Saturday nights, with plenty of local sounds. The restaurant is open at lunchtimes for drinks and light meals; set menu €12.50. Mon–Sat 1.30–3.30pm & 8pm–3am.

New High Club c/Naja 5; no phone. The city's most visible gay club, in the middle of the old town. In the main room, Spanish dance music is played, and in a small theatre upstairs XX-rated films are shown. There's a hyperactive "dark room" in the back. Mon–Thurs & Sun 8.30pm–3.30am, Fri & Sat 8.30pm–4.30am.

MUSIC AND THEATRE VENUES

Euskalduna Avda. Abondoibarra ☎ 944 035 000, ☯ euskalduna.net. Ultramodern structure, built on the ruins of the city's last shipyard, which serves as home to the Bilbao Symphony Orchestra, with a programme of opera and classical music, and theatrical performances. Box office Mon–Fri 9am–2pm & 4–7pm.

Teatro Arriaga Pl. Arriaga ☎ 944 163 333, ☯ www .teatroarriaga.com. This magnificent old-town landmark hosts dance and music events, as well as theatre.

DIRECTORY

Consulate The British consulate is at Alameda Urquijo 2 ☎ 902 109 356.

Football Athletico Bilbao (☯ athletic-club.net), known for their red-and-white-striped shirts as *Rojiblancos*, are famous for only fielding Basque players or products of their own youth system, and have never been relegated from the Primera División. Watch them play at the Campo de San Mamés.

Hospital Hospital de Basurto, Avda. de Montevideo 18

☎ 944 006 000 (ⓜ San Mamés). Call ambulances on ☎ 944 410 081 or ☎ 944 100 000 (24hr).

Internet access San Mamés Locutorio, Luís Briñas 25 (daily 11am–11pm), is opposite Termibus; Net-House, c/Villarias 6, opposite the Casco Viejo (daily 10.30am–10.30pm).

Post office Alameda Urquijo 19 (Mon–Fri 8am–9pm, Sat 9am–2pm; ⓜ Abando or Moyúa). There's another post office near the Guggenheim main entrance, Alameda Mazarredo 13 (same hours).

Vitoria-Gasteiz

The capital of the entire País Vasco, as well as of Araba (Alava), **VITORIA-GASTEIZ** is a fascinating and exceptionally friendly old city, all the better for lying off the tourist circuit, and well worth a couple of days' visit. Sancho el Sabio, King of Navarre, built a fortress here in 1181, on the site of the Basque village of **Gasteiz**. He renamed it **Vitoria** to celebrate his victories over Alfonso VIII of Castille, who promptly captured it back in 1200. Stretching along a low ridge in the heart of a fertile plain, Vitoria subsequently prospered as a trading centre for wool and iron, and still boasts an unusual concentration of Renaissance palaces and fine churches.

The streets of the city's Romanesque old town, the **Casco Medieval**, still circle like a spider's web around either side of the central hill, while a neater grid of later developments, Ensanche, lies below on the plain. All Vitoria's graceful mansions and churches are built from the same greyish-gold stone, and many of the medieval buildings are amazingly well preserved. The finest of Vitoria's buildings, on c/Fray Zacarías near the cathedral, include the **Palacio de Escoriaza-Esquibel**, with its sixteenth-century Plateresque portal, and the **Palacio de Montehermoso**, now run as a cultural and exhibition space. On the southern edge of the old town, the porticoed **Plaza de España** is a gem, while the neighbouring **Plaza de la Virgen Blanca** is more elegant, with glassed-in balconies. If you find the hill itself a bit of a challenge, Vitoria offers a remarkable feature: **moving stairways** climb it from both the east (Cantón de San Francisco Javier) and west (Cantón de la Soledad) sides.

Catedral de Santa María

Cathedral Guided tours: daily 11am–2pm & 5–8pm; booking essential • €6 • ☎ 945 255 135, ⓦ catedralvitoria.com **Visitor centre** Daily 10.30am–2pm & 4.30–8pm • Free

After nine centuries of tottering precariously at the highest point of Vitoria's old town, at the north end of the ridge, the venerable **Catedral de Santa María** had to be closed for reconstruction in 1994. It has now finally reopened for regular services, but the work is still ongoing, as are plans to display the fruits of twenty years of investigations into its fascinating history. A **visitor centre** off Plaza de la Burullería holds displays on the project, and can fill you in both on hard-hat **tours** of the site, and on plans to construct a museum immediately below the nave. During the last tour each evening, coloured lights are projected onto the superbly carved fourteenth-century west doorway, to reveal how it has changed in appearance over the centuries.

Museo Bibat de Naipes y Arqueología

C/Cuchillería 54 • Tues–Fri 10am–2pm & 4–6.30pm, Sat 10am–2pm, Sun 11am–2pm • Free

The word "Bibat" translates as "two in one", to denote the fact that this complex consists not only of two buildings fused together, but two distinct museums. The

---

VITORIA'S FESTIVALS

Vitoria's largest annual festival, the **Fiesta de la Virgen Blanca**, is celebrated from August 4 to August 9 each year. On the first day, head for the Plaza de la Virgen Blanca with a blue-and-white festival scarf, a bottle of champagne (or cava) and a cigar, and wearing old clothes. At 6pm, the umbrella-toting "Bajada del Celedón" – a life-size doll dressed in traditional costume – appears from the church tower and flies through the air over the plaza. This is the signal to spray champagne everywhere (hence the old clothes), light the cigar and put on your scarf – which the hard core don't take off until midnight on the 9th, when Celedón returns to his tower, signalling the end of the fiesta. In between, the town is engulfed in a continuous party.

During the third week of July, the city also hosts a **jazz festival** that attracts big-name performers (ⓦ jazzvitoria.com).

VITORIA-GASTEIZ

■ ACCOMMODATION	
La Casa de los Arquillos	2
Hostal La Bilbaina	1
Hotel Ciudad de Vitoria	3
Hotel Dato	6
NH Canciller Ayala	5
Pensión Amaia	4
Pensión Araba 2	7

● PINTXOS BARS & RESTAURANTS	
Asador Sagartoki	6
Ikea	7
La Malquerida	3
El Portalón	2
Saburdi	8
Toloño	5
El Tulipan de Oro	1
Virgen Blanca	4

first and more unusual, housed in a grand medieval mansion, is devoted to playing cards (*naipes*); many are rather beautiful, but by their very nature they're also small and repetitive, and in the absence of much contextual material it's not as interesting as you might hope.

The modern interconnected annexe holds well-presented displays of archeological artefacts found locally, ranging through prehistoric, Roman and early medieval times. One skull, dating from 2500 BC, still has a neatly chipped stone arrowhead embedded in its base.

Artium

C/Francia 24 • Tues–Thurs 11am–2pm & 5–8pm, Fri–Sun 11am–9pm • €6, Wed €0.01 • ☎ 945 209 000, �🌐 artium.org

East of the old town, not far from the bus station, the **Artium** is an attractive museum of contemporary art. It concentrates largely on temporary exhibitions of Basque and Spanish artists, for which it's able to draw on its own permanent collection of upwards of three thousand works.

Museo de Bellas Artes

Paseo de Fray Francisco de Vitoria • Tues–Fri 10am–2pm & 4–6.30pm, Sat 10am–2pm & 5–8pm, Sun 11am–2pm • Free

Southwest of Vitoria's centre, a magnificent mansion on the attractive, pedestrianized avenue in the Senda district holds the regional **Museo de Bellas Artes**. Its fine collection centres on the period from 1700 to 1950; highlights include *costumbrista* paintings, depicting Basque cultural and folk practices.

ARRIVAL AND INFORMATION VITORIA-GASTEIZ

6

By train Vitoria's RENFE train station is in the commercial district, a 10min walk south of the old town along the pedestrianized c/Dato. Services include to Madrid (5 daily; 3hr 45min–5hr 30min); Miranda del Ebro (12 daily; 20min); and Pamplona (4 daily; 1hr).

By bus The bus station is at c/Los Herrán 70, a 10min walk

east of the old town. Services run to: Bilbao (every 30min; 1hr 10min); Laguardia (4 daily; 1hr 45 min); Logroño (8 daily; 2hr); and Pamplona (10 daily; 1hr 30min).

Turismo Pl. de España 1 (July–Sept daily 10am–8pm; Oct–June Mon–Sat 10am–7pm, Sun 11am–2pm; ☎ 945 161 598, ☏ turismo.vitoria-gasteiz.org).

ACCOMMODATION

As Vitoria is not a major tourist destination, there's surprisingly little accommodation within the old town; on the plus side, rates are generally remarkably cheap. Budget hotels are concentrated near the train and bus stations, while more expensive options tend to be in Ensanche, south of the Casco Medieval.

⭐ **La Casa de los Arquillos** c/los Arquillos 1 ☎ 945 151 259, ☏ lacasadelosarquillos.com. Lovely little boutique hotel (which calls itself a B&B) in a superb central location in a medieval building converted to hold eight bright, stylish en-suite bedrooms. The one snag is that this spot can get a little noisy. **€74**

Hostal La Bilbaina c/Prudencio María de Verástegui 2 ☎ 945 254 400. Comfortable, modern rooms with bath and satellite TV above a large restaurant. All rooms have balconies, and they offer a substantial buffet breakfast. **€50**

Hotel Ciudad de Vitoria Portal de Castilla 8 ☎ 945 141 100, ☏ hoteles-silken.com. Opulently *belle époque*, this beautifully restored historic hotel, a short walk from the old town, opens to a vast central atrium, and offers comfortable lavishly appointed rooms with immaculate marble-clad bathrooms. Extras include a fitness centre, cocktail bar, good buffet breakfasts, and free street parking outside. **€70**

Hotel Dato c/Dato 28 ☎ 945 147 230, ☏ hoteldato.com. Beyond the gaudy mix of classical statues and gilded mirrors

in the stairwells, this cosy hotel, close to the station, has super-helpful staff and tastefully decorated rooms with colourful batik bedspreads and free wi-fi. All rooms have baths; pay a little extra for an enclosed balcony. **€54**

NH Canciller Ayala c/Ramón y Cajal 5 ☎ 945 130 000, ☏ nh-hotels.com. Modern, business-oriented hotel in a convenient and pleasant location on the edge of the Parque de la Florida. The super-comfortable rooms come with polished wood floors and smart, contemporary furniture and fittings. **€60**

Pensión Amaia c/La Paz 15 ☎ 945 255 497, ☏ pensionamaia.com. Friendly *pensión* just outside the old town, with seven somewhat faded double rooms, two triples and one single; all share the use of modern bathrooms. **€35**

Pensión Araba 2 c/Florida 25 ☎ 945 232 588, ☏ pensionaraba.com. An excellent-value *pensión* in an immaculately kept family home near the station, offering four clean en-suite rooms, each capable of sleeping up to four guests. **€45**

EATING AND DRINKING

Vitoria-Gasteiz has a solid selection of quality **restaurants** and **cafés**, aimed principally at a no-nonsense local clientele – plazas de España and Virgen Blanca hold particularly appealing arrays of outdoor cafés – while **pintxos bars** are spread throughout both Ensanche and the edges of the Casco Medieval. Look out for such regional specialities as potatoes with chorizo, *porrusalda* (leek soup) and *perretxikos* (wild mushrooms with egg). The city's dynamic **nightlife** is primarily fuelled by its student population. The main areas are the streets off c/Dato in Ensanche, and the pubs on the eastern side of the Casco Medieval, particularly on c/Cuchillería, where places such as *Bar El 7* at no. 3 have a more youthful, alternative feel.

PINTXOS BARS AND RESTAURANTS

⭐ **Asador Sagartoki** c/Prado 18 ☎ 945 288 876, ☏ sagartoki.es. Far and away the best *pintxos* in the city – beautiful to look at, and delicious to eat. Sample five, plus a glass of wine, for just €10.50. Behind the bar, a fully-fledged

restaurant/grill serves succulent meats such as *chuletillas* (steak) for €15–20, and a special cider-house *menú* (€40.45). Mon–Fri 10am–midnight, Sat & Sun 11am–midnight.

Ikea Portal de Castilla 27 ☎ 945 144 747, ☏ restaurant eikea.com. Don't be misled by the name; this is Vitoria's most

6

acclaimed restaurant, a chic and expensive dining room in a stone town house transformed by architect Javier Mariscal. It serves good Basque food with a contemporary spin; mains from around €25, five-course tasting menu €75. The liver pâté is highly recommended. Tues–Sat 1–3.30pm & 8.30–11.30pm, Sun 1–3.30pm; closed last 3 weeks of Aug.

La Malquerida c/Correría 10 ☎ 945 257 068. Hugely popular, hip, tapas bar, a few steps away from the Pl. de la Virgen Blanca. A chalked-up menu of innovative snacks and *raciones* is to be enjoyed both indoors and out, with crowds spilling out into the adjoining alleyways. Daily 11am–midnight.

El Portalón c/Correría 150 ☎ 945 142 755, ⓦ restauranteelportalon.com. Vitoria's most beautiful sixteenth-century house makes an atmospheric setting for this pricey restaurant specializing in traditional Basque cooking. It's very dependable, if not exceptional, with a €35 weekday lunch menu and dinner menus from €46, or €60 for the "theatrical" option with medieval-garbed staff. Mon–Sat 1.30–3.30pm & 8.30–11pm, Sun 1.30–3.30pm.

Saburdi c/Dato 32 ☎ 945 147 016 755, ⓦ saburdi.com. Busy, friendly tapas bar, with outdoor tables on the main pedestrian road up from the station, which serves great-value *pintxos* from €1.50 – try the cod with squash, or quail's egg with ham – and more substantial *raciones*. Daily 9am–11pm.

Toloño Cuesta San Francisco 3 ☎ 945 233 336, ⓦ tolonobar.com. Determinedly modern tapas bar on the edge of the old town, with bright coloured lighting and brisk service, free nibbles with each drink, and a good changing menu of €2–3 *pintxos*. Late-night DJs at weekends. Sun–Thurs noon–1am, Fri & Sat noon–3am.

El Tulipan de Oro c/Correría 157. Cosy tapas bar in an aged wood-beamed house, serving chorizo flambéed at the bar over pig-shaped alcohol burners, with a €10 weekday *menú*. Mon–Thurs 11.30am–4pm & 7–11pm, Fri & Sat 11.30–midnight, Sun 11.30am–11pm.

Virgen Blanca Pl. de la Virgen Blanca 3 ☎ 945 286 199. Restaurant/bar with the feel of a British gastropub, in a great location with a terrace perched at the top end of the plaza, plus an atmospheric dining room with exposed brick walls and wooden tables. *Raciones* and sandwiches, or €15.40 lunch menu, €30.50 dinner menu. Mon 6pm–2am, Tues–Sun 9am–2am.

Rioja Alavesa

Forty kilometres south of Vitoria-Gasteiz, across a range of high, little-populated hills, the wine-growing district of **Rioja Alavesa** feels a rather incongruous appendage to the Basque Country. The north side of the Ebro valley does, however, belong to **Araba**, the same province as Vitoria-Gasteiz. As a result, so too do several of the richest and most famous Rioja wineries, even though the province of La Rioja, as well as the largest town hereabouts, Logroño (see p.410), lies immediately across the river.

Assuming you have your own transport, exploring the picturesque villages and **bodegas** of Rioja Alavesa makes a wonderful way to spend a day. The pick of the towns is lovely old **Laguardia**, while competition between the wineries is so fierce that several have invested quite astonishing amounts of money to attract attention, most notably **Bodegas Ysios** with its Santiago Calatrava-designed headquarters, and **Marqués de Riscal**, where Frank Gehry has created an amazing showpiece hotel

If you drive down from Vitoria-Gasteiz, be sure to stop after 35km at the **Balcon de la Rioja**, a staggering hillside viewpoint that offers a first magnificent panorama over the plains below.

Laguardia

Though little more than a village, **LAGUARDIA**, 15km northwest of Logroño, is the largest community in Rioja Alavesa. Known to the Basques as Biasteri, it's a lovely spot, stretching along the crest of a low ridge overlooking the vineyards, and still surrounded by its medieval walls.

Within its stout gateways, a couple of slender cobbled lanes, lined with ancient mansions, connect the churches at either end. The finer of the two, **Santa María de los Reyes** to the north, boasts an ornately carved Gothic doorway. Much of the town itself is actually concealed from view; beneath the surface, the hilltop is riddled with subterranean cellars, hollowed out to store the wine on which its prosperity is based.

Bodegas Ysios

Tours Mon–Fri 11am, 1pm & 4pm, Sat & Sun 11am & 1pm; €3; reserve ahead • ☎ 945 600 640, ⓦ ysios.com

Framed by the hills that rise to the north, the mesmerizing **Bodegas Ysios** undulates through the vineyards 2km north of Laguardia, off the Vitoria-Gasteiz road. Its resemblance to an ancient temple is entirely deliberate; the name Ysios honours twin Egyptian deities Isis and Osiris, and no expense was spared when architect Santiago Calatrava, also responsible for Bilbao airport, was commissioned to construct a new winery in 2001. The aluminium roof surmounts a wooden structure that on a more mundane level looks like a row of wine barrels.

Bodegas Marqués de Riscal

Tours Tues–Sun; €10; must be reserved in advance • ☎ 945 606 590, ⓦ marquesderiscal.com

Just outside the appealing village of **ELCIEGO**, 5km southwest of Laguardia, the **Bodegas Marqués de Riscal** is one of the oldest and largest of the Rioja vineyards. Several tours each day provide the opportunity to learn all about its history, and explore every stage of manufacture, from pressing to bottling. After seeing the cellars, used to store every vintage since 1858, you also get to taste a white and a red. Although the *bodega* forms part of the so-called City of Wine, the major component of which is the extraordinary **hotel**, tours do not however go into the hotel itself, but simply admire it from a distance of around 50m.

ARRIVAL AND INFORMATION   RIOJA ALAVESA

By bus Laguardia is served by regular buses from Vitoria-Gasteiz (4 daily; 1hr 45min).

Turismo c/Mayor 52, Laguardia (Mon–Sat 10am–2pm & 4–7pm, Sun 10.45am–2pm; ☎ 945 600 845, ⓦ laguardia-alava.com). Can provide detailed information on the many local *bodegas*.

ACCOMMODATION AND EATING

LAGUARDIA

★ **Castillo el Collado** Bodegas Palacio ☎ 945 621 200, ⓦ hotelcollado.com. Elegant B&B inn, just south of town on the road to Elciego, with a dozen antique-furnished rooms, individually styled on such themes as "Love and Madness", and an intimate, top-notch restaurant. **€125**

Hospedería Los Parajes Pl. Mayor 46–48 ☎ 945 621 130, ⓦ hospederiadelosparajes.com. Fancy restaurant in the very heart of town, serving main courses like loin of venison or turbot with couscous for €18–22, or a set menu for €55. Daily 8.30–11pm.

Hostal/Bar Biazteri c/Berberana 2 ☎ 945 600 026, ⓦ biazteri.com. Simple good-value en-suite rooms at the south end of town, above a bar that serves €10 weekday lunches including a glass of Rioja, and also excellent tapas. **€53**

Hotel Villa de Laguardia Paseo San Raimundo 15 ☎ 945 600 560, ⓦ hotelvilladelaguardia.com. Large country-house hotel a short walk south of the town wall, with light, spacious rooms and a good restaurant. **€83**

ELCIEGO

Hotel Marqués de Riscal c/Torrea 1, Elciego ☎ 945 180 880, ⓦ hotel-marquesderiscal.com. Designed by Frank O. Gehry and echoing his Guggenheim Museum, this extraordinary hotel, swaddled in a baffling tangle of colossal multicoloured titanium ribbons, is an amazing structure to find in such a tiny place. Laid out to offer beautiful views of the ancient village nearby, it's absolutely breathtaking, but it's also smaller than you might expect. The 43 rooms themselves are large and opulent, but only half of them are in the main structure; the rest are set into the adjacent hillside, connected via a walkway. There are also two very classy restaurants. **€285**

6

Pamplona

A prosperous city of just under 200,000, **PAMPLONA** (Iruña) is a robust, visceral place, with a rough-hewn edge and a strong streak of macho self-confidence. Having started out as a powerful fortress town defending the northern approaches to Spain at the foothills of the Pyrenees (the city takes its name from the Roman general Pompey), it later became capital of Navarra – often a semi-autonomous state – and an important stop on the Camino de Santiago. With plenty to offer around its Casco Antiguo – enticing churches, a beautiful park and the massive citadel – Pamplona makes an appealing year-round destination, though for anyone who has been here during the thrilling week of the **Fiestas de San Fermín** a visit at any other time can only be an anticlimax.

Everything you're likely to want to see in Pamplona lies within its remarkably compact **Casco Antiguo**. Centring on the **Plaza del Castillo**, ringed with fashionable cafés, it's a glorious and very much lived-in jumble of buildings from all eras, where every twisting stone lane is worth exploring and intriguingly tatty old shops and bars lie concealed behind medieval shutters.

Catedral de Santa María

C/Curia s/n • Mon–Sat: mid-March to mid-Nov 10.30am–7pm; mid-Nov to mid-March 10.30am–5pm • €4 • Ⓦ catedraldepamplona.com

Built between the late fourteenth and the early sixteenth centuries, the **Catedral de Santa María** is basically Gothic. While it may not look promising at first, thanks to an unattractive facade added in the eighteenth century, it's worth paying to go inside. In the cathedral itself, the tomb of the recumbent Carlos III and his queen Eleanor, in the centre of the nave, dates from 1413. The fee also admits you to the appealing cloisters beyond, which hold several superbly sculpted doorways. The finest, the Puerta de la Preciosa, leads to what were originally the sleeping quarters, now home to a lovely exhibition celebrating the cathedral's musical heritage. Another opens onto a chapel with a lovely star vault, and another into the **Museo Diocesano**, a collection of Navarran sacred art housed in the former refectory and kitchen.

The city walls

Behind the cathedral, in one of the oldest parts of Pamplona, the most substantial remaining section of the **city walls** looks down over a loop of the Río Arga. If you head out through the gate here, the Portal de Zumalacárregui (or de Francia), you can take paths down to the river from where you get the full force of the impregnability of these defences.

Museo de Navarra

C/Santo Domingo 47 • Tues–Sat 9.30am–2pm & 5–7pm, Sun & public hols 11am–2pm • €2, free Sun • ⓦ cfnavarra.es/cultura/museo

A magnificent medieval hospital just inside the city walls now serves as the entrance to the **Museo de Navarra**, although most of its consistently beautiful treasures are displayed in the light, uncluttered galleries of a modern annexe. Prehistoric relics in the basement include a dyed-green skull found in (or near) an ancient copper mine; higher up there's a large mosaic floor taken from a Roman villa in Tudela. Other highlights include an ornately carved Muslim casket from 1004; a thirteenth-century ceiling fresco from a chapel in Olite; and fourteenth-century Gothic murals from Pamplona's own cathedral; and, amid the extensive collection of paintings, Goya's full-length portrait of the Marqués de San Adrián, from 1804.

ARRIVAL AND DEPARTURE   PAMPLONA

By train Pamplona's train station is 1.5km northwest of the old city on Avda. San Jorge, served by local bus #9. RENFE trains connect the city with Madrid (4 daily; 3hr 10min); San Sebastián (2 daily; 1hr 45min); Vitoria (4 daily; 1hr); and Zaragoza (5 daily; 2hr).

By bus The bus station is 250m south of the old town on c/Conde Oliveto. Connections include: Bilbao (6 daily; 2hr 15min); Irún (3 daily; 2hr); Ochagavía (daily except Sun; 2hr); Roncal (daily; 1hr 45min); San Sebastián (9 daily; 1–3hr); Zaragoza (2–3 daily; 4hr).

By car Drivers should leave their cars in the car parks either on c/Taconera or at the bullring.

INFORMATION

Turismo Pamplona's main *turismo* is outside the old town, close to the bullring at Roncesvalles 4 (June–Sept Mon–Sat 9am–7pm, Sun 10am–2pm; Sept–May Mon–Sat 10am–2pm & 4–7pm, Sun 10am–2pm; ☎848 420 420,

ⓦturismodepamplona.es). There's also a summer-only kiosk in Pl. Consistorial (May & June daily 10.30am–2pm & 4.30–8pm; July to mid-Sept daily 10am–8pm).

ACCOMMODATION

Much the most enjoyable area of Pamplona in which to stay is the Casco Antiguo, which holds a reasonable selection of accommodation in all price ranges. The rates below refer to the peak summer season but *not* San Fermín, when they double or even triple.

Alojamientos Acella Travesía de Acella 3 ☎948 261 000, ⓦhostalacella.com. A wide range of clean, modern but somewhat uninspiring double and single rooms, both sharing bathrooms and en suite (€20 extra), plus

apartments for rent, overlooking Parque Yamaguchi 1km southwest of the Casco Antiguo. A refuge during San Fermín, though rates triple. **€42**

Gran Hotel La Perla Pl. del Castillo 1 ☎948 223 000,

FIESTAS DE SAN FERMÍN

Pamplona's legendary **Fiestas de San Fermín**, or Sanfermines, known to the rest of the world as the **Running of the Bulls** and popularized by Ernest Hemingway's *The Sun Also Rises* (1926), lasts from noon on July 6 until midnight on July 14. The daily early-morning bull-run, or **encierro**, is just one component of nine days of riotous celebration, which also features bands, parades and 24-hour dancing in the streets. For details, see ⓦ **sanfermin.com**.

ACCOMMODATION AND SECURITY

Accommodation during the fiesta should be booked in advance – and be warned many hotels triple their rates. If you arrive without a reservation, head for the *turismo* opposite the bullring, where locals offer **rooms** at exorbitant prices. Many revellers simply sleep outdoors, on the ramparts, in the park or *plaza*. **Petty crime** soars, but valuables and luggage can be left at the bus station, which also holds showers.

The **campsite**, *Ezcaba*, 7km east (ⓣ 948 330 315, ⓦ campingezcaba.com), can be reserved in advance, and is connected by regular buses. Security is tight – admission is by pass only and a guard patrols all night. **ATMs** frequently run out of money during the festival, while **banks** are closed over the weekend.

EL ENCIERRO

The **encierro**, the Running of the Bulls, takes place every morning. Six bulls are released at 8am, to run from the Corralillos near Plaza Santo Domingo to the bullring, where they will fight that evening. They take around four minutes to race a fenced-off course of just over 800m, through Plaza Consistorial and along c/Estafeta; official *pastores* (shepherds) armed with sticks make sure they keep going. A second batch of more placid animals follows, to help round up stragglers. In front, around and occasionally beneath the bulls run the hundreds of locals and tourists who are foolish or drunk enough to test their daring against the horns.

To **watch** the *encierro* arrive early, by 6am. The best vantage points are near the start, or on the wall leading to the bullring. Try to get a spot on the outer of the two barriers – don't worry when the one in front fills up and blocks your view, as all these people will be moved on by police before the run.

The event divides into two parts. First comes the actual running of the bulls, when the object is to run with the bull or whack it with a rolled-up newspaper. Even if you don't see the bulls amid the runners, you'll sense the terror and excitement down on the ground; occasionally, if a bull manages to breach the wooden safety barriers, this spreads to the watching crowd.

ⓦ granhotellaperla.com. You simply can't beat Pamplona's grandest hotel for location, right on the main old-town square, or history – past guests include Hemingway and Chaplin. Spacious, well-restored rooms overlook either the square or lively c/Estafeta behind, with bargain rates for advance bookings. **€140**

Hostal Arriazu c/Comedías 14 ⓣ 948 210 202, ⓦ hostalarriazu.com. Conveniently central and surprisingly quiet *hostal*, offering comfortable en-suite rooms just a few steps from the main square. **€65**

Hostal Bearán c/San Nicolás 25 ⓣ 948 223 428, ⓦ hostalbearan.com. A clean *hostal* in the heart of the old town, whose simple en-suite rooms are perfectly acceptable for budget travellers who don't mind a bit of late-night noise so long as they're close to all the action. **€53**

Hostal Navarra c/Tudela 9, 2° ⓣ 948 225 164, ⓦ hostalnavarra.com. Well-established *hostal* near the bus station, going back more than forty years; all rooms have en-suite facilities and have been pleasantly refurbished, and there's a laundry. **€55**

Hotel Eslava Pl. Virgen de la O 7 ⓣ 948 222 270, ⓦ hotel-eslava.com. Cosy, welcoming hotel in a quiet corner of the old town, run by the Eslava family. Rooms are bright and en suite, albeit rather anonymous; some have balcony views overlooking the gardens to the south. Fifteen doubles and thirteen particularly well-priced singles, with a bar in the basement. **€73**

Hotel Yoldi Avda. de San Ignacio 11 ⓣ 948 224 800, ⓦ hotelyoldi.com. Old hotel with smart, stylish rooms, a few hundred metres south of the Casco Viejo, not far from the bullring – this is where the bullfighters stay during San Fermín. Garage parking. **€86**

Pensión Escaray c/Nueva 24, 1° ⓣ 948 227 825. Ageing but friendly place in a charming building in the old town. Rooms are small but clean, with wooden floors and shared bathrooms. **€45**

Pensión Sarasate Paseo Sarasate 30 ⓣ 948 223 084, ⓔ pensionsarasate@gmail.es. Simple little *pensión* on the edge of the old town, very nicely maintained in the finest old-school tradition. All the rooms are en suite and some have balconies. **€50**

Next, bullocks with padded horns are let loose on the crowd in the bullring. By then, the bullring is already too crowded for anyone who has watched the running to get in there; to see both, you'll have to go on two separate mornings – for the bullring, arrive at 6am to get the free lower seats. For a seat higher up, buy a ticket from the office outside, not from the touts inside. On Sunday, you have to pay.

If you do decide to **run** – and we strongly advise you not to – remember that although it's generally less dangerous than it looks, at least one person gets seriously injured (or killed) every year. Find someone who knows the ropes to guide you through the first time, and don't try any heroics. Don't get trapped hiding in a doorway, or come between a scared bull and the rest of the pack. Traditionally, women don't take part, though more and more do so. Under-18s are barred.

The only official way in is at the **starting point**, Plaza Santo Domingo, entered via Plaza San Saturnino. Shortly before the start, the rest of the course is cleared. Then, shortly before 8am, you're allowed to make your way to your own preferred starting point. To mark the start, two rockets are fired: one when the bulls are released, and the second when they are all out. As soon as the first goes, you can start to run, though if you do so you'll probably reach the ring well before the bulls and be booed for your trouble; if you wait a while, you're more likely to get close to the bulls. No one is allowed to stop altogether. There are plenty of **escape points**, but they're only for use in emergency – try to get out prematurely, and you'll be shoved back. A third rocket is fired when all the bulls are in the bullring, and a final fourth once they've all entered the corral within.

OTHER SAN FERMÍN EVENTS

Pamplona offers plenty of other hazardous pursuits. Many visitors have fun hurling themselves from the central **fountain** on Plaza Consistorial or surrounding buildings, in the all-too-often vain hope that their friends will catch them. Other events include live **music** nightly from midnight in the bars and at Plaza del Castillo, continuing until about 4am in the fairground on the Avenida de Bayona, 1km southwest of the centre. **Fireworks** go off every evening in the Ciudadela park (about 11pm), and there's a **funfair** on the open ground alongside. Competing **bands** stagger through the streets all day playing to anyone who'll listen.

Bullfights take place daily at 6.30pm. Tickets (€15–75) go on sale at the Plaza de Toros at 8am the day before. At the end of the week (midnight July 14), the festivities are officially wound up for another year with a mournful candlelit procession, the **Pobre De Mi** (Poor Me).

Among the best of the **other Basque towns** where fiestas involve some form of *encierro* are Tudela (July 24–28), Estella (first weekend of Aug, with no official ban on women participants), and Tafalla (mid-Aug).

EATING AND DRINKING

The greatest number of **restaurants** and raucous little **bars** are on c/San Nicolás and its continuation, c/San Gregorio, and also along c/Estafeta on the *encierro* route. For good, inexpensive *menús*, and a wide range of **pintxos** and *bocadillos*, head for the streets around c/Major, in particular c/San Lorenzo. Navarra is noted for its fine asparagus, red peppers and red wines.

PINTXOS BARS

Baserri c/San Nicolás 32 ☎948 222 021, ⓦrestaurantebaserri.com. Highly acclaimed tapas bar, with a huge wine list and a varied, innovative array of snacks. €24 buys a special *pintxos* menu featuring six award-winners, plus cheese, while you can get a set menu in the restaurant at the back, including wine, for €14. Sun–Thurs 1–4pm & 8–11pm, Fri & Sat 1–4pm & 8.30–11.15pm.

Bodegón Sarria c/Estafeta 50–52 ☎948 227 713, ⓦbodegonsarria.com. Tapas bar and restaurant, where the *pintxos* taste as good as they look – try the artichoke plate – hams hang from the beams, and the glossy brick walls are adorned with photos of Hemingway enjoying his favourite fiesta. Daily 9am–12.30am.

La Cepa c/San Lorenzo 2 ☎948 225 178. Earthy, lively local bar with a fine selection of tapas and *bocadillos*; set menus also available. Mon–Sat 1pm–1am.

Fitero c/Estafeta 58 ☎948 222 006, ⓦbarfitero.es. Award-winning, bustling and very friendly tapas bar, just off the main square, where the counter is lined with unusual concoctions including cod crêpes, and dumplings stuffed with almonds. Daily noon–midnight.

★ **Gaucho** Traversa de Espoz y Mina 1 ☎948 225 073, ⓦcafebargaucho.com. Excellent tapas bar, just off Pl. del Castillo, where a tremendous range of *pintxos*, using ingredients like sea urchin roe or foie gras, attracts a mixed crowd that spills out across the street at weekends. Daily 8am–2am.

★ **Mesón del Caballo Blanco** c/Redín ☎948 211 504. Perhaps the most atmospheric bar in town, well away from the bustle in a converted medieval church, with a tree-shaded terrace at the top of the city walls giving fantastic views of Pamplona and mountains beyond. Snacks range from nachos with guacamole for €4.20 up to *jamón ibérico* for €15, plus a long list of *tostadas*. Daily noon–midnight.

CAFÉS AND RESTAURANTS

Café Alt Wien Parque de la Taconera ☎650 486 569, ⓦcafevienes.com. Also known as *El Vienés*, this park café is a great place to eat a simple breakfast and relax in peaceful surroundings, though it can get crowded with families in the afternoon. Daily 9am–10pm, weekends only Oct–April.

★ **Café Iruña** Pl. del Castillo 44 ☎948 222 064, ⓦcafeiruna.com. Elegant *belle époque* café and bar, with fine *pintxos* and a €13.50 set menu. There's seating on the *plaza* or inside the grand old nineteenth-century dining room, with its huge mirrors and decorative pillars. Daily 8am–10pm.

Europa c/Espoz y Mina 11 ☎948 221 800, ⓦhreuropa.com. This hotel restaurant is considered one of the best dining rooms in Navarra, under the direction of local culinary star Pilar Idoate, who knocks out a carefully crafted seasonal menu featuring traditional and *nouvelle* dishes. Tasting *menús* €45 and €62. Mon–Sat 1–3pm & 8–11pm.

San Fermín c/San Nicolás 44 ☎948 222 191, ⓦrestaurantesanfermin.com. Simple, first-floor dining room serving up classics such as *ajoarriero*, a tasty cod dish, seasonal vegetables and sumptuous desserts. Mains from €30. Tues–Thurs & Sun 1–4pm, Fri & Sat 1–4pm & 9–11pm.

Sarasate c/San Nicolás 19–21 ☎948 225 727. This great vegetarian restaurant, hidden away upstairs on a lively old-town street, was established in the 1950s. Has a *menú* for €12.50 and a good list of organic wines. Sun & Mon 1–3pm, Tues–Sat 1–3pm & 9–11pm.

Sidrería Asador Zaldiko c/Santo Domingo 39 ☎948 222 277, ⓦzaldiko.com. Close to the Museo Navarra, this typical Navarran grill and cider house knocks out excellent grilled steaks and lamb for around €20, cooked over a wood-fired *parilla*. Mon–Sat 1–3pm & 9–midnight.

Southwest of Pamplona

Pamplona having long served as a gateway city to Spain, it's no surprise that the main route southwest towards the heart of the peninsula – by way of Logroño – holds some impressive medieval towns, including **Puente La Reina** and **Estela**.

Puente La Reina

Few towns so perfectly evoke the days of the great medieval pilgrimages as **PUENTE LA REINA** (Gares), 20km southwest of Pamplona. This is the meeting place of the two main Spanish routes: the Navarrese trail, via Roncesvalles and Pamplona, and the Aragonese one, via Jaca, Leyre and Sangüesa. From here on, all pilgrims followed the same path to Santiago.

The main historic thoroughfare through town, calle Mayor, is lined by tall buildings decorated with their original coats of arms. At its western end, the town's namesake **bridge** crosses the Río Arga. Spain's finest medieval bridge, it was built by royal command at the end of the eleventh century, and remains in use, though now by pedestrians and animals only.

At the eastern edge of town, a twelfth-century Templar church, the **Iglesia del Crucifijo** (open for services only) contains an unusual Y-shaped crucifix.

INFORMATION   PUENTE LA REINA

Turismo c/Mayor 105, near the bridge (June–Aug Tues–Sat 10am–2pm & 4–7pm, Sun 11am–2pm; ☎948 341 301, ⓦpuentelareina-gares.net).

ACCOMMODATION AND EATING

Hotel Bidean c/Mayor 20 ☎948 341 156, ⓦbidean.com. Charming hotel in a seventeenth-century mansion in the very heart of town, with a high standard of comfort in its modernized rooms, and a good restaurant in its cavernous cellars. Twenty percent reductions for pilgrims. **€120**

Joaquin c/Mayor 48 ☎948 340 931. The nicest place to eat in town, on the ground floor of one of its finest old houses.

Serves traditional Navarran cuisine, including *alubias* (kidney beans) at reasonable prices. Daily 1–3.30pm & 8–11pm.

Mesón del Peregrino c/Irunbidea s/n ☎948 340 075, ⓦhotelelperegrino.com. Highly opulent hotel, just east of town on the main road towards Pamplona, and offering twelve luxurious and individually decorated rooms, plus a pool and high-class restaurant. **€190**

Estella

The old town of **ESTELLA** (Lizarra), 20km west of Puente La Reina, boasts a fine crop of monuments. While strictly speaking its old quarter, centring on **Plaza de los Fueros**, lies cradled within a loop of the Río Ega, many of its most interesting buildings are across the river in Barrio San Pedro. The whole place is small enough to be explored thoroughly on foot; be sure to seek out such churches as the fortified **San Pedro de la Rúa**, just up the hill from the *turismo*, and long-abandoned **Santo Sepulcro**.

Palacio de los Reyes de Navarra

C/San Nicolás, Barrio San Pedro • Tues–Sat 11am–1pm & 5–7pm, Sun & hols 11am–1.30pm • Free • ⓦ museogustavodemaeztu.com

Navarra's only large-scale Romanesque civil edifice, the twelfth-century **Palacio de los Reyes de Navarra**, is now open as an art gallery devoted to the Navarrese painter Gustavo de Maeztu (1887–1947).

INFORMATION   ESTELLA

Turismo c/San Nicolás 1 (April–Aug Mon–Sat 9am–8pm, Sun 10am–2pm; Sept Mon–Sat 10am–2pm & 4–7pm, Sun 10am–2pm; Oct–March Mon–Sat 10am–5pm, Sun 10am–2pm; ⓣ 948 556 301, ⓦ www.estella-lizarra.com). The well-stocked *turismo* is next door to the Palacio de los Reyes de Navarra.

ACCOMMODATION

Hotel Tximista c/Zaldu 15 ⓣ 948 555 870, ⓦ hoteltximista.com. Rather striking modern hotel 1km northwest of the old town, imaginatively welded around a nineteenth-century industrial complex, but now offering very bright upscale rooms in a verdant garden setting. €90
Hotel Yerri Avda. Yerri 35 ⓣ 948 546 034, ⓦ www .hotelyerri.es. Clean if unexciting new hotel a short walk northwest of the old town, with easy parking and a decent standard of accommodation, as well as its own restaurant. €62
Pensión San Andrés Pl. Santiago 58, 1º ⓣ 948 554 158. Estella's cheapest accommodation is in an unbeatably central location, right on the main square in the old town. Assorted simple rooms, both with and without en-suite facilities. €35

EATING AND DRINKING

Asador Astarriaga Pl. de los Fueros 12 ⓣ 948 550 802, ⓦ asadorastarriaga.com. Decent restaurant in the heart of the old town, with extensive terrace seating as well as a stylish dining room. Mon–Sat 1–4pm & 8–10.30pm, Sun 1–4pm.
La Moderna c/Mayor 54 ⓣ 948 550 007. Central cafe-bar that opens early for breakfast, and serves a good array of *pintxos* later on. Daily 9am–11pm.

The Navarran Pyrenees

East of Pamplona, the **Navarran Pyrenees** bite a hundred-kilometre-wide chunk out of France. While the frontier itself is lined with jagged 2000m peaks, most of this area consists of lush green uplands rather than impenetrable mountain fastnesses. For travellers, it's most readily explored as a driving day-trip from Pamplona, though several of the pretty and fundamentally similar villages along the way can also make appealing overnight stops. Each tends to have at least one little hotel, to cope with the steady trickle of **pilgrims** en route to Santiago.

Ever since the Middle Ages, the obvious route between Navarra and France has been to follow the **Roncesvalles** pass. As immortalized in the *Song of Roland*, Charlemagne was retreating this way in 778, after laying Pamplona to waste, when Basque warriors ambushed his forces and killed the noblest of his French knights, Roland himself.

Auritz-Burguete

Having once managed to break free from Pamplona's infuriatingly labyrinthine ring-road, the N135 climbs steeply northeast along the Valle de Erro. With no need to huddle against the elements, each successive village straggles alongside the road and river. The first place it's worth pausing is **AURITZ-BURGUETE**, just after the road makes a sharp northwards turn and begins to climb towards the pass. With their ornate gingerbread trimmings, the traditional houses here epitomize the region's architectural style.

Hostal Burguete c/Única 51 ☎ 948 760 005, ⓦ hotel burguete.com. After a century as the focal point for the village – Ernest Hemingway stayed here while writing *Fiesta* – this old-fashioned but very presentable hotel is still going strong, with its large, plain and shiny-floored en-suite rooms and a simple, good-value dining room. **€55**

Loizu c/San Nicolás 13 ☎ 948 760 008, ⓦ hotelloizu.com. Large gabled house at the south end of town, holding 27 very pleasant, modernized en-suite rooms, and a fine restaurant, which serves good-value contemporary cuisine on *menús* that start at €20. Discounts for pilgrims. **€89**

Orreaga-Roncesvalles

Despite its fame as the traditional Spanish starting point of the Pilgrim Route to Santiago – roadsigns make it clear the Gallego city lies a leg-aching 790km west – **ORREAGA-RONCESVALLES** is no more than a small cluster of buildings beside the N135. As you approach from Spain, neither the avenue of trees that lines the 2km road from Auritz-Burguete nor the sloping hillside meadows around the hamlet itself hint at the peaks that soar to the east.

Colegiata de Santa María

Feb, March, Nov & Dec daily 10am–2pm & 3.30–5.30pm; April–Oct daily 10am–2pm & 3.30–7pm; closed Jan • Church free; cloister 2.60, with museum €4.20 • ⓦ www.roncesvalles.es

Orreaga-Roncesvalles centres on a venerable monastery complex that stretches northwards away from the road. Its various elements can be visited in different combinations, with free access to the brooding church known as the **Colegiata de Santa María**. You have to pay to see its elegant Gothic cloisters, however, while to learn more about the history of the pilgrimage, visit the small adjoining museum.

Silo de Carlomagno

A roadside chapel near the Colegiata de Santa María, named the **Silo de Carlomagno** for its resemblance to a granary, is said to mark the spot decreed by Charlemagne for the burial of Roland and his other fallen heroes. This site, however, only rose to prominence after the bishop of Pamplona built a pilgrimage hospital here in 1127.

Turismo Inside the monastery complex (Mon–Sat 10am–2pm & 4–7pm, Sun 10am–2pm; ☎ 948 760 301, ⓦ www.roncesvalles.es).

ACCOMMODATION AND EATING

Hostal Casa Sabina ☎ 948 760 012, ⓦ casasabina.es. Four rather spartan but clean en-suite rooms, above a welcoming little mountain restaurant/bar just in front of the tourist office. On weekdays, a €9 *menú* for pilgrims is served at 7pm & 8.30pm; the price for others is €14, or you can buy a plate of pasta and a glass of wine for €7. **€50**

La Posada de Roncesvalles ☎ 948 760 225, ⓦ laposada deroncesvalles.com. Large hostel run under the auspices of the monastery, with comfortable en-suite rooms; those that sleep four cost a little extra. The usual dinner menu costs €16, but there's a €9 version for pilgrims, who can also get discounted accommodation. **€55**

Ochagavía

If, instead of heading north into France from Orreaga-Roncesvalles, you retrace your steps to Auritz-Burguete and then turn east on to the NA140, you'll find yourself on a remote and rather lovely road that repeatedly undulates from valley to valley. Though

THE CAMINO DE SANTIAGO IN NAVARRA

The **Camino de Santiago** crosses into Navarra from France via the foothills of the Pyrenees, descending steeply to the historic monastery at **Orreaga-Roncesvalles**. As the mountains peter out, the path passes alongside trout-filled rivers lined with beech trees and through traditional whitewashed Basque villages graced with Romanesque churches.

Navarra has invested considerably in this section of the route, and its twenty or so *albergues* – all with comfortable, if basic, facilities – are among the best along the *camino*. The path mainly follows dirt farm-tracks, although some stretches have been paved, which makes the walking less messy but leaves pilgrims prone to blisters.

Traces of Charlemagne's tenth-century foray into Spain are everywhere in Navarra, from the pass before Roncesvalles by which he entered the country to a stone monument some 20km farther on that depicts the massive Stride of Roland, his favourite knight. The region also contains some of Hemingway's much-loved haunts; the *camino* passes through his trout-fishing base at **Auritz-Burguete**, just 3km from Roncesvalles, and lively **Pamplona**, another 40km into the walk.

There are a couple of stiff climbs, notably the 300m up to the **Alto de Perdón**, just outside Pamplona. Here, legend tells of an exhausted medieval pilgrim who stood firm against the Devil's offer of water in exchange for a renunciation of his Christian faith. The pilgrim was rewarded with the appearance of Santiago himself, who led him to a secret fountain.

Navarra boasts some of the finest Romanesque architecture in Spain, including the octagonal church at **Eunate**, 20km from Pamplona, thought to be the work of the Knights Templar, and the graceful bridge that gave its name to **Puente La Reina**, 4km farther on. The architectural highlight is undoubtedly the small town of **Estella**, where it's worth spending an afternoon exploring the Palacio de los Reyes de Navarra and the many lovely churches. The route from Estella is lined with vineyards, and Bodegas de Irache's free Fuente del Vino (wine fountain), just outside town, is said to fortify pilgrims for the journey on through the Rioja region to Santiago de Compostela. For practicalities on the *camino*, see p.556.

each is separated from the next by steep and densely wooded hills, the road never climbs above the treeline.

Just over 30km along, at the confluence of the Zatoia and Anduña rivers, the ancient settlement of **OCHAGAVÍA** makes the ideal spot to break a day-trip from Pamplona. The Anduña cuts a broad swathe through the heart of town, with a pleasant promenade stroll along both its banks, forested slopes looming to either end, and a fine old church on the hillside just above. For details of longer hikes in the vicinity – especially in the **Irati Forest** immediately north – pick up a trail map from the tourist office.

INFORMATION OCHAGAVÍA

Turismo c/de Izalzu, on the north bank of the river (mid-June to mid-Sept Mon–Sat 10am–2pm & 4.30–8.30pm, Sun 10am–2pm; mid-Sept to mid-June Mon–Sat 10am–2pm & 4.30–7.30pm, Sun 10am–2pm; ☎ 948 890 641, ⓦ ochagavia.com).

ACCOMMODATION AND EATING

Hostal Auñamendi Pl. Gúrpide ☎ 948 890 189, ⓦ hostalauniamendi.com. Slightly pricey but undeniably comfortable, well-maintained en-suite rooms, on an open square set slightly back south of the river. The pub-like restaurant on the ground floor (closed Sat eve & Sun) serves main courses from €8, including local trout with ham. **€81**

Hostal Orialde c/Urrutia 4 ☎ 948 890 027, ⓦ hostalorialde.com. Sturdy farmhouse, facing a footbridge on the river's south bank, that's now a hotel with a dozen antique-furnished rooms. Not all are en suite, but those that are only cost €5 extra. **€45**

Roncal

Twenty kilometres southeast of Ochagavía, the **Valle de Roncal** is perhaps the prettiest in the Navarran Pyrenees. In high summer it tends to be a bit too busy for comfort, but come spring or autumn its villages and meadows, wild flowers and trees, are a delight. The nicest place to get your bearings and grab a meal is the little community of **RONCAL** itself, clustered beside the NA137, 6km south of its junction with the NA140 at Isaba.

INFORMATION   RONCAL

Turismo c/Julian Gayarre (mid-June to mid-Sept Mon–Sat 10am–2pm & 4.30–8.30pm, Sun 10am–2pm; mid-Sept to mid-June Mon–Thurs & Sun 10am–2pm, Fri & Sat 10am–2pm & 4.30–8.30pm; ☎948 475 256, Ⓦvallederoncal.es). Doubles as a Nature Interpretation Centre, with details of hiking and other activities in the surrounding countryside.

ACCOMMODATION AND EATING

Hostal Zaltúa c/ Castilla 3 ☎948 475 008, Ⓦzaltua .com. Large white hotel, where the main road crosses the river, with eleven well-priced en-suite rooms; those with bath rather than shower cost €10 extra. There's also a decent restaurant, on a raised terrace with river views. **€55**

Monasterio de San Salvador de Leyre

Summer Mon–Fri 10.15am–2pm & 3.30–7pm, Sat & Sun 10.15am–2pm & 4–7pm; winter Mon–Fri 10.15am–2pm & 3.30–6pm, Sat & Sun 10.15am–2pm & 4–6.30pm • Services 5 daily 6am–9.10pm • Guided tours in Spanish only, minimum 15 people, every 45min; €2.50 • Ⓦwww.monasteriodeleyre.com

The **Monasterio de San Salvador de Leyre**, 50km southwest of Roncal, grew as the first stop in Navarra on one of the many different routes used by pilgrims heading from France to Santiago. To reach it from Roncal, you have to briefly dip southwards into the province of Aragón, then head west back into Navarra on the N240, the main road between Pamplona and Jaca.

The monastery itself stands amid mountainous country 4km northeast of **YESA**. Although the convent buildings are sixteenth to eighteenth century, the church is largely Romanesque; its tall, severe apses and belfry perched on the south apsidal roof are particularly impressive. After languishing in ruins for over a century, it was restored and reoccupied by the Benedictines in the 1950s and is now in immaculate condition. The crypt, with its sturdy little columns, is the highlight of the **guided tour**. You can also access the church by attending **services**, at most of which the twenty or so white-habited monks employ Gregorian chant.

ACCOMMODATION AND EATING   MONASTERIO DE SAN SALVADOR DE LEYRE

Hospedería de Leyre ☎948 884 100, Ⓦwww .monasteriodeleyre.com. Housed in the monastery's former hospice, this smart hotel holds a roughly equal mix of double and single (half-rate) rooms, all en suite, as well as a handful capable of accommodating three or four guests. Its restaurant serves a good-value €16 dinner *menú*. **€80**

Javier

Although tiny **JAVIER**, 5km south of Yesa, never had anything to do with the Pilgrim Route, it's a place of pilgrimage in its own right, as St Francis Xavier was born in its redoubtable **castle** in 1506. Javier itself, 500m beyond the castle, is predominantly modern, and holds nothing of interest.

Castillo de Javier

Daily 10am–1.30pm & 3.30–6.30pm • €2.50

The patron saint of Navarra, St Francis Xavier ranks among the most famous Jesuits. He travelled all over the Far East, dying in China in 1552. The restored **castle** that was his birthplace, originally built as a Moorish stronghold in the ninth century, now serves as an absorbing **museum** dedicated to the saint's life; labels are in Spanish only. With coachloads of pilgrims arriving daily, it's surrounded by spacious grounds that hold a large cafeteria as well as plenty of room for picnics.

Hotel Xabier ☎ 948 884 006, ⓦ hotelxabier.com. Rather grand but nonetheless relaxing hotel, facing the main entrance to Javier's castle, with rooms and a restaurant that serves a good-value €18 set menu. **€88**

Sangüesa

Once a major stop on the Pilgrim Route, the rather run-down little town of SANGÜESA, 8km southwest of Javier, can still boast a number of significant monuments, including several churches from the fourteenth century and earlier. Many of its streets can have changed little in centuries, and still hold some handsome mansions, the remains of a royal palace and a medieval hospital, as well as the seventeenth-century Palacio de Ongay Vallesantoro, which houses the *ayuntamiento*.

Santa María La Real

C/Mayor 1 • Mon–Sat 10am–1.30pm & 4–6pm • €2

The Romanesque church of **Santa María La Real**, pressed up against the Río Aragón at the west end of Sangüesa, dates from the twelfth century. Its finest feature is its southern facade, with a richly carved doorway and sculpted buttresses: God, the Virgin and the Apostles are depicted amid a chaotic company of warriors, musicians, craftsmen, wrestlers and animals.

Southern Navarra

South of Pamplona, the country changes rapidly; the mountains are left behind and the monotonous plains of central Spain begin to open out. The people are different, too – more akin to their southern neighbours than to the Basques of the north. Regular buses and trains run south to **Tudela**, the second city of Navarra, passing through Tafalla and **Olite**, once known as the "Flowers of Navarra", while attractive smaller towns and villages dot the area.

Olite

OLITE, 42km south of Pamplona, is as gorgeous a small town as you could ever hope to stumble across, all the more unexpected a pleasure in that its larger neighbour Tafalla is quite unremarkable, and the town itself is surrounded by ugly modern developments. Its dominant feature is a former royal palace, the **Palacio Real de Olite**, but it also holds a couple of fine old churches, Romanesque **San Pedro** and Gothic **Santa María**.

Olite's exuberant **Fiesta del Patronales** takes place from September 13 to 19, and there's a **medieval festival** the second weekend in August, leading up to the saint's day of Olite's patron, the "Virgin of the Cholera" on August 26, which commemorates the town's salvation from the cholera epidemic of 1885.

Palacio Real de Olite

April daily 10am–7pm; May, June & Sept Mon–Fri 10am–7pm, Sat & Sun 10am–8pm; July & Aug daily 10am–8pm; Oct–March daily 10am–6pm • €3.10 • ☎ 948 740 035, ⓦ palaciorealdeolite.com

The magnificent **Palacio Real de Olite**, which rambles along most of Olite's eastern flank, was commissioned in 1387 by Carlos III, the French-born king of Navarre. All fairytale turrets and grand halls, keeps and dungeons, it's such a colossal structure that it takes several hours to explore properly – and that's despite the fact that only its so-called "New Palace" section is open to visitors, as the oldest parts now house the local parador. The entire complex was originally sumptuously decorated, and painted in bright colours, but sadly few of its fixtures and trappings now remain; the appeal instead is largely architectural, supplemented by the consistently tremendous views over the rest of the old town.

6

6

Galerías Medievales

Pl. Carlos III • Mon–Fri 11am–1.30pm & 5–7.45pm, Sat & Sun 11am–2pm & 5–8pm • €1.75 • ☎ 948 741 885

Olite's central square, Plaza Carlos III, sits atop a series of impressive **Medieval Galleries**, whose existence was a local legend for centuries before they were unearthed in the 1980s. Their original purpose is still a mystery, although it is thought they could have been a market or crypt, or even part of a secret tunnel linking Olite with Tafalla. Now accessed via a spiral stairway that drops from the centre of the square, they house displays on the costumes and cuisine of the Navarran court, aimed largely at schoolchildren.

Museo del Vino

Pl. de los Teobaldos 10 • Easter–Sept Mon–Sat 10am–2pm & 4–7pm, Sun 10am–2pm; Oct–Easter Mon–Fri 10am–5pm, Sat & Sun 10am–2pm • €3.50 • �W guiartenavarra.com

Housed, along with the *turismo*, in one of Olite's abundant spare seventeenth-century palaces, the well-presented **Museo del Vino** celebrates the town's central role in the Navarran wine industry. Visitors who make their way through its three floors of high-tech displays on wine-making old and new are rewarded with a complimentary bottle; the rosé is especially recommended.

ARRIVAL AND INFORMATION   OLITE

By bus Olite is connected regularly by bus with Pamplona (12 daily; 50min) and Tudela (5 daily; 50min).
By train Four daily trains between Pamplona to the north (40min) and Tudela to the south (45min) stop at Olite.

Turismo Pl. de los Teobaldos 10, opposite the parador (Easter–Sept Mon–Sat 10am–2pm & 4–7pm, Sun 10am–2pm; Oct–Easter Mon–Fri 10am–5pm, Sat & Sun 10am–2pm; ☎ 948 741 703, �W www.olite.es).

ACCOMMODATION AND EATING

★ **Casa Zanito** c/Mayor 16 ☎ 948 740 002, �W casazanito.com. Atmospheric townhouse hotel, a few steps away from Pl. Carlos III, with quiet, well-appointed rooms reached via a maze of corridors, and a very good restaurant that serves a great €26 dinner menu, reduced to €17 for guests. **€67**
Hotel Merindad de Olite Rúa de la Judería 11 ☎ 948 740 735, �W hotel-merindaddeolite.com. Cosy hotel, virtually next door to the parador, in a reconstructed house

that's been kitted out in medieval style. There are ten individually themed rooms with balconies and en-suite facilities, plus a reasonable restaurant. **€78**
Parador de Olite Pl. de los Teobaldos 2 ☎ 948 740 000, �W parador.es. Olite's fabulous parador makes the most of its superb setting inside the Palacio Viejo, with stone staircases and ancient hallways that lead to lavishly comfortable rooms. The modern, street-level dining room has a €32 set menu. **€150**

Ujué

Twenty kilometres northeast of Olite, a lonesome, winding road branches off to the east at San Martín de Unx, and after 8km brings you to tiny, hilltop **UJUÉ**. One of the true jewels of Navarra, this perfect medieval defensive village is perched high on the terraced hillside above the harsh, arid landscape; it's impossibly narrow to drive into, and all but impossible to park once you get all the way in.

Ujué is dominated by the thirteenth-century Romanesque church of **Santa María**, where the heart of King Carlos II of Navarra is supposedly preserved inside the altar. Views from the church's balconied exterior extend over the whole southern Navarra region of La Ribera. It's also the destination of a notable **romería** (pilgrimage), on the first Sunday after St Mark's Day (April 25), when half the populace of Tafalla, among others, walk through the night to celebrate Mass here in commemoration of their town's reconquest from the Moors in 1043.

From the main square by the church, a couple of pedestrianized cobbled streets plunge down to another beautiful little square, Plaza Mayor, which holds a ramshackle old bar with a balcony terrace.

Parque Natural Bardenas Reales

Free • Information centre daily: July & Aug 9am–2pm & 5–8pm; Sept–June 10am–6pm • ☎ 946 830 308, ⓦ bardenasreales.es

The further south you travel in Navarra, the drier the landscape becomes, until it's hard to believe you're still in the Basque Country. Indeed, the extraordinary **Parque Natural Bardenas Reales** (Bardenas Reales Natural Park), 70km south of Pamplona, looks more like the deserts of the Wild West than anything you'd expect to find in Spain.

To reach these desolate, eerily beautiful badlands, detour east of the main north–south roads to reach the village of Arguedas, 20km north of Tudela, then follow the signs east. Entrance is free, but it's worth stopping to pick up maps and advice at the **information centre**, 6km along. With an hour to spare, drivers can complete a short dirt-road loop to admire some of the most spectacular formations, including stark mesas, jagged striated hills, and bizarre isolated hoodoos. Any longer, and you can venture further off the beaten track into the back country, or explore the various clearly marked hiking trails.

Tudela

Thousand-year-old **TUDELA**, on the banks of the Ebro 90km south of Pamplona, lies at the heart of the region known as La Ribera. Its old town, stretching north of the richly decorated **Plaza de los Fueros**, is a jumble of narrow, cobbled lanes that can have changed little since Alfonso I of Aragón ended the Moorish occupation of the city in 1119. On the edge of town, the bizarre thirteenth-century **Puente Sobre** over the Ebro looks as if it could never have carried the weight of an ox cart, let alone seven centuries of traffic on the main road to Zaragoza.

The Catedral and the Museo de Tudela

Mon–Fri 10am–1.30pm & 4–7pm, Sat 10am–1.30pm • €3 • ⓦ museodetudela.com

Enter through the main doorway of Tudela's sturdy, twelfth-century Gothic **Catedral**, and you'll find that you only have access to a small portion of the interior. To see the rest, you have to pay for admission to the adjoining **Museo de Tudela**, in what used to be the dean's palace. The various polychrome statues, paintings and altarpieces there are nicely displayed without being all that interesting, but the museum leads in turn to some impressive Romanesque cloisters. Adorned on all sides with deft primitive carvings, these also hold large placards explaining the city's Muslim and Jewish traditions. As for the cathedral itself, its intricately carved alabaster west doorway portrays a chilling vision of the Last Judgement, and is topped by a rose window, while inside there's an unusual *retablo* and some beautiful old tombs.

ARRIVAL AND INFORMATION

TUDELA

By bus Tudela is connected regularly by bus with Pamplona (9 daily; 1hr 30min).

By train Trains from Tudela run to Madrid (3 daily; 2hr 15min), Pamplona (7 daily; 1hr 10min) and Zaragoza (14 daily; 40min–1hr 20min).

Turismo c/Jucio 4, very close to the cathedral (Mon–Fri 9.30am–2pm & 4–8pm, Sat 10am–2pm & 4–8pm, Sun 10am–2pm; ☎ 948 848 058, ⓦ tudela.com).

ACCOMMODATION AND EATING

AC Ciudad de Tudela c/Misericordia ☎ 948 402 440, ⓦ ac-hotels.com. Tudela's classiest accommodation, in an imposing eighteenth-century mansion at the edge of the old town. It has smart, plushly furnished en-suite rooms, aimed primarily at business travellers, plus a restaurant. **€94**

Hostal Remigio c/Gaztambide 4 ☎ 948 820 850, ⓦ hostalremigio.com. Plain, light, en-suite rooms at reasonable prices, just off Pl. de los Fueros close to the old town, with a good modern restaurant downstairs. **€60**

Rancho Grande c/San Nicolás s/n ☎ 948 822 780. Simple, friendly little bar, a short walk from the tourist office, with lots of appetizing tapas spread out on the counter, and more substantial *raciones*, like stuffed onions or artichokes with *jámon*, for around €10. Daily except Wed noon–midnight.

Cantabria and Asturias

NARANJO DE BULNES, PICOS DE EUROPA (P.526)

Cantabria and Asturias

While the northern provinces of Cantabria and Asturias are popular holiday terrain for Spaniards and the French, they remain hardly touched by the mass tourism of the Mediterranean coast, mostly because of the somewhat unreliable weather. But the sea is warm enough for swimming in the summer months, and the sun does shine, if not every day; it's the warm, moist climate, too, that's responsible for the forests and rich vegetation that give the region its name, Costa Verde, or the Green Coast. The provinces also boast old and elegant seaside towns, and a dramatic landscape that features tiny, isolated coves along the coast and, inland, the fabulous Picos de Europa, with peaks, sheer gorges and some of Europe's most spectacular montane wildlife.

Cantabria, centred on the city of Santander and formerly part of Old Castile, was long a conservative bastion amid the separatist leanings of its coastal neighbours. **Santander** itself, the modern capital, is an elegant if highly conventional resort, linked by ferry to Plymouth and Portsmouth in Britain. Either side lie attractive, lower-key resorts, crowded and expensive in August especially, but quieter during the rest of the year. The best are **Castro Urdiales**, to the east, and **Comillas** and **San Vicente de la Barquera** to the west. Perhaps the pick of the province's towns, though, is the beautiful **Santillana del Mar**, overloaded with honey-coloured mansions and, at times, with tourists, too. Inland lies a series of **prehistoric caves**: the most famous, **Altamira**, is no longer open to the public but is explained by a great museum, while another can be seen at **Puente Viesgo**, near Santander.

To the west lie the towering cliffs and rugged coves of **Asturias**, a land with its own idiosyncratic traditions, which include status as a principality (the heir to the Spanish throne is known as the Príncipe de Asturias), and a distinctive culture that incorporates bagpipes and cider (*sidra* – served from above head-height to add fizz). Asturias has a base of heavy industry, especially mining and steelworks – and a long-time radical and maverick workforce – but for the most part, the coastline is a delight, with wide, rolling meadows leading down to the sea. Tourism here is largely local, with a succession of old-fashioned and very enjoyable **seaside towns** such as **Ribadesella**, **Llanes** and **Cudillero**. Asturias also holds three sizeable cities: **Oviedo**, a delightful regional capital with a recently restored old centre; **Avilés**, at its best during the wild Carnaval celebrations; and nearby **Gijón**, which enjoys a vibrant nightlife and cultural scene as well as good beaches.

Inland, everything is dominated by the **Picos de Europa**, which in fact take in parts of León, as well as Cantabria and Asturias, though for simplicity the whole national park is covered in this chapter. A quiet pleasure on the peripheries of the mountains, as in Cantabria, is the wealth of Romanesque, and even rare pre-Romanesque,

CUDILLERO

Highlights

❶ Playas From El Sardinero in Santander all the way west through Asturias, the region has over two hundred beaches to choose from, so you needn't worry about finding space for your towel. **See p.503**

❷ Santillana del Mar Wander the narrow streets of this chocolate-box village, with its picturesque houses and stunning Romanesque church. **See p.509**

❸ Picos de Europa With its soaring peaks, verdant hillsides, remote villages and medieval towns, all within a few kilometres of the coast, this compact mountain range should not be missed. **See p.515**

❹ Cares Gorge The finest hiking trail in the

Picos: a horizontal walk through the vertical world of the Desfiladero de Cares. **See p.524**

❺ Avilés Carnaval Experience Spain at its most vibrant during the Mardi Gras celebrations. **See p.535**

❻ Santa María del Naranco, Oviedo An enigmatic, jewel-like pre-Romanesque church. **See p.538**

❼ Sidra Asturias' national drink must be poured from a great height to attain optimum fizz. **See p.529**

❽ Cudillero This lovely little fishing port might have been airlifted straight from a Greek island. **See p.540**

HIGHLIGHTS ARE MARKED ON THE MAP ON P.500

> **THE FEVE RAILWAY**
>
> Communications in Cantabria and Asturias are generally slow, with the one main road following the coast through the foothills to the north of the Picos de Europa. If you're not in a hurry, you may want to make use of the narrow-gauge **FEVE rail line** (w feve.es), which is unmarked on many maps and independent of the main RENFE system; note that rail passes are not valid on this service. The FEVE line can be broadly split into three routes: Bilbao in the Basque Country to Santander; Santander to Oviedo (where local services serve the triangle of Gijón, Avilés and Oviedo); and Oviedo to Ferrol in Galicia. The route is, on the whole, breathtakingly beautiful, skirting beaches, crossing *rías* and snaking through a succession of limestone gorges, but you will need several days to see it in its entirety. An expensive "train hotel" runs at night, but with the scenery the main attraction of the route, it's not the most rational way to get around.

churches found in odd corners of the hills. These reflect the history of the old Asturian kingdom – the embryonic kingdom of Christian Spain – which had its first stronghold in the mountain fortress of **Covadonga**, and spread slowly south with the Reconquest.

Santander

Much the largest city in Cantabria, with a population approaching 200,000, **SANTANDER** is an elegant, refined resort with excellent transport connections. While its setting on the narrow Bahía de Santander is beautiful – from the heart of the city, you can enjoy clear views across the bay to rolling green hills and high mountains that seem

CANTABRIA & ASTURIAS

HIGHLIGHTS

1. Playas
2. Santillana del Mar
3. Picos de Europa
4. Cares Gorge
5. Avilés Carnaval
6. Santa Mariá del Naranco, Oviedo
7. Sidra
8. Cudillero

to glow at sunset, and superb sandy **beaches** line much of the shorefront – the city centre lost most of its finest buildings to a massive fire in 1941. Nonetheless, the narrow lanes of the **old town**, running parallel to the waterfront, still abound in atmospheric bars and restaurants. The local beaches – the best is sandy **El Sardinero**, facing the open sea a couple of kilometres east – are broad and clean enough for Santander to rival Biarritz and San Sebastián as a favourite summer retreat for sophisticated holiday-makers from the interior. Santander may have a much more bourgeois identity than many of its earthier northern neighbours – and away from the beaches there's not all that much actually to see or do – but it's really not a bad place to while away a day or two.

Old Town Santander

Most of what's known as the **old town** in Santander, a compact grid of streets that stretches along the shoreline of the bay, is actually not very old at all, as the area had to be entirely rebuilt after the fire of 1941 destroyed its medieval core. It doesn't look particularly modern, though, just slightly faded and dull. As you stroll around, the only area that holds any great appeal lies a block back from the waterfront, along the parallel lanes that connect the colonnaded **Plaza Porticada** in the west to the **Plaza de Pombo** and the **Plaza Montero**. At the time of writing, the basement level of the attractive Mercado del Este at c/Hernán Cortés 4 was being converted to re-house the city's **Museo Provincial de Prehistória**, whose displays on the province's prehistoric cave-dwellers are worth seeing if you plan to visit Altamira or Puente Viesgo.

There's nothing to see in the **Catedral**, a little further west toward the stations, apart from the Gothic-Romanesque **crypt** down below (daily 8am–1pm & 4–8pm).

7

FIESTAS

JANUARY

22: Saint's day fiesta at San Vicente de la Barquera.

FEBRUARY–APRIL

Start of Lent: Carnaval Week-long festivities in Avilés, Gijón, Oviedo, Mieres, Santoña – fireworks, fancy dress and live music.
Good Friday Re-enactment of the Passion at Castro Urdiales.
Easter Sunday and Monday: Bollo Cake festival at Avilés.
First weekend after Easter: La Folia Torch-lit procession at San Vicente de la Barquera; a statue of the Virgin Mary is carried through town on a fishing boat.

JUNE/JULY

29: La Amuravela Cudillero enacts an ironic review of the year – and then proceeds to obliterate memories.
Throughout July Weekly fiestas in Llanes, with Asturian dancers balancing pine trees on their shoulders and swerving through the streets. Also, tightrope walking and live bands down at the harbour.
First Friday: Coso Blanco Nocturnal parade at Castro Urdiales.
Mid-July: Festival de Folk Cultural fiesta at San Vicente de la Barquera.
15: Traditional festival at Comillas, with greased-pole climbs, goose chases and other such events.
25: Festival of St James Cangas de Onis.

AUGUST

Throughout August: Festival Internacional Music and cultural festival at Santander. This

Museo Municipal de Bellas Artes

C/Rubio 6 • Mid-June to mid-Sept Mon–Fri 11.15am–1pm & 5.30–9pm, Sat 10.30am–1pm; mid-Sept to mid-June Mon–Fri 10.15am–1pm & 5.30–9pm, Sat 10am–1pm • Free

Santander's **Museo Municipal de Bellas Artes** is located uphill to the northwest of the cathedral. Its collection is an eclectic mix of past and present, from Goya portraits to contemporary photos, including Philip-Lorca di Corcia's enigmatic and powerful *Head* portraits.

Museo Marítimo

Tues–Sun: May–Sept 10am–7.30pm; Oct–April 10am–6pm • €6 • Ⓦ museosdecantabria.com

Ten minutes' walk east of Santander's old town, beyond the **Puerto Chico** where the pleasure boats dock, the up-to-the-minute **Museo Marítimo** sets out to trace the history of Cantabria's involvement with the sea. If you don't read Spanish, enough captions are translated into English to provide a general overview, but you'll miss a lot of the detail, so only the aquarium that fills most of the basement is likely to hold your interest.

Palacio de la Magdalena

Unrestricted access • Free, tourist train €2 • Ⓦ palaciomagdalena.com • Bus #1 from Jardines del Pereda

Perched on its eponymous headland at the eastern tip of the city, the **Palacio de la Magdalena** affords magnificent views of the golden coastline. Built at the end of the nineteenth century by Alfonso XIII, whose residence was largely responsible for the town's fashionability, the grounds now make a popular retreat for families keen to escape the crowded beaches. A small, rather sad **zoo** now houses only a few penguins and some sea lions, but the real attraction is strolling around the gardens themselves. Should you find the hills hard work, a tourist train departs regularly from the park gates.

being one of the wealthiest cities of the north, you can usually depend on the festival featuring some prestigious acts.

First or second weekend: Descenso Internacional del Sella Mass canoe races from Arriondas to Ribadesella down the Río Sella, with fairs and festivities in both towns.
First Sunday: Asturias Day Celebrated above all at Gijón.
12: Fiesta at Llanes.
15: El Rosario The fishermen's fiesta at Luarca, when the Virgin is taken to the sea.
Last Friday: Battle of the Flowers At Laredo.
Last week: San Timoteo Fairly riotous festivities at Luarca: best on the final weekend of the month, with fireworks over the sea, people being thrown into the river and a Sunday *romería*.

SEPTEMBER

7–9: Running of the bulls at Ampuero (Santander).
19: Americas Day In Asturias, celebrating the thousands of local emigrants in Latin America; at Oviedo, there are floats, bands and groups representing every Latin American country. The exact date for this can vary.
21: Fiesta de San Mateo At Oviedo, usually a continuation of the above festival.
Last Sunday: Campoo Day Held at Reinosa, and featuring a parade in traditional dress.
29: Romería de San Miguel At Puente Viesgo.

NOVEMBER

First or second weekend: Orujo Local-liquor festival in Potes.
30: San Andrés Saint's day fiesta, celebrated with a small regatta at Castro Urdiales. The tradition is to sample sea bream and snails.

The beaches

The first of Santander's beaches, **Playa de la Magdalena**, lies on the southern side of Magdalena headland. A beautiful yellow strand, sheltered by cliffs and flanked by a summer **windsurfing** school, it is deservedly popular. Around the headland to the north, two smaller and often slightly quieter beaches, **Camello** and **La Concha**, precede the main event, **El Sardinero**, which stretches for two magnificent kilometres, and is itself divided at high tide into two separate sections, Primera to the south and Segunda to the north.

Somo

Water taxi departs Puerto Chico every 20min • €4 return

If you find all the city beaches too crowded, catch a **water taxi** across the bay to the long stretches of dunes at **Somo** – a major **surfing** destination where you'll find boards to rent and a summer **campsite** – and **Pedreña**.

ARRIVAL, DEPARTURE AND GETTING AROUND   SANTANDER

By plane The Aeropuerto de Santander, 4km south at Parayas on the Bilbao road, stands across the bay in full view of the city. Several car rental companies have outlets there; a taxi into town costs around €20, and buses run nonstop to the bus station (6.30am–10.45pm; €2).

By train The RENFE and FEVE train stations stand side by side on the Pl. Estaciónes, just back from the waterside 500m west of the old town, and in the shadow of an escarpment that hides the main roads. RENFE services include direct trains to Madrid (3 daily; 4hr 30min); change

at Palencia for east–west routes including León. FEVE run east to Bilbao and west towards Oviedo (2 daily; 4hr 45min).

By bus A largely subterranean bus station (☏ 942 211 995) faces the train stations across Pl. Estaciónes. An extensive network of city buses covers all areas; routes #1, #3, #4, #7 and #E shuttle between the centre and El Sardinero. Routes further afield are listed on ⓦ transportedecantabria.es.
Destinations Barcelona (3 daily; 9–10hr); Bilbao (every 30min; 1hr 30min); Oviedo (11 daily; 2hr 15min); Potes via

7

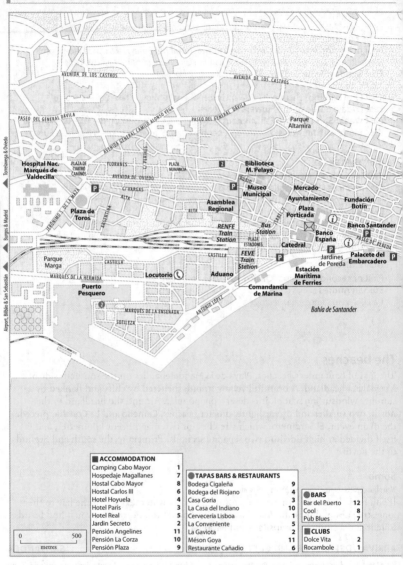

■ ACCOMMODATION	
Camping Cabo Mayor	1
Hospedaje Magallanes	7
Hostal Cabo Mayor	8
Hostal Carlos III	6
Hotel Hoyuela	4
Hotel Paris	3
Hotel Real	5
Jardin Secreto	2
Pensión Angelines	11
Pensión La Corza	10
Pensión Plaza	9

● TAPAS BARS & RESTAURANTS	
Bodega Cigaleña	9
Bodega del Riojano	4
Casa Goria	3
La Casa del Indiano	10
Cervecería Lisboa	1
La Conveniente	5
La Gaviota	2
Méson Goya	11
Restaurante Cañadio	6

● BARS	
Bar del Puerto	12
Cool	8
Pub Blues	7

■ CLUBS	
Dolce Vita	2
Rocambole	1

San Vicente and Unquera (3 daily; 2hr 30min); Santillana (7 daily; 40min).

By ferry Brittany Ferries (ⓦbrittany-ferries.co.uk) from England dock close to the stations.

INFORMATION

Turismo The municipal *turismo* stands in the Jardines de Pereda very near the ferry port (mid-June to mid-Sept daily 9am–9pm; mid-Sept to mid-June Mon–Fri 9am–7pm, Sat 10am–7pm, Sun 10am–2pm; ☏942 203 000, ⓦsantander.es). The Cantabrian regional *turismo* is one block north, at 4 c/Hernán Cortés in the Mercado del Este (daily: mid-June to mid-Sept 9am–9pm; mid-Sept to mid-June 9.30am–1.30pm & 4–7pm; ☏901 111 112, ⓦturismodecantabria.com).

ACCOMMODATION

July and August aside, Santander usually has enough **accommodation** to go round. The fundamental choice lies in whether you want to stay in the **old town** or near **El Sardinero** beach; they're a little too far apart for a hotel in either district to make a good base for visiting the other.

CENTRAL SANTANDER

Hospedaje Magallanes c/Magallanes 22 ☎942 371 421, ⓦhospedajemagallanes.com. Plain, neat rooms at bargain prices in anonymous modernized block, fifteen minutes' walk north of the train and bus stations. The cheapest options share bathrooms; pay €20 for en-suite facilities. €38

Hostal Cabo Mayor c/Cádiz 1 ☎942 211 181, ⓦhcabomayor.com. Six spotless little en-suite rooms across from the train stations, decorated in a modern palette of blacks and whites, with friendly management. €60

7

Pensión Angelines c/Atilano Rodríguez 9, 1° 25 ☎ 942 312 584, ⊛ pensionangelines.com. Basic but scrupulously clean rooms, in a busy location very near the train, bus and ferry, and sharing all washing and WC facilities. **€40**

Pensión La Corza c/Hernán Cortés 25 ☎ 942 212 950, ⊛ pension-la-corza-santander.com. Attractive central *pensión*, in an ideal position for enjoying Santander's bars and restaurants. Behind the old-fashioned public areas, the actual rooms are surprisingly modern and bright, and have en-suite bathrooms. **€55**

Pensión Plaza c/Cádiz 13 ☎ 942 212 967, ⊛ pension-plaza.com. Small, good-value modern *pensión* very near the train and bus stations, with eleven simple en-suite rooms. **€61**

THE REST OF THE CITY

Camping Cabo Mayor ☎ 942 391 542, ⊛ cabomayor .com. Well-equipped site with a swimming pool, 2km north of the casino on a bluff known as Cabo Mayor, 10min walk from Sardinero beach. Take bus #9 to Cueto from opposite the *ayuntamiento*. Closed mid-Oct to mid-April. Pitch for two plus car **€27.80**

Hostal Carlos III Avda. Reina Victoria 135 ☎ 942 271 616, ⊛ hostalcarlos3.com. Well-run *hostal* in a wonderful turreted old mansion overlooking Playa de la Magdalena. Some rooms have sea-view balconies. Closed Nov–March. **€79**

Hotel Hoyuela Avda. de los Hoteles 7 ☎ 942 282 628, ⊛ gruposardinero.com. Traditional, upmarket and expensive hotel, perfect for El Sardinero beach. Huge rooms, many with sea views, and good service. Rates drop enormously out of season. **€160**

Hotel Paris Avda. de los Hoteles 6 ☎ 942 272 350, ⊛ hotelparissantander.es. Upmarket nineteenth-century hotel, ageing gracefully and very near El Sardinero beach; some of its large, bright rooms have stylish sea-view balconies. Closed mid-Oct to mid-May. **€125**

Hotel Real Paseo Pérez Galdós 28 ☎ 942 272 550, ⊛ hotelreal.es. Elegant, upmarket hotel, 10min walk from the centre near Playa de la Magdalena; huge rooms with sea views, and a seawater spa. Expect old-fashioned grandeur, not every modern amenity. **€200**

Jardin Secreto c/Cardenal Cisneros 37 ☎ 942 070 714, ⊛ jardinsecretosantander.com. Small and very welcoming B&B, with six stylish rooms featuring exposed brickwork and attractive bed linens, and sharing use of the eponymous secret garden. **€75**

EATING, DRINKING AND NIGHTLIFE

Santander's old town holds the largest selection of **cafés**, **bars** and **restaurants**, though plenty more lie close to El Sardinero. As both a university town and an upscale resort, Santander also offers lively **nightlife**, especially on summer weekends. In the summer, the city hosts an international university, augmented by a **music and cultural festival** throughout August (⊛ festivalsantander.com).

TAPAS BARS AND RESTAURANTS

Bodega Cigaleña c/Daoiz y Velaverde 19 ☎ 942 213 062. Drop into this atmospheric, museum-like bar, decorated with old bottles, for tapas and a glass of wine, or linger over the traditional €35 dinner *menú*. Mon 9pm–midnight, Tues–Sat 1–4pm & 9pm–midnight; closed last week in May & Nov and first week in June & Dec.

Bodega del Riojano c/Río de la Pila 5 ☎ 942 216 750. Traditional *bodega* in a sixteenth-century wine cellar, serving good tapas, with a flagstone floor, beautifully painted casks and antique furniture. Daily 1.30–4pm & 8.30pm–midnight; closed Sun eve & Mon Sept–June.

Casa Goria Travesía La Pila ☎ 942 222 286. Traditional tiled tapas bar, just off c/Río de la Pila, where the ceiling is adorned with hanging Cantabrian hams. Wonderful empanadas and *pinchos*, with a dining room at the back, should the popular bar get claustrophobic. Daily 1–4pm & 8pm–midnight.

La Casa del Indiano Mercado del Este, c/Hernán Cortés 4 ☎ 942 074 660, ⊛ casadelindiano.com. Popular South American-style sit-down bar inside the flagstone-floored market. Open from breakfast onwards for drinks and snacks, with seating in the central patio as well as along the fine old counter, and a full restaurant menu (mains €10–20) plus a fine spread of *pintxos*. Daily 8am–midnight.

Cervecería Lisboa Pl. Italia, Sardinero ☎ 942 271 020. Of the clutch of restaurants in front of the casino, all with summer *terrazas*, this serves the best food, with a €24 *menú*. Daily 9am–1am.

★ **La Conveniente** c/Gómez Oreña 19 ☎ 942 212 887. Very old-fashioned and very atmospheric nineteenth-century *bodega* serving fried fish and other delicious, but pricey, snacks. Live music, too. Mon–Sat 7pm–1am.

La Gaviota c/Marqués de la Ensanada, Barrio de Puerto Pesquero ☎ 942 361 871. The best of several similarly busy, unpretentious seafood restaurants down by the port, featuring a street barbecue of spectacular, freshly caught seafood. You can spend anything, from a few euros for a *menú* or plate of sardines, to a small fortune for fishy exotica. Daily 12.30–4.15pm & 7pm–midnight.

Méson Goya c/Daoiz y Velaverde 25 ☎ 942 213 966, ⊛ mesongoya.com. Fine old house in the heart of the old town, with a tiled facade and a good range of traditional Spanish dishes, as tapas or on *menús* at €16 and €22. Daily except Wed 11am–5pm & 7pm–12.30am.

Restaurante Cañadio Pl. Cañadio ☎942 314 149, ⓦrestaurantecanadio.com. The city's most famous restaurant, known far and wide for the sublime fish and regional cooking of Paco Quirós. Typical main dishes cost €18–24, or you can simply join the foodies at the tables in the more modest bar, snacking on delicious *raciones* (€9–13), the €9 dish of the day, or the even cheaper *pinchos*. Daily 1–4pm & 9pm–midnight.

BARS

Bar del Puerto c/Hernán Cortés 63 ☎942 213 001, ⓦbardelpuerto.com. Swish bar and restaurant popular with the sailing crowd. Mon–Sat 1–4pm & 9pm–midnight, Sun 1–4pm.

Cool c/San Emeterio 3, no phone, ⓦcoolsantander.es.

Tiny, narrow and very hip bar, filled until late with a cool young crowd. Mon–Sat noon–4pm & 9pm–3am.

Pub Blues Pl. Cañadio ☎942 314 305. Popular blues and jazz music bar, with an expensive restaurant attached. Tues–Sat 7pm–3am.

CLUBS

Dolce Vita c/General Mola 45 ☎688 664 292. The biggest club in town, with two floors (dance/Latino) and a quieter bar area. Entrance fee for men, women free. Thurs–Sat 10pm–6am.

Rocambole c/Hernán Cortés 35 ☎942 364 025. Late-night club attracting a young and trendy crowd; Motown music and expensive drinks. Things tend not to get going before 3am. Daily 9pm until dawn.

7

East to Castro Urdiales

Easily accessible by car but still appealingly rural, the coast east of Santander is becoming ever more developed for tourism. The best-known resort is **Laredo**, with its enormous beach, but lower-key alternatives include the fishing ports of **Santoña** and **Castro Urdiales**.

Laredo

From its old core, sheltered behind a rocky promontory, **LAREDO**, poised 50km both east of Santander and west of Bilbao, has expanded westwards along the sandspit at the mouth of the Río Asón to become one of Cantabria's most popular resorts. In summer, the beaches and profusion of pubs, clubs and discos attract a young crowd keen to party, while there's enough of interest during the rest of the year to ensure that most of the hotels and restaurants remain open.

Laredo was Cantabria's provincial capital for a spell in the nineteenth century. Set well back from the overdeveloped beachfront, the village-like old town, the **Puebla Vieja**, stills retains the odd trace of its former walls and gates, climbing up towards a splendid thirteenth-century parish church, **Santa María de la Asunción** (daily 10am–1pm & 4–7.30pm). Beyond that, you can climb quickly out of town to the cliffs and to grand open countryside.

A five-minute walk from the old town leads down to the best **beach** this side of San Sebastián, also known as the **Playa de Salvé**. A gently shelving crescent of sand, well protected from the wind, it stretches for a full 5km.

Boat trips from the eastern end of Laredo's harbour, nearest the old town, run to Santoña, east to Castro Urdiales, or simply out into the sea (mid-June to mid-Sept; ☎608 392 666, ⓦexcursionesmaritimas.com).

INFORMATION AND ACTIVITIES   **LAREDO**

Turismo Laredo's well-stocked *turismo* is housed in a former radio station at the west end of the old town, close to the bus terminal (daily: summer 9am–9pm; winter 9.30am–1.30pm & 4–7pm; ☎942 611 096, ⓦlaredo.es).

Scuba diving Based in Laredo, Mundo Submarino (☎942 611 861, ⓦmundosubmarino.es) runs scuba-diving courses across the Cantabrian Sea.

ACCOMMODATION

Camping Laredo c/República de Filipinas 2 ☎942 605 035, ⓦwww.campinglaredo.com. Conveniently located just back from the beach, not far west of the town centre,

with separate adults' and kids' pools. Closed mid-Sept to May. Car and two adults €28

Hotel Montecristo c/Calvo Sotelo 2 ☎942 605 700,

whotelmontecristo.es. Not far back from the east end of the beach, a short walk from the old town. Behind its slightly drab facade, this hotel offers 28 plain but comfortable rooms and a pleasant garden terrace. €85

Hotel El Risco Blvd. Arenosa 2 ☎942 605 030, whotelrisco.com. Good-value rooms, perched atop a hill on the eastern outskirts of Laredo, with great views out to sea; the restaurant is nothing special, however. €85

EATING AND DRINKING

Guti c/Mayor 7 ☎942 605 674. The best of several options along the main street of the old town, serving good-value local cooking in a little dining room; mixed grills are the house speciality. Daily except Wed 1.30–4pm & 8.30pm–midnight.

El Pescador Avda. de la Victoria 2 ☎942 606 638, wrestaurantepescador.es. Good seafood restaurant, with a prime position on the beachfront not far from the old town; their catch of the day, costing around €20, always excellent. Daily noon–3pm & 7.30–11pm.

Santoña

West across the mouth of the estuary from Laredo, the compact little town of **SANTOÑA** is still a working fishing port, shielded from the open ocean by the mighty wooded hill of Monte Ganzo, and famous for its **anchovies**. You can watch the catch being unloaded before sampling it in the tiny bars grouped around the streets leading up from the port, particularly c/General Salinas.

INFORMATION SANTOÑA

Turismo Santoña's *turismo* is in the central Palacio Manzanedo (Mon–Sat 10am–2pm & 5–8pm, Sun

11am–2pm; ☎942 660 066, wturismosantona.es).

ACCOMMODATION, EATING AND DRINKING

Hotel Juan de la Cosa Playa de Berria 14 ☎942 661 238, whoteljuandelacosa.com. Modern hotel with large sea-view rooms and apartments, on the ocean side of the headland 2km west of central Santoña straight across from Berria beach. €91

Napoleon c/Alfonso XII 34 ☎942 662 347. This very good fish restaurant on the eastern edge of old-town Santoña is a great place to try the succulent local anchovies. Daily noon–4pm & 8–11pm.

Castro Urdiales

The congenial, handsome resort of **CASTRO URDIALES**, 20km east of Laredo, is only a short drive west from the huge conglomeration of Bilbao, and both hotel rooms and space on the beaches are at a premium in high season and at weekends.

Castro Urdiales retains a considerable fishing fleet, gathered around a beautiful natural **harbour**. Above this looms a massively buttressed Gothic church, **Santa María**, and a lighthouse, built within the shell of a Knights Templar castle. These are linked to the remains of an old hermitage by a dramatic reconstructed **bridge**, medieval in age, but known locally as the Puente Romano, under which the sea roars at high tide. The old quarter, the **Mediavilla**, is relatively well preserved, with arcaded streets and tall, glass-balconied houses.

Flavio Briga

Roman street July–Sept Mon–Fri 11am–2pm & 6–9pm, Sat & Sun 11am–2pm & 6–8pm; Oct–Dec Sat & Sun 11am–2pm & 4–7pm • Free

Castro Urdiales stands on the site of the Roman town of **Flavio Briga**, and a short stretch of ancient Roman street has been unearthed at c/Ardigales 5–7. You can simply admire it from the pavement outside, or enter to take a closer look at the foundations of assorted buildings.

The beaches

In high season, the main "town beach", **Playa del Brazomar**, a small strip of sand hemmed in by a cement esplanade, can be very busy. However, the crowds can be left behind by heading farther east to more secluded coves, or west to **Playa Ostende**, with its rough, dark sand. From this latter beach, there's an unusual walk back to town along the cliffs, with the sea pounding the rocks beneath you. In a tiny bay en route, the sea comes in under a spectacular overhang.

ARRIVAL AND INFORMATION CASTRO URDIALES

By bus The local bus terminal is a good half-hour walk east of the centre on c/Leonardo Rucabado, but town buses, and services to Bilbao, stop outside *Café-Bar Ronda* on Paseo Menendez Pelayo.
By car Finding a parking space in Castro Urdiales is

appallingly difficult; you'll spare yourself a lot of hassle if you settle for the first roadside space you see.
Turismo The *turismo* is in the castellated old town hall, at the head of the harbour (Mon–Sat 9am–2pm & 5–7pm; ☎942 871 512, ⊕www.castro-urdiales.net).

ACCOMMODATION

Castro Urdiales' best-value **accommodation** is scattered through the narrow, pedestrianized streets of the old town.

Hotel Las Rocas c/Flaviobriga 1 ☎942 860 400, ⊕lasrocashotel.com. Imposing, classy, pastel-yellow hotel, facing the beach in the newer part of the town. Comfortable upscale rooms with sea views, plus private parking; a real bargain for the price. **€93**
Pensión La Mar c/La Mar 27 ☎942 870 524, ⊕lamarcastro.es. Clean and presentable, if far from

distinguished, en-suite rooms, on a little shopping street just back from the sea in the heart of town. **€56**
Pensión La Sota c/La Correría 1 ☎942 871 188. Plain en-suite rooms, some with views over the port, in a fabulous central position (albeit one impossible to reach by car) beneath the seafront arches. **€65**

EATING AND DRINKING

Places to **eat** are clustered beneath the arches at the castle end of the harbour. Lively **Calle Ardigales**, a block inland from the Paseo del Mar and packed with *mesones* and *tabernas*, is the centre of the nightlife scene.

La Cierbanata c/La Correría 15 ☎942 781 195, ⊕lacierbanata.com. The pick of the row of old-fashioned tapas bars under the arcades just back from the harbour, with a fine tiled interior and a few outdoor tables. *Pintxos* for just €1 and *raciones* of mussels, razorshell clams and the like from just €4. Daily noon–midnight.
★ **Mesón Marinero** c/La Correría 23 ☎942 860 005. Top-notch fish restaurant, with harbour-facing tables beneath the arches of the big white waterfront monstrosity

(you'll know when you see it). Main courses cost upwards of €20, and there's a €28 *menú*, but you can dine well and cheaply on the *pintxos* set out along the bar. Daily 9am–midnight.
Sidrería Marcelo c/Ardigales 12 ☎942 867 058. Traditional cider-house across from the Roman ruins, with standing room at the barrels outside as well as great snacks or a good set *menú* for €27.40 inside – and fresh cider. Tues–Sun 1–3.30pm & 8–11pm.

Santillana del Mar and around

The outrageously picturesque village of **SANTILLANA DEL MAR** is the first major tourist destination west along the Cantabrian coast from Santander. No less an authority than Jean-Paul Sartre, in *Nausea*, hailed Santillana as "*le plus joli village d'Espagne*". The crowds that flock here in summer have unquestionably diminished its appeal, but on a quiet day it remains as beautiful as ever. Its cobbled lanes abound in gorgeous sandstone churches and mansions with flowery overhanging balconies, while the farms and fields that climb the adjacent hillsides give it a lovely rural atmosphere. Strolling is a delight, even if most of its ochre-coloured buildings now hold restaurants, hotels or souvenir shops.

Despite consisting of little more than two pedestrianized streets and a couple of plazas, Santillana feels more like a sizeable medieval town that never grew beyond its original core than a village. Its unusual name derives from a bastardization of "Santa Juliana", whose remains were brought here 1200 years ago after she was put to death by her husband for refusing to renounce her virginity. Referring to its literal translation, the locals jokily call it the "town of the three lies" – as it's neither very holy (*santi*) nor particularly flat (*llana*), and despite the *del Mar* actually stands a few kilometres back from the sea.

Many of the fifteenth- to eighteenth-century **mansions** clustered close to the Plaza Mayor still belong to the original families, but their noble owners have rarely visited in the last couple of centuries. Among the finest is the **Casa de los Hombrones**, on c/Cantón, named after the two moustached figures that flank its grandly sculpted escutcheon.

La Colegiata

Pl. Las Arenas • Tues–Sun: June–Sept 10am–1.30pm & 4–7.30pm; Oct–May 10am–1.30pm & 4–6.30pm • €3 with Museo Diocesano

Jutting out into the fields at the north end of the village, Santillana's elegantly proportioned village church, **La Colegiata**, is dedicated to Santa Juliana. Her recumbent tomb is in the central aisle of the church itself, which also holds a magnificent *retablo*. The most outstanding feature of the complex, however, is its ivy-drenched twelfth-century **Romanesque cloister**, where the squat, paired columns and lively capitals are carved with images of animals and hunting, as well as ornate patterns and religious scenes.

Museo Jesús Otero

Pl. Las Arenas • Daily 10am–1.30pm & 4–8pm, closed Mon Oct–May • Free

Assorted stone and wood carvings by local sculptor **Jesús Otero**, who was responsible for the bison in Santillana's Plaza Mayor, are collected in a modern building near the church that also holds the village's library and council offices. As well as horses and other animals influenced by the Altamiro cave paintings, there's a remarkable presentation of his family, completed when he was just 15.

Museo Diocesano Regina Coeli

El Cruce • Tues–Sun: June–Sept 10am–1.30pm & 4–7.30pm; Oct–May 10am–1.30pm & 4–6.30pm • €3 with La Colegiata • ⓦ santillanamuseodiocesano.com

On the main road just across from the village entrance, the seventeenth-century **Altamira Convento de Regina Coeli** houses the **Museo Diocesano Regina Coeli**, an exceptional museum of painted wooden figures and other religious art: pieces brilliantly restored by the nuns and displayed with great imagination to show the stylistic development of certain images, particularly of San Roque, a healing saint always depicted with his companion, a dog who licks the plague sore on his thigh. Supposedly, there's a resident ghost too, on the first floor.

The Caves of Altamira

Museum May–Oct Tues–Sat 9.30am–8pm, Sun 9.30am–3pm; Nov–April Tues–Sat 9.30am–6pm, Sun 9.30am–3pm • €3 • ☎ 942 818 815, ⓦ museodealtamira.mcu.es

The **Caves of Altamira**, which burrow into the hillside 2km west of Santillana, consist of an extraordinary series of caverns, adorned by prehistoric human inhabitants around fourteen thousand years ago with paintings of bulls, bison, boars and other animals. Etched in red and black with confident and impressionistic strokes, and sealed by a roof collapse a thousand years later, the murals were in near-perfect condition when rediscovered in the 1870s, their colours striking and vigorous; as Picasso put it, "After Altamira, everything is decadence". During the 1950s and 1960s, however, they seriously deteriorated due to the moisture released in the breath of visitors, and the caves are now **closed** to prevent further damage.

Alongside the site, the fascinating **Museo de Altamira** centres on a "Neocave", a large and very convincing replica of a portion of the caverns that gives a spine-tingling sense of how the paintings look *in situ*. Comprehensive displays in the adjoining galleries trace human history all the way back to Africa, with three-dimensional replicas and authentic finds from Altamira and other Spanish sites, and plentiful captions in English. No one knows exactly why the Paleolithic art at Altamira was created, but according to archeologists it was not primarily related to hunting, in that the specific animals depicted were not eaten any more than other species.

ARRIVAL AND INFORMATION   SANTILLANA DEL MAR

By bus Local buses stop on the main road near the tourist office; services include Santander (7 daily; 40min), and the nearest FEVE train station, 9km southeast in Torrelavega (20 daily; 20min).

Turismo c/Jesús Otero 20, just off the main road adjoining the village's largest car park (daily: June–Sept 9am–9pm; Oct–May 9am–1pm & 4–7pm; ☎942 818 812, ⓦsantillana-del-mar.com).

ACCOMMODATION

Santillana is not really a destination for budget travellers. If you're going to spend a night here, it's worth paying to stay in one of its many gorgeous upscale **hotels**, which uniquely include two **paradores**.

Camping Santillana Carretera Comillas km 6 ☎942 818 250, ⓦcampingsantillana.com. Santillana's large campsite, with a pool and good facilities, is located 1km northwest of the village along the Comillas road. Open all year, it also offers bungalows, studios and mobile homes for rent from €54. Two adults plus car **€30**.

Casa del Marqués c/Canton 26 ☎942 818 888, ⓦturismosantillanadelmar.com. Grand and very luxurious historic hotel, with sumptuous public spaces and tasteful, well-appointed rooms. **€97**

Casa del Organista c/Los Hornos 4 ☎942 840 452, ⓦcasadelorganista.com. This beautiful eighteenth-century B&B, just up from the central square, has very comfortable rooms, some with balconies, as well as nice public spaces, and also serves great breakfasts. Highest rates apply three weeks in August only. **€92**

Hotel Altamira c/Canton 1 ☎942 818 025,

ⓦhotelaltamira.com. Fine hotel opening off the corner of the main square, with 32 plush antique-furnished rooms and suites, lots of wood panelling, and several dining rooms. The front courtyard makes a delightful breakfast venue. **€104**

★ **Parador Gil Blas** Pl. Ramón Pelayo 11 ☎942 028 028, ⓦparador.es. Housed in a splendid mansion adjoining the main square, this definitive parador features a delightful terrace restaurant. **€180**

Parador Santillana Pl. Ramón Pelayo ☎942 818 000, ⓦparador.es. Santillana's other luxury parador stands in a tasteful modern building that's set slightly back from, and higher than, the central square. **€188**

Santa Juliana c/Carrera 19 ☎942 840 106, ⓦvisitsantillanadelmar.com. While ranking among Santillana's cheaper *posadas*, this still maintains high standards, and offers six attractive, beamed en-suite B&B rooms. **€60**

EATING AND DRINKING

Santillana is disappointingly short on tapas bars, while although it holds plenty of conventional **restaurants**, most tend to be expensive and relatively ordinary.

Los Blasones Pl. de la Gandara 8 ☎942 818 070, ⓦrestlosblasones.restaurantesok.com. Reliable restaurant, in a fine old building near the main car park, with *menús* from €18; the good-value €30 option features clams followed by steak or duck. Daily except Thurs 1–4pm & 8–11.30pm; closed mid-Dec to mid-March.

El Jardín del Marqués c/Canton 24 ☎942 840 363. Whether you want a coffee or a substantial salad, this relaxed café, sprawling along one side of surprisingly large

walled gardens across from the *Casa del Marqués* hotel, makes a great retreat in summer from the heat and bustle of the village. Daily noon–11.30pm.

Restaurante Castillo Pl. Mayor ☎942 818 377. Despite its deceptive frontage on the main square, where a couple of stone benches are great for an early-morning coffee, this place stretches way back, acting as a *sidrería* near the front and a more formal restaurant further back, with *menús* from €25. Daily 10am–4pm & 8–11pm.

Puente Viesgo: prehistoric caves

Las Monedas & El Castillo Daily: March to mid-June & mid-Sept to Oct 9.30am–2.30pm & 3.30–6.30pm; mid-June to mid-Sept 9.30am–2.30pm & 3.30–7.30pm; Nov–Feb 9.30am–3.30pm • €3 • ☎942 598 425, ⓦcuevas.culturadecantabria.com

Genuine **prehistoric caves** can still be visited just outside the attractive village of **PUENTE VIESGO**, set in a river gorge amid magnificent forested escarpments on the

N623 to Burgos, 15km southeast of Santillana or 24km southwest of Santander. Guided tours (in Spanish only) depart from an informative visitor centre located 1.5km up a winding mountain road from the village bus stop (served by SA Continental buses from the main station in Santander). Two of the four caves, 700 metres apart, are open to the public, **Las Monedas** and the slightly better **El Castillo**, but places are limited, and in summer it's best to book at least 24 hours in advance. The caves are magnificent, with weirdly shaped stalactites and stalagmites, and bizarre organ-like lithophones, natural features used by Paleolithic peoples to produce primitive music, while the astonishing paintings, depicting animals from mammoths to dogs, are clear precursors to the later developments at Altamira. Should you be unable to find a place on a tour, the visitor centre has an excellent digital exhibit enabling 360-degree views and interactive "tours".

La Anjana Corrobarceno 8 ☏ 942 598 526, ⓦ posadalaanjana.es. Spacious, well-equipped rooms at the south end of Puente Viesgo, where the price includes breakfast in the excellent restaurant. **€75**

Gran Hotel Balneario c/Manuel Pérez Mazo ☏ 942 598 061, ⓦ balneariodepuenteviesgo.com. Luxurious four-star hotel with its own lavish spa, set in magnificent grounds overlooking the glorious valley, and very close to the caves. **€120**

Pensión La Terraza c/General 49 ☏ 942 598 102. Squat little yellow-painted hotel, typical of several cheaper alternatives in Puente Viesgo, where the simple rooms share bathrooms. Closed Oct–June. **€60**

South of Santander: Reinosa and the Ebro

South of Santander, a large area of quiet Cantabrian countryside is dominated by an extensive reservoir, the Pantano del Ebro. The N611 to Palencia brushes its shores en route to the pleasant old town of **Reinosa**. To the east, the **Río Ebro** trails a lovely valley, past a succession of unspoilt villages, Romanesque architecture and cave churches.

Reinosa

REINOSA is a pretty, characteristically Cantabrian town with glass-fronted balconies and *casonas* – seventeenth-century townhouses – displaying the coats of arms of their original owners.

On the last Sunday in September – "**Campoo Day**" – the people of the Alto Campoo region, of which Reinosa is the capital, celebrate their unique folklore and traditions. Locals parade in distinctive alpine-style costume, complete with the unusual stilted clogs known as *albarcas*, and enjoy displays of traditional dance, typical foods and the usual late-night festivities.

Turismo Avda. Puente Carlos III 25 (mid-June to mid-Sept Mon–Fri 9.30am–2.30pm & 5–8pm, Sat & Sun 9.30am– 2.30pm; mid-Sept to mid-June Mon–Fri 9.30am–2.30pm; ☏ 942 755 215, ⓦ aytoreinosa.es).

Hotel Rubén c/Abrego 12 ☏ 942 754 914, ⓦ hotel ruben.es. Reasonably comfortable but rather dreary rooms, in an unbeatable location near the liveliest part of town. **€39**

Posada Rural de Fontibre El Molino 23, Fontibre ☏ 942 779 655, ⓦ posadafontibre.com. Rambling old mill, full of bizarre knick-knacks, near the source of the Ebro in a pretty little valley 5km west of Reinosa, with seven quirky, rather lovely bedrooms; breakfast costs extra. **€84**

EATING AND DRINKING

For a small town, Reinosa holds a wide range of traditional **bodegas** and **mesones**, concentrated around the central Pl. de la Constitución.

El Molino c/Deltebre 2 ☎ 942 752 227. Cosy, split-level, rural-themed restaurant, where the excellent home-made food attracts diners from miles around. On weekdays, there's a €16 lunch *menú*, otherwise expect to pay €15–20 for a main course. Daily except Wed 1.30–3.30pm & 9–11pm.

Pepe de los Vinos Avda. Puente Carlos III 29 ☎ 942 750 588. Central bar that makes a good venue for a glass of wine and a snack, and also offers more substantial meals. Daily noon–11pm.

The western Cantabrian coast

The coast west of Santillana, as far as drab little **Unquera** on the border with Asturias, is dotted with a succession of small, low-key resorts. Both the main towns, **Comillas** and **San Vicente de la Barquera**, are worth a visit, having retained a traditional, earthy feel long since abandoned elsewhere in a flood of high-rise hotels and apartments. The **FEVE line** runs inland along this stretch, but the towns are linked by regular bus services.

7

Comillas

COMILLAS, 16km west of Santillana del Mar, is a curious rural town with pretty cobbled streets and squares, which in its centre seems almost oblivious of the proximity of the sea. It nonetheless boasts a pair of superb beaches: **Playa de Comillas**, the closest, has a little anchorage for pleasure boats and a few beach cafés, while the longer and less developed **Playa de Oyambre** is 4km west out of town towards the cape.

El Capricho

Barrio de Sobrellano • Tues–Sat 10.30am–2pm & 3–7pm • €5 • ⓦ elcaprichodegaudi.com

Comillas is the unlikely location of the first house ever designed by architect **Antoni Gaudí**. Built in 1883, the villa known as **El Capricho** stands an easy walk from the centre. With its whimsical tower, adorned like most of the exterior with glazed hand made sunflower tiles, it has the incongruous air of a Hansel and Gretel gingerbread house. Until recently it was a restaurant, but now visitors can pay to wander through both house and gardens. The house itself curves around a greenhouse, which may well have stood here before Gaudí received his commission.

Palacio de Sobrellano

Daily: mid-June to mid-Sept 10am–9pm; mid-Sept to mid-June 9.40am–2.30pm & 3.30–6.20pm • Gardens free, palace €4, guided tour only

The enormous **Palacio de Sobrellano**, which stands all but next door to El Capricho but can only be accessed from the main road below, is another nineteenth-century *modernista* extravaganza. Designed by Gaudí's associate, Juan Martorell, it was home to the Marqués de Comillas, whose statue overlooks the beach from a nearby hillside. The Marqués, an industrialist friend of Alfonso XII, also commissioned the gargantuan **Universidad Pontífica**, on the hillside above, from Lluis Domenech i Montaner, another of the Barcelona *modernista* group; the gardens are open to the public.

ARRIVAL AND INFORMATION   **COMILLAS**

By bus Frequent buses use the main coast road through Comillas.
Destinations San Vicente (7 daily; 15min); Santander (7 daily; 45min); Santillana (4 daily; 35min).

Turismo c/La Aldea 2 (summer Mon–Sat 9am–9pm, Sun 11am–1pm & 5–8pm; winter Mon–Sat 9am–2pm & 4–6pm, Sun 9am–2pm; ☎ 942 722 591, ⓦ comillas.es).

ACCOMMODATION

The basic choice in Comillas is between paying a bit extra to stay right by the **beach**, or settling for the cheaper options up in **town**, which is where you'll probably choose to spend the evening anyway.

Camping Comillas ☏ 942 720 074, ⊛ campingcomillas .com. Attractive campsite in a great position, right above the beach on the headland at the east side of town. Closed Oct–May, except Easter. Car plus two adults **€25.50**

Hostal Esmeralda c/Antonio López 7 ☏ 942 720 097, ⊛ hostalesmeralda.com. Beautifully furnished place in a fine old building, with breathtaking sea views, though it's on a rather unattractive street at the east end of the old town. **€80**

Hotel Josein c/Manuel Noriega 27 ☏ 942 720 225, ⊛ www.hoteljosein.com. Custard-yellow hotel spilling down the hillside immediately above the Playa de Comillas; the lovely rooms have floor-to-ceiling sea-view windows and galleries that literally overhang the beach. The old town is an easy ten-minute walk away. Rates include breakfast. **€120**

Pensión La Aldea c/La Aldea 5 ☏ 942 721 046. Large, exceptionally inexpensive rooms in a welcoming and gloriously ancient house in the old town, with a superb restaurant on the ground floor. **€35**

EATING AND DRINKING

Bar El Siglo Pl. de la Constitución 11 ☏ 699 421 400. Lovely *mesón*, with tables on the square beside a huge, very plain church, and a cosy interior where you can enjoy hearty portions of ham and cheese, or seafood *raciones* such as squid for €6 or clams for €12. Daily noon–11pm;

closed Mon–Wed in winter.

Gurea c/Ignacio Fernández de Castro 11 ☏ 942 722 446. Good local cuisine in a large indoor dining room, with *menús* from €15 for lunch, €24 for dinner. Mon–Sat 11am–4pm & 7.30–11pm, Sun 11am–4pm.

San Vicente de la Barquera

The approach to **SAN VICENTE DE LA BARQUERA**, 12km west of Comillas, is dramatic: marooned on both sides by the sea, the town is entered via a long causeway across the Río Escudo, the Puente de la Maza. Local lore maintains that if you manage to hold your breath all the way across the bridge, your wish will come true. Inland, dark green, forested hills rise towards the Picos de Europa, strikingly silhouetted as the sun goes down.

The town itself, a thriving fishing port with a string of locally famed seafood restaurants, is functional rather than pretty, with not all that much left of its historic core. If you're looking for a **beach**, there's a good sweep of sand fifteen minutes' walk away, across the causeway on the east side of the river and flanked by a small forest.

A hot climb up from the modern town soon brings you to the remnants of the hilltop medieval town, which despite its intriguing setting and spectacular views turns out to be somewhat humdrum. At either end of the ridge, you'll find an impressive Renaissance **ducal palace** (Tues–Sun 11am–2pm & 5–8pm; €1.40) and a sturdy Romanesque-Gothic church, **Santa María de los Ángeles**. The latter, at the highest point, holds a famous reclining statue of the Inquisitor Corro, born here in 1472.

ARRIVAL AND INFORMATION   SAN VINCENTE DE LA BARQUERA

By train The nearest FEVE train station is 4km south at La Alcebasa.

By bus Buses stop 100m south of the old centre, at the bottom of Avda. Miramar near the west end of the causeway. Destinations Comillas (7 daily; 15min); Potes (3 daily; 1hr

20min); Santander (16 daily; 1hr 10min).

Turismo Avda. Generalísimo 20, in the heart of town (Mon–Fri 10am–1.30pm & 4.30–7.30pm, Sat 10am–1.30pm & 5–7.30pm, Sun 10.30am–1.30pm; ☏ 942 710 797, ⊛ sanvicentedelabarquera.org).

ACCOMMODATION AND EATING

Hotel Luzón Avda. Miramar 1 ☏ 942 710 050, ⊛ hotelluzon.net. A refined hotel close to the seafront, alongside the main square, with 36 pleasant rooms with large windows. **€70**

Pensión del Corro c/del Corro 1 ☏ 942 712 613, ⊛ pensionelcorro.com. On the steps leading from the back of the main square, this homely place, where the brightly painted rooms have slightly run-down bathrooms, is the cheapest central option. **€45**

El Pescador Avda. Generalísimo 26 ☏ 942 710 005. It's not immediately obvious when you peer into its cavernous interior from this street, but this large, rough-and-ready tapas-bar-cum-restaurant also offers open-air tables on the quayside around the back. A great array of seafood specialities, but full meals work out pricey, with special *menús* from €40 or a portion of rice with octopus and clams for €20. Daily noon–11pm.

The Picos de Europa

The **PICOS DE EUROPA** may not be the highest mountains in Spain, but they're the favourite of many walkers, trekkers and climbers. Declared a national park in its entirety in 1995, the range is a miniature masterpiece: a mere 40km across in either direction, shoehorned in between three great **river gorges**, and straddling the provinces of Asturias, León and Cantabria. Asturians see the mountains as a symbol of their national identity, and celebrate a cave-shrine at **Covadonga** in the west as the birthplace of Christian Spain.

Walks in the Picos are amazingly diverse, with trails to suit all levels, from a casual morning's stroll to two- or three-day treks. The most spectacular and popular routes are along the 12km **Cares Gorge** – which you can take in whole or part – and around the high peaks reached from the cable car at Fuente Dé and the subterranean funicular railway at Poncebos, though dozens of other paths and trails explore the river valleys or climb into the mountains. Take care if you go off the marked trails: the Picos can pose extreme challenges, with unstable weather and treacherous, unforgiving terrain, and what appears from a distance to be a slowly undulating plateau can too easily turn out to be a series of chasms and gorges.

As road access has opened up the gorges and peaks, the Picos have been brought increasingly into the mainstream of tourism, and the most popular areas get very crowded in July and August. If you have the choice, and are content with lower-level walks, spring is best, when the valleys are gorgeous and the peaks still snowcapped, although the changing colours of the beech forests in autumn give some competition.

You can **approach** – and leave – the Picos along half a dozen roads: from León, to the south; from Santander and the coast, to the north and northeast; and from Oviedo and Cangas de Onís, to the northwest. Public transport serves much of the park, but services are generally infrequent, even in summer.

The east: the Cantabrian Picos

If you're driving along the coast and want to dip briefly into the Picos, the Asturian portion of the range, covered on p.524 onwards, is the most readily accessible. It takes little more effort, however, to reach the **Cantabrian** section of the mountains, where following the valley of the Río Deva from **Potes** to **Fuente Dé** takes you into the very heart of the Picos. Villages such as **Espinama** make superb overnight stops, and the opportunities for **hiking** are endless.

WILDLIFE IN THE PICOS

Wildlife is a major attraction in the Picos de Europa. In the **Cares Gorge**, you may well see griffon vultures, black redstarts and ravens, though birdwatchers keep a special eye out for the red-winged, butterfly-like flight of the diminutive wallcreeper, named for the mouse-like way it creeps along the vertical cliff faces. Wild and domestic goats abound, with some unbelievably inaccessible high mountain pastures. **Wolves** are easy to imagine in the grey boulders of the passes, but bears, despite local gossip and their picturesque appearances on the tourist-board maps, are very seldom spotted. An inbred population of about a hundred specimens of *Ursus arctos pyrenaicus* (Cantabrian brown **bear**) remains in the southern Picos, most of them tagged with radio transmitters; another isolated group survives in western Asturias.

PICOS DE EUROPA

From the coast to Potes

The N621 heads inland from the coast at **Unquera**, at the mouth of the Deva on the Cantabria–Asturias border. Decision time comes 12km inland from there, at sleepy little **PANES**, where the C6312 forks west into Asturias, towards Arenas de Cabrales (see and Cangas de Onís, while the N621 continues south towards Potes.

Immediately south of Panes, you enter the eerily impressive gorge of the Río Deva, the **Desfiladero de La Hermida**, whose sheer sides are so high that they deny the village of **LA HERMIDA** any sunlight from November to April. From nearby **Urdón**, a path leads west to Sotres (see p.526); it's a pleasant few hours' walk, with mountains looming up around you.

Around 6km south of La Hermida, the village of **Lebeña** lies amid beautiful countryside, a very short detour east of the main road. Its church of **Santa María** (Tues–Sun 10am–1.30pm & 4–7.30pm; €1) built in the early tenth century by "Arabized" Christian craftsmen, is considered the supreme example of Mozarabic architecture, with its thoroughly Islamic geometric motifs and repetition of abstract forms.

Potes

POTES, the main road junction and travellers' base on the east side of the Picos, is still just 500m above sea level, but it's beautifully situated, at the confluence of the Deva and Quiviesa rivers in the shadow of tall white peaks. Once past its unpromising outskirts, at its core it's a very lovely medieval village, tumbling down to the Río Deva in higgledy-piggledy abandon.

While Potes can get very clogged indeed with traffic and sightseers in summer, don't let that put you off visiting. Away from the main road, the central lanes and riverbanks are truly attractive, and it's well worth taking a stroll along its roughly cobbled alleyways, lined with good little shops and bars as well as plenty of tourist tat. Several impressive timbered mansions stand hung with vines and geraniums. The **Casa de Cultura** on c/Sol 20 (March–Oct Tues–Sun 11am–2pm & 5–8pm; €5) holds an interesting **map museum**.

Torre del Infantado

Daily 10.30am–2pm & 3.30–6pm • Free • Ⓦ centrodeestudioslebaniegos.info

The thirteenth-century **Torre del Infantado**, the landmark tower in the centre of Potes, has been beautifully converted to hold a permanent exhibition called **Beato de Liébana y Los Beatos**. While the subject matter may seem arcane – the illuminated edition of the Apocalypse of St John that was produced by a ninth-century monk called Beato in the nearby monastery of Liébana – it's actually hugely enjoyable, learned and lurid at the same time, and gloriously colourful.

ARRIVAL AND INFORMATION   **POTES**

By bus In summer, daily Palomera buses run from Potes to Fuente Dé (Mon–Fri 3 daily, Sat & Sun daily). Services also run to Unquera, San Vicente and on to Santander three times a day, with two on Sunday.

Turismo Potes' *turismo* is in the bus station at the west end of town, on the road to Fuente Dé (Mon & Thurs–Sat 10am–2pm & 4–7pm, Sun 10am–2pm; ☏ 942 730 006).

ACCOMMODATION

Of Potes' abundant **accommodation** options, the best-value places are located on the banks of the Quiviesa in the heart of town.

Albergue El Portalón Vega de Liébana ☏ 942 736 048, Ⓦ albergue-el-portalon.com. Private hostel, in a fine old building 8km south of Potes. Activities range from paragliding and mountain biking to climbing and trekking. Dorm beds; rates include breakfast; full board also available. **€15**

Casa Cayo c/Cántabra 6 ☏ 942 730 150, Ⓦ casacayo .com. Very friendly and welcoming little hotel in Potes' most atmospheric old street, enjoying lovely river views, with a lively bar and excellent restaurant downstairs. Some of the rooms are tucked into the attic. **€60**

7

7

PICOS PRACTICALITIES

ACCOMMODATION

While options of all kinds abound in the more popular villages, it's always worth phoning ahead to book a room – especially in summer or at weekends, when whole towns can be booked solid. Alpine **refugios**, high in the mountains, range from organized hostels to free, unstaffed huts where you'll need to bring your own food. They provide blankets or hire out sleeping bags for around €1. In many places, guests have to leave their rucksacks outside the dorm, so bring a small padlock. **Camping** beside the *refugios* is accepted, and about half a dozen more campsites are scattered around the villages. Camping outside these sites is officially prohibited below 1600m, and subject to on-the-spot fines, but unofficially you won't be disturbed once away from populated areas.

ACTIVITY OPERATORS

Companies arranging activities of all kinds in the Picos, from canoeing and canyoneering to horseriding and mountain biking, include:

Cangas Aventura ⓦ cangasaventura.com; offices at Avda. Covadonga 17, Cangas de Onís ☎ 985 848 887, and Finca La Dehesa, Arriondas ☎ 985 841 699.

Jaire Aventura Avda. Covadonga 14, Cangas de Onís ☎ 985 841 464, ⓦ jairecanoas.com.

Montañas del Norte ☎ 985 841 035, ⓦ montanas delnorte.com; offices at El Muelle 26, Ribadesella, and

Pl. del Cañón 2, Arriondas.

Picos Tour c/San Roque 6, Potes ☎ 942 730 005, ⓦ picostour.com.

Torretours Arenas de Cabrales ☎ 985 846 640, ⓦ picosadventure.com.

Turaventura Caso de la Villa 50, Ribadesella ☎ 985 860 267, ⓦ turaventura.com.

CLIMATE

Good days for walking in the valleys occur even in the depths of winter, but at high altitudes the **walking season** lasts from late June to September, varying according to the preceding winter's snowfall. All year round, the weather is unstable, with brilliant sunshine rapidly turning to clouds, cold rain or dense mist; in summer, cloud often descends on the valleys, while higher up it remains bright and clear. Rain gear and a compass are highly advisable.

EQUIPMENT

Most trails in the Picos are stony, rugged and steep; **walking boots** are needed on all but the easiest routes. Safe, reliable water sources are sporadic, so carry a **bottle**. The routes given in this guide, unless mentioned otherwise, are straightforward and well marked; for walks at high altitude or off the marked trails, proper equipment and experience are essential, especially if you attempt any rock climbing.

★ **La Casa de las Chimeneas** Tudes ☎ 942 736 300, ⓦ lacasadelaschimeneas.es. Gorgeous complex of holiday apartments, in a converted farmstead in the lovely little hilltop village of Tudes, 9km south of Potes. The English owners also run a tiny bar/café opposite, *La Taberna del Inglés*. **€95**

Casa Gustavo Guesthouse Aliezo, 3km east of Potes ☎ 942732010, ⓦ picos-accommodation.co.uk. English-

owned farmhouse B&B, which arranges skiing and canoeing. A useful resource for help and advice on making the most of the Picos for visitors who don't speak Spanish. **€60**

Hostería Antigua c/Cántabra 9 ☎ 942 730 037, ⓔ hosterialaantigua@hotmail.com. Fine and very central old inn, with nice wooden balconies, on a narrow medieval lane. **€70**

EATING

Bar Chente Pl. Capitan Palacios ☎ 942 730 732. Perched above the river, with a relaxing open-air terrace just below the main road, this bustling place serves

good-value *menús* at €11 and €15. Daily noon–3pm & 7–11pm.

Café Llorente c/Cántabra 4 ☎ 942 738 165. The

GUIDED WALKS

Between July and September, the national park service runs free daily **guided walks** of easy to moderate standard, leaving from various points around the park's perimeter. These are an excellent way for novice walkers to get to know the Picos, although guides don't necessarily speak any English. Call or visit the park offices for details. The national park offices also have lists of **guiding companies** operating in each province; contact details are given below.

MAPS

Best are the **Adrados** editions, in two 1:25,000 sheets, one covering the western massif, the other the central and eastern massifs. Adrados also publish good walking and climbing guides. Maps are available in Cangas de Onís, Caín, Potes, Sotres, Bulnes and Arenas de Cabrales.

MOUNTAIN FEDERATIONS

For further information on trekking and climbing in the Picos, contact:

Federación de Montañismo de Asturias c/Julián Clavería 11, Oviedo ☎985 252 362, ⓦfempa.net.
Federación de Deportes de Montaña de Castilla y León c/Mariano Abril 8, Valladolid ☎983 360 295, ⓦfclm.com.

Federación Cántabra de Montaña y Escalada c/Concha Espina 3, Reinosa ☎942 755 294, ⓦfcdme.es.

NATIONAL PARK OFFICES

For **online information** on the Picos, see ⓦreddeparquesnacionales.mma.es. The **main park office** is at c/Arquitecto Reguera 13, Oviedo (☎985 241 412, Epicos@mma.es). Three **provincial offices** provide information on routes, activities and wildlife within the park, although each tends to be short of information on the other two regions: Casa Dago, Avda. Covadonga 43, Cangas de Onís, Asturias (☎985 848 614; see p.528); Calameño, Cantabria (☎942 730 555; and Posada de Valdeón, León (☎987 740 549; see p.522). **Information centres** also operate in summer in Poncebos, Fuente Dé, Los Lagos, and Panes. The huge **park visitor centre** (daily: July–Sept 9am–8pm; Oct–June 9am–6pm; ☎942 738 109, ❸gcantabria @oapn.mma.es) at **Sotama**, 6km south of **Lebeña**, offers comprehensive audio visual displays and exhibitions, plus information on guided walks.

TRANSPORT

No motorable **roads** cross the Picos (except the 4WD track from Espinama to Sotres), and circuits by road are long and slow; if you plan to trek across the range, make sure you allow sufficient time to get back to your starting point. **Bus** services along the main roads are limited to one or two a day, often at unsociable hours, and are very sketchy out of season. **Bikes** can be rented in Potes and other main towns.

wooden balcony of this busy bar, renowned for its good, cheap *raciones*, hangs high above the Quiviesa. Daily noon–3.30pm & 8–11pm.
Casa Cayo c/Cántabra 6 ☎942 730 150, ⓦcasacayo .com. Very nice hotel restaurant with a river-view dining room; portions are healthy and prices are reasonable, with starters at €6–9 and mains at €11–16. Daily except Thurs 1–4pm & 8–11pm.

Casa Susa c/Cántabra 5 ☎942 731 014. Lively, central tapas bar with a broad selection of tasty, well-priced *raciones*, and a *menú* for €10. Daily noon–midnight.
Taberna La Majada c/Independencia ☎942 731 044. Attractive little bar/restaurant, in an old cottage down by the river, with lots of outdoor tables. Snacks, dishes such as chicken with apple for €11, and inexpensive set meals. Daily 12.30–4pm & 7–11pm.

The Deva valley

A lovely little road, the CA185, heads west into the mountains from Potes, running beside the Río Deva below a grand sierra of peaks known as the Macizo Oriental. En route to the cliff-walled natural amphitheatre at Fuente Dé, it passes through several delightful villages.

Monasterio de Santo Toribio de Liébana

Daily 10am–1pm & 4–7pm • Free • ⓦ www.santotoribiodeliebana.com

Close by Turieno, on the south bank of the river above the main road from Potes, the eighth-century **Monasterio de Santo Toribio de Liébana** was one of the earliest and most influential monasteries in medieval Spain. Although much reconstructed, it preserves fine Romanesque and Gothic details, and the largest claimed piece of the True Cross. It was here during the ninth century that one monk, Beato, produced illustrations of the Apocalypse that were so influential that they inspired the creation of similar works – all known as "Beatos" – all over medieval Europe. A few reproductions of Beato's works are on show, but there's a much better exhibition in Potes; see p.517.

Turieno

TURIENO, across the river from the main road 3km west of Potes, is a quiet village where, once you're off the highway, you're as likely to share the road with a donkey as a car. Narrow mule tracks run to nearby hamlets that scarcely see a tourist from one year to the next; the walk to **Lon** and **Brez** is especially worthwhile, through a profusion of wild flowers and butterflies.

Cosgaya

The quiet and pretty village of **COSGAYA** lies 13km west of Potes and 6km east of Espinama. It's no more than a brief riverside strip, which remains idyllic despite the presence of two large hotels, one either side of the road.

Espinama

Twenty kilometres from Potes – far enough to feel that you're finally deep into the heart of the mountains – **ESPINAMA** is a charming little village, spilling down the hillside at the mouth of a slender gorge cut by the little Río Nevandi. Like Cosgaya, it straddles a busy road, but when the traffic dies down after dark it's a magical spot, and in the daytime there are plenty of walks (see box, p.521) in the nearby woods and meadows for those seeking rural tranquillity.

Fuente Dé

Teleférico Daily: summer 10am–8pm; shorter hours in winter • €9.20 one way, €15.50 return • ☎ 942 736 610

The road comes to a halt 4km past Espinama, hemmed in on three sides by towering sheer-sided walls of rock. This is the source of the Río Deva; debate as to whether its name should be Fuente de Deva or Fuente de Eva has left it called simply **FUENTE DÉ**. Most visitors to this lonely spot are here to ride the **teleférico**, a cable car that climbs almost vertically up 900m of cliff. It's an extremely popular excursion throughout the year, and though the cars set off every twenty minutes, you may well have a long wait to ascend, especially in the middle of the day. If that's the case, then you'll probably find yourself queuing again to come down, which in the mountain chill, 1900m above sea level, is not nearly so congenial.

The cable car provides easy access to an extraordinary mountainscape, well worth seeing even if you don't have time to **hike** any distance from the top. Many day-trippers simply wander around close to the upper station, known as **El Cable**, where they make an incongruous spectacle with their bathing suits and toddlers in tow. The views back down to the valley are amazing, while an enticing track immediately sets off higher into the wilderness – within a few minutes' walk there may not be another soul around.

ACCOMMODATION AND EATING
DEVA VALLEY

Camping La Isla Turieno ☎942 730 896, ⓔ campicoseuropa@terra.es. Very attractive campsite, tucked close to the river behind an orchard in Turieno, with

a swimming pool and pony-trekking. Closed Nov–March. Two adults and car **€20.50**

Camping El Redondo Fuente Dé ☎942 736 699,

HIKING IN THE EASTERN PICOS: FROM ESPINAMA AND FUENTE DÉ

The best starting point for hikes into the mountains from the Picos' eastern side has to be **Espinama**, though if you're at all pressed for time, taking the cable car up from **Fuente Dé** and then hiking back down to Espinama (10km; 3–4hr) makes a quick and relatively pain-free alternative.

A superb trek (12.5km; 5hr) follows a dirt track (also passable in 4WD vehicles) from Espinama to the village of **Sotres**, 8km east of Poncebos. Setting off north from Espinama beneath an arching balcony alongside the *Peña Vieja* bar, the track climbs stiffly, winding past hand-cut hay fields and through groups of barns, until tall cliffs rise on either side to form a natural gateway. Through this you enter a different landscape of rocky summer pasture and small streams. As you near the highest point, 4.5km or perhaps two hours along, the track divides at a small barn; the left-hand path leads up to the *Refugio de Aliva* (see below) and the top of the cable car, but for Sotres you should continue straight ahead, past a chapel (visible from the junction), up to the ridge forming the pass.

Over the divide the scenery changes again, into a mass of crumbling limestone. In spring and winter, the downhill stretch of track here is slippery and treacherous to all but goats. From the foot of the hill, where a seasonal bar sells drinks, you'll have to climb slightly once again to the east to reach Sotres itself, which, when it appears, has a grim, almost fortified feel, clinging to a cliff edge above a stark green valley. Alternatively, a zigzag climb to the west marks the start of the 5km route (around 2hr) to the more appealing village of **Bulnes** (see p.526).

Accommodation is available in both Sotres and Bulnes, but you can also stay higher up in the mountains in the hotel-like rooms of the remote *Refugio de Aliva* (**☎** 942 730 999; closed Oct–April; €50), which has a restaurant and its own fiesta, on July 2. That stands 4km northeast of the top of the Fuente Dé cable car, along the clearly signposted PR 24 trail, which then continues down another 2km to meet the track up from Espinama at the junction described above.

7

ⓦ elredondopicosdeeuropa.com. A 240-place campsite hidden away in a lovely wooded spot on the slopes above the road, with a shop and bar. Closed Oct–May. Two adults and car €20

Camping San Pelayo Baró **☎** 942 733 087, **ⓦ** campingsanpelayo.com. Pleasant family-oriented campsite, in a tiny village 10km up the valley west of Potes, with its own restaurant and a sizeable pool. Closed Nov–Easter. Two adults and car €18

Hostal Nevandi Espinama **☎** 942 736 608, **ⓦ** apartamentosnevandi.com. In the heart of the village, the *hostal* itself has ten plain but comfortable en-suite doubles, with large beds, but they also offer several larger self-catering apartments in the ravishing, even smaller hamlet of Pido just across the valley. Rooms €46, apartments €65

Hotel Cosgaya Cosgaya **☎** 942 733 230, **ⓦ** hotelcosgaya .es. The smaller of Cosgaya's two roadside hotels, housed in a sturdy alpine-looking stone-built mansion, offers 24 tasteful en-suite doubles, all with views, plus a pool. €70

Hotel del Oso Cosgaya **☎** 942 733 018, **ⓦ** hoteldeloso .com. Rather grand but extremely welcoming hotel, in a fine old house beside both road and river. The spacious terrace is a great place to lounge over a coffee or drink. Fifty spacious well-furnished rooms, plus a good dining room and an outdoor pool surrounded by lawns. €79

Hotel Rebeco Fuente Dé **☎** 942 736 600, **ⓦ** hotelrebeco .com. Perched at road's end in Fuente Dé, this modern hotel resembles a mountain lodge. Eleven of its thirty en-suite rooms are family sized, and its good-value restaurant stretches onto a nice mountain-view terrace. €65

Parador de Fuente Dé **☎** 942 736 651, **ⓦ** paradores.es. Modern parador set in a stunning mountain amphitheatre, near the foot of the cable car. The comfort inside belies the uninspiring exterior, there's a good restaurant, and bargain room rates are frequently available online. €100

Posada Javier Turieno **☎** 942 732 122, **ⓦ** posadajavier .com. Pretty little rural hotel, set well away from the main road amid the fields, and equipped with eight very pleasantly decorated (and centrally heated) en-suite rooms. €56

Puente Deva Espinama **☎** 942 736 658, **ⓦ** hostal puentedeva.com. The en-suite rooms belonging to this inviting little inn are actually in a separate building, 50m away; they're clean and correct, with valley views, but can get very cold out of season. The inn itself serves delicious food year-round; their steaks are fabulous. Restaurant daily 8–10pm. €42

Remoña Espinama **☎** 942 736 605, **ⓦ** remoña.com. Cosy en-suite rooms above an old tavern on the main road, where the dining room serves a decent traditional *menú* for €13, as well as self-contained apartments in a newly built structure nearby. Restaurant daily 8–10pm. €45

The south: the Leonese Picos

Although the southern flanks of the Picos de Europa lie in the region of **León** (otherwise covered in Chapter 5), visitors naturally experience the national park, and the mountains themselves, as a single unit. Exploring the southern side of the Picos from the north coast requires considerable time and effort, but those who do make the journey, or approach from the south, are rewarded with some of the mountains' most attractive little towns and villages, which also make a great approach to one of the finest hikes, along the **Cares Gorge**.

Posada de Valdeón

Whether you're literally coming from León, or simply touring the perimeter of the mountains, only one route leads into the heart of the Picos from the south. It starts from the pretty village of **POSADA DE VALDEÓN**, which stands at the junction of two minor roads. The village itself is a delightful spot, surrounded by soaring mountain slopes, and makes an ideal base for any number of hikes.

If you're approaching **from the east**, you'll get here by way of tiny **Portilla de la Reina**, a hamlet on the N621 that's served by León–Potes buses and lies 10km southeast of the high mountain pass known as the **Puerto de San Glorio**, a total of 38km southeast of Potes. The minor and quite enchanting LE243 runs 20km north from Portilla de la Reina to Posada, its last three ravishing kilometres as a narrow single-lane track. Coming **from the west**, LE244 leaves the N625 just south of another pass, the **Puerto del Pontón**, and a total of 45km south of Cangas de Onís; it remains broad and easy for its entire 23km run to Posada. Finally, it's also possible to reach the village **on foot** from Fuente Dé, in about four hours, over a mix of dirt tracks and footpaths.

Cordiñanes and Caín

The **Río Cares** runs through Posada del Valdeón, and its gorge begins just north of the village. Over its first section, as far as Caín, it remains relatively wide, running past brilliant green meadows at the base of the cliffs, and paralleled on its eastern side by a narrow paved road. The village of **CORDIÑANES**, 2km along – and also accessible on foot, via a dirt track on the western side of the river – makes for an especially peaceful night's stop. In summer, **CAÍN** itself, 6km further north, is uncomfortably full of hikers and day-trippers; a supermarket sells basic supplies.

INFORMATION   **POSADA DE VALDEÓN AND CAÍN**

National Park office Tucked away up from the road across from the *Cumbrés Valdeón* hotel in Posada del Valdeón (Mon–Fri 8am–2.30pm, Sat & Sun 9am–2pm & 4–7pm; ☎ 987 740 549).

ACCOMMODATION AND EATING

Albergue Cuesta-Valdeón c/San Sebastián, Posada del Valdeón ☎ 654 397 644, ⊚ alberguelacuesta.com. Simple, clean hostel on the northern outskirts of Posada, offering dorm beds with shared kitchen and bathrooms. **€10**

Cumbrés Valdeón Travesía de Soto, Posada del Valdeón ☎ 987 742 710, ⊚ cumbresvaldeon.com. Smart modern inn on the western edge of the village, where several of the comfortable rooms have mountain-view balconies. Closed mid-Dec to mid-Feb. **€53**

★ **Desván Valdeón** Travesía de Prada 10, Posada del Valdeón ☎ 987 742 733, ⊚ desvanvaldeon.com. Stylish, top-quality restaurant that serves exceptional food at affordable prices, including great salads and desserts, and delicious, delicate blue-cheese croquettes. All seating is

indoors, in a well-lit upstairs dining room that also has a mountain-view balcony. Daily 1–3pm & 8–10.30pm; closed Dec–Feb.

Hostal La Ruta Travesía del Cares 15, Caín ☎ 987 742 702. Right at the opening of the gorge path, this simple modern *hostal* offers rooms with and without en-suite bathrooms. Its inexpensive restaurant serves a €10 *menú* on a pleasant covered terrace. Closed mid-Oct to mid-March, restaurant open for all meals daily. **€40**

★ **Pensión Begoña** Pl. Cortina El Concejo 8, Posada del Valdeón ☎ 987 740 516. Very friendly, clean and homey place in the centre of the village, with simple rooms at great prices. The downstairs restaurant has outdoor tables, and serves delicious, inexpensive local food like wild

7

HIKING IN THE SOUTHERN PICOS: THE CARES GORGE

Deservedly the most popular walk in the Picos takes hikers into the heart of the central massif, along the **Cares Gorge** (**Desfiladero de Cares**). Its most enclosed section, between Caín and Poncebos – a massive cleft more than 1000m deep and some 12km long – bores through awesome terrain along an amazing footpath hacked out of the cliff face. Maintained in excellent condition by the water authorities, it's perfectly safe. Many day-trippers simply get a taste of it by walking as far as they choose to and from Caín, but with reasonable energy, it's perfectly possible to hike its full length – in both directions – in well under a day.

The **gorge** proper begins immediately north of Caín. Just beyond the end of the road, the valley briefly opens out, but then, as you follow the river downstream, it suddenly disappears – a solid mountain wall blocks all but a thin vertical cleft. In its early stages, the trail burrows dramatically through the rock, before emerging onto a broad, well-constructed and well-maintained footpath, which owes its existence to a long-established hydroelectric scheme. During busy periods, the first few kilometres of the trail tend to be thronged with day-trippers thrilling at the dripping tunnels and walkways. Once you get 4km or so from Caín, however, the crowds thin out, and the mountains command your total attention. They rise pale and jagged on either side, with griffon vultures and other birds of prey circling the crags. The river drops steeply, some 150m below you at the first bridge, but closer to 300m by the end.

A little over halfway along, the canyon bends to the right and gradually widens along the **descent to Poncebos**. Roughly 7km and 9km into the gorge, enterprising individuals run makeshift, summer-only refreshments stands, handy as there are no springs. For its final 3km, the main route climbs a dry, exposed hillside; an alternative riverside path can be reached by a steep side-trail that zigzags down the precipice.

It is, of course, equally possible to walk all or part of the gorge from the north, starting at Poncebos (see p.525).

---

boar stew and ultra-strong cheese. Restaurant open for all meals daily. **€40**

La Posada del Montañero Caín **☎** 985 742 711, **ⓦ** asturjoven.com/posada-montanero.html. Imposing

yellow-painted hotel, set back just off the road, with decent en-suite rooms and a good terrace restaurant. Three-night minimum in Aug. Closed Dec–Feb, restaurant open for all meals daily. **€56**

The Sella valley

The road running along the western end of the Picos, the N625 between Riaño and Cangas de Onís, is arguably as spectacular as the Cares Gorge. Mountains rear to all sides and for much of the way the road traces the gorge of the **Río Sella**. The central section of this, the **Desfiladero de los Beyos**, is said to be the narrowest motorable gorge in Europe – a feat of engineering rivalling anything in the Alps, and remarkable for the 1930s.

Not far south of the road's highest pass, the frequently foggy 1290-metre **Puerto del Pontón**, the exceptionally pretty village of **OSEJA DE SAJAMBRE** stands high on the steep slope of a broad and twisting valley. It currently lacks any facilities.

The north: the Asturian Picos

The most striking thing about the northern flanks of the Picos de Europa is just how near the mountains are to the sea. There's spectacular scenery to be enjoyed barely a dozen kilometres inland from resorts such as Ribadasella and Llanes. The AS114 highway runs parallel to the coast through the foothill area known as **Cabrales**, providing easy access to the mountain fastnesses that lie to the south, beyond **Poncebos** and **Covadonga**.

Arenas de Cabrales

The main village of this region, **ARENAS DE CABRALES** (shown on some maps as Las Arenas), might seem unremarkable if you simply scoot through, but stop for a while and you'll find it a cheerful, friendly little place. Not too commercialized, it holds a good selection of restaurants and inexpensive accommodation.

Cueva el Cares

Summer daily 10am–2pm & 4–8pm • 45min guided tour in Spanish €4.50

The Cabrales area is famed for its exceptionally strong cheese; gastronomes will want to check out the **Cueva el Cares**, a cheese-making museum a short way down the road towards Poncebos that has its own natural cave of fermenting cheese. On the last Sunday in August, Arenas hosts the **Asturian Cheese Festival**, an excuse for plenty of dancing and music but, oddly enough, not all that much cheese.

ARRIVAL AND INFORMATION   ARENAS DE CABRALES

By bus Three daily buses run from outside the *turismo* towards Cangas del Onís and Oviedo.

Turismo There's a helpful booth on the main street near the bridge (June–Sept Mon 9am–2pm & 4–9pm, Tues–Sun 9am–9pm; May & Oct Tues–Thurs 10am–2pm & 4–8pm, Fri–Sun 9am–9pm; ☎ 985 846 747, ⊚ cabrales.org).

ACCOMMODATION

Camping Naranjo de Bulnes ☎ 985 846 578, ⊚ campingnaranjodebulnes.com. Well-equipped campsite, with nicely shaded pitches set amid the woods and meadows 1km east of town. Closed Nov to mid-March. Two adults with car **€26.20**

Picos de Europa c/Mayor s/n ☎ 985 846 491, ⊚ hotelpicosdeeuropa.com. Large hotel, right by the river in the middle of town, painted an unmissable shade of orange, and offering well-equipped en-suite rooms plus a pool and a pleasant mountain-view terraza. **€75**

Torrecerredo Barrio de Vega s/n ☎ 985 846 640, ⊚ picosadventure.com. Cheerful hotel with an appealing hostel-like atmosphere, enjoying great mountain views from its perch amid the fields on the hillside a few hundred metres along a narrow lane from the west end of town. The English owners can arrange a wide range of mountain activities, including all-inclusive walking weeks. **€70**

Villa de Cabrales c/Mayor s/n ☎ 985 846 719, ⊚ hotelvilladecabrales.com. Prices at this elegant hotel, at the west end of town, drop considerably out of season, but it's good value even in summer. En-suite rooms (no. 31 is the best), a good bar, and a garden terrace with mountain views. **€75**

EATING AND DRINKING

Chigre el Orbayu c/Pedro Niembro ☎ 646 396 252. Funky little *sidrería* and café, with outdoor tables on a cobbled backstreet and an inexpensive daily *menú*. They even offer a cider-based *sangría*. Daily noon–3pm & 6–11pm.

Restaurante La Panera c/Sublayende 1 ☎ 985 846 810. Garden restaurant, a short climb up from the highway just east of the main intersection. Enjoy a €12 *menú del día* while admiring the mountain views; the local beans, *fabadas Asturianas*, are the speciality. Daily 1–3pm & 7.30–10pm; closed Jan.

★ **Sidrería Calluenga** Pl. Castañedo ☎ 985 846 719. Wonderful village restaurant, on a little square set well back from the main road and open on one side to a little stream. Fabulous local dishes include clams with wild mushrooms for €12, cod with potatoes for €10, or *cazuela de arroz*, a huge casserole of rice with Cabrales cheese, for €13. Daily 8am–midnight.

Poncebos

The dead-end AS264 branches south off AS114 at Arenas, climbing alongside the Cares river into the mountains. Most visitors simply go the first five, easy, kilometres to **PONCEBOS**, a gloomy little spot, too small to be considered even a village, that's home to an antiquated power plant and three unattractive and somewhat institutional hotels.

If you have your own transport, you're better off staying in Arenas or further afield, but for hikers Poncebos offers the twin advantages of lying at the northern end of the **Cares Gorge** which ranks among the Picos' very best trails, and at the foot of the steep, hour-and-a-half trek up the gorge of the Tejo stream to lovely little **Bulnes**.

Funicular de Bulnes

Daily: Easter & July–Sept 10am–8pm; rest of year 10am–12.30pm & 2–6pm; additional train Mon–Fri 8.30am • Adults one-way €16, round-trip €20.10; children one-way €3.90, round-trip €6.10; cash only

A bizarre **funicular railway** takes around twelve minutes to burrow 2km upwards through the rock from Poncebos, and emerge at a point 400m higher, just below **Bulnes**. You don't have to be a diehard mountaineer to feel there's something not quite right

7

HIKING IN THE NORTHERN PICOS: FROM PONCEBOS AND SOTRES

For visitors based on the northern flanks of the Picos, Poncebos and Sotres are the best spots from which to start hiking. As well as being the northern trailhead for the Cares Gorge, **Poncebos** also lies at the foot of the path up to Bulnes. Allow roughly 1hr 30min for that climb, which branches east from the Cares Gorge trail 1km south of Poncebos, across the photogenic medieval bridge of Jaya. While it's not a hard slog, you're better off taking the funicular if you have problems with vertigo.

Sotres, 9km east of Poncebos along the narrow CA 1, is not one of the more attractive Picos villages, but it lies at the northern end of the ravishing 12.5km hike from Espinama (see p.521), and thus makes a good overnight halt for walkers heading right across the central Picos. A direct trail connects Sotres with Bulnes in just 5km, by way of the broad, windy pass of **Pandébano** (which, with care, can also be reached along primitive roads by car). The high meadows at the top are still used for summer pasture by villagers from Bulnes, some of whom spend the summer there in simple stone dwellings. An old, steep, cobbled path leads down to Bulnes itself.

From both Bulnes village and the pass at Pandébano, well-used paths lead up to the **Vega de Urriello**, the high pasture at the base of the **Naranjo de Bulnes** (2519m). An immense slab of orange-hued rock, the Picos' trademark peak stands aloof from the jagged grey sierras around it. The approach from Pandébano is easier, a two- to three-hour hike along a track that passes the small *refugio* of **Terenosa** (☎985 252 362; no food; closed Oct–April). The direct path up from Bulnes is heavy going, and can take up six hours in bad conditions, with a slippery scree surface that's very difficult, and dangerous when wet. Once up on the plateau, you'll find another *refugio*, the **Vega de Urriello**, at an altitude of 1953m (☎985 925 200), and a permanent spring, as well as large numbers of campers and rock climbers, for whom the Naranjo is a popular target.

Experienced trekkers can stay the night in the *Vega de Urriello refugio* and then continue across the central massif, through a roller-coaster landscape unforgiving of mistakes, to the **Cabaña Veronica** *refugio*, which is for emergency use only, and has just three bunks. An easy descent from there brings you to the top of the **Fuente Dé** cable car. Alternatively, you can continue west through further challenging terrain to another *refugio* at **Collado Jermoso** (☎636 998 727, ��www.colladojermoso.com) before dropping down the ravine of Asotín takes you finally to Cordiñanes at the top of the **Cares Gorge**. The trek from Vega de Urriello should only be undertaken in a group equipped with proper maps and gear.

about an underground railway that tunnels through a beautiful mountain landscape without so much as a glimpse of light. For the casual visitor, however, it provides easy access to the inner recesses of the Picos massif, in a much less forbidding, and more picturesque, spot than the desolation encountered at the top of the Fuente Dé cable car.

Bulnes and around

The tiny but delightful stone-built mountain village of **BULNES** nestles in a cleft cut by the Río Tejo between two high peaks. Long the exclusive preserve of hardy hikers, it's still coming to terms with the daily influx of nonchalant sightseers who now arrive on the funicular from Poncebos – when you emerge from the railway tunnel, it lies just a couple of hundred metres up and to the left, along an easy footpath. Many visitors now bring baby-buggies, and romping infants contrast strangely with exhausted trekkers in the two streamside cafés in the heart of the village.

SOTRES, 5km east of Bulnes on foot and also accessible by road, 9km east of Poncebos along the narrow CA1, is not one of the more attractive Picos villages. As the trailhead for some superb hikes, however (see box, above), it's a well-established walkers' base.

ACCOMMODATION

BULNES AND SOTRES

Albergue Peña Castil Sotres ☎985 945 070, ⓦhotelpenacastil.com. Stone-built inn and hostel, in a dramatic mountain setting on the edge of Sotres. As well as two- and four-person private en-suite rooms, they also offer several four-person dorms, sharing bathrooms. Hiking and 4WD trips available. Closed Dec–March. Dorms **€15**, doubles **€60**

★ **La Casa del Chiflon** Bulnes ☎ 985 845 943, ⓦ casadelchiflon.com. Lovely little B&B, alongside the stream in the middle of Bulnes, offering simple en-suite rooms for two, three or four guests, and adjoining a cosy bar and restaurant. **€60**

Pensión Casa Cipriano Sotres ☎ 985 945 024, ⓦ casacipriano.com. Good-value little village hotel, with fourteen en-suite B&B rooms. They can also arrange hiking and 4WD expeditions, while the dining room is open for all meals daily. **€65**

Covadonga

High in the northern Picos, the pilgrimage site of **COVADONGA** is renowned as the place where the **Reconquist of Spain** began. Squeezed between enormously steep slopes, it's a stupendous spot, centring on a cave set into a high cliff face, from immediately below which a powerful waterfall spurts forth. It lies 5km up a spur road that parallels the Río Reinazo south into the mountains, 4km east of Cangas de Onís, or 28km west of Arenas de Cabrales.

According to Christian chronicles, in 718, the Visigothic King Pelayo and a small group of followers repelled the Moorish armies here at odds of 31 to 400,000. While the reality was slightly less dramatic, the Moors being little more than a weary and isolated expeditionary force, the symbolism of the event is at the heart of Asturian, and Spanish, national history, and the defeat allowed the Visigoths to regroup, slowly expanding Christian influence over the northern mountains of Spain and Portugal.

Although overwhelmed with tourists in summer, Covadonga remains a serious religious shrine. There's no village here, just a cluster of buildings dominated by a grandiose nineteenth-century pink-granite **basilica** that's more impressive from the outside than in. Alongside, the **Museo de Covadonga** (daily 10.30am–2pm & 4–7pm; €2.50) displays assorted paintings and engravings.

A short walk leads through cliff-face shrines to the **cave** itself (Mon–Fri 10am–6pm, Sat 9am–6pm; free). Daily Mass is celebrated in the stone chapel at the far end, next to Pelayo's sarcophagus.

7

ACCOMMODATION AND EATING   COVADONGA

Gran Hotel Pelayo ☎ 985 846 061, ⓦ arceahoteles .com. In truth this large hotel, located right next to the cave, is something of an eyesore, but once you're inside the views are tremendous, and the rooms are generally very comfortable. **€70**

Hospedería del Peregrino ☎ 985 846 047, ⓦ picosdeuropa.net/peregrino. Cheap and cosy little *fonda* on the main road below the cave town, with an excellent restaurant, open for lunch and dinner daily, that specializes in *fabada asturiana*. Closed Nov to mid-March. **€40**

Lago de Enol and Lago de la Ercina

Beyond Covadonga, the road climbs sharply, to reach the placid **mountain lakes** of **Enol** and **La Ercina** after 12km. To no specific schedule, however, it's often closed to all private traffic in summer, at which times visitors have to catch shuttle buses from Cangas de Onís.

The **Mirador de la Reina**, a short way before the lakes, gives an inspiring view of the assembled peaks. From the higher Lago de la Ercina, a good path leads east–southeast within three hours to the **Vega de Ario**, where there's a **refugio** (☎ 650 900 760; closed Nov–April), camping on the meadow, and unsurpassed **views** across the Cares Gorge to the highest peaks in the central Picos. Unless you have serious hiking experience for the steep descent to the Cares, this is something of a dead end, since to cross the bulk of the western peaks you'll need to backtrack at least to Lago de la Ercina to resume progress south.

Most walkers, however, trek south from the lakes to the **Vegarredonda** *refugio* (☎ 985 922 952). This popular route initially follows a dirt track but later becomes an actual path through a curious landscape of stunted oaks and turf. Vegarredonda, about three hours' walk, overlooks the very last patches of green on the Asturias side of the Cornión massif. From here the path continues west for another hour up to the viewing point, the **Mirador de Ordiales**.

Cangas de Onís

The busy market town of **CANGAS DE ONÍS** stands at the junction of the main routes between the Picos and central Asturias. The surrounding peaks provide a magnificent if distant backdrop to its big sight – the so-called **Puente Romano** (Roman Bridge), splashed across the front of many Asturian tourist brochures. Although this high-arched bridge, with its cross dangling beneath, has been rebuilt many times, it retains a good deal of charm.

As an early residence of the fugitive Asturian-Visigothic kings, Cangas lays claim to the title of "First Capital of Christian Spain". Today, however, it belies such history; only a small area of town, well east of the river, retains any of its medieval architecture. Instead it's a somewhat scruffy, workaday place, specializing in activity tourism, that's nonetheless ideal for a comfortable night, a drink in a nice little bar, and a solid meal after a spell in the mountains. It also abounds in souvenir stores selling local food and drink, such as cheese, cider and multicoloured *fabadas* (beans).

Capilla de Santa Cruz

Mon–Fri 10am–2pm & 4–7pm, Sat 10am–2pm & 4–7.30pm • Free

The curious little **Capilla de Santa Cruz** is a fifteenth-century rebuilding of an eighth-century chapel that counts as one of the earliest Christian sites in Spain. It was founded over a Celtic dolmen, now visible through an opening in the floor. To get there from the bridge, take the first left off the main road eastwards, the Avenida de Covadonga, and cross Río Güeña.

ARRIVAL AND INFORMATION

By bus Cangas is connected by bus with Arenas de Cabrales (4 daily; 45min); Covadonga (9 daily; 45min); and Posada de Valdeón (daily in summer; 2hr 15min);
Turismo Avda. de Covadonga 1, immediately east of the bridge (July–Sept daily 10am–10pm; Oct–June Mon–Sat 10am–2pm & 4–7pm, Sun 10am–2pm; ☎ 985 848 043, ⓦ cangasdeonis.com).
National Park office Casa Dago, Avda. de Covadonga 43 (Mon–Thurs 8am–2.30pm & 4–6pm, Fri 8am–2.30pm; ☎ 985 848 614, ⓦ reddeparquesnacionales.mma.es).

ACCOMMODATION

Hotel Covadonga Avda. de Castilla 38 ☎ 985 848 135, ⓦ hotel-covadonga.com. Simple but friendly hotel, 5min walk south of the centre, offering plain, good-value rooms with river views. **€60**
Hotel Nochendi Constantino González 4 ☎ 985 849 513, ⓦ hotelnochendi.com. Much the fanciest hotel in the middle of Cangas, with crisp, neat, modern rooms with stylish bathrooms, and its own good restaurant. Closed Jan. **€75**
Hotel Puente Romano Puente Romano 8 ☎ 985 849 339, ⓦ hotelimperion.com/puenteromano. Ochre-coloured villa in a great location beside the bridge on the west bank of the river, holding 27 sizeable, comfortable rooms. **€82**
Parador de Cangas de Onís Villanueva, Cangas de Onís ☎ 985 849 402, ⓦ parador.es. Spacious and very upscale parador, in the sumptuously restored monastery of La Vega, 2km north of town towards Arriondas. Look for offers online. **€161**
Pensión Labra Avda. de Castilla 1, 1° B ☎ 985 849 047. Inexpensive en-suite rooms, very close to the bridge, in an apartment in a modern block above the main-street shops. Not all rooms have windows. **€45**

EATING AND DRINKING

El Corcho c/Ángel Tarano 5 ☎ 985 849 477. The pick of several classic *sidrerías* in this small alleyway, just east of Pl. Ayuntamiento. Lots of outdoor tables (equipped with nifty cider-pouring devices), and a great range of snacks, like *patatas con Cabrales* for €5 or peppers stuffed with prawns and cod for €8. Daily except Tues 11am–4pm & 6pm–midnight.
La Golosa Avda. de Covadonga 4 ☎ 985 849 007, ⓦ confiterialagolosa.com. This stylish café-bakery, close to the bridge, is an elegant breakfast option with a good array of pastries. Tues–Sun 8am–10pm.
★**La Sifonería** c/San Pelayo 28 ☎ 985 849 055, ⓦ lasifoneria.es. Small *sidrería* and tapas bar, kitted out with a great collection of antique soda siphons, just off the southeast corner of the park on the south side of Avda. de Covadonga. With its attractive tiled decor and hearty mountain food, it's always packed with locals; be sure to try a delicious *sartén*, a single-pan melange of, for example, ham, eggs and potatoes. The same owners run a fully fledged restaurant two doors away. Daily noon–3pm & 7–11pm.

The Asturian coast: Llanes to Lastres

Once you get into Asturias, the coast becomes wilder and more rugged, as it parallels the **Picos de Europa** just 20km inland. The **FEVE line** hugs the shoreline as far as **Ribadesella**, an attractive little fishing port, before turning inland towards Oviedo. Beyond Ribadesella, towards Gijón, there are fewer appealing towns, though the fishing village of **Lastres** makes a pretty stop.

Llanes

Asturias' easternmost resort, **LLANES**, is a delightful seaside town, crammed between the foothills of the Picos and a particularly majestic stretch of the coast. To the east and west stretch sheer cliffs, little-known beaches and a series of beautiful coves, yours for the walking. The three town beaches are small but pleasant and very central, while the excellent **Playa Ballota** is only 3km to the east, with its own supply of spring water down on the sand (and a nudist stretch). A long *rambla*, the **Paseo de San Pedro**, runs along the top of the dramatic cliffs above the western town beach, the little **Playa del Sablón**.

In the centre of town, a tidal stream lined with cafés and seafood restaurants runs down into a small harbour. In the **old town** itself, a tangle of lanes twists around a small hill to the west and tall medieval walls shelter a number of impressive buildings in various stages of restoration or decay, which include the **Torre Medieval**, housing the *turismo*; the semi-ruined and overgrown Renaissance palaces of the **Duques de Estrada** and the **Casa del Cercau** (both closed to the public); and the **Basílica de Santa María**, built in the plain Gothic style imported from southern France.

ARRIVAL AND INFORMATION | LLANES

By train Llanes FEVE station is a short walk southwest of the centre.
Destinations Oviedo (4 daily; 2hr 30min); Ribadesella (5 daily; 35min); Santander (2 daily; 2hr 5min).
By bus The bus terminal is at the bottom end of c/Pidal, not far southeast of the stream.

Destinations Gijón (5 daily; 1hr 30min–2hr); Ribadesella (8 daily; 30min); San Vicente (4 daily; 30min).
Turismo Torre Medieval, c/Posada Herrera 15 (mid-June to mid-Sept daily 10am–2pm & 5–9pm; mid-Sept to mid-June Mon–Sat 10am–2pm & 4–6.30pm, Sun 10am–2pm; ☎ 985 400 164, ⓦ llanes.com).

ACCOMMODATION

Camping La Paz Playa de Vidiago ☎ 985 411 235, ⓦ campinglapaz.com. Wonderful ocean-view campsite, located on a dramatic headland overlooking a lovely, undeveloped sandy beach, 5km east of Llanes and just ten minutes' walk from the Vidiago FEVE stop. Closed mid-Oct to mid-April. Car and two adults €28

ASTURIAN FOOD AND DRINK

Asturian food is not for the faint-hearted, and it's certainly not for vegetarians. The signature dish is **fabada**, a dense haricot-bean stew floating with pungent chunks of meat: black pudding, *chorizo* and ham. It's served in a round terracotta dish, and you mop up the juice with the ubiquitous hunk of solid bread. **Seafood** is another feature, from sea urchins – particularly popular in Gijón – to sea bream and squid. The region produces a huge variety of **handmade cheeses**, most notably the veined and slightly spicy *cabrales*, which, in its purest form, is made with cow-, sheep- and goat-milk combined. Another variety is a small cone-shaped cheese, known as *afuega'l pitu*, which sometimes has a wrinkled exterior owing to its having been hung in cloth.

One sight you won't miss is waiters and punters pouring **sidra** (cider) – which you can only order by the bottle – from above their heads into wide-rimmed glasses. The idea is that you knock back the frothing brew in one go. Since it's a point of honour for the waiters to stare straight ahead rather than look at the glasses, and any residue that you don't drink within a minute or two is summarily discarded on the floor, it's hardly surprising the region seems to reek of stale cider.

El Habana Hotel de Campo La Pereda s/n, Llanes ☎985 402 526, ⓦelhabana.net. Large, very welcoming country-house hotel in a peaceful little village just 3km inland from Llanes, set against the foothills of the Picos. Spacious and nicely furnished rooms, plus a pool and a dining room for guests only. Closed Nov–March. €103

Posada del Rey c/Mayor 11 ☎985 401 332, ⓦlaposadadelrey.es. This attractive little hotel, in the heart of old Llanes, offers comfortable, pleasantly furnished en-suite rooms. €103

Sablón's Hotel Playa del Sablón 1 ☎985 401 987, ⓦhotelsablon.com. Modern hotel, perched in prime position on the bluff just above the Playa del Sablón, a short walk west of the old town. Most, but not quite all, of the spacious tiled-floor rooms have large sea-view windows. Look for discounts online. €100

EATING AND DRINKING

El Almacén c/Posada Herrera s/n ☎985 403 007, ⓦsidreria-el-almacen.com. Cosy *sidrería*, tucked away in a very quiet spot just inside the walls near the *turismo*, with outdoor tables and a wide selection of food, including all sorts of mushrooms, as well as €6 bottles of wine. Daily 1–3pm & 6–11pm.

★ **El Bodegón** Pl. de Siete Puertas ☎985 400 185. This characterful old-style tavern, spilling out onto benches in a pretty tree-shaded square near the harbour, is good for *sidra* and Asturian *raciones*, with its seafood specialities typically costing €7.50 to €11. Daily except Thurs noon–4pm & 7.30pm–midnight.

Confitería Vega c/Mercaderes 10 ☎985 400 822. This old-fashioned bakery and cake shop is a great place for takeaway goodies. Daily 8am–3pm & 4.30–9pm.

La Covadonga c/Manuel Cué 8 ☎985 400 891. White-tablecloth restaurant with some outdoor seating on an alley just up from the harbour, serving a great-value €11 *menú* that includes three courses plus wine. Tues–Sun 12.30–3.30pm & 7.30–10.30pm.

Ribadesella

RIBADESELLA, 18km west of Llanes, is an unaffected old port, split into two by the Sella river, and bridged by a long causeway. The attractive **old town**, crammed up against the hillside to the east, consists of successive, long stone alleyways, running parallel to the **fishing harbour** and bursting with great little bars and *comedores*. Freshly caught fish is still unloaded after midnight at the *lonja* and, although the catch is increasingly small, it's fun to hang out in the bars and watch it being hauled in. In the seafood joints lining the harbour you can sample delicacies such as *centolla* (spider crab) and *lubina* (sea bass), as well as Asturian specialities.

Across the bridge to the west, ten minutes' walk from the old town, the excellent town beach, **Playa Santa Marina**, is lined with the impressive nineteenth-century mansions built by returning emigrants who'd prospered in the Americas. The seafront itself is a pleasant pedestrian promenade.

Cueva Tito Bustillo

Cave Oct–March Wed–Sun first tour 10.15am, last 5pm; museum second fortnight of March & July to mid-Sept daily 10am–2.30pm & 4–8pm; April–June & second fortnight of Sept Wed–Sun 10am–2.30pm & 4–7pm; Oct–Dec Wed–Fri 10am–2.30pm & 3.30–6pm, Sat & Sun 10am–2.30pm & 4–7pm; cave and museum closed Aug 6 and Aug 7 • Cave and museum €7, no children under 7; museum only €5; both free Wed • Reservations ☎985 861 255 • ⓦcentrodearterupestredetitobustillo.com

Rediscovered in the late 1960s, the **Cueva Tito Bustillo** is adorned with a remarkable collection of **prehistoric paintings**, created between 25,000 BC and 10,000 BC. Best known for its vivid depictions of horses, it's also quite a natural wonder, with mighty stalactites hanging from the ceiling.

Located a short walk west of the old town – turn left along the riverbank from the west end of the bridge – the cave itself can only be visited on 45min guided tours. Only 350 visitors are allowed in each day, so unless you reserve far in advance you're unlikely to get in. Immediately in front, however, a modern **museum** holds excellent displays on ancient art and artefacts from all over the region.

ARRIVAL AND INFORMATION   RIBADESELLA

By train Ribadesella's FEVE station is a stiff climb up from the old town on c/Santander.

Destinations Llanes (5 daily; 35min); Oviedo (4 daily; 3hr); Santander (2 daily; 1hr 30min).

By bus The bus station is near the tourist office, at the east end of the bridge.

Turismo In the old town, on Paseo Princesa Letizia at the east end of the bridge (May, June & mid-Sept to Oct Mon–Sat 10am–2pm & 5–8pm, Sun 11am–2pm; July to mid-Sept daily 10am–10pm; Nov–April Tues–Sat 10am–2pm & 4–6.30pm, Sun 11am–2pm; ☎ 985 860 038, ⊛ ribadesella.es).

ACCOMMODATION

Albergue Ribadesella c/Ricardo Cangas 1 ☎ 985 861 105, ⊛ albergueribadesella.com. Not surprisingly, this gorgeous hostel, set in a beachfront mansion facing the Playa Santa Marina, is often booked out by groups. Rates include breakfast. Closed Nov. Dorm beds €13

Camping Ribadesella c/Sebreño ☎ 985 858 293, ⊛ camping-ribadesella.com. Ribadesella's best campsite is a few hundred metres from the sea, just south of the main road, beyond the west end of the beach, but has a great outdoor pool and a covered indoor one. Closed Oct–June except Easter. Car and two adults €27

★ **Covadonga** c/Manuel Caso de Villa 9 ☎ 985 860 110, ⊛ hotelcovadongaribadesella.com. Atmospheric old building just inland from the fish market. Several of the nicely revamped en-suite rooms have balconies overlooking the street; the *sidrería* downstairs has a boat-shaped bar. €60

Gran Hotel del Sella c/Ricardo Cangas 17 ☎ 985 860 150, ⊛ granhoteldelsella.com. One of the very grandest options beside the beach, set in a massive blue villa but with some cheaper rooms in a more recent extension. Fabulous sea views and a nice pool. €166

Pensión Arbidel c/Escura 1 ☎ 985 860 141, ⊛ arbidelpension.com. Inexpensive, cheerful little option, back from the sea at the south end of the old town and offering four pleasant en-suite rooms. Discounts for pilgrims. €60

Puente del Pilar c/Puente del Pilar ☎ 985 860 446, ⊛ desdeasturias.com/puentedelpilar. The best-value hotel on the west side of the bridge, albeit set 200m back from the sea beside a muddy stream. Sixteen very tasteful rooms, peaceful gardens, and a restaurant serving traditional Asturian food. Closed Oct–Easter. €80

EATING AND DRINKING

Casa Gaspar c/López Muñiz 6 ☎ 985 860 676. Very popular restaurant, with lots of outdoor tables on a pedestrian square in the heart of the old town, a few blocks inland. The great-value €10 lunch *menú* offers *fabadas asturianas* followed by a substantial meat or fish main course; dinner *menús* start at €15. Daily 11am–midnight.

Rompeolas c/Manuel Fernandez Juncos 9 ☎ 985 860 287. Classic old *sidrería*, with good food including a €12 *menú*, and tables in the courtyard at the back. Daily 1–4pm & 9pm–midnight.

Sidrería La Marina c/Manuel Caso de la Villa ☎ 985 861 219. Big, buzzy place, facing the port on a busy road and offering anything from full meals to tasty snacks. Tues–Sun 11.30am–midnight.

Lastres

LASTRES, off the Santander–Gijón highway 25km west of Ribadesella, below larger **Colunga**, is a tiny fishing village built dramatically on a steep and very verdant cliffside. Day-trippers huff and puff their way along its precipitous pedestrian lanes, down to the modern harbour, but it's a nice enough place to consider spending a night or two, with the bonus of a couple of good beaches on its outskirts.

ACCOMMODATION AND EATING
LASTRES

Casa Eutimio c/San Antonio s/n ☎ 985 850 012, ⊛ casaeutimio.com. Very nice en-suite rooms comfortably furnished in warm colours, in a great location above the port. Good seafood restaurant, serving all meals daily. €65

Costa Verde Playa la Griega ☎ 985 856 373. Large, well-maintained campsite, with grassy pitches set close to an excellent beach, 2km east of Llastres. Closed Oct–Easter. Car and two adults €24

Gijón

With 275,000 inhabitants, the port city of **GIJÓN** (Xixón) is the largest city in Asturias. Despite its industrial reputation, it remains largely surrounded by open green countryside, and it's a genuinely enjoyable place to visit, with its dynamic old core flanked either side by a huge curving **beach** and a vibrant pleasure port. Much of the city had to be rebuilt after the intensive bombardment it suffered during the Civil War, when miners armed with sticks of dynamite stormed the barracks of the Nationalist-declared army – the beleaguered colonel asked ships from his own side, anchored offshore, to bomb his men rather than let them be captured.

Gijón fans back along the coast in both directions from the stark rocky headland known as **Cimadevilla**, with the modern marina of the pretty **Puerto Deportivo** to the west (and the commercial port out of sight beyond that), and the town beach to the east. War damage has left little to see on Cimadevilla itself, though high up at the tip of the promontory a grassy park enjoys great views of the Cantabrian Sea, framed by Eduardo Chillida's sculpture *Elogio del Horizonte* (Eulogy to the Horizon). The epicentre of today's city lies at the narrow "neck" of the peninsula, immediately south

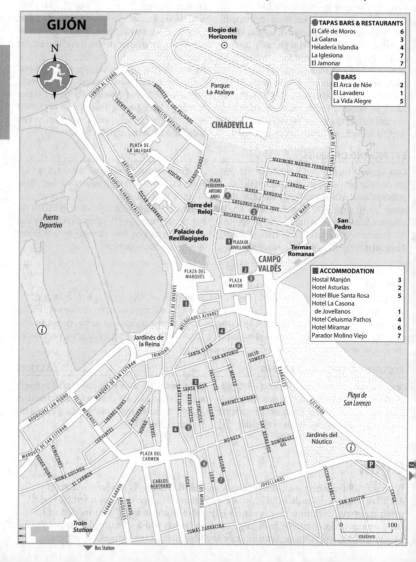

GIJÓN

● TAPAS BARS & RESTAURANTS
El Café de Moros | 6
La Galana | 3
Heladería Islandia | 4
La Iglesiona | 7
El Jamonar | 7

● BARS
El Arca de Nöe | 2
El Lavaderu | 1
La Vida Alegre | 5

■ ACCOMMODATION
Hostal Manjón | 3
Hotel Asturias | 2
Hotel Blue Santa Rosa | 5
Hotel La Casona de Jovellanos | 1
Hotel Celuisma Pathos | 4
Hotel Miramar | 6
Parador Molino Viejo | 7

of Cimadevilla. On its western side, the **Plaza del Marqués** holds a statue of Pelayo, the eighth-century king who began the Reconquest.

In the last week of July, the city hosts **Semana Negra** (ⓦsemananegra.org), officially an arts festival, but fast turning into another excuse for the locals to party. The hub of the action is around Gijón's El Moliñon football stadium in Parque Isabel La Católica, and while there are a host of poetry recitals, art displays and culture groups dotted around, these days you are just as likely to experience loud music, candyfloss and fairground rides.

Palacio de Revillagigedo

Pl. del Marqués • July & Aug Mon–Sat 11am–2pm & 6–9pm, Sun noon–2.30pm; Sept–June Mon–Sat 11am–2pm & 5–8pm, Sun noon–2.30pm • Free

Dominating the seafront Plaza del Marqués, the **Palacio de Revillagigedo** is a splendid mix of neo-Baroque and neo-Renaissance styles, and in its own way, its light modern interior is every bit as striking as the eighteenth-century facade. The complex is used for annual large-scale exhibitions, and also hosts music, theatre and other cultural events.

Termas Romanas de Campo Valdés

Tues–Fri 9.30am–2pm & 5–7.30pm, Sat & Sun 10am–2pm & 5–7.30pm • €2.50, free Sun • ⓦmuseos.gijon.es

An inconspicuous entrance from the seafront promenade just north of the end of the San Lorenzo beach, on the east side of the peninsula, leads to the remarkable **Termas Romanas** (Roman Baths) of ancient Gigia. Discovered during an aborted attempt to build an underground car park, they lie beneath an open park in front of the San Pedro church. A subterranean museum displays their history and use, while walkways allow visitors to crisscross the actual ruins.

Playa de San Lorenzo

The sands of the **Playa de San Lorenzo**, a lengthy golden beach reminiscent of the one at San Sebastián, curve 2km westwards from Campo Valdés. In the summer, the whole city seems to descend here on afternoons and weekends, which makes things pretty crowded when the strand dwindles at high tide. All year round, it's the focus of the evening *paseo*, and even on the gloomiest winter day some hardy surfer is usually braving the waves. At the far end of the beach, the tranquil Parque Isabel La Católica stretches back along the east bank of the Río Piles.

Museo del Pueblo de Asturias

C/La Guelga, off Paseo Dr Fleming • April–Sept Tues–Fri 10am–7pm, Sat & Sun 10.30am–7pm; Oct–March Tues–Fri 9.30am–6.30pm, Sat & Sun 10am–6.30pm • €2.50, free Sun • ⓦmuseos.gijon.es

East across the Río Piles from central Gijón, the **Museo del Pueblo de Asturias** incorporates a bagpipe museum, with an amazing array of instruments from all over the Celtic world and beyond.

ARRIVAL AND INFORMATION	**GIJÓN**
By train FEVE and local RENFE trains use the station on Pl. El Humedal, 300m south of the *turismo*; for all FEVE destinations east and west you have to change at El Berrón. Long-distance RENFE services arrive at a separate station on Avda. de Juan Carlos I, another 300m west. Destinations FEVE: Oviedo (every half-hour; 30min).	RENFE: León (6 daily; 2hr 30min); Madrid (4 daily; 5hr 45min); Oviedo (5 daily; 25min). **By bus** The wonderful Art Deco bus station is just south of the FEVE station, between c/Ribadesella and c/Llanes. The express bus from Asturias airport costs €7 (6am–11pm; 35min).

7

Turismo Gijón's *turismo* is on a broad jetty in the middle of the marina (daily: mid-July to Aug 10am–10pm; May to mid-July, Sept & Oct 10am–8pm; Nov–April 10am–2.30pm & 4.30–7.30pm; ☎ 985 341 771, ⓦ gijon.info). There's also a summer-only booth alongside the beach in the Jardines del Náutico. Both sell the Gijón Card, which gives free admission to the city's museums, free use of public transport, and many other discounts (€10/12/15 for 1/2/3 days; half-price on Tues).

ACCOMMODATION

Hostal Manjón Pl. del Marqués 1 ☎ 985 352 378. Adequate en-suite rooms at good prices, in a convenient location for both the old town and the harbour; the best rooms have sea views. **€50**

Hotel Asturias Pl. Mayor 11 ☎ 985 350 600, ⓦ hotelasturiasgijon.com. Friendly but pricey hotel on the attractive main square between the beach and port, with a choice between "modern" or "classic" rooms. **€104**

Hotel Blue Santa Rosa c/Santa Rosa 4 ☎ 985 091 919, ⓦ bluehoteles.es. Modern hotel in very central location near the old town, with an underground car park. The bedrooms are small, but they're dazzlingly bright and clean, with a/c and blue bed linens; some have galleried windows. **€105**

Hotel La Casona de Jovellanos Pl. de Jovellanos 1 ☎ 985 342 024, ⓦ lacasonadejovellanos.com. This atmospheric old building, in a great location on the neck of the peninsula, holds a dozen plain but acceptable en-suite rooms. The friendly bar downstairs spreads onto the square outside, and is often noisy on summer evenings. Parking nearby is €9, cheaper than city car parks. **€81**

Hotel Celuisma Pathos c/Santa Elena 6 ☎ 985 176 400, ⓦ celuisma.com. Very central hotel, where each of the crisp modern rooms is named in honour of a twentieth-century icon such as Che Guevara, and pop art adorns the public spaces. **€70**

Hotel Miramar c/Santa Lucía 9 ☎ 985 351 108, ⓦ hotelmiramargijon.com. Tastefully restored hotel, close to the action immediately south of the old town, with presentable rooms that are better value in low season. **€83**

Parador Molino Viejo Parque de Isabel La Católica ☎ 985 370 511, ⓦ parador.es. The usual luxurious standard of parador accommodation, set in a converted water mill in an attractive park 500m inland from the east end of the beach. **€163**

EATING

The streets around the seafront and immediately behind contain a mass of little **café-restaurants**, all reasonably priced and most with a *menú*. If in doubt, head to any of the *sidrerías* around Pl. Mayor.

El Café de Moros c/de los Moros 13, no phone. Spacious, old-fashioned, wooden-floored café, with a real homey feeling, set in a high-ceilinged former sewing-machine shop and using old sewing tables. Especially good for breakfast and strong coffee; no outdoor seating. Daily 8am–1am.

La Galana Pl. Mayor 10 ☎ 985 172 429. This great big bar/restaurant on the central square is Gijón's best-known rendezvous for cider and food, from snacks to full meals. Packed out every night, it's very friendly and welcoming, with inexpensive tiny tapas portions, or *raciones* for around €7. Daily noon–4pm & 7pm–1.30am.

Heladería Islandia c/San Antonio 4 ☎ 985 350 747, ⓦ laiglesiona.com. Inventive ice-cream joint offering (among others) *sidra, fabada* and *cabrales* cheese flavours. Daily 10am–2.30pm & 5–11pm.

La Iglesiona c/Begoña 34 ☎ 985 171 417, ⓦ laiglesiona .com. Among the larger of the enticing tapas bars that line "La Ruta", with a light, modernized feel and a fine array of hams hanging from the ceiling. Order a glass of wine and you'll be given some free snacks, or pay €17 for a plate of melt-in-your mouth *jamón iberico*. They also do a great line in *tortillas*, including *tortilla de bacalao* (cod). Tues–Sat 11am–4pm & 8pm–midnight, Sun 11am–4pm.

El Jamonar c/Begoña 38 ☎ 985 342 844. Atmospheric old-school tapas bar, serving *raciones* and good fish dishes, with a great-value three-course €8.50 *menú* on weekdays. Daily noon–2.30pm & 8pm–midnight.

NIGHTLIFE

At the weekend, a lively **nightlife** scene kicks off around the area known as **La Ruta**, a grid enclosed by c/Santa Lucía, c/Buen Suceso and c/Santa Rosa, a few hundred yards east of Pl. del Carmen. People also head to Cimadevilla, whose bars are crammed in summer, c/Rufo Rendueles and its extensions along the beach. The main **clubbing** area is focused around **El Náutico** farther north, and along the streets nearby, especially lively c/Jacobo Olañeta and c/San Agustín.

BARS

El Arca de Nöe c/Esculto Sebastián Miranda 1 ☎ 985 351 437. When you've had your fill of raucous *sidrerías*, get a cool taste of Montmartre at this arty jazz bar, with its open shuttered windows and fine wines; there's no food, though. Daily 6pm–1am.

El Lavaderu Pl. Periodista Arturo Arias 1 ☎ 985 359 380. Youthful crowds – and copious quantities of cider

– spill out from this charming old-fashioned bar, just up from the port, to fill the wide square outside, which as well as large tables holds a broad staircase ideal for soaking up the sun. Daily except Tues 11am–1am.

La Vida Alegre c/Buen Suceso 8, no phone. The most laidback bar on La Ruta, with fairy lights and exposed brick walls and a cool mambo soundtrack. Mon–Fri 9am–3pm & 7pm until late, Sat & Sun 7pm until late.

Avilés

Determined to consign its gritty, industrial reputation to the past, the city of **AVILÉS**, 23km west from Gijón, has greatly cleaned up its act in recent years. Its arcaded **old town**, on the west bank of the namesake Ría de Avilés, is looking spruce, while immediately across the river the new **Centro Oscar Niemeyer** is an architectural showcase sadly looks unlikely to match the impact of the Guggenheim in Bilbao.

The old town

Strewn with fourteenth- and fifteenth-century churches and palaces, Avilés' likeable **old town** is home to most of the city's shops, bars and places to stay, as well as the pretty, walled **Parque de Ferrera**.

Churches worth a closer look include the Romanesque **San Nicolás de Bari**, on c/San Francisco, and the thirteenth-century **Santo Tomás**. **La Iglesia de los Padres Franciscanos** contains the tomb of Don Pedro Menéndez de Avilés, the first governor of Spanish Florida, who founded the first European city in what is now the United States, St Augustine, in 1565.

There are also some superb palaces, especially the Baroque **Camposagrado**, in Plaza Camposagrado, built in 1663 and now serving as an art school, and the seventeenth-century **Palacio de Marqués de Ferrera** in Plaza de España, now an expensive hotel. Around the corner on c/San Francisco is the city's most distinctive monument, the seventeenth-century **Fuente de los Caños**, with its six grotesque heads spouting water.

CARNAVAL IN ASTURIAS

Carnaval, the Mardi Gras week of drinking, dancing and excess, usually takes place over late February and early March. In Spain, the celebrations are reckoned to be at their wildest in Tenerife, Cádiz and Asturias – and, in particular, **Avilés**. Events begin in Avilés on the **Saturday before Ash Wednesday**, when virtually the entire city dons fancy dress and takes to the streets. Many costumes are veritable works of art, ranging from toothbrushes to mattresses and packets of sweets. By nightfall, anyone without a costume is likely to be drenched in some form of liquid, as gangs of nuns, Red Indians and pirates roam the streets. On Calle Galiana, central to the action, the local fire brigade traditionally hoses down the street, and any passing revellers, with foam, while a parade of floats threads its way amid the frenzy.

The festivities, which include live music, fireworks and fancy-dress competitions, last till dawn. It's virtually impossible to find accommodation, but the celebrations continue throughout Asturias during the following week, so after a full night of revelling you can just head on to the next venue. Sunday is, in fact, a rest day before Carnaval continues in **Gijón** on the **Monday** night. Much the same ensues, and fancy dress is again essential; La Ruta is the place to be for the start of the night, with people and events shifting between Plaza Mayor and the harbour area till dawn. On **Tuesday** night, the scene shifts to **Oviedo**: the crowds are smaller here and events are less frantic, but a fair part of the city again dons costume. There's a parade along Calle Uría, a midnight fireworks display in the Plaza Escandelera, and live bands in the Plaza Mayor. Finally, on the **Friday after Ash Wednesday**, **Mieres**, a mining town just southeast of Oviedo, plays host to Carnaval. Celebrations take place in an area known as Calle del Vicio, which locals claim contains the highest concentration of bars in the entire province.

Centro Niemeyer

ⓦ centroniemeyer.org

The lynchpin of Avilés' urban regeneration project is the **Centro Niemeyer**, a multi-purpose cultural complex located on a former industrial site across the river from the old town. Designed by centenarian Brazilian architect Oscar Niemeyer, it opened on his 103rd birthday in 2010. Consisting of three stark geometric buildings – a dome, a tower encircled by a spiral staircase, and a long sinuous S-curve – set atop an enormous dazzling-white platform that's ideal for public events, it was intended to host a wide range of performances and temporary exhibitions. Despite a roster of big-name advisers including Kevin Spacey for theatre, Brad Pitt for architecture, and Woody Allen for cinema, at the time this book went to press it had already been forced to close for an indefinite period, due to alleged over-spending. Check the website to see whether it has re-opened.

ARRIVAL AND INFORMATION   AVILÉS

By plane Asturias airport, 14km west of Avilés, has all the usual car-rental outlets, and is connected to the city by express buses (6.30am–10.30pm; €1.40; 25min).
By train Both FEVE and RENFE trains use the same station on Avda. Telares, a short walk north of the old town, across Parque Muelle.

By bus The bus terminus is alongside the train station on Avda. Telares, just north of the centre.
Turismo c/Ruiz Gómez 21, off Pl. de España (July to mid-Sept daily 10am–8pm; mid-Sept to June Mon–Fri 9am–2pm & 4.30–6.30pm, Sat & Sun 10am–2pm; ☎ 985 544 325, ⓦ www.avilescomarca.info).

ACCOMMODATION

Hotel Don Pedro c/Fruta 22 ☎ 985 512 288, ⓦ hdonpedro.com. On a central pedestrian street, with 25 rather sumptuous, warm-toned rooms, many featuring exposed stone walls. The one potential drawback is late-night noise from the nearby bars. **€95**
El Magistral de Avilés c/Ponte Llano 4 ☎ 985 561 100, ⓦ magistralhoteles.com. Pleasant, good-value little renovated hotel, in prime position at the start of the bridge to the Niemeyer centre, and offering plain modern bedrooms with turquoise balconies. **€51**

Palacio de Marqués de Ferrera Pl. de España ☎ 985 129 080, ⓦ nh-hotels.com. This smart, central hotel, housed in a grand seventeenth-century mansion, is the most luxurious option in town, with spacious modernized rooms. Look for weekend discounts. **€105**
Pensión Puente Azud c/Acero 5 ☎ 985 550 177, ⓦ www.hostalpuenteazud.com. In truth, the small en-suite rooms of this simple *pensión*, 500m southeast of the centre, are no more exciting than its drab blue exterior, but they're the cheapest you're likely to find. **€45**

EATING AND DRINKING

Casa Alvarin c/las Alas 2 ☎ 985 540 113, ⓦ casaalvarin .com. Good old-fashioned *sidrería*, with a full range of hearty *raciones*, from beans with clams to octopus or succulent ham, and a €10 set *menú*. Daily 12.30–3.30pm & 8–11pm; closed 2nd half June and 1st half Oct.

Casa Tataguyo Pl. Carbayedo 6 ☎ 985 564 815, ⓦ tataguyo.com. This very charming 1840s *mesón*, one of several on the same square, is the oldest in town. Dependable local cuisine, at €15–20 for a main course. Daily noon–3.30pm & 8pm–midnight; closed mid-April to mid-May.

Oviedo

The bourgeois culture of **OVIEDO** is a contrast to the working-class ethos of its neighbours. As the Asturian capital, it has long been relatively wealthy, a history that can be traced through the grand, lovingly restored administrative and religious buildings that render the city among the most attractive in the north. The old quarter, all the better for being largely pedestrianized, is a knot of squares and narrow streets built in warm yellow stone, while the newer part is redeemed by a huge public park right in its centre. Throughout the city are excellent bars and restaurants, many aimed at the lively student population.

Oviedo also boasts three small **churches** that rank among the most remarkable in Spain, built in a style unique to Asturias. All date from the first half of the ninth century, a period of almost total isolation for the Asturian kingdom, which was then just 65km by

50km in area and the only part of Spain under Christian rule. Oviedo became the centre of this outpost in 810, as the base for King Alfonso II, son of the victorious Pelayo.

Around the cathedral, enclosed by scattered sections of the medieval town walls, a compact, attractive quarter preserves the remains of **Old Oviedo**. Much was destroyed in the Civil War when Republican Asturian miners laid siege to the Nationalist garrison; the defenders were relieved by a Gallego detachment when on the brink of surrender.

The Catedral

March–June & Oct Mon–Fri 10am–1pm & 4–7pm, Sat 10am–1pm & 4–6pm; July to mid-Sept Mon–Fri 10am–2pm & 4–8pm, Sat 10am–2.30pm & 4–6pm; second fortnight of Sept Mon–Fri 10am–2.30pm, Sat 10am–2.30pm & 4–6pm; Nov–Feb Mon–Sat 10am–1pm & 4–6pm • €3.50 for Cámara Santa & diocesan museum

In the ninth century, King Alfonso II built a chapel, the **Cámara Santa** (Holy Chamber), to house the holy relics rescued from Toledo when it fell to the Moors. Remodelled in the twelfth century, it now forms the inner sanctuary of Oviedo's unusually uncluttered Gothic **Catedral**. With its primitive capitals, the innermost of the Cámara Santa's pair of interconnecting chapels is thought to be Alfonso's original building. The antechapel is a quiet little triumph of Spanish Romanesque; each of the six columns supporting the vault is sculpted with a pair of superbly humanized Apostles.

Built around the attractive Gothic cloister, itself built on pre-Romanesque foundations, the **diocesan museum** holds a high-quality collection of devotional art and artefacts.

Museo de Bellas Artes

C/Santa Ana • July & Aug Tues–Sat 10.30am–2pm & 4.30–8pm, Sun 10.30am–2.30pm; Sept–June Tues–Fri 10.30am–2pm & 4.30–8.30pm, Sat 11.30am–2pm & 5–8pm, Sun 11.30am–2.30pm • Free • ⓦ museobbaa.com

The eighteenth-century Palacio de Velarde, immediately south of the cathedral, now houses the **Museo de Bellas Artes**. The highlights of the bold collection of contemporary Spanish art are on the top floor: Picasso's *Mosquetero con Espada y Amorcillo* is a gleeful take on historical portraiture, while Dalí's lyrical *Metamorfosis de Ángeles* has an unusually muted palette of browns and blues. The c/Santa Ana entrance brings you directly to another gem of the collection: El Greco's sombre portraits of the twelve Apostles (1585–90), which favour psychological depth over symbolism.

Museo Arqueológico

Pl. Alfonso II • Wed–Fri 9.30am–8pm, Sat 9.30am–2pm & 5–8pm, Sun 9.30am–3pm • Free • ⓦ museoarqueologicodeasturias.com

Oviedo's **Museo Arqueológico** occupies an impressively revamped modern structure behind the cathedral, built around the former convent of San Vicente and affording lots of views of otherwise inaccessible parts of the cathedral. Its comprehensive run-through of several thousand years of Asturian history is of most interest to locals – with only a few captions in English – but it does hold some very beautiful ancient artefacts. The section on the prehistoric cave of Tito Bustillo (see p.530) is especially interesting.

San Julián de los Prados

C/Gijón • May–Sept Mon 10am–12.30pm, Tues–Fri 10am–12.30pm & 4–5.30pm, Sat 9.30–noon & 3.30–5pm; Oct–April Mon 10am–12.30pm, Tues–Sat 9.30–11.30am • €1.20 guided tour in Spanish, free on Mon with no guide

The nearest of Oviedo's remarkable "Asturian-Visigoth" churches to the city, **San Julián de los Prados**, also known as **Santullano**, stands alongside a highway ten minutes' walk northeast of the centre, along c/Gijón. Built around 830, it is large and spacious, with an unusual "secret chamber" built into the outer wall. The original frescoes inside, still remarkably colourful, are executed in similar style to those of Roman villas – along with architectural motifs, you'll see two Latin crosses hung with the letters alpha and omega.

OVIEDO

San Julián, Airport, Gijón & Avilés

● EATING & DRINKING	
Gran Taberna	3
Los Lagos	2
La Más Barata	5
El Raitán	4
Tierra Astur	1

■ ACCOMMODATION	
Hotel Cristal Naranco	7
Hotel El Magistral	3
Hotel Ovetense	5
Hotel de la Reconquista	4
Hotel Santa Cruz	6
Hotel Vetusta	2
Pensión Riesgo	1

Santa María del Naranco

April–Sept Mon & Sun 9.30am–1pm, Tues–Sat 9.30am–1pm & 3.30–7pm; Oct–March Mon 10am–1pm, Tues–Sat 10am–12.30pm & 3–4.30pm, Sun 10am–12.30pm • €3 guided tour in Spanish, free on Mon with no guide

The greatest Asturian church, indeed the architectural gem of the principality, is **Santa María del Naranco**, majestically located amid the fields on a wooded slope 3km above the city. It's an easy signposted drive, or a 45min walk from the train station through the quiet suburb of Ciudad Naranco. The one drawback is that its impact is inevitably diminished by the huge tour groups that descend upon it in summer.

The initial glimpses of the warm stone and simple bold outline, in perfect harmony with its surroundings, led Jan Morris to describe it as "formidable beyond its scale". If you don't think it looks like a church, there's a good reason for that – it wasn't built as one. Instead it was designed as a palatial hunting lodge for Alfonso's successor, Ramiro I (842–52), and only converted into a church at the end of that century. Architecturally, the open porticoes at both ends predate later innovations in Byzantine churches, while thirty or so distinctive decorative medallions skirt the roof.

San Miguel de Lillo

April–Sept Mon & Sun 9.30am–1pm, Tues–Sat 9.30am–1pm & 3.30–7pm; Oct–March Mon 10am–1pm, Tues–Sat 10am–12.30pm & 3–4.30pm, Sun 10am–12.30pm • €3 guided tour in Spanish, free on Mon with no guide

King Ramiro's palace chapel, **San Miguel de Lillo**, stands a couple of hundred metres beyond Santa María. Built with soft golden sandstone and red tiles, it's generally assumed to be by the same architect – Tiodo – but its design is quite different. In fact, less than half of the original ninth-century church remains, the rest having been swept away by a landslide and clumsily rebuilt in the thirteenth century. The altar sits in Santa María del Naranco, and much of the interior sculpture has been removed to the Museo Arqueológico, but look for the window grilles carved from single slabs of limestone, and the superb Byzantine-style carved door frames depicting, incongruously enough, the investiture of a Roman consul, complete with circus-style festivities.

ARRIVAL AND DEPARTURE
OVIEDO

By plane Asturias airport is 50km northwest of the city; express buses to and from Oviedo cost €7 (7am–midnight; 40min).

By train Both the RENFE and FEVE train stations are in the same building on Avda. de Santander, northeast of the city centre.

Destinations RENFE: Barcelona (2 daily; 11hr); León (7 daily; 2–3hr); Madrid (4 daily; 5hr 15min). FEVE: Ferrol (2 daily; 6hr 30min); Ribadesella (5 daily; 2hr); Santander (2 daily; 4hr 45min).

By bus Oviedo's bus terminal (☏ 985 969 696, ⊚ estaciondeautobusesdeoviedo.com) is a short walk

northeast of the train stations, on c/Pepe Cosmen.
Destinations Avilés (every 30min; 30min–1hr); Cangas de Onís (10–14 daily; 1hr 20min); A Coruña via Betanzos (6 daily; 4hr–6hr 15min); Covadonga (5 daily; 1hr–1hr 45min); Cudillero (1–2 daily; 1hr 10min); Gijón (every 15min; 30min–1hr); León (8 daily; 1hr 30min–2hr); Lugo (3 daily; 4hr 15min–5hr); Madrid (15 daily; 5hr 30min); Pontevedra (2 daily; 7hr 30min); Ribadeo via Luarca (5 daily; 3hr); Ribadesella (7–10 daily; 1hr 20min–2hr); Santander (10 daily; 2hr 15min–3hr 45min); Santiago (7 daily; 5hr 30min); Valladolid (5 daily; 3hr 15min–4hr); Vigo (2 daily; 6hr 45min–8hr); Villaviciosa (12 daily; 30min–1hr).

INFORMATION

Turismo Oviedo's *turismo* is at Pl. de la Constitución 4 (daily: June 10am–7pm; July–Sept 9.30am–7.30pm; Oct–May 10am–2pm & 4.30–7pm; ☏ 985 086 060, ⊚ turismo .ayto-oviedo.es); there's also a booth at Marqués de Santa Cruz 1 (daily: July–Sept 9.30am–2pm & 4–7.30pm;

Oct–June 10am–2pm & 4.30–7pm; ☏ 985 227 586). A separate office at c/Cimadevilla 4 covers the whole of Asturias (July to mid-Sept Mon–Fri 10am–8pm, Sat 10am–7pm, Sun 10am–5pm; mid-Sept to June Mon–Sat 10am–6pm; ☏ 985 213 385, ⊚ infoasturias.com).

ACCOMMODATION

Oviedo has a good supply of **accommodation**, with cheaper *hostales* concentrated along c/Uría, opposite the train station, and along c/Nueve de Mayo and its continuation, c/de Caveda.

Hotel Cristal Naranco c/Carta Puebla 6 ☏ 985 220 012, ⊚ hcnaranco.com. Well-appointed, very modern little hotel with surprisingly large rooms, tucked down an alleyway at the south end of the old town. **€60**

Hotel El Magistral c/Jovellanos 3 ☏ 985 204 242, ⊚ elmagistral.com. Comfortable, ultramodern hotel in a very central location near the cathedral; the rooms themselves are less stylish than the flamboyant public spaces. **€74**

Hotel Ovetense c/San Juan 6 ☏ 985 220 840, ⊚ hotelovetense.com. Plain but great-value en-suite rooms in the old town, above a lively bar-restaurant – which is where you have your breakfast – near the cathedral and cider lanes. **€53**

Hotel de la Reconquista Gil de Jaz 16 ☏ 985 241 100, ⊚ hoteldelareconquista.com. Very comfortable accommodation with top-notch service and a price tag to match, in a

magnificent eighteenth-century hospital near Parque de San Francisco and the train station. **€149**

Hotel Santa Cruz c/Marqués de Santa Cruz 6 ☏ 985 223 711, ⊚ santacruzoviedo.com. Friendly place in a great location, with en-suite rooms overlooking Parque de San Francisco. Not as fancy as the website might suggest, but not bad for the price. **€65**

Hotel Vetusta c/Covadonga 2 ☏ 985 222 229, ⊚ hotelvetusta.com. Stylish modern hotel, with galleried upper storeys, on the northern edge of the old town near the cider lanes. Sixteen pleasant rooms, half of which have mini-saunas. **€58**

Pensión Riesgo c/Nueve de Mayo 16 ☏ 985 218 945. Small, good-value, family-run *pensión*, not too far from the bus and train stations, with plain but spotless little rooms. **€45**

EATING, DRINKING AND NIGHTLIFE

Oviedo's most renowned area for **eating and drinking** lies immediately north of the cathedral, just outside the pedestrian district, where lively **c/Gascona** is festooned with a large neon sign proclaiming it "El Bulevard de la Sidra"; the area is known for its spit-and-sawdust *sidrerías*, or **cider bars**. On weekend nights, the city is liable to fill up with huge crowds of teenage revellers, who commandeer many of its public spaces. If you prefer a less raucous atmosphere, head for the graceful arcaded **Plaza de Fontán** near the old market, ringed by Asturian restaurants and excellent speciality food shops.

Gran Taberna Pl. Porlier 1 ☏ 985 220 006, ⓦlagrantaberna.com. This classy place, on a pedestrian street leading west from the cathedral, makes a welcome retreat on Oviedo's more hectic nights. There's a good à la carte menu of tapas for around €7, *surtidos* for around €15, and solid grilled meat and fish for €20 and up, or you can just sip on a glass of wine in peace. Daily 8.30am–12.30am.

Los Lagos Pl. del Carbayón 4 ☏ 985 200 697, ⓦsidrerialoslagos.net. Excellent *sidrería*, beside a busy road near the cider lanes, and filled with the heady smell of strong Asturian foods, cider and sawdust. Good-value €15 set *menú*. There's another branch at c/Cervantes 7. Mon–Sat 11am–midnight.

La Más Barata c/Cimadevilla 2 ☏ 985 213 606, ⓦlamasbarata.com. Despite the name, this large, very bright bar/restaurant is far from the cheapest place in Oviedo – as you might guess from its stylish decor and prime location, beside the tourist office on the main pedestrian alley through the old town. Enjoy fine wines by the glass in the large open bar area, along with €3 tapas like *patatas cabrales*, or full meals such as an entire squid for €11, plus good rice dishes, in the more formal dining area. Daily noon–2am.

El Raitán Pl. Trascorrales 6 ☏ 985 214 218, ⓦelraitan.es. Superb, atmospheric restaurant in a delightful square off Pl. Mayor. The wide selection of *menús* ranges from €18 for a vegetarian meal to the huge *menú degustación* de cocina *asturiana* for €36, which includes crab soup, *fabada*, and onion-stuffed boar. Mon & Wed–Sat 1–3pm & 7pm–midnight, Sun 1–3pm.

Tierra Astur c/Gascona 1 ☏ 985 203 411, ⓦtierra-astur.com. At the top of "El Bulevard de la Sidra", this bustling place is the best and most salubrious *sidrería* hereabouts, with a large indoor dining room and an enclosed wooden terrace as well as its own large deli. Enormous platters of local cheeses and meats, rich Asturian cuisine, and, of course, large quantities of cider. Daily 11am–1am.

West to Galicia

The coast west of Avilés, as far as the Río Navia, is rugged, with scarcely more than a handful of resorts carved out from the cliffs. The most appealing are the old port and resort of **Luarca**, and pretty little **Cudillero**. West again from the Río Navia, the coast becomes marshy and largely unexceptional.

Cudillero

CUDILLERO is a delightful, picturesque little fishing port, squeezed so tightly into a narrow, corkscrewing valley 25km west of Avilés that none of its buildings manage to face directly out to sea. Nonetheless, the brightly coloured arcaded houses that rise, one above the other, up the steep horseshoe of cliffs that surround the port give it the feel, and appeal, of a Greek island village, and it's usually thronged with visitors in summer. As you climb the twisting main street away from the water, the architecture becomes grittier, but the whole town still oozes character. There's no beach here, however – the nearest is the lovely cove at **Playa Aguilar**, 3km east – so the most obvious attractions are the **fish tavernas** in the cobbled plaza just above the seafront.

ARRIVAL AND INFORMATION   CUDILLERO

By train The FEVE station is atop the cliffs, well above town.

By bus Cudillero is connected with Avilés (8 daily; 50min) and Gijón (8daily; 1hr 15min).

By car The most direct route down into Cudillero is a precipitous and very narrow road that twists its way down the cliffs from the FEVE station, a stiff 25min walk or a hair-raising drive. Motorists would do better to follow the longer road that leaves the N632 a couple of kilometres further west, and approaches the village along the coast; the only sizeable car park is a few hundred metres west of the centre.

Turismo In a modern building facing the harbour, just west of the village centre (Mon–Fri 10am–2pm & 4–7pm, Sat 11am–2pm & 4–7pm, Sun 11am–2pm; ☏ 985 591 377, ⓦcudillero.org).

ACCOMMODATION

Camping Cudillero c/Playa Aguilar ☏ 985 590 663, ⓦcampingcudillero.com. Rural campsite, set well back from the clifftops east of town, a steep 1.4km walk above gorgeous Aguilar beach, with a snack bar and shop, plus rental bungalows and a pool. Closed mid-Sept to mid-April. Car and two adults **€23**, bungalows from **€73**

★ **La Casona de Pío** c/Riofrío 3 ☎ 985 591 512, ⓦ lacasonadepio.com. Cudillero's nicest hotel, set just back from the main seafront square. Lovely, very comfortably furnished en-suite rooms with galleried windows (though not quite sea views), room service and a good restaurant

downstairs. The excellent breakfast costs €7 extra. Closed Jan. **€92**

Pensión Alver c/García de la Concha 8 ☎ 985 590 005, ⓦ pensionalver.com. Pleasant little *pensión*, up the hill from the port and offering good-value en-suite doubles plus some large family rooms. Closed Oct–Easter. **€50**

EATING AND DRINKING

Restaurante Isabel c/la Ribera 1 ☎ 985 590 211. The closest of Cudillero's restaurants to the sea, just a few metres back from the water. Despite the appealing harbourfront tables, you'll get a bit more peace, and better views, if you head for the upstairs dining room. Good seafood, on *menús* starting from €12 at lunch. Daily:

June–Sept 1–3.30pm & 8–11pm; Oct–May 1–3.30pm.

Rincón Pixueto Pl. Principal ☎ 650 112 032. It's hard to choose from the many restaurants on Cudillero's focal main square, but this friendly little place has lots of outdoor seating, and serves great *raciones*, like baby squid for €8 or prawns for €14. Daily noon–11pm.

Luarca

Beyond Cudillero, the N632 leaps over viaducts spanning deep, pine-wooded gorges. About 50km west, the attractive port of **LUARCA** is accessed from the N632 by a road that dips down steeply to the coast. A mellow place, it's built around an S-shaped cove surrounded by sheer cliffs. Down below, the town is bisected by a small, winding river, and knitted together by numerous narrow bridges.

Luarca is a seaside resort in a modest, faded sort of way, which has defiantly retained its traditional character, including a few *chigres* – old-fashioned Asturian taverns – where you can be initiated into the art of *sidra* drinking. The fishing-harbour area is the heartbeat of the town: cross the bridge from the plaza, and follow the river. You can watch the small fishing boats returning at around midnight and see the catch auctioned off at the *lonja* at around 3pm the following afternoon. The town **beach** is divided in two: the closer strip is narrower but more protected, while the broader one beyond the jetty is subject to seaweed litter.

From the *turismo*, c/de la Carril leads up to the cliffs overlooking the port where you will find a decorative cemetery considered by many the most distinctive in Asturias, a hermitage chapel and a lighthouse.

ARRIVAL AND INFORMATION   LUARCA

By train The FEVE station is 2km east of town.

By bus The bus station, just off c/del Crucero on the river, is connected with Oviedo (4 daily; 1hr 30min) and Ribadeo (4 daily; 1hr 25min).

By car Central Luarca is very short on parking; it's best to park on the edge of town as soon as you arrive.

Turismo c/Caleros 11 (July–Sept Mon–Sat 10.30am–2pm & 4.30–8pm, Sun 11am–2pm & 5–7pm; Oct–June Tues–Fri 10.30am–2pm & 4.30–6.30pm, Sat 10.30am–2pm & 5–7pm, Sun noon–2pm; ☎ 985 640 083, ⓦ turismoluarcavaldes.com). There's also a summer kiosk on Pl. Alfonso X (daily 11am–3pm & 4–8pm).

ACCOMMODATION AND EATING

Camping Los Cantiles Valdes ☎ 985 640 938, ⓦ campingloscantiles.com. A year-round campsite, facing the lighthouse across a rocky cove from the clifftop east of town, with facilities to match its superb setting, including a shop and summer-only café. Car and two adults **€17.20**

Hotel Rico Pl. Alfonso 6 ☎ 985 470 559, ⓦ hotelrico .com. Small, modern, good-value hotel in the very centre of town, where the rather minimal en-suite rooms do at least have large galleried windows. **€70**

Villa La Argentina Villar s/n ☎ 985 640 102,

ⓦ villalaargentina.com. Grand and very comfortable rooms, in a sumptuous *belle époque* mansion, with spacious formal gardens, a fifteen-minute walk east of the centre in the hillside Villar district. **€98**

Villa Blanca Avda. de Galicia 27 ☎ 985 641 035, ⓦ araz. net/villablanca. Smart, formal gourmet restaurant in the heart of town, with a hard-earned reputation for serving the best in traditional Asturian cuisine; the emphasis, naturally, is on seafood. Daily 1–3pm & 8–11pm; closed Mon in winter.

7

Galicia

SANTUARIO DA VIRXE DA BARCA, MUXÍA (P.570)

Galicia

Passionately entangled with the Atlantic Ocean, at the northwest corner of the Iberian Peninsula, Galicia feels far removed from the rest of Spain. Everywhere is green, from the high forested hills to the rolling fields, a patchwork of tiny plots still farmed by hand. Indeed, with its craggy coast and mild, wet climate, Galicia is more like Ireland than Andalucía. Its people take pride in their Celtic heritage, and cherish the survival of their language, Galego. It's hardly off the beaten track, however. Santiago de Compostela ranked during the Middle Ages as the third city of Christendom, and pilgrims have been making their way here along the Camino de Santiago for well over a thousand years.

Santiago itself remains the chief attraction for visitors. Still focused around its unspoiled medieval core, a delightful labyrinth of ancient arcades and alleyways, it's an unmissable gem. Galicia's other major selling point is its endlessly indented **shoreline**, slashed by the powerful sea into the deep, narrow estuaries known here as *rías*, and framed by steep green hillsides. Sadly, however, a lack of planning controls has meant that much of the coast is depressingly overbuilt, albeit with dreary villas and apartments rather than high-rise hotels. With each town tending to merge into the next, those few resorts that remain recognizable as sturdy little medieval fishing villages, such as **Cambados**, **Muros** and **Baiona**, come as welcome highlights. Pretty, secluded sandy beaches do exist, but they take a bit of finding these days, and often require a drive away from the built-up areas.

Broadly speaking, of the distinct coastal stretches, the **Rías Altas** in the north are wilder and emptier, while the picturesque **Rías Baixas**, neighbouring Portugal, are warmer and more developed, and consequently attract many more visitors. In between the two lie the dunes and headlands of the more rugged **Costa da Morte**. Only a couple of the seafront towns have grown to become cities: the modern ports of **A Coruña**, with its elegant glass-encased balconies, and **Vigo**, perched alongside a magnificent bay. Further inland, the settlements are more spread out, and the river valleys of the Miño and the Sil remain beautifully unspoiled, while the attractive provincial capitals of **Pontevedra**, **Ourense** and **Lugo** seem little changed since the Middle Ages.

Again like the Irish, the Galegos are renowned for having **emigrated** all over the world. Between 1836 and 1960, around two million Galegos – roughly half the total population – left the region, thanks largely to the demographic pressure on agricultural land. Half of them ended up in Argentina, where Buenos Aires is often called the largest city in Galicia. An untranslatable Galego word, *morriña*, describes the exiles' particular sense of homesick, nostalgic longing. That Celtic melancholy has its counterpart in the exuberant devotion to the land, its culture and its produce that you'll encounter in Galicia itself, as evinced in its music, – they even play the bagpipes (or *gaita galega*) – literature and festivals. Above all, Galegos view their **food** and **wine**

ILLA DO FARO, ILLAS CÍES

Highlights

❶ Santiago de Compostela The goal of pilgrims for over a thousand years, this ravishing cathedral city is a labyrinth of ancient lanes and dramatic squares. **See p.546**

❷ Sunset at Fisterra Fantastic views over the Atlantic, from the very edge of the world. See p.570

❸ Pimientos de Padrón Once tasted, these randomly piquant green peppers, fried in hot oil and sprinkled with sea salt, are never forgotten. See p.573

❹ Seafood and white wine Galicia is renowned for its delicious *mariscos* and unique Ribeiro and Albariño wines. **See p.575**

❺ Pontevedra Pontevedra's sleepy *zona monumental* metamorphoses into a lively party zone after dark. **See p.579**

❻ The Illas Cíes The pristine sands of these three islets make for an irresistible day-trip. See p.585

❼ The parador at Baiona This fabulous hotel enjoys an unsurpassable setting; look out for special offers on room rates. **See p.586**

❽ Cañón de Río Sil A truly staggering gorge, carved by the Romans into still-functioning vine-growing terraces. **See p.590**

HIGHLIGHTS ARE MARKED ON THE MAP ON P.546

almost as sacraments; share in a feast of the fresh local seafood, washed down with a crisp white Albariño, and you may find the *morriña* gets a hold on you, too.

Santiago de Compostela

The ancient pilgrimage centre of **SANTIAGO DE COMPOSTELA** ranks among the most beautiful cities in all Spain. A superb ensemble of twisting stone lanes, majestic squares and ancient churches, interspersed with countless hidden nooks and crannies, its medieval core remains a remarkably integrated whole, all the better for being very largely pedestrianized. Hewn from time-weathered granite, splashed with gold and silver lichen and sprouting vegetation from the unlikeliest crevices, the buildings and plazas, arcades and flagstones seem to blend imperceptibly into the next. Warrens of honey-coloured streets wind their way past a succession of beautiful monasteries and convents, culminating in the approach to the immense **Praza do Obradoiro**, flanked by the magnificent **Catedral**, the supposed resting place of the remains of St James. To

HIGHLIGHTS
1. Santiago de Compostela
2. Sunset at Fisterra
3. Pimientos de Padrón
4. Seafood and white wine
5. Pontevedra
6. The Illas Cíes
7. The Parador at Baiona
8. Cañyon de Río Sil

GALICIA

GALEGO FOOD

Galegos boast that their **seafood** is the best in the world, and for quality and sheer diversity it's certainly hard to match. Local wonders to look out for include *vieiras* (the scallops whose shells became the symbol of St James), *mejillones* (the rich orange mussels from the *rías*), *cigallas* (Dublin Bay prawns, though often inadequately translated as shrimp), *anguilas* (little eels from the Río Miño), *zamburiñas* (little scallops), *xoubas* (sardines), *navajas* (razor-shell clams), *percebes* (barnacles), *nécoras* (shore crabs) and *centollas* (spider crabs). *Pulpo* (octopus) is so much a part of Galego eating that there are special *pulperías* cooking it in the traditional copper pots, and it is a mainstay of local country fiestas. In the province of Pontevedra alone, Vilanova de Arousa has its own mussel festival (first Sun in Aug), Arcade has one devoted to oysters (first weekend in April), and O Grove goes all the way, with a generalized seafood fiesta. When eaten as tapas or *raciones*, seafood is not overly expensive, though you should always be wary of items like *navajas* and *percebes* that are sold by weight – a small plateful can cost as much as €50. Superb **markets** can be found everywhere; the coastal towns have their rows of seafront stalls with supremely fresh fish, while cities such as Santiago hold grand old arcaded market halls, piled high with farm produce from the surrounding countryside.

Another speciality, imported from the second Galego homeland of Argentina, is the **churrasquería** (grill house). Often unmarked and needing local assistance to find, these serve up immense *churrascos* – a term that in Galicia usually refers to huge portions of beef or pork ribs, cooked on a traditional open grill (*parrilla*). While Galegos don't normally like their food highly spiced, *churrascos* are usually served with a devastating garlic-based *salsa picante*. Other common dishes are *caldo galego*, a thick stew of cabbage and potatoes in a meat-based broth; *caldeirada*, a filling fish soup; *lacon con grelos*, ham boiled with turnip greens; and the ubiquitous *empanada*, a flat light-crusted pie, often filled with tuna and tomato. Should you be around during the summer months, be sure to try *pimientos de Padrón*, sweet green peppers fried in oil, served as a kind of lucky dip with a few memorably spicy ones in each serving.

8

enjoy an overall impression of the whole ensemble, take a walk along the promenade of the **Paseo da Ferradura** (Paseo de la Herradura), in the spacious **Alameda** just southwest of the old quarter.

To this day, locals and visitors alike continue to flock to the old quarter for its round-the-clock sense of life and vibrancy, making it far more than a mere historical curiosity. Modern tourists are as likely to be attracted by its food, drink and history as by religion, but pilgrims still arrive in large numbers, sporting their *vieira* (scallop shell) symbol. Each year at the **Festival of St James** on July 25, a ceremony at his shrine re-dedicates the country and government to the saint. Those years in which the saint's day falls on a Sunday are designated "Holy Years", and the activity becomes even more intense. The next will be in 2021.

For all its fame, however, Santiago remains surprisingly small. Its total population is estimated at 116,000, of whom 33,000 are students at its venerable university. Almost everything of interest to visitors is contained within the densely packed historic core, known as the *zona monumental*, which takes roughly fifteen minutes to cross on foot but several days to explore thoroughly. Most of the commercial activities and infrastructure lie a short distance downhill to the south, in the less appealing modern quarter, which is also where the students tend to live. A high hillside 2km southeast of the city is topped by an unfinished 400-million-euro extravaganza known as the City of Culture (ⓦwww.cidadedacultura.org), which will at some point hold a museum and performance centre. Wander away from the *zona monumental* in most other directions, however, and you can quickly reach open countryside.

Uniquely, Santiago is a city that's at its best in the rain; situated in the wettest fold of the Galego hills, it suffers brief but frequent showers. Water glistens on the facades, gushes from the innumerable gargoyles and flows down the streets.

FIESTAS

JANUARY
1: Livestock fair at Betanzos.
6: Los Reyes Horseback procession of the Three Kings in Baiona.

MARCH
1: San Rosendo Celanova's big festival, at the monastery.
Pre-Lent: *Carnavales* throughout the region.

APRIL/MAY
Semana Santa (Holy Week) Celebrations include a symbolic *descendimiento* (descent from the Cross) at Viveiro on Good Friday and a Resurrection procession at Fisterra. On Palm Sunday, there are Stations of the Cross at Monte San Tecla, near A Guarda.
Sunday after Easter: Fiesta de Angula Elver festival at Tui.
Second Monday after Easter: Fiesta San Telmo At Tui.
Late April–early May (dates vary) Festival at Ribadavia celebrating and promoting Ribeiro wines.
May 1: *Romería* at Pontevedra marks the start of a month-long festival.
Last week: Vino de la Ribeira Sacra Festival at Monforte de Lemos.

JULY
First weekend: Rapa das Bestas The capture and breaking in of wild mountain horses at Viveiro.
11: Fiesta de San Benito At Pontevedra, with river processions, and folk groups, and a smaller *romería* at Cambados.
Second weekend: Medieval de Betanzos Three-day fair at Betanzos, reliving the town's time under Andrade rule.
Second weekend: International Festival of the Celtic World Galicia's most important music festival is held in Ortigueira (⒲festivaldeortigueira.com); pipe bands from all the Celtic lands perform, alongside musicians from around the world, and every event is free.
16: Virgen del Carmen Sea processions at Muros and Corcubión.
24–25: St James (Sant Yago) Two days of celebration in many places, with processions of bigheads and *gigantones* on the 24th and spectacular parades with fireworks and bands through the following evening.
25: Santiago Galicia's major fiesta, at its height in Santiago de Compostela. The evening before, there's a fireworks display and symbolic burning of a cardboard effigy of the mosque at Córdoba. The festival – also designated "Galicia Day" – has become a nationalist event with traditional separatist marches and an extensive programme of political and cultural events for about a week on either side.

AUGUST
First Sunday Albariño wine festival at Cambados; bagpipe festival at Ribadeo; Virgen de la Roca observances outside Baiona; pimiento festival at Padrón; Navaja (razor shell) festival at Fisterra.
16: Fiesta de San Roque Festivals at all churches that bear his name: at Betanzos, there's a Battle of the Flowers on the river and the launching of the Fiesta del Globo.
24: Fiesta (and bullfights) at Noia.
25: Fiesta de San Ginés At Sanxenxo.

SEPTEMBER
6–10: Fiestas del Portal At Ribadavia.
14: Fiesta do Marisco Seafood festival at O Grove.

OCTOBER
13: Fiesta de la Exaltación del Marisco At O Grove – literally, "A Celebration in Praise of Shellfish".

NOVEMBER
11: Fiesta de San Martín At Bueu.
17: Magosto castaña Chestnut festival at Ourense.

The Catedral

Daily: summer 9am–8pm; winter 9am–7pm • ⓦ www.catedraldesantiago.es

All roads in Santiago lead to the **Catedral**. You first appreciate the sheer grandeur of the cathedral upon venturing into the vast expanse of the Praza do Obradoiro. Directly ahead stands a fantastic Baroque pyramid of granite, flanked by immense bell towers and everywhere adorned with statues of St James in his familiar pilgrim guise with staff, broad hat and scallop-shell badge. This is the famous **Obradoiro facade**, built between 1738 and 1750 in the efflorescent style known as Churrigueresque by an obscure Santiago-born architect, Fernando de Casas. No other work of Spanish Baroque can compare with it, nor with what Edwin Mullins sublimely called its "hat-in-the-air exuberance".

Behind the facade, the main body of the cathedral is Romanesque, rebuilt in the eleventh and twelfth centuries after a devastating raid by the Muslim vizier of Córdoba, al-Mansur, in 977. Although, perhaps not surprisingly, he failed to find the body of the saint, he forced the citizens to carry the bells of the tower to the mosque at Córdoba – a coup that was later dramatically reversed (see p.313).

Pórtico de Gloria

The acknowledged highlight of Santiago's cathedral – indeed, one of the great triumphs of medieval art – is the **Pórtico de Gloria**, the original west front, which now stands just inside the main doors, immediately behind the Obradoiro facade. As this book was researched, it was undergoing extensive renovation, which may not be complete by the time you read this.

Completed in 1188 under the supervision of Maestro Mateo, the Pórtico represented both the culmination of all Romanesque sculpture and a precursor of the new Gothic realism, each of its host of figures being strikingly relaxed and quietly humanized. The real mastery is in the assured marshalling of the ensemble. Above the side doors are representations of Purgatory and the Last Judgement, while Christ presides in glory over the main door, flanked by his Apostles, and surrounded by the 24 Elders of the Apocalypse playing celestial music. St James sits on the central column, beneath Christ and just above eye level. To either side are the Prophets of the Old Testament.

So many millions of pilgrims have given thanks at journey's end, by praying with the fingers of one hand pressed into the roots of the Tree of Jesse below the saint, that five deep and shiny holes have been worn into the solid marble. Finally, for wisdom, they would lower their heads to touch the brow of Maestro Mateo, the humble squatting figure on the other side.

The High Altar

The spiritual climax of each pilgrimage to Santiago comes when pilgrims climb the steps that lead up behind the **High Altar** – an extraordinary gilded riot of eighteenth-century Churrigueresque – embrace the Most Sacred Image of Santiago, and kiss his bejewelled cape. The whole process is rounded off by the pilgrims making their confession and attending a High Mass.

The Botafumeiro

An elaborate pulley system in front of the altar serves to move the immense "**Botafumeiro**" (incense burner), which, operated by eight priests (*tiraboleiros*), is swung in a vast thirty-metre ceiling-to-ceiling arc across the transept. Originally designed to fumigate bedraggled pilgrims, the Botafumeiro is now used only at certain services – ask whether there's one during your visit.

The crypt

The saint's bones, kept in a **crypt** beneath the altar, are also visited by a steady procession of pilgrims. Lost for a second time in 1700, after being hidden before an

8

SANTIAGO DE COMPOSTELA

■ ACCOMMODATION
As Artes	2
A Casa do Peregrino	6
Hospedería San Martín Pinario	5
Hospedaje La Tita	11
Hostal Alameda	8
Hostal La Estela	7
Hostal Mapoula	12
Hostal dos Reis Católicos	4
Hostal Suso	10
Hotel Costa Vella	1
Hotel Hortas	3
Hotel A Tafona Do Peregrino	9

● BARS & CAFÉS
O Beiro	9
Bierzo Enxebre	4
Cafeteria	2
Café Casino	11
Café Derby	18
Café Literarios	6
O Filandón	5
Momo	14
Paraiso Perdido	7

Convento de San Francisco

RÚA DAS GALERAS

RÚA DE ENTERRÍOS

COSTA DE SAN FRANCISCO

RÚA DE SAN FRANCISCO

RÚA DO VAL DE DEUS

RÚA DE CARRETAS

TRAVESA DÚAS PORTAS

Hostal dos Reis Católicos

RÚA DAS HORTAS

Igrexa de San Fructuoso

PRAZA DO OBRADOIRO

Pazo de Raxoi

Pazo de Xelmírez

PRAZA DA INMACULADA

Catedral Museum

Catedral

PASEO DA FERRADURA

RÚA DO POMBAL

RÚA DA TRINIDADE

RÚA DE RAXOI

PR. DA QUINTANA

Colexio de S. Jerónimo

CAMPO DE SAN CLEMENTE

Colexio de Fonseca

TRAVESA DE FONSECA

PR. DAS PRATERÍAS

Casa de Conga

RÚA DA CONGA

AV. DE RODRIGO DE PADRON

PR. DE FONSECA

RÚA DA REINA

Casa del Cabildo

RÚA DE XELMÍREZ

Casa del Deán

Colexio de San Clemente

RÚA DO FRANCO

Casa das Pomas

Alameda

AVENIDA DE FIGUEROA

ENTRECERCAS

RÚA DO VILAR

Palacio de Mondragón

Colexio dos Irlandeses

RÚA NOVA

Igrexa de Santa María Salomé

RÚA DA CALDEIRERÍA

PRAZA DA UNIVERSIDADE

Pontevedra

AV. XOÁN CARLOS

Porta de Faxeiras

BAUTIZADOS

ENTREMURAS

PRAZA DO TOURAL

Pazo de Bendaña

TRAS DE SALOMÉ

RÚA DAS ORFAS

Igrexa da Universidade

PRAZA MAZARELOS

CARDEAL PAYA

RÚA DA SENRA

C / ENTREMURALLAS

Porta da Mámoa

TRANS. DE LOS GRAMÁTICOS

Arco de Mazarelos

Casa de Valderrama

FONTE DE SANTO ANTONIO

RÚA DO PEXIGO DE ABAIXO

PRAZA DE GALICIA

CONCEPCIÓN ARENAL

RÚA DO HORREO

RÚA DO PATIO DE MADRES

Convento das Madres Mercedarias

Patio de Madres

RÚA DE GARCÍA BLANCO

▼ Train Station

0 — 100 metres

8

TAPAS BARS & RESTAURANTS	
Don Gaiferos	16
Enxebre	3
O Gato Negro	12
Maria Castaña	13
San Jaime	8
Sant Yago	10
Los Sobriños del Padre la Casa del Buen Pulpo	1
A Taberna do Bispo	15
A Tulla	17

Zona Monumental

THE HISTORY OF THE PILGRIMAGE TO SANTIAGO

The great medieval **pilgrimage to Santiago** was arguably Europe's first exercise in mass tourism. Home to the supposed shrine of St James the Apostle (Santiago to the Spanish, Saint Jacques to the French), the city became the third holiest site in Christendom, after Jerusalem and Rome. Following in the footsteps of Godescale of Puy, who arrived in 951, an estimated half-million pilgrims turned up each year during the eleventh and twelfth centuries.

Although the shrine was visited by the great – Fernando and Isabel, Carlos V, Francis of Assisi – you didn't have to be rich to come. The various roads through France and northern Spain that led here, collectively known as **El Camino de Santiago** (The Way of St James, or the Pilgrim Route), were lined with monasteries and charitable hospices. Villages sprang up along the route, and an order of knights was founded for the pilgrims' protection. There was even a guidebook – the world's first – written by a French monk called Aymery Picaud, which recorded, along with water sources and places to stay, such facts as the bizarre sexual habits of the Navarrese Basques (said to expose themselves when excited, and protect their mules from their neighbours with chastity belts). It was an extraordinary phenomenon in an age when most people never ventured beyond their own town or village.

Why did they come? Some, like Chaucer's Wife of Bath, who had "been in Galicia at Seynt Jame", had their own private reasons: social fashion, adventure, the opportunities for marriage or even for crime. But for most pilgrims, it was a question of faith. Thanks to the miraculous power of **St James**, they knew the journey guaranteed a remission of half their time in Purgatory. Few doubted that the tomb beneath Santiago's high cathedral altar held the mortal remains of James, son of Zebedee and Salome and first cousin of Jesus Christ. It seems scarcely credible that the whole business was an immense **ecclesiastical fraud**.

Yet the legend, at each point of its development, has no apparent basis in fact. It begins with the claim, unsubstantiated by the Bible, that St James visited Spain after the Crucifixion, to spread the gospel. He is said, for example, to have had a vision of the Virgin in Zaragoza. He then returned to Jerusalem, where he was undoubtedly beheaded by Herod Agrippa. But the legend relates that two of James's followers removed his corpse to Jaffa, where a boat appeared, without sails or crew, and whisked them in just seven days to Padrón, 20km downstream from Santiago.

The body was then buried, lost and forgotten for 750 years, before being rediscovered at Compostela in 813, at a time of great significance for the Spanish Church. Over the preceding century, the Moors had swept across the Iberian Peninsula, gaining control over all but the northern mountain kingdom of Asturias. They drew great strength from the inspiration of their champion, the Prophet Muhammad, whose death (in 632) still lay within popular memory, and a bone from whose arm was preserved in La Mesquita in Córdoba. Thus the discovery of the bones of St James, under a buried altar on a site traditionally linked with his name, was singularly opportune. It occurred after a hermit was attracted to a hillside by visions of stars; the hill was known thereafter as Compostela, meaning "field of stars". Alfonso II, king of Asturias, came to pay his respects and built a chapel, and the saint was adopted as the champion of Christian Spain against the infidel.

Within decades, the saint had appeared on the battlefield. Ramiro I, Alfonso's successor, swore that James had fought alongside him at the Battle of Clavijo (844), and that the saint had personally slaughtered 60,000 Moors. Over the next six centuries Santiago Matamoros (Moor-killer) manifested himself at some forty battles, assisting, for example, in the massacre of the Inca armies in Peru. While that may seem an odd role for the fisherman-evangelist, it presented no problems to the Christian propagandists who portrayed him most frequently as a knight on horseback in the act of dispatching whole clutches of swarthy, bearded Arabs with a single thrust of his long sword. (With consummate irony, when Franco brought his crack Moroccan troops to Compostela to dedicate themselves to the overthrow of the Spanish Republic, all such statues were discreetly hidden under sheets.)

English invasion, they were rediscovered during building work in 1879. In fact, the workers found three skeletons, which were naturally held to be those of St James and his two followers. The only problem was identifying which one was the Apostle. This was fortuitously resolved as a church in Tuscany possessed a piece of Santiago's skull that exactly fitted a gap in one of those here.

The cathedral museum

June–Sept Mon–Sat 10am–2pm & 4–8pm, Sun 10am–2pm; Oct–May Mon–Sat 10am–1.30pm & 4–6.30pm, Sun 10am–1.30pm • €5

Santiago's cathedral **museum** comprises several distinct sections, which you can visit in any order; each sells the combined admission ticket. The museum proper has its own entrance to the right of the main cathedral facade. Its ground floor holds archeological displays, while upstairs you'll find assorted relics of the cathedral's history, including the Botafumeiro itself when it's not in use. From there you can walk into the late Gothic cloisters, the courtyard of which offers a wonderful prospect of the riotous mixture of the exterior. Back inside, the tapestry rooms on the topmost floor include pieces based on Goya paintings, and open onto a long open-air gallery with similarly good views over the Praza do Obradoiro.

Doors from both the cloisters and the cathedral itself lead into the **Treasury**, where the highlight is a huge carved altarpiece depicting the legend of St James. The final component of the museum is Mateo's beautiful **Crypt of the Portico**, accessed beneath the cathedral's main entry staircase (and distinct from the crypt that holds James' relics). That, however, is currently undergoing a long-term restoration, so only a virtual version is on display.

Las Cubiertas and the Pazo de Xelmírez

Tues–Sun hourly departures 10am–2pm & 4–8pm • €10 • ☏ 981 552 985 • ⓦ archicompostela.org

A unique attraction of Santiago's cathedral is that it's possible to take a guided tour of its **roof**, known as **Las Cubiertas**. It's an experience not to be missed; the climb up leads through the upper floors of the cathedral interior (when no service is taking place), while the roof itself, which consists of shallow granite steps, offers superb views over the rest of the city, as well, of course, as the cathedral's own towers and embellishments. Every way you turn, it's crawling with pagodas, pawns, domes, obelisks, battlements, scallop shells and cornucopias.

The tours start by visiting the **Pazo de Xelmírez** (Palacio Arzobispal Gelmírez), which adjoins the cathedral to the north and is entered to the left of the main stairs. Archbishop Xelmírez was a seminal figure in Santiago's development. He rebuilt the cathedral in the twelfth century, raised the see to an archbishopric and "discovered" a ninth-century deed that gave annual dues to St James' shrine of one bushel of corn from each acre of Spain reconquered from the Moors – a decree that was repealed only in 1834. His appropriately opulent palace features a vaulted twelfth-century kitchen and a thirteenth-century synodal hall, along with plenty of ancient statues.

Note that the standard tour features a quick-fire Spanish commentary that may well leave you floundering; to arrange an English-language tour, at no extra charge, call five days in advance in summer, or two days in low season.

Praza do Obradoiro

You could easily spend several hours exploring the squares around the cathedral. The **Praza do Obradoiro**, in front of the main facade, is Santiago's most formal and impressive public space. Its northern side is dominated by the elegant Renaissance **Hostal dos Reis Católicos** (Hostal de los Reyes Católicos). As late as the thirteenth century the cathedral was used to accommodate pilgrims, but slowly its place was taken by convents around the city. Fernando and Isabel, in gratitude for their conquest of Granada, added to these facilities by building this superb hostel for the poor and sick. Now a parador, it's very much *the* place to stay if you can afford it. Even if you're not staying here, stroll in to take a look at its four lovely courtyards or the chapel with magnificent Gothic stone carvings, or simply to have a drink or meal.

Praza da Quintana

Equally large as the Praza do Obradoiro, but somehow more intimate, the **Praza da Quintana** has a flight of broad steps joining the back of the cathedral to the high walls of the **Convento de San Paio**, which serves around the clock as an impromptu bench for students and backpackers. The "Porta Santa" doorway here is only opened during Holy Years (see p.547).

Praza das Praterías

The **Praza das Praterías**, the Silversmiths' Square, centres on an ornate fountain of four horses with webbed feet, and features the seventy-metre-high Berenguela, or **clock tower**. On its west side, the extraordinarily narrow **Casa del Cabildo** was built in 1758 to fill the remaining gap and ornamentally complete the square – you'd never know to look at it, but it's a mere facade, with nothing behind it.

San Martiño Pinario

Praza da Inmaculada • July–Sept daily 11am–7pm; Oct–June daily 11am–1.30pm & 4–6.30pm• €2.50 • Ⓦ museosanmartinpinario.com

The **Praza da Inmaculada**, on the cathedral's northern side, is dominated by the grand Baroque frontage of the Benedictine monastery of **San Martiño Pinario**. At 20,000 square metres, this ranks among the largest religious buildings in Spain. Its left flank, as you face it, is now run as a hotel, while the monastery church to the right holds a quite extraordinary **museum**. The church itself is filled with magnificent Baroque altarpieces, while the various chapels and rooms to the side display bejewelled treasures and sculptures. Upstairs, things take a surprising twist: the monks' natural history collection includes a grotesque stuffed sloth, sharing space with an echidna and a pangolin, and there's also an apothecary they put together to treat pilgrims.

Museo das Peregrinacións

Praza de San Martiño • Tues–Fri 10am–8pm, Sat 10.30am–1.30pm & 5–8pm, Sun 10.30am–1.30pm • Free • Ⓦ mdperegrinacions.com

Santiago's **Museo das Peregrinacións** relates the story of pilgrimage not only here but also to religious shrines the world over. For the moment, it's housed in the sixteenth-century Pazo de Don Pedro, a short way east of San Martiño Pinario, though it's due to move to new premises in the Praza das Praterías. Excellent models and displays cover the *camino*, the city and cathedral, and there's a comprehensive (and free) guide in English. Look out for the room that explores how depictions of St James himself have changed over the centuries, to reflect his changing image.

Museo do Pobo Galego

C/San Domingos de Bonaval • Tues–Sat 10am–2pm & 4–8pm, Sun 11am–2pm • Free • Ⓦ museodopobo.es

Immediately northeast of the old quarter, the convent and church of **Santo Domingo** contains a unique seventeenth-century triple stairway, each spiral of which leads to different storeys of a single tower. Set off up different flights, and you may lose each other for hours. The convent houses the fascinating **Museo do Pobo Galego**, which features a diverse overview of Galego crafts and traditions, with a moving account of Galicia's history of emigration. Many aspects of the way of life displayed haven't yet entirely disappeared, though you're today unlikely to see *corozas*, straw suits worn into the last century by mountain shepherds. The convent chapel serves as the **Panteón de Galegos Ilustres**, home to the mortal remains of such local heroes as the poet Rosalía

CLOCKWISE FROM TOP SANTIAGO CATEDRAL; PRAZA DA QUINTANA; PILGRIM SOUVENIRS

PRACTICALITIES OF THE CAMINO DE SANTIAGO

Most pilgrims stay in hostels, called **albergues** or **refugios**, conveniently spaced anywhere from 10 to 20km apart. These provide simple accommodation in dormitories, are usually equipped with hot showers, sometimes have kitchen facilities and charge either a nominal fee of a few euros or ask for a donation. *Albergues* can get crowded in the summer months, and pilgrims sometimes have to sleep on mattresses on the floor. For those who crave a little more comfort, more upmarket choices are often available along the route. As a pilgrim, you'll also receive special treatment at restaurants – most will have a pilgrim *menú* for about €8 – and meals are served earlier than the Spanish norm, at about 8pm.

To prove your pilgrim status at the *albergues*, you'll need a **credencial** (pilgrim passport); it's best to get one in advance from your local pilgrim association (see below), although you can also pick one up at the *albergue* in Roncesvalles. You can then collect *sellos* (stamps, as proof of your pilgrimage) from *albergues*, churches and even some enterprising cafés, and finally show your stamped *credencial* in Santiago in order to get a *compostela* (certificate of pilgrimage). According to the official rules, you need only walk the final 100km of the route, or cycle the last 200km, to be entitled to a *compostela*. If your motives are other than strictly religious, apply for a *certificado* rather than a *compostela*.

It's difficult to lose your way. The *camino* sticks to good tracks and minor roads, is clearly marked with yellow arrows, and mostly passes through populated areas where locals can steer you in the direction of Santiago. Spring and autumn are the **best seasons**, as the route is quieter than in the busy summer months; most *albergues* are open, and you'll miss the weather extremes of the *meseta* and the mountains. If you're fit and healthy, you can walk from Roncesvalles to Santiago de Compostela in about a month, covering around 25km a day. Nevertheless, allow extra time for rest days, unforeseen injuries or just a whimsical decision to linger in one of the lovely towns en route.

The most useful website for information on the *camino* is ⓦ csj.org.uk. Run by the UK-based **Confraternity of St James**, it publishes route guides, maintains a busy online forum, and has links to similar organizations and **pilgrim associations** all over the world.

de Castro and the essayist and caricaturist Castelao. Gardens and orchards stretch up the hillside behind, offering a wonderful spot for a break from sightseeing.

Centro Galego de Arte Contemporánea

C/San Domingos de Bonaval • Tues–Sun 11am–8pm • Free

Opposite the convent, the **Centro Galego de Arte Contemporánea**, a modern addition to Santiago's heritage by the Portuguese architect Álvaro Siza, is a gloriously light and large exhibition space. It generally stages temporary shows of contemporary art and sculpture.

ARRIVAL AND DEPARTURE
SANTIAGO DE COMPOSTELA

By plane Santiago's airport is 13km east of the city in Lavacolla, on the road to Lugo, and is served by Ryanair flights from London Stansted. Frequent local buses (every half-hour; €3) connect the airport with the **bus station** and Rúa Doctour Teixeiro – the closest stop to the old town, just south of Praza de Galicia. Taxis into town charge a flat rate of €20.

By train The train station is a 10 min walk south of the old town at Rúa de Horreo 75.

Destinations A Coruña (16 daily; 35min); Burgos (daily; 8hr); Donostía/San Sebastian (daily; 10hr 30min); León (daily; 5hr 30min); Madrid (2 daily; 7–10hr); Medina del Campo (2 daily; 5hr 20min); Ourense (4 daily; 1hr 30min–2hr); Palencia (1 daily; 7hr); Pontevedra (15 daily; 1hr); Vigo (15 daily; 1hr 30min).

By bus Santiago's bus station is in an inconvenient and very urbanized location, ten minutes' walk northeast of the old town. For schedules see ⓦwww.monbus.es.

Destinations A Coruña (hourly; 1hr 15min); Barcelona (daily; 17hr); Betanzos (7 daily; 1hr 30min); Camariñas (4 daily; 3hr); Cambados (5 daily; 2hr); Donostía/San Sebastian (2 daily; 12hr); Fisterra (4 daily; 3hr); León (daily; 6hr); Lugo (9 daily; 2hr); Madrid (3–6 daily; 9hr 30min); Muros (hourly; 1hr 30min); Muxía (2 daily; 2hr); Noia (hourly; 50min); Ourense (7 daily; 2hr); Oviedo (6 daily; 5hr 30min); Padrón (every 30min; 45min); Pontevedra (hourly; 1hr); Vigo (hourly; 1hr 30min–2hr).

By car Drivers have little choice but to use one of the large car parks (ⓦtussa.org) on the periphery, as almost all the streets in the old quarter are pedestrianized, and very few hotels offer parking facilities. The closest to the cathedral is the huge Xóan XXIII car park, a short distance north, which is also where all coach tours pull in.

INFORMATION

Turismo Rúa do Vilar 63 (June–Sept daily 9am–9pm; Oct–May Mon–Fri 9am–7pm, Sat & Sun 9am–2pm & 4–7pm; ☎981 555 129, ⓦsantiagoturismo.com) in the old town, also sells stamps. A separate office nearby at Rúa do Vilar 43 (Mon–Fri 10am–8pm, Sat 11am–2pm & 5–7pm, Sun 11am–2pm; ☎981 584 081, ⓦturgalicia.es) provides information on Galicia as a whole.

THE CAMINO DE SANTIAGO

The **Camino de Santiago**, or Pilgrim Route, is the longest-established "tourist" route in Europe, and its final section through Galicia provides echoes of the medieval pilgrimage to the thousands who walk it every year, armed with the traditional staff and the scallop-shell emblem of St James. Today's pilgrims seldom walk from their homes to Santiago de Compostela and back; most follow one of the half a dozen or so standard pilgrimage routes through Spain and France. The most popular, the 750km **Camino Francés**, heads westward from Roncesvalles (or Orreaga-Roncesvalles in Basque) in the Pyrenees across northern Spain. You don't have to be Christian, or even religious, to follow the route. For roughly half of all pilgrims, the journey to Santiago is prompted by their religious faith, while others want to experience their own spiritual quest, or simply to immerse themselves in Spanish history and culture. Whatever the motivation, the *camino*'s popularity has exploded in recent decades; while only a handful of people walked to Santiago in the 1960s, the route now attracts well over 100,000 pilgrims a year, half of whom are Spanish.

THE CAMINO DE SANTIAGO IN GALICIA

The Camino de Santiago in Galicia passes few tourist sights, meandering instead through countless tiny villages. Pilgrims work a little harder on this last leg as the route clambers up and down steep hills and valleys, but the scenery is gorgeous compensation: green with oak forests and patchworked fields. Galicia is green for a reason, however; the region gets a lot of rain, and you can get caught in a storm even in summer.

The Galician government has made a huge effort to promote the *camino*, maintaining an extensive network of pilgrim hostels along the eight separate routes that converge on Santiago – all are listed on the website ⓦxacobeo.es. The **Camino Francés** enters Galicia at the Pedrafita do Cebreiro pass, a desolate spot where hundreds of English soldiers froze or starved to death during Sir John Moore's retreat towards A Coruña in 1809. It's a fierce 30km climb from Villafranca del Bierzo in León up cobbled paths often slick with mud and dung to the mountain village of **O Cebreiro**. There can be snow here in winter, and fog often obscures the spectacular views, but it's a magical place, with round, thatched-roof *pallozas* (stone huts) and intricate *horréos* (granaries).

The *camino* is naturally at its most crowded in Galicia. The volume of pilgrims reaches a crescendo at **Sarría**, 115km from Santiago, which is the last major town where you can start walking and still earn a *compostela*; 12km southeast of here, the moss-covered **Monasterio de Samos** (daily 10.30am–1pm & 4.30–7pm; free), famous for its library in the Middle Ages, is one of the few surviving ancient buildings along the route.

The closer you get to Santiago, the more pilgrim rituals you'll encounter. Medieval pilgrims would wash themselves in the river at **Lavacolla**, 12km east of the city and now the site of its airport, to prepare for their arrival. During this ritual cleansing – often the first bath since leaving home – they'd pay extra attention to their private parts; *lavacolla* is said to mean scrotum-washing. From there, they'd race 5km to **Monte de Gozo** (Mount of Joy), where the first to cry *"mon joie"* on spotting Santiago's cathedral spires was declared the king of the group.

Although most people end their pilgrimage at **Santiago de Compostela**, some walk another 75km to Fisterra (Finisterra), a Celtic route towards the setting sun that predates the medieval pilgrimage by at least a millennium. The quiet, well-marked rural route ends at **Cabo Fisterra**, the westernmost point of mainland Europe. Below the lighthouse, at a small bronze sculpture of a pair of walking boots, pilgrims traditionally burn their clothes after a dip in the sea to celebrate the end of the journey.

ACCOMMODATION

Santiago offers an enormous array of **accommodation** to suit all budgets, ranging from its gorgeous parador down to the many inexpensive *hostales* aimed at pilgrims and young travellers. Your priority should definitely be to stay in the old quarter, which holds the biggest concentration of options. Even during the July festival, this is rarely a problem, as half the bars in the city rent out rooms. **Compostur**, the city's official tourist agency, offers discount bookings and last-minute availability via a website and toll-free phone line (☎902 190 160, ⓦsantiagoreservas.com).

★ **As Artes** Travesa Dúas Portas 2 ☎981 572 590, ⓦasartes.com. Very attractive little hotel near the cathedral. Each of its seven en-suite rooms is named after a specific artist, and decorated in a distinctive but traditional and very cosy style. The larger ones are significantly nicer. **€98**

A Casa do Peregrino Rúa Azabachería 2 ☎981 573 931, ⓦacasadoperegrino.com. You wouldn't expect it from the ice-cream shop downstairs, but this ancient house holds eleven attractive rooms, with exposed stonework including moulded basins. Modern features include soundproofing, walk-in showers and wi-fi. **€85**

Hospedaje La Tita Rúa Nova 46 ☎981 583 981. Five pleasant, bare-bones and very inexpensive rooms, sharing a bathroom and WC, above a bar in the old quarter. Single rooms half-price. **€40**

Hospedería San Martin Pinario Praza da Inmaculada ☎981 560 282, ⓦsanmartinpinario.eu. Part of this colossal and very central monastery was converted into a stylish contemporary hotel in 2010. The rooms are still recognizably cells, with minimal furnishings and no TVs, but the beds are extremely comfortable, with luxurious linens. A hugely atmospheric and remarkably quiet location, it also offers all meals in its cavernous ancient dining rooms, open to non guests as well. Lower midweek rates; ask about pilgrim discounts. **€90**

Hostal Alameda Rúa do San Clemente 32 ☎981 588 100. Presentable if somewhat dated rooms – all except one en suite – with polished floors and large windows, and a good restaurant. Pleasantly located by the Alameda. Very reasonable prices, especially for single travellers. **€55**

Hostal La Estela Rúa Raxoi 1 ☎981 582 796, ⓔhostallaestela@yahoo.es. This stunningly located *hostal*, on a pretty street that drops from one corner of the Praza do Obradoiro, offers excellent value for both en-suite and shared-bath rooms. Ask for one at the front, for great views of the cathedral. **€40.**

Hostal Mapoula Rúa do Entremurallas 10 ☎981 580 124, ⓦmapoula.com. Clean, friendly, third-storey *hostal*, with spacious, en-suite rooms; some sleep three or four guests. It's close to the heart of the action, near good cafés and bars, so don't be put off by the slightly dingy alleyway. **€50**

★ **Hostal dos Reis Católicos** Praza do Obradoiro 1 ☎981 582 200, ⓦparador.es. Santiago's magnificent parador, facing the cathedral, is one of the world's most famous – and possibly oldest – hotels. Its 136 irresistibly luxurious rooms are arranged around four separate tranquil courtyards, and there are also two restaurants and a plush bar. It's worth every penny, especially if you get a multi-day discount. **€180**

Hostal Suso Rúa do Vilar 65 ☎981 586 611. A neat, comfortable *hostal*, above a good bar-restaurant and alongside the *turismo* in a lively arcaded street. Wi-fi in the common area and some rooms, too. **€49**

★ **Hotel Costa Vella** Rúa da Porta da Peña 17 ☎981 569 530, ⓦcostavella.com. Welcoming, very comfortable and beautifully furnished hotel on the northern edge of the old quarter, with views over the rooftops. Rates include breakfast, served in the small flower-filled garden in summer, which stays open as a bar all day. Paying a little extra gets you a larger room with a delightful balcony. **€81**

Hotel Hortas Rúa Hortas 30 ☎881 359 018, ⓦhotelhortas.com. Tasteful conversion of a typical townhouse, a short walk from the cathedral down a quiet street, into a seven-room hotel. Sparkling modern bathrooms, plus a café downstairs. **€85**

Hotel A Tafona do Peregrino Rúa Virxe da Cerca 7 ☎981 568 923, ⓦatafonadoperegrino.com. Old house turned hip modern hotel, immediately east of the old quarter – across the road from the marketplace – featuring lots of exposed stonework and gleaming tiles. Smart bedrooms, two lounges, and a bar-café downstairs. **€130**

CAMPING

As Cancelas Rúa de 25 de Julio 35 ☎981 580 266, ⓦcampingascancelas.com. Located well outside the old town, a half-hour walk uphill northeast from the cathedral, this year-round campsite has tent pitches and some four-person rental bungalows (€80). Served by buses #8 and #9, as well as the airport bus, it's reached via the road to A Coruña, branching off at the Avda. del Camino Francés. Tent pitches **€6.50**

As Sirenas ☎981 898 688, ⓦcomarcasantiago.com/sirenas.htm. A reasonable second choice for drivers, this small and inexpensive campsite, 11km northwest on the Santa Comba road, has children's and adults' pools, and its own *pensión*. Closed mid-Sept to June. Tent pitches **€3.50**

8

EATING, DRINKING AND NIGHTLIFE

Galego food is plentiful and excellent in Santiago, with a plethora of great **places to eat**. The two main concentrations lie along the parallel rúas Franco and Raiña, which can get very busy in summer, and northeast of the cathedral on the quieter rúas da Troia and Porta da Peña, where there's much more outdoor seating. Traditional **tapas bars**, with small dishes spread out on the counter, are outnumbered by informal *mesones*, serving substantial and consistently superb seafood *raciones* for around €8–10. There are also plenty of more formal **restaurants**. With all those students to keep the city buzzing, countless bars remain alive with drinkers long into the night. Locals were recently up in arms at proposals that all bars should close at 5.30am. Santiago is also the best place in Galicia to hear Celtic **music**, played either by solo performers on *gaitas* (bagpipes), or by student ensembles known as *tunas*, who stroll the streets in historic garb at night, especially in summer, playing assorted guitars, mandolins and fiddles.

FOOD SHOPPING IN SANTIAGO

If you're shopping for your own food, don't miss the large covered **Mercado de Abastos**, held daily until 3pm in and around the venerable stone halls of the Praza de Abastos, on the southeast edge of the old city. Thursday is the main market day, but it's also bustling on Saturdays. In addition, tiny delicatessens throughout town sell the traditional breast-shaped **cheese**, *queso de tetilla*, as well as flat *tarta de Santiago* almond cakes, adorned with crosses in honour of the Apostle; the *tartas* at *El Coral* at Dr Teixeiro 32 are particularly renowned.

TAPAS BARS AND RESTAURANTS

Don Gaiferos Rúa Nova 23 ☎981 583 984. Traditional restaurant, formal without being stuffy, in attractive cellar-like surroundings. The speciality is superb seafood cuisine, with simple but delicious fish dishes from €21. Tues–Sat 1.15–3.45pm & 8.15–11.30pm, Sun 1.15–3.45pm.

Enxebre Hostal dos Reis Católicos, Praza do Obradoiro 1 ☎981 582 200. The less formal of the parador's two restaurants, housed in the attractive former cellars and with its own entrance just off the square, serves tasty variations on traditional Galego cuisine, with tapas-sized portions as well as daily specials for around €15. Daily 1–4pm & 8–11.30pm.

O Gato Negro Rúa da Raiña s/n ☎981 583 105. Either join the crowds jostling at the plain white bar, or push past to find a table in the back room, then settle down to enjoy classic Galego specialities such as empanada or peppers for around €3, or shellfish of all kinds. Mon–Sat noon–3pm & 8pm–midnight.

★ **Maria Castaña** Rúa da Raiña 19 ☎981 560 137. This delightful, cosy bar/restaurant, with rough-hewn tables and exposed stone, serves delicious food at reasonable rather than rock-bottom prices, from simple seafood tapas or soft cheese wrapped in anchovies to paella-like fish *cazolos* from €26, plus bottles of fine Galego wine at very affordable prices. Daily 1–4pm & 7–11pm.

San Jaime Rúa da Raiña 4 ☎981 572 257. All the usual *raciones* are available inside this little bar, and there's a set lunch *menú* for €12.50, but the best reason to come is to nab one of the few tables on the pretty Praza de Fonseca, and enjoy the finest *chocolate con churros* in town. Daily 10am–11pm.

★ **Sant Yago** Rúa da Raiña 12 ☎981 582 444, ��sant -yago.com. Smoked hams and cheese are the speciality at this friendly, charming little tapas bar, but the *tortillas* and seafood are every bit as good, and very well priced, with almost nothing costing over €10, and a €13 *menú del día*. Aim to eat in the bar rather than the upstairs dining room. Daily noon–11pm.

★ **Los Sobriños del Padre la Casa del Buen Pulpo** Fonte de San Miguel 7. The long-winded name belies the simplicity, and quality, of the *pulpo* (octopus), *tortilla* and other *raciones* at this very plain little local restaurant, which has pavement tables and serves white china jugs full of wine for just €4. If you only eat *pulpo* once in your life, make it here. Mon–Sat noon–3pm & 7–11pm.

A Taberna do Bispo Rúa do Franco 37 ☎981 586 045, ⓦatabernadobispo.com. This smart, busy tapas bar on the main tourist thoroughfare stands out for its brightly-lit counter display of appetizing goodies, with lots of cheese and meat snacks as well as its €3–5 seafood offerings. Daily noon–midnight.

A Tulla Callejon de Entre Rúas 1 ☎981 580 889, ⓦrestaurante-atulla.com. Small, very friendly bar-restaurant, shoehorned into a tiny square up an even tinier alley between rúas Nova and Vilar. Wonderful home cooking, from the bread and wide array of vegetables to the meat and seafood main dishes, almost all priced at €10 or less. Daily except Wed 1–4pm & 8.30pm–midnight.

BARS AND CAFÉS

O Beiro Rúa da Raiña 3 ☎981 581 370, ⓦobeiro.com. The back room in this *vinoteca*, very close to the cathedral, is a friendly and relaxing place to sample the finest local wines by the glass, or buy bottles to take home. There's also an upstairs dining room. Daily 11am–3.30pm & 6pm–1am.

Bierzo Enxebre Rúa do Troia 10 ☎981 581 909, ⓦbierzoenxebre.es. Sprawling out across an old stone alleyway, this ranks among the city's nicest places to drink outside; there's also a decent, good-value dining room indoors. Daily 1–3pm & 6pm–midnight.

Cafetería Hostal dos Reis Católicos, Praza do Obradoiro 1. On a summer evening, the outdoor terrace at the parador, with views back towards the cathedral and out to the green hills, is the ideal spot to linger over a sunset cocktail. Daily 1pm– midnight.

Café Casino Rúa do Vilar 35 ☎981 577 503. With its deep sofas and wood panelling, plus outdoor seating on the old stone lane, this venerable café/tearoom has a real old-world charm. Mon–Wed 8.30am–midnight, Thurs 8.30am–1am, Fri & Sat 11am–2am, Sun 9am–midnight.

Café Derby Rúa das Orfas 29 ☎981 586 417. This classic old café-bar between the old quarter and the Praza da Galicia, kitted out with dark-wood panelling, green leather bar stools and bentwood chairs, has been a favourite local rendezvous for over eighty years. Daily 8am–midnight.

Café Literarios Praza da Quintana ☎ 981 565 630. The terrace of this popular café, at the top of the broad stairs in the square behind the cathedral, makes a perfect venue for peaceful people-watching. Daily 10am–1am.

O Filandón Rúa da Azabachería 6 ☎ 981 572 738. Thread your way through the simple cheese and wine shop to reach the narrow, bustling bar in the cave-like space at the back, where students and wine-lovers enjoy cheap, high-quality local *vinos* and free morsels. Mon–Sat 8pm–1am.

Momo Virxe da Cerca 23 ☎ 981 565 580, ⓦ pubmomo .com. A popular hangout with wide-ranging appeal, full of students during term-time. Fantastic and varied decor includes Parisian-style mini café-bars, an outdoor terrace and a jungle dancefloor. Daily 4pm–4am.

Paraíso Perdido Rúa Antealtares 3 ☎ 981 560 930. Cavernous, mysterious bar that tunnels deeply away from a tiny square not far east of Praza da Quintana, with endless eclectically decorated subterranean nooks and crannies. The €4.50 *mojitos* are recommended. Daily 7pm–1am.

The Rías Altas

Galicia's north coast has been ravaged by the ocean into a series of dramatic bays and estuaries known as the **Rías Altas** (High Estuaries). As you approach from Asturias, the coastline becomes noticeably more desolate, the road twisting around rocky inlets where wind-lashed villages cling to the shore, backed by eucalyptus forests and wild-looking hills. Driving is slow, though the final westward stretch of the **FEVE railway**, from Luarca to Ferrol, is perhaps the most picturesque of the entire route.

Ribadeo

RIBADEO, the easternmost Galego town and *ría*, has little to offer beyond a certain crumbling charm. Its finest architecture is concentrated around the Praza de España, where the **Palacio del Marquès de Sargadelos**, with its unusual decorative tower, is the town's main monument.

Thanks to its succession of fine beaches, the coast immediately west of Ribadeo has been subject to almost continuous low-level strip development. It's well worth stopping at the **Praia As Catedrais**, however, 6km along, where low tide reveals a procession of extraordinary natural arches, towering from a stark sandscape. The waves are usually too strong for swimming, but it's an unforgettable spot for coastal hiking, along a network of boardwalks.

ARRIVAL AND INFORMATION   RIBADEO

By train Ribadeo is served by FEVE trains along the coast, east towards Cudillero (2 daily; 2hr) and west towards Viveiro (4 daily; 1 hr 5min).

Turismo Rúa Gamalo Fierros 7 (July & Aug Mon–Sat

10.30am–2pm & 4–8pm, Sun 10.30am–2pm; Sept–June Mon–Fri 10.30am–2pm & 4–7pm, Sat 10.30am–2pm & 4–8pm, Sun 10.30am–2pm; ☎ 982 128 689, ⓦ ribadeo .org), near the parador.

ACCOMMODATION, EATING AND DRINKING

Mediante Praza de España 16 ☎ 982 130 453, ⓦ hotelmediante.com. The best-value alternative to the parador, on a pedestrian street in the centre of town. Several of its twenty rooms have balconies overlooking the main square. **€64**

Parador de Ribadeo Rúa Amador Fernández 7 ☎ 982 128 825, ⓦ parador.es. Ribadeo's modern parador, a short way south of the centre, faces the green fields of

Asturias across the Eo estuary. Its rooms spill down the riverbank in successive sunny tiers, each with its own glassed-in gallery. **€112**

San Miguel Porto do Porcillán ☎ 982 129 717, ⓦ restaurantesanmiguel.org. Superb if somewhat expensive seafood restaurant, immediately beneath the main road bridge across from Asturias, a short walk from Ribadeo's tiny and somewhat faded harbour. Daily 1–3pm & 7–11pm.

Viveiro

VIVEIRO, 60km west of the Asturian border, is now much more of a tourist centre than the port it used to be, with holiday homes spreading up the hillsides of the *ría* and along its many **beaches**. The old town, however, remains protected by the vestiges of its Renaissance walls. Largely closed to traffic, its narrow streets are lined with glass-fronted houses in delicate wooden frames.

The large **Praia de Covas** is a good ten minutes' walk from town across a causeway, while the pick of several more peaceful beaches around the bay is the **Praia de Faro**, further up towards the open sea.

ARRIVAL AND INFORMATION
VIVEIRO

By train and bus Both the bus station and the FEVE station (3–4 trains daily in each direction to Ribadeo and Ferrol) are across the harbour from the old town, five minutes' walk apart.

Turismo Avda. Ramón Canosa (mid-June to mid-Sept Mon–Fri 11am–2pm & 4.30–7.30pm, Sat 11am–2pm & 5–7pm, Sun 11.30am–1.30pm; mid-Sept to mid-June Mon–Fri 11am–2pm & 4.30–7pm, Sat 11am–2pm & 5–7pm; ☎ 982 560 879, ⓦ viveiro.es), on the edge of the old town on the waterfront.

ACCOMMODATION

With no hotels in the heart of the old town, there's something to be said for staying near the beaches, across the harbour.

Camping Vivero Praia de Covas ☎ 982 560 004. Viveiro's spacious, well-shaded campsite is located just behind the largest local beach. Closed Oct–May. Two adults plus car €16.

Hostal Vila Rúa Nicolás Montenegro 57 ☎ 982 561 331, ⓦ hotel-vila.net. Plain but clean and perfectly adequate hotel, in a drab street just outside the walls at the Porta del Vallado. €60

Hotel As Areas Rúa Granxas 84 ☎ 982 560 605, ⓦ hotelasareas.com. Comfortable hotel, set just back from the long Praia de Covas beach around twenty minutes' walk from town. Free parking. €64

Hotel Orfeo Rúa Navia Castrillón 2 ☎ 982 562 101, ⓦ hotelorfeo.net. Smart but characterless rooms overlooking the bay just south of the old town. €70

EATING AND DRINKING

O Asador Rúa Melitòn Cortiñas 15 ☎ 982 560 688, ⓦ oasador.com. Not far southwest of the main square in the old town, this formal restaurant offers excellent but reasonably priced seafood. Daily 1–3pm & 8–10.30pm.

O Muro Rúa Margarita Pardo de Cela 28 ☎ 982 560 823. This busy, functional *pulpería* and grill serves a wide menu of fish and meats, and even pizzas. Tues–Sun 1–3.30pm & 7.30–10pm.

Porto do Barqueiro and Ortigueira

West of Viveiro, shorefront development finally thins out, and the scenery grows ever more dramatic. The next two *ría* villages (and FEVE stops) are **PORTO DO BARQUEIRO**, 16km along, a tiny and very picturesque fishing port of slate-roofed houses near Spain's northernmost point, and the larger **ORTIGUEIRA**, 14km farther on, set amid a dark mass of pines and host to July's musical extravaganza, the International Festival of the Celtic World (ⓦ festivaldeortigueira.com).

ACCOMMODATION
PORTO DO BARQUEIRO AND ORTIGUEIRA

El Castaño Dormilón O Baleo 15, Ortigueira ☎ 981 400 994, ⓦ elcastanodormilon.es. Former school, a short way inland 4km east of Ortigueira, which has been exquisitely converted into a bright, great-value and exceptionally comfortable rural inn. Rates include breakfast. €80

Hotel Porto do Barqueiro Porto do Barqueiro ☎ 981 414 098, ⓦ hramarina.com. The best value among a handful of hotels dotted around the tiny harbour at Porto do Barqueiro; the rooms are undeniably plain, but the views are great. €50

La Perla Avda. la Penela, Ortigueira ☎ 981 400 150. This 20 room hotel, on the main coast road as it approaches Ortigueira from the northeast, offers decent en-suite doubles and is close to the heart of the festival action. €58

San Andrés de Teixido

While the FEVE heads inland after Ortigueira, drivers can make a worthwhile side-trip to the hermitage at **SAN ANDRÉS DE TEIXIDO**, the so-called Mecca of the

Galegos. The tortuous road up here leaves the main AC862 at **Mera**, 9km west of Ortigueira, and climbs for a magnificent 12km farther, high above the coast, threading in and out of the pine forests into rolling clifftop meadows and bare heathland. The cliffs at **Vixia de Herbeira**, just short of the sanctuary, are said to be the tallest in Europe, at over 600m, while the church itself perches high above the ocean. Like so many of Galicia's sanctuaries, it is based on a pre-Christian religious site, but a monastery was already in place by the twelfth century. It now welcomes coachloads of Galego pilgrims, so the adjoining hamlet holds a café as well as plenty of souvenir stalls.

Cedeira

CEDEIRA, 12km southwest of San Andrés in its own attractive little *ría*, is a graceful port where elegant houses and pleasant tapas bars line the shaded, canalized mouth of a little stream, while a huge beach sweeps south.

ACCOMMODATION   CEDEIRA

Hotel Herbeira Lugar de Cordobelas ☎ 981 492 167, ⊛ hotelherbeira.com. This startling modern hotel, on a hillside 1km south of town, looks like a stack of boxes; each holds a bright, beautifully equipped room with great views of both beach and town, and there's a large pool. **€80**

Pensión Brisas Rúa Calvo Sotelo 19 ☎ 981 481 054. This simple little place offers the best-priced rooms in central Cedeira. **€40**

Betanzos

As the navy-dominated port of Ferrol, birthplace of General Franco, is best avoided, the final stop worth making in the Rías Altas is the ancient town of **BETANZOS**. Twenty kilometres southeast of A Coruña, at the head of the **Ría de Betanzos**, it was built on a pre-Roman site so old that what was once a steep seafront hill is now located well inland at the confluence of the Mendo and Mandeo rivers. The base of the hill is surrounded by fragments of medieval walls, now largely built over.

Betanzos' attractive main square, **Praza dos Irmáns García Naveira**, is just below its appealing hill-top old quarter. A short walk up from here brings you to the much smaller Praza da Constitución, home to the Gothic church of Santiago. Within the mass of twisting and tunnelling narrow streets immediately below stands the twelfth-century church of **Santa María do Azougue**, while the tomb of Conde Fernán Perez de Andrade "O Boo" (The Good), who commissioned its construction, lies in the Gothic **Igrexa de San Francisco** opposite.

If you're in Betanzos on August 16, don't miss the **Fiesta del Globo**, the highlight of which is the midnight launch, from the Torre de Santo Domingo in the main square, of the world's largest paper balloon, daubed with political slogans. There is also a medieval **festival** in the second weekend of July, when the town is transported back to the times of the Andrade lords.

Museo das Mariñas

Rúa Emilio Romay • June–Sept Mon–Fri 10am–2pm & 4–8pm, Sat 10.30am–1pm • €1.20

Just behind Betanzos' main square, the excellent **Museo das Mariñas** provides a fascinating insight into the history of the town and neighbouring *mariñas* (sea-facing villages), and includes a colourful collection of period costumes.

ARRIVAL AND DEPARTURE   BETANZOS

By train and bus The Betanzos Ciudad RENFE train station, ten minutes' walk south of the centre, is only used by the four daily trains between Ferrol and A Coruña. Other trains use the Betanzos Infesta station, 2.5km away at the top of a steep climb. Buses from A Coruña pull up just behind the square.

By car Driving in central Betanzos is all but impossible; park down by the river, and walk up from there.

INFORMATION

Turismo Praza de Galicia 1, just off the main square (mid-June to mid-Sept Mon–Fri 10am–2pm & 5–8pm, Sat & Sun 11am–2pm & 5–7pm; mid-Sept to mid-June Mon–Fri 10am–2pm & 4.30–7.30pm, Sat 10.30am–1pm; ☎ 981 776 666, ⓦ betanzos.net).

ACCOMMODATION

Hotel Los Garelos Rúa Afonso IX 8 ☎ 981 775 922, ⓦ hotelgarelos.com. A short walk west of the main square, just outside the hill-top centre, this jazzed-up town hotel offers smart, modernized en-suite rooms at slightly inflated prices. **€70**

Hotel San Roque Rúa Afonso IX 8 ☎ 981 775 555, ⓦ complejosanroque.es. Large hotel/restaurant complex in a converted boarding house on the main road into town from the south, 300m from the central square. Reasonable but unexciting rooms, and good food downstairs. **€70**

EATING AND DRINKING

Eating and drinking possibilities in Betanzos centre on the row of attractive bars under the stone arcades of the main square, and the two tiny alleys that drop down between them.

★ **Casa Carmen** Rúa da Fonte de Unta 12 ☎ 696 255 365. Delightful old *mesón*, with several tables beneath the venerable stone arches that lead down from the central square. There's a great range of seafood *raciones* and a €10 lunch *menú*; and the speciality is *tortilla de Betanzos*, an omelette that sandwiches layers of spinach and tomato. Daily noon–4pm & 7–11pm.

O Pote Travesía do Progreso 9 ☎ 981 770 414. Betanzos'

finest tapas bar, tucked down a narrow alleyway, with a wide range of tasty snacks and a buzzy atmosphere. Daily 11.30am–4pm & 8pm–midnight.

Vinoteca Versailles Venela del Campo ☎ 981 772 910. Lovely Modernist café, right on the main square itself, with decorative dark wood-panelling. Ideal for morning coffee, or fine wines later in the day. Daily 10am–11pm.

A Coruña

The fine port of **A CORUÑA** centres on a narrow peninsula that juts from Galicia's northern coast, 64km north of Santiago. A broad headland curves in both directions from the end of that peninsula to create two large bays: one faces across to Ferrol, and shelters a large harbour, while the other lies open to the Atlantic, and is lined by a long sandy beach. In the dynamic city in between, a five-minute walk takes you from a bustling modern port to a relaxed resort, by way of old stone alleyways where tantalizing restaurants, tapas bars and nightspots jostle for attention.

The distinctive glass-fronted galleries of the sea-facing buildings, rising six storeys high along the Avenida da Marina in front of the port, form a magnificent ensemble. They were originally designed so local residents, whose lives were intertwined with the ocean, could watch the activity of the harbour in shelter.

Praza de María Pita

The heart of A Coruña, poised between the old city and its modern sprawl just inland from the port, is the colonnaded **Praza de María Pita**. The city's role as the departure point for the Spanish Armada in 1588 earned it a retaliatory visit from Sir Francis Drake the following year. His attack was only repelled when a humble local heroine, María Pita, killed the English standard-bearer; her spear-waving statue now dominates the square.

The old town

East of the Praza de María Pita, the narrow and atmospheric streets of the **old town** wind around the Romanesque churches of **Santiago** and **Santa María del Campo**, and are shielded from the sea by a high wall. A small walled garden, the **Xardín de San Carlos**, holds the tomb of English general Sir John Moore, who died in battle near A

Arteixo, Fisterra & Carballo

A CORUÑA

ACCOMMODATION

Hesperia Finisterre	7
Hostal Sol	5
Hotel Avenida	1
Hotel Nido	2
Pension Alborán	6
Pension Centro Gallego	3
Pensión Roma	4

TAPAS BARS & RESTAURANTS

Bar Suso	2
Coral	5
Mesón do Pulpo	6
El Serrano	4

BARS

Cova Celtica	1
Retro Pub	3

CALVO SOTELO
PRAZA DE PORTUGAL
Casa das Ciencias
AV. DE LUGO
Palacio de Congresos
AV. DE FISTERRA
ALFREDO VICENTI
AV. B. AIRES
JUAN FLÓREZ
AVENIDA DE PEDRO
Praia do Razor
PRAZA DE VIGO
EL FERROL
FONTÁN
BELANZOS
FONSECA
COMPOSTELA
PRAZA DE PONTEVEDRA
La Coraza
Enseada do Orzán
AV. LINARES RIVAS
PRAZA DE OURENSE
Casa Museo Picasso
PIERAO UNIFICADO SANTA LUCÍA Y LINARES RIVAS
SÁNCHEZ BREGUA
C. JUANA DE VEGA
DURÁN LORIGA
Rosaleda
LOS CANTÓNS
ESTRELL
RUA ALTA
Praia do Orzán
PIERAO DE LA BATERÍA
Xardins de Méndez Núñez
RUA NUEVA
BARRIE DE LA MAZA
JUAN CANALEJO
La Terraza
Igrexa de S. Andrés
ROTONDA DO MATADERO
PEIRAO DE CALVO SOTELO
Estación Marítima
Kiosko Alfonso
OLMOS
GALERA
DEL ORZÁN
CORRALÓN
DE SAN ANDRÉS
SOL
C. DEL HOSPITAL SAN ROQUE
Gobierno Civil
REAL
RUA DA BARRERA
DE ZALAETA
PEIRAO DE TRANSATLÁNTICOS
Porto da Coruña
Conv. de las Capuchinas
S. NICOLÁS
S. Nicolás
CANAADEIRAS
Dársena da Marina
AV. DA MARINA
RIEGO DE AGUA
PL. DE S. AGUSTÍN
Mercado
MERCADO
PR. DE ESPAÑA
Puerta Real
FRANJA
Galerías Coruñesas
S. Jorge
Palacio Municipal
PRAZA DE MARÍA PITA
SANTIAGO
M. ASTRAY
TABERNAS
PASEO DE LA DÁRSENA
Igrexa de Santiago
NTRA. SRA. DEL ROSARIO
PASEO MARÍTIMO
Torre de Hercules
Colegiata de Santa María del Campo
ZAPATERÍA
HERRERÍAS
MAESTRANZA
VERAMAR
OLD TOWN
P. DEL PARROTE
Casa de la Cultura
CORTADURÍA
Museo Arqueolóxico e Histórico
Hospital Militar
S. FRANCISCO
Museo Militar
Convento de Santo Domingo
Enseada de San Amaro
Xardín de San Carlos
Xardíns da Maestranza
PASEO SIR JOHN MOORE
Casino Club Náutico

Aquarium, Museo Domus & Palais do Orzán & de Riazor

0   100
metres

8

Coruña in 1809 during the British retreat from the French during the Peninsular Wars. A wall nearby holds poet Charles Wolfe's contemporary lines describing his original hasty battlefield burial – "Not a drum was heard, not a funeral note" – along with a similarly melancholic offering by Galicia's most famous poet, Rosalía de Castro.

Museo Arqueolóxico e Histórico

July & Aug Tues–Sat 10am–9pm, Sun 10am–3pm; Sept–June Tues–Sat 10am–7.30pm, Sun 10am–2.30pm • €2, Sat free

On a former island at the port entrance, the restored Castelo San Antón used to be a garrison and, until the 1960s, a military and political prison; today, it houses the **Museo Arqueolóxico e Histórico**. As well as fascinating ancient finds, including pre-Christian gold jewellery, it holds an unusual full-size replica of an Iron Age wicker-and-leather boat.

Torre de Hercules

April–June & Sept daily 10am–6.45pm; July & Aug Mon–Thurs & Sun 10am–8.45pm, Fri & Sat 10am–11.45pm; Oct–March daily 10am–5.45pm • €3, free Mon • ⓦ torredeherculesacoruna.es

During the Iron Age, the site of A Coruña was home to the Artabri tribe, one of whose hillforts can still be seen at nearby Elviña. It was the Romans, however, who built the landmark **Torre de Hercules**. Said to be the world's only still-functioning Roman lighthouse, it dominates the northern tip of the headland, amid a sweeping expanse of grass and heather. It's an impressive spectacle, though it was rebuilt in the eighteenth century and only a few foundation stones from the Roman era remain on show. The views from the top, out over the Atlantic and back to the city, are superb.

Aquarium Finisterrae

Jan–April Mon–Fri 10am–6pm, Sat & Sun 11am–8pm; May, June & Sept–Dec Mon–Fri 10am–7pm, Sat & Sun 11am–8pm; July & Aug daily 10am–9pm • €10 • ⓦ casaciencias.org

The state-of-the-art **Aquarium Finisterrae** stands on the next headland along from the Torre de Hercules. Far more than just a series of fish tanks, it offers a vast array of interactive displays that will delight adults and children alike, as well as the 4.5-million-litre *Nautilus* tank, which plunges visitors into a world filled with the marine life of the Atlantic coast.

Museo Domus

Rúa Santa Teresa 1 • Jan–April Mon–Fri 10am–6pm, Sat & Sun 11am–7pm; May, June & Sept–Dec Mon–Fri 10am–7pm, Sat & Sun 11am–7pm; July & Aug daily 10am–8pm • €2, cinema €4 • ⓦ casaciencias.org

Just above the Paseo Marítimo, further anti-clockwise around the headland, the **Museo Domus**, or Museum of Mankind, takes visitors on an educational trip around the workings of the human body. A large and superbly designed new building, it's aimed more at local schoolkids than tourists, and many of the displays do not have English captions. Besides lots of models explaining pregnancy and childbirth, and even a pair of pickled Siamese twins, it holds some fascinating interactive exhibits, including "mindball", a counter-intuitive game in which you beat your opponent by being more relaxed. Films in its 3D cinema cost extra.

Casa das Ciencias

Jan–April Mon–Fri 10am–6pm, Sat & Sun 11am–7pm; May, June & Sept–Dec Mon–Fri 10am–7pm, Sat & Sun 11am–7pm; July & Aug daily 10am–8pm • €2, planetarium €2 • ⓦ casaciencias.org

At the inland end of the peninsula, south of the city centre, a tower atop a hill in the lovely little Parque de Santa Margarita holds the **Casa das Ciencias**, or House of

Science. Filled with gadgets to play with, this enjoyable science museum is intended mainly for kids, and also features a planetarium.

The beaches

The sweeping golden arc of the city's main beaches, **Praia do Orzán** and the contiguous **Praia de Riazor**, line the opposite side of the peninsula from the Dársena. Considering how very close they are to the city centre, they're surprisingly clean and unpolluted, and you need to arrive early in summer to grab a prime spot.

Casa Museo Picasso

Payó Gómez 14 • Wed & Sun 10.30am–2pm, Thurs–Sat 10.30am–2pm & 5.30–8pm• Free • ☎ 981 184 278

Pablo Picasso lived in A Coruña between the ages of 9 and 13, and produced his first oil paintings here. The **Casa Museo Picasso**, his former home just north of the city centre, is a typical galleried townhouse. It's of interest mainly for its authentic (but not original) period furnishings rather than the few reproduced paintings by both Pablo and his father.

ARRIVAL AND DEPARTURE   A CORUÑA

By train A Coruña's train station is south of the city, where Avda. Alcalde Alfonso Molina meets the ring road, Ronda de Outeiro; it's a half-hour walk to the centre, or you can take buses #5 or #11.

Destinations Barcelona (2 daily; 14hr); Betanzos (2 daily; 30min); Bilbao (daily; 11hr); Burgos (4 daily; 8–9hr); León (3 daily; 6hr); Lugo (4 daily; 1hr 45min); Madrid (2 daily; 8–10hr); Ourense (4 daily; 2hr); Santiago de Compostela (16 daily; 35min); Vigo (15 daily; 2hr); Zaragoza (2 daily; 12hr).

By bus The bus station faces the train station, 2km south of the centre.

Destinations Betanzos (every 30min; 45min); Camariñas

(3 daily; 2hr); Fisterra (5 daily; 2hr 10min); Laxe (3 daily; 1hr 50min); Lugo (8–14 daily; 1hr 15min); Madrid (8 daily; 7hr); Ourense (5 daily; 2hr 30min); Oviedo (4 daily; 3hr 45min–6hr); Pontevedra (10 daily; 1hr 45min); Santiago de Compostela (hourly; 1hr 15min); Vigo (9 daily; 2hr 15min); Viveiro (1 daily; 3hr 30min).

By car Driving in A Coruña is extremely difficult and unrewarding; no map could do justice to the tangle of dead-end and one-way streets in the old quarter. Drive out to the Torre de Hercules, but otherwise it's best to park as soon as possible, ideally in the central, underground Los Cantones car park.

INFORMATION

City turismo Praza de María Pita 6 (Mon–Fri 9am–8.30pm, Sat 10am–2pm & 4–8pm, Sun 10am–3pm; ☎ 981 923 093, ⓦ turismocoruna.com). The regional

turismo is on the Dársena de la Marina (Mon–Fri 10am–2pm & 4–7pm, Sat 11am–2pm & 5–7pm, Sun 11am–2pm; ☎ 981 221 822, ⓦ turgalicia.es).

ACCOMMODATION

Whatever your budget, the pedestrian streets that approach Praza María Pita and the old town are the best hunting grounds for **accommodation**, though if you're driving you won't be able to park nearby.

Hesperia Finisterre Paseo del Parrote 2 ☎ 981 205 400, ⓦ hesperia-finisterre.com. The top option in town, this vast orange waterfront five-star, in easy reach of everything, comes complete with tennis courts, Olympic-size swimming pool and every conceivable luxury. **€139**

Hostal Sol Rúa Sol 10 ☎ 981 210 362, ⓦ hotelsolcoruna .com. Behind the unprepossessing modern exterior, with its bordello-style flashing sign, the rooms in this central option are stylish and comfortable. Rates include parking, which is a major plus for drivers. **€70**

Hotel Avenida Rúa Alvaro Cunqueiro 1 ☎ 981 249 466,

ⓦ hotelavenida.com. Stylish modern hotel, in a not especially attractive neighbourhood well south of the centre, but surprisingly quiet and offering a high standard for the price. **€78**

Hotel Nido Rúa San Andrés 146 ☎ 981 213 201, ⓦ hotel-nido-coruna.com. On central Coruña's main street, close to all the action, with fifty smart, shiny if unexciting rooms; for a quieter night, ask for one facing the courtyard. **€60**

Pensión Alborán Rúa Riego de Agua 14 ☎ 981 226 579, ⓦ hostalalboran.es. Excellent location near Praza

8

María Pita, with thirty comfortable rooms, all with bath and wi-fi, and some with balconies overlooking the attractive pedestrianized street. **€50**

Pensión Centro Gallego Rúa Estrella 2 ☎ 981 222 236, ⓦ pensioncentrogallego.com. The simple rooms at this budget hotel above a bar, some of which have balconies, are great value for such a central location. **€50**

Pensión Roma Rúa Nueva 3 ☎ 981 228 075, ⓦ pensionroma.com. Good-value, clean, modern en-suite rooms, plus use of computers, in a convenient central location. Closed Oct–June. **€52**

EATING

The small streets leading west from Praza de María Pita, from Rúa da Franxa through to Rúa La Galera, Rúa Los Olmos and Rúa Estrella, are crowded with bars that offer some of Spain's tastiest **seafood**.

Bar Suso Rúa la Galera 31 ☎ 981 200 957. The best of several seafood tapas bars along this central alleyway, with a set lunch *menú* for just €7 and a €1 snack of the day. Daily 11am–midnight.

Coral Rúa da Estacada 9 ☎ 981 200 569. A Coruña's best formal restaurant, set very slightly back from the main portside boulevard in a tiny square. Typical meat main dishes cost €16–18, fish upwards from €20. Daily 1–4pm & 9pm–midnight.

Mesón do Pulpo Rúa da Franxa 9 ☎ 981 202 444. In the

cluster of *marisquerías* just off Praza de María Pita, with no outside seating. Ultra-fresh seafood is the speciality; a full *ración* of its trademark octopus, sprinkled with paprika, costs €10.80, but half-portions are available. Mon–Sat noon–11pm.

El Serrano Rúa la Galera 23 ☎ 981 220 353, ⓦ elserrano.es. A cornucopia for carnivores, this fine old *jamonería* serves ham platters for €8 to €20, plus all kinds of sausage as well, and there's also a full menu of *raciones*. Mon–11am–4pm & 7pm–midnight.

DRINKING AND NIGHTLIFE

In summer, the beachfront **bars** across the peninsula do a roaring trade, while bar-filled Rúa Orillamar is a good place to start the evening.

Cova Celtica Rúa do Orzan 82 ☎ 981 915 140. Celtic pub with exposed stone walls that's a popular rendezvous for folky students. Besides beers and a devastating coffee liqueur, it also serves snacks, and often has live Galego music. Mon–Thurs 7.30pm–2am, Fri & Sat 7.30pm–3.30am.

Retro Pub Rúa do Orzan 19. Lively late-night pub in the heart of old-town Coruña's busiest nightlife district, with a classic rock soundtrack and live bands at weekends. Daily 8pm–2am.

The Costa da Morte

Wild, windy and at times desolate, the **Costa da Morte**, west of A Coruña, is often passed over by tourists heading south to the beaches of the Rías Baixas. But while the Costa da Morte lacks both the climate and the infrastructure for large-scale tourism, it's not nearly as overdeveloped as the regions to the south, while boasting similarly beautiful coves, tiny fishing villages huddled against the headlands, and forested mountain slopes aplenty.

Its fearsome name, which means Coast of Death, stems from the constant buffeting the shoreline receives from the Atlantic waves. The most notorious of the countless **shipwrecks** that litter the sea bed is the oil tanker *Prestige*, which snapped in two following a ferocious storm in 2002. Although 77,000 tonnes of crude oil were released into the ocean, barely a trace of oil remained just twelve months later.

The coast from **Camariñas** to **Fisterra** is the most exposed and westerly stretch of all. Ever since a Roman expedition under Lucius Florus Brutus was brought up short by what seemed to be an endless sea, it has been known as *finis terrae* (the end of the world), and it is not hard to see why. This is prime territory, however, for hunting *percebes* (barnacles), one of Galicia's most popular and expensive seafood delicacies, which have to be scooped up from the very waterline. Collectors are

---

GETTING AROUND THE COSTA DA MORTE

While it's well worth following the coastal road west around the Costa da Morte all the way to Fisterra, you'll need to allow plenty of time. **Driving** is slow, and, with no train lines, **buses** offer the only public transport. They're predominantly operated by Monbus (ⓦwww.monbus .es), whose routes include Camariñas to Cée via Muxía (2 daily; 1hr 30min), and Fisterra to Santiago via Cée, Carnota, Muros and Noia (3 daily; 3hr).

---

commonly swept away by the dreaded "seventh wave", which can appear out of nowhere from a calm sea.

Even where the isolated coves do shelter fine beaches, you will rarely find resort facilities. While the beaches may look splendid, braving the water is recommended for only the strongest of swimmers, and the climate is significantly wetter and windier here than it is a mere 100km or so further south.

Malpica de Bergantiños

Few potential stopping points lie immediately west of A Coruña. If you're driving, take the toll motorway to its end at the busy inland road junction of **Carballo**. Heading north from there for 15km brings you to **MALPICA DE BERGANTIÑOS**, the first of a succession of tiny seaside ports. Crammed onto the neck of a narrow peninsula, Malpica consists of a harbour on one side and a marvellous – though exposed – beach hardly 100m away on the other.

The best local beach, the sheltered **Praia de Niñons**, is roughly 6km west. Follow signs for **Corme**, then turn right at the village of Niñons, from where narrow lanes thread through fields of maize to the sea. A granite church with a *fuente* (fountain) stands guard just above the beach itself, a crescent of thick sand that stretches out to either side of a little stream. Young Spaniards set up fireside campsites here in summer, but the solitary bar isn't open at night.

ACCOMMODATION, EATING AND DRINKING   MALPICA DE BERGANTIÑOS

Hostal Panchito Praza Villar Amigo 6 ☎981 720 307, ⓦhostalpanchito.com. Smart en-suite rooms in the heart of the tiny port, all facing the harbour and overlooking the fishing boats. **€43**

San Francisco Rúa Eduardo Pondal 5 ☎981 720 489. Good seafood restaurant in a tiny fishing village, where you can choose your dinner from a tankful of live sea creatures. Daily 12.30–3.30pm & 7.30–10.30pm.

Laxe

Some 24km southwest from Malpica, having crossed the River Anllóns via an ancient bridge at **Ponteceso**, the coast road reaches **LAXE** (pronounced "la-shay"), which offers the area's safest swimming. A formidable sea wall protects a small harbour, while the long sweep of fine, clean sand is backed by café-lined streets.

Just outside Laxe are two beaches, the deserted **Praia de Soesto**, which, though exposed, more than rivals the town beach; and a perfect cove, the **Praia de Arnado**. There's another massively long beach, the **Praia de Traba**, 6km south; remote as anything, it's backed by sand dunes and a jigsaw of mini-fields.

ACCOMMODATION, EATING AND DRINKING   LAXE

Casa do Arco Praza de Ramón Juega 1 ☎981 706 904, ⓦcasadoarco.es. This fine restaurant is housed in an ancient archway that leads off Laxe's attractive little seafront square. Most fish and meat dishes cost around €20, while there's a €20 set *menú* on weekdays. They also run a cheaper *méson* and tapas bar, and offer simple

rooms (€40). Daily except Tues 12.30–3.30pm & 7.30–11pm.

Hostal Bahía Avda. Besugueira 24 ☎981 728 304, ⓦbahialaxe.com. Laxe's most appealing hotel is right in the port, above a burger bar. Several of its en-suite rooms have spacious balconies with sea views, costing €20 extra. **€50**

8

Camariñas

Although the seafront buildings of **CAMARIÑAS**, 25km southwest of Laxe, are almost entirely modern, it's still an attractive village, curled around a harbour that holds a fishing fleet as well as the yachts of well-heeled visitors.

Camariñas marks the start of Galicia's wild west, at the region's westernmost extremity. A 5km trek from town leads to the lighthouse at **Cabo Vilán**, guarding the treacherous shore on a rocky outcrop; climb the adjacent rocks for a stunning sea view. Winds whip viciously around the cape, and the huge, sci-fi propellers of the adjacent wind farm spin eerily, lit by the searchlight beam of the lighthouse once darkness falls.

ACCOMMODATION, EATING AND DRINKING   CAMARIÑAS

Café Bar Playa Avda. Ambrosio Feijoo 3 ☎635 523 002. This simple village bar, across from the harbour, serves great tapas and *raciones* at rock-bottom prices – €2 for a generous serving of peppers, €1.20 for empanada, €5 for octopus – and their bread is wonderful too. Daily noon–3.30pm & 7–11pm.

Hostal Gaviota Rúa do Rio 15 ☎981 736 030, ⊕hostalgaviota.en.eresmas.com. Modern hotel, set slightly back from the sea, with a dozen plain but reasonably pleasant rooms. €40

★ **Hotel Puerto Arnela** Praza del Carmen 20 ☎981 705 477. This lovely little flower-bedecked hotel, in one of Camariñas' few ancient houses, faces the sea from the far end of the port. The nicest rooms have their own balconies; there's also a small restaurant, and the owners are exceptionally friendly. Rates include breakfast. €55

Muxía

On the tip of a rocky promontory across the *ría* from Camariñas, the small fishing port of **MUXÍA** is nothing special. Make your way up to the Romanesque church on the hill above, though, and there's a fabulous view to either side of the headland. Paths lead down to the eighteenth-century **Santuario da Virxe da Barca**, where a massive sea-level church marks what was once an important site of Galicia's pre-Christian animist cult. The cult was centred around the strange granite rocks at the farthest point of the headland, some of which are precariously balanced and said to make wonderful sounds when struck correctly; others supposedly have healing power. In later times, the rocks were reinterpreted as being the remains of the stone ship that brought the Virgin to the aid of Santiago, an obvious echo of the saint's own landing at Padrón.

ACCOMMODATION, EATING AND DRINKING   MUXÍA

Casa Marujita Rúa Virxe da Barca 15 ☎981 742 546. Tiny, tumbledown restaurant that's renowned for its excellent and inexpensive seafood. It's immediately inland at the far end of the seafront road, where the road to the headland begins. Daily 1–3pm & 8–10.30pm.

Hostal A Cruz Rúa Lopez Abente ☎981 742 084. This imposing glass-galleried hotel, facing the sea at the southern approach to Muxía and an easy walk from the beach, offers clean, comfortable rooms. €55

Hotel Tira da Barca Baluca–Moraime ☎981 742 323. Pleasant rustic hotel 1km south of Muxía, not far from the beach, with well-priced rooms and a restaurant. €50

Fisterra

Famed until the time of Columbus as the western limit of the world, the town of **FISTERRA (Finisterre)** still looks like it's about to drop off the end of the earth. On a misty, out-of-season day, it can feel no more than a grey clump of houses wedged into the rocks, but it puts on a cheerier face in the summer sunshine.

Just beyond the southern end of Fisterra's long harbour wall, a tiny bay cradles an appealing beach, overlooked by the pretty little eighteenth-century **Castelo de San Carlos**. Originally an artillery post, this now holds a museum of fishing (May–Aug daily 11am–2.30pm & 4–8pm; Sept–April Tues–Sat 10.30am–1.30pm & 3.30–6.30pm, Sun 10.30am–1.30pm; €2). Beside the road south out of town, **Santa María das Areas** is a small but atmospheric church. Its beautiful carved altar, like the strange weathered tombs left of the main door, is considerably older than the rest of the building.

ACCOMMODATION   FISTERRA

Albergue de Paz Rúa Victor Cardalda ☎ 981 740 332, ⓦ alberguedepaz.com. Fisterra's cheapest accommodation, near the little castle at the south end of the port, with individual beds in two- to five-person dorms. **€10**

Casa Velay Praza Cerca ☎ 981 740 127. Poised above the northern end of Fisterra's little in-town beach, this friendly establishment offers bargain-priced rooms, and also has a good-value bar/restaurant, with outdoor sea-view tables. Restaurant daily 1–4pm & 8.30pm–midnight. **€35**

Hostal Praia de Estorde Praia de Estorde ☎ 981 745 585. Delightful if somewhat isolated *hostal*/restaurant, commanding a fine white-sand beach that nestles in a small cove 7km east of Fisterra, 1km beyond the village of Sardiñeiro. They also run a small summer-only *campsite*, *Ruta de Finisterre*, in the woods across the road. Tent plus car **€16.50**; *hostal* **€72**

Hotel Rural Prado da Viña Camino Barcia ☎ 981 740 326, ⓦ hotelruralpradodavina.com. Very comfortable little purpose-built B&B, on the hillside a short way north of central Fisterra, with nice en-suite rooms and a small swimming pool. Rates include breakfast. **€80**

Fisterra Lighthouse

Thanks to the shape of the headland, the **Fisterra Lighthouse**, which marks the final point of the Camino de Santiago, is actually 4km south of Fisterra itself. The road there leads first along a heathered mountainside, then through a pine-forest plantation; the squat, square lighthouse perches high above the waves at the tip of the cape. When, as so often, the whole place is shrouded in thick mist and the mournful foghorn wails across the sea, it's an eerie spot. Traditionally, this is where pilgrims would burn their clothes, signalling the end of the pilgrimage, and also collect their scallop shell; the wearing of a scallop throughout the journey is a relatively recent phenomenon.

ACCOMMODATION, EATING AND DRINKING   FISTERRA LIGHTHOUSE   8

★ **Semaforo** Faro de Fisterra ☎ 981 725 869, ⓦ finisterrae.com/semaforo. Small hotel/restaurant, a few metres before the lighthouse and the only place to stay right at the cape itself, which charges something over the odds for its five upscale guest rooms. The restaurant serves a €20 lunch *menú*, or you can get cheaper tapas at *O Refuxio*, the bar below. Closed Nov; restaurant open daily 1.30–4pm & 8.30pm–midnight. **€110**

Ezaro, O Pindo and Carnota

Around **EZARO**, where the Río Xallas meets the sea 30km east of Fisterra, the scenery is marvellous. The rocks of the sheer escarpments above the road are so rich in minerals that they are multicoloured, and glisten beneath innumerable tiny waterfalls. Upstream there are warm, natural lagoons and more cascades. Another couple of kilometres on, the little (though far from picturesque) port of **O PINDO**, beneath a stony but thickly wooded hill dotted with old houses, also has a small beach.

Towards Carnota, another 12km south, the series of short beaches finally joins together into one long, unbroken line of dunes, swept by the Atlantic winds. The village of **CARNOTA** is a couple of kilometres from the shore, but its palm trees and old church are still thoroughly caked in salt. To get to the beach, you have to follow a long wooden boardwalk across the marshes.

ACCOMMODATION   O PINDO

Pensión Sol E Mar Praia do San Pedro, O Pindo ☎ 981 760 298. Good-value sea-view hotel on the main coast road, a short walk from the beach and with eight comfortable en-suite rooms. **€50**

Ría de Muros e Noia

The **Rías Baixas**, much the most touristed portion of Galicia's coastline, starts in the north with the **Ría de Muros e Noia**. In truth, it's so close to the Costa da Morte that there's little difference in climate or appearance, and it remains relatively underdeveloped, but unspoiled little **Muros** is well worth visiting.

Muros

Some of the best traditional Galego architecture outside Pontevedra can be found in the old town of **MUROS**, enhanced by a marvellous natural setting at the widest point of the Ría de Muros, just before it meets the sea. The town rises in tiers of narrow streets from the curving waterfront, where fishing boats unload their catch, to the Romanesque **Iglesia de San Pedro**. Everywhere you look are squat granite columns and arches, flights of wide steps, and benches and stone porches built into the house fronts. There's also a nice – though small – **beach** on the edge of town next to the road to Fisterra.

ARRIVAL AND INFORMATION   MUROS

By bus Monbus services stop across from the *Ría de Muros* hotel (see below).
Turismo The seasonal *turismo* is located in the central

square, where the coast road bends (July to mid-Sept Mon–Fri 10am–2pm & 4–7pm, Sat 10.30am–3pm, Sun 11am–2pm & 4–9pm; ☎ 981 826 050, ⊛ muros.es).

ACCOMMODATION

★ **Hostal Ría de Muros** Rúa Castelao 53 ☎ 981 826 056. A real unexpected gem; behind its unprepossessing exterior on the coast road through town, this eight-room hotel offers fantastic value. The six rooms away from the road are smart but unexceptional, but the seafront doubles on the top storey, which cost €10 extra, are breathtaking: spacious and tastefully furnished, with glorious balconies

facing across the harbour and bay. €50
★ **Jallambau Rural** Lugar de Millaflores ☎ 981 826 056, ⊛ jallambaurural.com. Commanding a majestic panorama of the bay from the hillside above town, reached via a ferociously steep, narrow road, this superbly equipped and positioned four-room B&B can also be rented in its entirety as a holiday home. €95

EATING AND DRINKING

Pulpería Pachanga Rúa Castelao 29 ☎ 981 826 048. Right on the seafront, with outdoor seating in its own little precinct, this excellent *raciones* bar/restaurant has a stone-vaulted interior, and serves fresh seafood and grilled meats. Daily 11am–11pm.

Xamonería O Varadoiro Rúa A Canavala 2, Praza da Pescadería ☎ 981 826 331. This cheap ham, cheese and tapas place is one of several good café-restaurants on a little inland square, a block back from the seafront behind the Ría de Muros. Daily noon–3pm & 7.30–11pm.

Noia

NOIA (Noya), 25km east of Muros near the head of the *ría*, is, according to a legend fanciful even by Galego standards, named after Noah, whose Ark is supposed to have struck land nearby. Scarcely less absurd is Noia's claim to be a "Little Florence", on the strength of a couple of nice churches and an arcaded street or two. Nonetheless, there is a lot to like about Noia. Developed in the Middle Ages to serve as Santiago's port, and now connected to it by a fast motorway, it has recently experienced a major overhaul which has reinvigorated its medieval core. The single most impressive building, the church of **San Martino**, dominates a delightful ancient square.

ACCOMMODATION, EATING AND DRINKING   NOIA

Hotel Elisardo Rúa Costa do Perrador 15 ☎ 981 820 130. Small townhouse offering ten simple but very presentable en-suite rooms, on the edge of the old core. €40
Tasca Típica Rúa Cantón 15 ☎ 981 821 842. Hugely

atmospheric tapas bar, spreading from a fourteenth-century mansion onto tables tucked beneath imposing stone arches, and serving a great array of Galego specialities. Daily 10.30am–3.30pm & 8–10.30pm.

Castro de Baroña

From Noia the AC301 heads inland through deep, lush gorges towards Padrón. To trace the southern side of the Ría da Noia, sometimes called the "Cockle Coast", follow the C550 as it winds past dunes that serve in good weather as excellent beaches.

From the roadside *Castro de Baroña* restaurant, just outside **BAROÑA** (Basonas) 18km along, a fifteen-minute walk down through the woods leads to a lovely little beach.

Built on top of a rocky outcrop that juts from the sand into the sea, and somehow spared by the mighty Atlantic waves for the last two millennia, are the remains of the **Castro de Baroña** itself. This once-impregnable pre-Roman settlement consists of the circular stone foundations of several thatched dwellings, as also seen at A Guarda farther south, which were in turn enclosed behind a fortified wall.

Ría de Arousa

Tourism on a significant scale starts to make its presence felt in the next *ría* south, the **RÍA DE AROUSA**. The most popular destination is the old port of **O Grove** – linked by bridge to the island of **A Toxa**, which holds a very upscale enclave of luxury hotels – while much the nicest of the old towns hereabouts is **Cambados**, renowned for its beautiful central plaza. Sadly, both are bypassed by the rail line south from Santiago to Pontevedra and Vigo.

While strip development mars much of the coast, the hillsides just inland are a patchwork of tiny fields, primarily planted with the grapes that go into the delicious local **Albariño wine**. Gourmets will want to sample authentic *pimientos* in the village of **Padrón**.

Padrón

According to legend, St James completed his miraculous posthumous voyage to Galicia by sailing up the Ría de Arousa as far as **PADRÓN**. Accumulated silt from the Río Ulla having left it stranded 12km inland, Padrón is no longer even on the sea, and the old town now consists of a handful of narrow pedestrian lanes squeezed between two busy roads. There's surprisingly little to show for the years of pilgrimage, except an imposing seventeenth-century church of Santiago, where the *padrón* (mooring post) to which the vessel was tied supposedly resides under the high altar.

Padrón is best known as the source of the small green peppers known as **pimientos de Padrón**. Available in summer only, they're served whole, shallow-fried in oil and liberally sprinkled with sea salt. Most are sweet, but around one in ten is memorably hot.

Rosalía de Castro museum

A Matanza • June–Sept Tues–Sat 10am–2pm & 4–8pm, Sun 10am–1.30pm; Oct–May Tues–Sat 10am–1.30pm & 4–7pm, Sun 10am–1.30pm • €2 • ⑳ rosaliadecastro.org

Not far east of old Padrón, just across the tracks from the pink-painted RENFE station, the house of nineteenth-century Galego poet **Rosalía de Castro** is now a **museum**. Unless you're a devotee of her work, the jumble of texts, photographs and bric-a-brac may not hold much interest, but the low-ceilinged rooms furnished in period style have character, and the gardens are pleasant.

INFORMATION   PADRÓN

Turismo Avda. de Compostela (Tues–Sat 10am–1.30pm & 4.15–7pm, Sun 10am–1.30pm; ☎ 627 210 777, ⑳ concellodepadron.es).

ACCOMMODATION, EATING AND DRINKING

O Pementeiro Praza do Castro 3 ☎ 981 810 641, ⑳ restauranteopementeiro.es. Though it serves a full regional menu, this central restaurant is especially renowned for its local peppers. Daily 12.30–2.30pm & 7–11pm.

Pensión Jardín Rúa Salgado Araújo 3 ☎ 981 810 950. The best-value place to stay in Padrón; a beautiful eighteenth-century house, overlooking the park on the edge of the old town. €50

Pulpería Rial Praza das Travesas 13 ☎ 981 811 624. Friendly and attractive octopus and seafood restaurant, on a tiny little square in the heart of the old town. Daily noon–3pm & 6–10.30pm.

8

RÍAS BAIXAS

Catoira

Rianxo

Boiro

Vilagarcía
de Arousa

Caldas
de Reis

Santa Uxía
de Ribeira

Vilaxoán

Río Umia

Vilanova de
Arousa

Ría de Arousa

Illa de
Arousa

Cambados

A Toxa

O Grove

Río Lerez

Reboredo

Lerez

San Vicente
do Mar

Poio

Praia La
Lanzada

Combarro

Pontevedra

Sanxenxo

Marín

Portonovo

Mogor

Illa de
Ons

Lago
Castiñeiras

Ría de Pontevedra

Arcade

Cabo
Udra

San
Simón

Soutomaior

Bueu

Aldan

Moaña

Hío

Cangas

Redondela

Mondariz

Donón

Illas
Cíes

Ría de Vigo

Vigo

Ponteareas

Canido

Porriño

Panxón

Praia de América

Baiona

Gondomar

Salvaterra
do Minho

Ramallosa

Tui

Mougás

Valença
do Minho

PORTUGAL

Oia

Loureza

Goián

N

0   25
kilometres

A Guarda

Río Miño

Monte
SantaTecla

Camposancos

8

Illa de Arousa

The first two towns on the southern shore of the Ría de Arousa, **Vilagarcía de Arousa** and **Vilaxoán**, just over 20km southwest of Padrón, are too industrialized to make worthwhile stops. A little further south, however, a 2km road bridge leads out to the wooded **ILLA DE AROUSA**, which holds some great beaches. Effectively part of the mainland, the island holds a sizeable permanent population, concentrated in the eponymous fishing port at its northern end. Turn south as soon as you cross the bridge to reach a small "natural park", the **Parque Carreirón**. If you're driving, you'll have to leave your car at the point where the island narrows to a mere 50m wide, but you can walk on from here to reach half a dozen fine, isolated beaches, backed by trees and saltwater marshes much loved by migratory water birds.

ACCOMMODATION   **ILLA DE AROUSA**

Camping El Edén Praia do Concerrado ☎ 986 527 378, ⓦ eledencampingplaya.com. The nicest campsite on the island, just before the end of the road to the Parque Carreirón, with rental bungalows (€50) and its own tapas bar. Closed mid-Sept to mid-April. Two people plus car **€22.50**

Hostal Benalua Rúa Méndez Núñez ☎ 986 551 335. Well-equipped if unremarkable hotel, close to the waterfront in the island's only town and offering simple but comfortable en-suite double rooms. **€50**

Cambados

By contrast with most of its neighbours, the village of **CAMBADOS**, 5km south of the Illa de Arousa bridge, is exquisite. Only its historic core, however, set a couple of hundred metres back from the waterfront and easily missed altogether if you're driving along the coast road, deserves such praise. The paved stone **Praza de Fefiñáns** here is an idyllic little spot, overlooked by a seventeenth-century church and lined on all sides with beautiful buildings, several of which hold wine shops and *bodegas*. As the vines crammed into its every spare square centimetre testify, Cambados is the main production centre for Galicia's excellent **Albariño wine**.

The seafront itself is unremarkable, though a small island at its southern end holds the vestiges of a watchtower originally erected to look out for Viking raiders, while the

8

THE WINES OF GALICIA

Thanks largely to the international success of its crisp, dry **Albariño**, which has become the best known of all Spanish white wines, Galicia is now recognized as a premium wine-producing region. The Romans first introduced vines two thousand years ago, growing them on high terraces sculpted by slaves into the banks of rivers like the Miño and Sil. With its mild climate and high rainfall, Galicia is more akin to Portugal than to the rest of Spain – Galego wines, and especially Ribeiro, were much exported to Britain during the seventeenth and eighteenth centuries, before declining relations between Britain and Spain led the Portuguese to develop their own wineries, which produce similar wines to this day.

Technically, "Albariño" is the name of a grape variety, introduced to Galicia by monks who followed the Camino de Santiago all the way from the Rhine during the twelfth century – it translates literally as "white wine from the Rhine". Albariño cultivation centres around the **Rías Baixas** (ⓦ doriasbaixas.com), where around five thousand farmers grow grapes on tiny, scattered plots, often banding together and forming co-operatives to bottle and market their wine. The largest co-operative winery, **Condes de Albarei**, on the main road 2km south of Cambados, is open for guided tours and visits (☎ 986 543 535, ⓦ condesdealbarei.com).

The best-selling wine in Galicia itself is **Ribeiro**, produced in the region around **Ribadavia** on the Río Miño. It comes in both white and red, from such grape varieties as Treixadura, Torrontés and Loureira. The recent success of Albariño having spurred greater quality control, white Ribeiro has lost its previous trademark cloudiness, and is seen as the closest Spanish approximation to the dry Muscadet of France. Ribadavia's tourist office (ⓦ ribadavia .net) organizes guided tours, and can also provide maps and listings for free, self-guided winery visits.

Only the **Ribeira Sacra** region, concentrated along the stunning canyon of the Río Sil (see p.590), produces more red than white wine. That it's not better known is largely because two thirds of it never reaches the market but is drunk by the producers themselves. There are no large wineries or even co-operatives, but the three thousand or so farmers who create it have instigated a tourist route through the region and its vineyards (ⓦ ribeirasacrata.com).

vast seaweed-strewn flats exposed at each low tide play host to legions of redoubtable freelance clam- and cockle-pickers known as *mariscadoras*.

INFORMATION   CAMBADOS

Turismo Praza do Concello (June–Sept daily 10am–2pm & 5–8.30pm; Oct–May Tues–Sat 10am–2pm & 4.30–7.30pm, Sun 10am–2pm; ☎986 520 786, ⓦ cambados.es), close to the ocean.

ACCOMMODATION

Os Pasos Rúa Eduardo Pondal 1 ☎986 542 020, ⓦ hotelospazos.es. Ordinary but perfectly comfortable family-run hotel, in the newer part of town. **€45**

Parador del Albariño Praza Clazada ☎986 542 250, ⓦ parador.es. Centred on a much-expanded seventeenth-century *pazo*, or manor house, just off the waterfront road at the edge of the old town, Cambados' fine parador offers very comfortable rooms and some lovely suites, plus a courtyard bar and a very good restaurant, with a €32 set dinner *menú*. **€193**

EATING AND DRINKING

Bar Laya Praza de Fefiñáns ☎986 542 436. With lots of tree-shaded tables out on the main square, this *bodega* makes a great place to stop for a liquid lunch, sampling the local wines. Daily 10am–1pm.

★ **O'Arco** Rúa Real 14 ☎986 543 355, ⓦ restaurante oarco.es. Extremely welcoming little restaurant, with a few tables out on the street in full view of the nearby Praza de Fefiñáns. The €11 lunch *menú* offers phenomenal value, with a large plate of mixed seafood (including the normally expensive *percebes*) and a delicious *churrasco* (grilled ribs). Daily 1–3pm & 7–10pm.

8 O Grove and A Toxa

At the northern tip of the peninsula that lies across the bay from Cambados, **O GROVE** exists primarily as a family resort. Inexpensive bars and restaurants compete for the attention of summer influx of visitors, while dozens of hotels line the waterfront Rúa Teniente Domínguez and its continuation, Rúa Castelao. The town plays host to a huge Fiesta do Marisco, or Shellfish Festival, on September 14 each year.

Across the bridge, the pine-covered islet of **A TOXA** (La Toja) caters for a completely different clientele. It's very explicitly a playground for the wealthy, with luxury holiday homes and three huge and very expensive hotels set in the forest clearings, and a nine-hole golf course so guests can practise their swing.

Acquariumgalicia

Aquarium June to mid-Oct daily 10am–9pm; mid-Oct to May Fri–Sun 10am–8pm • €10 **Glass-bottomed boats** April–June & Oct 2–4 daily; July–Sept every 30min 10.30am–7.30pm • €15

Just before the village of **Reboredo**, 3km west of O Grove, the **Acquariumgalicia** is among the largest aquariums in Spain. As well as displaying a huge selection of Atlantic marine life, it arranges ninety-minute trips on the *ría* in glass-bottomed boats.

INFORMATION   O GROVE AND A TOXA

Turismo There's a small kiosk by the port of O Grove (June Mon–Sat 10am–2pm & 5–7pm, Sun 11am–2pm; July & Aug Mon–Sat 10am–8pm, Sun 10am–2pm; Sept–May Tues–Sat 10am–2pm & 5–7pm, Sun 11am–2pm; ☎986 731 415, ⓦ turismogrove.com).

ACCOMMODATION

Though **O Grove** holds plenty of accommodation options, those along the seafront tend to be pricey in summer. Even more exclusive and expensive hotels lie across the bridge on **A Toxa**, while the pretty village of **San Vicente do Mar**, 6km west, offers cheaper and quieter alternatives.

Casa Angelina Rúa Torre 4, San Vicente ☎986 738 167, ⓦ casaangelina.com. This attractive modern house, close to the beach at the western end of the peninsula, offers ten comfortable en-suite rooms, the nicest of which have sea-view balconies. **€50**

Gran Hotel Hesperia La Toja A Toxa ☎986 730 050,

ⓦ granhotelhesperia-latoja.com. The most luxurious of A Toxa's three hotels, with extravagant sea-view rooms and three fine restaurants. Spa facilities include a dazzling turquoise indoor pool with a cascading waterfall, while treatments on offer involve liberal use of mineral salts and mud. For a particularly decadent massage, you can even have yourself rubbed with chocolate oil, then given a chocolate body mask. **€179**

Hotel Puente de la Toja Rúa Castelao 206, O Grove ☎ 986 730 761, ⓦ hotelpuentedelatoja.com. The smartest waterfront hotel in O Grove, facing the bridge to the island, can be great value in low season. Rates include breakfast. **€119**

CAMPING

Moreiras Rúa Reboredo 26, Moreiras ☎ 986 731 691, ⓦ campingmoreiras.com. Well-shaded beachfront camp site near the tip of a little inlet 3km west of O Grove, with its own restaurant and shop. They also have bungalows, starting at €59 for two persons. Camping for two with car **€24.45**

Paisaxe II Praia de Area Grande ☎ 986 738 331, ⓦ campingplayapaisaxe.com. Large campsite, just back from the beach near San Vicente, 5km west of O Grove, with rental bungalows from €90 and a restaurant. Closed Nov–March. Camping for two with car **€22**

EATING AND DRINKING

Although the waterfront by the port in O Grove is chock solid with the inevitable *marisquerías*, it holds disappointingly few tapas places.

O Lavandeiro Rúa Hospital 2, O Grove ☎ 986 731 956. Cheap but dependable fishy restaurant, in an appealing little square set slightly back from the port, with a good-value €10 lunch *menú*. Tues–Sun 9am–4pm & 7–11pm.

Ría de Pontevedra

8

Of all the Rías Baixas, the long, narrow **Ría de Pontevedra** is the archetype, its steep and forested sides closely resembling a Scandinavian fjord. **Pontevedra** itself is a lovely old city, set slightly back from the sea at the point where the Río Lérez begins to widen out into the bay. Though it lacks a beach of its own, it makes a good base for excursions along either shore of its *ría*. The **north coast** is the more popular with tourists, with **Sanxenxo** (Sanjenjo) as its best-known resort, but if you want to avoid the crowds, head for the **south coast**, which stretches out past secluded beaches towards the rugged headland, ideal for camping in privacy.

Praia La Lanzada and the north-shore beaches

The southern side of the narrow neck of the peninsula that holds O Grove is adorned with the region's largest beach, the vast golden arc of **PRAIA LA LANZADA**. Packed with sun worshippers in summer and a favourite of windsurfers in winter, the whole strand is best admired from the sloping hillside of the peninsula at its western end. The mainland to the east holds several more excellent **beaches**, often far less crowded than La Lanzada. Most have campsites nearby.

Sanxenxo

The coastal resort of **SANXENXO** (Sanjenjo) lies 10km southeast of La Lanzada, or 17km west of Pontevedra. Together with the barely distinguishable suburb of **Portonovo**, 3km west, it forms the epicentre for Galicia's one real exercise in mass tourism. Not that there's any real large-scale development, just a long succession of little beaches, each with its own crop of largely seasonal small **hotels**. Individually they tend to be nice enough, but cumulatively they're overwhelming, especially as the major attraction for Spanish visitors is the summer **nightlife**, so they're interspersed with bars and clubs that keep going from 10pm until 8am nightly.

Turismo In the marina at the east end of the main Praia de Silgar beach (June–Sept daily 9am–9pm; May–Oct Tues– Sun 9am–2pm & 4–7pm; ☎ 986 720 825, ⓦ sanxenxo.es).

ACCOMMODATION

Antiga Casa de Reis Lugar de Reis 39, Padriñan ☎ 986 690 550, ⓦ antigacasadereis.com. This lovely B&B, set in a restored farmhouse up in the hills 2km northeast of Sanxenxo, offers a great change of pace. All its seven antique-furnished rooms (including one single at €75) have en-suite facilities, and are named for particular grape varieties; this is prime wine-growing territory. **€114**

Hotel Farsund Praia de Areas 54 ☎ 986 729 000, ⓦ hotelfarsund.es. Friendly little hotel, with simple but perfectly adequate rooms, in a quiet area a very short walk from the beach west of central Sanxenxo. Closed Nov–April. **€50**

Illa de Ons

The beautiful **ILLA DE ONS** lies out on the ocean at the mouth of the Ría de Pontevedra. Wilder and more windswept than the nearby Illas Cíes, it's home to a community of fishermen and some interesting birdlife. Good walking tracks here provide terrific views of coast and sea; you can hike round the entire island in about three hours, or climb to the lighthouse and back in just over an hour.

While you arrive at the pretty Praia das Dornas, the eastern shore is indented with half a dozen small but very sandy **beaches**, so it's easy enough to escape the crowds and find your own patch of paradise. The best of the lot is the **Praia de Melide**, a gorgeous stretch of white sand near the northern tip. There are no hotels or other facilities, but it is possible to **camp** for free, within a designated area.

By ferry Ferries run to Illa de Ons daily between mid-July and mid-September, and weekends-only between May and September, costing €14 return. Naviera Mar de Ons sail from Sanxenxo and Portonovo (☎ 986 225 272, ⓦ mardeons.com), as do Cruceiros Rías Baixas (☎ 986 731 343, ⓦ crucerosriasbaixas.com), while Vio Viajes depart from Portonovo and Bueu (☎ 986 320 048, ⓦ isladeons.net).

Combarro and Poio

The fishing village of **COMBARRO**, 7km west of Pontevedra, boasts the largest collection of **hórreos** (stone granaries) in Galicia, lining the waterfront and looking out across the *ría* to Marín. A path cut into the rocks leads from the main square behind the *hórreos*, littered with souvenir shops and poky but atmospheric bars and tavernas, several of which have outdoor tables. During Combarro's **sardine festival**, on June 23, the fish are grilled in the open air on the shore. Inland, the tight streets are lined with little houses, each with Baroque stone balconies and galleries, winding claustrophobically towards the chapel of San Roque at the heart of town.

Monasterio de Poio

Mon–Sat 10.30am–1.30pm & 4.30–8pm, Sun 4.30–8pm • €1.50

Two kilometres east of Combarro, above the modern town of **POIO**, the seventeenth-century Benedictine **MONASTERIO DE POIO** is a haven of calm. Its cloister features a million-piece mosaic mural of the Camino de Santiago, created between 1989 and 1992 by Czech artist Anton Machourek, and there's also an eccentric little museum of tiny books.

Casa Solla Avda. Sineiro 7 ☎ 986 872 884, ⓦ nove.biz /es/solla. Very fancy, expensive modern restaurant, on the main road through Poio, offering delicious gourmet food and good views over the fields. The set tasting *menú* costs €61, and there's a gourmet version at €85. Tues, Wed, Fri & Sat 1.30–3.45pm & 9–11.30pm, Thurs & Sun 1.30–3.45pm.

Monasterio de Poio ☎ 986 770 000, ⊛ mercedarios
.com. The stately monastery of Poio also contains a
wonderful *hospedaría*, modern and efficient despite the
age and beauty of its setting, and with a *cafetería* that
serves all meals daily. Cafeteria daily 8am–8pm. **€45**

Pontevedra

Compact, charming and very tourist friendly, **PONTEVEDRA** is the quintessential old
Galego town. Located just short of its namesake *ría*, at the last bend in the Río Lérez, it
was supposedly founded by a Greek hero returning from the Trojan War, and later
became a prosperous medieval fishing port. Although it has lost its ancient walls, it still
centres on an attractive *zona monumental*. A maze of pedestrianized flagstoned
alleyways, interspersed with colonnaded squares, granite crosses and squat stone houses

PONTEVEDRA

ACCOMMODATION

Boa Vila	2
Casa Alicia	5
Casa Maruja	4
Hotel Madrid	6
Hotel Rúas	3
Parador Casa del Barón	1

TAPAS, CAFÉS & RESTAURANTS

La Carabela	6
O Cortello	2
Fidel O Pulpeiro	1
Jaqueyvi	5
Os Maristas	4
La Tienda da Clara	3

8

with floral balconies, the old quarter is always lively, making it perfect for a night out enjoying the local food and drink.

Prazas da Peregrina and da Ferrería

Two adjoining squares connect Pontevedra's old and new quarters. The **Praza da Peregrina** holds a pilgrim chapel, the **Santuario de la Peregrina**, a tall, eye-catching Baroque structure with a floor plan in the shape of a scallop shell, while the **Praza da Ferrería** is a paved square lined by arcades on one side and rose trees on the other. On its eastern side, the town's main church, **San Francisco**, is best admired from outside. Amid the surrounding fountains, gardens, and open-air cafés, all the daily rituals of life in a small town take place, especially during the Sunday *paseo*, when the entire population hits the streets. It's also the prime location for the city's many festivals, the busiest of which, **Os Maios**, lasts through the whole of May.

Museo de Pontevedra

Praza da Leña • June–Sept Tues–Sat 10am–9pm, Sun 11am–2pm; Oct–May Tues–Sat 10am–2pm & 4–7pm, Sun 11am–2pm • Free • Ⓦ museo.depo.es

Pontevedra's **zona monumental** can be accessed via any of the narrow lanes that lead north from Praza da Ferrería. Rúa Figueroa swiftly reaches the attractive little complex of old stone houses adjoining the picture-postcard **Praza da Leña**, which holds the elegant and well-conceived **Museo de Pontevedra**. This traces local history from megaliths and hand axes, via pre-Roman gold and silver, to the modern era.

As well as a large model of Christopher Columbus' flagship, the *Santa María*, which was built in Pontevedra and is also known, here at any rate, as *La Galega*, there's also a strange underground chamber remodelled to evoke the officers' room of the *Numancia*, Spain's first battleship, built in 1862. Three rooms are dedicated to the artist and writer Alfonso Castelao, who was driven into exile during the Franco years, and died in Argentina in 1950. His beautifully observed paintings, drawings and cartoons, at their most moving when depicting pre war poverty and the horror of the Civil War, celebrate the strength and resilience of the Galego people.

The Alameda and around

Leading down from Praza de España towards the sea, the **Alameda** is a grand promenade watched over by magnificent buildings and dotted with monuments commemorating largely naval achievements. Slightly off the Alameda stands a **statue of Christopher Columbus**. Some locals even claim the navigator was a native son who decided to pass himself off as Genoese.

ARRIVAL AND DEPARTURE   PONTEVEDRA

By train and bus Both stations are about 1km southeast of the centre, side by side, and connected to the town centre by half-hourly buses from the bus station (€1). At least one local bus hourly connects the bus station with each of Cambados, Cangas, O Grove and Vigo; each route takes an hour or less.

By car If you're driving, you won't be able to penetrate the historic core; it's best to park on the fringes, in the big car parks under Rúa Santa Clara and Praza de España.

INFORMATION

Turismo Praza da Verdura, in the old town (summer daily 9am–2pm & 4–8pm; winter Mon–Sat 9.30am–2pm & 4.30–7.30pm, Sun 10am–2pm; Ⓦ visit-pontevedra.com, Ⓣ 986 090 890).

ACCOMMODATION

Finding good **accommodation** in Pontevedra is a little challenging. While it's definitely preferable to stay in the winding streets of the **zona monumental**, where there is at least a good parador, that area holds very few mid-range options, so you may well have to settle for a plain, simple budget alternative. Hotels in the new town tend to be characterless and overpriced.

Boa Vila Rúa Real 4–6 ☎986 105 265 ⓦhotelboavila .es. Housed above a bar/restaurant in an attractive townhouse in the heart of old Pontevedra, this nicely decorated ten-room B&B features exposed stonework and period furnishings. Rates include breakfast. **€60**

Casa Alicia Avda. de Santa María 5 ☎986 857 079. Four good-value, well-kept rooms, all en suite, in a pleasant house on the edge of the old quarter. **€40**

Casa Maruja Avda. de Santa María 12 ☎986 854 901. Very plain but clean and perfectly acceptable en-suite rooms, just inside the old quarter; the garish bathrooms are far from soothing at the end of a hard day. **€38**

Hotel Madrid Rúa Andrés Mellado 5 ☎986 865 180, ⓦhotelmadrid.org. A somewhat anonymous hotel, a short walk south of La Peregrina in the newer part of town.

Its standard modern rooms are light and spacious, making it a good-value alternative. **€50**

Hotel Rúas Rúa Figueroa 5 ☎986 846 416, ⓦhotelruas.net. This handsome building is in an excellent location, near the museum and tourist office with entrances on two of Pontevedra's squares, and has its own good restaurant. Many of its en-suite rooms are a little small – though some sleep four – and if you want a quiet night you're better off choosing one without an external window. **€55**

Parador Casa del Barón Rúa del Barón 19 ☎986 855 800, ⓦparador.es. Elegant but delightfully cosy and well-priced parador, housed in a historic stone mansion that's tucked into a tiny square in the heart of the old quarter, with a little off-street parking. **€110**

EATING AND DRINKING

The twisting streets of old Pontevedra are packed with tiny **bars** and **restaurants**, especially jammed with late-night revellers at weekends. When it comes to **tapas bars**, the choice is almost overwhelming. Prime areas to start exploring include the *zona*'s prettiest squares: the tiny **Praza da Cinco Rúas** is a central hub, from which five streets lined with bars run spoke-like in all directions; the arcaded **Praza da Verdura** is a lively nightlife centre, where several bars have open-air tables; and the elegant **Praza Teucro**, with its orange trees, holds some grown-up wine bars.

La Carabela Praza da Ferrería ☎986 581 245. Named for Columbus' flagship, this grand old café has been the favourite rendezvous on Pontevedra's central square for generations; huddle over morning coffee inside, or savour evening drinks and free peanuts at the numerous outdoor tables. Daily 8am–1am.

O Cortello Rúa Isabel II 36 ☎986 840 043. This dark, rustic tapas bar, tucked just behind the Santa María church, takes a little finding. Filled with quirky, witchy junk, it's totally wonderful and remarkably cheap, selling *raciones* of seafood empanada for €3, all kinds of shellfish for well under €10, and cheap wine in china cups and jugs. Daily noon–3.30pm & 7–10.30pm.

Fidel O Pulpeiro Rúa San Nicolás 7 ☎986 851 234. Central, simple *mesón*, just off the Praza da Cinco Rúas, with glaring lights and white tables but big helpings of fabulous fresh octopus and seafood. Daily 1–3pm & 7–11pm.

Jaqueyvi Rúa Dona Tareixa 1 ☎986 861 820. When you've had your fill of seafood, come to this smart bar, in front of the Teátro Municipal, for traditional Galician hams and cheeses. Friendly and intimate, with the odd formal touch, it serves mixed platters at good prices, along with excellent local wines. Daily 11am–4pm & 6pm–12.30am.

★ **Os Maristas** Praza da Verdura 5 ☎986 844 075. Busy bar with a lot of outdoor seating, that serves a full menu of *raciones* but is renowned for the astonishing liqueur, Tumba Dios, an esoteric but fearsome blend of *aguardiente* (firewater) and *vino de pasas* (raisin wine), laced with coffee plus sundry secret herbs and spices. Daily 10am–3pm & 7pm–midnight.

La Tienda da Clara Praza de Teucro 16 ☎986 102 071. The town's fanciest upscale tapas, as well as fine wines and beer, to be relished at outdoor tables that spread out across Rúa Princesa onto the attractive Praza de Teucro. Daily 1–3.30pm & 7pm–2am.

The southern shore

Though the first stretch of the Ría de Pontevedra's southern side is extremely ugly, those who press on beyond the military town of **Marín**, 7km southwest of Pontevedra, will be amply rewarded with a series of gorgeous and largely deserted little bays. **Buses** from Pontevedra's Praza de Galicia run right around the headland and along the southern shore of the *ría*.

Praia de Mogor

Beyond Marín the bay broadens into a series of breathtaking sandy coves. A narrow side-road drops away from the main coast road immediately beyond the naval academy outside Marín, leading to three beaches. The second of these, the **Praia de Mogor**, is perfect, with fields of green corn as the backdrop to a crescent of fine, clean sand, one end of which is shielded by a thick headland of dark green pines. There are a couple of seasonal bar-cum-restaurants overgrown with vines, and the villagers' rowing boats are pulled up in the shade of the trees.

Ría de Vigo

The **Ría de Vigo** ranks among the most sublime natural harbours in the world. Its narrowest point is spanned by a vast suspension bridge that carries the Vigo–Pontevedra highway; you'll see its twin towers from all around the bay. On the inland side is what amounts to a saltwater lake, the inlet of **San Simón**. The road and railway from Pontevedra run beside it to **Redondela**, separated from the sea by just a thin strip of green fields, and pass close to the tiny San Martín islands, once a leper colony and used during the Civil War as an internment centre for Republicans. Beneath these waters lies a fleet of Spanish bullion galleons, sunk by a combined Anglo-Dutch force at the Battle of Rande in 1703.

The city of **Vigo** looks very appealing, spread along the waterfront, but although it makes a good base for trips along the south shore to **Baiona**, across the bay to **Cangas**, and, especially, out to the wonderful **Illas Cíes**, it has few attractions of its own.

Cangas

The prime reason to visit the ever-growing resort of **CANGAS**, facing Vigo across the *ría*, is to enjoy the superb twenty-minute **ferry** ride from Vigo. During the crossing, watch out for the *mejilloneiras* – ramshackle rafts, perched on the bay like water-spiders and sometimes topped by little wooden huts, which are used for cultivating mussels.

Cangas is at its most lively during the Friday **market**, when the seafront gardens are filled with stalls. Otherwise, the **Praia de Rodeira**, a ten-minute walk from the ferry jetty – turn right as you get off, then follow the seafront – is a beautiful five-hundred-metre sandy beach with majestic views.

The beaches and hills west of Cangas are stunning and all but deserted. The best target is the **Praia de Melide**, at the tip of the peninsula 2km beyond **Donón**. An isolated cove backed by woods and a lighthouse, it offers superb walks along the cape.

ARRIVAL AND INFORMATION | CANGAS

By bus and ferry Frequent ferry services between Cangas and Vigo operate daily (from Vigo 6.30am–10.30pm; from Cangas 6am–10pm; €4.10 return, €3 if the outbound trip is before 9am; ⓦ mardeons.es). Ferries to the Illas Cíes also leave from here in summer (June–Sept 4 daily; 1hr;

€18.50), and there's a bus station alongside the jetty used by buses to and from Pontevedra and Vigo.
Turismo Cangas' *turismo* is right where the ferries dock (daily 10am–2pm & 4–8pm; ⓣ 986 300 875, ⓦ cangas.org).

ACCOMMODATION AND EATING

A considerable main cluster of **bars and restaurants** surrounds the port in Cangas.

Bar Celta Rúa Alfredo Saralegui 28 ⓣ 986 300 088. Excellent old-fashioned tapas bar, looking out over the bay from the steps that rise slightly to the left of the jetty as you face the town, serving fresh seafood *raciones* at good prices. Daily noon–11pm.
Hostal Prado Viejo Rúa Ramón Cabanillas 16, Moaña ⓣ 986 311 634, ⓦ pradoviejo.com. Pleasant hotel in Cangas' closest neighbour, Moana, 5km east, which has

stylish en-suite rooms with floor-to-ceiling windows, a smart seafood restaurant, and private parking. **€55**
Hotel Airiños Avda. Eugenio Sequeiros 30, Cangas ⓣ 986 304 000, ⓦ airinos.com. This modern hotel offers comfortable sea-view rooms on the inland side of Cangas' waterfront public park, and also holds a decent restaurant. **€85**
Hotel Playa Avda. Ourense 78, Cangas ⓣ 986 301 363,

⚐ hotel-playa.com. Good-value hotel, right on the beach in the middle of the Praia de Rodeira, and open year-round.

As well as tasteful, well-equipped rooms, they also offer self-catering apartments of various sizes. **€63**

Castillo de Soutomaior

Daily except Mon: summer 11am–2pm & 5–9pm, winter 11am–2pm & 4–7pm• €1.50 • ⚐ cameliagalicia.com

A worthwhile detour 2km east of the village of Arcade, north of Vigo on the old road to Pontevedra, leads to the twelfth-century hill-top **castle of Soutomaior**. The rambling halls and towers of the castle itself are used for temporary exhibitions, while its superb landscaped grounds are planted with mighty sequoias and other exotic species. One former inhabitant travelled to Samarkand early in the fifteenth century, as ambassador to the court of Tamerlane the Great.

ACCOMMODATION   **CASTLE OF SOUTOMAIOR**

Pousada del Castillo de Soutomaior ☎ 986 705 105, ⚐ hotelpousadadelcastillo.com. This lovely rural hotel, in the grounds of the castle, makes a gorgeous place to stay, even though very few of its rooms have the views you'd expect of such a location. **€80**

Vigo

Few cities enjoy such a magnificent natural setting as **VIGO**. Arrayed along the sloping southern shoreline of its namesake estuary, it enjoys superb views not only of the bay itself, surrounded by green forest ridges, but also out towards the ocean. While it's undeniably magnificent when seen from a ship entering the harbour, once ashore it fails to live up to that initial promise, and few visitors use it as anything more than an overnight stop.

Although Vigo is now the largest city in Galicia, home to some 300,000 people, Baiona, closer to the mouth of the *ría*, was the principal port hereabouts until the nineteenth century. Then the railways arrived, and Vigo became the first Galego town to industrialize, with the opening of several sardine canneries. It's now Spain's chief fishing port, with wharves and quays that stretch almost 5km along the shore.

Pride of place in the middle still belongs to the passenger port where generations of Galego emigrants have embarked for the Americas. These days, cruise passengers mingle with tourists arriving at the **Estación Marítima de Ría** off the Cangas ferry, and set off to explore the steep, cobbled streets that climb up into the old city, known as **O Berbés** and crammed with shops, bars and restaurants.

Along the seafront early in the morning, kiosks revive fishermen with strong coffee, while there and in the lively daily market hall nearby, the **Mercado da Pedra**, their catch is sold. Immediately below, on the aptly named **Rúa da Pescadería**, women set out plates of fresh oysters on permanent granite tables to tempt passers-by. On **Rúa Carral**, shops sell kitsch marine souvenirs.

Castro hill

A stiff but enjoyable climb up from the old town, mostly along stone staircases, brings you to the top of the **Castro hill**. So named for the circular ancient ruins still visible on one side, and also the site of a seventeenth-century castle, the hill enjoys comprehensive views.

Museo Quiñones de León

Tues, Thurs & Fri 10am–1.30pm & 5–8pm, Wed 10am–8pm, Sat 5–8pm, Sun 10am–1.30pm • Free • ⚐ museodevigo.org

The **Museo Quiñones de León** is the focal point of the large **Parque de Castrelos**, the extensive formal gardens and woodlands of which begin 2km southwest of Castro hill. Set in an attractive old manor house, it's one of Galicia's best museums, covering both

8

the archeology and history of Vigo and its region. It also boasts a fine collection of Galego art.

The beaches

Most of the **beaches** near Vigo are crowded and unappealing. Farther south, however, the beach at **Samil** is better, while those at **Vao** and **Canido**, further on, are also quite reasonable, and are equipped with campsites.

ARRIVAL AND DEPARTURE   VIGO

By plane Vigo's airport, 9km east of the city on bus route #9A, is served by Vueling flights from London Gatwick and Barcelona (ⓦ vueling.com).

By train Vigo's RENFE station is 500m southeast of the old town.

Destinations A Coruña (15 daily; 2hr); Barcelona (2 daily; 14–15hr); Burgos (4 daily; 7–8hr); Irún (daily; 11hr 30min); León (5 daily; 6hr); Madrid (2 daily; 7hr 30min–10hr); Ponferrada (6 daily; 4–5hr); Pontevedra (15–18 daily; 30min); Santiago de Compostela (15 daily; 1hr 30min).

By bus Vigo's bus station is 500m south of the RENFE station, making it 1km southeast of the old town. Local buses #12 and #12B (all €1; ⓦ vitrasa.es) run via the train station to the Porta do Sol in the old town.

Destinations A Coruña (9 daily; 2hr 15min); Baiona (every 15min; 1hr); Cangas (20 daily; 1hr); Lugo (5–6 daily; 3hr); Madrid (3 daily; 8hr); O Grove (2 daily; 1hr 15min); Oporto and Lisbon (3 weekly; 3hr 30min/6hr); Ourense (13 daily; 2hr); Oviedo (daily; 6hr 15min); Pontevedra (every 30min; 30min–1hr); Ribadavia (13 daily; 1hr 30min); Santiago de Compostela (hourly; 1hr 30min–2hr); Tui (every 30min; 45min).

By car The most convenient central car parks are on the seafront at Rúa das Avenidas, and beneath the Porta do Sol.

INFORMATION

Turismo Avda. Cánovas del Castillo 22, just up from the port (July & Aug Mon–Fri 9.30am–2pm & 4.30–7.30pm, Sat 10am–1.30pm; Sept–June Mon–Fri 9.30am–2pm & 4.30–6.30pm, Sat 10am–1.30pm; ☎ 986 430 577, ⓦ www.turismodevigo.es).

ACCOMMODATION

Vigo's **hotels** are concentrated in two main areas: around the old town, down by the port, which is close to the best restaurants and bars; and in the less atmospheric streets up by the train station.

Hostal Ancla Dorada Rúa Irmandiños 2 ☎ 986 223 403, ⓦ ancladorada.com. Welcoming family hotel, 200m west from the train station towards the old town, with clean, simple rooms, some with shared bathrooms and some sleeping up to four. Free wi-fi. **€43**

Hotel Águila Rúa Victoria 6 ☎ 986 431 398, ⓦ hotelaguila.com. Old-fashioned but well-equipped hotel near the Porta do Sol, with bags of charm. All rooms are en suite, though some are a bit small. Rates include breakfast. **€50**

★ **Hotel Puerta Gamboa** Rúa Gamboa 12 ☎ 986 228 674, ⓦ hotelpuertagamboa.com. Very friendly family-run hotel, set in a charming nineteenth-century house in the old town, just a few steps from the ferry port. All eleven rooms are en suite, with good facilities including wi-fi; some have large balconies. Rates include breakfast, and drop considerably in low season. **€105**

Hotel Puerta del Sol Rúa Porta do Sol 14 ☎ 986 222 364, ⓦ alojamientosvigo.com. Clean, very central hotel that offers small but pleasant en-suite rooms, with TV and wi-fi, plus a couple of five-person apartments. Good off-season and weekend discounts. **€72**

EATING AND DRINKING

Virtually all of the **bars** in Vigo's old quarter serve great tapas. Rúa da Pescadería is the liveliest place for **lunch**, at an outdoor table among the oyster sellers.

Marisquería Bahía Rúa da Pescadería ☎ 986 449 655, ⓦ marisqueriabahia.com. Taking up most of one side of the so-called "street of oysters", this is said to be allegedly the largest seafood restaurant in Spain. Decorated with an odd mixture of underwater scenes and antelope heads, it serves predictably excellent seafood, and prices aren't too steep, starting at around €15. Daily 11am–5pm & 8.30pm–12am, closed Wed in winter.

El Mosquito Praza da Pedra 4 ☎ 986 433 570, ⓦ elmosquitovigo.com. Crowds flock to this intimate family-run restaurant for the city's finest Gallego cuisine, with seafood the speciality; just be prepared to pay significantly more than you would in a typical raciones place. Mon–Sat 1.30–4pm & 8pm–midnight, closed mid-Aug to mid-Sept.

Taberna da Curuxa Rúa dos Cesteiros 7 ☎986 438 857. Top-quality *raciones*, from *pimientos* to squid in all forms, in a deliberately rustic setting just off Praza de Constitución in the heart of the old town. Daily except Tues 11.30am–4.30pm & 8.30pm–midnight.

The Illas Cíes

The most irresistible sands of the Ría de Vigo adorn the three islands of the **Illas Cíes**, which can be reached by boat from Vigo, and (less regularly) from Baiona and Cangas. Sprawling across the entrance to the *ría*, battered by the open Atlantic on one side but sheltering delightful sandy beaches where they face the mainland, the islands were long used by raiders such as Sir Francis Drake as hide-outs from which to ambush Spanish shipping, but are now a nature reserve. The most southerly, **Illa de San Martiño**, is an off-limits bird sanctuary; the other two, **Illa do Monte Ayudo** and **Illa do Faro**, are joined by a narrow causeway of sand, which cradles a placid lagoon on its inland side.

Most visitors stay on the sands, with their sprinkling of bars and a campsite in the trees, so if you want to escape the crowds, it's easy to find a deserted spot – particularly on the Atlantic side. From the beach, a long climb up a winding rocky path across desolate country leads to a lighthouse with a commanding ocean view. The islands' campsite has a small shop and restaurant, but if you're on a budget you're better off taking your own supplies.

ARRIVAL AND DEPARTURE   ILLAS CÍES   **8**

Ferries Mar de Ons ferries (40min; €18.50 return; ☎986 438 358, ⓦmardeons.com) run from Estación Marítima in Vigo from July until the second Sunday of September (12 daily; first leaves Vigo at 9.15am, last leaves Cíes at 8pm), and less frequently from the last weekend in May to end of June, and during the second half of September (4 daily; first leaves Vigo at 10.15am, last leaves Cíes at 7pm). From Cangas and Baiona, they run only between July and the first week of September (4 daily from each; first leaves Cangas at 9.45am, last return leaves Cíes at 7pm; first leaves Baiona at 10am, last return leaves Cíes at 6.45pm). Only a certain number of visitors are allowed to visit the Cíes on any one day, so aim for an early boat.

ACCOMMODATION

Camping Islas Cíes ☎986 687 630, ⓦcampingislascies .com. This gloriously sited campsite is the only accommodation option on the islands; if you want to stay in mid-season, book ahead to make sure there's space. It has its own shop, café and restaurant. Closed Oct–May. Per person **€8**

Baiona

BAIONA (Bayona), 21km south of Vigo, is situated just before the open sea at the head of a miniature *ría*, the smallest and southernmost in Galicia. This small and colourful port, which nowadays makes a healthy living from its upscale tourist trade, was the first place in Europe to hear of the discovery of the New World. On March 1, 1493, Columbus' *Pinta* made its triumphant return to Spain; the event is commemorated by numerous sculptures scattered around the town. An exact replica of the *Pinta* (daily 10am–8.30pm; €2) is moored in the harbour, which these days contains pleasure yachts rather than fishing boats.

The **medieval walls** that surround the wooded promontory adjoining Baiona enclose an idyllic parador (see p.586). It's definitely worth paying the €1 fee to walk around the parapet, which provides a series of changing, unobstructed views across the *ría* to the chain of rocky islets that leads to the Illas Cíes. Another hugely enjoyable footpath circles beneath the walls at sea level, and provides access to several diminutive beaches. These are not visible from the town proper, which despite its fine esplanade has only a small, if attractive, patch of sand.

Praia de América

Galicia's best-known **beach** lies 2km east of Baiona, across the mouth of the bay. The **Praia de América** is a superb, long curve of clean sand that remains surprisingly underdeveloped considering its reputation, lined at a discreet distance by imposing suburban villas, only a few of which hold hotels or other businesses. A coastal footpath leads north to the beach from the village of **Ramallosa**, on the seafront Vigo–Baiona highway, near the spot where a splendid little Roman bridge crosses the Río Miñor.

ARRIVAL AND INFORMATION   BAIONA

By bus Buses between Vigo and A Guarda stop near the seafront, close to the tourist office and parador.
Turismo Baiona's seafront *turismo* is alongside the gate that leads up to the *parador* (April, May & Sept–Dec

Mon–Fri 10am–2pm & 3–7pm; June Mon–Sat 10am–2pm & 4–8pm, Sun 11am–2pm & 4–8pm; July & Aug daily 10am–3pm & 4–9pm; ☎ 986 687 067, ⊚ baiona.org).

ACCOMMODATION

Hotel Tres Carabelas Rúa Ventura Misa 61 ☎ 986 355 133, ⊚ hoteltrescarabelas.com. Good-value hotel in a narrow pedestrianized street one block inland, where each of the ten en-suite rooms honours a particular hero of the sea, from Robinson Crusoe to Moby Dick. **€88**
★ **Parador Conde de Gondomar** Monte Real ☎ 986 355 000, ⊚ parador.es. It's hard to imagine any better location than Baiona's gorgeous parador, which, though totally surrounded on the headland by genuine medieval walls, is actually a modern version of a traditional Galego manor house. The rooms are spacious and comfortable, with superb views, and as well as two restaurants, it holds a couple of bars, both open to non-residents, one of which stands alone in the grounds. **€150**
Pazo de Mendoza Rúa Elduayen 1 ☎ 986 385 014, ⊚ pazodemendoza.com. Appealing twelve-room hotel,

in a converted manor house adjoining the Praza Pedro de Castro on Baiona's seafront esplanade with sea views. **€109**

CAMPING

Bayona Playa Praia Ladeira, Sabaris ☎ 986 350 035, ⊚ www.campingbayona.com. While the beach itself isn't as good as Praia de América, the waterfront setting of this campsite, 1km east of town on a long spit of land with the sea to one side and an inland lagoon to the other, is magnificent. Bungalows from **€144**. Pitches with car **€21.50**
Playa América Nigran ☎ 986 365 404, ⊚ campingplayaamerica.com. Huge campsite beside Baiona's best beach, 2km across the bay. Rates for the plentiful rental bungalows start at **€105**. Mid-March to mid-Oct. Pitches with car **€20**

EATING AND DRINKING

Seafood **restaurants** abound on Praza Pedro de Castro and along Rúa Ventura Misa, most with tanks stuffed full of doomed marine creatures. Ventura Misa is also the hub of the town's **nightlife**, with several bars and pubs staying open late.

Jaqueyvi Rúa de Reloxo 2 ☎ 986 356 773. Smart little restaurant that specializes in rice with fish. Daily 11am–4pm & 6pm–midnight.
El Túnel Rúa Ventura Misa 21 ☎ 986 355 109,

⊚ restauranteeltunel.com. Top-quality seafood place, with outdoor seating on a pleasant, sheltered square just off the seafront. Daily noon–3.30pm & 7.30–10.30pm.

Oia

The C550 highway continues due south for 30km from Baiona to the mouth of the Río Miño, which marks the frontier with **Portugal**. Once a windswept wilderness, this straight stretch of coastline is now scattered with *hostales* and hotels. There are no beaches, but the sight of the ocean foaming through the rocks is mightily impressive.

Immediately around the first curve from Baiona, a massive granite statue known as the **Virgen de la Roca** towers above the sea; on appropriately solemn religious occasions, devotees climb up inside it and onto the boat she holds in her right hand. Halfway between Baiona and A Guarda, beneath the town of **OIA** – itself little more than a very tight bend in the road – nestles a remarkable Baroque **monastery**, with its sheer stone facade surviving the constant battering of the ocean.

ACCOMMODATION OIA

Talaso Atlántico As Mariñas, Mougas ☎ 986 385 090, ⓦ talasoatlantico.com. Facing dramatically out to sea from the hillside above the monastery at Oia, this spa-hotel specializes in thalassotherapy, or seawater treatment. Between relaxing in the large, heated indoor seawater pool, with its huge picture windows and assorted high-pressure jets, guests can sample a wide range of seaweed wraps and beauty treatments. **€160**

A Guarda

Just short of the mouth of the Miño, the workaday port of **A GUARDA** (La Guardia) is largely the modern creation of emigrants returned from Puerto Rico. The extensive remains of a **celta** – a pre-Roman fortified hill settlement – stand just above the town in the thick pine woods of **Monte Santa Tecla**, reached by a stiff thirty-minute climb or an easy drive.

Monte Santa Tecla
Archeological museum March–Nov daily 9.30am–11pm • €1

Occupied between roughly 600 and 200 BC, the *celta* was abandoned when the Romans established control over the north. The site consists of the foundations of well over a hundred circular dwellings, crammed tightly inside an encircling wall. A couple of them have been restored as full-size thatched huts; most are excavated to a metre or so, though some are still buried. On the north slope of the mountain there is also a large **cromlech**, or stone circle, while continuing upwards you pass along an avenue of much more recent construction, lined with the Stations of the Cross, and best seen looming out of a mountain mist. Five minutes farther on, at the top, are a church, a small **archeological museum** of Celtic finds from the mountain, two restaurants and a hotel.

Camposancos
While A Guarda itself has a couple of small **beaches**, there's a better stretch of sand at the village of **Camposancos** about 4km south, facing Portugal and a small islet capped by the ruins of a fortified Franciscan monastery.

ARRIVAL AND INFORMATION A GUARDA

By bus ATSA buses (every 30min from Tui; 2 daily from Baiona) arrive at the small Praza Avelino Vicente, well above the port.
By ferry Camposancos is connected by ferry across the Río Miño with Caminha in Portugal (daily: every 30min summer 9.30am–10.30pm, winter until 7.30pm; pedestrians €1, car & driver €3 one way).
Turismo A Guarda has a seasonal *turismo* at Rúa Praza do Reló 1 (June–Sept daily 9am–3pm & 7–9pm; ☎ 986 614 546, ⓦ aguarda.es).

ACOMMODATION, EATING AND DRINKING

Anduriña Rúa do Porto 58 ☎ 986 611 108, ⓦ restauranteandurinha.com. Friendly, high-quality seafood restaurant, the pick of the crop along the seafront in the heart of town. Daily 1–4.30pm & 7.30–11.30pm; closed Sun in low season, plus all Nov.
Hotel Convento de San Benito Praza San Benito ☎ 986 611 166, ⓦ hotelsanbenito.es. Much the best hotel in A Guarda, in the beautiful old Benedictine convent right by the port. The ten antique-furnished rooms have great sea views. **€77**
Hotel Pazo Santa Tecla Monte Santa Tecla ☎ 986 610 002. One-star hotel, poised above the *celta* at the top of Monte Santa Tecla, and boasting glorious views along the coast and the Río Miño; all rooms are en suite. **€65**

8

Tui

TUI (Tuy, pronounced *twee*), 24km inland along the Miño from A Guarda and roughly the same distance south of Vigo, is the principal Galego frontier town on the river, staring across to the neat ramparts of Portuguese **Valença do Minho**. While Valença is a much more compelling destination – its old quarter is positively delightful – Tui does have its moments. The old town stands back from the river, tiered amid trees and stretches of ancient walls above the fertile riverbank. Sloping lanes, paved with huge slabs of granite, climb to the imposing fortress-like **Catedral** dedicated to San Telmo, patron saint of fishermen, while a pair of enticing little river beaches lie on the far side of the old town from the main street.

A fifteen-minute walk out of town leads to the Portuguese border, by way of an iron bridge designed by Eiffel. The ravishing little town of **VALENÇA DO MINHO**, dwarfed behind its mighty ramparts, lies a similar distance beyond. There's no border control at the bridge: just stroll (or drive) across and head up the hill to the centre.

ARRIVAL AND INFORMATION   TUI

By train If you're coming by train from Ribadavia or Ourense, it's much quicker to go to Guillarei station, a 3km taxi ride east of town, than to wait for a connection to Tui itself.

By bus Tui has regular bus connections with Vigo and A Guarda.

Turismo Praza do Concello 1 (April–Dec Mon–Fri 10am–8pm, Sat & Sun 10am–2.30pm & 3.30–7.30pm; ☎677 418 405).

ACCOMMODATION

Hostal La Generosa Paseo Calvo Sotelo 37 ☎986 600 055. The simple rooms at this gracefully ageing hotel, on old Tui's acacia-lined main street opposite the bus stop, offer amazing value for budget travellers. **€30**

Hotel Colón Rúa Colón 11 ☎986 600 223, ⓦhotelcolontuy.com. Modern hotel with large,

comfortable rooms, a pool and great views across to Valença. Rates include breakfast. **€92**

Parador San Telmo Avda. Portugal s/n ☎986 600 300, ⓦparador.es. Tui's imposing parador, out near the border with Portugal, features extensive landscaped grounds with a good swimming pool and tennis courts. **€161**

EATING AND DRINKING

O Novo Cabalo Furado Praza do Concello 3 ☎986 602 263, ⓦonovocabalofurado.com. Next to the cathedral, the more formal offshoot of the *Vello Cabalo* is the best of Tui's surprisingly small handful of restaurants. If money's no object, this is the place to sample the local speciality,

angulas, baby eels from the river. Daily noon–3pm & 8–11pm.

O Vello Cabalo Furado Rúa Seixas 2 ☎986 603 800. Good and very affordable *raciones*, a block down from the cathedral. Daily noon–4pm & 8pm–midnight.

Inland Galicia

While most visitors to Galicia concentrate their attentions on Santiago and the coast, the interior of the region can be both spectacular and intriguing. The **Romans** were always more interested in mining gold from inland Galicia than they were in its coastline, and some remarkable vestiges of their ancient occupation still survive, including the terraced vineyards along the stupendous **canyon of the Río Sil**, and the intact walls of unspoiled **Lugo**. The obvious route for exploring the region is the one used by the Romans, following the beautiful **Río Miño** upstream, via towns such as **Ribadavia** and **Ourense**, and through the wine regions of **Ribeiro** and **Ribeira Sacra**.

Ribadavia

Roughly 60km east of either Vigo or Tui along the A52 motorway, but more pleasantly approached by following the N120 highway or the train line up the lovely valley of the

Miño – which tends to fill with mist every morning – the riverside town of **RIBADAVIA** is a good deal grander than its size might promise. Centre for a thousand years of the Ribeiro wine industry, it's home to a number of several fine churches and a sprawling **Dominican monastery**.

Ribadeo also holds an interesting **Barrio Xudeo** (Jewish Quarter), dating back to the eleventh century, when the town's first Jewish immigrants arrived. By the fourteenth century, Jews had become half the town's population, and formed one of the most important and prosperous Jewish communities in Spain, although many were forced to convert to Catholicism during the Inquisition.

Head for the tiny square behind the Iglesia de la Magdalena for a wonderful view of the hillside terraces. Immediately above the central Praza Maior, which is home to several good bar-restaurants, look out for the remains of the small but quaint **Castillo de los Condes de Ribadavia**.

INFORMATION   RIBADAVIA

Turismo Ribadavia's *turismo* is in a Baroque former palace on the central Praza Maior (July–Sept daily 9.30am–1.30pm & 4–8pm; Oct–June Mon–Fri 9.30am–2.30pm & 4–6.30pm, Sat 10.30am–2.30pm & 4–6.30pm, Sun 10.30am–2.30pm; ☎ 988 471 275, ⓦ ribadavia.travel).

ACCOMMODATION

Hostal Plaza Praza Maior 15 ☎ 988 470 576, ⓦ hostalplazaribadavia.com. The only hotel in the old town, with good en-suite rooms and its own restaurant. €40

Celanova

Monastery daily 9am–2pm & 4–7pm, tours hourly • €1.50 • ☎ 988 432 201

Little **CELANOVA**, 35km southeast of Ribadavia and best reached along the high and winding road that follows the south bank of the Miño, is hardly more than a village. Its long, narrow main square is appealingly overshadowed by a vast and palatial **Benedictine monastery**, officially known as the Monasterio de San Salvador. Felipe V retired into monastic life here, having spent much of his reign securing the throne in the War of the Spanish Succession (1701–13). The monastery is now a school, but you can explore its two superb cloisters – one Renaissance, the other Baroque – and the cathedral-sized church. Most beautiful of all is the tiny, tenth-century Mozarabic chapel of **San Miguel** in the garden.

Ourense

Set slightly back from the Miño atop a low hill, the historic core of **OURENSE** (Orense), one of Galicia's four provincial capitals, is more attractive and personable than you might expect from the dispiriting urban sprawl that surrounds it. While not a place to spend more than one night – or to break a train or bus journey, as both stations are a considerable way out, across the river – the old quarter does at least offer a handsome and lovingly restored tangle of stepped streets, patrician mansions with escutcheoned doorways, and grand little churches squeezed into miniature arcaded squares. Its centrepiece is a squat, dark **Catedral**, an imitation of the one in Santiago, which contains a museum of religious odds and ends that's not really worth bothering with.

A bewildering number of bridges cross the River Miño as it curves extravagantly through Ourense. The oldest is the thirteenth-century **Ponte Romana**, but the most visually impressive is the new **Ponte Milenio**, a futuristic road bridge with an undulating pedestrian loop that provides great views.

By train Ourense's train station is north of the river, 2.5 km from the old town and served by local buses.

Destinations A Coruña (4 daily; 2hr); Burgos (5 daily; 5hr 30min); León (4 daily; 4hr); Madrid (2 daily; 5hr 30min–7hr 30min); Monforte de Lemos (5 daily; 40min); Pontevedra (2 daily; 2hr 45min); Ribadavia (daily; 20min); Santiago de Compostela (4 daily; 1hr 30min–2hr); Vigo (8 daily; 2hr).

By bus The long-distance bus station is north of the river, 2.5 km from the old town; change to a local bus to reach the centre.

Destinations A Coruña (5 daily; 2hr 30min); Celanova (8 daily; 1hr 30min); Lugo (5 daily; 2hr); Santiago de Compostela (7 daily; 2hr); Vigo (12 daily; 2hr).

Turismo Pl. de Eugenio Montes, on the edge of the old town (Mon–Fri 9am–2pm & 4–8pm, Sat & Sun 11am –2pm; ☏ 988 366 064, ⊛ turismodeourense.com).

ACCOMMODATION

Gran Hotel San Martín Rúa Curras Enriquez 1 ☏ 988 371 811, ⊛ gh-hoteles.com. Ourense's most luxurious hotel is a smart modern high-rise near the river in an unexciting part of town, a few minutes' walk from the old quarter. Spacious and very comfortable rooms at reasonable rates. €65

Hostal Candido Rúa Hermanos Villar 15 ☏ 988 229 607, ⊛ hostalcandido.es. Nine basic en-suite rooms, located above an old-fashioned *chocolatería* near the cathedral. €36

Hotel Zarampallo Rúa Hermanos Villar 19 ☏ 988 230 008, ⊛ zarampallo.com. Smart, modern little doubles, with either shower or bath, the heart of the old town, plus a restaurant downstairs. €50

EATING AND DRINKING

Bar Mundial Praza Maior 17 ☏ 988 221 041. This well-priced tapas bar, on the old town's sleepy, arcaded main square, makes a great place to relax on a sunny summer's afternoon. Daily noon–midnight.

Casa de María Andrea Rúa San Miguel 7 ☏ 988 277 045. Great-value old-town restaurant, with balcony seating above a pretty little square, and a €10 *menú*. Daily 1–4pm & 9pm–midnight.

Cañon de Río Sil

Inland Galicia's most spectacular scenery can be admired not far northeast of Ourense, though it's only practicable to explore this area by car, and you can expect the driving to be slow. Follow the N120 out of the city, alongside the Río Miño, and after 20km you'll reach the confluence of the Miño with the lesser **Río Sil**. For roughly 50km east from here, the final stretch of the Sil is quite extraordinarily picturesque and dramatic, flowing through a stunning canyon known as the **Gargantas del Sil**.

This magnificent gorge is the heartland of the **Ribeira Sacra wine** region – the only place in Galicia that produces more red than white wine – and even where they're all but vertical, the river cliffs are almost always terraced with grape vines. That phenomenal landscaping project was started by the Romans, and has continued for two millennia. A high mountain road climbs east from the N120 just before the confluence, then winds along the topmost ridge of the canyon's southern flank, passing through a succession of lovely villages.

Castro Caldelas

Around 50km northeast of Ourense, the village of **CASTRO CALDELAS** surmounts a small hilltop a few kilometres south of the canyon itself. The medieval castle at the very top (daily 10am–2pm & 4–8pm; free) gives tremendous views over the town and surrounding countryside.

Just before the village, a side road drops back down to the river, where a small jetty is the base for **boat trips** on the Sil (daily in summer, schedules vary; €14; ☏ 902 100 403, ⊛ hemisferios.es).

Doade

A steep and precipitous winding road, LU903, climbs 4km up the northern slopes of the Sil gorge from the boat jetty, to reach the village of **DOADE**. Shortly before the village, a dirt road leads an amazing viewpoint over the canyon and its ancient vineyards. A statue of a woman grape harvester, officially entitled the **Spatium Interpretationis Riveyra Sacrata**, commemorates nine centuries of viniculture.

INFORMATION AND TOURS CAÑON DE RÍO SIL

Turismo Castro Caldelas has a useful *turismo* in the hilltop castle (daily 10am–2pm & 4–8pm; ☎988 203 358, ⓦwww.castrocaldelas.es).

Outdoor activities such as rafting, canoeing, canyoneering and horseriding in the canyon are offered by Galitur Sport (☎988 269 544, ⓦgalitursport.com).

ACCOMMODATION, EATING AND DRINKING

Hotel Rustico A Forxa Luintra ☎988 201 025, ⓦhotelaforxa.com. Attractive country-house hotel in a pretty village near San Estevo. Its nine rooms vary widely in facilities and price, but all are en suite, and there's a decent restaurant with *menús* from €12 and garden seating. Restaurant daily 1–3pm & 8–10pm. €36

Hotel Vicente Risco rúa Grande 4, Castro Caldelas ☎988 203 360, ⓦpousadavicenterisco.com. Very nice little eight-room hotel in the heart of the village, with eight attractive and good-value en-suite rooms, and a good restaurant. Restaurant daily 1–3pm & 7.30–9.30pm. €55

Parador of Santo Estevo de Ribas de Sil Nogueira de Ramuín ☎988 010 110, ⓦparador.es. One of the newest and nicest paradors in the country, 8km east of the main road, and housed within a magnificently converted tenth-century monastery. The ancient cloisters remain intact, but it also boasts ultramodern spa facilities, including a whirlpool bath set on an outdoor terrace, and a beautifully styled contemporary restaurant. €130

★ **Reitoral de Chandrexa** Parada do Sil ☎988 208 099, ⓦchandrexa.com. Higgledy-piggledy old farmhouse, with magnificently uneven oak floors and exposed beams, tucked away down a very rural lane 6km north of the village of A Teixeira. All its three delightful B&B rooms are similarly priced though only some have en-suite facilities. The friendly owner prepares fabulous dinners on demand, with produce from his own fields. €52

8

Monforte de Lemos

A dozen kilometres north of Doade, or 66km south of Lugo along the C546, the rail junction of **MONFORTE DE LEMOS** makes a satisfyingly unspoiled and ancient overnight stop. The town proper, which is home to an incongruously gigantic yet elegant Renaissance **Colegio**, encircles a hill of largely tumbledown old houses. The surprisingly rural area at the top of the hill holds a rambling ensemble which includes the **Torre de Homenaxe** and a four-hundred-year-old monastery that's home to an imposing parador.

INFORMATION MONFORTE DE LEMOS

Turismo Monforte's *turismo*, alongside the Colegio (daily 10am–2pm & 4–7pm; ☎982 404 715, ⓦconcellodemon forte.com), can advise on tours of the Ribeira Sacra wine region and its Romanesque monuments.

ACCOMMODATION, EATING AND DRINKING

★ **O Grelo** c/Campo de la Virgen s/n ☎982 404 701, ⓦresgrelo.com. This fabulous restaurant, a short way down the hillside from the parador, offers an inventive if expensive take on traditional Galego cuisine. Mon–Sat 1–4.30pm & 8.30pm–midnight, Sun 1–4.30pm.

Hostal Puente Romano Praza Dr Goyanes 6 ☎982 403 551, ⓦhpuenteromano.com. Light, good-value hotel, beside the river in the town proper, with large, nicely-furnished en-suite rooms. €48

Parador de Monforte de Lemos Pl. Luis de Góngora y Argote ☎982 418 484, ⓦparador.es. Stately parador, housed in a grand Benedictine monastery, on the highest point not only in town but for a considerable distance around. Fifty spacious rooms, with tiled floors and huge comfortable beds, plus a pool and restaurant. €110

Lugo

The oldest city in Galicia, and as "Lucus Augusti" the region's first capital, two thousand years ago, **LUGO** is, these days, a small town that's chiefly remarkable for its stout **Roman walls**. Rated as the finest late Roman military fortifications to survive anywhere, the walls with which the Romans enclosed this hilltop, overlooking the

Miño river, still form a complete loop around the old town. Few traces remain of the 71 semicircular towers that once punctuated the perimeter; instead, a broad footpath now runs atop the full 2.5km length of the ramparts, so a thirty-minute walk takes you all the way around, to admire the city core from every angle.

Sadly, insensitive building and a busy loop road make it impossible to appreciate the walls from any distance outside, but the road does at least keep traffic out of the centre, which maintains an enjoyable if slightly neglected medley of medieval and eighteenth-century buildings. The most dramatic of the old city gates, the **Porta de Santiago**, in the southwest, offers access to an especially impressive stretch of wall, leading past the **Catedral**.

Catedral de Santa María
Daily 8am–8.30pm • Free

The large and very mossy Catedral de Santa María, tucked into a corner of the walled city, was originally Romanesque when built in the twelfth century. Since then, it has been repeatedly rebuilt, with flamboyant Churrigueresque flourishes still conspicuous despite the more recent Neoclassical facade. The interior is remarkable for being entirely split down the middle, its two separate aisles running either side of a succession of chapels and altars.

Museo Provincial
Rúa Nova • July & Aug Mon–Fri 11am–2pm & 5–8pm, Sat 10am–2pm; Sept–June Mon–Fri 10.30am–2pm & 4.30–8.30pm, Sat 10.30am–2pm & 4.30–8pm, Sun 11am–2pm • Free • ⓦ museolugo.org

Lugo's excellent **Museo Provincial** is partly housed in the old Convento de San Francisco. It holds a well-displayed collection of Galego art, contemporary Spanish work swiped from the Prado, and an early collection of Galicia's Sargadelos china, alongside the more predictable Roman remains and ecclesiastical knick-knacks.

ARRIVAL AND INFORMATION   LUGO

By train Lugo's train station is 600m northeast of the old town.
Destinations A Coruña (4 daily; 1hr 40min); Madrid (1 daily; 9hr).
By bus The bus station is just south of the walls, on Praza da Constitucíon.

Destinations A Coruña (hourly; 2hr); Ourense (5 daily; 2hr); Pontevedra (5 daily; 2hr); Santiago de Compostela (9 daily; 2hr); Vigo (5 daily; 3hr); Viveiro (4 daily; 2–3hr).
Turismo Praza do Campo 11, in the old town (daily 10.30am–2pm & 4.30–8pm; ☎ 982 251 658, ⓦ lugoturismo .com).

ACCOMMODATION

Hostal Mar de Plata Ronda de Muralla 5 ☎ 982 228 910. Pleasant budget hotel, outside the walls next to the bus station, offering plain but adequate en-suite rooms. **€38**
Méndez Núñez Rúa Raiña 1 ☎ 982 230 711, ⓦ www

.hotelmendeznunez.com. Upscale hotel, in a modern building with large balconies, within the walls immediately north of the central Praza Maior. Crisply minimal furnishings but a good standard of comfort. **€60**

EATING AND DRINKING

Mesón de Alberto Rúa da Cruz 4 ☎ 982 228 310, ⓦ www.mesondealberto.com. Fancy old-town restaurant, which specializes in rice dishes to share – expect to pay around €40 per head for a full meal. There's also a good tapas bar at the front, where €14 buys you two sizeable tapas and a dessert. Daily 10.30am–4pm & 8pm–midnight.
Mesón O Castelo Rúa Nova 23 ☎ 982 253 486, ⓦ pulperiaocastelo.webcindario.com. One of the very best bar/restaurants on the old town's busiest lane,

facing the provincial museum. A great range of inexpensive tapas and *raciones*: *pulpo* costs €9.80, while you can get a substantial meat dish for €7, or try a delicious local sausage for €2.30. Daily noon–3pm & 7pm–midnight.
Os Tres Pes Rúa Nova 17 ☎ 982 228 803. Good tapas bar in the old town, which serves a great-value €9 *menú*, or portions of seafood delights like langoustines or little scallops for €7–9. Daily noon–3.30pm & 7.30–11pm.

Sobrado dos Monxes

Mon–Sat 10am–1pm & 4.30–7.30pm, Sun 12.15–1pm & 4.30–7pm • €1

The twelfth-century Cistercian monastery of **Sobrado dos Monxes** makes a highly worthwhile detour en route between Lugo and Santiago. The range of the abbey buildings proclaims past royal patronage, their scale emphasized by the tiny village below, while the huge church itself sprouts flowers and foliage from every niche and crevice, its honey-coloured stone blossoming with lichens and mosses. Within, all is immensely grand – long, uncluttered vistas, mannerist Baroque, and romantic gloom; there are superb, worm-endangered choir stalls (once in Santiago's cathedral) and, through an arch in the north transept, a tiny, ruined Romanesque chapel. A community of monks maintains the monastery and operates a small shop.

8

Aragón

BASÍLICA DE NUESTRA SEÑORA DEL PILAR, ZARAGOZA (P.598)

9

Aragón

Politically and historically Aragón has close links with Catalunya, with which it formed a powerful alliance in medieval times, exerting influence over the Mediterranean as far away as Athens. Locked in on all sides by mountains, it has always had its own identity, with traditional *fueros* like the Basques and a written Aragonese language existing alongside Castilian. The modern *autonomía* – containing the provinces of Zaragoza, Teruel and Huesca – is well out of the Spanish political mainstream, especially in the rural south, where Teruel is the least populated region in Spain. Coming from Catalunya or the Basque Country, you'll find the Aragonese pace in general noticeably slower.

It is the **Pyrenees** that draw most visitors to Aragón, with their sculpted valleys, stone-built farming villages and excellent trekking. Some valleys have been built up with expensive ski resorts, but they still reveal the stunning wilderness of the **Parque Nacional de Ordesa** and the **Parque Natural de Posets-Maladeta**, with their panoply of canyons, waterfalls and peaks. Aragón's Pyrenean towns are also renowned for their sacred architecture; **Jaca** has one of the country's oldest Romanesque cathedrals.

The most interesting monuments of central and southern Aragón are, by contrast, Mudéjar: a series of churches, towers and mansions built by Muslim workers in the early decades of Christian rule, which have been on UNESCO's World Heritage list since 2001. In addition to its absorbing Roman remains, **Zaragoza**, the Aragonese capital and the only place of any real size, sets the tone with its remarkable Aljafería palace. Other examples are to be found in a string of smaller towns, in particular **Tarazona**, **Calatayud** and – above all – the southern provincial capital of **Teruel**. In southern Aragón, the captivating walled village of **Albarracín** is incredibly picturesque, while to the east lies the isolated region encompassing the **Sierra de Gúdar** and **El Maestrazgo**, a rugged countryside stamped with dark peaks and gorges.

Zaragoza, Teruel and southern Aragón

The city of **Zaragoza** houses nearly half of Aragón's 1.5 million population, and most of its industry. It's a big but enjoyable place, with a lively zone of bars and restaurants tucked in among remarkable monuments, and it's a handy transport nexus, too, for both Aragón and beyond. Its province includes the Mudéjar towns of **Tarazona**, **Calatayud** and **Daroca**, and, along the border with Navarra, the old **Cinco Villas**, a series of lovely mountain villages, of which the most interesting is **Sos del Rey Católico**. Wine enthusiasts can also follow the **Ruta de los Vinos**, south from Zaragoza through Cariñena to Daroca.

Teruel province is a lot more remote, and even the capital doesn't see too many passing visitors. It is unjustly neglected, considering its superb Mudéjar monuments, and if you have transport of your own, there are some wonderful rural routes to

LOS ARCOS AQUEDUCT, TERUEL

Highlights

❶ **Basílica de Nuestra Señora del Pilar, Zaragoza** The majestic shrine of one of the most revered patron saints of Spain. **See p.598**

❷ **Aljafería, Zaragoza** Step into the Moorish past at this magnificent palace. **See p.604**

❸ **Cinco Villas** Experience small-town Aragón as it once was in these lovely "five villages", where you might go all day hearing nothing but pealing church bells in the mountain stillness. See p.609

❹ **Teruel** Not only does this historic provincial capital feature majestic Mudéjar architecture,

but you can often have it all to yourself – Teruel is refreshingly off the tourist trail. **See p.613**

❺ **Albarracín** Wander medieval lanes past balconied houses in this postcard town. **See p.617**

❻ **Monasterio de San Juan de la Peña** Built right into a craggy mountain, it's hard to tell where the rock face ends and the monastery begins. In a word – stunning. **See p.631**

❼ **Parque Nacional de Ordesa** Dramatic, canyon-slashed landscape for fine high-altitude hiking. **See p.634**

HIGHLIGHTS ARE MARKED ON THE MAP ON P.599

9

explore: especially west, through **Albarracín** to Cuenca, or south to Valencia. The valleys and villages of the **Sierra de Gúdar** and **El Maestrazgo**, which borders Valencia province, are the most remote of the lot: a region largely untouched by tourism, and where transport of your own is a big help.

Zaragoza

ZARAGOZA is an inviting city that has managed to absorb its rapid growth with a rare grace. Its centre reflects an air of prosperity in its wide, modern boulevards, and stylish shops and bars. Highlights include the spectacular Moorish **Aljafería**, an impressive collection of **Roman ruins** and an awesome basilica, devoted to one of Spain's most famous incarnations of the Virgin Mary, **Nuestra Señora del Pilar**.

The city's **fiestas** in honour of the revered saint – which take place throughout the second week of October – are well worth planning a trip around, so long as you can find accommodation. In addition to the religious processions (which focus on the 12th), the local council lays on a brilliant programme of cultural events, featuring top rock, jazz and folk bands, floats, bullfights and traditional *jota* dancing.

The **Plaza del Pilar** is the obvious point to start exploring Zaragoza. The square, paved in a brilliant, pale stone, was remodelled in 1991, creating a vast, airy expanse from **La Seo**, past the great Basílica de Nuestra Señora del Pilar, and over to Avda. César Augusto. The *plaza* spans the city's entire history: Roman ruins at both ends; between the churches, a Renaissance exchange house, the **Lonja**; and at the centre, some modern statuary and the **Fuente de la Hispanidad**, a giant waterfall shaped like a section of Central America and the Caribbean to commemorate 1492.

Basílica de Nuestra Señora del Pilar

Pl. del Pilar • Daily 6.45am–9.30pm, until 8.30pm in winter • Free • ⓦ cabildodezaragoza.org

Majestically fronting the Río Ebro, the **Basílica de Nuestra Señora del Pilar** is one of Spain's greatest and most revered religious buildings. It takes its name from a **pillar** – the centrepiece of the church – on which the Virgin Mary is said to have descended from heaven in an apparition before St James the Apostle. The structure around this shrine is truly monumental, with great corner towers and a central dome flanked by ten brightly tiled cupolas; it was designed in the late seventeenth century by Francisco Herrera el Mozo and built by Ventura Rodríguez in the 1750s and 60s.

The pillar, topped by a diminutive image of the Virgin, is constantly surrounded by pilgrims, who line up to touch an exposed (and thoroughly worn) section, encased in a marble surround. Elsewhere, the main artistic treasure of the cathedral is a magnificent alabaster reredos on the high altar, a masterpiece sculpted by Damián Forment in the first decades of the sixteenth century.

Museo Pilarista and Torre

Museo Mon–Fri 9am–1.30pm & 4–5.30pm, Sat 9am–1.30pm • €2 **Torre** Summer Mon–Thurs & Sat 9.30am–2pm & 4–7pm; winter 10am–1.30pm & 4–6.30pm • €3

Off the north aisle is the **Museo Pilarista**, where you can inspect at close quarters the original sketches for the decoration of the domes by Goya, Velázquez, and Francisco and Ramón Bayeu. Your ticket also admits you to the **Sacristía Mayor**, off the opposite aisle, with a collection of religious paintings and tapestries. You'll have to pay extra, however, if you want to enjoy the panoramic views from the **Torre**, the tower at the northwest corner of the church.

Torreón de la Zuda

Glorieta de Pío XII • Mon–Sat 10am–1.30pm & 4.30–7.30pm, Sun 10am–1.30pm • Free

Near the basilica looms the **Torreón de la Zuda**, part of Zaragoza's impressive medieval fortifications. The tower was built atop the **Roman walls** and after the Reconquest it

ARAGÓN

FRANCE

PYRENEES

NAVARRA

CASTILLA-LA MANCHA

CATALUNYA

VALENCIA

LOS MONEGROS

SIERRA DE GUARA

PARQUE NACIONAL DE ORDESA

PARC NATURAL POSETS-MALADETA

SIERRA DE GÚDAR

EL MAESTRAZGO

RINCÓN DE ADEMUZ

San Sebastián
Pau
Vielha
Pamplona
Canfranc-Estación
Ansó
Siresa
Echo
Jaca
Torla
Broto
Bielsa
Benasque
Castejón de Sos
El Pont de Suert
Sabiñánigo
Sos del Rey Católico
Santa Cruz de la Serós
San Juan de la Peña
Los Mallos
Riglos
Ainsa
Uncastillo
Loarre
Ayerbe
Sádaba
Ejea de los Caballeros
Huesca
Alquézar
Graus
Tudela
Tardienta
Barbastro
Monzón
Tarazona
Tauste
Binéfar
Borja
Monasterio de Veruela
Sariñena
Río Ebro
Río Duero
Zaragoza
Lleida
Fraga
Muel
La Ermita de Nuestra Señora de La Fuente
Calatayud
Cariñena
Fuendetodos
Belchite
Casa Natal de Goya
Monasterio de Piedra
Nuévalos
Daroca
Hijar
Caspe
Tortosa
Molina
Calamocha
Alcañiz
Valdeltormo
Calanda
Centro Buñuel
Alcorisa
Montalbán
Valderrobres
Ejulve
Morella
Villarluengo
Vinarós
Albarracín
Dinópolis (Theme Park)
Teruel
Cedrillas
Mirambel
Cantavieja
La Iglesuela del Cid
Villafranca del Cid
Villel
Mora de Rubielos
Linares de Mora
Mosqueruela
Rubielos de Mora
Cuenca
Ademuz
Castellón de la Plana
Valencia

Río Ebro

HIGHLIGHTS
1. Basílica de Nuestra Señora del Pilar
2. Aljafería
3. Cinco Villas
4. Teruel
5. Albarracín
6. Monasterio de San Juan de la Peña
7. Parque Nacional de Ordesa

0   25
kilometres

N

9

FIESTAS

MAY

First Friday: Battle of Vitoria Commemorated in Jaca with processions and folkloric events.
Monday of Pentecost: Romería Nuestra Señora de Calentuñana At Sos del Rey Católico.

JUNE

Nearest Sunday to the 19th: Fiesta de los Mozos Celebrated in Cantavieja with a serious religious event but also with dancing and the usual fairground activities.
25: Fiesta de Santa Orosia In Jaca.

JULY

First and second week: Vaquilla del Ángel One of Aragón's major festivals sees Teruel burst into ten days of festivities.
Last two weeks: Pireneos Sur World music festival at Sallent de Gallego and Lanuza (ⓦ pirineos-sur.es).

AUGUST

Early August: Fiesta de San Lorenzo In Huesca.
14–15: Fiestas del Barrio Street markets and parties in Jaca.
16 Patron saint's festival at Biescas – "bigheads" and eats.
27–28 *Encierros* – crazy local bull-running – at Cantavieja.

SEPTEMBER

Early September: Feria de Teruel Annual town fair.
4–8 Fiesta at Barbastro includes *jota* dancing, bullfights and sports competitions.
8 Virgin's birthday prompts fairs at Echo and Calatayud.
8–14 Bull-running and general celebrations at Albarracín.

OCTOBER

Second week Aragón's most important festival, in honour of the Virgen del Pilar. Much of the province closes down around the 12th, and at Zaragoza there are floats, bullfights and *jota* dancing.

---

formed part of the stately residential palace of various Aragón monarchs, from Alfonso I el Batallador to Jaime I.

Lonja

Pl. del Pilar • Usually only open for exhibitions • ☎ 973 397 239 • Free

The sixteenth-century **Lonja**, the old exchange building, is a Florentine-influenced structure, with an interior of elegant Ionic columns and a soaring, vaulted ceiling. A recurring motif throughout the building is the Zaragoza city shield. La Lonja opens periodically for art exhibitions and other temporary shows.

La Seo

Pl. del Pilar • Summer Mon–Fri 10am–8.30pm, Sat 10am–noon & 3–8.30pm, Sun 10am–11.30pm & 2–8.30pm; winter Tues–Fri 10am–2pm & 4–6pm; Sat & Sun 10am–noon & 4–6pm; sometimes closed for special occasions; last entry 30min before closing • €4, includes Tapestry Museum

The old cathedral, Catedral de San Salvador, known as **La Seo**, stands at the far end of Plaza del Pilar. The gleaming exterior is essentially Gothic-Mudéjar with minor Baroque and Plateresque additions, while to the left of the main entrance is a Mudéjar wall with elaborate geometric patterns. Inside, the superb *retablo mayor* contains some recognizably Teutonic figures executed by the German Renaissance sculptor, Hans of Swabia. Also housed within La Seo, the **Museo de Tapices** features a formidable collection of Flemish and French tapestries from the fourteenth to seventeenth centuries.

The Roman Route

Ruta Romano ticket €7 • See ⓦ zaragoza.es for up-to-date information on the Roman sites

Zaragoza has an impressive Roman history, which can be explored via a variety of museums and architectural remains. If you plan on visiting all the sights, you can buy a combined **Ruta Romano** ticket at the *turismo* or at any of the Roman sights.

Museo del Foro de Caesaraugusta

Pl. de la Seo 2 • Tues–Sat 9am–8pm, Sun 9am–2pm • €3, or Ruta Romano ticket

Just outside the cathedral, marked by a striking entrance portal lined with onyx, is the **Museo del Foro de Caesaraugusta** – Zaragoza's name derives from that of Caesar Augustus (César Augusto in the Spanish form). The museum comprises the ruins (primarily foundations) of the old Roman forum, located in an impressive underground chamber beneath the *plaza*, as well as a small exhibition with displays of artefacts found on site.

Museo del Teatro de Caesaraugusta

C/San Jorge 12 • Tues–Thurs 9am–9pm, Fri–Sat 9am–10.30pm, Sun 10am–1.30pm • €3.50, or Ruta Romano ticket

Near Plaza de San Pedro Nolasco, a vast modern canopy covers the ruins of the Roman theatre, which are the highlight of the **Museo del Teatro de Caesaraugusta**. The exhibit features audiovisual displays, collections of archeological finds and a walk through the theatre and its vaulted galleries, which gives you a sense of its former glory and grandeur.

Museo de las Termas Públicas and Museo del Puerto Fluvial

Museo de las Termas Públicas c/San Juan y San Pedro 3–7 • Tues–Sat 9am–8pm, Sun 9am–2pm • €3, or Ruta Romano ticket **Museo del Puerto Fluvial** Pl. San Bruno 8 • Tues–Thurs 9am–9pm, Fri & Sat 9am–10.30pm, Sun 10am–1.30pm • €2.50, or Ruta Romano ticket

The **Museo de las Termas Públicas** displays the remains of the foundations of the city's Roman baths, along with a scale model. The **Museo del Puerto Fluvial** preserves the vestiges of the Roman river-port buildings and installations, and also features audiovisuals that delve into their history.

Museo Ibercaja Camón Aznar

C/Espoz y Mina 23 • Tues–Sat 10am–1.45pm & 5–8.45pm, Sun 10am–1.45pm • Free

A block south of the Plaza del Pilar, in the impeccably restored Palacio de los Pardo, is the **Museo Ibercaja Camón Aznar**, which houses the private collections of José Camón Aznar, one of the most distinguished scholars of Spanish art. Highlights include a permanent display of most of Goya's prints (the artist was born at nearby Fuendetodos; see p.608).

Museo Pablo Gargallo

Pl. San Felipe 3 • Tues–Sat 9am–8pm, Sun 9am–2pm • €4

On the western side of the *casco viejo*, the **Museo Pablo Gargallo** is housed in the attractive Renaissance Palacio Argillo and features the work of the celebrated Aragonese sculptor, including striking sculptures, engravings and the moulds he used. Some of Gargallo's sculptures reveal hints of Cubism, while others are more traditional renderings in bronze and marble.

Santa María Magdalena

Pl. de Magdalena • Usually only open for exhibitions • ☎ 976 299 598

The handsome church of **Santa María Magdalena** features the finest of Zaragoza's several Mudéjar towers. It's considered the city's best remaining example of civil Mudéjar architecture from the fifteenth century. It occasionally hosts temporary exhibits on local history and cultures.

9

ZARAGOZA

N

Pamplona (A68) ▲

Grancasa, Expo Zaragoza & Acuario de Zaragoza ▲

PLAZA DE LAS COMUNIDADES EUROPEAS

PASEO DE ECHEGARAY Y CABALLERO

SANTA LUCÍA

SANTA INÉS

PLAZA DE SANTO DOMINGO

1 PREDICADORES

CASTA ÁLVAREZ

AGUADORES

ARMAS

Aljafería

SAN BLAS

SAN PABLO

BASILIO BOGGIERO

2

San Pablo

CONDE DE ARANDA

AVENIDA DE MADRID **2**

PLAZA DEL PORTILLO

MARIANO CEREZO

CONDE DE ARANDA

PLAZA DE LA VICTORIA

Plaza de Toros

RAMÓN PIGNATELLI

S. MARTÍN

FUENTERRABÍA

MADRE RAFOLS

SANTIAGO RAMÓN Y CAJAL

PLAZA SAN LAMBERTO **ℹ**

San Ildefonso

DOCTOR FLEMING

PASEO MARÍA AGUSTÍN

JOSÉ LUIS

AVENIDA DE CÉSAR AUGUSTO

PLAZA DE NTRA. SRA. DEL CARMEN

9 **P**

ALBAREDA

MANUEL ESCORIAZA Y FABRO

JOSÉ ANSELMO CLAVÉ

IAACC Pablo Serrano

MADRE SACRAMENTO

CALLE DE CANFRANC

CALLE DE PÓNCIANO PONZANO

PLAZA DE ARAGÓN

Puerta del Carmen

HERNÁN CORTÉS

PIZARRO

PASEO DE PAMPLONA

PASEO DE TERUEL

ALMAGRO

PLAZA DE BASILIO PARAÍSO

AVDA. PINTOR FRANCISCO GOYA

Antigua Facultad de Medicina y Ciencias

GRAN VÍA

◄ 2 & Zaragoza Airport

◄ Train Station & Bus Station

10 (1km) & Teruel (A23) ▼

Teruel (A23) & La Romareda (1km) ▼

■ **HOTELS AND PENSIÓS**
Catalonia El Pilar	3
Hotel Palafox	9
Hotel Reino de Aragón	7
Hotel Sauce	5
Hotel Vía Romana	4
Hotel Zentro Zaragoza	8
Pensión La Peña	6

■ **HOSTELS AND CAMPING**
Albergue Juvenil Baltasar Gracián	10
Camping Ciudad de Zaragoza	2
Zaragoza Hostel	1

■ **CLUBS AND LIVE MUSIC**
La Campana de los Perdidos	1
La Casa del Loco	4
Daluxe	3
Oasis	2

● **CAFES, TAPAS BARS AND RESTAURANTS**
Bodegas Almau	7
Bodegón Azoque	11
La Bodeguilla de Santa Cruz	5
El Calamar Bravo	9
Casa Emilio	2
La Cueva en Aragón	6
El Fuelle	8
Gran Café Zaragoza	4
Montal	3

● **BARS**
Bull McCabe's	10
Cucaracha	1

Centro de Historia de Zaragoza

Pl. San Agustín 2 • Tues–Sat 10am–2pm & 5–8pm • Free • ☎ 976 205 640

The **Centro de Historia de Zaragoza**, housed in the old convent of San Agustín, has innovative galleries on Zaragoza's history, organized thematically, including on the city's rich array of lively festivals and its role as a bustling trade centre. The museum is also often used for contemporary art exhibitions, both local and international.

Museo de Zaragoza and around

Museum Pl. de los Sitios 6 • Tues–Sat 10am–1.45pm & 5–7.45pm, Sun 10am–1.45pm • Free **San Miguel** c/San Miguel **Santa Engracia**
Pl. de Santa Engracia • Enquire at museum about church opening hours

The well-curated **Museo de Zaragoza** features works by famous Aragonese son
Goya, along with other exhibits that span the city's Iberian, Roman and Moorish
past. Nearby is a pair of interesting churches: **San Miguel**, with a minor *retablo*

9

by Forment and a Mudéjar tower, and **Santa Engracia**, with a splendid Plateresque portal.

IAACC Pablo Serrano

Paseo María Agustín 20 • Tues–Sat 10am–2pm & 6–9pm, Sun 10am–2pm • Free; guided tours €3 • ☎ 976 280 659, ⊛ iaacc.es

The eye-catching **Aragonés de Arte y Cultura Contemporáneos Instituto** (Aragón Institute of Contemporary Arts and Cultures), or **IAACC**, has recently been expanded with a sleek design by acclaimed Aragonese architect José Manuel Pérez Latorre. The institute features a wide range of exhibits on contemporary art, architecture, design and sculpture. The centre is named after Pablo Serrano, a well-known Aragonese abstract sculptor whose works are also shown here.

The Aljafería

Avda. de Madrid, Parque de Aljafería • April–Oct daily 10am–1.30pm & 4.30–7.30pm; Nov–March Mon–Sat 10am–2pm & 4–6.30pm, Sun 10am–2pm; closed some Thurs & Fri mornings (when meetings are in session) • Guided tours 10.30am, 11.30am, 12.30pm, 4.30pm, 5.30pm (summer only) & 6.30pm • €3, includes guided tour • ☎ 976 289 683

Moorish Spain was never very unified, and from the tenth to the eleventh century Zaragoza was the centre of an independent dynasty, the Beni Kasim. Their palace, the **Aljafería**, was built in the heyday of their rule in the mid-eleventh century, and as such predates the Alhambra in Granada and Seville's Alcázar. Much, however, was added later, under twelfth- to fifteenth-century Christian rule, when the palace was adapted and used by the *reconquista* kings of Aragón. Since 1987, the Aragonese parliament has met here.

The foremost relics from the original design are a tiny and beautiful **mosque**, adjacent to the entrance, and farther on an intricately decorated court, the **Patio de Santa Isabella**. From here, the **Grand Staircase** (added in 1492) leads to a succession of mainly fourteenth-century rooms, remarkable for their carved *artesonado* ceilings; the most beautiful is in the Throne Room.

Expo Zaragoza

On and around Avda. de Ranillas • ⊛ expozaragozaempresarial.com

In 2008, Zaragoza hosted the splashy **Expo Zaragoza**, based around the theme of water and sustainable development. The gleaming Expo site, unfolding along the river just northwest of the city centre, featured plenty of intriguing architecture, some of which is still standing, including the iconic **Water Tower**, looming at nearly 76m tall; and a sleek bridge pavilion designed by Zaha Hadid. The Expo site now functions as a business district, where occasional conferences are hosted.

Acuario de Zaragoza

Avda. de Ranillas • Summer daily 10am–8pm; winter hours vary – consult website; last entry 45min before closing • €14 • ⊛ acuariodezaragoza.com

The Expo site is also home to the **Acuario de Zaragoza** (Zaragoza Aquarium), the largest freshwater aquarium in Europe, with over three hundred river species from around the world. It's very kid-friendly, and often packed with schoolchildren on excursion.

ARRIVAL AND DEPARTURE   ZARAGOZA

By air Zaragoza's airport, serving domestic flights and services from London, Milan and other cities, is 10km northwest of the city centre; an airport bus plies back and forth in conjunction with flights (Mon–Sat every 30min 6am–10.30pm, Sun hourly 6am–10pm; €1.60). Taxis cost around €20.

By train Trains use the intermodal Estación Delicias, just over 3km from the centre. Catch bus #51 from right outside the station to Paseo Constitución. There's also a small *turismo* booth (daily 10am–8pm), which can supply you with a map.

Destinations Regular and AVE trains zip throughout the day to Barcelona (16 daily; 4–5hr; AVE 2hr) and Madrid (12 daily; AVE; 3hr). There are also services to Bilbao (4 daily; 5hr); Burgos (5 daily; 4hr); Cáceres (daily; 7hr); Cádiz (daily; 9hr); Córdoba (2 daily; 6–8hr); Girona (daily; 6hr 30min); Huesca

(4–7 daily; 50min–1hr); Jaca (3 daily; 3hr 20min); León (3 daily; 6hr); Lleida (10–12 daily; 1hr 40min); Logroño (9 daily; 2hr); Málaga (daily; 11hr); Pamplona (7 daily; 2–3hr); Salamanca (3 daily; 4hr 30min–8hr); San Sebastián (4 daily; 4hr); Seville (daily; 7hr); Tarragona (5–10 daily; 3hr; AVE to Tarragona Camps 1hr 30min); and Teruel (3 daily; 3hr).

By bus Buses arrive at the intermodal train station, including Agreda and Alsa services from Asturias, Barcelona, Bilbao, Galicia, León, Madrid and several destinations in Old Castile; Agreda services to Huesca and Jaca; and Eurolines buses and services south to Daroca, Cariñena (45min) and Muel (30min).

Destinations A Coruña (daily; 12hr); Barcelona (hourly; 3hr 45min); Belchite (3–4 daily; 1hr); Bilbao (9 daily; 4hr); Burgos (3 daily; 4hr 15min); Huesca (every 30min; 1hr); Jaca (6 daily; 2hr 15min); León (3 daily; 7hr); Lleida (5 daily; 2hr 30min); Logroño (3 daily; 2hr 15min); Madrid (hourly; 3hr 45min); Salamanca (2 daily; 7hr); Santiago de Compostela (daily; 13hr); Sos del Rey Católico (daily; 2hr 15min); Tarragona (7 daily; 2hr 45min); and Valladolid (5 daily; 5hr).

By car Car rental is available from Atesa, Avda. Valencia 6 ☎ 976 350 408; Avis, Paseo Fernando el Católico 9 ☎ 976 489 236; and Hertz, Avda. de Goya 61–63 ☎ 976 320 400.

By taxi Radio-Taxi Aragón ☎ 976 383 838; Radio-Taxi Zaragoza ☎ 976 424 242.

INFORMATION AND TOURS

Turismo The main *turismo* is opposite the basilica on Pl. del Pilar (Easter–Sept daily 9am–9pm; Oct–Easter 10am–8pm; ☎ 976 201 200, ⓦ turismozaragoza.com). This caters for the city, while a well-equipped office on Avda. César Augusto 25 (Mon–Fri 10am–2pm & 5–8pm, Sat 10am–2pm & 5–8pm, Sun 10am–2pm; ☎ 976 282 181, ⓦ turismodearagon.com) has information on the Zaragoza province. There's also a *turismo* booth at the train station.

Tours The tourist office offers several different walking tours around town. The Bus Turístico (Tourist Bus) travels between all the main sights every 15min, departing from c/Don Jaime, next to the Lonja (summer daily; winter weekends only; €6; ☎ 976 201 200).

Discount card The tourist office sells the Zaragoza Card (ⓦ zaragozacard.com; 24hr €15, 48hr €20, 72hr €24), which offers access to the main sights around town, a certain number of free rides on public transport, discounts at hotels and restaurants, and a free ride on the Bus Turístico.

ACCOMMODATION

Zaragoza offers a decent range of accommodation, from simple *pensiones* to well-appointed hotels. The central, atmospheric *casco viejo* houses many of the *pensiones,* both around Pl. del Pilar and the small streets off c/Méndez Núñez. You'll also find a good number of hotels dotted around east of Pl. de España.

HOTELS AND PENSIONES

★ **Catalonia El Pilar** c/Manifestación 16 ☎ 976 205 858, ⓦ hoteles-catalonia.es. Inside a lovely *modernista* building on the edge of the old town, this hotel blends contemporary design with traditional features such as a wrought-iron lift. Rooms feature designer furnishings and a simple, understated colour scheme. **€85**

Hotel Palafox Marqués de Casa Jiménez ☎ 976 237 700, ⓦ palafoxhoteles.com. One of the closest five-stars to the *casco viejo*, this sleek spot sports a blend of contemporary, Aragonese and Mudéjar design by Pascua Ortega. Excellent facilities, including parking, a fine restaurant (closed Sun & Aug) and an outdoor pool. **€79**

Hotel Reino de Aragón c/Coso 80 ☎ 976 468 200, ⓦ hotelreinodearagon.com. Smart Silken chain hotel with a boutique feel. Rooms combine classical and contemporary style with satellite TV and marble-clad bathrooms. Sometimes offers good online deals in low season. **€95**

Hotel Sauce c/Espoz y Mina 33 ☎ 976 205 050, ⓦ hotelsauce.com. Along with its great name, this hotel has a central location – 100m from Pl. del Pilar – and well-maintained, attractively furnished rooms to offer. **€58**

Hotel Vía Romana c/Don Jaime I 54 ☎ 976 398 215, ⓦ hotelhusaviaromana.com. Smart mid-range option, just off the Pl. del Pilar, in a well-restored building with neat, comfortable rooms, some with city views, and cheap weekend deals. Good online discounts. **€50**

Hotel Zentro Zaragoza c/Coso 86 ☎ 976 703 300, ⓦ hotelzentrozaragoza.com. This upmarket hotel, also from Silken, reveals a *modernista* facade and an elegant, cool-toned lobby (from which you can peer down at the underground Roman remains) that gives way to handsome rooms. Check the website for good last-minute or low-season offers. **€70**

Pensión La Peña c/Cinegio 3, 1º ☎ 976 299 089. Comfortable, simple, inexpensive rooms at this family-run *pensión*. The facilities are basic, but it's central and clean. **€30**

HOSTELS AND CAMPING

Albergue Juvenil Baltasar Gracián c/Franco y López 4, off Avda. de Valencia ☎ 976 306 692, reservations ☎ 902 088 905, ⓦ reaj.com. This well-run hostel, about 500m from the train station, has basic but clean rooms sleeping two, four or eight people on bunk beds, and breakfast in the simple dining room included. €4 discount for under-26s. From **€17**

Camping Ciudad de Zaragoza c/San Juan Bautista de la Salle, about 6km southwest of the city ☎ 976 753 870, ⓦ campingzaragoza.com. This well-tended

9

ARAGONESE CUISINE

Aragonese cuisine in many ways reflects the region: rugged, hearty, traditional. In a word: meat. Popular dishes include roast lamb (**ternasco**, derived from the word *tierno*, or tender); plump coils of pork sausages, such as **longaniza**; and, of course, **ham**, particularly from Teruel, whose dry but cold winds create an ideal climate for curing. The region is also known for its stews, such as **chilindrón**, which gets its name from the heavy pot in which it's cooked. Multiple varieties exist – the traditional version is a fragrant mix of bell peppers, chicken and cured ham. **Migas** ("breadcrumbs"), based on day-old bread cooked with garlic, peppers and other ingredients, is a popular dish throughout central Spain; the Aragón recipe calls for sausage and grapes. As for fish, fresh river **trout** from the Pyrenees often appears on menus, while sweets include the region's famous **frutas de Aragón**: candied fruits covered in chocolate. Aragón also has several **wine-growing regions**, including Somontano, Campo de Borja, Cariñena and Calatayud.

campsite, between the outer neighbourhoods of Valdefierro, Rosales del Canal and Montecanal, has good facilities, including a pool, organized kids' activities, bungalows (with kitchen and outdoor terrace) and a café/restaurant (for campers) with a €10 *menú del día* (€18 on weekends). Tent plus adult €10; four-person bungalow €100

Zaragoza Hostel c/Predicadores 70 ☎976 282 043, ⓦalberguezaragoza.com. Central, spacious, lively hostel built in a solid, medieval building near the banks of the Ebro. Doubles and dorm rooms, free internet, kitchen use and breakfast included. Dorms €18, rooms €40

EATING

The *casco viejo* features an array of economic restaurants, *comedores* and bars. As you'd expect in a place of this size, you'll also find upmarket restaurants scattered throughout the rest of the city. For tapas – and plenty of late-night drinking – head to **El Tubo**, the series of narrow streets near Pl. de España, particularly Estébanes, Cuatro de Agosto and La Libertad; also try the areas around Pl. de Santa Marta or Pl. de San Pedro Nolasco.

CAFÉS, TAPAS BARS AND RESTAURANTS

Bodegas Almau Estébanes 9 ☎976 299 834, ⓦbodegasalmau.es. Spirited tapas bar established in 1870, with a handsome, tiled interior that gives way to a bustling outdoor area strewn with pebbles and barrel-tables. A range of tasty tapas includes their speciality of anchovies. Mon–Sat 11am–2pm & 7pm–midnight.

Bodegón Azoque Casa Jiménez 6 ☎976 220 320, ⓦbodegonazoque.com. Upmarket tapas bar, catering to a smart business crowd sipping quality wine at the rustic, wood-encased bar. Barrels of wine stand at the door, while diners graze on sardines and the celebrated *jamón de Jabugo*. Daily 11.30am–midnight.

La Bodeguilla de Santa Cruz c/Santa Cruz 3 ☎976 200 018. A characterful bar that looks like a cross between Aladdin's cave and an old apothecary, serving a creative selection of beautifully presented tapas and *raciones*. Mon–Fri 8pm–midnight, Sat 1–3.30pm & 8pm–midnight.

★ **El Calamar Bravo** c/Cinco de Marzo 14 ☎976 794 264. A hugely popular and inexpensive stand-up tapas bar with outstanding *calamares* sandwiches and *patatas bravas* (€2–3), all smothered in mayonnaise and spicy salsa. Daily 11am–3pm & 6–11pm.

Casa Emilio Avda. Madrid 3–5 ☎976 435 839. For a taste of old-world Aragón, try this longtime, family-run

restaurant, popular with local writers and journalists, that serves up traditional Aragonese cuisine, like tender roast lamb. Dishes are in the €10–20 range. Daily 1–4pm, plus Tues–Sat & 8.30–11pm.

La Cueva en Aragón c/La Libertad 16 ☎976 204 645. Lively tapas joint that's also known as "El Champi" for its signature *tapa* – succulent mushrooms topped with a powerful garlic sauce. Usually daily noon until late.

El Fuelle c/Mayor 59 ☎976 398 033, ⓦel-fuelle.com. Earthy local *cocina*, specializing in no-frills Aragonese cuisine, especially meat dishes. Great atmosphere and value for money. Daily except Mon 1–4pm & 8–11pm; closed Sun eve.

★ **Gran Café Zaragoza** c/Alfonso I 25 ☎976 394 125. Historic, genteel café; the nineteenth-century interior features dark-wood ceilings, a burnished wooden bar, and large windows overlooking the street. Daily 8.30am–10pm.

Montal Torre Nueva 29 ☎976 298 998, ⓦmontal.es. An old shop dating from 1919 that also has an alluring restaurant. Relax on a Renaissance balcony for an elegant dinner of regional cuisine (*menú* €59 per person). Reservations essential. Mon–Fri 1.30–3.30pm & 8.30–11pm (or until last diner), Sat dinner only. Closed Aug.

DRINKING AND NIGHTLIFE

The *casco viejo* has several hopping *zonas* of music-and-tapas bars and nightclubs, including the area around c/Contamina and c/Temple, which hits its stride at the weekends after midnight.

BARS

Bull McCabe's c/Cádiz ☎976 225 016, ⓦbullmccabes .net. One of the most popular of Zaragoza's Irish bars, with two floors and reasonably priced pints of the black stuff. Mon–Fri 9.30am–12.30pm, Sat 2pm–2.30am, Sun 5pm–2am.

Cucaracha c/Temple 25, no phone. Raucous place in the heart of *casco viejo*'s bar district, especially popular for its range of mind-numbing shots. Tends to get busy well after midnight. Wed–Sat from 9pm.

CLUBS AND LIVE MUSIC

La Campana de los Perdidos c/Prudencio 7. Wonderfully unique bar with an old-time, traditional decor, a cave-like cellar and a great line-up of local performers, from jazz to folk music. Generally Thurs, Fri & Sun from

9pm for gigs, plus other days depending on live music programme.

La Casa del Loco c/Mayor 10 ☎976 396 771, ⓦlacasadelloco_com. Rock pub with plenty of live acts, and a mix of the latest English and Spanish sounds, along with the occasional Ibiza-style foam party. Cover €7–10 for live shows. Thurs–Sat 9.30pm–6am.

Daluxe Pl. del Pilar 12 ⓦdaluxe.es. Plush *discoteca*, home to the late-night party crowd, just behind the main *turismo*. Usually Thurs–Sat from 8–10pm to 5 or 6am, Sun 6pm–midnight.

Oasis c/Boggiero 28 ☎976 439 534, ⓦoasisclubteatro .com. A grand old concert hall with a glitzy disco and pub, and live shows that sometimes include drag acts. Fri & Sat from 9pm.

DIRECTORY

Banks Barclays has numerous branches in the city: Paseo María Augustín 3; c/San Vincente Mártir 18; Avda. de Madrid 141–143. Citibank is at Paseo de Sagasta 9.

Cinema Filmoteca de Zaragoza, Pl. de San Carlos 4 (ⓦfilmotecazaragoza.com), has an arts programme, including original-language movies.

Football Real Zaragoza (ⓦrealzaragoza.com) plays at La Romareda stadium in the south of the city.

Hospital Miguel Servet, Pl. Isabel la Católica 1 ☎976 765 500.

Post office The main *Correos* is at Paseo de la Independencia 33 (Mon–Fri 8.30am–8.30pm, Sat 8.30am–2pm).

Shops The big shopping street is Paseo de la Independencia, south of Pl. de España, lined with chain stores including a branch of El Corte Inglés. Northwest of the city lies the Grancasa (ⓦgrancasa.es), one of Zaragoza's largest shopping centres.

The wine route and Goya trail

Few tourists spend much time exploring the sights and towns around Zaragoza, and with the Pyrenees just a step to the north, it is perhaps no wonder. However, wine buffs heading south might want to follow the **Ruta de los Vinos** through **Cariñena**. There are vineyards dotted all over Aragón, but some of the best wines – strong, throaty reds and good whites – come from this region, whose towns and villages are best explored with your own transport.

Goya enthusiasts will be interested in **Muel**, and his birthplace in **Fuendetodos**. Nearby lies **Belchite**, one of Spain's most poignant reminders of the Civil War. Buses travel from Zaragoza to several towns in this area, including Cariñena, Muel and Belchite.

Muel: La Ermita de Nuestra Señora de la Fuente

Hermitage Mon–Sat 10am–2pm & 4–7pm, Sun 10am–2pm • Free

MUEL marks the northernmost point of the region and was once a renowned pottery centre. It has seen much better days, however, and few trains stop here any more. The town's interest lies in a Roman fountain and a hermitage, **La Ermita de Nuestra Señora de la Fuente**, which has some early frescoes of saints by Goya painted in 1772. It's signposted on the edge of town, with a small car park nearby.

9

Fuendetodos

Buses run 1–2 times daily from Zaragoza to Fuendetodos (55min)

Francisco Goya, who became court painter to Carlos IV, spent his early childhood in the quiet village of **FUENDETODOS**, 24km southeast of Muel. The small, pretty town, with stone houses and flowers sprouting on balconies, features Goya's home, which has been turned into a charming museum.

Casa Natal de Goya and Museo del Grabado de Goya

C/Zuloaga • Tues–Sun 11am–2pm & 4–7pm • €3 • ⓦ fundacionfuendetodosgoya.org

The **Casa Natal de Goya** is the eighteenth-century labourer's house where Goya was born in 1746; it has been faithfully restored, complete with rustic, period decor. Entry is included with tickets to the **Museo del Grabado de Goya**, 100m farther along c/Zuloaga at no. 3, which exhibits four of the artist's print series: *Caprichos* (Caprices), *Desashres* (Disasters), *Tauromaquia* (Bullfighting) and *Disparates* (Absurdities). *Caprichos* and *Disparates* represent a savage attack on the follies Goya perceived in Spanish society at the time, while *Tauromaquia* reflects the artist's genuine passion for bullfighting.

Belchite

Autocares Hife buses (☎ 902 119 814, ⓦ hife.es) run from Zaragoza (3–4 daily)

Of all the reminders of the Spanish Civil War, the war-torn town of **Belchite**, 20km east of Fuendetodos and 50km southeast of Zaragoza, is perhaps the most haunting. It's also the most unforgettable, which is why this casualty of war was left untouched after it was bombed by Franco's forces. Residents built up a new Belchite 1km away from its ravaged sibling.

The sign at the entrance for the bombed-out Belchite reads simply "*Belchite, Pueblo Viejo*". Dusty streets are lined with abandoned houses, their twisted wrought-iron balconies dangling askew. Peeling shutters creak in the wind, while crumbling walls bear bulletholes. The church is especially affecting, with jagged holes in the ceiling gaping at the sky, and crushed rocks in place of where the pews used to be. The only signs of life are the occasional shepherd and his flock, weaving through the silent ruins to the green fields beyond.

Cariñena

Twenty-four kilometres west of Fuendetodos, just off the main A23 highway, **CARIÑENA** is the capital of the Campo de Borja *comarca*. The town was named after the Cariñena grape and is home to a small wine museum and a clutch of **bodegas**, where you can taste and buy wine.

Museo del Vino

Camino de la Platero 1 • Tues–Fri 10am–2pm & 4–6pm, Sat 11am–2pm & 5–7pm, Sun 11am–2pm • €2 • ⓦ docarinena.com

This well-run **Museo del Vino** explores the Cariñena wine region through a variety of exhibits, including old wine-making instruments, photos of ancient *bodegas* and vineyards of the region and audiovisual displays. The museum can also supply information about touring the local vineyards.

Grandes Vinos y Viñedos

Shop usually Mon–Fri 8am–2pm & 4–6pm • Tours €6, includes a commemorative bottle of wine; call ahead (tours fixed when ten or more people sign up) • ☎ 976 621 261, ⓦ grandesvinos.com • To reach it, follow the N330 north towards Zaragoza and after 3km turn left at the sign for Santuario de Ntra. Sra. de Lagunas

A good place to taste and buy wine is the *tienda* at **Grandes Vinos y Viñedos**, one of the largest *bodegas* in Aragón. They offer tours, which includes a visit to the blending building, the modern bottling plant and the ageing section, as well as a tasting at the end. You can also visit the small on-site **museum**.

The Cinco Villas

9

North of Zaragoza, the **Cinco Villas** stretch for some 90km along the border with Navarra and comprise Tauste, Ejea de los Caballeros, Sádaba, Uncastillo and Sos del Rey Católico, all set in delightful, scarcely visited countryside. The title of Cinco Villas is owed to Felipe V, who awarded it for their services in the War of the Spanish Succession (1701–14). For those en route to the Pyrenees (the road past Sos continues to Roncal in Navarra) or to Pamplona, the Cinco Villas make a pleasant stopoff. **Sos**, the most interesting of the five, attracts the majority of visitors.

Tauste, Ejea de los Caballeros and Sádaba

TAUSTE, closest of the "towns" to Zaragoza, has an interesting parish church built in the Mudéjar style. Nearby **EJEA DE LOS CABALLEROS** retains elements of Romanesque architecture in its churches. Twenty kilometres northwest, remote, tranquil **SÁDABA** boasts an impressive thirteenth-century castle, as well as the remains of an early synagogue.

Uncastillo

UNCASTILLO, 15km northwest of Sádaba, also has a handsome castle, as its name suggests, this time dating from the twelfth century, and the remains of an aqueduct. In the castle is the small **Museo de la Torre** (July to mid-Sept daily 11am–2pm & 5–8pm; rest of the year Wed–Fri 11am–2pm, Sat & Sun 11am–2pm & 4–6pm; free; ☎ 976 679 121), with simple exhibits on the castle and Uncastillo's history.

Sos del Rey Católico

SOS DEL REY CATÓLICO, 120km from Zaragoza, derives its name from Fernando II, El Rey Católico, born here in 1452 and as powerful a local-boy-made-good as any Aragonese town could hope for. The narrow cobbled streets of the *centro histórico*, like so many in Aragón, are packed with marvellously grand mansions. Sos also features a lovely Romanesque **church** and the ruined **Castillo de la Peña Felizana**, which offers magnificent views over the village's terracotta rooftops and surrounding countryside. The excellent parador has memorable vistas and might entice you to spend at least one night.

Casa Palacio de Sada

Pl. Hispanidad 1 • June to mid-Sept daily 10am–2pm & 4–8pm; mid-Sept to May Wed–Fri 10am–1pm & 4–6pm, Sat & Sun 10am–2pm & 4–7pm • Tours daily at 10am, 11am & 1pm

At the heart of the *centro histórico* is the stately **Casa Palacio de Sada**, where Fernando el Católico was reputed to have been born in 1452. The grand palace houses the tourist office (see below), and also has exhibits on the history of the impressive Aragonese monarchy.

Iglesia de San Esteban

Pl. de la Iglesia • Mon–Sat 10am–1pm & 4–6pm, Sun 10am–noon & 4–6pm (3.30–5.30pm in winter) • Free

The Romanesque parish church of **San Esteban** dates back to the eleventh century and has an impressive northern facade. Its unusual lower chapel, dedicated to Santa María del Perdón, features apses with well-preserved fourteenth-century frescoes and detailed capitals.

ARRIVAL, INFORMATION AND TOURS   **THE CINCO VILLAS**

By bus Generally only one bus a day makes it up from Zaragoza to Sos (2hr 15min), so you'll need your own transport if you want to explore further.

Turismo Palacio de Sada, Pl. Hispanidad 1, Sos (June to mid-Sept daily 10am–2pm & 4–8pm; mid-Sept to May

Wed–Fri 10am–1pm & 4–6pm, Sat & Sun 10am–2pm & 4–7pm; ☎ 948 888 524).

Tours In addition to the tour of the Palacio de Sada, Sos' tourist office also offers a guided walk through the village (€4).

9

ACCOMMODATION

One of the best bases for the area is the parador in Sos, but the other villages have a few choices, while the surrounding countryside features a number of quaint *casas rurales* – the website ⓦ civitur.es offers a good overview.

UNCASTILLO

Posada la Pastora Behind the Santa María church ☏ 976 679 499, ⓦ lapastora.net. Uncastillo has a few charming spots, including this lovingly renovated, excellent-value posada with country-style rooms. **€80**

SOS DEL REY CATÓLICO

Albergue de Sos c/Meca ☏ 948 888 480, ⓦ alberguedesos.com. The cheapest accommodation in town is the handsome, well-maintained *Albergue de Sos* in a medieval *torre*, with stone walls, brightly patterned furnishings and spacious, clean public areas. Under-26s €2.50 discount. Dorm **€17.50**

Hotel Triskel c/de las Afueras 9 ☏ 948 888 570, ⓦ hoteltriskel.com. This comfortable though otherwise characterless hotel overlooks the old town, with a lovely view – get one with a balcony. The cosy restaurant serves regional cuisine. **€80**

★ **Parador Sos del Rey Católico** c/Arquitecto Sainz de Vicuña ☏ 948 888 011, ⓦ parador.es. This superb hotel is well worth a splurge. In the finest parador tradition, it's a lovely blend of historic and modern architecture – with spectacular panoramic views across the hills. The elegant restaurant features Aragonese specialities, such as *ternasco*, or young lamb, and wine from the Campo de Borja region. Closed mid-Jan to early Feb. **€138**

Tarazona and around

The Aragonese plains are dotted with reminders of the Moorish occupation, and nowhere more so than at **TARAZONA**, a wonderfully atmospheric old town loaded with Mudéjar architecture. If you're en route to Soria or Burgos, it's an ideal place to break the journey. Don't miss out, either, on the tranquil Cistercian monastery of **Veruela**, 15km southeast.

Tarazona's most absorbing sights lie in the old upper town, incorporating the **Judería** and **Morería** (Jewish and Moorish quarters, respectively), which stands on a hill overlooking the river, with medieval houses and mansions lining the *callejas* and *pasadizos* – the lanes and alleyways.

If you're around for the **fiesta** on August 27, watch out for "El Cipotegato" (ⓦ cipotegato.com), a luckless character dressed in jester-like red, green and yellow stripy pyjamas who runs through the streets while everyone pelts him with tomatoes. He kicks off the town's annual week-long festivities, during which there are street parties, live music and bullfights.

Ayuntamiento

Pl. de España

At the heart of the old town is **Plaza de España**, flanked by a magnificent sixteenth-century **ayuntamiento**, with a facade of coats of arms, sculpted heads and figures in high relief. A frieze, representing the triumphal procession of Carlos V after his coronation as Holy Roman Emperor in Bologna, runs the length of the building, while the large figures underneath represent Hercules and other classical heroes performing feats of mythological proportions.

Santa María Magdalena and around

C/Conde • Open for services only

The Mudéjar tower of the church of **Santa María Magdalena** dominates the town. Within the church, look for the interesting fifteenth-century wooden lectern, carved in a geometric pattern. From the entrance there are especially good views of the eighteenth-century **Plaza de Toros** below – an octagonal terrace of houses, with balconies from which spectators could view the *corrida*. From the church you can continue uphill to the sixteenth-century convent church of **La Concepción** on c/Concepción, again with a slender brick tower.

Catedral

C/de la Verónica • Tues–Sat 11am–2pm & 5–7pm, Sun 11am–2pm, plus mid-June to mid-Sept 4–6pm; sometimes closed Tues • €4 • ☎ 976 640 271, ⓦ catedraldetarazona.es

In the lower town, the principal sight is the **Catedral**, built mainly in the fourteenth and fifteenth centuries. It's a typical example of the decorative use of brick in the Gothic-Mudéjar style, with a dome built to the same design as that of the old cathedral in Zaragoza, and Mudéjar cloisters. Parts of the interior may be closed for renovation.

ARRIVAL AND INFORMATION   TARAZONA

By bus Regular buses travel between Zaragoza and Tarazona (1hr 15min).

Turismo Pl. de San Francisco (daily 9.30am–2pm & 4–7pm; closes at 6.30pm in winter; ☎ 976 640 074,

ⓦ turiaso.com). The *turismo*, in the main square below the cathedral, runs guided tours of the town (€3/1hr or €5/2hr) on Sat at 5pm (6pm June–Aug) and Sun at noon.

ACCOMMODATION

Condes de Visconti c/Visconti 15 ☎ 976 644 908, ⓦ www.condesdevisconti.com. Lovely sixteenth-century *palacete* with individually decorated rooms, some with hardwood floors and wood-beam ceilings. **€90**

Hostal Palacete de los Arcedianos Pl. Arcedianos 1 ☎ 976 642 303, ⓦ palacetearcedianos.com. Basic hotel near Pl. de España, with simple rooms in a refurbished sixteenth-century building. **€42**

★ **Hostal Santa Agueda** c/Visconti 26 ☎ 976 640 054, ⓦ santaagueda.com. This welcoming *hostal* is set in a lovingly restored historic home, with lovely period

furnishings. The *hostal* also houses a small exhibit on Tarazona 1920s singer and vaudeville performer Raquel Meller. **€55**

★ **La Merced de la Concordia** Pl. de la Merced 2 ☎ 976 199 344, ⓦ lamerced.info. Handsome hotel in a 1501 *palacete* with modern flourishes that juxtapose nicely with the historic interior: pale-wood floors, recessed lights and sleek furnishings meet stone walls and restored rustic ceilings. Enjoy creatively prepared regional fare in the elegant, soft-toned restaurant (closed Sun dinner & Mon). **€70**

EATING AND DRINKING

El Caserón 2 Reino Aragón 2 ☎ 976 642 312. Just north of the old town, this friendly bar has haunches of ham dangling over the bar, and serves up traditional cuisine. Daily 1–3.30pm & 9–11pm (closed Sun dinner).

El Galeón Avda. La Paz 1 ☎ 976 642 965. In the lower town, this mid-priced restaurant serves good traditional food, including grilled *ternasco* (lamb) and seafood. Daily 1–4pm & 9pm–midnight (closed Sun dinner).

Monasterio de Veruela

Daily: April–Sept 10.30am–8.30pm; Oct–March 10.30am–6.30pm • €2

The **Monasterio de Veruela**, isolated in a fold of the hills 15km to the southeast of Tarazona, and standing within a massively fortified perimeter, is one of Spain's great religious houses. The monastery is uninhabited now, but the magnificent church, built in the severe twelfth-century Transitional style of the Carthusians, is kept open. The monastery admission ticket also gives access to the fourteenth-century cloisters and convent buildings.

Museo del Vino

Daily except Tues: April–Sept 10.30am–8.30pm; Oct–March 10.30am–6.30pm • ⓦ campodeborja.com

Housd within the monastery complex (and also covered by the monastery ticket) is a well-run **Museo del Vino**, which offers several floors of snazzy exhibits that trace Campo de Borja wine from grape to glass. You can also enjoy the wine tastings at high tables overlooking the ancient monastery.

Calatayud

Like Tarazona, **CALATAYUD** is a town of Moorish foundation with some stunning Mudéjar towers. It's worth climbing up to the old upper town where, amid a maze of alleys, stand

9

the church of **San Andrés** (generally closed; enquire at *turismo*) and **Colegiata de Santa María** (closed for renovations) both of which have ornate Mudéjar towers. Santa María, the collegiate church, also has a beautifully decorative Plateresque doorway, while towards the river, at c/Valentín Gómez 3, **San Juan el Real** (daily 10am–1pm & 4–8pm; free) features paintings attributed to the young Goya. The ruins of a Moorish **castle** (open access; free) survive on high ground at the opposite end of town from the train station. The views from here are lovely, and you can walk around the evocative ruins and parts of the city wall.

Museo de Calatayud

Pl. de Santa Teresa 3 · Mon–Sat 9.30am–1.30pm & 4–8pm, Sun 9.30am–1.30pm · Free · ☎ 976 897 816

The latest addition to the cultural scene in Calatayud is the well-curated **Museo de Calatayud**, housed in the historic Convento de la Orden del Carmelo. The interior is a pleasing blend of classic and contemporary architecture, and exhibits and audiovisual displays explore Calatayud's culture and history, with a focus on archeological finds, including Roman remains and ceramics from the nearby Roman site of Augusta Bilbilis.

ARRIVAL AND INFORMATION — CALATAYUD

By bus Regular buses travel between Zaragoza and Calatayud (1hr).

Turismo Museo del Calatayud, Pl. de Santa Teresa 3 (Mon–Sat 9.30am–1.30pm & 4–8pm, Sun 9.30am–1.30pm; ☎ 976 886 322, ⊛ turismocalatayud).

ACCOMMODATION

Hospedería Mesón la Dolores Pl. Mesones 4 ☎ 976 889 055, ⊛ mesonladolores.com. Comfortable hotel in a rustic eighteenth-century building with stone arches, tiled floors and dark wood ceilings. The restaurant serves a hearty *menú del día* (Mon–Fri €12.50, weekend €20), which includes gazpacho and grilled meats. **€81**

Hotel Castillo de Ayud Avda. de la Diputación 8 ☎ 976 880 088, ⊛ hotelcastillodeayud.com. This stylish, luxury *belle époque* complex has two adjoining places to stay – the beautifully renovated, traditional *Chalet de los Sánchez* and a contemporary three-star hotel, the *Castilo de Ayud* itself – as well as a soothing spa. The simple but good restaurant in the modern hotel has a surprisingly well-priced weekly lunch *menú* for €9 (€15 at the weekends) while there's also a more upmarket restaurant in the *Chalet* (open Fri dinner, Sat lunch & dinner, Sun lunch only), with a tasting menu for €35. *Castilo de Ayud* from **€60**, *Chalet de los Sánchez* **€144**

Monasterio de Piedra

Gardens daily 9am–8pm, until 6pm in winter · €13.50 · ☎ 902 196 052, ⊛ monasteriopiedra.com

The **Monasterio de Piedra** – "The Stone Monastery" – lies 20km south of Calatayud, 4km from the village of **NUÉVALOS**. The monastic buildings, once part of a grand Cistercian complex, are a ruin, but they stand amid lush park-like **gardens**, which seem all the more verdant in this otherwise harsh, dry landscape. The entrance fee includes a guided tour of the monastery's cloisters, church, wine cellar, refectory and kitchens. Red arrows mark out a route through the park and take you past a series of waterfalls, grottoes and lakes.

ARRIVAL AND DEPARTURE — MONASTERIO DE PIEDRA

By bus In summer a daily bus generally runs from Zaragoza to Nuévalos (2hr 30min). In winter it usually only runs twice during the week and on the weekends.

ACCOMMODATION

Hotel Monasterio de Piedra Near the park entrance ☎ 976 849 011, ⊛ monasteriopiedra.com. For the full experience, stay in this handsome abbey-turned-hotel, where you can sleep in the Cisterian monks' rooms, which have been plushly renovated. **€136**

Hotel Río Piedra Carretera del Monasterio de Piedra, Nuévalos ☎ 976 849 007, ⊛ www.hotelriopiedra.com. This family-run hotel, at the foot of the road up to the monastery, has a range of rooms, some with terraces. The restaurant serves well-prepared regional cuisine. **€80**

Hotel Las Truchas Carretera del Monasterio de Piedra, Nuévalos ☎ 976 849 040, ⊛ hotellastruchas.com. This family-run, reasonably priced hotel has simply furnished but clean rooms, and a pool. **€65**

Daroca

9

DAROCA, 38km southeast of Calatayud, is a charming old town, set within an impressive run of **walls** that include no fewer than 114 towers and enclose an area far greater than that needed by the present population of around 2200. The last major restoration of the walls was in the fifteenth century, but though largely in ruins today, they are still striking.

You enter the town through its original gates, the **Puerta Alta** or stout **Puerta Baja**, the latter decorated with the coat of arms of Carlos I. Within, c/Mayor runs between the two gates, past ancient streets dotted with Romanesque, Gothic and Mudéjar **churches**.

Colegial de Santa María

Pl. de España • Tues–Sun 11am–1pm & 5.30–8pm; in winter closes at 7pm • €3

The appeal of Daroca lies more in the whole ensemble rather than any specific monuments, though the principal church, the Renaissance **Colegial de Santa María**, on the main street off Plaza de España, does have a small museum of religious artefacts, including robes, silverwork, *retablos* and paintings.

ARRIVAL AND INFORMATION

DAROCA

By bus Daroca is connected to Calatayud, Teruel and Cariñena/Zaragoza by a couple of daily bus services; buses pull in on the c/Mayor close to the Puerta Baja.

Turismo c/Mayor 44 (daily 10am–2pm & 4–7.30pm; ☎ 976 800 129). The small *turismo* offer tours for groups of six (Tues–Sun 11.15am; €3 per person).

ACCOMMODATION AND EATING

Hotel Cien Balcones c/Mayor 88 ☎ 976 545 071, ⓦ cienbalcones.com. As the name suggests, this welcoming hotel has balconies galore, many fronted by wrought-iron handiwork, and overlooking a breezy patio. Ask about their creative packages, one of which includes a horse ride into the countryside. The elegant *Ruejo* restaurant serves regional cuisine. Breakfast included. **€80**

La Posada del Almudí c/Grajera 7, near Pl. Santiago, off c/Mayor ☎ 976 800 606, ⓦ posadadelalmudi.es. This place has two types of room to choose from: those in the restored fifteenth- to sixteenth-century mansion house; or those in a modern, stylish annexe across the street. There's also a bar and good restaurant (best to reserve; dinner for hotel guests only). **€65**

Teruel

The provincial capital of **TERUEL** offers an appealing glimpse into this rugged and sparsely populated wedge of Aragón. Because it's often overlooked, the region came up with the playful slogan "*Teruel existe*" ("Teruel exists"). If you're looking for remote, you're in the right region, with its back-of-beyond villages and medieval sights that haven't been prettified. The land, too, is high and harsh, with the coldest winters in the country.

Teruel the town is a likeable and impressively monumental place, with some of the finest **Mudéjar** work in Spain. Like Zaragoza, it was an important Moorish city and retained significant Muslim and Jewish communities after its Reconquest by Alfonso II in 1171. As you approach town, the Mudéjar towers, built by Moorish craftsmen over three centuries, are immediately apparent, and – like the fabulous Mudéjar ceiling in the cathedral – should not be missed.

The **centro histórico**, on a hill above the Río Turia, has Plaza del Torico at its heart, and is enclosed by a few remains of fortified walls, with a viaduct linking it to the modern quarter to the south. Leading off to the north is a sixteenth-century aqueduct, **Los Arcos**, a slender and elegant piece of monumental engineering.

La Escalinata

From the train station, you'll see straight ahead of you **La Escalinata**, a flight of steps decorated with bricks, tiles and turrets that is pure civic Mudéjar in style – note the iron gap in the wall to the left, where a lift (free) shoots up to the *paseo*, part of the extensive redevelopment of the site in 2004 by British architect David Chipperfield.

9

Torre de El Salvador and Torre de San Martín

Torre de El Salvador c/El Salvador 5 • Daily 11am–2pm & 4.30–7.30pm • €2.50

From the top of La Escalinata, c/El Salvador leads to the **Torre de El Salvador**, the finest of the town's four Mudéjar towers. It's covered with intricately patterned and proportioned coloured tiles to stunning effect, echoed closely in its more modest sister tower, **Torre de San Martín** (exterior only), best reached via c/de los Amantes. A common feature of all the towers is that they stand separate from the main body of the church to which they belong, a design most probably influenced by the freestanding minarets of the Muslim world.

Catedral de Santa María de Mediavilla

Pl. de la Catedral • Daily 11am–2pm & 4–8pm, until 7pm in winter; last entry 30min before closing • €3, or covered by joint ticket with Museo Diocesano

The **Catedral de Santa María de Mediavilla**, built in the twelfth century but gracefully adapted over subsequent years, boasts another fine Mudéjar tower, incorporating Romanesque windows and a lantern that combines Renaissance and Mudéjar features. The interior follows a more standard Gothic-Mudéjar pattern and at first sight seems unremarkable, save for its brilliant Renaissance *retablo*. Climb the stairs by the door, however, and put money in the illuminations box, and the fabulous **artesonado ceiling** is revealed. Completed between 1260 and 1314 by Moorish craftsmen, it's a gorgeous and fascinating mix of geometric Islamic motifs and medieval painting of courtly life.

EATING AND DRINKING
Los Aljibes	4
Bar Gregori	7
Lennon	6
La Menta	3
Mesón Óvalo	5
La Tierreta	1
Yaín	2

ACCOMMODATION
La Casa del Canónigo	1
Hostal Aragón	2
Hotel Gargallo Reina Cristina	5
Hotel El Mudayyan	4
Hotel Plaza Boulevard	6
Parador de Teruel	3

Museo Diocesano

Pl. de la Catedral • Daily 11am–2pm & 4–8pm, until 7pm in winter; last entry 30min before closing • €3, joint ticket with cathedral

Standing next to the cathedral, the sixteenth-century Palacio Episcopal houses the **Museo Diocesano**. Inside, look out for the *Calvario*, a beautiful woodcarving of Jesus (whose arms are missing), St John and the Virgin Mary, carved in the fifteenth century but for many years hidden behind a wall in a church in Sarrón, where it was discovered in 1946. Another highlight is the *Arbol de la Vida*, a striking seventeenth-century ivory carving of Christ.

Museo de Teruel

Pl. Fray Anselmo • Tues–Fri 10am–2pm & 4–7pm, Sat & Sun 10am–2pm • Free • ⓦ museo.deteruel.es

The well-run **Museo de Teruel** is worth a peek for its range of exhibits on local folklore and traditional rural life, including pottery, silverwork, clothing and a reconstructed interior of an eighteenth-century chemist shop. The museum also has interesting temporary exhibitions, including contemporary photography.

San Pedro and Mausoleo de los Amantes

Daily: Aug 10am–8pm; rest of year 10am–2pm & 4–8pm • **San Pedro** c/Matías Abad 3 • €2 • **Mausoleo de los Amantes** €4, combined ticket of church, tower and mausoleum €7 • ⓦ amantesdeteruel.es

Just beyond Plaza del Torico, which is flanked by a trio of *modernista* houses, is the church of **San Pedro**, endowed with a lovely Mudéjar tower which you can visit. Its claim to fame, however, relates to the nearby **Mausoleo de los Amantes**, a chapel containing the alabaster tomb of the Lovers of Teruel, Isabel de Segura and Juan Diego Martínez de Marcilla. This pair's thirteenth-century tale of thwarted love is a legend throughout Spain. The story goes that Diego, ordered by his lover's family to go away and prove himself worthy, left Teruel for five years, returning only to find that Isabel was to be married that same day. He asked for a last kiss, was refused and expired, heartbroken; Isabel, not to be outdone, arranged his funeral at San Pedro, kissed the corpse and died in its arms. The lovers' (reputed) bodies were exhumed in 1955 and now lie illuminated for all to see – a macabre yet popular pilgrimage for newlyweds.

Dinópolis

Daily 10am–8pm • €24, under-12s €19 • ⓦ dinopolis.com

Travellers with children might want to check out **Dinópolis**, a lively dinosaur theme park on the outskirts of town, replete with rides, guides dressed (and acting) like mad professors and oodles of dinosaur exhibits. Dinópolis also run a number of other similarly themed parks in the region, including the Bosque Pétreo (Petrified Forest); enquire at the ticket office for details.

ARRIVAL AND INFORMATION   TERUEL

By train Trains run regularly from Zaragoza (2hr 15min) and Valencia (2hr 30min). The station is on the fringes of the *centro histórico*; from the train station, walk up La Escalinata and c/Nueva into town.

By bus The bus station is also on the eastern edge of town; walk north a short way up the ring road, taking the first left to Pl. Judería. There are a number of bus companies, so check the timetables in the windows before buying a ticket, as some buses are considerably slower than others. All services are reduced on Sun.

Destinations Ademuz (daily; 45min); Albarracín (daily; 2hr); Barcelona (daily; 5hr); Valencia (5 daily; 2hr); Zaragoza (7 daily; 2hr).

Turismo Pl. de los Amantes 6 (daily 10am–2pm & 4–8pm; Aug daily 10am–8pm; ☎ 978 624 105, ⓦ teruel.es).

Regional tourist office c/San Francisco, near the La Escalinata (Mon–Sat 9am–2pm & 4.30–8pm, Sun 10am–2pm & 4.30–8pm; ☎ 978 602 279).

ACCOMMODATION

La Casa del Canónigo c/San Martín ☎ 978 607 199, ⓦ casadelcanonigo.com. Well-preserved *casa* in the

middle of the old town, set in a seventeenth-century mansion that was acquired by the *canónigo* (canon) of the

9

Teruel cathedral in 1698. There are six well-furnished apartments, all with kitchens. Two-person apartment €60

Hostal Aragón c/Santa María 4 ☎978 601 387, ⓦhostalaragon.org. This basic spot has small but comfortable rooms, both with (€15 extra) and without bathroom. Note that the thin walls mean it can get noisy in the evenings. €29

Hotel Gargallo Reina Cristina Paseo del Óvalo 1 ☎978 606 860, ⓦgargallohotels.es. This attractive hotel by the Torre del Salvador has modern if unexciting rooms, as well as an excellent restaurant that serves regional cuisine, from the famous local ham to a dessert of *arroz con leche caramelizado* (rice with caramelized milk). Breakfast included. €85

Hotel El Mudayyan c/Nueva 18 ☎978 623 042, ⓦelmudayyan.com. Lovely, petite hotel where you can – quite literally – explore underground Teruel: medieval tunnels, once used by priests to travel to and from the sacristy, extend below the hotel, and intrepid guests can venture into them (as far as they dare), led by the owners who can expound on Teruel's history. *El Mudayyan*'s eight rooms are snug but individually decorated with Mudéjar touches, while a small Moroccan-style tearoom makes for a relaxing afternoon. Breakfast included. €70

Hotel Plaza Boulevard Pl. Tremedal 3 ☎978 608 817, ⓦbacohoteles.com. This smart hotel near Pl. San Juan has modern rooms with wooden floors and king-size beds. €54

Parador de Teruel Carretera Sagunto-Burgos, 2km out of town ☎978 601 800, ⓦparador.es. This modern building, on a wooded hillside overlooking the town and towers, has a swimming pool and tennis courts but not much in the way of character. €133

EATING AND DRINKING

Jamón de Teruel is the town's most celebrated gastronomic creation – the region's dry but cold winds create an ideal climate for curing. You'll find the tasty, fat-streaked *jamón* in shops and served up in tapas bars and restaurants all over the old town. The main areas for restaurants are on the eastern side of the old town, principally Pl. Judería, c/Bartolomé Esteban, c/Abadía and c/San Esteban, though you'll also find lively cafés on Pl. del Torico. For bars, check out the streets around Pl. Judería and Pl. Bolamar.

Los Aljíbes c/Yagüe de Salas 3. A buzzing café and *bodega* specializing in Aragonese and Navarran cuisine such as *migas a la Pastora* and juicy lamb (entrees €12–15), with a well-stocked tapas counter and an extensive wine list featuring local vintages. Daily 8am–11pm; closed Sun in Aug & Sept, plus last 2 weeks of July.

Bar Gregori Paseo del Óvalo 6 ☎978 608 063. This friendly tapas bar serves all the favourites, including Teruel's famous *jamón* and pigs' ears. Outside tables, plus good, keenly priced wine and *sangría* make for a chilled place to pass the evening. Daily from late morning until 1am.

Lennon c/San Andrés 23 ☎978 601 970. A vast, laid-back bar with several rooms, comfy chairs and sofas, occasional live music and a pool table. Tues–Sun 3pm–midnight, or later.

La Menta c/Bartolomé Esteban 10 ☎978 605 804. One of the city's top restaurants, with a carefully constructed menu that changes weekly, and sumptuous dishes of Aragonese classics for €15–18 and up. Daily except Sun 1.30–3pm & 9–11pm.

Mesón Óvalo Paseo del Óvalo 2 ☎978 618 235, ⓦmesonovalo.es. A very popular *mesón* with warm, tangerine-coloured walls, quality cooking (the trout dishes are excellent) and a range of Maestrazgo specialities from around €14. Tues–Sat 10am–5pm & 8.30–11.30pm, Sun 10am–5pm; closed Mon.

La Tierreta Francisco Piquer 6 ☎978 617 923,

EL RINCÓN DE ADEMUZ

El Rincón de Ademuz (ⓦwww.rincondeademuz.com), 30km due south of Teruel, is a strange little region: a Valencian province enclosed within Aragonese territory. It's a very remote corner of Spain, with a bleak kind of grandeur, and scarcely a tourist from one year to the next.

The place to head for – and if you're bussing it, the only realistic place to get to from Teruel – is **ADEMUZ** itself, without doubt Spain's tiniest and least significant provincial capital. Strung along a craggy hill at the confluence of two long rivers, this could make a beautiful base for walking, and there's a fascination just in wandering the streets with their dark stone cottages and occasional Baroque towers.

For energetic **trekking**, Torre Baja lies to the north along the Río Turia, and beyond it the beautiful village of Castielfabib. The most interesting of these little Ademuz hamlets, Puebla de San Miguel, is to the east, in the Sierra Tortajada, easily accessible by road from Valencia, but also from a minor road just out of Ademuz in the Teruel direction, east over the Río Turia bridge and signposted to Sabina, Sesga and Mas del Olmo.

latierreta.com. Tucked away behind the cathedral is this elegant restaurant, with pale-wood walls and white curtains. The innovative dishes (€14–20) are rooted in regional produce, such as monkfish flavoured with saffron culled from the nearby Monreal del Campo and wild sea bass with seasonal mushrooms. Daily 1.30–4pm, plus Tues–Sat 9–11pm.

★ **Yaín** Pl. de la Judería 9 ☎ 978 624 076, ⓦyain.es. Proof that creative, gourmet fare has a place in Teruel. The sleek restaurant (named after the Hebrew word for "wine", because of its location on Pl. de la Judería) reveals gleaming dark wood, alabaster lamps and an impressive wine cellar. Regional dishes (€13–19) with a twist include *pimiento del piquillo* (bright-red peppers shaped like a *piquillo*, or "little beak") stuffed with cod and quail with a *garbanzo* puree. The tasting *menú* (€30) makes for a memorable splurge. Daily except Mon 1.30–3pm, plus Wed–Sat 9–11pm.

Albarracín

ALBARRACÍN, 37km west of Teruel, is one of the more accessible targets in rural southern Aragón – and also one of the most picturesque towns in the province, poised above the Río Guadalaviar and retaining, virtually intact, its medieval streets and tall, balconied houses. There's a historical curiosity here, too, in that from 1165 to 1333, the town formed the centre of a small independent state, the kingdom of the Azagras.

Despite its growing appeal as a tourist destination, Albarracín's dark, enclosed lanes and ancient buildings adorned with splendid coats of arms still make for an intriguing wander – reminders of past eras. Approaching from Teruel, you may imagine that you're about to come upon a large town, for the **medieval walls** swoop back over the hillside – protecting, with the loop of the river, a far greater area than the extent of the town, past or present.

Moving on from Albarracín, if you have transport, you could take a fabulous route west to Cuenca through beautiful country, by way of Frías de Albarracín and the source of the Río Tajo (see p.184).

Catedral and Museo Diocesano

C/Catedral • Mon–Sat 10.30am–2pm & 4.30–6.30pm (until 6pm in winter), Sun 10.30am–2pm; may be closed for renovations • €2.50, includes entry to museum

The **Catedral**, a medieval building remodelled in the sixteenth to eighteenth centuries, rises over a small square, and features an eye-catching gilded altarpiece. The newly renovated **Museo Diocesano**, housed in the attached Palacio Obispal, displays religious and sacred art from around the region, including painting, sculpture, metalwork and musical instruments.

Museo de Albarracín

C/San Juan 18 • Mon–Sat 10.30am–2pm & 4.30–6.30pm, Sun 10.30am–2pm • €3.50

The well-curated **Museo de Albarracín** is housed in an eighteenth-century hospital that was also used as a prison after the Civil War. It features a range of exhibits and audiovisual displays on the history, art and culture of Albarracín, including rare archeological finds like eleventh-century ceramics.

Castillo de Albarracín

Tours: summer daily 11am, noon, 1pm, 5pm, 6pm & 7pm; less regular in winter • €2.50

The crumbling but atmospheric **castle**, in the southern part of town, forms part of Albarracín's impressive remains, and dates from the ninth century when the town was a fortified Islamic outpost. Among its remains are parts of a tenth-century Moorish palace and various lookout points along the ancient walls.

Torre Blanca and Torre del Andador

Torre Blanca Daily: summer 10.30–2pm & 5–8pm; winter usually daily 1–2pm & 7–8pm, but sometimes only open weekends • €1.50 • ☎ 978 704 035 **Torre Andador** Open access • Free

The **Torre Blanca**, near the castle, houses temporary changing exhibits on everything from portrait paintings to contemporary photography, and you can climb to a lookout

9

ALBARRACÍN'S MUSEUMS

If you plan on seeing most of Albarracín's sights, opt for a **joint ticket** for €7, that allows access to all the main sights, including the Museo Diocesano, Museo de Albarracín, the castle and Torre Blanca. For €9, the ticket includes a guided tour of town. Tickets are on sale at the Centro de información, and at all the sights.

---

point within the tower to survey the surrounding landscape. The **Torre del Andador** looms over the northern part of town.

ARRIVAL AND INFORMATION
ALBARRACÍN

Bys bus Regular buses run from Teruel (45min) and Cuenca (3hr).

Turismo c/San Antonio, next to the main bridge (Mon–Sat 10am–2pm & 4–8pm, Sun 10am–2pm & 4–7pm; ☎ 978 710 262, ⍉ comarcadelasierradealbarracin.es), has information on both the town and the surrounding region.

Centro de Información c/Catedral, next to the cathedral (daily: summer 10am–2pm & 4–8pm; till 6.30 or 7pm in winter; ☎ 978 704 035, ⍉ fundacionsantamariadeal barracin.com). The centre offers guided tours (1hr 30min; €2) of Albarracín that depart at various times of the day; enquire within.

ACCOMMODATION AND EATING

Albergue Juventud Rosa Bríos c/Santa María 5 ☎ 978 710 005, reservations ☎ 902 088 905, ⍉ reaj .com. This youth hostel, just past the cathedral, is set in a medieval mansion, with comfortable dorm rooms and a basic dining hall; they can also organize excursions into the surrounding countryside. Breakfast included. Dorms €16

★ **Casa Santiago** Subida a las Torres 11 ☎ 978 700 316, ⍉ www.casadesantiago.net. The inviting, family-run *Casa Santiago* is set in a restored country house at the top of a stone staircase near the Pl. Mayor, with cosy, individually decorated rooms – with colourful quilts and wood-beamed ceilings – and sun-lit sitting rooms where

you can gaze over the brightly tiled roofs of Albarracín. The restaurant serves local cuisine. €70

El Hostal Los Palacios c/Los Palacios, beyond the Portal de Molina ☎ 978 700 327, ⍉ www .montepalacios.com. This welcoming hotel features well-cared-for rooms, some with rustic brick walls, and a casual terrace restaurant-bar serving hearty regional cuisine like roast lamb, and a *menú del día* for €16. €45

Posada del Adarve c/Portal de Molina 23 ☎ 978 700 304, ⍉ posadadeladarve.com. Relax in handsome, carefully renovated rooms, some with wood-beam ceilings and rustic furniture, in a historic townhouse, right near the Portal de Molina. €60

Sierra de Gúdar

The mountains of the **Sierra de Gúdar** and nearby El Maestrazgo (see p.620), to the east and northeast of Teruel, are an area of great variety and striking, often wild, beauty, with severe peaks, deep gorges and lush meadows. One hundred years ago, this now impoverished region had four times the number of inhabitants it does today. Defeated in their attempts to make a living from agriculture, many left to seek their fortunes in the cities, leaving behind the crumbling remains of once grand, honey-hued farmhouses that dot the landscape and stone-walled terraces etched into the steep-sided hills.

A landscape of sharp, rocky crags, Sierra de Gúdar is easy to access by following the N234 southeast from Teruel and then heading northeast into the mountains along the A232. This will bring you to the lovely medieval villages of **Mora de Rubielos**, 42km from Teruel, and its even lovelier twin, **Rubielos de Mora**. Head north from here for **Linares de Mora** and **Mosqueruela**, also charming and remote mountain villages.

Mora de Rubielos and Rubielos de Mora

These confusingly named villages both have fine collections of medieval houses, with small, wrought-iron balconies, often bedecked with flowers. Both are lovely places to while away an afternoon of wandering about. **Mora de Rubielos** has an impressive castle, while **Rubielos de Mora**, 14km from Mora, features handsome *palacios* with finely carved wooden eaves, a small art museum and the **Ex Colegiata de Santa María la Mayor**, on Plaza de Marqués de Tosos, with an ostentatious tiered bell tower. If you want to see inside, enquire at the *turismo*.

Castillo de Mora de Rubielos

Mora de Rubielos • Tues–Fri 10am–2pm & 5–7.30pm, Sat & Sun 10am–2pm & 5–8pm • €2

For such a small place, Mora de Rubielos has an extremely grand **castle**, built in a luminous pinkish-gold stone, which during the Middle Ages served as both defensive fort and noble residence, and was the heart of town life. Inside, several fairly nondescript rooms, squeezed between the castle's outer and inner walls, are set around a courtyard of pointed arches. One room hosts a small **Museo Etnológico**, a motley collection of rustic antiquities. If it's open, it's worth having a peek inside the bulky, Gothic **Ex Colegiata de Santa María** below the castle.

Fundación Museo Salvador Victoria

C/Hospital 13, Rubielos de Mora • Mon–Fri 10am–2pm & 5–7.30pm, Sat & Sun 10am–2pm & 4–8pm • Free • ☎ 978 804 034, ⓦ salvadorvictoria.com

Housed in the eighteenth-century Hospital de Gracia, the **Fundación Museo Salvador Victoria** in Rubielos de Mora features an in-depth collection of work by Salvador Victoria (1928–1994), from lithographs to luminous paintings. The museum also has a well-curated collection of contemporary Spanish art from the second half of the twentieth century, including works by Lucio Muñoz, Rafael Canogar and Manuel Rivera.

ARRIVAL AND DEPARTURE | MORA DE RUBIELOS AND RUBIELOS DE MORA

By bus Buses are infrequent in this area, but most villages are connected with each other and/or Teruel once a day. A bus (Mon–Fri) leaves Teruel in the afternoon for Mosquentela via Mora de Rubielos, Rubielos de Mora and Linares de Mora, returning in the early morning.

INFORMATION

Mora de Rubielos c/Hispanoamericano 5 (Tues–Fri 10am–2pm & 5–7.30pm, Sat & Sun 5–8pm; ☎ 978 800 000, ⓦ moraderubielos.com).

Rubielos de Mora In the *ayuntamiento* on Pl. de Hispano América (July–Sept 10am–2pm & 5–8pm; till 7.30m Oct–June; ☎ 978 804 001, ⓦ rubielosdemora.es).

ACCOMMODATION AND EATING

MORA DE RUBIELOS

Hotel Jaime I Pl. de la Villa near the ayuntamiento ☎ 978 800 092, ⓦ hoteljaime.com. This attractively restored hotel has elegantly rustic rooms in an old mansion, some with wood beams, as well as a restaurant with good regional cuisine. **€79**

Hotel La Trufa Negra Avda. Ibañez Martín 10 ☎ 978 807 144, ⓦ latrufanegra.com. This swanky hotel has stylish rooms full of amenities, a luxurious spa and an upmarket restaurant serving excellent local cuisine. This area of the Maestrazgo is famous for its truffles (*trufas*) which, unusually, are rooted out by dogs rather than pigs. The hotel offers packages where you can go out into the countryside with truffle-hunters and their dogs, and then enjoy the fragrant truffles on the tasting menu in the restaurant. **€139**

RUBIELOS DE MORA

Hotel de la Villa Pl. del Carmen ☎ 978 804 640, ⓦ hotel-de-la-villa.com. This handsome hotel has a restored sixteenth-century facade, a stone-arch entrance, elegant rooms with wooden furnishings and beamed ceilings, and a fine restaurant with a €15 *menú del día*. **€90**

★ **Los Leones** Pl. Igual y Gil 3 ☎ 978 804 477, ⓦ losleones.info. A well-restored seventeenth-century palace near the church, complete with antique bedsteads and heavy wooden doors. Also has a smart restaurant serving an excellent array of regional specialities. **€70**

Linares de Mora

The vegetation becomes scrubbier and the views more dramatic as the road climbs north 23km from Rubielos to **LINARES DE MORA**, a beguiling place, with houses piled higgledy-piggledy up the mountainside and glorious views. Its ruined castle is situated, rather precariously, on a jutting rock above the village, while another promontory hosts a church.

9

El Portalico c/Portalico ☎978 802 110, ⊛hostal elportalico.com. Sitting on the edge of the old quarter, this basic but clean *hostal* is set in a historic mansion and has pleasant, simply furnished rooms with wrought-iron beds. Breakfast included. €32

Mosquerela

A couple of kilometres beyond Linares de Mora, the superbly positioned **Mirador del Puerto de Linares** (1555m) affords hair-raising views down an almost vertical slope to the village below. Continuing northeast along the A1701, you'll come to **MOSQUERUELA**. With its ramshackle streets and back-of-beyond charm, this sleepy village feels as if it hasn't changed much since its foundation in 1262, and it's not uncommon to see flocks of sheep being herded through the centre. The village boasts an attractive, porticoed **Plaza Mayor** and a couple of pretty churches, but there's not much more to detain you.

Southern Maestrazgo

Unfolding northeast of Teruel, the **Maestrazgo** is dry, windswept, rugged terrain dominated (and named after) the Maestrazgo mountain range. In keeping with the rest of the region, the Maestrazgo is sparsely populated and often seems stuck in time, particularly if you wander the quiet, cobbled streets of its ancient mountain villages. Approaching the region from Teruel, you pass nearby **Cedrillas** with its conspicuous, ridge-top castle ruin. From here the road starts climbing into the hills, scaling high mountain passes and affording tantalizing views of the valleys. The first village of any size is **Cantavieja**, which makes a useful base for exploring – or walking in – the region, while to the southeast lies the fairly well-preserved **La Iglesuela del Cid**.

Cantavieja

CANTAVIEJA, dramatically situated by the edge of an escarpment at an altitude of 1300m, is a little livelier and larger than most Maestrazgo villages, though its population is still under a thousand. The beautiful, porticoed **Plaza de Cristo Rey**, halfway up c/Mayor from Plaza de España, is typical of the region, and the escutcheoned *ayuntamiento* bears a Latin inscription with suitably lofty sentiments: "This House hates wrongdoing, loves peace, punishes crimes, upholds the laws and honours the upright."

Museo de las Guerras Carlistas de Cantavieja

C/Mayor • June–Aug daily 10am–2pm & 4–8pm; rest of year Wed 4–7pm, Thurs–Sat 10am–2pm & 4–7pm, Sun 10am–2pm • €1.50

In the same building as the *turismo*, the small but well-curated **Museo de las Guerras Carlistas de Cantavieja** documents the nineteenth-century Carlist Wars in Cantavieja via panels, scale models, old uniforms, newspaper clippings and weapons. They also have audiovisual displays on the theme of "El Maestrazgo en Tiempos de Cambio" ("Maestrazgo in Times of Change"), which covers the cultural and geographical evolution of this mountainous region, focusing on the Carlist Wars era.

Mirambel

The best views of Cantavieja can be found on the rough and narrow road to **MIRAMBEL**, 15km to the northeast and walkable in about four hours. The village preserves a timeless atmosphere with its ancient walls, gateways and stone houses. It was temporarily thrown into a whirl of excitement when Ken Loach filmed *Land and Freedom* (1995) here, but these days it's back to its usual, sleepy self.

La Iglesuela del Cid

LA IGLESUELA DEL CID, 11km to the southeast of Cantavieja, is another fine walk along a rough country road. The village's name bears witness to the exploits of **El Cid**

Campeador, who came charging through the Maestrazgo in his fight against the infidel, though other than the El Cid *romería*, a fiesta organized by the village, forty days after Easter (usually in May), there's nothing else to commemorate the legendary hero.

The village's ochre-red, dry-stone walls, ubiquitous coats of arms and stream, now little more than a trickle cutting through the village, are picturesque enough in this remote countryside, but there's not much else to see. The central, compact Plaza de la Iglesia is enclosed by the old *ayuntamiento*, the attractive **Iglesia Parroquial de la Purificacíon** and a restored eighteenth-century *palacio*, now home to an upmarket hotel (see below).

Villarluengo and beyond

Another dramatic, almost alpine, route is in store if you head 30km northwest from Cantavieja, past Cañada de Benatanduz to **VILLARLUENGO**, an enchanting village of ancient houses stacked on a terraced hillside.

Continue 6km farther north, over the Villarluengo Pass (1132m), and you'll come to the wonderfully atmospheric *Hostal de la Trucha*. A further 19km, over another pass and past the striking jagged limestone ridges known as **Los Órganos de Montoro**, the road drops down to the small village of **Ejulve**, and then 11km north to the N211 between Montalbán and Alcañiz.

ARRIVAL AND INFORMATION
SOUTHERN MAESTRAZGO

By bus The main approaches to El Maestrazgo are from Teruel, and there are daily buses to Cantavieja and La Iglesuela del Cid, or from Morella in the province of Castellón. Note that bus schedules can vary, so confirm with the *turismo* in Teruel.

Turismo c/Mayor, Cantavieja (mid-July to mid-Sept daily 10am–2pm & 4–7pm; rest of the year usually Sat & Sun only; ☎964 185 414, ⍵cantavieja.es).
Online For more general information on the Maestrazgo, check out ⍵elmaestrazgo.com.

ACCOMMODATION AND EATING

CANTAVIEJA

Buj Avda. Maestrazgo 6 ☎964 185 033. Cantavieja is home to this unexpectedly chic restaurant, specializing in refined Aragonese cuisine with a twist. Daily 1.30–3pm.
Hotel Balfagón Avda. Maestrazgo 20 ☎964 185 076, ⍵hotelbalfagon.com. This stylish and modern hotel, on the main road at the southern edge of town, has comfortable rooms, as well as an excellent restaurant that serves traditional cuisine (closed Sun dinner in winter). **€67**

MIRAMBEL

Guimera c/Agustín Pastor 28 ☎964 178 269, ⍵hostalguimera.com. Excellent little *fonda* with cosy rooms, comfy beds and a good-quality, popular restaurant serving home-cooked dishes, like *judías blancas con chorizo* (white beans with sausage) and a variety of good-priced *menús*. **€35**

LA IGLESUELA DEL CID

Casa Amada c/Fuente Nueva 10 ☎964 443 373. This

simple *hostal*, on the main road through the village, has basic rooms and a restaurant (closed Sun dinner) which serves well-priced, substantial country cooking. **€40**
★ **Hospedería La Iglesuela del Cid** c/Ondevilla 4 ☎964 443 476, ⍵www.hospederiasdearagon.com. Lovely luxury hotel, set in the eighteenth-century Palacio Matutano-Daudén, with well-appointed rooms. The restaurant serves regional cuisine and offers a *menú del día* for €15. Breakfast included. **€68**

VILLARLUENGO AND BEYOND

Fonda Villarluengo Pl. Castel 1, Villarluengo ☎978 773 014. Friendly *hostal* with well-maintained rooms above a bar and a *comedor* serving simple meals (closed Tues). **€35**
Hostal de la Trucha c/Las Fábricas, 6km north of Villarluengo ☎978 773 008, ⍵gargallo-hotels.com. Set in an old farmhouse on the banks of the tranquil Río Pitarque, this wonderfully atmospheric *hostal* has a restaurant that serves trout caught a few metres away. **€50**

Northern Maestrazgo

The northern limits of the Maestrazgo edge into Tarragona province in Catalunya, and can be approached from Tarragona/Gandesa, or from Zaragoza via Alcañiz, where the N232 forks: east to the lovely town of **Valderrobres**, with its superb castle and

9

elegant Gothic church, and south to **Calanda** and a new centre dedicated to film-maker Luis Buñuel.

Calanda: Centro Buñuel

C/Mayor 48, on the edge of town • Tues–Sun 10.30am–1.30pm & 4–8pm • €3.50 • ⓦ cbcvirtual.com

Just 15km beyond Alcorisa, **CALANDA** is home to the **Centro Buñuel**, dedicated to surrealist filmmaker Luis Buñuel, who was born here in 1900. Buñuel left Spain in the 1930s, spending his most creative periods in France and then Mexico, where he died in 1983, but remained fond of his home town throughout his life. The centre houses a series of innovative displays on the man and his movies, and also has an extensive film library.

Valderrobres

VALDERROBRES is one of the Maestrazgo's most attractive towns. It stands 53km from Calanda, near the border with Catalunya and astride the Río Matarraña, whose crystal waters, flanked by lush valleys, teem with trout. The old quarter sits north of the river, connected to the new town by Avda. Hispanidad and the Puente de Piedra, with the unassuming seventeenth-century **ayuntamiento** on Plaza España just over the bridge – this was considered so characteristic of the region that it was reproduced in Barcelona's Poble Espanyol open-air museum in 1929.

A short walk from here and dominating the town are the **Castillo-Palacio** (summer Tues–Sat 10.30–2pm & 5–8.30pm, limited hours in winter; enquire at *turismo*; €3), once owned by the archbishops of Zaragoza, and a Gothic parish church – **Santa María** – which has a fine rose window (open during services only).

ARRIVAL AND INFORMATION · NORTHERN MAESTRAZGO

By bus Buses run between Valderrobres and Alcañiz (50min) and Tortosa (1hr).
Turismo Avda. Cortes de Aragón 7, near the iron bridge (July & Aug Tues–Sat 9.30am–2pm & 5–7.30pm, Sun 9.30am–2pm; Sept–June Wed–Sat 10am–2pm & 4–6pm, Sun 10am–2pm; ☎ 978 890 886).

ACCOMMODATION AND EATING

Fonda La Plaza Pl. España 8, opposite the ayuntamiento ☎ 978 850 106, ⓦ posadalaplaza.com. Longtime *fonda* in the old quarter, which has atmospheric rooms set in a medieval mansion. The restaurant serves a *menú del día* for €12 during the week, and €12–20 on the weekend. **€50**
Hostal Querol Just up Avda. Hispanidad from the bridge ☎ 978 850 192, ⓦ hostalquerol.com. This plain but adequate *hostal* has simple, clean rooms and a bar and *comedor* (closed Sun) serving local cuisine. **€50**
El Salt Elvira Hidalgo 14 ☎ 978 890 865, ⓦ hotelelsalt .com. In the new town, this is one of the more comfortable options. It's not far from the river, and has well-maintained rooms. **€50**

The Aragonese Pyrenees

The **Aragonese Pyrenees** seem to define all the superlatives associated with the soaring Pyrenean mountains: the peaks here are the highest, the wildest and, in the eyes of many, the most beautiful of the Spanish Pyrenees. From the snowy mountain tips piercing the blue sky to lushly forested valleys and thundering rivers, the Aragonese Pyrenees are one of the country's national treasures. And you can lace up your ski or hiking boots, and take to the verdant valleys or snow slopes – the mountains offer adventure throughout the seasons.

Huesca and Jaca are the two biggest cities, with plenty of bus connections into the Pyrenees. **Huesca**, the provincial capital, is a good jumping-off point for the splendid castle of **Loarre**, the relatively under-the-radar **Sierra de Guara**, with sculpted gorges, and the surreal rock formations of **Los Mallos**. East of Huesca, **Barbastro** is the centre of the fertile Somontano wine region. Amiable **Jaca**, with a formidable cathedral and decent array of hotels and *hostales*, makes for a popular base, particularly for the busy **ski resorts** to the north, Astún and Candanchú. As for summer activities, hiking trails traverse the entire range, including in the gorgeous **Ansó** and **Hecho** valleys and the magnificent **Parque Nacional de Ordesa y Monte Perdido**.

Huesca

Capital of one of the three provinces that make up Aragón, **Huesca** is a pleasant mix of urban and rustic, with modern apartment buildings lining its perimeter and a dark, atmospheric old quarter with outdoor cafés and drinking dens. Huesca's history is impressive: the Romans settled here first, calling it Osca, followed by the Moors who took Huesca in 718, just seven years after their arrival in Spain, and ruled it for almost four hundred years. In 1096, it became the capital of the Aragón kingdom until power was transferred to Zaragoza in the early twelfth century. Huesca was hit particularly hard during the Spanish Civil War and witnessed several years of fierce battles between the Republicans and Franco's forces.

Catedral and Museo Diocesano

Pl. de la Catedral · **Catedral and Museo** Mon–Fri 10.30am–2pm & 4–8pm, Sat 10.30am–2pm · €3 · **Catedral only** Services Sat 4.30–6.30pm, Sun 9am–1pm & 4.30–6.30pm · Free

The **Catedral**, looming majestically over the old town, beautifully reveals the city's past, including everything from brick Mudéjar to soaring Gothic. It features a superb sixteenth-century alabaster *retablo* by the legendary Renaissance artist Damián Forment, with a triptych detailing scenes from the Crucifixion. The **Museo Diocesano** exhibits well-preserved religious works, including sacred art, from medieval to Baroque, culled from across the region.

Ayuntamiento

Pl. de la Catedral 1 · Contact *turismo* for opening times · €2

The **Ayuntamiento** features a Baroque staircase and a famous nineteenth-century painting, *The Bell of Huesca*, which depicts one of the more macabre moments in Huesca's history. As the legend goes, in the twelfth century King Ramiro II ordered the beheading of a group of noblemen who had apparently committed treason. He then

9

had their heads laid out in a circle, forming the base of the bell, and suspended one of the heads on a rope over the circle, as the bell's clapper. It is this Ramiro II is who is buried in San Pedro del Viejo (see below).

Museo Provincial de Huesca
Pl. de la Universidad • Tues–Sat 10am–2pm & 5–8pm, Sun 10am–2pm • Free

The **Museo Provincial de Huesca** showcases a wide variety of archeological items from around the province, including ruins of a Roman necropolis; lithographs by Goya; and paintings by Aragonese artists, including Huesca native Ramón Acín. The museum is built around a unique octagonal courtyard.

San Pedro el Viejo
Pl. de San Pedro • Mon–Sat 10am–1.30pm & 4–7.30pm, Sun 11am–12.15 & 1–1.45pm • €2.50

Founded as a Benedictine monastery in the eleventh century, the church of **San Pedro el Viejo** houses the tombs of Aragonese royalty King Alfonso I and his son Ramiro II. It also features a lovely, well-maintained Romanesque cloister with beautifully carved capitals.

ARRIVAL AND INFORMATION   HUESCA

By train and bus The intermodal train and bus station is on c/Zaragoza, south of town. Huesca is well connected by bus and train to the region and beyond: regular Alosa buses (𝖜 alosa.es) connect the town with Zaragoza (just over 1hr), Jaca (just over 1hr), Barbastro (50min), Lleida (just

over 2hr) and Barcelona (4hr). Numerous trains run daily to Zaragoza (just over 1hr) and Teruel (3hr 15min). AVE trains also run to Zaragoza (40min) and Madrid (just over 2hr).
Turismo Pl. López Allué (daily 9am–2pm & 4–8pm; 𝕿 974 292 170, 𝖜 huescaturismo.com).

ACCOMMODATION

Hostal Joaquín Costa c/Joaquín Costa 20 𝕿 974 241 774, 𝖜 hostaljoaquincosta.com. Centrally located, this amiable *hostal* has rooms in a white-and-grey colour scheme and bathrooms revealing designer flair. €50
Hostal San Marcos c/San Orencio 10 𝕿 974 222 931, 𝖜 hostalsanmarcos.es. Friendly *hostal* with low-frills but well-maintained rooms. Within easy walking distance of Huesca's main sights. €37
Hotel Sancho Abarca Coso Alto 52 𝕿 974 220 650,

𝖜 hotelsanchoabarca.com. A notch above the other accommodation in town, this hotel (renovated in 2010) has modern, crisp rooms with decently sized bathrooms, a spa and fitness centre with a sauna, and a restaurant (closed Sun dinner) serving Aragonese cuisine. €80
La Posada de la Luna c/Joaquín Costa 10 𝕿 974 240 857, 𝖜 posadadelaluna.com. Petite, colourful, boutique-style hotel with cosy rooms and well-outfitted bathrooms. €69

EATING AND DRINKING

La Bodeguita del Centro c/Sancho Ramírez 3 𝕿 974 226 823. Handsome basement restaurant, with stone walls and wood ceilings, and a menu of local cuisine, from juicy sirloin to duck breast. They also run a street-level bar dishing up *raciones* and a good selection of wine. Daily except Mon 1.30–4pm & 8.30–11pm.
★ **Gastrologica** c/La Palma 7 𝕿 974 111 974, 𝖜 gastrologica.es. Quirky, progressive restaurant and "gastrobar" that produces unique dishes rooted in seasonal, local produce. In the upstairs restaurant, a tasting menu is offered for €40, while the downstairs *bar de tapas* features small plates (€4–9), which are a great way to casually sample the breadth of the menu. Daily except Mon noon–4pm & 8pm–midnight; closed Sun night.
Hervi c/Santa Paciencia 𝕿 974 240 333. This lively restaurant draws a local crowd and serves hearty dishes, including grilled meats and seafood, and nicely priced

regional wines. Generally 1.30–3.30pm & 8.30–10.30pm.
Taberna de Lillas Pastia Pl. Navarra 4 𝕿 974 211 691. Dine on gourmet Aragonese cuisine, from suckling pig to *arroz negro* (rice cooked in squid ink) topped with tender octopus, at this delightful restaurant. The wine selection is chosen from local vineyards, including the Somontano region. Splurge on the tasting menu (€56) or the equally delicious though less elaborate *menú Carmen*, for €32. Daily except Mon 1.30–3.30pm & 9.30–11pm; closed Sun night.
Las Torres c/María Auxiliadora 3 𝕿 974 228 213, 𝖜 lastorres-restaurante.com. Innovative cuisine finds inspiration in the local bounty, from freshwater fish to pig's trotters to aromatic herb sauces. The dining room is grandly elegant, with white linen tablecloths and sparkling crystal glasses. Expect to pay around €60 per person. Usually daily lunch & dinner but call ahead.

PARQUE NACIONAL DE ORDESA (P.634) >

9

Around Huesca

The mountainous terrain around Huesca reveals several eye-catching sights, including the imposing, eleventh-century **Castillo de Loarre** and **Los Mallos**, a series of rock formations that jut into the sky.

Castillo de Loarre

March to mid-June & mid-Sept to Oct & 10am–2pm & 4–7pm; mid-June to mid-Sept daily 10am–2pm & 4–8pm; Nov–Feb 11am–5.30pm • €3.30, or €4.80 with guided tour • ☎ 974 342 161, ⓦ castillodeloarre.es

From afar, the scene looks like little more than rocky outcrops punctuating the Aragonese landscape. As you draw closer, the eleventh-century **Castillo de Loarre** comes into magnificent focus, glowering from its hilltop perch. The castle was constructed in the eleventh century by Sancho Ramírez, king of Aragón and Navarra. The dark and mysterious, mazelike interior makes for great exploring: tunnels lead down to dark cellars, and narrow stairs wind up to lookout towers that command wonderful views over the far-reaching fields. The castle's two main **towers** are the imposing Torre de la Reina, and the Torre del Homenaje, which features a huge fireplace. You can also peer into a quiet Romanesque **church**, with detailed, carved capitals in the apse.

The castle lies 36km northwest of Huesca, and just 4km beyond the village of **Loarre**.

ARRIVAL AND DEPARTURE	CASTILLO DE LOARRE
By bus During the week, two buses run daily from Huesca to Loarre (40min), with one service on Sat. **By train** Ayerbe, 7km southwest of Loarre, has the closest	train station, with services from Huesca (30min), though schedules vary; check ahead. A bus makes the 10min trip between Ayerbe and Loarre daily during the week.

ACCOMMODATION	
Camping La Banera 1.5km out of Ayerbe on the road to Loarre ☎ 974 380 242. This decent campsite has a well-maintained camping area and a small bar-restaurant (open to campers only). Closed Oct–March. Tent plus adult **€7** **Hospedería de Loarre** Pl. Miguel Moya ☎ 974 382	706, ⓦ hospederiadeloarre.com. Restored seventeenth-century *hospedería* with comfortable rooms and a respected restaurant serving Aragonese cuisine (*menú* from €17). Breakfast included. **€98**

Los Mallos and Riglos

Just north of Ayerbe you'll see otherworldly towering rock formations off in the distance. These are **Los Mallos** (The Mallets), which are popular with rock-climbers. A good base from which to access them – and to take photos – is the nearby village of **Riglos**, about 45km from Huesca.

ACCOMMODATION	LOS MALLOS AND RIGLOS
Refugio de Riglos At the entrance to Riglos ☎ 974 383 051, ⓦ refugioderiglos.es. Catering to climbers and trekkers, this *refugio* has two-, six- and eight-bed rooms	and a fitness room with a climbing wall, so you can warm up before doing the real thing. The restaurant serves hearty Aragonese food. Dorm from **€15.90**

Sierra de Guara

The bird's-eye view of the **Sierra de Guara** shows an arid, almost desolate terrain cleaved by over two hundred canyons and gorges that look like giant, angry slashes in the earth. This is canyoning (*barranquismo*) country: the eastern half of Sierra de Guara is the most popular section for outdoor activities, and the pleasant town of **Alquézar**, in the southeastern corner, functions as the Guara's hub.

Alquézar

Tackling the great outdoors and brushing up your Aragonese history are prime draws in small but well-preserved **Alquézar**, which lies about 45km from Huesca and 20km northwest of Barbastro. In town the streets are dotted with outdoor operators and

CANYONING IN THE SIERRA DE GUARA

Alquézar has a range of quality canyoning operators who cater to all levels, and offer everything from thrilling descents into dark, echoing caves to treks along gaping gorges to river rafting. Average cost is around €49–65 per person/per day, with prices varying depending on the level of difficulty and size of tour group.

OUTDOOR OPERATORS IN ALQUÉZAR
Avalancha c/Arrabal s/n ☎ 974 318 299, ⊛ avalancha.org. This well-regarded operator organizes canyoning, rafting, hiking and skiing trips. Daily 9am–2pm & 5–9pm; closed Dec–Feb.

Guias Boira Paseo San Hipólito ☎ 974 318 974, ⊛ guiasboira.com. This friendly operator offers a wide range of guided trips, including canyoning, rafting and *escalada en hielo* (ice-climbing). Early April to Oct: daily 9am–9pm.

tour companies that specialize in canyoning, mountain-climbing and hiking excursions (see box above).

Colegiata de Santa María del Mayor

Daily except Tues: April–Sept 11am–1.30pm & 4.30–7.30pm; Oct–March 11am–1.30pm & 4–6pm • €2.50, €3 includes Casa Fabián • ⊛ alquezar.es

Keeping watch over Alquézar, the imposing **Colegiata de Santa María del Mayor** was originally built as a Moorish citadel in the eighth century. It was then conquered by the Christians, who adapted it into a monastery and fortress complex in the twelfth century. Reflecting its long and varied history, the Colegiata reveals art and architecture from throughout the ages: the Romanesque cloister has detailed capitals and frescoes depicting the New Testament that were created in the fifteenth to eighteenth centuries, while the Gothic-Renaissance church is heavy on Baroque art, but also has a simple yet powerful wooden Crucifixion dating back to the thirteenth century.

Museo Etnológico "Casa Fabián"

C/Baja 13 • April–Oct Wed–Sun 10.30am–1.30pm & 4–8pm; Nov–May Tues–Sun 10.30am–1.30pm & 4.30–7pm • €1.50 • ☎ 974 318 913, ⊛ alquezar.org

For a glimpse into *la vida cotidiana* (daily life) of historic Alquézar, browse the tidy **Casa Fabián**, an ethnological museum housed in a seventeenth-century building. Exhibits cover folk art and culture, an overview of the agricultural trade of the region, household items and other ethnological and archeological finds.

ARRIVAL AND INFORMATION   ALQUÉZAR

By bus Buses generally run daily to Alquézar from Huesca (50min) and Barbastro (30min); times vary, so confirm with the tourist office.

Turismo c/Arrabal, on the edge of the old town (daily 9am–1.30pm & 4.30–8pm; Aug daily 9am–8pm; sometimes limited hours in winter; ☎ 974 318 940, ⊛ alquezar.org).

ACCOMMODATION

Albergue Rural de Guara c/Pilaseras ☎ 974 318 956, ⊛ albergueruraldeguara.com. Sturdy, simple *refugio* above town with views over the countryside and simple rooms with bunk beds. Sometimes closed in winter. Dorm **€14**

Camping Alquézar Off the Carretera Barbastro, just under 1km south of Alquézar ☎ 974 318 300, ⊛ alquezar.com. Friendly site with a range of services and amenities, including outdoor activities and a restaurant-bar for campers. They also have well-maintained bungalows. Tent plus adult from **€10.70**; two-person bungalow **€50**

Hotel Maribel c/Arrabal ☎ 974 318 979, ⊛ hotelmaribel.es. This colourful, quirky – and slightly kitsch – hotel has

rooms named (and decorated) after different types of grape, like the Moscatel room with a canopied bed and crystal lamp, or the Moristel with a forged-iron headboard and wallpaper in a colour "similar to the water in the river Vero." They also have a full house you can rent in town (€350 per night, enquire for details) and run a good restaurant, *Casa Gervasio* (see p.628). Breakfast included. **€120**

Hotel Villa de Alquézar c/Pedro Arnal Cavero 12 ☎ 974 318 416, ⊛ villadealquezar.com. A stone arch graces the front door at this artfully renovated hotel with wood-beam ceilings and a terrace with views of the Colegiata and the Río Vero canyon. **€68**

9

EATING AND DRINKING

Casa Gervasio c/Arnal Cavero 13 ☎ 974 318 282. Decent restaurant with a breezy terrace with pots of flowers and stone walls – a creative take on local cuisine. The menu might include *longaniza* (sausage), chickpeas with shellfish or rabbit in almond sauce; dishes €14–20. Daily 1.30–3.30pm & 8–11pm; more limited hours in winter.

Casa Pardina c/Medio ☎ 974 318 425. Handsome, rustic restaurant with modern touches, and a lovely terrace that overlooks the Guara countryside. Average price €30–35 per person. Easter to Oct daily except Tues 1.30–3.30pm & 8.30–10.30pm; Nov–Easter usually open Fri–Sun only.

Barbastro

Barbastro's formidable history put it on the map, but it's the rich local wines that have given this small town its staying power as a tourist destination. For over three centuries, the Moors ruled Barbastro as one of its chief outposts in the far north. In 1137, it was here that the marriage of Petronia, daughter of Ramiro of Aragón, to Count Ramón Berenguer IV of Barcelona established the union of Aragón and Catalunya. As for the *vino*: Barbastro is capital of the **Somontano** wine region, and makes for an ideal jumping-off point for tastings at the thirty-plus *bodegas* and vineyards clustered around town (see box, p.629).

The old town

Barbastro's old town exudes a certain faded glory and is presided over by a sturdy Gothic cathedral. In **Plaza de la Constitución** sits the fifteenth-century *ayuntamiento*. Nearby are the arcaded **Plaza del Mercado** and the shaded **Paseo del Coso**, where you can ease into the evening over a drink or three at the outdoor bars.

Catedral

Pl. Palacio • **Catedral** Daily 10am–2pm & 4.30–7.30pm, Sun 10am–noon; may have limited hours in winter • €2, €4.50 includes Museo Diocesano **Museo** Tues–Sat 10am–1pm & 4–7pm (June–Sept 5–8pm), Sun 11am–2pm • €4 • ⓦ museodiocesano.es

The handsome sixteenth-century **Catedral** features an alabaster *retablo* by Damián Forment. He left the work unfinished when he died in 1540, and the remainder was completed by his student, Liceire, two decades later. The cathedral bell tower has been well preserved, while inside the cathedral are elegant ribbed vaults and a nave with carved columns. The **Museo Diocesano** features a well-maintained collection of sacred art from Aragón's rural medieval churches, archeological remains from the Moorish era, and an array of Gothic and Romanesque murals, including several beautiful depictions of Madonna and Child.

ARRIVAL AND INFORMATION

BARBASTRO

By bus Regular buses operate to Huesca (50min), where you can make connections to Jaca and Zaragoza. Buses also travel to Lleida (1hr 30min), Benasque (2hr) and Alquézar (30min).

Turismo Avda. de la Merced 64 (July & Aug Mon–Sat 10am–8pm, Sun 10am–2pm & 4.30–7.30pm; Sept–June Mon–Sat 10am–2pm & 4.30–7.30pm; ☎ 974 308 350, ⓦ barbastro.org).

ACCOMMODATION

La Alcoba de Baco c/Mayor, next to the Palacio de los Argensola ☎ 974 316 342, ⓦ viajesenoturismo.es. Handsome, central apartments with full kitchens, that cater to those visiting Somontano for *enoturismo* (wine tourism). They often offer good weekend packages that include wine tastings and dinner. **€75**

Hostal Pirineos c/General Ricardos 13 ☎ 974 310 000. Simple *hostal* with basic, well-maintained rooms. The restaurant serves good food, with a *menú* starting at €14.

Daily 1–3.30pm & 9–10.30 pm, closed Sun dinner. **€50**

Hotel San Ramón del Somontano c/Academia Cerbuna 2 ☎ 974 312 825, ⓦ hotelsanramonso montano.com. This beautiful four-star hotel is set in a 1903 Modernist *hostal* that hosted everyone from George Orwell to Miguel de Unamuno. The elegant original design has been artfully incorporated into the modern hotel. The restaurant (see p.629) serves Aragonese cuisine. **€125**

SOMONTANO WINE

Somontano has become one of Aragón's most distinguished D.O. – Denominación de Origen – wine regions, with over thirty vineyards producing superb red, white and rosés from a variety of local and international grapes. The **Espacio del Vino** interpretation centre (Mon–Sat 10am–2pm & 4.30–7.30pm) is in the same building as the Barbastro tourist office, and features a short film on the history of Somontano wine, along with a shop.

The organization **Ruta del Vinos Somontano** (Somontano Wine Routes; ⓦrutadelvinosomontano.com) offers myriad tours, including a morning tasting through three of the region's most emblematic *bodegas*, including **Enate** (ⓦenate.es), **Viñas del Vero** (ⓦvinasdelvero.es) and **Pirineos** (ⓦbodegapirineos.com). Tours run from Monday to Saturday, and cost €10–15; check the website or call ☎974 316 342 to reserve.

Many of the vineyards are also individually open to visitors (generally Mon–Sat, morning to early evening), and offer tours (ranging from free to €5). The Barbastro tourist office has a wealth of information on routes, vineyards and itineraries.

EATING AND DRINKING

Flor c/Goya 3 ☎974 311 056. Dine on creative cuisine, from hake and cod in fragrant sauces to suckling pig, at this elegant, well-regarded restaurant. Excellent Somontano wine list. Dishes €19–24. Daily except Mon 1–3.30pm & 9–11pm; closed Sun night.

San Ramón del Somontano c/Academia Cerbuna 2 ☎974 312 825, ⓦhotelsanramonsomontano.com. The well-appointed restaurant in this historic hotel serves tasty regional cuisine based on locally sourced ingredients, plus an array of Somontano wines. Daily 1.30–3.30pm & 9–11pm.

Jaca

The busy industrial town of **Jaca** is one of the main crossroads and transport hubs of northern Aragón, and first impressions are not great. Venture into the city centre, however, and you'll find a bevy of sights that powerfully evoke the town's long history, including a magnificent cathedral. Extending south of the cathedral is Jaca's *casco antiguo* (old town), which includes atmospheric little *plazas* and streets, and the fifteenth-century Torre de Reloj (watchtower).

Jaca was founded by the Romans and then conquered by the Moors in the early eighth century. Later in the century, it was won back by the Christians in a victory that's celebrated annually on the first Friday in May. In an interesting twist, the Moorish armies were driven back thanks to an immense – and brave – effort by the town's women, and the festival includes a parade that pays homage to these brave Jaca ladies. In the eleventh century, Jaca became the first capital of the Aragón kingdom, though by the end of the century the power had shifted to Huesca.

Jaca makes for a good jumping-off point for outdoor adventure in the Pyrenees, including skiing at Astún and Candanchu, just 30km away (see box, p.634). During the **Festival Folklórico de los Pirineos** (ⓦjaca.es/festival), held in early August every odd-numbered year, people stream in from all over the Pyrenees to show off their cultural traditions with religious dances, performances and food. Also in August, over a two-week period, is the annual **Festival Internacional en el Camino de Santiago** (ⓦfestival caminosantiago.com), featuring religious and classical music concerts at different venues, including the famous cathedral, as well as a medieval market in the city centre.

Catedral and Museo Diocesano

Pl. de San Pedro • **Catedral** Daily 8am–2pm & 4–8pm • Free • ☎974 356 241 **Museo Diocesano** July & Aug Tues–Sun 10am–1.30pm & 4–8pm; Sept–June Tues–Fri 10am–1.30pm & 4–7pm, Sat 10am–1.30pm & 4–8pm, Sun 10am–1.30pm • €6, €7.50 with guided tour • ⓦdiocesisdejaca.org

The jewel of Jaca is its eleventh-century **Catedral**, one of the oldest in Spain, and perhaps the city's finest reminder of its years as the seat of the Aragonese kingdom.

9

JACA: CASCO ANTIGUO

The cathedral's incredible history and staying power is revealed through its gorgeous amalgam of styles, from French Romanesque to Gothic. And, while the original Romanesque design has been largely built over – the original ceilings were in wood, which were replaced by double-barrel vaults – you'll still find vestiges of it, such as the simple main door. Within the cathedral are elegant carvings gracing the capitals, a sixteenth-century statue of Santiago and a central apse painted in 1792 by Aragonese artist Manuel Bayeu, who was Francisco Goya's brother-in-law. A highlight is the shrine of Santa Orosía, the patron saint of Jaca. Adjoining the cathedral is the **Museo Diocesano**, which displays an extensive collection of religious art, artefacts and frescoes from mountain churches throughout the area.

Ciudadela

Avda. del Primer Viernes de Mayo • Tues–Sun 11am–2pm & 5–8pm, closed for part of Nov • €10, includes museum • ⓦ ciudadeladejaca.es

The impressive star-shaped **Ciudadela** (also called Castillo de San Pedro) looms just east of the centre of town, and is still partly used by the military. Wander along the fortified walls for lovely views of the surrounding mountains and countryside. The **Museo de Miniatura Militares** (Museum of Military Miniatures) within is a remarkable – almost mesmerizing – collection of over 35,000 toy soldiers, dioramas, models and more. The tiny lead soldiers, measuring 2cm in height, are depicted in historical battles from around the world, from the Crusades to the Crown of Aragón era.

Puente San Miguel

The fifteenth-century **Puente San Miguel** arches across the river west of the Ciudadela. It was the main entrance to Jaca used by pilgrims on the Camino Aragonés, a branch of the Camino de Santiago. In tribute to this history, the town celebrates with the Festival Internacional en el Camino de Santiago (see p.629).

ARRIVAL AND INFORMATION

By bus Regular buses travel daily from the central bus station, on Pl. de Biscós, to Huesca (1hr 25min), Zaragoza (4hr) and to Pamplona (just under 2hr).
By train The train station, on c/Ferrocarril, is about a 15min walk from the town centre. Regular trains run to

Zaragoza (4hr) and other regional towns.
Turismo Pl. de San Pedro (summer Mon–Sat 9am–9pm, Sun 9am–3pm; winter Mon–Fri 9am–1.30 & 4.30–7pm, Sat 10am–1pm & 5–7pm; ☎ 974 360 098, ⓦ jaca.es).

ACCOMMODATION

★ **Barrose** c/Estiras 4, Barós ☎ 974 360 582, ⓦ barosse.com. This wonderfully unique *casa rural*, in a village 2km south of Jaca, blends designer style with rustic appeal. Each room is named after traditional edifices, like the Romanesque-style Ermita (hermitage), with stone, gleaming woods and elegant drapes. **€115**
Hostal La Casa del Arco c/San Nicolás 4 ☎ 974 364 448, ⓦ lacasadelarco.net. Historic hotel in the *casco histórico*, with simple but well-maintained rooms and, unusually for this part of Spain, a vegetarian restaurant. **€30**

Hotel Conde Aznar Paseo de la Constitución 3 ☎ 974 361 050, ⓦ condeaznar.com. This welcoming three-star hotel has rooms done up in elegant, old-fashioned decor. The restaurant, *La Cocina Aragonesa* (closed Tues night & Wed in low season), serves tasty Aragonese cuisine. **€70**
Hotel Mur c/Santa Orosía 1 ☎ 974 360 100, ⓦ hotelmur.com. Famed writers and artists from Pío Baroja to Santiago Ramón y Cajal have warmed the beds at this historic hotel, which originated in 1875. Rooms are a bit dated, but handsomely maintained. **€120**

EATING AND DRINKING

La Casa del Arco c/San Nicolás 4 ☎ 974 364 448, ⓦ lacasadelarco.net. This charmingly offbeat spot serves creative vegetarian cuisine, with a focus on organic products. The weekday *menú* is a good deal at €12. Daily except Sun 1.30–3.30pm & 8.30–10.30pm.
Meson Cobarcho Ramiro I 2 ☎ 974 363 643. Aragón is meat country – and you can get a hearty taste of it at this friendly spot: grilled and roasted lamb chops and T-bone steaks, suckling pig, duck and more are on the menu at equally friendly prices, including a *menú del día* for €15. Daily except Mon 1–4pm & 8.30–11pm.
Restaurante Biarritz Avda. Primer Viernes de Mayo 12 ☎ 974 361 632, ⓦ restaurantebiarritz.com. The

speciality at this welcoming restaurant is *carnes a la brasa* (grilled meats), from thick, juicy steaks to tender veal. Pair your meat with fresh salads of goat cheese and *bacalao* (cod). The *menú* starts at €12–15. Daily except Wed 1–4pm & 7.30–11pm.
La Tasca de Ana Ramiro I 3 ☎ 974 364 726. It can get crowded and loud, but if you're going to do tapas in Jaca, this long-running spot is the place to go. It draws a healthy mix of locals and visitors, all here to chow on the delicious small bites from grilled squid to pungent cheeses and cured hams to the perennially popular *langostinos* (prawns). Usually noon to late.

San Juan de la Peña and around

March–May & Sept to mid-Oct 10am–2pm & 3.30–7pm; June to mid-July daily 10am–2pm & 3–8pm; mid-July to Aug daily 10am–8pm; mid-Oct to Feb 10am–3.30pm; €6.50, or €8.50 for access to both interpretation centres; all admission includes Santa María church • ☎ 974 355 119, ⓦ monasteriosanjuan.com

The **Monasterio de San Juan de la Peña**, set amid protected natural parkland 21km south of Jaca, is one of the most stunning sacred buildings in Aragón, if not in Spain. Tucked protectively under the overhang of a massive boulder, it's built right into a rocky mountain: from certain angles, it's hard to tell where man-made structure ends and nature begins. Dating from the ninth century, the monastery is named after a hermit who lived in solitude atop the towering cliff (*peña*). The monastery features a Romanesque church with twelfth-century murals and the Gothic San Victorián chapel, but the real standout is the elegant twelfth-century cloister, shaded by the bulging rock face that looms over it. The cloister has ornate capitals, some fully ringed by saints and apostles, depicting different scenes from the Bible.

In 1675, a fire in the monastery forced the monks to leave and build a newer one, which sits further up the hill. The **Monasterio Nuevo** (same hours as old monastery) features a helpful visitors' centre and two interpretation centres, which chronicle the history of the monastery and the eventful lives of the Aragón's kings and queens.

9

Church of Santa María

Daily 10am–2pm & 3–8pm • €2, or included in admission to San Juan de la Peña

From San Juan de la Peña, a series of trails fan out through the forest, including a popular path to the nearest village, **Santa Cruz de Serós**, 7km away, which is home to the eleventh-century Romanesque church of **Santa María**, formerly a monastery and featuring an elegant vaulted nave. The trail is signposted near the church.

ARRIVAL AND DEPARTURE SAN JUAN DE LA PEÑA AND AROUND

By bus There is no scheduled bus from Jaca, but in high season a bus occasionally connects Santa Cruz de Serós to the monastery; call the monastery to confirm.

ACCOMMODATION

Hospedería Monasterio de San Juan de la Peña ☎ 974 374 422, ⊛ www.hospederiasdearagon.com. Forming part of the Monasterio Nuevo, this handsome, four-star hotel features elegant rooms, lovely gardens, a rustic restaurant and also a spa. **€150**

Valles de Echo and Ansó

Wild and beautiful, the **Ansó and Echo valleys**, northwest of Jaca, burrow deep into the Pyrenees. The terrain is by turns desolate and fecund and the tiny mountain villages are as quaint as they come. But perhaps the main allure? Fewer visitors than elsewhere in the Pyrenees. Summer can get busy, but in the off-season you can often have an entire trail (if not an entire valley) largely to yourself. In fact, if there is activity on the slopes, it's usually the local **wildlife** – the forested mountains, especially in the Valle de Echo, are home to creatures large and small, from chamois to red squirrels to a small population of brown bear. Also, keep an eye out for all sorts of birds, including the lammergeier. The valley's main towns are the charming Echo and Ansó, while scattered about are tiny villages, often with their own parish church, like Siresa. Elsewhere, natural wonders abound, including **La Selva de Oza** (about 5km from Siresa), a spruce and pine forest crossed by the rushing Río Aragón Subordán, which is thick with Pyrenean trout.

Echo and around

Lovely **Echo**, the main town of the valley of the same name, is the very definition of rustic Aragón. Stone houses with wrought-iron balconies cast shadows on cobbled streets, the scene framed by vivid green valleys and elegant peaks. The village made its mark in history as the *sede* (seat) of the young Aragonese kingdom, and is also where King Alfonso I was born. Here, locals speak "Cheso", a dialect of Aragonese.

Two kilometres north of Echo lies the pretty little village of **Siresa**, which is crowned by the ninth-century monastic **Iglesia de San Pedro** (daily 11am–1pm & 5–8pm; €1.50).

Arte Contemporáneo al Aire Libre

Carretera Oza • Open access • Free

Echo also has an arty angle: until the mid-1980s, the town hosted an annual symposium on contemporary sculpture, founded by artist Pedro Tramulas. One of its legacies is the **Arte Contemporáneo al Aire Libre**, an open-air sculpture park near the entrance to town, featuring striking contemporary stone pieces – the juxtaposition of modern art and historic town makes for a memorable scene. Adjoining the park, sharing the *turismo* building, is a small exhibition of modern woodworks and paintings (mid-June to mid-Oct daily 10am–2pm & 4–8pm; usually closed mid-Oct to mid-June; free).

Museo Etnológico Casa Mazo

C/Aire • Daily 10.30–1.30pm & 6–9pm • €1

The **Museo Etnológico Casa Mazo** explores the rural life of villagers in the valleys, with an overview of the agricultural history of the region, via an array of displays, including re-creations of dwellings, furnishings and old photographs depicting *la vida cotidiana* (daily life).

ARRIVAL AND INFORMATION
ECHO AND AROUND

By bus Buses from Jaca service Echo and Siresa (both around 1hr) generally once daily (except Sun).

Turismo In the sculpture park, Carretera Oza (mid-June to mid-Oct daily 10am–2pm & 4–8pm; usually closed mid-Oct to mid-June; ☎974 375 505, ⚘valledehecho.net).

ACCOMMODATION

Albergue Siresa c/Reclusa, Siresa, 2km north of Echo ☎974 375 385, ⚘alberguesiresa.com. This basic, friendly *albergue*, in the heart of small Siresa, has comfortable bunk-bedded dorms and plenty of information on exploring the surrounding mountains, including books and mountain gear rental; they can also arrange guided hikes. Breakfast included. Dorms from €15

Borda Bisaltico Carretera Gabardito, 6km north of town ☎974 375 388 or 974 375 098, ⚘bordabisaltico .com. This well-tended complex features a campsite, an *albergue* with four-, six- and eight-person dorms, and basic apartments (€80). Pitch plus adult €9.20, dorm from €14

Camping Valle de Hecho Carretera Puenta la Reina ☎974 375 361, ⚘www.campinghecho.com. This well-run campground has a range of amenities, including an outdoor pool, a restaurant, a cafeteria and organized activities, including hiking excursions. They also have wooden bungalows (€100). Pitch plus adult €8.60

Casa Blasquico Pl. Palacio de la Fuente 1 ☎974 375 007, ⚘casablasquico.com. Lovingly cared for rooms, each named after a flower or herb, feature comfortable beds, hardwood floors and clean bathrooms. The hotel also has the acclaimed *Restaurante Gaby*. €50

Hotel Castillo d'Acher Pl. Mayor ☎974 375 313. Basic, well-maintained rooms in the centre of the village. The restaurant serves decent regional cuisine, including *conejo con caracoles* (rabbit with snails), tripe with chickpeas and grilled meats. €54

EATING AND DRINKING

Restaurante Gaby Pl. Palacio de la Fuente 1 ☎974 375 007, ⚘casablasquico.com. This lovely restaurant is a town institution – and for good reason. It's the model of mountain charm: low, wood-beamed ceilings; walls hanging with old photos; and excellent regional cuisine, including grilled *conejo* (rabbit), crêpes with mushrooms and a superb wine list, with a particular focus on Aragón's Somontano wines. Daily 1.30–3.30pm & 8.30–10pm; may have limited hours in winter.

Ansó

Ansó rivals Echo for rustic, alpine appeal: red-roofed stone houses stand out against a backdrop of lush greenery, with the big, blue sky opening above. As with many mountain villages in the Pyrenees, the pleasure here is to just wander the cobbled streets and Plaza Mayor, and perhaps to take some shade along the banks of the river, the Río Veral.

ARRIVAL AND INFORMATION
ANSÓ

By bus Buses from Jaca service Ansó 1–2 times daily.

Turismo Pl. Mayor (Easter & summer daily 9am–1.30pm & 5–8pm; sometimes closed in winter; ☎974 370 049).

ACCOMMODATION

Casa Mina c/Mayor 38 ☎639 118 184, ⚘www .casamina.es. This small *casa*, on Ansó's main street, has plain but well-cared-for rooms with a few rustic-chic touches like hardwood floors. €75

El Pajar de Pierra Avda. Pedro Cativiela 3a & 3b ☎619 224 539 or ☎660 836 220, ⚘elpajardepierra. com. Two side-by-side *casa rural*-style houses done up as an elegant farmhouse, featuring cosy interiors and lovely mountain views throughout, especially from the breezy garden. Groups and families can rent out the full house (each includes 5 bedrooms, 3 bathrooms, and a fully equipped kitchen) by the day (€175) or week (€800). €55

Posada Magoria c/Milagro 32 ☎974 370 049, ⚘posadamagoria.com. This inviting *posada* has been beautifully restored, with wood-beam ceilings, solid furniture and comfortable beds. The restaurant (reserved for guests) serves organic vegetarian cuisine using vegetables grown in the garden, including squash and aubergine. €55

9

HIT THE SLOPES IN ARAGÓN

Skiing in the Aragon Pyrenees matches that of Catalunya and, increasingly, of France. Overall, the **ski resorts** are well maintained and cater to all levels, from downhill daredevils to wobbly first-timers. Note that, as in the Catalan Pyrenees, some of the best discounts are via pre-trip package deals offered by hotels, agencies or the resorts themselves. But even if you don't book a package ahead of time, you can often find on-site deals once you've arrived, offered by the *turismos* as well as the hotels and the resorts.

In the west are **Candanchú** (wcandanchu.com), with a well-known ski school, and **Astún** (wastun.com), which lies just 4km away, and has a wide range of pistes, including plenty for beginners. The main hub for accommodation and the like is **Jaca**. Partly funded by the Aragón government, the Aramón group (waramon.com) now manages a group of formerly independently run ski resorts. Of these, **Formigal** is one of the larger, with 93 runs and 21 lifts, and caters to all levels. **Panticosa** is smaller but also less crowded, as daily numbers are limited to 3500 people per day. In the Pyrenees' easternmost section, sleek **Cerler** attracts seasoned skiers, with several ski centres totalling about 52km, altitudes up to 2630m, 61 runs and 18 lifts. Cerler also offers equipment rental and ski and snowboard schools. **Benasque** is a popular hub for Cerler, with a decent array of accommodation.

Parque Nacional de Ordesa y Monte Perdido and around

The best of Aragón's natural wonders all seem to converge with climactic glory in the **Parque Nacional de Ordesa y Monte Perdido**. Presiding over the park's greenery is the Monte Perdido (Lost Mountain) range, the largest limestone chain in Western Europe. Verdant valleys blanketed in beech, fir and pine cut through the terrain, and clear blue streams and gushing waterfalls keep the fields fertile. After the snow melts, honeysuckle, primroses and irises bloom in rocky crevices and on sun-speckled slopes. As for wildlife, the park is teeming with it: Egyptian vultures and golden eagles soar overhead; Pyrenean chamois scamper up hillsides; and trout dart through ice-cold streams.

Many of the deep valleys were created by massive glaciers, at the heads of which are cirques: basins shaped roughly like an amphitheatre with steep walls of rock. Elsewhere, tiny alpine villages, with stone houses crowned with sandstone-tile roofs and conical chimneys, dot the mountainsides and make for pleasant stops along the many routes that meander through the park. The park is divided roughly into three main sections: **Ordesa** (to the west), **Añisclo** (to the south) and **Escuaín** (to the east). The chief town of **Torla**, 3km south of the park's southwest border, is one of the more popular gateways, from where trails lead into the park.

INFORMATION

Centro de Visitantes The park is well serviced with a number of tourist information offices, including a gleaming new Centro de Visitantes and interpretation centre in the car park at Torla (see p.635). There is also a Centro de Visitantes in Tella, in the fairly remote Escuaín section in the east.

Turismo Tourist offices in various towns near the park,

including Aínsa and Bielsa, are generally well stocked with info on park conditions, trails, maps and more.

Maps and guides Editorial Alpina (weditorialalpina .com) has good maps of the park. Cicerone (wcicerone .co.uk) publishes in-depth trekking guides, including one on the Spanish Pyrenees and the GR11 trail.

Online wordesa.net.

ACCOMMODATION

Hotels The towns around the park generally have a decent mix of hotels and budget beds. In high season, it's a good idea to book ahead, whether you're staying in a hotel at one of the nearby towns or a park refuge.

Refuges The park has a number of basic stone refuges

(€15–30 per person), where you can stay when on longer treks. Note that refuges will often be closed for a part of the low season; enquire before setting out.

Camping Camping is prohibited inside the park.

Torla

Torla in many ways exemplifies the modern-day Pyrenean town: turn down one cobbled street in the old town, and you're rewarded with the alluring sight of stone houses prettily framed by bright-green valleys and naked peaks; turn the other way, and you run smack into a high-rise hotel or a belching tour bus pulling into a car park. It is however this very mix of low-key village life and tourist-friendly amenities that makes Torla a good base for exploring the park.

ARRIVAL AND DEPARTURE   TORLA

By bus One bus per day from Sabiñánigo, a transport hub for the area, to Aínsa stops at Torla (1hr). There are additional weekday services in July and August between Sabiñánigo and Torla. In the summer, a shuttle runs from Torla town to the park entrance. Several daily buses operate from Jaca to Sabiñánigo.

By car Outside of high season (Easter week and July to mid-Sept) you can drive to the park border, northwest from Torla. Otherwise you'll have to leave your vehicle in the Torla car park and board a shuttle (every 15min: daily around 6am–9/10pm; €3/€4.50 one way/return) to the park.

INFORMATION

Centro de Visitantes In Torla car park (daily: summer 9am–1pm & 4.15–8pm; winter 9am–2pm & 4–7pm; ☏ 974 486 472). The visitor and interpretation centre has an ascending ramp that simulates climbing a mountain,

featuring a different rock face on each floor. A lookout point at the top offers views of the Aragonese landscape.
Turismo c/Fatás, in the old town (mid-June to mid-Sept Mon–Sat 9.30–1.30pm & 5–9pm; ☏ 974 486 378).

ACCOMMODATION AND EATING

Camping Río Ara 300m from Torla, on the road to Ordesa, signposted from road ☏ 974 486 248, ⓦ campingrioara.com. There are several campsites around Torla, and this is one of the closest to town, set in a verdant riverside area. There's a café/bar and information on trekking into the park can be provided. Open Easter–Oct. Tent plus adult €8.20
Camping y Refugio Valle de Bujaruelo 7km north of Torla, off the A-135, in the Valle de Bujaruelo ☏ 974 486 348, ⓦ campingvalledebujaruelo.com. Well-maintained alpine complex, surrounded by the leafy Valle de Bujaruelo, with a range of accommodation, including camping, three- and four-person dorms in the refuge and bungalows. Open Easter–Oct. Tent plus adult €9, dorm from €14, bungalow €100
Hotel Villa Russell c/Principal s/n ☏ 974 486 770, ⓦ hotelvillarussell.com. This established, amiable spot,

on Torla's main drag, offers basic (and rather dated) but well-cared-for rooms with an alpine feel, like wooden furnishings and cosy blankets. Some rooms come with a small kitchenette, so you can do self-catering. €104
Refugio Luicen Briet c/Francia ☏ 974 486 221, ⓦ refugiolucienbriet.com. Long-running, stone-walled refuge-style hostel with well-maintained dorm rooms and doubles. They also run the nearby restaurant, La Brecha, with simple, local cuisine from Navarran trout to grilled rabbit. Dorm €10, double €40
Villa de Torla Pl. Aragón 1 ☏ 974 486 156, ⓦ hotelvilladetorla.com. The handsome alpine hotel has fairly straightforward rooms with the occasional rustic touch (hardwood floors, old-fashioned furniture) but it's the surprising discovery that there's a pool – surrounded by mountain greenery – that makes it a notch above the others. €69

Hikes in the park

The park offers a wide range of hikes, from half-day ambles to multi-day treks, all of which take you past natural wonders, including crashing waterfalls, gaping canyons and bright-green valleys. You can access the park on foot from Torla on the well-marked GR15 path from town, which eventually links up with the GR11, a right fork of which goes to **Pradera de Ordesa**, entrance to the **Cañón de Ordesa** and the starting point for most of the popular hikes further into the park. The whole trek from Torla to Pradera takes about two hours.

Circo de Soaso

The **Circo de Soaso** trek is one of the park's main crowd-pleasers – and for good reason. It offers a lovely overview of the park's natural highlights – gorgeous greenery, tumbling waterfalls – but is not too challenging, and it can be completed in a day. From Pradera

9

de Ordesa the route leads through forest, followed by a steep climb up the **Senda de los Cazadores** (Hunters' Path), which then flattens out as the Faja de Pelay path to the beautiful **Cola de Caballo** (Horsetail Waterfall). The journey takes about three to four hours (around 6–7hr roundtrip).

Circo de Cotatuero

This trek also has a lovely waterfall as a reward, and takes you along the northern crest of the impressive **Valle de Ordesa**. The full round-trip hike takes about 5 to 6 hours. Park officials warn that the hike should only be done in the summer or early autumn; in the winter and spring, there is the risk of avalanches. From Pradera de Ordesa, the hike starts steeply and eventually leads to a lookout point below the thundering **Cascada de Cotatuero** (for an onward route from the Cascada, see Brecha de Rolando, below). To return from the Cascada, head downhill and then continue on the Cotatuero *circo* back to the Pradera de Ordesa.

Refugio Góriz and Monte Perdido

From Pradera de Ordesa, trek along the GR11 to Circo de Soaso (about 3hr) and then up to the **Refugio Góriz** (2169m; see box), the traditional jumping-off point to climb **Monte Perdido** (3355m). The trek up Monte Perdido (about 5hr) requires intermediate mountaineering skills, crampons and other professional equipment.

Brecha de Rolando and Refuge des Sarradets

If you have a head for heights, try this memorable onward route from the Cascada de Cotatuero: from the waterfalls, on the Cotatuero cirque, you can climb, via a series of iron pegs in a wall, the **Clavijas de Cotatuero**. Note that you don't need any special climbing equipment but you should be fit and have the aforementioned affinity for heights. Once you've done the climb, it's about a two- to three-hour trek to the **Brecha de Rolando**, a large natural gap in the Cirque de Gavarnie on the French border. From the Brecha, it's then a steep climb (about 500m) to the **Refuge des Sarradets** (2587m; see box), across the border in France.

Parc National des Pyrénées and Gavarnie village

The northern section of the park is adjacent to France's **Parc National des Pyrénées**, which in total runs for about 100km along the Spain–France border. The French side offers more of the same wild Pyrenean landscape, and a popular trek with hikers is to cross northwest into the French park and on to the pretty village of **Gavarnie**. Many will do this hike over the course of a couple of days. From Torla, hike along the GR15.2 to **Puente de los Navarros** and then continue on the GR11 to San Nicolás de Bujaruelo (roughly 7km from Torla), which is marked by a medieval bridge. Here you'll find the **Refugio Valle de Bujaruelo** (see box). From the San Nicolás bridge, you can trek over mountains and into France and Garvarnie – about a six- to eight-hour hike.

REFUGES IN THE PARQUE NACIONAL DE ORDESA

Refugio Góriz ☎974 341 201, ⊛goriz.es. This refuge has a well-maintained interior, comfortable mattresses and a restaurant. It's always a good idea to book ahead in summer. Note that if you're making reservations more than three days in advance of your stay, you can only reserve online; otherwise, you can call to book a space. **€15.90**

Refuge des Sarradets ☎+33 06 83 38 13 24. Simply furnished, well-run refuge with great views,

that gets busy in summer. Generally staffed Easter–Oct only. Half-board **€39**; when unstaffed **€6**

Refugio Valle de Bujaruelo ☎974 486 412, ⊛mesondebujaruelo.com. Comfortable refuge with meal service and camping. Can arrange guided treks with the well-run Grupo Explora Casteret (⊛casteretgrupoexplora.com). Open weekends from mid-March to end of summer; limited opening times rest of year. Dorm **€14**, double **€25**, tent/car **€4**

Cañón de Añísclo and Garganta de Escuaín

The canyons of **Añísclo** and **Escuaín** dramatically carve up the terrain in the southeast corner of Ordesa. These canyons draw considerably fewer tourists than the Cañón de Ordesa, in part because it can be a tough area to penetrate, with no public transport and minimal accommodation.

Cañón de Añísclo

From the north, the **Cañón de Añísclo** – filled with jagged cliffs, quiet forests of looming trees and gurgling brooks – is a day-hike from *Refugio Góriz*. If you have your own transport, you can reach it from the south. About 13km from tiny **Escalona**, 10km north of Aínsa, in the direction of Sarvisé is a trail that leads into the canyon; it's five-hour round-trip trek through the most verdant section of the gorge to the clearing, **La Ripareta**.

Garganta de Escuaín

Centro de Visitantes, Tella: April–Nov 9am–2pm & 4–7pm, though times vary • ☎ 974 243 361

The **Garganta Escuaín**, in the Río Yaga valley, is smaller than Añísclo but also spectacular. It's best accessed from the village of **Lafortunada**, 17km northeast of Aínsa. From Lafortunada, you can trek the GR15 trail for the two-hour trip to the pretty village of **Tella**, which has a **park information office**. Just beyond the village, a trail leads to tiny **Escuaín**, from where it's about an hour into the gorge. With your own transport, you can also reach Escuaín from a small road off the Escalona–Sarvisé road.

Aínsa and around

In certain lights of day, the medieval stone village of **AÍNSA** looks like it has sprouted of the earth itself, with its cobbled streets, rooftops in varying shades of rust and grey and tendrils of green hanging out of flowerpots on wrought-iron balconies. The village is perched on a hill and views of the surrounding looming mountains greet you around every turn. Aínsa also has a decent selection of accommodation and makes an ideal base for exploring the park, as it lies about 10km from the trail into the **Cañón de Añísclo**

Iglesia de Santa María

Pl. Mayor • Generally daily 10am–2 & 4–9pm • Belfry entry €1

The exceptional Romanesque **Iglesia de Santa María** rises over the Plaza Mayor, and features a simple entryway with four archivolts (decorative arches). Inside are a triangular cloister and a fortified four-storeyed belfry, which you can ascend for far-reaching views from the top.

Bielsa

Some 33km north of Aínsa lies the small town of **Bielsa**, west of which sits the well-appointed *Parador de Bielsa* (see p.638), which is also a good jumping-off point for exploring the park. Bielsa sits at the confluence of the Cinca and Barrosa rivers, and northeast of town, in the park, unfolds the lush Valle de Pineta and the glassy Lago de Marboré. From the parador, which sits at the park's edge, you can trek – 4 to 5 hours one way – through the valley to Marboré Lake.

ARRIVAL AND INFORMATION   AÍNSA AND AROUND

By bus One bus daily runs to Aínsa from Barbastro (1hr) and Torla (1hr); in July and Aug, there are two buses daily. Three times a week (daily in summer) there's also a service to Bielsa (just under 1hr).

Turismo Avda. Pirenaica (daily 9am–2.30pm & 4–8.30pm; in summer Sat 9am–8pm; sometimes shorter hours and closed Sun in winter; ☎ 974 500 767).

Regional tourist office Pl. del Castillo Torre Nordeste (Mon–Thurs 9.30am–1.30 or 2pm & 4.30–7.30 or 8pm, Fri–Sun 9.30am–1.30pm & 4–8pm, limited hours in winter; ☎ 974 500 512, ⊛ turismosobrarbe.com).

9

ACCOMMODATION

Albergue Mora de Nuei Portal de Abajo 2, Aínsa ☎ 974 510 614, ⓦ alberguemoradenuei.com. Top-notch hostel, featuring well-maintained dorms with sturdy wooden bunks, clean bathrooms and a snack bar. They also have comfortable doubles. Dorms €17, Doubles €120

Parador de Bielsa Valle de Pineta, 14km northwest of Bielsa ☎ 974 501 011, ⓦ parador.es. This inviting rustic parador has handsome rooms and lovely views. It sits on the eastern slopes of the park, and is a comfortable base for

exploring the area. The restaurant serves regional cuisine, including Aragón's version of *migas*, with sausage and grapes. Note that there is no public transport between the parador and Bielsa, but taxis are available between the two (around €20 one way). 138

Los Siete Reyes Pl. Mayor 27, Aínsa ☎ 974 500 681, ⓦ lossietereyes.com. Wonderfully rustic hotel right on the Pl. Mayor, with inviting rooms that blend old and new – stone walls, colourful art, crisp linens. €90

EATING

Bodegas de Sobrarbe c/Mayor 2 ☎ 974 500 237. The area around the Pl. Mayor is dotted with restaurants and cafés, including this *bodega*, set in an ancient building and exuding a medieval feel – stone arches, wooden tables and hearty Aragonese meats. Daily 12.30–3.30pm & 8.30–10.30pm.

Bodegón de Mallacán Pl. Mayor ☎ 974 500 977. This amiable spot serves grilled meats and other mountain fare in a cosy dining room with wood-beam ceilings. Daily 2–4pm & 8–11pm.

Benasque and around

East of Bielsa lies the small town of **Benasque**, spectacularly set in the spacious green Ésera valley and ringed by rocky mountains. Much of the surrounding area is protected as the **Parque Natural Posets-Maladeta**, and numerous trails snake through the valleys and up the mountains. A lively crossroads, the town of Benasque itself is hardly untouched – it's often crammed with adventure-seeking tourists in high season – but this also means that it has plenty of outdoor sports services and tours, mountaineer-friendly accommodation and decently priced restaurants where you can refuel over robust meals.

Benasque is especially popular with avid climbers and trekkers who wish to ascend the Pyrenees' highest peaks, **Aneto** (3404m) and **Posets** (3371m). To do this you'll need all the proper equipment: crampons, ice-axe, rope and a helmet to guard against falling rocks. If you're less experienced, your best bet is to go on a trek with one of the

HIKES AND REFUGES AROUND BENASQUE

Benasque falls more or less in the middle of the trans-Pyrenean GR11 trail, making the town a popular resting spot for hikers, whether for one or more nights. One of the best ways of exploring the surrounding wilderness is to use the many refuges dotted around Benasque as your base.

One of the more popular treks is northwest of Benasque, along the Estós valley to the **Refugio de Estós**, a three-hour trek. You can then continue over the Puerto de Gistaín to the **Refugio de Viadós**, which takes another 5 hours. Viadós is a base for treks up Posets, but again, this is a serious undertaking, and you'll need all the proper equipment to do this climb.

An alternative to this route (though best if you're in tip-top shape, because it can be challenging) is northwest up the Eriste valley, 4km southwest of Benasque, and then over the **Collado de Eriste** before descending to Viadós. Along this route, you can stop at the **Refugio Ángel Órus**.

North of Benasque lies the lush **Upper Esera valley** and massive **Maladeta massif**. A small hub is **La Besurta**, about 16km northeast of Benasque (and linked by buses in summer), which has parking and a small hut/bar with food and supplies (summer only) and is a gateway to hikes in the area. A good base is *Hotel-Spa Hospital de Benasque* (see p.639), about 3km before you reach La Besurta. In the summer, buses connect Benasque to La Besurta (€11 round trip) and also to Valle de Vallibierna and the **Refugio Pescadores**, 11km northwest of Benasque.

REFUGES AROUND BENASQUE

Refugio Ángel Órus ☎ 974 344 044, ⓦ turism obenasque.com. Open year-round. Bunk bed €15.90

Refugio de Estós ☎ 974 344 515, ⓦ turism obenasque.com. Open year-round. Half-board is €36.40.

Bunk bed €15

Refugio Pescadores Open all year; not staffed. Free

Refugio de Viadós ☎ 974 506 163 or 974 506 082. Open in Easter & summer. Breakfast is €5.50 extra. Bunks €11

ADVENTURE OPERATORS IN BENASQUE

Benasque is filled with a wide variety of adventure operators and gear shops; the tourist office can direct you to recommended outfits. The prices for guided outdoor trips, from mountain treks to snowboarding courses, are similar to other Pyrenean destinations, ranging around €49–65 per person per day, with prices varying depending on the level of difficulty and size of tour group.

All Radical Mountain Avda. Francia ☎974 551 425. This well-run outfit specializes in snowboarding and other winter sports; they rent out skis and snowboards and other gear and equipment, and offer ski and snowboard classes. Mon–Sat 8.30am–11.30pm & 4–8.30pm, Sun 8.30am–1.30pm & 3.30–8.30pm.

Barrabés Avda. Francia ☎974 551 351, ⓦbarrabes .com. Large, well-regarded adventure retailer that rents

out gear, guidebooks, maps and more. Keep an eye out for their ongoing *rebajas* (sales). Daily 10.30–1.30pm & 4.30–8pm.

Compañía de Guías Valle de Benasque Based in the All Radical Mountain shop, Avda. Francia ☎974 551 425, ⓦguiasbenasque.com. This long-running operator offers all manner of guided climbs, treks and hikes through all the seasons – and for all levels.

many operators in town (see box, above). Either way, the tourist office is well equipped with maps and can update you on weather and trail conditions. As for snow sports, there's a popular ski hub in the area at **Cerler** (see box, p.634).

ARRIVAL AND INFORMATION

By bus Regular buses run from Barbastro (2hr) and Huesca (2hr 45min). Buses from other towns in the region, including Aínsa, also run to Benasque but via connections in Barbastro.

BENASQUE AND AROUND

Turismo c/San Sebastián, on the southeast edge of town (daily in summer 9.30–1pm & 4.30–8pm; may have limited hours in winter; ☎974 551 289, ⓦturismobenasque.com).

ACCOMMODATION

Hotel Aneto Carretera de Francia 4 ☎974 551 061, ⓦhotelesvalero.com. One of the first four-star hotels in the area, *Hotel Aneto* has spacious, well-appointed rooms and fetching mountain views, and they can help you arrange hiking and ski trips. €145

Hotel Aragüells Avda. Los Tilos ☎974 551 619, ⓦhotelaraguells.com. Well-maintained rooms as well as a restaurant serving regional cuisine; they also offer nearby apartments (call ahead for prices). €85

Hotel Ciria Avda. Los Tilos ☎974 551 612 or 974 551 080, ⓦhotelciria.com. Long-time, family-run hotel in the middle of town with cosy rooms with sturdy furnishings. They can also arrange for guided treks into the mountains.

The popular restaurant *El Fogaril* (see below) serves hearty mountain cuisine. Hotel closed two weeks around Easter (when ski season ends) and in mid-Oct. €94

Hotel-Spa Hospital de Benasque Camino Real de Francia, Los Llanos del Hospital, about 3km from La Besurta ☎974 552 012, ⓦllanosdelhospital.com. Los Llanos del Hospital is a mountain resort and ski centre anchored by a large, handsome alpine lodge with a wide range of rooms and services. The resort is a great jumping-off point for exploring the Parque Natural Posets-Maladeta, with a range of activities throughout the year, from skiing in winter to hiking and mountain biking in summer. Regular buses connect the resort with La Besurta. €84

EATING AND DRINKING

El Fogaril Hotel Ciria, Avda. Los Tilos ☎974 551 612 or 974 551 080, ⓦhotelciria.com. The Ciria brothers, who are avid hunters and fishermen, bring back their prey and catch to this well-regarded restaurant, which is known for serving game and meat dishes that you often won't find elsewhere, from wild boar to partridge to *sarrio* (Pyrenean mountain goat), all of which are sometimes roasted in a wood oven. Expect to pay €18–25 per person. Daily 1.30–3.30pm & 8.30–10.30pm.

La Llardana Camino de San Anton, at the entrance to Benasque ☎974 551 687. This amiable *casa rural*

has a top-notch restaurant, with beautiful views, which features local cuisine with a modern twist, and may include ravioli with pine nuts, roast lamb with wild mushrooms, and quail. The tasting menu is around €30–35. They also have comfortable rooms (€60). Daily 1–3.30pm & 8–11pm; sometimes closed Mon or Wed in winter.

Restaurante La Parrilla Carretera Francia ☎974 551 134. Enjoy traditional mountain cuisine, from wild rice to rich Magret duck to grilled meats, at this friendly restaurant. Daily 1–4pm & 9–11.30pm.

Barcelona

PARC GÜELL (P.678)

Barcelona

Barcelona – Spain's second city, and the self-confident capital of Catalunya – vibrates with life, and there's certainly not another city in the country to touch it for sheer style, looks or energy. It's long had the reputation of being the avant-garde capital of Spain, its art museums are world-class, its football team sublime, while its designer restaurants, bars, galleries and shops lead from the front. And in Antoni Gaudí's extraordinary church of the Sagrada Família, the winding alleys and ageing mansions of the picture-postcard Gothic Quarter, and the world-famous boulevard that is the Ramblas, you have three sights that are high up any Spanish sightseeing list. As a thriving port, prosperous commercial centre and buzzing cultural capital of three million people, the city is almost impossible to exhaust – even in a lengthy visit you will likely only scrape the surface.

Everyone starts with the **Ramblas**, and then dives straight into the medieval nucleus of the city, the **Barri Gòtic** (Gothic Quarter), but there are plenty of other central old-town neighbourhoods to explore, from **La Ribera** – home to the celebrated **Museu Picasso** – to funky **El Raval**, where cool bars, restaurants and boutiques have mushroomed in the wake of the striking contemporary art museum, **MACBA**. Even if you think you know these heavily touristed neighbourhoods well, there's always something else to discover – tapas bars hidden down alleys little changed for a century or two, designer boutiques in gentrified old-town quarters, bargain lunches in workers' taverns, unmarked gourmet restaurants, craft outlets and workshops, *fin-de-siècle* cafés, restored medieval palaces and neighbourhood markets.

But endlessly fascinating as these districts are, Barcelona is so much more than just its old-town areas. The fortress-topped hill of **Montjuïc**, for example, contains the Olympic stadium used for the 1992 Games as well as some of the city's best art museums, notably **MNAC**, ie the Museu Nacional d'Art de Catalunya – note the word "nacional", which tells you all you need to know about Catalunya's strong sense of identity. Other museums too explore the work of internationally famous Catalan artists, from Joan Miró to Antoni Tàpies, while in the nineteenth-century, uptown extension of the city – the **Eixample** – are found most of Barcelona's celebrated *modernista* architectural wonders, from private houses to Gaudí's peerless church.

MNAC

Highlights

❶ Las Golondrinas Jump on a sightseeing boat around the harbour and local coast to see Barcelona at its best. **See p.656**

❷ La Boqueria If you're not hungry when you visit the city's – some say Spain's – greatest market, you soon will be. **See p.650**

❸ Fundació Joan Miró The life's work of the iconic Catalan artist is housed in the city's best-looking gallery. **See p.667**

❹ FC Barcelona at Camp Nou The world's greatest football team? Only *madrileños* will argue with you. **See p.679**

❺ MNAC A thousand years of Catalan art is contained within the superb Museu Nacional d'Art de Catalunya, the flagship gallery on the slopes of Montjuïc. **See p.666**

❻ Sagrada Família The *modernista* works of architect Antoni Gaudí define the city – his famous church is a virtuoso masterpiece. See **p.673**

❼ Bar hopping, El Raval Barcelona's coolest neighbourhood is the best place for a night on the tiles. **See p.694**

❽ Parc Güell If you visit only one city park, make it Gaudí's extraordinary flight of fancy. See **p.678**

HIGHLIGHTS ARE MARKED ON THE MAP ON P.644

If Barcelona sounds a bit too much like hard cultural work, then simply look instead for entertainment to the city's harbour, parks, gardens and beaches. Indeed, it's remarkably easy to forget you're in a big city at all some times – just to take one example, walking from the **Port Vell** harbour takes you along the marina, through the old fishing and restaurant quarter of **Barceloneta**, past the leafy **Parc de la Ciutadella**, and out along the beachside promenade to the bar-and-restaurant zone that is the **Port Olímpic**. Other easy city jaunts include a trip out to the

Diagonal Mar conference and exhibition district for the new natural science museum, or up to the distinctive neighbourhood of **Gràcia**, with its small squares, lively bars and Gaudí's amazing **Parc Güell**. If you're saving yourself for just one aerial view of Barcelona, wait for a clear day and head for **Tibidabo**, a mountain-top amusement park backed by the Collserola hills, while beyond the city limits the one day-trip everyone should make is to the mountain-top monastery of **Montserrat**, 40km northwest.

■ **ACCOMMODATION**	
Barcelona Urbany	1
Equity Point Sea	3
Hotel Arts Barcelona	2
W Barcelona	4

● **BAR**	
Gimlet	1

● **CAFÉ & RESTAURANT**	
Agua	2

■ **CLUBS**	
Bikini	3
Sala Razzmatazz	1
Universal	2

HIGHLIGHTS
❶ Las Golondrinas
❷ La Boqueria
❸ Fundació Joan Miró
❹ FC Barcelona at Camp Nou
❺ MNAC
❻ Sagrada Fauilia
❼ Bar hopping, El Raval
❽ Parc Güell

10

FESTIVALS IN BARCELONA

FEBRUARY

Festes de Santa Eulàlia A week's worth of music, dances, parades of *gegants* (giants), *castellers* (human castle-builders) and fireworks in honour of one of Barcelona's patron saints – the saint's day falls on February 12.

EASTER

Semana Santa (Holy Week) There's a procession from the church of Sant Agustí on c/de l'Hospital (El Raval) to La Seu, starting at 4pm on Good Friday, while Palm Sunday sees the blessing of the palms at La Seu.

APRIL

23: Día de Sant Jordi St George's Day, dedicated to Catalunya's dragon-slaying patron saint – the city fills with roses and books, exchanged by sweethearts as gifts.

MAY

Last week: Primavera Sound The city's hottest music festival heralds a massive three-day bash, attracting top names in rock, indie and electronica.
Last week: Festival de Flamenco de Ciutat Vella Five days of guitar recitals, singing and dancing, plus DJ sessions and chill-out zone.

JUNE

Usually 2nd or 3rd week: Sónar Europe's most cutting-edge electronic music, multimedia and urban art festival attracts up to 100,000 visitors for three days of brilliant noise and spectacle. By day, the focus is on events at MACBA/CCCB; by night, the action shifts to out-of-town L'Hospitalet, with all-night buses running from the city to the Sónar bars and clubs.
23/24: Verbena/Día de Sant Joan The "eve" and "day" of St John is the city's wildest annual celebration, with bonfires and fireworks (particularly on Montjuïc), drinking and dancing, and watching the sun come up on the beach. The day itself (24th) is a public holiday.
End June to August: Festival de Barcelona Grec The summer's foremost arts and music festival, with main performances at Montjuïc's open-air Greek theatre – see feature on p.667.

JULY

First week: Montjuïc de Nit Once a year, Montjuïc's galleries throw open their doors for the night, while parks, spaces and buildings across the whole hillside throb with free gigs, dance, theatre, films, street art and family events.

AUGUST

Mid-month: Festa Major de Gràcia Music, dancing, fireworks and *castellers* in the neighbourhood's streets and squares.

SEPTEMBER

11: Diada Nacional The Catalan national day is a public holiday in Barcelona.
24: Festes de la Mercè The city's biggest traditional festival lasts for a week around the 24th – the 24th itself is a public holiday (and there's free entry that day to city museums). Highlights include costumed giants, breathtaking firework displays and competing teams of *castellers*.

OCTOBER/NOVEMBER

Third week: Festival de Tardor Ribermúsica Wide-ranging four-day music festival held in the Born, with free concerts in historic and picturesque locations.
End October to November: Festival de Jazz The biggest annual jazz festival in town highlights big-name solo artists and bands.

DECEMBER

1–22: Fira de Santa Llúcia A Christmas market and crafts fair outside La Seu.

Along the Ramblas

It is a telling comment on Barcelona's character that one can recommend a single street – the **Ramblas** – as a highlight. No day in the city seems complete without a stroll down at least part of what, for Spanish poet Federico García Lorca, was "the only street in the world which I wish would never end". Lined with cafés, restaurants, souvenir shops, flower stalls and newspaper kiosks, it's at the heart of Barcelona's life and self-image.

The Ramblas splits the old-town areas of Barcelona in half, with the Barri Gòtic on the east flank of the avenue and El Raval on the west. It also actually comprises five separate sections strung head to tail – from north to south, Rambla Canaletes, Estudis, Sant Josep, Caputxins and Santa Mònica – though you'll rarely hear them referred to as such. Here, under the plane trees, you'll find pet canaries, tropical fish, flowers, plants, postcards and books. You can buy jewellery, have your palm read and your portrait painted, play cards with a man on an upturned cardboard box (not a good idea), or while away time with the buskers and human statues.

10

Plaça de Catalunya

Ⓜ Catalunya

Plaça de Catalunya lies at the heart of the city, with the old town and port below it, and the planned Eixample district above and beyond. It was laid out in its present form in the 1920s, centred on a formal arrangement of statues, circular fountains and trees, and is the focal point for local events and demonstrations – notably the mass gathering here on New Year's Eve. It's the site of the main tourist office, while principal landmark is the massive **El Corte Inglés** department store, which has some stupendous views from its ninth-floor café. On the southwest side, over the road from the top of the Ramblas, is **El Triangle** shopping centre, whose ground-floor **Café Zurich** is a traditional Barcelona meeting place.

Església de Betlem and around

Ramblas 107 • Daily 8am–6pm • Free • Ⓜ Liceu

The **Església de Betlem** was built in 1681 in Baroque style for the Jesuits, but was completely gutted in 1937 as anarchists sacked the city's churches at will. It seems hard to believe, but this part of the Ramblas was a war zone during the Spanish Civil War, when the city erupted into factionalism. As he recounted in *Homage to Catalonia*, **George Orwell** was caught in the crossfire between the nearby *Café Moka* (Ramblas 126) – the current café of the same name is a modern replacement – and the Poliorama cinema opposite, now the **Teatre Poliorama** (Ramblas 115).

Palau de la Virreina

Ramblas 99 • Tiquet Rambles office daily 10am–8.30pm; galleries Tues–Sun noon–8pm • Gallery admission usually free • ☎ 933 161 000, Ⓦ bcn.cat/virreinacentredelaimatge • Ⓜ Liceu

The graceful eighteenth-century **Palau de la Virreina** is used by the city council's culture department, and has a useful ground-floor **information centre** called "Tiquet Rambles"

THE RAMBLAS STATUES

You can't move for **human statues** on the Ramblas, standing on their little home-made plinths. Classical figures and movie characters have always formed part of the parade, but there's also some real wit and invention on display, like "Fruit Lady", a one-woman mobile market stall, or the twin "Bicycling Skeletons". Then there's just the plain weird, like "Lady Under Rock", crushed under a boulder, issuing plaintive shrieks at passers-by. And quite what demons drive "Man Sitting on Toilet", only he can say.

10

THE OLD TOWN

SHOPS

Almacens del Pilar	15
Almacén Marabí	7
L'Arca del Avia	10
Artesania Catalunya	13
Bubó	17
Camper	2
Casa Gispert	11
La Central del Raval	5
Cereria Subirà	9
El Corte Inglés	1
Custo Barcelona	14
Discos Castelló	3

Espai Drap Art	21
Etnomusic	4
Fantastik	6
Formatgeria	12
La Seu	23
Forn Baluard	16
La Manual	19
Alpargatera	
Naifa	8
Papabubble	22
U-Casas	18
Vila Viniteca	20

CLUBS

Jamboree	4
Jazz Sí Club	1
Karma	3
La Macarena	5
Moog	6
Sidecar	2
Tarantos	4

▲ Parc Zoològic

10

■ ACCOMMODATION
Barceló Raval	21
Bonic Barcelona	24
Chic & Basic Born	4
Equity Point Gothic	10
Hostal Benidorm	22
Hostal Fernando	14
Hostal Gat Raval	5
Hostal Gat Xino	16
Hostal Mare Nostrum	15
Hostal Nuevo Colón	13
Hostal Rembrandt	8
Hosteria Grau	2
Hotel Banys Orientals	12
Hotel Canton	23
Hotel España	19
Hotel H1898	7
Hotel El Jardi	11
Hotel Peninsular	18
Itaca Hostel	3
Le Méridien Barcelona	6
Neri Hotel	20
Pensió Alamar	9
Pensió 2000	1
Pensión Mari-Luz	17

● CAFÉS, TAPAS & RESTAURANTS
Antiga Casa Figueres	29
El Atril	5
Arc Café	42
Bar del Pi	17
Bar Pinotxo	22
Bar Ra	21
La Bascula	39
Biblioteca	12
Biocenter	43
Bodega La Plata	26
Café de l'Acadèmia	34
Café de l'Opera	2
Caj Chai	18
Cal Pep	27
Can Majó	49
Can Maño	46
Casa Delfin	13
Casa Mari y Rufo	6
Comerç 24	1
Cova Fumada	48
Dos Palillos	8
Dulcinea	15
Granja M. Viader	10
Jai-Ca	44
El Jardi	31
Mosquito	3
Romesco	35
Senyor Parellada	19
Taller de Tapas	25
Venus	14
Delicatessen	37
El Xampanyet	20

■ BARS
Almirall	9
L'Ascensor	32
Betty Ford's	7
Bosc de la Fades	47
Can Paixano	40
Casa Paco	4
Espai Barroc	14
La Fianna	16
Glaciar	36
Luz de Gas	45
Marmalade	41
Marsella	38
Milk	24
Muy Buenas	28
Resolís	33
Schilling	43
La Vinya del	
Senyor	30

where you can find out about upcoming events and buy tickets. Various galleries and studios also present an interesting mix of changing **exhibitions** highlighting La Virreina's role as the "Centre de la Imatge". Duck into the courtyard to see the city's two official **Carnival giants** (*gegants vells*) representing the celebrated thirteenth-century Catalan king, Jaume I, and his wife Violant. The origin of Catalunya's outsized (five-metre-high) wood-and-plaster Carnival figures is unclear, though they probably once formed part of the entertainment at medieval travelling fairs.

Mercat de la Boqueria

Ramblas 91 • Mon–Sat 8am–8.30pm • ☎ 933 182 584, ⓦ boqueria.info • Ⓜ Liceu

Beyond the Palau de la Virreina lies the city's most famous market, known locally as **La Boqueria**, though officially the Mercat Sant Josep. While others might protest, the market really can claim to be the best in Spain. Built between 1836 and 1840, it's a riot of noise and colour, with great piles of fruit and vegetables, dried herbs, exotic mushrooms, cured meats and an amazing variety of fish and seafood. If you're going to buy, do some browsing first, as the flagship fruit and veg stalls by the entrance tend to have higher prices than those farther inside. There are some excellent stand-up snack bars in here, open from dawn onwards for the traders – *Pinotxo* near the Ramblas entrance is the most famous.

Gran Teatre del Liceu

Ramblas 51–59 • Tours daily 10am, 11.30am, noon, 12.30pm & 1pm, English spoken • 10am tour €9, later tours €4.20 • ☎ 934 859 914, ⓦ liceubarcelona.com • Ⓜ Liceu

Barcelona's celebrated opera house, the **Gran Teatre del Liceu**, was first founded as a private theatre in 1847. Tours of the lavish interior depart from the modern extension, the Espai Liceu – you'll learn most on the more expensive, hour-long 10am guided tour; the other, cheaper tours are self-guided and last only twenty minutes. Highlights include the classically inspired **Saló dels Miralls** (Salon of Mirrors) and the impressive gilded auditorium containing almost 2300 seats – making it one of the world's largest opera houses. Meanwhile, the traditional meeting place for post-performance refreshments for audience and performers alike is the famous *Cafè de l'Òpera*, just across the Ramblas.

Arts Santa Mònica

Ramblas 7 • Tues–Sun & hols 11am–9pm • Free • ☎ 935 671 110, ⓦ artssantamonica.cat • Ⓜ Drassanes

The Augustinian **convent of Santa Mònica** dates originally from 1626, making it the oldest building on the Ramblas. It was remodelled in the 1980s as a contemporary **arts centre**, known as **Arts Santa Mònica,** and hosts regularly changing exhibitions in its

---

ON THE MIRÓ TRAIL

Halfway down the Ramblas, just past La Boqueria, look down at the pavement – that's right, the large circular mural under your feet is by **Joan Miró**. The famous Catalan artist was born just a couple of minutes' walk off the Ramblas in the Barri Gòtic (there's a plaque to mark the building on Passatge del Crèdit, off c/de Ferran) – and when you've seen one Miró in Barcelona, well, you start to see them everywhere, whether it's T-shirts for tourists or branding for businesses. There's another large ceramic mural at the airport, for a start, while Miró designed the starfish logo for the Caixa de Pensions savings bank (there's one splashed across the Caixa Forum arts centre on Montjuïc). And this is all on top of the Montjuïc museum devoted to his life's work (see p.667). In many ways, it's a Miró city, whatever Picasso fans might think.

grand, echoing galleries – it's an unusual gallery space dedicated to "artistic creation, science, thought and communication" so there's usually something worth seeing.

Museu de la Cera

Ramblas 4–6, entrance on Ptge. de Banca • July–Sept daily 10am–10pm; Oct–June Mon–Fri 10am–1.30pm & 4–7.30pm, Sat & Sun 11am–2pm & 4.30–8.30pm • €15, under-11s €9 • ☎ 933 172 649, 🅦 museocerabcn.com • Ⓜ Drassanes

Final stop at the bottom of the Ramblas is the city's wax museum, the **Museu de la Cera**, housed in an impressive nineteenth-century bank building. Needless to say, it's extremely ropey and enormously amusing, culminating in cheesy underwater and space capsules and an unpleasant "Terror" room. You also won't want to miss the museum's extraordinary grotto-bar, the *Bosc de les Fades* ("Forest of the Fairies").

Barri Gòtic

The **Barri Gòtic**, or Gothic Quarter, forms the very heart of the old town, spreading out from the east side of the Ramblas. It's a remarkable concentration of medieval buildings principally dating from the fourteenth and fifteenth centuries, when Barcelona reached the height of its commercial prosperity before being absorbed into the burgeoning kingdom of Castile. It takes the best part of a day to see everything here, with the cathedral – La Seu – a particular highlight, and you certainly won't want to miss the archeological remains at the Museu d'Història de la Ciutat or the eclectic collections of the Museu Frederic Marès. That said, sauntering through the atmospheric alleys or simply sitting at a café table in one of the lovely squares is just as much an attraction.

The picture-postcard images of the Barri Gòtic are largely based on the streets north of c/de Ferran and c/de Jaume I, where tourists throng the boutiques, bars, restaurants, museums and galleries. South of here – from Plaça Reial and c/d'Avinyó to the harbour – the Barri Gòtic is rather more traditional (or sometimes just plain run-down).

La Seu

Pl. de la Seu • Mon–Fri 8am–12.45pm & 5.15–7.30pm, Sat 8am–12.45pm & 5.15–8pm, Sun 8am–1.45pm & 5.15–8pm • Cathedral and cloister free during general admission times, otherwise tourist admission charge obligatory 1–5pm, €6, but includes entrance to all sections • 🅦 catedralbcn.org • Ⓜ Jaume I

Barcelona's cathedral, **La Seu**, is one of the great Gothic buildings of Spain. Located on a site previously occupied by a Roman temple and then an early Christian basilica, it was begun in 1298 and finished in 1448, save for the principal facade, which wasn't finally completed until the 1880s. The cathedral is dedicated to the city's co-patroness, **Santa Eulàlia**, martyred by the Romans for daring to prefer Christianity, and her tomb rests in a crypt beneath the high altar. The rest of the interior is typically ornate, with no fewer than 29 side chapels, but the most magnificent part of the cathedral is its fourteenth-century **cloister**, which looks over a lush garden complete with soaring palm trees and – more unusually – a gaggle of honking geese. White geese have been kept here for over five hundred years, either (depending on which story you believe) to reflect the virginity of Santa Eulàlia or as a reminder of the erstwhile Roman splendour of Barcelona (geese having been kept on the Capitoline Hill in Rome).

Visit in the morning or late afternoon, and admission to the church interior and cloister is free. However, to see everything, it's better to visit during 1pm and 5pm when the obligatory admission charge includes entry to all sections of the cathedral, including the treasury, as well as areas like the choir and various side-chapels that are not open to the public during the general admission times.

Dalí Barcelona

C/dels Arcs 5 • Daily 10am–10pm • €10 • ☎ 933 181 774, ⓦ dalibarcelona.com • Ⓜ Jaume I

The handsome Gothic palace housing the Real Circle Artístic (Royal Artistic Circle) hosts various exhibitions and concerts, though the big draw is **Dalí Barcelona**, a collection of 44 wildly original bronze sculptures by Salvador Dalí, completed in the 1970s as a private commission for a wealthy Catalan businessman. The sculptures, large and small, are theatrically displayed under Gothic arches, behind swags of red velvet curtain, and depict various themes that fascinated Dalí throughout his life: the sea, women, horses, mythology, religion and so on.

10

Plaça del Rei

Ⓜ Jaume I

The harmonious enclosed square of **Plaça del Rei**, behind the cathedral apse, was once the courtyard of the palace of the counts of Barcelona, later the residence of the count-kings of Aragón. The palace buildings themselves are steeped in history, and include the romantic Renaissance **Torre del Rei Martí**, the main hall known as the **Saló del Tinell**, and the fourteenth-century **Santa Agata chapel** – there's no public access to the tower, though the interiors of both hall and chapel can usually be seen during a visit to the Museu d'Història de Barcelona (see below). The square itself, meanwhile, was the scene of one of Barcelona's greatest historic set-pieces, since it was from the steps of the exterior stone staircase that Ferdinand and Isabella received Christopher Columbus on his triumphant return from his famous voyage of 1492.

Museu d'Història de Barcelona (MUHBA)

Pl. del Rei, entrance on c/del Veguer • Tues–Sat 10am–8pm (Oct–March 10am–2pm & 4–7pm), Sun 10am–8pm, hols 10am–3pm • €7, includes entry to other MUHBA sites, free Sun after 3pm • ☎ 932 562 100, ⓦ museuhistoria.bcn.cat • Ⓜ Jaume I

The **Museu d'Història de Barcelona** (Barcelona History Museum) comprises half a dozen sites across the city, though its crucial draw is its underground archeological section – nothing less than the extensive remains of the Roman city of Barcino, stretching under the surrounding streets as far as the cathedral. The remains date from the first to the sixth centuries AD and reflect the transition from Roman to Visigothic rule. Not much survives above chest height, but explanatory diagrams show the extent of the streets, walls and buildings, while models, mosaics, murals and displays of excavated goods help flesh out the reality of daily life in Barcino. Plaça del Rei's **Saló del Tinell** and the beautiful **Capella de Santa Agata** are also part of the history museum, and are usually open for visits with your museum ticket, though there's sometimes an extra charge for special exhibitions held in the Saló del Tinell.

BOHO BARCELONA AND THE FOUR CATS

There's not much to see in the shopping zone north of the cathedral, but a century or so ago a tavern called **Els Quatre Gats** (The Four Cats; c/Montsió 3, ⓦ www.4gats.com) burned brightly as the epicentre of Barcelona's bohemian in-crowd. It was opened in 1897 as a gathering place for artists and literary types, with the building gloriously decorated in exuberant Catalan Art Nouveau style. *Els Quatre Gats* soon thrived as the scene of poetry readings and the venue for cultural debate, while a young Picasso designed the menu. Today, a modern restoration displays something of its former glory, with the bar-restaurant overseen by a copy of Ramon Casas' famous wall-painting of himself and café founder Pere Romeu on a tandem bicycle (the original is in MNAC).

Museu Frederic Marès

Pl. de Sant Iu 5–6, off c/dels Comtes • Tues–Sat 10am–7pm, Sun & hols 11am–8pm • €4.20, free Sun after 3pm & first Sun of the month • ☎ 932 563 500, Ⓦ museumares.bcn.cat • Ⓜ Jaume I

One of the old town's most fascinating museums, the **Museu Frederic Marès** occupies a wing of the old royal palace, behind Plaça del Rei. It celebrates the diverse passions of sculptor, painter and restorer Frederic Marès (1893–1991), whose beautifully presented collection of ancient and medieval sculpture does little to prepare visitors for Marès' true obsession, namely a kaleidoscopic array of curios and collectibles. These present an incredible retrospective jumble gathered during fifty years of travel, with entire rooms devoted to keys and locks, cigarette cards and snuff boxes, fans, gloves and brooches, playing cards, walking sticks, dolls' houses, toy theatres and archaic bicycles, to name just a sample of what's on show. The museum's summer café (April–Sept; closed Mon) occupies the romantic courtyard, with seats under the orange trees.

Església de Santa María del Pi and around

Ⓜ Liceu

The fourteenth-century **Església de Santa María del Pi** stands at the centre of three delightful little squares, five minutes' walk from the cathedral or just two minutes from the Ramblas. The church stands on the middle square, **Plaça Sant Josep Oriol**, the prettiest of the three, overhung with balconies and scattered with seats from the *Bar del Pi*. This whole area becomes an **artists' market** at the weekend (Sat 11am–8pm, Sun 11am–2pm), while buskers and street performers often appear here, too. A **farmers' market** spills across Plaça del Pi on the last Saturday and Sunday of the month (Oct–May only), selling honey, cheese, cakes and other produce, while the cafés of **Carrer de Petritxol** (off Plaça del Pi) are the place to come for a cup of hot chocolate – *Dulcinea* at no. 2 is the traditional choice.

Palau de la Generalitat

Pl. de Sant Jaume, entrance on c/de Sant Honorat • 1hr guided tours on 2nd and 4th Sun of the month (except Aug), every 30min–1hr, 10am–2pm (only 1 or 2 each day in English), also on April 23, and Sept 11 & 24 • Free, passport or ID required • ☎ 934 024 600, Ⓦ gencat.cat • Ⓜ Jaume I

On the north side of **Plaça de Sant Jaume** – the square that marks the very centre of the Barri Gòtic – rises the **Palau de la Generalitat**, traditional home of the Catalan government, from where the short-lived Catalan Republic was proclaimed in April 1931. There's a beautiful cloister on the first floor, while opening off this is the chapel of Sant Jordi (St George, patron saint of Catalunya as well as England), and an upper

---

A TOUR OF JEWISH BARCELONA

Barcelona's medieval Jewish quarter lay nestled in the shadow of the cathedral – under the Church's careful scrutiny. It was centred on c/Sant Domènec del Call, where you'll find the most notable surviving landmark, the **Antiga Sinagoga** (c/Marlet 5, corner with c/Sant Domènec del Call; Mon–Fri 10.30am–5.30pm, Sat & Sun 10.30am–3pm, sometimes closed Sat for ceremonies; €2.50; ☎ 933 170 790, Ⓦ calldebarcelona.org; Ⓜ Liceu) – not many people stop by, and if you do, you'll get a personalized tour of the small room by a member of the local Jewish community. The prosperous settlement persisted until the pogrom and forced conversion of 1391, after which most of the buildings used by the Jews were torn down. However, a plaque further down c/Marlet (junction with c/Arc Sant Ramon del Call) marks the site of the former rabbi's house, while in nearby Plaçeta Manuel Ribé another house – originally belonging to a veil-maker – now serves as a small museum, the **Centre d'Interpretació del Call** (Pl. Manuel Ribé; Wed–Fri 11am–2pm, Sat 11am–6pm, Sun & hols 11am–2pm; free; ☎ 932 562 100, Ⓦ museuhistoria.bcn.cat; Ⓜ Liceu).

courtyard planted with orange trees, overhung by gargoyles and peppered with presidential busts. Aside from the guided tours on alternate Sundays, the Generalitat is also traditionally open to the public on April 23 – **Día de Sant Jordi** (St George's Day) – when the whole square is festooned with bookstalls and rose sellers.

Ajuntament de Barcelona

Pl. de Sant Jaume, entrance on c/Font de Sant Miquel • Public admission Sun 10am–2pm • Free, English-language leaflet provided • ☎ 934 027 000, ⓦ bcn.cat • Ⓜ Jaume I

On the south side of Plaça de Sant Jaume stands Barcelona's City Hall, the **Ajuntament**, parts of which date from as early as 1373, though the Neoclassical facade was added in the nineteenth century when the square was laid out. On Sundays you're allowed into the building for a self-guided tour around the rather splendid marble halls, galleries and staircases. The highlights are the magnificent restored fourteenth-century council chamber, known as the **Saló de Cent**, and the dramatic historical murals by Josep María Sert in the **Saló de les Cròniques** (Hall of Chronicles), while the ground-floor courtyard features sculptural works by some of the most famous Catalan artists.

Palau Moxó

Pl. de Sant Just 4 • Guided tours on Fridays at noon, English spoken, €10; Thursday concerts at 8pm, €20; reservations essential for tours and concerts • ☎ 933 152 238, ⓦ palaumoxo.com • Ⓜ Jaume I

Near the *ajuntament*, down c/d'Hercules, **Plaça de Sant Just** is a handsome little corner of the old town, sporting a remarkable Baroque palace. Built in 1770 for a wealthy land-owning family, the **Palau Moxó** has been in the hands of the Moxó family ever since, which makes it unique in Barcelona – doubly so, in fact, since most of the city's other Baroque residences were destroyed during the Civil War. Weekly guided tours show you the grand salons and intimate chambers, while Thursday-evening **concerts** provide another way to soak up something of the noble life. The square, too, is a particularly nice spot for an alfresco lunch at the excellent *Café de l'Acadèmia*.

Museu d'Idees i Invents de Barcelona (miba)

C/Ciutat 7 • Tues–Fri 10am–7pm, Sat 10am–8pm, Sun & hols 10am–2pm • €7 • ☎ 933 327 930, ⓦ mibamuseum.com • Ⓜ Jaume I

The impressive buildings of the Barri Gòtic have many grand entrances, from exterior stone staircases to courtyards into which you can drive a coach-and-four – but there's only one where you get to slide down an enclosed steel chute, water-park style, into the vaulted bowels of the building. That would be Catalan inventor Pep Torres' brain-boggling Barcelona Museum of Ideas and Inventions, known as **miba**, which presents a mixture of his own inventions and those of budding and established creative inventors worldwide.

Plaça Reial and around

Ⓜ Liceu

Of all the old-town squares, the most popular with visitors is the elegant nineteenth-century **Plaça Reial**, just off the Ramblas. It's studded with tall palm trees and decorated iron lamps (made by the young Antoni Gaudí), bordered by high, pastel-coloured arcaded buildings, and centred on a fountain depicting the Three Graces. It used to be a bit dodgy here, but most of the really unsavoury characters have been driven off over the years and predatory, menu-toting waiters are usually the biggest nuisance these days.

The alleys on the south side of Plaça Reial emerge on c/dels Escudellers – still with a late-night seediness about it, but teetering on the edge of respectability. Bars and restaurants around here attract a youthful crowd, nowhere more so than those flanking funky **Plaça George Orwell**, at the eastern end of c/dels Escudellers. To the south, down **Carrer d'Avinyó** is the harbourside neighbourhood known as **La Mercè**, formerly the home of merchants enriched by Barcelona's maritime trade. Carrer de la Mercè and the surrounding streets (particularly Ample, d'en Gignas and Regomir) are home to a series of old-style **taverns** that provide one of the old town's more authentic experiences.

10 Port Vell

Perhaps the greatest recent transformation in the city has been along the waterfront, where harbour and Mediterranean have once again been placed at the heart of Barcelona. The glistening harbourside merges seamlessly with the old town, with the tourist attractions of **Port Vell** (ie, Old Port) just steps from the bottom of the Ramblas. Meanwhile, the pleasant walk around the harbour along the waterfront to Barceloneta takes you past the **marina**, where a boat has been converted into a floating bar, the *Luz de Gas*, which is a particularly good place for a sundowner.

Mirador de Colón

Pl. del Portal de la Pau • Daily 8.30am–8.30pm • €4 • ⓜ Drassanes

At the foot of the Ramblas, in the middle of swirling traffic, stands the striking **Mirador de Colón**, which commemorates the visit made by Christopher Columbus (known locally as Cristóbal Colón) to Barcelona in June 1493. A lift whisks you up to the enclosed *mirador* at Columbus' feet for terrific 360-degree city views.

Museu Marítim

Avgda. de les Drassanes • **Museum** daily 10am–8pm • Reduced museum admission during renovation works €2.50, free on Sun after 3pm • Santa Eulàlia Tues–Fri noon–5.30pm, Sat, Sun & hols 10am–5.30pm, €1, free with Museu Marítim ticket • ☎ 933 429 920, ⓦ mmb.cat • ⓜ Drassanes

Barcelona's medieval shipyards, or **Drassanes**, date from the thirteenth century, and were originally used as a dry dock to fit and arm Catalunya's war fleet in the days when the Catalan-Aragonese crown was vying with Venice and Genoa for control of the Mediterranean. The unique stone-vaulted buildings make a fitting home for the city's **Museu Marítim** (Maritime Museum), though a large-scale renovation project means access is restricted, probably until 2013. In the meantime, there's cut-price admission to one or two changing exhibitions that draw on the museum collections, and continued access to the shop and café. Your ticket also allows a quick tour of the

---

HARBOUR TOURS

It's often easy to forget – exploring the medieval old-town streets or uptown boutiques – that Barcelona is, esentially, a **maritime city**, built on its Mediterranean location and trade. For a reminder, jump on one of the sightseeing boats that tie up in the inner harbour, just at the bottom of the Ramblas (ⓜ Drassanes).

Catamaran Orsom ☎ 934 410 537, ⓦ barcelona-orsom.com. Afternoon catamaran trips around the port (€12.95) and evening jazz cruises (€14.90), with departures Easter week & June–Sept daily, May & Oct daily except Tues & Wed. There's a ticket kiosk at the quayside opposite the Columbus statue, but you should call in advance to be certain of departures.

Las Golondrinas ☎ 934 423 106, ⓦ lasgolondrinas.com. Daily sightseeing boats depart from Pl. Portal de la Pau, behind the Columbus monument – trips are either around the port (35min; €6.80, under-10s €2.60, under-4s free), or port and coast including the Port Olímpic and Diagonal Mar (90min; €14, under-10s €5, under-4s free). Departures are at least hourly June–Sept, less frequently Oct–May but still daily.

Santa Eulàlia, moored over on the Moll de la Fusta, a three-masted ocean schooner that once made the run between Barcelona and Cuba.

Rambla de Mar and Maremàgnum

Moll d'Espanya • Daily 10am–10pm • Free • Ⓦ maremagnum.es • Ⓜ Drassanes

The old wharves and warehouses of the inner harbour have been replaced by an entertainment zone that is reached by the wooden **Rambla de Mar** swing bridge. This stretches across the harbour to **Maremàgnum**, two floors of gift shops and boutiques, plus outdoor seating and park areas that provide fantastic views back across the harbour to the city.

L'Aquàrium

Moll d'Espanya • July & Aug daily 9.30am–11pm; Sept–June daily 9.30am–9pm, until 9.30pm at weekends • €18, under-12s €13, under-4s free, online discounts available • ☏ 932 217 474, Ⓦ aquariumbcn.com • Ⓜ Drassanes/Barceloneta

L'Aquàrium drags in families and school parties to see 11,000 fish and sea creatures in 35 themed tanks representing underwater caves, tidal areas, tropical reefs, the planet's oceans and other maritime habitats. It's vastly overpriced, and despite the claims of excellence it offers few new experiences, save perhaps the eighty-metre-long walk-through underwater tunnel, which brings you face to face with rays and sharks.

Museu d'Història de Catalunya

Pl. de Pau Vila 3 • Tues–Sat 10am–7pm (Wed until 8pm), Sun & hols 10am–2.30pm • €4, first Sun of month free • ☏ 932 254 700, Ⓦ mhcat.net • Ⓜ Barceloneta

The only surviving warehouse on the Port Vell harbourside is known as the Palau de Mar, home to the **Museu d'Història de Catalunya**, which entertainingly traces the history of Catalunya from the Stone Age to the present day. On the fourth floor, the café-bar boasts a glorious view from its huge terrace.

El Raval

The old-town area west of the Ramblas is known as **El Raval** (from the Arabic word for "suburb"). In medieval times, it was the site of hospitals, churches and monasteries, but by the twentieth century it had acquired a reputation as the city's main red-light district, known to all as the Barri Xinès – China Town. Even today in the backstreets around c/de Sant Pau and c/Nou de la Rambla are found pockets of sleaze, while a handful of old bars trade on their former reputations as bohemian hangouts. Over the last two decades, however, El Raval has changed markedly, particularly in the "upper Raval" around Barcelona's contemporary art museum, MACBA. Cutting-edge galleries, designer restaurants and fashionable bars are all part of the scene these days, although you'd hesitate to call El Raval gentrified, as it clearly still has its rough edges.

Museu d'Art Contemporani de Barcelona (MACBA)

Pl. dels Àngels 1 • Mon & Wed–Fri 11am–7.30pm (mid-June to mid-Sept till 8pm), Sat 10am–8pm, Sun & hols 10am–3pm; closed Tues all year; tours of the permanent collection in English currently Mon & Wed–Sat at 4pm • €6 or €7.50, depending on exhibition; tour included in admission fee • ☏ 934 120 810, Ⓦ macba.cat • Ⓜ Catalunya

Anchoring the upper Raval is the huge, luminous **Museu d'Art Contemporani de Barcelona**, known as **MACBA**. Once inside, a series of swooping ramps from the ground floor to the fourth floor afford continuous views of the square below – usually full of careering skateboarders. The collection represents the main movements in contemporary art since 1945, mainly in Catalunya and Spain but with a good smattering of foreign artists as well. The pieces are shown in rotating exhibitions, so you may catch works by Joan Miró, Antoni Tàpies, Eduardo Chillida, Alexander Calder, Robert Rauschenberg or Paul Klee. Joan Brossa, leading light of the Catalan avant-garde "Dau al Set" group, has work here, too, as do contemporary Catalan conceptual and abstract artists.

10 Centre de Cultura Contemporània de Barcelona (CCCB)

C/de Montalegre 5 • Tues–Sun 11am–8pm, Thurs until 10pm • €5 or €7 depending on exhibition, reduced entry €3/5 on Wed & on Thurs after 8pm, free on Sun after 3pm; *C3* bar daily 9am–9pm • ☎ 933 064 100, ⓦ cccb.org • Ⓜ Catalunya

Adjoining MACBA is the **Centre de Cultura Contemporània de Barcelona**, or **CCCB**, which hosts temporary art and city-related exhibitions as well as supporting a cinema and a varied concert and festival programme. At the back of the building, the *C3* café-bar has a sunny terrassa on the modern square joining the CCCB to MACBA.

Hospital de la Santa Creu

Entrances on c/del Carme and c/de l'Hospital • Garden daily 10am–dusk • Free • La Capella, c/de l'Hospital 56, exhibition information on ⓦ bcn.cat/lacapella • Ⓜ Liceu

The **Hospital de la Santa Creu** occupies a large site between c/del Carme and c/de l'Hospital. The attractive complex of Gothic buildings was founded as the city's main hospital in 1402, a role that it retained until 1930. The fifteenth-century hospital wards were subsequently converted for cultural and educational use, and now hold the Royal Academy of Medicine, an art and design school, and two libraries, including the Catalan national library, the Biblioteca de Catalunya. Visitors can wander freely through the charming medieval cloistered **garden** (access from either street), while the hospital's former chapel, **La Capella** (entered separately from c/de l'Hospital) is an exhibition space for new contemporary artists. There's also the rather nice *El Jardí* **café** in the garden at the c/de l'Hospital side.

Rambla de Raval and around

Ⓜ Liceu

The most obvious manifestation of the changing character of El Raval is the **Rambla de Raval**, a palm-lined boulevard that strikes through the centre of the district between c/de l'Hospital and c/de Sant Pau. The *rambla* has a distinct character that's all its own – signature building, halfway down, is the glow-in-the-dark designer *Barceló Raval* **hotel**, while on either side are kebab joints and grocery stores, and an increasing number of fashionable cafés and bars. A Saturday **street market** (selling anything from samosas to hammocks) adds a bit more character, while the two

---

HIGH SOCIETY AT THE HOTEL ESPAÑA

There's a hidden gem tucked around the back of the Liceu opera house, on the otherwise fairly shabby c/de Sant Pau, where some of the most influential names in Catalan architecture and design came together at the beginning of the twentieth century to transform the **Hotel España** (c/de Sant Pau 9–11; ⓦ www.hotelespanya.com; Ⓜ Liceu) into one of the city's most lavish addresses. With a wonderfully tiled dining room designed by Lluís Domènech i Montaner, a bar with an amazing marble fireplace by Eusebi Arnau, and a bathing area with glass roof (now the breakfast room) whose marine murals were executed by Ramon Casas, the hotel was the fashionable sensation of its day. A century later it's back in vogue, following a remarkable contemporary restoration, and lunch or dinner in the original *modernista* dining room (known as the Fonda España) is a real in-the-know treat.

extremes of the *rambla* offer a snapshot of the changing neighbourhood. At the bottom end, off **c/de Sant Pau**, the *barri*'s remaining prostitutes accost passers-by as they head back towards the Liceu and the Ramblas. The top end, meanwhile, leads you straight into **c/de la Riera Baixa**, a narrow street that's at the centre of the city's secondhand and vintage clothing scene.

Palau Güell

C/Nou de la Rambla 3–5 • Tues–Sun & hols 10am–8pm (Nov–March until 5.30pm) • €10 • ☎ 933 173 974, ⓦ palauguell.cat • Ⓜ Liceu

El Raval's outstanding building is the **Palau Güell**, an extraordinary townhouse designed (1886–90) by the young Antoni Gaudí for wealthy ship-owner and industrialist Eusebi Güell i Bacigalupi. At a time when architects sought to conceal the iron supports within buildings, Gaudí turned them to his advantage, displaying them as decorative features in the grand rooms on the **main floor**, which are lined with dark marble hewn from the Güell family quarries. Meanwhile the famous **roof terrace** culminates in a fantastical series of chimneys decorated with swirling patterns made from fragments of glazed tile, glass and earthenware.

A painstaking restoration has returned the building to its original state and it's one of Barcelona's most popular attractions – numbers are limited and your ticket will be for a specific time-slot for a one-hour visit.

Sant Pere

The Barri Gòtic is bordered on its eastern side by Via Laietana, which was cut through the old town at the beginning of the twentieth century. Across it to the east stretches the quiet neighbourhood of **Sant Pere**, home to two remarkable buildings, the Palau de la Música Catalana concert hall and the restored neighbourhood market, Mercat Santa Caterina.

Palau de la Música Catalana

C/Sant Pere Més Alt • Guided tours (in English on the hour) daily 10am–3.30pm, plus Easter week & Aug 10am–6pm • €12; tour tickets available by phone, online, or at the box office, up to a week in advance • ☎ 902 475 485, ⓦ palaumusica.org • Ⓜ Urquinaona

Lluís Domènech i Montaner's stupendous **Palau de la Música Catalana** barely seems to have enough space to breathe in the narrow c/Sant Pere Més Alt. Built in 1908, its bare brick structure is lined with tiles and mosaics, the highly elaborate facade resting on three great columns, like an elephant's legs. The stunning interior, meanwhile, incorporates a bulbous stained-glass skylight capping the second-storey auditorium – which contemporary critics claimed to be an engineering impossibility. Successive extensions and interior remodelling have opened up the original site – to the side, an enveloping glass facade provides the main public access to the box office, terrace restaurant and foyer bar. This is where you come to buy tickets for the fifty-minute-long **guided tours** of the original interior – as visitor numbers are limited you'll almost certainly have to book a day or two in advance.

Mercat Santa Caterina

Avgda. Francesc Cambò 16 • Mon 7.30am–2pm, Tues, Wed & Sat 7.30am–3.30pm, Thurs & Fri 7.30am–8.30pm, July & Aug open mornings only • ☎ 933 195 740, ⓦ mercatsantacaterina.net • Ⓜ Jaume I

At the very heart of Sant Pere is the **Mercat Santa Caterina** whose splendid restoration has retained its nineteenth-century balustraded walls and added a dramatic multi-coloured wave roof. During the renovation work, the foundations of a major medieval convent were discovered on the site – parts of the walls are visible behind glass at the

10

rear of the market. Santa Caterina is one of the best places in the city to come and shop for food, and its market restaurant and bar is definitely worth a visit in any case.

La Ribera

South of Sant Pere, across c/de la Princesa, **La Ribera** sports Barcelona's biggest single tourist attraction, the Museu Picasso. The sheer number of visitors in this neighbourhood rivals the busiest streets of the Barri Gòtic, and this has had a knock-on effect in terms of the bars, shops and restaurants found here. La Ribera is at its most hip, and most enjoyable, in the area around the Passeig del Born, the elongated square leading from Santa María church to the old Born market. This area – widely known as the Born – is one of the city's premier nightlife centres.

Museu Picasso

C/de Montcada 15–23 • Tues–Sun & hols 10am–8pm; guided tours in English (Tues at 4.30pm & Thurs at 5.30pm), advance bookings essential, by phone or by email through the website • €10, exhibitions €6, under-16s free, plus free Sun after 3pm & first Sun of month • ☏ 932 563 000, ⓦ museupicasso.bcn.cat • Ⓜ Jaume I

The celebrated **Museu Picasso** is housed in a series of medieval palaces converted specifically for the museum. It's one of the most important collections of Picasso's work in the world, but even so, some visitors are disappointed: the museum contains none of his best-known works, and few in the Cubist style. But what is here provides a unique opportunity to trace Picasso's development from his early paintings as a young boy to the major works of later years.

The highlights

Particularly fascinating are the **early drawings**, in which Picasso – still signing with his full name, Pablo Ruíz Picasso – attempted to copy the nature paintings in which his father specialized. Paintings from his art-school days in Barcelona (1895–97) show tantalizing glimpses of the city that the young Picasso was beginning to know well – the Gothic old town, the cloisters of Sant Pau del Camp, Barceloneta beach – and even at the ages of 15 and 16 he was producing serious work. Later, there are paintings from the famous **Blue Period** (1901–04), the Pink Period (1904–06) and from his Cubist (1907–20) and Neoclassical (1920–25) stages. The large gaps in the main collection (for example, nothing from 1905 until the celebrated *Harlequin* of 1917) only underline Picasso's extraordinary changes of style and mood. This is best illustrated by the large jump to 1957, a year represented by his 44 interpretations of Velázquez's masterpiece **Las Meninas**, in which Picasso brilliantly deconstructed the individual portraits and compositions that make up Velázquez's work.

PICASSO IN BARCELONA

Although born in Málaga, **Pablo Picasso** (1881–1973) spent much of his youth – from the age of 14 to 23 – in Barcelona, and there are echoes of the great artist at various sites throughout the old town. Not too far from the museum, you can still see many of the buildings in which Picasso lived and worked, notably the Escola de Belles Arts de Llotja (c/Consolat del Mar, near Estació de França), where his father taught drawing and where Picasso himself absorbed an academic training. The apartments where the family lived when they first arrived in Barcelona – Pg. d'Isabel II 4 and c/Cristina 3, both opposite the Escola – can also be seen, though only from the outside. Less tangible is to take a walk down c/d'Avinyó, which cuts south from c/de Ferran to c/Ample. Large houses along here were converted into brothels at the turn of the twentieth century, and Picasso used to haunt the street, sketching what he saw – women at one of the brothels inspired his seminal Cubist work, *Les Demoiselles d'Avignon*.

Disseny Hub Barcelona (DHUB)

C/de Montcada 12 • Tues–Fri 11am–7pm, Sat, Sun & hols 11am–8pm • Some exhibitions free, otherwise €5, free Sun after 3pm & first Sun of the month • ☎ 932 562 300, ⓦ dhub-bcn.cat • Ⓜ Jaume I

The city's unparalleled design (*disseny*) and applied art collections are currently on display at the Palau Reial at Pedralbes (see p.679) pending the construction of a new Design Centre. In the meantime, the umbrella organization, known as **Disseny Hub Barcelona** (**DHUB**), hosts thought-provoking temporary exhibitions in the fourteenth-century palace that used to be the old Textile Museum building and covering anything from aspects of *modernista* design to 3D printing techniques. The ticket is also valid for the Palau Reial collections, and there's a handy courtyard café here too.

10

Museu Barbier-Mueller

C/de Montcada 14 • Tues–Fri 11am–7pm, Sat & Sun 11am–7pm, hols 11am–3pm • €3.50, first Sun of month free • ☎ 933 104 516, ⓦ barbier-mueller.ch • Ⓜ Jaume I

The **Museu Barbier-Mueller** is a terrific collection of pre-Columbian art housed in the renovated sixteenth-century Palau Nadal. Temporary exhibitions highlight wide-ranging themes, and draw on a peerless collection of sculpture, pottery, jewellery, textiles and everyday items, with some pieces dating back as far as the third century BC.

Església de Santa María del Mar

Pl. de Santa María • Mon–Sat 9am–1.30pm & 4.30–8pm, Sun 9.30am–1.45pm & 4.30–8.45pm; choral Mass Sun at 1pm • Free • Ⓜ Jaume I

La Ribera's flagship church of **Santa María del Mar** is the city's most exquisite example of pure Catalan-Gothic architecture. Conceived as thanks for the Catalan conquest of Sardinia in 1324, work on the church began in 1329 and was finished in just over half a century, which is pretty rapid for medieval church construction (and also explains its consistency of style). Its wide nave, narrow aisles, massive buttresses and octagonal, flat-topped towers are all typically Catalan-Gothic features, while its later Baroque trappings were destroyed during the Civil War, which is probably all to the good. Subsequent restoration work has concentrated on showing off the simple bare spaces of the interior and the stained glass, especially, is beautiful.

Passeig del Born

Ⓜ Jaume I/Barceloneta

Fronting Santa María church is the fashionable **Passeig del Born**, an avenue lined with a parade of plane trees shading a host of classy bars, delis and shops. Shoppers scour the narrow, vaulted medieval alleys on either side for boutiques and craft workshops, while at night the Born becomes one of Barcelona's biggest bar zones. At the end of the avenue stands the hulking skeleton of the **Antic Mercat del Born**, which served as the city's main wholesale fruit and veg market until 1971. The former market stands directly on top of the remains of part of the eighteenth-century city, and the massive cast-iron frame now protects the surviving metre-high walls of period shops, factories, houses and taverns. Work is still ongoing, but the eventual plan is to retain the archeological remains within a neighbourhood cultural centre.

Parc de la Ciutadella

Park entrances on Pg. de Picasso (Ⓜ Barceloneta, or a short walk from La Ribera) and Pg. de Pujades (Ⓜ Arc de Triomf); use Ⓜ Ciutadella-Vila Olímpica for direct access to the zoo • Daily 8am–dusk • Park entrance free

East of La Ribera, across Passeig de Picasso, the **Parc de la Ciutadella** is the largest green space in the city centre. It's also the meeting place of the Catalan parliament (no public access), occupying part of a fortress-like structure right at the centre of the park, the surviving portion of the star-shaped Bourbon citadel from which the park takes its name. In 1888, the park was chosen as the site of the Universal Exhibition, and the city's *modernista* architects left their mark here in a series of eye-catching buildings and monuments, not least the giant brick Arc de Triomf that dominates the avenue at the top of the park.

10 Cascada

Parc de la Ciutadella • Ⓜ Arc de Triomf

The first of the major projects undertaken inside the park was the **Cascada**, the monumental fountain in the northeast corner. Assistant to the principal park architect was the young Antoni Gaudí, then a student, and the Baroque extravagance of the fountain is suggestive of the flamboyant decoration that was later to become Gaudí's trademark. Incidentally, Gaudí is also thought to have had a hand in the design of the Ciutadella's iron park gates.

Museu de Ciències Naturals

Pg. de Picasso • Plant houses open daily 8am–dusk • Free • Ⓦ museuciencies.bcn.cat • Ⓜ Arc de Triomf

The city's Natural Science Museum has its public showcase, the Museu Blau, over at the Diagonal Mar Fòrum site (see p.664), but its genesis lies in two buildings in Parc de la Ciutadella that are currently undergoing major renovation (completion expected in 2012). The Neoclassical **Museu Martorell** formerly housed the city's geological collections, though the new permanent exhibition here will concentrate on the development of the natural sciences in Barcelona. The other building, a whimsical red-brick confection that was long the zoology museum, is universally known as the **Castell dels Tres Dragons** (Three Dragons Castle). It's going to become the research, study and conservation centre for the Natural Science Museum's geology and zoology collections. Meanwhile, the two real unsung glories of Ciutadella are its plant houses, the **Umbracle** (Palm House) and **Hivernacle** (Conservatory), arranged either side of the Museu Martorell.

Parc Zoològic

Main entrance on c/de Wellington • Daily: March–May & Oct 10am–6pm; June–Sept 10am–7pm; Nov–Feb 10am–5pm • €16.50, under-12s €9.90, under-3s free • ☎ 932 256 780, Ⓦ zoobarcelona.cat • Signposted from Ⓜ Ciutadella-Vila Olímpica, or tram #T4 stops outside

Ciutadella's most popular attraction by far is the city's zoo, the **Parc Zoològic**, taking up most of the southeast of the park. It boasts 7500 animals from over 400 different species – simply too many for a zoo that is still essentially nineteenth century in character, confined to the formal grounds of a public park. However, the zoo's days in its current form are numbered, since there's been a belated recognition that it needs to modernize. Over the next few years its animal areas and habitats will be completely remodelled as the zoo attempts to expand its education, conservation and research facilities, and there are also advanced plans to move the marine animals to a new coastal zoo and wetlands area at the Diagonal Mar seashore.

Barceloneta

There's no finer place for lunch on a sunny day than **Barceloneta**, an eighteenth-century neighbourhood of tightly packed streets with the harbour on one side and a **beach** on the other. It was laid out in 1755 – a classic eighteenth-century grid of streets where previously there had been mudflats – and the long, narrow streets are still very much as they were planned, broken at intervals by small squares and lined with

THE CROSS-HARBOUR CABLE CAR

The most thrilling ride in the city centre is **across the inner harbour on the cable car**, the Trasbordador Aeri, which sweeps from the Torre Sant Sebastià, at the foot of Barceloneta, to the Torre Miramar in Montjuïc, with a stop in the middle at Torre de Jaume I (though this middle stop is currently closed for long-term repairs). Departures are every fifteen minutes (daily 10.30am–6pm, June–Sept until 8pm), though in summer and at weekends you may have to wait for a while at the top of the towers for a ride, as the cars only carry about twenty people at a time. Tickets cost €10 one way or €15 return.

10

multi-windowed houses. The local market, **Mercat de la Barceloneta**, was stylishly refurbished in 2007, while at Barceloneta's famous seafood restaurants – most characteristically lined along the harbourside **Passeig Joan de Borbó** – for most of the year you can sit outside and enjoy your meal.

La Fàbrica del Sol

C/de Ginebra 52 • Tues–Fri 10am–2pm & 4–8pm, Sat 10am–2pm & 4–7pm (Aug Tues–Fri 10am–2pm only) • Free • ☎ 932 564 430, ⓦ bcn.cat/mediambient • ⓜ Barceloneta

Inside the yellow-painted, red-brick building on the edge of the Parc de la Barceloneta – once the city's gas works – the local council's **La Fàbrica del Sol** is a sustainable eco-centre that takes a close look at green living in all its guises, from recycling to transport. Although it's all in Catalan, the displays, gadgets and exhibits are all fairly self-explanatory – you've got to love the elevator that weighs its passengers so as to use only the exact amount of energy required to lift them up to the roof terrace to see the building's garden and solar thermal system.

Platja de Sant Sebastià and Passeig Marítim

ⓜ Barceloneta

Barceloneta's beach, **Platja de Sant Sebastià**, is the first in the series of sandy **city beaches** that stretches northeast from here along the coast. It curves out to the landmark, sail-shaped *W Barcelona* hotel (designed by Catalan architect Ricardo Bofill). Meanwhile, at the Barceloneta end there are beach bars, outdoor cafés and public sculptures, while a double row of palms backs the **Passeig Marítim** esplanade that runs above the sands as far as the Port Olímpic (a 15min walk).

Port Olímpic

ⓜ Ciutadella-Vila Olímpica

Approaching the **Port Olímpic** along the Passeig Marítim, the shimmering golden mirage above the promenade slowly reveals itself to be a **huge copper fish** (courtesy of Frank O. Gehry, architect of the Bilbao Guggenheim). It's the emblem of the huge seafront development constructed for the 1992 Olympics, and is backed by the city's two tallest buildings – the **Torre Mapfre** and the steel-framed **Hotel Arts Barcelona** – while the surrounding area has filled up with restaurants, cafés and bars. The whole zone turns into a full-on resort in summer, backed by a series of class-conscious clubs along Passeig Marítim that appeal to the local rich kids and A-list celebs.

Beyond the Port Olímpic, the **city beaches** are split into separate named sections (Nova Icària, Bogatell, Mar Bella, Nova Mar Bella and Llevant), each with showers, playgrounds and open-air café-bars. It's a pretty extraordinary leisure facility to find so close to a city centre – the sands are regularly swept and replenished, while joggers, cyclists and bladers have one of the Med's best views for company.

10

Diagonal Mar

ⓂEl Maresme Fòrum, or tram #T4 to Fòrum via Glòries and Avgda. Diagonal

The waterfront convention-and-business district of **Diagonal Mar** was developed in the wake of the Universal Forum of Cultures Expo, held here in 2004. Everything is on a grand scale, starting with Jacques Herzog's dazzling blue biscuit-tin of a building hovering – seemingly unsupported – above the ground. This houses the main exhibitions of the Natural Science Museum (the **Museu Blau**), while the vast, landscaped area beyond is one of the city's showpiece urban leisure projects, the **Parc del Fòrum**.

Museu Blau

Pl. Leonardo da Vinci 4–5, Parc del Fòrum · June–Sept Tues–Sun & hols 10am–9pm; Oct–May Tues–Fri 10am–7pm, Sat, Sun & hols 10am–8pm · €7, includes entrance to Jardí Botànic at Montjuïc, under-16s free, plus free first Sun of the month & every Sun after 3pm · ☎932 652 200, Ⓦmuseuciencies.bcn.cat · ⓂEl Maresme Fòrum, or tram #T4 to Fòrum

To unravel the mysteries of life, the universe and everything, you need travel no further than the Natural Science Museum's bold re-boot of its heritage collections, which were previously displayed in Parc de la Ciutadella. The million-strong collection of rocks, fossils, plants and animals have a state-of-the-art home in the visually stunning **Museu Blau** (Blue Museum), whose permanent exhibition – Planeta Vida (Planet Life) – plots a journey through the history of life on earth. It's heavily focused on evolutionary, whole-earth, Gaia principles, with plenty of interactive bells and whistles to guide you through topics as diverse as sex and reproduction and conservation of the environment.

Parc del Fòrum

ⓂEl Maresme Fòrum, or tram #T4 to Fòrum via Glòries and Avgda. Diagonal

The boast about Diagonal Mar's main open space, the **Parc del Fòrum**, is that it's the second largest space in the world (150,000 square metres) after Beijing's Tiananmen Square. This immense, undulating expanse spreads towards the sea, culminating in a giant solar-panelled canopy that overlooks the marina, beach and park areas. The space can still seem a bit soulless at times – hot as Hades in summer, buffeted by biting winter winds – but it's worth the metro ride if you're interested in heroic-scale public projects. In summer, temporary bars, dancefloors, open-air cinema and chill-out zones are established, while the city authorities have shifted some of the bigger annual music festivals and events down here to inject a bit of life outside convention time.

Montjuïc

You'll need to reserve at least a day to see **Montjuïc**, the steep hill and park rising over the city to the southwest. There's been a castle on the heights since the mid-seventeenth century, but since it was chosen as the site of the **International Exhibition** of 1929 Montjuïc has been firmly positioned as a cultural leisure park, anchored around the heavyweight art collections in the **Museu Nacional d'Art de Catalunya (MNAC)**. This unsurpassed national collection of Catalan art is supplemented by works in two other superb galleries, namely international contemporary art in the CaixaForum and that of the famous Catalan artist Joan Miró in the Fundació Joan Miró. In addition, there are several other minor museums, quite apart from the buildings and stadiums associated with the 1992 Olympics, which was centred on the heights of Montjuïc.

10

GETTING AROUND MONTJUÏC

Metro The quickest way to Montjuïc is by metro (Ⓜ Espanya; follow exit signs for "Fira/Exposició"), which deposits you at Plaça d'Espanya, for easy walking access to CaixaForum, Poble Espanyol and MNAC – the Olympic area can then be reached by escalators behind MNAC. But there are several other ways of getting there and getting around.

Funicular The Funicular de Montjuïc (every 10min; Mon–Fri 7.30am–8pm, Sat, Sun & hols 9am–8pm, April–Oct daily until 10pm; €1.45, transport tickets and passes valid; ⓦ tmb .cat) departs from Ⓜ Paral.lel and takes a couple of minutes to ascend the hill. The upper station on Avgda. de Miramar is only a few minutes' walk from the Fundació Joan Miró, or you can switch to the Montjuïc cable car or bus services.

Cross-harbour cable car The Transbordador Aeri from Barceloneta (departures every 15min, daily 10.30am–6pm,

June–Sept until 8pm; €10 one way/€15 return; ☎ 932 414 820) drops you by the Jardins de Miramar, from where it's a ten-minute walk to the Montjuïc cable car and funicular stations, and another five to the Fundació Joan Miró.

Montjuïc cable car The Telefèric de Montjuïc (daily: June–Sept 10am–9pm; April, May & Oct 10am–7pm; Nov–March 10am–6pm; €6.50 one way/€9.30 return, under-12s €5/6.70, under-4s free; ⓦ tmb.net), from Avgda. de Miramar whisks you up to the castle and back.

Bus services City bus #193 (transport tickets and passes valid) stops at the main Montjuïc attractions, departing from a stop on Avgda. de la Reina María Cristina, outside Ⓜ Espanya. The sightseeing, hop-on, hop-off Bus Turístic follows a similar route.

Font Màgica

Pl. de Carles Buïgas • May–Sept Thurs–Sun 9–11.30pm; Oct–April Fri & Sat only at 7pm, 7.30pm, 8pm & 8.30pm • Free • Ⓜ Espanya

Walk up from the landmark Plaça d'Espanya, past the square's 47-metre-high twin towers and the vast exhibition halls, to the **Font Màgica** at the foot of the Montjuïc steps. On selected evenings, the "Magic Fountain" forms the centrepiece of an admittedly impressive, if slightly kitsch, sound-and-light show, with sprays and sheets of brightly coloured water dancing to the strains of Holst and Abba.

CaixaForum

Avgda. de Francesc Ferrer i Guàrdia 6–8 • Daily 10am–8pm (Sat until 10pm) • Free • ☎ 934 768 600, ⓦ fundacio.lacaixa.es • Ⓜ Espanya

CaixaForum is a terrific arts and cultural centre set within the old Casamarona textile factory, built in 1911. The undulating roof offers unique views, while the high Casamarona tower, etched in blue and yellow tiling, is as readily recognizable as the huge Miró starfish logos emblazoned across the building. The centre houses the Fundació La Caixa's celebrated contemporary art collection, focusing on the period from the 1980s to the present, with hundreds of artists represented, from Antoni Abad to Rachel Whiteread. Works are shown in partial rotation, along with an excellent free programme of changing **exhibitions** across all aspects of the arts. The café occupies an airy converted space within the old factory walls.

Poble Espanyol

Avgda. de Francesc Ferrer i Guàrdia 13 • Mon 9am–8pm, Tues–Thurs 9am–2am, Fri 9am–4am, Sat 9am–5am, Sun 9am–midnight • €9, under-4s free, family ticket €20, night ticket €5.50, combined ticket with MNAC €12 • ☎ 935 086 300, ⓦ poble-espanyol.com • Ⓜ Espanya and 800m walk, or bus #193 or #50 from Avgda. de la Reina María Cristina

The **Poble Espanyol**, or "Spanish Village", was designed for the International Exhibition, and its streets and squares consist of famous or characteristic buildings from all over the country. "Get to know Spain in one hour" is what's promised – and it's nowhere near as cheesy as you might think. As a crash-course introduction to Spanish architecture it's not at all bad: everything is well labelled and at least reasonably accurate. The echoing main square is lined with cafés, while the streets, alleys and buildings off here contain around forty workshops where you can see engraving, weaving, pottery and other crafts. Get there as it opens if you want to enjoy the village in relatively crowd-free circumstances – once the tour groups arrive, it becomes a bit of a scrum.

Museu Nacional d'Art de Catalunya (MNAC)

Palau Nacional • Tues–Sat 10am–7pm, Sun & hols 10am–2.30pm • €8.50, ticket valid 48hr, under-16s & first Sun of the month free; special exhibitions, varied charges apply • ☎ 936 220 376, ⓦ mnac.cat • Ⓜ Espanya, or bus #193 from Avgda. de la Reina María Cristina

The towering Palau Nacional, centrepiece of Barcelona's 1929 International Exhibition, is home to one of Spain's great museums, the **Museu Nacional d'Art de Catalunya (MNAC)**, showcasing a thousand years of Catalan art in stupendous surroundings. Its scope is such that it can be difficult to know where to start, but if time is limited it's recommended you concentrate on the medieval collection, which you'll be able to see in an afternoon. This is split into two main sections, one dedicated to **Romanesque** art and the other to **Gothic** – periods in which Catalunya's artists were pre-eminent in Spain. The collection of Romanesque frescoes in particular is the museum's pride and joy, while MNAC also has impressive holdings of European Renaissance and Baroque art, as well as an unsurpassed collection of "modern" (ie nineteenth- and twentieth-century) Catalan art up until the 1940s – everything from the 1950s and later is covered by MACBA. In addition, temporary blockbuster exhibitions (separate admission charge) change every two to four months.

Romanesque collection

The **Romanesque collection** is the best of its kind in the world. From the eleventh century, the Catalan villagers of the high Pyrenees built sturdy stone churches, which were then lavishly painted in vibrantly coloured frescoes. To save them from degradation, the frescoes were moved to the museum and now are imaginatively presented in reconstructions of their original church settings. Still luminescent after eight hundred years, the frescoes have a vibrant, raw quality, best exemplified by those taken from churches in the Boí valley in the Catalan Pyrenees – such as the work of the anonymous "Master of Taüll" in the church of Sant Climent; look out for details such as the leper, to the left of the Sant Climent altar, patiently suffering a dog to lick his sores.

Gothic collection

The evolution from the Romanesque to the Gothic period was marked by a move from murals to painting on wood, and by the depiction of more naturalistic figures in scenes of the lives of saints and royalty. By the time of fifteenth-century Catalan artists like **Jaume Huguet** and **Lluís Dalmau**, works showed the strong influence of contemporary Flemish painting, in the use of denser colours, the depiction of crowd scenes and a concern for perspective. The last Catalan Gothic-era artist of note is the so-called **Master of La Seu d'Urgell**, responsible for a fine series of six paintings (Christ, the Virgin Mary, Saints Peter, Paul and Sebastian, and Mary Magdalene) that once formed the covers of an organ.

Renaissance and Baroque collections

Major European artists displayed include Rubens, Goya, El Greco, Zurbarán and Velázquez, though the museum is of course keen to play up Catalan works of the period, which largely absorbed the prevailing European influences – thus Barcelona artist **Antoni Viladomat** (1678–1755), whose twenty paintings of St Francis, executed for a monastery, are shown here in their entirety. However, more familiar to most will be the masterpieces of the Spanish Golden Age, notably Velázquez's *Saint Paul*.

Modern art collection

MNAC ends on a high note with its **modern Catalan art** collection, which is particularly good on *modernista* and *noucentista* painting and sculpture, the two dominant schools of the nineteenth and early twentieth centuries. Rooms highlight individual artists and genres, shedding light on the development of art in an exciting period of Catalunya's history, while there are fascinating diversions into *modernista* interior design (with some pieces by Gaudí), avant-garde sculpture and historical photography.

Fundació Joan Miró

Parc de Montjuïc • Tues–Sat 10am–7pm, July–Sept until 8pm, Thurs until 9.30pm, Sun & hols 10am–2.30pm • General admission €9, exhibitions €4, Espai 13 €4 • ☎ 934 439 470, ⓦ fundaciomiro-bcn.org • ⓜ Paral.lel, then Funicular de Montjuïc and 5min walk, or bus #193 or #50 from Avgda. de la Reina María Cristina

Montjuïc's highlight for many is the **Fundació Joan Miró**, Barcelona's most adventurous art museum, opened in 1975 and set among gardens overlooking the city. Joan Miró (1893–1983) was one of the greatest of Catalan artists, establishing an international

---

TEATRE GREC AND THE BARCELONA FESTIVAL

Montjuïc takes centre-stage each year during Barcelona's annual summer cultural festival (ⓦ barcelonafestival.com), known locally as the Grec, when arias soar from the open-air stage of the **Teatre Grec**, a Greek theatre cut into a former quarry on the Poble Sec side of the hill. Starting in late June (and running throughout July and August), the festival incorporates drama, music and dance, with the opening sessions and some of the most atmospheric events staged in the theatre, from Shakespearean productions to shows by avant-garde performance artists. These can be magical nights – a true Barcelona experience – though you'll need to be quick off the mark for tickets (which usually go on sale in May).

10

reputation while never severing his links with his homeland. He showed a childlike delight in colours and shapes and developed a free, highly decorative style – the paintings and drawings, in particular, are instantly recognizable, among the chief links between Surrealism and abstract art. Miró had his first exhibition in 1918, and after that spent his summers in Catalunya (and the rest of the time in France) before moving to Mallorca in 1956, where he died.

Inside the museum

Miró's friend, the architect Josep Lluís Sert, designed the beautiful building that now houses the museum, a permanent collection of paintings, graphics, tapestries and sculptures donated by Miró himself and covering the period from 1914 to 1978. For a rapid appraisal of Miró's entire *oeuvre*, look in on the museum's **Sala K**, whose 23 works are on long-term loan from a Japanese collector. Here, in a kind of potted retrospective, you can trace Miró's development as an artist, from his early Impressionist landscapes (1914) to the minimal renderings of the 1970s. Other exhibits include his enormous bright tapestries (he donated nine to the museum), pencil drawings and sculpture outside in the gardens. Young experimental artists have their own space in the **Espai 13** gallery. There's also a bookshop, and a café-restaurant (lunch 1.30–3pm, otherwise drinks, pastries and sandwiches) with outdoor tables on a sunny patio – you don't have to pay to get into the museum to use this.

Castell de Montjuïc

Carretera de Montjuïc • Grounds open Tues–Sun 9am–7pm (April–Sept until 9pm) • Free • ☎ 932 564 445, ⓦ bcn.cat/castelldemontjuic • Direct access by Telefèric de Montjuïc, or bus #193 from Avgda. de la Reina María Cristina

Marking the top of Montjuïc and the end of the line is Barcelona's **castle** – and the best way up is by the **Telefèric de Montjuïc** (cable car), which tacks up the hillside, offering magnificent views on the way, before depositing you within the forbidding eighteenth-century walls. The fortress served as a military base and prison for decades, and was where the last president of the pre war Generalitat, **Lluís Companys i Jover**, was executed on Franco's orders on October 15, 1940.

In 2008 the castle was symbolically handed over to the city, and restoration work is now transforming the site into a combined peace museum, memorial space and Montjuïc interpretation centre. Something of its design and its brutal past are touched on in an exhibition in the Santa Amàlia bastion, in the inner keep, which also explains the future use to which the castle will be put. The cable-car ride and dramatic location merit a visit in any case, while the ramparts and grounds are free to enter.

Below the castle walls, a panoramic pathway – the **Camí del Mar** – has been cut from the cliff edge, providing scintillating views. The path is just over 1km long and ends at the back of the castle battlements near the **Mirador del Migdia**.

Jardí Botànic de Barcelona

C/Dr Font i Quer 2 • Daily: June–Aug 10am–8pm; April, May & Sept 10am–7pm; Oct–March 10am–6pm • €3.50, or €7 combination ticket with Museu Blau, free Sun after 3pm & last Sun of month • ☎ 932 564 160, ⓦ museuciencies.bcn.cat • ⓜ Espanya and 20min walk via escalators, or bus #193 or #50 from Avgda. de la Reina María Cristina

Principal among Montjuïc's many gardens is the city's botanical garden, the **Jardí Botànic de Barcelona**, laid out on terraced slopes that offer fine views across the city. The Montjuïc buses run here directly, or the entrance is just a five-minute walk around the back of the Olympic stadium. It's a beautifully kept contemporary garden, where wide, easy-to-follow paths wind through landscaped zones representing the flora of the Mediterranean, Canary Islands, California, Chile, North and South Africa and Australia.

The Eixample

The vast nineteenth-century street grid north of Plaça de Catalunya is the city's main shopping and business district. It was designed as part of a revolutionary urban plan – the **Eixample** in Catalan (pronounced aye-sham-pla, the "Extension" or "Widening") – that divided districts into regular blocks, whose characteristic wide streets and shaved corners survive today. It's not a neighbourhood as such – and, in fact, is further split into two distinct sections, namely the Dreta de l'Eixample (ie, the right-hand side) and Esquerra de l'Eixample (left-hand side), which fall either side of the two central parallel avenues, Passeig de Gràcia and Rambla de Catalunya. It's on and around Passeig de Gràcia, above all, that the bulk of the city's show-stopping *modernista* (Catalan Art Nouveau) buildings are found, along with an array of classy galleries and some of the city's most fashionable hotels, shops and boutiques.

Museu del Modernisme Català

C/de Balmes 48 • Mon–Sat 10am–8pm, Sun & hols 10am–2pm • €10 • ☎ 932 722 896, ⓦ mmcat.cat • ⓜ Passeig de Gràcia

Barcelona's traditional "gallery district", around c/Consell de Cent, just off Rambla de Catalunya, is a fitting location for the stupendous *modernista* collection housed in the **Museu del Modernisme Català**. There are two exhibition floors in a restored building that was once a textile warehouse – the grand, vaulted basement contains paintings and sculpture while on the ground floor is *modernista* furniture, from screens to sofas. There are paintings and works by many famous names, whether oils by Ramon Casa i Carbó, or sinuous mirrors and tables by Antoni Gaudí (originally made for the casas Batlló and Calvet). But above all, this is a rare opportunity to examine extraordinary Art Nouveau fixtures, fittings and furniture – as a crash course in the varied facets of Catalan *modernisme*, beyond the iconic buildings themselves, it's invaluable.

Casa Amatller

Fundació Amatller, Pg. de Gràcia 41 • Check website for current guided tour details • €10, reservations essential, in person, by phone or email • ☎ 934 961 245, ✉ amatller@amatller.org, ⓦ amatller.org • ⓜ Passeig de Gràcia

First standout building on Passeig de Gràcia is Josep Puig i Cadafalch's striking **Casa Amatller** apartment block (1900), designed for Antoni Amatller, a Catalan chocolate

10

manufacturer, art collector, photographer and traveller. The house has kept much of its original Art Nouveau furniture and interior design, and is currently being restored as a *modernista* cultural centre, but **guided tours** continue to operate on various days, subject to the progress of the renovation works (the tours include a visit to Amatller's photographic studio and chocolate-tasting in the original kitchen).

Casa Batlló

Pg. de Gràcia 43 • Daily 9am–8pm, access occasionally restricted due to private events • €18.15, under-18s €14.55, under-6s free; advance-purchase tickets advised, in person or by phone • ☎ 932 160 306, Ⓦ casabatllo.es • Ⓜ Passeig de Gràcia

Perhaps the most extraordinary of all the private *modernista* mansions on Passeig de Gràcia stands right next door to Casa Amatller, namely the **Casa Batlló** – designed for the industrialist Josep Batlló – whose original construction was considered dull by contemporaries. Antoni Gaudí was hired to give it a facelift and created a naturalistic masterpiece: the stone facade hangs in folds, like skin, while on the rooftop sprout the celebrated mosaic chimneys and a little tower topped with a three-dimensional cross.

The sinuous house interior too resembles some great organism, complete with window frames, doorways and staircases that display not a straight line between them. Self-guided audio tours show you the main floor, the patio and rear facade, the ribbed attic and the rooftop.

Fundació Antoni Tàpies

C/Aragó 255 • Tues–Sun 10am–7pm • €7 • ☎ 934 870 315, ⓦ fundaciotapies.org • Ⓜ Passeig de Gràcia

The definitive collection of the work of Catalan abstract artist **Antoni Tàpies** is housed in *modernista* architect Lluís Domènech i Montaner's first important building, the **Casa Montaner i Simon** (1880), which was converted in 1990 to house the **Fundació Antoni Tàpies**. The artist was born in the city in 1923 and was a founding member (1948) of the influential avant-garde grouping known as Dau al Set ("Die at Seven"). He was interested in collage and engraving techniques from an early age, and later developed an abstract style that matured during the 1950s. His large works are deceptively simple, though underlying messages and themes are signalled by the

10

BUILDING A DESIGNER CITY

As Barcelona grew more prosperous throughout the nineteenth century, it was clear that the city had to expand beyond the Barri Gòtic. A contest was held to design the city's new quarters and the winning plan was that of utopian engineer and urban planner **Ildefons Cerdà i Sunyer**, who drew up a grid-shaped town marching off to the north, intersected by long, straight streets and cut by broad, angled avenues. Work started in 1859 and the Eixample immediately became the fashionable area in which to live, as the moneyed classes moved into luxurious apartments on the wide new avenues. As the money in the city moved north, so did a new class of architects who began to pepper the Eixample with ever more striking examples of their work, inspired by *modernisme*, the Catalan offshoot of Art Nouveau. Three **architects** in particular came to prominence in Barcelona and, in doing so, introduced a building style that has given the city a look like no other.

ANTONI GAUDÍ I CORNET

Born in Reus, near Tarragona, to a family of artisans, the work of **Antoni Gaudí i Cornet** (1852–1926) was never strictly *modernista* in style, but the imaginative impetus he provided was incalculable. Fantasy, spiritual symbolism and Catalan pride are evident in every building he designed, while his architectural influences were Moorish and Gothic, embellished with elements from the natural world. Gaudí rarely wrote a word about the theory of his art, preferring the buildings to demand reaction – no one stands mute in front of an Antoni Gaudí masterpiece.

LLUÍS DOMÈNECH I MONTANER

With Gaudí in a class of his own, it was **Lluís Domènech i Montaner** (1850–1923) who was perhaps the greatest pure *modernista* architect. Drawing on the rich Catalan Romanesque and Gothic traditions, his work combined traditional craft methods with modern technological experiments, seen to triumphant effect in his masterpiece, the Palau de la Música Catalana.

JOSEP PUIG I CADAFALCH

Like other *modernista* architects, the work of **Josep Puig i Cadafalch** (1867–1957) also contains a wildly inventive use of ceramic tiles, ironwork, stained glass and stone carving. His first commission, the Casa Martí, housed the famous *Els Quatre Gats* tavern for the city's avant-garde artists and hangers-on, while in various Eixample mansions Puig i Cadafalch brought to bear distinct Gothic and medieval influences.

OTHER MODERNISTA CRAFTSMEN

Modernisme was often a true collaborative effort between the architects and their artisans. Antoni Gaudí, for example, always worked with skilled craftsmen, including his longtime collaborator – and a master of mosaic decoration – **Josep María Jujol i Gilbert** (1879–1949). The other significant name is that of **Eusebi Arnau i Mascort** (1864–1933), who provided meticulous carvings for all the main *modernista* architects – much loved is his tour-de-force carved fireplace in the Raval's *Hotel Espanya*. Some projects brought together the cream of craft talent, so at Domènech i Montaner's Palau de la Música Catalana, for example, the glorious stained glass by Antoni Rigalt and elaborate facade sculpture by Miquel Blay form an integral part of the whole.

inclusion of everyday objects, unusual materials and symbols on the canvas. Tàpies' work is not immediately accessible (in the way of, say, Miró), and you're either going to love or hate the gallery: temporary exhibitions focus on selections of his work from every period, while special exhibitions highlight works and installations by other contemporary artists.

Museu Egipci de Barcelona

C/de València 284 • Mon–Sat 10am–8pm, Sun 10am–2pm • €11 • ☎ 934 880 188, ⓦ museuegipci.com • Ⓜ Passeig de Gràcia

Half a block east of Passeig de Gràcia, the **Museu Egipci de Barcelona** is an exceptional collection of artefacts from ancient Egypt, ranging from the earliest kingdoms to the era of Cleopatra. The emphasis is on the shape and character of Egyptian society, and a serendipitous wander is a real pleasure, turning up items such as a wood and leather bed of the First and Second Dynasties (2920–2649 BC), some examples of cat mummies of the Late Period (715–332 BC) or a rare figurine of a spoonbill (ibis) representing an Egyptian god (though archeologists aren't yet sure which).

Palau Montaner

10

C/de Mallorca 278 • Guided visits Sat at 10.30am in English, plus 11.30am & 12.30pm, and Sun at 10.30am, 11.30am & 12.30pm, in Spanish/Catalan • €6 • ☎ 933 177 652, ⓦ rutadelmodernisme.com • Ⓜ Passeig de Gràcia

The **Palau Montaner** has an unusual dual personality. After the original architect quit, *modernista* architect Lluís Domènech i Montaner took over halfway through construction, and the top half of the facade is clearly more elaborate than the lower part. Meanwhile, the period's most celebrated craftsmen were set to work on the interior, which sports rich mosaic floors, painted glass, carved woodwork and a monumental staircase. The weekend **guided tours** explain something of the house's history and show you the lavish public rooms, grand dining room and courtyard.

La Pedrera

Pg. de Gràcia 92, tour entrance on c/Provença • **Self-guided visits** daily 9am–6.30pm (March–Oct until 8pm), closed first week Jan • €11, or €15 with audio-guide, under-12s free • **Exhibitions** Daily 10am–8pm • Free • **Pedrera de Nit** Fri & Sat nights, June–Aug • €25 • Advance booking essential, at the ticket office or from TelEntrada ☎ 902 101 212, ⓦ telentrada.com • ☎ 902 400 973, ⓦ lapedreraeducacio.org • Ⓜ Diagonal

Gaudí's weird and wonderful apartment building is simply not to be missed – though you can expect queues whenever you visit. Constructed as the Casa Milà between 1905 and 1911, and popularly known as **La Pedrera**, or the Stone Quarry, it was declared a UNESCO World Heritage Site in 1984. Its rippling facade, which curves around the street corner in one smooth sweep, is said to have been inspired by the mountain of Montserrat, and the apartments themselves, whose balconies of tangled metal drip over the facade, resemble eroded cave dwellings.

The self-guided visit includes a trip up to the extraordinary **roof terrace** (closed if it's raining) to see at close quarters the enigmatic chimneys, as well as an informative exhibition about Gaudí's work installed under the 270 curved brick arches of the attic. El Pis ("The Apartment") on the building's fourth floor re-creates the design and style of a *modernista*-era bourgeois apartment in a series of rooms that flow seamlessly from one to another. Casa Milà itself is still split into private apartments, while the whole building is administered by the Fundació Caixa de Catalunya. Through the main entrance on Passeig de Gràcia there's access to the Fundació's **exhibition hall** which hosts temporary art shows of works by major international artists.

Perhaps the best experience of all is the summer evening concert season known as **La Pedrera de Nit**, when you can enjoy the rooftop and night-time cityscape with a complimentary glass of cava and music from jazz groups and chamber ensembles.

Sagrada Família

C/Mallorca 401 • April–Sept daily 9am–8pm; Oct–March daily 9am–6pm; 60min guided tours (no advance purchase) run daily, in English at 11am, noon (not weekdays Nov to May) & 1pm • €12.50 (under-10s free) or €16.50 including guided tour or audio-guide; combination ticket with Casa Museu Gaudí at Parc Güell €14.50 • ☎ 932 073 031, ⓦ sagradafamilia.cat • Ⓜ Sagrada Família

Nothing – really, nothing – prepares you for the impact of the **Temple Expiatori de la Sagrada Família** which occupies an entire city block between c/de Mallorca and c/de Provença, north of the Diagonal; the metro drops you right outside. In many ways

10

the overpowering church of the "Sacred Family" has become a kind of symbol for the city. It is the most fantastic of the modern architectural creations in which Barcelona excels – even the coldest hearts will find the Sagrada Família inspirational in form and spirit.

Some history
Although the church survived the Civil War, Gaudí's plans and models were destroyed in 1936 by the anarchists. Nonetheless, work restarted in the late 1950s amid great controversy, and has continued ever since – as have the arguments. On balance, it's probably safe enough to assume that Gaudí saw the struggle to finish the building as at least as important as the method and style. However, the current work has attracted criticism for infringing Gaudí's original spirit, while tunnelling under the temple for the high-speed AVE train line has kicked up a huge stink among critics who claim that the church will be put at risk (not so, say the tunnel engineers). All in all, though the project might be drawing inexorably towards completion (within the next twenty years, it's said), there's still plenty more time for argument.

Visiting the building
Towers and museum open same hours as the church • Towers €2.50, timed elevator tickets available from main ticket office; museum free

The size alone is startling – Gaudí's original plan was to build a church to seat over 10,000 people, while the iconic **towers** rise to over 100m high. A precise symbolism pervades the facades, each of which is divided into three porches devoted to Faith, Hope and Charity. Gaudí made extensive use of human, plant and animal models in order to produce exactly the sculptural likenesses he sought – the spreading stone leaves of the roof in the church interior, for example, were inspired by the city's plane trees. Although parts of the interior still resemble a giant building site, and the **Glory facade** remains unfinished, the whole church will be roofed in due course, with a 170-metre-high central dome and tower to follow (which will then make the church the tallest building in Barcelona).

There are eight towers at the Sagrada Família, four on each current facade, though following Gaudí's design there will eventually be eighteen – twelve symbolizing the Apostles, four dedicated to the Evangelists and one each for Mary and Jesus. They have been likened to everything from perforated cigars to celestial billiard cues, and to see them at close quarters take one of the separate **elevators** that run up the Passion and Nativity facades. Your entrance ticket also gives you access to the **museum**, which traces the career of the architect and the history of the church.

CLOCKWISE FROM TOP LEFT PARC GÜELL (P.678); SAGRADA FAMÍLIA; CASA BATLLÓ (P.670).; LA PEDRERA (P.673)>

Hospital de la Santa Creu i de Sant Pau

C/de Sant Antoni María Claret 167, at c/Dos de Maig • Information point open daily 9.30am–1.30pm, admission free • Tours daily in English at 10am, 11am, noon & 1pm, plus others in Spanish/Catalan, €10 • ☎ 933 177 652, ⓦ rutadelmodernisme.com • Ⓜ Hospital de Sant Pau

Lluís Domènech i Montaner's *modernista* public hospital, the **Hospital de la Santa Creu i de Sant Pau**, is possibly the one building in town that can rival the Sagrada Família for size and invention. The hospital has its own metro stop, but it's far better to walk up the four-block-long Avinguda de Gaudí from the church, which gives terrific views back over the spires of the Sagrada Família.

Work started in 1902, the brief being to replace the city's medieval hospital buildings in the Raval. The architect spent ten years working on the project and left his trademarks all over it, notably the whimsical pavilions, turrets and towers covered with sculpture, mosaics, stained glass and ironwork. These days, the old buildings have been superseded by the modern hospital behind, though a painstaking restoration of the *modernista* pavilions is currently under way. Informative **tours** of the site tell you more about the six-hundred-year history of the hospital and the current renovation project.

Plaça de les Glòries Catalanes

Ⓜ Glòries

Barcelona's major avenues all meet at the **Plaça de les Glòries Catalanes**, a glorified roundabout dedicated to the "Catalan glories", from architecture to literature. It's now at the centre of the city's latest bout of regeneration, which plans to tunnel the traffic underground, thus opening up a grand pedestrianized park containing a design centre to house the city's applied art collections. Signature building on the roundabout is Jean Nouvel's cigar-shaped **Torre Agbar** (142m), a highly distinctive aluminium-and-glass tower with no fewer than four thousand windows, housing the headquarters of the local water company. Nouvel also designed the **Parc del Centre del Poble Nou** further down the Diagonal (10min walk from Glòries or tram stop Pere IV), an eye-catching contemporary park set on another former industrial site – a surviving brick chimney stands in the centre, surrounded by willow trees.

Teatre Nacional de Catalunya

Pl. de les Arts 1 • Tours currently Tues & Thurs 10am–1pm, on the hour • €5, reservations required • ☎ 933 065 700, ⓦ tnc.cat • Ⓜ Glòries or tram #T4

Off to the southwest of Glòries, Catalunya's national theatre – the **Teatre Nacional de Catalunya** – presents the neighbourhood with a soaring glass box encased within a Greek temple on a raised dais, surrounded by manicured lawns. There are guided building and backstage **tours** for anyone interested in learning more, as well as a bar and restaurant that are open in the evening – a summer evening's drink on the open-air terrassa is a nice way to take in the grandiose surroundings.

TREASURE-HUNTING AT ELS ENCANTS VELLS

At the city's traditional open-air flea market, **Els Encants Vells** (c/del Dos de Maig; Mon, Wed, Fri & Sat 7am–3pm, plus same times Sun & hols from Dec 1–Jan 5; ⓦ encantsbcn.com; Ⓜ Encants/Glòries), you name it, you can buy it: old sewing machines, cheese graters, photograph albums, cutlery, lawnmowers, clothes, shoes, CDs, antiques, furniture and out-and-out junk. It's best in the early morning, and haggling for any "old charms" (*encants vells*) you might fancy is de rigueur, but you're up against experts. The market is due a new home with the completion of the Glòries renovations, so access, hours and location are subject to change over the next few years.

L'Auditori and the Museu de la Música

L'Auditori c/Lepant 150 • ⓦ auditori.cat • **Museu de la Música** c/Padilla 155 • Mon & Wed–Sat 10am–6pm, Sun & hols 10am–8pm •
€4, free first Sun of the month & every Sun after 3pm • ☎ 932 563 650, ⓦ museumusica.bcn.cat • ⓜ Glòries/Marina

Forming a sort of cultural enclave, **L'Auditori** is the city's contemporary city concert
hall, within which is housed the **Museu de la Música**. It's all very impressive, with
soaring glass-walled display cases, and yet it struggles to engage, partly because of the
sheer number and variety of instruments and partly because of the impenetrable
commentary, with sections called things like "The humanist spirit and the
predominance of polyphony". Make of that what you will, or the chronological
"timeline" that runs from Pythagoras in the fifth century BC to 2007 when "the
Rolling Stones continue to play".

Parc Joan Miró

C/de Tarragona • Daily 10am–dusk • Free • ⓜ Tarragona

The main attraction on the left-hand side of the Eixample is the **Parc Joan Miró**, which
features a raised piazza marked only by Joan Miró's gigantic mosaic sculpture *Dona i
Ocell* ("Woman and Bird"), towering above a shallow reflecting pool. The rear of the
park is given over to games areas and landscaped sections of palms and firs, with a
kiosk café and some outdoor tables found in among the trees.

Arenas de Barcelona

Gran Vía de les Corts Catalanes 373–385, at Pl. d'Espanya • ⓦ arenasdebarcelona.com **Museu del Rock** 4th Floor • Tues & Wed 10am–
10pm, Thurs & Fri 10am–4pm, €5, under-12s €3; Thurs & Fri 4–10pm, Sat & Sun 10am–10pm, €9, under-12s €5 • ⓦ museudelrock.com
• ⓜ Espanya

The **Arenas de Barcelona**, the fabulous Moorish-style bullring, was originally built in
1900 but re-imagined as a swish shopping and leisure centre that opened in 2011.
Conceived by architect Richard Rogers as a gateway to the city centre, and preserving
the beautiful brick exterior, the various retail levels at Arenas are hung in sweeping,
circular galleries, while right on top is a wide walk-around exterior promenade circling
the dome, offering 360-degree views of the western side of the city. Also at Arenas is
the city's **Museu del Rock** – a "greatest hits" collection of gold records, musical
instruments, stage clothes and music-history ephemera, from Spanish rockers and
international superstars alike.

Gràcia

Gràcia – the closest neighbourhood to the Eixample – was a village for much of its early
existence before being annexed as a city suburb in the late nineteenth century. There's
still a genuine small-town atmosphere here, very distinct from the old-town
neighbourhoods, while Gràcia's vibrant cultural scene and nightlife counters the notion
that Barcelona begins and ends on the Ramblas. That said, there's not that much to see,
but wander the narrow, gridded streets, catch a film or hit one of the excellent local
bars or restaurants, and you'll soon get the feel of a neighbourhood that – unlike some
in Barcelona – still has a soul. Most of the boutiques, galleries, cinemas and cafés are
near pretty **Plaça de la Virreina**, with **c/Verdi** in particular always worth a stroll. A short
walk to the southwest, **Plaça del Sol** is the beating heart of much of the district's
nightlife, while **Plaça Rius i Taulet**, the "clock-tower square", a couple of minutes to the
south, is another popular place to meet for brunch. However, the one unmissable
attraction is just on the neighbourhood fringe, namely the surreal Parc Güell, by
architectural genius Antoni Gaudí.

Parc Güell

Main entrance c/d'Olot • Daily: March & Oct 10am–7pm; April & Sept 10am–8pm; May–Aug 10am–9pm; Nov–Feb 10am–6pm • Free

Antoni Gaudí's extraordinary urban park on the outskirts of Gràcia, **Parc Güell** was originally planned as a private housing estate of sixty dwellings, furnished with ornamental paths, recreational areas and decorative monuments. Gaudí worked on the project between 1900 and 1914 but in the end only two houses were actually built, and the park was officially opened to the public instead in 1922. Laid out on a hill, which provides fabulous views back across the city, the park is an almost hallucinatory expression of the imagination. Pavilions of contorted stone, giant decorative lizards, a vast Hall of Columns (intended to be the estate's market), the meanderings of a huge ceramic bench – all combine in one manic swirl of ideas and excesses.

Casa Museu Gaudí

Inside Parc Güell • Daily 10am–6pm (April–Sept until 8pm) • €5.50, combination ticket with Sagrada Família €14.50 • ☎ 932 193 811, ⓦ casamuseugaudi.org

One of Gaudí's collaborators, Francesc Berenguer, designed and built a turreted house within the park for the architect. In the **Casa Museu Gaudí**, his ascetic study and bedroom have been kept much as they were in his day, while other rooms display a diverting collection of furniture he designed for other projects – a typical mixture of wild originality and brilliant engineering.

ARRIVAL AND DEPARTURE   GRÀCIA AND PARC GÜELL

By metro and train For Gràcia, the best metro stations are Ⓜ Diagonal (south), Ⓜ Fontana (north) or Ⓜ Joanic (east). For Parc Güell use Ⓜ Vallcarca, walk a few hundred metres down Avgda. de Vallcarca until you see the mechanical escalators on your left, ascending Baixada de la Glòria. Follow these right to the western-side park entrance (15min).

By bus Bus #24 from Plaça de Catalunya or Passeig de Gràcia stops on Carretera del Carmel at the eastern side gate of Parc Güell. The Bus Turístic stops at the bottom end of c/de Larrard, on c/de la Mare de Deu de la Salut.
On foot Gràcia is a 30min walk from Plaça de Catalunya. From any of the neighbourhood stations, it's around a five-hundred-metre walk to Gràcia's central squares. Walking to Parc Güell from Gràcia (ⓂLesseps), turn right along Travessera de Dalt and then left up steep c/de Larrard, which leads straight to the main entrance of the park on c/Olot (10min).

Les Corts and Pedralbes

To the northwest of the city centre, what was once the village of Les Corts is now largely indistinguishable from the rest of the modern city, save for the hallowed precincts of Camp Nou, FC Barcelona's stupendous football stadium. Nearby, across Avinguda Diagonal, the Palau Reial de Pedralbes combines the city's applied art collections (of clothes and textiles, decorative arts and ceramics), while a half-day's excursion can be made by walking from the palace, past the Gaudí dragon gate at Pavellons Güell to the calm cloister at the Gothic monastery of Pedralbes.

Camp Nou and FC Barcelona

Avgda. Arístides Maillol • ☎ 902 189 900 or 934 963 600, ⓦ fcbarcelona.com • Ⓜ Collblanc/María Cristina plus 10min walk

It's no exaggeration to say that football in Barcelona is a genuine obsession, with support for the local giants **FC (Futbol Club) Barcelona** raised to an art form. "More than just a club" is the proud boast, and certainly during the dictatorship years the club stood as a Catalan symbol around which people could rally. Arch-rivals, Real Madrid, on the other hand, were always seen as Franco's club. The swashbuckling players in the famous "blaugrana" (claret and blue) shirts have transcended national barriers to become every football fan's second favourite team; indeed, the four-times European champions (most recently in 2011) – mercurial masters of the elegant *tiki-taka*, pass-and-move style – are often hailed as the world's best team.

Museum and stadium tour

Museu del Futbol, entrance on Avgda. Arístides Maillol, through Gates (Accés) 7 and 9 • April–Oct Mon–Sat 10am–8pm, rest of the year until 6.30pm, Sun & hols 10am–2.30pm, last tour 1hr before closing, no tours on match days • €19, under-13s €15.50, under-5s free • ☎ 902 189 900 or 934 963 600, ⓦ fcbarcelona.com

Together, the 98,000-seat stadium and museum – billed as the "Camp Nou Experience" – provide a magnificent celebration of Spain's national sport. The **self-guided tour**, complete with audio-guide, winds through the changing rooms and players' tunnel onto the pitch and up to the press gallery and directors' box for stunning views. The **museum** is jammed full of silverware and memorabilia, including the six cups won in 2009 alone, Barcelona's *annus mirabilis*, while a cracking multimedia zone profiles historic games and famous players and relives the match-day atmosphere. Finally, you're directed into the **FC Botiga** megastore, where you can buy anything from a replica shirt down to a branded bottle of wine.

Palau Reial de Pedralbes

Avgda. Diagonal 686 • Gardens daily 10am–dusk • Free • Museums Tues–Sun 10am–6pm • €5, ticket valid for all Palau Reial museums, free Sun after 3pm & first Sun of the month • Ⓜ Palau Reial or tram #T1, #T2 or #T3

Opposite the university on Avinguda Diagonal, the **Palau Reial de Pedralbes** is an Italianate palace set in formal grounds. The **gardens** are a calm oasis, while – until the projected Centre del Disseny (Design Centre) at Glòries is completed – the palace rooms contain separate museums devoted to the city's **applied art collections**, namely of ceramics, decorative arts, and textiles and clothing, all of which can be visited on the same ticket (note that all are closed on Mondays). The Decorative Arts Museum is probably the highlight for anyone with just a general interest in applied art, but you can easily whip around all three museums in an hour or two.

Pavellons Güell

Avgda. de Pedralbes 7 • Tours Sat & Sun at 10.15am & 12.15pm in English, plus 11.15am & 1.15pm in Spanish/Catalan • €6 • ☎ 933 177 652, ⓦ rutadelmodernisme.com • Ⓜ Palau Reial and 5min walk

As an early test of his capabilities, Antoni Gaudí was asked by his patron, Eusebi Güell, to rework the entrance, gatehouse and stables of the Güell summer residence, which was sited on a large working estate well away from the filth and unruly mobs of downtown Barcelona. The brick-and-tile stables and outbuildings – known as the **Pavellons Güell** – survive as Gaudí created them, though it's the gateway that's the most famous element. An extraordinary winged dragon made of twisted iron snarls at the passers-by, its razor-toothed jaws spread wide in a fearsome roar.

Monestir de Pedralbes

Baixada del Monestir 9 • Tues–Sat 10am–2pm (April–Sept until 5pm), Sun 10am–8pm, hols 10am–3pm • €7, includes entry to other Museu d'Història de Barcelona sites, free Sun after 3pm • ☎ 932 563 434, ⓦ museuhistoria.bcn.cat • Ⓜ Palau Reial and 20min walk; or FGC Reina Elisenda (frequent trains from Pl. de Catalunya) and 10min walk; or bus #64 from Pl. Universitat

Founded in 1326 for the nuns of the Order of St Clare, the Gothic **Monestir de Pedralbes** is, in effect, an entire monastic village preserved on the outskirts of the city, within medieval walls that completely shut out the clamour of the twenty-first century. After 600 years of isolation, the monastery was sequestered by the Generalitat during the Civil War and it later opened as a museum in 1983 – a new adjacent convent was built as part of the deal, where the Clare nuns still reside. The **cloisters** are the finest in the city, adorned by the slenderest of columns, with the only sound the tinkling water from the fountain. Side rooms and chambers give a clear impression of medieval convent life, from the chapter house and austere refectory to a fully equipped kitchen and infirmary. While the nuns themselves eschewed personal trappings, the monastery acquired valuable art and other possessions over the centuries – including pieces of Gothic furniture, paintings by Flemish artists, and some outstanding illuminated choir books. In the adjacent **church** the foundation's sponsor, **Elisenda de Montcada**, wife of Jaume II, lies in a superb, carved marble tomb.

Tibidabo and Parc de Collserola

The views from the heights of **Tibidabo** (550m), the peak that signals the northwestern boundary of the city, are legendary. On a clear day you can see across to the Pyrenees and out to sea even as far as Mallorca. However, while many make the tram and funicular ride up to Tibidabo's wonderfully old-fashioned amusement park, few realize that beyond stretches the **Parc de Collserola**, an area of peaks, wooded river valleys and hiking paths – one of Barcelona's best-kept secrets. Meanwhile, don't miss **CosmoCaixa**, the city's excellent science museum, which can easily be seen on the way to or from Tibidabo.

CosmoCaixa

C/Teodor Roviralta 47–51 • Tues–Sun 10am–8pm • €3, under-18s €2, under-7s & first Sun of month free, children's activities €2, planetarium €2 • ☎ 932 126 050, ⓦ cosmocaixa.com • FGC Avinguda del Tibidabo (trains from Pl. de Catalunya) and 10min walk, or Tramvia Blau stops close by

A dramatic refurbishment in 2005 transformed the city's science museum into **CosmoCaixa**, a must-see attraction, certainly if you've got children in tow – it's an easy place to spend a couple of hours. Hands-on experiments and displays investigate life, the universe and everything, "from bacteria to Shakespeare", with the two big draws being the 100 tonnes of "sliced" rock in the **Mur Geològic** (Geological Wall) and, best of all, the **Bosc Inundat** – nothing less than a thousand square metres of real Amazonian rainforest, complete with croc-filled mangroves, anacondas and giant catfish.

Parc d'Atraccions Tibidabo

10

Pl. del Tibidabo • Days and hours vary, but basically June–Sept & hols Wed–Sun, rest of the year Sat, Sun & hols only, closed Jan & Feb, park open from noon until 7–11pm depending on season • Skywalk ticket €12, full admission €26, plus family/discount tickets • ☎ 932 117 942, ⓦ tibidabo.es

Barcelona's self-styled "magic mountain" amusement park – the **Parc d'Atraccions** – has been thrilling the citizens for over a century. It's a mix of traditional rides, plus an influx of high-tech roller-coasters and free-fall drops, laid out around several levels of the mountaintop, connected by landscaped paths and gardens. Some of the most famous historic attractions are grouped under the discounted "Skywalk" ticket, like the aeroplane – spinning since 1928 – the carousel, and the quirky Museu d'Autòmates, a collection of coin-operated antique fairground machines in working order. Summer weekends finish with parades, concerts and a noisy *correfoc*, a theatrical fireworks display.

ARRIVAL AND DEPARTURE   TIBIDABO

By train, tram and funicular Take the FGC train (Tibidabo line 7) from Plaça de Catalunya station to Avinguda del Tibidabo (the last stop). From across the road an antique tram service, the Tramvia Blau (departures every 15–30min: mid-June to mid-Sept daily 10am–8pm, rest of year weekends & hols, plus Christmas and Easter weeks 10am–6pm; €2.90 one way, €4.50 return) runs up the hill to Plaça del Doctor Andreu; there's a bus service instead out of season during the week. By the tram and bus stop on Plaça Doctor Andreu (where there are several café-bars and restaurants), change to the Funicular del Tibidabo, with connections to Tibidabo at the top (every 15min, operates when the Parc d'Attracions is open, €4 return, fare reimbursed with park admission). The whole journey takes about 1hr.

By bus The Bus Turístic stops at Avinguda del Tibidabo, where you can change for the Tramvia Blau. Alternatively, the special Tibibus runs direct to Tibidabo from Plaça de Catalunya (from 10.30am, every day the park is open; €3, fare reimbursed with park admission).

Parc de Collserola

Centre d'Informació • Daily 9.30am–3pm • ☎ 932 803 552, ⓦ parcnaturalcollserola.cat • FGC Baixada de Vallvidrera (on the Sabadell or Terrassa line from Pl. de Catalunya; 15min)

Given a half-decent day, local bikers, hikers and outdoors enthusiasts all make a beeline for the city's ring of wooded hills beyond Tibidabo, the **Parc de Collserola**. The **park information centre** lies in oak and pine woods, an easy, signposted ten-minute walk up through the trees from the FGC Baixada de Vallvidrera train station. There's a bar-restaurant here with an outdoor terrace, plus an exhibition on the park's history, flora and fauna, while the staff hand out English-language leaflets detailing the various walks, which range from a fifteen-minute stroll to the Vallvidrera dam to a couple of hours circling the hills.

ARRIVAL AND DEPARTURE   BARCELONA

Barcelona's main points of arrival are all fairly convenient, even the airport, and have useful train and metro stations for onward travel. In most cases, you can be off the plane, train, bus or ferry and in your hotel room within the hour. Note that some budget-airline "Barcelona" flights are no such thing: for Ryanair arrivals at Girona airport (90km north of Barcelona), there's a connecting bus service (see p.737) to Barcelona Nord bus station, and there are also connecting buses from Reus airport (110km south, near Tarragona; see p.783) to Barcelona Sants train station.

10

BY PLANE

Barcelona Airport Barcelona's airport (general information ☏ 902 404 704, ☝ aena.es) is 18km southwest of the city at El Prat de Llobregat. A taxi to the city centre costs up to €30, including the airport surcharge.

Airport train The airport train service (daily 5.42am–11.38pm; journey time 19min; €3.15) runs every thirty minutes to Barcelona Sants (the main train station), and continues on to Passeig de Gràcia (best stop for Eixample, Plaça de Catalunya and the Ramblas). It departs from Terminal T2, and there's a free shuttle-bus to the station from T1 which takes around ten minutes. Trains back to the airport run from Barcelona Sants on a similar half-hourly schedule. City travel passes (*targetes*) and the Barcelona Card are valid.

Aerobus The Aerobus (daily 6am–5am; €5.30 one way, €9.15 return; departures every 5–10min; ☝ aerobusbcn .com) departs from both T1 and T2, stopping in the city at Plaça d'Espanya, Plaça Universitat, Plaça de Catalunya and Passeig de Gràcia. It takes 35–40min to reach Plaça de Catalunya, longer in the rush hour. Departures back to the airport from Plaça de Catalunya (in front of El Corte Inglés department store) – note that there are separate services to either Terminal T1 or T2.

BY TRAIN

Barcelona Sants The main station for national and international arrivals is Barcelona Sants (Ⓜ Sants Estació), 3km west of the centre. From Sants, metro line 3 runs direct to Drassanes and Liceu (for the Ramblas), Catalunya (for Plaça de Catalunya) and Passeig de Gràcia (Eixample), while line 5 runs to Diagonal (Eixample and Gràcia).

AVE services The high-speed AVE line between Barcelona and Madrid (via Tarragona and Zaragoza) has cut journey times in half between the two cities (2hr 45min–3hr 25min, depending on the service). Arrivals and departures are at Barcelona Sants, though a second high-speed station is currently being built at La Sagrera, east of the centre beyond Glòries (completion date estimated 2013).

Estació de França Some inter-city services and international trains also stop at Estació de França, 1km east of the Ramblas and close to Ⓜ Barceloneta.

Regional and provincial trains Other possible arrival points by train are Plaça de Catalunya, at the top of the Ramblas (for trains from coastal towns north of the city, and towns on the Puigcerdà–Vic line), and Passeig de Gràcia (Catalunya provincial destinations).

Destinations Figueres (hourly; 1hr 40min); Girona (at least hourly; 1hr 15min); Lleida (9 daily; 2hr 30min–3hr); Madrid (AVE up to 20 daily, every 30–60min at peak times, 2hr 45min–3hr 25min; other services 8 daily, 5–9hr); Portbou (hourly; 2hr 20min); Puigcerdà (7 daily; 3hr 20min); Ripoll (hourly; 2hr); Sitges (every 30min; 25–40min); Tarragona (AVE up to 14 daily, 35min; other services every 15–30min, 1hr); Valencia (16 daily; 4–5hr); Vic (hourly; 1hr 15min);

Zaragoza (AVE 14 daily, 1hr 30min–1hr 50min; other services up to 8 daily, 3hr 45min–5hr 30min).

BY BUS

Barcelona Nord The main bus terminal is on c/Ali-Bei (☏ 902 260 606, ☝ barcelonanord.com; Ⓜ Arc de Triomf), four blocks north of Parc de la Ciutadella. There's a bus information desk on the ground floor (daily 7am–9pm), with the ticket offices above at street level (advanced booking advised on long-distance routes). Some inter-city and international services also make a stop at the bus terminal behind Barcelona Sants station on c/de Viriat (Ⓜ Sants Estació). Either way, you're only a short metro ride from the city centre.

Destinations Andorra (2 daily; 4hr 30min); Banyoles (2–3 daily; 1hr 30min); Besalú (2–3 daily; 1hr 45min); Cadaqués (2–5 daily; 2hr 20min); Girona (Mon–Sat 6–9 daily, Sun 3 daily; 1hr 30min); Lleida (Mon–Sat 12 daily, Sun 4 daily; 2hr 15min); Lloret de Mar (July to mid-Sept 10 daily; 1hr 15min); Madrid (15 daily; 8hr); Olot (2–3 daily; 2hr 10min); Palafrugell (8 daily; 2hr); La Seu d'Urgell (2 daily; 4hr); Tarragona (18 daily; 1hr 30min); Tossa de Mar (July to mid-Sept 12 daily; 1hr 35min); Valencia (10 daily; 5hr 30min); Zaragoza (11 daily; 4hr 30min).

BY FERRY

Estació Marítima Ferries from the Balearics dock at the terminal in Port Vell, at the bottom of Avinguda Paral.lel (Ⓜ Drassanes), not far from the Ramblas. There are ticket offices inside the terminal (July & Aug are very busy) for services to Palma de Mallorca, Mahón and Ibiza, with Trasmediterranea (☝ trasmediterranea.es), Iscomar (☝ iscomar.com) and Balearia (☝ balearia.net). Navi Grandi Veloci (☝ 1.gnv.it) has a year-round service to Genoa, Italy, and Tangiers, Morocco.

BY CAR

Driving into Barcelona Head for the Ronda Litoral, the southern half of the city's ring road. Following signs for "Port Vell" takes you towards the main exit for the old town; exits for Gran Vía de les Corts Catalanes and Avinguda Diagonal will suit better if uptown Barcelona is your destination.

Parking City-centre garages and car parks (up to €25 for 24hr) are linked to display boards that indicate where there are free spaces. There are cheaper BSM (Barcelona Serveis Municipals) **long-term car parks** for residents and visitors, best option being the large Plaça del Fòrum car park at Diagonal Mar (Ⓜ El Maresme-Fòrum), where parking for one to five days costs €33.75, plus €7 for each additional day. Closer to the centre, the 24-hour BSM car park at Barcelona Nord bus station (c/d'Ali-Bei 54; Ⓜ Arc de Triomf) costs €16.85 per day. Otherwise, the ubiquitous Área Verda meter-zones throughout the city allow pay-and-display parking for visitors (around €3 per hour, one- or two-hour maximum stay).

INFORMATION

The city tourist board, Turisme de Barcelona (☎807 117 222 if calling from within Spain, ☎932 853 834 if calling from abroad, ⓦbarcelonaturisme.com), has a very useful English-language website, plus offices in the city centre as well as at the airport and Barcelona Sants station. There are also **staffed kiosks** in main tourist areas, such as on the Ramblas and outside the Sagrada Família, which sell discount passes and entrance tickets for popular attractions.

Turisme de Barcelona Main tourist office is at Pl. de Catalunya 17, opposite El Corte Inglés, ⓜCatalunya (daily 8.30am–8.30pm); also a Barri Gòtic office at Pl. de Sant Jaume, entrance at c/Ciutat 2, ⓜJaume I (Mon–Fri 8.30am–8.30pm, Sat 9am–7pm, Sun & hols 9am–2pm). The main office is always busy – frustrating if you just want a quick answer to a question. There's also an accommodation desk, tour and ticket sales, and a gift shop. **Institut de Cultura** Palau de la Virreina, Ramblas 99, ⓜLiceu ☎933 161 000, ⓦbcn.cat/cultura (daily 10am–8.30pm). Cultural information office, for events, concerts, exhibitions and festivals; you can also buy tickets here.

Centre d'Informació de Catalunya Palau Robert, Pg. de Gràcia 107, Eixample, ⓜDiagonal ☎932 388 091 or ☎012, ⓦgencat.cat/palaurobert (Mon–Sat 10am–7pm, Sun & hols 10am–2.30pm). Information about travel in Catalunya, plus exhibitions and events relating to all matters Catalan.
City Information Service The Ajuntament (City Hall)'s 24-hour ☎010 telephone enquiries service (English-speaking staff available) can help with transport queries, public services and other matters, while their website (ⓦbcn.cat) and that of the regional government; (Generalitat, ⓦgencat.cat) are absolute mines of information about every aspect of cultural, social and working life in Barcelona; both have English-language versions.

GETTING AROUND

Much of what you'll want to see in the city centre can be reached on foot in under twenty minutes from Plaça de Catalunya. But Barcelona also has an excellent integrated **public-transport system**, which comprises the metro, buses, trams, local trains and a network of funicular railways and cable cars. The local transport authority, **Transports Metropolitans de Barcelona** (TMB; ⓦtmb.net, English-language version available), has a very useful website, while route and ticket information is posted at major bus stops and all metro and tram stations. A transit plan divides the province into six zones, but as the entire metropolitan area of Barcelona (including the airport) falls within Zone 1, that's the only one you'll normally need to worry about.

TICKETS AND TRAVEL PASSES

Tickets On all the city's public transport (including night buses and funiculars) you can buy a single ticket every time you ride (€1.45).

Targetes It's much cheaper to buy a *targeta* (discount ticket-strip), available at metro, train, tram and funicular stations,

but not on the buses. The T-10 ("tay day-oo" in Catalan) gives you ten journeys for €8.25, and can be used by more than one person at a time – just feed it through the barrier for each person travelling. Changing methods of transport within 1hr 15min counts as one journey with the T-10 (re-punch the ticket – it only registers once). There's also a single-person,

SIGHTSEEING DISCOUNT CARDS

If you're going to do a lot of sightseeing in a short amount of time, you can save yourself money by buying one of the widely available **discount cards**. Choose carefully, since some are targeted at very specific interests, or cover things like transport that you might already have paid for – and bear in mind that there's plenty to do in town for free.

Barcelona Card (2 days €27.50, 3 days €33.50, 4 days €38 or 5 days €45, full details on ⓦbarcelonaturisme .com). Free public transport, plus big discounts at museums, venues, shops and restaurants. It's available at points of arrival, tourist offices and kiosks, and other outlets, though there's a ten-percent discount if you buy online.

Articket (€22, valid six months; ⓦarticketbcn.org). Free admission into seven major art centres and galleries (MNAC, MACBA, CCCB, Museu Picasso, Fundació Antoni Tàpies, Fundació Joan Miró, and Centre Cultural Caixa

Catalunya at La Pedrera). Buy at participating galleries, at Barcelona tourist offices and kiosks, or online.
Ruta del Modernisme (€12, valid one year; ⓦrutadelmodernisme.com). English-language guide-book, map and discount-voucher package that covers 115 *modernista* buildings in Barcelona and other Catalan towns. It's also packaged with *Let's Go Out*, a guide to *modernista* bars and restaurants (total package €18), with both available from the Centre del Modernisme desk at the main Plaça de Catalunya tourist office.

10

one-day T-Día at €6.20 for unlimited travel within Zone 1, plus combinations up to the 5-Dies (5 days; €25).

Out of town Heading for Sitges, Montserrat and other out-of-town destinations, you'll need to buy a specific ticket or relevant zoned *targeta*.

METRO, BUSES AND TRAMS

Metro The metro runs on eight lines (with major extensions across the city centre and out to the airport currently under construction). Hours of operation are Monday until Thursday, plus Sunday and public holidays 5am to midnight; Friday 5am to 2am; Saturday and the day before a public holiday 24hr.

Buses Bus routes operate daily, roughly from 4/5am until 10.30pm, though some lines stop earlier and some run on until after midnight. Night buses fill in the gaps on all main routes, with services every twenty minutes to an hour from around 10pm to 4am. Many bus routes (including all night buses) stop in or near Plaça de Catalunya.

Trams Lines #T1, #T2 and #T3 (daily 5am–midnight, every 8–20min) depart from Plaça Francesc Macià and run along the uptown part of Avinguda Diagonal to suburban destinations in the northwest – useful tourist stops are at L'Illa shopping centre and the María Cristina and Palau Reial metro stations. There's also the handy Line #T4 from Ciutadella-Vila Olímpica (where there's also a metro station), up to Glòries and then down Avinguda Diagonal to Diagonal Mar and the Parc del Fòrum.

TRAINS

FGC The city's commuter train line – **Ferrocarrils de la Generalitat de Catalunya** (FGC; ☎ 932 051 515, ⓦ fgc.cat) – has its main stations at Plaça de Catalunya and Plaça d'Espanya. You'll need this for Montserrat and Tibidabo.

RENFE The national rail service, RENFE (☎ 902 320 320, ⓦ renfe.com), runs all other services out of Barcelona, with local lines – north to the Costa Maresme and south to Sitges – designated as **Rodiales/Cercanías**. The hub is Barcelona Sants, with services also passing through Plaça Catalunya (heading north) and Passeig de Gràcia (south).

TAXIS

Black-and-yellow **taxis** have a green roof light on when available for hire – most short journeys across town run to around €9. There's a minimum charge of €2 and after that it's €0.90 per kilometre (€1.15 after 8pm, and on Sat, Sun & hols), with surcharges for baggage and picking up from Barcelona Sants station and the airport. Taxis have meters, so prices are transparent; asking for a receipt (*rebut*) should clear up any confusion. They can be called on the following numbers (though English is unlikely to be spoken): ☎ 933 577 755, ☎ 933 033 033, ☎ 933 300 300, ☎ 934 208 088.

CYCLING AND BIKE RENTAL

The city council's Bicing pick-up and drop-off scheme (ⓦ bicing.com) is touted as Barcelona's new public transport system. You'll see the red bikes and bike stations all over the city, but Bicing is not aimed at tourists, rather at locals who are encouraged to use the bikes for short trips. However, there are plenty of bike-rental outfits more geared to tourist requirements. Rental costs around €20, while many bike tour companies (see "City tours", below) can also fix you up with a rental bike.

Bike rental outfits Biciclot, Pg. Marítim 33–35, Port Olímpic (ⓜ Ciutadella-Vila Olímpica), ☎ 932 219 778, ⓦ biciclot.net; Un Coxte Menys/Bicicleta Barcelona, c/Esparteria 3, La Ribera (ⓜ Barceloneta), ☎ 932 682 105, ⓦ bicicletabarcelona.com.

CITY TOURS

You can see the sights in Barcelona on anything from a Segway to a hot-air balloon. Walking tours and bike tours in particular are hugely popular, while other operators offer tapas-bar crawls, party nights and out-of-town excursions. Highest profile are the open-top sightseeing bus tours, whose board-at-will services stop outside every attraction in the city.

Barcelona Walking Tours ☎ 932 853 832, ⓦ barcelonaturisme.com. The tourist office coordinates a popular series of walks and tours, including a 90min tour of the Barri Gòtic (daily 10am; €13), a 90min Picasso tour (Tues, Thurs & Sat at 4pm; €19.50, includes entry to Picasso Museum), or a two-hour Modernisme tour (Fri & Sat, May–Oct at 3pm, June–Sept at 6pm; €13). Times given are for the current English-language tours, advance booking essential.

Bike Tours Barcelona ☎ 932 682 105, ⓦ bike toursbarcelona.com. Find the red-T-shirted guides in Plaça de Sant Jaume in the Barri Gòtic (top of c/de la Ciutat) – tours last three hours (daily 11am, plus April–Sept Fri–Mon 4.30pm; €22), no reservations required.

Bus Turístic ⓦ barcelonabusturistic.cat. The main official sightseeing service (departures every 5–25min) with over forty stops on three combined routes, linking all the main tourist sights. Northern (red) and southern (blue) routes depart from Plaça de Catalunya (daily 9am–7pm, April–Sept 9am–8pm), and a full circuit on either route takes two hours. The green Fòrum route (daily April–Sept 9.30am–8pm) runs from Port Olímpic to Diagonal Mar and back via the beaches, and takes 40 minutes. Tickets available on board and online, at Sants station or at any tourist office: €23 for one day, €30 for two days (children aged 4–12 €14/18 respectively; under 4 free.

10

BARCELONA TRANSPORT

Line 1
Line 2
Line 3
Line 4
Line 5
Line 9
Line 10
Line 11
Tram
Tramvia Blau
Funicular
Cable car
Interchange station
FGC
Connection with RENFE

10

My Favourite Things ☎ 637 265 405, ⓦ myft.net. Highly individual tours – whether it's where and what the locals eat, Art Nouveau discoveries or ecofriendly Barcelona. Tours (in English) cost €26 per person and last around four hours, advance bookings essential – call or email for latest information or tailor-made requests.

ACCOMMODATION

Finding a **hotel** vacancy in Barcelona can be very difficult, so it's always best to book in advance, especially at Easter, in summer and during festivals or trade fairs. Prices are high for Spain – absolute cheapest rooms in a simple family-run hotel, sharing a bathroom, cost around €50 (singles from €30), though for private facilities €70–80 a night is more realistic. Places with a bit of boutique styling start at around €100, while for Barcelona's most fashionable hotels, count on €250 to €400 a night. In youth hostels, or cheap hotels with dorms, a bed goes for between €15 and €30 a night, depending on the season. You can **reserve** hotel accommodation online with the city tourist board or make same-day bookings in person only at their **tourist offices** (see p.683). For apartments, try Barcelona On-Line (ⓦ barcelona-on-line.es) or Inside-BCN (ⓦ inside-bcn.com), while Barcelona-based **My Favourite Things** (ⓦ myft.net) has an eye for offbeat rooms and apartments in private houses.

THE RAMBLAS

★ **Hostal Benidorm** Ramblas 37 ☎ 933 022 054, ⓦ hostalbenidorm.com; ⓜ Drassanes; map p.648. Refurbished *pensión* opposite Plaça Reial that offers real value for money. Plain rooms available for one to five people, all with bathtubs or showers, and a balcony or Ramblas view if you're prepared to pay a bit more. €75

Hostal Mare Nostrum Ramblas 67, entrance on c/Sant Pau ☎ 933 185 340, ⓦ hostalmarenostrum.com; ⓜ Liceu; map p.648. A cheery Ramblas *pensión* whose English-speaking management offers comfortable double, triple and family rooms (€10 less for share-bathroom) – nothing flashy, but reasonably modern and double-glazed against the noise. €95

★ **Hotel H1898** Ramblas 109, entrance on c/Pintor Fortuny ☎ 935 529 552, ⓦ hotel1898.com; ⓜ Catalunya; map p.648. The former HQ of the Philippines Tobacco Company has four grades of eye-popping boutique rooms (the standard is "Classic") in deep red, green or black. Public areas are similarly dramatic, like the neo-colonial lounge and bar, and the fanciest *Starbucks* in town. There are both outdoor and indoor pools and a glam spa, too. Special rates from €160. €255

Le Méridien Barcelona Ramblas 111 ☎ 933 186 200, ⓦ lemeridienbarcelona.com; ⓜ Catalunya; map p.648. A big-money makeover for the high-end, five-star Ramblas stalwart has sharpened up both rooms and public areas – with "deluxe" as the norm you can expect your bedroom to feature designer leather furniture, an iPod-dock and a splash-TV screen in the marble bathroom. €189

BARRI GÒTIC

Hostal Fernando c/de Ferran 31 ☎ 933 017 993, ⓦ hfernando.com; ⓜ Liceu; map p.648. Light, modern rooms all with a/c and private bathroom (some cheaper singles share facilities). Straightforward dorm accommodation also available in en-suite rooms that sleep four to eight. Dorms €26, rooms €80

★ **Hostal Rembrandt** c/Portaferrissa 23 ☎ 933 181 011, ⓦ hostalrembrandt.com; ⓜ Liceu; map p.648. A safe, old-town budget *pensión*. Simple tile-floored rooms (a bit cheaper without private bathroom) have a street-side balcony or little patio, while larger rooms are more versatile and can sleep up to four. €65

Hotel Cantón c/Nou de Sant Francesc 40 ☎ 933 173 019, ⓦ hotelcanton-bcn.com; ⓜ Drassanes; map p.648. A

WHAT'S THE NEIGHBOURHOOD LIKE?

First things first: if you hanker after a **Ramblas** view, you'll pay for the privilege – generally speaking, there are much better deals to be had either side of the famous boulevard, often just a minute's walk away. Most of Barcelona's cheapest accommodation (as well as some classy boutique choices) is found in the **Barri Gòtic** and **El Raval** neighbourhoods, which can both still have their rough edges – be careful (without being paranoid) when coming and going after dark. East of the Barri Gòtic, in **Sant Pere** and **La Ribera**, there are a number of safely sited budget, mid-range and boutique options, handy for the Picasso museum and Born nightlife area. North of Plaça de Catalunya, the **Eixample** has some of the city's most fashionable hotels, often housed in converted palaces and mansions and located just a few minutes' walk from the *modernista* architectural masterpieces. For waterfront views look at **Port Vell** at the end of the Ramblas, and at the **Port Olímpic** southeast of the old town. If you prefer neighbourhood living, then **Gràcia** is the best base, as you're only ever a short walk away from its bars, restaurants and clubs.

modest one-star hotel that's only two blocks off the Ramblas and close to the harbour and Port Vell. Forty rooms feature uniform blue-and-white trim curtains and bedspreads, central heating and a/c, fridge and wardrobe. **€85**

Hotel El Jardí Pl. Sant Josep Oriol 1 ☎ 933 015 900, ⓦ eljardi-barcelona.com; Ⓜ Liceu; map p.648. The hotel's location, overlooking the charming Plaça del Pi, is what sells this place – and explains the steepish prices for rooms that can seem a bit bare and poky. But the best (the top ones have terraces, €10 extra) do look directly onto the square. **€85**

Itaca Hostel c/Ripoll 21 ☎ 933 019 751, ⓦ itacahostel .com; Ⓜ Jaume I; map p.648. Bright and breezy converted house close to the cathedral, offering spacious hostel rooms (sleeping eight or twelve) with balconies. Dorms are mixed, though you can also reserve a private room or apartment (sleeps up to 6, €100–150). Dorms **€26**, rooms **€65**

★ **Neri Hotel** c/de Sant Sever 5 ☎ 933 040 655, ⓦ hotelneri.com; Ⓜ Liceu/Jaume I; map p.648. A delightful eighteenth-century palace close to the cathedral houses this stunning boutique hotel of just 22 rooms and suites, featuring swags of flowing material, rescued timber, granite-toned bathrooms and lofty proportions. Breakfast is served bento-box style, out in the courtyard in summer. **€285**

Pensió Alamar c/Comtessa de Sobradiel 1 ☎ 933 025 012; ⓦ pensioalamar.com; Ⓜ Liceu/Jaume I; map p.648. If you don't mind sharing a bathroom then this makes a convenient base. There are twelve rooms (including five singles), most with little balconies, and while space is tight, there's a friendly welcome, laundry service and use of a kitchen. No credit cards. **€45**

★ **Pensión Mari-Luz** c/del Palau 4, 2º ☎ 933 173 463, ⓦ pensionmariluz.com; Ⓜ Jaume I/Liceu; map p.648. This old mansion, on a quieter-than-usual Barri Gòtic street, offers inexpensive rooms (shared bathrooms) and small dorms, plus a more personal touch than many other places of its kind. It can be a tight squeeze when full, but a dozen apartments (sleeping 2–6, €65–125) a few minutes' walk away in the Raval offer more space. Dorms **€24**, rooms **€65**

PORT VELL

★ **Bonic Barcelona** c/Josep Anselm Clavé 9 ☎ 626 053 434, ⓦ bonic-barcelona.com; Ⓜ Drassanes; map p.648. Chic and charming "urban guesthouse", just a few steps from the Ramblas. Rooms are simply furnished, and the three bathrooms are shared, but a maximum of six guests at any one time ensures peace and privacy. Advance reservations essential; minimum two-night stay required. **€90**

EL RAVAL

Barceló Raval Rambla de Raval 17–21 ☎ 933 201 490, ⓦ barceloraval.com; Ⓜ Liceu/Sant Antoni; map p.648. Neighbourhood landmark is this glow-in-the-dark tower, with sophisticated, open-plan rooms plus

360-degree top-floor terrace with plunge pool and sensational city views. **€100**

★ **Hostal Gat Raval** c/Joaquín Costa 44, 2º ☎ 934 816 670, ⓦ gatrooms.com; Ⓜ Universitat; map p.648. At the boutique end of the budget market, with each room boasting a signature backlit street photograph and artwork that doubles as a reading light. Only six of the 24 rooms are en suite (an extra €10), but communal facilities are good. **€60**

Hostal Gat Xino c/Hospital 149–155 ☎ 933 248 833, ⓦ gatrooms.com; Ⓜ Sant Antoni; map p.648. The sister hotel to the *Gat Raval* shares the same kind of style, but all the rooms here are en suite while four suites (€10 more) have more space and bigger bathrooms (and one has a terrace, from €100). **€75**

★ **Hosteria Grau** c/Ramelleres 27 ☎ 933 018 135, ⓦ hostalgrau.com; Ⓜ Catalunya; map p.648. A really friendly *pensión* with attractive rooms on several floors; you'll pay around €15 less for a room with shared facilities or €15 more for superior rooms with balconies, while six private apartments in the same building (sleeping 2 to 4, available by the night, €100) offer a bit more independence. **€80**

★ **Hotel España** c/de Sant Pau 9–11 ☎ 935 500 000, ⓦ hotelespanya.com; Ⓜ Liceu; map p.648. The *modernista* icon has been sumptuously restored as a four-star-plus hotel, and the gem-like interior – colourful tiles, bright mosaics, sculpted marble, iron swirls and marine motifs – has no equal in Barcelona. Guest rooms are a perfectly judged boutique blend of earth tones and designer style, and there's a plunge pool and chill-out deck on the roof terrace. The handsome house restaurant – known as *Fonda España* – offers contemporary Catalan bistro dishes by hot chef Martín Berasategui. **€135**

Hotel Peninsular c/de Sant Pau 34 ☎ 933 023 138, ⓦ hotelpeninsular.net; Ⓜ Liceu; map p.648. This interesting old building originally belonged to a priestly order, which explains the slightly cell-like quality of the rooms. However, there's nothing spartan about the galleried inner courtyard, while breakfast is served in the arcaded dining room. **€80**

★ **Market Hotel** c/Comte Borrell 68, at Ptge. Sant Antoni Abat ☎ 933 251 205, ⓦ markethotel.com.es; Ⓜ Sant Antoni; map p.665. The designer-budget *Market* makes a definite splash with its part Japanese, part neo-colonial look. There's also an impressive restaurant, where the food is exceptionally good value, while the hotel's vintage Asian-style *Bar Rosso* is a bit of a local hipsters' haunt. **€100**

SANT PERE

★ **Pensió 2000** c/Sant Pere Més Alt 6, 1º ☎ 933 107 466, ⓦ pensio2000.com; Ⓜ Urquinaona; map p.648. As close to a traditional, family-style B&B as Barcelona gets – seven en-suite rooms (some overlook the Palau de la Música Catalana, across the street) in a welcoming mansion

10

10

apartment strewn with books, plants and pictures. A third person could easily share most rooms (€20 supplement). **€80**

LA RIBERA

★ **Chic & Basic Born** c/de la Princesa 50 ☎ 932 954 652, ⌨ chicandbasic.com; Ⓜ Jaume I; map p.648. Punchily boutique and in-your-face, from the open-plan, all-in-white decor to laugh-aloud conceits like adjustable mood-lighting, sashaying plastic curtains and mirrored walls. There are other Chic & Basic outlets in the Raval, one on c/Tallers (near Pl. Universitat) and the other off the bottom of the Ramblas, and some Barri Gòtic apartments too (details on the website). **€110**

Equity Point Gothic c/Vigatans 5, online bookings only ⌨ equity-point.com, hostel information ☎ 932 312 045; Ⓜ Jaume I; map p.648. Of the three Equity Point hostels, this is the most backpacker-orientated, which might or might not be a good thing, depending on your view, age and capacity for company. Dorms **€25**

★ **Hostal Nuevo Colón** Avgda. Marquès de l'Argentera 19, 1º ☎ 933 195 077, ⌨ hostalnuevocolon .com; Ⓜ Barceloneta; map p.648. Well-kept *pensión* sporting spacious rooms kitted out with directors' chairs and double glazing – you'll save around €20 if you forgo a private bathroom. Sunny front rooms, lounge and terrace all have side views to Parc de la Ciutadella. **€70**

Hotel Banys Orientals c/de l'Argenteria 37 ☎ 932 688 460, ⌨ hotelbanysorientals.com; Ⓜ Jaume I; map p.648. Funky boutique hotel with 43 minimalist rooms, plus some more spacious duplex suites (€130) in a nearby building. Hardwood floors, crisp white sheets, sharp marble bathrooms and urban-chic decor – not to mention bargain prices for this sort of style – make it a hugely popular choice. **€100**

BARCELONETA

Equity Point Sea Pl. del Mar 1–4, online bookings only ⌨ equity-point.com, hostel information ☎ 932 312 045; Ⓜ Barceloneta; map p.644. The budget beachside choice. Neat little en-suite bunk rooms sleep six or seven, while the attached café looks right out onto the boardwalk and palm trees. Dorms **€26**

★ **W Barcelona** Pl. de la Rosa dels Vents ☎ 932 952 800, ⌨ w-barcelona.com.com; Ⓜ Barceloneta; map p.644. Signature building on the Barceloneta seafront is the stupendously cool, wave-shaped *W Barcelona*. There's a hip, resort feel, with direct beach access, while open-plan designer rooms have fantastic views through floor-to-ceiling windows, and facilities are first rate, iPod docks to infinity pool. Dining in hotel restaurant *Bravo* is courtesy of creative Barcelona chef Carles Abellan. **€245**

PORT OLÍMPIC

Hotel Arts Barcelona c/Marina 19–21, Port Olímpic ☎ 932 211 000, ⌨ ritzcarlton.com/hotels/barcelona; Ⓜ Ciutadella-Vila Olímpica; map p.644. Thirty-three floors of five-star-plus designer luxury, with fabulous views of the port and sea. Service and standards are first-rate, and the rooms feature floor-to-ceiling windows and enormous marble bathrooms. Seafront gardens encompass an open-air pool and hot tub, and there's a 43rd-floor spa. **€385**

EIXAMPLE

★ **Barcelona Urbany** Avgda. Meridiana 97 ☎ 932 458 414, ⌨ barcelonaurbany.com; Ⓜ Clot; map p.644. Huge steel-and-glass 400-bed hostel that's on handy metro and airport train routes (it's an easy ride in to Plaça de Catalunya). The rooms are boxy en-suites with pull-down beds (sleeping 2 to 8) that are just as viable for couples on a budget as backpackers. Rates vary according to season, but go as low as €15 for dorms and €50 for rooms. Bar and terrace, plus free health club and pool entry in the same building. Dorms **€30**, private rooms **€84**

★ **BCN Fashion House** c/Bruc 13 ☎ 637 904 044, ⌨ bcnfashionhouse.com; Ⓜ Urquinaona; map p.670. Italian owners have added a touch of chic flair to what was formerly an *atelier* in Barcelona's "garment district", and the seven spacious, high-ceilinged rooms (some with veranda) are lightened with prints, sculptures and artefacts from their travels. **€82**

★ **Equity Point Centric** Pg. de Gràcia 33, online bookings only ⌨ equity-point.com, hostel information ☎ 932 312 045; Ⓜ Passeig de Gràcia; map p.670. Bills itself as "one of the most spectacular hostels in Europe" and it's hard to disagree, with around 450 beds spread across several storeys of a refurbished *modernista* building in a swish midtown location. Dorms sleep up to 12, while private rooms are also available (sleeping 2–4, low-season rates from €80), all with lockers and en-suite shower room, and many with balcony and views. Dorms **€22**, rooms **€110**

Hostal Girona c/Girona 24, 1º ☎ 932 650 259, ⌨ hostalgirona.com; Ⓜ Urquinaona; map p.670. Delightful, family-run *pensión* with a wide range of cosy, traditional rooms (not all en suite, from as low as €60), plus corridors laid with rugs, polished wooden doors, antique paintings and restored furniture throughout. **€90**

Hostal San Remo c/Ausias Marc 19, 2º ☎ 933 021 989, ⌨ hostalsanremo.com; Ⓜ Urquinaona; map p.670. As basic *pensiones* go, the doubles aren't a bad size for the money and the small tiled bathrooms are pretty good for this price range. You'll get more peace at the back – though the internal rooms aren't nearly as appealing as those with balconies. **€65**

Hotel Axel c/d'Aribau 33 ☎ 933 239 393, ⌨ axelhotels .com; Ⓜ Universitat; map p.670. The *Axel's* snazzy "heterofriendly" boutique stylings are a real hit with gay visitors. It's a hip but relaxed space with designer rooms (featuring complimentary beauty products), a bar and restaurant that are part of the local scene, plus fabulous terrace pool and "Skybar". **€170**

Hotel Omm c/Rosselló 265 ☎934 454 000, ⓦhotelomm.es; ⓜDiagonal; map p.670. The glam designer experience that is *Omm* means minimalist rooms, a studiously chic bar, Michelin-starred restaurant (closed Sun & Aug), plus terrace, pool and Spaciomm "relaxation centre", not to mention fearsomely handsome staff. €220

Mandarin Oriental Pg. de Gràcia 38–40 ☎931 518 888, ⓦmandarinoriental.com/Barcelona; ⓜPasseig de Gràcia; map p.670. The latest designer addition to Barcelona's most prestigious avenue fills the premises of a former bank building with a soaring white atrium and a serene selection of gorgeously light rooms. There's the obligatory superstar restaurant, *Moments*, while bar, spa, mimosa garden and rooftop "dipping pool" combine oriental tranquillity and Euro cool. €300

Residencia Australia Ronda Universitat 11, 4° ☎933 174 177, ⓦresidenciaustralia.com; ⓜUniversitat; map p.670. A very welcoming budget *pensión*, overseen by Thomas, fount of city knowledge, musician and cheery host. Three of the four rooms have basins and balconies, and share two nice bathrooms; the other is classed as a suite with private bathroom (€60–85, depending on season) and there are more similarly priced suites just down the street. €53

★ **Somnio Barcelona** c/Diputació 251 ☎932 725 308, ⓦsomniohostels.com; ⓜPasseig de Gràcia; map p.670. Simple but smart rooms with wood-block floors cater for singles, couples and friends (it's especially welcoming for women visitors), and there are two six-bed, single-sex dorms. You'll pay another €10 for an en-suite room, while there's more inexpensive shared budget accommodation at their new sister hostel in the same district. Dorms €26, rooms €78

★ **The5Rooms** c/Pau Claris 72, 2° ☎933 427 880, ⓦthefiverooms.com; ⓜUrquinaona; map p.670. The owner's impeccable taste and fashion background is evident in gorgeous contemporary-styled B&B rooms and apartments (from €175 for 2 people), where the feel is house party rather than hotel – breakfast is served whenever you like, and owner Jessica is happy to sit down and talk you through her favourite bars, restaurants and galleries. €145

GRÀCIA

Hostal HMB c/Bonavista 21 ☎933 682 013, ⓦhostalhmb.com; ⓜDiagonal; map p.678. Tucked away at the bottom of the neighbourhood is this chic little budget *pensión*, with a range of rooms including some family and friends "suites" (ie, bigger rooms with a sofa bed, from €90). Add €10 per night for a weekend stay. €60

EATING

You'll probably do most of your **eating** where you do most of your sightseeing. However, if you venture no farther than the Ramblas, or the streets around La Seu, you are not going to experience the best of the city's cuisine – in the main tourist areas, food and service can be indifferent and prices high. Instead, explore the backstreets of neighbourhoods like Sant Pere, La Ribera, El Raval and Poble Sec, where you'll find excellent restaurants, some little more than hole-in-the-wall taverns, others surprisingly funky and chic. Most of the big-ticket, destination-dining restaurants are found in the Eixample, while Gràcia is a pleasant place to spend the evening, with plenty of good mid-range restaurants. For fish and seafood, you're best off in the harbourside Barceloneta district or at the Port Olímpic.

Most cafés are open from 7 or 8am until midnight, or much later – so whether it's coffee first thing or a late-night nibble, you'll find somewhere to cater for you. Restaurants generally open 1 to 4pm and 8.30 to 11pm, though in tourist zones like the Ramblas and Port Olímpic, restaurants tend to stay open all day.

RAMBLAS

CAFÉS

Antiga Casa Figueras Ramblas 83 ☎933 016 027, ⓦescriba.es; ⓜLiceu; map p.648. Classy, historic *modernista*-designed pastry shop near the Boqueria market that many rate as the best bakery in Barcelona. Mon–Sat 9am–3pm & 5–8.30pm.

★ **Cafè de l'Òpera** Ramblas 74 ☎933 177 585,

WHAT'S COOKING IN BARCELONA?

The minimalist, food-as-chemistry approach, pioneered by Catalan super-chef Ferran Adrià (of *El Bulli* fame), has Barcelona in a vice-like grip. The best local chefs continue to reinterpret classic Catalan dishes in innovative ways, and while prices in these gastro-temples are high there's a trend towards more economic, bistro-style dining even by the hottest chefs. Current fad is the fusion of Mediterranean and Asian flavours – a so-called **"Mediterrasian" cuisine** – that combines local, market-fresh ingredients with more exotic tastes. It rears its head especially in the world of tapas, since although there are still plenty of traditional tapas bars (particularly in the Barri Gòtic, along c/Ample, c/de la Mercè, and their offshoots), there's also a real sense of adventure in new-wave places that are deadly serious about their food – you're as likely to get shrimp tempura or a yucca chip as a garlic mushroom in Barcelona these days.

10

@ cafeoperabcn.com; @ Liceu; map p.648. If you're going to pay through the nose for a Ramblas seat, it may as well be at this famous old café-bar opposite the opera house, with its sought-after pavement tables. Daily 8.30am–2.30am.

Café Zurich Pl. Catalunya 1 @ 933 179 153; @ Catalunya; map p.648. The most famous meet-and-greet café in town, right at the top of the Ramblas underneath El Triangle shopping centre. Sit inside if you don't want to be bothered by endless rounds of buskers and beggars. Mon–Fri 8am–11pm, Sat & Sun 10am–11pm (June–Sept open until 1am).

TAPAS BARS

★ **Bar Pinotxo** Mercat de la Boqueria, Ramblas 91 @ 933 171 731; @ Liceu; map p.648. The market's most renowned refuelling stop – just inside the main entrance on the right. Let the cheery staff steer you towards the tapas and daily specials (€5–15), anything from a slice of *tortilla* to fried baby squid. Mon–Sat 6am–5pm; closed Aug.

BARRI GÒTIC
CAFÉS

Bar del Pi Pl. Sant Josep Oriol 1 @ 933 022 123; @ Liceu; map p.648. Best known for its terrace tables on one of Barcelona's prettiest squares. Linger over drinks and sandwiches as the old town reveals its charms, especially during the weekend artists' market. Mon–Sat 9am–11pm, Sun 10am–10pm; closed 2 weeks in Jan, & Aug.

★ **Caj Chai** c/Sant Domènec del Call 12 @ 933 019 592, @ cajchai.com; map p.648. This refined backstreet boudoir offers a menu of painstakingly prepared teas, from Moroccan mint to organic Nepalese *oolong*. Mon 3–10pm, Tues–Sun 10.30am–10pm.

Dulcinea c/Petritxol 2 @ 932 311 756; @ Liceu; map p.648. One of the old town's age-old treats is to come here for a thick hot chocolate, slathered in cream. It's a bygone-era kind of place, with dickie-bow-wearing waiters patrolling the beamed and panelled room. Daily 9am–1pm & 5–9pm; closed Aug.

TAPAS BARS

★ **Bodega La Plata** c/de la Mercè 28 @ 933 151 009; @ Drassanes; map p.648. A classic taste of the old town, with a marble counter open to the street and dirt-cheap wine served straight from the barrel. For €5 or so you can get a couple of drinks and a dish of the speciality anchovies. Daily 10am–4pm & 8–11pm.

Taller de Tapas Pl. Sant Josep Oriol 9 @ 933 018 020, @ tallerdetapas.com; @ Liceu; map p.648. The fashionable "tapas workshop" sucks in tourists with its pretty location by the church of Santa María del Pi. The open kitchen turns out market-fresh tapas, with fish a speciality at dinner, from grilled langoustine to seared tuna (most tapas €4–12). Daily noon–midnight (Fri & Sat until 1am).

RESTAURANTS

Arc Café c/Carabassa 19 @ 933 025 204, @ arccafe .com; @ Drassanes; map p.648. Chilled-out bistro-bar where the kitchen is open all day, serving a seasonally changing menu (most mains around €10) of hearty soups, Mediterranean salads, spring rolls, pastas and Thai curries (with Thurs & Fri nights designated Thai food nights). Mon–Thurs noon–1am, Fri & Sat noon–2am.

★ **Café de l'Acadèmia** c/Lledó 1 @ 933 198 253; @ Jaume I; map p.648. Great for a date or a lazy lunch, with creative Catalan cooking served in a romantic stone-flagged restaurant or outside in the medieval square. Prices are pretty reasonable (mains €11–18) and it's always busy, so dinner reservations essential. Mon–Fri 1.30–4pm & 8.45–11.30pm; closed 2 weeks in Aug.

EL RAVAL
CAFÉS

★ **Federal** c/Parlament 39 @ 931 873 607, @ federalcafe.es; @ Sant Antoni; map p.665. Effortlessly cool café, squished into a corner townhouse with a great little roof-garden on top. Australian owners have imported their own funky vibe, so whether you're looking for a bacon butty, a glass of New Zealand *sav blanc* or a dandelion soy latte, you can guarantee that there's nowhere else quite like this in Barcelona. Tues–Thurs 8am–10pm, Fri & Sat 8am–1am, Sun 9am–5.30pm.

Granja M. Viader c/Xuclà 4–6 @ 933 183 486, @ granjaviader.cat; @ Liceu; map p.648. The oldest traditional *granja* (milk bar) in town has a pavement plaque outside for services to the city. Signature drink is their own invention "Cacaolat" (a popular chocolate drink), or try *mel i mató* (curd cheese and honey) or *llet Mallorquina* (fresh milk with cinnamon and lemon rind). Mon 5–8.30pm, Tues–Sat 9am–1.30pm & 5–8.30pm; closed 2 weeks in Aug.

★ **El Jardí** c/de l'Hospital 56 @ 933 291 550, @ eljardibarcelona.es; map p.648. The "garden bar", hidden in the elegant courtyard of the Gothic Hospital de la Santa Creu is a real away-from-the-bustle find – drinks, snacks, salads and sandwiches during the day, plus a decent lunch menu and a changing list of market-fresh tapas. Mon–Sat 8am–11pm.

TAPAS BARS

★ **Dos Palillos** c/Elisabets 9 @ 933 040 513, @ dospalillos.com; @ Catalunya; map p.648. Flag-waver for Asian fusion tapas is this hipster hangout, which offers a la carte *dim sum* in the front bar (steamed dumplings to grilled oysters and stir-fried prawns, mostly €5–7) and a back-room, counter-style Asian bar where tasting menus (€50 and €65, reservations required) wade their way through the highlights. Tues & Wed 7.30–11.30pm, Thurs–Sat 1.30–3.30pm & 7.30–11.30pm; closed 2 Weeks in Jan & 3 weeks in Aug.

RESTAURANTS

Bar Ra Pl. de la Garduña 3 📞615 959 872, 🌐ratown
.com; 🚇Liceu; map p.648. A hip little corner behind the
Boqueria market, with a groove-ridden music policy, a
funky feel and a sunny terrassa. The menu is eclectic to say
the least – veggie lasagne to tuna with wasabi and
avocado – but it's all good stuff. Around €25. Daily
9am–1am, closed Sun Nov–March.

★ **Biblioteca** c/Junta del Comerç 28 📞934 126 221,
🌐bibliotecarestaurant.com; 🚇Liceu; map p.648. A stylish
place for creative Barcelona cuisine, with an open kitchen
turning out fish dishes that might be cooked Japanese- or
Basque-style, robust lamb given the local treatment (with
parsnip and turnip), or the signature dish of venison pie served
with a zippy veg purée of the day (mains €13–19). Mon–Sat
8pm–midnight; closed 2 weeks in Aug.

Romesco c/de l'Arc de Sant Agustí 📞934 189 381;
🚇Liceu; map p.648. As long as you accept the limitations
(dining under strip-lights, gruff waiters) you can hardly go
wrong, as the most expensive thing on the menu in this
simple diner is a €9 grilled sirloin and most dishes go for
€6 or less. Mon–Sat 1–11.30pm; closed Aug.

SANT PERE

TAPAS BARS

★ **Mosquito** c/dels Carders 46 📞932 687 569,
🌐mosquitotapas.com; 🚇Jaume 1; map p.648. A funky
Asian tapas bar, festooned with hanging paper lanterns,
which pours artisan beers and offers an authentic, made-
to-order *dim sum* menu (dishes €3–5), from shrimp
dumplings to tofu rolls. Mon 7.30pm–12.30am, Tues–
Sun 1pm–12.30am (Fri & Sat until 2.30am).

RESTAURANTS

★ **El Atril** c/dels Carders 23 📞933 101 220,
🌐atrilbarcelona.com; 🚇Jaume 1; map p.648. Aussie-
owned bistro-bar with a popular summer terrassa – lunch
is always a steal, with tapas served at other times, and
dinner from 7pm, from a menu that ranges from *moules
frites* to Thai red curry (mains €10–15). Mon 6pm–
midnight, Tues–Sun noon–midnight.

Casa Mari y Rufo c/Freixures 11 📞933 197 302;
🚇Jaume 1; map p.648. A great place for no-frills market
cooking, with a busy family turning out quick-fried
sardines, grilled Catalan sausage, steak and chips and the
like – or ask what's good from the fish stalls that day. With
lunch for an unbeatable €12 and dinner around €30, the
locals know a good deal when they see one. Mon–Wed
1–4pm, Thurs–Sat 1–4pm & 8–11pm.

Comerç 24 c/Comerc 24 📞933 192 102, 🌐carlesabellan
.com; 🚇Jaume 1/Arc de Triomf; map p.648. Chef Carles
Abellan calls his cutting-edge cuisine "glocal" (ie, global +
local) and in the oh-so-cool interior you're presented with
tapas-style dishes, mixing flavours and textures with

seeming abandon but to calculated effect (such as *foie gras*
and truffle hamburger, shot glasses of frothy soup, and tuna
sashimi on pizza). Around €80 a head. Tues–Sat 1.30–
3.30pm & 8.30–11pm; closed 2 weeks in Aug.

LA RIBERA

TAPAS BARS

★ **Cal Pep** Pl. de les Olles 8 📞933 107 961, 🌐calpep
.com; 🚇Barceloneta; map p.648. You may have to queue
for this famous tapas bar (there are no reservations), and
prices are high for what's effectively a bar meal (up to €50 a
head) but it's definitely worth it for the likes of impeccably
fried shrimp, grilled sea bass, Catalan sausage and beans,
and baby squid and chickpeas. Mon 7.30–11.30pm,
Tues–Fri 1–3.45pm & 7.30–11.30pm, Sat 1.15–
3.45pm; closed Easter week & Aug.

El Xampanyet c/de Montcada 22 📞933 197 003;
🚇Jaume 1; map p.648. Traditional blue-tiled bar doing a
roaring trade in sparkling cava, cider and tapas *(anchovies are
the speciality, but there's also marinaded tuna, spicy mussels,
sun-dried tomatoes, sliced meats and cheese). Tues–Sat
noon–4pm & 6.30–11pm, Sun noon–4pm; closed Aug.

RESTAURANTS

★ **Casa Delfín** Pg. del Born 36 📞933 195 088;
🚇Jaume 1; map p.648. Bubbly, updated taverna, with a
sunny *terrassa* outside the old market and a long menu that
takes a loving look at traditional Catalan dishes, from
sausage and beans to chickpeas and squid, crispy artichokes
to roast mountain lamb. It's served tapas-style, with dishes
from €5–20. Daily noon–1am.

Senyor Parellada c/Argenteria 37 📞933 105 094,
🌐senyorparellada.com; 🚇Jaume 1; map p.648. An
utterly gorgeous renovation of an eighteenth-century
building is the mellow backdrop for genuine home-style
Catalan cuisine – cuttlefish and cod, stuffed cabbage rolls,
duck with figs. Most dishes cost between €8 and €15. Daily
1–3.45pm & 8.30–11.30pm.

BARCELONETA

TAPAS BARS

★ **Cova Fumada** c/Baluard 56 📞932 214 061;
🚇Barceloneta; map p.648. Behind brown wooden doors
on Barceloneta's market square (there's no sign), this
rough-and-ready tavern may not look like much but the
food's great – market-fresh tapas (€2–10), from griddled
prawns to the house speciality, the *bomba* (spicy potato-
meatball). Mon–Wed & Sat 9am–3pm, Thurs & Fri
9am–3pm & 6–8pm; closed Aug.

Jai-Ca c/Ginebra 13 📞932 683 265; 🚇Barceloneta;
map p.648. Always a winning choice for seafood tapas
(dishes up to €10), with bundles of razor clams, plump
anchovies, stuffed mussels and other platters piled high on
the bar. Daily 10am–11pm.

10

RESTAURANTS

Can Majo c/Almirall Aixada 23 ☎932 215 455, ⓦcanmajo.es; Ⓜ Barceloneta; map p.648. A lovely summer terrassa by the beach promenade, where you can tuck into wonderful rice dishes, *fideuà* (noodles with seafood), *suquet* (fish stew) or grilled fish – €40–50 a head. Tues–Sat 1–3.30pm & 8–11.30pm, Sun 1–3.30pm.

★ **Can Maño** c/Baluard 12 ☎933 193 082; Ⓜ Barceloneta; map p.648. There's rarely a tourist in sight in this old-fashioned diner, packed with noisy locals around formica tables. Expect fried or grilled fish, roughhouse wine and absolutely no frills, but it's an authentic experience, which should cost less than €15 a head. Mon–Fri 8–11am, 12.15–4pm & 8–11pm, Sat 8–11am & 12.15–4pm; closed Aug.

PORT OLÍMPIC
RESTAURANTS

Agua Pg. Marítim 30 ☎932 251 272, ⓦgrupotragaluz .com; Ⓜ Ciutadella-Vila Olímpica; map p.644. Much the nicest boardwalk restaurant on the beachfront strip, perfect for brunch, with a seasonal, contemporary Mediterranean menu – grills, *risotti*, pasta, salads and tapas (most dishes €9–23). Daily 1–3.45pm & 8–11.30pm, Fri & Sat until 4.30pm & 12.30am.

POBLE SEC
TAPAS BARS

★ **Quimet i Quimet** c/Poeta Cabanyes 25 ☎934 423 142; Ⓜ Paral.lel; map p.665. In Poble Sec's cosiest tapas bar, little plates of classy finger-food (mostly €3–10) are served reverently from the minuscule counter – things like roast onions, marinated mushrooms, stuffed cherry tomatoes and anchovy-wrapped olives. Tues–Sat noon–4pm & 7–11pm, Sun noon–4pm; closed Aug.

Tickets & 41° Avgda. Paral.lel 164; no phone, online reservations only ⓦticketsbar.es, ⓦ41grados.es; Ⓜ Poble Sec; map p.665. Swank tapas bar under the star-studded helm of pastry-chef supremo Albert Adrià and his *El Bulli*-famed brother Ferran Adrià. It's terrifically classy (dishes €5–20 each, expect to spend €70), but with only 100 covers a night, and online reservations up to three months in advance, you can't guarantee a table, though you might bag a seat at *41°* (or 41 Grados, ie 41 Degrees), the adjacent, sleek cocktail and oyster bar. Tues–Sat 7–11pm, Sun 1–3pm; *41°* Tues–Sat 6pm–2am (snacks until 11pm); closed 2 weeks in Aug.

RESTAURANTS

Bella Napoli c/Margarit 14 ☎934 425 056; Ⓜ Poble Sec; map p.665. The pizzas – the best in the city – come straight from the depths of a beehive-shaped oven, or there's a big range of pastas, *risotti* and veal *scaloppine*, with almost everything priced between €9 and €15. Tues 8.30pm–midnight, Wed–Sun 1.30–4.30pm & 8.30pm–midnight.

★ **La Tomaquera** c/Margarit 58, no phone; Ⓜ Poble Sec; map p.665. Chatter-filled tavern where the grilled chicken is sensational and the *entrecôtes* enormous (most mains €8–15). Locals limber up with an appetizer of pan-fried snails with *chorizo* and tomato. Tues–Sat 1.30–3.45pm & 8.30–10.45pm; closed Aug.

EIXAMPLE
CAFÉS

Fast Vínic c/de la Diputació 251 ☎934 873 241, ⓦfastvinic.com; Ⓜ Passeig de Gràcia; map p.670. Designer sandwich bar with an emphasis on top-of-the-range ingredients from sustainable sources (sandwiches mostly €5–10), plus a range of more than twenty Catalan wines, starting at pocket-money prices. Mon–Sat noon–midnight.

TAPAS BARS

★ **Tapas24** c/Diputació 269 ☎934 880 977, ⓦcarlesabellan.com; Ⓜ Passeig de Gràcia; map p.670. Carles Abellan, king of pared-down designer cuisine at his famed restaurant *Comerç 24*, offers a simpler tapas menu at this retro basement bar-diner, serving *patatas bravas*, Andalucian-style fried fish, meatballs, *chorizo* and fried eggs, fried squid and the like. Most tapas cost €4–16. Mon–Sat 9am–midnight.

RESTAURANTS

Casa Calvet c/de Casp 48 ☎934 124 012, ⓦcasacalvet .es; Ⓜ Catalunya/Urquinaona; map p.670. The wonderfully decorated townhouse that a young Antoni Gaudí built for a Catalan industrialist makes for a truly glam night out. It offers a seasonally changing modern Catalan menu, with mains around the €30 mark, lunch at €40 or tasting menus from €55 to €70. Mon–Sat 1–3.30pm & 8.30–11pm.

Cinc Sentits c/Aribau 58 ☎933 239 490, ⓦcincsentits .com; Ⓜ Universitat; map p.670. Contemporary Catalan cuisine that touches the "Five Senses" – six- and eight-course tasting menus (around €60 and €80, matching wines available) use rigorously sourced ingredients (wild fish, mountain lamb, seasonal vegetables, farmhouse cheeses) in elegant, pared-down dishes that are all about flavour. Tues–Sat 1.30–3pm & 8.30–10pm; closed 2 weeks in Aug.

★ **La Flauta** c/d'Aribau 23 ☎933 237 038; Ⓜ Universitat; map p.670. One of the city's best-value lunch menus sees diners queuing for tables early – get there before 2pm to avoid the rush. Meals are served tapas-style, day and night (dishes €4–10), based on seasonal market produce, wild mushrooms to locally landed fish. Mon–Sat 8am–1am; closed 3 weeks in Aug.

★ **Gaig** c/Aragó 214 ☎934 291 017, ⓦrestaurantgaig .com; Ⓜ Universitat; map p.670. Its towering reputation (and Michelin star) rests on innovative reinterpretations of traditional Catalan dishes, so a typical *arròs* (rice) dish

10

BARCELONA'S VEGETARIAN RESTAURANTS

Vegetarians will find themselves pleasantly surprised by the choice available in Barcelona if they've spent any time in other areas of Spain. The restaurants listed below are reliable places for a good veggie meal, but you'll also be able to do pretty well for yourself in tapas bars and modern Catalan brasseries and restaurants.

La Báscula c/Flassaders 30 ☎933 199 866; Ⓜ Jaume I; map p.648. An old chocolate factory in the backstreets has been given a hippy-chic makeover by a local co-operative and serves up veggie pastas, turnovers, couscous, quiches and salads (dishes around €8.50). Wed–Sat 1pm–midnight, Sun 1–8pm.

Biocenter c/Pintor Fortuny 25 ☎933 014 583, Ⓦ restaurantebiocenter.es; Ⓜ Liceu; map p.648. One of the longest-running strictly veggie places in town, with a popular fixed-price lunch menu (€10, weekends €12.50). For dinner, they dim the lights, add candles and sounds, and turn out a few more exotic dishes, from red veg curry to ginger tofu (mains around €12). Daily 1–5pm & 8–11.15pm.

Sesamo c/Sant Antoni Abat 52 ☎934 416 411; Ⓜ Sant Antoni; map p.648. Classy tapas place (bar at the front, restaurant tables at the back) that offers up a heavily vegetarian-orientated chalkboard menu of innovative dishes – think Catalan sushi of stuffed courgette rolls, slow-roast tomato tart, or a daily risotto and pasta dish, all in the range €7–15. Tues–Sun 7.30pm–2.30am; closed 3 weeks in Aug.

Venus Delicatessen c/Avinyó 25 ☎933 011 585; Ⓜ Liceu/Jaume I; map p.648. Not a deli, despite the name, but it's a handy place serving Mediterranean bistro cuisine throughout the day and night. Things like lasagne, couscous, moussaka and salads are mostly meat-free and cost around €7–10. Daily noon–midnight.

might combine *foie gras*, endive and citrus. But when starters can cost €35, and the *menú degustació* is over €100, you're talking about a true special-occasion place. Mon 9–11pm, Tues–Sat 1–3.30pm & 9–11pm; closed Easter week & 3 weeks in Aug.

GRÀCIA

TAPAS BARS

Bo Pl. Rius i Taulet 11 ☎933 683 529; Ⓦ borestaurant .com; Ⓜ Diagonal; map p.678. Gràcia´s nicest square also has its best selection of café-bars, including this contemporary *tasca* that serves tapas and stuffed sandwiches all day and night. You can easily rustle up a decent meal here, from mussels to Caesar salad (most dishes €5–8). Daily 10am–1am (Fri & Sat until 2am).

RESTAURANTS

★ **Flash, Flash** c/de la Granada del Penedès 25 ☎932 370 990; Ⓜ Diagonal; map p.678. A classic 1970s' survivor, *Flash* does *tortillas* (€6–9) served any time you

like, any way you like, from plain and simple to elaborately stuffed, with sweet ones for dessert. Chances are you'll love the original white leatherette booths and monotone "models-with-cameras" cutouts – very Austin Powers. Daily 1pm–1.30am, bar open 11am–2am.

Goliard c/Progrés ☎932 073 175; Ⓜ Diagonal; map p.678. Smart but casual *Goliard* offers a pared-down dining experience in a contemporary foodie bistro that looks like it should cost three times as much. Although the menu is divided into starters and mains (most things €7–15), there are smaller portions available if you want to mix and match. Mon–Fri 1–3.30pm & 9–11.30pm, Sat 9–11.30pm.

La Singular c/Francesc Giner 50 ☎932 375 098; Ⓜ Diagonal; map p.678. The tiniest of kitchens turns out refined Mediterranean food at moderate prices – say, aubergine and smoked fish salad, or chicken stuffed with dates and ham, with most dishes costing €9–15. Mon–Fri 1.30–4pm & 9pm–midnight (Fri until 1am), Sat 9pm–1am; closed 2 weeks in Aug/Sept.

DRINKING AND NIGHTLIFE

Whatever you're looking for from a night out, you'll find it somewhere in Barcelona – bohemian boozer, underground club, cocktail bar, summer dance palace, techno temple, Irish pub or designer bar, you name it. Best known of the city's **nightlife haunts** are its hip designer **bars**, while there's a stylish **club and music scene** that goes from strength to strength fuelled by a potent mix of resident and guest DJs, local bands and visiting superstars. Local listings magazines *Guía del Ocio* (Ⓦ guiadelociobcn.com) and *Time Out Barcelona* (Ⓦ timeout.cat) cover current openings, hours and club nights, and most bars, cafés and music stores carry flyers and free magazines containing news and reviews. For the Barcelona music scene, check out the websites Ⓦ atiza.com and Ⓦ barcelonarocks.com.

Opening hours and closing days Most bars stay open until 2am, or 3am at weekends, while clubs tend not to open much before midnight and stay open until 5am, or even later at weekends – fair enough, as they've often

10

barely got started by 3am. Unlike restaurants, bars and clubs generally stay open throughout August.

Admission charges Some clubs are free before a certain time, usually around midnight. Otherwise, expect to pay €10–20, though this usually includes your first drink (if there is free entry, don't be surprised to find that there's a minimum drinks' charge of anything up to €10). Tickets for gigs run from €20 to €50, depending on the act though there are cheaper gigs (€5–20) almost every night of the year at a variety of smaller clubs and bars.

BARS
RAMBLAS
Bosc de les Fades Ptge. de la Banca 5 ☎933 172 649, ⓦ museocerabcn.com; ⓜDrassanes; map p.648. Tucked away in an alley off the Ramblas, by the wax museum, the "Forest of the Fairies" is festooned with gnarled plaster tree trunks, fountains and stalactites. It's a cheesy location for a cocktail or two. Mon–Thurs & Sun 10am–1am, Fri & Sat 10am–2am.

BARRI GÒTIC
★ **L'Ascensor** c/Bellafila 3 ☎933 185 347; ⓜJaume I; map p.648. Sliding, antique wooden elevator doors announce the entrance to "The Lift", but it's no theme bar – just an easy-going local hangout, great for a late-night drink. Daily 7pm–3am.

Glaciar Pl. Reial 3 ☎933 021 163; ⓜLiceu; map p.648. At this traditional Barcelona meeting point the terrace seating is packed most sunny evenings and at weekends. Mon–Sat 4pm–2am (Fri & Sat until 3am), Sun 9am–2am.

★ **Milk** c/Gignàs 21 ☎932 680 922, ⓦmilkbarcelona .com; ⓜJaume I; map p.648. Irish-owned bar and bistro that's carved a real niche as a welcoming neighbourhood hangout. Get there early for the famously relaxed brunch (Thurs–Sun 10am–4pm), or there's dinner and cocktails every night to a funky soundtrack. Mon–Wed 6pm–3am, Thurs–Sun 10am–3am.

Schilling c/de Ferran 23 ☎933 176 787, ⓦcafeschilling .com; ⓜLiceu; map p.648. Something of a haven on this heavily touristed drag, *Schilling* has a certain European "grand-café" style, with its high ceilings, big windows and upmarket feel. Mon–Sat 10am–3am, Sun noon–3am.

EL RAVAL
Almirall c/de Joaquin Costa 33 ☎933 189 917; ⓜUniversitat; map p.648. Dating from 1860, Barcelona's oldest bar is a *modernista* design classic – check out the doors, counter, and stupendous glittering bar. Daily 6pm–2am (Fri & Sat until 3am).

Betty Ford's c/de Joaquin Costa 56 ☎933 041 368; ⓜUniversitat; map p.648. With a vibe somewhere between a student lounge and a beach bar, *Betty's* is a bouncy place full of bouncy young things, sipping colourful cocktails and

cold Australian beer. Daily 6pm–1am (Fri & Sat until 2am).

Marmalade c/de Riera Alta 4–6 ☎934 423 966, ⓦmarmaladebarcelona.com; ⓜSant Antoni; map p.648. A hugely glam facelift for the old Muebles Navarro furniture store goes for big, church-like spaces and a back-lit Art Deco bar that resembles a high altar. Cocktails, bistro meals and gourmet burgers pull in a relaxed dine-and-lounge crowd, and there's a popular weekend brunch too. Mon–Fri 7pm–3am, Sat & Sun 10am–3am.

★ **Marsella** c/de Sant Pau 65 ☎934 427 263; ⓜLiceu; map p.648. Authentic, atmospheric 1930s bar – named for the French port of Marseilles – that featured in Woody Allen's *Vicky Cristina Barcelona*, so expect a spirited mix of film fans, oddball locals and young dudes. Mon–Sat 10pm–3am; closed 2 weeks in Aug.

Muy Buenas c/del Carme 63 ☎934 425 053; ⓜLiceu; map p.648. Arguably the Raval's nicest traditional watering-hole, with a restored *modernista* interior and eager-to-please staff making things go with a swing. Tues–Sat 9am–3am.

★ **Resolis** c/Riera Baixa 22 ☎934 412 948; ⓜSant Antoni; map p.648. A cool hangout with decent tapas, where punters spill out of the door on to "secondhand clothes street" and a good time is had by all. Mon–Wed 1pm–1am, Thurs–Sat 1pm–2.30am.

SANT PERE
★ **Casa Paco** c/d'Allada Vermell 10 ☎935 073 719; ⓜJaume I; map p.648. The *barri's* signature bar is this cool music joint that's a hit on the weekend DJ scene – the tagline "not a disco, just a bar with good music" says it all. Daily 9am–2am (Fri & Sat until 3am), Oct to March opens at 6pm.

LA RIBERA
Espai Barroc c/de Montcada 20 ☎933 100 673; ⓜJaume I; map p.648. Every evening the doors are thrown open at the Palau Dalmases for drinks and cocktails in a remodelled medieval mansion known as the *Espai Barroc*, or "Baroque Space". Come on Thursday and you'll catch singers belting out arias as you sip fine wines under the chandeliers (recital at 11pm, €20, first drink included). Tues–Sat 8pm–2am, Sun 6–10pm.

★ **La Fianna** c/Banys Vells 19 ☎933 151 810, ⓦlafianna.com; ⓜJaume I; map p.648. Flickering candelabras, parchment lampshades, rough plaster walls and deep colours set the Gothic mood in this stylish lounge-bar that's "putting the beat in the Born". Mon–Wed & Sun 6pm–1.30am, Thurs–Sat 6pm–2.30am.

La Vinya del Senyor Pl. Santa María 5 ☎933 103 379; ⓜJaume I; map p.648. A great wine bar with front-row seats onto the lovely church of Santa María del Mar. The wine list is really good and there's classy tapas available. Tues–Thurs noon–1am, Fri & Sat noon–2am, Sun noon–midnight.

PORT VELL

★ **Can Paixano** c/Reina Cristina 7 ☎933 100 839, ⓦcanpaixano.com; ⓜBarceloneta; map p.648. A must on everyone's itinerary is this crowded backstreet joint where the drink of choice – all right, the only drink – is cava (Catalan champagne). Don't go thinking sophistication – the drinks might come in traditional champagne saucers (the sort of thing Dean Martin used to stack in a pyramid and then pour wine over), but this is a counter-only joint where there's fizz, tapas and tapas-in-sandwiches and that's your lot. And who could want more? Mon–Sat 9am–10.30pm; closed 1 week in Feb & 2 weeks in Aug.

Luz de Gas Moll de Diposit, in front of Palau de Mar ☎934 842 326, ⓦluzdegas.com; ⓜBarceloneta; map p.648. Sip a chilled drink on the polished deck of the moored boat, and soak up some great marina and harbour views. It's especially nice at dusk as the city lights begin to twinkle. March–Oct daily noon–3am.

POBLE SEC

★ **Bar Seco** Pg. Montjuïc 74 ☎933 296 374; ⓜParal.lel; map p.665. The "Dry Bar" is a local hit, with its mellow vibe, freshly squeezed juices, Free Trade drinks and artisan beers. Mon 9am–8pm, Tues–Thurs 9am–1am (Nov–April Tues & Wed closes at 8pm), Fri 9am–2am, Sat 10am–2am, Sun 10am–1am.

Xix Bar c/Rocafort 19 ☎934 234 314, ⓦxixbar.com; ⓜPoble Sec; map p.665. "Chicks" is an old *granja* (milk bar) turned candlelit, but completely unstuffy, cocktail bar. Gin's the big drink here (they claim over 100 varieties), and they even have their own specialist gin shop on site. Mon–Sat 5pm–2.30am (Fri & Sat until 3am).

EIXAMPLE

Belchica c/Villarroel 60 ☎934 511 355, ⓦbelchica.es; ⓜUrgell; map p.670. Barcelona's first Belgian beer bar guarantees a range of decent brews (including hard-to-find Trappist ales). It's also a muso's joint, playing electronica, new jazz, lounge, reggae and other left-field sounds. Mon–Fri 6pm–3am, Sat 7pm–3am.

Dry Martini c/Aribau 166 ☎932 175 072, ⓦdrymartinibcn.com; ⓜDiagonal; map p.670. White-jacketed bartenders, dark wood and brass fittings, a self-satisfied air – it could only be the city's legendary uptown cocktail bar. Best drink to order? The clue's in the bar name. Mon–Fri 1pm–2.30am (open 6.30pm in Aug), Sat & Sun 6.30pm–3am.

★ **Velódromo** c/Muntaner 213 ☎934 306 022; ⓜHospital Clinic; map p.670. A glam Art Deco gem, with a lofty, Parisian feel, a swooping staircase and a gleaming bar. It's ideal for swish drinks and cocktails, though with fancy breakfasts, brunch and a tapas-and-bistro menu it's also made for early starts and later dinners. Daily 6am–2.30am.

GRÀCIA

Cafè del Sol Pl. del Sol 16 ☎934 155 663; ⓜFontana; map p.678. The grandaddy of the Plaça del Sol scene sees action day and night. On summer evenings, when the square is packed, there's not an outdoor table to be had. Daily 1pm–2.30am.

★ **Canigó** Pl. de la Revolució 10, no phone; ⓜFontana; map p.678. Family-run neighbourhood bar now entering its third generation. It's not much to look at, but the drinks are cheap and it's a real Gràcia institution, packed out at weekends with a young, hip and largely local crowd. Tues–Sun 8pm–2am.

★ **Vinilo** c/Matilde 2 ☎626 464 759; ⓜDiagonal; map p.678. Wear a beret, are surgically attached to your ipod and drool over *Blade Runner*, Jeff Buckley and Band of Horses? This hipster music joint is just for you. Daily 7pm–2am (Fri & Sat until 3am).

Virreina Pl. de la Virreina 1 ☎932 379 880, ⓦvirreinabar.com; ⓜFontana; map p.678. On one of the neighbourhood's prettiest squares, with a very popular summer terrassa. It's one of those places where you drop by for a quick drink and find yourself staying for hours. Daily 10am–1am (Fri & Sat until 2am).

LES CORTS, PEDRALBES AND SARRIÀ-SANT GERVASI

Gimlet c/Santaló 46 ☎932 015 306; FGC Muntaner; map p.644. Especially popular in summertime, when the street-side tables offer a great vantage-point for watching the party unfold. There are also two or three other late-opening bars on the same stretch. Daily 7.30pm–3am.

CLUBS AND LIVE MUSIC

BARRI GÒTIC

Jamboree Pl. Reial 17 ☎933 191 789, ⓦmasimas.com; ⓜLiceu; map p.648. Nightly jazz gigs (from €10) pull in the crowds, while the wild Monday-night WTF jazz, funk and hip-hop jam session (from 9pm, €5) is a city fixture. Stay on for the club, which kicks in after midnight (entry €10) and you get funky sounds until the small hours. Gigs daily at 9pm & 11pm, club daily midnight–5am.

Karma Pl. Reial 10 ☎933 025 680, ⓦkarmadisco.com; ⓜLiceu; map p.648. Old-school studenty basement place spinning indie, Britpop and US college, while a lively crowd gathers at the square-side bar and terrassa. Club admission around €10. Tues–Sun midnight–5am.

La Macarena c/Nou de Sant Francesc 5; no phone; ⓦmacarenaclub.com; ⓜDrassanes; map p.648. Once a place where flamenco tunes were offered up to La Macarena, the Virgin of Seville – now a heaving temple to all things electro. Entry free until around 1am, then from €5. Daily midnight–4.30am (Fri & Sat until 5am).

★ **Sidecar** Pl. Reial 7 ☎933 021 586, ⓦsidecarfactoryclub.com; ⓜLiceu; map p.648. The

10

THE BEAT FROM THE STREET

The Barcelona sound – *mestiza* – is a cross-cultural musical fusion whose heartland is the immigrant melting-pot of the Raval. The local postcode – **08001** – lends a name to the sound's hippest flagbearers, while also typically "Raval" is the collective called **Cheb Balowski**, an Algerian-Catalan fusion band. The biggest star on the scene is the Parisian-born, Barcelona-resident **Manu Chao**, whose infectious, multi-million-selling album *Clandestino* (1998) kick-started the whole genre. He's widely known abroad, and influenced many Barcelona bands, including the world music festival favourites **Ojos de Brujo** (Eyes of the Wizard), who present a fusion reinvention of flamenco and Catalan rumba. Other hot sounds come from the Latin American dub and reggae band **GoLem System**, and the fusion-freestyle merchants **LA Kinky Beat**.

hippest concert space in the old town has nightly gigs and DJs that champion rock, indie, roots, electronica and fusion acts. Entry €7–10, though some gigs up to €20. Tues–Sun 8pm–5am, gigs usually at 10.30pm, DJs at 12.30am.

★ **Tarantos** Pl. Reial 17, Barri Gòtic ☎ 933 191 789, ⓦ masimas.com; ⓜ Liceu; map p.648. Some purists are sniffy about the experience, but for a cheap flamenco taster you can't beat this small bar in front of a stage where young performers appear nightly at 8.30pm, 9.30pm & 10.30pm (plus extra nightly session in July & Aug). Entry €7. It's the sister club to jazz/dance club *Jamboree*, at the same address.

EL RAVAL

★ **Jazz Sí Club** c/Requesens 2 ☎ 933 290 020, ⓦ tallerdemusics.com; ⓜ Sant Antoni; map p.648. A great place for inexpensive (€5–8) gigs. Every night from around 8.30 or 9pm there's something different, from exuberant rock, blues, jazz and jam sessions to the popular weekly Cuban (Thursday) and flamenco (Friday) nights. Daily 8–11.30pm.

★ **Moog** c/Arc del Teatre 3 ☎ 933 017 282, ⓦ masimas.com; ⓜ Drassanes; map p.648. One of the most influential clubs around for electronic sounds, playing techno, electro, drum'n'bass and trance to a cool but up-for-it crowd. Admission €10. Daily midnight–5am.

POBLE NOU

Sala Razzmatazz c/Pamplona 88 ☎ 933 208 200, ⓦ salarazzmatazz.com; ⓜ Bogatell; map p.644. *Razzmatazz* hosts the biggest in-town rock gigs, while at weekends the former warehouse turns into "five clubs in one", spinning indie, rock, pop, techno, electro, retro and more in variously named music bars like "The Loft", "Pop Bar" or "Lolita". Admission €15, gets you entrance to all the bars. Fri & Sat 1–6am.

MONTJUÏC

El Tablao de Carmen Avgda. Francesc Ferrer i Guàrdia, Poble Espanyol, Montjuïc ☎ 933 256 895, ⓦ tablaodecarmen.com; ⓜ Espanya; map p.665. The long-standing flamenco club in the Poble Espanyol at least

looks the real deal, sited in a replica Andalucian street. From €35 for the show and a drink, rising to €70 for the show plus dinner. Advance reservations essential. Tues–Sun, shows at 7.30pm & 10pm.

La Terrrazza Avgda. Francesc Ferrer i Guàrdia, Poble Espanyol ☎ 932 724 980, ⓦ laterrrazza.com; ⓜ Espanya; map p.665. Open-air summer club that's *the* place to be in Barcelona. Nonstop dance, house and techno, though don't get there until at least 3am, and be prepared for the style police. May–Oct Thurs–Sat midnight–6am.

POBLE SEC

★ **Maumau** c/Fontrodona 33 ☎ 934 418 015, ⓦ maumaunderground.com; ⓜ Paral.lel; map p.665. A great underground lounge-club, cultural centre and chill-out space with nightly film and video projections, exhibitions, and a roster of guest DJs playing deep, soulful grooves. Strictly speaking it's a private club, but they tend to let foreign visitors in for free. Thurs–Sat 11pm–2.30am.

Sala Apolo c/Nou de la Rambla 113 ☎ 934 414 001, ⓦ sala-apolo.com; ⓜ Paral.lel; map p.665. Old-time ballroom turned hip concert venue with gigs on two stages (local acts to big names) and an eclectic series of club nights with names to reckon with (Nasty Mondays, Crappy Tuesdays etc). Gigs €10–35, club nights €10–15. Daily midnight–5am.

GRÀCIA

★ **Heliogabal** c/Ramon i Cajal 80 ⓦ heliogabal.com; ⓜ Joanic; map p.678. A cool, twenty-something crowd flocks here for the live poetry and music – expect something different every night (Catalan versifying, jazz jam sessions and earnest singer-songwriters), starting at 10pm. Admission €3–10. Tues–Sun 9pm–2am (Fri & Sat until 3am).

Otto Zutz c/de Lincoln 15 ☎ 932 380 722, ⓦ ottozutz.com; FGC Gràcia; map p.678. It first opened in 1985 and has since lost some of its glam cachet, but this three-storey former textile factory still has a shed-load of pretensions. Admission €15. Wed–Sat midnight–6am.

LES CORTS, PEDRALBES AND SARRIÀ-SANT GERVASI

★ **Bikini** Avgda. Diagonal 547 ☎ 933 220 800, ⓦ bikinibcn.com; Ⓜ Les Corts/María Cristina; map p.644. This traditional landmark of Barcelona nightlife offers a regular diet of great indie, rock, roots and world gigs, followed by club sounds. Admission €15–25, though some gigs up to €40. Wed–Sun midnight–5am; closed Aug.

Universal c/Marià Cubí 182 ☎ 934 146 362, ⓦ universalbcn.com; FGC Muntaner; map p.644. A classic designer music bar and dance club that's been at the cutting edge of Barcelona style since 1985 – and there are still queues. Admission charged weekends, from €10. Mon–Thurs 11pm–3.30am, Fri & Sat 11pm–5am.

ARTS AND CULTURE

10

As you would expect from a city of its size, Barcelona has a busy entertainment calendar – throughout the year there'll be something worth catching, whether it's a contemporary dance performance, cabaret show or night at the opera. Classical and contemporary music, in particular, gets an airing in some stunning auditoriums, while the city boasts a long tradition of street and performance art, right down to the human statues plying their trade on the Ramblas. A useful first stop for tickets and information is the **Palau de la Virreina**, Ramblas 99 (daily 10am–8.30pm; ☎ 933 161 000; Ⓜ Liceu). **ServiCaixa** (☎ 902 332 211, ⓦ servicaixa.com) and **TelEntrada** (☎ 902 101 212, ⓦ telentrada.com) are the main advance booking agencies.

The city council's Institute of Culture website, ⓦ **bcn.cat/cultura**, covers every aspect of art and culture in the city. Otherwise, the best **listings magazines** are the weekly *Guía del Ocio* (ⓦ guiadelociobcn.com) and *Time Out Barcelona* (ⓦ timeout.cat), online or from any newspaper stand.

GAY AND LESBIAN BARCELONA

There's a vibrant local **gay and lesbian** crowd in Barcelona, not to mention the lure of nearby Sitges (see p.772), mainland Spain's biggest gay resort. There's a particular concentration of bars, restaurants and clubs in the so-called **Gaixample**, the "Gay Eixample", an area of a few square blocks just northwest of the main university in the Eixample. The biggest event of the year is Carnival in Sitges, while the main city bash is Barcelona's annual LGBT **Pride** festival (ⓦ pridebarcelona.org), which has events running over ten days each June, from street parades to Tibidabo fun-fair parties.

There's a **lesbian and gay city telephone hotline** on ☎ 900 601 601 (daily 6–10pm). Aside from the weekly bar and club listings in *Guía del Ocio* and *Time Out Barcelona*, there's also a good free **magazine** called *Nois* (ⓦ www.revistanois.com), which carries an up-to-date review of the scene. Single best English-language website is the excellent 60by80 (ⓦ 60by80.com/Barcelona), which has its finger on the pulse of all things hot, from shopping to partying.

GAY BARS AND CLUBS

Aire c/de Valencia 236, Eixample ☎ 934 515 812, ⓦ arenadisco.com; Ⓜ Passeig de Gràcia; map p.670. The hottest, most stylish lesbian bar in town is a relaxed place for a drink and a dance to pop, house and retro sounds. Thurs–Sat 11pm–3am, July & Aug also Tues & Wed.

Arena Madre c/de Balmes 32, Eixample; Classic c/de la Diputació 233; VIP Grand Vía de les Corts Catalanes 593; Dandy Grand Vía de les Corts Catalanes 593; ☎ 934 878 342, ⓦ arenadisco.com; Ⓜ Passeig de Gràcia; map p.670. The *Madre* "mother" club sits at the helm of the Arena empire, all within a city block (pay for one, get in to all) – frenetic house at *Arena Madre*, high disco antics at *Arena Classic*, more of the same plus dance, R&B, pop and rock at the more mixed *Arena VIP*, and vintage chart hits at *Arena Dandy*. Fri & Sat 12.30–6am, Madre daily till 5.30am.

Dietrich c/Consell de Cent 255, Eixample ☎ 934 517 707, Ⓜ Universitat; map p.670. Well-known music bar and "teatro-café" – *tranquilo* during the week, but ever more hedonistic as the weekend wears on, with drag shows, acrobats and dancers punctuating the DJ sets. Daily 10pm–2.30am (Fri & Sat until 3am).

Metro c/Sepúlveda 158, Eixample ☎ 933 235 227, ⓦ metrodiscobcn.com; Ⓜ Universitat; map p.670. A gay institution in Barcelona, with extremely crowded club nights at weekends, playing current dance, techno and retro disco. Daily midnight–5am (Fri & Sat until 6am).

Punto BCN c/Muntaner 63–65, Eixample ☎ 934 536 123, ⓦ arenadisco.com; Ⓜ Universitat; map p.670. A Gaixample classic that attracts a lively crowd for drinks, chat and music. Wednesday happy hour is a blast, while Friday night is party night. Daily 6pm–2.30am.

10

CLASSICAL MUSIC AND OPERA

Most of Barcelona's classical-music concerts take place in the extravagantly decorated Palau de la Música Catalana or at the purpose-built, contemporary L'Auditori, while opera is performed at its traditional home, the Gran Teatre del Liceu on the Ramblas. Notable **festivals** include the annual contemporary music festival known as Nous Sons ("New Sounds", March–April), the Festival de Música Antiga (May) and the scores of free concerts held every year on June 21, the so-called Festa de la Música. There are also free classical concerts in Barcelona's parks each July.

★ **Ateneu Barcelonès** c/Canuda 6, Barri Gòtic ☎ 933 426 121, ⓦ ateneubcn.org, concert information ☎ 933 191 789; ⓦ masimas.com; ⓜ Catalunya. There's an excellent chamber music programme at the 150-year-old Ateneu cultural association, with cheap 30-minute performances on Friday, Saturday and Sundays at 6pm, 7pm & 8pm; entry €8.

L'Auditori c/Lepant 150, Glòries ☎ 932 479 300, ⓦ auditori.cat; ⓜ Marina/Glòries. The city's main concert hall is home to the Orquestra Simfònica de Barcelona i Nacional de Catalunya (OBC), whose weekend concert season runs Sept–May. Also other orchestral and chamber works, jazz and world gigs, and music for children and families.

Gran Teatre del Liceu Ramblas 51–59 ☎ 934 859 900; box office c/de Sant Pau 1 ☎ 934 859 913, ⓦ liceubarcelona.com; ⓜ Liceu. Hosts a wide-ranging programme of opera and dance productions, plus other concerts and recitals. The season runs from Sept to June – note that sales for the next season go on general sale in mid-July. Box office Mon–Fri 1.30–8pm, Sat & Sun 1hr before performance.

★ **Palau de la Música Catalana** c/Palau de la Música 4–6, off c/Sant Pere Més Alt, Sant Pere ☎ 932 957 200 or 902 442 882, ⓦ palaumusica.org; ⓜ Urquinaona. Home to the Orfeó Català choral group, and venue for concerts by the Orquestra Ciutat de Barcelona among others, though over a season (Sept–June) you can catch anything, from *sardanes* to pop concerts.

DANCE

Barcelona is very much a **contemporary dance** city, with regular performances at theatre venues across the city. Meanwhile, the **Dies de Dansa** (Days of Dance) festival in July offers up brief (10- to 20-minute) contemporary dance performances in courtyards at places like MACBA, CCCB, CaixaForum and the Miró museum.

Mercat de les Flors c/de Lleida 59, Montjuïc ☎ 934 261 875, ⓦ mercatflors.cat; ⓜ Poble Sec. The city's old flower market serves as the "national centre for movement arts", with dance the central focus of its varied programme – from Asian performance art to European contemporary dance.

FILM

At most of the larger cinemas and multiplexes films are usually shown dubbed into Spanish or Catalan, though several cinemas do screen mostly **original-language** ("V.O.") foreign films. Tickets cost around €8, and most cinemas have one night (usually Mon or Wed) when entry is **discounted**, usually to around €6. Many cinemas also feature **late-night** screenings (*madrugadas*) on Friday and Saturday nights, which begin at 12.30am or 1am.

Cinema Maldà c/del Pi 5, Barri Gòtic ☎ 933 019 350, ⓦ cinemamalda.net; ⓜ Liceu. Hidden away in a little shopping centre, just up from Plaça del Pi, the Maldà is a great place for independent movies and festival winners, all in V.O.

FilmoTeca Avgda. de Sarrià 33, Eixample ☎ 934 107 590, ⓦ gencat.cat/cultura/iciC/filmoteca; ⓜ Hospital Clínic. Run by the Catalan goverment, the FilmoTeca shows three or four different films (often foreign-language, and usually in V.O.) every day – themed programming and

---

CELEBRATING CATALAN-STYLE

Catalunya's national folk dance, the **sardana**, is danced every week in front of La Seu, in Plaça de la Seu (every Sunday at noon, plus every Saturday at 6pm from Easter until the end of November). Mocked in the rest of Spain, the Catalans claim theirs is a very democratic dance. Participants (there's no limit on numbers) all hold hands in a circle, each puts something in the middle as a sign of community and sharing, and since it is not overly energetic (hence the jibes), old and young can join in equally.

The main event in a **traditional Catalan festival** is usually a parade, either promenading behind a revered holy image (as on saints' days or at Easter) or a more celebratory costumed affair that's the centrepiece of a neighbourhood festival. At the main Eulàlia (Feb), Gràcia (Aug) and Mercè (Sept) festivals, and others, you'll encounter parades of *gegants*, five-metre-high giants with papier-mâché heads based on historical or traditional figures. Also typically Catalan is the **correfoc** ("fire-running"), where brigades of drummers, dragons and devils with spark-shooting flares fitted to pitchforks cavort in the streets. Perhaps most peculiar of all are the **castellers**, the human tower-builders who draw crowds at every traditional festival, piling person upon person, feet on shoulders, to see who can construct the highest, most aesthetically pleasing tower (ten human storeys is the record).

retrospectives are its stock-in-trade. Tickets are just €3 per film, or there's a €40 pass allowing entry to twenty films.
Sala Montjuïc Castell de Montjuïc ☎ 933 023 553, ⓦ salamontjuic.org, ⓦ servicaixa.com; cable car (Telefèric de Montjuïc) or cinema bus (normal tickets and passes valid) from Pl. d'Espanya (Ⓜ Espanya), departures from 8.30pm, returns when film finishes. Every July there's a giant-screen open-air cinema at Montjuïc castle (Mon, Wed & Fri night; live music from 9pm, films at 10.15pm, tickets €5) – bring a picnic. Screenings are in the original language, with Spanish subtitles.
Verdi c/Verdi 32, and **Verdi Park** c/Torrijos 49, Gràcia ☎ 932 387 990, ⓦ cines-verdi.com; Ⓜ Fontana; map p.678. Sister cinemas in adjacent streets showing independent, art-house and V.O. movies.

THEATRE AND CABARET
The Teatre Nacional de Catalunya (Catalan National Theatre) was conceived as a venue to promote Catalan productions, and features a programme of translated classics (such as Shakespeare in Catalan), original works and productions by guest companies. The other big local theatrical project is the Ciutat del Teatre (Theatre City) on Montjuïc, which incorporates the progressive Teatre Lliure and the Insitut del Teatre theatre and dance school. Some theatres draw on the city's strong cabaret tradition – more music-hall entertainment than stand-up comedy, and thus more accessible to non-Catalan/Spanish speakers. For last-minute tickets visit the Palau de la Virreina (Ramblas 99; Mon–Sat 10am–8.30pm), which offers same-day **half-price tickets** from three hours before the show.

L'Antic Teatre c/Verdaguer i Callis 12, Sant Pere ☎ 933 152 354, ⓦ lanticteatre.com; Ⓜ Urquinaona. Independent theatre with a wildly original programme of events, many free, from video shows to offbeat cabaret performances. In the end though, the best bit may just be the summer garden bar (open daily 4–11pm).
★ **Cafè Teatre Llantiol** c/Riereta 7, El Raval ☎ 933 299 009, ⓦ llantiol.com; Ⓜ Sant Antoni. Idiosyncratic cabaret café-theatre offering a mix of mime, song, clowning, magic and dance. Shows (€10–15) normally at 9pm & 11pm (6pm & 9pm on Sundays), with an additional late-night Saturday special. Closed Mon.
El Molino c/Vila i Vilà 99, Avgda. Paral.lel, Poble Sec ☎ 932 055 111, ⓦ elmolinobcn.com; Ⓜ Paral.lel. One of Barcelona's most famous old cabaret theatres – the self-styled "Little Moulin Rouge" – has a classy new look for its traditional burlesque and music stage shows. Performances daily from Wednesday to Sunday (show and drink from €40, show plus dinner from €80), plus Monday tango and Tuesday flamenco nights (varied prices).
Teatre Lliure Pl. Margarida Xirgu, Montjuïc ☎ 932 892 770, ⓦ teatrelliure.cat; Ⓜ Poble Sec. The "Free Theatre" performs the work of contemporary Catalan and Spanish playwrights, as well as re-workings of the classics, from Shakespeare to David Mamet (some productions have English subtitles).
Teatre Nacional de Catalunya (TNC) Pl. de les Arts 1, Glòries ☎ 933 065 700, ⓦ tnc.cat; Ⓜ Glòries. Features major productions by Catalan, Spanish and European companies, as well as smaller-scale plays, experimental works and dance productions.

SHOPPING

While not on a par with Paris or the world's other style capitals, Barcelona still leads the way in Spain when it comes to **shopping**. It's the country's fashion and publishing capital, and there's a long tradition of innovative *disseny* (design), from clothes and accessories to crafts and household goods. The annual sales (*rebaixes*; *rebajas* in Castilian) follow the main fashion seasons – mid-January until the end of February, and throughout July and August.

ANTIQUES, ARTS, CRAFTS AND GIFTS
The best area for antiques browsing is around c/de Palla, between La Seu and Plaça del Pí, combined with the antique market on Thursdays in front of La Seu. The **Tallers Oberts**, or Open Workshops (ⓦ tallersoberts.net), are usually held over the last two weekends of May, when there are studio visits, exhibitions and other events.
Almacenes del Pilar c/Boqueria 43, Barri Gòtic ☎ 933 177 984, ⓦ almacenesdelpilar.com; Ⓜ Liceu; map p.648. A world of frills, lace, cloth and materials used in the making of Spain's traditional regional costumes – pick up a decorated fan for just a few euros. Mon–Sat 10am–2pm & 4.30–8pm; closed Aug.
★ **Almacen Marabi** c/Flassaders 30, La Ribera; no phone, ⓦ almacenmarabi.blogspot.com; Ⓜ Jaume I; map p.648. Mariela Marabi makes handmade felt finger

dolls, mobiles, puppets and animals of extraordinary invention. Her eye-popping workshop also has limited-edition pieces by other selected artists and designers. Tues–Sat noon–2.30pm & 5–8.30pm.
L'Arca del Avia c/Banys Nous 20, Barri Gòtic ☎ 933 021 598, ⓦ larcadelavia.com; Ⓜ Liceu; map p.648. Catalan brides used to fill up their nuptial trunk (*arca*) with embroidered bed linen and lace, and this shop is a treasure-trove of vintage and antique textiles. Mon–Fri 10am–2pm & 5–8pm, Sat 10am–2pm; closed Aug.
Artesanía Catalunya c/Banys Nous 11, Barri Gòtic ☎ 934 674 660, ⓦ artesania-catalunya.com; Ⓜ Liceu; map p.648. Changing exhibitions in the showroom of the local government's arts and crafts promotion board, from contemporary basketwork to colourful glassware. Mon–Sat 10am–8pm, Sun 10am–2pm.

10

Cereria Subirà Bxda. Llibreteria 7, Barri Gòtic ☎ 933 152 606, Ⓜ Jaume I; map p.648. Barcelona's oldest shop (since 1760) has a beautiful interior, selling hand-crafted candles. Mon–Fri 9am–1.30pm & 4–7.30pm, Sat 9am–1.30pm.

★ **Espai Drap Art** c/Groc 1, Barri Gòtic ☎ 932 684 889, Ⓦ drapart.org; Ⓜ Jaume I; map p.648. The Drap-Art creative recycling organization has a shop and exhibition space for artists to show their wildly inventive wares, from trash-bangles to tin bags. Tues–Fri 11am–2pm & 5–8pm, Sat 6–9pm.

★ **Fantastik** c/Joaquin Costa 62, El Raval ☎ 933 013 068, Ⓦ fantastik.es; Ⓜ Universitat; map p.648. You'll never know how you lived without such beguiling gifts, whether it's Chinese robots, African baskets, Russian domino sets or Vietnamese kitchen scales. Mon–Thurs 11am–2pm & 4–9pm, Fri & Sat 11am–9pm.

BOOKS

You'll find English-language **books**, newspapers and magazines at the stalls along the Ramblas.

Altaïr Gran Vía de les Corts Catalanes 616, Eixample ☎ 933 427 171, Ⓦ altair.es; Ⓜ Universitat; map p.670. Europe's biggest travel superstore has a massive selection of travel books, guides, maps and world music, plus a programme of travel-related talks and exhibitions. Mon–Sat 10am–8.30pm.

★ **La Central del Raval** c/Elisabets 6, El Raval ☎ 902 884 990, Ⓦ lacentral.com; Ⓜ Catalunya; map p.648. Occupying a unique space in the former Misericordia chapel, La Central is a fantastically stocked arts and humanities treasure-trove, with books piled high in every nook and cranny. Mon–Fri 9.30am–9pm, Sat 10am–9pm.

Hibernian Books c/Montseny 17, Gràcia ☎ 932 174 796, Ⓦ hibernian-books.com; Ⓜ Fontana; map p.678. Barcelona's best secondhand English bookstore has around 40,000 titles in stock –you can part-exchange, and there are always plenty of giveaway bargains available. Mon 4–8.30pm, Tues–Sat 10.30am–8.30pm.

CLOTHES, SHOES AND ACCESSORIES

New designers can be found in the medieval streets and alleys of La Ribera, around Passeig del Born, but also down c/d'Avinyó in the Barri Gòtic, between c/del Carme and MACBA in El Raval, and along c/Verdi in Gràcia. For secondhand and vintage clothing, stores line the whole of c/de la Riera Baixa (El Raval), with others nearby on c/del Carme and c/de l'Hospital, and on Saturdays there's a street market there.

Antonio Miró c/Consell de Cent 349, Eixample ☎ 934 870 670, Ⓦ antoniomiro.es; Ⓜ Passeig de Gràcia; map p.670. Barcelona's most innovative designer, especially good for classy suits, though now also branding accessories and household design items. Mon–Sat 10.30am–8.30pm.

Camper c/Pelai 13–37, El Triangle, Eixample ☎ 933 024 124, Ⓦ camper.com; Ⓜ Catalunya; map p.648.

Spain's favourite shoe store opened its first shop in Barcelona in 1981. Providing hip, well-made, casual city footwear at a good price has been the cornerstone of its success. Mon–Sat 10am–9pm.

Custo Barcelona Pl. de les Olles 7, La Ribera ☎ 932 687 893, Ⓦ custo-barcelona.com; Ⓜ Barceloneta; map p.648. Where the stars get their T-shirts. Hugely colourful designer tops and sweaters for men and women. There are other branches around town. Mon–Sat 10am–9pm, Sun noon–8pm.

★ **Lailo** c/Riera Baixa 20, El Raval ☎ 934 413 749, Ⓜ Liceu; map p.648. Secondhand and vintage clothes shop with a massively wide-ranging stock, plus fancy dress costumes, tuxes and gowns available for hire. If you don't find what you want, just move on down the street to the neighbouring stores and outlets. Mon–Sat 11am–2pm & 5–8.30pm.

Mango Pg. de Gràcia 8–10, Eixample ☎ 934 121 599, Ⓦ mango.com; Ⓜ Passeig de Gràcia; map p.670. Now available worldwide, Barcelona is where Mango began and prices here are generally a bit cheaper than in North America or other European countries. Mon–Sat 10.15am–9.30pm.

Mango Outlet c/Girona 37, Eixample ☎ 934 122 935, Ⓦ mangooutlet.com; Ⓜ Girona; map p.670. Last season's Mango gear at unbeatable prices, with items starting at just a few euros. The shop is in the city's "garment district" and there are other outlet stores in the same neighbourhood. Mon–Sat 10.15am–9pm.

★ **La Manual Alpargatera** c/d'Avinyó 7, Barri Gòtic ☎ 933 010 172, Ⓦ lamanualalpargatera.com; Ⓜ Liceu; map p.648. Traditional workshop making *alpargatas* (espadrilles) to order, as well as other straw, rope and basketwork. Mon–Fri 9.30am–1.30pm & 4.30–8pm, Sat 10am–1.30pm & 4.30–8pm.

Naifa c/Doctor Joaquim Dou 11, El Raval ☎ 933 024 005; Ⓜ Liceu; map p.648. Original, colourful and informal men's and women's collections by Argentinian designer Paula Guillaumin. Mon–Sat 11.30am–3pm & 4.30–9pm.

U-Casas c/Espaseria 4, La Ribera ☎ 933 100 046, Ⓦ casasclub.com; Ⓜ Jaume I; map p.648. Never mind the funky shoes, the stores are pretty spectacular, especially at the branch in the Born where an enormous shoe-shaped bench-cum-sofa takes centre-stage. Mon–Thurs 10.30am–8.30pm, Fri & Sat 10.30am–9pm.

DEPARTMENT STORES AND MALLS

Department stores and shopping malls are open Monday to Saturday 10am–10pm, though the cafés and leisure outlets in malls often open later, and on Sunday.

Arenas de Barcelona Gran Via de les Corts Catalanes 373–385, Eixample ☎ 932 890 244, Ⓦ arenasdebarcelona .com; Ⓜ Espanya; map p.670. The city's newest designer mall is a glam refit of a former bullring, and while it's bigger on leisure facilities than shops and boutiques, you won't want to miss the view from the circular rooftop promenade. Mon–Sat 10am–10pm.

El Corte Inglés Pl. de Catalunya 14, Eixample ☎ 933 063 800, ⓦ elcorteingles.es; Ⓜ Catalunya; map p.648. The city's largest department store has outlets all over the city – visit the flagship Pl. de Catalunya branch for nine storeys of clothes, accessories, cosmetics, household goods, toys and top-floor café. Mon–Sat 10am–10pm.

L'Illa Avgda. Diagonal 545–559, Les Corts ☎ 934 440 000, ⓦ lilla.com; Ⓜ María Cristina; map p.670. The landmark uptown shopping mall is stuffed full of designer fashion (including the local Custo), plus Camper (shoes), FNAC (music, film and books), Decathlon (sports), El Corte Inglés (department store), Caprabo (supermarket), gourmet food hall and much more. Mon–Sat 10am–9.30pm.

DESIGN AND STYLE

Cubiña c/Mallorca 291, Eixample ☎ 934 765 721, ⓦ cubinya.es; Ⓜ Verdaguer; map p.670. The building itself is stupendous – Domènech i Montaner's *modernista* Casa Thomas – while inside holds the very latest in household design, from slinky CD racks to €5000 dining tables. Mon–Sat 10am–2pm & 4.30–8.30pm.

★ **Vinçon** Pg. de Gràcia 96, Eixample ☎ 932 156 050, ⓦ vincon.com; Ⓜ Passeig de Gràcia; map p.670. The grandaddy of household style, with various separate street entrances and separate sections for bedroom and kitchen stuff, plus temporary art and design exhibitions in La Sala Vinçon. Mon–Sat 10am–8.30pm.

FOOD AND DRINK

The main local supermarket chain is Caprabo (ⓦ caprabo .es), which has a useful branch in the Mercat de la Barceloneta, though most other branches are located in residential neighbourhoods, away from the tourist sights. The most convenient downtown supermarket is that in the basement of El Corte Inglés (Pl. de Catalunya), and there's also the fairly basic Carrefour Express at Ramblas 113.

Bubó c/Caputxes 10, La Ribera ☎ 932 687 224, ⓦ bubo .ws; Ⓜ Jaume I; map p.648. There are chocolates and then there are Bubó chocolates – jewel-like creations and playful desserts by pastry maestro Carles Mampel. Daily 10am–1pm (Fri & Sat until 1am).

★ **Casa Gispert** c/Sombrerers 23, La Ribera ☎ 933 197 535, ⓦ casagispert.com; Ⓜ Jaume I; map p.648.

Roasters of nuts, coffee and spices for over 150 years. It's a truly delectable store of wooden boxes, baskets, stacked shelves and tantalizing smells. Tues–Fri 9.30am–2pm & 4–7.30pm (also Mon, same times, in Oct, Nov & Dec), Sat 10am–2pm & 5–8pm.

★ **Formatgeria La Seu** c/Dagueria 16, Barri Gòtic ☎ 934 126 548, ⓦ formatgerialaseu.com; Ⓜ Jaume I; map p.648. Chatty Scottish owner Katherine is usually on hand to advise about her best farmhouse cheeses, and you can try before you buy with a €2.50 tasting plate. Tues–Thurs 10am–2pm & 5–8pm, Fri & Sat 10am–3.30pm & 5–8pm; closed Aug.

Forn Baluard c/Baluard 38–40, Barceloneta ☎ 932 211 208, ⓦ baluardbarceloneta.com; Ⓜ Barceloneta; map p.648. There are scores of bakeries in Barcelona, but when push comes to shove, foodies pick the Baluard, right next to Barceloneta market, whose passion for artisan bread, cakes and pastries knows no bounds. Mon–Sat 8am–9pm.

Papabubble c/Ample 28, Barri Gòtic ☎ 932 688 625, ⓦ papabubble.com; Ⓜ Drassanes; map p.648. Groovy young things rolling out home-made candy to a chill-out soundtrack. Mon–Fri 10am–2pm & 4–8.30pm, Sat 10am–8.30pm; closed Aug.

Vila Viniteca c/Agullers 7 & 9, La Ribera ☎ 937 777 017, ⓦ vilaviniteca.es; Ⓜ Barceloneta; map p.648. A very knowledgeable specialist in Catalan and Spanish wines. Pick your vintage and then nip over the road for the gourmet deli part of the operation. Mon–Sat 8.30am–8.30pm (closes Sat at 2.30pm in July & Aug).

MUSIC

Independent music and CD stores are concentrated around c/dels Tallers (El Raval), off the Ramblas.

Discos Castelló c/Tallers 3, El Raval ☎ 933 182 041, and c/Tallers 7 ☎ 933 025 946, ⓦ castellodiscos.com; Ⓜ Catalunya; map p.648. You can track down pretty much anything you want from the c/Tallers music stores, including classical recordings at no. 3 and pop, rock, *mestiza*, electronica, hardcore, and Spanish and Catalan sounds at no. 7. Mon–Sat 10am–8pm.

★ **Etnomusic** c/del Bonsuccés 6, El Raval ☎ 933 011 884, ⓦ etnomusic.com; Ⓜ Catalunya; map p.648. World-music specialist, especially good for *mestiza*, reggae, Latin and all types of South American music. Mon–Sat 11am–2pm & 5–8pm.

DIRECTORY

Banks and exchange For out-of-hours exchange offices, look down the Ramblas, or go to Barcelona Sants (daily 8am–8pm); El Corte Inglés, Pl. de Catalunya (Mon–Sat 10am–9.30pm); or Turisme de Catalunya tourist office, Pl. de Catalunya 17 (Mon–Sat 9am–9pm, Sun 9am–2pm).

Consulates Australia, Avgda. Diagonal 458, Esquerra de l'Eixample ☎ 934 909 013, ⓦ spain.embassy.gov.au;

Ⓜ Diagonal; Britain, Avgda. Diagonal 477, Eixample ☎ 933 666 200, ⓦ ukinspain.com, Ⓜ Hospital Clinic; Canada, c/Elisenda de Pinós 10, Sarrià ☎ 932 042 700, ⓦ canadainternational.gc.ca, FGC Reina Elisenda; Republic of Ireland, Gran Vía Carles III 94, Les Corts ☎ 934 915 021, Ⓜ María Cristina/Les Corts; New Zealand, Ⓜ Avgda. de Gràcia 64, Gràcia ☎ 932 090 399, ⓦ nzembassy.com, FGC

10

Gràcia; USA Pg. de la Reina Elisenda 23, Sarrià ☎ 932 802 227, ⊕ barcelona.usconsulate.gov, FGC Reina Elisenda.

Hospitals The following have 24hr accident and emergency services: Centre Perecamps, Avgda. Drassanes 13–15, El Raval ☎ 934 410 600, Ⓜ Drassanes; Hospital Clínic i Provincial, c/Villaroel 170, Eixample ☎ 932 275 400, Ⓜ Hospital Clínic; Hospital del Mar, Pg. Marítím 25–29, Vila Olímpica ☎ 932 483 000, Ⓜ Ciutadella-Vila Olímpica; Hospital de la Santa Creu i Sant Pau, c/Sant Antoni María Claret, Eixample ☎ 932 919 000, Ⓜ Hospital de Sant Pau.

Laundries Lavomatic, Pl. Joaquim Xirau 1, Barri Gòtic ☎ 933 425 119, Ⓜ Drassanes, and c/Consolat del Mar 43–45, Pl. del Palau, La Ribera ☎ 932 684 768, Ⓜ Barceloneta (both Mon–Sat 9am–9pm); and LavaExpress, at nine locations, including c/Ferlandina 34, El Raval ☎ 933 183 018, ⊕ lavaxpres.com, Ⓜ Universitat (daily 8am–11pm). At La Lavandería de Ana, c/Carme 63, El Raval ☎ 639 957 046, ⊕ lalavanderiadeana.com, Ⓜ Liceu (Mon–Sat 9am–8pm), you can leave your laundry for a wash-and-dry (from €8).

Left luggage Barcelona Sants (daily 7am–11pm; €3–4.50 per day). There are lockers at the Estació de França, Passeig de Gràcia station and Barcelona Nord (all 6am–11.30pm; €3–4.50).

Pharmacies Usual hours are weekdays 9am to 1pm and 4pm to 8pm. At least one in each neighbourhood is open daily 24hr (and marked as such) – *Farmacia Clapies*, Ramblas 98 ☎ 933 012 843, ⊕ farmaciaclapes.com, Ⓜ Liceu, is convenient.

Police Guàrdia Urbana station at Ramblas 43, opposite Pl. Reial ☎ 932 562 430, Ⓜ Liceu (24hr; English spoken). To get a police report for your insurance, go to the Mossos d'Esquadra (Catalan police force) station at c/Nou de la Rambla 76–80, El Raval ☎ 933 062 300, Ⓜ Paral.lel (take your passport). Contact the police on: Mossos d'Esquadra ☎ 088, Policía Nacional ☎ 091, Guàrdia Urbana ☎ 092.

Post offices Main post office (*Correus*), Pl. d'Antoni López, Barri Gòtic ☎ 934 868 302, ⊕ correos.es, Ⓜ Barceloneta/ Jaume I (Mon–Fri 8.30am–9.30pm, Sat 8.30am–2pm).

Swimming pools The city's most spectacular pool is the open-air Piscina Municipal de Montjuïc, Avgda. Miramar 31, Montjuïc, Funicular de Montjuïc (mid-June to early Sept daily 11am–6.30pm; €5). Indoor and outdoor beachside pools at Club Natació Atlètic Barceloneta, Pl. del Mar, Ⓜ Barceloneta (Mon–Fri 6.30am–11pm, Sat 7am–11pm, Sun 8am–5pm, until 8pm mid-May to Sept; full-day €11).

Telephone offices *Locutorios*, which specialize in discounted overseas connections – are scattered through the old city, particularly in El Raval.

Montserrat

The mountain of **Montserrat**, with its strangely shaped crags of rock, its monastery and ruined hermitage caves, stands just 40km northwest of Barcelona, off the road to Lleida. It's the most popular day-trip from the city, reached in around ninety minutes by train and then cable car or rack railway for a thrilling ride up to the monastery. Once there, you can visit the basilica and monastery buildings, and complete your day with a walk around the woods and crags, using the two funicular railways that depart from the monastery complex. Inevitably, monastery and mountain are ruthlessly exploited as a tourist trip from the city or the Costa Brava, while the main **pilgrimages** take place on April 27 and September 8, but don't be put off – the place itself is still magical and well worth a visit.

Monestir de Montserrat

Legends hang easily upon Montserrat. Fifty years after the birth of Christ, St Peter is said to have deposited an image of the Virgin carved by St Luke in one of the mountain caves. The so-called Black Virgin (La Moreneta) icon was subsequently lost in the early eighth century, after being hidden during the Muslim invasion, but reappeared in 880, accompanied by the customary visions and celestial music. A chapel was built to house it, superseded in 976 by a Benedictine monastery, the Monestir de Montserrat, set at an altitude of nearly 1000m. Miracles abounded and the Virgin of Montserrat soon became the chief cult image of Catalunya and a pilgrimage centre second in Spain only to Santiago de Compostela. Its fortunes declined in the nineteenth century, though in recent decades Montserrat's popularity has again become established. Today, in addition to the tourists, tens of thousands of newly married couples come here to seek La Moreneta's blessing.

The monastery's various outbuildings – including hotel and restaurant, post office, souvenir shop, self-service cafeteria and bar – fan out around an open square, and there are extraordinary mountain views from the terrace.

Basílica

Daily 7.30am–8pm, access to La Moreneta 8–10.30am & noon–6.30pm • Boys' choir Mon–Fri at 1pm & 6.45pm, Sun at noon & 6.45pm,
not Sat and not during school holidays at Christmas/New Year and from late June to mid-Aug • Free

Of the religious buildings, only the Renaissance **Basílica** is open to the public. **La
Moreneta** stands above the high altar, and the approach to this beautiful icon reveals
the enormous wealth of the monastery, as you queue along a corridor leading through
the back of the basilica's rich side-chapels. The best time to visit the basilica is when
Montserrat's world-famous **boys' choir** sings. The boys belong to the Escolania, a
choral school established in the fourteenth century and unchanged in musical style
since its foundation.

Museu de Montserrat

Daily 10am–5.30pm • €6.50

The **Museu de Montserrat** presents a few archeological finds brought back by travelling
monks, together with paintings and sculpture dating from as early as the thirteenth
century, including works by Old Masters, French Impressionists and Catalan
modernistas. There's also a collection of Byzantine icons, though other religious items
are in short supply, as most of the monastery's valuables were carried off by Napoleon's
troops, who sacked the complex in 1811.

Mountain walks

Funicular departures every 20min, daily 10am–6pm, weekends only Oct–March • Santa Cova €3 return, Sant Joan €7.50 return,
combination ticket €8.50

Following the mountain tracks to the nearby caves and hermitages, you can contemplate
Goethe's observation of 1816: "Nowhere but in his own Montserrat will a man find
happiness and peace." One funicular drops to the path for **Santa Cova**, a seventeenth-
century chapel built where the La Moreneta icon is said to have been found. It's an easy
walk there and back, which takes less than an hour. The other funicular rises steeply to
the hermitage of **Sant Joan**, from where it's a tougher 45-minute walk to the **Sant Jeroni**
hermitage, and another fifteen minutes to the **Sant Jeroni summit** at 1236m.

ARRIVAL AND INFORMATION   MONTSERRAT

There are two ways to reach Montserrat by public transport: either by cable car or mountain railway, but in the first instance
you need to take the **FGC train** (line R5, direction Manresa), which leaves Barcelona's Plaça d'Espanya (⑩ Espanya) daily
at hourly intervals from 8.36am.

By cable car Get off the train at Montserrat Aeri (52min)
for the connecting cable car, the Aeri de Montserrat
(departures every 15min, March–Oct daily 9.40am–2pm &
2.30–7pm, Nov–Feb daily 10.10am–2pm & 2.30–5.45pm;
☎ 938 350 005, ⑩ aeridemontserrat.com). You may have
to queue for fifteen minutes or so, but then it's an
exhilarating five-minute swoop up the sheer mountainside
to a terrace just below the monastery.

By mountain railway The Montserrat mountain railway,
the Cremallera de Montserrat (departures hourly, daily
8.48am–5.38pm, until 7.38pm at weekends April–Oct plus
daily July–Sept; ☎ 902 312 020, ⑩ cremallerademontserrat
.cat), departs from Monistrol de Montserrat (the next stop
after Montserrat Aeri, another 4min), and takes twenty
minutes to complete the climb.

Tickets Return through-tickets from Barcelona cost
around €20, either for the train/cable car or train/mountain
railway. There are also two combination tickets available:

the Trans Montserrat (€25), which includes all transport
services, including unlimited use of the mountain
funiculars, and entry to the audiovisual exhibit; and the Tot
Montserrat (€40), which includes the same plus monastery
museum entry and a cafeteria lunch.

By car Take the A2 motorway as far as the Martorell exit,
and then follow the N11 and C55 to the Montserrat turn-off
– or park at either the cable-car or the mountain-railway
station and take the rides up instead. All-in cable-car/
cremallera/Montserrat attraction combo tickets are
available at the station for drivers who park-and-ride.

Visitor Centre ☎ 938 777 701, ⑩ montserratvisita
.com; daily 9am–5.45pm, Sat, Sun & July–Sept until
6.45pm. You can pick up maps of the complex and
mountain, and they can also advise about the
accommodation options, from camping to staying at the
three-star *Abat Cisneros* hotel.

Catalunya

TEATRE-MUSEU DALÍ, FIGUERES (P.739)

Catalunya

Barcelona may make the biggest splash with visitors, but it's the rest of Catalunya that defines the region's distinct – and proud – identity. Out of the city – and especially in rural areas – you'll hear Catalan spoken more often and find better Catalan food. Towns and villages are surprisingly prosperous, a relic of the early industrial era when Catalunya developed more rapidly than most of Spain. There's a confidence in being Catalan that dates back to the fourteenth-century Golden Age, when it was a kingdom that ruled the Balearics, Valencia, the French border regions, and even Sardinia. Today, Catalunya is officially a semi-autonomous *comunidad*, but it can still feel like a separate country – cross the borders into Valencia or Aragón and you soon sense the difference.

11

Catalunya (Cataluña in Castilian Spanish, Catalonia in English) is a spectacular study in contrasts, from the soaring peaks of the Pyrenees to the sparkling blue water of the Mediterranean's shallow coves. The showy swagger of Costa Brava's mega-resorts, meanwhile, mixes alluringly with the stillness of ancient parish churches hidden deep in the heartland. Despite this diversity, however, Catalunya is relatively compact, so it's possible – as many a local will proudly point out – to ski in the morning and sunbathe on the beach in the afternoon.

On the whole everything is easily reached from Barcelona; the city is linked to most main centres by excellent bus and train services. The obvious targets are the **coasts** north and south of the city, and the various **provincial capitals** (Girona, Tarragona and Lleida), destinations that make a series of comfortable day-trips. Even on a short trip, you can take in the medieval city of **Girona** and the surrounding area, which includes the extraordinary volcanic **Garrotxa** region, as well as the best of the beach towns on the **Costa Brava**, which runs up to the French border. This was one of the first stretches of Spanish coast to be developed for mass tourism, and though that's no great recommendation, the large, brash resorts are tempered by some more isolated beaches and lower-key holiday and fishing villages, such as **Cadaqués**. Just inland from the coast, **Figueres** contains the Teatre-Museu Dalí, Catalunya's biggest tourist attraction.

SITGES

Highlights

① Cadaqués Experience the Costa Brava as it once was at this lovely, quirky seaside town. **See p.728**

② Girona This beautiful, labyrinthine city boasts a two-thousand-year-old history, including one of the best-preserved medieval Jewish quarters in the country. **See p.733**

③ Teatre-Museu Dalí Explore the life and work of the flamboyant artist at this shrine to Surrealism. **See p.739**

④ Rafting on the Noguera Pallaresa Grab a paddle: the Noguera Pallaresa offers the best rafting in Spain. **See p.759**

⑤ The Romanesque Trail The Pyrenean Vall de Boí is an open-air Romanesque museum, featuring many of the finest churches from that era in Spain. **See p.765**

⑥ Cava country Sip Spain's magnificent bubbly at one of the modernista vineyards around Sant Sadurní d'Anoia. **See p.771**

⑦ Sitges Sample the frenetic nightlife or, better still, the Carnaval, of chic Sitges. **See p.772**

⑧ Roman Tarragona This ancient city reveals some of the country's most important remains of the Roman occupation. **See p.776**

HIGHLIGHTS ARE MARKED ON THE MAP ON PP.710–711

With more time, you can head for the **Catalan Pyrenees**, which offer magnificent and relatively isolated hiking territory, particularly in and around the **Parc Nacional de Aigüestortes**, and good skiing in winter. South of Barcelona, the **Costa Daurada** features a fine beach at **Sitges** and the attractive coastal town of **Tarragona**; inland, the appealing cava **vineyards** around Sant Sadurní d'Anoia or the romantic monastery of **Poblet** figure as approaches to the enjoyable provincial capital of **Lleida**.

Brief history

The **Catalan people** have an individual and deeply felt historical and cultural identity, seen most clearly in the language, which takes precedence over Castilian on street names and signs. Despite being banned for over thirty years during the Franco dictatorship, Catalan survived behind closed doors and has staged a dramatic comeback since the Generalísimo's death. As in the Basque Country, though, regionalism goes back much farther than this.

11

Early origins to the twentieth century

On the expulsion of the Moors in 874, Guifré el Pelós (Wilfred the Hairy) established himself as the first independent **Count of Barcelona**; his kingdom flourished and the region became famous for its seafaring, mercantile and commercial skills, characteristics that to some extent still set the region apart. In the twelfth century came union with Aragón, though the Catalans kept many of their traditional, hard-won rights (*usatges*). From then until the fourteenth century marked Catalunya's **Golden Age**, and in 1359 the Catalan Generalitat – Europe's first parliamentary government – was established.

In 1469, through the marriage of Fernando V (of Aragón) to Isabel I (of Castile), the region was added on to the rest of the emergent Spanish state. Throughout the following centuries the Catalans made various attempts to secede from the stifling grasp of central bureaucracy, which saw the Catalan enterprise as merely another means of filling the state coffers. Early industrialization, which was centred here and in the Basque Country,

CATALÀ

Your main problem throughout Catalunya is likely to be the **language** – Català (Catalan). Català has more or less taken over from Castilian, a phenomenon known as the *venganza* (revenge), though few visitors realize how ingrained and widespread the language is and sometimes commit the error of calling it a dialect. On paper, Català looks like a cross between French and Spanish and is generally easy to understand if you know those two but, spoken, it has a distinct, rounded sound and is far harder to come to grips with, especially away from Barcelona, where accents are stronger.

When Franco came to power, publishing houses, bookshops and libraries were raided and Català books destroyed. While this was followed by a let-up in the mid-1940s, the language was still banned from the radio, TV, daily press and, most importantly, schools, which is why many older people today cannot necessarily write Català (even if they speak it all the time). As for Castilian, in Barcelona virtually everyone can speak it, while in country areas, many people can sometimes only understand, not speak, it.

Català is spoken in Catalunya proper, part of Aragón, much of Valencia, the Balearic Islands, the Principality of Andorra and in parts of the French Pyrenees, albeit with variations of dialect (it is thus much more widely spoken than several better-known languages such as Danish, Finnish and Norwegian). It is a Romance language, stemming from Latin and, more directly, from medieval Provençal and *lemosi*, the literary French of Occitania. Spaniards in the rest of the country tend to belittle it by saying that to get a Català word you just cut a Castilian one in half. In fact, the grammar is much more complicated than Castilian, and the language has eight vowel sounds (including three diphthongs). In the text we've tried to keep to Català names (with Castilian in parentheses where necessary) – not least because street signs and *turisme* maps are in Català. Either way, you're unlikely to get confused as the difference is usually only slight: ie Girona (Gerona) and Lleida (Lérida). For a Catalan glossary, see p.927.

only intensified political disaffection, and in the 1920s and 1930s anarchist, communist and socialist parties all established major power bases in Catalunya.

The Civil War to the present day
In 1931, after the fall of the dictator General Primo de Rivera, a **Catalan Republic** was proclaimed and its autonomous powers guaranteed by the new Republican government. Any incipient separatism collapsed, however, with the outbreak of the Civil War, during which Catalunya was a bastion of the Republican cause, Barcelona holding out until January 1939. In revenge, Franco pursued a policy of harsh suppression, attempting to wipe out all evidence of Catalan cultural and economic primacy. Among his more subtle methods was the encouragement of immigration from other parts of Spain in order to dilute regional identity. Even so, Catalunya remained obstinate, the scene of protests and demonstrations throughout the dictatorship, and after Franco's death a **Catalan government** was formally reinstated in 1979. This, the semi-autonomous **Generalitat**, enjoys a high profile and is gradually extending its power, and the local police, or Mossos d'Esquadra, continue to replace the national forces.

11

The Costa Brava

Stretching from Blanes, 60km north of Barcelona, to the French border, the unfairly maligned **Costa Brava** (Rugged Coast) boasts wooded coves, high cliffs, pretty beaches and deep blue water. Struggling under its image as the first developed package-tour coast in Spain, it is very determinedly shifting away from mass tourism. It is undeniable that the unharnessed tourist boom wreaked damage in some areas, but the old *sangría*-and-chips image is giving way to greater prominence for the area's natural beauty and fascinating cultural heritage.

Broadly, the coast is split into three areas: **La Selva** at the southern tip, clustered around brash **Lloret de Mar**, and the medieval walled town of **Tossa de Mar**; the stylish central area of **Baix Empordà** between Sant Feliu de Guíxols and Pals, popular with the chic Barcelona crowd, which boasts some wonderfully scenic stretches of rolling coastline around Palamós, the beaches and villages of inland Palafrugell and hill-top Begur; and the more rugged **Alt Empordà** in the north. This area is marked by the broad sweep of the Golf de Roses, site of a nature reserve, the Parc Natural dels Aiguamolls de l'Empordà, and the alluring peace of the ancient Greek and Roman settlement of Empúries, and extends to the bohemian Cadaqués, which attracts an arty crowd paying tribute to Salvador Dalí; the artist lived most of his life in the labyrinthine warren of converted fishermen's huts in a neighbouring cove, now a fabulous museum.

GETTING AROUND   COSTA BRAVA

By car Driving is the easiest way to get around and gives you access to some of the more remote parts of the coast, though expect the smaller coastal roads to be very busy in summer and parking to be tricky in the major towns.

By bus Buses in the region are almost all operated by Sarfa (ⓦ sarfa.com), which has offices in the bigger towns and offers an efficient service the length of the coast. Teisa (ⓦ teisa-bus.com) also operates some routes in the area. You could consider using Girona or Figueres as a base for lateral trips to the coast, as both have big bus termini and are within an hour of the beach.

By train The train from Barcelona to the French border runs inland most of the time, serving Girona and Figueres, but emerging on the coast itself only at Llançà. The new

AVE train, which is faster but pricier, now operates from Perpignan in France to Figueres; it will eventually extend from Figueres to Barcelona, sections of which are due to begin operating in 2012 though this may change.

By boat Between Easter and Sept, there are daily boat services (*cruceros*), which cover short hops along the coast; there are generally services between Lloret de Mar, Tossa de Mar and Sant Feliu de Guíxols, among other coastal towns. Tourist offices have up-to-date information on companies and schedules; timetables and routes can vary yearly.

By foot Finally, you can access some of the lovelier coves by walking all or just parts of the fabulous Camí de Ronda necklace of footpaths that runs along almost all of the coastline.

FRANCE

Perpignan

Port Vendres

ur de Carol

Llívia

La Molina

La Masella

Alp

erda

Toses

Queralbs

Núria

Ribes de Freser

La Jonquera
Rabós
Espolla
Portbou
El Port de la Selva
Mollet
Llançà
Portlligat
Maçanet
Cadaqués
Molló
Beget
Tregurá
Camprodon
Sant Martí d'Ogassa
Sadernes
Darnius
Sant Pere de Rodes
Roses
Sant Llorenç
Figueres
Castelló d'Empúries

GARROTXA

Ripoll

Berga

Borredà

Sant Joan de les Abadesses
Olot
Castellfollit
Besalú
Siurana d'Empordà
PARC NATURAL DELS AIGUAMOLLS DE L'EMPORDÀ

PARC NATURAL DE LA ZONA VOLCÀNICA

Santa Pau
Banyoles
Empúries
L'Escala

Riu Freser

Riu Ter

Girona

L'Estartit

Costa Brava

Torroella de Montgrí
Bordils
Ullastret
Sa Riera
Púbol
Pals
Peratallada
Begur
La Bisbal
Aiguablava
Tamariu
Palafrugell
Llafranc
Palamós
Calella de Palafrugell

Vic

Sant Hilari Sacalm

Santa Coloma de Farners

Viladrau
Arbúcies

SERRA DEL MONTSENY

Hostalric

Platja d'Aro
S'Agaró
Sant Feliu de Guíxols

Costa Brava

Tossa de Mar
Lloret de Mar
Blanes

Manresa

Riu Llobregat

C25

Terrassa

Sabadell
Granollers
Calella
Sant Pol de Mar

serrat

Mataró

Costa Maresme

Barcelona

Castelldefels

tges

urada

MAR MEDITERRÁNEO

HIGHLIGHTS
❶ Cadaqués
❷ Girona
❸ Teatre-Museu Dalí
❹ Rafting on the Noguera Pallaresa
❺ The Romanesque Trail
❻ Cava country
❼ Sitges
❽ Roman Tarragona

0   kilometres   25

N

FIESTAS

FEBRUARY/MARCH/APRIL

Lent: Carnaval Sitges has Catalunya's best celebrations.
Easter: Semana Santa (Holy Week) Celebrations at Besalú, Girona and La Pobla de Segur.
April 23: Semana Medieval de Sant Jordi St George is celebrated throughout Catalunya, with a week of exhibitions, dances and medieval music in Montblanc, among other places (ⓦsetmanamedieval.org).

MAY/JUNE

Throughout May and June: Festival de Jazz In Vic.
First fortnight: Festa de la Lana Annual wool fair in Ripoll.
Third week of May: Fires i Festes de la Santa Creu Processions and music in Figueres.
Corpus Christi (variable): Festa de Corpus Christi Big processions in Sitges, plus the massive **Patum** festival in Berga.
June 21–23: Festa de Sant Patllari In Camprodon.
June 24: Dia de Sant Joan Celebrated everywhere; watch out for things shutting down for a day on either side.

JULY/AUGUST

Early July to late August: Ripoll International Music Festival Classical music in Ripoll.
Third week: Festa de Santa Cristina At Lloret de Mar.
19: Festa de Sant Magi In Tarragona.
July/early Aug: Festival Internacional de Música In Torroella de Montgrí.
Mid-July to late Aug: Festival Jardins de Cap Roig In Calella de Palafrugell.
Late July to late Aug: Festival de Música de Begur In Begur.

SEPTEMBER

8: The Virgin's Birth celebrated in Cadaqués, Núria and L'Escala, among other towns.
22: Sant Maurici At his *ermita* in the national park above Espot.
Nearest weekend to 24: Festa de Sant Primuns and Felician At Besalú.
Third week: Mercat de Música Viva festival in Vic.
Third week: Festa de Santa Tecla Human castles (*castells*) and processions of *gegants* (giant puppets) in Tarragona.

OCTOBER

8: Feria de Vielha Annual fair.
Last week: Fires i Festes de Sant Narcis In Girona.

NOVEMBER

1: Sant Ermengol Celebrations in La Seu d'Urgell.

DECEMBER

Early Dec: Mercat Medieval de Vic Re-creation of a medieval market in Vic.

Lloret de Mar

Some 66km northeast of Barcelona, tourist-central **LLORET DE MAR** is everything you've ever heard about it – and more. Yet underneath its undeniably brash commercialism and gaudy nightlife is a centuries-old town trying to make itself known; the result is one of Europe's highest concentrations of clubs clustered around a delightful fifteenth-century church, high-rise monstrosities alongside genteel mansions, and a packed main beach that belies some splendid rocky coves tucked away either side of town. Any sightseeing in Lloret is centred on the warren of streets in the **old town**, amid the sometimes overwhelming hustle of T-shirt shops and tourist paraphernalia.

Church of Sant Romà and Capella del Santíssim

Pl. de l'Església • **Sant Romà** Open for services only • **Capella del Santíssim** Daily 10am–2pm & 5–8pm; confirm with *turisme*

Holding court over the old town is the colourful church of **Sant Romà**, originally built in Gothic style in 1522. A *modernista* renovation was begun in 1914, but much of this work was destroyed in the Civil War; only the adjacent **Capella del Santíssim**, with its Byzantine cupolas, Mudéjar and Renaissance influences, remains.

Museu del Mar

Pg. Camprodon i Arrieta • March–May, Oct & Nov Mon–Sat 9am–1pm & 4–7pm, Sun 10am–1pm & 4–7pm; June–Sept Mon–Sat 10am–1pm & 4–8pm, Sun 10am–1pm & 4–7pm; Dec–Feb Mon–Sat 9am–1.30pm & 3.30–6pm, Sun 9am–2pm; last admission usually 45min before closing time • €4 • ⓦ lloretdemar.org

You can explore Lloret's maritime legacy – illustrated by ship models and a replica of an 1848 figurehead – and other aspects of the town's history in the well-run **Museu del Mar**, sharing space with the town's *turisme* in one of Lloret's few remaining nineteenth-century mansions on the town's stately promenade.

The beaches

Lloret's main **beach** and neighbouring Fenals beach, where many of the hotels are grouped, get packed and noisy; the south end of Fenals, backed by a pine wood, is much less crowded. Farther afield are a number of tiny **coves** favoured by local bathers. Cala Santa Cristina and the adjacent Cala Treumal are the best, while the lovely Cala Boadella is popular with nudists; all are off the Blanes road.

Jardins de Santa Clotilde

Daily: April–Sept 10am–8pm; Oct–March 10am–5pm; last admission 1hr before closing time • Year-round guided tours Sun 10.30pm • €4

On a headland above the last beach are the surprisingly tranquil **Jardins de Santa Clotilde**, ornamental gardens laid out in *modernista* style in 1919 and offering fabulous views over the Mediterranean. Visitor numbers are limited to fifty at a time but you're most likely to find yourself alone, even in August. In spring and summer, you can sometimes catch live jazz on the weekends in the gardens; ask at the tourist office for details.

ARRIVAL AND INFORMATION
LLORET DE MAR

By bus The bus station is north of the town centre, on Carretera de Blanes. As well as frequent services from nearby Tossa, there are regular buses from Barcelona (8–10 daily; 1hr 15min), Girona (5 daily; 1hr 20min), Palafrugell (2 daily; 1hr) and Platja d'Aro (2–4 daily; 50min), among others.

By boat *Cruceros* and other coastal boats dock at the beach, which is where the ticket offices are too. In summer there are around a dozen daily services up and down the coast.

Turisme The most central *turisme* is on the seafront at Pg. Camprodon i Arrieta 1 (March–May Mon–Sat 9am–1pm & 4–7pm, Sun 10am–1pm & 4–7pm; June–Sept Mon–Sat 9am–8pm, Sun 10am–1pm & 4–7pm; Oct & Nov daily 9am–1pm & 4–7pm; Dec–Feb 9am–1.30pm & 3.30–6pm, Sun 10am–3pm; ☏ 972 364 735, ⓦ lloretdemar.org).

ACCOMMODATION

Most **hotels** in Lloret are block-booked by agents, so it's a good idea to book in advance, especially in the summer. As you'd expect, there are lots of high-rise hotels, but you'll also find some decent smaller spots in the old part of town, not far from the beach.

Hostal La Habana c/Les Taronges 11 ☏ 972 367 707, ⓦ lahabanalloret.com. Smart, family-run *pensió* on a narrow street leading from the beach to the old town, with bright, well-maintained rooms. **€70**

Hotel Santi Marta Platja de Santa Cristina ☏ 972 364 904, ⓦ hstamarta.com. A tranquil escape, this luxurious hotel sits above a quiet beach and the Ermita de Santa Cristina, between Lloret and Blanes, with elegant rooms and lovely views of the sea. **€226**

EATING AND DRINKING

Although you're never going to be far from a fast-food joint, there's still a reasonably good choice of places to **eat** in the old town. **Clubs** are mainly centred around Avgda. Just Marlés, the main road into town running perpendicular to the seafront, while lively **bars** dot the streets around Pl. d'Espanya and Pl. del Carme, just behind the beach.

11

CUINA CATALANA

"Catalunya has a fantastic climate, a rich plurality of products and diverse geography – the sea, the mountains, and the plains. There are few parts of the world this fertile."
Ferran Adrià

That's how the famous Catalan chef describes his home region's geographical bounty, source of its rich *cuina Catalana*. Culled from "**mar i muntanya**" (sea and mountain), Catalunya's cuisine matches fresh seafood on the coast with hearty meats (particularly sausages) inland, while fragrant fruits and vegetables provide ballast to every meal.

The **seafood** variety is impressive, and includes plump shrimp and langoustine; eel from the Ebro delta; trout from Pyrenean rivers; and the ever-present *bacallà* (cod). **Sausages**, most using pork as a base, include *botifarra*, *fuet* (a thin, dried sausage) and *llonganissa* (cured sausage). Catalunya has taken **mushrooms** to a high art, not least aromatic *bolets* (wild mushrooms), which are picked and prepared in autumn. In late winter and early spring, *calçots* (large, tender, sweet spring onions) are roasted over coals and dipped in a **romesco** sauce, which is made with tomatoes, peppers, onions, almonds, garlic and olive oil.

Perhaps Catalunya's best-loved export is **pa amb tomàquet**, bread rubbed with tomato and drizzled in olive oil, which is not only ubiquitous throughout the region, but in the rest of Spain. As for dessert: Catalunya's answer to *crème brûlée* is the custard-style **crema Catalana**. And when it comes time to celebrate, do so with **cava** (see p.771), a sparkling wine that rivals champagne, but is significantly cheaper.

CATALAN CHEFS

Contemporary Catalan cuisine has become synonymous with **Ferran Adrià**, who transformed (and transfixed) the culinary world with his famous scented *espumas* (foams) and "molecular gastronomy" (or, as Ferran prefers to describe it, *cocina de vanguardia*). The effects have gone far beyond the dazzling laboratory of a kitchen in his former restaurant **El Bulli** on the Costa Brava. (Ferran closed *El Bulli* in July 2011 to launch a nonprofit culinary foundation; see box, p.728). Chefs across the region have been inspired by Ferran, each adding their own spin, including (in Barcelona) Carles Abellán, as well as Albert Adrià who, with older brother Ferran, opened the excellent tapas bar *Tickets* (see p.692) in 2011. The region is also home to two legendary restaurants: *El Celler de Can Roca* (see p.738) and *El Motel* (see p.741).

Calamic Carnisseria Velle 5 ☎ 972 367 857, ⓦ calamic. com. Feast on robust seafood dishes – such as *merluza*, or hake, with clams – and a good weekday lunch *menú* for €10.50 at this friendly, homespun restaurant. Tues–Sun 1–3.30pm, plus 8–11pm Thurs–Sun.

Can Tarradas Pl. d'Espanya 7 ☎ 972 366 121, ⓦ restaurantecantarradas.com. This welcoming restaurant features a range of dishes, including seafood from sea bass to squid and salmon, grilled meats, and simple pizzas and pastas at mid-range prices. Daily except Wed 1–5pm & 7pm–midnight.

Tossa de Mar

TOSSA DE MAR is quite a sight upon arrival by boat: medieval walls and the turrets of the old quarter, **Vila Vella**, rise pale and shimmering on the hill above the modern town. Tossa has managed to escape the full-blown tourism of Lloret, 13km to the south, and balances comfortably between a restful holiday hub and working town. Founded originally by the Romans, the town has twelfth-century walls that surround the old quarter – a maze of cobbled streets, whitewashed houses and flower boxes – and climb the headland, offering terrific views over beach and bay.

Far de Tossa and around

Pg. de la Vila Vella • Tues–Sun 10am–5pm, sometimes open longer hours in summer • €3

Towering over the Vila Vella is the nineteenth-century **Far de Tossa**, home to an innovative exhibition on Mediterranean lighthouses. Just below here, not far from the ruins of the town's fifteenth-century Gothic church, stands a **statue of Ava Gardner**, who made the town famous in the 1950 film, *Pandora and the Flying Dutchman*.

Museu Municipal

Pl. Roig i Soler 1 • June–Sept Tues–Sat 10am–8pm, Sun & Mon 10am–2pm & 4–8pm; Oct–May Tues–Sat 10am–2pm & 4–8pm, Sun 10am–2pm • €3

In the old quarter, the **Museu Municipal** features a Roman mosaic and remnants, including ceramic vases, from a nearby excavated Roman villa, and a Chagall painting, *Celestial Violinist*. Chagall spent summers here for four decades, and evocatively called Tossa the "blue paradise".

The beaches

Tossa's best beach is the **Platja de la Mar Menuda**, around the headland away from the old town and very popular with divers; look for a natural pink cross in the rock, supposedly marking where Sant Ramon de Penyafort gave a dying man his absolution in 1235. The central **Platja Gran**, though pleasant, gets crowded; if you have your own transport, make for the tiny coves north and south of the town, which are much more rewarding. Booths on the main beach sell tickets for **boat trips** (Easter–Oct) around the surrounding coastline; the trip to Sant Feliu is especially good.

11

ARRIVAL AND INFORMATION   TOSSA DE MAR

By bus The bus station is at Avgda. del Pelegrí 25, behind the *turisme*. To reach the centre, and the beaches, head straight down the road opposite the bus station and turn right along Avgda. Costa Brava. Tossa is an easy day-trip from Barcelona (up to 8 daily; 1hr 30min); Lloret (generally every 30min; 15min); and Girona (up to 2 daily; 1hr).

By boat *Crucero* boats stop right at the centre of the beach, with the ticket offices nearby. Boats travel to Sant Feliu (up to 5 daily; 45min), and Platja d'Aro/Sant Antoni de Calonge/Palamós (up to 4 daily; 1hr 15min/1hr 25min/1hr 45min).

Turisme Avgda. del Pelegrí 25, in front of the bus station (April, May & Oct Mon–Sat 10am–2pm & 4–8pm; June–Sept Mon–Sat 10am–8pm; Nov–March Mon–Sat 10am–2pm & 4–7pm; ☎ 972 340 108, ⊛ infotossa.com).

ACCOMMODATION

There's plenty of accommodation in the warren of tiny streets around Sant Vicenç church and below the old city walls. There are five local campsites, all within 2–4km of the centre.

HOTELS AND PENSIÓS

Can Lluna c/Roqueta 20 ☎972 340 365, ⊛fondalluna.com. Basic, tidy *pensió* – white-walled rooms and tiled floors – run by an amiable family, and tucked away in the old town. Some rooms have views of the stone turrets and the sea beyond, while the roof also offers lovely vistas. **€44**

Gran Hotel Reymar Platja de Mar Menuda ☎972 340 312, ⊛ghreymar.com. Sumptuous beachfront hotel across the bay from the Vila Vella. Modern rooms come with marble-clad bathrooms and terraces overlooking the sea. It has its own car park. Closed Nov–April. **€224**

Hotel Cap d'Or Pg. del Mar 1 ☎972 340 081, ⊛capdor.com. Relaxed, friendly, ivy-clad *pensió* on the seafront – in the home of the family who has managed it since 1954 – nestled beneath the walls of the old town. Closed Nov–April. Rate includes breakfast. **€80**

Hotel Capri Pg. del Mar 17 ☎972 340 358, ⊛hotelcapritossa.com. Considering its proximity to the sea, this simple hotel is good value. Rooms are plain but comfortable, and many have terraces. A buffet breakfast is included. Closed Dec–Feb. **€86**

Hotel Diana Pl. d'Espanya 6 ☎972 341 886, ⊛hotelesdante.com. Nicely located hotel in a *modernista* mansion on an attractive square, and with a bar on the seafront behind. Large rooms have sea or *plaça* (cheaper) views and tiled floors. Closed Nov–Easter. Includes breakfast. **€140**

Hotel Sant March Avgda. del Pelegrí 2 ☎972 340 078, ⊛hotelsantmarch.com. This amiable, family-run hotel has simple, clean rooms – many of which receive plenty of outdoor light – overlooking a breezy garden. They also have a small outdoor swimming pool. **€75**

CAMPING

Cala Llevadó 3km out of town, off the road to Lloret ☎972 340 314, ⊛calallevado.com. This is one of the better local campsites, with good facilities – swimming pool, bar-restaurant – plus plenty of outdoor activities, from windsurfing to minigolf. They also have bungalows (from €75). Closed Oct–April. One adult plus tent pitch **€19.90**

Pola 4km north off the corniche road to Sant Feliu ☎972 341 050, ⊛campingpola.es. This campsite sits in a pretty cove, has good facilities and can organize outdoor activities. Closed Oct–May. Tent pitch plus car **€18.10**

EATING AND DRINKING

Tossa offers a range of restaurants, from top-notch seafood spots to simple *sangría*-and-tapas joints. Pg. del Mar and the road behind it, c/Portal, are brimming with alfresco options. Come evening, c/de Sant Josep gets lively with revellers hitting the bars.

Bahía Pg. del Mar 19 ☎ 972 340 322. A welcoming interior and breezy terrace are the comfortable setting for tasty seafood meals (*menús* from €16–18 weekdays). Summer daily 1–3.30pm & 7.30–10.30pm; winter lunch only.

Bar Vila Vella On the main path up to the lighthouse ☎ 972 340 288. The outdoor stone terrace, featuring superb views of the town and beach, fills with a mix of visitors and locals, especially when the vats of *sangría* come tumbling out. Tapas €5–15. Daily 11am–9pm.

Castell Vell c/Pintor Roig i Soler ☎ 972 341 030. In a tranquil corner of the old town, this spot serves tasty mid-priced fish and seafood on a terrace shaded with vines. March–Oct usually daily 1.30–3.30pm & 8.30–10.30pm (closed Mon lunch); closed Nov–Feb.

★ **La Cuina de Can Simon** c/Portal 24 ☎ 972 341 269, ⓦ lacuinadecansimon.es. This venerable joint turns out classic regional dishes in an elegant dining room of linen-topped tables, stone walls and oil paintings. The menu features a *mar i muntanya* (sea and mountain) section, including fresh clams and grilled lamb. Main courses range €16–25. April to mid-Oct Wed–Sat 1–4pm & 8–11pm, Sun 1–4pm; closed mid-Oct to March.

Cuina Viva Avgda. de Sant Raimon Penyafort 13 ☎ 972 342 510, ⓦ cuinaviva.es. Enjoy creative, international-influenced Spanish fare made with a personal touch, from a fragrant seafood risotto to paella, at this breezy, family-run restaurant with views of the sea. *Menú* from €15. Daily 11am–4pm & 7–10.30pm, Sat & Sun 12.30–10.30pm; sometimes closed Mon, plus Nov–Feb some years.

Baix Empordà

While there are still one or two touristy places, the **Baix Empordà**, north from La Selva, feels less like a package holiday hotspot, with more stylish towns with a greater local flavour. Known as the Triangle d'Or (Golden Triangle), as the rising property prices and burgeoning number of four- and five-star hotels will bear out, it is much favoured by chic Catalans and foreign visitors seeking less mass-tourism-oriented delights. The first part includes a smarter version of Lloret in **Platja d'Aro** – with a particularly lively nightlife, popular with weekenders from Barcelona – and the more family-friendly Sant Antoni de Calonge, bookended by the working fishing ports of **Sant Feliu de Guíxols** and **Palamós**, both of which remain largely aloof from their boisterous neighbours. Farther north, the area around **Palafrugell** boasts some fabulous cove towns, while hill-top **Begur** stands over a string of lovely little coves. **Inland** lures include the medieval towns of Pals and Peratallada, atmospheric Iberian ruins at Ullastret and the pottery industry of La Bisbal.

Sant Feliu de Guíxols and around

Separated from Tossa by 22km and, reputedly, 365 curves of stunning corniche, **SANT FELIU DE GUÍXOLS** is a bustling town with a decent beach and a cluster of handsome *modernista* buildings, evidence of its prosperous nineteenth-century cork industry. Its origins go back to the tenth century, when a settlement grew up around a Benedictine **monastery**, whose ruins, including the arched Porta Ferrada, still stand in Plaça Monestir.

Sant Feliu's old-world style is at its most apparent in the *modernista* **Casa Patxot** (built in 1917 and now home to the Chamber of Commerce) at Pg. del Mar 40, on the corner of Rambla Portalet, and the curious Moorish-style **Nou Casino La Constància** nearby at Pg. dels Guíxols 1–3, which was begun in 1851 and later adorned with *modernista* touches and brightly coloured swooping arches. The *passeig* follows the sweep of the coarse sand **beach** and yachting marina, while the streets back from the sea are great for a stroll past the shops and bars and the eighteenth-century **Plaça del Mercat**, with its bustling daily market.

Church of Sant Feliu es la Mare de Déu dels Àngels and Museu d'Història de la Ciutat

Pl. del Monestir • Museum July–Sept Tues–Sat 11am–2pm & 5–8pm, Sun 11am–2pm; Oct–June Tues–Sat 11am–2pm & 4–7pm • Free

The **church of Sant Feliu es la Mare de Déu dels Àngels** has a Romanesque facade and beautifully crafted crucifix dating from the same period as the Benedictine monastery, though it was rebuilt in Gothic style in the fourteenth century. The church is open for services only, while the rest of the complex is part of the **Museu d'Història de la Ciutat**, which contains absorbing exhibitions on the history of the town, including local archeological finds.

S'Agaró

On a headland north of Sant Feliu is the curious village of **S'AGARÓ**, created in the 1920s, where every house was built in the *modernista* style by Rafael Masó, a student of Antoni Gaudí. The short Camí de Ronda leading to the fabulous **Platja Sa Conca** is the best way to explore and take in a swim.

ARRIVAL AND INFORMATION SANT FELIU DE GUÍXOLS

By bus Teisa bus services to and from Girona stop opposite the monastery, while the Sarfa bus station (for buses to and from Palafrugell, Girona and Barcelona) is a 5min walk north of the centre on the main Carretera de Girona, at the junction with c/Llibertat.
Destinations Barcelona (8 daily; 1hr 30min); Girona (July–Sept 11 daily; 2hr); Lloret de Mar (July & Aug 2 daily; 40min); Palafrugell (15 daily; 45min); Palamós (15 daily;

30min); Platja d'Aro (17 daily; 15min).
By boat *Cruceros* boats dock on the main beach, where you'll also find the various ticket offices.
Turisme Pl. del Mercat 28, behind the main promenade (June–Sept daily 10am–2pm & 4–8pm; Oct–May Mon–Sat 10am–1pm & 4–7pm, Sun 10am–2pm; ☎972 820 051, ⊚guixols.cat).

ACCOMMODATION

Hostal de La Gavina Pujada de l'Hostal, S'Agaró ☎972 321 100, ⊚lagavina.com. Sitting in calm grounds overlooking Platja Sant Pol at the southern end of S'Agaró, this five-star *hotel* features palatial, marble-floored rooms adorned with elegant hand-carved furniture and fine antique rugs and lamps; the luxury continues with wood-panelled

dining rooms, bars, terraces, a saltwater pool and spa. **€325**
Hotel Plaça Pl. del Mercat 22 ☎972 325 155, ⊚hotelplaza.org. You'll find a score of family-run *hostals* and hotels in the old town, most within walking distance of the sea, including this friendly hotel that's set back from the water in the market square. **€113**

EATING

Cau del Pescador c/Sant Domènec 11 ☎972 324 052, ⊚caudelpescador.com. This atmospheric spot has a generous choice of seafood, from Sant Feliu anchovies to shrimp and squid, at mid-range prices. Daily 1–4pm & 8–11pm; Sept–June closed Mon dinner & Tues.
El Dorado Rambla Vidal 17 ☎972 821 414, ⊚grupoeldorado.com. The *El Dorado* mini-empire offers a range of dining in Sant Feliu, starting with this stylish location, which serves creative Catalan dishes. Next door is their tapas establishment, *El Dorado Pintxos*, with a range

of well-priced, fresh tapas that you can enjoy on the breezy terrace. El Dorado daily 1–4pm & 8pm–midnight; El Dorado Pintxos usually daily 1pm–midnight; both closed Mon in winter.
El Dorado Mar President Irla 15 ☎972 326 286, ⊚grupoeldorado.com. Dine on fresh seafood, from clams to cod, at this sister *El Dorado* restaurant overlooking the harbour at the southern end of the beach. *Menú* starts at €18. Daily 1–4pm & 8pm–midnight; closed Wed in winter.

Platja d'Aro and around

A few kilometres to the north of S'Agaró, **PLATJA D'ARO** is a neon strip of bars and shops running parallel to, but hidden from, a long sandy beach. It's by no means picturesque, but it does offer excellent **nightlife**, a great **beach** and some stylish **shopping**.

Beyond Platja d'Aro, the road leads to the more family-oriented but not terribly pretty town of **Sant Antoni de Calonge**; more enticing are the **coves** and beaches strung out between the two towns, all of which can be reached on foot by the serpentine and at times tricky **Camí de Ronda** or by a number of footpaths descending from the main road.

ARRIVAL AND INFORMATION PLATJA D'ARO AND AROUND

By bus Regular Sarfa buses travel to Platja d'Aro from around the Costa Brava, including Girona (just under 2hr).
Turisme Cinto Verdaguer 4, on the junction with central

Avgda. S'Agaró (July & Aug 8am–9pm, rest of year daily 9am–1pm & 4–7pm; ☎972 817 179, ⊚platjadaro.com).

ACCOMMODATION AND EATING

Platja d'Aro is filled with the usual assortment of tourist-friendly restaurants, with the cheapest ones on the main road through town.

Can Poldo Hotel Costa Brava, Punta d'en Ramis 17 ☎ 972 817 308, ⓦ hotelcostabrava.com. Serves fresh seafood and tasty Catalan dishes. The views rival the cuisine: the restaurant is beautifully situated, perched on a rock at the end of the beach. *Menú* starts at €20; dishes €16–25. Daily 1–3pm & 8–10pm; sometimes closed during the week in winter – call ahead.

Hotel Bell Repòs c/Nostra Senora del Carme 18 ☎ 972 817 100, ⓦ hotelbellrepos.com. The family-run, well-maintained hotel, with clean, basic rooms, is near the main beach. It also offers tickets for a well-priced €12 *menú*, which you can use at a handful of local restaurants. **€95**

Palamós and around

Immediately northeast of Sant Antoni de Calonge, **Palamós** was founded in 1277 and sacked by Barbarossa in 1543. Though the town is low on sights, its pleasant old quarter, set apart from the new on a promontory at the eastern end of the bay, makes for a pleasant afternoon wander and an evening at one of the breezy outdoor restaurant terraces.

Museu de la Pesca

Mid-June to mid-Sept Tues–Sun 10am–9pm; mid-Sept to mid-June Tues–Sat 10am–1.30pm & 3–7pm, Sun 10am–2pm & 4–7pm • €3 • ☎ 972 600 424, ⓦ museudelapesca.org

The working fishing port here is home to the mildly interesting **Museu de la Pesca**, chronicling the town's fishing and maritime history via audiovisual exhibits and archeological finds. The museum also organizes a variety of activities, many targeted at kids, including sailing.

The beaches

Accessible from Palamós by road or along the Camí de Ronda are two fabulous **beaches**. The first, the idyllic **Cala S'Alguer**, is framed by nineteenth-century fishermen's huts, while the larger **Platja de Castell** was rescued from the clutches of property developers thanks to a local referendum. Perched on the headland at the northern tip of Platja de Castell are the tranquil ruins of an Iberian settlement, visited by surprisingly few people.

ARRIVAL AND INFORMATION

PALAMÓS AND AROUND

By bus Regular Sarfa buses travel to Palamós from around the Costa Brava, including Girona (1hr 30min).

Turisme Pg. del Mar (summer daily 9am–9pm; winter Mon–Sat 10am–2pm & 4–7pm, Sun 10am–2pm; ☎ 972 600 550, ⓦ palamos.org).

EATING AND DRINKING

The town hosts a variety of good traditional restaurants. **Nightlife** is generally a fun and spontaneous affair; the best places are between the old town and the port in the La Planassa area (towards the end of the promontory).

Maria de Cadaqués c/Tauler i Servià 6 ☎ 972 314 009, ⓦ mariadecadaques.cat. This locally renowned restaurant, just off the marina, has an impressive history: it was founded in 1936 as a fishermen's tavern, and continues to serve excellent – though pricey – shellfish and *calamares*. Daily lunch & dinner; closed Sun eve.

La Plata Pl. San Pere 11, no phone. At *La Plata* you can enjoy cocktails and conversation in the lively downstairs bar and leafy terrace upstairs. Later, night owls decamp to the string of bars at the marina, a short walk east. Fri & Sat usually from 8 or 9pm; sometimes also open during the week.

Palafrugell

Seven kilometres north of Palamós, and 4km inland from a delightful coastline, lies the old town of **PALAFRUGELL**, comprising a cluster of streets and shops around a sixteenth-century church. It's at its liveliest during the morning produce market (daily except Mon), which on Sunday expands to include clothing, toys and other items.

Fundació Vila Casas Can Mario

Pl. Can Mario 7 • Tues–Sun 5–9pm • €5 • ☎ 972 306 246, ⊚ fundaciovilacasas.com

This sleek modern art centre, set in an old cork factory, features temporary exhibits with a focus on contemporary sculpture by Catalan and Spanish artists. The well-curated centre is run by the nonprofit Fundació Vila Casas, headquartered in Barcelona, which has the primary goal of promoting contemporary Catalan art.

ARRIVAL AND INFORMATION

PALAFRUGELL

By bus Buses arrive at Palafrugell's Sarfa bus terminal at c/Luís Companys 2, a 10min walk from the town centre. Palafrugell is also well connected by bus to other cities in the region, including to Barcelona (8 daily; 2hr); Figueres (5 daily; 1hr 30min); Girona (15 daily; 1hr); L'Escala (4 daily; 35min); Lloret de Mar (2 daily; 1hr 30min); Palamós (15 daily; 15min); Pals (4 daily; 10min); and Sant Feliu (17 daily; 45min).

Turisme c/Carrilet 2, near the terminal (May, June & Sept Mon–Sat 10am–1pm & 5–8pm, Sun 10am–1pm; July & Aug Mon–Sat 9am–9pm, Sun 10am–1pm; Oct–April Mon–Sat 10am–1pm & 4–7pm, Sun 10am–1pm; ☎ 972 300 228, ⊚ visitpalafrugell.cat). There's also a *turisme* in the centre at c/de Sta. Margarida 1 (Easter–Oct Mon–Sat 10am–1pm & 5–8pm, Sun 10am–1pm; same phone number).

ACCOMMODATION

There are places to stay at any of the nearby beaches, though rooms are expensive and zealously sought after. In the summer, it's usually easier and cheaper to stay in Palafrugell itself and get the bus to the beach: it's still wise to try and book ahead.

Café del Centre Bed & Breakfast c/dels Valls 26 ☎ 972 308 092, ⊚ grupgretelicafedelcentre.com. Five simple, clean rooms, sharing one bathroom, sitting above an inviting café. Rates include breakfast; they offer better deals for longer stays, and can also rent out all five rooms to one group. **€63**

Hostal L'Estrella c/de les Quatre Cases 13 ☎ 972 300 005, ⊚ hostal-estrella.com. A decent budget choice, on a little street near the main Pl. Nova. The basic rooms are arranged around a cloistered courtyard dating from 1605. **€62**

Hostal Plaja c/Sant Sebastià 34, on Pl. Nova ☎ 972 610 828, ⊚ hostalplaja.com. This decent spot is similar but slightly pricier than the others, with plain but comfortable and well-maintained rooms. They sometimes offer discounts for longer stays. **€66**

EATING AND DRINKING

Mas Oliver Avgda. d'Espanya (outside town on the ring road) ☎ 972 301 041. Similarly priced to *La Xicra*, with praised Catalan cuisine, including excellent grilled fish and meats. In warm weather dine on the outdoor terrace. Daily 1.30–4pm & 8–11pm; closed Tues lunch and usually Nov & Dec.

Pa i Raim c/Torres i Jonama 56 ☎ 972 304 572, ⊚ pairaim.com. Inviting, elegant restaurant featuring excellent Catalan cuisine with a twist, including monkfish

with sautéed artichoke, and roast veal scented with vanilla. €18–25 for mains. Daily except Mon 1.30–3pm & 8–10pm; closed Tues lunch in Aug, plus Sun in winter.

La Xicra c/de Sant Antoni 17 ☎ 972 305 630, ⊚ restaurantlaxicra.com. A pleasant Catalan restaurant, where the menu centres on local produce, including in-season mushrooms, as well as fresh seafood. A meal will run to €35 a head. Daily 1–4pm & 8–11pm; closed Wed lunch in summer; closed Sun dinner, Tues & Wed in winter.

Around Palafrugell

The area around Palafrugell boasts tranquil, pine-covered slopes, which back three of the most alluring villages on the Costa Brava – **Calella**, **Llafranc** and **Tamariu** – each with a distinct character and all with scintillatingly turquoise waters. With no true coastal road, the beach development here has been generally mild – low-rise, whitewashed apartments and hotels – and although a fair number of foreign visitors come in season, it's also where many of the better-off Barcelonans have a villa for weekend and August escapes. All this makes for one of the most appealing (though hardly undiscovered) stretches of the Costa Brava.

Calella de Palafrugell

Captivating **Calella de Palafrugell** possesses a gloriously rocky coastline punctuated by several tiny sand and rocky **beaches** with a backdrop of whitewashed arches and *fin-de-siècle* villas. From the charming area around the minuscule main beaches, the town stretches southwards along a winding Camí de Ronda to the hidden **El Golfet** beach.

11

CHEERS TO CREMAT

Catalan sailors returning from Cuba and the Antilles in the nineteenth century brought back more than soulful *havaneres* songs. They also brought back Caribbean rum, which forms the basis for **cremat**, a typical drink of the fishing villages in this region, particularly Calella and neighboring Llafranc.

The potent concoction contains rum, sugar, lemon peel, coffee grounds and sometimes a cinnamon stick. The ritual of drinking *cremat* is a big part of the experience: it's brought out in an earthenware bowl and you have to set fire to it, occasionally stirring until (after a few minutes) it's ready to drink. Also part of the ritual… to sing *havaneres* while drinking.

Calella hosts a **Cantada de Havaneres** on the first Saturday of July, with five groups performing *havaneres* (tickets €30). Check in with the *turismes* in Palafrugell (see p.719) or Calella (see below).

Jardí Botanic de Cap Roig

Daily: June–Sept 9am–8pm; Oct–May 9am–6pm • €6 • ⓦ jardins.caproig.cat

Above the El Golfet beach, the Cap Roig headland is home to the **Jardí Botanic de Cap Roig**, a cliff-top botanical garden and castle begun in 1927 by an exiled colonel from the tsar's army and his aristocrat English wife. This is also the site of the superb music festival **Festival Jardins de Cap Roig** (mid-July to late Aug), which features everything from jazz to rock, and has hosted such big names as Bob Dylan, Diana Ross, Elvis Costello and Leonard Cohen.

Llafranc

A gentle, hilly, twenty-minute walk high above the rocks along the Camí de Ronda brings you to **Llaranc**, tucked into the next bay from Calella de Palafrugell, with a good (if packed) stretch of **beach** and a glittering **marina**. A little more upmarket than Calella, it's a self-consciously opulent place with expensive beachside restaurants and hillside villas glinting in the sun. Steps lead up from the port for the winding climb through residential streets to the **Far de Sant Sebastià**, a lighthouse where you'll be rewarded with some terrific views.

Tamariu, Platja d'Aiguablava and Fornells

Tamariu, 4km north of Llafranc, is quieter and a great favourite with well-heeled Catalan families. The town's action is focused on the small seafront, and the **promenade** – lined with tamarind trees, the source of the town's name – has a hushed but inviting atmosphere, with small shops, pavement restaurants and neighbours sitting on their front porches. Geared more towards the summer-home crowd, the town has fewer hotels than other towns on the coast, but most are good.

It's a pleasant drive along the coast from here to Begur, passing **Platja d'Aiguablava**, with the lovely *Parador de Aiguablava* (see opposite). Just 1km north is the tiny and exclusive cove of **Fornells**, 3km from Begur.

ARRIVAL AND INFORMATION

By bus From June to Sept, buses run regularly from Palafrugell to Calella and then on to Llafranc (July & Aug every 30min; June & Sept roughly hourly), reducing to around four times daily from Oct to May. A less frequent service runs to the more distant beach at Tamariu (June–Sept; 3–4 daily).

AROUND PALAFRUGELL

Turisme c/de les Voltes 6, Calella de Palafrugell (July & Aug daily 10am–8pm; Easter–June & Sept–mid-Oct Mon–Sat 10am–2pm & 5–8pm, Sun 10am–1pm; ☎ 972 614 475, ⓦ visitpalafrugell.cat).

ACCOMMODATION

CALELLA DE PALAFRUGELL

Hotel Sant Roc Pl. Atlàntic 2 ☎ 972 614 250, ⓦ santroc .com. This plush hotel sits perched over the sea, with superb views of the coves. The restaurant, *El Balcó del Calella*, serves tasty Mediterranean cuisine (closed Tues in winter). **€135**

Mediterrani c/Francesc Estrabau 40 ☎ 972 614 500,

w hotelmediterrani.com. Friendly, family-run hotel with comfortable rooms featuring lovely sea views, as well as a breezy terrace. Closed Oct–April. **€130**

LLAFRANC

Hotel Casamar c/del Nero 3 ☎972 300 104, w hotelcasamar.net. This friendly hotel has cool-toned bright rooms; those with balconies feature lovely views of the bay. **€107**

Hotel El Far Far de Sant Sebastià ☎972 301 639, w elfar.net. This sumptuous hotel sits on a cliff, and the elegant rooms each have a panoramic balcony. The alluring restaurant (closed Jan) serves fresh seafood and a good selection of paella, rice and *fideuà* (thin noodles) dishes. **€245**

Hotel Terramar Pg. Cipsela 1 ☎972 300 200, w hterramar.com. On the seafront, this comfortable hotel is run by the fourth generation of the same family, and has simple yet elegant rooms overlooking the beach. **€115**

TAMARIU

Tamariu Pg. del Mar 2 ☎972 620 031, w tamariu.com. The seafront *Tamariu*, originally a fishermen's tavern in the 1920s, has simple but comfortable rooms with terrace. **€149**

PLATJA D'AIGUABLAVA

Parador de Aiguablava ☎972 622 162, w parador.es. Set on a craggy headland jutting out into the sea, this modern hotel may lack the character of historic paradores, but has good facilities and large windows throughout to show off the magnificent views. The restaurant serves up a range of local dishes, including *anchoas* (anchovies) from L'Escala, and dishes rooted in Catalunya's *mar i muntanya* cuisine. **€150**

EATING AND DRINKING

CALELLA DE PALAFRUGELL

La Gavina c/Gravina 7 ☎972 614 554, w lagavinacalella.com. Excellent traditional Catalan cooking and a wide selection of fish and seafood for around €15–20; enjoy the sea breezes on the open, shaded terrace. Summer daily 8–11pm; usually closed Oct–March.

LLAFRANC

La Llagosta Hostal La Llagosta, c/Francesc Blanes 24 ☎972 300 115, w hostallallagosta.com. This comfortable spot on the seafront serves decently priced regional fare, including fresh seafood and *llagosta* (lobster). April–Sept daily 1.30–3.30pm & 8–10.30pm; usually closed Oct–March.

Llevant Hotel Llevant, c/Francesc Blanes 5 ☎972 300 366, w hotel-llevant.com. For good seafood, from shrimp to cod, dine at this welcoming spot which offers a hearty €25 *menú*. Daily 1.30–3.30pm & 8.30–10.30pm; Jan–March closed Sun dinner & Mon; closed mid-Nov to Dec.

Begur and around

In the lee of a ruined hill-top castle, chic **BEGUR**, about 7km from Palafrugell and slightly inland, stands at the centre of a web of winding roads leading down to its tranquil and equally stylish **beaches**. Narrow streets lead to the simple exterior and surprisingly ornate Gothic interior of the **Església Parroquial de Sant Pere**; most remarkable is the odd contrast between statuary and architecture, especially the simplicity of the alabaster *Madonna and Child* compared with the busy altarpiece. Watching over it all, the thrice-destroyed **Castell de Begur** offers fabulous perspectives of the rocky coves to the south and the curving swathe of the Golf de Roses to the north. The annual **Festival de Música de Begur**, generally from late July to late August, features everything from classical music to swing and jazz.

From here roads lead east to the **Cap de Begur**, with its spectacular *mirador*, the coves of **Sa Tuna** and **Aiguafreda**, linked by a scenic footpath (1km), and the pretty hamlet of **SA RIERA**, where you can walk to **Platja del Raco** and **Platja Illa Roja**, some of the best beaches on the coast.

ARRIVAL AND INFORMATION

BEGUR AND AROUND

By bus Sarfa buses travel to Begur from around the Costa Brava, including nearby Palafrugell (10min), and once a day from Girona (1hr 15min). The beaches are connected to the town by summer minibus services.

Turisme Avgda. Onze de Setembre 7, just south of Begur's main square, Pl. de la Villa (daily: spring and autumn 9am–2pm & 4–7pm; summer 9am–2pm & 4–9pm; winter 9am–2pm; ☎972 624 520, w visitbegur.cat).

ACCOMMODATION AND EATING

There are a few fairly expensive hotels at the beaches, while beyond the pleasant *Fonda Caner*, you'll find further options for a meal or a drink at plenty of beachside spots and in town around the Pl. del la Villa.

Fonda Caner c/Pi i Ralló 10 ☎ 972 622 391, ⓦ hotel-rosa.com. The *Hotel Rosa* owners run this nearby, inviting restaurant with tiled floors and partially exposed stone walls. *Cuina Catalana* includes a *menú* for €21. April–Oct Mon–Fri 8–10.30pm, Sat & Sun 1–3.30pm & 8–10.30pm, also open lunch Mon–Fri in Aug; closed Nov–March.

Hotel Rosa c/Pi i Ralló 19 ☎ 972 623 015, ⓦ hotel-rosa .com. In Begur itself is this charming family-owned spot, with comfortable rooms and a cheerful atmosphere. **€105**

Pals

Turisme: Pl. Major 7, in the old town (daily: June–Aug 10am–2pm & 5–8pm; rest of year 10am–2pm & 4–7pm; ☎ 972 637 380, ⓦ pals.es).

The 7km journey north from Palafrugell to Torroella de Montgrí can be broken at **PALS**, also 7km from Begur. This fortified medieval village was long neglected until it was painstakingly restored by a local doctor after the Civil War, which has earned it the rather unfortunate side effect of being invaded by scores of day-trippers. Even so, its fourteenth-century streets and hill-top setting make it an enjoyable place for a stroll. The golden-brown buildings cluster around a stark tower, all that remains of the town's Romanesque **castle**; below is the beautifully vaulted Gothic **Església de Sant Pere** and Romanesque **Torre de les Hores**.

La Bisbal

LA BISBAL, 12km northwest of Palafrugell on the main road to Girona, is a medieval market town in an attractive river setting. Since the seventeenth century, La Bisbal has specialized in the production of **ceramics**, and pottery shops line the main road through town (c/de L'Aigüeta), great for browsing and picking up some terrific local pieces.

Ceramics apart, La Bisbal is a pleasant stop anyway, as its handsome old centre retains many impressive mansions, the architectural remnants of a once thriving Jewish quarter and the fortified medieval **Castell Palau de la Bisbal**.

Terracotta Museu

C/Sis d'Octubre 99 • June–Sept Mon–Sat 11am–2pm & 4.30–8.30pm, Sun 11am–2pm • €3 • ⓦ museuscostabrava.cat

If the industry grabs you, the **Terracotta Museu**, housed in one of the oldest ceramic tile factories in the region, makes for an interesting diversion, featuring a historical overview, a colourful array of pottery pieces and tools and equipment. The museum has been closed for renovation, but should have reopened by the time you read this.

Castell Palau de la Bisbal

Tues–Sat 11am–2pm & 5–8pm, Sun 11am–2pm • €2, guided tour €3

La Bisbal's most important historical building is the fortified **Castell Palau**, built for the bishops of Girona. The sturdy castle, which dates back to the eleventh and twelfth centuries, has been in continuous use since it was built, including a spell as a prison during the Spanish Civil War. Inside, you'll learn about medieval Catalunya while touring its various sections.

ACCOMMODATION AND EATING   LA BISBAL

Arcs de Monells c/Vilanova 1, Monells ☎ 972 630 304, ⓦ hotelarcsmonells.com. This lovely hotel, set in a fourteenth-century hospital 3km northwest of town, is a lavish base, with a beautifully renovated interior and comfortable rooms. **€200**

★ **Hotel Castell d'Empordà** ☎ 972 646 254, ⓦ castelldemporda.com. This 800-year-old castle, perched on top of a hill 3km north of the town with beautiful views of the surrounding countryside, is now a sumptuous hotel. You're in good company: a captain for Christopher Columbus stayed here, and Dalí once tried to buy it. The restaurant celebrates the local bounty, and serves creative Catalan cuisine and excellent regional wines. **€165**

Peratallada and Ullastret

Five kilometres northeast of La Bisbal, the medieval walled town of **PERATALLADA** has preserved a rustic feel, with the help of its tiny cobbled streets, stone arches and shaded squares. An influx of small hotels and restaurants has proved to be surprisingly in keeping with their thirteenth-century Romanesque setting, making it a fabulous base away from the beach. The focal point is the **Castell de Peratallada** (closed to visitors), whose origins have been dated to pre-Roman times.

Museu d'Arqueologia de Ullastret

Puig de Sant Andreu d'Ullastret • Summer Tues–Sun 10am–8pm; winter 10am–2pm & 3–6pm • €2.30

Six kilometres northeast lie the remains of the Iberian settlement of **Puig de Sant Andreu d'Ullastret**, a lovely, peaceful ruin with an archeological museum, with excavated artefacts from the area. The site is just north of the friendly, historic village of **Ullastret**, signposted off the main road.

INFORMATION	PERATALLADA AND ULLASTRET

Turisme Pl. del Castell, in front of the Castell de Peratallada (summer daily noon–2pm & 3–8pm; winter generally Sat & Sun only; ☎ 872 987 030, ⓦ visitlabisbal.cat).

ACCOMMODATION	

Hostal La Riera Pl. les Voltes 3, Peratallada ☎ 972 634 142, ⓦ lariera.es. Cosy *hostal*, comfortably housed in a seventeenth-century building – and one of the area's more economical options. Rate includes breakfast. **€80**

Torroella de Montgrí

TORROELLA DE MONTGRÍ, 8km from Ullastret and 9km beyond Pals, was once an important medieval port, but today has been left high and dry by the receding Mediterranean. It now stands 5km inland, beneath the shell of the huge, crenellated **Castell de Montgrí** (at 302m, a stiff thirty-minute walk away), built by King Jaume II between 1294 and 1301 but never completed. The town itself remains distinctly medieval in appearance with its narrow streets, fine mansions and fourteenth-century parish church of **Sant Genís** (daily 4–6pm; sometimes open in mornings as well). The town is probably best known for its **Festival Internacional de Música** (ⓦ en. festivaldetorroella.com), held each July and August in the main square and church, which features an excellent line-up of classical music.

Centre Cultural de la Mediterrània

C/d'Ullà • July & Aug daily 10am–2pm & 6–9pm; Sept–June Mon & Wed–Sat 10am–2pm & 5–8pm, Sun 10am–2pm • Free • ⓦ museudelamediterrania.org

The **Centre Cultural de la Mediterrània**, in the historic Can Quintana house, has displays on local geography, history and culture, including a mural map of the Mediterranean, interactive displays, old photographs of the region and audiovisual exhibits.

ARRIVAL AND INFORMATION	TORROELLA DE MONTGRÍ

By bus Regular buses travel between Torroella and Barcelona (just under 2hr), as well as to L'Estartit (15min).
Turisme Centre Cultural, c/d'Ullà (July & Aug daily 10am–2pm & 6–9pm; Sept–June Mon & Wed–Sat 10am–2pm & 5–8pm, Sun 10am–2pm; ☎ 972 755 180, ⓦ visitestartit.com/en).

ACCOMMODATION	

Fonda Mitja c/Església 14 ☎ 972 758 003, ⓦ fondamitja.com. If you decide to stay, this homely hotel, just off Pl. de la Vila, has comfortable rooms and a cosy restaurant providing breakfast or full board. **€75**

Palau Lo Mirador Pg. de l'Església 1 ☎ 972 758 063, ⓦ palaulomirador.com. This handsome, historic hotel features a palatial interior, but it can get noisy during weddings and events, which they host often, so ask before booking. **€120**

L'Estartit and the Illes Medes

The nearest beach to Torroella is 6km to the east at **L'ESTARTIT**, an otherwise unexceptional resort town. Call into the *turisme* for information about the nearby **Illes Medes**, Catalunya's only offshore islands – kiosks in the area sell boat trips in the summer. The tiny islands form a protected nature reserve, hosting the most important colony of herring gulls in the Mediterranean, numbering some eight thousand pairs, and offer some of the best **diving** and snorkelling on the coast.

ARRIVAL AND INFORMATION	L'ESTARTIT AND THE ILLES MEDES

By bus Hourly buses travel here from Torroella de Montgrí (15min).

Turisme At the northern end of Passeig Marítim, which

runs along the seafront (summer daily 9.30am–2pm; rest of year Mon–Fri 9am–1pm & 3–6pm, Sat & Sun 10am–2pm; ☎ 972 751 910, ⓦ visitestartit.com).

ACCOMMODATION AND EATING

Hotel Les Illes c/Illes 55 ☎ 972 751 239, ⓦ hotellesilles .com. This amiable hotel, with comfortable, well-maintained rooms, also organizes its own popular diving excursions. **€108**

Restaurant Bravo Pg. Marítim 82–86 ☎ 972 752 116.

You'll find plenty of bars and restaurants along the seafront, like this restaurant, which serves mid-priced fresh seafood and rice dishes on a breezy terrace. Summer usually daily 1–4pm & 8–10pm; sometimes limited hours in winter.

Alt Empordà

Beyond Torroella de Montgrí, the scenery changes quite abruptly as you move into the fertile plains and wetlands of the southern part of the **Alt Empordà**, dominated by the broad swathe of the **Golf de Roses**. Coves give way to long stretches of sand as far north as **Roses**, which nestles in its own closed-in bay. The gulf is backed for the most part by flat, rural land, well watered by the Muga and Fluvià rivers. Having been left to its own quiet devices for centuries, this section of coast is distinct from the otherwise touristy Costa Brava, and has really only suffered the attentions of the developers in towns at either end of the bay, most notably in the few kilometres between Roses and the giant marina-cum-resort of Empuriabrava.

At the southern end of the gulf is the pleasant old fishing port of **L'Escala**, made more remarkable by the presence of **Empúries**, a ruined Greek and Roman settlement and one of Spain's most important archeological sites. Beyond Roses, the familiar crashing rocks and deeply indented coves return with a vengeance in the wild Cap de Creus headland. The jewel in the crown here is **Cadaqués**, eternally linked to **Salvador Dalí**, who lived for years in the neighbouring fishermen's village of **Portlligat**, now home to an absorbing museum in his bizarre former residence. For the final run to the French border, the road swoops along the coast through quieter villages such as whitewashed **El Port de la Selva**.

L'Escala

At the southernmost end of the sweeping billhook of the Golf de Roses, **L'ESCALA** is split between its shabby but picturesque *nucli antic*, or **old town**, favoured by local holiday-makers, and the more commercial **Riells** quarter, which has a beach and is the haunt of foreign visitors. Infinitely more appealing, the narrow pedestrianized streets of the old town huddle around the ancient port, where you'll find medieval mooring posts

---

THE ART OF ANCHOVIES

There are anchovies, and then there are **Catalan anchovies**. Most think of anchovies as oily, limp little items, but here on the Catalan coast, and most famously in **L'Escala**, *anchoas* (*anxoves* in Catalan) are succulent, pale in colour, and plump – almost double the size of what you may be used to. L'Escala is widely known for its canning factories where Catalunya's best anchovies are packaged.

You can sample them in most bars and restaurants – and there may be nothing better than a plate of anchovies, a hunk of bread (the better to soak up the aromatic olive oil-laced juices) and a *cerveza* or three, enjoyed at a seaside *terraza*. And bring the taste home with you: plenty of grocery shops around town sell little jars and cans that you can pack into your bags.

and a cannonball embedded in the wall of the house at c/Joan Massanet 2 (close to the seafront at the end of c/Pintor de Massanet), fired from a ship in May 1809.

A further enticement is L'Escala's proximity to the ancient site of Empúries, which lies just a couple of kilometres out of town.

ARRIVAL AND INFORMATION   L'ESCALA

By bus Buses stop on Avgda. Girona, just down the road from the *turisme*. Regular services travel to Barcelona (3 daily; 2hr 40min); Figueres (4 daily; 45min); Girona (2 daily; 1hr); Palafrugell (4 daily; 45min); and Pals (4 daily; 35min).
By car Parking is tricky, although there are a number of small car parks around the centre or meters along the

promenade between the old port and Riells.
Turisme Pl. de las Escoles 1, on the edge of the old town (mid-June to mid-Sept Mon–Sat 9am–8pm, Sun 10am–1pm; mid-Sept to mid-June Mon–Fri 9am–1pm & 4–7pm, Sat 10am–1pm & 4–7pm, Sun 10am–1pm; ☎ 972 770 603, ⓦ lescala.cat).

ACCOMMODATION

Hostal Empúries Platja de Portitxol s/n ☎ 972 770 207, ⓦ hostalempuries.com. A lovingly run, well-located hotel, facing the beach and near the main entrance to Empúries. There are two sections: the cheaper, older, historic section and the newer, sleeker spa rooms, with

terraces overlooking the sea (€191). The attahed *Potritxol* restaurant serves tasty local cuisine. **€145**
Hotel Voramar Pg. Lluis Albert 2 ☎ 972 770 108, ⓦ hotelvoramar.com. Decent if slightly faded rooms, plus a pretty pool and bar above the waves. **€118**

EATING AND DRINKING

Freshly caught fish and seafood, particularly anchovies are the speciality of the town's **restaurants**, with a good choice in the port and the old town. For a **drink**, head to the *nucli antic*, where you'll find a range from fishermen's taverns and bars.

Restaurant l'Avi Freu Paseo Lluis Albert 7 ☎ 972 771 241. This established restaurant serves a daily *menú* focusing on *arroces* (rice dishes) starting at €16, as well as fresh seafood and other regional fare. Daily 1–4pm & 7.30–10.30pm; weekends only in winter.

Restaurant Potritxol Hostal Empúries ☎ 972 770 207, ⓦ hostalempuries.com. Feast on fresh local fare, such as monkfish with artichokes. They offer a *menú* for €23, except in the summer when it's only à la carte. Dishes €16–21. Daily 1–3.30pm & 8–10.30pm.

Empúries

Daily: Easter & June–Sept 10am–8pm; rest of year 10am–6pm • €3 • A "tourist train" sometimes runs in summer from L'Escala to Empúries (€2); contact the tourist office in L'Escala

The archeological site of **Empúries**, which lies behind a sandy bay about 2km north of L'Escala, has immense historical significance, being the first entry point of classical Mediterranean culture into Iberian Spain – its fascination derives from its distinct Greek and Roman quarters showing how one culture steadily usurped the other. You can see the ruins in a leisurely afternoon, spending the rest of your time on the pleasant duned stretch of sand nearby.

Empúries was the ancient Greek Emporion (literally "trading station"), founded in the early sixth century BC by merchants who, for three centuries, conducted a vigorous trade throughout the Mediterranean. In 218 BC, their settlement was taken by Scipio, and a Roman city – more splendid than the Greek, with an amphitheatre, fine villas and a broad marketplace – grew up above the old Greek town. The Romans were replaced in turn by the Visigoths, who built several basilicas, and Emporion disappears from the records only in the ninth century when, it is assumed, it was wrecked by either Saracen or Norman pirates.

The Greek colony

You can enter the **site** via the beach in summer, but at other times the main entrance and car park lie on the road farther inland. The remains of the original **Greek colony**, destroyed by a Frankish raid in the third century AD – at which stage all inhabitants moved to the Roman city – occupy the lower part of the site. Among the ruins of several **temples**, to the south on raised ground is one dedicated to Asklepios, the Greek healing god whose cult was centred on Epidauros and the island of Kos. The temple is marked by a replica of a fine third-century-BC statue of the god, the original of which (along with many finds from the site) is in the Museu Arqueològic in Barcelona. Nearby are several large water filters: Emporion had no aqueduct so water was stored here to be filtered and purified and then supplied to the town by means of long pipes, one of which has been reconstructed. Remains of the town gate, the **agora** (or central marketplace) and several streets can easily be made out, along with a mass of house foundations, some with mosaics, and the ruins of Visigoth basilicas. A small **museum** stands above, with helpful models and diagrams of the excavations, as well as some of the lesser finds, and an excellent audiovisual display giving a brief history of the settlement.

The Roman town

Beyond the museum stretches the vast but only partially excavated **Roman town**. Here, two luxurious villas have been uncovered, and you can see their entrance halls, porticoed gardens and magnificent mosaic floors. Farther on are the remains of the **forum**, **amphitheatre** and outer walls.

Parc Natural dels Aiguamolls de l'Empordà

Daily • Free

Halfway around the Golf de Roses, in two parcels of land on either side of the resort of Empuriabrava, is one of Spain's more accessible nature reserves. The **Parc Natural dels Aiguamolls de l'Empordà** is an important wetland reserve, created by the Catalan government in 1983 to save what remained of the Empordà marshland, which once covered the entire plain here but gradually reduced over the centuries as a result of agricultural developments and cattle-raising. The park attracts a wonderful selection of birds to both its coastal terrain and the paddy fields typical of the area.

The park

There are two main **paths** around the lagoons and marshes: the first takes around two hours, while a second five-hour trek crosses more open land and can be cycled. Hides have been created along the way; morning and early evening are the best times for **birdwatching** and you'll spy the largest number of species during the migration periods (March–May & Aug–Oct). You'll almost certainly see marsh harriers and various waterfowl, and might spot bee-eaters and the rare glossy ibis.

Sant Pere Pescador

The nearest village to the visitors' centre at El Cortalet is **Sant Pere Pescador**, 6km south, pleasant enough but surrounded by a glut of sprawling, extremely busy campsites. You can rent bikes here, handy given the flat countryside, but the hordes of tourists make Castelló d'Empúries, 8km farther on, a more attractive base.

ARRIVAL AND INFORMATION   **PARC NATURAL DELS AIGUAMOLLS DE L'EMPORDÀ**

By bus Sarfa buses travel to Sant Pere Pescador from Castelló d'Empúries, L'Escala and Figueres.
Visitor centre El Cortalet (daily: April–Sept 9.30am–2pm

& 4.30–7pm; Oct–March 9.30am–2pm & 3.30–6pm; ☎ 972 454 222, ⌨ parcsdecatalunya.net). Here you can pick up a brochure marking the recommended routes in the park.

ACCOMMODATION

Can Ceret c/Mar 1 ☎ 972 530 433, ⌨ canceret.com. If you decide to stay in Sant Pere Pescador, try this well-maintained eighteenth-century farmhouse, which offers comfortable rooms and good meals. **€115**
Nautic Almatà In the Parc Natural dels Aiguamolls de

l'Empordà ☎ 972 454 477, ⌨ almata.com. This massive campsite is one of the best for access to the park. It has well-maintained facilities and can organize outdoor excursions. Closed Oct to mid-May. Tent pitch for six people, plus car/caravan **€46**

Castelló d'Empúries

Formerly the capital of the counts of Empúries, the delightful small town of **CASTELLÓ D'EMPÚRIES**, halfway between the beach at Roses and Figueres, is also midway between the two halves of the Parc Natural dels Aiguamolls. A five-minute walk from where the bus halts takes you into a small medieval conglomeration that's lost little of its genteel charm. The town's narrow alleys and streets conceal some fine preserved buildings, a medieval bridge and fine church.

Church of Santa María

Church and museum: daily 10am–2pm & 4–8pm • Museum €1.50

The towering thirteenth-century church, **Santa María**, has an ornate doorway and alabaster altarpiece which alone are reward enough for the trip. Known as the Cathedral of the Empordà, the church was intended to be the centre of an episcopal see, but opposition from the bishopric of Girona meant this was never to be, thus leaving Castelló with a church out of proportion to the town. The church's **Museu Parroquial de Santa María** contains a mildly interesting collection of silver and gold religious artefacts.

11

ARRIVAL AND INFORMATION   CASTELLÓ D'EMPÚRIES

By bus Daily Sarfa buses service Castelló d'Empúries from Figueres (15min), Cadaqués (1hr) and Barcelona (1hr 30min). It's a 10min walk from the bus stop into town.

Turisme Pl. Jaume I (summer daily 9am–9pm; rest of year Mon–Sat 9am–2pm & 4–6pm, Sun 10am–1pm; ☎ 972 156 233, ⓦ castelloempuriabrava.com).

ACCOMMODATION AND EATING

Hotel Canet Pl. Joc de la Pilota 2 ☎ 972 250 340, ⓦ hotelcanet.com. If you're looking for budget beds, try this hotel with simple, economical rooms – plus a restaurant (closed Mon in winter) that serves Catalan fare, including seafood, grilled meats and local produce. **€85**

Hotel de la Moneda Pl. de la Moneda 8–10 ☎ 972 158 602, ⓦ hoteldelamoneda.com. Elegant seventeenth-

century mansion, run by the same owners as *Hotel Canet*, with cosy, brightly painted rooms. **€110**

El Molí 8km west of Castelló d'Empúries ☎ 972 525 139, ⓦ elmolidesiurana.com. Lovely *El Molí* is one of several *casas rurales* in the area. It's set among vast gardens with oaks and laurel trees, near the village of Siurana d'Empordà, between Figueres and Sant Pere Pescador. Includes breakfast. **€85**

Roses

ROSES, 9km from Castello, enjoys a lovely situation beneath medieval fortress walls at the head of the grand, sweeping bay. It's a site that's been inhabited for over three thousand years – the Greeks called the place Rhoda when they set up a trading colony around the excellent natural harbour in the ninth century BC – but apart from the ruined **Castell de la Trinitat** and the Citadel, which contains the absorbing **Museu de la Ciutadella**, there's little in present-day Roses to hint at its long history. Instead, Roses is a full-blown package resort that trades exclusively on its 4km of sandy beach, which has fostered a large and popular watersports industry. If you're staying, don't skip a day-trip to Cadaqués, which you can reach via a short bus ride over the hill.

Citadel and the Museu de la Ciutadella

Tues–Sun: April–Sept daily 10am–9pm; Oct–March 10am–6pm • €4

You can walk around the **Citadel**, which contains the remains of the Greek settlement of Rhoda, an ancient Roman villa and the **Museu de la Ciutadella**, which explores the Citadel's history – and its role in the evolution of Roses – via exhibits and photographs.

ARRIVAL AND INFORMATION   ROSES

By bus The bus station is on the corner of c/Gran Vía Pau Casals and Rambla Ginjolers. Sarfa buses travel regularly to and from Barcelona (2hr 15min) and Figueres (30min).

Turisme On the seafront promenade near the citadel

(mid-June to mid-Sept 9am–9pm; rest of year Mon–Fri 9am–6pm, Sat 10am–2pm & 3–6pm, Sun 10am–1pm; ☎ 972 257 331, ⓦ roses.cat). Has an extensive accommodation list.

THE EVOLUTION OF EL BULLI

Why did the most famous chef in the world close his restaurant at the height of its popularity? The answer to that explains who Catalan chef Ferran Adrià is.

Adrià's legendary "molecular gastronomy" restaurant **El Bulli**, near the town of Roses, was voted best restaurant in the world for five years – twice in 2010 – by *Restaurant* magazine, the arbiters of such things. At its apex, there were two million reservation requests per year – and eight thousand granted. Adrià closed *El Bulli* in July 2011, and in its place is setting up a nonprofit culinary foundation and centre, due to open in 2014, in pursuit of what he calls "constant evolution" and "a permanent commitment to creativity". For up-to-date information, including information on visiting, check the website: ⓦ elbulli.com. In the meantime, though *El Bulli* has now closed its doors, you can visit the lively tapas bar, **Tickets**, Ferran opened in 2011 with his brother Albert in Barcelona (see p.692).

Adrià is perhaps best known for his "foams" (*espumas*), scented with everything from carrot to pine nuts to smoke. One of his culinary signatures has been to re-create traditional Mediterranean flavours via very non-traditional methods, his wizardry yielding such concoctions as liquid ravioli; spherified olives; parmesan ice cream; and "caviaroli" – caviar made with *allioli*. As Adrià has said of his cuisine: "Nothing is as it seems." Adrià is also famous for his deconstruction of Spain's comfort dishes, like *tortilla de patatas*. Hot potato is transformed into foam, onion made into a thick purée and egg white becomes a whipped sabayon. It's served in a tiny sherry glass with a spoon: the flavours fill the mouth – intense, warm and startlingly familiar.

The **El Bulli Foundation** will occupy the same space as the restaurant, which is perched over the quiet cove of **Montjoi**, at the end of a long and winding road above Roses. It's a lovely, isolated spot – a far cry from the thronged Costa Brava and its laminated, quadrilingual menus. The land on which it sits was originally purchased by a German couple, who opened a beach bar which was followed by a restaurant, which they named after their pet French bulldogs – *El Bulli*. Adrià joined the staff in 1984, and contemporary Catalan cuisine has never been quite the same since.

Adrià is sometimes compared to another famous native son of Catalunya: Salvador Dalí. One is a surrealist on canvas, the other a surrealist in the kitchen. We asked Adrià about the parallel, if any, between art and cuisine, and he summed it up like this:

The dialogue between art and cuisine is still young. But in the end, it's not that important if cuisine is art, but if it changes the way you look at the world.

ACCOMMODATION AND EATING

Almadraba Park Hotel Avgda. Díaz Pacheco 70, Platja de l'Almadraba ☎ 972 256 550, ⓦ almadrabapark.com. For a splurge stay at this classy spot, which has retained its history and elegance even amid the overbuilt Costa Brava. The hotel features pretty views of the sea and stylishly comfortable rooms, while the restaurant (closed mid-Oct to March) is worth a visit in itself: it's helmed by the well-known chef Jaume Subirós of the *Hotel Empordá* (see p.741), and serves creative Catalan cuisine; the *menú* is €43, and dishes start at €24. **€164**

Cadaqués

CADAQUÉS is by far the most pleasant place to stay on the northern Costa Brava, reached only by the winding road over the hills from either Roses (16km) or Port de la Selva (12km) and consequently retaining an air of isolation. With whitewashed and bougainvillea-festooned houses lining narrow, hilly streets, a tree-lined promenade and craggy headlands on either side of a working fishing port, it's genuinely picturesque. Already by the 1920s and 1930s the place had begun to attract the likes of Picasso, Man Ray, Lorca, Buñuel, Thomas Mann and Einstein, but Cadaqués really "arrived" as an **artistic-literary colony** after World War II when Surrealist painter **Salvador Dalí** and his wife Gala settled at nearby Portlligat, attracting for some years a floating bohemian community. Today, a seafront statue of Dalí provides the town's physical and spiritual focal point, haughtily gazing on the artists, well-heeled Barcelonans and art-seeking foreigners who have rolled up in his wake.

CADAQUÉS; GIRONA (P.733) >

With its art galleries and studios, smart restaurants and trendy clothes shops, Cadaqués makes for an interesting stroll. At the top of the hill is the austere-looking sixteenth-century **Església de Santa María**, containing an ornate eighteenth-century altarpiece and a side chapel on the left painted by Dalí. Local **beaches** are all tiny and pebbly, but there are some enjoyable walks around the harbour and nearby coves; the helpful tourist office has further information and maps.

Museu de Cadaqués

C/Narcis Monturiol 15 • April–June Mon–Sat 10am–1.30pm & 4–7pm; July to mid-Sept Mon, Tues & Thurs–Sun 10am–8pm, Wed 10am–1.30pm & 4–7pm; mid-Sept to Dec Mon, Tues & Thurs–Sat 10.30am–1.30pm & 3.30–6.30pm, Wed 10am–3pm; generally closed Jan–March • Entry fee varies • ☎ 972 258 877

Below the church, the **Museu de Cadaqués** features temporary exhibitions by local artists and intriguing displays relating to aspects of Dalí's work. They also occasionally showcase exhibits on other artists connected to Cadaqués, including Picasso.

11 | ARRIVAL AND INFORMATION | CADAQUÉS

By bus Sarfa buses arrive at the little bus office on c/Sant Vicenç, on the edge of town, next to a large pay car park. From here, you can walk along c/Unió and c/Vigilant to the seafront or climb up through the old streets to reach it. Buses run to Barcelona (2 daily; 2hr 20min); Castelló d'Empúries (4 daily; 1hr); Figueres (3 daily; 1hr 5min); and Roses (4 daily; 30min).

Turisme c/des Cotxe 2, just back from Pl. Frederic Rahola on the promenade (late June to mid-Sept Mon–Sat 9am–9pm, Sun 10am–1pm & 5–8pm; mid-Sept to late June Mon–Sat 9am–1pm & 3–7pm; ☎ 972 258 315, ⓦ visitcadaques.org).

ACCOMMODATION

Cadaqués can get very busy in the peak season, and it's a good idea to book in advance if possible. Note that many hotels close in low season, from Nov to Feb, so it's always a good idea to call ahead if you're visiting in winter.

L'Hostalet de Cadaqués c/Miquel Rosset 13 ☎ 972 258 206, ⓦ hostaletcadaques.com. Pleasant, small hotel with a stone-and-iron facade that gives way to stylish rooms, each named after a different *cala*, or cove; a glossy, commissioned photo of each cove hangs over the bed. **€65**

Hostal La Residència c/Caritat Serinyana 1 ☎ 972 258 312, ⓦ laresidencia.net. Handsome building, built in 1904 (the year that Dalí was born) and loaded with character, though the rooms are relatively ordinary – the suites are elaborately decorated with Dalí in mind, however, and the balconies have stunning views. **€95**

★ **Hostal Vehí** c/Església 6 ☎ 972 258 470, ⓦ hostalvehi.com. Friendly and family-owned, this excellent-value *pensió* has a lovely central location near the church and well-tended rooms, and is consequently very popular. Closed Nov–Feb. **€70**

Hotel Blaumar c/Massa d'Or 21 ☎ 972 159 020, ⓦ hotelblaumar.com. If you've come to Cadaqués for some quiet afternoons of sprawling poolside, *Blaumar* delivers. It's about a 10min walk from the centre of town, but that gives it an intimate, tucked-away feel. Rooms are simple but

well-kept-up, most with terraces, and the staff are helpful and accommodating. Closed Nov to mid-March. **€119**

Llané Petit c/Dr Bartomeus 37 ☎ 972 251 020, ⓦ llanepetit.com. Friendly, relaxing hotel at the southern end of the town. Most room have terraces with sea views, and you can splash in the well-maintained pool. Closed Jan & Feb. **€124**

Misty Carretera Portlligat ☎ 972 258 962, ⓦ hotel-misty.com. Hacienda-style hotel set around a garden and swimming pool on the road to Portlligat, on the edge of town. Extras include small pool, tennis court and tranquil garden. Breakfast included. Closed Nov–April. **€85**

Playa Sol Platja Pianc 3 ☎ 972 258 100, ⓦ playasol.com. Set in a curve of the seafront, this quiet, charming hotel offers simply furnished but comfortable rooms affording superb views of the town or over tranquil gardens. Closed Dec. **€157**

Sol i Xent Paratje Els Caials, c/Sant Baldiri 10 ☎ 972 251 043, ⓦ hotelsolixent.com. Classy, light-filled hotel with boutique touches, elegant rooms, breezy terraces and a pool. It sits on the outskirts of town, on the coast, giving it an intimate feel. **€130**

EATING AND DRINKING

Moderately priced seafood **restaurants**, any of which are worth trying, are strung along the seafront, while dotted about the old town and along c/Miquel Rosset are places to suit a wide range of tastes and budgets. **Nightlife** is a pleasurable blend of laidback idling at the beachside terraces and stylish hobnobbing around the bars and restaurants on c/Miguel Rosset.

Can Tito c/Vigilant ☎ 972 259 070. Managed by part of the same family that runs *Casa Anita*, *Can Tito* specializes in Catalan cuisine, with many dishes featuring seafood, including grilled anchovies and a robust shellfish paella. *Menú* starts at €15. April–Sept daily 1.30–3pm & 9–10pm, closed Mon lunch; Oct weekends only; closed Nov–March.

Casa Anita c/Miquel Rosset 16 ☎ 972 258 471. Cadaqués marches to the beat of its own drum, and this quirky institution is a good example. Seating is at communal tables and there are generally no menus – just the family staff rattling off the day's specials of superb mid- to upper-priced Catalan cuisine. Best to reserve ahead. Daily except Mon 1.30–4pm & 8.30–10pm; closed Nov.

Casa Nun Pl. de Portitxó 6 ☎ 972 258 856. This lovely restaurant offers top-notch regional fish and meat dishes, and a €22 *menú*, which you can enjoy on the small, sunny terrace perched above the Pl. des Portitxó. Easter–Oct daily lunch & dinner; Nov–Easter Fri & Sat lunch & dinner, plus Sun lunch.

Es Baluard Riba Nemesi Llorens ☎ 972 258 183, ⓦ esbaluard-cadaques.net. This friendly spot has the hallmarks of traditional Cadaqués: it's family-run, seafood reigns supreme and it's built into the old sea wall (*baluard* means bastion). Mid-range prices. Mid-Feb to Oct daily lunch & dinner.

L'Hostal Pg. del Mar 8, no phone. This dark, atmospheric and slightly surreal bar was one of Dalí's supposed haunts, and it features live bands. Daily 8pm–late; more limited hours in winter.

La Sirena c/Es Call ☎ 972 258 974. Tucked away in the old town, this appropriately named restaurant – "*sirena*" means "mermaid" – serves some of the best seafood in town. *Menú* starts around €15. Daily lunch & dinner; limited hours in winter.

Casa-Museu Salvador Dalí

Mid-June to mid-Sept daily 9.30am–9pm; rest of year Tues–Sun 10.30am–6pm; closed Jan 7 to mid-Feb; last entry 50min before closing • Tour €11; visits must be booked in advance by phone or via the website • ☎ 972 251 015, ⓦ dali-estate.org

A well-signposted twenty-minute walk north of Cadaqués and 3km by road is the tiny harbour of **PORTLLIGAT**, former home of Salvador Dalí. The artist had spent much of his childhood and youth in Cadaqués, and later, with his wife and muse, Gala, he converted a series of waterside fishermen's cottages in Portlligat into a sumptuous home that has all the quirks you would expect of the couple, such as speckled rooftop eggs and a giant fish painted on the ground outside. The house is now open to the public as the **Casa-Museu Salvador Dalí**, and although there's not much to see in the way of art, it's worth the visit to see first-hand how the bizarre couple lived until Gala's death in 1982, after which Dalí moved to Figueres. Visitor numbers are strictly controlled and you have to **book a visit** beforehand.

Tours take in most of the house, and include Dalí's studio, the exotically draped model's room, the couple's master bedroom and bathroom, a secondary workshop in an olive grove and, perhaps best of all, the oval-shaped sitting room that Dalí designed for Gala, which, apparently by accident, boasts stunning acoustics. You'll also see the garden and swimming pool where the couple entertained guests – they didn't like too many strangers trooping through their living quarters. The phallic-shaped pool and its various decorative features, including a giant snake and a stuffed lion, are a treat.

THE DALÍ TRIANGLE

There are three museums in the Costa Brava devoted to the life and work of **Salvador Dalí** and they're known locally as the Dalí Triangle. The **Teatre-Museu Dalí** in Figueres (see p.739) provides a display of the breadth of his art and his consummate creative skill, whereas the **Casa-Museu Castell Gala Dalí** (see p.738), northwest of Girona, reveals the artist's complex personal relationship with his Russian wife and muse, Gala. Famously, he was only allowed to enter her home with permission; he repaid her with mischief by painting false radiators on the covers she had insisted he install to hide the real ones. You can also gain insight into the artist at **Casa-Museu Salvador Dalí** (see p.731) in Portlligat, next to Cadaqués, which was his only fixed home from 1930 until 1982, when he moved into Gala's castle. The *casa* is a tortuous maze of a home made up of fishermen's huts that were successively acquired and strung together.

Cap de Creus

Museum Summer Mon–Wed, Sat & Sun 10am–7pm, Thurs & Fri 10am–2pm & 3.30–6.30pm; rest of the year Mon–Fri 9am–4.30pm, Sat & Sun 9am–5pm • Free, or small entry fee depending on the exhibit • **Creuers Cadaqués** ☎ 972 159 462, ⊕ creuerscadaques.cat

A road winds 8km from Dalí's house past glimpses of wave-plundered coves to the wind-buffeted **Cap de Creus** headland, the easternmost tip of the Iberian Peninsula, providing breathtaking views of the coast and topped by a lighthouse built in 1853. It's now occupied by the **Museu Espai Cap de Creus**, with a small exhibition on the surrounding *parc natural*. If you fancy viewing the Cap de Creus from the sea, you'll find a few **boats** along the seafront that do excursions, including those run by Creuers Cadaqués.

EATING AND DRINKING

Bar Restaurant Cap de Creus ☎ 972 199 005. The old building on the clifftop behind the lighthouse houses a bar and restaurant, which serves simple meals. On summer evenings, they often host live music, from jazz to flamenco. Usually daily for lunch and dinner, and until late when there's live music.

11 El Port de la Selva and around

Thirteen kilometres northwest of Cadaqués, **EL PORT DE LA SELVA** is centred on its fishing and pleasure **ports**, while either side is a ribbon of lovely **coves** with some of the cleanest water in the Mediterranean: those to the north are far more rugged and reached on foot or by sea, while the ones to the west are easier to get to and, therefore, more popular.

Sant Pere de Rodes

Tues–Sun: June–Sept 10am–7.30pm; Oct–May 10am–5pm, though check hours with Cadaqués' turisme • €5, Tues free

It's 8km up the paved **road** from El Port de la Selva, via Selva de Mar, to the Benedictine monastery of **Sant Pere de Rodes**, just below the 670m-high summit of the Serra de Roda; approaching **by foot**, use the marked trail (1hr 30min) through the Vall de Santa Creu, which begins at Molí de la Vall.

The first written record of the monastery dates back to 879, and in 934 it became independent, answerable only to Rome: in these early years, and thanks especially to the Roman connection, the monks became tremendously rich and powerful. As the monastery was enlarged it was also fortified against attack, starting a period of splendour that lasted four hundred years before terminal decline set in. Many fine treasures were looted when it was finally abandoned in 1789, and it was also pillaged by the French during the Peninsular War; some of the rescued silver can be seen in Girona's Museu d'Art.

Once one of the most romantic ruins in all of Catalunya, its central church universally recognized to be the precursor of the Catalan Romanesque style, the monastery is being robbed of a great deal of its charm by overzealous restoration. No original columns or capitals remain in the cloister and some of the work looks too clinical. The redeeming feature, apart from the view, is the **cathedral**, which retains its original stonework from the tenth to fourteenth centuries, including eleventh-century column capitals carved with wolves' and dogs' heads. Nearby is the peaceful pre-Romanesque church of **Santa Elena**, all that remains of the small rural community that grew up around the monastery.

Castell de Sant Salvador

Above the monastery (and contemporary with it) stands the much more atmospheric, ruined **Castell de Sant Salvador**, a thirty-minute scramble up a steep, narrow path. This provided the perfect lookout site for the frequent invasions (French or Moorish), which normally came from the sea; in the event of attack, fires were lit on the hill to warn the whole surrounding area.

ARRIVAL AND DEPARTURE   EL PORT DE LA SELVA AND AROUND

By bus A daily bus travels from Figueres to El Port de la Selva (30min), though there's currently no public transport to Sant Pere de Rodes.

ACCOMMODATION AND EATING

Hostal La Tina c/Mayor 15 ☎ 972 387 149, ⓦ hostal latina.cat. Comfortable and central *hostal*, with a simple, brick-arched restaurant (closed Sun in Oct, and sometimes in winter) serving local cuisine, from grilled meats to seafood. **€80**

Hotel Porto Cristo c/Major 59 ☎ 972 387 062, ⓦ hotelportocristo.com. Elegant rooms, well-outfitted bathrooms and the pleasant restaurant *Monterrey*, which

features local cuisine, including fresh seafood and seasonal produce. *Menú del día* €22. Closed late Dec to mid-Feb. **€160**

Port de la Vall Carretera de Llanca, km 6 ☎ 972 387 186, ⓦ www.campingportdelavall.com. There are a few campsites within 2km of the beach, the best being *Port de la Vall*, with well-maintained grounds. Closed Oct–Easter. Car and pitch **€31.80**

Girona and around

Accessible within an hour from the sea, medieval **Girona** offers a refreshing change from the sun-and-sand hedonism of the Costa Brava. This elegant, provincial capital features a beautiful walled medieval quarter, **Barri Vell**, perched on a hill above the city – a delight to explore, with narrow cobbled alleyways, balconied houses and shady little *plaças*. Clinging to the banks of the Ríu Onyar, as it meanders through the centre of town, is a long row of picturesque pastel-hued houses, the **Cases de l'Onyar**.

Historically, Girona has seen it all – at least by Spanish standards. The Romans settled here, and called the town Gerunda. Girona then became an Islamic town after the Moors conquered Spain. A vibrant Jewish community also flourished here for more than six centuries, and Girona's **Call**, the medieval Jewish quarter, remains one of the best preserved in Spain. Elsewhere, you'll spy a fetching mix of architectural styles, from Romanesque to *modernisme*. Girona also features a range of excellent museums, a lovely cathedral and lively arts and music festivals. **Rambla de la Llibertat**, running along the river, is the city's grand promenade, where locals take their daily *paseo* past a bustling strip of shops and restaurants.

Northwest of Girona, in the town of Púbol, rises the **Casa-Museu Castell Gala Dalí**, a medieval castle-turned-museum about surreal master Salvador Dalí and his wife Gala.

Catedral

Pl. de la Catedral • Daily: April–Oct 10am–8pm; Nov–March 10am–7pm; hours may vary • €5, free Sun • ☎ 972 214 426, ⓦ catedraldegirona.org

Looming majestically over the old quarter, Girona's **Catedral** is an elegant amalgamation of architectural styles. The Romanesque cloister and tower are the only parts remaining from the original eleventh-century building, and the cathedral was continually rebuilt and expanded up to and throughout the eighteenth century. The splendid Gothic nave, dating from the fifteenth and sixteenth centuries, is the second widest of its kind in the world (after St Peter's in Rome). Also impressive are the fourteenth-century silver altarpiece and Gothic tombs.

It's well worth visiting the twelfth-century **cloister** (same hours as cathedral), and the Tresor Capitular (Chapter Treasury), which features a wealth of religious artefacts, including medieval gold pieces, a fifteenth-century bible and the ornate

GIRONAMUSEUS CARD

The **GironaMuseus** card (ⓦ gironamuseus.cat) offers discounted entry to five of Girona's museums – the Museu d'Arqueologia de Catalunya, Museu d'Art, Museu d'Història de la Ciutat, Museu d'Història dels Jueus and Museu del Cinema. Pay regular entry at any of the five, pick up the card and then you'll receive fifty percent discount to the other museums. You can get the card at any of the museums covered by the card, or at the *turisme* (see p.737).

GIRONA

11

Parc de la Devesa

Sant Nicolau

Església de Sant Feliu

Banys Àrabs

Museu Arqueologia (Monestir de Sant Pere de Galligants)

Catedral

Entry to City Wall

Museu d'Història de la Ciutat

Museu d'Art

Jardins dels Alemanys

CALL

Museu d'Història dels Jueus

Museu del Cinema

City Wall

Train Station & Bus Station

ACCOMMODATION			
Can Carreras de Mas	1		
Casa Cúndaro	3		
Equity Point Hostel	8		
Hostal Bellmirall	5		
Hotel Carlemany	9		
Hotel Ciutat de Girona	6		
Hotel Històric	4		
Mas de la Roda	2		
Pensió Viladomat	7		

CLUB	
Blau Club	1

● BAR	
Lola Café	3

● RESTAURANTS	
Albereda	5
Café Le Bistrot	4
Celler de San Roca	1
Els Jardins de la Mercè	2
Mimolet	6

sixteenth-century *retablo* of Santa Elena. The main attraction is a splendid Italian tapestry, which dates back to the twelfth century and depicts the Creation.

Museu d'Art

Pujada de la Catedral 12 • Tues–Sat 10am–7pm (Oct–Feb until 6pm), Sun 10am–2pm • €2 • ⓦ museuart.com

Housed in the Palau Episcopal (Bishop's Palace) near the cathedral, Girona's **Museu d'Art** features a wide-ranging collection of Romanesque, Gothic and modern art. The museum's five storeys encompass a wide variety of Romanesque and Gothic art, including beautifully preserved murals from local churches, fifteenth-century embroidery and rare stained-glass tables. Don't miss the tenth-century portable altar from Sant Pere de Rodes and the impressive collection of modern Catalan art, such as sculptures by Olot artist Miquel Blay.

Església de Sant Feliu

Pl. de Sant Feliu • Mon–Sat 9.30am–2pm & 4–7pm, Sun 10am–noon • Free

The large **Església de Sant Feliu** is one of Girona's most iconic churches, and it reveals an interesting transition between the Romanesque and Gothic styles. The thirteenth-century Romanesque interior is topped by a grand Gothic nave, and a Baroque tower looms over the western facade. The highlight is the Catalan Gothic statue, *Crist Jacent* (Recumbent Christ).

Banys Àrabs

C/Ferran el Catòlic • April–Sept Mon–Sat 10am–7pm, Sun 10am–2pm; Oct–March Mon–Sat 10am–2pm • €2 • ⓦ banysarabs.org

Built in the twelfth century, the **Banys Àrabs** (Arab baths) were inspired by the Romans' public bathhouses, and are among the best preserved of their type in Spain. The Moorish-tinged Romanesque building contains several graceful rooms, each with its own pool: the frigidarium (cold-water room), whose elegant columns support a central dome; the tepidarium (warm-water room); and the caldarium, the steam room, which was heated by a roaring fire burning underneath. Also on view is the apodyterium (changing room), and there's an outdoor terrace, a good vantage point to view both the building's exterior and the surrounding Girona cityscape.

Museu Arqueologia de Catalunya

C/Santa Llúcia 8 • June–Sept Tues–Sat 10.30am–1.30pm & 4–7pm, Sun 10am–2pm; Oct–May Tues–Sat 10am–2pm & 4–6pm, Sun 10am–2pm • €2.30 • ⓦ mac.cat

The impressive **Monestir de Sant Pere de Galligants**, a Romanesque Benedictine monastery near the baths, houses the **Museu Arqueologia de Catalunya**. It features a large collection of finds from Girona excavations, including beautiful Hebrew tombstones, sections of Roman pillars and Bronze Age metalworks.

Passeig de la Muralla

Daily 10am–8pm • Free

One of the finest vantage points over Girona is from the **Passeig de la Muralla**, also known as the Passeig Arqueològic, a walkway along the ramparts and medieval city wall. You can gain access to it from various points, including from near the Museu Arqueologia. As you trudge along the perimeter of the walls, you can enjoy lovely views of Girona – over the colourful rooftops to the river snaking through the centre – and the surrounding Ter valley. The walkway has several exits along the way, and it ends at Plaça Catalunya, where you can descend and amble back into the old town.

JEWISH GIRONA

A Jewish community first settled in Girona in the late ninth century; by the tenth century, the Jews had become a prosperous and influential sector of the city's society, but this all changed in the thirteenth century, when Gironan Jews became the victims of severe and unrelenting persecution. The entire Jewish quarter became a constant target of racist attacks and eventually became an isolated ghetto, in which the residents were virtually imprisoned, confined within neighbourhood limits and banned from the rest of the city. This continued until 1492, when all Jews were expelled from Spain. Life in the Call was bleak and presented an immense daily challenge: out of desperate necessity, residents created an underground community of tiny alleys and courtyards within which to survive.

Carrer de la Força and the Jewish Quarter

Girona's Jewish community, known as the **Call** or the **Aljama**, existed for more than six hundred years, and the warren of narrow streets and alleyways around **Carrer de la Força** is widely regarded to be one of the finest preserved Jewish neighbourhoods in Europe.

Centre Bonastruc ça Porta and Museu d'Història dels Jueus

C/de la Força 8 • July & Aug Mon–Sat 10am–8pm, Sun 10am–2pm; Sept–June Mon–Sat 10am–6pm, Sun 10am–1pm • €3 • ☎ 972 216 761, ⓦ ajgirona.org/call

The well-run **Centre Bonastruc ça Porta**, housed in a former synagogue, is home to the **Museu d'Història dels Jueus**, which does an excellent job of curating archeological and ethnological finds from Girona's Jewish heritage. The exhibition covers themes such as festivals and tradition; the synagogue and cemetery; the diaspora; and the Inquisition, which features a display of original documents ordering the expulsion of all Jews from Spain. Other highlights include a gilded seal used for making Passover bread; a fourteenth-century limestone slab inscribed with Jewish law from a local synagogue; and a unique belt buckle, dating to between the thirteenth and fifteenth centuries, engraved with what is believed to be the mythical Leviathan, which features in the Hebrew Bible.

Museu d'Història de la Ciutat

C/de la Força 27 • Tues–Sat 10am–2pm & 5–7pm, Sun 10am–2pm • €3 • ⓦ ajuntament.gi/museuciutat

Girona's history is formidable, and the excellent **Museu d'Història de la Ciutat** offers a well-organized overview under one roof. There's a wide range of Roman remains and modern arts and crafts on show, and the museum includes exhibits on the old fortified walls – and those who attacked them to plunder Girona; the history of the Catalan *sardana* dance and other folkloric traditions; and contemporary paintings by regional artists.

Museu del Cinema

C/Sèquia 1 • May, June & Sept Tues–Sat 10am–8pm, Sun 11am–3pm; July & Aug daily 10am–8pm; Oct–April Tues–Fri 10am–6pm, Sat 10am–8pm, Sun 11am–3pm • €5 • ⓦ museudelcinema.cat

Film through the ages, from the Lumière brothers' first cinema in the late 1800s to bulky projectors and cameras from the 1930s and '40s is celebrated at the surprisingly entertaining **Museu del Cinema**. The museum is rooted in the private collection of Girona film director Tomàs Mallol. Exhibits include rudimentary yet colourful children's short films, East Asian shadow puppetry and up to 1200 historic pieces, such as a camera obscura and old film reels.

ARRIVAL AND INFORMATION

GIRONA

By plane Girona-Costa Brava airport (ⓦ barcelona-girona-airport.com), 13km south of the city, handles flights by discount airlines from throughout Europe. Sagalés Barcelona Bus regularly does the 25min trip between the airport and the Girona bus station, and also to Barcelona's Estació del Nord (1hr 10min). A taxi from the airport to central Girona costs around €20.

By train The train station is in the modern section of the city, near Pl. d'Espanya, a 15–25min walk southwest from the Barri Vell. Girona is well connected by train; it's on the train line between Barcelona (1hr 30min), Figueres

(40min) and Portbou (1hr). The Madrid–Paris AVE high-speed train line, which will stop in Girona and Figueres, is currently being constructed; opening dates vary, but some sections are due to begin operating in 2012.

By bus The bus station is next to the train station. Teisa buses operate regularly to regional cities, including Besalú (50min) and Olot (a little over an hour). Sarfa runs several buses in the summer from the airport to the coast, including Roses (1hr 30min) and Tossa de Mar (1hr).

Turisme c/Joan Maragall 2 (Mon–Sat 9am–8pm, Sun 9am–2pm; ☎ 972 226 575, ⓦ girona.cat/turisme).

ACCOMMODATION

Girona has a wide variety of accommodation, from well-maintained hostels to historic hotels, many of which are central and within an easy stroll to the old quarter. In the surrounding countryside, you'll also find a range of comfortable **cases de pages**, including in the rustic hamlet of **Bordils**, which lies 10km northeast of town.

THE CITY

★ **Casa Cúndaro** Pujada de la Catedral 9 ☎ 972 223 583, ⓦ casacundaro.com. Top off your experience of medieval Girona by staying at this family-run hotel, which features elegantly restored rooms and apartments in a historic Jewish home a short stroll from the cathedral. It's an artful blend of old and new, from wood-beam ceilings and stone walls to leather sofas and, in the apartments, gleaming kitchens. €80

Equity Point Hostel Pl. Catalunya 23 ☎ 972 41 78 40, ⓦ equity-point.com. This well-run hostel mini-chain has now set up shop in Girona. The bright hostel, with unisex dorms with shared bathrooms, and private rooms, features all the *Equity Point* characteristics – clean, friendly, central – plus welcoming details like free breakfast, complimentary wi-fi and common room with table football. Dorm €19, doubles €60

Hostal Bellmirall c/Bellmirall 3 ☎ 972 204 009, ⓦ bellmirall.cat. Housed in a renovated fifteenth-century building, with comfortable rooms, stone walls, a communal living room and a hearty continental breakfast. It's right near the cathedral, so light sleepers may be woken up by the bell chimes. €65

Hotel Carlemany Pl. Miquel Santaló ☎ 972 211 212, ⓦ thecarlemanyhotel.com. Modern four-star hotel, geared more towards business travellers, but handily

within walking distance of the train station. The *El Pati Verd* restaurant serves tasty Catalan cuisine. €100

Hotel Ciutat de Girona c/Nord 2 ☎ 972 483 038, ⓦ hotel-ciutatdegirona.com. This boutique hotel in the centre of town has modern rooms in muted greys and red. The sleek *Blanc* restaurant serves creative Mediterranean fare, including grilled tuna with sesame. €150

Hotel Històric c/Bellmirall 4a ☎ 972 223 583, ⓦ hotelhistoric.com. This aptly named and inviting hotel is indeed historic, set in a lovingly renovated ninth-century house in the centre of the old town. The rooms are simple and comfortable, some with wood beams. €100

Pensió Viladomat c/Ciutadans 5 ☎ 972 203 176, ⓦ pensioviladomat.com. A good economical choice is this well-run *pensió*, with simple but clean rooms in the old town, near the Rambla and the cathedral. €56

BORDILS

Can Carreras del Mas c/Creu 34, Bordils ☎ 972 490 276, ⓦ cancarrerasdelmas.com. This welcoming, rustic *casa rural* has stone walls, brick-arched ceilings and contemporary amenities, including a swimming pool. €85

Mas de la Roda c/Creu 31, Bordils ☎ 972 490 052, ⓦ masdelaroda.com. This cared-for stone house is a good place to relax, with a fireplace, four ample rooms and home-made meals made from locally sourced ingredients. €76

EATING, DRINKING AND NIGHTLIFE

Girona has a diversity of **restaurants**, including a top-notch selection serving Catalan cuisine, most famously at the *Celler de San Roca*, just out of town. The area around c/de la Força and c/Ballesteries is dotted with restaurants, while you'll find breezy outdoor cafés along Rambla de la Llibertat and Pl. del Vi. Girona's nightlife caters to the sizeable university crowd, with rustic **bars** in Pl. de la Independencia and across the river along Rambla de la Llibertat, and splashier **clubs** (like *Blau Club*) further afield. The suburb of Pedret, about 700m north of the old town, also heats up at night with a string of clubs, while in the summer, everyone heads to the open-air bars, **Les Carpes**, which operate in the Parc de la Devesa, on the west side of the river in the modern part of town.

RESTAURANTS

Albereda c/Albereda 7 ☎972 226 002, ⓦrestaurant albereda.com. Dine on excellent Catalan cuisine – with a twist – at the long-running *Albereda*, in an elegant dining room of wooden floors, brick arches, and linen-topped tables. Dishes start at €19. Daily except Sun 1.30–3.30pm & 8–10.30pm; sometimes closed for part of the winter.

Café Le Bistrot Pujada Sant Domènec 4 ☎972 218 803. Inviting restaurant with a *belle époque* interior and tables outside, where you can fill up on Catalan cuisine at decent prices – the weekday *menú* is €14. Daily 1–4pm & 8–midnight; sometimes later at weekends.

★ **Celler de Car Roca** Can Sunyer 48, about 2.5km northwest of town off the Taialà road ☎972 222 157, ⓦcellercanroca.com. The Roca brothers – Joan, Josep and Jordi – have become household names in Spain, and for good reason. Their beautiful restaurant is consistently ranked among the top in country, with Ferran Adrià-style renderings of Catalan cuisine, from caramelized olives that arrive hanging from a small tree to steak tartare with mustard ice-cream. For a superb sampling, try the "signature dishes" menu for €105. Reservations essential. Daily 1–3.30pm & 9–11pm; closed three weeks around Christmas, 1 week in Aug and for Easter.

Els Jardins de la Mercè Pujada de la Mercè 10 ☎972 226 845, ⓦelsjardinsdelamerce.com. Comfortable restaurant, with black-and-white tiled floors and a youthful appeal, in the centre of town. Enjoy well-priced, market-fresh Catalan cuisine and alfresco dining in the patio garden. Usually daily 1.30–3.30pm & 8.30–10.30pm; sometimes limited hours in winter.

Mimolet c/Pou Rodó 12 ☎972 202 124, ⓦmimolet .net. Classy, welcoming restaurant with a Catalan menu built around local produce, including monkfish with olives and duck with glazed apple. A seasonal menu is €36.50, while individual dishes range €18–24. Tues–Sat 1–3pm & 8.30–10.30pm.

BAR

Lola Café c/Força 7 ☎972 228 824. This friendly, Latin-themed bar, in the middle of the old town, serves tasty tropical cocktails – *mojitos, caipirinhas* – and heats up with occasional live music, from rumba to salsa and more. Usually daily 6pm–3am.

CLUB

Blau Club Camp de les Lloses 8 ⓦblauclub.com. About 2km south of town, this is where the cool kids come to groove and flirt, with DJs spinning all night long on the weekends. Fri & Sat 11pm/midnight until late.

Púbol

Salvador Dalí had many obsessions, but none quite like Gala, his beloved wife and lifelong muse, who he met when she was visiting Cadaqués in 1929 with her husband, French poet Paul Eluard. Dalí and Gala fell in love and married in 1934. Dalí lavished many gifts on her, including, in 1969, the medieval castle of Casa Púbol, which rises near the small village of **Púbol**, about 20km northeast from Girona. Gala lived here, and rumour has it that she entertained a string of lovers all the while, and imposed strict rules on Dalí, who supposedly had to get permission before he could visit. She stayed here until her death in 1982, when **Dalí** moved in. The artist made this his permanent base until 1984 when fire struck parts of the castle, prompting him to move to Figueres.

Casa Púbol is one of three Dalí sights in this region; the other two are the museum in Figueres and the house in Portlligat near Cadaqués.

Casa-Museu Castell Gala Dalí

Mid-March to mid-June & mid-Sept to Oct Tues–Sun 10am–6pm; mid-June to mid-Sept daily 10am–8pm; Nov & Dec Tues–Sun 10am–5pm; closed Jan to mid-March • €8 • ☎972 488 655, ⓦsalvador-dali.org • Regular Sarfa-run Girona–Palafrugell buses stop in La Pera, from where it's 2km to Púbol (you'll need to walk or take a taxi); the Barcelona–Portbou train stops in Flaça, which is 4km from Púbol

The castle, which is now the **Casa-Museu Castell Gala Dalí**, is decorated in vintage Dalí style, though parts of it are considerably more understated than other Dalí sights. Stuffed animal heads protrude from walls, and dome ceilings are painted in quasi-religious motifs, but there are also quietly stark rooms with simple wood floors. Exhibits feature a supremely entertaining array of Dalí photos, particularly from his 1930s–40s heyday, while outside is an atmospheric swimming pool and garden, populated by sculptures of Richard Wagner, one of Dalí's favourite composers.

Figueres

It is a testament to **Dalí**'s enduring popularity that his eponymous museum, in the middle of **Figueres**, 35km northeast of Girona, is the most visited sight in Spain after Madrid's Prado and Bilbao's Guggenheim. There's more to Figueres, of course, but you wouldn't immediately know it from the crowds tripping over themselves to get to the museum. Native son Dalí returned to Figueres specifically to create this homage to Surrealism, and what an homage it is: wonderfully bizarre and cheekily interactive, the museum is all you'd expect from the world's most celebrated Surrealist.

By all means make the museum your first stop – but leave yourself some time to roam Figueres afterwards, and enjoy the pleasant capital of the Alt Empordà region. Cutting a wide swath through the centre of town is **La Rambla de Figueres**, a graceful, leafy pedestrian street lined with modern houses and outdoor cafés. The **Museu de l'Empordà** features local archeological finds and the nearby **Castell de Sant Ferran** is a massive fortification on sprawling grounds.

11

Teatre-Museu Dalí

Teatre-Museu Dalí Pl. Gala i Salvador Dalí · **Dalí Joies** Corner of c/María Àngels Vayreda and Pujada del Castell · Both daily: March–June 9.30–6pm, July–Sept 9am–8pm, Oct 9.30am–6pm, Nov–Feb 10.30–6pm; last admission 45min before closing · €12, includes entry to Dalí Joies · ☎ 972 677 500, ⓦ salvador-dali.org

One thing is certain: you won't have trouble spotting the **Teatre-Museu Dalí**. Just look for a roof topped with giant eggs and a red facade with protruding bread loaves. Housed in a former theatre – which is particularly apt, for this most theatrical of artists – the museum is designed around a large courtyard with white ceramic sinks and gold mannequins inspired by Oscar statues. Light streams in to the building through a transparent, geodesic dome ceiling that resembles the eye of a fly, in a nod to Dalí's fixation with insects. Incidentally, the artist had no problem with flies, but was supposedly repulsed by ants, which he depicted crawling out of eyeballs and such in his paintings.

> **DALÍ BY NIGHT**
>
> The **Dalí Museum** may be surreal by day, but is even more so at night (and especially after a glass of cava). In the summer, generally from late July to late August, the museum opens its doors at night (10pm–1am; last entry at 12.30am). For an admission price of €13, visitors are offered a glass of cava on one of the terraces, where they also show a film on Dalí. There is limited capacity, so it's worth booking ahead, which you can do on the museum website (🖥 salvador-dali.org).

Dalí created the museum to be an all-round sensory – and surreal – experience. Look through binoculars to see *Gala Nude Looking at the Sea Which at Twenty Metres is Transformed into a Portrait of Abraham Lincoln*, or revive a "dead" body in a coffin made of circuit boards. And check out *The Face of Mae West That Can Be Used as a Drawing Room*, in which Mae's giant nose has a fireplace (complete with logs) built into each nostril, and her fleshy red lips are a couch.

The **Sala de Tresor** houses many of Dalí's better-known works, including *The Spectre of Sex Appeal*, which explores his famous sex phobia. Other emblematic works include *Soft Self-Portrait with Fried Bacon*, in which Dalí's dripping visage is held up by little sticks, and *Venus de Milo with Drawers*.

Dalí, fittingly, is buried in his fantastical museum. By 1984, he had moved to the nearby **Torre Galtea**, where he died in 1989. His body now lies behind a simple granite slab in a basement gallery of the museum. The museum ticket includes entry to the nearby **Dalí Joies** exhibit, featuring jewels designed by Dalí.

Museu de l'Empordà

Rambla 2 • May–Oct Tues–Sat 11am–8pm, Sun 11am–2pm; Nov–April Tues–Sat 11am–7pm, Sun 11am–2pm • €4, or free with Teatre-Museu Dalí ticket • ☎ 972 502 305, 🖥 museuemporda.org

The **Museu de l'Empordà** explores the region's history, with exhibits covering Greek and Roman archeological remains, frescoes and sacred art. It also features a well-curated collection of nineteenth- and twentieth-century art by an assortment of well-known Catalan and Spanish artists, from Sorolla and Miró to Tàpies to Dalí.

Museu del Joguet de Catalunya

Hotel Paris, c/de Sant Pere 1 • June–Sept daily 10am–1pm & 4–7pm; Oct–May Tues–Sat 10am–6pm, Sun 11am–2pm • €5 • ☎ 972 504 508, 🖥 mjc.cat

From ancient toy wooden tops and bronze Roman rattles to candy-red cars, miniature circuses and twentieth-century optical-illusion games, the **Museu del Joguet de Catalunya** (Toy Museum of Catalunya) offers a playful glimpse into the history of having fun. Particularly curious are the religious items, which include altar boys' clothes from 1905 and mini-churches with tiny movable priest figures. Don't miss the traditional *caganers*, little figurines of squatting peasants taking a break to "fertilize the earth", who are cheekily hidden in the back of Catalan nativity scenes. The museum also hosts lively temporary exhibits, such as the recent "Salvador Dalí: the first twenty years".

Castell de Sant Ferran

Daily: March–June & mid-Sept to Oct 10.30am–2pm & 4–6pm; July to mid-Sept 10.30am–8pm; Nov–Feb 10.30am–2pm; last admission 1hr before closing • €3 • 🖥 castillosanfernando.org

The impressive eighteenth-century fortified **Castell de Sant Ferran**, one of the largest in Europe, stands 1km northwest of Figueres. Explore the sprawling castle grounds and walk its 4km perimeter and you'll get a sense of just how massive it is. It was at Sant Ferran that the last official meeting of Spain's Republican parliament took place, on

February 1, 1939, before it surrendered to Franco's forces. More recently, Colonel Tejero was imprisoned here after his failed coup attempt in 1981.

ARRIVAL AND INFORMATION   FIGUERES

By train The train station is just east of the city centre. Figueres is on the train line from Barcelona, via Girona, to Portbou on the French border. Services run regularly between Figueres and Girona (up to 20 daily; 40min), and Barcelona (3–6 daily; just over 2hr). The French TGV now operates from Perpignan to Figueres, stopping at Figueres-Vilafant, 2km west of Figueres; the TGV will eventually (from late 2012, or

later) connect to the AVE, which will run from Figueres to Barcelona. Teisa buses (€1.10) run from the city centre, and the bus and train stations, to Figueres-Vilafant station.
Turisme Pl. del Sol (late June to mid-Sept Mon–Sat 9am–8pm, Sun 10am–3pm; rest of year generally Mon–Sat 10am–2pm & 4–7pm, Sun 10am–2pm; ☎972 503 155, ⓦfigueresciutat.com).

ACCOMMODATION

Hotel Los Àngeles c/Barceloneta 10 ☎972 510 662, ⓦhotelangeles.com. This basic hotel is slightly dated (with chintzy figurines and the like) but has decent, comfortable rooms and good-sized bathrooms. €60
Hotel Duran c/Lausaca 5 ☎972 501 250, ⓦhotelduran .com. Long-running hotel – Dalí and Gala were frequent visitors – that has been artfully updated, with inviting rooms of polished wood floors, muted colours and modern baths. Keep an eye out for original Dalí works displayed throughout. The restaurant serves tasty Catalan cuisine (see below). €69
Hotel Empordá Av. Salvador Dalí i Domènech 170, 1km northwest of Figueres ☎972 500 562, ⓦhotelemporda.com. While it's the restaurant that receives the accolades (see below), the hotel itself is also

historical and welcoming, with comfortable rooms and a breezy terrace. It's important to book ahead. €95
★ **Hotel Plaza Inn** Pujada del Castell 14 ☎972 514 540, ⓦplazainn.es. Bright, friendly hotel right in the centre, next to the museum, with a quirky, art-filled decor, well-maintained rooms and a small rooftop terrace overlooking the Figueres rooftops. €65
Hotel Rambla Rambla 33 ☎972 67 60 20, ⓦhotelrambla.net. Central and comfortable, this hotel rises over the main thoroughfare, and features simple but crisply clean rooms and a well-maintained 1860 facade. €58
Hotel Ronda Av. Salvador Dalí 17 ☎972 503 911, ⓦhotelronda.com. It looks a bit antiseptic from the outside, but this modern hotel has elegant rooms, and a friendly restaurant with terrace. €82

EATING AND DRINKING

Figueres, particularly in high season, can be crammed with visitors. This translates into a slew of restaurants, especially in the streets around the Museu Dalí, that cater to tourists, often with mediocre menus at inflated prices. You will find some good choices, though, slightly beyond the centre. Also, if you have your own wheels, you can opt for heading to one of the villages around Figueres, several of which have lovely, old farmhouse restaurants, such as *Mas Pau.*

Hotel Duran c/Lausaca 5 ☎972 501 250, ⓦhotelduran .com. You're in good company: Dalí used to have his own dining room here, where creative regional cuisine has been prepared by the Duran family for generations. *Mar i muntanya* (sea and mountain) dishes might include cuttlefish and meatballs or prawns and sausage. The weekday *menú* generally starts at €19. Daily 12.30–4pm & 8.30–11pm.
Mas Pau Carretera de Figueres a Besalú ☎972 546 154, ⓦmaspau.com. Splendid Catalan fare in a sixteenth-century farmhouse surrounded by lush gardens, 5km southwest of town. The restaurant, which opened in 1960 and is now managed by two Ferran Adrià disciples, celebrates the seasons and regional produce, and might include local anchovies, suckling lamb from Ripoll with cauliflower and couscous, and spring onion soup with *calçotada romesco* fritters. They also operate as a comfortable hotel. Dishes start at €26–30 or it's €89 for a full *menú*. The restaurant is on the road to Besalú near the turning for Avinyonet de Puigventós. Mid-March to Dec

Wed–Sat 1.30–3.30pm & 8.30–10.30pm; Sun open lunch only; Tues open dinner only; closed Mon & Jan to mid-March.
★ **El Motel** Hotel Empordà, Av. Salvador Dalí i Domènech 170, 1km northwest of Figueres ☎972 500 562, ⓦelmotel.cat. Before the foams of Ferran Adrià and the "emotional cuisine" of the Roca brothers, there was the *Hotel Empordà* (originally called the *Motel Ampurdan*, in part because it sits on a busy roadway), where chef Jaume Subirós is credited with elevating traditional cooking from home kitchen to restaurant quality. Considered the birthplace of modern Catalan cuisine, *El Motel* (as the restaurant is now called in homage to its roots) continues to serve some of the finest and most innovative food in the region. The chefs find inspiration in the sea, with dishes like wild sea bass from Cadaqués with lime leaves and polenta, rock lobster from Cap de Creus with fragrant rice, shrimp from Roses, and sea cucumbers. Dishes start at €24. Book ahead. Daily 1–3.30pm & 8.30–10.30pm.

11

Onix c/Sant Llátzer 8 ☎ 972 505 848. This small yet stylish spot stands out from the other touristy spots with a good *menú* (€13) of Catalan cuisine and a friendly, family atmosphere. Tues–Sun 1–3.30pm & 8.30–10.30pm; sometimes closed for part of winter.

La Garrotxa

The fertile landscape of **La Garrotxa**, which unfolds west of Girona and Figueres, is anchored by the historic capital of **Olot**. To the east lies lovely, quiet **Besalú**; to the north, mountain peaks march along the French border; and to the south extends the **Parc Natural de la Zona Volcànica**, a verdant, hilly terrain punctuated by volcanic cones and craters.

Besalú

Medieval **Besalú**, about 50km north of Girona, is a captivating sight: the impressive eleventh-century Romanesque **Pont Fortificat** spans the River Fluvià at the entrance to the town, beyond which rise church towers amid stone houses. These days, Besalú is a small, humble town, but its beautifully preserved core, with dark little streets, arcaded shops and elegant historic architecture, is testament to its formidable past. Roman, Visigothic and Muslim rulers all passed through, but Besalú's most important role came between the tenth and twelfth centuries, when it served as the capital of the region until power was transferred to Barcelona.

Església de Sant Pere and around

The thirteenth-century **Casa de la Vila**, which now houses the *ajuntament*, rises over Plaça de la Llibertat. To the west of Llibertat lies a spacious *plaça*, the Prat de Sant Pere, which is presided over by the tenth-century Benedictine monastery **Església de San Pere**. Keep an eye out for the beautiful Gothic window on the west facade. The nearby Romanesque **Església de Sant Vicenç** features impressive Gothic capitals. Both churches are usually only open for services, but guided tours are sometimes organized by the *turisme*.

Miqvé

Baixada de Mikwe • Guided tours: summer usually daily noon, 1.30pm, 4.30pm & 6pm; check with *turisme* and for times the rest of the year

Similar to Girona, Besalú had a Jewish community from the ninth century onwards, until the Jews were forced out of town in 1436 due to Christian persecution. Their **Miqvé**, said to be the only existing Jewish ritual bath in Spain, sits near the river, and features a barrel-vaulted underground stone room. The bath was also once connected to the town's **synagogue**, the remains of which were discovered nearby.

ARRIVAL AND INFORMATION BESALÚ

By bus The bus stop is on the main Olot–Girona road; there are regular buses to and from Figueres (30min) and Girona (50min).
Turisme Pl. de la Llibertat (daily 10am–2pm & 4–7pm;

☎ 972 591 240, ⓦ besalu.cat). In addition to guided tours of the churches and Miqvé, the *turisme* also offers tours encompassing all of Besalú's sights, usually daily at 5pm, but hours are subject to change.

ACCOMMODATION

Hotel Comte Tallaferro c/Ganganell 2 ☎ 972 591 609, ⓦ grupcalparent.com. This historic hotel features elegant, well-furnished rooms with wood floors, and a restaurant (open daily lunch and dinner) serving regional fare. **€118**

Els Jardins de la Martana Pont 2 ☎ 972 590 009, ⓦ lamartana.com. For a true feel of Besalú's history, bed down in this antique mansion, with graceful rooms and leafy gardens, that sits across from the Pont Fortificat. **€120**

EATING

Cal Parent Hotel Fonda Siqués, Av. Lluís Companys 6–8 ☎ 972 590 110, ⓦ grupcalparent.com/siques.html.

Sample tasty local cuisine at around €35 per person, from grilled meats to fresh local produce, at this comfortable

restaurant. Mon–Sat 1–4pm & 8.30–10pm, Sun 1–4pm only; closed Mon in winter.
★ **Cúria Reial** Pl. de la Llibertat 14 ☎972 590 263, ⓦ curiareial.com. Enjoy the twin pleasures of top-notch local

cuisine and the beautiful outdoors at this friendly, mid-priced restaurant, where you can dine alfresco at outdoor tables overlooking the historic bridge. Daily except Tues 12.30–4pm & 8.30–10.30pm; closed Mon dinner in winter.

Beget

The tiny village of **BEGET**, about 30km northwest of Besalú, is nestled so deeply in a valley that you don't see it until you're almost upon it. And when you do, it's a handsome sight: Beget looks much as it did centuries ago, with narrow cobbled streets, little bridges and stone houses. A stillness fills the graceful twelfth-century church, **Sant Cristòfor**, which rises over the village. The church (sporadic opening times; enquire in the village) is notable for its *Majestat*, a carved-wood figure of Christ in a full-length tunic, arms outstretched.

ARRIVAL AND DEPARTURE   BEGET

By bus and taxi It's hard to reach Beget without your own transport. The best option is to take a bus to

Camprodon (see p.750), and then hire a taxi.

11

ACCOMMODATION AND EATING

Les Barnedes Veïnat dels Grells in the village of Molló, 11km northwest of Beget ☎656 925 816 or 676 157 806, ⓦ barnedes.com. This *casa rural* has rustic, self-catering two- and three-bedroom apartments, each equipped with a full kitchen, fireplace and a garden. In July and Aug, the apartments rent out only by the week (€775). **€155**
Can Jeroni c/Bellaire 17–19 ☎972 741 239, ⓦ canjeroni.net. Friendly, family-run restaurant serving

seasonal Catalan cuisine (€20-plus à la carte), with seating near an old bridge and views of the church. Usually daily 1.30–3.30pm & 8.30–10.30pm; limited hours in winter.
Hostal El Forn c/Josep Duñach ☎972 741 230. This cosy *hostal* is one of the better budget choices in town. It's set in a rustic stone house and features brightly coloured rooms. Rate includes breakfast. **€42**

Olot

La Garrotxa's provincial capital, **OLOT**, is an amiable, mid-sized town with busy shopping streets and a breezy Plaça Mayor. Passeig d'en Blay, the central *rambla*, is flanked by lovely historic buildings and dotted with lively cafés. Olot's varied countryside, marked by sheer cliffs, verdant valleys and extinct volcanic cones and craters, inspired the highly respected nineteenth- and twentieth-century **Olot School** of landscape painters, whose works you can view in the town's Museu Comarcal.

Museu Comarcal de la Garrotxa

C/Hospici 8 • Summer Tues–Sat 11am–2pm & 4–7pm, Sun 11am–2pm; rest of year Tues–Fri 10am–1pm & 3–6pm, Sat 11am–2pm & 4–7pm, Sun 11am–2pm • €3
Nature was at the core of the Olot School of painters, who explored Garrotxa's unique landscape on canvas, from rolling, pastoral hills to desolate terrain punctuated by stark trees. The school, founded by Joaquim Vayreda i Vila, was also influenced by the French Impressionists. You can view many of its striking works in the well-curated **Museu Comarcal de la Garrotxa**, housed in a renovated eighteenth-century hospital. The museum also features *modernista* sculptures by Miquel Blay and Josep Clarà, and exhibits on the history of Olot and Catalan arts and crafts.

Parc Nou

Avgda. Santa Coloma, 1km southwest of town centre • Jardí Botànic Daily April–Sept 9am–9pm; Oct–March 9am–7pm (sometimes 6pm) • Free Museu dels Volcans July–Sept Tues–Sat 10am–2pm & 4–7pm, Sun 10am–2pm; Oct–June Tues–Fri 10am–2pm & 3–6pm, Sat 10am–2pm & 4–7pm, Sun 10am–2pm • €3
Parc Nou is a nine-acre municipal park that encompasses the well-tended, leafy **Jardí Botànic** and the **Casal dels Volcans**, a Palladian building that houses the helpful Centro

d'Informació del Parc Natural de la Zona Volcànica, where you can pick up park maps and other information. Also here is the **Museu dels Volcans**, which features exhibits on the volcanic history of the region, including rock samples and photos.

ARRIVAL AND INFORMATION   OLOT

By bus The bus station is at the east end of c/Bisbe Lorenzana, the main thoroughfare. Teisa runs regular buses to and from Barcelona (just under 3hr) and Girona (just over 1hr).

Turisme c/Hospici 8, inside the Museu Comarcal (summer Mon–Sat 10am–2pm & 4–7pm, Sun 10am–2pm; rest of

year Mon–Sat 9am–2pm & 4–6pm, Sun 10am–2pm; ☎ 972 260 141, ⓦ turismeolot.cat). The tourist office has up-to-date lists of local accommodation and transport timetables, and also sells a joint ticket to the museums in the area (€4–6 depending on number of museums you visit).

ACCOMMODATION

Olot has a range of decent hotels and hostels in town, but some of the most appealing accommodation options are the manors and B&Bs in the surrounding countryside, many of which make the most of their proximity to the volcanic park with terraces, hearty breakfasts to fuel your hiking, and bikes for hire.

OLOT

Hostal Olot c/Sant Pere Martir 29 ☎ 972 261 212, ⓦ hostalolot.com. Modern, well-maintained hotel right on the edge of the old town. Rooms are on the small side, but other perks make up for it, including a decent breakfast (included). Also nice: fair prices for single rooms (€44). **€72**

Torre Malagrida Pg. de Barcelona 15 ☎ 972 264 200, ⓦ xanascat.cat. This central, well-kept youth hostel with simple dorms is housed in a nineteenth-century tower set amid gardens. **€21.75**

OUTSIDE TOWN

Can Blanc Passatges de la Deu, around 1.5km south of town ☎ 972 276 020, ⓦ canblanc.es. The location here is the big draw: it's in the Parque Natural, and surrounded by greenery, yet still within easy reach of town (around

30min on foot, should you want to walk). Rooms are comfortable, and nearby is the historic *La Deu Restaurant* (see below). **€50**

Hostal Sant Bernat Carretera de les Feixes 29–31 ☎ 972 261 919, ⓦ hostalsantbernat.com. If you're looking for something calm, simple and slightly out of the town, this is a decent choice: the *hostal* lies just a few hundred metres northeast of the city centre with views over the volcanic hills, and basic but clean rooms – more hostel than hotel. Popular with hikers and trekkers. **€64**

Mas El Guitart Vall de Bianya, 7km northwest of Olot, just above Sant Andreu de Socarrats village ☎ 972 292 140, ⓦ guitartrural.com. Comfortable country house, with hardwood-floor rooms and cabins, and, somewhat unusually, a lovingly run spa, with therapies including hot-stone massages and reflexology. **€70**

EATING

The volcanic Garrotxa region, famed for its fertile soil, has become known for its rich **Cuina Volcànica** (ⓦ cuinavolcanica .cat). Traditional ingredients – all locally produced – include Santa Pau haricot beans, black radishes, mushrooms and sheep's cheese. Olot has several good Cuina Volcànica restaurants, though it's in the surrounding villages, like Besalú and Santa Pau, that you'll find the best renditions.

Les Cols Carretera de la Canya, on the northern outskirts of town ☎ 973 269 209, ⓦ lescols.com. Fresh produce reigns supreme at this elegant restaurant, where the menu ranges from wild mushrooms and sweetcorn to fresh river trout. Pricey but worth it. Reservations advised. Wed–Sat 1–3.30pm & 8.30–10.30pm, Sun 1–3.30pm. Closed Mon, Tues & sometimes two weeks in summer.

La Deu Restaurant Carretera de la Deu s/n, near Can Blanc, about 1.5km south of Olot ☎ 972 261 004, ⓦ ladeu.es. This established restaurant, which sits in the

Parque Natural and dates back to 1885, is helmed by the fourth and fifth generations of the Reixac family. The menu is rooted in Cuina Volcànica, and includes their signature La Deu potatoes; *escalivada*, a typical Catalan dish of grilled vegetables; and pig's trotters. The *menú* is €11.60. Daily 1.30–3.30pm & 8–10.30pm; closed Sun dinner.

La Garrotxa c/Serra i Ginesta 14 ☎ 972 261 604. This casual, mid-priced Cuina Volcànica restaurant features an array of delicious local dishes, from roast pork cheek to rabbit stew. Daily 1–4pm, plus Sat dinner.

Parc Natural de la Zona Volcànica

The sprawling **Parc Natural de la Zona Volcànica** makes up much of the **Baixa Garrotxa** region. You won't see lava flows and smoke-snorting volcanoes, though – the last eruption was almost 11,000 years ago, and the park in fact largely green and verdant, with a remarkably fertile soil. The volcanic landscape comes in the shape of the park's forty cones, which vary widely in size, the bigger ones topping 170m.

There are numerous trails through the park – if you're short on time, you can opt to take shorter trails to several of the volcanoes that start at car parks around Olot. Posted signs point out those that lead to the two easiest cones to access from town: **Volcà del Croscat**, the youngest cone in the park, and **Volcà de Santa Margarida**.

Santa Pau

Medieval **Santa Pau**, 9km southwest of Olot, sits right in the middle of the volcanic region, and is a great jumping-off point for exploration. The beautifully preserved village features stone houses, narrow lanes, ancient archways and the thirteenth-century **Plaça Mayor**, once the Firal dels Bous (Cattle Market). Santa Pau is also known for its *fesols* (haricot beans), which figure prominently in the local cuisine. The village celebrates its beloved bean in the Fira de Sant Antonic, also known as the **Fira de Fesol** (Fesol Festival) in mid- or late January.

11

ARRIVAL AND INFORMATION

Accessing the park You'll need your own wheels to access the park; there is a regular Teisa bus service between Girona and Olot.

Centro d'Informació del Parc Natural de la Zona Volcànica Casal del Volcans, Olot (Mon–Sat 10am–2pm

PARC NATURAL DE LA ZONA VOLCÀNICA

& 4–6pm, Sun 10am–2pm; ☎ 972 268 112, ⓦ gencat.cat/parcs/garrotxa). The main park information office is in Parc Nou in Olot, where you can pick up helpful hiking maps.

Turisme Pl. Mayor, Santa Pau (Mon & Wed–Sat noon–6pm, Sun 11am–3pm; ☎ 972 680 349).

ACCOMMODATION AND EATING

Cal Sastre c/Cases Noves, near Plaçeta dels Balls, Santa Pau ☎ 972 680 049, ⓦ calsastre.com. For a taste of the famous Santa Pau *fesols*, dine at this established Catalan restaurant, which also doubles as a handsome hotel (from €90, includes breakfast). Daily except Mon 1–3.30pm & 9–10.30pm, closed Sun night; closed Feb.

Can Menció Pl. Major 17, Santa Pau ☎ 972 680 014, ⓦ canmencio.com. This inviting hotel is one of the better

picks in town, with alpine-style rooms and an inviting, breezy café-bar (open daily) right on the *plaça*. **€50**

Ecologic Lava Carretera Santa Pau, 3km west of Santa Pau ☎ 972 680 358. This well-maintained campsite, near two volcanic cones, has tents and basic bungalows, and offers information on hikes in the area. Tent pitch from **€5**, bungalows **€120**

Vic

The Serra del Montseny, a towering granite mountain range with lushly forested slopes, looms southwest of Girona. On the west of the range, 34km southwest of Olot and easily accessible as a day-trip from Barcelona, is the amiable, well-preserved town of **Vic**. Vic is considered one of the more quintessential Catalan towns, both because the locals have especially strong Catalan pride, and also because it's near the Ripoll area, cradle of Catalan history. Vic was once the capital of an Iberian tribe, and in the second century became a Roman settlement – you'll spy various Roman remains, including parts of a temple, scattered around town.

Vic also hosted a prosperous medieval market, and the town has a yearly **Mercat Medieval de Vic** (ⓦ firesifestes.com) in its old quarter in early December, celebrating its medieval past. Vic is defined by its elegant, enormous **Plaça Mayor**, ringed by historic, porticoed buildings, which features a colourful **food market** twice a week (Tues & Sat) – and if there's one thing to buy, it's Vic's famous sausages (*llonganissa* or *fuet*), which are heralded throughout Catalunya and perfect for tossing into the suitcase to bring home.

MÚSICA IN VIC

Raucous rumba tunes, melancholy classics by string quartets, quirky improvisational jazz bands, and a Catalan songstress singing in her native tongue … you'll see it all at the superb festival **Mercat de Música Viva**, or Live Music Market (w mmvv.net), in mid-September, which showcases international groups in venues around town. Equally entertaining is the **Festival de Jazz** (w jazzcava.com), generally in May and June, which draws local and global jazz bands.

Catedral and Museu Episcopal

Catedral Pl. de la Catedral • Daily 10am–1pm & 4–7pm • €2 for cloister and crypt **Museu Episcopal** Pl. Bisbe Oliba 3 • April–Sept Tues–Sat 10am–7pm, Sun 10am–2pm; Oct–March Tues–Fri 10am–1pm & 3–6pm, Sat 10am–7pm, Sun 10am–2pm • €5 • w museuepiscopalvic.com

Vic's Neoclassical **Catedral** looms over the centre of town; inside, striking murals depict scenes from the Bible by Catalan artist Josep Maria Sert. The nearby **Museu Episcopal** features a superb collection of sacred art from the eleventh to thirteenth centuries, including an alabaster altarpiece depicting the Passion, Resurrection and Ascension of Christ. The museum also showcases an array of art and religious artefacts culled from Pyrenean churches, making it one of the most important collections of Catalan Romanesque art outside of the Museu d'Art de Catalunya in Barcelona.

Museu de l'Art de la Pell

C/de l'Arquebisbe Alemany 5 • Tues–Sat 11am–2pm & 5–8pm, Sun 11am–2pm • €3

Housed in an old convent, the well-curated **Museu de l'Art de la Pell** displays the collection of long-time leather tailor Andreu Colomer Munmany. Exhibits explore the history of leather and other local crafts in and around Vic, and include numerous decorative leather items.

ARRIVAL AND INFORMATION   VIC

By train and bus Trains and Sagalés buses run regularly to and from Barcelona (1hr 20min). It's a short walk east from the (adjacent) train and bus stations to the centre of town.

Turisme Just off Pl. Mayor (Mon–Fri & Sat 10am–2pm & 4–7pm, Sun 10.30am–1.30pm; ☎ 938 862 091, w victurisme.cat).

ACCOMMODATION AND EATING

HOTEL

Estació del Nord Pl. de l'Estació 4 ☎ 935 166 292, w estaciodelnord.com. It's hard to get any more convenient than the sleek little boutique hotel on the upper level of Vic's train station. The fully refurbished hotel has well-maintained rooms, with lots of white and pale, earthy colours. **€75**

RESTAURANTS

★ **D.O. Vic** c/de Sant Miquel dels Sants 16 ☎ 938 832 396, w restaurante-do-vic.com. This creative, *cuina*

Catalana restaurant lives up to its name of "Denominació d'Origen", focusing on locally sourced ingredients. Dishes might include artichoke hearts with cod, tuna tartare with golden apples, and duck breast. Tasting *menú* €32. Daily 1.30–3.30pm, plus Wed–Sat 8.30–10.30pm.

El Jardinet c/Corretgers 8 ☎ 938 862 877. Dine on seasonal Mediterranean cuisine at this welcoming restaurant which has a well-priced weekday lunchtime *menú del día* for €13, and €24 for dinner. Usually daily 1.30–3.30pm, plus Tues–Sat 8.30–10.30pm.

Cardona and Salsona

Seventy kilometres west of Vic, and further into the rustic heartland of Catalunya, rises the splendid, ancient castle of **Cardona**, which is now an elegant parador. Nearby is the medieval town of **Solsona**.

Cardona

The first glimpse of **CARDONA** is an impressive one: a brooding medieval castle sits, like a protective parent, on the hillside above the village. The castle has been converted into a four-star **parador**, which is well worth a visit to stroll the grounds even if you're not staying here. Elsewhere, the town's casual, small-town ambience and tiny medieval centre make it an enjoyable place for a wander.

Salina de Cardona

Els Escorials • Usually mid-March to July & Sept–Dec Tues–Fri 10am–3pm (guided tours 11.30am & 1.30pm), Sat & Sun 10am–6pm (guided tours usually every 30min); Aug daily 10am–7pm (guided tours every 30min); limited hours or closed Dec to mid-March (check with *turisme*); last visit at least 1hr before closing • €10 • ⓦ salineradecardona.com

Salt mining formed an important part of Cardona's past, as evidenced by the **Salina**, or salt mountain, a massive saline deposit near the river. On a tour, you'll don a hard hat, explore caves and visit a museum detailing the history of the salt mine, which functioned from 1929 to 1990.

ARRIVAL AND DEPARTURE

CARDONA

By train Regular trains run from Barcelona to Manresa (1hr 20min), from which Alsina Graells buses travel to Cardona (30min).

By bus Alsina Graells buses run direct from Barcelona to Cardona (2hr).

ACCOMMODATION

★ **Cardona Parador** Castell de Cardona ☎ 938 691 275, ⓦ parador.es. A prime example of just how impressive the parador experience can be: spacious rooms feature all the amenities, while throughout, the ancient ambience has been carefully preserved, from stone arches to an eleventh-century chapel that contains the tombs of the counts of Cardona. The handsome restaurant looks right out of a medieval knight's tale. **€204**

Hotel Bremon c/Cambres 15 ☎ 938 684 902, ⓦ hotelbremon.com. While the parador is the top bet for staying the night, Cardona now also has this fetching hotel, set in a former nineteenth-century convent and school that was run by the Carmelite nuns. The interior has been lovingly renovated, with comfortable rooms and a lovely terrace overlooking Cardona's medieval core. **€105**

Solsona

The unspoiled medieval town of **SOLSONA**, 16km west of Cardona, is capital of El Solsonès, the "region of 1000 farms". Dating from the tenth century, Solsona has maintained its ancient infrastructure particularly well, with impressive ancient walls and a maze-like old town. Towns and villages across Catalunya celebrate their **festa major** once a year – and Solsona is one such place to catch a glimpse into small-town life: its *festa major* is September 7–11, when the streets fill with *gegants*, dragons and *trabucaires* (armed men), all traditional folklore figures dating from the seventeenth century.

Catedral

Cathedral and museum: usually Tues–Sat 10am–1pm & 4.30pm–7pm (Oct–April 4–6pm), Sun 10am–2pm • €3

The Gothic **Catedral** features a notable Baroque altarpiece and one of the oldest organs in Catalunya. Its star attraction is its twelfth-century miniature Virgin carved of black stone – the Mare de Déu del Claustre, the patron of Solsona. Originally attached to a column, the statue inclines forward at an angle, revealing that the sculptor signed it in Latin on the back: *Gilabertus Me Fecit* ("Gilabertus made me").

Museu Diocesà

Adjoining the cathedral is the **Museu Diocesà**, whose excellent collection includes fifteenth-century processional crosses and Gothic stone statues. Because the Diocesan Museum is one of Catalunya's oldest – it was founded in 1896 – Solsona has managed to hold on to its religious and artistic treasures.

ARRIVAL AND INFORMATION

By bus Alsina Graells buses travel from Barcelona through nearby Cardona to Solsona (2hr 30min), and then continue on to La Seu d'Urgell.

Turisme c/Bassella 1 (Mon–Fri 9am–1pm & 4–7pm, Sat 10.30am–1.30pm & 4–7pm, Sun 10.30am–1.30pm; ☎973 481 009, ⓦsolsonaturisme.com).

ACCOMMODATION AND EATING

Hotel Sant Roc Pl. de Sant Roc 2 ☎973 480 006, ⓦhotelsantroc.com. This charming boutique hotel has a small spa while the hotel's *El Bufí* restaurant serves creative regional cuisine, from sea bass with seasonal mushrooms to duck with a purée of chestnuts. **€105**

The Catalan Pyrenees

Looming gracefully over northern Catalunya, the snow-tipped Pyrenees form a mighty barrier between the Iberian Peninsula and the rest of Europe. You can ski and hike throughout these mountains, making use of a range of ski centres and vast stretches of natural parkland. Imposing peaks reach more than 3400m, while fierce rivers cleave the green valleys; tucked away in the valleys and clinging to the mountains are centuries-old alpine villages, each with its own Romanesque church, collectively forming an open-air rural museum of early medieval architecture, particularly in the beautiful **Vall de Boí**.

The Pyrenees are easy to reach from Barcelona – **Ripoll**, a gateway town to the mountains, is accessible in less than three hours. The ski scene dominates the mountains northwest of Ripoll, while summer draws hikers and trekkers. North of Ripoll is the village of **Ribes de Freser**, where you can board the famous **cremallera** railway which snakes its way up to the small ski town and pilgrimage site of **Núria** – one of the most magnificent journeys in the Pyrenees.

West of here unfolds the formidable **Serra del Cadí**, which offers superb hiking and trekking around one of Catalunya's most recognizable peaks, the **Pedraforca**. To the north, along the French boder, is **La Cerdanya**, a lush, sunny Pyrenean valley that's especially popular in the summer with outdoor enthusiasts. Cerdanya's capital is the lively town of **Puigcerdà**, while just across the border sits the geographical oddity of **Llívia**, a Spanish town fully enclosed by France. In winter, skiers flock to **La Molina** and **Masella**, the two big ski resorts in the area.

The mountainous terrain around **La Seu d'Urgell**, still further west, offers some of the best trekking in the Pyrenees. White-water aficionados get their adrenalin rush in the **Noguera Pallaresa** valley, where churning rivers offer the best rafting in the region. Finally, in the far northwest unfolds the rugged **Parc Nacional d'Aigüestortes i Estany de Sant Maurici**, and lush **Val d'Aran**, one of Spain's most chic and finest ski resorts.

THE GR11 AND THE HRP

Running roughly parallel to the GR10, which runs on the French side, the **GR11** is a network of long-distance hiking trails which traverses the Spanish Pyrenees from one end to the other. Estimated to be about 850–900km in length, it runs from the Golfo de Vizcaya (Bay of Biscay) in the Basque region to the west to Cap de Creus, near Cadaqués in the east. For seasoned trekkers, there is also the **HRP** (Haute Randonnée Pyrénéenne), which follows a higher and wilder course in the Pyrenees, crisscrossing the Spanish–French border along the way. It runs largely through the Parc National des Pyrénées in France but also takes in parts of the Parc Nacional d'Aigüestortes i Estany de Sant Maurici. In Spain, you can get more general information about the GR routes from the Federación Española de Deportes de Montaña y Escalada (FEDME; Spanish Mountain Sports Federation; ⓦfedme.es), though the website is mostly in Spanish only. Tourist offices, refuges, and many hotels in the Pyrenees can also supply maps, info on accommodation along the route and more.

THE LEGEND OF THE BLOODY FLAG

Many legends swirl around the colourful **Guifré el Pélos** ("Wilfred the Hairy"), who established himself as the first count of Barcelona in the ninth century. One such story is the bloody creation of the **Catalan flag**. As the legend goes: Guifré el Pélos was mortally wounded in a battle against the Normans (some say the battle was against the Moors). The Frankish king Charles the Bald wanted to pay tribute to the dying Guifré's bravery by awarding him a coat of arms on the battlefield. The king is said to have dipped Guifré's hands in his own freshly drawn blood, and then ran his fingers across the golden shield; hence the four bands of red on a yellow background.

Ripoll

The quiet mountain town of **RIPOLL**, which serves as a good starting point for exploring the Pyrenees, is known as the cradle of Catalunya, as it was here that founding father Guifré el Pélos (Wilfred the Hairy) staked his claim to what became the Autonomous Community of Catalunya. The chief reason to visit is to view the impressive Benedictine Monestir de Santa Maria, founded in 888 by Wilfred the Hairy – and where he is buried. Ripoll holds an international **music festival** in July and August in the fourteenth-century church of Sant Pere, which rises over the Plaça Abat Oliba.

Monestir de Santa Maria

Monastery Pl. Abat Oliba • Daily 10am–1pm & 3–7pm (till 6pm Oct–March) • €3

One of the few parts to survive a tragic fire, the splendid twelfth-century facade of the west portal of the **Monestir de Santa Maria**, founded some four hundred years earlier, is considered one of Spain's great works of Romanesque art. The portal showcases a series of sculptures depicting the Creation and other Biblical scenes in gorgeous detail – singing angels, the stories of Moses and Solomon and mythical beasts representing the Apostles, among other scenes – giving it its nickname as the "Stone Bible" or "Ripoll Bible". The cloister has also aged beautifully, while the nave is a replica of the original structure that was built over Guifré el Pélos' tomb.

Museu Etnogràfic de Ripoll

Pl. Abat Oliba • Mon–Sat 10am–1.30pm & 4–6pm (July & Aug open till 7pm), Sun 10am–2pm • €4 • ⓦ museuderipoll.org

Reopened in 2011 after ten years of closure, the **Museu Etnogràfic de Ripoll** explores the history of Ripoll and inland Catalunya through its culture, society, religion and trades, with exhibits on everything from farming methods to folklore. Ripoll had a thriving metalworking industry in the Middle Ages, and later became a production centre for weapons and firearms, and exhibits include ancient keys, forged ironwork and early rifles and other weapons.

ARRIVAL AND INFORMATION
RIPOLL

By train and bus The train and bus stations are near each other, a 10min walk from the centre of town. Regular trains from Barcelona stop in Ripoll (2hr) en route to Puigcerdà.

Turisme Pl. Abat Oliba, near the monastery (Mon–Sat 9.30am–1.30pm & 4–7pm (sometimes 8pm in Aug), Sun 10am–2pm; ☏ 972 702 351, ⓦ ripoll.cat).

ACCOMMODATION

Ca La Paula c/Pirineus 6 ☏ 972 700 011. Pickings in town are slim but for budget beds try this basic *hostal*, which sits next to the monastery and offers decent, simple rooms. **€45**

Masia Jaume Coll Borredà, 20km west of Ripoll, on Carretera C-26, the road to Berga ☏ 938 239 095 or 670 964 751. Inviting, stone-walled *casa de pagès* ("peasant's house") in the tiny village of Borredà. They also have a small café-restaurant for guests. **€55**

Sant Joan de les Abadesses

Sitting in the verdant Ríu Tur valley 1km northeast of Ripoll, the petite town of **SANT JOAN DE LES ABADESSES** was built around the monastery of the same name, which was founded by Guifré el Pélos in 887 and named after his daughter. Sant Joan is a pleasant place for a stroll, particularly through the Plaça Major to the Gothic bridge over the Ríu Ter.

The monastery and museum

Monastery and museum daily 10am–7pm · €3

The twelfth-century **monastery** features an elegant single-nave church, a Gothic cloister and a thirteenth-century wooden sculpture depicting Christ's descent from the cross. Also a highlight is the beautiful alabaster Gothic altarpiece of Santa María la Blanca, dating from the fourteenth century. The **Museu de Monestir** offers a well-curated overview of the town's formidable religious history, with sacred artefacts and detailed embroidery and silverware.

ARRIVAL AND INFORMATION   SANT JOAN DE LES ABADESSES

By bus Teisa buses run regularly to Sant Joan de les Abadesses (4–6 times daily, sometimes less often on weekends) on the Girona–Olot–Ripoll route.

Turisme Palau de l'Abadia, next to the Museu del Monestir (Mon–Sat 10am–2pm & 4–7pm, Sun 10am–2pm; ☏ 972 720 599, ⓦ santjoandelesabadesses.cat).

ACCOMMODATION

Sant Joan, while pleasant for an overnight stop, has minimal accommodation. A better bet is to venture into the countryside, where you'll find several excellent rustic houses.

Can Janpere c/Mestre Andreu 3 ☏ 972 720 077, ⓦ elripolles.com/fondajanpere. This is one of the few budget spots in town; the rooms are simple, with somewhat dated furnishings, but they're clean and well maintained, as are the bathrooms. They also offer a dinner *menú*. **€50**

★ **Mas Mitjavila** 10km northwest of Sant Joan, in Sant Martí d'Ogassa ☏ 972 722 020, ⓦ masmitjavila.es. Stone farmhouse that was once, along with the adjacent tenth-century church of Sant Martí, a dependency of the Sant Joan monastery. The lovely rooms are the picture of

rustic-chic, with lots of gleaming dark wood – from the furnishings to the beamed ceilings – and views of the surrounding green valley. **€76**

El Reixac 3km north of town ☏ 972 720 373, ⓦ elreixac.com. Signposted from town, this friendly, family-run farmhouse has cottages and apartments with comfortable, rustic rooms and a swimming pool. The surrounding area is prime hiking territory, and they have lots of information on local trails. Cottages for four are €100. Apartments **€70**

Camprodon

CAMPRODON, 12km east of Sant Joan de les Abadesses, is where you really start to feel like you're in the mountains: the peaks loom in the distance, the air is crisp and the streets are dotted with ski- and outdoor-gear shops. Camprodon also has an upscale, alpine-holiday air to it, particularly along the broad promenade of **Passeig Maristany**, where many well-off Catalans have mountain villas. Camprodon's handsome centrepiece is the sixteenth-century **Pont Nou**, which spans the Ríu Ter in the middle of town. From here, the main street leads to the lovely Romanesque **Sant Pere church**, open generally for services only.

Museu Isaac Albéniz

Plaça d'Espanya 1 · Daily except Tues 11am–2pm & 4–7pm · €2.40 · ⓦ albeniz.cat

Composer and pianist Isaac Albéniz (1860–1909) was born in Camprodon, and was known for his pieces that evoked Catalan and Spanish folk songs. The small **Museu Isaac Albéniz** showcases his life and times via photographs and documents. Camprodon also hosts a music **festival** in July that celebrates Albéniz, with a range of classical music concerts.

ARRIVAL AND INFORMATION

By bus Regular Teisa buses from Ripoll stop at a shelter at the southeast edge of town.

Turisme Pl. d'Espanya 1 (Tues–Sat 10am–2pm & 4–7pm, Sun 10am–2pm; ☎ 972 740 010, ⓦ valldecamprodon.org).

ACCOMMODATION

Camprodon gets busy in the peak season, when it's advisable to make reservations. You'll also find some good accommodation out of town in the Ter valley.

Hotel de Camprodon Pl. Dr Robert 3 ☎ 972 740 013, ⓦ hotelcamprodon.com. This handsome hotel, in a *modernista* building, has a graceful interior and well-maintained rooms. **€130**

Hotel Maristany Avdga. Maristany 20, just north of town ☎ 972 130 078, ⓦ hotelmaristany.com. Historic building with landscaped gardens and stylish rooms. The restaurant (reserve in advance) serves local cuisine, such as veal with mushrooms and duck with cherries. Closed Jan & Feb. **€70**

EATING AND DRINKING

El Pont 9 Cami Cerdanya ☎ 972 740 521, ⓦ restaurantelpont9.com. Worth a splurge, with lovely views of the bridge, and superb market-fresh Catalan cuisine, from pungent sheep cheeses to cod and *caragols* (snails). The daily *menú* starts at €17–20. Daily 12.30–4pm, plus Wed & Thurs 8–10pm, Fri & Sat 8.30–10.30pm.

Taverna Fraxanet c/Freixenet 8 ☎ 972 740 724. This welcoming *taverna* has rustic stone walls and serves mid-priced hearty grilled meats and other regional cuisine. Daily 1–4pm & 8–11pm; usually closed Tues Nov–March.

Around Camprodon

Beyond Camprodon, appealing mountain villages and trekking trails dot the peaks and **Ter valley**. This is hiking territory, and many visitors come to this area for outdoor adventure, whether on the trails in summer, or on the slopes of **Vallter2000** in winter. The best way to explore is with your own wheels, though a few buses crawl through the valley. **Villalonga de Ter**, 5km from Camprodon, makes for an amiable stopover in your explorations of the valley, with a Romanesque church, Sant Martí, on the main *plaza*. Also a pleasant stop is the hill-top **Tregurá de Dalt**, 6km beyond Villalonga, with stone houses lining cobbled streets and lovely views of the valley and peaks. Both have good accommodation options.

Vallter2000

ⓦ vallter2000.com

If you're looking to ski in the area, try the well-run **Vallter2000**, which overlooks the Ter valley and has a decent range of pistes. Check the website before visiting, though, because snowfall can vary. The resort also offers plenty of summer activities, from hiking to horseriding.

ACCOMMODATION

Fonda Rigà Carretera de Tregurà, Tregurà de Dalt ☎ 972 136 000, ⓦ fondariga.com. Family-run rustic inn with inviting rooms, some with wood-beamed ceilings. The restaurant (call ahead to check opening times), with picture windows overlooking the sloping valley, serves hearty Catalan cuisine. Breakfast included. **€45**

Hostal Pastoret Pl. Constitució 10, Villalonga de Ter ☎ 972 740 319, ⓦ hostalpastoret.com. This comfortable hotel has simply furnished, well-cared-for rooms, some with small wrought-iron balconies and views of the mountains. They can also arrange trekking excursions and other outdoor activities. Half-board **€100**

Ribes de Freser, Núria and around

The Freser valley extends north of Ripoll to the mountain village of **Ribes de Freser** and Queralbs before unfolding eastward through a stunning gorge. Ribes de Freser sits at the confluence of three rivers, hemmed in by verdant valleys, and features a small old

THE CREMALLERA

The journey of the Cremallera de Vall de Núria, most often just known as the **cremallera** railway ("zipper" in Catalan), built in 1931, is spectacular: the little train follows the rushing Ríu Freser and then, quite suddenly, begins to scale steep mountainsides along stomach-churning switchbacks, from where you're rewarded with beautiful views of the river and valley far below. Trains depart from the Ribes-Enllaç station, in the southern part of Ribes, daily year-round except November, when it's closed. In high season (July to mid-Sept, plus winter hols), trains run 10–13 times a day; in low season, it's around 6–7 times. One-way journey time is 35 minutes; tickets are €21.25 round-trip in high season, €17.75 in low season. For the latest information, visit ⓦ valldenuria.cat or call ☎ 972 732 020.

town and the **church of Santa María**, which dates back to the eleventh century but was then rebuilt in the 1900s in a modernist style. The village is best known as the starting point for the famous rack-and-pinion **cremallera** train (see box above), which snakes up the mountain to the sanctuary of **Núria** and its neighbouring ski centre, offering tantalizing views along the way. Ribes de Freser also makes for a pleasant Pyrenean base, thanks to its proximity to the mountains and decent array of accommodation.

Santuari de la Mare de Déu

The Núria valley has long been visited by pilgrims, and the **Santuari de la Mare de Déu** had its beginnings in a visit by **Sant Gil of Nîmes**, who came here on retreat in the seventh century. Gil left behind a wooden statue of the Virgin Mary, which became an object of veneration, and eventually a patron saint among local shepherds. The sanctuary consists basically of a parochial **church** (built in 1911) and a hermitage – a small, ancient-looking mountain church, built in 1615 and refurbished over the years. The overall complex itself is rather plain – it includes the sanctuary, plus several straightforward bars, restaurants and self-catering apartments. Pilgrims still come to visit, and the church holds daily Mass for locals, but the devout are usually outnumbered by skiers in winter and hikers in summer.

Hiking and skiing

Vall de Núria ski centre ⓦ valldenuria.cat

The area abounds with good **hikes**, including the popular trek along the river gorge from Núria to the village of Queralbs (2hr 30min). Those with more stamina can go on a full-day hike through the **Gorges of Freser**, trekking on the GR11.7 and then returning on another signposted trail. You can stop along the way at **Refugi Coma de Vaca** (see p.753).

The **Vall de Núria ski centre** has plenty of activities for kids, so is popular with families.

ARRIVAL AND INFORMATION

By train Regular trains on the Barcelona–Puigcerdà line stop at the Ribes de Freser (2hr 30min), where you can catch the *cremallera* train (see box above).

RIBES DE FRESER, NÚRIA AND AROUND

Turisme Pl. de l'Ajuntament 3, Ribes de Freser (Mon–Sat 10am–2pm & 5–8pm, Sun 10am–1pm; ☎ 972 727 728, ⓦ vallderibes.cat). Can assist in finding a bed for the night.

ACCOMMODATION AND EATING

RIBES DE FRESER

Hotel Caçadors c/Balandrau 24–26 ☎ 972 727 006, ⓦ hotelsderibes.com. This hotel has well-maintained, good-sized rooms in an earthy colour scheme. The restaurant serves tasty, mid-priced Catalan cuisine with a creative twist – and hearty portions. Meals are best value if you opt for half-board (€140). **€94**

Hotel Resguard dels Vents Camí de Ventaiola, 1km

north of town. Stylish little hotel with airy rooms, views of the surrounding quiet mountains and a small, peaceful spa. **€84**

NÚRIA

Albergue Pic de l'Àliga ☎ 972 732 048, ⓦ xanascat .cat. Location is the big draw at this youth hostel, which sits at the top of the cable-car line of the ski centre. Basic dorms, large communal spaces, and they can help arrange outdoor activities. Dorm €26

Hotel Vall de Núria ☎ 972 732 030, ⓦ valdenuria.com. This comfortable spot, with clean rooms and self-catering apartments, is decent but a bit expensive for what you get. Rate includes breakfast; half-board also available. €128

GORGES OF FRESER

Refugi Coma de Vaca ☎ 972 198 082, ⓦ comadevaca .com. This well-maintained refuge has bunk-bed dorms, an inviting common room with wooden tables and lovely mountain views. Staffed Easter & mid-June to mid-Sept, but call ahead to confirm. €15

The Serra del Cadí

Unfolding in the eastern section of the Western Pyrenees, the verdant **Parc Natural Cadí-Moixeró** encompasses the massive **Serra del Cadí**, which has the area's best hiking and trekking around one of Catalunya's most recognizable mountains, **Pedraforca**. The village of **Bagà** houses the park's tourist office. The park has a number of staffed refuges, which you can access via treks from the surrounding mountain villages. There are also superb birding opportunities, and you may spy Tengmalm's owls and the black woodpecker, the park symbol. It's best to have your own transport, as buses pass only intermittently through the outer villages.

Bagà

The village of **BAGÀ** makes for a good base in the area, and is home to the park's well-stocked main tourist office. Bagà also has a tidy little medieval quarter, centred on Plaça Porxada, and a pretty Romanesque-Gothic church.

Gòsol

Surrounded by the leafy Gòsol valley, the village of **Gòsol**, 10km to the west of Saldes (see p.754), is also a good base. The remains of an eleventh-century castle loom over the village, which is dotted with a few places to stay and a good campsite nearby. Gòsol celebrates its popular annual festival on August 15, with local folk dances, music and cuisine.

DRAGONS AND DEVILS

Pleasant **BERGA**, 30km west of Ripoll, is the main town in the *comarca* of **Berguedà**. Berga has the usual historical draws – an old town, the remains of a castle – but the reason that it's on the map, so to speak, is as host of one of Catalunya's most famous festivals, the **Festa del Patum**, during Corpus Christi week. During the festival, Berga's otherwise staid streets fill with parade floats of pagans and fantasy creatures – the famous *gegants*, devils, dragons spewing fireworks and dragon-slayers – while revellers dance on the sidelines and behind the floats. The festival is said to be named after the sound of the drum, and you'll hear the crowd chanting "pa-tum, pa-tum!" throughout. If you can't make it to the festival, you can catch a glimpse of the festival at the simple **La Casa de Patum** (summer Thurs–Sun 11am–2pm & 6–8pm; winter only open on weekend, same hours; free), which features a video of the festival and various costumes. During Patum, you must book accommodation at least a month in advance.

INFORMATION

Turisme c/dels Àngels 7, in the middle of the old town (Mon–Sat 10am–2pm & 6–8pm, Sun 11am–2pm & 6–8pm; ☎ 938 211 384, ⓦ turismeberga.cat).

ACCOMMODATION AND EATING

Hotel Estel Carretera Sant Fruitós 39 ☎ 938 213 463, ⓦ hotelestel.com. This *hostal* has basic but comfortable rooms. €55

Hotel HCC Ciutat de Berga Pg. de la Industria 11 ☎ 938 214 422, ⓦ hcchotels.es. This modern hotel geared to business travellers may be a touch antiseptic but it's also central, with friendly staff and a decent restaurant – and it's a good overnight base if you're here for the Patum festival. €60

Sala Pg. de la Pau ☎ 938 211 185, ⓦ restaurantsala .com. One of Berga's best-known restaurants – and for good reason – this excellent though pricey restaurant serves creative, seasonal cuisine, including expertly grilled game, fresh salads and a bounty of mushrooms in autumn. Expect to pay around €55–60 per person. Wed–Sat 1.30–3pm & 8.30–11pm, plus Sun 1.30–3pm.

11

REFUGES AND HIKES 0N PEDRAFORCA

One of the best ways to negotiate the Pedraforca is by using the refuges as your nightly base – or as refuelling pit-stops. A ninety-minute trek from Saldes brings you near **Refugi Lluís Estasen** (1647m; important to reserve ahead in summer), from where you can ascend the 2491m Pedraforca (the full trek up and down takes about 5–6hr). The hike up the mountain reaches the divide between the two summits, where you'll connect with the path coming up from Gòsol. You'll find a number of refuges on the mountain; the tourist office in Bagà has up-to-date information on all of them. One popular day-hike from the *Refugi Lluís Estasen* is to the **Refugi Sant Jordi** (1570m; staffed generally only in summer) to the east, with the mountain peaks rising up all around you.

REFUGES

Refugi Lluís Estasen ☎608 315 312. Generally staffed only in summer; call ahead or enquire at park information office. Dorm from €15

Refugi Sant Jordi ☎619 239 860. Generally staffed only in summer; call ahead or enquire at park information office. Dorm from €15

Pedraforca and around

Gaze up at the mighty **Pedraforca**, which rises east of Gòsol, and it's easy to see why it has become Catalunya's most iconic peak. Its name means "stone pitchfork" because the looming mountain appears cleaved down the middle, resulting in two impressive peaks. The Pedraforca is a boon for hikers; most people access it from **Saldes**, a village at the foot of the mountain.

ARRIVAL AND INFORMATION

By bus Alsa buses travel several times daily from Barcelona via Berga to Bagà (2hr 30min); buses drop you off near the centre of Bagà.

Park information office c/la Vinya 1, Bagà (summer

THE SERRA DEL CADÍ

Mon–Fri 9am–1.30pm & 4–7pm, Sat 9am–1.30pm & 4–6.30pm, Sun 9am–1pm; winter Mon–Fri 8am–3pm, Sat 9am–1.30pm & 4–6.30pm, Sun 9am–1pm; ☎938 244 151). You can pick up maps and a list of refuges here.

ACCOMMODATION AND EATING

BAGÀ

Hotel Ca L'Amagat c/Clota 4 ☎938 244 032, ⓦhotelcalamagat.com. Near the centre of town, this cosy spot has comfortable rooms and a stone-and-wood-walled restaurant (closed Mon in winter) with hearty Catalan cuisine. €75

Molí del Casó 2km south of town ☎938 244 076, ⓦmolidelcaso.es. Welcoming *casa rural* with cosy rooms, a vegetable garden and dining room (for guests only) serving regional cuisine. €140

GÒSOL

Cadí Southwest of Gòsol, off the road to Tuixént ☎973 370 143, ⓦcadivacances.com. This well-maintained complex has both a camping area and bungalows, as well as a swimming pool and restaurant with fireplace. Tent pitch and car €17, bungalows €110

Cal Triuet Pl. Major 4 ☎973 370 072. This longtime hotel has decent rooms; they can offer info on hikes into the surrounding mountains. The restaurant (closed Tues in winter) serves good mid-priced regional cuisine. Hotel closed Dec–Feb. €50

La Cerdanya

The verdant **Cerdanya valley**, hemmed in by looming peaks to the north and south, has long shared a geo-cultural affinity with France. The border snakes its way through the middle of the valley, but you can hardly tell where Spain ends and France begins. Catalan is spoken on both sides of the border, and in many ways, Cerdanya seems to function as an independent entity, with customs all its own. As the locals say, it's not quite Spain, and it's not quite France – it's simply La Cerdanya. The only Pyrenean valley running east–west, the Cerdanya is showered with more sunlight than any other part of the range, and is therefore a popular summer spot for hikers and mountain-bikers. In winter, skiers flock to **La Molina** and **Masella**, the two big ski resorts.

Puigcerdà, the capital of Cerdanya, is the transport hub for the area, from where you can catch a train that continues into France – the only still-running trans-Pyrenean rail route, and offering lovely views along the way.

Toses

The small village of **TOSES**, about 18km west of Ribes de Freser, is perched at 1450m. Its highlight is the church of **San Cristòfol**, dating from the tenth to twelfth centuries (open usually for services only). The church is modest but well restored, with a handsome nave, rectangular belfry and reproduction frescoes. You'll also find several good places to stay in town as well as restaurants serving hearty regional cuisine.

ACCOMMODATION AND EATING · TOSES

Ca la Martra c/de l'Església ☎ 972 736 398 or 618 475 511, ⓦ calamartra.com. Comfortable, rustic apartments with views of the leafy hills. Usually a minimum two-night stay. Apartment (per night) **€100**

Cal Racó Carretera La Molina ☎ 972 736 226. This amiable restaurant serves a daily *menú* that ranges from €12 to €16, and features grilled meats and other substantial alpine fare. Daily 8am–midnight; closed Mon in winter.

Les Forques d'en Pep Pl. Estudi 2 ☎ 972 736 125. Fill up here on mid-priced regional cuisine, from steak and lamb to root vegetables and rice dishes. Summer usually daily 1.30–3.30pm & 8.30–10.30pm; weekends only in winter.

La Molina and La Masella

ⓦ lamolina.com; ⓦ masella.com

The combined ski resorts of **La Molina** and **La Masella** comprise one of the larger ski areas in the Spanish Pyrenees, with pistes on **Tosa d'Alp** (2537m; 15km south of Puigcerdà) and a total of 101 runs. If you're new to skiing, try La Molina, which caters to beginners and has a good ski school. La Masella also has a ski school, and offers extensive runs that appeal to more skilled skiers.

ARRIVAL AND ACCOMMODATION · LA MOLINA AND LA MASELLA

By bus It's easiest to get around with your own transport, though in the ski season there is an intermittent bus from Puigcerdà (generally departing once in the morning to the resort, and twice in the afternoon back to Puigcerdà).

ACCOMMODATION

You'll find a few options in the area. Many skiers, if they have their own transport, opt to stay in Puigcerdà or other villages in the region.

Hotel Adserà La Molina ☎ 972 892 001, ⓦ hoteladsera .com. This alpine hotel has simple but comfortable rooms, an on-site restaurant with regional food and views of the Cerdanya valley. Ask about discounts and packages, which they offer for ski classes and lift passes. **€60**

SKIING THE CATALAN PYRENEES

There's a good reason the Spanish royal family and other luminaries choose to ski in the Catalan Pyrenees – it's home to some of the best resorts in Spain. As with most ski regions, often the best way to save is through the **package deals** offered by many hotels, which include discounts on lift tickets. General prices are €14–24 a day for ski gear (skis, boots, poles), and €26–48 daily for lift passes, with prices varying with the length of time you buy passes for, whether it's a weekday or the weekend and the quality of the resort. Note, also, that it's well worth checking ahead to find out the level of snow, especially in the spring.

The Catalan Pyrenees offer a surprising variety of resorts, catering both to first-timers and advanced skiers. Intermediate skiers will find plenty of thrilling terrain at **La Masella** in La Cerdanya; **Boí-Taüll** on the western boundary of Aigüestortes; and **Baqueira-Beret** in the Val d'Aran. The best resorts for newbies and families are **Espot Esquí** on the eastern boundary of the Parc Nacional de Aigüestortes i Estany de Sant Maurici; and **La Molina** near La Masella.

Puigcerdà

Perched above the breezy union of the rivers Segre and Querol (*puig* is Catalan for "hill"; *cerdà* comes from Cerdanya), with the Pyrenees looming grandly above, hill-top **Puigcerdà** is one of the prettier border towns you'll come across. With its cluster of budget lodgings and proximity to ski resorts, the town is a busy stopover for skiers, hikers and mountain-bikers.

Founded in 1177, Puigcerdà has a rich history, but sadly most of its old buildings were destroyed in the Civil War, and its aged roots are best reflected in the layout and design of its narrow streets and *plaças*. Among the monuments that were spared is the *campanaria* (bell tower) in graceful **Plaça de Santa Maria**, while the well-preserved Plaça Cabrinetty (near Plaça de l'Ajuntament) has beautiful balconies and porticoes.

Church of Sant Domènec and around

Pg. 10 d'Abril • Generally open for services only: daily 8pm, plus Sun mornings and occasional weekday mornings; church opens 1hr before the service

11

The **church of Sant Domènec** was built in 1291 and restored after the Civil War. The church features an elegant portal, while inside is a series of fourteenth-century Gothic paintings. Next door sits the convent of Sant Domènec, which now houses a library, a historical archive and sacred artefacts.

ARRIVAL AND INFORMATION

By train and bus The train and bus stations sit at the bottom of the hill, from which a free funicular (daily 5.30am–midnight) travels up to Pl. de l'Ajuntament in the middle of town. Several trains daily connect Puigcerdà with Barcelona (3hr), via Vic and Ripoll. *Rodalies* (local) trains also run 4–5 times daily from Puigcerdà to Latour de Carol

in France (10min), from which there are connections to Toulouse (2hr 30min–3hr).

Turisme c/Querol 1, near the Pl. de l'Ajuntament (June to mid-Sept Mon–Fri 9.30am–1pm & 4–7pm, Sat 10am–1pm & 4–7pm, Sun 10am–1pm; rest of the year closed Sun & Mon; ☎972 880 542).

ACCOMMODATION

Fonda Cerdanya c/Ramon Cosp 7 ☎972 880 010, ⊛es.fondacerdanya.es. Among the cheapest beds in town is this basic *fonda*, with simple but clean rooms. **€50**

Hospes Villa Paulita Avgda. Pons i Gasch 15 ☎972 884 622, ⊛hospes.com. This boutique hotel, housed in a nineteenth-century summer villa, has cheery rooms and a good restaurant (closed Mon & Tues, plus Sun dinner) serving regional cuisine. Hearty breakfast included. **€156**

Hotel del Lago Avgda. Dr Piguillem 7 ☎972 881 000,

⊛hoteldellago.com. Blessed with a breezy garden, this hotel features alpine-style rooms, and a small spa offering massages and facials. **€124**

Sant Marc In the village of Les Pereres, 1.5km south of Puigcerdà ☎972 880 007, ⊛santmarc.es. If you have your own transport, stay at one of the *casas rurales* in the area, like this well-preserved mansion, which features spacious sitting rooms, cosy fireplaces, wood-floored rooms and a stone-walled restaurant with filling regional fare. **€80**

EATING AND DRINKING

Puigcerdà has a range of restaurants, most tending towards homely regional cuisine; take a twirl around Pl. de Santa Maria, which has plenty of eating spots.

El Caliu c/Alfons Primer 1 ☎972 140 825, ⊛elcaliu.com. Everything from beef tenderloin to salmon and sardines is served at this inviting spot, where dishes run between €10 and €15. Daily 1–3.30pm & 8.30–10.30pm; sometimes closed Wed.

El Secret de la Cerdanya Pl. del Call ☎639 056 008. For post-dinner drinks, head to this central bar and club for

cocktails and occasional live music. Daily evening until late.

Taberna del Call Pl. del Call ☎972 141 036. Fill up on tasty, mid-priced regional fare, including grilled fish and meats, at this welcoming *taberna*, which is popular with locals and has a terrace overlooking the *plaça*. Daily 1–3.30pm & 8.30–10.30pm.

Llívia

In 1659, the town of **LLÍVIA** officially became a Spanish enclave within France, a geographical oddity that has garnered a mention in guidebooks ever since. Though the

Spanish ceded 33 villages to France that year, tiny Llívia, deemed a town, remained Spanish. Just 6km from Puigcerdà, it's easy to reach on foot, or you can take a bus. Either way, Llívia makes for a lovely day-trip, if only to lose yourself in the town's medieval aura, which becomes increasingly more apparent the higher you climb the steep streets.

Mare de Déu dels Àngels

C/dels Forns 13 • Usually daily in summer 10am–1pm & 3–7pm; more limited hours in winter – check with turisme • ☎ 972 896 301

This sturdy church, dating to the fifteenth century, features Doric columns and a Baroque *retablo*. The best time to visit is during the long-running Llívia **music festival** (since 1982), which is held in and around the church on August weekends, and features orchestras, choirs and sometimes big-name stars (Catalan opera great Montserrat Caballé once performed here).

Museu Municipal

C/dels Forns 12 • Mon–Sat 10am–1pm & 3–6pm • Entry fee to be determined upon reopening • ☎ 972 896 011

The **Museu Municipal** has long been closed for renovations, but is scheduled to reopen in 2012. It features sections of what is thought to be the oldest pharmacy in Europe, founded in the early fifteenth century. Look out for the ancient pharmaceutical implements, as well as an impressive collection of Renaissance coffers, with portraits of saints.

11

ARRIVAL AND INFORMATION LLÍVIA

By bus Buses leave for Llívia from in front of Puigcerdà's train station at least twice daily on weekdays, and once daily on weekends.

Turisme c/dels Forns 10 (Mon–Fri 9am–1pm & 4–7pm, Sat 10am–1.30pm & 4–7pm, Sun 10am–1pm; shorter hours in winter; ☎ 972 896 313).

ACCOMMODATION AND EATING

Fonda Mercè c/Estavar 29, east side of old town ☎ 972 897 001, ⓦ fondamerce.com. Simple *fonda* with hardwood floors, as well as a Catalan-cuisine restaurant (closed Tues in winter) that serves tapas and hearty grilled meats. €85

★ **La Formatgeria de Llívia** Pla Ro, Gorguja ☎ 972 146 279, ⓦ laformatgeria.com. This inviting restaurant on the town's eastern edge is housed in a former cheese factory, and accordingly serves superb, gooey fondues and raclettes, as well as seasonal Catalan cuisine. Mon & Thurs–Sun lunch & dinner; may close in Aug.

Hotel Bernat de So Cereja 5, just north of town ☎ 972 146 206, ⓦ hotelbernatdeso.com. This handsome hotel is a lovely blend of rustic and elegant, with a breezy outdoor garden, a pool and a comfortable living room with a fireplace. €126

Hotel L'Esquirol Av. de Catalunya ☎ 972 146 363, ⓦ hotelesquirol.net. This comfortable spot has basic, well-maintained rooms with wood furnishings, and also a small café-bar and a living room with a fireplace where you can snuggle up on cold winter nights. €90

Bellver de Cerdanya

The Pyrenean atmosphere is very evident in the historic village of **BELLVER DE CERDANYA**, where rustic, slate-roofed chalets line the cobbled streets. About 25km west of Puigcerdà, Bellver overlooks the rushing Ríu Segre – and trout fishing was once a major local industry. The elegant **Plaça Major** is graced with impressive porticoes, while nearby rises the Gothic church of **Sant Jaume**. South of town is the twelfth-century Romanesque church of **Santa Maria de Talió**, presided over by a wooden Virgin.

ARRIVAL AND INFORMATION BELLVER DE CERDANYA

By bus Bellver is one of the first stops on the bus route between Puigcerdà (25min) and La Seu d'Urgell (35min).

Turisme Pl. de Sant Roc 9 (mid-June to mid-Sept Mon–Sat 11am–1pm & 6–8pm, Sun 11am–1pm; ☎ 973 510 229).

ACCOMMODATION

Cal Mateuet c/Església, Travesseres ☎ 973 515 170, ⓦ calmateuet.com. This *casa rural*, in a village 9km west of Bellver de Cerdanya, offers three stone-walled cottage-apartments – for four, six and eight people – with wooden furnishings, fully equipped kitchen and lovely views of the Serra del Cadí. Four-person cottage €150

Fonda Biayna c/de Sant Roc 11 ☎973 510 475, ⓦfondabiayna.com. It takes less than half a day – if that – to explore town, but this delightful, wood-floored *fonda* may entice you to stay. The cosy rooms are done up in period furniture, and you can fill up on hearty Catalan cuisine in the simple restaurant (open for guests only). **€60**

La Seu d'Urgell

Known to locals simply as Seu, the pleasant town of **La Seu d'Urgell**, capital of the *comarca* of Alt Urgell, sits amid looming peaks, with Andorra just 10km to the north and the valleys of the rocky Serra del Cadí nearby. As the seat (*seu*) of the regional archbishopric since the sixth century and home to an outdoor market held continuously since 1029 (on Tues and Sat), Seu has a formidable history, which is revealed in its well-preserved medieval quarter, twisting alleys and imposing cathedral.

The pleasantly mysterious medieval quarter is a small warren of narrow, arcaded streets. **Carrer dels Canonges**, the oldest street, cuts through its heart, lined with centuries-old buildings like **Cal Roger**, believed to have been a pilgrim's hostel, and which reveals wooden ceiling beams and some fourteenth-century Gothic carvings (enquire at the *turisme* about visiting).

Catedral de Santa Maria

Plaça dels Oms • June–Aug Mon–Sat 10am–1pm & 4–7pm, Sun 10am–1pm; Oct–May Mon–Sat 11am–1pm & 4–6pm, Sun 11am–1pm • €3, includes cloister and Museu Diocesà

Seu's twelfth-century **Catedral de Santa Maria**, just off Plaça dels Oms, is a wonderfully preserved example of Romanesque architecture, with a thirteenth-century cloister which has columns topped with sculpted figures from medieval mythology, and the adjoining eleventh-century chapel of San Miquel. The **Museu Diocesà** features superbly preserved reliquaries and fragments of the sarcophagus of Bishop Abril Pérez.

Espai Ermengol–Museu de la Ciutat

C/Major 8 • Summer Mon–Fri 9am–7pm, Sat 10am–2pm & 4–7pm, Sun 10am–2pm; rest of year Mon–Sat 10am–2pm & 4–6pm, Sun 10am–2pm • Free, but may start charging a small entrance fee

The helpful, well-stocked *turisme*, in sparkling new digs next to the cathedral, shares the building with a small **city museum** that features four floors of exhibits on La Seu's history. Exhibits include archeological remains, videos and interactive maps and an in-depth look at local products such as the region's well-known Cadí cheese. On the top floor, you can enjoy lovely views over the rooftops of town.

ARRIVAL AND INFORMATION

LA SEU D'ARGELL

By bus The bus station is on c/Joan Garriga Massó, just north of the old town. Alsina Graells runs buses to Barcelona (3–5 daily; 3hr 30min), Puigcerdà (3 daily; 1hr) and Lleida (1 daily, 2hr 30min).

Turisme c/Major 8 (summer Mon–Fri 9am–7pm, Sat 10am–2pm & 4–7pm, Sun 10am–2pm; rest of year Mon–Sat 10am–2pm & 4–6pm, Sun 10am–2pm; ☎973 351 511, ⓦturismeseu.com).

ACCOMMODATION

Seu has a number of mid-range hotels, but limited choices in the budget category. If you have your own wheels, try one of the many *casas rurales* in the area, as most are reasonably priced and have the bonus of an inviting homespun ambience. The *turisme* also has a list of recommended country hotels in the area.

Casa Rural Vall del Cadí Camí del Salit, about 2km south of town ☎973 350 390, ⓦvalldelcadi.com. Friendly *casa rural* with wood-beamed ceilings, wrought-iron bed frames and bucolic countryside views. To reach it cross the Ríu Segre, then head east toward Ortedò/Tuixent. **€70**

El Castell de Ciutat 1.5km west of La Seu, at the foot of the Castellciutat citadel ☎973 350 000, ⓦhotel-castell-ciutat.com. This luxurious Relais & Châteaux hotel and spa is set in an ancient castle, and features elegant rooms, sumptuous spa treatments and excellent Mediterranean cuisine, which you can enjoy on the breezy terrace overlooking the Urgellet valley. Usually closed first two weeks in Nov. **€225**

WHITEWATER ADRENALINE RUSH

The **Noguera Pallaresa**'s mighty flow is legendary, and draws thrill-seekers from around Spain and further afield. The original rafts were primitive – logs lashed together – but could withstand the frothy waters, and were ridden by *raiers* (rafters) to the sawmills of La Pobla de Segur. These days, the rafts are of the inflatable variety, and exciting whitewater trips are offered by operators throughout the region.

The most popular section of the river is between **Llavorsí** and **Rialp**, but tour companies offer a range of trips, each more rugged and scenic than the last. The rafting **season** is from April to early September; some outfitters also offer rafting programmes in March and October. In season, trips are run daily, usually in the late morning and lasting 1–2 hours on the water. Two-hour trips start at €35, and go up to €70–80 for longer rides, including lunch. The tourist office has a list of recommended **rafting operators**, including those listed below. Most offer other activities as well:

SORT

Rubber River Diputación 14 ☎ 973 620 220, ⓦ rubber-river.com. Sort is filled with rafting and adventure shops, including this reputable outfitter, which offers everything from rafting, kayaking (€70 for a 3hr class) and canoeing to bungee-jumping (€25 per jump) and horseriding. Offices open daily 9am–1pm & 5–9pm; closed mid-Oct to April.

LLAVORSÍ

Rafting Llavorsí Camí de Riberies ☎ 973 622 158, ⓦ raftingllavorsi.com. This established operator offers rafting, kayaking (€80 for 2 days of instruction; 2hr per

day) and multiple other aquatic adventures; in the winter, they can arrange snowshoe treks. Daily 9am–8pm.

Roc Roi Pl. Nostra Senyora de Biuse ☎ 973 622 035, ⓦ rocroi.com. This friendly operator runs a multitude of river sports plus trekking and horseriding. Mid-Oct to Easter daily 9am–9pm.

Yeti Emotions Pl. Nostra Senyora de Biuse ☎ 973 622 201, ⓦ yetiemotions.com. This longtime outfitter, which shares the same office and is under the same management as Roc Roi, offers a wide range of river and land sports, both summer and winter. Snowshoe treks from €80. Mid-Oct to Easter daily 9am–9pm.

11

Hotel Avenida Avgda. Pau Claris 24 ☎ 973 350 104, ⓦ avenhotel.com. Decent hotel near the town centre with basic and rather musty rooms. The restaurant, *Miscela* (closed dinner Sun & Mon), serves regional fare, like peppers stuffed with cod. The *menú del día* is €9, while a more elaborate *menú* is €16. **€75**

Parador Seu d'Urgell c/Sant Domènec 6 ☎ 973 352 000, ⓦ parador.es. This welcoming parador has a blend of old and new – the spacious ground floor incorporates a Romanesque cloister strewn with sofas, while rooms are modern with pale woods. **€138**

EATING AND DRINKING

El Menjador c/Major 4 ☎ 34/606 922 133, ⓦ elmenjador .com. This inviting, quirky restaurant, set in a former inn and decorated with flowers and colourful local art, features market-fresh cuisine, including trout from the Ríu Segre, chicken from local farms and cheeses from Cadí's co-operative. *Menú* €19. Daily except Sun 1.30–3.30pm & dinner (starts at 9pm; reserve ahead); call ahead to check times.

Restaurant Creperia Ignasi c/Capdevila 17 ☎ 973

352 719. Locals fill up on crêpes, with savoury fillings like Gruyère and ham, at this cheap and friendly spot, which also serves more robust fare such as duck and seafood. Mon–Thurs 1–4pm & 8–10.30pm, Fri & Sat 8–10.30pm.

Les Tres Portes Av Joan Garriga i Massó 7 ☎ 973 355 658. Mid-priced grilled meats, such as pork tenderloin with mushrooms, and well-prepared seafood served in a breezy garden. Daily 1–4pm & 8–11pm.

The Noguera Pallaresa valley

Catalunya's most famous whitewater-rafting river, the **Noguera Pallaresa**, churns through the lush valley of the same name. The river has long been an important source of hydroelectric power, and large power plants sit at various points along its banks. The *raiers* (logger-raftsmen) of **La Pobla de Segur** used to ride rafts of logs from the Pallars Forest all the way south to the lowlands.

The town of **Sort**, north of La Pobla de Segur, has become the region's whitewater-rafting hub, with a host of aquatic-adventure shops. If you're using public transport,

TREN DELS LLACS

"Nostalgia y paisaje" ("nostalgia and landscape") is what the historic **Tren dels Llacs** (Lake Train) promises, as it makes the 90km journey between Lleida and La Pobla de Segur. The train, comprised of refurbished old-fashioned steam and diesel locomotives, chugs over 31 bridges and through 41 tunnels, along cliffs, mountain passes and, of course, lakes. The train (1hr 50min one way, €24 round trip) operates from April to October, generally only on the weekends or on holidays. You can buy tickets only at the tourist offices in Lleida or La Pobla de Segur, or La Tienda de FGC in Barcelona on Carrer Pelai. For details, check the website: ⍟trendelsllacs.cat.

you'll likely arrive or depart from La Pobla de Segur, which has most of the valley's connections to and from Barcelona and Lleida.

La Pobla de Segur

The amiable town of **La Pobla de Segur** is one of the largest in the Vall de la Noguera, and a good base for river rafting or relaxing amid valley scenery for a few days. You'll find a decent selection of simple accommodation, plus regular train and bus services.

ARRIVAL AND INFORMATION   LA POBLA DE SEGUR

By train Regular trains connect La Pobla de Segur with Lleida (1hr 50min) and Barcelona (4hr; via Lleida).
By bus Regular buses run between La Pobla de Segur and Lleida and Barcelona. Buses also head west to El Pont de Suert, Boí and Capdella, where you can access the Parc Nacional d'Aigüestortes i Estany de Sant Maurici; and

north to Sort and Llavorsí, from where you can also access the park.
Turisme Avgda. Verdaguer 35, at the north end of town, by the *ajuntament* (Mon–Sat 9am–2pm; ☎973 680 257, ⍟pobladesegur.cat).

ACCOMMODATION AND EATING

Fonda Can Frasersia c/Major 4 ☎973 680 245, ⍟canfasersia.com. This former boarding house in the middle of the old town is one of several simple *fondas*, and has comfortable rooms. €53
Lo Racó del Pont ☎973 681 195. For a traditional,

mid-priced meal, from grilled meats to snails, dine out at this refurbished country house on the outskirts of town, near Pont de Claverol and the river. Daily 11.30–4pm (except Mon) & 7.30–1pm; in winter, open lunch only Mon–Fri.

Gerri de la Sal

Thirteen kilometres north from La Pobla de Segur toward Sort, you'll come to the petite village of **GERRI DE LA SAL**, named after the nearby salt mines. Next to the village, an old stone bridge leads to the beautiful twelfth-century **Monasterio de Sant Maria**. Though it's closed to the public, the area around it is lovely for a wander. Just beyond Gerri de la Sal is a tunnel, alongside which the old road hugs the rocky side of the mountain and is open to hikers and bikers.

Sort

The capital of the *comarca* of Upper Pallars, **SORT** is a pleasant mix of old and new, with an ancient core and modern facilities catering to the outdoor adventurers (see box, p.759) who descend in the spring and summer. Every year in early July, the town hosts the **Raiers (Rafters) Festival**, celebrating the log-rafters of the past.

ARRIVAL AND INFORMATION   SORT

By bus One Alsina Graells bus departs Barcelona daily for Sort, Rialp, Llavorsí and Esterri d'Àneu. Buses stop at a shelter north of town.
Turisme Camí de la Cabanera (July & Aug Mon–Fri 9am–8pm, Sat 10am–2pm & 3–8pm, Sun 10am–1pm;

Sept–June Mon–Thurs 9am–3pm, Fri 9am–3pm & 4–6.30pm, Sat 10am–2.30pm; ☎973 621 002, ⍟pallarssobira.cat). Has information on the region, and is helpful in directing you to recommended river-rafting operators.

ACCOMMODATION

Hotel Florido Pl. Joan Carles Dolcet ☎973 620 727, ⓦhotelfloridol.com. Run by the friendly folks at the adventure operator Rubber River (see p.759), this spacious hotel is geared towards outdoor enthusiasts, with a pool, volleyball courts, equipment rental and basic but well-maintained rooms. Closed mid-Oct to April. **€45**

Rialp and Port-Ainé

Tiny **RIALP**, which lies just 3km north of Sort, is an atmospheric jumble of old houses and new chalets. **Port-Ainé** (ⓦgranpallars.com), 15km northeast of Rialp, features good beginner and intermediate skiing on its thirty-plus runs, and also a dedicated children's slope. Snow conditions are generally top-notch, even in the spring.

ACCOMMODATION · RIALP AND PORT-AINÉ

Hotel Marvel Condes del Pallars Av. Flora Cadena 2, Rialp ☎973 620 350, ⓦmarvelhotels.com. This long-established resort-style hotel, popular with families, may be a bit faded around the edges, but has plenty of amenities, including a restaurant (guests only), a small gym and a kids' activity centre. Full board, with three meals, is a good deal at €140. Rate includes breakfast. **€100**

Hotel Port Ainé 2000 Port-Ainé, at the bottom of the ski lifts ☎973 627 627. At 2000m, this is one of the higher hotels in the Pyrenees, and offers awesome views of the surrounding peaks and countryside. **€95**

Llavorsí

Regular buses run from Barcelona to Llavorsí (5hr 30min) via Sort and Rialp

A rugged mountain landscape surrounds the riverside **LLAVORSÍ**, 10km north of Rialp. With an attractive mix of stone houses, modern accommodation and established outdoor operators, the town makes for a good base. Sports operators offer a wide range of activities, including rafting, mountain biking, canyoning and rock climbing.

ACCOMMODATION AND EATING · LLAVORSÍ

Aigües Braves 1km north of Llavorsí ☎973 622 153, ⓦcampingaiguesbraves.com. This campsite has a variety of facilities, including pool, bar and arranged activities. Closed Oct–April. Adult plus tent pitch **€10**

Hostal Noguera ☎973 622 012, ⓦhostalnoguera .info. Large rooms with wood floors and beamed ceilings, some with balconies overlooking the river. Their restaurant (closed Jan & Feb) serves regional cuisine, and also has nice views. **€58**

Hotel Riberies ☎973 622 051, ⓦriberies.com. This hotel features elegant rooms, a small spa with jacuzzi and a good restaurant serving regional cuisine, from river trout to duck with pears. Breakfast included. **€75**

Riberies Camí de Riberies, just east of town ☎973 622 151, ⓦcampingriberies.cat. This well-maintained campsite has a pool and bar, and they can set up outdoor activities. Closed mid-Sept to mid-June. Adult plus tent pitch **€10.60**

Vall d'Àneu and Esterri d'Àneu

The **Vall d'Àneu** stretches north of Llavorsí, sitting at the head of the Noguera Pallaresa river. The rugged valley is well placed for access to the region's great outdoors, from hiking in the Parc Nacional d'Aigüestortes i Estany de Sant Maurici to skiing at the Espot resort to the west and Baqueira-Beret to the north. The Vall d'Àneu is made up of a smattering of villages and towns, most comprising a mix of modern chalets catering to the ski crowd and traditional homes and restaurants.

Esterri d'Àneu

Once a rustic mountain community, **Esterri d'Àneu** is now angled as an alpine resort, with both contemporary apartment buildings and hotels. It has a well-restored **old town**, over which rises the elegant **Sant Vicenç** church. A lovely Romanesque bridge, dating to the early thirteenth century, arches over the river, along whose banks you can walk and take in the surrounding mountain scenery.

ARRIVAL AND INFORMATION

ESTERRI D'ÀNEU

By bus Regular buses travel between Esterri d'Àneu and Barcelona (5hr 30min) and Lleida (3hr).
Turisme c/Major 62 (summer Mon 10am–1.45pm, Tues–Sun 10am–1.45pm & 4–8.20pm; rest of year usually Sat & Sun only; ☎973 626 345, ⓦvallsdaneu.org). Has information on the valley and outdoor activities.

ACCOMMODATION AND EATING

Hostal Vall d'Àneu c/Major 46 ☎973 626 097, ⓦhostalvalldaneu.com. This central refurbished inn has simple, well-tended rooms and a restaurant serving regional fare. €42
Pensió La Creu c/Major 3 ☎973 626 437, ⓦwww .pensiolacreu.com. In the centre of town, this *pensió* has basic but clean rooms. Breakfast included. €52
Els Puis Av. del Dr Morell 13 ☎973 626 160. Fill up on robust, mid-priced Catalan cuisine, from steak and lamb to rice dishes, at this friendly restaurant. Daily 1.30–3.30pm & 9–10.30pm; closed Mon in winter.

Parc Nacional d'Aigüestortes i Estany de Sant Maurici

ⓦgencat.cat/parcs/aiguestortes

One of nine in Spain, Catalunya's largest national park, the **Parc Nacional d'Aigüestortes i Estany de Sant Maurici**, encompasses soaring peaks topping 3000m and lush meadows irrigated by more than four hundred lakes, streams, waterfalls and impressive glacial valleys. Established in 1955, the park is comprised of valleys blanketed in pine and fir forests, while wild animals like the isard, a small antelope also known as the chamois, roam the terrain. You might even spot a golden eagle or black woodpecker, both common here.

Hiking and trekking opportunities abound, from easy walks around sparkling lakes to serious treks up the mountain. The **Sant Nicolas valley** in the west features numerous glacial lakes, as well as the meanders of **Aigüestortes** (Twisted Waters). In the east lies the massive **Estany de Sant Maurici** (Sant Maurici Lake), at the head of the Escrita valley. In the winter, you can also **cross-country ski** through the park, though there are no marked trails.

The park's western sector is best reached from the **Vall de Boí** – to explore Aigüestortes, the approach is generally from Boí via **El Pont de Suert**; the eastern portion, including Lake Sant Maurici, is accessed via **Espot**, which lies just beyond the eastern border of the park. The easiest starting point for the higher mountains is **Capdella**, south of the park. If you'll be hiking for several days at a time between June and September, you can stay at any of the **refuges** throughout the park (see p.764). Either visitor centre can give you a list.

PRACTICALITIES

Access Private cars are not allowed in the park, but taxis regularly travel to the park's entrance from Espot (see p.764) and Boí (see box, p.766). If you drive, the closest you can get are the car parks 4km west of Espot or the La Molina or La Farga car parks, near Boí in the west. It's important to keep track of the weather, as it can greatly affect accessibility. In the cold season, it can be difficult to access certain roads.

Information You can pick up trail guides and park maps at the visitor centres in Boí (see p.766) and Espot (see p.764).
Maps Editorial Alpina (ⓦeditorialalpina.com) has excellent, detailed topographical maps of the park.
Entrance Entry to the park is free.
Safety It's always a good idea to alert the refuge staff before you set out on treks, any time of year.

ACCOMMODATION

Refuges Accommodation in and around the park encompasses sixteen refuges, with six within the park and ten in the peripheral zone. The refuges usually open in the summer (when most are staffed), Easter and sometimes Christmas, as well as on selected weekends and school holidays during the rest of the year. Refuges are usually equipped with bunk beds and have a basic meal service.

Prices generally range between €13 and €20 per person. Most refuges are fully booked during July and August, so you'll need to reserve ahead, which you can do via ⓦlacentralderefugis.com or by calling ☎973 641 681.
Camping Camping in the park is officially forbidden, though you can camp in the peripheral zone.

HIKES AND RIDES FROM CAPDELLA

There are a number of popular **treks** from Capdella, including the half-day hike to the inviting *Refugi Colomina*, set amid mountain lakes (see box, p.764). You'll find various treks around the *Refugi Colomina*, including to Estany Llong, by way of Estany Tort. You can also access the park on the **teleférico** (cable car; July–Sept; departs daily 8am, 9am & 3pm, returns 1 & 6pm; €6 round trip). The cable car travels from the Saliente reservoir (about 7km north of Capdella) to the Estany Gento, which is near an entrance of the park – on its fifteen-minute trip, the cable car climbs 450m. It was originally constructed in 1981 to transport materials and workers while the Saliente power station was being built, and it's said to be one of the cable cars with the greatest transport capacities in Europe; it was opened to the public in 1991.

Vall de Fosca

The verdant **Vall de Fosca**, which extends just south of the park, received its name Fosca ("dark") because it's surrounded by steep slopes that obscure the sun. Tiny **Capdella** is perched at its northernmost point, and at 1420m, is the highest of the fifteen or so tiny villages and settlements that are sprinkled south through the valley, including **Espui** and **La Torre de Capdella**, which has the valley's tourist office. Capdella makes for a good jumping-off point into the park, and is the village closest to the **teleférico** (cable car; see box above).

11

ARRIVAL AND INFORMATION   VALL DE FOSCA

By bus Buses travel from La Pobla de Segur to Capdella (30min).

Turisme The Vall de Fosca *turisme* is in the *ajuntament* of

Torre de Capdella on the Pl. Major (daily Mon–Fri 9am–3pm, Mon & Thurs also 4.30–8.30pm; ☎973 663 001, ⓦvallfosca.net), 4km south of Espui.

ACCOMMODATION

Casa Sastre Near the village of Espui, about 4km south of Capdella; signposted from road ☎973 663 082. Renovated stone house with rustic rooms, some with slanting wooden ceilings. Guests are also allowed access to the kitchen. **€40**

Hotel Montseny Near the village of Espui, about 4km

south of Capdella; signposted from road ☎973 663 060, ⓦmontseny.com. This amiable, alpine-style hotel has cosy rooms, a swimming pool, and a bar/restaurant (open for lunch and dinner for guests; lunch only for non-guests). Breakfast included. Hotel and restaurant closed from late Dec to Easter. **€90**

Espot, Espot Esquí and around

Espot is a cosy mountain town hemmed in by a lovely green valley, which has increasingly been built up as a tourist centre. In the winter, skiers pass through on their way to **Espot Esquí** (ⓦgranpallars.com), just south of town, with nearly thirty alpine trails.

CHARIOTS OF FIRE

If you're up for a challenge, try trekking the **Carros de Foc** (Chariots of Fire; ⓦcarrosdefoc .com) route. The itinerary is simple: to hike a circular loop that passes nine of the park's refuges (both in the park and on the periphery), including *Colomers, Estany Llong* and *Josep Maria Blanc* (see box, p.764). The hard part? To do it within one day.

The Carros de Foc challenge began in the summer of 1987, when a group of park guards came up with the route, and the goal to do it in a day. A few succeeded, and the Carros de Foc was born. These days, it's less about tackling the trek in one day – few can do so – as it is about celebrating the outdoors.

The Carros de Foc website has a good map outlining the entire route: it lists the walking distance between each refuge which, for the average hiker, ranges between two and four hours. Each of the *refugios* stamps trekkers' Carros de Foc documents with the date and time of their arrival. As for the most impressive times, check the website for the annual champions – in 2010, the fastest time clocked in was 9 hours 32 minutes.

POPULAR HIKES AND REFUGES

One of the most popular (though challenging in parts) hikes is to traverse the park from east to west, starting at the **Estany de Sant Maurici**. The full trek, all the way to **Boí**, takes about 9–10 hours, but you can shorten the trek by hopping on taxis for the last part from the park entrance to Boí. Roughly halfway along this trek sits the **Refugi de Estany Llong**.

The northern section of the park offers a wealth of treks for the adventurous and well-equipped – the Espot park information office has detailed maps of trails – as well as refuges, including the top-notch **Refugi de Colomèrs**, the **Refugi de Restanca** and the **Joan Ventosa i Calvell**, near Estany Negre.

Another good hike from the east is to **Refugi Josep Maria Blanc**, which lies southwest of Espot and is surrounded by lush valleys. The hike from Espot to the refuge takes 3–4 hours. From here, the hike continues to the **Colomina** refuge, which you can reach in another 3–4 hours.

REFUGES

Refugi de Colomèrs 973 253 008, refugicolomers.com. Daily Easter & mid-June to late Sept, weekends Feb & March. €15

Refugi Colomina 973 252 000. Early Feb, mid-March to mid-April & mid-June to mid-Sept; call ahead to confirm. From €15

Refugi de Estany Llong 973 299 545. Late Feb, Easter & June to mid-Oct. From €15

Refugi Josep Maria Blanc 973 250 108, jmblanc.com. Late May to mid-Oct. €17

Refugi de Restanca 608 035 559, restanca.com. Weekends most of the year, plus daily Easter week & mid-June to late Sept. €17

Refugi Joan Ventosa i Calvell 873 297 090, refugiventosa.com. Mid-June to late Sept & some winter weekends. €17

You can access the park from Espot, which lies about 7km from the **Estany de Sant Maurici**. Upon arrival at the *estany* (lake), you'll want to get your camera out: it's a beautiful scene, the lake fringed by wilderness and dominated by the spires of **Els Encants** ("The Enchanted Ones"; 2700m).

ARRIVAL, GETTING AROUND AND INFORMATION ESPOT, ESPOT ESQUÍ AND AROUND

By bus and taxi The daily buses from Barcelona, Lleida and La Pobla de Segur to Esterri d'Àneu stop at the Espot turn-off. From there, it's a steep 8km uphill walk to Espot, and then another similar distance to get to the park.

By taxi The quickest and easiest way to the park is by taxi, which travel from Espot to Estany de Sant Maurici. Taxis generally depart from the park information offices (July–Sept 8am–6pm or 7pm, rest of year 9am–6pm; from around €6 one way).

Casa del Parc information office c/de Sant Maurici 5, at the edge of Espot (June–Sept daily 9am–1pm & 3.30–6.45pm; Oct–May Mon–Sat 9am–2pm & 3.30–5.45pm; Sun 9am–2pm; 973 624 036). Has maps of the park and up-to-date weather reports.

ACCOMMODATION AND EATING

Camping La Mola Carretera Estany de Sant Maurici, 3km east of Espot 973 624 024, campinglamola.com. This quality campsite features a range of amenities, including a pool, a bar and a small supermarket. They also have apartments with kitchens (with bedsheets and towels available to rent). Open Easter & July–Sept. Pitch plus car €12; apartment (for four people) €100

Casa Felip c/Felip 973 624 093, casafelip.com. One of the better deals in Espot, with comfortable rooms and a small front garden. €50

Juquim Pl. Sant Martí 1 973 624 009. In the centre of Espot, try this friendly restaurant which serves filling mountain fare, including grilled meats and sausages (€9–14). Generally daily 1.30–3.30pm & 8.30–10.30pm; sometimes closes for part of winter.

El Pont de Suert

Regular buses service the village, including Alsina Graells from Barcelona (5hr) via Lleida (2hr 30min)

EL PONT DE SUERT, 41km northwest of La Pobla de Segur, features a pleasant old town, a handsome main *plaça*, an arcaded c/Mayor and the elegant fifteenth-century **Palau Abadial**, a former residence of abbots. The town also receives fairly regular buses, so you'll pass through if you're arriving at the park from the west.

ACCOMMODATION	EL PONT DE SUERT

Hotel Cotori Pl. Mercadal 8 ☎973 690 096, ⓦhotelcotori.com. This hotel, in the heart of the old town, has elegant, wood-beamed rooms with views of the Pl. Mercadal or the river valley. They also have an inviting café, and can arrange trekking and mountain-biking excursions. **€60**

Vall de Boí

Extending just west of the national park is the lush **Vall de Boí**, anchored by the mountain village of **Boí**. The highlights of the valley are its lovely **Romanesque churches**, the most remarkable of their kind in Catalunya. In 2000, the churches were designated a World Heritage Site by UNESCO, who described them as "an especially pure and consistent example of Romanesque art in a virtually untouched rural setting". And it is this setting that leaves the lasting impression – the beautiful simplicity of the early Romanesque architecture is magnified by the utter alpine stillness surrounding them. The churches, all built between the eleventh and fourteenth centuries, were constructed of local materials, like stone, slate and wood – and their most striking features are their elegant belfries which, in the case of **Taüll**, rises an impressive six storeys. Note that many of the church frescoes are reproductions – though excellent ones, to be sure – because the originals have been moved to MNAC in Barcelona. In addition to the valley's two finest churches in Taüll, other Romanesque beauties worth a visit are Sant Feliu in **Barruera**, Nativitat in **Durro** and Santa Eulàlia in **Erill la Vall**.

11

Boí

The pleasant town of **Boí** serves as a good embarking point for exploring the surrounding region, both for the Romanesque churches – you can walk a variety of signposted trails from Boí to neighboring churches – and also the national park, an entrance to which lies 3.5km from town. Boí also has a helpful park information office, and its own Romanesque church, the twelfth-century **Sant Joan**, with parts of the original belfry still intact, and three naves. As with other churches in the area, the frescoes are reproductions but nonetheless eye-catching, and include images of mythical animals.

Estany de Cavallers

Northwest of the *Caldes de Boí*, 5km north of Boí, is the **Estany de Cavallers** (Cavallers Lake), where you can pick up trails towards the lake-filled landscape in the northwest section of the park, which are presided over by the Besiberri and Montrarto peaks. A good refuge in the northwest of the park is *Joan Ventosa i Calvell* (see p.764).

Taüll

Taüll, 3km east of Boí, is home to two of the valley's best-known Romanesque churches. **Sant Climent**, consecrated in 1123, features an exquisite six-storey square belfry that rises gracefully above the town. The church's emblematic Romanesque murals were created by the so-called Master of Taüll, and transferred to Barcelona in 1922. Particularly striking is the image of Pantocrator (Christ in Majesty) in the apse. Taüll's second Romanesque icon is the church of **Santa Maria** (daily 10am–8pm; free), with a four-storey belfry.

ROMANESQUE CHURCHES IN THE VALL DE BOÍ

Pick up information on all the Romanesque churches at the **Centre d'Interpretació del Romànic**, on c/del Batalló in **Erill la Vall** (Mon–Sat 9am–2pm & 5–7pm, Sun 10am–2pm; ☎973 696 715, ⓦcentreromanic.com), in the centre of the valley. All churches, except for Santa Maria de Taüll, have the same hours: July to early Sept daily 10am–2pm & 4–8pm; rest of the year daily 10am–2pm & 4–7pm. Individual churches are €1.50, or €6 for a combined ticket to all churches; Santa Maria de Taüll is free.

INTO THE PARK FROM BOÍ

When you arrive at the park entrance from Boí (3.5km) it's then about another 3.5km to the crashing waterfalls of **Aigüestortes**. There are **park information** booths at the entrance and also above the waterfalls (both generally open July–Sept daily 9.30am–2pm & 4–7pm).

4WD taxis travel from the main square in Boí to the information booth at the entrance; taxis operate July to Sept 15 (8 or 9am–7pm) and rest of the year (9am–6pm) from €5.10 one way. The closest you can get to the park in your car is La Molina car park, near the boundary. When this fills up, try the La Farga car park, about 1.5km east. You can arrange for a 4WD taxi to take you from either car park further uphill.

Boí-Taüll

☎ 902 406 640, ⊕ boitaullresort.es

The valley is also home to a ski centre, **Boí-Taüll**, which lies 11km southeast of Taüll. The resort has nearly fifty pistes, lifts that reach up to 2750m and covers an area of about 45km. They offer an array of classes for beginners, and a good family ski programme. Call ahead, as the resort may be undergoing some changes and have limited hours.

ARRIVAL AND INFORMATION

By bus Buses from Barcelona to La Pobla de Segur run up to three times daily throughout the year. From July to mid-Sept, a connecting bus travels from La Pobla de Segur to El Pont de Suert and from there to Barruera and the Boí turn-off, about 1km before Boí.

VALL DE BOÍ

Park information office c/de les Graieres 2, Boí (July & Aug daily 9am–2pm & 3.30–6pm; rest of year closed Sun afternoon; ☎ 973 696 189). Has route information, maps and a list of the refuges in the park. There are also information booths both at the park entrance and above the Aigüestortes waterfalls (see box above).

ACCOMMODATION AND EATING

BOÍ

Hotel Pey Pl. Treio 3 ☎ 973 696 036, ⊕ hotelpey.com. This comfortable hotel has a range of rooms and prices, as well as fully equipped apartments (€80 for 2–3 people). They also have a friendly restaurant, where you can refuel over hearty meat dishes. **€70**

CALDES DE BOÍ

Caldes de Boí 5km north of Boí ☎ 973 696 201, ⊕ caldesdeboi.com. If you'd like some pampering, head to this lovely spot, considered one of the best spas in the Spanish Pyrenees, with a wide range of treatments, from natural springs to massages, and two accompanying hotels, the *Manantial* and the *Caldes*, both comfortable and well maintained. Both are closed Jan–March. *Manantial* **€102**, *Caldes* **€77**

TAÜLL

Hostal Rural Santa Maria Cap del Riu 3 ☎ 973 696 170, ⊕ taull.com. This beautifully renovated house features cosy, wood-beamed rooms, a dining room with a fireplace, and a breezy garden. **€110**

El Xalet de Taüll c/El Como 5 ☎ 973 696 095, ⊕ elxaletdetaull.com. This inviting chalet has wood-panelled rooms, mountain views and a summer garden. May be closed for part of winter so call ahead. **€115**

BOÍ-TAÜLL

Boí-Taüll Resort Pla de l'Ermita s/n ☎ 902 406 640, ⊕ boitaullresort.com. Decent hotel, with comfortable if slightly worn rooms, as well as a pool, and a restaurant for guests; they can also supply you with info on outdoor activities, from hiking in summer to skiing in winter. Hotel sometimes closes for part of the year; call ahead to confirm. **€68**

Val d'Aran

Nudging the French border in the far northwest of the Catalan Pyrenees, the lush **Val d'Aran** has long been geographically and culturally distinct from the rest of the Pyrenees. You can see the disparity of its architecture – French-style chalets dot the mountains – and you can hear it on the streets: the language here is Aranés, a mix of Gascon French and Catalan. The valley drains toward the Atlantic and splits into the Garonne River, whose waters eventually feed the vineyards of Bordeaux.

The Val d'Aran joined Catalunya-Aragón in the twelfth century and was fully given over to Catalunya in 1389. Completely ringed by high peaks, however – some reaching over 3000m – it has always been difficult to access. For most of the valley's history, the only routes in from the Spanish side crossed the tricky **Bonaigua** or Bossòst passes, both accessible only in summer. This changed only in 1948, when the first Vielha Tunnel opened on the N230 highway.

The valley's capital and commercial centre is **Vielha**, a beautiful alpine town with one foot in the past and the other in the very contemporary present, as a luxury resort. In winter, the Val d'Aran becomes upscale **skiing** country, drawing folks from all over Spain and France. While the area still reveals pockets of traditional life, it has undergone a massive shift in the last several decades, with upmarket apartments replacing family dwellings, and much of the retail catering to slick skiers. The Spanish royal family, along with the fit and fabulous, frequent **Baqueira-Beret**, one of Spain's premier ski resorts.

The Val d'Aran is divided into three sectors: **Vielha e Mijaran** (Middle Aran), **Baish Aran** (Lower Aran; northwest of Vielha near the French border) and **Nau Aran** (Upper Aran; east of Vielha). Both Upper and Lower Aran are ripe for exploration, each of their mountain villages more lovely than the last. You'll find plenty of hiking and trekking opportunities – trails meander all over the valley. You could easily spend a day or two hiking from one tiny village to the next, enjoying a country meal at one, and bedding down in a rustic farmhouse in the next. **Salardú** and **Arties** make for pleasant stopovers in Nau Aran.

Vielha

The valley centres on the bustling town of **VIELHA**, which goes through a metamorphosis in winter: when the snow descends, so too do the slickly outfitted skiers, who crowd the slopes, gear shops and restaurants. After the snow melts, Vielha reverts to its small-town self, when the hilly streets get quiet, and the bars are again the domain of the locals. The tiny old quarter features the parish church of **Sant Miquèu**, with a twelfth-century wooden *Crist de Mijaran,* a superb example of Romanesque art.

Museu dera Val d'Aran

C/Major 26 • Tues–Sat 10am–1pm & 5–8pm, Sun 11am–2pm • €2

The small **Museu dera Val d'Aran**, housed in a seventeenth-century building in the old town, features an overview of Aranese history, folklore and ethnology, from prehistoric times to today, including exhibits of old photographs, period furnishings and more.

ARRIVAL AND INFORMATION   VIELHA

By bus A couple of Alsina Graells buses travel daily between Barcelona and Vielha (5hr 30min), via Lleida and El Pont de Suert. From June to Sept, one daily service also runs from Barcelona to Vielha via La Pobla de Segur, Llavorsí and Salardú.

Turisme c/Sarriulera 6 (daily 9am–9pm; ☎973 640 110, ⓦ visitvaldaran.com). Has up-to-date lists of accommodation in the valley.

ACCOMMODATION

Hotel El Ciervo Pl. de San Orenç 3 ☎973 640 165, ⓦ hotelelciervo.net. This cheerful hotel has well-maintained rooms, each individually decorated. €70

Hotel Fonfreda Pg. de la Llibertat 18 ☎973 640 486. Simple, creaky-floored hotel that feels refreshingly quaint compared to the big, shiny resorts. Some of the rooms are a bit faded, but comfortable, and the price is right. €75

Marvel Vielha Just south of town on the Carretera Baqueira ☎902 027 447, ⓦ www.hotelmarvelvielha

.com. This 33-room alpine hotel has cosy rooms, a pool, a small spa and a ski locker room. It's well placed for easy access to the ski resort. €80

Parador de Vielha Carretera del Túnel ☎973 640 100, ⓦ parador.es. The draw at this modern parador is the lovely views of the mountain peaks. The granite building is very contemporary looking – no historic charm here – but the rooms are warmly done up in the trademark parador style, with wooden furniture. €168

EATING AND DRINKING

Basteret c/Major 6 ☎973 640 714. Central and casual, with simple local food, including river trout and tasty tapas. Daily 1.30–3.30pm & 8.30–10.30pm.

Casa Turnay 2km east, in the village of Escunhau ☎973 640 292. Rustic, stone-walled Aranese restaurant with hearty local food, from grilled rabbit to trout fished from local rivers to *butifarra negra* (Catalan sausage). Dishes €10–15. Daily except Sun 1.30–3.30pm & 8–11pm.

Era Mòla c/Marrec 14 ☎973 642 419. This perennially popular restaurant (also called *Restaurant Gustavo*) serves rich, French-influenced Catalan fare, including a superb duck breast with wild mushrooms. Dishes start at €24. Mon, Tues, Thurs & Fri 8–11pm, Sat & Sun 1.30–3.30pm & 8–11pm.

Saxo Blu c/Marrec 6 ⓦsaxoblu.com. For cocktails and occasional live music, try this lively bar which has decently priced drinks and draws a mix of locals and visitors. Daily 7pm–2.30am.

Baqueira-Beret

☎973 639 010, ⓦbaqueira.es

The massive **Baqueira-Beret** ski resort has more development than any other in the area and imbues the valley with a stylish sheen. It's one of Spain's choicest resorts, and has the crowd to match. Discriminating skiers, most famously Spain's king himself, flock to its 72 pistes, which cover up to 105km – making it one of Spain's largest resorts. The resort amenities – groomed pistes, numerous chairlifts, a top-notch ski staff – rival the Pyrenean scenery of frosted peaks piercing the bright blue sky. If you don't want to go for the pricey resort accommodation, do what many do: stay for considerably less at a nearby village, including Salardú or Vielha.

Salardú

The Val d'Aran contains over thirty hillside villages, most with their own Romanesque church. **SALARDÚ**, which lies just west of Baqueira-Beret, is one of the largest of the valley's settlements, with the thirteenth-century **church of Sant Andreu** (open for services; enquire at *turisme* about other times) standing tall in its centre. Take a look at the detailed portal and, inside, the carefully restored frescoes.

Salardú makes for a good overnight spot, with a decent tourist infrastructure – several options for lodging and food – but also a rugged alpine personality. Call ahead to your hotel in the non-snow season, as they sometimes close.

PyrenMuseu

Pl. Major • Mon–Sat 10.30am–1.30pm & 4.30–7.30pm; hours can be extended on request • €5 • ☎973 645 814, ⓦpyrenmuseu.com

One of the oldest places to stay in town, **Refugi Rosta** (see also p.770) now also doubles as a charming small **museum** – and has therefore created the slogan, "Ahora puedes alojarte en un museo" ("Now you can sleep in a museum"). The museum, which is spread out among the *refugi's* well-preserved rooms, hallways, bar and other spaces, is the first of its kind, exploring the unique history of tourism in the Val d'Aran, with exhibits featuring period furnishings and art, old photographs and maps, a timeline of the development of the famous ski resort Baqueira-Beret and more. Entry to the museum includes a glass of wine in the atmospheric bar.

ARRIVAL AND INFORMATION	SALARDÚ

By bus From June to Sept, one daily service runs from Barcelona to Vielha via La Pobla de Segur, Llavorsí and Salardú (about 5hr 30min).

Turisme c/des Estudis (daily 9am–1pm & 4–7pm, off-season hours may be limited; ☎973 645 197, ⓦvisitvaldaran.com).

ACCOMMODATION

Alberg Era Garona Carretera de Vielha ☎973 645 271, ⓦtojuaran.com. Basic but fairly spacious youth hostel in a stone-and-slate building. Rooms, which have up to four beds, each have their own bathroom. **€26**

Hotel Colomèrs Dera Mola 8 ☎973 644 556,

ⓦhotelcolomers.es. Modern alpine hotel with lots of rustic wood (floors, ceiling, furnishings) and a comfortable living room with fireplace where you can ease into the evening after a day of skiing. **€110**

Hotel Deth Pais Pl. Dera Pica ☎973 645 836,

ⓦ hoteldethpais.com. This comfortable, slate-roofed hotel in the village centre has clean rooms with balconies. They also run the *Prat Aloy* restaurant across the river. **€80**

Refugi Rosta Pl. Major 1 ☎ 973 645 308. Comfortable

EATING AND DRINKING

Borda Benjamin Pl. La Pica ☎ 973 645 113, ⓦ bordabenjamin.com. This established spot serves Aranese cuisine, from grilled meats to seasonal vegetables, for about €18 per person. Daily noon–4pm & 8–10pm; closed Nov and after Easter for a month.

Prat Aloy Dera Mola ☎ 973 644 179. Run by *Hotel deth Pais*, *Prat Aloy* serves good local cuisine like grilled steak, lamb and sausages; main dishes €17–25. Daily 1–4pm & 9–11pm; usually closed March, Oct & Nov.

★ **Refugi Rosta** Pl. Major 1 ☎ 973 645 308. *Refugi*

refuge in a three-hundred-year-old building on the main plaza, catering to trekkers and skiers on a budget. It also doubles as a lovely museum (see p.769). Breakfast included. Sometimes closed March, Oct & Nov. **€23**

Rosta serves mid-priced Pyrenean cuisine in a lovely, traditional dining room, and is also home to one of the more appealing bars in town, *Delicatesen*, which now forms part of the *refugi*'s museum. They also have several creative offers including the PyrenCena (€20; Mon–Sat 8.30pm, but call ahead to reserve), which includes a traditional Pyrenean meal in the *refugi*'s historic dining room. Restaurant open daily for dinner 8–10pm ; bar daily late morning to 11pm or later; closed March, Oct & Nov.

Arties

ARTIES, 3km west of Salardú, offers a charming mix of Pyrenean history and the chance to join the locals in dining (and drinking) out. Its old town is pleasant for a stroll, featuring the signature slate-roof houses of the valley, and you can take in the Romanesque-Gothic **Santa Maria** (open for services), which has a barrel-vaulted nave and a five-storey belfry.

ACCOMMODATION AND EATING   ARTIES

Casa Irene c/Major 3 ☎ 973 644 364, ⓦ hotelcasairene .com. This well-regarded restaurant (closed Mon & late Sept to early Dec) serves mountain cuisine, from grilled rabbit to thick Aranese stews; prices range from €17 to €27 for mains. They also have an adjoining hotel, with elegant, individually decorated wood-floored rooms, and a small

but well-run spa. **€156**

Eth Clòt Pl. Sant Orenç, no phone. Arties is known for a fairly lively bar scene, with local music and a convivial after-dark atmosphere, including this popular bar, with rustic stone walls, a wooden bar and an amiable crowd. Evenings only; hours vary.

The south

The great triangle of land south of Barcelona may be one of the lesser-visited wedges of Catalunya – but it shouldn't be. This wonderfully varied area encompasses a sun-speckled coast, a trinity of medieval monasteries and the historically rich provincial capitals of Tarragona and Lleida.

West of Barcelona lies **cava country**, where you can tour Catalunya's best-known cava producers, especially around **Sant Sadurní d'Anoia**. On the coast, just south of Barcelona, sits vibrant **Sitges**, a major gay summer destination that's also home to some fine *modernista* architecture. Beyond this is the **Costa Daurada** – the coastline that stretches from just north of Tarragona to the Delta de l'Ebre – which suffered less exploitation than the Costa Brava. It's easy enough to see why it was so neglected – the shoreline can be drab, with beaches that are narrow and characterless, backed by sparse villages – but there are exceptions, and if all you want to do is relax by a beach for a while, there are several down-to-earth and perfectly functional possibilities, including **Cambrils**.

The Costa Daurada really begins to pay dividends, however, if you can forget about the beaches temporarily and spend a couple of days in **Tarragona**. It's a city with a solid Roman past – reflected in an array of impressive ruins and monuments – and makes a handy springboard for trips inland into Lleida province. South of Tarragona, Catalunya peters out in the lagoons and marshes of the **Delta de l'Ebre**, a riverine wetland rich in bird life – perfect for slow boat trips, fishing and sampling the local seafood.

CAVA COUNTRY

Cava – Spain's answer to champagne – is grown largely in the Penedès region, which also produces quality white wines and sturdy reds. "Cava" simply means cellar, and was the word chosen when the French objected to the word champagne. The eminently drinkable, and very affordable, sparkling wine is usually defined by its sugar content: *seco* (literally "dry") has around half the sugar of a *semi-seco* ("very sweet"). In addition to selling cheap bottles of bubbly, the region's famous *bodegas* often offer informative tours and tastings, and are located in stunning properties, attractions in themselves. Most can be found in the Penedès region near the town of **Sant Sadurní d'Anoia**, about 30km west of Barcelona, and easily accessible via the highway that zips right past it. The countryside around **Vilafranca de Penedès**, 15km southwest of Sant Sadurní, is also dotted with wineries, including wine giant Torres. There are regular trains from Estació-Sants Barcelona to Sant Sadurní (40min) and Vilafranca de Penedès (50min).

AROUND SANT SADURNÍ D'ANOIA

Codorníu Avgda. Jaume Codorníu, just outside Sant Sadurní d'Anoia ☎ 938 913 342, ⓦ codorniu.com. Codorníu, one of Spain's best-known cava brands, is credited with bringing champagne production to Spain in 1872. On a tour, you'll explore the cellars, view the beautiful *modernista* premises designed by Josep Maria Puig i Cadafalch and enjoy a tasting at the end. Reservations are essential – you can call, email or book online. The winery is about 2km from the highway and well signposted. Tours €6. Mon–Fri 9am–5pm, Sat & Sun 9am–1pm.

Freixenet c/Joan Sala 2, visible from the highway ☎ 938 917 096, ⓦ freixenet.com. This celebrated producer offers interesting tours which include a visit to their oldest cellars, originally excavated in 1922, a ride on a tourist train around the winery and samples of bubbly. There's also a well-stocked shop. Tours must be booked in advance, either by phone or the website. Tours €6.10. Consult the website for information on hours.

Jean Leon Pago Jean Leon, El Pla del Penedès, 10km west of Sant Sadurní d'Anoia ☎ 938 995 512, ⓦ jeanleon.com. Owned by Torres, the boutique wine-maker Jean Leon features an American-modernist-inspired visitor centre set in particularly bucolic surroundings. Tours include a visit to the vineyards, the wine cellars, ageing barrels and a small museum, followed by a tasting. They also offer Segway tours for groups. Book in advance, via phone or web. Tours €10. Mon–Fri 9am–6pm, Sun 9am–1pm.

AROUND VILAFRANCA DEL PENEDÈS

Bodegas Torres Finca el Maset, Pacs del Penedès, 3km northwest of town ☎ 938 177 487, ⓦ torres.es. Torres, one of Spain's big-name wine producers, leads well-organized tours, which include trundling through the fragrant vineyards in a small tourist train, slick audiovisual presentations and a tasting at the end. Oenophiles can opt for a more in-depth experience with wine-tasting classes on Saturdays (4–6.30pm; €22). Tours €6.10. Mon–Sat 9.15am–4.45pm, Sun 9.15am–1pm.

11

Inland attractions are fewer, and many travelling this way are inclined to head on out of Catalunya altogether, not stopping until they reach Zaragoza. It's true that much of the region is flat, rural and dull, but nonetheless it would be a mistake to miss the outstanding monastery at **Poblet**, only an hour or so inland from Tarragona. A couple of other nearby towns and monasteries – notably medieval **Montblanc** and **Santes Creus** – add a bit more interest to the region, while by the time you've rattled across the huge plain that encircles the provincial capital of **Lleida** you'll have earned a night's rest. Pretty much off the tourist trail, Lleida is the start of the dramatic road and train routes into the western foothills of the Catalan Pyrenees, and is only two and a half hours from Zaragoza.

Vilafranca del Penedès

Pleasant **VILAFRANCA DEL PENEDÈS**, capital of the *comarca* of Alt Penedès, lies about 45km southwest of Barcelona, and offers the twin pleasures of history and wine. It was founded in the eleventh century in an attempt to attract settlers to land retaken from the expelled Moors and in time became a prosperous market centre. This character is still in evidence today, with a compact old town with narrow streets and arcaded squares adorned with restored medieval mansions. In the centre, around Plaça de Sant Joan, a Saturday market sells everything from farm-fresh produce to clothes, household goods and handicrafts. The **vineyards** of Vilafranca are all scattered in the countryside out of town – one of the closest (and most famous) is Torres (see box, p.771).

The **Festa Major** (ⓦfestamajor.info), at the end of August and the first couple of days in September, brings the place to a standstill. Dances and parades clog the streets, while the festival is most widely known for its display of *castellers* – teams of people competing to build human towers (see box, p.778).

Museu de Vilafranca-Museu del Vi

Pl. Jaume I • June–Aug Tues–Sat 10am–7pm, Sun 10am–2pm; Sept–May Tues–Sat 10am–2pm & 4–7pm, Sun 10am–2pm • €5 • ⓦ museosdelvino.es

Opposite the much-restored Gothic church of Santa Maria, the **Museu de Vilafranca-Museu del Vi** is housed in a twelfth-century palace and worth visiting largely for its impressive exhibits on the region's wine industry. Highlights include antique casks, a reproduction of a wine cellar, wine-themed art through the ages, and most notably one of the region's more extensive collections of ceramics used in wine-making in Catalunya.

ARRIVAL AND INFORMATION — VILAFRANCA DEL PENEDÈS

By train Regular trains travel from Barcelona to Vilafranca (50min).

Turisme c/Cort 14 (Mon 4–7pm, Tues–Fri 9am–1pm & 4–7pm, Sat 9.30am–1.30pm & 4–7pm, Sun 10am–1pm; ☎938 181 254, ⓦturismevilafranca.com). For a taste of history and wine, you can opt for one of their evening guided tours each Sat (July 8.30pm, Aug 8pm & Sept 7pm; €4.30) that head up to the town's belltower where you can enjoy the views – and a glass of Penedès wine.

ACCOMMODATION, EATING AND DRINKING

Casa Torner i Güell Rambla de Sant Francesc 26 ☎938 174 755, ⓦcasatorneriguell.com. For the full Penedès experience, bed down in this graceful *modernista* boutique hotel in the heart of the charming old town. The elegant, light-filled rooms feature gleaming woods and sleek furnishings. Take in breezes in the leafy garden, sip local wines in the handsome cocktail lounge and dine on local cuisine, from cod and wild sea bass to roast lamb, in the sophisticated restaurant: a choice of two *menús* at €25 and 35. **€140**

Inzolia c/de la Palma 21, just off c/de Sant Joan ☎938 181 938, ⓦinzolia.com. An agreeable place in town to wine-taste: a range of cavas and wines are sold by the glass, and there's a good wine shop attached. Tues–Sat 10am–2pm & 5–10pm, Sun 5–10pm.

Sitges

SITGES, 40km from Barcelona, is definitely the highlight of this stretch of coast. Established in the 1960s as a holiday town, whose liberal attitudes openly challenged the rigidity of Franco's Spain, it has now become the great weekend escape for young Barcelonans, who have created a resort very much in their own image. It's also a noted gay holiday destination, with the nightlife to match. Indeed, if you don't like vigorous action of all kinds, you'd be wise to avoid Sitges in the summer – staid it isn't. Finding a place to stay in peak season can be a challenge, unless you arrive early in the day or book well in advance. None of this deters the varied and generally well-heeled visitors, however – nor should it, since Sitges as a sort of Barcelona-on-Sea is definitely worth experiencing for at least one night.

CARNAVAL IN SITGES

Carnaval in Sitges (Feb/March) is outrageous, thanks largely to the gay populace. The official programme of parades and masked balls is complemented by an unwritten but widely recognized schedule of events. The climax is the Tuesday late-night parade, in which exquisitely dressed drag queens swan about the streets in high heels, twirling lacy parasols and coyly fanning themselves. Bar doors stand wide open, bands play, and processions and celebrations go on until four in the morning.

CAFÉS & BARS			RESTAURANTS			CLUBS			ACCOMMODATION	
B Side	2		Al Fresco	8		L'Atlántida	5		Hotel Alenti	3
Bourbons	1		Mare Nostrum	11		The Organic	2		Hotel Antemare	7
Café-Bar Roy	5		La Nansa	10		Pacha Sitges	1		Hotel Celimar	5
Montroig Café	4		El Trull	7		Privilege	3		Hotel Romàntic	2
Parrots Pub	6		El Velero	9		Sweet Pacha	4		Hotel Terramar	6
El Piano	3								Hotel El Xalet	1
									Pensió Bonaire	4

The town itself is appealing and attractive: a former fishing village whose well-maintained houses and narrow streets have attracted artists and opted-out intellectuals for a century or so. The beaches, though crowded, are far from oppressive, and there's a smattering of cultural interest.

If you're a fan of fantasy, a date worth noting in your diary is the annual **Sitges Film Festival** (Ⓦcinemasitges.com), one of the world's premiere fantasy and horror film festivals. The festival has also expanded to embrace other genres and attracts some big-name actors and directors. It takes place over ten days in late October at venues around the town (information and venues from the *turisme*). In the summer, the city government usually hosts **outdoor concerts** at the various museums and gardens, including opera, jazz and classical guitar. Enquire at the tourist office.

The beaches

It's the **beach** that brings most people to Sitges, and it's not hard to find, with two strands right in town, to the west of the church. From here, a succession of *platjas* of varying quality and crowdedness stretches west for a couple of kilometres down the coast. A long seafront promenade, the **Passeig Marítim**, flanks the beach, and all along there are beach bars, restaurants, showers and watersports facilities. Towards the end of the western stretch of beach, you'll reach nudist beaches, a couple of which are exclusively gay.

Museu Cau Ferrat

C/de Fonollar · ☎ 938 930 464

In town, climb up the knoll overlooking the beaches, which is topped by the Baroque parish church – known as La Punta – and a street of old whitewashed mansions, locally called the Corner of Calm. One contains the **Museu Cau Ferrat**, home and workshop to the artist and writer Santiago Rusiñol (1861–1931). Its two floors contain a massive jumble of his own paintings, as well as sculpture, painted tiles, ceramic, glasswork, drawings and various collected odds and ends, such as the decorative ironwork (over 800 pieces) Rusiñol brought back in bulk from throughout Catalunya. Two of his better buys were the minor El Grecos at the top of the stairs on either side of a crucifix. The museum also contains works by the artist's friends (including Picasso) who used to meet in the *Els Quatre Gats* bar in Barcelona. The museum has been going through major renovations, to be reopened at the end of 2012, so call ahead or check at the *turisme*.

11 Museu Maricel de Mar

C/de Fonollar · ☎ 938 940 364

The **Museu Maricel de Mar** has some minor artworks, medieval to modern, and maintains an impressive collection of Catalan ceramics and sculpture. The museum has been going through major renovations, to be reopened at the end of 2012; call ahead or check at the *turisme*.

Museu Romàntic

C/Sant Gaudenci 1 · Visits only via guided tour, every hour on the hour · €3.50 · ☎ 938 942 969

The **Museu Romàntic** aims to show the lifestyle of a rich Sitges family in the eighteenth and nineteenth centuries by displaying some of their furniture and possessions. It's full of nineteenth-century knick-knacks, including a set of working music boxes and a collection of antique dolls.

Fundació Stämpfli Museu d'Art Contemporani

Pl. Ajuntament · Fri & Sat 9.30am–2pm & 4–7pm (Oct–June 3.30–6.30pm), Sun 10am–3pm · €3.50 · ⓦ fundacio-stampfli.org

This impressive addition to the Sitges museum scene, opened in late 2010, was founded by the acclaimed art foundation **La Fundació Stämpfli**, helmed by Swiss artist Peter Stämpfli, who has worked in the Catalan art world for decades. The museum, which occupies two adjoining historic buildings, one of which was the old fish market, houses over seventy artworks (around 30 to 40 are on display at any one time) from around the globe, from bold, colourful paintings to wooden assemblage sculptures.

Casa Bacardi

Pl. Ajuntament 11 · Guided tours Fri–Sun 11am–7.15pm (generally one in the morning and two in the afternoon); reserve by phone or via website · €5 · ☎ 938 948 151, ⓦ casabacardi.es

The founder of Bacardi rum, Facundo Bacardí Massó, was born in Sitges and raised here until his mid-teens, when he emigrated to Cuba in 1830. The **Casa Bacardi**, housed in the historic Mercat Vell, explores the history of Bacardi rum – and its connection to Sitges – culminating in a rum tasting.

ARRIVAL AND INFORMATION   SITGES

By train Trains to Sitges leave Barcelona's Estació-Sants every 30min throughout the day (trip length 25–40min). The train station is a 10min walk from the town centre and seafront. For current timetables and ticket information, consult RENFE (☎ 902 240 202, ⓦ renfe.es).

By bus Buses stop in front of the train station, except those to and from Barcelona, which stop outside the main

turisme. MonBus (☎ 938 937 511, ⓦ monbus.cat) runs throughout the day (until about 10.30pm) from Sitges to Barcelona airport and the city centre.

Turisme c/Sínia Morera 1 (July–Sept Mon–Sat 9am–2pm & 4–8pm, Sun 10am–2pm; rest of year Mon–Fri 10am–2pm & 4–7pm, Sun 10am–2pm; ☎ 938 944 251, ⓦ sitgestur.com).

ACCOMMODATION

There are dozens of hotels of all types and prices in Sitges, but it's a good idea to reserve in high season as they fill up quickly. If you arrive without a reservation, a short walk through the central streets and along the front (particularly Passeig de la Ribera) reveals most of the possibilities. Come out of season (after Oct and before May) and the high prices tend to soften a little, though in midwinter it may be a challenge to find accommodation that's open, especially at the budget end of the scale.

Hotel Alenti c/1er de Maig ☎938 114 790, ⓦhotelalenti.com. Sleek boutique hotel, in an all-white, cube-shaped building, with plenty of pale woods and picture windows that let in the Sitges sunshine. Restaurant with a terrace directly onto the "Street of Sin". **€190**

Hotel Antemare c/Mare de Déu del Montserrat 50 ☎938 947 000, ⓦantemare.com. One street back from the sea, about 1.5km from the centre, this classy hotel has stylish rooms at reasonable rates. Also has a thalassotherapy (seawater) spa, with massages and body wraps. **€115**

Hotel Celimar Pg. de la Ribera 20 ☎938 110 170, ⓦhotelcelimar.com. Pleasant seafront hotel, worth trying for a balconied room with a view. Breakfast included. **€129**

Hotel Romàntic c/Sant Isidre 33 ☎938 948 375, ⓦwww.hotelromantic.com. Attractive converted nineteenth-century villa in the quiet streets away from the front, not far from the train station, with ornate, *modernista* touches and rooms with plenty of character; some have a terrace overlooking the palm-shaded gardens. It's a favourite with gay visitors. Breakfast included. Closed Nov–March. **€122**

Hotel Terramar Pg. Marítim 80 ☎938 940 050, ⓦhotelterramar.com. Well placed at the end of the long promenade, with lovely views from its large, balconied rooms, though it can be a long trudge back from the best bars. **€147**

Hotel El Xalet c/Illa de Cuba 35 ☎938 110 070, ⓦelxalet.com. This longtime hotel has a pretty *modernista* design, though is a bit faded. Rooms are decent, there's a charming little interior courtyard and it's near the train station. **€100**

Pensió Bonaire c/Bonaire 31 ☎938 945 326, ⓦbonairehostalsitges.com. This small *pensió* is basic, but it sits just back from the sea and the price is right. Closed Oct–March. **€60**

EATING, DRINKING AND NIGHTLIFE

Most of the **restaurants** along the promenade feature seaview terraces and serve paella and seafood, while the side streets are also dotted with inviting spots. You can get picnic supplies at the town's **market**, the Mercat Municipal, near the train station, on Avgda. Artur Carbonell. Late-opening **bars** centre on pedestrianized c/1er (Primer) de Maig (popularly known as *Calle del Pecado*, or Street of Sin) and its continuation, c/Marqués de Montroig, while c/de les Parellades and c/Bonaire complete the block. In summer, this is basically one long run of disco-bars, pumping music out into the late evening, interspersed with the odd restaurant or fancier cocktail bar, all with outdoor tables vying for your custom. If you're looking for more genteel nightspots, try those on the seafront. Sitges also has several music-pounding **clubs** just outside of town, where cocktail-fuelled crowds dance all night long, especially in the summer.

RESTAURANTS

Al Fresco c/Pau Barrabeitg 4 ☎938 940 600, ⓦalfrescorestaurante.es. This inviting restaurant serves Mediterranean cuisine with a twist, from lamb with black olives to chicken curry with green mango. Mains €15–22, €35 for two courses. Summer daily 8.30–11.30pm; closed Mon & Tues in winter.

Mare Nostrum Pg. de la Ribera 60 ☎938 943 393, ⓦrestaurantmarenostrum.com. Long-established fish restaurant on the seafront, with a menu that changes according to the catch and season. Around €35 a head, unless you stick to the *platos del día*. March to late Dec daily except Wed 1–4pm & 8–11pm; closed late Dec to Feb.

La Nansa c/Carreta 24 ☎938 941 927, ⓦrestaurantlanansa.com. A *nansa* (fishing net) hangs in this amiable, family-run restaurant, which has wood-panelled walls, brass lanterns and maritime paintings. The top-notch seafood- and fish-focused menu (mains €16–26) includes the regional favourite, *arroz a la Sitgetana* (rice with meat, prawns, clams, and a generous splash of Sitges Malvasia wine). Daily except Tues 1.30–4pm & 8.30–11pm; also closed Wed lunch & all Jan.

El Trull Ptge. Mossèn Félix Clarà 3, off c/Major ☎938 944 705. Fairly pricey French-style restaurant in the old town, with exceptional foie gras and sumptuous fish casserole. Mon, Tues, Thurs & Fri 7.30–11pm, Sat & Sun 1.30–4.30pm & 7.30–11pm; closed Wed & all Jan.

El Velero Ptge. de la Ribera 38 ☎938 942 051, ⓦrestauentevelero.com. One of the town's most celebrated restaurants, right on the promenade with a glass terrace at the front and an elegant interior. Large menu offers plenty of seafood and classic paellas; pricey but worth it. Daily except Mon 1.30–4pm & 8.30–10.30pm; closed Sun eve (except July to mid-Sept).

CAFÉS AND BARS

Café-Bar Roy c/de les Parellades 9 ☎938 110 269. An old-fashioned café with dressed-up waiters and marble tables. Watch the world go by from its prime streetside perch, over a glass of cava or a fancy snack. Daily noon till late.

11

SITGES' GAY SCENE

The frenetic and ever-changing **gay scene** in Sitges is chronicled on a gay map and guide available from *Parrots Pub*, as well as from several other bars and clubs. Most of the bars and clubs are centred around Plaça Indústria and in the triangle made up by c/Espalter, c/Sant Francesc and c/Parellades. Sitges' clubs are liveliest in the summer, when they're open Friday and Saturday nights and sometimes during the week; in winter, hours vary and may be limited. Most clubs open no earlier than midnight and stay hopping until the wee hours; check websites to confirm.

Parrots Pub (see below) is a good place to start any time of day, but especially for early evening cocktails. Other lively bars include **El Piano**, c/Sant Bonaventura 37; **B Side** at c/Sant Gaudenci 7; and **Bourbons**, c/Sant Buenaventura 13. Popular gay clubs include **Privilege**, c/Bonaire 24, with theme nights, including 70s and 90s disco; and **The Organic** at c/Bonaire 15 (opens at 2.30am). For more information, check out ⓦgogayguide.com.

Montroig Café c/Marqués de Montroig 11 ☎938 948 439, ⓦmontroigcafe.com. Large, two-level, buzzy café with a shady courtyard out back, where you can sip *cerveza* or *café con leche* while soaking up the sun and the social scene. Daily 9am–2am; closed mid-Dec to mid-Jan.

Parrots Pub Pl. de la Indústria ☎938 111 219, ⓦparrotspub.com. One of the town's best-known gay bars, at the top of c/1er de Maig, and a required stop for practically everyone at some point in the day or night; it's just one place you can pick up the free gay map of Sitges. Front bar: summer usually daily 10am until late; the rest of the pub 5pm until late.

CLUBS

L'Atlántida Platja de les Coves, Sector Terramar, 3km out of town ☎635 442 560, ⓦclubatlantida.com. The town's – if not the Mediterranean coast's – favourite club, with a huge open-air dance floor. Recently renovated, its enthusiastic fans say that the *discoteca* rivals the best of Ibiza. In summer generally open 2 nights during the week plus Fri & Sat, until late; limited hours in winter; check website for up-to-date times.

Pacha Sitges c/San Dídac, Urb Valpineda, 1.5km north of town ☎938 943 812, ⓦpachasitges.com. Mother of all *Pachas*, opening in 1967 and spawning a global dynasty of mega-clubs; fans won't be disappointed – there are two massive dancefloors, a huge sound system and big-name resident and visiting DJs. Summer generally Fri, Sat & sometimes Sun till late; winter hours depend on events.

Sweet Pacha Port Esportiu d'Aiguadolç ☎938 943 812, ⓦsweetpacha.com. *Sweet Pacha* offers a more chic-lounge experience than *Pacha Sitges*, with plenty of white leather, a back-lit bar, DJ tunes and a dancefloor, a seafood restaurant (*Sweet Mar*) and sea views. Summer daily 8.30pm–1am; winter hours vary.

Tarragona

Sited on a rocky hill, sheer above the sea, **TARRAGONA** has a formidable ancient past. Settled originally by Iberians and then Carthaginians, it was later used as the base for the Roman conquest of the peninsula, which began in 218 BC with Scipio's march south against Hannibal. The fortified city became an imperial resort and, under Augustus, **Tarraco** was named capital of Rome's eastern Iberian province – the most elegant and cultured city of Roman Spain, boasting at its peak a quarter of a million inhabitants. Temples and monuments were built in and around the city and, despite a history of seemingly constant sacking and looting since Roman times, it's this distinguished past which still asserts itself throughout modern Tarragona.

Time spent in the handsome upper town quickly shows what attracted the emperors to the city: strategically – and beautifully – placed, it's a fine setting for some splendid Roman remains and a few excellent museums. There's an attractive medieval section, too, while the rocky coastline below conceals a couple of reasonable beaches. If there's a downside, it's that Tarragona is today the second-largest port in Catalunya, so the views aren't always unencumbered – though the fish in the Serrallo fishing quarter is consistently good and fresh. Furthermore, the city's ugly outskirts to the south have been steadily degraded by new industries – chemical and oil refineries and a nuclear power station – which do little for Tarragona's character as a resort.

Orientation

The city divides clearly into two parts: a predominantly medieval, walled upper town (where you'll spend most of your time) known as **La Part Alta**, and the prosperous modern centre below, referred to as **Eixample**, or the Centre Urbà. Between the two cuts is the **Rambla Nova**, a sturdy provincial rival to Barcelona's, lined with fashionable cafés and restaurants, culminating at its southern end with the lovely **Balcó del Mediterràni**, overlooking the sea. Parallel, and to the east, lies the **Rambla Vella**,

11

TARRAGONA

0   100
metres

PASSEIG DE TORROJA

Passeig
Arqueológic
Muralles

PASSEIG DE TORROJA

City Walls

Passeig
Arqueológic
Muralles

PLAÇA MN.
PERFECTE
C PINTOR
L. MALLOL

AVINGUDA MARIA CRISTINA

City Walls

Cloisters

CARRER SANT PAU

C PORTAL DEL CARRO

C ESCORXADOR

PUIG D'EN SITGES

CARRER LLORENS

C DESCALZOS

PLAÇA DE
SANT ANTONI

Museu
Diocesà

PLAÇA
DE PAU

C MARE

C GUITARRA

Catedral

PLAÇA
DE LA SEU

C NOU PATRIARCA

PLAÇA
PESCATERIES
VELLES

ARC DE
SANT BERNAT

C CARME

C ESCRIVANIES VELLES

C VIDRE

CARRER CIVADEIRA

C GA

PGE ST. MIQUEL

C MISSER SITGES

C MEDIONA

C MOLES

C ABAT

C ENDRÓDICS

PLAÇA S.
ROSSIGNOL

CARRER MERCERIA

CALDERERS

C SANT PERE CLAVERS

C VERTALLOLS

PLAÇA ANGELS

PLAÇA DE
TROVELLET

Portal del
Roser

AVINGUDA DE CATALUNYA

Maqueta
Tárraco

C COMTE

P DE R. POU

PLAÇA
DEL
PALLOL

CARRER CAVALLERS

Casa
Castellarnau

C FERRERS

CARRER MAJOR

C CUIRATERIES

C CRESTALL

CARRER NOU

C VILA-ROMA

PLAÇA
DEL REI

Museu
Nacional
Arqueológic

Pretori

C ENRAJOLAT

C TRINQUET VELL

Circ
Roma

Casa de
la Festa

PASSEIG DE SANT ANTONI

VIA DE L'IMPERI ROMA

RERE SANT DOMÈNEC

C SALINES

C SANT DOMÈNEC

C LA PALMA

C PORTALET

C CÓS DEL BOU

C TRINQUET NOU

C OLEGUER

PLAÇA DE LA FONT

VIA AUGUSTA

ESCALES DEL MIRACLE

Parc del
Miracle

Ajuntament

HOTELS & PENSIÓS

RAMBLA VELLA

Amfiteatre

PASSEIG DE LES PALMERES

Hostal Noria   4
Hotel Astari   1
Hotel Ciutat de
  Tarragona   3
Hotel Husa
  Imperial Tarraco 7
Hotel Lauria   6
Hotel Nuria   8
Hotel Plaça de la Font 2
Hotel Urbis Centre 5

CARRER COMTE DE RIUS

C. J. MARAGALL

C SANTA CLARA

C SANT AGUSTÍ

ROGER DE LLÚRIA

PLAÇA
VERDAGUER

CARRER AUGUST

CAMPING

Camping Las Palmeras 3

Balcó del
Mediterràni

CARRER COMTE DE RIUS

CARRER SANT FRANCESC

CARRER ASSALT

RAMBLA NOVA

RAMBLA NOVA

Roger de
Llúria statue

PASSEIG MARÍTIM MARE DE CASANOVA

Platja del
Miracle

	RESTAURANTS	
	AQ Restaurant	1
	Els Arcs	5
	Les Coques	3
	Palau del Baró	4
	La Puda	10
	Sadoll	2
	Sol-Ric	6
	Les Voltes	8
	CAFÉS & BARS	
	El Candil	9
	El Cau	7

Fórums, Bus Station & Necropolis

Platja Arrabassada

Platja del Miracle

Fórum Local, Necropolis,
Aqüeducte de les Ferreres & AVE Station

Train Station & Serrallo

marking – as its name suggests – the start of the old town. To either side of the *rambles* are scattered a profusion of relics from Tarragona's Roman past, including various temples and parts of the forum, theatre and amphitheatre. Note that some of the most impressive monuments are a fair way out, but there's enough within walking distance to occupy a good day's sightseeing and to provide a vivid impression of life in Tarragona in imperial Roman times.

Passeig Arqueològic Muralles

Portal del Roser, Avgda. Catalunya • Easter–Sept Tues–Sat 9am–9pm, Sun 9am–3pm; Oct–Easter Tues–Sat 9am–7pm, Sun 10am–3pm • €3, or Tarragona Card • ☎ 977 245 796, ⓦ museutgn.com

The **Passeig Arqueològic Muralles** is a promenade that encircles the northern half of the old town. From the entrance at the Portal del Roser, a path runs between **Roman walls** of the third century BC and the sloping, **outer fortifications** erected by the British in 1709 to secure the city during the War of the Spanish Succession. Megalithic walls built by the Iberians are excellently preserved in places, too, particularly two awesome gateways; the huge blocks used in their construction are quite distinct from the more refined Roman additions. Vantage points (and occasional telescopes) give views across the plain behind the city and around to the sea, while various objects are displayed within the *passeig*: several Roman columns, a fine bronze statue of Augustus and eighteenth-century cannons still defending the city's heights. Just beyond the entrance on the right, a small doorway leads up to the battlements where you get fine views of the old city.

The Necropolis

Museum Avgda. Ramón i Cajal 78 • March–May & Oct Tues–Sat 9.30am–1.30pm & 3–6pm, Sun 10am–2pm; June–Sept Tues–Sat 10am–1.30pm & 4–8pm, Sun 10am–2pm; Nov–Feb Tues–Sat 9.30am–1.30pm & 3–5.30pm, Sun 10am–2pm • €3, or Tarragona Card • ⓦ mnat.cat • Walk 20min out of the centre down Avgda. Ramón i Cajal, which runs west off Rambla Nova

The most interesting remains in town are those of the ancient **Necropolis**. Here, both pagan and Christian tombs have been uncovered, spanning a period from the third to the sixth century AD. The small **Museu i Necropolis Paleocristians** features sarcophagi and some of the most fascinating finds, such as an ivory doll with moveable arms and legs, and you can peek at the main burial grounds through the fence. Most of the relics attest to Tarragona's importance as a centre of Christianity: St Paul preached here, and the city became an important Visigothic bishopric after the break-up of Roman power.

Forum

Easter–Sept Tues–Sat 9am–9pm, Sun 9am–3pm; Oct–Easter Tues–Sat 9am–7pm, Sun 10am–3pm • €3, or Tarragona Card • ☎ 977 242 501, ⓦ museutgn.com

In the centre of town, the Roman forum, or rather forums, have also survived, since – as provincial capital – Tarragona sustained both a ceremonial **Forum Provincial** (the

---

HUMAN CASTLES

It's not often that you'll come across a group of grown men and women who willingly climb onto each other's back to form a tall, if a bit wobbly, human tower. But when you do, it's a sight to behold. Catalunya's famous *castellers* – teams of people competing to build human towers – originated in **Valls**, near Tarragona, at the end of the eighteenth century. Over time, the rest of Catalunya embraced the tradition, and *castells* now form a part of festivals throughout the region. The impressive *castells* can loom up to ten human storeys tall, and are completed by a small child scrambling to the very top.

Castells are a feature of Tarragona's annual **Festival of Santa Tecla** in mid-September. To learn more about the history, pay a visit to Tarragona's **Casa de la Festa**, Via Augusta 4 (end June to end Sept Tues–Sat 11am–2pm & 5–9pm, Sun 11am–2pm; rest of year Tues & Wed 9am–1pm, Thurs & Fri 9am–1pm & 5–7pm, Sat 10am–2pm & 5–7pm, Sun 11am–2pm; free; ☎ 977 220 086). The Festa Major of Vilafranca del Penedès in late August (see p.772) also showcases *castells*.

> **TARRAGONA CARD**
>
> If you plan on seeing most of Tarragona's sights, then it's well worth picking up a **Tarragona Card** (€15), which is valid for 48 hours, and allows entry into the city's main museums and sights, along with discounts at select restaurants and shops, free rides on municipal transport and more. The card comes with a guide detailing all the participating venues. You can buy it at the tourist offices and select hotels; for more information see ⓦ tarragonaturisme.cat.
>
> Note, too, that the main Roman sights – Passeig Arqueològic Muralles, Forum de la Colonia, Amfiteatre, Circ Roma and Casa Castellarnau – also have their own joint ticket for €10, though it's an overall better deal to go for the Tarragona Card. To get a lay of the Roman land, stop in to the **Maqueta Tàrraco**, Pl. del Pallol 3 (Easter–Sept Mon 9am–2pm, Tues–Sat 9am–9pm, Sun 9am–3pm; Oct–Easter Mon 9am–2pm, Tues–Sat 9am–7pm, Sun 9am–3pm; free; ⓦ museutgn .com), which displays a model of Roman Tarragona.

scant remnants of which are displayed on Plaça del Forum) and a **Forum de la Colonia** on c/Lleida, whose more substantial remains are on the western side of Rambla Nova, near the Mercat Central. Located on the flat land near the port, this was the commercial centre of imperial Tarraco and the main meeting place for locals for three centuries. The site, which contained temples and small shops ranged around a porticoed square, has been split by a main road: a footbridge now connects the two halves where you can see a water cistern, house foundations, fragments of stone inscriptions and four elegant columns.

Amfiteatre

Parc del Miracle • Easter–Sept Tues–Sat 9am–9pm, Sun 9am–3pm; Oct–Easter Tues–Sat 9am–7pm, Sun 10am–3pm • €3, or Tarragona Card • ⓦ museutgn.com

A group of Tarragona's tangible Roman remains lie close to each other at the seaward end of the Rambla Vella. Most rewarding is the **Amfiteatre**, built into the green slopes of Parc del Miracle. The tiered seats backing onto the sea are original, and from the top you can look north, up the coast, to the headland; the rest of the seating was reconstructed in 1969–70, along with the surviving tunnels and structural buildings.

Circ Roma and Pretori

Rambla Vella, Pl. del Rei • Easter–Sept Tues–Sat 9am–9pm, Sun 9am–3pm; Oct–Easter Tues–Sat 9am–7pm, Sun 10am–3pm • €3, or Tarragona Card • ⓦ museutgn.com

The **Circ Roma**, or Roman Circus, was the site of chariot races. The visible sections encompass vaults that are set back from the street under the gloom of the surrounding buildings. You can exit through the Roman **Pretori** tower on Plaça del Rei.

Museu Nacional Arqueològic

Pl. del Rei • June–Sept Tues–Sat 9.30am–8.30pm, Sun 10am–2pm; Oct–May Tues–Sat 9.30am–6pm & 4–7pm, Sun 10am–2pm • €3.50, or Tarragona Card • ☎ 977 236 209, ⓦ mnat.es

The most stimulating exhibition in town is housed in adjacent buildings off Plaça del Rei, opposite the entrance to the Pretori and Circ Roma. The splendid **Museu Nacional Arqueològic** is a marvellous reflection of the richness of imperial Tarraco. Its huge collection is well laid out, starting in the basement with a section of the old Roman wall preserved *in situ*. On other floors are thematic displays on the various remains and buildings around the city, accompanied by pictures, text and relics, as well as whole rooms devoted to inscriptions, sculpture, ceramics, jewellery – even a series of anchors retrieved from the sea. More importantly, there's an unusually complete collection of mosaics, exemplifying the stages of development from the plain black and white patterns of the first century AD to the elaborate polychrome pictures of the second and third centuries.

Catedral

Pl. de Palau 2 • Mid-March to mid-Oct Mon 3–6pm, Tues–Sat 10am–6pm; mid-Oct to mid-March Mon–Sat 10am–2pm • €3.50, or Tarragona Card • ⓦ arquebisbattarragona.cat

The central c/Major climbs to the quarter's focal point, the **Catedral**, which sits at the top of a broad flight of steps. This, quite apart from its own grand beauty, is a perfect example of the transition from Romanesque to Gothic forms. You'll see the change highlighted in the main facade, where a soaring Gothic portal is framed by Romanesque doors, surmounted by a cross and an elaborate rose window. Except for services, entrance to the cathedral is through the **cloisters** (*claustre*; signposted up a street to the left of the facade), themselves superbly executed with pointed Gothic arches softened by smaller round divisions. The cloister also has several oddly sculpted capitals, one of which represents a cat's funeral being directed by rats. Note that the cathedral has been undergoing renovations, so parts of it may be closed to the public, and entry fee may therefore be reduced. The ticket also gives access to the **Museu Diocesà**, piled high with ecclesiastical treasures.

Casa Castellarnau

C/Cavallers 14 • Easter–Sept Tues–Sat 9am–9pm, Sun 9am–3pm; Oct–Easter Tues–Sat 9am–7pm, Sun 10am–3pm • €3, or Tarragona Card • ⓦ museutgn.com

Strolling the old town's streets will also enable you to track down one of Tarragona's finest medieval mansions and lesser-known museums, the **Casa Castellarnau**. The interior courtyard alone rewards a visit, with its arches and stone coats of arms built over Roman vaults. Otherwise, the small-scale collections are largely archeological and historical (Roman jars and the like), rescued from banality by some rich eighteenth-century Catalan furniture and furnishings on the upper floor.

Serrallo

A fifteen-minute walk west along the industrial harbour front from the train station (or the same distance south from the Necropolis) takes you to the working port of **Serrallo**, Tarragona's so-called "fishermen's quarter". Built a century ago, the harbour here isn't particularly attractive, though it's authentic enough – fishing smacks tied up, nets laid out on the ground for mending. The real interest for visitors is the line of **seafood restaurants** which fronts the main Moll dels Pescadors. The warehouses nearby, back towards town, have been given a face-lift, as has the Estació Marítima (cruise-ship terminal).

Museu Port de Tarragona

Moll de Costa, Port de Tarragona • June–Sept 10am–2pm & 5–8pm, Sun 11am–2pm; Oct–May Tues–Sat 10am–2pm & 4–7pm, Sun 11am–2pm • €2, or Tarragona Card

The mildly interesting **Museu Port de Tarragona**, which occupies part of a massive maritime warehouse, traces the port's history from Roman times to the present, giving an overview of life on the docks. Exhibits include restored fishing boats and vessels, and the museum also includes entry to the port's **Far de la Banya** (Banya Lighthouse; Sun 11am–2pm only), which contains old maritime instruments and covers the history of the lighthouse.

ARRIVAL AND DEPARTURE **TARRAGONA**

By train The train station is on Pg. de Espanya (☏ 902 432 343), from which it's an easy walk into town. In addition to the regular trains, there are pricier hourly high-speed AVE trains from Barcelona Sants (35min), which arrive at the Camp de Tarragona AVE station, a 10min taxi ride from the centre.
Destinations Barcelona (every 30min; 1hr); Cambrils (12 daily; 20min); Lleida (12 daily; 2hr, *talgo* 1hr, AVE 30min);

Sitges (direct every 30min; 1hr); Tortosa (13 daily; 1hr); Valencia (16 daily; 4hr, *talgo* 2hr 15min); Zaragoza (12 daily; 3hr 30min).
By bus The bus terminal is at the end of Rambla Nova, at Pl. Imperial Tarraco.
Destinations Barcelona (18 daily; 1hr 30min); Berga (July & Aug 1 daily, rest of year Sat & Sun only; 3hr 10min); La Seu d'Urgell (daily at 8am; 3hr 45min); Lleida

(6 daily; 1hr 45min); Montblanc (3 daily; 50min); Poblet (Mon–Sat 3 daily; 1hr 5min); Tortosa (Mon–Fri 1 daily; 1hr 30min); Valencia (7 daily; 3hr 30min); Zaragoza (4 daily; 4hr).

INFORMATION

Turisme c/Major 39 (July–Sept Mon–Sat 9am–9pm, Sun 10am–2pm; Oct–June Mon–Sat 10am–2pm & 4–7pm, Sun 10am–2pm; ☎977 250 795, ⓦtarragonaturisme.cat). There are a few other information booths/offices, including on Rambla Nova (summer daily 10am–8pm; winter Mon–Sat 10am–2pm & 4–7pm, Sun 10am–2pm).

Regional tourist office c/Fortuny 4, just south of Rambla Nova (Mon–Fri 9am–2pm & 4–6.30pm, Sat 9am–2pm; ☎977 233 415, ⓦtarragonaturisme.cat). If you're travelling farther afield you might find the regional tourist office handy.

ACCOMMODATION

HOTELS AND PENSIÓS

Hostal Noria Pl. de la Font 53 ☎977 238 717, ⓦhotelpdelafont.com. Decent *pensió* above a no-frills bar popular with locals, with small but clean singles and doubles. Same owners as (and book via) *Hotel Plaça de la Font*. **€49**

Hotel Astari Vía Augusta 95–97 ☎977 236 900, ⓦhotelastari.com. Friendly hotel with modern rooms, a marble-floor lobby, a decent swimming pool and pleasant garden. It's a 15min walk from the old town, and less than a 10min stroll from the nearest beach. **€96**

Hotel Ciutat de Tarragona Pl. Imperial Tarraco 5 ☎977 250 999, ⓦsbhotels.es. Somewhat impersonal but very comfortable hotel on the main roundabout at the entrance to Rambla Nova. Good last-minute rates online. **€100**

Hotel Husa Imperial Tarraco Pg. de les Palmeres ☎977 233 040, ⓦhusa.es. One of the city's finer hotels, modern but beautifully positioned, sitting on top of the cliff and facing out to sea. Relax in the breezy garden or lounge by the pool. Good online rates. **€110**

Hotel Lauria Rambla Nova 20 ☎977 236 712, ⓦhotel-lauria.com. Well-located three-star just off the main *rambla* with modern if functional rooms, some smartly refurbished,

and a small outdoor pool. Good online rates. **€84**

Hotel Núria Vía Augusta 145 ☎977 235 011, ⓦhotelnuria.com. Amiable hotel near Arrabassada beach, 1km northeast of Tarragona – the *playa* stretches right nearby, and town is about a 25min walk away (or you can opt for one of the regular buses). The decor tends towards minimalist, and there's a restaurant-café, with a weekday lunchtime *menú* for €13. **€95**

Hotel Plaça de la Font Pl. de la Font 26 ☎977 246 134, ⓦhotelpdelafont.com. Central, cosy hotel with simple, well-scrubbed rooms, and a small restaurant with a cheery terrace on the *plaça* (closed Sun & Dec). **€70**

Hotel Urbis Centre Pl. Corsini 10 ☎977 240 116, ⓦhotelurbiscentre.com. This central hotel has a contemporary style, with white marble floors in the lobby. The simple rooms are well maintained, and the regional-cuisine restaurant (closed Sun) serves a good selection of local wines. **€90**

CAMPING

Camping Las Palmeras ☎977 208 081, ⓦlaspalmeras.com. There are a number of campsites east of town including this well-maintained site at Platja Llarga, 3km northeast along the coast. Pitches from **€22**

EATING AND DRINKING

There are plenty of good **restaurants** in the centre of Tarragona; many – particularly in and around Pl. de la Font – have outdoor seating in the summer. Alternatively, you could try the fish and seafood places down in Serrallo – not cheap, but the food is as fresh as can be and you can find some *menús* for around €15–20 in the narrow street behind the main Moll dels Pescadors. *Pescado romesco* is the regional speciality and you'll find it on several *menús* around town: *romesco* sauce has a base of peppers, almonds and/or hazelnuts, olive oil, garlic and sometimes wine. Beyond this there are many variations, as cooks tend to add their own secret ingredients. Tarragona's marina (Port Esportiu) features several **clubs and bars**, which generally heat up in the summer – though note that they come and go with great regularity. It's in town – around the old quarter and the cathedral and in the streets between the train station and Rambla Nova – that you'll find spots with more historical, local appeal.

RESTAURANTS

★ **AQ Restaurant** c/Les Coques 7 ☎977 215 954, ⓦaq-restaurant.com. Glossy restaurant – the sky-lit dining room sports honey-hued walls and sleek furnishings – with impressive cuisine to match (main dishes €18–25). Husband-and-wife team Quintín and Ana (after whom the restaurant is named) serve up seasonal fare with flair including superb

fresh fish and shellfish. Tues–Sat 1.30–3.30pm & 9–11pm; usually closed second two weeks of Dec.

Els Arcs Misser Sitges 13 ☎977 218 040, ⓦrestaurantarcs.com. Ancient, graceful stone arches – hence the name – preside over a cosy dining room. Fresh Mediterranean dishes include cod with a Cabrales cheese sauce and duck with sweet-and-sour cherry preserves.

11

Expect to pay around €40 per person, without drinks. Tues–Sat 1.30–3.30pm & 8.30–10.30pm.

Les Coques c/Sant Llorenç 15 ☎977 228 300, ⓦlescoques.com. Top-notch Catalan fare in a comfortable restaurant near the cathedral, with a weekday lunch *menú* for €25. Daily except Sun 1.30–4pm & 9–10.30pm.

Palau del Baró c/Santa Anna 3 ☎977 241 464, ⓦpalaudelbaro.com. Dining rooms set in an eighteenth-century mansion with a lovely courtyard area. Well-prepared regional food includes shellfish in *romesco* sauce and *fideuà* (Catalan noodles) with clams and monkfish. Good-value €15 weekday lunch *menú*, and €18 dinner *menú*. Daily except Mon 1–4pm & 8–11pm; closed Sun eve.

La Puda Moll dels Pescadors 25 ☎977 211 070. In the Serrallo quarter, this popular fish restaurant has tables overlooking the harbour inside and out. There's a short selection of seafood tapas, and *menús* starting at €25. Usually daily 1.30–3.30pm & 8.30–10.30pm; sometimes limited hours in winter.

Sadoll c/Mare de Déu de la Mercè 1 ☎ 977 244 404, ⓦsadollrestaurant.com. Inviting restaurant tucked away in a quiet corner near the cathedral, and featuring fresh, creative dishes in an elegant Art Nouveau dining room.

Average price per dish: €15. Daily except Sun 1.30–3.30pm & 8.30–10.30pm.

Sol-Ric Vía Augusta 227, about 1km east of the city ☎977 232 032, ⓦrestaurantesolric.es. Feast on seafood and grilled meats at this amiable restaurant set in an old house with antique furniture and wooden beams. Daily except Mon 1–4pm & 8.30–11pm; also closed Sun dinner.

★ **Les Voltes** c/Trinquet Vell 12 ☎977 230 651, ⓦrestaurantlesvoltes.cat. Atmospheric, mid-priced restaurant, with a fabulous location within Roman vaults, and recommended for its hearty seafood and meats. Daily except Mon 1–3.30pm & 8–10.30pm; closed Sun eve.

CAFÉS AND BARS

El Candil Pl. de la Font 13 ☎977 240 516. Fashionable, friendly café by day, which transforms into a cellar bar with tapas at night. Serves a wide selection of herbal teas, hot chocolate and coffees as well as beer and cava. Daily 11am–3pm & 5pm–midnight.

El Cau c/Trinquet Vell 2 ☎977 231 212. Situated in an underground Roman vault in the old town, this dark venue has live indie-pop or rock every Sat night. Daily 10pm–4am.

Around Tarragona

The coast between Tarragona and the historic town of **Altafulla**, 11km east, is littered with additional Roman remains, well worth checking out, though for all but the Roman **aqueduct** you'll need your own transport. West of Tarragona, the pleasant town of **Reus** features an entertaining museum on master Catalan architect Antoni Gaudí.

Aqüeducte de les Ferreres

Free • Parking on site; a bus marked "Sant Salvador" (every 20min; last bus back at around 10.45pm; journey time 10min), departs from a stop outside Avgda. Prat de la Riba 11, off Avgda. Ramón i Cajal, which runs west off Rambla Nova

Perhaps the most remarkable (and least visited) of Tarragona's monuments stands 4km outside the original city walls, reached via a small, signposted road off the main Lleida highway. This is the Roman **Aqüeducte de les Ferreres**, which brought water from the Ríu Gayo, some 32km distant. The most impressive extant section, nearly 220m long and 27m high, lies in an overgrown valley in the middle of nowhere: the utilitarian beauty of the aqueduct is surpassed only by the one at Segovia and the Pont du Gard, in the south of France. Popularly, it is known as El Pont del Diable (Devil's Bridge) because, remarked Richard Ford, of the Spanish habit of "giving all praise to 'the Devil', as Pontifex Maximus".

Torre dels Escipions, Pedrera Romana del Medol and Arc de Berà

Pedrera Romana del Medol Easter–Sept Tues–Sat 9am–8pm, Sun 9am–3pm; Oct–Easter Tues–Sat 10am–4pm, Sun 10am–3pm • Free

Other local Roman monuments of similar grandeur line the main road north towards Barcelona (N340) – keep an eye out for signs as they can be easy to miss. The square, three-storey **Torre dels Escipions**, a funerary monument built in the second century AD and nearly 10m high, stands just off the N340, 6km northeast of Tarragona.

A couple of kilometres farther north, at the Altafulla junction, you'll see signs to the **Pedrera Romana del Medol**, an excavated quarry that provided much of the stone used in Tarragona's constructions.

Keep heading towards Barcelona, and 20km from Tarragona, near the town of Creixell, rears the triumphal **Arc de Berà**, built over the great Via Maxima in the second century AD.

Reus

Gaudí aficionados (and particularly those with children in tow) might want to take a spin through the small, handsome city of **Reus**, 14km west of Tarragona, where the Modernisme master, Gaudí, was born in 1852. While Reus has no Gaudí buildings – he left at the age of 16 – it does feature a smattering of other *modernista* buildings, all of which form part of the town's **Ruta del Modernisme**. Besides Gaudí, Reus is popular for its good shopping, especially clothing, thanks in part to the town's once-thriving textile industry.

Gaudí Centre

Pl. del Mercadal • Mid-June to mid-Sept Mon–Sat 10am–8pm, Sun 11am–2pm; mid-Sept to mid-June Mon–Sat 10am–2pm & 4–8pm, Sun 11am–2pm • €7 • ⓦ gaudicentre.com

The sleek **Gaudí Centre** offers an engaging overview of the great artist via three floors of tactile and sensory exhibits. The first floor focuses on young Gaudí and his connection with Reus; look for what is believed to be the only hand-written notebook by Gaudí still in existence. The second floor, called "Gaudí the Innovator", focuses on his progressive designs. The top floor shows a film on Gaudí and covers his influence on architecture around the globe.

11

ARRIVAL AND INFORMATION

REUS

By bus Regular trains and buses connect Reus with Tarragona (15min) and Barcelona (1hr 40min). Buses also travel regularly between the Barcelona airport and Reus airport, which lies about 6km east of Reus and handles various budget European airlines.

Turisme Inside the Gaudí Centre (mid-June to mid-Sept Mon–Sat 9.30am–8pm, Sun 11am–2pm; mid-Sept to mid-June Mon–Sat 9.30am–2pm & 4–7pm, Sun 10am–2pm; ⓣ 977 010 670, ⓦ reus.cat/turisme). You can pick up a map at the helpful tourist office.

Tours The tourist office offers a variety of good guided tours of the city, which sometimes include access to *modernista* buildings otherwise closed to the public.

ACCOMMODATION AND EATING

HOTELS

Hotel Gaudí Raval de Robuster 49 ⓣ 977 345 545, ⓦ gargallohotels.es. This comfortable, mid-range hotel, one of several decent options in the city, has modern rooms in muted colours, a casual cafeteria and a lobby with a Gaudí-style decor. **€60**

Mas Passamaner Camí de la Serra 52, La Selva del Camp, 5km northwest of Reus ⓣ 977 766 333, ⓦ maspassamaner.com. For a further taste of Modernisme, consider staying at this hotel designed by the master

architect Lluis Domènech i Montaner in 1922, and converted into a five-star hotel, with elegant rooms, a pool and a spa. **€222**

RESTAURANT

GaudíR Top floor of the Gaudí Centre ⓣ 977 127 702. One of the finer dining options in the city, with a breezy terrace overlooking Reus' rooftops, it serves up creative regional fare, including fragrant fish and rice specialities. Daily except Sun 1.30–4pm & 8.30–11pm; also closed Mon eve.

Altafulla

ALTAFULLA makes a reasonable stop for a wander about the old town, with its 400-year-old castle (privately owned), the Baroque **Església Parroquial de Sant Martí** (open for services only), completed in 1705 with its distinctive octagonal dome, and a pair of gateways left standing from the original medieval walls.

Villa Romana dels Munts

C/Villa Romana • March–May Tues–Sat 10am–1.30pm & 3–6pm, Sun 10am–2pm; June–Sept Tues–Sat 10am–1.30pm & 4–8pm, Sun 10am–1.30pm; Nov–Feb Tues–Sat 10am–1.30 & 3–5.30pm, Sun 10am–2pm • €1.85

Nearer the beach and surrounded by a sleepy estate of holiday homes, the **Villa Romana dels Munts** is one of the more important finds in the region, primarily because of the exceptional mosaics and paintings that decorated its rooms and thermal baths

– indicating an owner of high standing. The mosaics are preserved in the Museu Nacional Arqueològic in Tarragona and today the villa is worth a look chiefly for the ruins of its thermal baths, which include a remarkably well-preserved arch and water tank.

ARRIVAL AND INFORMATION
ALTAFULLA

By bus and train Regular buses and trains connect Altafulla with Tarragona (10min).
Turisme c/Marqués de Tamarit 16 ⓦ altafulla.cat (Jan–March Mon–Fri 9am–3pm; May, June & Sept–Dec Mon–Thurs 9am–3pm, Fri & Sat 4–7pm; July & Aug daily 10am–2pm & 4–8pm; ☏ 977 651 426); Pl. dels Vents (summer only; ☏ 977 650 752). Note that hours change depending on city budget.

ACCOMMODATION

Hotel Gran Claustre c/del Cup 2, near the castle ☏ 977 651 557, ⓦ granclaustre.com. Ideal for the splurge, the *Hotel Gran Claustre* features luxurious rooms combining contemporary style with historical elegance, all within an enchanting mansion built in 1746; there's also an extremely swish pool facing the castle walls and a rooftop jacuzzi. **€194**

11

Costa Daurada

The coast south of Tarragona is an uninspiring prospect. The occasional beaches are hard to reach by public transport, and few of them have anything to encourage a stop. This part of the Costa Daurada, however, does boast the gigantic **PortAventura** theme park, and the pretty harbour town of **Cambrils**.

PortAventura

PortAventura Daily: mid-April to mid-June, Sept, Oct & parts of Dec daily 10am–7/8pm; mid-June to Aug daily 10am–midnight; Nov & parts of Dec Sat & Sun only 10am–7/8pm; closed Jan to mid-April; check website for exact details • €44 per day, €69 for 2 days, €79 for 3 days; Aquatic Park included **Aquatic Park** Daily: late May to June & first two weeks Sept 10am–6pm; July & Aug 10.30am–7pm • €24 per day, or joint ticket with PortAventura • ⓦ portaventura.es • The park has its own RENFE station

Just outside the resort of Salou lies **PortAventura**, one of the largest theme parks in Europe. The razzle-dazzle consists of PortAventura Park, an amusement park comprising five themed "lands" including China and the Wild West, each offering death-defying rides, garish restaurants and live entertainment; an **Aquatic Park**; and several pricey hotels.

Cambrils

CAMBRILS, set back from a large harbour, still has working boats and fishing nets interspersed among its restaurants and hotels. In summer, it's as full as anywhere along the Catalan coast, and is probably better seen as a day-trip from Tarragona, only fifteen minutes to the north. Out of season, though, it can be wonderfully relaxed.

Museu Torre del Port

Pg. Miramar 31 • Open only when there's an exhibition – check with turisme • €1.50–2

The small **Museu Torre del Port** is housed in the seventeenth-century circular watchtower in the harbour, and features temporary maritime exhibits, some of which explore local fishing history. The view from the top is lovely, showing off not just the town's port but also nearby beaches.

ARRIVAL AND INFORMATION
CAMBRILS

By train Regular trains travel from Tarragona (25min). Upon arrival, it's a 15min walk from the inland part of town down to Cambrils-Port and the harbour.
Turisme Pg. de les Palmeres 1 (May, June, Sept & Oct daily 9.30am–2pm & 4.30–7pm; July & Aug Mon–Fri 9.30am–2pm & 5.30–9pm, Sat & Sun 10am–1.30pm & 5.30–9pm; Nov–April Mon–Fri 9am–2pm & 4–6pm, Sat & Sun 9.30am–2pm; ☏ 977 792 307, ⓦ cambrils-tourism.com).

ACCOMMODATION AND EATING

There are plenty of **hotels** in town, but as with all places on the coast you'll need to reserve in high season, especially if you want to be on the harbour. There are several **campsites** in and around Cambrils, up the coast in both directions; the *turisme* has a map showing where they all are. For a meal, there's plenty of choice and some splendid fish **restaurants** along the harbour. Expect to pay around €15–20 for a good *menú*, though à la carte seafood at some of the harbour-front restaurants comes in at considerably more than that.

Don Camilo Avgda. Diputació 42 ☎977 361 490, ⓦplayacambrils.com. One of the closest campsites to the centre, with a range of facilities including two swimming pools, a bar-restaurant, a playground and plenty of kid-friendly activities. Closed Nov–April. Pitches from €25
Hotel Princep c/Narcís Monturiol 2 ☎977 361 127, ⓦhotelprincep.com. This hotel, one street in from the sea, looks fairly plain from the outside, but is comfortable

and clean within. €75
Joan Gatell Pg. Miramar 26 ☎977 360 057, ⓦjoangatell.com. A main draw for food-lovers, this is one of the best-known restaurants on this stretch of coast. The seafood, which is delivered twice daily, is so fresh it's practically flopping on your plate. Expensive, but worth it for a Catalan maritime feast. Daily except Mon 1–4pm & 8.30–11pm, closed Sun night & Dec.

Tortosa

The only town of any size in Catalunya's deep south is **TORTOSA**, slightly inland astride the Ríu Ebre. In the Civil War the front was outside Tortosa for several months until the Nationalists eventually took the town in April 1938. The battle cost 35,000 lives, and is commemorated by a gaunt metal monument on a huge stone plinth in the middle of the river in town. The fighting took its toll in other ways, too: there's little left of the medieval quarter, the *barri antic*, which lies on the east bank of the Ebro, north of the modern commercial district.

Catedral de Santa Maria
C/Portal del Palau • Tues–Sat 10am–1pm & 4.30–7pm, Sun usually 12.30–2pm

The **Catedral de Santa Maria** is worth a look. Founded originally in the twelfth century on the site of an earlier mosque, it was rebuilt in the fourteenth century, and its Gothic interior and quiet cloister – although much worn – are both lovely.

La Suda and the Jardins del Príncep
Jardins del Príncep May to mid-Sept Tues–Sat 10am–1.30pm & 4.30–7.30pm, Sun 11am–1.30pm; mid-Sept to April 10am–1.30pm & 3.30–6.30pm, Sun 11–1.30pm • €3

Tortosa's brightest point is also its highest. **La Suda**, the old castle, sits perched above the cathedral, glowering from behind its battlements at the Ebre valley below and the mountains beyond. Like so many in Spain, the castle has been converted into a luxury parador, but there's nothing to stop you climbing up for a

---

TOURING THE PRIORAT

Around 35km west of Tarragona lies one of Spain's emerging wine regions, the **Priorat**, which was awarded its DOC in 2001. The red wine produced here, and in the adjacent Montsany DOC, is highly sought after, and the *cellers* have started to follow their more established competitors in La Rioja by cashing in with wine tours and tastings. The *turisme* in Tarragona has up-to-date information, or you can try the local office in Falset (Mon–Fri 9am–3pm & 4–7pm, Sat 10am–2pm, Sun 11am–2pm; ☎977 831 023, ⓦturismepriorat.org). Most tours cost €5–7, and many have English-speaking guides – reservations are essential.

La Conreria de Scala Dei c/Mitja Galta 32, Scala Dei, just south of La Morera de Montsant ☎977 827 027, ⓦvinslaconreria.com. This established winery, named after the Carthusian monks of Scala Dei, offers tours through its cellars and vineyards followed by tastings. Book tours in advance, via phone or website. Tours €10. Mon–Fri 11am–5pm, Sat & Sun 11am–2pm.

Costers del Siurana Camí Manyetes, Gratallops ☎977 839 276, ⓦcostersdelsiurana.com. This highly regarded winery offers tours through the cellars, and also runs the charming, small *Cellers de Gratallop* restaurant nearby, which serves regional cuisine – and Priorat wine, of course. Call or email ahead to enquire about tour hours and prices.

11

magnificent view from the walls, or from going into the plush bar and having a drink.

The breezy **Jardins del Príncep**, which sit at the base of the castle, feature an impressive collection of sculptures of the human figure by Santiago de Santiago.

ARRIVAL AND INFORMATION	TORTOSA

By train Tortosa is connected by regular trains to Barcelona (2hr) and Tarragona (1hr).
By bus Buses run from Tortosa to Vinaròs (in Castellón province to the south), from where you can reach the wonderful inland mountain town of Morella; and to

Tarragona and the Delta de l'Ebre area.
Turisme Jardins del Príncep (May to mid-Sept Tues–Sat 10am–1.30pm & 4.30–7.30pm, Sun 11am–1.30pm; mid-Sept to April 10am–1.30pm & 3.30–6.30pm, Sun 11am–1.30pm; ☎ 977 442 005, ☒ tortosaturisme.cat).

ACCOMMODATION AND EATING

El Celler d'en Panxampla Carretera d'Alfara, 7km west of Tortosa in the hamlet of Els Reguers ☎ 977 474 135, ☒ elcellerdenpanxampla.com. For a taste of the Tortosa countryside, try this comfortable *hotel rural* with elegant rooms with stone walls and wood-beam ceilings. The rustic restaurant (closed Mon) serves Catalan cuisine. Breakfast included. **€100**

Hotel Virginia Avgda. de la Generalitat 139 ☎ 977 444

186, ☒ hotelvirginia.net. For plain but clean budget rooms, try the amiable *Hotel Virginia*. **€45**
Parador Nacional Castell de la Suda ☎ 977 444 450, ☒ parador.es. For a splurge, it's well worth opting for this splendid parador, where you'll feel like you've stepped into the medieval era. It also has one of the better restaurants in town, open to non-guests and specializing in fish from the Ebro delta. **€110**

The Delta de l'Ebre

In the bottom corner of Catalunya is the **Delta de l'Ebre** (Ebro Delta), 320 square kilometres of sandy delta constituting the biggest wetland in Catalunya and one of the most important aquatic habitats in the western Mediterranean. Designated a natural park, its brackish lagoons, marshes, dunes and reed beds are home to thousands of wintering birds and provide excellent fishing; around fifteen percent of the total Catalan catch comes from this area. The scenery is unique in Catalunya, with low roads running through field after field of rice paddies, punctuated by solitary houses and small villages, before emerging onto dune-lined beaches. Since much of the area of the **Parc Natural de Delta de l'Ebre** is a protected zone, access is limited, and it's best to visit with your own transport. Check in with the well-stocked tourist office about birdwatching opportunities and other nature tours and treks.

Deltebre

The best place to start to get a good sense of the area is the town of **Deltebre**, at the centre of the delta, 30km from Tortosa. There's also an interesting **Ecomuseum**, in the park information centre (Mon–Sat 10am–2pm & 3–7pm, Sun 10am–2pm, until 6pm in winter, Sun 10am–2pm; €1.20), with an aquarium displaying species found in the delta.

Riumar

The town of **Riumar**, 10km east of Deltebre, also makes for a good base, with a couple of restaurants and good, if windy, bathing on a sandy beach, connected to the road by duckboards winding through the dunes, and more remote beaches accessible to the north.

CRUISES IN THE DELTA DE L'EBRE

A river cruise is a good way to experience the delta. Several boat companies, including the **Santa Susana** (☎ 629 204 117) and **Olmos** (☎ 977 48 05 48) operate from Deltebre for the hour-or-so trip on the river. Enquire at the tourist office or call ahead, because the boats sometimes only operate for groups; prices start at around €8 for a trip.

INFORMATION

DELTA DE L'EBRE

Park information centre Martí Buera 22, on the main highway, on the edge of Deltebre (Mon–Sat 10am–2pm & 3–7pm, Sun 10am–2pm, until 6pm in winter; ☎ 977 489 679, ⊛ deltebre.net). The well-signposted information centre can provide you with a map of the delta and has information about tours and local walks.

ACCOMMODATION

Delta Hotel Avgda. del Canal, on the outskirts of Deltebre towards Riumar ☎ 977 480 046, ⊛ deltahotel.net. This comfortable hotel has well-cared-for, rustic rooms, some with wood-beam ceilings, as well as a breezy garden. **€90**

Mediterrani Blau c/de l'Eucaliptus, 11km south of Deltebre towards the sea ☎ 977 479 079, ⊛ mediterraniblau.com. This blocky, white hotel is filled with modern if rather impersonal rooms, and a restaurant serving local seafood, duck and rice dishes. Hotel and restaurant usually closed Nov–Feb. **€92**

EATING

Casa Núri Final Goles de Ebre, Riumar ☎ 977 480 128. Here you can sample a wide range of seafood, as well as the local speciality, *arròs a banda* – similar to paella except that the rice is brought before the seafood. Daily 10am–10.30pm; lunch only in winter.

Los Hortets c/Doctor Joan Bonet 111, Deltebre ☎ 664 333 383, ⊛ restaurantloshortets.com. Feast on paella at this cheery restaurant, which has yellow-and-slate walls and plenty of leafy plants. Daily 1–4pm & 8.30–11pm; closed Mon in winter.

Inland: the route to Lleida

From Tarragona, the train trip inland is a fairly monotonous ride northwest across the flat lands to **Lleida**. The Tarragona–Lleida bus is a slightly more attractive proposition than the train, if only because it climbs the odd bluff and ridge on the way for good views over the plain. The bus also takes you directly to the region's only major attraction, the monastery of **Poblet**, which you could see in half a day and then move on to Lleida. Access to the monastery by train is possible, but means walking some of the way along a signposted footpath through farmland. Since it lies on the same line, it's easy enough to combine a trip to Poblet with a stopoff at **Montblanc**.

Montblanc

The walled medieval town of **MONTBLANC**, 8km before the turning to the monastery at Poblet, is a surprisingly beautiful place to discover in the middle of nowhere. The Plaça Major is picturesque, and livens up for the evening *passeig*, while there are many fine little Romanesque and Gothic monuments contained within the town's tight circle of old streets; all are marked on the map in front of the town's medieval gateway, the **Torre-portal de Bové**, which is just 100m or so up from the train station. On the southern side of the walls, the **Torre-portal de Sant Jordi** marks the spot where San Jordi, or St George (patron saint of Catalunya as well as England), slew the dragon, an event commemorated with a fiesta on April 23.

Santa Maria la Major

Pl. Major • Mon–Sat 11am–1pm & 4–6pm, Sun 11am–2pm • Free

Just above the central square, Plaça Major, stands the grand Gothic parish church of **Santa Maria la Major**; its elaborate facade has lions' faces on either side of the main doorway and cherubs swarming up the pillars. There's a fine view from the once-fortified mound that rises behind the church (known as the Pla de Santa Bàrbara – over the rooftops, defensive towers and walls, and away across the plain.

Sant Miquel

Pl. St Miquel • Open only as part of a guided tour

East from Santa Maria along c/Major, the church of **Sant Miquel** dates from the fourteenth century, and has Romanesque and Gothic elements, an impressive coffered ceiling and lovely Gothic lateral chapels. The church was the seat of the Catalan courts from 1307 to 1370.

> ## MEDIEVAL MONTBLANC
>
> The tourist office runs a top-notch variety of informative **guided tours** of medieval Montblanc, including a general tour through town (€5, including a glass of cava); a walk along the medieval walls (€3, or €8 with tapas and wine); and screenings of the 3D film *El Misteri de San Jordi* about Catalunya's patron saint (€2). For those who prefer to go on their own, the *turisme* also offers walking tours you can follow on an iPad-style tablet with GPS (€3), or it's 99c to download the tour to your smartphone. Tours are offered throughout the week; for more information, check at the *turisme* or ⓦ montblancmedieval.org.

Museu Comarcal de la Conca de Barberà

Just off Pl. Major • Tues–Sat 10am–2pm & 4–7pm, Sun 10am–2pm • €2.90 • ⓦ mccb.cat

This fine local **history museum**, set in a medieval home dating from the thirteenth century, has well-curated exhibits on the history and culture of the region, including on the art of glassmaking, and features a reproduction of an old chemist's shop.

ARRIVAL AND INFORMATION   MONTBLANC

By bus Regular trains and buses connect Montblanc to Tarragona (50min) and Lleida (50min).
Turisme At the eastern end of c/Major (Mon–Sat

10am–1.30pm & 3–6.30pm, Sun 10am–2pm; ☎ 977 861 733, ⓦ montblancmedieval.org). Helpful *turisme* in the old church of Sant Francesc, just outside the walls.

ACCCOMMODATION

Fonda Cal Blasi c/Alenyà 11–13 ☎ 977 861 336, ⓦ fondacalblasi.com. This friendly *fonda* is in a restored

nineteenth-century stone townhouse, just a short walk from Pl. Major; they also serve meals. <u>**€75**</u>

The Monestir de Poblet

Mon–Sat 10am–12.40pm & 3–5.25pm (mid-June to mid-Sept till 5.50pm), plus mid-March to mid-Oct only Sun 10am–12.25pm & 3–5.25pm • €7, guided tour (1hr) obligatory, departs roughly every 30min • ☎ 977 870 254, ⓦ larutadelcister.info

There are few ruins more stirring than the **Monestir de Poblet**, lying in glorious open country, vast and sprawling within massive battlemented walls and towered gateways. Once *the* great monastery of Catalunya, it was in effect a complete manorial village and enjoyed scarcely credible rights, powers and wealth. Founded in 1151 by Ramón Berenguer IV, who united the kingdoms of Catalunya and Aragón, it was planned from the beginning on an immensely grand scale. The kings of Aragón-Catalunya chose to be buried in its chapel and for three centuries diverted huge sums for its endowment, a munificence that was inevitably corrupting. By the late Middle Ages Poblet had become a byword for decadence – there are lewder stories about this than any other Cistercian monastery – and so it continued, hated by the local peasantry, until the Carlist revolution of 1835 when a mob burned and tore it apart. The monastery was repopulated by Italian Cistercians in 1940 and over the decades since then it's been subject to continual – and superb – maintenance and restoration.

The cloisters

As so often, the **cloisters**, focus of monastic life, are the most evocative and beautiful part. Late Romanesque, and sporting a pavilion and fountain, they open onto a series of rooms: a splendid Gothic **chapterhouse** (with the former abbots' tombs set in the floor), wine cellars, a parlour, a **kitchen** equipped with ranges and copper pots, and a sombre, wood-panelled **refectory**.

The chapel

Beyond, you enter the **chapel** in which the twelfth- and thirteenth-century tombs of the kings of Aragón have been meticulously restored by Frederico Marès, the manic collector of Barcelona. They lie in marble sarcophagi on either side of the nave, focusing attention on the central sixteenth-century altarpiece.

VISITING THE MONASTERIES

If you plan on visiting all three monasteries in the area – Poblet, Reial Monestir de Santes Creus and Monestir de Vallbona de les Monges – you can purchase a **joint ticket** available at any of the three, for €9. For more information, check ⓦ larutadelcister.info.

The dormitory

You'll also be shown the vast old **dormitory**, to which there's direct access from the chapel choir, a poignant reminder of Cistercian discipline. From the dormitory (half of which is sealed off since it's still in use), a door leads out onto the cloister roof for views down into the cloister itself and up the chapel towers.

ARRIVAL AND INFORMATION   MONESTIR DE POBLET

By bus Two to three buses a day (Mon–Sat only) run to Poblet from Tarragona or Lleida, passing right by the monastery. It's an easy day-trip from either city.

By train By train, you get off at the ruined station of L'Espluga de Francolí, from where it's a beautiful 3km walk to the monastery, much of it along a signposted country track.

Turisme Pg. Abat Conill 9, Poblet (summer Tues–Sat 10am–1.30pm & 3–6pm, Sun 10am–2pm; winter Tues–Fri 10am–2pm & 2.30–5pm, Sat 10am–1.30pm & 3–6.30pm, Sun 10am–2pm; ☏ 977 871 247).

ACCOMMODATION AND EATING

Staying overnight at **Poblet** is an attractive proposition if you have your own transport, since it makes a good base for excursion into the surrounding countryside. A kilometre up the road from Poblet, around the walls, the hamlet of **Les Masies** has a couple of hotels and restaurants, while **L'Espluga**, 2km northwest, also has a few places to stay.

POBLET

★ **Hospedería del Monasterio de Poblet** ☏ 977 871 201, ⓦ poblet.cat. For the full monastic experience, stay at the lovely new *hospedería*, opened in 2010, which rises up alongside the monastery. Designed by Spanish architect Mariano Bayón, the building blends harmoniously with its surroundings, featuring honey-hued stone, a cloister and a courtyard planted with olive trees. The monastic philosophy extends to all parts of the *hospedería*, which is quiet and soothing, with no TVs in the simply furnished rooms. Guests are invited to participate in the monastery's liturgy and services, and the restaurant even serves dishes inspired by historical monastic menus, like cod with *allioli de membrillo* (quince). Breakfast included. **€90**

Hostal Fonoll Outside the main gate of the monastery ☏ 977 870 333, ⓦ hostalfonoll.com. Adequate, modern rooms with a dark-wood decor; the restaurant (closed Thurs & mid-Dec to mid-Jan) has a €15 weekday *menú* (and €20 weekend *menú*) and serves rustic dishes like roast chicken with apples and prunes. **€70**

LES MASIES

Villa Engràcia ☏ 977 870 308, ⓦ villaengracia.com. This attractive former spa built in 1888, set in pleasant, leafy grounds, has elegant, well-outfitted rooms, an outdoor pool and tennis courts. **€155**

L'ESPLUGA DE FRANCOLÍ

Hostal del Senglar Pl. Montserrat Canals ☏ 977 870 121, ⓦ hostaldelsenglar.com. This welcoming *hostal* has cosy, comfortable rooms and a charming garden with tiled benches and towering trees. **€79**

Prades

If you have time and transport, a couple of excursions into the countryside surrounding Poblet are well worth making. The red-stone walled village of **PRADES**, in the Serra de Prades, 20km from the monastery, is a beautifully sited and tranquil place that needs no other excuse for a visit. It's also the place to be during the second weekend of July, when they replace the water in the fountain with cava, and you can join in and help yourself – or order a bottle of bubbly at a terrace bar in the porticoed *plaza* and enjoy the scene. The area around Poblet is also home to two more twelfth-century Cistercian monasteries.

Reial Monestir de Santes Creus

Tues–Sun 10am–5pm, June–Sept till 6.30pm • €4.50, or part of joint monastery ticket • ⓦ larutadelcister.info

The **Reial Monestir de Santes Creus** is the easier to reach, 7km north of the Barcelona–Lleida highway, and clearly signposted from there. It's built in Transitional style, with a grand Gothic cloister and some Romanesque traces, and you can explore the dormitory, chapterhouse and main church.

Monestir de Vallbona de les Monges

Tues–Sat 10.30am–1.30pm & 4.30–6.45pm, Sun noon–1.30pm & 4.30–6.45pm; Nov–Feb closes 6pm • €3.50, or part of joint monastery ticket • ⓦ larutadelcister.info

Trickier to find, though worth the drive, is the **Monestir de Vallbona de les Monges**, about 16km north of Poblet, reached via Montblanc. This monastery of *monges* (nuns) has been occupied continuously for over 800 years. The church, built over the twelfth to fourteenth centuries, is a particularly noteworthy example of the transition between Romanesque and Gothic, and has a rectangular nave and elegant cloisters.

Lleida

LLEIDA (Lérida), at the heart of a fertile plain in inland Catalunya, has a rich history. First a *municipium* under the Roman Empire and later the centre of a small Arab kingdom, it was reconquered by the Catalans and became the seat of a bishopric in 1149. Little of those periods survives in today's city but there is one building of outstanding interest, the old cathedral, which is sufficient justification in itself to visit. Several interesting museums and a steep set of old-town streets will easily occupy any remaining time. Rooms are easy to come by, and the students at the local university fill the streets and bars on weekend evenings, including at the breezy Plaça de Sant Joan, in good-natured throngs.

Seu Vella and Castillo del Rey

Cathedral Summer Tues–Sat 10am–7.30pm, Sun 10am–3pm; winter Tues–Fri 10am–1.30 & 3–5.30pm, Sat 10am–5.30pm, Sun 10am–3pm; last entry 30min before closing • ⓦ turoseuvella.cat **Castillo del Rey** Summer Tues–Sat 10.30am–2pm & 4–7.30pm, Sun 10am–3pm; winter Tues–Sat 10am–1.30 & 3–5.30pm, Sun 10am–3pm; last entry 30min before closing • €4 for cathedral and castle

The **Seu Vella**, or old cathedral, is enclosed within the walls of the ruined Castillo del Rey (also called La Suda), high above the Ríu Segre, a twenty-minute climb from the centre of town. It's a peculiar fortified building, which in 1707 was deconsecrated and taken over by the military, remaining in their hands until 1940. Enormous damage was inflicted over the years but the church remains a notable example of the Transitional style, similar in many respects to the cathedral of Tarragona. The Gothic cloisters are masterly, each walk comprising arches different in size and shape but sharing delicate stone tracery. They served the military as a canteen and kitchen. You can also visit parts of the reconstructed **castle**, such as the fortified walls – the views from the walls over the plain are stupendous.

Seu Nova

Mon–Fri 9.30am–1pm & 5.30–7.30pm, Sat & Sun 9.30am–1pm & 5.30–8.30pm • Free

You can climb back down from the old cathedral towards the river by way of the new cathedral, **La Seu Nova**. It's an austere eighteenth-century building with Neoclassical doorways, a main facade topped by a large crest of the Casa de Borbón and a series of minuscule, high stained-glass windows.

Museu de Lleida

C/Sant Crist 1 • Tues–Sun 10am–2pm & 4–7pm (June–Sept till 8pm) • €4 • ⓦ museudelleida.cat

The spacious **Museu de Lleida** is the city's flagship museum. Two floors show off ancient finds from throughout Lleida and Catalunya, including Romanesque altarpieces, a Visigoth baptismal font and stone sculptures from the Seu Vella.

Museu d'Art Jaume Morera

C/Mayor 31 • Tues–Sat 11am–2pm & 5–8pm, Sun 11am–2pm • Free

The **Museu d'Art Jaume Morera**, housed in the same building as the tourist office, focuses on twentieth-century Catalan art (particularly Lleida artists), and displays everything from paintings and sculptures to photography and graphic design. One of the museum highlights is the vast collection of works by Catalan Surrealist sculptor Leandre Cristòfol.

Centre d'Art La Panera

Pl. de la Panera 2 • Tues–Fri 10am–2pm & 4–7pm (5–8pm in July), Sat 11am–2pm & 5–8pm, Sun 11am–2pm • Free • ☎ 973 262 185, Ⓦ www.lapanera.cat

For top-notch exhibits of contemporary art, check out the creative **Centre d'Art La Panera**. The building's history is as interesting as the art inside: it dates back to the twelfth century, when it was Lleida's trading exchange and market, and you can still see evidence of its medieval roots in the original colonnade, made up of a line of 21 stone columns. In the early 1600s, the building was acquired by the canonry of the cathedral, who used it to store and sell food products – hence its official name, La Panera dels Canonges, or The Canons' Pantry.

ARRIVAL AND INFORMATION   LLEIDA

By train Trains regularly connect Lleida to Barcelona via Valls or Reus/Tarragona (17 daily; 2hr–4hr 15min, AVE 1hr). There are also services to: La Pobla de Segur (3 daily; 2hr 10min); Tarragona (8 daily; 1hr 30min–2hr); and Zaragoza (20 daily; 1hr 50min). For current timetables and ticket information, consult RENFE (☎ 902 240 202, Ⓦ renfe.es). It's a 15–20min walk east of the train station to Pl. de Sant Joan.

By bus Lleida has regular buses to Barcelona (Mon–Sat 10 daily, Sun 4; 2hr 15min); Huesca (5 daily; 2hr 30min); La Seu d'Urgell (2 daily; 3hr); Montblanc (6 daily; 1hr 30min); Pobla de Segur (daily; 2hr); Poblet (Mon–Sat 3 daily; 1hr 15min); Tarragona (3 daily; 2hr); Vielha, via Túnel de Vielha (2 daily; 3hr); and Zaragoza (Mon–Sat 6 daily, Sun 2; 2hr

30min). It's a 15–20min walk west of the bus station, down Avgda. de Blondel, to Pl. de Sant Joan.

By plane The new Lleida-Alguaire airport (☎ 973 032 700, Ⓦ aeroportlleida.cat), 15km northwest of Lleida, is a regional hub with flights to Barcelona, Madrid, the Balearics and a few European cities, including Frankfurt. UK charter flights also occasionally fly here, ferrying skiers to the Pyrenees. Buses travel to the airport from Lleida's bus station Fridays (3 departures; €3.50 one way) and Sundays (2 departures; €4 one way), though the schedule is subject to changes in the flight timetable.

Turisme c/Mayor 31 (Mon–Sat 10am–2pm & 4–7pm, Sun 10am–2pm; ☎ 973 700 402, Ⓦ turismedelleida.com).

ACCOMMODATION

There are a couple of places to stay right outside the train station, and more along the road straight ahead – Rambla Ferran – which leads into the centre. Otherwise, press on to the central Pl. Sant Joan, around which there are several possibilities.

Alberg Sant Anastasi Rambla d'Aragó 11 ☎ 973 266 099, Ⓦ xanascat.cat. Lleida's youth hostel is well run and central. Dorm bed from **€18**

Hotel Real Avgda. Blondel 22 ☎ 973 239 405, Ⓦ hotelrealllleida.com. One of the more comfortable hotels in the old town, in a great location facing the river.

Rooms have a simple, modern design and tiled bathrooms. **€65**

Hotel Sansi Lleida c/Alcade Porqueras 4–6 ☎ 973 244 000, Ⓦ sansihotels.com. A smart, modern hotel on the north side of the old town with hassle-free parking and plenty of bars nearby. **€60**

EATING AND DRINKING

Lleida is famous for its **snails**, roasted over a wood fire with peppers and garlic (*caragols a la llauna*). The block of streets north of the church of Sant Martí holds a range of restaurants; the university is close by, and this is where the students come to eat and, as night falls, to hang out at the loud **music-bars** along the block formed by c/Sant Martí, c/Camp de Mart, c/Balmes and Avgda. Prat de la Riba.

El Celler del Roser c/Cavallers 24 ☎ 973 239 070. One of the better spots to sample the celebrated snails is at this amiable restaurant, with wood tables and exposed brick. Daily except Sun 1–4pm & 8.30–11pm.

Gardeny c/Salmerón 10 ☎ 973 234 510. Traditional, Lleida cuisine in an elegant restaurant, serving a hearty weekday lunchtime *menú* for €13.50, dinner €16. Summer daily 1–3.30pm, plus Fri & Sat 9–10pm. Winter daily except

Tues 1–3.30pm & 9–10pm; also closed Mon dinner.

La Huerta Avgda. Tortosa 7 ☎ 973 245 040. For market-fresh regional cuisine, don't miss this established restaurant out of the centre of town, near the river and east of the train station. Specialities include the savoury *escalivada*, made with grilled peppers, onions and aubergine. Daily 1–4pm & 8.30–11.30pm.

Valencia and Murcia

PEÑÍSCOLA (P.820)

Valencia and Murcia

Named "El Levante" after the rising sun, this lush region is the part of Spain that wakes up first. Valencia has the Mediterranean Sea as its front yard, while the inland *huerta* is one of the most fertile in Europe, crowded with orange and lemon groves, date-palm plantations and rice fields still irrigated by systems devised by the Moors. Paella originated in these parts, and a juicy orange is named after Valencia. Evidence of the lengthy Moorish occupation can be seen throughout, in the castles, crops and place names – Benidorm, Alicante and Alcoy are all derived from Arabic. The region also encompasses the historical Murcia, which offers a fascinating contrast to the sun-and-sand debauchery on the water. Explored from one end to the other, this is a land of ancient and modern, of beauty and beastliness.

The growing self-assurance of the region is evident in the increasing presence of Valenciano – a dialect of Catalan – which challenges Castilian as the main language of education and broadcasting in the area. There are even a few extreme trains of thought that challenge the dialect's Catalan origins, but those beliefs have remained largely on the margins.

Murcia is quite distinct, a *comunidad autónoma* in its own right, and there could hardly be a more severe contrast with the richness of the Valencian *huerta*. This southeastern corner of Spain is virtually a desert and is some of the driest territory in Europe. It was fought over for centuries by Phoenicians, Greeks, Carthaginians and Romans, but there survives almost no physical evidence of their presence – or of five hundred years of Moorish rule, beyond an Arabic feel to some of the small towns and the odd date-palm here and there. The province's capital city of **Murcia**, with its lovely cathedral and terrace tapas bars, makes for a comfortable base for exploring the region.

Much of the **coast** is marred by heavy overdevelopment, with concrete apartment blocks and sprawling holiday complexes looming over many of the best beaches. However, away from the big resorts, particularly around **Denia** and **Xàbia** (Jávea) in Valencia, there are some attractive isolated coves, while the historic hilltop settlements of **Altea** and **Peñíscola** are undeniably picturesque, if touristy. In Murcia, the resorts of the **Mar Menor** are reasonably attractive and very popular with Spanish families in high season; the best beaches are in the extreme south, around **Águilas**, where you'll find some dazzling unspoilt coves. The increasingly vibrant cities of **Valencia** and **Alicante** are the major urban centres, and there are several delightful historic small towns and villages a short way inland, such as **Morella**, **Xàtiva** and **Lorca**.

The Valencia area has a powerful tradition of **fiestas**, and there are a couple of elements unique to this part of the country. Above all, throughout the year and more

Valencian cuisine p.796	Horchata p.812
Fiestas p.798	Gay Valencia p.813
The Valencia card p.802	All pulped out: La Tomatina p.815
CAC: Tickets and transport p.802	Festival Internacional de Benicàssim p.819
Las Fallas: Valencia on Fire p.804	Benidorm's water parks p.827
The port and the playas p.807	Fiestas de Moros y Cristianos p.829
Valencia by bike p.809	Turrón p.835
Fashion forward p.810	Earthquake in Lorka p.846

MORELLA

Highlights

❶ Las Fallas Witness giant effigies going up in an explosion of flames – this is one of Spain's most famous festivals. **See p.804**

❷ La Ciudad de las Artes y Ciencias Europe's largest cultural centre and the architectural definition of Valencia: progressive, playful, breathtaking. **See p.799**

❸ Horchata Cool your throat with a chilled glass of Valencia's own tiger-nut shake. **See p.812**

❹ Paella Feast on Spain's most iconic dish in its birthplace. **See p.814**

❺ Morella Step into medieval Spain in this fortified town crowned by a fairytale castle. **See p.821**

❻ Alicante A city that seems to capture the Mediterranean: elegant esplanades, *sangría* at terrace cafés, and silky-sand beaches. **See p.829**

❼ Festival Benicàssim Huge annual music festival featuring the biggest names in alternative pop. **See p.819**

❽ Cuatro calas Águilas' gorgeous cove beaches offer an inviting blend of sun, sea and, on some stretches in low season, solitude. **See p.845**

HIGHLIGHTS ARE MARKED ON THE MAP ON P.797

VALENCIAN CUISINE

Gastronomy is of great cultural importance to the Valencians. Rice is the dominant ingredient in dishes of the region, grown locally in paddy fields still irrigated by the Moorish canal system (*acequias*). Gourmets tend to agree that the best **paellas** are to be found around (but not *in*) Valencia, the city where the dish originated. The genuine version doesn't mix fish and meat – it typically contains chicken, rabbit, green beans, *garrofón* (large butter beans), snails, artichokes and saffron – and should be prepared fresh and cooked over wood (*leña*), not scooped from some vast, sticky vat; most places will make it for a minimum of two people, with advance notice.

Other **rice-based dishes** vary around the region: *arroz negro* is rice cooked with squid complete with ink, which gives the dish its colour, and served with *all i oli*, a powerful garlic mayonnaise. *Arroz al horno* is drier, baked with chickpeas. *Fideuà* is seafood and noodles cooked paella-style. The most famous, *arroz a banda*, is found on the south coast around Denia – it's rice cooked with seafood, served as two separate dishes: soup, then rice. Around Alicante, you can try *arroz con costra*, which is a meat-based paella topped with a baked egg crust. Apart from rice, **vegetables** (best *a la plancha*, brushed with olive oil and garlic) are always fresh and plentiful.

The sweet-toothed should try **turrón** (see box, p.835), a nuts-and-honey nougat, which you could follow with a **horchata** (or *orxata*; see box, p.812), a rich drink made from tiger nuts (*chufas*) or almonds (*almendras*).

or less wherever you go, there are mock battles between Muslims and Christians (Moros y Cristianos). Recalling the Christian Reconquest of the country – whether through symbolic processions or re-creations of specific battles – they're some of the most elaborate and colourful festivities to be seen anywhere, above all in Alcoy (see box, p.839). The other recurring feature is the *fallas* (bonfires) in which giant carnival floats and figures are paraded through the streets before being ceremoniously burned.

Getting around by public transport is relatively straightforward with frequent train and bus services, though you'll need your own transport to really explore the area. The motorway network is excellent, but tolls are quite pricey.

Valencia

For many, **VALENCIA**'s enviable perch on the Mediterranean would be enough of a draw. Not so for the city itself: Valencia has been reinventing itself at a heady pace, and shows no signs of slowing down. Well on the way to equalling – indeed, eclipsing in some instances – the cosmopolitan vitality of Barcelona and the cultural variety of Madrid, Spain's third-largest city has finally shaken off its slightly provincial former reputation. In the last decade and a half, a vast, iconic **La Ciudad de las Artes y Ciencias** cultural complex has been established, the state-of-the-art metro has continued to expand and dozens of hip new bars, restaurants and boutiques have injected new life into the historic centre. Valencia has also fully redeveloped its beach and port area, in part sparked by its hosting of prestigious yachting jamboree, the America's Cup. Nevertheless, despite its size and *stylista* cachet, Valencia retains an unpretentious if tangibly charged air.

Always an important city, Valencia was fought over for the agricultural wealth of its surrounding *huerta*. After Romans and Visigoths, it was occupied by the Moors for over four centuries with only a brief interruption (1094–1101) when **El Cid** recaptured it. He died here in 1099, but his body, propped on a horse and led out through the gates, was still enough to cause the Moorish armies – previously encouraged by news of his death – to flee in terror. It wasn't until 1238 that Jaime I of Aragón permanently wrested Valencia back. It has remained one of Spain's largest and richest cities ever since.

Valencia has long boasted some of the best **nightlife** in mainland Spain. *Vivir Sin Dormir* (Live Without Sleep) is the name of one of its bars, and it could be taken as a Valencian mantra. The city is alive with noise and colour throughout the year, with explosions of

VALENCIA & MURCIA

0 — 50
kilometres

N

Madrid

Cuenca

Teruel

Ademuz

Montanejos

EL MAESTRAZGO

Morella

Tarragona & Barcelona

Vinaròs

Benicarló

Peñíscola

Vilafamés

Oropesa

Benicàssim

Castellón de la Plana

Jérica

Segorbe

Vall d'Uixó

Madrid

Llíria

El Puig

Sagunto

Requena

Buñol

Chiva

Moncada

El Palmar

El Saler

Valencia

Horchata

El Perelló

Parellonet

La Albufera

Paella

Sueca

Alcudia de Carlet

Algemesí

Cullera

Alcira

VALENCIA

Ayora

Xàtiva

Gandia

Oliva

Albacete

Chinchilla de Monte-Aragón

Almansa

Ontenient

Denia

Xàbia

Ibiza

Jaén

Bocariente

Cocentaina

Quatretondeta

Alcoy

Callosa d'En Sarrià

Guadalest

Calpe

Villena

Jijona

Altea

Yecla

Benidorm

Hellín

Jumilla

Elda

Villajoyosa

Costa Blanca

San Juan de Alicante

Alicante

Moratalla

Cieza

Elche

Isle de Tabarca

El Caravaca de la Cruz

Cabezo de Torres

Orihuela

Mula

Torrevieja

MURCIA

Alhama de Murcia

Murcia

PARQUE NATURAL DE ESPUÑA

San Javier

Santiago de la Ribera

Los Alcázares

Mar Menor

Lorca

Mazarrón

Cartagena

El Puerto de Mazarrón

Almería

Águilas

Ibiza & Mallorca

HIGHLIGHTS
1 Las Fallas
2 La Ciudad de las Artes y Ciencias
3 Horchata
4 Paella
5 Morella
6 Alicante
7 Festival Benicàssim
8 Cuatro calas

FIESTAS

FEBRUARY

Week before Lent: Carnaval Águilas' *carnaval* is one of the wildest in the country. Vinaròs also has good *carnaval* celebrations.

MARCH/APRIL

12–19 March: Las Fallas de San José (see box, p.804) Valencia's Las Fallas is by far the biggest of the bonfire festivals, and indeed one of the most important fiestas in all Spain. The whole thing costs over €1 million, most of which goes up in smoke (literally) on the final *Nit de Foc* when the grotesque caricatures, fashioned from papier-mâché and wood, are burned. Throughout, there are bullfights, music and stupendous fireworks.

19 March: Día de San José Smaller *fallas* festivals in Xàtiva, Benidorm and Denia.

Third Sun of Lent: Fiesta de la Magdalena Castellón de la Plana celebrates the end of Moorish rule with pilgrimages and processions of huge floats.

Semana Santa (Holy Week) In Elche, there are, naturally, big Palm Sunday celebrations making use of the local palms, while throughout the week there are also religious processions in Cartagena, Lorca, Orihuela and Valencia. The **Easter processions** in Murcia are particularly famous, and they continue into the following week with, on the Tuesday, the Bando de la Huerta, a huge parade of floats celebrating local agriculture, and, on the Saturday evening, the riotous "Burial of the Sardine" which marks the end of these spring festivals.

April 22–24: Moros y Cristianos After a colourful procession in Alcoy, a huge battle commences between the two sides in the main square.

MAY

1–5: Fiestas de los Mayos Fiesta in Alhama de Murcia, and Moros y Cristianos in Caravaca de la Cruz.

Second Sun: La Virgen de los Desamparados The climax of this celebration in Valencia is when the statue of the Virgin is transferred from her basilica to the cathedral.

Third Sun: Moros y Cristianos In Altea.

JUNE

23–24: Noche de San Juan Magnificent *hogueras* festival in Alicante (and San Juan de Alicante) with processions and fireworks, culminating as huge effigies and bonfires are burnt in

gunpowder, fireworks and festivities punctuating the calendar. Valencia's **fiestas** are some of the most riotous in Spain and the best is Las Fallas, March 12–19, which culminates in a massive bonfire where all the processional floats are burned.

The most atmospheric area of the city is undoubtedly the maze-like **Barrio del Carmen** (in Valenciano "de Carmé"), roughly north of the Mercado Central to the Río Turia, extending up to the Torres de Serranos and west to the Torres de Quart. This once-neglected quarter continues to undergo regeneration, as buildings are renovated and stylish cafés open up next to crumbling townhouses, all of which makes for an incredibly vibrant, alternative neighbourhood. The **city walls**, which, judging from the two surviving gates, must have been magnificent, were pulled down in 1871 to make way for a ring road, and the beautiful church of **Santo Domingo**, in Plaza de Tetuan, has been converted into a barracks – it was from here that General Milans del Bosch ordered his tanks onto the streets during the abortive coup of 1981. This incident, however, isn't representative of the city's political inclination, which has traditionally been to the left – Valencia was the seat of the Republican government during the Civil War after it fled Madrid, and was the last city to fall to Franco.

The oldest part of Valencia is almost entirely encircled by a great loop of the **Río Turia**, which is now a landscaped **riverbed park**. In 1956, after serious flooding damaged much of the old town, the river was diverted. The ancient stone bridges remain, but the riverbed now houses cycle ways, footpaths and football pitches, as well as the astonishing Ciudad de las Artes y Ciencias, Europe's largest cultural complex. As the streets at midnight. It's celebrated on a smaller scale on the beaches of Valencia (Malvarossa, Cabanyal and Aloboraya) with bonfire-jumping. Altea also celebrates with a popular tree-bearing procession and a bonfire in the old town.

JULY
Early July: Fiestas de la Santísima Sangre Dancing in the streets of Denia, plus music and mock battles.
15–20: Moros y Cristianos In Orihuela.
Second week: Feria de Julio Valencia hosts music, bullfights and above all fireworks, ending with the Battle of the Flowers in the Alameda.
Penultimate weekend: FIB Benicàssim's international music festival, a massive party bringing together the major names in alternative and electronic music.
25–31: Moros y Cristianos Villajoyosa sees battles by both land and sea.

AUGUST
4: Festa del Cristo de la Salut Festival in El Palmar with processions by boat into the lake.
Mid-Aug: Misteri d'Eix Elche presents a mystery play, based on a drama dating back to medieval times.
14–20: Feria de Agosto Xàtiva's fair has a very extensive cultural dimension including concerts, plays and exhibitions, plus bullfights and barrages of fireworks.
15 Local festivities in Denia.
Last week: La Tomatina A riotous free-for-all of tomato-throwing takes place in Buñol on the last Wednesday of the month. There's also a music festival in Morella.
Last Wed Local fiesta in Sagunto, and at the same time the great Moros y Cristianos festival and a mystery play in Elche.

SEPTEMBER
4–9: Moros y Cristianos In Villena.
Second week: Bull-running through Segorbe's streets.
8–9: Les Danses Celebrations in Peñíscola's old quarter include a human tower construction.
22: Fiesta de Santo Tomás In Benicàssim with bands and a "blazing bull".

OCTOBER
Second Sun: La Virgen de Suffrage Benidorm celebrates its patron saint's day.

further proof that Valencia is ever inventing itself, the city is now getting its own Central Park. The 23-hectare Valencia Parque Central is currently being built on old rail lines, in the area of the new Sorolla train station, and is one of the city's – if not Spain's – largest redevelopment projects to date. The massive park will include *plazas*, promenades, children's gardens, an art centre, an amphitheatre and more.

Valencia's main beach is the **Playa de la Malvarrosa** to the east of the city centre, which becomes **Playa de las Arenas** at its southern end.

La Ciudad de las Artes y las Ciencias

Avda. Autopista del Saler • ☎ 902 100 031, ⓦ cac.es

More than any other project, the breathtaking **Ciudad de las Artes y las Ciencias** (City of Arts and Sciences, or CAC), rising from the riverbed, symbolizes the autonomous government's vision for Valencia and its quest to establish the city as a prime tourist destination. The giant complex – Europe's largest cultural centre – consists of a series of futuristic edifices designed mainly by Valencian architect Santiago Calatrava.

The architecture itself is simply stunning. Even if you only have a day or two in the city, it's well worth the effort getting here to take in the eye-catching buildings surrounded by huge, shallow pools. Calatrava's designs adopt an organic form, his technical and engineering brilliance providing the basis for his pioneering concrete, steel and glass creations. However, despite near-universal acclaim for its architecture, the complex has

12

VALENCIA

ACCOMMODATION

La Casa Azul	9
Center Valencia Youth Hostel	4
El Coso del Mar	19
Hôme Backpackers	2
Hôme Youth Hostel	6
Hospes Palau de Mar	13
Hostal Antigua Morellana	7
Hostal El Globo	18
Hostal Venecia	14
Hotel Acta del Carmen	1
Hotel Ad Hoc	3
Hotel Las Arenas	20
Hotel Husa Dimar	15
Hotel Neptuno	17
Hotel Palacio Marqués del Caro	5
Hotel Sorolla Centro	16
Pensión Paris	12
Purple Nest	8
Red Nest	10
Vincci Palace	11

EATING

El Alto de Colón	19
Arrop	11
Bar Pilar	9
La Bodeguilla del Gato	10
Burdeos in Love	16
Ca' Sento	21
Casa Montaña	20
Kaymus	1
Ocho y Medio	14
Palau Fesol	18
La Pepica	22
La Salvaora	7
La Sucursal	2

CLUBS

Las Ánimas	9
Las Ánimas Puerto	8
La Bolseria	6
Deseo 54	1
Fox Congo	4
Jimmy Glass	2
The Music Box	3
Pacha	10
Velvet	7
Venial	5

BARS

Café de las Horas	3
Café Madrid	17
Cafe del Negrito and Cava del Negret	8
Café Tocado	25
Cava Siglos	4
Destino 56	24
Johnny Marracas	5
Radio City	15
Sant Jaume	6
El Tornillo	12
L'Umbracle Terraza	26
Vinicius Pub	13
Vivir Sin Dormir	23

0 —————— 200
metres

Alicante & Albacete

THE VALENCIA CARD

If you plan on exploring the city extensively, consider buying a **Valencia Card** (€12/18/22 for one, two or three days; ☎900 701 818, ⓦvalenciatouristcard.com), which gives you unlimited access to the entire transport system and discounted entry to many museums, and for bike rental and guided tours, as well as money off your bill at bars and restaurants – you can buy one at most *turismo* offices, at major hotels and newspaper kiosks.

---

not completely escaped criticism. Some feel that the vast cost of constructing it should have been used to tackle the city's pressing social issues, while others have been less than overwhelmed by some of the content inside the Ciudad's startling structures.

In your explorations, stroll through the **Umbracle**, a series of eighteen-metre-high arches towering over a landscaped walkway shaded with vegetation from throughout the region, including palms, honeysuckle, bougainvillea and, of course, orange trees.

Hemisfèric

Normally 10am–7pm, open later in summer • €7.70

The **Hemisfèric**, one of the more astonishing buildings of the complex, is a striking eye-shaped concrete structure – complete with lashes, and an eyeball that forms a huge concave screen used to project IMAX movies, laser shows, nature documentaries and more.

Museo de las Ciencias

Daily 10am–7pm, July to mid-Sept till 9pm • €7.70

The colossal **Museo de las Ciencias** (Science Museum), whose protruding supports make the building resemble a giant sun-bleached carcass, is crammed with interactive exhibits about science, sport and the human body that are sure to appeal to children, from a colourful 3D representation of DNA to a Foucault Pendulum, which at 34m is one of the longest in the world.

Parque Oceanográfico

Mid-June to mid-July daily 10am–8pm; mid-July to Aug daily 10am–midnight; Sept to mid-Oct Mon–Fri & Sun 10am–7pm, Sat 10am–8pm; rest of the year Mon–Fri & Sun 10am–6pm, Sat 10am–8pm • €24.50, shark encounter €300 per dive

The **Parque Oceanográfico**, designed by Félix Candela, is one of the world's largest aquariums. It's divided into multiple zones, with beluga whales in the Arctic area, Japanese spider crabs in the temperate zone and a kaleidoscopic collection of reef fish, sharks and turtles in the seventy-metre tunnel that forms the tropical zone. The park also has all manner of splashy events, including the thrilling (though pricey) **Encuentro con Tiburones** (Shark Encounter), where you can scuba-dive with sharks; and a **penguin visit**, popular with kids, where you can feed Humboldt penguins and view their hatchery and rearing area. In the summer, the aquarium sometimes opens for night visits, while the restaurant is a sleek underwater space where you dine with fish darting past your table.

CIUDAD DE LAS ARTES: TICKETS AND TRANSPORT

You can buy tickets for the Ciudad de las Artes y las Ciencias individually at each sight, or opt for one of several discounted **ticket options**. A combined entrance to all three main attractions is €32.40, and is valid for one, two or three (not necessarily consecutive) days; you'll need at least one full day to see everything. The CAC also offers a walking tour (€7.70; daily 10:30am, 12:30pm & 4:30pm, plus 6:30pm in summer; English tours available).

There are several **transport links** to the CAC, including the bus #35 (a special tourist route) from Avda. Marqués de Sotelo, just south of the Plaza del Ayuntamiento. You can also catch #95 at the Torres de Serrano or Plaza de América. The closest **metro** stop is Alameda (20min walk). If you drive, you can park at the Umbracle car park (€2/hr).

12

Palacio de les Arts Reina Sofía and L'Ágora

Guided tours daily at 11.30am & 1pm · €8 · Box office ☎ 902 202 383, ⓦ lesarts.com

The majestic pistachio-nut-shaped **Palacio de las Artes** is a high-tech performing arts palace, with renowned musical director Lorin Maazel at the helm. Stages and halls of varying sizes – all with splendid acoustics – host ballet, opera and classical-music concerts, among others. Performances are staged throughout the year, and it's well worth snagging a ticket to see one. The equally impressive 80m L'Ágora (open for events only), is a multifunctional space inaugurated in November 2009 to host the Valencia 500 Open tennis tournament, and now features various events, from sports meets to the glittering annual Valencia Fashion Week.

Plaza Ayuntamiento

Museo Histórico Municipal Mon–Fri 9am–2pm · Free · ☎ 963 525 478

In the heart of Valencia, just north of the train station, the **Plaza del Ayuntamiento** is a handsome central square lined with flower stalls, and an impressive floodlit fountain. The *ayuntamiento* itself houses the **Museo Histórico Municipal**, whose library has an impressive eighteenth-century map of Valencia showing the city walls intact.

Estación del Norte

Built in 1917, the **Estación del Norte**, just south of the Plaza del Ayuntamiento on c/Xàtiva, is another of the city's lovely, and surprisingly well preserved, *modernista* buildings. Peer around at the detailed ceramic mosaics, tiled ceilings and carved wooden doorways, both in the main foyer and in a few side-rooms.

12

Museo Nacional de Cerámica

Poeta Querol 2 · Tues–Sat 10am–2pm & 4–8pm, Sun 10am–2pm · €3, free Sat afternoon & Sun · ☎ 963 516 392

The distinctive feature of Valencian architecture is its wealth of elaborate Baroque facades – you'll see them on almost every old building in town, but none so extraordinary or rich as the **Palacio del Marqués de Dos Aguas**. Hipólito Rovira, who designed its amazing alabaster doorway, died insane in 1740, which should come as no surprise to anyone who sees it. Inside the *palacio* is the **Museo Nacional de Cerámica**, with a vast collection of ceramics from all over Spain, and particularly Valencia, itself a major ceramics centre, largely owing to the size of its *morisco* population. Apart from an impressive display of *azulejos*, the collection contains some stunning plates with gold and copper varnishes (*reflejos*) and a trio of evocatively ornate eighteenth-century carriages.

Plaza Patriarca

Colegio del Patriarca Daily 11am–1.30pm · €2 · ☎ 963 514 176

Rising over the Plaza Patriarca is the Neoclassical former **Universidad**, with lovely cloisters where free classical concerts are sometimes held in the summer, and the beautiful Renaissance **Colegio del Patriarca**, with a small **art museum** that includes works by El Greco, Morales and Ribalta. The university **library** contains the first book printed in Spain, *Les Trobes*, in 1474.

Catedral and around

Pl. de la Reina · **Catedral** daily 8.30am–8.30pm · Free **Museum** Mon–Sat 10am–5.30pm, Sun 2–5.30pm · €4, includes entry to cathedral **Miguelete tower** Mon–Fri 10am–7.30, Sun 10am–1pm & 5–7.30pm · €2 · ☎ 963 918 127

The café-rich **Plaza de la Reina** is overlooked by the florid spire of the church of Santa Catalina and octagonal tower of Valencia's **Catedral**. Founded in the

FALLAS: VALENCIA ON FIRE

Valencia erupts in a blaze of colour and noise for the Fiesta de las Fallas, March 12 to 19. During the year, each *barrio* or neighbourhood builds satirical caricatures or *fallas*, some as tall as buildings. These begin to appear in the plazas at the beginning of March and are judged and awarded prizes before being set alight at midnight on March 19, the **Nit de Foc** – traditionally, carpenters celebrated the beginning of spring by decorating the torches (*foc* in Valenciano) they used over winter and adding them to a ritual bonfire. The *fallas* are ignited in succession – and the last to go up are the prize winners. Each *falla* has a small model or *ninot* beside it, usually created by the children of the *barrio*. These are exhibited in La Lonja before the fiesta begins, and the best displayed in the Museu Fallero (see p.807); the rest are burned with the *fallas*.

During the fiesta, **processions** of *falleros*, dressed in traditional costume and accompanied by bands, carry flowers to the Plaza de la Virgen, where they are massed to create the skirt of a huge statue of La Virgen. The daily Las Mascaletas **firecracker display** (2pm in the Plaza del Ayuntamiento) sees the whole city racing to this central square for a ten-minute series of body-shuddering explosions. There are also nightly fireworks, bullfights, paella contests in the streets and *chocolate y buñuelos* stalls. Finally, around 1am on March 19, the *falla* of the Plaza del Ayuntamiento goes up in flames, followed by the last thunderous firework display of the Nit de Foc.

thirteenth century, the cathedral embraces an eclectic combination of architectural styles, with the lavishly ornate Baroque main entrance leading to a largely Gothic-built interior. It's an exhausting climb up the tower, known as the **Miguelete**, but the spectacular views of the city and its many blue-domed churches more than compensate. The **museum** contains more paintings and also a 2300-kilo tabernacle made from gold, silver and jewels donated by the Valencian people. Above the structure's crossing, the cathedral's fourteenth-century lantern is another fine feature, as are its soaring windows glazed with thin sheets of alabaster to let in the Valencian light.

Many visitors, however, come just for the cathedral's most celebrated religious icon: a gold-and-agate chalice (the Santo Cáliz), said to be the one used by Christ at the Last Supper – the **Holy Grail** itself, and no mean asset in an era of post-*Da Vinci Code* fever. It's certainly old and, hidden away throughout the Dark Ages in a monastery in northern Aragón, it really did inspire many of the legends associated with the Grail. Other treasures include the two Goya paintings of the San Francisco chapel, one of which depicts an exorcism (the corpse was originally naked, but after Goya's death a sheet was painted over it).

Plaza de la Virgen

Leaving the cathedral through the Puerta de los Apóstoles, you enter the **Plaza de la Virgen**. Here, close to the doorway, the Tribunal de las Aguas (the black-clad regulatory body of Valencia's water users) meets at noon every Thursday to judge grievances about the irrigation system of the *huertas*. The practice dates back to Moorish times, and Blasco Ibáñez (1867–1928) describes their workings in detail in his novel *La Barraca*, which is about peasant life in the Valencian *huerta* and remains the best guide to the life of the region at that time.

Nuestra Señora de los Desamparados

Pl. de la Virgen • Mon–Fri 6.45am–1.45pm & 4.30–8.45pm, Sat & Sun 7.30–1.45pm–4.30–8.45pm • Free • ☎ 963 918 611

Two footbridges allow the clergy (only) to go straight from the cathedral into the archbishop's palace and on to the domed basilica of **Nuestra Señora de los Desamparados**, also on the Plaza de la Virgen, where thousands of candles constantly burn in front of the image of the Virgin, patron of Valencia.

Palau de la Generalitat

C/Caballeros • Only open via reservation; enquire at the *turismo*

From the Plaza de la Virgen, c/Caballeros leads to the **Palau de la Generalitat**, which dates from the fifteenth century and today is the seat of the Valencian autonomous government. Inside, you can see beautifully painted ceilings and frescoes depicting a meeting of the assembly (1592) in the Salón Dorado, as well as the tiled Salón de Cortés.

La Lonja

Pl. del Mercado • Tues–Sat 10am–2pm & 4.30–8.30pm, Sun 10am–3pm • Free • ☎ 963 525 478

If you tire of Baroque excesses, you could head for the wonderfully sombre interior of the Gothic **La Lonja** (also known as La Lonja de la Seda, or the Silk Exchange). The main focus of this UNESCO-listed building is its superb main hall, with an elegant rib-vaulted ceiling supported by slender, spiralling columns; the wooden trading tables are now used on Sundays by coin and stamp collectors.

Mercado Central

Pl. del Mercado • Mon–Sat 8am–2.30pm • ☎ 963 829 101

The enormous **Mercado Central**, a *modernista* iron, girder and glass structure built in 1928, is embellished with a collage of tiles and mosaics, and crowned with swordfish and parrot weather vanes. It's one of the biggest markets in Europe – fitting for *huerta* country – with almost a thousand stalls selling fruit and vegetables, meat and seafood.

Mercado Colón

C/Cirilo Amorós • Daily 7am–1.30pm • ☎ 963 525 478

About 1km southeast of the Mercado Central, Valencia's other market, the renovated **Mercado Colón**, is an even more impressive *modernista* building. Its open-sided rectangular design loosely resembles a church, with slim wrought-iron columns supporting a steep pitched roof, and monumental arched facades at either end. However, it's the building's detail that's really outstanding, combining two-tone brickwork with broken-tile mosaic chimneys, features that reveal the influence of *modernista* architect Antoni Gaudí – indeed, the market's architect, Francisco Mora, was a close friend of the Catalan genius. The Mercado Colón also houses colourful flower stalls, a bookstore, upmarket cafés and the lovely restaurant *El Alto de Colón* (see p.811), with a vaulted ceiling of a Valencian mosaic, and large windows that offer glimpses of the market's eye-catching *modernista* ironwork.

Museu de Bellas Artes and the Jardines del Real

C/San Pío V 9 **Museu de Belles Artes** Tues–Sun 10am–8pm • Free • ☎ 963 870 300 • **Jardines del Real** Daily 8am–sunset • Free

The **Museu de Belles Artes**, on the far side of the river, has one of the best general collections in Spain, with works by Bosch, El Greco, Goya, Velázquez, Ribera and Ribalta, as well as quantities of modern Valencian art. The museum takes up the southwest corner of the **Jardines del Real** (also called Los Viveros). The lovely gardens – the largest of Valencia's parks – are well worth a stroll, and host various outdoor concerts in the summer.

Torres Serranos

Pl. de los Fueros • Tues–Sat 10am–2pm & 4.30–8.30pm, Sun 10am–3pm • €2, free Sun • ☎ 963 919 070

The fourteenth-century **Torres Serranos**, once part of Valencia's fortified walls, is an impressive gateway defending the entrance to town across the Río Turia. Climb up to the top for panoramic views over the city; to the west, you can pick out another gateway, the Torres de Quart, which dates from the fifteenth century.

THE PORT AND THE PLAYAS

Barcelona famously transformed its waterfront from drab to dazzling, and Valencia has done something similar to its city coastline, having significantly spruced up its beaches and boardwalk over the last decade. In 2007, Valencia became the first European port since 1851 to host the America's Cup (which was staged here again in 2010), and to celebrate the event, parts of the forgotten waterfront were redeveloped, with a gleaming new **marina** and the eye-catching **Veles e Vents** ("Sails and Winds") structure designed by British architect David Chipperfield helping to transform the area. The Valencia Street Circuit was also constructed in the port area as the race site of the 2008 **Formula One European Grand Prix**, which will continue to be held here until 2014.

As for **beaches**, you can catch some rays on the soft sand of the broad and breezy playas Malvarrosa and Las Arenas, which are backed by the Paseo Marítimo and extend along the waterfront. The outdoor cafés, bars and clubs here are particularly popular in the summer months. There are a number of ways to get to Malvarrosa and Las Arenas, but one easy route is to take the #5 metro at the central Colón station to Marítim Serrería, and switch to the #6 line to Neptú, from where you can walk north along the boardwalk to the sands. You can also catch buses from Plaza del Ayuntamiento, often supplemented during the summer by buses from various points in the centre; ask at the tourist office.

El Salér, 10km south of the city, is also a pleasant beach: a long, wide stretch of sand with pine trees behind. Autocares Herca buses (☎ 963 491 250, ⓦ autocaresherca) leave from various points around town, including the corner of Gran Vía Germanías and c/Sueca, and Plaza Cánovas (May–Sept every 30min; Oct–April hourly; 30min).

Instituto Valenciano de Arte Moderno

12

C/Guillém de Castro 118 • Tues–Sun 10am–8pm, till 9pm July & Aug • €2, free Sun • ⓦ ivam.es

The **Instituto Valenciano de Arte Moderno (IVAM)** features a permanent display of works by sculptor Julio González, as well as many excellent temporary exhibitions by mainly Spanish contemporary artists. It also has a smaller gallery near Plaza del Carmen at c/Museu 2 (opening dependent on exhibitions; free), currently devoted to temporary shows. In keeping with other well-known modern-art museums, IVAM also features an excellent restaurant, *La Sucursal* (see p.812).

Casa-Museo José Benlliure

C/Blanquerias 23 • Tues–Sat 10am–2pm & 4.30–8pm, Sun 10am–3pm • €2 • ☎ 963 916 662

Set in the beautifully renovated home of Valencian painter and sculptor José Benlliure, the **Casa-Museo José Benlliure** displays historical and religious works, from paintings and drawings to sculptures and ceramics. Pieces by his son, Pepino, are also on show, as are works by his brother, the established sculptor Mariano Benlliure, and there's a lovely flower garden out back.

Museu Fallero

Pl. Monteolivete 4 • Tues–Sat 10am–2pm & 4.30–8.30pm, Sun 10am–3pm • €2 • ☎ 963 525 478

Ten minutes' walk from Plaza de la Reina, the **Museu Fallero** offers a fascinating insight into Valencia's Fiesta de las Fallas. On display are an array of *ninots* that have been voted the best of their year, and consequently saved from the flames.

Museo del Gremio de Artistas Falleros

Avda. San José Artesano 17 • Mon–Fri 10am–2pm & 4–7pm, Sat 10am–2pm; closed Aug • €2.50 • ☎ 963 479 623, ⓦ gremiodeartistasfalleros.com • Bus #12 from c/Cerdan de Tallada, near the Palacio de Justicia.

If you can't get enough of *ninots*, the **Museo del Gremio de Artistas Falleros** houses the ones-that-got-away by permission of the Guild of Fallas Artists, and a photo exhibition.

Bioparc

Avda. Pío Baroja • Daily: summer 10am–9pm; rest of year until 6/9pm • €20, under 12 €15 • ☎ 902 250 340, ⊚ bioparcvalencia.es • Metro lines #3 and #5 to Nou d'Octubre (10min walk); or buses #7, #17, #29 and #95 from various different points

If you're travelling with kids, the city's relatively new **Bioparc**, an open-air zoo west of the city centre, might entice. As far as zoos go, this well-maintained specimen tries to be a different sort of animal. The creators have made serious attempts to be as eco-aware and animal-friendly as possible, with re-created African savanna and Malagasy landscapes that are home to roaming rhinos, giraffes, antelopes, gorillas, leopards, elephants and lions.

Casa-Museo de Vicente Blasco Ibáñez

C/Isabel de Villena • Tues–Sat 10am–2pm & 4.30–8.30pm, Sun 10am–3pm • €2, free on Sun • ☎ 963 525 478

The **Casa-Museo de Vicente Blasco Ibáñez** explores the life of the celebrated Valencian author, journalist and political activist Vicente Blasco Ibáñez (1867–1928). An outspoken antimonarchist, he was best known in the English-speaking world for his World War I novel *Los Cuatro Jinetes del Apocalipsis* (The Four Horsemen of the Apocalypse), which was later made into a film. His renovated home, on Malvarrosa beach, has been turned into an in-depth museum featuring personal mementos, photographs, documents and more, all of which offer insight both into Blasco Ibáñez himself and the political history of Valencia and Spain during his era.

ARRIVAL AND DEPARTURE VALENCIA

12

BY PLANE

Valencia airport (☎ 961 598 500, ⊚ aena.es) is 8km west of town, and served by metro lines #1 & #3; the most convenient stop for the centre is Colón. Alternatively, a taxi will set you back around €14. EasyJet and Ryanair fly to and from the UK, while other airlines, including Air Europa, Air Berlin and Vueling, fly to other parts of Europe and Spain.

BY TRAIN

Estación del Norte is close to the town centre; walk north along Avda. Marqués de Sotelo to the Pl. del Ayuntamiento, the central square.

Destinations Alicante (12 daily; 1hr 30min–2hr 15min); Barcelona (14 daily; 2hr 50min–4hr 45min); Benicàssim (8 daily; 1hr 10min); Castellón de la Plana (every 30min; 45min–1hr); El Puig (every 20min; 20min); Gandía (every 30min; 50min); Madrid (10–14 daily; 3hr 30min–4hr 30min); Málaga (6 daily; 9hr); Murcia (12 daily; 3hr 25min); Orihuela (12 daily; 3hr); Peñíscola (9 daily; 1hr 30min); Sagunto (every 30min; 30min); Segorbe (3 daily; 1hr); Teruel (3 daily; 2hr 25min); Xàtiva (every 30min; 1hr); and Zaragoza (2 daily; 5hr–6hr 45min).

Estación Joaquín Sorolla (☎ 902 432 343, ⊚ adif.es), just south of Estación del Norte, is the new station for the Madrid–Levante high-speed AVE line. There are free shuttles from Estación del Norte to Sorolla for AVE ticket holders. There's also a metro stop, Joaquín Sorolla Station, nearby, and a taxi rank just outside. When fully operational, the AVE line will also serve Alicante, Castellón, Murcia and Cartagena.
Destinations Madrid (around 15 daily; 1hr 40min).

BY BUS

Valencia's bus station is some way out on the north side of the river; take local bus #8 or #79 or the metro to Turia, or allow a half-hour if you decide to walk. Regular buses travel from Valencia to:

Destinations Alicante (15–21 daily; 2hr 30min–3hr 30min); Barcelona (17–19 daily; 4hr 15min–5hr); Benidorm (15–20 daily; 2hr 30min); Bilbao (3 daily; 9hr); Castellón de la Plana (4–9 daily; 1hr 30min–2hr); Cuenca (3 daily; 4hr); Denia (10–11 daily; 1hr 45min); Gandía (11–14 daily; 1hr); Madrid (16–19 daily; 4hr); Murcia (11–14 daily; 3hr 15min); and Sagunto (25 daily; 45min).

BY FERRY

Puerto de Valencia The Balearic ferry terminal connects with Pl. del Ayuntamiento via bus #4 and with the train station via bus #19. Ferries are operated by Acciona Trasmediterránea (☎ 902 454 645, ⊚ trasmediterranea .es), Iscomar (☎ 902 119 128, ⊚ iscomar.com) and Balèaria (☎ 902 160 180, ⊚ balearia.com).

Destinations Acciona Trasmediterránea: Palma de Mallorca (June–Sept 2 daily; 5hr 45min & 7hr 15min; Oct–May weekly; 9hr); Ibiza (June–Sept daily; 2hr 45min; Oct–May weekly; 4hr 45min); Maó, Menorca (Sat; 14hr).
Iscomar: Palma (5 weekly; 9hr 30min).
Balèaria: Ibiza (daily; 3hr 45min); Palma (daily; 6hr 45min).

VALENCIA BY BIKE

With its famously balmy weather, relatively flat terrain and network of well-maintained bike lanes (including in the Río Turia riverbed park and near the beaches), Valencia is a great place to explore by bike. The city's new **public bike scheme**, ValenBiSi (ⓦ valenbisi.es), features 2750 cycles distributed across 275 stations throughout the city, including the centre and Barrio del Carmen. There are several options if you want to hop on one of the bikes – the shortest is the seven-day subscription (€10). Once you have a subscription, the first 30min is free, and then it's €1 for the next 30min. After that, it's €3/hr. Credit cards are accepted.

Another option is to rent a bike from the well-run Orange Bikes, c/Santa Teresa 8 (ⓣ 963 917 551, ⓦ orangebikes.net), with bicycles for €9–15 per day; they also do repairs.

GETTING AROUND

By metro, bus and on foot Most of Valencia's sights are centrally located and can be reached on foot, but the city also has an efficient, well-maintained public transport system – metro, trams and buses – which are helpful for reaching outlying neighbourhoods and sights (including the Ciudad de las Artes y Ciencias) and the beaches. Metro stations in the city centre include Xàtiva and Colón, where you can connect with several metro lines. Local EMT buses (ⓦ emtvalencia.es) cost €1.30 per journey, and they also sell various discount multi-use tickets; trams and metro are €1.40 for inner zone A, which covers central Valencia (more info on the metro system at ⓦ metrovalencia.com). If you plan on using public transport regularly, a Valencia Card

(see below) is a good way to save. The hop-on, hop-off Valencia Bus Turístic (ⓣ 963 414 400, ⓦ valenciabusturistic.com; €15/24hr, €18/48hr) offers various routes around the city, including Historic or Maritime Valencia, as well as to Albufera (see p.814).

By car Rental companies in Valencia include Avis (airport & Gran Vía de Ramón y Cajal 2, among other locations; ⓣ 963 510 734, ⓦ avis.com); Hertz (airport & c/Segorbe 7 ⓣ 963 415 036, ⓦ hertz.com); and Atesa (airport & Estación del Norte ⓣ 963 517 145, ⓦ atesa.es).

By taxi Radio Taxi ⓣ 963 703 333; Tele Taxi ⓣ 963 571 313; Valencia Taxi ⓣ 963 740 202.

INFORMATION AND TOURS

Turismo The main *turismo* is at Pl. de la Reina 19 (Mon–Sat 9am–7pm, Sun 10am–2pm; ⓣ 963 153 931, ⓦ turisvalencia.es). There are also branches in Pl. del Ayuntamiento (same hours; ⓣ 963 524 908, ⓦ turisvalencia.es), at the airport and at the Joaquín Sorolla train station. Valencia has several helpful regional offices including at c/Paz 48 (Mon–Fri 9am–7pm, Sat 10am–2pm & Sun 11am–2pm; ⓣ 963 986

422, ⓦ comunitatvalenciana.com) and c/Poeta Querol (Mon–Fri 9.30am–7pm, Sat 10am–2pm, Sun 11am–2pm; ⓣ 963 514 907, ⓦ valenciaterraimar.org).

Tours Valencia Guías, Paseo de la Pechina 32 (ⓣ 963 850 827, ⓦ valenciaguias.com), offers a range of excellent tours in many languages, including by bike.

ACCOMMODATION

Valencia offers a huge range of **accommodation**, from historical hotels to hip hostels and sunny beachfront properties. The city centre, between the train station and the Río Turia, is sprinkled with budget hotels and hostels, while you'll find a number of comfortable spots overlooking the beaches.

THE CITY CENTRE AND AROUND

La Casa Azul Vinos & Rooms Palafox 7, cnr Pl. del Mercado ⓣ 963 153 705, ⓦ lacasaazulvinosandrooms.com. Curl up on an opium bed at this quirky, three-room hotel run by local jeweller Vicente Gracia. Spanish royalty wear his unique brooches and necklaces, and the rooms are designed with the same kind of flair, though bathrooms can be small. The roof terrace is a great place to enjoy a glass of wine overlooking the old town. **€118**

Center Valencia Youth Hostel c/Samaniego 18 ⓣ 963 914 915, ⓦ center-valencia.com. Just about as central as you can get, this amiable hostel sits in Barrio del Carmen, just a stumble away from a slew of bars and cafés. **€19**

Hôme Youth Hostel & Hôme Backpackers c/La Lonja 4 ⓣ 963 916 229 & Pl. Vicente Iborra ⓣ 963 913 797, ⓦ likeathome.net. These lively backpacker hostels are in the historic quarter and feature retro-chic furnishings and clean dorms, plus double rooms. Full kitchen, laundry, internet. *Hôme Youth Hostel*: dorms **€17**, doubles **€46**; *Hôme Backpackers*: dorms **€12**, doubles **€46**

Hospes Palau de Mar Navarro Reverter 14 ⓣ 963 162 884, ⓦ hospes.com. Set in a nineteenth-century baronial mansion, this handsome hotel exudes a lovely blend of old and new, from the renovated historic facade to the sleek, white interior that borders on minimalist. Get pampered at the Bodyna Spa, and then dine on Mediterranean fare at

12

the *Senzone*. Restaurant Tues–Sat 1.30–4pm & 8.30–11pm. **€115**

Hostal Antigua Morellana c/En Bou 2 ⊙ 963 915 773, ⓦ hostalam.com. The quiet rooms at this cheerful, well-maintained hotel close to the Barrio del Carmen offers quiet excellent value. Book ahead. **€55**

Hostal Venecia c/En Llop 5 ⊙ 963 524 267, ⓦ hotelvenecia.com. Don't be fooled by the *hostal* tag: this is a stylish, well-managed, central hotel. Some rooms come with views over the Pl. del Ayuntamiento, and all are clean and comfy. **€59**

Hotel Acta del Carmen Blanquerías 11 ⊙ 962 057 700, ⓦ hotel-carmenvalencia.com. This colourful, boutique-style hotel – quirky art, walls painted in red and blue – sits in the middle of the Barrio del Carmen's bustle. **€65**

Hotel Ad Hoc c/Boix 4 ⊙ 963 919 140, ⓦ adhochoteles .com. One of Valencia's first boutique hotels, this is suitably comfortable and elegant, with exposed brick walls and textile wall-hangings, in a building with plenty of period character. **€96**

Hotel Husa Dimar Gran Vía del Marqués del Turia 80 ⊙ 963 951 030. Comfy, stylish rooms, and a fairly central location, on the edge of the old town. **€80**

Hotel Palacio Marqués del Caro Almirante 14 ⊙ 963 925 566, ⓦ marquesdecaro.com. This luxury boutique hotel, in a thirteenth-century palace, reveals a gorgeous blend of history and *haute* style. The owners (one of whom is a descendant of the last Moorish King of Valencia) discovered a large section of Moorish wall when renovating the building, and incorporated it into the design of the hotel; the result is a bewitching glimpse into Valencia of the past, with upscale amenities that are very much from the present.

Hotel Sorolla Centro Convento Santa Clara 5 ⊙ 963 523 392, ⓦ hotelsorolla.com. Comfortable, slightly Asian-influenced rooms – and well-placed for the new Joaquín Sorolla high-speed train station, which is 600m away. **€86**

Pensión Paris c/Salvá 12 ⊙ 963 526 766, ⓦ pensionparis.com. Inviting, family-owned *pensión*. Clean, comfy rooms (some with en-suite bathrooms, others with shower and shared bathroom) are simply furnished but well tended, and have tightly focused views of the old university. **€34**, with bathroom **€42**

Red Nest & Purple Nest c/de la Paz 36 ⊙ 963 427 168 & Pl. Tetuan 5 ⊙ 963 532 561, ⓦ nesthostelsvalencia .com. Bright, cheery, sister backpacker hostels with well-maintained dorms and doubles, and a youthful energy. *Purple Nest* has its own bar, which makes for a particularly social atmosphere. Dorm **€15**, doubles **€46**

★ **Vincci Palace** La Paz 42 ⊙ 962 062 377, ⓦ vinccihoteles.com. Well-heeled hotel with the history to match, housed in a former *palacete* that offered safe lodging to intellectuals during the Civil War, with a lovely facade fronted by wrought-iron balconies. Comfortable rooms, soft beds, spic-and-span bathrooms and all the amenities. **€96**

THE PORT AND THE BEACHES

El Coso del Mar Paseo Neptuno 12 ⊙ 963 728 213, ⓦ elcosodelmar.com. If you're in Valencia for the *playa*, then you'll like the location of this beachside hotel, with easy access to Playa Malvarrosa. Rooms are decent, though ask for a beachside view when booking, as only certain rooms have them. It's about a half-hour journey into town, walking to and hopping on the tram. **€109**

Devesa Gardens Near El Saler beach and La Albufera ⊙ 961 611 136, ⓦ devesagardens.com. Some 15km southeast of Valencia, with spacious grounds surrounded by pine forest, and great amenities including a swimming pool, tennis courts and also simple wooden bungalows. Adults **€5.60** plus **€5.60** per tent; bungalows **€79.50**

Hostal El Globo Paseo de Neptuno 42–44 ⊙ 963 727 777, ⓦ hostalelglobo.com. Friendly place with simple, funkily furnished rooms – some with great views – near the beach. They also run the long-established bar *Vivir Sin Dormir* (see p.813). **€75**

Hotel Las Arenas Eugenia Viñes 22–24 ⊙ 963 120 600, ⓦ hotel-lasarenas.com. Valencia's only five-star beachside

12

FASHION FORWARD

Move over Madrid and Barcelona, and make room for fashion diva Valencia. The city has a rich and vibrant **fashion culture**, and twice a year, in spring and autumn, the glossy Valencia Fashion Week (ⓦ www.valenciafashionweek.com) sees catwalk shows from all the latest and greatest local and national designers. Valencia's home-grown designers have made a splash in the international scene: look out for the flamboyant, gypsy-inspired pieces of Francis Montesinos; the sexy styles of Alex Vida; the urban look of Alejandro Sáez de la Torre; bold, geometric swimwear from Dolores Cortés; Higinio Mateu's frisky dresses; and the avant-garde, flouncy threads of Tonuca. Shoes and accessories rival the clothes, with such renowned designers as jeweller Vicente Gracia, whose reinvented antique brooches have been worn by the Queen of Spain herself.

Where to shop? You can find both local and international designs throughout Valencia, from small boutiques to big department stores, particularly around the old town and city centre, including the Eixample (Ensanche) district, between Calle Colón and Gran Vía del Marqués del Turia; and Calle Jorge Juan by Mercado Colón.

hotel maximizes its proximity to the sea: the morning light fills the cream and dark-wood rooms; sun-speckled terraces face the sea; and it's a short stroll to the beach. **€190**
Hotel Neptuno Paseo de Neptuno 2 ☏963 567 777, ⓦhotelneptunovalencia.com. Light-flooded hotel with a minimalist, modern look: white furnishings, a glass lift,

gleaming hardwood floors and a beach-facing terrace strewn with low sofas and plump red pillows – a prime spot to ease into the Valencia evening. The top-notch *Tridente* restaurant serves up creative Valencian cuisine. Rates include breakfast. Restaurant daily 1–4pm & 8.30–11pm; closed Sun dinner. **€120**

EATING

As befits Spain's third-largest city, Valencia's cuisine scene is wonderfully varied and suits all budgets. For **tapas** and cheap eats, head to the area around the Mercado Central, where there are plenty of places offering set meals for under €15; Barrio del Carmen is also sprinkled with lively tapas bars. The once-gritty, now-hip Russafa, just south of the centre, has continued to evolve into one of Valencia's liveliest multi ethnic neighbourhoods, where you can find everything from Arabic tearooms to Halal butchers.

Valencia has also marched into the gourmet culinary echelons with style and swagger: witness such standouts as *Arrop* and *Ca' Sento*. And while the city is the home of **paella**, the finest places to eat it are, in fact, out of town, in Perellonet or El Palmar (see p.815), or along the city beach – Paseo Neptuno is lined with small paella and *marisco* restaurants.

RESTAURANTS

El Alto de Colón Mercado Colón ☏963 530 900, ⓦgrupoelalto.com. Elegant, vaulted restaurant with a high-end Mediterranean menu (at high-end prices) that features lots of innovative flourishes, such as fresh shellfish heaped on sticky rice. Mon–Fri 2–4pm & 9–11pm, 9–11pm; closed Aug.

★ **Arrop** Hotel Palacio Marqués de Caro, c/Almirante 14 ☏963 155 287, ⓦarrop.com. Valencian cuisine is taken to a high art at this new Michelin-starred restaurant. The superb dishes – traditional with a twist – reveal chef Ricard Camarena's prowess in the kitchen, from a shellfish broth draped delicately with flower petals to *calamari* bathed in its own ink. The tasting *menú* (€78) celebrates the newest dishes; there's also a classics *menú* (€59) or, perhaps the best deal, a weekday lunch *menú* for €30. Tues–Sat 1.30–3.30pm & 9–10.30pm.

Burdeos in Love c/Mar 4 ☏963 914 350, ⓦburdeosinlove.com. Giant forks speared with wine corks flank the doorway of this stylish restaurant, where rich, creative dishes like cod with a parmesan mousse, and a mini veal burger topped with a quail egg, pair beautifully with robust Spanish reds. €30 *menú*. Mon–Sat 1.30–4pm & 8.30–11.30pm.

★ **Ca' Sento** c/Méndez Núñez 17 ☏963 301 775, ⓦcasento.net. Tucked away in a low-key, portside neighbourhood west of the centre, *Ca' Sento*'s discreet appearance belies the creative prowess in the kitchen. The menu hinges on the freshest *frutas del mar*, with innovative chef Raúl Aleixandre teasing out natural, sea-soaked flavours and adding unique accompaniments: tender squid quivers under a spray of caramelized onion purée and asparagus arrives with a dollop of warm mayonnaise foam and trout eggs. The elaborate €110 tasting *menú* provides the full experience; other excellent *menús* range from €50 to €90 per person. Ⓜ Metro Marítim-Serrería, then a 15min walk. Reservations essential. Tues–Sat 2–4pm & 9–11pm; closed early Aug & slate March.

Kaymus Avda. del Mestre Rodrigo 44 ☏963 486 666, ⓦkaymus.es. This classy restaurant just north of the city centre fuses modern and traditional – try the superb *arroces* (rice dishes), like cod and cauliflower. The crisp dining room, with paintings in modern stripes and swirls that play against the white walls, caters to the growing business district near the gleaming Palacio de Congresos (conference centre). Tasting *menú* €45; lunch and dinner *menú* €28/€32. Daily 2–4pm & 9–11pm, closed Mon dinner.

Ocho y Medio Pl. Lope de Vega 5 ☏963 922 022, ⓦelochoymedio.com. Named after the Fellini film, this bi-level restaurant with dusky peach walls, blonde-wood floors and views of the Santa Catalina church, excels at innovative French-tinged Mediterranean fare, from their speciality of rich foie gras to aromatic paellas or grilled squid with black risotto. Mains €17–25. Daily noon–midnight; hours can vary in winter.

★ **Palau Fesol** Hernán Cortés 7 ☏963 529 323, ⓦpalacefesol.com. Feast on plump sardines, fragrant *arroces* and superb wines (at mid-range to expensive prices) at this graceful restaurant, which turned 100 in 2009 – proof that things do get better with age. The rustic dining room boasts a colourful mosaic, beamed ceiling and stone walls, while the gracious owner is the consummate host. Daily 1–6pm, dinner generally group reservations only; closed second half of Aug.

La Pepica Paseo Neptuno 6 ☏963 710 366, ⓦlapepica.com. Founded in 1898, this inviting, spacious paella restaurant has undeniable staying power: over the decades, it has hosted plenty of the rich and famous, from Hemingway and Orson Welles to swaggering bullfighters and the Spanish royal family. Settle in on the sun-speckled terrace and tuck into fresh fish and seafood or aromatic paellas. Daily 1–4pm & 8.30–11pm; closed second half of Nov.

La Salvaora c/Calatrava 19 ☏963 921 484, ⓦlasalvaora.com. This slender Andalucian restaurant, with high, dark-wood tables and white marble floors, pays homage to flamenco singers and stars via black-and-white

12

photos on the walls. The creative fare includes tripe tossed with red peppers and steak with a port reduction. Their weekday lunch *menú* is excellent value at €11 (Mon–Thurs). Daily 1.30–3.30pm & 8.30–11.30pm, closed Mon lunch.

La Sucursal c/Guillém de Castro 118 ☎963 746 665. Valencia's IVAM gallery features a superb restaurant that matches (if not sometimes trumps) the art within. The elegant, sparse *La Sucursal* features artisanal cuisine with a twist, from saffron-scented rice studded with lobster to a cauliflower mousse. Mains are €21–35. Daily 2–3.30pm & 9–11pm, closed Sat lunch, Sun and second half of Aug.

TAPAS BARS

★ **Bar Pilar** Cnr c/Moro Zeit 13, off Pl. del Esparto ☎963 910 497. This boisterous joint, which has been around since 1917, gets packed most nights, with the beer-happy crowd spilling out onto the pavement. The speciality is *clochinas* (mussels), which you can slurp at the bar, tossing the shells into buckets on the floor. Daily noon–midnight.

La Bodeguilla del Gato c/Catalans 10 ☎963 918 235. Yes, it can sometimes seem like there are more tourists than locals, but this is an authentically lively tapas bar nonetheless, with exposed brick-and-mustard walls hung with bullfighting posters. Munch on *pulpo a la Gallega*, octopus dusted with paprika, and crisp *flamenquines*, croquettes of pork, ham and cheese. Daily 8.30pm–midnight.

Casa Montaña c/José Benlliure 69 ☎963 672 314, ⓦemilianobodega.com. This vintage, cheery tapas bar in the Cabañal fishermen's quarter is one of the oldest (and best) in the city, with one of Valencia's most impressive wine cellars to boot. Graze on a wonderful array of tapas from anchovies and *michirones* (fava beans) to cod croquettes, which get a nutty kick from pine nuts. Daily 1–3.30pm & 8–11.30pm, closed Sun dinner & second half of Aug.

DRINKING AND NIGHTLIFE

The heady days of *La Ruta del Bacalao* (when people drove hundreds of kilometres to party in Valencia's out-of-town warehouses) may be long gone, but the city still takes its **nightlife** seriously. The **Barrio del Carmen** is one of the liveliest areas at night, especially around c/Caballeros, with scores of small cafés, music bars and restaurants. The whole area between Pl. de la Reina, Pl. Santa Ursula and Pl. Portal Nueva is heaving at the weekend. Calle Juan Llorenç, west of the city centre, is another popular area to bar- and club-hop, with lively Latin and salsa-style clubs. Russafa, southeast of the city centre, has evolved into one of the funkier, still relatively untouristed neighbourhoods, and bustles with cafés and bars. Across the Río Turia, near the **university**, particularly on and around c/Blasco Ibáñez; and just north, around Pl. Benicalmet, you'll find a more studenty, alternative-music-style nightlife, especially during the school year.

In **summer**, the bars lining the **Malvarrosa beach** are the places to be. Many Valencian bars serve *Agua de Valencia* – the classic Valencian cocktail, made with orange juice, cava and vodka, and served by the jug.

To get a grip on **what's going on**, you can check out local English-language websites like ⓦthisisvalencia.com and ⓦvalenciavalencia.com, which both offer updated overviews of nightlife and restaurants. For a Spanish-language lowdown on the club scene, check out *A Little Beat* magazine (ⓦalittlebeat.com). Note that the big nightclubs are generally open Thursday to Saturday, and usually get going after midnight.

HORCHATA

Valencia is known for its **horchata** – a drink made from *chufas* (tiger nuts) served either liquid or *granizada* (slightly frozen), and accompanied by long, thin cakes called *fartons*. Legend has it that the name *horchata* was coined by Jaume I, shortly after he conquered Valencia. He was admiring the *huerta* one hot afternoon, and an Arab girl offered him a drink so refreshing that he exclaimed, "*Aixó es or, xata*" (this is gold, girl).

There are **horchaterías** all over the city: the two oldest are *Santa Catalina* (daily 8am–9pm; ☎963 912 379) and *El Siglo* (daily generally 8am–9pm; ☎963 918 466), both in Plaza Santa Catalina. One of the better-known spots to cool your throat is *Daniel*, Avda. de la Horchata 41 (daily 10am–1am; closed mid-Dec to Feb; ☎961 858 866, ⓦhorchateria-daniel.es; ⓜPalmaret), where you can sit on the breezy terrace. In the historic Mercado de Colón, try the excellent *La Casa de l'Orxata* (daily Mon–Fri 7.30am–10.30pm, Sat & Sun until 2am; ☎963 527 307, ⓦwww.casadelaorxata.com), who make their smooth *horchata* with traditional methods and organic ingredients, and sell it from street carts around town.

Traditionally, however, the best *horchata* comes from **Alboraya**, formerly a village in the Valencian suburbs, now absorbed into the city – take metro line #3. One old-time spot is *Subies*, Carretera de Barcelona in the Almássera neighborhood of Alboraya (daily 8.30am–11pm; ☎961 854 673, ⓦhorchatasubies.es), where three generations have been honing their craft.

BARS

Café de las Horas Conde de Almodóvar 1 ☎ 963 917 336. Baroque-tinged, gay-friendly bar with a gurgling fountain, tiled floors and a marble bar. Drop in early evening for a romantic glass of wine, or later in the night join the crowds getting tipsy on chilled jugs of *Agua de Valencia*. Mon–Thurs 4pm–1.30am, Fri–Sun 4pm–3am.

★ **Café Madrid** c/de la Abadía de San Martín 10, no phone. This two-storey haunt is considered the birthplace of *Agua de Valencia* – and, as you might expect, the bartenders are true connoisseurs at making this fruity cocktail. The welcoming bar has managed to maintain a wonderfully old-fashioned air – dark wood, burgundy walls, antique mirrors – while still drawing a buzzy, stylish set until the small hours. Mon–Thurs 7pm–2am, Fri & Sat 7pm–3.30am.

Café del Negrito & **Cava del Negret** Pl. del Negrito 1 & c/Calatrava 15 ☎ 963 914 233. These sociable bars sit on one of Valencia's loveliest plazas, perfect for an outdoor cocktail. Come evening, a bohemian crowd gathers for conversation and *cervezas al aire libre*. Mon–Thurs & Sun 5pm–3am, Fri & Sat 5pm–3.30am.

Café Tocado c/Cádiz 44 ☎ 650 390 232. Enjoy cocktails and conversation at this fun, longstanding Russafa café, with a decor inspired by Paris cabarets. Daily 7pm–midnight.

Cava Siglos c/Caballeros 12 ☎ 963 916 271, ⓦ cavasiglos.com. Stylish, minimalist wine bar, with a "look neoyorquino" ("New York look"), serving a creative selection of wine and cava, plus *bocadillos*. Mon noon–5pm, Tues–Sun noon–1.30am.

Destino 56 Avda. Neptuno, Playa de las Arenas ☎ 689 979 416, ⓦ destino56.com. Ease into the Valencia night over cocktails with views of the beach, followed by grooving on the dancefloor. Summer Thurs–Fri 10pm–midnight; check website for updates.

Johnny Marracas c/Caballeros 39 ☎ 963 915 266. Stylish locals flirt over strong cocktails at this smooth lounge. Mon–Thurs 7pm–3am, Fri–Sun 7pm–4am.

Radio City c/Santa Teresa 19 ☎ 963 914 15. This veteran drinking den hosts poetry, films and live music, with full-on flamenco on Tues. Daily 10.30pm–3.30am.

★ **Sant Jaume** c/Caballeros 51 ☎ 963 912 401. Of the many bars on this main drag, the characterful *Sant Jaume*, set in a small converted pharmacy with aged mirrors and tiles, is one of the most popular, with a great terrace that packs in the crowds nightly. Daily noon–1.30am.

El Tornillo Campoamor 42 ☎ 639 403 148, ⓦ eltornillo .com. Bohemian student hangout spinning indie, alternative and left-field electronica. Look for the *tornillo* (screw) that marks the spot outside. Open Tues & Wed 8.30pm–2.30am, Thurs–Sat 8.30pm–3.30am.

L'Umbracle Terraza L'Umbracle, La Ciudad de las Artes y las Ciencias ☎ 671 668 000, ⓦ umbracleterraza.com. Sexy lounge where you can sip tasty cocktails under palm trees and the twinkling stars, and then head to the downstairs dance club *Mya* to finish off the night. Summer Thurs–Sat 10/11pm–late.

Vinicius Pub c/Bolsería 11 ☎ 607 723 219, ⓦ vini ciuspub.com. Sip potent cocktails, from *Agua de Valencia* to *caipirinhas*, to a playlist of international and Spanish pop, funk and house. Wed–Sat 10pm–3.30am.

Vivir Sin Dormir Paseo Neptuno 42 ☎ 963 727 777, ⓦ vivirsindormir. Once a legend, and now a lively pub-club with a long bar and an outdoor terrace, particularly popular with travellers. Daily 9pm–3am.

CLUBS

Las Ánimas & **Las Ánimas Puerto** c/Pizarro 31 & Paseo Neptuno ☎ 902 108 527, ⓦ grupolasanimas .com. The hopping *Las Ánimas* is the city-centre location of the popular chain; there's another busy branch at the port. Check the website for details of upcoming DJ sessions and events. Usually Thurs–Sat midnight–late.

La Bolsería Bolsería 41 ☎ 963 918 903. Sleek nightspot that can sometimes take itself too seriously. That said, it's a comfortably swish place to enjoy Valencia's nightlife, with excellent cocktails, a cool house and pop soundtrack, and a mature crowd. Daily 8pm–4am.

Fox Congo c/Caballeros 35 ☎ 963 925 527. On the barrio's main strip, this dimly lit, funky club reveals a sexy interior of copper pillars, black banquettes and glowing

12

onyx bar. Dance tunes and good cocktails, too. Daily 11pm–late.

Jimmy Glass c/Baja 28, no phone, ⓦ jimmyglassjazz .net. Authentically smoky, shoebox-shaped jazz club putting on quality live acts for a studenty audience. Daily 8pm–3am.

The Music Box Pinto Zariñena 16 ☎ 963 914 151. The cool crowd heats up the dancefloor at this busy club that pumps out soul and swing, indie and electro. Daily 1am–7am.

Pacha c/San Vicente 305, no phone, ⓦ pachavalencia .com. South of the city centre, the Valencian branch of the Spanish superclub features booming house tunes and two floors of writhing dancers in party gear. Check the website for up-to-date information. Thurs–Sat 11pm–late.

Velvet Campoamor 58, no phone. Lively student-jammed club, with tunes ranging from indie rock to Spanish pop or electronica. Tues–Sat 9pm–late.

DIRECTORY

Consulates UK c/Colón 22, 5-H ☎ 963 520 710; USA c/Dr Romagosa 1, 2-J ☎ 963 516 973.

Hospital Hospital General, Avda. del Cid, at the Tres Cruces junction ☎ 961 972 00; ⓜ Avenida del Cid.

Internet access Most hostels and hotels offer internet access, whether wi-fi or an internet centre. Workcenter,

c/Colón 84 (Mon–Fri 7am–11pm, Sat & Sun noon–9pm; ☎ 963 536 919, ⓦ workcenter.es), also offers internet, among other office services.

Police c/Los Mestres 2 ☎ 963 920 607.

Post office Pl. del Ayuntamiento 24 (Mon–Fri 8.30am–8.30pm, Sat 9.30am–2pm).

Around Valencia

There are a number of good **day-trips** to be made from Valencia, including a visit to the monastery at El Puig or a meal at some of the region's very best paella restaurants at El Palmar, El Perelló or El Perellonet.

Real Monasterio del Puig de Santa María

Guided visits Tues–Sat 10am, 11am, noon, 4pm & 5pm • €4 • ☎ 961 470 200, ⓦ monasteriodelpuig.es.tl • Trains (every 30min; 20min) and buses (hourly; 30min) from Valencia

Eighteen kilometres north of Valencia on the road to Sagunto is the small town of **El Puig** (pronounced "pooch"), where it's well worth spending a couple of hours visiting the impressive **Real Monasterio del Puig de Santa María**, a huge fort-like structure flanked by four towers that dominates the town and surrounding countryside. The Orden de la Merced – the order that acts as guardians of the sanctuary – was founded by Pedro Nalaso in 1237 after he'd seen a vision of the Virgin Mary on the nearby hill. It is a favourite pilgrimage destination for Valencians and royalty alike, from Jaime I to the present monarchs Juan Carlos I and Doña Sofía, although in Franco's time it was put to a rather different use – as a prison.

Museum of Print and Graphics

In the lower cloister, the **Museum of Print and Graphics** (one of the most important in Europe) contains a wealth of artefacts, including the smallest book in the world – the size of a thumbnail. Looking at it through a magnifying glass reveals the Padre Nuestro (Lord's Prayer) in half a dozen languages. Other star exhibits include a copy of the Gutenberg Bible and a wonderful pictorial atlas of natural history, both from the sixteenth century. In the upper cloister, the **ceramics room** houses various Roman pieces, but its real treasures are the fourteenth-century plates, bowls and jars recovered from the seabed close to El Puig. Keep an eye out, too, for the neck manacles that the monks use as candle holders throughout the monastery.

La Albufera and the paella villages

La Albufera, just 12km south from Valencia, is a vast lagoon separated from the sea by a sandbank and surrounded by rice fields. Being one of the largest bodies of fresh water in Spain, it constitutes an important wetland, and attracts tens of thousands of migratory birds – a throng composed of 250 species, of which ninety breed here regularly. In the Middle Ages, it was ten times its present size but the surrounding paddies have gradually reduced it. After growing contamination by industrial waste, domestic sewage and insecticide, the area was turned into a natural park. Whether you're into birdwatching or not, the lagoon area makes a relaxing change from the city.

It's possible to "hop on, hop off" the Valencia Bus Turístic and tuck into a lunch of **paella**, or eels with *all i pebre* (piquant sauce), in the lakeside village of **EL PALMAR**, which is packed with restaurants. On August 4, El Palmar celebrates its **fiesta**; the image of Christ on the Cross is taken out onto the lake in a procession of boats to the *illuent*, or centre, of the lake, where hymns are sung. Another 2km farther along the road to El Perelló is the tiny village of **EL PERELLONET**, where you can also sample some of the best paella in Spain.

ARRIVAL AND DEPARTURE
LA ALBUFERA AND THE PAELLA VILLAGES

By bus If you're pressed for time, one of the easiest ways to do La Albufera is to jump aboard the Valencia Bus Turístic, which leaves from various points in the city (every 30min in winter, every 20min in summer; €15; ☎963 414 400, ⓦvalenciabusturistic.com*)*; the trip includes a short boat ride on the lake. Additionally, regular Autocares Herca buses travel to El Saler and on to the lagoon, El Palmar and El Perelló.

EATING AND DRINKING

Blayet Avda. Gaviotas 17, El Perellonet ☎961 777 184, ⓦblayet.com. Since 1935, this inviting spot has been ladling out fragrant paellas and fresh seafood. Book ahead on weekends. Tues–Sun: Aug 1–4pm & 9–11pm; rest of the year 1–4pm.

Nou Raco Del Palmar 21, El Palmar ☎961 620 172. Traditional cuisine meets a modern sensibility (and decor) at this welcoming restaurant where seafood is the speciality, along with paella, of course. Tues–Sun 1.30–3.30pm, plus Fri & Sat 8.30–11.30pm in summer.

12

ALL PULPED OUT: LA TOMATINA

La Tomatina – the tomato-throwing festival of Buñol – is about as wild and excessive as Spanish fiestas get. Picture this: 30,000 people descend on a small provincial town, at the same time as a fleet of municipal trucks, carrying 120,000 tonnes of tomatoes. Tension builds. "To-ma-te, to-ma-te" yell the crowds. And then the truckers let them have it, hurling the ripe, pulpy fruit at everyone present. And everyone goes crazy, hurling the pulp back at the trucks, at each other, in the air … for an hour. It's a fantasy battle made flesh: exhausting, not pretty and not to everyone's taste. But it is Buñol's contribution to fiesta culture, and most participants will tell you that it is just about as much fun as it is possible to have with your clothes on. Not that you should wear a great deal.

La Tomatina has been going since 1944 but has got a lot bigger in recent years, following a string of articles in the press in Spain and abroad. The novelist Louis de Bernières was one of the first foreign writers to cover the event: he wrote a superb account that is reprinted in *Spain: Travelers' Tales*, and concluded that, if he planned his life well and kept his health, he could attend another nineteen Tomatinas, before he would be too enfeebled for the occasion.

If the idea appeals, then you'll need to visit Buñol on the **last Wednesday of August** (but call the Valencia tourist office just to check, as some years it takes place a week early). You can get there from the city by train or bus in around an hour, but try to arrive early, with a spare set of clothing that you should leave at a bar. The tomato trucks appear on the central Plaza del Ayuntamiento at around noon, and then the battle commences: this is no spectator sport – everyone is considered fair game. At 1pm, an explosion signals the end of the battle and nobody hurls another speck of tomato for the next twelve months. Instead, the local fire brigade arrives to hose down the combatants, buildings and streets, and a lull comes over the town. And then, miraculously, within the hour, everyone arrives back on the street, perfectly turned out, to enjoy the rest of the fiesta, which, oddly enough, includes such refined pursuits as orchestral concerts in the town's open-air auditorium. For more information, check out the festival website ⓦlatomatina.es, or try the town's own website ⓦbunyol.es.

As Buñol's **accommodation** options are limited, most people take in the fiesta as a day-trip from Valencia; but if you want to stay, try *Hotel Condes de Buñol*, Avda. Blasco Ibañez 13 (☎962 504 852, ⓦcondesdebunol.com; €48, or €90 during Tomatina, when it's a three-night minimum).

North of Valencia: the Costa del Alzahar

Most of the Costa del Alzahar north of Valencia is dotted with **beach resorts**, with some of the best sands around **Benicàssim**, north of the provincial capital, **Castellón de la Plana**. Farther north still, the historic walled city of **Peñíscola** commands a spectacular cliff-top location, while **Vinaròs** is more port than resort. Apart from the appeal of the coastline, there are fine Roman ruins at **Sagunto**, sweeping mountain scenery and good hiking around **Segorbe** and **Montanejos**, while the fortified town of **Morella** is definitely worth a visit for its castle and Gothic architecture.

Sagunto

Twenty-four kilometres north of Valencia are the fine Roman remains of **SAGUNTO** (Sagunt). This town passed into Spanish legend when, in 219 BC, it was attacked by Hannibal in one of the first acts of the war waged by Carthage on the Roman Empire. Its citizens withstood a nine-month siege before burning the city and themselves rather than surrendering. When belated help from Rome arrived, the city was recaptured and rebuilding eventually got under way. Today, Sagunto has several restored buildings to explore, especially in the well-preserved Jewish quarter, where you'll find medieval houses lining the cobbled alleyways.

Teatro Romano

May–Sept Tues–Sat 10am–8pm, Sun 10am–2pm; Oct–April Tues–Sat 10am–6pm, Sun 10am–2pm • Free

Chief among the ruins is the second-century Roman amphitheatre, the **Teatro Romano**, the basic shape of which survives intact. After years of (occasionally controversial) renovation, it's now functional, and in the summer (usually Aug) you can take in plays and concerts, from *Hamlet* to classical music and ballet. The views from its seats are wonderful, encompassing a vast span of history – Roman stones all around, a ramshackle Moorish castle on the hill behind, medieval churches in the town below and, across the plain towards the sea, the black smoke of modern industry.

Museu Històric de Sagunt

C/de Castillo • Summer Tues–Sat 11am–8pm, Sun 11am–3pm; winter Tues–Sat 11am–6pm, Sun 11am–3pm • Free • ☎ 962 664 096

The **Museu Històric de Sagunt**, which occupies two storeys of a fourteenth-century medieval house, features archeological finds from Sagunto and around, including Latin and Hebrew inscriptions and sculptures, detailed mosaics, vases, ceramics and more.

Centro de Recepción de Visitantes

Casa dels Berenguer • Summer Mon–Sat 9am–1.30 & 5.30–9pm, Sun 9am–1.30; winter Mon–Sat 10.30–5.30, Sun 10am–2pm • Free

Displays at the **Centro de Recepción de Visitantes**, near the Iglesia de Santa María, offer a good overview of the city's history. Exhibits include ancient books and manuscripts, artworks and archeological finds from throughout the region, including the remains of fourteenth-century ritual baths from Sagunto's Jewish quarter.

ARRIVAL AND INFORMATION · SAGUNTO

By train and bus There are half-hourly trains and frequent buses between Sagunto and Valencia; the town centre is a 25min walk from the train station.

Turismo The main office is at Pl. Cronista Chabret (summer Mon 10am–2.30pm & 4.30–7.30pm, Tues–Fri 9am–2.30 & 4.30–7.30pm, Sat 10.30am–2pm & 4–6.30pm, Sun 10am–2pm; winter Mon–Fri 9am–2pm & 4–6.30pm, Sat & Sun 9am–2pm; ☎ 962 655 859, ⓦ saguntoturismo.es).

There's another office at the Puerto de Sagunto, Avda. Mediterráneo 67 (summer Mon–Fri 9.30am–2pm & 5.30–8.30pm, Sat 10.30–2pm & 4–6.30pm, Sun 10am–2pm; winter 9.30am–2pm & 4–6.30pm, Sat 9am–2pm; ☎ 962 690 402, ⓦ saguntoturismo.es), while the Centro de Recepción de Visitantes also has information on Sagunto and the surrounding region.

ACCOMMODATION

Complejo Turístico La Pinada 3km out of town, on the road to Teruel ☎ 962 660 850, ⓦ complejoturisticolapinada.com. This well-maintained hotel and leisure complex has plenty of amenities, including swimming pools and saunas. **€45**

Vall d'Uixo

Daily: Jan–May & Oct–Dec 11am–1.15pm & 3.30–5.45pm; June, July & Sept 11am–1.15pm & 3.30–6.30pm; Aug 11am–1.15pm & 3.30–7.15 • €9.50 • ⓦ riosubterraneo.com • Frequent buses from Sagunto pass through Vall d'Uixo

Twenty-eight kilometres north of Sagunto, at **Vall d'Uixo**, is the underground river of San José, featuring caves with wonderful stalactites. Along with boat trips through the caves, the attendant tourist complex also has a swimming pool, restaurant, and an auditorium which holds summer concerts.

Segorbe

About 30km inland from Sagunto is **SEGORBE**, the Roman Segóbriga, which is worth a visit more for its tranquillity and surrounding scenery than its sights, though part of the old city wall remains. It lies in the valley of the Río Palancia, among medlar and lemon orchards. Segorbe has its **fiestas** at the beginning of September, when the Entrada de Toros y Caballos takes place, and bulls are run through the town by horses. One kilometre outside town on the road to Jérica, the so-called **fountain of the provinces** has fifty spouts, one for each province of Spain, each labelled with the coat of arms.

Cathedral and museum

Tues–Sat 11am–1.30pm & 5–7pm, Sun 11am–1.30pm & 4.30–6pm • €3, but this may vary

Segorbe's **cathedral** was begun in the thirteenth century, but suffered in the Neoclassical reforms, and only the cloister is original. Its **museum** contains a few pieces of Gothic Valencian art, with *retablos* by Vicente Maçip and his son; Flemish artwork; and a Madonna with Child in marble by the Italian master Donatello.

ARRIVAL AND INFORMATION   SEGORBE

By train and bus There are daily trains and buses between Valencia and Segorbe.

Turismo The tourist office is next to the *ayuntamiento* (Mon–Fri 9am–2pm & 5–7pm, Sat 10am–2pm & 5–7pm, Sun 10.30–1.30pm; ☎ 964 713 254, ⓦ turismo.segorbe.es).

ACCOMMODATION

Hospedería el Palen c/Franco Ricart 9 ☎ 964 710 740, ⓦ elpalen.com. This renovated *hospedería*, set in a historic building in the centre of town, has comfortable rooms. **€50**

Montanejos

Some 38km from Segorbe, tiny **MONTANEJOS** (not to be mistaken for Montan, the village just before) is popular with visitors for its hot springs, **Fuente de Baños**, where the water emerges at 25°C and has medicinal properties. **Walks** around the village join up with the nationwide GR (Gran Recorrido) network of trails.

ARRIVAL AND INFORMATION   MONTANEJOS

By bus Regular buses travel from Segorbe.

Information Visit ⓦ montanejos.com for information.

ACCOMMODATION

Hotel Gil Avda. Fuente de Baños 28 ☎ 964 131 380, ⓦ hotelgil.com. Comfortable rooms with views of the river and mountains, and a variety of spa treatments on offer. **€28**

Hotel Rosaleda del Mijares Carretera de Tales 28 ☎ 964 131 079, ⓦ hotelesrosaleda.com. Well-appointed hotel with a spa that provides a range of therapies. **€80**

12

Castellón de la Plana

CASTELLÓN DE LA PLANA is a provincial capital and one of the main cities in the Costa del Azahar area. It's a prosperous enough place, with a sight or two, but there's no real reason to linger long here, except perhaps for the nearby beaches. In the centre of town, there's a fine seventeenth-century **ayuntamiento**, and nearby is the sixteenth-century **El Fadrí** bell tower. Next to the tower is the neo-Gothic **Concatedral de Santa María** – the original eleventh-century building was destroyed in the Civil War.

You'll find **beaches** at Castellón's *grau* (port), 5km east of the centre, but the best stretches are along the coastal road north to Benicàssim.

Museo de Bellas Artes

Avda. Hermanos Bou 28 • Tues–Sat 10am–8pm, Sun 10am–2pm • Free • ☎ 964 727 500, ⓦ culturalcas.com

The impressive contemporary premises of the **Museo de Bellas Artes** features some valuable works by Francisco Zurbarán and Sorrolla, ceramics and sculptures, and other paintings and works by a variety of regional and Spanish artists.

ARRIVAL AND INFORMATION

CASTELLÓN DE LA PLANA

By train and bus Buses and trains to and from destinations north and south, plus Morella, arrive at the combined station on Avda. Pintor Oliet. Buses for the port and beaches leave regularly from Pl. Borrull, and from nearby Pl. Farrell to Benicàssim.

Turismo Pl. María Agustina (summer Mon–Fri 9am–7pm, Sat 10am–2pm; winter Mon–Fri 9am–2pm & 4–7pm, Sat 10am–2pm; ☎ 964 358 688, ⓦ comunitatvalenciana. com), with a wealth of information about the city and the whole province.

ACCOMMODATION, EATING AND DRINKING

There are plenty of **places to eat**, especially in the streets just south of Pl. Santa Cruz.

AC Hotel Castellón Carcagente ☎ 964 723 825, ⓦ espanol.marriott.com. Sleek, if somewhat antiseptic large hotel, in the city centre. Rooms are on the smaller side, but outfitted with all the amenities. **€55**

Hotel Herreros Avda. del Puerto 28 ☎ 964 284 264, ⓦ hotelherreros.com. This well-run hotel, about 2km from the beach, has simple, comfy rooms. **€43**

Rafael c/Churruca 28 ☎ 964 282 185. By the port, this restaurant offers an excellent, if somewhat pricey, selection of seafood, hauled in fresh daily. Mon–Sat 1.30–4pm & 8.30–11pm.

Vilafamés

VILAFAMÉS, 24km inland from Castellón, is an attractive hill town that successfully mixes the medieval, Renaissance and modern. In the highest part of town, there's an ancient ruined castle, conquered by Jaime I in 1233.

Museo de Arte Contemporáneo

Diputación Provincial 20 • Tues–Fri 10am–1.30pm & 4–7pm, Sat & Sun 10.30am–2pm & 4–7pm, in summer usually open until 8pm • €2 • ☎ 964 329 152, ⓦ turismodecastellon.com

The fifteenth-century Palau del Batlle houses the **Museo de Arte Contemporáneo**, a collection of over five hundred sculptures and paintings, from the late 1920s onwards, including works by Miró, Lozano, Mompó and Barjola.

ACCOMMODATION AND EATING

VILAFAMÉS

El Jardin Vertical c/Nou 15 ☎ 964 329 938, ⓦ eljardinvertical.com. This welcoming *casa rural*, in a seventeenth-century stone-walled house, reveals views of the rolling countryside and lovely, rustic rooms. The restaurant serves up a tasting dinner *menú* for €35; non-guests should book ahead. Restaurant generally daily 1.30–3.30pm & 8.30–10.30pm, closed Mon–Fri in winter. **€135–155**

El Rullo c/de la Fuente 2 ☎ 964 329 384. Clean, wood-beamed rooms, and also a restaurant, with a weekday *menú* for €10. Daily lunch & dinner; hours sometimes limited in winter. **€60**

Benicàssim and around

It's music that draws the masses to **BENICÀSSIM**, a few kilometres north of Castellón, which hosts the annual, highly acclaimed alt-music **Festival Internacional de Benicàssim**. Beyond the festival, Benicàssim is also a popular summer resort for Spaniards, with sun-speckled beaches, and a well-oiled tourist infrastructure.

Bodegas Carmelitano

C/Bodolz 10, off Avda. Castellón • Summer 9am–1.30pm & 3.30–7.30pm; winter 9am–1.30pm & 3–6.30pm • Tours €2.50 • ☎ 964 300 849, ⓦ carmelitnao.com

The Benicàssim area was well known as a centre for the production of Moscatel wine; very few vineyards remain today, but you can take a wine-tasting tour at **Bodegas Carmelitano**, named after the local Carmelite monks who produced an acclaimed aromatic herb liqueur here in the late seventeenth century. The *bodegas* continue to make the liqueur, using the same process and recipes as the monks, as well as Moscatel and other wines. Tours include the history of the *bodega*, a visit to the cellar and wine and liqueur tasting. Note that you have to book tours in advance.

Aquarama

Mid-June to early Sept daily 11am–7pm • Full day €20.50, €14.50 for children under 1.4m tall; half-day €13.50/€9.80 • ☎ 964 303 321, ⓦ aquarama.net

As befits a vacation spot, Benicàssim boasts the massive Aquarama water park just south of town, with all the usual pools, water slides, overpriced snacks and screaming (but happy) kids.

Desierto de las Palmas

Six kilometres inland from Benicàssim, the **Desierto de las Palmas** is a nature reserve with a scattering of ruins (including the atmospheric *monasterio antiguo*, abandoned in the late eighteenth century) and walking circuits. The name was coined by Carmelite monks whose presence in the area dates back to 1697.

ARRIVAL AND INFORMATION

BENICÀSSIM

By train and bus Trains for both Vinaròs and Castellón leave fairly regularly from the small station, ten minutes' walk north of the *turismo*. There's a regular bus service between Castellón and Benicàssim: buses leave from the bus stop on Avda. Pintor Oliet roughly every fifteen minutes in summer, every thirty minutes in winter. There are also five daily buses to and from Vinaròs, two of which stop at Peñíscola en route.

Turismo c/Santo Tomás 74–76 (summer Mon–Fri 9am–2pm & 5–8pm, Sat & Sun 10.30am–1.30pm & 5–8pm; winter Mon–Sat 9am–2pm & 4–7pm, Sun 9am–2pm; ☎ 964 300 102, ⓦ benicassim.org).

ACCOMMODATION

Although Benicàssim is heavily developed for package tourism, budget accommodation is fairly easy to come by in the streets around the *turismo*.

Camping Florida Sigalero 34 ☎ 964 392 385, ⓦ camping florida.net. Well-run campsite close to the beach, with a pool and tennis courts. Adults €5.50, plus €8.50 per pitch

Hotel Montreal c/Les Barraques 5 ☎ 964 300 681, ⓦ hotelmontreal.es. Comfy, polished-floor rooms near Terrers beach, plus a swimming pool, sun-dappled garden

FESTIVAL INTERNACIONAL DE BENICÀSSIM

The annual **Festival Internacional de Benicàssim** (FIB; ⓦ fiberfib.com) in late July draws tens of thousands to hear the world's biggest names in alternative pop and rock. Over the years, it has pulled in everyone from Depeche Mode to Oasis and, more recently, The Strokes and Arctic Monkeys. The dance tents are generally just as buzzing as the live-music stages, with DJs playing all night long. A four-day festival ticket is €165, or €240 with free camping for eight days around the event at the massive campsite.

12

terrace and a buffet-style restaurant. Closed Oct to Semana Santa. **€129**

Hotel Residencia Canada c/La Pau 1 ☏ 964 304 611, ⓦ hotelcanadabenicassim.com. Sunny, well-kept rooms in the city centre, about a 20min stroll to the beach. **€39**

Hotel Termas Marinas Palasiet c/Pontazgo 11 ☏ 964 300 250, ⓦ palasiet.com. For the utmost in pampering (and prices) try this spa-hotel overlooking Playa Voramar, about 3km from town. In addition to elegant, pale-toned rooms, there's a thermal centre with thalassotherapy treatments – think whirlpools with algae – along with sweet-chocolate facial peels and onyx-stone massages. **€230**

Hotel Voramar Paseo Pilar Coloma 1 ☏ 964 300 150, ⓦ voramar.net. This friendly, family-run hotel is a refreshing departure from the typical tourist trap, and also has an enviable perch right on the beach. The restaurant serves local dishes and seafood, and looks out at the sea. Restaurant daily 1.30–4pm & 8.30–11pm. **€145**

EATING AND DRINKING

There are plenty of restaurants in the town centre, particularly on and around c/Tomás. As for nightlife, Benicàssim has its fare share of party spots: c/de los Dolores is dotted with pubs, and for *discotecas* head to Avda. Gimeno Tomás.

Casa Teresa c/Estatut 23 ☏ 964 301 327. Dine on mid-priced paella, seafood, grilled meats and other regional cuisine at this family-run restaurant. Daily 1–3.30, Fri & Sat 8.30–11pm.

Peñíscola

There's not much else along the stretch of coast north of Benicàssim until you reach **PEÑÍSCOLA**, 60km away. The setting is one of Spain's most stunning: a heavily fortified promontory jutting out into the Mediterranean, zealously shielding its warren of alleys and lanes with perfectly preserved medieval walls. Yet it's also one of the starkest – immediately below the old walls, the requisite line of eyesore high-rises snakes out along the seafront like a besieging army.

The breezy Paseo Marítimo is a pleasant place from which to take in views of the sea, and the resort's slender **beach** is well kept, if busy. The farther north you get from the castle, the quieter it becomes. There's also a smaller cove beach, Playa Sur, 200m west of the old town.

The castle

Daily: summer 9.30am–9.30pm; winter 10.30am–5.30pm • €3.50

Peñíscola's **castle**, where part of *El Cid* was filmed, is well worth a visit to admire the colossal vaulted guards' quarters, basilica and the views from its roof. There was once a Phoenician settlement here, and later it was occupied by Greek, Carthaginian, Roman and Moorish rulers, but the present castle was built by the Knights Templar, with alterations by Pedro de la Luna. Pope Benedict XIII (Papa Luna) lived here for six years after he had been deposed from the papacy during the fifteenth-century Church schisms.

Museo del Mar

C/Principe • April–June daily 10am–2pm & 4–8pm; July–Sept daily 10am–2pm & 5–9pm; Oct–March Tues–Sun 10am–2pm & 4–6pm • Free • ☏ 964 481 603

Peñíscola's **Museo de Mar** explores the town's rich maritime history, from ancient seafaring and archeological finds – including ancient anchors, old bronze diving helmets and pottery – to the fishing industry and the area's underwater flora and fauna. The museum also has several aquariums filled with local fish species.

ARRIVAL AND INFORMATION PEÑÍSCOLA

By bus Buses shuttle between Peñíscola and Vinaròs every half-hour between 7.30am and 11pm, stopping at various points along Avda. Papa Luna. For points south, you'll have to change bus at Benicarló (c/San Francisco).

Turismo Paseo Marítimo (summer Mon–Fri 9.30am–8pm, Sat 10am–1pm & 5–8pm, Sun 10am–1pm; winter Mon–Fri 10am–1pm & 4–7pm, Sat 10am–1pm & 4–7pm, Sun 10am–1pm; ☏ 964 480 208, ⓦ peniscola.es); there's also a small kiosk just below the entrance to the walled city. Both provide a good map and accommodation information.

ACCOMMODATION

Dios Esta Bien c/San Roque 22 y 24 ☎ 964 482 253, ⓦ diosestabien.com. One of the better choices in town: inviting and rustic, with comfortable rooms and a terrace; they also have an apartment with a private kitchen that's good for small groups. **€65**, apartment **€80**

Hostal Aranda c/General Aranda 3 ☎ 964 480 816, ⓦ hostalaranda.com. This comfortable spot has clean rooms with pastel walls and tiled floors. **€75**

Hotel Restaurante Simó c/Porteta 5 ☎ 964 480 620, ⓦ restaurantesimo.es. If you want to be within striking distance of the beach, try this spot in the shadow of the walls, whose bright rooms have sea views. The restaurant has decent local cuisine; rates include breakfast. Restaurant 1–4pm & 8–11pm. **€69**

EATING AND DRINKING

The area just below the old town is thick with **restaurants**, many serving local dishes such as *suquet de peix* (fish stew).

Mandarina Avda. Papa Luna 1 ☎ 964 467 650, ⓦ mandarinaclub.net. This restaurant-lounge gets crowded in summer, but if you can nab a seat on the breezy terrace, you enjoy everything from salads and sushi to seafood and pasta – and then ease into the warm evening over cocktails. Mains €13–22, sushi tasting *menú* €25. Daily noon until late; generally closed Nov–April.

El Peñón c/Santos Mártires 22 ☎ 964 480 716. This rustic, long-established restaurant serves quality seafood and other hearty local dishes. Daily 1–3.30pm & 8–11pm; closed late Dec to March.

Vinaròs

The **beaches** of the scruffy port-cum-resort **VINARÒS**, next along the coast, are small but rarely packed, and in town there's an elaborate Baroque church, with an excellent local produce market nearby. In the early evening, it's worth going down to the dockside **market** to watch the day's catch being auctioned and packed off to restaurants all over the region. Locally caught fish is excellent, with the *langostinos* reputedly the best in Spain. In mid-August, Vinaròs celebrates the **Fiestas del Langostino**, with plenty of outdoor seafood feasts.

12

ARRIVAL AND INFORMATION

By train The train station, some 2km west of the centre, has eight daily services to and from Valencia (via Castellón) and nine connecting to Barcelona (via Tarragona).

By bus There are two buses to Morella (8am & 4pm Mon–Fri), leaving from Pl. de Sant Esteve. Both the half-hourly service to Peñíscola, and the six daily buses to Castellón (three of which stop at Benicàssim) leave from

VINARÒS

the corner of Avda. de Leopold Querol and Passeig del 29 de Setembre.

Turismo Near the seafront, the *turismo* (summer daily 10am–1.30pm & 5.30–8pm; winter Mon–Sat 10am–1.30pm & 5.30–6.45pm, Sun 10.30am–1.30pm; ☎ 964 453 334, ⓦ vinaros.org) has decent maps and will help to locate accommodation.

ACCOMMODATION, EATING AND DRINKING

Bar Folet c/Costa y Borràs 58 ☎ 964 453 145. Almost overlooking the portside action, this is a wonderfully friendly spot for local seafood dishes and a glass of wine. Daily 10.30am–4pm & 7.30–midnight, closed Tues lunch; closes around 10.30pm in winter.

El Faro Zona Portuaria ☎ 964 456 362. This converted lighthouse serves creative seafood cuisine, including an array of tapas; it can be quite pricey, but the seafood is top-notch and fresh. Generally daily 1.30–3.30pm & 8.30–10.30pm; limited hours in winter.

Hotel Nou Casablanca c/Santa 30 ☎ 964 450 425, ✉ noucasablanca@gmail.com. Central, family-run hotel with comfortable rooms. They also run the next-door *Pensión Casablanca*, which has simple rooms and a roof terrace. Rooms **€50**, *pensión* **€30**

Morella

MORELLA, 62km inland on the road from the coast to Zaragoza, is one of the most attractive – and possibly most friendly – towns in the Castellón province. A medieval fortress town, it rises from the plain around a small hill crowned by a tall, rocky spur and a virtually impregnable **castle** that dominates the surrounding countryside. A perfectly preserved ring of ancient walls defends its lower reaches. The city was recovered from the Moors in the thirteenth century by the steward of Jaime I. He was reluctant to hand it over to the Crown, and it's said that the king came to blows with him over possession of the town. Today, Morella hosts an annual **festival of classical music** in the first two weeks of August.

Basílica de Santa María la Mayor
Pl. Arciprestal • Tues–Sun: summer 11am–2pm & 4–7pm; winter 11am–2pm & 4–6pm • Free

Chief among the town's monuments is this beautiful church, a fourteenth-century Gothic construction with carved doorways and an unusual raised *coro* reached by a marble spiral stairway, with detailed reliefs that depict the different stages in the life of Christ.

The castle
Daily: summer 11am–7pm; winter 11am–5pm • €3

Though it's in ruins, Morello's **castle** is still impressive. It's a tiring climb up, but there are tremendous views in every direction from the crumbling courtyard at the top – down over the monastery, bullring and town walls to the plains. In the distance are the remains of the peculiar Gothic **aqueduct** that once supplied the town's water. The splendid and newly restored Palacio del Gobernador features an exhibit on the history of the castle and of Morella.

Museo Tiempo de los Dinosaurios
Pl. de San Miguel • Tues–Sun 11am–2pm & 4–7pm, Oct–April closes 6pm • €2

Across from the tourist office, the curious **Museo Tiempo de los Dinosaurios** features a wide array of dinosaur fossils, from carnivores to herbivores, discovered in the area, along with audiovisual displays and exhibits on geological finds. Look out especially for the full-scale replica of an Iguanodon.

ARRIVAL AND INFORMATION   MORELLA

By bus Buses run between Morella and Vinaròs (Mon–Fri 2 daily) and Castellón (Mon–Fri 2 daily, Sat daily). Morella is one possible approach to the Maestrazgo region of southern Aragón – buses leave for Alcañiz (Mon & Fri 10am) and Cantavieja/Villafranca del Cid (Mon–Fri daily, early evening departure).

Turismo Pl. de San Miguel (summer daily 10am–2pm & 4–7pm; winter Tues–Sat 10am–2pm & 4–6pm, Sun 10am–2pm; ☎ 964 173 032, ⓦ morellaturistica.com).

ACCOMMODATION

At the foot of the castle, the restored Convento de San Francisco has been undergoing a long-term conversion to a parador. There have been a number of delays, but it's due to open by 2014; check with the tourist office for an update.

La Fonda Moreno c/Sant Nicolau 12 ☎ 964 160 105, ⓦ lafondamoreno.com. Pleasant, colourful rooms, along with an inviting restaurant serving regional cuisine. Restaurant daily 1–3.30pm & 9– 10pm, closed Sun dinner. €60

Hostal La Muralla c/Muralla 12 ☎ 964 160 243. Relax in clean, well-kept rooms with views of the hills. Rates include breakfast. €52

Hotel El Cid Puerta San Mateo 3 ☎ 964 160 125, ⓦ hotelelcidmorella.com. Modern, comfortable rooms with balconies. They also have a restaurant with nicely priced *menús* (weekdays €9.50 and weekends €12). Restaurant daily 1–3.30pm & 9–10.30pm; closed Sunday. €54

Hotel del Pastor San Julián 12 ☎ 964 161 016, ⓦ hoteldelpastor.com. Welcoming hotel with wood-beam ceilings and cosy rooms; they also run the excellent restaurant *Mesón del Pastor*. Rates include breakfast. €73

EATING AND DRINKING

Morella's porticoed main street, Els Porxos, bisected by steep steps leading down to the lower walls, is the place for **food**, with bars, bakeries and cafés. Ask for *flaons*, a local pastry made from cinnamon, cheese and almonds. Morella is prime **truffle** country – the best time to try them is February and early March, when many of the restaurants serve truffles, and the town hosts a gastronomic festival celebrating this aromatic delicacy.

Casa Roque Cuesta San Juan 1 ☎ 964 160 336. For local *trufa negra* and other gourmet-rustic delicacies, head to this inviting restaurant. Generally daily 1.30–3.30pm & 8.30–10.30pm, closed Sun eve & Mon.

Mesón del Pastor Cuesta Jovani 5 y 7 ☎ 964 160 249. Fill up on robust dishes of grilled meats, wild mushrooms and the region's famous truffles, when in season. Daily 1–4pm & 10pm until last diners leave; closed Sun dinner.

The Costa Blanca

Stretching south of Valencia, the **Costa Blanca** (White Coast), boasts some of the **best beaches** on this coast, especially between Gandía and Benidorm. Much of it, though, suffers from the worst excesses of **package tourism**, with concrete building projects looming over the sand. It pays to book ahead in summer, particularly in August. Campers have it somewhat easier – there are hundreds of campsites – but driving can be a nightmare unless you stick to the toll roads. If you're taking the inland route as far as **Gandía**, you'll get the opportunity to see the historic town of **Xátiva**.

Xàtiva

The ancient town of **XÀTIVA** (Játiva), 50km south of Valencia, was probably founded by the Phoenicians and certainly inhabited by the Romans. Today, it's a scenic, tranquil place and makes a good day-trip. Medieval Xàtiva was the birthplace of Alfonso de Borja, who became Pope Calixtus III, and his nephew Rodrigo, father of the infamous Lucrezia and Cesare Borgia. When Rodrigo became Pope Alexander VI, the family moved to Italy.

Xàtiva has a fine collection of mansions scattered around town, but most are private and cannot be entered. Many of the churches, though, have been recently renovated, and the **old town** is a pleasant place to wander. **Fiestas** are held during Semana Santa and in the second half of August, when the Feria de Agosto is celebrated with bullfights and livestock fairs.

Keep an eye open for **arnadí** in the bakeries – a local speciality of Moorish origin, it's a rich (and expensive) sweet made with pumpkin, cinnamon, almonds, eggs and pine nuts.

12

Museo del Almudín

Corretgeria 46 • Mid-June to mid-Sept Tues–Fri 9.30am–2.30pm, Sat & Sun 10am–2pm; mid-Sept to mid-June Tues–Fri 10am–2pm & 4–6pm, Sat & Sun 10am–2pm • €2.40, or €3.10 with the castle • ☎ 962 276 597

In the centre of town, the **Museo del Almudín** features both an archeological collection and an art museum. The latter includes several pictures by José Ribera (who was born here in 1591) and engravings by Goya – *Caprichos* and *Los Proverbios*. A portrait of Felipe V is hung upside down in retribution for his having set fire to the town in the War of the Spanish Succession and for changing its name (temporarily) to San Felipe.

The castle

Tues–Sun 10am–7pm; Nov–Feb closes 6pm • €2.40, or €3.10 for a joint ticket with the Museo del Almudín

From town, it's a long and tiring walk up a steep hill (there's the option of a tourist train for €4.20) to Xátiva's sturdy tenth-century **castle** – follow signposts from the main square, Plaza del Españoleto, or take a taxi from outside the *turismo* (€11 one way). At the castle you can wander around the fortified grounds and leafy gardens, enjoy views of the surrounding town and countryside, and see a chapel that houses the tomb of the Count of Urgell.

Església de Sant Feliu

Tues–Sat 10am–1pm & 4–7pm, Nov–March 3–6pm, Sun 10am–1pm • Free

On the way to the castle, you'll pass the thirteenth-century **Església de Sant Feliu**, a hermitage built in transitional Romanesque-Gothic style, and the oldest church in Xàtiva. The interior boasts ancient pillars, fine capitals and a magnificent Gothic *retablo*.

By bus and train Xàtiva is served by buses and trains to and from Valencia; the train (1hr) is cheaper, and leaves every half-hour. There are also connections with Gandía (by bus) and Alicante (by train).

Turismo c/Alameda Jaume I (summer Tues–Fri 10am–2pm & 5–7.30pm, Sat & Sun 10am–2pm; winter Tues–Fri 10am–1.30pm & 4–6pm, Sat & Sun 10am–2pm; ☏ 962 273 346, ⓦ comunitatvalenciana.com). There's also a seasonal office in front of the *ayuntamiento* (summer daily 10am–2pm; same phone).

Casa La Abuela c/Reina 17 ☏ 962 281 085, ⓦ casalaabuela.es. Feast on traditional fare, from robust rice dishes to stews, at this welcoming restaurant that draws plenty of locals. The *menú del día* is €15, while mains are €9–17. Daily 1–4pm & 8.30–10.30pm, closed Tues, and Wed & Friday dinner.

Hostería de Mont Sant ☏ 962 275 081, ⓦ mont-sant .com. If you'd like to go the deluxe route, opt for this lovely hotel on the way up to the castle, which has stunning gardens and a pool. €83

Hotel Murta c/Ángel Lacalle ☏ 962 276 611, ⓦ hotelmurta.com. If you're enjoying Xàtiva's peace and quiet and are looking for a decently priced spot, try this comfortable hotel. They also have a restaurant (guests only, though they can arrange dinner for groups) specializing in local cuisine. €55

Gandía and around

GANDÍA, 65km south of Valencia, is a historical town and lively resort area. The main town features the impressive Borja palace, a quiet old quarter, and plenty of shops and restaurants, while the long, sun-splashed **Gandía Playa** sprawls along the coast 4km away, and draws crowds of vacationing Spaniards in the summer.

Palacio Ducal de los Borja

Mon–Sat 10am–2pm & 4–8pm, Sun 10am–2pm; rest of the year Mon–Sat 10am–2pm & 3–7pm • All visits are by guided tour, €6 • ☏ 962 871 4 65, ⓦ palauducal.com

Gandía was once important enough to have its own university, but the only real testimony to its heyday is the **Palacio Ducal de los Borja**, built in the fourteenth century, with Renaissance and Baroque additions and modifications. Duke Francisco de Borja was much responsible for the golden age of the town (late fifteenth to early sixteenth century) in terms of urban and cultural development. Learned and pious, the duke opened colleges all over Spain and Europe, and was eventually canonized. The palace contains his paintings, tapestries and books, but parts of the building itself are of equal interest, such as the *artesonado* ceilings and the pine window shutters, so perfectly preserved by prolonged burial in soil and manure that resin still oozes from them when the hot sun beats down. There are also several beautiful sets of *azulejos*, but these are outshone by the fourteenth-century Arabesque wall tiles, whose brilliant lustre is irreparable as it was derived from pigments of plants that became extinct soon after the Muslims left. The palace also occasionally hosts excellent contemporary and international arts and theatre programmes.

By train and bus The joint bus and train station is on Avda. Marqués de Campo. Trains and buses run regularly to and from Valencia. The AVE train now connects Gandía with Madrid (via Valencia) in just over 3hr; trains run a couple times a day in each direction; schedules may be limited in winter; contact RENFE (ⓦ renfe.com) for current updates.

Getting around Buses run every fifteen to twenty minutes (6am–11.30pm) from the tourist office in town to Gandía Playa.

Turismo The main *turismo* is opposite the station (summer Mon–Fri 9.30am–2.30pm & 4–8pm, Sat 9.30am–2.30pm; winter Mon–Fri 9.30am–1.30pm & 3.30pm–7.30pm, Sat 9.30am–1.30pm; ☏ 962 877 788, ⓦ gandiaturismo.com).

There's a second office at Paseo Neptuno 45, Gandía Playa (summer Mon–Sat 9.30am–8.30pm, Sun 9.30am–1.30pm; winter Tues, Thurs & Fri 9.30am–2.30 & 3.30–6.30pm, Sat 9.30–1.30; ☏ 962 842 407).

ACCOMMODATION

Albergue Mar i Vent 10km south of Gandía Town ☎ 962 831 748. This exceptionally pleasant hostel is on the beachfront at Playa de Piles. In summer, about six daily buses run there from outside the train station; in winter, there are fewer buses, and they drop you off about 1km from the hostel. Dorms **€10.50** under-25s, **€14.50** over-25s

Hostal Residencia Clibomar c/Alcoy 24, Playa de Gandía ☎ 962 840 237. Comfortable, well-kept rooms, a short stroll to the beach. Usually closed in winter. **€65**

Hotel Bayren Paseo de Neptuno 62 ☎ 962 840 300, ⓦ hotelesrh.com. Big, glossy four-star beach hotel – if you're in Gandía for the sun and sand, then this place delivers. Most of the rooms have balconies, plus there's a pool, restaurant/terrace and plenty of activities for kids. **€105**

Hotel Los Naranjos c/Avda. del Grau 67 ☎ 962 873 143, ⓦ losnaranjoshotel.com. In the middle of town, this decent hotel has clean, if rather faded, rooms. **€40**

EATING AND DRINKING

Gandía Town has a range of restaurants, from traditional spots with a *menú del día* to tapas, while the beach zone is a good place for **seafood** and paellas; don't miss *fideuà*, a seafood paella cooked with vermicelli instead of rice.

La Gamba Carretera Nazaret-Oliva ☎ 962 841 310, ⓦ gambamarisqueria.com. A few blocks back from Gandía Playa, with a breezy terrace in the summer. Fill up on fresh seafood, from *cigalas* (crayfish) and lobster to, yes, *gambas* (shrimp). The daily *menú* is €30, and mains are €15–20. Daily 1.30–3.30pm, plus 8.30–10.30pm in summer; closed Mon.

L'Ullal c/Benicanena 12 ☎ 962 877 382. The chefs here use local ingredients to creative use, with a tasty range of seafood, grilled meats and the regional speciality of *fideuà*. Tasting *menús* €28–35. Just west of the old town. Generally daily 1.30–3.30pm & 8.30–10.30pm, closed Sun, and dinner Mon & Tues.

NIGHTLIFE

For **nightlife**, head just slightly inland to Pl. del Castell for cocktails at one of the busy bars, then make for the beach area clubs, most of which are liveliest on summer weekends; some open in the low season for events and parties.

CocoLoco Paseo de Neptuno 53, no phone, ⓦ cocoloco .es. The crowds here get hot and sweaty, dancing to everything from Latin beats to techno. The owners also run several other spicy nightspots, including poolside beach

club *Agua de Coco* and the sleek *Luna*, both on Paseo Neptuno (ⓦ lunagandia.com).

Discoteca Bacarra c/Legazpi 7, no phone. Groove to DJ-spun tunes surrounded by fresh-off-the beach locals.

Around the cape: Gandía to Altea

A string of attractive little towns and beaches stretches from **Gandía** to **Altea**, before you reach the developments of Benidorm and Alicante, but your own transport is essential to enjoy the best of them, and accommodation can be pricey. The least expensive option along this coast is to camp – there are scores of decent **campsites**, and a useful booklet listing them is available from local *turismos*.

Denia

DENIA, at the foot of Parque Natural Montgó, is a sizeable, sprawling town even without its summer visitors. Beneath the wooded capes beyond, bypassed by the main road, stretch probably the most beautiful **beaches** on this coastline – it's easier if you have a car to get to most of them, though there are a couple of buses that make the trip from the port.

ARRIVAL AND DEPARTURE   DENIA

By train and bus Trains depart regularly for Benidorm, where you can then connect to a tram to Alicante. Buses also run hourly to and from Alicante, departing from Pl. Archiduque Carlos, among other spots.

By ferry Daily ferries service Mallorca and Ibiza: for

information, contact Baleària (☎ 902 191 068, ⓦ balearia .com), or Iscomar (☎ 902 119 108, ⓦ iscomar.com). Departures Sant Antoni, Ibiza (2 daily; 2hr 15min); Ibiza Town (3 daily; 2hr); Palma (4 daily; 5hr); Formentera (daily; 3hr 45min).

12

ACCOMMODATION

Hostal Residencia Loreto c/Loreto 12 ☎ 966 435 419, ⓦ hostalloreto.com. Simple and slightly dated place, though the rooms have a certain rustic style. **€79**

La Posada del Amar Pl. Drassanes, at the port ☎ 966 432 966, ⓦ laposadadelmar.com. Set in a nicely renovated thirteenth-century building that was a former customs house, this hotel blends old and new with elegant aplomb. **€130**

Xàbia

At the heart of this area, very near the easternmost Cabo de la Nao, is **XÀBIA** (Jávea), an attractive, prosperous town surrounded by hillside villas, with a fine beach and a very pleasant old town. In summer, both Denia and Xàbia are lively in the evenings, especially at weekends, as they're popular with Valencianos. There are plenty of idyllic cove beaches close to Xàbia; one of the best is **Cala Portitxol** (also known as Playa la Barraca), a wonderful sand-and-pebble bay backed by high cliffs.

ACCOMMODATION   XÀBIA

Hotel Xàbia Pío X 5 ☎ 965 795 461, ⓦ www.hotel-javea.com. Elegant rooms by the port, with a touch of a maritime theme and balmy sea views. **€82**

Parador de Jávea Avda. del Mediterráneo ☎ 965 790 200, ⓦ parador.es. With an enviable perch overlooking the sea and great views, this modern place has all the parador hallmarks, including a restaurant serving local cuisine. **€170**

EATING AND DRINKING

Nightlife is centred on the beach bars. Later in the evening, the crowds move to the out-of-town clubs on the road to Cabo de San Antonio.

La Bohême Playa Arenal ☎ 965 791 600, ⓦ bohemejavea .com. Restaurants come and go with great frequency in Xàbia, but *La Bohême* has stayed around. The Mediterranean fare has international touches – a seafood casserole with basmati rice, or fresh tuna drizzled in teriyaki sauce. The lunch *menú* is a good deal at just under €15. Daily noon–11.30pm.

La Bomboneria Lepanto 20 ☎ 965 791 647. Enjoy uniquely prepared Mediterranean cuisine and fresh seafood at this friendly port restaurant. The daily *menú* is around €18, and there's a gourmet version for €29. Daily 1–3.30pm & 8–11pm.

Altea

Heading southeast, you pass the dramatic rocky outcrop known as the **Peñón de Ifach**, its natural beauty offering a stark contrast to the concrete towers of the neighbouring package resort of **Calpe** (Calp). If you'd like to enjoy the coast for a night or two, **ALTEA**, just 11km to the south, is a more attractive proposition: a small resort set below a historic hilltop village, with views overlooking the whole stretch of coastline. Tourist development is centred on the seafront, where there's a pebble beach and attractive promenade of low-rise apartment buildings interspersed with tottering old fishermen's houses.

The old village, or *poble antic*, up the hill, is even more picturesque, with its steep lanes, white houses, blue-domed church and profuse blossoms. In summer, the entire quarter is packed with pavement diners and boutique browsers.

INFORMATION   ALTEA

Turismo c/San Pedro 9 (summer usually Mon–Fri 9.30am–2pm & 5–7.30pm, Sat 10am–1pm & 5–8pm; rest of the year reduced hours; ☎ 965 844 114, ⓦ altea.es).

ACCOMMODATION

It's a good idea to book ahead in the summer. Beyond staying in town, the verdant interior reveals a number of comfortable and unique *casas rurales*.

Hotel Altaya c/San Pedro 28 ☎ 965 840 800, ⓦ hotelaltaya.com. This swanky place on the seafront has prime sea views from balustraded balconies. **€65**

El Naranjal Cami dels Morers 15 ☎ 965 792 989,

ⓦcampingelnaranjal.com. Well-run campsite 1.5km south of Xàbia with plenty of facilities, including a pool and bar and, in the summer, live music and other events. Adults **€6.15**, pitches **€11.45**
Refugio Marnes Sierra de Bernia, Benissa ☏637 063 003, ⓦrefugiomarnes.com. Some 15km northwest of

Calp, this rural *finca* (country estate), covering 50 acres, has three types of accommodation: a restored old farmhouse, a private cottage and a luxurious Bedouin tent (both available for weekly rentals only) which brings new meaning to "glamping". Farmhouse rooms **€81**, tent and cottage **€500–€630** weekly

EATING AND DRINKING

It's a treat **to eat** in the old town, with most of the alfresco dining centred on Pl. de la Iglesia; there are also plenty of cafés and restaurants along the seafront. The best places to **drink** are to be found around the main square of the old village.

Oustau c/Mayor 5 ☏965 842 078, ⓦoustau.es. If you're feeling flush, try the French-influenced cuisine at this quality restaurant – it's one of the better-known old-town options. Daily 7am–1pm; usually closed Mon in winter.
Restaurante La Capella c/San Pablo 1 ☏966 880 484. Lovely restaurant in a historic building with stone walls and a breezy terrace with views of the surrounding countryside.

Traditional mid-priced cuisine, from *arroz a la banda* to salads bursting with local produce. Daily noon–4 & 8–midnight; closed Wed dinner, & last two weeks in Sept, Nov & Feb.
Sant Pere 24 c/Sant Pere 24 ☏965 844 972. By the seafront, this comfortable spot serves up delicious seafood and rice combinations, including fresh shrimp, lobster and the catch of the day. Mains €10–15. Daily 1–11.30pm.

Benidorm

Hugely high-rise, vaguely Vegas and definitely dodgy, **BENIDORM** is the beach resort that everyone loves to hate. Nonetheless, the crowds keep coming, and if you're looking for package tourism at its apex, then Benidorm is king (in fact, it's not only king, but also emperor, sultan and president). Decades ago, British writer Rose Macaulay described Benidorm as a small village "crowded very beautifully round its domed and tiled church on a rocky peninsula". The old part's still here, but it's so overshadowed by the kilometres of towering concrete that you'll be hard-pressed to find it. If you want hordes of British, German and Scandinavian holiday-makers who are lobster-red from the sun (and, often, the drink); laminated, quadrilingual menus of overpriced, mediocre food; "English" pubs screening football and rugby; pulsating discos and bar-clubs; and bacon, eggs and watery coffee for breakfast – Benidorm has all of it. But it also has its sun-splashed coast, which is what brought everyone here in the first place. **Playa de la Levante**, Benidorm's biggest highlight, is 2km of golden sand, and undeniably pleasant when you can see it through the hordes of roasting bodies. A little farther from the centre is the slightly more relaxed and less exposed **Playa de Ponienete**, which has slightly more Spanish flavour.

One of the better ways to take in Benidorm is as a day-trip from Alicante: the connection via tram is quick and easy. This way, you can enjoy the beach, the bars, and the boisterous atmosphere and, best of all, when you've had enough, you can leave.

ARRIVAL AND INFORMATION   BENIDORM

By train, bus and tram Trains arrive at the top of town, off Avda. de Beniarda, while the main bus stop is at the junction of Avda. de Europa and c/Gerona. Moving on to Alicante, you can either take the FGV tram or a bus,

but the tram is quicker and more convenient. There's also a night-train service that runs along the coast to Alicante in July and August. Regular buses travel to and from Valencia.

BENIDORM'S WATER PARKS

If you're travelling with kids (or just want to get in touch with your inner child), you're spoilt for choice in Benidorm, where each amusement park seems to eclipse the next: there's the "mythical" theme park **Terra Mítica** (Mythic Land; ⓦterramiticapark.com); the wildlife theme park **Terra Natura** (ⓦterranatura.com); the **Aqualandia** water park (ⓦaqualandia.net); and, well, you get the idea.

Turismo Pl. del Torrejó, in the old town (Mon–Fri 9am–9pm, mid-Sept to mid-June until 8pm, Sat 10am–1pm; ☎ 965 851 311, ⊛ benidorm.org).

ACCOMMODATION

With tens of thousands of hotel beds and hundreds of apartments, finding a **place to stay** isn't a problem (except perhaps in Aug). Budget places are clustered around the old town, and out of season many of the giant hotels slash their prices drastically, making Benidorm a cheap base from which to explore the surrounding area.

Barceló Asia Gardens Glorieta del Fuego, Mítica ☎ 966 818 400, ⊛ barceloasiagardens.com. If you're looking to splurge in Benidorm, this elegant, five-star hotel is the place to do it. Set back from the sea (2km from the beach) in massive grounds on the slopes of the Sierra Cortina, it boasts Balinese-style furnishings, Thai massages in the spa and two good Asian-themed restaurants. **€275**

Gran Hotel Bali c/Luís Prendes ☎ 966 815 200, ⊛ granhotelbali.com. It's hard to miss this towering deluxe landmark, one of Europe's highest hotels – and the preferred choice of visiting rock royalty. Prices can plummet by half in the low season. **€150**

Hotel Iris c/Palma 47 ☎ 965 865 251, ⊛ iris-hotel.net. Comfortable, simple budget hotel. It's a nice price regardless, but especially reasonable if you consider its central location in the middle of the old town. **€40**

Hotel Rocamar c/Cuatro Esquinas 18 ☎ 965 850 552, ⊛ hotelrocamarbenidorm.es. Smack in the heart of the old town, with simple rooms boasting touches of boutique style. **€88**

Hotel Santa Faz c/Santa Faç 18 ☎ 965 854 063, ⊛ santafazhotel.com. Basic but well kept, and one of the better budget options in town. **€80**

Villa Venecia Pl. San Jaume 1 ☎ 965 855 466, ⊛ hotelvillavenecia.com. Fully updated and renovated, this welcoming beachfront property is now a five-star boutique hotel, with a breezy, light-filled interior, a sun-speckled terrace overlooking the sea, and a restaurant serving innovative local dishes, from fragrant rice to seafood. Restaurant daily 1.30–4pm & 8.30–11pm. **€226**

CAMPSITE

Camping Raco Avda. Doctor Ochoa 19 ☎ 965 868 552, ⊛ campingraco.com. One of the best – and greenest – of Benidorm's myriad campsites. Adults **€6.60**, pitches **€7.70**

EATING

Fish and chips dominate in Benidorm, along with dubiously "authentic" Spanish cuisine that's often much pricier than it needs to be. But you'll still find local restaurants here and there, including in the old town around Calle Santo Domingo.

Club Náutico Benidorm Paseo Colón ☎ 965 855 425, ⊛ cnbenidorm.com. For a departure from the Benidorm crowds and cacophony, amble down to this quiet waterfront restaurant south of the centre, where you can sample fresh seafood on a breezy terrace to the sounds of water slapping against the sides of boats in the dock. Daily 1–4pm & 8–11pm.

La Picaeta de Matias c/L'Alt 3 ☎ 687 239 466. Basic and friendly spot, if a bit touristy, with tasty tapas and fish. Mains €8–12. Mon–Sat 8pm–midnight.

Posada del Mar Paseo Colón ☎ 965 851 373. Usually crammed to the gills, this is a lively seafood spot, where you can tuck into freshly caught fish, prawns and the like. Daily 1–4pm & 8–midnight; may have limited hours in winter.

La Tasca del Pueblo c/Marqués de Comillas ☎ 966 806 312. For tapas, follow the natives to a checked-tablecloth-and-antlers joint that serves quality, reasonably priced *platos*. Daily noon–1am.

Inland from Benidorm

In total contrast to the coastal strip, the remote mountainous terrain **inland from Benidorm** harbours some of the most traditional and isolated villages in the Valencia region. Better roads and local government grants (which encourage the conversion of rural properties into guesthouses) are slowly opening up this area to tourism, but for now the austere *pueblos* retain a fairly untouched character, Castilian is very much a second language and the main visitors are hikers. The area is rich in **birdlife**, with golden eagles, and, in autumn, griffon vultures, often spotted soaring over the limestone ridges. There's no bus or train service, other than links to Alcoy and **Guadalest** (generally only once daily to and from Benidorm), so you'll need your own wheels to get around – and a leisurely drive to take it all in is well worth it. Heading

FIESTAS DE MOROS Y CRISTIANOS

Fiestas de Moros y Cristianos are some of the most important fiestas in the region, and the three-day Fiesta de Moros y Cristianos in **Alcoy**, about 60km from Alicante, is perhaps the biggest of the lot. It's held for three days around St George's Day (Día de San Jordi); usually April 23 but this can vary slightly according to when Easter falls. Magnificent processions and mock battles for the castle culminate in the decisive intervention of St George himself – a legend that originated in the Battle of Alcoy (1276), when the town was attacked by a Muslim army. New costumes are made each year and prizes are awarded for the best, which then go into the local museum, the **Museo Alcoyano de la Fiesta**, at c/San Miguel 60–62 (Tues–Sat 10.30am–2pm & 4–7pm, Sun 11am–2pm; €3; ☎965 540 812).

On the first day, the Christians make their entrance in the morning, the Moors in the afternoon; day two is dedicated to St George, with several religious processions; day three sees a gunpowder battle, leading to the saint's appearance on the battlements. Access from Alicante is easy, with five buses a day. If you decide to stay in town, you can try *Hostal Savoy*, c/Casablanca 9 (☎965 547 272, ⊚hostalsavoy.com; €100), or the *Hotel Reconquista*, Puente San Jorge 1 (☎965 330 900, ⊚hotelreconquista.es; €66, during fiestas €150). The *turismo*, c/Sant Llorenç 2, next to the *ayuntamiento* (Mon–Fri 10am–2pm & 4–6pm, Sat & Sun 11am–2pm; ☎965 537 155, ⊚alcoy.org/turismo), can also offer suggestions for accommodation. After Alcoy's fiesta, the Moros y Cristianos fiestas in **Villena** (beginning of Sept) and **Elche** (Aug) are two of the best.

west along the well-maintained highway to **Alcoy**, the contrast between the hedonistic sun-and-sand coast and quiet, rural inland is memorable. The road continues westward up the valley after Guadalest, passing the village of Confrides and following a serpentine route towards Alcoy.

Guadalest

Twenty-one kilometres west of Benidorm, **GUADALEST** is one of the more popular tourist attractions in the area. The sixteenth-century Moorish castle town is built into the surrounding rock, and you enter through a gateway tunnelled into the mountain. If you can put up with the slew of tourists and gift shops, it's worth visiting for the view down to the reservoir (accessible via the village of Beniarda just to the west) and across the valley.

Casa Típica

C/Iglesia 1 • Mon–Fri & Sun: summer 10am–7pm; winter 10am–6pm • €2

Set in an eighteenth-century house on the main street, **Casa Típica** explores local history via exhibits of antique tools and agricultural methods, plus audiovisual accompaniments and displays that explain the production process of local foods, such as "from olives to olive oil".

INFORMATION AND TOURS   GUADALEST

Turismo The office on Avda. de Alicante (generally summer Mon–Sun 10.30am–2pm & 3–7.30pm; winter Mon–Fri 10.30–2pm & 3–7.30pm, Sun 10.30am–1pm; ☎965 885 298, ⊚guadalest.es) has maps of the town and can arrange trips on a solar-powered tourist boat which centre on the local flora and fauna.

Alicante (Alacant)

In the minds of many, **Alicante** (**ALACANT**) is often lumped together with the other brash Costa Blanca resorts. It shouldn't be. Valencia's second-largest city, the thoroughly Spanish Alicante has a decidedly elegant Mediterranean air. Seafront *paseos* and wide, breezy esplanades, such as the Rambla Méndez Núñez, are peppered with cosy bars and terrace cafés; a series of well-curated museums feature everything from ancient

12

ALICANTE (ALICANT)

SAN CARLOS

E. Y MINA

C. ADOLFO BLANCH

CALLE DEL PINTOR MURILLO

CALLE TORRES QUEVEDO

BERNARDO LÓPEZ GARCÍA

GARCÍA GUTIÉRREZ

CALLE DEL DOCTOR SAPENA

MARQ

Plaza de Toros

PLAZA DE ESPAÑA

PLAZA DE STA. TERESA

PLAZA MISERICORDIA

CUESTA DE LA FÁBRICA

CALLE DEL PADRE MARIANA

NUEVA BAJA

NUEVA ALTA

M. OLCADE

CALLE JUAN DE HERRERA

CALLE PARAÍSO

CALLE DE LA HUERTA

Parque de la Ereta

GLORIA

C. MANUEL ANTÓN

CALLE DE TRAFALGAR

CALLE DE LA ESPERANZA

OLVIDO

CALLE DEL OVID

PELIGROS

DESENGAÑO

VALCÁRCEL

EMPEDRADO

PLATOS

GALLO

CALLE CONCEPCIÓN

P

Mercado Central

T

Castillo de Santa Bárbara

Lift to Castle

DIPUTADO

AUSSET

SAN BARTOLOMÉ

MUCHAMIEL

ÁLVAREZ

ARGENSOLA

PL. DEL CARMEN

C. ROQUE

TOLEDO

PLAZA DEL PUENTE

Teatro Principal

PL. DE S. CRISTÓBAL

CARMEN

PLAZA QUIJANO

BARRIO VIEJO

VIRGEN DE BELÉN

C/SANTO TOMÁS

SAN ANDRÉS

SAN PASCUAL

C. SAN AGUSTÍN

C. MONJAS

Real Colegio de la Compañía de Jesús

C. MALDONADO

PL. ARQ MIGUEL LÓPEZ

Museo de Arte Moderno

LUCETUM

FRAY JUAN RICO

AVENIDA DE JOVELLANOS

Catedral de S. Nicolás

SAN JOSÉ

PLAZA STA.FAZ

C. VILAVIEJA

PL. STA. MARÍA

Iglesia de Sta. María

MIGUEL SOLER

S. NICOLÁS

CALLE JORGE JUAN

Pº RAMIRO

CALLE MAYOR

PORTAL DE ELCHE

Ayuntamiento

PLAZA AYUNTA-MIENTO

CERVANTES

CALLE DE GRAVINA

PASEO DE GOMIZ

★ **Bus to Airport**

C. RAFAEL ALTAMIRA

CAPITÁN MECA

JUAN BAUTISTA LAFORA

PUERTA DEL MAR

Hotel Meliá

Playa del Postiguet

Puerto

EXPLANADA DE ESPAÑA

PASEO CONDE DE VALLELLANO

P P P

12

Valencia

Playa de San Juan de Alicante

0 — 200 metres

Estación Marítima

■ **ACCOMMODATION**
La City Hotel 3
Eurostars Lucentum 2
Guest House 1
Hospes Amérigo 7
Hostal La Milagrosa 5
Hostal Les Monges 4
Hotel Bahia 6

● **EATING**
César Anca 12
El Cisne de Oro 2
Dársena 13
Mesón de Labradores 3
Monastrell 10
Nou Manolín 6
Piripi 9
El Rebujito 8
Restaurante La Ereta 1
La Taberna del Gourmet 11

■ **CLUBS**
Desdén 1
Jazboree 2
Z Klub 3

● **BARS**
Celestial Copas 5
Desafinado 4
El Forat 7

archeology to contemporary art; the city's cuisine scene is making a name for itself, just as its healthy nightlife did long ago; and its long, sandy beaches are sunkissed for much of the year.

Founded by the Romans, who named it Lucentum (City of Light), and dominated by the Arabs in the second half of the eighth century, Alicante was finally reconquered by Alfonso X in 1246 for the Castilian Crown. In 1308, Jaime III incorporated Alicante into the kingdom of Valencia.

Today, the main **fiesta**, Las Hogueras, is at the end of June, and ignites a series of cracking celebrations second only to Las Fallas in Valencia.

Castillo de Santa Bárbara

Castle Daily: April–Sept 10am–10pm; Oct–March 10am–8pm • Free • **Lift** Daily: April–Sept 10am–8pm; Oct–March 10am–7.30pm • €2.40

The rambling **Castillo de Santa Bárbara**, an imposing medieval fortress located on the bare rocky hill above the town beach, is Alicante's main historical sight. It's best approached from the seaward side where a 205-metre shaft has been cut straight up through the hill to get you to the top; the **lift** entrance is on Avda. de Jovellanos. Almost opposite are the Iberian and Roman remains that have been found on the site, but most of the present layout dates from the sixteenth century. The castle itself is home to the **Museo de la Ciudad de Alicante (MUSA)**, which explores the history of Alicante and the surrounding region via a variety of exhibits. The grounds, or **Parque de la Ereta**, are attractively landscaped, with olive groves, pathways, a café and tremendous views of the city.

Museo de Arte Moderno

Pl. de Santa María 3 • Tues–Sat 10am–8pm, Sun 10am–2pm • Free • ☎ 965 213 156

North of the impressive *ayuntamiento* and next to the Santa María basilica, the **Museo de Arte Moderno** is housed in the city's oldest surviving civil building, a Baroque affair dating back to 1685. It was originally designed as a cereal warehouse, but served as a business school before finally becoming a museum. After a long closure, the fully renovated museum opened in spring 2011, and houses an important collection of contemporary art, including works by Chillida, Picasso, Dalí and Miró.

Museo Arqueológico

Pl. Dr Gómez Ulla • Tues–Sat 10am–7pm, Sun 10am–2pm • €3, €2 to El Tossa archeological site, or €4 for joint ticket • ☎ 965 149 000, ⒲ marqalicante.com • Bus routes #2, #6, #9, #20 and #23 pass by the museum

The impressive, stylish **Museo Arqueológico (MARQ)** features locally found relics from the Iberian to medieval periods. The museum also manages **El Tossal de Manises**, the remains of the ancient Roman settlement of Lucentum, in the suburb of Albufereta, and can arrange visits to the site.

Beaches

The city's well-maintained beach – **Playa del Postiguet** – gets very crowded in summer. The beaches at **San Juan de Alicante**, about 6km out, are also quite built up, and can be reached either by bus #21 or #22 from the Plaza del Mar or via the FGV tram (get off at the Costa Blanca stop). **Playa Arenales**, backed by sand dunes, is more pleasant; it's 12km south of the city and reachable by an hourly bus from the main bus station.

Isle de Tabarca

Boats June–Sept 6 daily; limited service in winter • ☎ 965 216 396

Isle de Tabarca, a small island and marine reserve to the south of the city, makes a nice day-trip from Alicante. You can relax on the decent, sunny beach, which has basic facilities but does tend to get very cramped and crowded during the summer. Weather permitting, boats leave from the Explanada de España; call to clarify sailing times and fares.

Museu de Fogueres

C/Teniente Álvarez Soto • Summer Tues–Sat 10am–2pm & 6–9pm, Sun 10am–2pm; winter Tues–Sat 10am–2pm & 5–8pm, Sun 10am–2pm • Free • ☎ 965 146 828, ⍾ hogueras.org

The exhibits at the **Museu de Fogueres** delve into the history of the raucous Fiesta de San Joan, Alicante's version of Valencia's Las Fallas. Exhibits include impressively detailed satirical effigies that are burned during the festivities, plus elaborate costumes and photographs documenting the festival's history.

ARRIVAL AND DEPARTURE   ALICANTE

By plane The airport is 12km south of the centre, in El Altet, and is served by charter, discount and other airlines from around Spain and Europe. The much-improved C6 shuttle bus, which now departs roughly every 20min (daily 5am–10 or 11pm; €2.65) travels into town, dropping off at Pl. del Mar, La Rambla and other city-centre spots.

By train Estación de Madrid, Avda. Salamanca, has direct connections to Madrid, Albacete, Murcia and Valencia. By 2013, the high-speed AVE railway, on the Madrid–Levante route, is expected to reach Alicante; for the latest updates, consult RENFE (☎ 902 240 202, ⍾ renfe.es). There are also plans to build a new combined train, bus and tram station to replace Estación de Madrid; ask at the *turismo* for an update. Destinations Albacete (9 daily; 1hr 30min); Benidorm (half-hourly to hourly; 1hr 10min); Denia (half-hourly to

hourly; 2hr 15min); Madrid (9 daily; 3hr 45min); Murcia (14–23 daily; 1hr 15min); Valencia (10 daily; 1hr 30min–2hr 15min); and Xàtiva (5 daily; 1hr 20min).

By bus The bus station, c/Portugal 13 (☎ 965 130 700), handles local and long-distance services. Destinations Albacete (9 daily; 2hr 30min); Almería (5 daily; 5hr 30min); Barcelona (11 daily; 8hr); Cartagena (8 daily; 2hr); Granada (6 daily; 5hr); Madrid (8 daily; 6hr); Málaga (6 daily; 8hr); Murcia (8 daily; 1hr 45min).

By tram Alicante's ever-expanding and efficient FGV tram system (⍾ fgvalicante.com) zips to Benidorm and Denia via the red #1 line, picking it up at various points in the city including the main terminus at Pl. Luceros or Mercado Central; fares start at €1.25, and there's also a variety of multi-use discount tickets.

INFORMATION

Turismo Avda. Rambla Méndez Núñez 23 (Mon–Fri 9am–8pm, Sat 10am–8pm, Sun 10am–2pm; ☎ 965 200

000, ⍾ alicanteturismo.com). There's also a branch on Explanada de España (Mon–Fri 10am–7pm, Sat 10am–2pm).

ACCOMMODATION

Alicante has a wide range of **accommodation**, with plenty of hotels concentrated at the lower end of town, above the attractively tiled seafront walk, Explanada de España.

La City Hotel Avda. de Salamanca 16 ☎ 965 131 973, ⍾ lacityhotel.com. Bright, modern hotel near the train station, with a cool-toned lobby that gives way to comfortable rooms with crisp bedspreads and blonde-wood furnishings. Good value for the price – and ideal for those with an early-morning train to catch. **€70**

Eurostars Lucentum Avda. Alfonso X El Sabio 11 ☎ 902 932 424, ⍾ eurostarslucentum.com. Sleek and central addition to the Eurostars chain, with plenty of blonde wood, gleaming marble lobby floors, recessed lights and business-friendly amenities. **€70**

Guest House c/Segura 20 ☎ 650 718 353,

⍾ guesthousealicante.com. A perennial budget favourite among travellers – and with good reason – this inviting, cheery guesthouse is lovingly cared for by the amiable owner. Individually decorated, spic-and-span rooms and apartments reveal personal touches, such as complimentary coffee and tea. **€50**

★ **Hospes Amérigo** Rafael Altamira 7 ☎ 965 146 570, ⍾ hospes.es. Past meets present in this upscale hotel, housed in a magnificently restored seventeenth-century convent. The rooms reveal gleaming hardwood floors and delicate white curtains, while the breezy rooftop deck has a pool, sauna and spa, and a chill-out zone where you can

12

relax under the night sky. One of the city's better restaurants, *Monastrell*, is on site. **€120**

Hostal La Milagrosa c/Villavieja 8 ☎ 965 216 918, ⓦ hostallamilagrosa.com. Efficiently run, often busy *pensión* with great-value rooms that are simple, spotless and inviting. A roof terrace seals the deal. **€40**

★ **Hostal Les Monges** c/San Agustín 4 ☎ 965 215 046, ⓦ lesmonges.net. Named after the convent of cloistered nuns (*monges*) that sits across the street, this is one of the better – and more original – deals in Alicante, with lovely, strikingly styled rooms. Some are antique-chic, while others are Japanese influenced, and are accessed from corridors lined with vibrant *azulejos*, oddball curios and unlikely paintings – a true labour of love. Ask for an upstairs room if you're a light sleeper. **€52**

Hotel Bahia c/Juan Bautista Lafora 8 ☎ 965 206 522, ⓦ hotelbahia.es. This friendly, unpretentious hotel on the seafront has a bright reception and unassuming, coolly comfortable rooms, some with sea views. **€50**

CAMPING

Camping El Jardín El Campello ☎ 965 657 580, ⓦ campingeljardin.com. One of many campsites along the coast here, this inviting site is near a quiet beach, accessible by tram and also has fetching little bungalows. **€5.65** per adult, plus **€7** per pitch, bungalows **€106**

Internacional La Marina 29km out on the Carretera. Alicante–Cartagena ☎ 965 419 200, ⓦ campinglamarina.com. A pleasant location in the woods, close to a good beach, and with excellent facilities: everything from a gym to live music. **€8** per adult, pitches start at **€26**

EATING

Alicante boasts a rich variety of restaurants, and has emerged as a culinary destination to watch in recent years: uniquely, a good number of the city's well-known chefs are women, such as María José San Román of *Monastrell* (see below), who is nicknamed the "Saffron Queen" for her prowess with rice dishes. Restaurants are concentrated in and around the old town, with **tapas** places on c/San Francisco. If you want to fashion your own meals, there's no better place than the enormous **Mercado Central**, housed in a wonderful old *modernista* building on Avda. Alfonso X El Sabio. Another market (a major outdoor event) is held by the Pl. de Toros (Thurs & Sat 9am–2pm).

César Anca c/Ojeda 1, Pl. Gabriel Miró ☎ 965 201 580, ⓦ cesarancahosteleria.com. Elegant restaurant where rising star César Anca reinvents Mediterranean cuisine, with mains at €15–25. Wines from the on-site *bodega*, including an excellent selection of Valencia and Alicante *vinos*, are matched to the superb food. For creative tapas, try the adjoining *La Barra de César Anca*. Daily 1.30--4pm & 9–11pm, Fri & Sat till midnight; closed Sun lunch & Mon dinner; in winter, also closed Sun dinner.

El Cisne de Oro c/del Teatro 5 23 ☎ 965 141 427. Locals crowd around the curved bar at this lively little tapas bar to munch on the justifiably popular signature grilled pork loin, with mushrooms, pepper and mayonnaise. Also on the menu is the regional speciality of *mojama* (salted tuna). Generally noon–late.

Dársena Muelle de Levante 6 ☎ 965 207 589, ⓦ darsena.com. This handsome restaurant on the waterfront serves aromatic paellas and top-notch seafood in a genteel setting. It's pricey – but the paella is the real deal. Daily 1–4pm & 8–11pm.

Mesón de Labradores c/Labradores 19 ☎ 965 204 846. Buzzing bar where you can graze on tasty tapas, from fresh seafood bites and ham, and wash it down with jugs of *sangría*. Tues–Sun 7.30pm–1am.

★ **Monastrell** Amérigo Hotel, c/Rafael Altamira 7 ☎ 965 200 363, ⓦ monastrell.com. Acclaimed chef María José San Román creates delicious Spanish cuisine with a twist, from monkfish with rye-bread crumbs and saffron-scented tomato sauce to a superb variety of rice dishes, including one topped with red Denia prawns and white truffles. *Menú* is €38, tasting *menú* is €65. Tues–Sat noon–4pm & 8pm–midnight.

Nou Manolín c/Villegas 3 ☎ 965 200 368, ⓦ noumanolin.com. Feast on market-fresh regional fare, including superb shellfish and paella, or keep it casual at the atmospheric tapas bar. Mains are €18–27. Daily 1–4pm & 8–midnight.

Piripi Avda. Oscar Esplá 30 ☎ 965 227 940, ⓦ noumanolin.com. This long-established restaurant, run by the same owners as *Nou Manolín*, features top-notch tapas, excellent rice dishes prepared with fresh seasonal produce and a good selection of wines. Daily 1–4pm & 8pm–midnight.

El Rebujito c/San Francisco ☎ 965 210 796. Lively little Andalucian bar-restaurant, where in the true tapas tradition, dining out is as much a social occasion as a gastronomic one. Seating is at the bar or at big barrels-turned-tables, and the menu is scrawled on a chalkboard. Try a plate of shrimp with a bottle of wine for €15, or opt for a glass of beer or sangría for the nice price of €1.50–2. Daily noon–late; may close for part of summer.

Restaurante La Ereta Parque de la Ereta ☎ 965 143 250, ⓦ laereta.es. The memorable city views are matched by the locally sourced cuisine with a designer touch, from razor clams and quivering ruby-red hunks of tuna to cubes of watermelon sangría. Surrounded by the greenery of Parque de la Ereta, the restaurant offers a refreshing change from the bustle of the city. Tasting *menú* €56. Mon–Sat 8.30–11pm.

TURRÓN

Spaniards have a sweet spot for **turrón** (*torró* in Catalan/Valenciano), a nougat candy with almonds and honey that's perhaps most popular in the Alicante region. *Turrón* is believed to have originated as a Moorish delicacy in the town of **Jijona** (Xixona), about 20km north of Alicante. You can sink your teeth into two varieties: crunchy (often called Alicante) and soft (Jijona), which has a smooth consistency almost like peanut butter. The two leading brands are Lobo and 1880, though you'll find many others throughout Spain, including small-batch boutique producers; and you'll see *turrón* for sale in sweet shops throughout the region, including along c/Mayor in Alicante. The **Museo del Turrón** in Jijona (Jan–June Mon–Fri 10am–1.30pm & 4–7.30, Sat 10am–1pm & 4–7pm, Sun 10am–1pm & 5–7pm; July–Dec Mon–Fri 10am–7.30, Sat 10am–1pm & 4–7pm, Sun 10am–1pm & 5–7pm; €3; ☎ 965 610 712, Ⓦ museodelturron.com), traces *turrón's* impressive timeline – it can be traced back to the Middle Ages – and includes a view of the modern production plant on site.

La Taberna del Gourmet c/San Fernando 10 ☎ 965 204 233. Stylish haunt with an eye-catching rocky facade, which serves some of the more creative tapas and organic wines in Alicante, including lamb sweetbreads, chorizo croquettes and scrambled eggs with cod. It's run by the same owners as *Monastrell*. Tapas and *montaditos* €4–5, mains €17–25. Tapas *menú* is €25; tasting *menú* is €50. Daily 1pm–midnight.

NIGHTLIFE

For hitting the bars and **drinking** with locals, the old town – or El Barrio, as it's called – still rules, with everything from dark, cosy bars to jazz joints. Alicante also has a decent number of **gay clubs and bars**, both in the old town and just south of it, around c/de San Fernando.

BARS
Celestial Copas c/San Pascual, no phone. Knock back a few cocktails in this deliciously strange and arty bar. Summer daily 10pm–3am; winter generally Thurs 10pm–3am, Fri & Sat 10pm–4am.

Desafinado c/Santo Tomás 6 ☎ 965 142 671. This lively pub heats up with live music and friendly banter. Generally Tues–Sun 8.30–4.30am.

El Forat Pl. Santa Faz, no phone. Wildly popular gay (but very straight-friendly) bar with an over-the-top decor of twinkling lights, huge bunches of fake flowers and caricatures of divas and record covers on the walls. Generally Fri & Sat 11pm–late.

CLUBS
Desdén c/Labradores 22 ☎ 965 143 323. Groove to a range of music, from jazz and house to dance and funk. Generally Thurs–Sat 11pm–late.

Jazboree c/San José 10 ☎ 616 971 325. Music club with all sorts of live acts: jazz, ska, roots and sometimes even flamenco. Generally Thurs–Sat 11pm–late.

Z Klub c/San Fernando ☎ 965 210 646. This stylish club spins laidback dance sounds, and draws a lively, youngish crowd. Generally Thurs–Sat 11pm–late.

DIRECTORY

Consulates UK, Pl. Calvo Sotelo 1–2 ☎ 965 216 022.

Police c/Médico Pascual Pérez 27 ☎ 965 148 888.

Around Alicante

For a distinct change from Alicante's sun and sea, head inland to the lush palm forest at the lovely town of **Elche**. Further south, explore the region's formidable history in elegant **Orihuela**, which features three medieval churches and a well-preserved old quarter.

Elche

ELCHE (ELX), 20km inland and south from Alicante, is famed throughout Spain for its exotic **palm forest** and for the ancient stone bust known as *La Dama de Elche*, discovered here in 1897 (and now in the Museo Arqueológico in Madrid). The palm trees, originally planted by the Moors, are still the town's chief industry – not only do they attract tourists, but the female trees produce dates, and the fronds from the males are in demand all over the country for use in Palm Sunday processions and as charms against lightning.

Elche is also the home of a remarkable **fiesta** in the first two weeks of August, which culminates in a centuries-old mystery play – *Misteri*, held in the eighteenth-century **Basílica Menor de Santa María** over August 14–15. Additional celebrations include one of the best examples of the Moros y Cristianos mock battles (see box, p.829).

Huerto del Cura

Porta de la Morera 49 • Daily: Jan–Feb & Nov–Dec Mon–Sat 10am–5pm, Sun 10am–3pm; May–Aug 10am–8.30pm; March, April, Sept & Oct Mon–Sat 10am–7.30pm, Sun 10am–6pm • €5 • ☎ 965 451 936, ⓦ turismedelx.com

Elche's palm forests, unique in Europe, are all around the outskirts of the city; the finest trees are those in the **Huerto del Cura**, a beautifully landscaped private garden, where you can stroll among the sun-warmed groves.

Museu del Palmeral

Porta de la Morera 12 • Tues–Sat 10am–1.30pm & 4.30–8pm, Sun 10.30am–1.30pm • €3 • ☎ 965 422 240, ⓦ turismedelx.com

Set in a traditional farmhouse near the Huerto del Cura, the **Museu del Palmeral** explores the origins, history and evolution of the beautiful palm groves via exhibits, videos and touch screens. A visit also includes a walk through the lush, adjacent palm grove and orchard.

12

ARRIVAL AND INFORMATION ELCHE

By train and bus Trains and buses run more or less hourly between Alicante and Elche.

Turismo c/Filet de Fora 1 (Mon–Fri 9am–7pm, Sat 10am–7pm, Sun 10am–2pm; ☎966 658 140, ⓦ turismedelx.com).

ACCOMMODATION

Hostal Candilejas c/Doctor Ferran 19 ☎965 466 512, ⓦ hostalcandilejas.com. If you're looking for budget beds, try this simple, clean *hostal* near the centre of town. **€40**

Hotel Huerto del Cura Porta de la Morera 14 ☎966 612 050, ⓦ hotelhuertodelcura.com. One of Elche's most elegant hotels, just south of the Huerto del Cura, with wood-beamed rooms leading onto stunning gardens, and a graceful ambiance throughout. **€90**

EATING AND DRINKING

Keep an eye out for *arroz con costra*, a local speciality (literally "rice and crust"), made with rice, eggs, *embutidos*, chicken and rabbit, which is served at a number of the local restaurants.

El Granaino c/José María Buch 40 ☎966 664 080, ⓦ mesongranaino.com. For Levantine and Andalucian delicacies, head to this acclaimed restaurant, where the chefs incorporate seasonal produce in the well-crafted dishes. Pricey but worth it. Daily 1–4pm & 8–11pm, closed Sun.

Restaurant El Parque Municipal Parque Municipal ☎965 453 415. This massive restaurant, set amid the leafy town park, serves tasty traditional cuisine, from rice dishes to quality seafood and meats. Mains 14–20. Daily 1–4pm & 8.30–11pm.

Orihuela

Just over 50km southwest of Alicante lies **ORIHUELA**, capital of the Vega Baja district, where Los Reyes Católicos held court in 1488. The town's aristocratic past is reflected in the restored old quarter, but despite its proximity to the coast, Orihuela retains its provincial charm and is worth a wander. It also has a natural attraction in **El Palmeral**, the second-largest palm forest in Spain, which lies beyond the Colegio de Santo Domingo, about a 20min walk out of town.

One of Orihuela's hidden treasures, the Baroque **Monastario de la Visitación Salesas** on c/Salesas Marqués Arneva has several paintings by the nineteenth-century artist

Vincente López displayed in its cloisters. The building is currently closed to the public, but occasionally opens temporarily; enquire at the turismo.

Catedral de Orihuela
C/Doctor Sarget • Tues–Fri 10am–2pm & 4–7pm, Sat & Sun 10am–2pm; in winter hours may vary • €2

Right in the centre of the old town is the medieval **Catedral**, no bigger than the average parish church, built with spiralling, twisted pillars and vaulting. A painting by Velázquez, *The Temptation of St Thomas*, hangs in a small museum in the nave – and don't overlook the Mudéjar-influenced, fourteenth-century Puerta de las Cadenas.

Museo Diocesano de Arte Sacro
C/Ramón y Cajal • Tues–Fri 10am–2pm & 4–7pm, Sat & Sun 10am–2pm • €4 • ☎ 966 743 627

The **Palacio Episcopal**, with its impressive Baroque exterior, is home to the **Museo Diocesano de Arte Sacro**, which explores the city's formidable religious past via an unexpectedly rich collection of art and sacred treasures from throughout the town and the region, including works by the early Renaissance painter Pablo de San Leocadio.

Iglesia de Santiago
Pl. de Santiago • Tues–Fri 10am–2pm & 4–7pm, Sat & Sun 10am–2pm • Free

The **Iglesia de Santiago** is one of the town's three medieval churches – all of which are Catalan Gothic (subsequently altered), a style you won't find any farther south. The oldest part of the church is the front portal, the Puerta de Santiago, a spectacular example of late fifteenth-century Isabelline style. Inside, the furniture is Baroque, and there's a *retablo* by Francisco Salzillo.

Iglesia de Santas Justa y Rufina
Pl. Salesas • Generally Tues–Fri 10am–2pm & 4–7pm, Sat & Sun 10am–2pm • Free

In the town centre, just past the *ayuntamiento*, rises another of Orihuela's medieval churches, the **Iglesia de Santas Justa y Rufina** – its tower is the oldest construction in the parish and has excellent gargoyle sculptures.

Museo de Semana Santa
Pl. de la Merced 1 • Tues–Sat 10am–2pm & 4–7pm, Sun 10am–2pm • €2 • ☎ 966 744 089

Housed in the Iglesia de Nuestra Señora de la Merced, the **Museo de Semana Santa** explores the history of the Semana Santa celebrations, with exhibits on the elaborate costumes and rituals, plus audiovisual presentations and photographs that trace the long timeline of Semana Santa.

Museo de la Muralla
C/del Río • Tues–Sat 10am–2pm & 4–7pm, Sun 10am–2pm • Free • ☎ 965 304 698

Set within the grounds of the Universidad Miguel Hernández, the **Museo de la Muralla** is centred on the extensive underground remains of Orihuela's impressive city walls, plus a well-preserved *baños Árabes* (Arab baths), which includes a room where the water was heated. There's also a Gothic palace and a Baroque building dating from the eighteenth century, plus displays of ancient ceramics.

Museo Fundación Pedrera
C/López Pozas 4 • Currently open only for temporary exhibitions; enquire at the *turismo* • ☎ 966 736 106

The latest addition to Orihuela's museum circuit is the impressive new **Museo Fundación Pedrera**, set in the eighteenth-century Palacio de Sorzano de Tejada. At the time of writing, the building was open only for temporary exhibitions, though it does have a rich permanent collection that includes works by many of the Spanish greats, including Sorolla, Picasso, Murillo, Zurbarán, Goya and Dalí.

Colegio de Santo Domingo

C/Adolfo Claravana • Tues–Sat 10am–2pm & 4–7pm, 5–8pm in summer, Sun 10am–2pm; confirm hours at the *turismo* • Free

The Baroque **Colegio de Santo Domingo**, at the entrance to town near the palm forest, was originally a Dominican monastery. It was converted into a university in 1569 by Pope Pius V, then closed down by Fernando VII in 1824. The two cloisters are well worth seeing, along with the fine eighteenth-century Valencian tiles in the refectory. For a view of the town and surrounding plains, walk up to the seminary on top of the hill – from Plaza Caturla in the centre of town, take the road leading up on the right; not far from the top, there are a couple of steeper shortcuts to the right.

ARRIVAL AND INFORMATION ORIHUELA

By train and bus Orihuela is connected by regular trains and buses to Alicante and Murcia, which arrive and depart from the combined station at the bottom of Avda. de Teodomiro.
Turismo Pl. Marqués de Rafal, near the cathedral (summer

Mon 8am–3pm, Tues–Fri 8am–3pm & 4–8pm, Sat & Sun 10am–2pm & 5–8pm; winter Mon 8am–4pm, Tues–Fri 8am–3pm & 4–7pm Sat & Sun 10am–2pm & 4–7pm; ☎ 965 304 645, ⓦ orihuelaturistica.es).

ACCOMMODATION AND EATING

Hostal Rey Teodomiro Avda. Teodomiro 10 ☎ 966 743 348. Convenient for the bus station, and just five blocks straight up from the train station, this decent *hostal* has clean, bright, unpretentious rooms. **€51**
Hotel Melia Palacio de Tudemir c/Alfonso XIII 1 ☎ 966 738 010, ⓦ hotelpalaciodetudemir.com. This handsome hotel is suitably palatial, with wall-mounted excavations inscribed in ancient Arabic, and calming rooms and corridors; the restaurant serves regional fare.

Restaurant daily 1.30–4pm & 8.30–11pm. **€70**
Restaurante Casa Corro Avda. Doctor Garcia Rogel 23, El Palmeral ☎ 965 302 963. Tuck into traditional cuisine such as the local speciality of *arroz con costra*, at this long-established restaurant 1km out of town. The lunchtime *menú del día* is €10. They also operate a basic hotel, with simple, well-kept rooms. Restaurant Tues–Sun 1.30–4pm & 9–11pm. **€40**

Murcia

MURCIA, according to the nineteenth-century writer Augustus Hare, would "from the stagnation of its long existence, be the only place Adam would recognize if he returned to Earth". Things have certainly changed – today, Murcia is the commercial hub of the region and boasts a lively cultural scene. Founded by the Moors in the ninth century on the banks of the Río Segura (no more than a trickle now), the city soon became an important trading centre and, four centuries later, the regional capital. It was extensively rebuilt in the eighteenth century, and the buildings in the old quarter are still mostly of this era. Today, a substantial student population ensures that there's a thriving bar and club scene, plus plenty of tapas bars and restaurants to suit all budgets.

The Catedral

Pl. Hernández Amores • **Catedral** Daily: summer 7am–1pm & 6–8pm; winter 7am–1pm & 6–9pm • Free • **Museum** Summer Tues–Sat 9am–2pm, Sun 10am–1pm; winter Tues–Sat 10am–1pm & 5–8pm, Sun 10am–2pm • €2–3 • ☎ 968 219 713

The **Catedral** towers over the mansions and plazas of the centre. Begun in the fourteenth century and finally completed in the eighteenth, it's a strange mix of styles, dubbed "Mediterranean Gothic". The outside is more interesting architecturally, particularly the west side with its Baroque facade, and the tower rising on the north, which you can climb for great views of the city. Inside, the most remarkable aspect is the florid Plateresque decoration of the chapels – particularly the **Capilla de los Vélez** (1491–1505). Originally designed as a funeral area, but never completed, it's one of the finest examples of medieval art in Murcia and one of the most interesting pieces of Hispanic Gothic; an urn in the niche of the main altar contains the heart of Alfonso the Wise. The **museum** has some fine primitive sculptures and, above all, a giant

12

MURCIA

ACCOMMODATION
Hotel Arco de San Juan	4
Hotel Hispano	1
Hotel Rincón de Pepe	3
Hotel Zenit Murcia	2
Pensión Campoy	5

● **EATING**
El Grumete	5
Hotel Rincón de Pepe	12
Mesón Las Viandas	10
Las Mulas	6
Restaurante La Plaza	13
La Tapa	7
Los Ventanales	3

● **BARS**
El Ahorcado Feliz	8
Atomic Bar	9
El Bosque Animado	2
Kennedy Bar	1
El Refugio	11
	4

● **CLUBS**
El Garaje de la Tía María	1
Mundaka	2

processional monstrance – 600kg of gold and silver twirling like a musical box on its revolving stand.

The ayuntamiento

Pl. Cardenal Belluga • Generally closed to the public – enquire at the *turismo*

Looming across the Plaza Cardenal Belluga is the newest addition to Murcia's architectural heritage. Architect Rafael Moneo's extension to the **ayuntamiento** closes the square with a strikingly contemporary building that faces the cathedral facade with a rhythmic twentieth-century version of the Baroque *retablo*.

Museo Salzillo

Pl. de San Agustín 1 • Summer Mon–Sat 10am–2pm; winter Mon–Sat 10am–5pm, Sun 11am–1.30pm • €5 • ☎ 968 291 893, ⓦ museosalzillo.es

The **Museo Salzillo**, west of the centre in Plaza San Agustín, has an extraordinary collection of the figures carried in Murcia's renowned Semana Santa procession. They were carved in the eighteenth century by Francisco Salzillo and display all the cloying sentimentality and delight in the "rustic" of that age.

Museo Arqueológico

Gran Vía Alfonso X 5 • Tues–Fri 10am–2pm & 5–8pm, Sat 11am–2pm & 5–8pm, Sun 11am–2pm; in summer open mornings only • Free • ☎ 968 234 602, ⓦ museosdemurcia.com

The **Museo Arqueológico**, housed in the Casa de Cultura, features an extensive collection of ceramics and potsherds (broken fragments of pottery), as well as other archeological finds from around the region, including well-preserved religious and sacred art.

The casino

C/Trapería 22 • Daily 11.30am–9pm, in Aug sometimes closed Sat afternoon & Sun • €5 • ☎ 968 215 399, ⓦ casinomurcia.com

Murcia's **casino** is a quirky delight and well worth a visit. The building dates from 1847 and combines an Arabic-style patio and vestibule, an English-style library reading room, a Pompeiian patio with Ionic columns, a billiard room and French ballroom. The neo-Baroque ladies' powder room (open to all) has a ceiling which depicts angelic ladies among the clouds, powdering their noses and tidying their hair.

Museo de Bellas Artes

C/Obispo Frutos 12 • Tues–Sat 10am–9pm, Oct–April until 8.30pm, Sun 10am–2pm • Free • ☎ 968 239 346, ⓦ museosdemurcia.com

The **Museo de Bellas Artes (MUBAM)**, founded in 1910 and designed by the Murcian architect Pedro Cerdán Martínez, features a representative collection of Renaissance and Golden Age art, contemporary sculpture and even an esoterically carved door said to have belonged to a Portuguese witch.

ARRIVAL AND INFORMATION   MURCIA

By plane The town's airport is 45km away in San Javier on the Mar Menor (☎ 968 172 000). Ryanair, easyJet and some charters fly to the UK, and there are limited internal flights to Almería, Barcelona and Madrid. City buses run to and from the airport three times a day; taxi fares into town start at €40.

By train The train station is at the southern edge of town, about a 20min walk into the centre.

Destinations Águilas (3–5 daily; 2hr); Alicante (14–23 daily; 1hr 30min); Barcelona (4 daily; 7hr); Cartagena (8 daily; 1hr); Lorca (12–18 daily; 1hr); Madrid (5 daily; 4hr 30min); Orihuela (14–23 daily; 20min).

By bus The bus station (☎ 968 292 211, ⓦ www .estaciondeautobusesdemurcia.com) is just west of the centre, within walking distance.

Destinations Águilas (3–6 daily; 2hr); Albacete (11 daily; 2hr 30min); Alicante (8 daily; 1hr 45min); Almería (4–6 daily; 3hr 30min); Barcelona (9 daily; 8hr); Cartagena (17–26 daily; 1hr); El Puerto de Mazarrón (3–4 daily; 1hr 30min); Granada (6 daily; 6hr); Lorca (6–17 daily; 1hr 15min); Madrid (12 daily; 6hr 30min); Málaga (5 daily; 7hr); Orihuela (5–16 daily; 1hr); Valencia (4–7 daily; 4hr 45min).

Turismo Pl. Cardenal Belluga, near the cathedral (April–Oct Mon–Sat 10am–2pm & 5–9pm, Sun 10am–2pm; Oct–March Mon–Sat 10am–2pm & 4.30–8.30pm, Sun 10am–2pm; ☎ 968 358 749, ⍟ murciaciudad.com). For regional info, visit ⍟ murciaturistica.es.

ACCOMMODATION

Hotel Arco de San Juan Pl. de Ceballos 10 ☎ 968 210 455, ⍟ arcosanjuan.com. A Neoclassical palace turned hotel. The rooms can be slightly frumpy – but the handsome facade may be worth the price alone, and the acclaimed *Restaurant La Plaza* is on site. **€50**

Hotel Hispano c/Radio Murcia 3 ☎ 968 216 152, ⍟ hotelhispano.net. A welcoming mid-range hotel, with basic, comfortable rooms and a restaurant serving decent local cuisine. **€50**

★ **Hotel Rincón de Pepe** c/Apósteles 34 ☎ 968 212 239, ⍟ nh-hotels.com. One of the finer hotels in Murcia, paved with pink Portuguese marble and featuring suitably plush rooms plus a well-regarded downstairs restaurant and bar. Discounted weekend rates. **€65**

Hotel Zenit Murcia Pl. San Pedro 5–6 ☎ 968 214 742, ⍟ zenithoteles.com. Comfortable, three-star hotel that sits in the thick of things, a few paces from lively Pl. de las Flores. A cool-toned lobby, tidy rooms and all the amenities. **€50**

Pensión Campoy c/Diego Hernández 32 ☎ 968 254 591, ⍟ pensioncampoy.com. This basic *pensión* has clean, if somewhat spartan rooms. Perfectly situated for the train station. **€32**

EATING

Murcia is known as *la huerta de Europa* (the orchard of Europe), and although this might be a slight exaggeration, you'll find local produce on most restaurant menus: vegetable soups, grills and paellas are the main specialities. It's also an important rice-growing region, and the local variety, Calasparra, which ripens very slowly, is the variety used to make paella. When talk turns to **tapas**, Murcia doesn't often come up; it should. Come evening, do as the locals and *ir de tapeo* in and around Pl. de las Flores, Pl. Santa Catalina and along Gran Vía Alfonso X. For well-priced traditional Spanish, it's also worth checking out the *mesones* in the Pl. de Julián Romea (beside the theatre) and on and around Pl. San Juan.

El Grumete c/Vara de Rey 6 ☎ 968 220 807. If you're in the mood for seafood, this is the spot for tasty, fresh *mariscos*, served by weight, should you choose. Generally Tues–Sun 1.30–3.30pm & 8.30–10.30pm, closed part of summer.

Hotel Rincón de Pepe c/Apósteles 34 ☎ 968 212 239, ⍟ nh-hotels.com. This elegant restaurant is *the* place for a Murcian gastronomic experience. Expect to pay around €55 a head for a meal, which will invariably include some inspired combinations of local produce – be sure to leave room for the desserts. Daily noon–4pm & 8–midnight; closed Sun dinner and Mon, in July & Aug closed Fri & Sat.

Mesón Las Viandas c/Pascual ☎ 968 221 188. Friendly local restaurant with straightforward, hearty food. *Menú del día* from €15. Daily 7am–midnight, closed Sun in Aug.

Las Mulas c/Ruiperez 5 ☎ 968 220 561. An earthy tapas experience, with a delicious *patatas Real Murcia*, a scrambled egg and potato concoction named after the local football team. Daily 9am–midnight.

Restaurante La Plaza *Hotel Arco de San Juan*, Pl. San Juan ☎ 968 221 200, ⍟ laplazarestaurante.com. Regional cuisine with a modern twist, from succulent duck with a mandarin liqueur to artisanal desserts. Various *menús*, from €18 to €25. Daily 7.30am–4pm & 8.30–11.30pm, closed Sun, & dinner Mon & Tues.

La Tapa Pl. de las Flores 13 ☎ 968 211 317. For outdoor tapas, settle in at one of the tables scattered near the plaza fountain, and graze on tasty bites including young eel tossed with potatoes and grilled *pulpo*. Daily noon–5pm & 8pm–midnight.

Los Ventanales c/Alejandro Seiquer ☎ 968 214 338, ⍟ losventanales.com. The most central of several citywide branches of this popular tapas place, cooking up five different varieties of *patatas a lo pobre*. Mon–Fri 8am–4.30pm & 7pm–midnight, Sat 10am–4.30pm & 7.30–1am, Sun 10am–4.30pm & 7–11.30pm.

DRINKING AND NIGHTLIFE

As a university town, Murcia has a disarmingly vibrant and diverse **nightlife** during term time, and a scene that hasn't yet succumbed to style-bar uniformity. To get a grip on what's hot, pick up a copy of the free listings magazines such as *Guía de Ocio*. One of the liveliest areas for **bars** is around the university, near the Museo de Bellas Artes, in particular c/Dr Fleming, c/de Saavedra Fajardo and the side streets off them.

BARS

El Ahorcado Feliz c/Cánovas del Castillo ☎968 934 986. This hopping bar pulls in an amiable local crowd and has decently priced beer and cocktails. Generally Mon–Thurs 2.30pm–2.30am, Fri & Sat 2.30pm–3am.

Atomic Bar c/Simón García ☎968 957 767, ⓦatomicbar.es. Happening bar with live music, from blues to rock, amid low leather chairs and velvet drapes. Generally Mon–Sat 6pm–late.

El Bosque Animado Pl. Cristo del Rescate ☎968 905 342, ⓦelbosqueanimado.es. This central, aptly named "Animated Forest" has outdoor tables for evening cocktails (try the great *mojitos*) on the breezy plaza and, inside, artificial trees twinkling with lights. Generally Mon–Sat 6pm–late.

Kennedy Bar Callejón Burruezo ☎968 291 680. Irish-style pubs may be ubiquitous in Spain, but this amiable spot just west of Jardín San Esteban is worth seeking out. Original stone arches grace the spacious interior, and a long bar invites conversation; check out, too, the elevated church pulpit brought over from England, which makes for a romantic drinking nook. They also host comedy shows – ask at the bar for dates – which sometimes feature well-known names. Mon–Thurs 3pm–2am, Fri & Sat 3pm–3am, Sun 4pm–midnight.

★ **La Muralla** *Hotel Rincón de Pepe* c/Apósteles 34 ☎968 212 239. This underground, low-lit bar below the hotel is one of Murcia's more memorable places to drink – sip cocktails in the shadow of the original Moorish city walls. They also host regular jazz sessions. Mon, Tues & Wed 3.30pm–1am, Thurs–Sat 3pm–4am.

El Refugio Pl. de las Balsas, no phone. The terrace of this bar is more or less at the centre of the action for cocktails and conversation, and makes a good place to start off the evening. Generally Mon–Sat 6pm–late.

CLUBS

El Garaje de la Tía Maria Avda. Miguel de Cervantes, no phone. The action here gets going around 2am, and the music policy mashes up everything from electrodisco to Nirvana and Vivaldi. Generally Thurs–Sat midnight–late.

Mundaka Carretera Catalina 26. This funky club is a premier house and techno venue, hosting national and international DJs. Generally Thurs–Sat midnight–late.

DIRECTORY

Car rental Europcar, Avda. Miguel de Cervantes 7 ☎968 283 086, ⓦeuropcar.es; Atesa, c/Azarbe del Papel 16 ☎968 200 337, ⓦatesa.es.

Hospitals Hospital General Universitario "Reina Sofia", Avda. Intendente Jorge Palacios ☎968 359 000; Red Cross ☎968 355 339.

Market The Mercado Las Verónicas, c/Verónicas (Mon–Sat 8am–2pm), has stacks of wonderful local produce.

Police Avda. San Juan de la Cruz ☎968 358 750.

The coast south of Torrevieja

The stretch of coast around the south of **Torrevieja** has been developed at a rapid rate, and is now home to a wide mix of Europeans alongside the locals. Just to the south is a series of pleasant beaches, known collectively as **Las Playas de Orihuela** (as they come within Orihuela's provincial boundary). Both Playa La Zenía and Playa Cabo Roig are good, clean options with car parks and cafés (the restaurant at Cabo Roig is also exceptionally good and enjoys wide views over the harbour).

Santiago de la Ribera

The Murcian Costa Cálida starts at **Mar Menor** (Lesser Sea), a broad lagoon whose shallow waters (ideal for kids) warm up early in the year, making this a good out-of-season destination. With its high-rise hotels, the "sleeve" (*la manga*) looks like a diminutive Benidorm; the resort of **SANTIAGO DE LA RIBERA** on the land side of the lagoon is a more appealing place to spend a day or two by the coast, and is popular with *murcíanos*. There's a good sandy beach, an attractive promenade and an important sailing club here – the calm sea is perfect for novices.

ARRIVAL AND INFORMATION   SANTIAGO DE LA RIBERA

By train The nearest train station is Balsicas (connected with Murcia, San Pedro and Santiago by hourly buses). Trains run direct between Barcelona, Valencia and Madrid.

By bus Buses run regularly to and from Cartagena.

Turismo c/Padre Juan, 300m back from the seafront (summer Mon–Fri 10am–2pm & 5.30–8.30pm, Sat & Sun 10.30am–1.30pm; winter Mon–Fri 10am–2pm & 5–7pm, Sat & Sun 10am–1.30pm; ☎ 968 571 704).

ACCOMMODATION, EATING AND DRINKING

Hotel El Marino Explanada Barnuevo 13 ☎ 968 572 121, ⓦ elmarino.es. This family-owned, nautical-themed hotel has homely rooms with good sea views. **€46**

Lonja Mar Menor Paseo Colón ☎ 968 573 657. This lively restaurant near the beach is the perfect spot for a seafood feast. Try a plate of *fritura*, or small fried fish, or go all out with a generous – and pricey – *mariscada*, with shrimp, clams and prawns. Daily 1–5pm & 8pm–midnight.

Cartagena

Whether you're approaching **CARTAGENA** from one of the numerous resorts along Mar Menor, inland from Murcia, or from Almería to the south, it's not a pretty sight, even if the rusting mineworks that scar the landscape have their own austere appeal. It's only when you reach the old part of town down by the port, with its narrow medieval streets, packed with bars and restaurants, that the city's real character emerges.

Cartagena was Hannibal's capital city on the Iberian peninsula, named after his Carthage in North Africa, and a strategic port and administrative centre for the Romans. International Nautical Week is celebrated here in June. In July, the Mar de Músicas festival presents some of the best in world music, and in November the city hosts both a nationally famous jazz festival and an International Festival of Nautical Cinema. The **fiestas** of Semana Santa are some of the most elaborate in Spain, with processions leaving from the church of Santa María de Gracia in the early hours of Good Friday morning.

The best way to get a feel of the city's rich past is to stroll the streets: you'll see a large number of *modernista* buildings. Most of these are the work of former Cartagenian and disciple of Gaudí, Victor Beltri (1865–1935). In particular, have a look at **Casa Maestre** in Plaza San Francisco; **Casa Cervantes**, c/Mayor 15; and the old **Hotel Zapata**, Plaza de España.

Castillo de la Concepción

July to mid-Sept Mon–Sat 10am–2.30pm & 4–8.30pm; mid-Sept to Nov 1, Easter & mid-March–June Tues–Sun 10am–2.30pm & 4–7.30pm; Nov to mid-March Tues–Sun 10am–5.30pm • €3.75, or €4.25 with lift • ☎ 968 500 093

Reached by a signposted path or a lift, the impressive **Castillo de la Concepción** has interesting displays exploring Cartagena's history, and you can also wander around the old walls, where look-out points afford panoramic views of the town and surrounding landscape.

Museo Naval

C/Menéndez Pelayo 6 • Tues–Sun 10am–1.30pm • Free • ☎ 968 127 138

The vast military **Arsenal** that dominates the old part of the city dates from the mid-eighteenth century. Set in its walls, the well-curated **Museo Naval** provides an in-depth look at Cartagena's naval history, from exhibits on nautical maps and navigational charts to model ships, uniforms, artillery, and a section dedicated to Cartagena-born Isaac Peral, the inventor of the submarine.

Museo Nacional de Arqueología Subacuática (ARQUA)

Paseo Alfonso XII 22 • Mid-April to mid-Oct Tues–Thurs 10am–9pm, Fri & Sat 10am–10pm, Sun 10am–3pm; mid-Oct to mid-April Tues–Sat 10am–7.30pm, Sun 10am–3pm • €3 • ☎ 968 121 166, ⓦ museoarqua.mcu.es

The **Museo Nacional de Arqueología Subacuática (ARQUA)**, on the outer walls of the Arsenal on the way to the lighthouse, has a reconstructed Roman galley and lots of

12

interesting exhibits, including one section focused on naval history and navigation, and another on Mediterranean ports and items salvaged from shipwrecks.

Museo Archeológico Municipal

C/Ramón y Cajal 45 • Tues–Fri 10am–2pm & 5–8pm, Sat & Sun 11am–2pm • Free • ☎ 968 539 027

The **Museo Archeológico Municipal** is built on a Roman burial ground and offers a good introduction to the ancient history of the city. The excellent collection of Roman artefacts includes an impressive display of glass, plus Romanesque art and sculptures.

Muralla Púnica

C/San Diego • July to mid-Sept daily 10am–2.30pm & 4–8.30pm; mid-Sept to Nov 1, Easter & mid-March to June Tues–Sun 10am–2.30pm & 4–7.30pm; Nov 2 to mid-March Tues–Sun 10am–5.30pm • €3.50 • ☎ 968 500 093

The **Muralla Púnica** visitor and interpretation centre, built on and around one of the city's old Punic walls, explores the city's Carthaginian and Roman history via exhibits, audiovisuals and more. It also provides helpful information on other sights around the city and can suggest good itineraries to follow.

ARRIVAL AND INFORMATION

By train and bus The FEVE train station (with services connecting Cartagena with Los Nietos on the Mar Menor) is almost next door to the bus station, on c/Trovero Marín, and the RENFE station nearby at the end of Avda. América. **Turismo** Pl. del Ayuntamiento, in the Palacio Consistorial (Mon–Sat 10.30am–1.30pm & 5.30–7.30pm, Sun 10.30am–1.30pm; ☎ 968 521 427 or 968 128 950, ⒲ cartagena.es). The Muralla Púnica also offers local information, and offers tours and discount tickets through Cartagena Puerto de Culturas (☎ 968 500 093, ⒲ cartagenapuertodeculturas.com).

CARTAGENA

ACCOMMODATION

Hotel Los Habaneros c/San Diego 60 ☎ 968 505 250, ⒲ hotelhabaneros.com. Comfortable, well-maintained rooms, and a very central location near both the bus and train stations. **€50**

NH Cartagena Real 2, Pl. Héroes de Cavite ☎ 968 120 908, ⒲ nh-hotels.com. Smart place with elegant rooms, plus one of the chain's signature *NHube* restaurants, serving creative regional fare. **€65**

Pensión Oriente c/Jara 27 ☎ 968 502 469, ⒲ pensionoriente.com. Long-established *pensión*, with basic, clean, budget rooms in a central location. **€34**

EATING AND DRINKING

Mare Nostrum Paseo de Alfonso XII ☎ 968 522 131, ⒲ marenostrum.es. Dine on excellent seafood dishes (€16–20) by the port, including *mero marinera*, grouper with clams, and crayfish. Daily 1–4pm & 7–11pm.

El Mejillonera c/Mayor 4 ☎ 968 521 179. This lively spot does tasty *mejillones* (mussels) and Gallego-style *pulpo*. Generally daily 1.30–3.30pm & 8.30–10.30pm.

The Golfo de Mazarrón

South of Cartagena, much of the scenic coastline down to the border with Andalucia is undeveloped, with a succession of fine coves lying beneath a backdrop of arid, serrated hills. The region's main resorts, **El Puerto de Mazarrón** and **Águilas**, are both fairly small scale and easy going, mainly attracting Spanish families. Public transport is limited, however, so you'll need your own vehicle to get to the better beaches.

El Puerto de Mazarrón

Despite a fair amount of development, **EL PUERTO DE MAZARRÓN** is pretty quiet even in season, and, with five **buses** a day from Cartagena, fairly accessible. There are great

beaches within easy reach of town. Buses head 6km southwest along the coast to Bolnuevo, where there's a superb stretch of sand. West of Bolnuevo, the route becomes a dirt track, with access to several coves popular with nudists, until you reach the headland of Punta Calnegre, 15km from El Puerto de Mazarrón, where there are more good stretches of sand. Alternatively, if you head northeast from El Puerto de Mazarrón the best beaches are around Cabo Tiñoso, 13km away. If you get tired of sunbathing, the nature reserve at **La Rambla de Moreras**, 2km north of Bolnuevo, has a lagoon that attracts a variety of migratory birds.

INFORMATION

EL PUERTO DE MAZARRÓN

Turismo Pl. Toneleros 1 (Mon–Fri 9am–2pm & 5–8pm, Sat 10am–1pm & 5–7pm; summer also Sun 9.30am–1.30pm; ☏ 968 594 426, ⊚ mazarron.es).

ACCOMMODATION AND EATING

La Barraca c/Santiago 3 ☏ 968 594 402. Enjoy fresh seafood, from lobster and shrimp to sea bream, as well as hearty paellas at this long-established restaurant near the port. Mains €16–25. Daily 1–3.30pm & 8.30–10.30pm; closed Wed dinner & mid-Jan to mid-Feb.

Hotel Bahía Playa de la Reya ☏ 968 594 000, ⊚ hotelbahia.net. It may look fairly generic and concrete from the outside, but it's near the beach, and offers decent rooms, a plant-filled lobby and a terrace. €77

Playa de Mazarrón Carretera Bolnuevo ☏ 968 150 660, ⊚ playamazarron.com. This well-maintained, massive campsite, with good facilities, is open year-round. Two adults, including car €24

Águilas

12

ÁGUILAS, 47km from Mazarrón and almost on the border with Andalucia, is hemmed in by the parched hills of the Sierra del Contar. Along with the cultivation of tomatoes – one of the few things that can grow in this arid region – fishing is the mainstay of the economy here, and a fish auction is held at around 5pm every day in the port's large warehouse. **Carnaval** is especially wild in Águilas, and for three days and nights in February, the entire population lets its hair down with processions, floats and general fancy-dress mayhem.

Águilas is also popular for its plentiful **beaches**, and the area has a superb year-round climate. The town itself has managed to escape the worst excesses of tourism, and retains much of its rural charm and character.

The beaches

You'll find sandy **beaches**, and over thirty small *calas* (coves) in the vicinity – those to the north are rockier and more often backed by low cliffs, while the best are the wonderful, fairly undeveloped **cuatro calas** south of town. You'll need your own wheels to reach these beaches, which get better the farther you get away from Águilas, but all are signposted. The first two, **Calarreona** and **La Higuérica**, have fine sands and are backed by dunes and the odd villa, but 6km south of Águilas where the coast is completely wild, the ravishing back-to-back sandy coves of **Cala Carolina** and **Cala Cocedores** are simply superb.

If you don't have your own transport, you're better heading for the chain of beaches north of Águilas served by regular buses (generally mid-July to end of Aug only). **Playa Hornillo** is a nice beach with a couple of bars (and you could actually reach it by walking from the train station), while **Playa Amarillo** is decent but in a built-up area. The bus also passes *playas* Arroz, La Cola and finally Calabardina (7km from town). If you feel energetic, you could head across **Cabo Cope** to yet another chain of beaches beginning at Ruinas Torre Cope.

ACCOMMODATION AND EATING

ÁGUILAS

Hotel Restaurante El Paso c/Cartagena 13 ☏ 968 447 125, ⊚ hotelelpasoaguilas.com. This amiable small hotel has simple but well-maintained rooms, a central interior courtyard and a bar-restaurant for guests. €72

Restaurante la Veleta c/Blas Rosique Blaya 6 ☎ 968 411 798. Dine on fresh seafood, from mussels to octopus to plump shrimp, as well as grilled meats and aromatic rice dishes at this inviting restaurant. Daily *menú* €16; tasting *menú* €45. Daily 1–4pm & 8pm–midnight; closed March.

Lorca and around

Many of the historic villages of inland Murcia are accessible only with your own transport, but one place you can reach easily is **LORCA**, an attractive former frontier town whose historic centre, on the hill between c/López Gisbert and the castle, still has a distinct aura of the past. For a time, it was part of the Córdoba caliphate, but it was retaken by the Christians in 1243, after which Muslim raids were a feature of life until the fall of Granada, the last Muslim stronghold. Most of the town's notable buildings – churches and ancestral homes – date from the sixteenth century onwards.

Today, Lorca is famed for its **Semana Santa** celebrations, which outdo those of both Murcia and Cartagena, the next best in the region. There's a distinctly operatic splendour about the dramatization of the triumph of Christianity, with characters such as Cleopatra, Julius Caesar and the royalty of Persia and Babylon attired in embroidered costumes of velvet and silk. The high point is the afternoon and evening of Good Friday.

Casa de los Guevara

C/Lope Gisbert • Mon–Fri 9.30am–2pm & 4.30–7.30pm, Sat & Sun 11am–2pm • €3 • ☎ 968 441 914

The **Casa de los Guevara** is an excellent example of civic eighteenth-century Baroque architecture and features all the historical hallmarks of a luxurious mansion, including a lovely patio and well-appointed rooms with paintings and period furniture. The building was closed for post-earthquake repairs at the time of writing, so you might want to call ahead for an update before visiting.

Calle Corredera

On the corner of Plaza San Vicente and **Calle Corredera**, the main shopping artery, is the **Columna Milenaria**, a Roman column dating from around 10 BC which marked the distance between Lorca and Cartagena on the *via Heraclea*, the Roman road from the Pyrenees to Cádiz. The Gothic **Porche de San Antonio**, the only gate remaining from the old city walls, lies at the far end of c/Corredera.

Plaza de España

Colegiata de San Patricio Daily 11am–1pm & 4.30–6.30pm, Sat & Sun until 8pm • Free

The **Plaza de España** is the focal point of Lorca life, and holds the imposing **Colegiata de San Patricio**, with its enormous proto-Baroque facade, built between the sixteenth

---

EARTHQUAKE IN LORCA

On May 11, 2011, Lorca was shaken by a 5.2-magnitude **earthquake**, said to be the most serious tremor to hit Spain in fifty years. Parts of town – particularly the old quarter – were levelled, and ten people were killed. While some tourist sights have reopened, a number are still being repaired, and you may encounter construction as the town rebuilds.

and eighteenth centuries – there's a marked contrast between the outside and the sober, refined interior, which is largely Renaissance. Nearby is the **ayuntamiento**, with its seventeenth- to eighteenth-century facade. An equally impressive front is presented by the sixteenth-century **Posito**, down a nearby side-street – originally an old grain storehouse, it's now the municipal archive.

Castillo

Easter & mid-July to Sept Tues–Sun 10.30am–6.30pm; reduced hours rest of the year• €8, including miniature train and Centro de Visitantes • Night visits Tues–Sat at 8.30pm • €8, or €20 with dinner

Lorca's brooding thirteenth- to fourteenth-century **Castillo**, overlooking the town, has been turned into a medieval-themed tourist attraction, which may or may not be your cup of tea: think actors prancing around in medieval costume, and re-enacted battle scenes. To be fair, however, there are also some well-presented exhibits about the castle's undoubtedly formidable history.

Note that though the miniature train goes up to the castle, it's perfectly possible to walk (or drive) up via the *barrio antiguo* above the Colegiata de San Patricio.

Museo del Paso Azul

C/Nogalte • Mon–Sat 10am–2pm & 5–8pm, in Aug Mon–Fri 10am–2pm • €3 • Guided tours 12.30pm & 6.30pm

Timing your visit to coincide with Lorca's famous Semana Santa festivities is an unforgettable experience, but if you can't experience the real thing, it's still worth visiting the **Museo del Paso Azul** to get some insight into the elaborate costumes, history, and the incredible devotion that the festival is known for.

Centro de Artesanía

C/Lope Gisbert • Mon–Fri 9am–2pm & 5.30–7.30pm, Sat 11am–1.30pm & 6–8pm • Free • ☎ 968 463 912, ⓦ carm.es

If you're looking to pick up some souvenirs, it's worth popping into the spacious **Centro de Artesanía**, in the Palacio de Guevara, which displays and sells traditional crafts, and has an area where you can watch local artists at work.

ARRIVAL AND INFORMATION

LORCA

By train and bus Hourly trains and buses connect Lorca with Murcia, although the train is cheaper and a little quicker.

Turismo Due to the 2011 earthquake, the *turismo* has relocated to the Centro de Visitantes, in the Antiguo Convento de la Merced on c/Puerta de San Ginés (summer Mon–Sat 9.30am–2pm & 5–8pm, Sun 10am–2.30pm; winter Mon–Sat 9.30am–2pm & 5.30–7.30pm, Sun 10am–2pm; ☎ 902 400 047, ⓦ ayuntalorca.es).

ACCOMMODATION, EATING AND DRINKING

Note that hotel rates go up around the time of Semana Santa, and you'll have to book accommodation at least three months in advance for the festival – or stay in Murcia or Águilas.

Hotel Alameda c/Musso Valiente 8 ☎ 968 406 600, ⓦ hotel-alameda.com. You can't get more central than this simple but friendly hotel, which sits smack in the centre of town. The rooms are decent and have a bird's-eye view of the Semana Santa parades; rates include breakfast. **€60**, during Semana Santa **€100**

Jardines de Lorca Alameda Rafael Méndez ☎ 968 470 599, ⓦ hotelesdemurcia.com. This hotel sits in a restful residential zone, near the leafy park after which it's named. Prices dip to nearly half in low season. **€70**, during Semana Santa **€165**

La Parrilla de San Vicente Pl. San Vicente ☎ 968 471 287. For hearty Lorcan cuisine, including excellent grilled meats, head to this friendly, central restaurant. Weekday *menú del día* €10. Daily 1–4pm & 8–11pm; July & Aug closed Sat.

12

The Balearic Islands

CALA TURQUETA, MENORCA (P.889)

13

The Balearic Islands

East of the Spanish mainland, the four chief Balearic Islands – Ibiza, Formentera, Mallorca and Menorca – maintain a character distinct from the rest of Spain and from each other. Ibiza is wholly unique, its capital Ibiza Town is loaded with historic interest and a draw for thousands of clubbers and gay visitors, while the north of the island has a distinctly bohemian character. Tiny Formentera has even better beaches than its neighbour and makes up in rustic charm what it lacks in cultural interest. Mallorca, the largest and best-known Balearic, battles with its image as an island of little more than sun, booze and high-rise hotels. In reality, you'll find all the clichés, most of them crammed into the mega-resorts of the Bay of Palma and the east coast, but there's lots more besides: mountains, lovely old towns, some beautiful coves, and the Balearics' one real city, Palma. Mallorca is, in fact, the one island in the group you might come to other than for beaches and nightlife, with scope for plenty of hiking. And finally, to the east, there's Menorca – more subdued in its clientele, and here, at least, the modern resorts are kept at a safe distance from the two main towns, the capital Maó, which boasts the deepest harbour in the Med, and the charming, pocket-sized port of Ciutadella.

Access to the islands is easy from Britain and mainland Spain, with plenty of bargain-priced flights in summer, though in winter only Mallorca is really well connected. In addition, ferries and catamarans link Barcelona, Valencia and Denia with the islands, and there are plenty of inter-island ferries, too, though these can be pricey and fully booked in summer. For fuller details on **routes**, see the "Arrival and Departure" sections for individual ports and cities.

The main fly in the ointment is cost: as prime "holiday islands", the Balearics charge considerably above mainland prices for rooms and eating out can be expensive. Rental **cars** can also be hard to come by at this time. Travelling around by **bus**, **moped**, **scooter** and **bicycle** are all perfectly feasible, but note that car-rental companies do not allow their vehicles to be taken from one island to another.

Catalan is spoken throughout the Balearics, and each of the three main islands has a different dialect, though locals all speak Castilian (Spanish). For the visitor, confusion arises from the difference between the islands' road signs and street names – which are almost exclusively in Catalan – and many of the maps on sale, which are in Castilian. In particular, note that Menorca now calls its capital Maó rather than Mahón, while both the island and town of Ibiza are usually referred to as Eivissa. In this chapter we give the Catalan name for towns, beaches and streets, except for Ibiza and Ibiza Town which are not widely known by their Catalan names outside Spain.

PALMA CATHEDRAL, MAJORCA

Highlights

❶ A stroll through Dalt Vila Explore Ibiza Town's souk-like walled city, a UNESCO World Heritage Site. **See p.854**

❷ World clubbing capital Lose yourself to the music of the globe's most sought after DJs at one of the island's legendary club nights. **See p.858**

❸ Explore Ibiza's hidden calas Hire a bike and spend a day cycling between exquisite cove beaches, including Benirràs and Cala Mastella. **See p.859**

❹ Formentera's beaches Sweeping white-sand beaches and pellucid waters. **See p.863**

❺ Palma's old town Charming Renaissance mansions cluster this delightful part of Mallorca's capital city. **See p.866**

❻ Deià, Mallorca One of Mallorca's prettiest villages, perched high above the ocean. **See p.874**

❼ Downtown Ciutadella A delightful little Menorcan town of mazy lanes and fine old mansions. **See p.886**

HIGHLIGHTS ARE MARKED ON THE MAP ON P.853

13

AIRLINES AND FERRY COMPANIES

Most inter-island **flights** are operated by either Iberia (☎902 400 500, ✆iberia.com), Span Air (☎807 001 700, ✆spanair.com) or Air Berlin (☎902 320 737, ✆airberlin.com).

Ferries and **catamarans** between the islands and to the Spanish mainland are operated by Trasmediterránea (☎902 454 645, ✆trasmediterranea.es), Baleària (☎902 191 068, ✆balearia.com) and Iscomar (☎902 119 128, ✆iscomar.com). Trasmapi (☎902 314 433, ✆trasmapi.com) run ferries from Ibiza Town to Formentera.

Ibiza

IBIZA, or **Eivissa** in Catalan, is an island of excess – beautiful, and blessed with scores of stunning cove beaches and dense pine forests. Nevertheless, it's the islanders (*eivissencs*) and their visitors who make it special. Ibiza has long attracted hedonistic characters and wealthy bohemians, and the locals remain determinedly blasé about the mullet-haired fashionistas and celebrities who flock to the island today.

For years, Ibiza was *the* European hippie escape, but nowadays it's the extraordinary clubbing scene that most people come here to experience. The island can lay a strong claim to being the globe's **clubbing capital**, with virtually all of the world's top house DJs and many more minor players performing here during the summer season. However, visit between October and May, and you'll find a much more peaceful island – just one club (*Pacha*) and a few funky bars remain open through the winter.

Ibiza Town, the capital, is the obvious place to base yourself: only a short bus ride from two great beaches – **Ses Salines** and **Es Cavallet** – and crammed with bars, restaurants and boutiques. The town of **Sant Antoni** is, for the most part, a sprawling concrete mass of seedy bars and unappealing restaurants, and is best avoided beyond a few choice bars and clubs. The more pleasant town of **Santa Eulària** is a good base for exploring the north of the island. Around the entire shoreline, you'll find dozens of exquisite **cove beaches** (*calas*), many all but deserted even in high season, though you'll need your own transport to reach the best spots. **Inland**, the scenery is hilly and thickly wooded, dotted with a series of tiny hamlets.

Brief history

The **Carthaginians**, who founded Ibiza Town in about 654 BC, transformed the island into a major trading port, with salt the main export. The **Romans** arrived in 123 BC and the island continued to prosper. After the fall of the Roman Empire, Ibiza was

---

BALEARIC CUISINE

The influx of the sea-and-sun-seeking masses has brought an **international flavour** – or lack thereof – to many Balearic cafés and restaurants. There are, perhaps, notably few dishes which are unique to the islands but that's hardly surprising given their history of foreign invasion. Typical dishes, which are often of Catalan descent, consist of hearty stews, soups and spiced meats.

Fish and shellfish are the mainstay of most menus. *Caldereta de llagosta* (a lobster stew cooked with tomatoes) is a common speciality, especially in Menorca, as is salted cod, grilled squid and prawns cooked in antisocial – but delicious – amounts of garlic.

As in mainland Spain, the most enjoyable way to experiment with local cuisine is by sampling smaller portions in the form of tapas, or *pintxos* (typical of the Basque country). *Pa amb oli* (bread rubbed with olive oil) is an obvious cheap eat and is typically eaten for lunch or breakfast. For the sweeter-toothed, another source of Balearic culinary pride is a spiral pastry dusted with icing sugar called an **ensaimada**.

Menorcans were inspired into gin-making by the British, and Xoriguer gin made in Maó has a potent kick – it's often drunk as a *pomada* (gin with lemonade). Mallorcan wine – particularly red Binissalem – is experiencing something of a resurgence and is worth seeking out.

THE BALEARICS

MAINLAND SPAIN

Valencia

Denia

Alicante

0 — 50
kilometres

N

MEDITERRANEAN SEA

Barcelona

Barcelona

Menorca

Fornells
Maó
Ciutadella ⑦

Mallorca

Port d'Alcúdia
Pollença
Port de Sóller
Deià ⑥
Valldemossa
PALMA ⑤

Cabrera

Ibiza

Santa Eulària
Sant Antoni ②
③
Ibiza Town ①
La Savina ④
Formentera

HIGHLIGHTS
① A stroll through Dalt Vila
② World clubbing capital
③ Explore Ibiza's hidden calas
④ Formentera's beaches
⑤ Palma's old town
⑥ Deià, Mallorca
⑦ Downtown Ciutadella

13

IBIZA

Portinatx
Cala Xuclar
Cala Xarraca
Cala d'en Serra
Cala Sant Vicent
Aigües Blanques
Illa de Tagomago
Cova de Can Marça
Sant Joan
403m
Es Figueral
Benirràs
Es Portitxol
Cala d'Aubarca
Port de Sant Miquel
Sant Miquel
Cap d'Albarca
Sant Carles
Cala Boix
Cala Mastella
Cala Llenya
Sant Llorenç de Balàfia
Es Canar
Punta Arabí
Sant Mateu d'Albarca
Santa Agnès de Corona
Santa Gertrudis
Santa Eulària des Riu
Cala Salada
Sant Antoni de Portmany
Port des Torrent
Cala Bassa
Sa Conillera
Cala Conta
Sant Rafel
Jesús
Talamanca
Cala Tarida
Sant Agustí
Sant Josep
IBIZA TOWN
Figueretes
Cala Vadella
436m
Sant Jordi
Platja d'en Bossa
MEDITERRANEAN SEA
Es Cubells
Salt Flats
Cala d'Hort
Cala Jondal
Ses Salines
Es Cavellet
Es Vedrà
Ses Salines
Illa d'es Penjats
S'Espardell
S'Espalmador

CLUBS
Amnesia	3
Las Dalias	1
Privilege	2
Space	4

0   5
kilometres

conquered by the Moors in the ninth century, and their five-hundred-year reign is still evident in the island's architecture and traditional dress. But thereafter a gradual decline set in, and it wasn't until Beatniks discovered the island in the 1950s that Ibiza began to reinvent itself as one of the most chic locations in the Mediterranean.

Today more than four million tourists flock to the much-revered "white isle" every year. However, Ibiza's tourism-driven prosperity has seen more and more coastline consumed by **rampant development**. The balance between keeping the tourists coming and maintaining the island's natural allure is keenly felt by the islanders but, for now at least, it's not hard to find a pristine cove or a quiet forested trail if you make the effort.

Ibiza Town

IBIZA TOWN (Ciutat d'Eivissa) is easily the most attractive settlement on the island. Colossal medieval walls guard the maze of cobbled streets of the UNESCO-listed old town quarter of **Dalt Vila**. The walls reach a dramatic climax at the main archway entrance, the imposing **Portal de ses Taules**. Just beyond is the elegant **Plaça de Vila**, which is lined with restaurants and cafés and makes a delightful setting for some tapas or a meal. It's well worth the walk up the steep, winding streets to the cathedral, if only to enjoy the wonderful views out over the harbour.

13

During summer nights, the whitewashed streets of the port area are packed with people darting between chic boutiques, street market stalls and hip bars. In winter, things are much more peaceful, and the focus of activity shifts to the area around the graceful boulevard Passeig de Vara de Rey.

Catedral

Daily 9.30am–1.30pm & 5–8pm; closed Mon & Sun afternoons • Free

Today's thirteenth-century **Catedral** stands at the highest point in Dalt Vila. It's pleasingly austere, with sombre, sturdy Gothic lines supported by giant buttresses, though inside the white-washed decor contains somewhat trite Baroque embellishments.

Museu Arqueològic d'Eivissa i Formentera

April–Sept Tues–Sat 10am–2pm & 6–8pm, Sun 10am–2pm; Oct–March Tues–Sat, 9am–3pm, Sun 10am–2pm • €2.40 • ☎ 971 301 231

Opposite the Catedral, the recently refurbished **Museu Arqueològic d'Eivissa i Formentera** has some interesting Phoenician and Carthaginian exhibits, including images of the fertility goddess Tanit. Ibiza's Moorish period is dealt with in the Centro de Interpretación Madina Yabisa (same hours; €2) inside La Cúria, a converted courthouse that has some flashy video displays and fine ceramics.

Outside the walls

The port areas of **Sa Penya** and **La Marina** snuggle between the harbour and the ramparts, a maze of raked passages and narrow lanes crimped by balconied, whitewashed houses. This highly atmospheric quarter is packed with boutiques, bars and restaurants. Farther to the west, the **new town** is generally of less interest, but the boulevard-like Passeig de Vara de Rey and the leafy, pedestrianized Plaça des Parc just to the south both host some fine cafés and restaurants.

Punic necropolis

Tues–Sat 10am–2pm & 6–8pm, Sun 10am–2pm • Free • ☎ 971 301 771

Set on a rocky hillside off Vía Romana are the remains of a huge **Punic necropolis**. There's not that much to see today – though you can descend into some of the tombs – but thousands of terracotta pieces, amphorae and amulets have been uncovered here. Ibiza functioned as an A-list burial site, with wealthy Carthaginians paying by special minted currency for the shipment of their bodies to the island upon death.

ARRIVAL AND DEPARTURE   IBIZA TOWN

By plane Ibiza's international airport is situated 6km southwest of Ibiza Town; buses leave for Ibiza Town (€3.20) and also for Sant Antoni (June–Sept only, hourly 7am–3am) and Santa Eulària (June–Sept only, every 2hr 8am–9pm).
Destinations Palma (8–10 daily; 45min) and Maó (4 weekly; 50min).

By bus The town's bus station – which is little more than an office next to where the buses pull up – is about 1.5km northwest of the centre, just off the inner ring road on Avgda. d'Isidor Macabich; regular buses run from here to the port area. Full timetables and ticket costs are available at ⊕ ibizabus.com. There's a good bus service between Ibiza Town, Sant Antoni, Santa Eulària, Portinatx, the airport and a few of the larger beaches. Note that services are less frequent from Nov–April.
Destinations Airport (every 20min 6.20am–12.20am,

every 15min July & Aug; 20min); Figueretes (every 30min; 5min); Platja d'en Bossa (every 20min; 10min); Portinatx (2–3 daily; 45min); Sant Antoni (every 15–30min; 30min); Santa Eulària (every 30min; 25min); Sant Joan (2–7 daily; 35min); Sant Josep (5 daily; 20min); Sant Miquel (3–8 daily; 30min); Ses Salines (hourly; 20min).

By ferry There are two ferry terminals: one on Avgda. Santa Eulària (for Formentera), and the other on Passeig des Moll (mainland and Mallorca). All Ibiza destinations run from May–Oct only and mainland services are less frequent in winter.
Destinations Barcelona (1–2 daily; 5–8hr); Denia (daily; 3hr); Es Canar (5 daily; 55min); Formentera (every 30min; 35min); Palma (3–4 daily; 2–4hr); Platja d'en Bossa (7 daily; 20min); Santa Eulària (7 daily; 45min); Talamanca (every 20min; 5min); Valencia (1–2 daily; 5hr).

IBIZA TOWN

CLUBS	
Anfora	2
Pacha	1

EATING & DRINKING

Bar Dado	3
Bide Bide	1
Bon Profit	11
La Brasa	10
Comidas Bar San Juan	6
El Olivo	12
Madagascar	8
Lo Cura	5
Los Pasajeros	2
Rock Bar	4
Sunrise	7
Sunset	9

ACCOMMODATION

Hostal Giramundo	9
Hostal Juanito	3
Hostal Las Nieves	4
Hostal Residencia Parque	7
Hostal Residencia Sol y Brisa	5
Hostal Residencia La Ventana	8
Hotel Lux Isla	2
Hotel Ocean Drive	1
Vara de Rey Guest House	6

INFORMATION

Turisme Passeig de Vara de Rey (June–Sept Mon–Fri 9am–8pm, Sat 9am–7pm & Sun 9am–2pm; Oct–May Mon–Fri 8.30am–1.30pm & 4.30–7pm; ☎ 971 301 900).

Helpful English-speaking staff with good maps and leaflets. The excellent website ⊛ ibiza-spotlight.com is also highly informative.

ACCOMMODATION

Most of the **budget accommodation** is in the port area, particularly around Passeig de Vara de Rey. In the height of the tourist season, prices rocket and last-minute vacancies are hard to come by. Hotel staff can be flummoxed by visitors turning up on spec, so it's generally worth booking ahead, and you're often most likely to find the best deals online.

Hostal Giramundo c/Ramón Muntaner 55, Figueretes ☎ 971 307 640, ⊛ hostalgiramundoibiza.com. A brightly coloured, backpacker haven that's very close to Figueretes beach and a 15min walk from the centre. Bonuses include lockers, a DVD room and a popular in-house bar. Room prices drop significantly in winter months. Double **€80**, dorm **€28**

Hostal Juanito & Hostal Las Nieves c/Joan d'Austria 18 ☎ 971 190 319, ⊛ hostalibiza.com. Two well-established *hostales* run by the same management.

Unimaginative but clean rooms, some en suite, on a quiet street a 5min walk from the main drag. Prices at *Juanito* are slightly cheaper. Closed Nov–Easter. **€50**

Hostal Residencia Parque Caieta Soler s/n ☎971 301 358, ⓦhostalparque.com. Stylish, smart hotel in an excellent central location, with superb views of Dalt Vila from the pricey penthouse suites. All doubles are en suite with a/c and TVs. Also has a pleasant patio café. **€130**

Hostal Residencia Sol y Brisa Avgda. Bartomeu Vicente Ramón 15 ☎971 310 818, ⓦhostalsolybrisa .es. A quiet, family-run *hostal* which boasts impeccably clean singles, doubles and triples; most bathrooms are shared. Situated in a handy central location, the *Sol y Brisa* is excellent value for money. **€60**

Hostal Residencia La Ventana Sa Carrossa 13 ☎971 390 857, ⓦlaventanaibiza.com. Classy hotel inside Dalt Vila, with thirteen beautifully furnished rooms with four-poster beds and great views, as well as an excellent restaurant (open May–Oct) and roof terrace. All rooms have satellite TV and most have private balconies. **€178**

Hotel Lux Isla c/Josep Pla 1, Talamanca ☎971 313 469, ⓦluxisla.com. Just off the beach in Talamanca, 1.5km from Ibiza Town's marina, this is a well-run, excellent-value modern hotel with spacious, comfortable rooms, most with sea-view balconies and a/c. Staff are happy to help with your holiday plans. **€125**

Hotel Ocean Drive Port Deportiu, Marina Botafoch, on the north side of Ibiza's harbour ☎971 318 112, ⓦoceandrive.es. This luxury boutique hotel is one of Ibiza's most stylish. Its pristine, tasteful rooms are located across the bay from Dalt Vila. Perks include getting your name on the guest lists at the island's most sought after club nights. **€320**

★ **Vara de Rey Guest House** Passeig de Vara de Rey 7 ☎971 301 376, ⓦhibiza.com. Housed in an attractive former mansion, the creatively decorated rooms echo the building's grandiose charm. You'll need to climb several flights of stairs but there's a winch for your bags. Rooms all have washbasins; most bathrooms are shared. **€80**

EATING

The maze of streets in the port area is packed with lively **bars and restaurants**, with touts competing for custom. Generally speaking, prices are high for varying standards with most restaurants offering seafood specialities along with a selection of international dishes. For an atmospheric evening meal, head to Dalt Vila.

★ **Bide Bide** c/Felipe II 13 ☎971 312 680. Lively, modern bar with a superb choice of *pintxos* from about €3; sample dishes include delicious strips of pork cooked in beer to peppers stuffed with salted cod, as well as classics like *patatas bravas*. Try the excellent house red to wash them down. Open 7pm–late.

Bon Profit Plaça des Parc 5 ☎971 313 866. Bustling canteen-style place with a bargain-priced menu and really hearty, flavoursome food. Try the grilled squid (€8.40). No reservations taken and tables fill up fast but the service is extremely efficient. Mon–Sat 1–3pm and 8–10pm; closed Jan.

La Brasa c/Pere Sala 3 ☎971 301 202, ⓦlabrasaibiza .com. Classy restaurant with a delightful garden terrace shaded by plants and palm trees. The innovative menu concentrates on Mediterranean fish and grilled meat. It's a good place to splash out, particularly on the Ibiza sea crab, which goes for €26.50. Mon–Sat 1pm–late & Sun 6.30pm–late.

★ **Comidas Bar San Juan** c/G. de Montgri 8 ☎971 311 603. Cosy, atmospheric, bistro restaurant with dimly lit rooms and excellent-value Spanish and Ibizan cuisine. Expect to share tables. The Spanish omelette is a bargain at €4. Closed Sun.

El Olivo Plaça de Vila 9 ☎971 300 680, ⓦelolivoibiza .org. For a memorable meal in historic surrounds, this sophisticated Dalt Vila restaurant with a choice of Mediterranean and international cuisine comes highly recommended. If you want to sit on the terrace, reserve in advance. Ibiza skate with capers €20. Daily from 7pm; closed Mon Sept–June.

Los Pasajeros c/Vicent Soler s/n. Inexpensive first-floor restaurant that's a kind of staff canteen for the hard-core club crowd. You may have to queue for a table but the atmosphere is always sociable. Spanish food and cheap wine. Dishes €6.50–8. May–Oct only, open until 2am.

DRINKING AND NIGHTLIFE

Ibiza's **bar and club scene** is nothing short of incendiary. Drink prices at the island's clubs are astronomical but Ibiza Town offers no shortage of reasonably priced bars to get the night started. Stylish bars line the eastern end of c/Garijo, while the café/bars of Plaça des Parc are best for a quiet beer.

BARS

Bar Dado c/de la Verge 40. Just along the street from the more flamboyant drinking holes of Ibiza's gay quarter, this friendly bar draws a sociable crowd. Cocktails (€6–7) are cheaper than the bars closer to the port. May–Oct 9pm–late.

13

CLUBBING ON IBIZA

Some of the globe's most spectacular **clubs** are spread across the southern half of Ibiza. Clubs cost around €30–70 to get in, and are open between midnight and 6am – try to blag a guest pass from one of the bars. The Discobus (midnight–6.30am; €3) ferries partygoers from Ibiza Town to the island's major clubs, leaving from the main port.

Lo Cura c/Antonio Marí Ribas 4. Opposite *Comidas Bar San Juan*, this is a quirky local hangout. Space is limited but it's fantastic for people-watching over a frozen margarita (€8). May–Oct 9pm–late.

Rock Bar c/Garijo 14 ⓦtherockbaribiza.com. This British-run island institution is a second home for a crowd of characterful expats. Staff are friendly and you're guaranteed to meet fellow fun-seekers before hitting the clubs. May–Oct daily from 7pm.

Sunrise c/de la Verge 44. Popular and stylish bar, though nothing gets going until around midnight. It's dubbed the only lesbian bar in town but actually attracts a mixed clientele. May–Oct 10pm–late.

Sunset Plaça des Parc. Down-to-earth and relaxed café/bar with tables out onto the square. *Bocadillos*, pizzas and juices on offer, in addition to beers and cocktails. Open from 8am.

Teatro Pereyra c/Comte de Rosselló 3. A breath of fresh air – and alternative music – among the town's clubland-focused nightlife. A lively bar and a superb calendar of blues, reggae, rock and jazz acts. Free entry. Daily from 8pm.

CLUBS

Amnesia Ibiza Town–Sant Antoni road, km 5 ☎971 198 041, ⓦamnesia.es. Historically Ibiza's most innovative club, and the setting for the acid-house revolution. The atmosphere can be explosive; the best nights are Cream, Tonight, and legendary gay night La Troya. Daily June–Sept.

Anfora c/Sant Carles 7, Dalt Vila ☎971 302 893, ⓦdisco-anfora.com. Intimate gay club located in a cave in Dalt Vila. Unpretentious, and the drinks prices are moderate. Disco night on Thursdays is popular. Daily May–Oct.

★ **Las Dalias** Ibiza Town–Sant Carles road, km 12 ☎971 326 825, ⓦlasdalias.es. This bar-cum-venue has a legendary place in Ibiza's hippie scene past and present. Its chilled-out garden terrace attracts rock stars and locals alike. Namaste night on Wednesdays is a must-do. Bar daily 8am–midnight; lounge event days from 7pm; disco hours vary.

Pacha Avgda. 8 d'Agost, Ibiza Town ☎971 313 600, ⓦpacha.com. The *grande dame* of the scene and a world-renowned clubbing brand. Multiple rooms playing dance, funk and soul as well as a beautiful garden terrace. Regular DJs including Erick Morillo, David Guetta and Pete Tong spin tunes here. April–Sept daily; Oct–March weekends only.

Privilege Ibiza Town–Sant Antoni road, km 7 ☎971 198 160, ⓦprivilegeibiza.com. Gargantuan club with a hangar-like main room, fourteen bars, a garden terrace, pool, chill-out dome and café. Rarely busy though. Daily June–Sept.

Space Platja d'en Bossa ☎971 396 793, ⓦspace-ibiza.es. One of Ibiza's most modern clubs with a vast main room, two huge terraces and a plethora of other chill-out zones and alternative rooms. June–Oct daily from 10pm; sometimes earlier.

DIRECTORY

Car rental Avis (☎971 809 176) and Hertz (☎971 809 178) are at the airport. Class Rent-a-Car, Avgda. Cala Llonga (☎971 196 285) is also recommended.

Consulates UK, Avgda. d'Isidor Macabich 45 ☎971 301 818 (Mon–Fri 8.30am–1pm).

Hospital Hospital C'an Misses, 2km west of the port (☎971 397 000).

Internet access Chill, Vía Púnica 49 (Mon–Fri

9.30am–9.30pm, Sat 8am–2.30pm).

Laundry Wash & Dry, Avgda. d'Espanya 53 (Mon–Fri 10am–1.30pm & 5–8.30pm, Sat 10am–2pm).

Moped and bike rental Motos Valentín, Bartomeu Vicent Ramón 19 (☎971 310 822).

Post office Avgda. d'Isidor Macabich 67 (☎971 399 769; Mon–Fri 8.30am–8.30pm, Sat 8.30am–2pm).

The beaches around Ibiza Town

There's sea and sand close to Ibiza Town at **Figueretes**, **Platja d'en Bossa** and **Talamanca** beaches, but the first two of these are built-up continuations of the capital and only at Talamanca is there any peace and quiet. Figueretes is just a 15min walk from Ibiza Town and regular buses run to all three.

Ses Salines and Es Cavallet

To the **south of Ibiza Town**, stretching from the airport to the sea, are thousands of acres of **salt flats**. For two thousand years, Ibiza's prosperity was dependent on these salt fields (*salines*), a trade that was vital to the Carthaginians. Even today, some salt production continues. Buses from the Ibiza Town bus station leave regularly for the gorgeous beach of **SES SALINES**, whose fine white sand arcs around a bay, the crystal-clear waters fringed by pines and dunes. The beach also has a handful of superb beach bars – Sa Trinxa at the far end is the pick of the bunch. From Ses Salines, it's a brief walk through the dunes to **ES CAVALLET**, a popular nudist beach that's also favoured by gay visitors.

The east coast

Heading northeast from Ibiza Town, it's 15km to **SANTA EULÀRIA DES RIU**, a pleasant town with a plush marina but few obvious sights. Though it does boast an attractive **church** – a fortified whitewashed sixteenth-century construction perched on a hilltop to the west of the town centre, **SANT CARLES**, 7km to the north, is an agreeable one-horse village.

East of Sant Carles the road passes through burnt-red fields of olive, almond and carob trees to several almost untouched beaches. **Cala Llenya**, a broad sandy cove with sparkling waters, is the nearest, and is popular with families. Tiny **Cala Mastella**, 2km farther north, is a supremely peaceful spot, with a diminutive sandy beach and crystal-clear sheltered water. Just north of Cala Mastella, **Cala Boix** is another stunning sandy cove, a little larger and more exposed.

Continuing north from Cala Boix, the coastal road follows an exhilarating, serpentine route above the shore, through thick pine forests and past the lonely nudist beach of **Aigües Blanques**.

ACCOMMODATION	THE EAST COAST
Hostal Cala Boix Cala Boix ☎971 335 224, ⓦhostalcalaboix.com. A wonderfully tranquil setting with unexciting but spacious rooms just metres from a	quiet beach, all rooms have a/c and private bathrooms. Half-and-full board options available. **€70**

EATING AND DRINKING

Anita's Bar Sant Carles, on the main through road ☎971 335 090. A milestone in Ibiza's hippy past, this vine-shaded patio is a shadow of its former self but remains a popular meeting point and has a menu of burgers, pizza, tapas and a good range of drinks. Daily 9.30am–late.

El Bigotes Cala Mastella, no phone. Perched on a rocky outcrop a short walk from the beach (follow the signs), this simple fish restaurant offers a daily sitting at 2pm, serving up the catch of the day (€21). It's a beautiful setting but a bit of a tourist trap. In high season, you have to book a table in person in advance.

Restaurante Cala Boix ☎971 335 408. Next door to the *hostal* of the same name, this family-run establishment offers limited choices but the fish is excellent – with dishes starting from €10. Their shaded patio area is the perfect place for a cold beer. Daily 10am–midnight.

The north

Twenty kilometres from Ibiza Town, **SANT JOAN** is a pretty hilltop village home to a typically minimalist, whitewashed Ibizan church, and a sprinkling of café-bars. North of the village are some wonderful beaches, especially remote **Cala d'en Serra**, a tiny, exquisite sandy cove, with turquoise waters perfect for snorkelling. **Benirràs**, 9km northwest of Sant Joan, is another beautiful bay, backed by high, wooded cliffs. This is one of Ibiza's prime hippie-centric beaches – dozens gather here to burn herbs and pound drums to the setting sun on Sundays.

The next village to the west is **SANT MIQUEL**, where there's an imposing fortified church, and a number of simple tapas bars – try *Es Pi Ver* for an inexpensive meal. The once astonishingly beautiful inlet at **PORT DE SANT MIQUEL**, 3km north of the village,

13

has been badly mauled by the developers, but outside high season it's not too packed here, and the sheltered bay is great for children.

ACCOMMODATION THE NORTH

Atzaró Sant Joan, km15 ☎ 971 338 838, ⓦ atzaro.com. Serene countryside retreat dotted with orange trees, complete with a heavenly spa, sushi lounge and a

top-notch restaurant. Rooms are exquisitely decorated and the grounds breathtakingly beautiful. **€360**

The west and south coast

For years unchallenged at the top of Europe's *costa hooligania* league table, the package resort of **SANT ANTONI DE PORTMANY** on the island's west coast is trying hard to shake off its tarnished image. The high-rise concrete skyline and gritty British pubs of the "West End" aren't at all enticing, but the Sunset Strip on the western side of town is an appealing place for a drink. Hordes of young British clubbers flock to San An for its plethora of bars within easy staggering distance.

Beaches near Sant Antoni

Heading south of Sant Antoni, it's just a few kilometres to some exquisite coves. Sheltered **Cala Bassa** gets packed with holidaying families in high season, but it does have a campsite, while the more exposed beach of **Cala Conta** is less crowded, and is a beautiful spot to while away an afternoon. The most beguiling beach in the Balearics, **Cala d'Hort**, is in the extreme southwest of the island, with a lovely quiet sand-and-pebble shoreline plus three good, moderately priced seafood restaurants. From the shore there are mesmeric vistas of **Es Vedrà**, an incisor-shaped 378-metre-high islet that's revered by islanders and island hippies alike, and is the subject of various myths and legends – including a claim to be Homer's island of the sirens.

Taking the scenic southern road to Ibiza Town you pass via **SANT JOSEP**, a pretty village with a selection of café-restaurants. Some 7km southwest of Sant Josep, **Cala Jondal**, is a popular pebble beach.

ARRIVAL AND DEPARTURE THE WEST AND SOUTH COAST

By bus The modern bus station at c/Paris in Sant Antoni is located just behind the main street, at the corner where the main road parallel to the beach meets the road that runs alongside the marina.

Destinations Buses leave Sant Antoni for Ibiza Town every 15–30min from 7am–11.30pm, and there are frequent departures to the *calas* Vedella, Conta and Tarida (May–Oct).

By ferry Most ferry services to the island arrive and depart from Ibiza Town but there are a number of mainland services which call at Sant Antoni. The port is easily accessible at the end of the marina on the north side of the bay.

Destinations Barcelona (1–2 daily; 7hr 30min); Denia (2 daily; 3hr); Valencia (1–2 daily; 3hr 20min).

ACCOMMODATION

Cala Bassa ☎ 971 344 599, ⓦ campingcalabassa.com. Just 250m from the beach, this well-established campsite caters for tents and caravans, and mobile homes for four

people €95 per night. Two adults camping with a car costs €25. Closed Oct–March.

EATING

Blue Marlin Playa Es Jondal ☎ 971 410 230, ⓦ bluemarlinibiza.com. A suave beach club in an idyllic spot, attracting top DJs. If your budget allows, the cuisine is excellent, though unsurprisingly pricey: sea bass with sesame and spinach, for example, costs €36. Daily April–Oct 10am–4am.

El Destino c/Atalaya 15, Sant Josep ☎ 971 800 341. Tasty tapas bar with an excellent range of fresh meat, fish and vegetable dishes. Fills up fast and groups will need to book in advance. Tapas from €8. Mon–Sat 1pm–1am.
Racó Verd Pl. de la Iglesia, Sant Josep ☎ 971 800 267, ⓦ racoverdibiza.es. A healthy food paradise that is perfect

13

for getting you through the morning after the night before. Delicious fresh juices for €4–5, as well as wraps and salads.

DRINKING AND NIGHTLIFE

Café Mambo c/Vara de Rey 38, Sant Antoni ☎ 971 346 638, ☗ cafemamboibiza.com. A classic haunt on the Sunset Strip with a deserved reputation for ambient tunes, blissful sunsets and strong cocktails (about €11). Great place to start a night out. April–Oct daily 8am–late.

Eden Avgda. Calle Salvador Espriu ☎ 971 340 212, ☗ edenibiza.com. It looks like a psychedelic mosque from the outside and is a favourite of young British clubbers, with regular big-name DJ nights and a 5000 capacity. There's a dress code banning football shirts and

Also doubles as a live music and cultural venue. April–Sept Mon–Sat 10am–3am; Oct–March Thurs–Sat 6pm–late.

beachwear. Open May–Sept.

Ibiza Rocks c/Cervantes. Combining hotel, bar and fantastic venue, *Ibiza Rocks* hosts big-name gigs and showcases up-and-coming acts. Club nights begin at 7am. May–Sept daily from 7pm.

Sunset Ashram Cala Conta ☎ 661 347 222, ☗ sunsetashram.com. Looking out over the beach, this is a beautiful spot to sup a cocktail and watch the sun sink into the Med. International dishes from €19. March–Oct daily 10am–noon.

Formentera

Just eleven nautical miles south of Ibiza Town, **FORMENTERA** (population 8212) is the smallest of the four main Balearic Islands, measuring just 20km from east to west. Formentera's history more or less parallels that of Ibiza, though between 1348 and 1697 it was left uninhabited for fear of pirate raids. Like Ibiza, it was a key part of the 1960s hippie trail (Pink Floyd made an album here), and the island retains a bohemian character.

Formentera is very arid, and mainly covered in rosemary, which grows wild everywhere; it also crawls with thousands of brilliant-green **Ibiza wall lizards** (*Podarcis pityusensis*), which flourish in parched scrubland. The economy is tourism-based, taking advantage of some of Spain's longest, whitest and least-crowded beaches. Development has been limited, and visitors come here seeking escape rather than sophistication. Nude sunbathing is the norm just about everywhere, except in Es Pujols.

La Savina

There's nothing much to keep visitors in **LA SAVINA**, Formentera's only port. Along from the ferry port, there's a smart marina which fills with a fleet of gleaming yachts in the summer. Beyond that, though, it's a rather functional place with little more than car rental kiosks and unappealing wholesale stores.

Sant Francesc Xavier

The island capital, **SANT FRANCESC XAVIER**, is 4km inland and serves as Formentera's commercial and shopping centre with a handful of restaurants, cafés, street stalls and a supermarket, plus the island's main post office, at Plaça de sa Constitució 1. The only real sight here is the mighty fortified **church**, now stripped of its defensive cannon, that sits in the large central square.

Sant Ferran and Es Pujols

The sleepy village of **SANT FERRAN** is home to *Pepe*, a long-established and laidback bohemian bar-cum-restaurant, and a small nineteenth-century church. From Sant Ferran, a side road leads to **ES PUJOLS**, Formentera's main resort development – though it's tiny, and tame by mainland standards. Here you'll find two fine sandy beaches and clear, shallow waters, plenty of good seafood restaurants and some late-night bars.

The finest beaches

Northwest of Es Pujols are the absolutely spectacular sands of **Platja de Ses Illetes**, and, across a narrow channel, the uninhabited island of **Espalmador**, where there's another great beach, and water turquoise enough to trump any Caribbean brochure. It's possible to wade across most of the year, or you can get to Espalmador on one of the regular boats from La Savina (May–Oct only; €10 return).

Taking up most of Formentera's southern coastline, **Platja de Migjorn** is a sweeping bay with 5km of pale sands and crystalline waters.

The East

Heading eastwards from Sant Ferran, dusty pathways and tracks – well worth exploration – dart off from the main island road to quieter spots along Platja de Migjorn. After about 6km, the road passes through **Es Caló de Sant Agustí**, a tiny inlet with a café, restaurant and hotel. The road continues eastwards through pine forests as it skirts the northern flanks of **La Mola**, at 192m the island's highest point. After the drowsy little town of **EL PILAR**, the road straightens for the final two-kilometre dash to the **Far de La Mola** (lighthouse), which stands on cliffs high above the blue ocean. It was here that Jules Verne was inspired to write his *Journey Round the Solar System* as he gazed into the clear night sky.

ARRIVAL AND INFORMATION   FORMENTERA

Ferries (return €32–41) make the crossing from Ibiza. **Destinations** Denia (June–Sept daily; 4hr); Ibiza (daily; every 30min; 35min–1hr).

Turisme Inside the ferry port building in La Savina (April–Sept Mon–Fri 10am–7pm & Sat 10am–3pm; Oct–May Mon–Fri 10am–2pm & 5–7pm, Sat 10am–3pm; 971 322 057, formentera.es), can help with accommodation and cycle routes, and provide maps.

GETTING AROUND

By bus There's a basic bus service from the port of arrival, La Savina, to the main settlements.

By bike, scooter and car Getting about by bicycle is very popular, since apart from the hill of La Mola, the island is extremely flat; there are several rental places by the ferry dock, and in Es Pujols (€10–12 per day). Scooters and cars are also available but be warned that some of the tracks down to the beaches are very uneven and sand-covered terrain.

ACCOMMODATION

It's almost essential to make an **advance reservation** between late June and September, as the bulk of the island's limited supply of beds is snapped up early. Camping is not permitted anywhere on the island.

Gecko Beach Club Platja de Migjorn 971 328 024, geckobeachclub.com. If you want to enjoy Formentera's simple charms from a sophisticated base, this stylish hotel is one of the island's best. A picture-postcard location on the beach with gleaming floors, a garden-like pool area, an excellent restaurant, yoga classes and massage sessions. **€295**

Hostal Pepe c/Major 68, Sant Ferran 971 328 033. Situated on the village's main street, opposite the *Pepe* bar, these no-frills rooms are not particularly enticing but are immaculately clean. Breakfast is included. Closed Nov–March. **€75**

Hostal Rafalet Es Caló 971 327 016, hostal-rafalet.com. Overlooking a tiny fishing harbour, this hotel's spacious rooms afford magnificent sea views. With welcoming staff and a good bar and restaurant, it's the perfect place to unwind. Closed Nov–March. **€105**

Hostal Residencia Illes Pitiüses Sant Ferran 971 328 189, illespitiuses.com. A long-established family-run hotel located right on the main cross-island road. Rooms are comfortable but rather old-fashioned, all have satellite TV, private bathrooms and a/c. **€123**

Hostal Residencia Mayans Es Pujols, c/Puntaprima 971 328 724, hrmayans@terra.es. Good-value, modern hotel with a large pool and shaded patio café/bar area. Breakfast included. Apartments also available on the same site. Closed Nov–March. **€100**

13

EATING AND DRINKING

Most of Formentera's *hostales* serve **meals**, or you can get your own supplies from the SYP supermarket in Sant Francesc Xavier. This is not the place for sophisticated **nightlife** though cocktails and beer flow at the island's **beachside bars** or *chiringuitos*.

Blue Bar Platja de Migjorn ☎971 187 011, ⓦbluebarformentera.com. Chilled-out beachside bar with ambient tunes and a perfect place to enjoy a cocktail under the stars. Groups should book ahead to dine. May & Oct 1–10.30pm; June–Sept 1–5pm & 7pm–midnight.

Cafetería Espardell Es Pujols ☎971 328 357, ⓦespardell.com. Popular café/bar tourist haunt on the seafront with quality, international fare and a good selection of cakes and pastries. Pasta dishes from €8. Daily from 8.30am–2am. Closed Nov–March.

Fonda Platé San Francesc Xavier. A pleasant café next to the church with a vine-shaded patio, serving up snacks, sandwiches and light meals – the vanilla milkshakes (€3.80) are very refreshing.

Macondo Sant Ferran, no phone. At the end of the main street, this highly recommended pizzeria has modern decor, an outside terrace and a smart-looking bar area. Gets lively in the evenings. Closed Nov–March.

El Mirador On the main road to La Mola ☎971 327 037. It is the exceptional views rather than the food that brings people here in droves but the specialities are paella and fish. Daily 1–4pm & 7–11pm.

Restaurant Rafalet Caló de Sant Agustí ☎971 327 077. Inside the *Hostal Rafalet*, this restaurant with Carribean-esque views across the cove has a reputation for excellent fish, with mains from €23. For lighter meals, try the adjacent bar – under the same management – with *pa amb coses* (bread and things) at €14. Closed Nov–March.

DIRECTORY

Car rental Autos Ca Marí, ☎971 328 855, ⓦautoscamariformentera.com. Offices in La Savina, Ca Marí and Es Caló.

Emergencies For the police, call ☎092 and fire brigade, dial ☎112.

Taxi Radiotaxi ☎971 322 342.

Mallorca

Few Mediterranean holiday spots are as often and as unfairly maligned as **MALLORCA**. The island is commonly perceived as little more than sun, sex, booze and high-rise. It's an image spawned by the helter-skelter development of the 1960s, yet it takes no account of Mallorca's beguiling diversity. In fact, the spread of development, even after fifty years, is essentially confined to the **Badia de Palma** (Bay of Palma), a thirty-kilometre strip flanking the island capital, and a handful of mega-resorts notching the east coast.

Elsewhere, things are very different. **Palma** itself, the Balearics' one real city, is a bustling, historic place whose grand mansions and magnificent Gothic cathedral defy the expectations of many visitors. And so does the northwest coast, where visitors delight in the rearing peaks of the rugged **Serra de Tramuntana**, beautiful cove beaches, monasteries at Valldemossa and Lluc, and a string of delightful old towns and villages – such as Deià, Sóller and Pollença. There's a startling variety and physical beauty to the land, which has drawn tourists to visit and well-heeled expatriates to settle here since the nineteenth century, including artists and writers of many descriptions, from Robert Graves to Roger McGough.

GETTING AROUND   MALLORCA

Public transport Palma lies at the hub of an extensive public transport system, with bus services linking the capital to all Mallorca's principal settlements and even a couple of train lines – one, a beautiful ride up through the mountains to Sóller (see p.873), is an attraction in itself. And with your own transport, Palma is within two hours' drive of anywhere on the island. Hiring a bike is also a popular way to seek out the island's quieter spots.

Taxis can work out a reasonable deal, too, if you're travelling in a group – the fare for the thirty-kilometre trip from Palma to Sóller is about €45, for instance.

ACCOMMODATION

The main constraint for travellers is **accommodation**, or lack of it. In high season (May–Oct) rooms are far less booked out in inland towns and villages. Everything is quieter in the winter months but many hotels in the main resorts close. Bear in mind also that several of Mallorca's former **monasteries** rent out renovated cells at exceptionally inexpensive rates – reckon on €22–50 per double room per night. The Monastir de Nostra Senyora at Lluc (see p.877) and the Ermita de Nostra Senyora del Puig outside Pollença (see p.878) are both reachable by public transport.

Palma

In 1983, **PALMA** became the capital of the newly established Balearic Islands autonomous region, since when it has developed into a go-ahead and cosmopolitan commercial hub of almost 400,000 people. The new self-confidence is plain to see in the city centre, a vibrant place – and a world away from the heaving tourist enclaves of the surrounding bay.

Finding your way around Palma is fairly straightforward once you're in the city centre. The obvious landmark is the **Catedral**, which dominates the waterfront and backs onto the oldest part of the city, a cluster of alleys and narrow lanes whose northern and eastern limits are marked by the zigzag of avenues built beside – or in place of – the city walls. On the west side of the Catedral, Avgda. d'Antoni Maura/Passeig d'es Born cuts up from the seafront to intersect with Avgda. Jaume III/Unio at Plaça Rei Joan Carles I. These busy thoroughfares form the core of the modern town.

13 The Catedral

April-May Mon–Fri 10am–5.15pm, Sat 10am–2.15pm; June–Sept Mon–Fri 10am–6.15pm, Sat 10am–2.15pm; Nov–March Mon–Fri 10am–3.15pm, Sat 10am–2.15pm • €4 including the Museu de la Catedral

Five hundred years in the making, Palma's **Catedral** is a magnificent building – the equal of almost any on the mainland – and a surprising one, too, with its interior featuring *modernista* touches designed by Antoni Gaudí. The original church was built following the Christian Reconquest of the city, and the site taken, in fulfilment of a vow by Jaume I, was that of the Moorish Great Mosque. Essentially Gothic, with massive exterior buttresses to take the weight off the pillars within, the church derives its effect through its sheer height, impressive from any angle but startling when glimpsed from the waterside esplanade.

The nave

In the central nave, fourteen beautifully aligned, pencil-thin pillars rise to 21m before their ribs branch out – like fronded palm trees – to support the single-span, vaulted roof. The **nave**, at 44m high, is one of the tallest Gothic structures in Europe, and its length – 121m – is of matching grandeur. This open, hangar-like construction, typical of Catalan Gothic architecture, was designed to make the high altar visible to the entire congregation, and to express the mystery of the Christian faith, with kaleidoscopic floods of light filtering in through the **stained-glass windows**. For once, the light isn't trapped by the central *coro* (choir) that normally blocks the centre of Spanish cathedrals. The innovative though controversial sidelining of the *coro*, and the fantastic forms of the lighting system above the altar, were Gaudí's work, undertaken between 1904 and 1914.

Museu de la Catedral

On the way into the church, you pass through three rooms of assorted ecclesiastical bric-a-brac, which comprise the **Museu de la Catedral**. The first room's most valuable exhibit, in the glass case in the middle, is a gilded silver monstrance of extraordinary delicacy, its fairy-tale decoration dating from the late sixteenth century. The second room is mainly devoted to the Gothic works of the **Mallorcan Primitives**, a school of painters who flourished on the island in the fourteenth and fifteenth centuries, producing strikingly naive works of bold colours and cartoon-like detail.

Palau de l'Almudaina

April–Sept Mon–Fri 10am–5.45pm, Sat 10am–1pm; Oct–March Mon–Fri 10am–1pm & 4–5pm, Sat 10am–1pm • €4, plus €2.50 for audio-guide; free entry on Wed to EU citizens showing their passport

Opposite the cathedral entrance stands the **Palau de l'Almudaina**, originally the palace of the Moorish *walis* (governors) and later of the Mallorcan kings. The interior has been painstakingly restored, but its rabbit warren of rooms and corridors has been left comparatively bare, the main decorative highlight being a handful of admirable Flemish tapestries, each devoted to classical themes.

Palau March Museu

Mon–Fri 10am–6.30pm, Nov–March until 5pm, Sat 10am–2pm • €3.60

Along c/Palau Reial stands the opulent 1930s townhouse of the Mallorcan magnate and speculator Joan March (1880–1962), now opened to the public as the **Palau March Museu**. The highlight here is the splendid Italianate courtyard, which is used to display a potpourri of modern art drawn from the March collection. There are two Henry Moore sculptures, a Rodin torso and a fetchingly eccentric *Orgue del Mar* (*Organ of the Sea*) by Xavier Corbero.

Museu de Mallorca

C/Portella 5 • Tues–Sat 10am–7pm, Sun 10am–2pm • €3

Within the medina-like maze of **old-town** streets at the back of the cathedral is the **Museu de Mallorca**. Occupying one of the many fifteenth- and sixteenth-century patrician mansions that dot this section of town, the museum holds an extensive collection of Mallorcan archeological finds as well as some exceptionally fine medieval religious paintings, including further examples of the work of the Mallorcan Primitives.

Basílica de Sant Francesc

Daily 9.30am–12.30pm & 3.30–6pm, but closed Sun pm • €1

Occupying, oddly enough, the site of the old Moorish soap factory, the **Basílica de Sant Francesc** is the finest among the city's bevy of medieval churches. It's a substantial building, founded towards the end of the thirteenth century, and the main facade displays a stunning severity of style, with a great sheet of dressed sandstone stretching up to an arcaded balcony and pierced by a gigantic rose window. Entered via a fine trapezoidal Gothic cloister, the cavernous interior is a little disappointing, but you can't miss the monumental **high altar**, a gaudy affair illustrative of High Baroque.

Santa Eulàlia

Mon–Fri 9.30am–midday & 6.30–8.30pm, Sat 10.30am–1pm & 6.30–8.30pm, Sun 9.30am–1pm & 6.30–7.30pm • Free

From the basilica, it's a couple of minutes' walk west to **Santa Eulàlia**, the first church to be built after King Jaume's arrival, a typically Gothic construction with a yawning nave originally designed – as in the cathedral – to give the entire congregation a view of the high altar. Close by, the **Ajuntament** (town hall) is a debonair example of the late Renaissance style, with a grand and self-assured foyer.

Baluard Museu d'Art Modern i Contemporani

Tues–Sun 10am–9pm, Oct–May until 8pm, Fridays in July & Aug until midnight • €6, entry by donation on Fri • ⓦ esbaluard.org

On the west side of the city centre, the **Passeig Mallorca** is bisected by the deep, walled watercourse that once served as the city moat and is now an especially handsome feature of the city. One of the old bastions overlooking the watercourse, on Plaça Porta Santa Catalina, has recently been turned into the **Baluard Museu d'Art Modern i Contemporani** (Modern & Contemporary Art Museum), where pride of place goes to a rare and unusual sample of Picasso ceramics, most memorably a striking, white, ochre and black vase-like piece entitled *Big Bird Corrida*.

ARRIVAL AND DEPARTURE PALMA

By plane Mallorca's whopping international airport is 11km east of Palma. It has car rental outlets, 24-hour ATMs and currency exchange facilities among the package tour operator helpdesks. The airport is linked to the city and the Bay of Palma resorts by a busy highway. Bus #1 leaves for Palma every fifteen minutes from the main entrance of the terminal building, just behind the taxi rank (6am–2.10am; €2), and goes to Plaça Espanya, on the north side of the city centre. A taxi from the airport to the city centre will set you back around €18.

Destinations Ibiza (8–10 daily; 45min) and Maó (6–12 daily; 40min).

By bus Buses from outside Palma arrive and depart from the city's transport hub at Plaça Espanya. Go down the escalators and follow the signs.

Destinations Andratx (hourly; 1hr); Deià (3–5 daily; 45min); Pollença (2–5 daily; 1hr 10min); Port de Pollença (2–5 daily; 1hr 15min); Port de Sóller (via the tunnel:

Mon–Fri hourly, Sat & Sun every 1–2hr, 35min; via Valldemossa: 3–5 daily, 1hr 30min); Sóller (via Valldemossa: 3–5 daily, 1hr 15min; via the tunnel: Mon–Fri hourly, Sat & Sun every 1–2hr, 30min); Valldemossa (4–9 daily; 30min).

By ferry The Palma ferry terminal is about 4km west of the city centre. Bus #1 leaves every fifteen minutes from outside Terminal 2 (6am–2.10am; €2) bound for the Plaça Espanya. The taxi fare for the same journey is about €12.

Destinations Barcelona (2–3 daily; 7–8hr); Denia (1–2 daily; 5hr) Ibiza (3–4 daily; 2–4hr) Maó (1 weekly; 6hr 30min); Valencia (2 daily; 7–8hr).

By train Palma has two train lines. The scenic trip on the Tren de Sóller is the most popular (see p.873) but a more functional service also runs from the modern Palma train station (☎ 971 177 777, ⓦ tib.caib.es), off Plaça Espanya.

Destinations Binissalem (every 25min; 30min) and Inca (every 25min; 45 min).

13

CENTRAL PALMA

0 100 metres

Bus Station, Inca & Sa Pobla Train Station (400m)

Main Train Station

Sóller Train Station

JOAN MARCH
PLAÇA ESPANYA
MARIE CURIE
PORTA PINTADA
JOAN XXIII
SANT MIQUEL
CAPUTXINS
VILANOVA
Mercat de l'Olivar
VOLTA DE LA MERÉ
SANTA FOU I DE L'EBRER
MOLINERS
CAN VALLORI
SINDICAT
HOSTAL DE L'ESTEL
LLOTGETA
HOSTALS
CORDERIA
QUINTANA

FRANCESC DE BORJA MOLL
CAN MAÇANET
CAN PERPINYÀ
MISSIÓ
SANT MIQUEL
Sant Miquel
Teatre Principal
PL. MAJOR
PL. MARQUÉS DEL PALMER
BOSSERIA
ARGENTERIA

CECILI METEL
MONTEROS
OMS
SANT ELIES
CARDENAL POU
SANT MIQUEL
MISSIÓ
TERESES
POSADA DE LA REAL
CARME
HORTS
RIERA
L'Àguila
Can Rei
COLOM
BARTOMEU
JAUME II
SINDI
PL. CAN TAGAMENT

PL. BISBE BERENGUER DE PALOU
JERONI ANTIC
P. DE JESÚS
OMS
PASSEIG DE LA RAMBLA
CAN OLIVA
CAN PUEYO
Gran Hotel
PL. WEYLER
CAPUTXINS
CAN JAQUOTOT
C. CAMPANER
ROSA
UNIÓ
PL. CAN SANTA CÍLIA
VALDO
CAN DAMÚS
BROSSA
QUINT

BARÓ DE PINOPAR
VIA ROMA
CAMPINS
BOTIA
SANTIAGO RUSIÑOL
MISERICÒRDIA
BISBE
PL. STA. MAGDALENA
C. DE STA. MAGDALENA
ÀNGELS
BISBE
SASTRE ROIG
SANT JAUME
PALMA
SACRISTIA DE SANT JAUME
C. FAMENGOL
CAN SERINYA
Can Balaguer
CAN BRONDO
SANT NICOLAU
SANT VERÍ
PESCADORIA
PARAÍSOS

IOAQUIM
PL. HOSPITAL
CATANY
JARDÍ BOTÀNIC
C. TORRELLA
GAVARRERA
SANT JAUME
PL. MERCAT
QUIRÀNERA
JOVELLANOS

Hospital General
MISERICÒRDIA
CAVALLERIA
ERMITA
CONCEPCIÓ
PL. REI JOAN CARLES I
Can Solleric
PARAÍSOS

BISBE
DIETAI
SANT MARTÍ
MONTCADES
AIGUA
GAIETA
SANT
GRANADA
CAN CIFRE
Can Moner
SANT FELIU

CONCEPCIÓ
RUBÉN DARÍO
CERDANYA
CONFLENT
OMELADES
CARLADES
BERENGUER SANT JOAN
HUG DE RIBESALTES
ARAGONÉS
CREMONA
BONAIRE
ANTIGE MATAR
CAN RIBERA
AVINGUDA JAUME III
AVINGUDA JAUME III
PAU
BERENGUER
Can Pavesi
EL PUIG DE SANT PERE
CAN SALES
VI
SANT LLORENÇ

AVINGUDA DE PORTUGAL
PASSEIG MALLORCA
PASSEIG MALLORCA
JOAN DE SEPÚLVEDA
STA. MARIA DEL SEPULCRE

CA'AL
MATEU OBRADOR
EIVISSA
RAMON
I
RUIZ DE ALDA
POLVORA
PL. PORTA DE SANTA CATALINA
Es Baluard Museu
C. D'OLIVERA
B. DE BOU
PASSEIG MALLORCA
AVINGUDA DE L'ARGENTINA
AVINGUDA DE L'ARGENTINA

N

13

Badia de Palma

Parc de la Mar

13

INFORMATION

Turisme In the city centre, the *turisme* nearest the old town is just off the Passeig d'es Born at Plaça de la Reina 2 (Mon–Fri 9am–8pm, Sat 9am–2pm; ☎971 173 990).
Municipal office The main office on the north edge of Plaça Espanya not far from the main bus/train station (daily 9am–9pm; ☎971 754 329). Both provide island-wide information.

ACCOMMODATION

The bulk of Palma's **accommodation** is dotted around the city centre – fortunately enough, as this is by far the most engaging part of the city. Note that particularly in high season some places insist on a minimum stay of two or three nights.

Hostal Brondo c/Ca'n Brondo 1 ☎971 719 043, ⓦhostalbrondo.com. A stylish little place in a central but quiet location, with Mallorcan antiques and newly done-up rooms. It's probably the best bang for your buck in town. Both en-suite and shared-facility doubles. €55

★ **Hostal Ritzi** c/Apuntadors 6 ☎971 714 610, ⓦhostalritzi.com. Superbly located in a fantastic five-storey former mansion off the Passeig d'es Born, the *Ritzi* is an excellent meeting point for other travellers. Ask for a room which doesn't back onto the main street as it can get noisy at night. Dorm €20, Double €55

Hotel Araxa c/Pilar Juncosa 22 ☎971 731 640, ⓦhotelaraxa.com. About 2km west of the centre, this attractive four-storey modern hotel has pleasant gardens and an outdoor swimming pool. Most rooms have balconies. To get there, take EMT bus #6 and get off at c/Marquès de la Sènia, just before the start of Avgda. Joan Miró; it's a 5–10min walk from the bus stop. €140

★ **Hotel Born** c/Sant Jaume 3 ☎971 712 942, ⓦhotelborn.com. Comfortable and justifiably popular hotel in an excellent downtown location. It's a sixteenth-century refurbished mansion and has marvellous high-ceiling rooms and grand communal areas as well as a courtyard café. €105

★ **Hotel Dalt Murada** c/Almudaina 6 ☎971 425 300, ⓦdaltmurada.com. Set inside a former manor house with period architecture and artwork, and all modern comforts and conveniences. Great central location, too – just behind the town hall. €157

Hotel Palau Sa Font c/Apuntadors 38 ☎971 712 277, ⓦpalausafont.com. This smooth and polished four-star hotel, decorated in earthy Italian colours and graced by sculptures and other modern works of art, manages to be both stylish and welcoming. There's a roof terrace with inspiring views of the cathedral. €167

Hotel Saratoga Pg. Mallorca 6 ☎971 727 240, ⓦhotelsaratoga.es. An excellent modern hotel with swimming pool. Most rooms have balconies overlooking either the boulevard (a bit noisy) or the interior courtyard and pool (quieter). Pluses include an in-house spa and jazz bar. €180

EATING

Eating in Palma is less pricey – or can be – than anywhere else in the Balearics. Inexpensive **cafés** and **tapas bars** are liberally distributed around the city centre, with a particular concentration in the side streets off the Passeig d'es Born and Avgda. Antoni Maura. In central Palma, especially along the harbourfront and around Plaça Llotja, many **restaurants** are unashamedly geared to the tourist trade. At all but the most expensive of places, €25–40 will cover the cost of a starter, main course and half a bottle of wine.

CAFÉS AND TAPAS BARS

Bar Bosch Plaça Rei Joan Carles I. One of the most popular and inexpensive cafés in town, the traditional haunt of intellectuals, and usually humming with conversation. At peak times, you'll need to be assertive to get served. *Horchata* €2.50. Daily 8am–late.

★ **Bar Dia** c/Apuntadores 18 ☎971 716 264. Bustling tapas bar with delicious Spanish cuisine at reasonable prices. Often standing room only and you'll need to sharpen your elbows to get to the bar. Try the prawns in garlic, €12. Tues–Sun 1pm–late.

★ **Ca'n Joan de S'Aigo** c/Can Sanç 10. In a tiny alley near Plaça Santa Eulàlia, this long-established coffee house has wonderful, freshly baked *ensaimadas* (sweet spiral pastry buns). Charmingly formal, period-piece decor. Daily except Tues 8am–9pm.

La Taberna del Caracol c/Sant Alonso 2 ☎971 714 908. Deep in the depths of the old town, this smashing tapas bar occupies charming old premises – all wooden beams and ancient arches. A first-rate range of tapas begins at just €6. Reservations advised at peak times. Mon–Sat 7.30–11.30pm.

RESTAURANTS

Bon Lloc c/Sant Feliu 7 ☎971 718 617, ⓦbonlloc restaurant.com. One of the few vegetarian restaurants on the island, centrally situated off the Passeig d'es Born, with an informal atmosphere and good food at low prices. Good-value lunch menu €14.50. Mon–Sat 1–4pm.

Ca n'Eduardo c/Contramoll Mollet 4 ☎971 721 182, ⓦcaneduardo.com. Spic-and-span restaurant located upstairs in one of the plain modern buildings looking out above the fish dock. There's an enjoyable view of the harbour, but the real treat is the fresh fish – a wonderful range, all simply prepared; the monkfish bouillabaisse (€28) is superb. The restaurant is just across from – and east of – the foot of Avgda. Argentina. Tues–Sat 1–3.30pm & 8–11pm.

Celler Pagès Off c/Apuntadors at c/Felip Bauza 2 ☎ 971 726 036. Small, inexpensive restaurant with an easy-going family atmosphere serving traditional Mallorcan food – try the stuffed marrows with home-made mayonnaise. Good-value lunch menu at €13. Reserve at weekends. Mon–Sat 1–3.30pm & 8–11pm.

Mangiafuoco Plaça Vapor 4, Santa Catalina ☎ 971 451 072. Tuscan-owned restaurant-cum-wine bar offering top-notch Italian food and specializing in dishes featuring truffles. Try the *tagliatelle al tartuffo* and prepare to be wowed. Attractive setting, too – metres from the top of the low ridge that overlooks the harbourfront. Daily except Tues 1.30–3.30pm & 8–11pm.

Restaurant del Museu Es Baluard Museu, Plaça Porta Santa Catalina s/n ☎ 971 908 199, ⊛ esbaluard restaurant.com. Adjacent to the Es Baluard gallery, this excellent restaurant occupies two modernist glass cubes with views out across the bay. The menu is full of international flavour and portions are generous. Main courses cost around €16 in the evening, and are slightly less during the day. Tues–Sun noon–3.30pm & 8–11pm.

DRINKING AND NIGHTLIFE

There's a cluster of lively **late-night bars** – mostly with music as the backdrop rather than the main event – among the narrow side-streets backing onto Plaça Llotja. The **club scene** in Palma is small but worth investigating after around midnight; entry charges are between €6 and €24, depending on the night and what's happening.

BARS

Abaco c/Sant Joan 1 ☎ 971 714 939. Easily Palma's most unusual bar, with fruits cascading down its stairway, caged birds hidden amid patio foliage, elegant music and a daily flower bill you could live on for a month. Cocktails start at €16, but you're never hurried into buying one. Everyone is often so mesmerised by the bizarre surroundings that the atmosphere is rather sedate. Sun–Thurs 8pm–1am, Fri & Sat 8pm–3am; closed most of Jan.

Agua Bar Jaume Ferrer 6 ⊛ aguabar.com. Friendly New-Yorker run bar with a good range of beer, an impressive collection of rock and roll and a relaxed vibe. Open-mic night on Sundays attracts a crowd. Daily from 7pm–late.

L'Ambigú c/Carnisseria 1 ☎ 971 572 151. Just behind Santa Eulàlia, this modern bar with wall-to-wall contemporary artwork attracts a young professional crowd. It's hidden just away from the tourist droves so is generally speaking a peaceful place for a relaxed drink. Flavourful tapas too. Mon–Sat from 7pm.

La Lonja c/Llotja de Mar 2 ☎ 971 722 799. A popular, well-established expat haunt, with revolving doors and pleasantly old-fashioned decor; the background music caters for (almost) all tastes. Tapas are served, too; don't miss the dates wrapped in bacon (€3). Mon–Thurs 10am–1am, Sat 11am–3am, Sun 11am–1pm.

CLUBS

Tito's Plaça Gomila 3 ☎ 971 730 017, ⊛ titosmallorca .com. With its stainless steel, neon lighting and glass exterior, this long-established nightspot looks a bit like something from a sci-fi film. Outdoor lifts carry you up from Avgda. Gabriel Roca (the back entrance) to the dancefloor, which plays anything from hardcore dance to mainstream pop. Entry €30 but try to get on the guest list. June to early Sept daily 11pm–5am; Oct–May Fri–Sun 11pm–5am.

DIRECTORY

Car rental Hertz (☎ 971 789 670) and Avis (☎ 902 110 261) have offices in the city and at Palma airport.
Hospital Son Dureta Hospital, Andrea Doria 55, ☎ 971 175 000.

Internet access Azul Computer Group, c/Soledat 4, ☎ 971 712 927.
Post office c/Constitució 6, ☎ 971 721 867.

Around Palma

Anywhere in the west or centre of the island is readily accessible as a **day-trip** from Palma. If you're after a quick **swim** the most convenient option is to stick to the resorts strung along the neighbouring **Badia de Palma** (Bay of Palma). Locals tend to go east on the #15 bus (every 10min; 30min) from Plaça Espanya to **S'Arenal**, where there's an enormously long, albeit very crowded, sandy beach.

13

Castell de Bellver

April–Sept Mon–Sat 8.30am–8.30pm, Sun 10am–6.30pm; Oct–March Mon–Sat 8.30am–7pm, Sun 10am–5pm • €2, free on Sun

An appealing option, though there are no buses to it, is the **Castell de Bellver**, a strikingly well-preserved fortress of canny circular design built for Jaume II at the beginning of the fourteenth century. The castle perches on a wooded hilltop some 3km west of the city centre and offers superb views of Palma and its harbour.

Andratx, Sant Elm and Sa Dragonera

Inland from the Bay of Palma, you could spend an hour or two exploring **ANDRATX**, a small, undeveloped town huddled among the hills to the west of the city – there are hourly buses. From here, it's another short bus ride through a pretty, orchard-covered landscape to low-key **SANT ELM**.

With more time to spare, you can catch a **boat** across from Sant Elm's minuscule harbour to the austere offshore islet of **Sa Dragonera**, an uninhabited chunk of rock some 4km long and 700m wide, with an imposing ridge of sea cliffs dominating its northwestern shore; the main pull here – apart from hiking on this traffic-free islet – is the birdlife; the ferry trip takes fifteen minutes each way and the return fare is €15.

ACCOMMODATION AND EATING

SANT ELM

Hostal Dragonera ☎ 971 239 086, ⓦ hostaldragonera .net. A highly recommended operation is this very reasonably priced *hostal* situated right on the seafront with simple but comfortable rooms, most of which offer sea views. Closed March & April. **€57**

Vista Mar c/Jaime I 46 ☎ 971 239 044. Harbourside restaurant with a beautiful terrace and delicious paella and fish dishes. Reckon on at least €40 for a complete meal, including house wine. Opens lunch & dinner.

Northern Mallorca

Mallorca is at its scenic best in the gnarled ridge of the **Serra de Tramuntana**, the imposing mountain range that stretches the length of the island's western shore, its soaring peaks and plunging sea cliffs intermittently intercepted by valleys of olive and citrus groves and dotted with some of the island's most attractive towns and villages. An enjoyable way to admire this spectacular scenery at a leisurely pace is to drive or cycle along the coastal road Ma-10, which runs from Andratx to Pollença – though be aware that some of the twists and turns are quite precarious. If you're reliant on public transport, the easiest way to explore the north is to travel up from Palma to Sóller and use this town as a base, making selected forays along the coastal road. Sóller is within easy striking distance of the mountain village of **Deià** and the monastery of **Valldemossa** to the southwest, or it's a short haul northeast to the monastery of **Lluc**, the quaint town of **Pollença** and the resort of **Port de Pollença**.

As far as **beaches** are concerned, most of the region's coastal villages have a tiny, shingly strip, and only around the bays of Pollença and Alcúdia are there more

HIKING IN NORTHERN MALLORCA

The **Serra de Tramuntana** provides the best walking on Mallorca, with scores of hiking trails latticing the mountains. Generally speaking, paths are well marked, though apt to be clogged with thorn bushes. There are trails to suit all levels of fitness, from the easiest of strolls to the most gruelling of long-distance treks, but in all cases you should come properly equipped – certainly with an appropriate hiking **map** (available in Palma and at the Sóller *turisme*), and, for the more difficult routes, a **compass**. Spring and autumn are the best times to embark on the longer trails; in midsummer, the heat can be enervating and water is scarce. Bear in mind also that the mountains are prone to mists, though they usually lift at some point in the day.

substantial offerings. The resorts edging these bays have the greatest number of hotel and *hostal* rooms, but elsewhere **accommodation** requires some forethought.

Sóller

If you're arriving by train at **SÓLLER**, the obvious option is to take the **tram to the port.** If you do pass straight through, however, you'll miss one of the most laidback and enjoyable towns on Mallorca, though it's the general flavour of the place that appeals rather than any specific sight: the town's narrow, sloping lanes are cramped by eighteenth- and nineteenth-century stone houses, whose fancy grilles and big wooden doors once housed the region's well-heeled fruit merchants.

Plaça Constitució

All streets lead to the main square, **Plaça Constitució**, an informal, pint-sized affair of crowded cafés just down the hill from the train station. The square is dominated by the hulking mass of the church of **Sant Bartomeu**, a crude but still somehow rather engaging neo-Gothic remodelling of the medieval original, its main saving grace being the enormous rose window cut high in the main facade.

ARRIVAL AND DEPARTURE

SÓLLER

By bus Buses to and from Port de Sóller to Palma, Deià, Valldemossa and north Mallorca call en-route at the Sóller bus station at c/Cetre – about a 5min walk west of the centre.
Destinations Deià (4–7 daily; 25min); Palma (via Valldemossa: 3–5 daily, 1hr 25min; via the tunnel: Mon–Fri hourly, Sat & Sun every 1–2hr, 35min); Port de Sóller (4–7 daily; 5min); Valldemossa (3–5 daily; 55min).
By train Easily the best way to cross the Serra de Tramuntana is to take the train (W trendesoller.com, T 971 630 130) from Palma to Sóller, a 28-kilometre journey that takes about one

hour on antique rolling stock that seems to have come straight out of an Agatha Christie novel. The rail line, constructed on the profits of the nineteenth-century orange and lemon trade, dips and twists through the mountains and across fertile valleys, offering magnificent views.
Destinations Palma (6–7 daily; 1hr; 10 one way, €17 return).
By tram Trams leave (7am–9pm, every 30min–1hr; 15min; €4 each way) from outside the station down to the seashore at Port de Sóller, just 5km away.

INFORMATION

Turisme Located inside an old tram carriage on Plaça de Espanya and has a good supply of leaflets as well as a list of accommodation (Mon–Fri 9.45am–2pm & 3.15–5pm; Sat

9.15am–1pm; T 971 638 008). The website W sollernet .com is also an excellent source of information.

ACCOMMODATION

Casa Margarita c/Reial 3 T 971 634 214, W sollernet .com/casamargarita. A family-run guesthouse with basic but comfortable rooms decorated with antique furniture. The more expensive rooms have access to an outdoor terrace. The lady of the house is warm and welcoming. €33
Hotel Ca'l Bisbe c/Bisbe Nadal 10 T 971 631 228, W hotelcalbisbe.com. Upmarket hotel in an immaculately restored old mansion with spacious rooms, all with a/c and

cable TV, set around an attractive pool area. Check their website for bargain. Closed Nov–Jan. €115
Hotel El Guía c/Castanyer 2 T 971 630 227, W sollernet.com/elguia. First opened in 1880, this smart-looking hotel just metres from the train station is a family-run Sóller institution. Expect – and revel in – plenty of old-world charm but few mod cons. Closed Dec–April. €89

EATING AND DRINKING

Restaurant El Guía c/Castanyer T 971 630 227. In the hotel of the same name, this period dining room boasts smartly-clad waiters and linen-draped tables. Cuisine is typically Mallorcan with simply prepared but excellent fish dishes – ask for the daily specials. Menú €18. Daily 1.45–3.15pm & 8–10pm.

Sa Fàbrica de Gelats Romaguera 12 T 971 631 708, W gelatsoller.com. Heavenly ice-cream parlour with a choice of 40 flavours. It's famed for its hugely refreshing orange ice-cream. Takeaway or enjoy in the garden terrace. Two scoops go for €2.50. Mon–Sat 9am–7pm.

13

Port de Sóller

PORT DE SÓLLER is one of the most popular and family-orientated resorts on the west coast, and its horseshoe-shaped bay must be the most photographed spot on the island after the package resorts around Palma. The best **swimming** is along the pedestrianized area of **Platja d'en Repic**, where the water is clear and the beach clean and well maintained. Also good fun is the fifty-minute walk up to the **lighthouse**, which guards the cliffs above the entrance to Port de Sóller's harbour. It's a steep climb but the views out over the wild and rocky coast are spectacular, especially at sunset. Directions couldn't be easier: from the centre of the resort, walk round the southern side of the bay past the Platja d'en Repic beach and keep going.

ARRIVAL AND INFORMATION
PORT DE SÓLLER

By tram Trams from Sóller clank to a halt beside the waterfront, bang in the centre of town and a couple of minutes' walk from the *turisme*.

By bus Buses arrive and depart from c/Església, just around the corner from the tourist office.

Destinations Deià (3–5 daily; 30min); Palma (via Valldemossa: 3–5 daily, 1hr 30min; via the tunnel: Mon–Fri hourly, Sat & Sun every 1–2hr, 35min);

Pollença (May–Oct Mon–Sat 2 daily; 2hr); Port de Pollença (April–Oct Mon–Sat 2 daily; 2hr 10min); Sóller (Mon–Fri hourly, Sat & Sun every 1–2hr; 5min); Valldemossa (3–5 daily; 1hr).

Turisme Located beside the church on c/Canonge Oliver (March–Oct Mon–Fri 9.15am–1pm & 2.45–5pm; ☎ 971 633 042). They can provide a full list of local hotels and *hostales*.

ACCOMMODATION

Hotel Marina ☎ 971 631 461. The pick from the string of modern waterfront hotels, and just a stone's throw from the crowded but pleasant enough beach. There are clean, functional rooms and a swimming pool. **€85**

★ **Hotel Es Port** c/Antonio Montis s/n ☎ 971 631 650, ⓦ hotelesport.com. Outside peak season, there's a good chance of a reasonably priced room at the attractive *Hotel Es Port*, which occupies a huge old mansion with lovely gardens set back from the main part of the port. **€124**

EATING AND DRINKING

Es Faro Cap Gros de Moleta ☎ 971 633 752. It's quite a climb up around the bay to this restaurant perched high on the cliff; to reach it, follow the Passeig de Sa Platja and keep going up. It's not cheap – expect to pay at least €50 for two courses but the views are spectacular. The menu is limited but the daily selection of fresh fish is exquisitely prepared. Open noon–4pm & 7–11pm.

So Caprichos Sant Ramon de Penyafor 15 ☎ 971 630 095. A gem among the rather overpriced harbourside options. Large slabs of hot-stone-cooked meat are the speciality among a good choice of Mallorcan and international cuisine, served up on a shaded terrace by attentive staff. Set menu €14. Daily 8am–late.

Deià

It's a dramatic, ten-kilometre journey southwest from Sóller along the Ma-10 to the beautiful village of **DEIÀ**, where the mighty Puig des Teix mountain ramps down to the coast. At times, this thoroughfare is too congested to be much fun, but the tiny heart of the village, tumbling over a high and narrow ridge on the seaward side of the road, still preserves a surprising tranquillity. Here, labyrinthine alleys of old peasant houses curl up to a pretty country in the precincts of which stands the grave of **Robert Graves** (1895–1985), the village's most famous resident – marked simply "Robert Graves: Poeta, E.P.D." (*En Paz Descanse*: "Rest In Peace"). From the graveyard, the views out over the coast are truly memorable.

Ca N'Alluny

April–Oct Mon–Fri 10am–5pm & Sat 10am–3pm; Nov, Feb & March Mon–Fri 9am–4pm & Sat 9am–2pm • €5; includes a short film about Graves' life • ☎ 971 636 185 • ⓦ fundaciorobertgraves.com

Graves put Deià on the international map, and his old home, **Ca N'Alluny**, a substantial stone building beside the main road about 500m east of the village, was opened to the public in 2006. Graves first lived here in the 1930s and returned after World War II to remain in the village until his death. For the most part, the house has been returned to its 1940s appearance, and its rooms are decorated with Graves' own furnishings and fittings. The study, where he produced much of his finest work, is of particular interest.

13

Cala de Deià

Cala de Deià, the nearest thing the village has to a beach, comprises some 200m of shingle at the back of a handsome rocky cove of jagged cliffs, boulders and white-crested surf. It's a great place for a swim, the water clean, deep and cool, and there's a ramshackle beach bar. It takes about thirty minutes to walk from the village to the *cala*, a delightful stroll down a wooded ravine – or a five-minute drive.

ARRIVAL AND INFORMATION

DEIÀ

By bus The Palma–Port de Sóller bus scoots through Deià five times daily in each direction, dropping passengers on the main street.

Information There's no *turisme* but a useful website with information about the village is ⓦ deia.info.

ACCOMMODATION

★ **Es Molí** ☎971 639 000, ⓦesmoli.com. One of the most agreeable hotels on Mallorca, the *Es Molí* is a supremely comfortable establishment in an immaculately maintained building with superb gardens overlooking the main road at the west end of the village. Closed Nov–March. **€342**

★ **Pensión Miramar** c/Ca'n Oliver s/n ☎971 639 084, ⓦpensionmiramar.com. A slightly run-down-looking *pensión* in lush surroundings, reached by a short, steep walk up above the main road. Rooms are unimaginative but perfectly adequate, and there are smashing views over the village from the terrace. Closed Dec–April. **€64**

EATING AND DRINKING

Café Sa Fonda Arxiduc Lluis Salvador 5. Up a few steps from the main street, this popular café/bar with a patio bar gets lively at night. The selection of salads and *bocadillos* are also excellent value – and surprisingly good. Pear and rocket salad €6. Mon–Sat noon–late.

Restaurant Jaume Arxiduc Lluis Salvador 22 ☎971 639 029, ⓦrestaurantejaume-deia.com. Mouthwatering Mallorcan cuisine with exquisite presentation and a patio with stunning views of the tree-covered valley. The rack of lamb wrapped in black olives and almonds with set you back €39. Open 1pm–late; closed Thurs.

Valldemossa

Some 10km **southwest of Deià** along the Ma-10 lies the ancient and intriguing hill town of **VALLDEMOSSA**, a sloping jumble of rusticated houses and monastic buildings set in a lovely valley and backclothed by mountains. The origins of Valldemossa date to the early fourteenth century, when the asthmatic King Sancho built a royal palace here in the hills, where the air was easier to breathe. Later, in 1399, the palace was given to Carthusian monks from Tarragona, who converted and extended the original buildings into a **monastery**, now the island's most visited building after Palma Catedral.

Real Cartuja de Jesús de Nazaret

Mon–Sat 9.30am–5.30pm, June–Sept until 6.30pm, Nov–Feb until 4pm, Sun 10am–1pm • €7.50

Remodelled on several occasions, most of the present complex, the **Real Cartuja de Jesús de Nazaret**, as it's formally named, is of seventeenth- and eighteenth-century construction, its square and heavy church leading to the shadowy corridors of the cloisters beyond. The monastery owes its present fame almost entirely to the novelist and republican polemicist **George Sand**, who, with her companion, the composer **Frédéric Chopin**, lived here for four months during 1838–39 in a commodious set of vacant cells – their stay is commemorated in Sand's self-important work, *A Winter in Majorca*.

A visit begins in the gloomy, aisleless **church**, which is distinguished by its fanciful bishop's throne, and then continues in the adjoining cloisters, where the **prior's cell** is, despite its name, a comfortable suite of bright, sizeable rooms with splendid views

13

down the valley. Farther along the corridor, **cells no. 2 and 4** exhibit miscellaneous curios relating to Chopin and Sand, from portraits and a lock of hair to musical scores and letters. Upstairs, there's a small but outstanding collection of **modern art**, including work by Miró, Picasso, Francis Bacon and Henry Moore. And be sure also to take the doorway beside the prior's cell that leads outside the cloisters to the enjoyable **Palace of King Sancho**. It's not the original palace at all – that disappeared long ago – but it is the oldest part of the complex, and its fortified walls, mostly dating from the sixteenth century, accommodate a string of handsome period rooms.

ARRIVAL AND DEPARTURE — VALLDEMOSSA

By bus Valldemossa is easily reached by **bus** from Deià, Sóller and Palma. Buses stop beside the bypass at the west end of town; from here, it's just a couple of minutes' walk to the monastery – cross the bypass and keep straight.

Destinations Andratx (weekly; 1hr 15min); Deià (3–5 daily; 15min); Palma (4–9 daily; 30min); Port de Sóller (3–5 daily; 55min).

ACCOMMODATION AND EATING

C'an Molinas Via Blanquerna 15 ☎ 971 612 247. Long-established café with a lovely garden and a display counter bursting with delicious pastries and sandwiches, all available to take away. Serves good, strong coffee and *ensaimadas* (sugar-dusted pastries) for €1.50. Daily 8am–8pm. Popular with walkers seeking evening comforts. **€127**

Hotel Valldemossa ☎ 971 612 626, ⓦ hotelvalldemossa .com. A 5min-walk south along the Old Palma Road, this

hotel is the height of luxury with an indoor and outdoor pool, beautiful gardens and a gourmet restaurant. Given the astronomical prices, though, the rooms are not particularly enticing. **€355**

★ **Es Petit Hotel** c/Uetam 1 ☎ 971 612 479, ⓦ espetithotel-valldemossa.com. Spacious and tastefully decorated rooms in a refurbished old house. All have a/c, satellite TV and include an excellent buffet breakfast.

Lluc

Without doubt, the most interesting approach to the northernmost tip of the island is the 35km stretch of the Ma-10 northeast from Sóller to **LLUC**. The road slips through the highest and harshest section of the **Serra de Tramuntana**. Tucked away in a remote mountain valley, Lluc was Mallorca's most important place of pilgrimage from the middle of the thirteenth century, supposedly after a shepherd boy named Lluc (Luke) stumbled across a tiny, brightly painted statue of the Madonna here in the wood.

Monestir de Nostra Senyora

Daily 10am–11pm, until 8pm in winter • Free

Lluc is dominated by the austere, high-sided dormitories of the **Monestir de Nostra Senyora**. At the centre of the monastery is the main shrine and architectural highlight, the **Basílica de la Mare de Déu de Lluc**, a dark and gaudily decorated church, whose heaviness is partly relieved by a dome over the central crossing. On either side of the nave, stone steps extend the aisles round the back of the Baroque high altar to a little chapel. This is the holy of holies, built to display the much-venerated statue of the Virgin, commonly known as **La Moreneta** ("The Little Dark-Skinned One") ever since the original paintwork peeled off in the fifteenth century to reveal brown stone underneath.

Museu de Lluc and the Camí dels Misteris del Rosari

Museu Daily 10am–1.30pm, closed Sat • €4 • ☎ 971 871 525

Allow time for a visit to the monastery museum, the **Museu de Lluc**, which includes a fascinating display of archeological finds and gifts offered to the Virgin, and for a stroll along the **Camí dels Misteris del Rosari** (Way of the Mysteries of the Rosary), a broad pilgrims' footpath that winds its way up the rocky hillside behind the monastery.

ARRIVAL AND DEPARTURE

Buses stop at a large car park just a few minutes' walk from the monastery's main entrance.
Destinations Palma (2 daily; 1hr 10min); Pollença (2 daily;

50min); Port de Alcúdia (2 daily; 1hr 15min); Port de Sóller (2 daily; 1hr 20min); Sóller (2 daily; 1hr 10min).

ACCOMMODATION

Santuari de Lluc ✆ 971 871 525, ⊕ lluc.net. Spending the night at the monastery provides the perfect opportunity to experience the peace and quiet that has been sought here for centuries. Rooms are basic but comfortable; apartments

are available for two to six people. Note the kitchens are not equipped with utensils. Gates shut at midnight. Double **€35**; apartment for 2–3 **€50**

EATING AND DRINKING

Sa Fonda Inside the monastery. Atmospheric and grander than you might expect from a former monks' refectory, this is the pick of Lluc's dining experiences. Lamb

is the speciality. Mains about €15. Wed–Sun 8am–10pm, 1–3.30pm & 7–9pm.

Pollença

Heading northeast from Lluc, the Ma-10 twists through the mountains to travel the 20km on to **POLLENÇA**, a pretty and ancient little town that nestles among a trio of hillocks where the Serra de Tramuntana fades into the coastal flatlands. Following standard Mallorcan practice, the town was established a few kilometres from the seashore to protect it against sudden pirate attack, with its harbour, Port de Pollença (see p.878), left as an unprotected outpost. For once, the stratagem worked. Unlike most of Mallorca's old towns, Pollença avoided destruction, and the austere stone houses that cramp the twisting lanes of the centre mostly date from the eighteenth century. In the middle, **Plaça Major**, the main square, accommodates a cluster of laidback cafés and the dour facade of the church of **Nostra Senyora dels Àngels**, a sheer cliff-face of sun-bleached stone pierced by a rose window.

Via Crucis

Pollença's pride and joy is its **Via Crucis** (Way of the Cross), a long, steep and beautiful stone stairway, graced by ancient cypress trees, which ascends **El Calvari** (Calvary Hill) directly north of the principal square. At the top, a much-revered statue of the **Mare de Déu del Peu de la Creu** (Mother of God at the Foot of the Cross) is lodged in a courtyard of the simple **Oratori** (Chapel), whose whitewashed walls sport some of the worst religious paintings imaginable. On Good Friday, a figure of Jesus is slowly carried by torchlight down from the Oratori to the church of Nostra Senyora dels Àngels, in the **Davallament** (Lowering), one of the most moving religious celebrations on the island.

Ermita de Nostra Senyora del Puig

There are magnificent views from the **Ermita de Nostra Senyora del Puig**, a rambling, mostly eighteenth-century monastery that occupies a serene and beautiful spot on top of the Puig de María, a 320-metre-high hump facing the south end of town. The Benedictines now own the place, but the monks are gone and today a custodian supplements the order's income by renting out cells to tourists. To get to the monastery, take the signposted turning left off the main Pollença–Inca road just south of town, then head up this steep, 1.5-kilometre lane until it fizzles out, to be replaced by a cobbled footpath that winds up to the monastery entrance. It's possible to drive to the top of the lane, but unless you've got nerves of steel, you're better off leaving your vehicle by the turning near the foot of the hill. Allow just over an hour each way if you're walking from the centre of town.

13

ARRIVAL AND INFORMATION
POLLENÇA

Buses to Pollença from Palma and Port de Pollença halt immediately to the south of Plaça Major, just along the road from the *turisme*. But, inconveniently, buses from Lluc and Sóller drop off passengers about 1km north of the centre on the main Ma-10 road.
Destinations Palma (every 1hr; 1hr 10min); Sóller (May–Oct Mon–Sat 2 daily; 1hr 50min); Lluc (2 daily; 50min); Port de Pollença (every 20min; 15min).

Turisme c/Sant Domingo 17, a few blocks south of the main plaza (Mon–Fri 9am–1.30pm & 2–4pm, Sun 10am–1pm; ☎ 971 865 467, ⊕ pollensa.com).

ACCOMMODATION

Ermita de Nostra Senyora del Puig ☎ 971 184 132. It's back to basics in the old monks' cells but the views are spectacular. Be warned, though, that it can get cold and windy at night, and the refectory food is mediocre. Call ahead to be sure of a room. Double €22
Hotel Juma Plaça Major 9 ☎ 971 535 002, ⊕ hoteljuma.com. The most central place to stay is the *Hotel Juma*, a medium-sized hotel with comfortable, air-

conditioned modern bedrooms above a café. Closed Nov–Feb. €120
La Posada de Lluc c/Roser Vell 11 ☎ 971 535 220, ⊕ posadalluc.com. A welcoming hotel occupying an intelligently revamped old mansion where the Lluc monks once used to stay when they were in town. Rooms are bright and homely. €142

EATING AND DRINKING

Café Espanyol Plaça Major 2. One of the less tourist-centred cafés around the main square, offering snacks, simple meals and strong coffee. Good choice of *bocadillos* for €3.50. Daily 8am–late.
★ **Manzanas y Peras** c/Jesús 38, ☎ 971 533 835, ⊕ manzanasyperas.es. Tiny, arty café/restaurant just to

the right after the first flight of steps towards El Calvari. Dishes are innovative, tasty and excellent value. Try the pork, apple and sage burger (€7) and the heavenly chocolate fudge cake. Daily 11am–4pm; until 11pm Tues–Thurs. Closed Sat.

Port de Pollença

Over at **PORT DE POLLENÇA** things are a little more touristy, though still pleasantly low-key. With the mountains as a backdrop, the resort arches through the flatlands behind the Badia de Pollença, a deeply indented bay whose sheltered waters are ideal for swimming. The **beach** is the focus of attention, a narrow, elongated sliver of sand that's easily long enough to accommodate the crowds.

Excursions

For a change of scene, passenger **ferries** shuttle between the marina and the Platja de Formentor (April–Oct 5 daily; 30min), one of Mallorca's most attractive beaches, while **boat trips** cruise the bay (June to mid-Oct Mon–Sat daily; 2hr 30min) or work their way along to Cap de Formentor (Mon–Wed & Fri daily; 1hr). There's also a delightful three-kilometre (each way) **hike** across the neck of the Península de Formentor to the remote shingle beach of **Cala Boquer**.

ARRIVAL AND INFORMATION
PORT DE POLLENÇA

Buses to Port de Pollença stop by the marina right in the centre of town – and metres from the seafront *turisme*.
Destinations Palma (2–5 daily; 1hr 15min); Pollença (every 15min to 1hr; 15min); Port de Sóller (April–Oct Mon–Sat 2 daily; 2hr 10min); Sóller (May–Oct Mon–Sat 2 daily; 2hr).
Turisme Located on the seafront by the bus station (Mon–

Fri 8am–8pm & Sat 9am–4pm; ☎ 971 865 467).
Bike rental The flatlands edging the Badia de Pollença make for easy, scenic cycling, and mountain bikes can be rented from March at c/Joan XXIII 89 (☎ 971 864 784, ⊕ rentmarch.com).

ACCOMMODATION

Hostal Bahía Pg. Voramar 31, ☎ 971 866 562, ⊕ hoposa.es. A few minutes' walk north of the marina, this peaceful hotel is a good choice with small but pleasant

rooms and an excellent restaurant. Expect to pay extra for a sea view. Closed Nov–March. €100
Hotel Can Llenaire Carretera Llenaire ☎ 971 535 251,

hotelllenaire.com. The *Can Llenaire* occupies an imposing Mallorcan manor house on the brow of a hill with wide views over the Badia de Pollença. There are just eleven rooms, each decked out in period style, and the hotel is clearly signposted down a country lane from the main coastal road just east of the centre of the resort. **€275**

EATING AND DRINKING

Restaurant Stay On the Moll Nou jetty ☎ 971 864 013, stayrestaurant.com. A chic and popular place that features the freshest of seafood and a specials menu that changes weekly. Three-course menu available for €33.80; the highly-recommended sea bass goes for €21. Reservations are advised. Noon–10.30pm.

★ **Restaurant Bahía** ☎ 971 866 562. Located in the hotel of the same name, this stylish restaurant boasts attentive service, divine fish dishes and doors which open up to allow a sense and sight of the sea's proximity. Mains about €22. Tues–Sun 1–3.30pm & 8–10pm.

Península de Formentor

Travelling northeast out of Port de Pollença, the road soon weaves up into the craggy hills of the twenty-kilometre-long **Península de Formentor**, the final spur of the Serra de Tramuntana. At first, the road (which suffers a surfeit of tourists from mid-morning to mid-afternoon) travels inland, out of sight of the true grandeur of the scenery, but after about 4km the **Mirador de Mal Pas** rectifies matters with a string of lookout points perched on the edge of plunging, north-facing sea cliffs. From here, it's another couple of kilometres to the woods backing onto the **Platja de Formentor**, a pine-clad beach of golden sand in a pretty cove. In the summer, buses make the trip from Port de Pollença four times per day.

Alcúdia

It's just 10km round the bay from Port de Pollença to the pint-sized town of **ALCÚDIA**, whose main claim to fame is its impeccably restored medieval walls and incredibly popular open-air market (Tues & Sun), with everything from souvenir trinkets to fruit and veg. Situated on a neck of land separating two large, sheltered bays, the site's strategic value was first recognized by the Phoenicians, and later by the Romans, who built their island capital, Pollentia, here in the first century AD.

Pollentia

Tues–Fri 10am–3pm, Nov–June until 4pm, Sat & Sun 10.30am–1pm • €2

It only takes an hour or so to walk around the antique lanes of Alcúdia's compact centre, and to explore the town walls and their fortified gates. This pleasant stroll can be extended by a visit to the meagre remains of Roman **Pollentia**, whose broken pillars and mashed foundations lie just outside the town walls. The entrance ticket includes admission to the small but excellent **Museu Monogràfic** nearby – just inside the walls.

ARRIVAL AND DEPARTURE   ALCÚDIA

Buses to Alcúdia stop beside – and immediately to the south of – the town walls on Avgda. dels Princeps d'Espanya.

Destinations Lluc (2 daily; 1hr); Palma (3–4 daily; 1hr 10min); Pollença (2 daily; 45min); Sóller (daily; 2hr 5min).

EATING AND DRINKING

Restaurant Sa Plaça Plaça Constitució 1, ☎ 971 546 278. Smart-fronted restaurant with a beautiful dining room – the perfect place to treat yourself to a sophisticated evening meal. It specializes in *bacalao* (cod) dishes with mains at around €23 and six-selection tapas for €20. Daily 11am–11pm.

Port d'Alcúdia

PORT D'ALCÚDIA, 3km south of Alcúdia, is easily the biggest and busiest of the resorts on the Badia d'Alcúdia, its raft of restaurants and café-bars attracting crowds from a seemingly interminable string of high-rise hotels and apartment buildings. The tower blocks are, however, relatively well distributed and the streets neat and tidy. Predictably,

13

the daytime focus is the **beach**, a superb arc of pine-studded golden sand, which stretches south for 10km from the combined marina and fishing harbour.

ARRIVAL AND DEPARTURE
PORT DE ALCÚDIA

By bus Port d'Alcúdia acts as northern Mallorca's summertime transport hub, with frequent **bus** services to and from all the neighbouring towns and resorts, plus Palma. Destinations Alcúdia (2 daily; 5min); Lluc (2 daily; 1hr15min); Palma (5–8 daily; 1hr 10min); Pollença (2 daily; 50min); Sóller (1hr 20min).

By ferry Ferries depart from the modern ferry building on the eastern side of the bay to make the crossing to Ciutadella in Menorca.

Destination Ciutadella (3–5 daily; 1–2hr 30min).

INFORMATION

Turisme Situated in a kiosk on Carretera d'Artà, about 2km south round the bay from the marina (Easter to Oct Mon–Sat 9am–7pm; ☎ 971 892 615). It can supply all sorts of information, most usefully free maps marked with all the resort's hotels and apartments, but bear in mind that in winter almost everywhere is closed.

Car and bike rental There's a plethora of car, moped and bicycle rental companies strung out along Carretera d'Artà.

Parc Natural de S'Albufera

Daily: April–Sept 9am–6pm; Oct–March 9am–5pm • Free • Buses from Port d'Alcúdia to Ca'n Picafort (2–3 daily; 30min) stop beside the entrance

Heading south around the bay from Port d'Alcúdia, it's about 6km to the **Parc Natural de S'Albufera**, a slice of protected wetland, which is all that remains of the marshes that once extended round most of the bay. The signposted entrance to the park is on the Ma-12, but access is only on foot or cycle – so if you're driving, you'll need to use the small car park near the entrance. About 1km from the entrance, you come to the park's **reception centre**, from where footpaths radiate out into the reedy, watery tract beyond. It's a superb habitat, with ten well-appointed hides allowing excellent **birdwatching**. Over two hundred species have been spotted: resident wetland-loving birds, autumn and/or springtime migrants, and wintering species and birds of prey in their scores.

Menorca

The second largest of the Balearic Islands, boomerang-shaped **MENORCA** is the least plagued by unsavoury development. An essentially rural island, it features rolling fields, wooded ravines and humpy hills filling out the interior in between its two main – but still notably small – towns of **Maó** and **Ciutadella**. Much of this landscape looks pretty much as it did at the turn of the twentieth century, and only around the edges of the island, and then only in parts, have its rocky coves been colonized by sprawling villa complexes. Neither is the development likely to spread: determined to protect their island from the worst excesses of the tourist industry, the Menorcans have clearly demarcated development areas and are also pushing ahead with a variety of environmental schemes – the island was declared a UNESCO Biosphere Reserve in 1993, and over forty percent of it now enjoys official protection.

Menorca is also dotted with **prehistoric monuments**, weatherworn stone remains that are evidence of a sophisticated culture. Little is known of the island's prehistory, but the monuments are thought to be linked to those of Sardinia and are classified as examples of the **Talayotic culture**, which is usually considered to have ended with arrival of the Romans in 123 BC. **Talayots** are the rock mounds found all over the island – popular belief has it that they functioned as watchtowers, but it's a theory few experts accept. The megalithic **taulas** – huge stones topped with another to form a T, around 4m high and unique to Menorca – are even more puzzling. They have no obvious function, and they are almost always found alongside a *talayot*. Some of the best-preserved *talayot* and

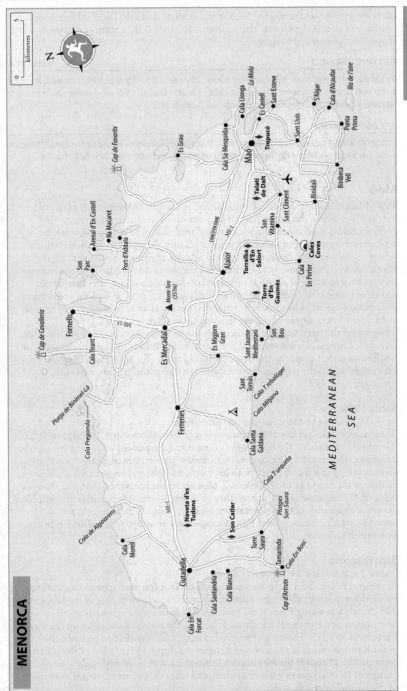

MENORCA

13

taula remains are on the edge of Maó at the **Talatí de Dalt** site. The third prehistoric structure of note is the **naveta** (dating from 1400 to 800 BC), stone-slab constructions shaped like an inverted bread tin.

GETTING AROUND
MENORCA

By bus Bus routes are distinctly limited, adhering mostly to the main central road between Maó and Ciutadella, occasionally branching off to the larger coastal resorts.

By car You'll need your own vehicle to reach any of the emptier beaches, which are sometimes down a track fit only for 4WD.

ACCOMMODATION

Accommodation is at a premium, with limited options outside Maó and Ciutadella – and you can count on all the beds in all the resorts being block-booked by the tour operators from the beginning to the end of the season (May–Oct).

Maó

MAÓ (Mahón in Castilian), the island capital, is likely to be your first port of call. Perched high above the largest natural harbour in the Mediterranean, the town's compact centre is no more than ten minutes' walk from one end to the other. Its architecture consists of an unusual hybrid of classical Georgian townhouses, which reflect a strong British connection, and tall Spanish apartment blocks shading the narrow streets. Port it may be, but there's no real gritty side to Maó, and the harbour is now home to a string of slick – if rather sedate – restaurants and cafés that attract droves of tourists. Wandering the maze of alleyways and peering into the gateways of the city's collection of handsome old mansions are its charm, rather than any specific sight, and you can explore the place thoroughly in a day.

From near the ferry terminal, set beneath the cliff that supports the remains of the city wall, a generous stone stairway, the **Costa de Ses Voltes**, leads up to the series of small squares that comprise the heart of the old town. The first, **Plaça Espanya**, offers views right across the port and bay, and houses Maó's bustling fish market, in operation since 1927.

Santa María
Mon–Sat 7.30am–12.30pm & 6–8.30pm; organ concert Mon–Sat at 1pm • Free

The Plaça Constitució boasts the town's main church, **Santa María**, founded in 1287 by Alfonso III to celebrate the island's Reconquest and remodelled on several subsequent occasions. The church's pride and joy is its **organ**, a monumental piece of woodwork, all trumpeting angels and pipes, built in Austria in 1810 and lugged across half of Europe at the height of the Napoleonic Wars under the concerned charge of Britain's Admiral Collingwood. Daily concerts are held here Monday to Saturday at 1pm. Next door, the eighteenth-century **ajuntament** benefited from British largesse, too, its attractive arcaded facade graced by a clock that was presented to the islanders by the first British governor.

Sant Francesc
C/Isabel II • Daily 10am–12.30pm & 5–7pm • Free

At the end of c/Isabel II, the Baroque facade of **Sant Francesc** appears as a cliff face of pale golden stone set above the rounded, Romanesque-style arches of its doorway. The church was a long time in the making, its construction spread over the seventeenth and eighteenth centuries following the razing of the town by the piratical Barbarossa in 1535. The nave is poorly lit, but it's still possible to pick out the pinkish tint in much of the stone and the unusual spiral decoration of the pillars. In contrast, the **Chapel of the Immaculate Conception** is flooded with light – an octagonal wonderland of garlanded vines and roses that offers an exquisite example of the Churrigueresque style.

MAÓ

0 — 100 — metres

N

ILLA PINTO

Naval Base

PORT DE MAÓ

MOLL DE PONENT

MOLL DE LLEVANT

Ferry Terminal

COSTA D'ES GENERAL

Gobierno Militar

Ajuntament

Santa Maria

Claustre del Carme

Indoor Market

Fish Market

Esglèsia del Carme

Museu de Menorca

Sant Francesc

Teatre Principal

Bus Station

■ ACCOMMODATION
Hostal La Isla   1
Hotel Port-Mahón   3
Posada Orsi   2

● EATING & DRINKING
Café Ars   4
Café Mirador   3
Cristina y Gradinata 1
La Minerva   2

@ Biblioteca

PLAÇA BARCELONA
BELLAVISTA
SANTA CECILIA
SANT NICOLAU
SANTA ROSA
SANTA CATERINA
SANT SEBASTIÀ
SANT JOAN
PLANA
CONCEPCIÓ
SANTA TERESA
SANTA ANNA
ST. ELIES
CARME
PLAÇA MIRANDA
PLAÇA PRÍNCEP
CAMÍ D'ES CASTELL
COMERÇ
NORD
ANUNCIVAY
PLAÇA CARME
PLAÇA ESPANYA
PORTAL DE MAR
SARA VALLETA
INFANTA
VERGE DE GRACIA
PLAÇA REIAL
COSTA DE SES VOLTES
PLAÇA CONQUESTA
NOU
DEIÀ
PLAÇA COLÓN
HANNOVER
PL. CONSTITUCIÓ
ROSARI
ESGLÈSIA
BON AIRE
ST. ROC
ALAIOR
BASTIÓ
PLAÇA BASTIÓ
SANT JORDI
ES CÒS DE GRACIA
ISABEL II
SANT JAUME
FORN
SA ROVELLADA DE BAIX
ROVELLADA DE DALT
MORERIES
SANT JOSEP
ES FABRELS
S'ARRAVAL
AVGDA DR. GUARDIA
PLAÇA S'ESPLANADA
AV. JOSEP MARIA QUADRADO
VASALLO

Airport

Sant Lluís

Trepucó

13

Museu de Menorca
April–Oct Tues–Sat 10am–2pm & 6–8.30pm, Sun 10am–2pm • €2.40, free Sat & Sun pm

The monastic buildings adjacent to Sant Francesc now house the **Museu de Menorca**, easily the island's biggest and best museum, holding a wide sample of prehistoric artefacts, beginning with bits and pieces left by the Neolithic pastoralists who settled here around 4000 BC; there's also an extensive range of material from the Talayotic period.

Trepucó
Tues–Fri 9am–2.30pm, Sat & Sun 9am–3pm • €1.80; open access outside of these times

It's a 35min walk south from the Museu de Menorca to the prehistoric remains of **Trepucó**. To get there, follow c/Moreres from the eastern corner of Plaça S'Esplanada, take the first right down c/Cós de Gràcia and then go straight, streaming onto c/Verge de Gràcia just before the ring road. At the ring road, go straight over the roundabout and follow the twisting lane in front of you, past the cemetery, and thereafter follow the signs.

Surrounded by olive trees and dry-stone walls, the tiny site's focal point is a 4.2-metre-high and 2.75-metre-wide **taula**, one of the largest and best preserved of these T-shaped monoliths on the island. The *taula* stands inside a circular compound that is edged by the remains of several broadly circular buildings. These were thoroughly excavated by a team of archeologists from Cambridge University in the late 1920s, but even they couldn't work out how the complex was structured. There are two cone-shaped **talayots** close by, the larger one accessible, the other not.

ARRIVAL AND DEPARTURE

MAÓ

By air Menorca's airport, just 5km southwest of Maó, has a handful of car-rental outlets. There are buses (€1.60) every 30min to Maó bus station; the taxi fare about €10.
Destinations Mallorca (6–12 daily; 40min) and Ibiza (4 weekly; 50min).
By bus The station is on the west side of Plaça S'Esplanada.
Destinations Ciutadella (Mon–Fri hourly, Sat & Sun 6 daily; 50min); Es Mercadal (Mon–Fri hourly, Sat & Sun 6 daily; 30min).
By ferry Ferries sail right up the inlet to Maó harbour, mooring directly beneath the town centre. From behind the ferry dock, it's a five-minute walk up the wide stone stairway to the old part of town.
Destinations Barcelona (2 daily; 8–9hr) and Palma (1 weekly; 5hr 30min).

INFORMATION

Turisme Down on the harbourfront, just along from the ferry terminal (daily 8am–8.30pm; ☎ 971 355 952). It can provide maps of the island and free leaflets giving the lowdown on almost everything. The island's official website is ⓦ e-menorca.org.

ACCOMMODATION

Maó has a limited supply of **accommodation**, and excessive demand tends to inflate prices at the height of the season. Despite this, along with Ciutadella it remains the best Menorcan bet for bargain lodgings, with a small concentration of **hostales**. None of these places is inspiring, but they're reasonable enough, and convenient.

MAYONNAISE AND FOOD INFLUENCES FROM ABROAD

Maó has a place in culinary history as the eighteenth-century birthplace of **mayonnaise** (*mahonesa*). Various legends, all of them involving the **French**, claim to identify its inventor: take your pick from the chef of the French commander besieging Maó; a peasant woman dressing a salad for another French general; or a housekeeper disguising rancid meat from the taste buds of a French officer. The French also changed the way the Menorcans bake their bread, while the **British** started the dairy industry and encouraged the roasting of meat.

Hostal La Isla c/Santa Caterina 4 ☎971 366 492. Rooms at this amenable *hostal* may be on the small side, but they are reasonably attractive, and all have private bathroom and TV. There's a popular bar and restaurant downstairs, too. **€50**

Hotel Port-Mahón Avgda. Fort de l'Eau 13 ☎971 362 600, ⓦsethotels.com. An elegant colonial-style hotel in a superb location overlooking the Maó inlet, with a swimming pool and all mod cons. It's located a 20min walk east of the town centre along c/Carme. Room prices vary enormously. **€150**

Posada Orsi c/Infanta 19 ☎971 364 751, ⓦposadaorsi .es. In an old terrace house a couple of minutes' walk from Plaça Reial, this one-star *hostal* has sixteen rooms, nine doubles, three singles and five triples, mostly with shared facilities. The rooms are quite small, but you couldn't possibly complain about the colour scheme – bright pinks, reds, greens and blues throughout. There's a rooftop terrace, too. **€47**

EATING AND DRINKING

Tourist-oriented **restaurants** are mainly spread out along the harbourside – the Moll de Ponent west of the main stairway, the Moll de Llevant to the east. There's also a smattering of cheaper restaurants and **coffee bars** in the centre of town. **Nightlife** is not Maó's forte, though there are some fairly lively **bars** along the harbourfront that stay open until around 2am on summer weekends.

★ **Café Ars** Plaça Príncipe, ☎971 351 879, ⓦarscafe .info. The menu here may be simple but it's superbly executed – try one of the risottos from €10.50. The dining area is across several levels, allowing for a romantic dinner in an atmospheric setting. Also hosts musical and cultural events. Open Mon–Sat noon–4.30pm & 7.30–11.30pm, until 4am on Fri & Sat.

Café Mirador Plaça Espanya 2. Located a few steps from the fish market, this appealing café-bar offers a good range of snacks and tapas, and has great views over the harbour from its terrace. Jazz is the favoured background music. Daily 10am–late.

★ **Cristinal y Gradinata** c/Isabel II 124 ☎971 363 316. A collection of old radios, hats and beer bottles adorn the shelves of this delightful bistro bar. The delicious sandwiches are among the tastiest on the island and a snip at about €2. Also, a good selection of wines and beer. Tues–Fri 8.30am–3pm & 7–11.30pm, Sat noon–3pm & 7.30–11.30pm.

La Minerva Moll de Llevant 87 ☎971 351 995. One of the more polished restaurants in town, with a menu focused on seafood. The paella is outstanding and so is the *menú*, a relative snip at €15. Reservations well-nigh essential at the height of the season. Good-value tapas too. Daily 12.30–3.30pm & 7–11.30pm.

DIRECTORY

Hospital Hospital Verge del Toro, c/de Barcelona 3 ☎ 971 157 700.

Internet c/Sant Elies 54 ☎971 360 701.
Post office c/Bonaire 13.

Across the island

The road from Maó to Ciutadella, the **Me-1**, forms the backbone of Menorca, and what little industry the island enjoys – a few shoe factories and cheese plants – is strung along it. Here also is the island's highest peak, **Monte Toro**, from the top of which there are wondrous views.

Talatí de Dalt

May–Sept daily 10am–sunset • €3 • Oct–April open access • Free

Just 4km out of Maó on the Me-1, you pass the short and clearly signposted country lane that leads to **Talatí de Dalt**, another illuminating Talayotic remnant. Much larger than Trepucó, the site is enclosed by a Cyclopean wall and features an imposing *taula*, which is adjacent to the heaped stones of the main *talayot*. All around are the scant remains of prehistoric dwellings. The rustic setting is charming – olive and carob trees abound and a tribe of semi-wild boar root around the undergrowth.

Es Mercadal and Monte Toro

The old market town of **ES MERCADAL** squats among the hills at the very centre of the island about 20km west of Maó. It's an amiable little place of whitewashed houses and trim allotments, whose antique centre straddles a quaint watercourse.

13

Monte Toro

From Es Mercadal, you can set off on the ascent of **Monte Toro**, a steep 3.2-kilometre climb along a serpentine road. At 357m, the summit is the island's highest point and offers wonderful vistas. It has been a place of pilgrimage since medieval times, and the Augustinians plonked a monastery on the summit in the seventeenth century. Bits of this original construction survive in the convent there today, though much of the convent area is closed to visitors.

From this lofty vantage point, Menorca's geological division becomes apparent: to the north, Devonian rock (mostly reddish sandstone) supports a rolling, sparsely populated landscape edged by a ragged coastline; to the south, limestone predominates in a rippling plain that boasts both the island's best farmland and, as it approaches the south coast, its deepest valleys.

Naveta d'es Tudons

May–Sept daily 10am–sunset • €3 • Oct–April open access • Free

Heading on from Es Mercadal, the Me-1 swings past the village of **FERRERIES** before sliding across the agricultural flatlands of the western part of the island. There are prehistoric remains to either side of the road, but easily the most interesting is the **Naveta d'es Tudons**, Menorca's best example of a *naveta*, located just 6km short of Ciutadella. Seven metres high and fourteen long, the structure is made of massive stone blocks slotted together in a sophisticated dry-stone technique. The narrow entrance leads into a small antechamber, which was once sealed off by a stone slab; beyond lies the main chamber where the bones of the dead were stashed away after the flesh had been removed.

Ciutadella

Like Maó, **CIUTADELLA** sits high above its harbour, though navigation is far more difficult here, up a narrow channel too slender for anything but the smallest of cargo ships. Despite this nautical inconvenience, Ciutadella has been the island's capital for most of its history, the narrow, cobbled streets of its compact, fortified centre brimming with fine old palaces, hidden away behind high walls, and a set of Baroque and Gothic churches very much in the Spanish tradition.

The main plazas, accommodation and points of interest are all within a few strides of each other, on and around the main square, **Plaça d'es Born**, in the middle of which a soaring obelisk commemorates the town's futile defence against the marauding Turks in 1558. To the northwest, the square is bordered by the steep harbour walls, and in the northeast lies the vast nineteenth-century Palau Torresaura. Like many of the city's grand aristocratic mansions, it is still privately owned and off limits to visitors.

Allow at least a couple of days, more if you seek out one of the charming cove beaches within easy striking distance of town – **Cala Turqueta** is the pick of the bunch.

Catedral

May–Oct Mon–Sat 10.30am–1.30pm & 4–7pm • €4 includes entry to Museu Diocesà

From beside Palau Torresaura, c/Major d'es Born leads through to the **Catedral**, built by Alfonso III at the end of the thirteenth century on the site of the town's chief mosque. Built so soon after the Reconquest, its construction is fortress-like, with windows set high above the ground – though the effect is somewhat disturbed by the flashy columns of the Neoclassical west doorway, the principal entrance.

Església del Roser

May–Oct Mon–Sat 11am–1pm & 6–9pm; Nov–April 10.30am–1pm & 5.30–8pm • Free

Cutting down c/Roser from the cathedral, you'll pass the tiny **Església del Roser**, whose striking Churrigueresque facade, which dates back to between the seventeenth and

CIUTADELLA

■ **ACCOMMODATION**
Hostal-Residencia Oasis	1
Hotel Géminis	3
Hotel Hesperia Patricia	2

● **EATING & DRINKING**
La Guitarra	3
Restaurant Aurora	1
Restaurant Café Balear	2

eighteenth centuries, boasts a quartet of pillars engulfed by intricate tracery. Nowadays, the church is used as a cultural and exhibition centre, mostly displaying contemporary arts and crafts.

Museu Diocesà de Menorca

Tues–Fri 10.30am–2pm • €3 • ☎ 971 481 297, ⓦ bisbatdemenorca.com

At the end of c/Roser, turn left and then left again for c/Seminari and the **Museu Diocesà de Menorca**, housed in an old and dignified convent. Inside, the museum's collection comprises a hotchpotch of Talayotic and early Classical archeological finds, notably a superbly crafted miniature bull and a similarly exquisite little mermaid, both Greek bronzes dating from the fifth century BC.

The mercat

Plaça Llibertat

The green-and-white-tiled **mercat** (market) is another delightful corner of the old town, where fresh fruit, vegetable and fish stalls mingle with lively and inexpensive

13

cafés selling the freshest of *ensaimadas*. The benches and café patios are great for people-watching but the market square lacks the atmospheric chaos, bustle and colour of a typical Spanish town, though the produce on sale is second to none.

North of the centre

C/Seminari proceeds north from the Museu Dicesà to intersect with the narrow, pedestrianized main street running through the old town – here **c/J.M. Quadrado**, though it goes under various names along its route. To the east of this intersection is a parade of whitewashed, vaulted arches, **Ses Voltes**, distinctly Moorish in inspiration and a suitable setting for several attractive shops and busy cafés. c/J.M. Quadrado then leads into **Plaça Nova**, a minuscule square edged by some of the most popular pavement cafés in town. Continuing east along c/Maó, you leave the cramped alleys of the old town at Plaça Alfons III.

ARRIVAL AND DEPARTURE

CIUTADELLA

By bus Buses from Maó and points east pull in on the south side of Plaça de Menorca, southwest of the town centre. Local buses shuttle up and down the west coast from the north side of Plaça dels Pins.
Destinations Es Mercadal (Mon–Fri hourly, Sat & Sun 6 daily; 30min); Maó (Mon–Fri hourly, Sat & Sun 6 daily; 50min).

By ferry Car ferries dock at the port about 4km south of the centre. Buses meet the boats to ferry passengers to the town centre (€1.40).
Destinations Alcúdia (3–5 daily; 1–2hr 30min); Barcelona (4 weekly; 4hr).

INFORMATION

Turisme Opposite the cathedral on Plaça Catedral (May–Oct Mon–Fri 8.30am–8.30pm, Sat 9am–1pm; Nov–April Mon–Fri 9am–1pm & 5–7pm, Sat 9am–1pm; ☎971 382 693), has buckets of information on Menorca as a whole and Ciutadella in particular. Bike hire is available at Velos Joan, c/Sant Isidre 32–34 (☎971 381 576, ⓦvelosjoan.com).

ACCOMMODATION

Hostal-Residencia Oasis c/Sant Isidre 33 ☎971 382 197. Just a few metres from Plaça Artrutx, this old-fashioned, one-star *hostal* has nine simple rooms next door to a courtyard-restaurant. The building itself is looking slightly tired but the owners are friendly and helpful. Closed Oct–March. **€70**
Hotel Géminis c/Josepa Rossinyol 4 ☎971 384 644, ⓦhotelgeminismenorca.com. Distinctively painted in pink and white, this well-tended, very comfortable two-star hotel on a quiet residential street has thirty rooms, each decorated in bright modern style. Closed mid-Dec to Feb. **€80**
★ **Hotel Hesperia Patricia** Pg. Sant Nicolau 90 ☎971 385 511, ⓦhoteles-hesperia.es. The smartest hotel in town, popular with business folk and handy for the centre. The comfortable, modern rooms come with all facilities and there's an outside pool. Prices vary considerably. **€114**

EATING AND DRINKING

For an early **breakfast**, make your way to the **market** on Plaça Llibertat, where a couple of simple cafés serve coffee and fresh pastries. Later in the day, around **lunchtime**, aim for c/J.M. Quadrado, Plaça Nova or Plaça Alfons III, which together hold a good selection of inexpensive café-bars, offering tapas and light meals. In the summer evenings, head to the bars around the harbour for a taste of Ciutadella nightlife.

★ **La Guitarra** c/Nostra Senyora dels Dolors 1 ☎971 381 355. Located a short walk from the cathedral, this is arguably the best restaurant in town, a family-run affair featuring the very best of Menorcan cuisine, with main courses – anything from seafood to lamb to snails – averaging a very reasonable €14–20. Daily noon–3.30pm & 7.30–11pm.
Restaurant Aurora Plaça Ses Palmeres 3 ☎971 481 994. In one of the quieter squares, opposite the windmill, this popular restaurant cooks up a mix of international and Spanish cuisine with the *menú* good value at €21. Tapas too. Daily noon–4pm & 7–11pm.
★ **Restaurant Café Balear** Es Pla de Sant Joan 15 ☎971 380 005. Justifiably popular, this attractively decorated restaurant sits at the back of the harbour by the bridge. The terrace is the best place to eat, but there are tables inside, too. The food is first-rate, with shellfish and fish the big deals – mains average around €20. Closed Mon.

Southeast of Ciutadella: Cala Turqueta

13

Beginning at the traffic island on c/Alfons V, the cross-country **Camí de Sant Joan de Missa** runs southeast from Ciutadella to the remote coves of the south coast. The one to head for is **Cala Turqueta**, a lovely cove flanked by wooded limestone cliffs. About 3km from town, you reach the clearly marked farmhouse of **Son Vivó**, where the road branches into two with the more easterly (signposted) road leading to the **Ermita de Sant Joan de Missa**, a brightly whitewashed church with a dinky little belltower. There's a fork here, too, but the signs are easy to follow, and you keep straight with the road slicing across the countryside before swerving round the **Marjal Vella** farmhouse. Shortly afterwards, about 4.3km from the church, you turn at the sign, going through the gateway to reach the car park for Cala Turqueta. The beach, a sheltered horseshoe of white sand, slopes gently into the sea and is ideal for swimming.

CHRISTOPHER COLUMBUS RECEIVED BY THE CATHOLIC MONARC

Contexts

History

The first Europeans of whom we have knowledge lived in southern Spain. A recent series of spectacular discoveries at Orce, 115km northeast of Granada, rocked the archeological world, as the date for the arrival of early humans in Europe was pushed back from around 700,000 years ago to perhaps a million years before this, making Orce – if the findings are scientifically confirmed – the earliest known site of human occupation in Europe by a long way. Other finds of early human remains around 800,000 years old in the Sierra de Atapuerca are further confirmation of early activity on the peninsula. Evidence of occupation by Stone Age societies stretching back some 400,000 years was already known about from discoveries at Venta Micena, close to Orce, where early inhabitants hunted elephant and rhino and left behind tools and camp fires. Some of the earliest human fossils found on the Iberian peninsula were unearthed inside the Gibraltar caves, with evidence of Neanderthals dating from around 100,000 BC.

In the Paleolithic period, the first **homo sapiens** arrived on the Iberian Peninsula from southern France, settling around the Bay of Biscay as well as in the south. They were cave dwellers and hunter-gatherers, and, at **Altamira** in the Cordillera Cantábrica near Santander, and the Pileta and Nerja caves near Málaga, left behind remarkable **cave paintings** and deftly stylized cave murals depicting the animals they hunted. The finest examples (created about 12,000 BC) are at Altamira – now closed for general visits, though you can see similar paintings at Puente Viesgo nearby. During the later Neolithic phase, a sophisticated material culture developed in southern Spain, attested to by the finds of *esparto* sandals and baskets as well as jewellery in the **Cueva de los Murciélagos** in Granada. This period also saw the construction of **megalithic tombs** (dolmens) along the perimeter of the Iberian Peninsula, including the superbly preserved examples at Romanya de la Selva, in Catalunya, and **Antequera**, near Málaga.

Subsequent prehistory is more complex and confused. There does not appear to have been any great development in the cave cultures of the north. Instead, the focus shifts south to Almería, which was settled around 5000–4000 BC by the "Iberians", **Neolithic** colonists from North Africa. They had already assimilated into their culture many of the changes that had developed in Egypt and the Near East. Settling in villages, they introduced pastoral and agricultural ways of life and exploited the plentiful supply of copper. Around 1500 BC, with the onset of the **Bronze Age**, they began to spread outwards into fortified villages on the central *meseta*, the high plateau of modern Castile. At the turn of the millennium, they were joined by numerous waves of **Celtic** and **Germanic** peoples. Here, Spain's divisive physical make-up – with its network of mountain ranges – determined its social nature. The

1.5 million years ago	25,000 BC	12,000 BC
Early humans active at Orce in the province of Granada after arriving from Africa	Cave dwellers occupy caves in Málaga province	Cave paintings made at Altamira in Cantabria and dolmens constructed in Catalunya and Málaga.

incoming tribes formed distinct and isolated groups, conquering and sometimes absorbing each other but only on a very limited and local scale. Hence the Celtic "urnfield people" established themselves in Catalunya, the **Vascones** in the Basque Country and, near them along the Atlantic coast, the **Astures**. Pockets of earlier cultures survived, too, particularly in Galicia with its *citanias* of beehive huts.

First colonies

The Spanish coast, meanwhile, attracted colonists from different regions of the Mediterranean. The **Phoenicians** founded the port of Gadir (Cádiz) around 1100 BC and traded intensively in the metals of the Guadalquivir valley. Their wealth and success gave rise to a Spanish "Atlantis" myth, based on the lost kingdom of Tartessus, mentioned in the Bible and probably sited near Huelva; the sophisticated jewellery it produced is on display in Seville's archeological museum. Market rivalry later brought the **Greeks**, who established their trading colonies along the eastern coast – the modern Costa Brava. There's a fine surviving site at Empúries, near Barcelona.

More significant, however, was the arrival of the **Carthaginians** in the third century BC. Expelled from Sicily by the Romans, they saw in Spain a new base for their empire, from which to regain strength and strike back at their rivals. Although making little impact inland, they occupied most of Andalucía and expanded along the Mediterranean seaboard to establish a new capital at Cartagena ("New Carthage"). Under Hannibal they prepared to invade Italy, and in 219 BC attacked Saguntum, a strategic outpost of the Roman world. It was a disastrous move, precipitating the **Second Punic War**; by 210 BC, only Cádiz remained in their control and they were forced to accept terms. A new and very different age had begun.

Romans and Visigoths

The **Roman colonization** of the peninsula was far more intense than anything previously experienced and met with great resistance from the Celtiberian tribes of the north and centre. It was almost two centuries before the conquest was complete, and indeed the Basques, although defeated, were never fully Romanized.

Nonetheless, Spain became the most important centre of the Roman Empire after Italy itself, producing no fewer than three emperors, along with the writers Seneca, Lucan, Martial and Quintilian. Again, geography dictated an uneven spread of influence, at its strongest in Andalucía, southern Portugal and on the Catalan coast around Tarragona. In the first two centuries AD, the Spanish mines and the granaries of Andalucía brought unprecedented wealth and Roman Spain enjoyed a brief "**Golden Age**". The finest monuments were built in the great provincial capitals – Córdoba, Mérida (which boasts the most impressive remains) and Tarragona – but across the country more practical construction was undertaken: roads, bridges and aqueducts. Many of the latter were still used well into recent centuries – perhaps the most remarkable being those of Segovia and Tarragona – and quite a few bridges, such as that crossing the Guadalquivir in Córdoba, remain in use even today.

Towards the third century, however, the Roman political framework began to show signs of decadence and corruption. Although it didn't totally collapse until the Muslim invasions

2500 BC	c1100 BC	c1000 BC	c9th–4th century BC
Chalcolithic (Copper Age) sites flourish in Almería	Phoenicians found Cádiz	Semi-mythical kingdom of Tartessus flourishes in the southwest of the peninsula.	Celts settle in the north and west of the peninsula. Greeks establish trading posts along east coast

of the early eighth century, it became increasingly vulnerable to **barbarian incursions** from northern Europe. The Franks and the Suevi (Swabians) swept across the Pyrenees between 264 and 276, leaving devastation in their wake. They were followed two centuries later by further waves of Suevi, Alans and Vandals. Internal strife was heightened by the arrival of the **Visigoths** from Gaul, allies of Rome and already Romanized to a large degree. The triumph of Visigothic strength in the fifth century resulted in a period of spurious unity, based upon an exclusive military rule from their capital at Toledo, but their numbers were never great and their order was often fragmentary and nominal, with the bulk of the subject people kept in a state of disconsolate servility and the military elite divided by constant plots and factions – exacerbated by the Visigothic system of elected monarchy and by their adherence to the heretical Arian doctrine. In 589, **King Recared** converted to Catholicism but religious strife was only multiplied: forced conversions, especially within the Jewish enclaves, maintained a constant simmering of discontent.

Moorish Spain

In contrast to the drawn-out Roman campaigns, **Moorish conquest** of the peninsula was effected with extraordinary speed. This was a characteristic phenomenon of the spread of Islam – Muhammad left Mecca in 622 and by 705 his followers had established control over all of North Africa. Spain, with its political instability, wealth and fertile climate, was an inevitable extension of their aims. In 711, Tariq, governor of Tangier, led a force of seven thousand Berbers across the straits and routed the Visigothic army of King Roderic; two years later, the Visigoths made a last desperate stand at Mérida, and within a decade the Moors had conquered all but the wild mountains of Asturias. The land under their authority was dubbed "**al-Andalus**", a fluid term that expanded and shrank with the intermittent gains and losses of the Reconquest. According to region, the Moors were to remain in control for the next three to eight centuries.

It was not simply a military conquest. The Moors (a collective term for the numerous waves of Arab and Berber settlers from North Africa) were often content to grant a limited autonomy in exchange for payment of tribute; their administrative system was tolerant and easily absorbed both Jews and Christians, those who retained their religion being known as "Mozarabs". And al-Andalus was a distinctly Spanish state of Islam. Though at first politically subject to the Eastern Caliphate (or empire) of Baghdad, it was soon virtually independent. In the tenth century, at the peak of its power and expansion, Abd-ar-Rahman III asserted total independence, proclaiming himself caliph of a new **Western Islamic empire**. Its capital was Córdoba – the largest, most prosperous and most civilized city in Europe. This was the great age of Muslim Spain: its scholarship, philosophy, architecture and craftsmanship were without rival and there was an unparalleled growth in urban life, in trade and in agriculture, aided by magnificent irrigation projects. These and other engineering feats were not, on the whole, instigated by the Moors, who instead took basic Roman models and adapted them to a new level of sophistication. In **architecture** and the **decorative arts**, however, their contribution was original and unique – as may be seen in the fabulous monuments of Seville, Córdoba and Granada.

The Córdoban Caliphate for a while created a remarkable degree of unity. But its rulers were to become decadent and out of touch, prompting the brilliant but

c500–300 BC	c5th century BC	c214 BC
Greeks establish trading colonies along the Mediterranean coast	Carthage colonizes southern Spain. Celto-Iberian culture develops, with Greek influence	Second Punic War with Rome

---

ALMOHAD ARCHITECTURE

In the eleventh century, Andalucía fragmented into rival kingdoms or *taifas*, allowing successive waves of Moorish invaders to move into the power vacuum. One of these, the ultra-fundamentalist **Almohads**, left behind a number of remarkable buildings of which the foremost is the magnificent **Giralda** tower in Seville, the surviving minaret of the Friday mosque demolished to construct the Gothic cathedral. At 100m high with elaborate *sebka* brickwork panels adorning its exterior walls, it was started in 1184 under architect Ahmed ibn Baso and completed twelve years later.

---

dictatorial **al-Mansur** to usurp control. Under this extraordinary ruler, Moorish power actually reached new heights, pushing the Christian kingdom of Asturias-León back into the Cordillera Cantábrica and sacking its most holy shrine, Santiago de Compostela. However, after his death the caliphate quickly lost its authority, and in 1031 it disintegrated into a series of small independent kingdoms, or *taifas*, the strongest of which was Seville.

Internal divisions among the *taifas* weakened their resistance to the Christian kingdoms that were rallying in the north, and twice North Africa had to be turned to for reinforcement. This resulted in two distinct new waves of Moorish invasion – first by the fanatically Islamic **Almoravids** (1086) and later by the **Almohads** (1147), who restored effective Muslim authority until their defeat at the battle of Las Navas de Tolosa in 1212.

The Christian Reconquest

The **Reconquest** of land and influence from the Moors was a slow and intermittent process. It began with a symbolic victory by a small force of Christians at Covadonga in Asturias (722) and was not completed until 1492 with the conquest of Granada by Fernando and Isabel.

The victory at Covadonga resulted in the formation of the tiny Christian kingdom of **Asturias**. Initially just 50 by 65km in area, it had by 914 reclaimed León and most of Galicia and northern Portugal. At this point, progress was temporarily halted by the devastating campaigns of al-Mansur. However, with the fall of the Córdoban Caliphate and the divine aid of Spain's Moor-slaying patron, St James the Apostle, or Santiago (see p.532), the Reconquest moved into a new and powerful phase.

The frontier castles built against Arab attack gave their name to Castile, founded in the tenth century as a county of León-Asturias. Under **Ferdinand I** (1037–65), it achieved the status of a kingdom and became the main thrust and focus of the Reconquest. Other kingdoms were being defined in the north at the same time: the Basques founded **Navarra** (Navarre), while dynastic marriage merged **Catalunya** with **Aragón**. In 1085, this period of confident Christian expansion reached its zenith with the capture of the great Moorish city of Toledo. The following year, however, the Almoravids arrived on invitation from Seville, and military activity was effectively frozen – except, that is, for the exploits of the legendary El Cid (see p.420), a Castilian nobleman who won considerable lands around Valencia in 1095.

The next concerted phase of the Reconquest began as a response to the threat imposed by the Almohads. The kings of León, Castile, Aragón and Navarra united in a general

210 BC	27 BC	c409–15	c5th–7th century
Roman colonization begins	Octavian-Augustus becomes first Roman emperor	Vandals invade Spain	Visigoths arrive and take control of most of Spain

crusade that resulted in the great victory at Las Navas de Tolosa (1212). Thereafter, Muslim power was effectively paralyzed, and the Christian armies moved on to take most of al-Andalus. Ferdinand III ("El Santo", The Saint) led Castilian soldiers into Córdoba in 1236 and twelve years later into Seville. Meanwhile, the kingdom of Portugal had expanded to more or less its present size, while Jaime I of Aragón was to conquer Valencia, Alicante, Murcia and the Balearic Islands. By the end of the thirteenth century, only the kingdom of Granada remained under Muslim authority, and for much of the following two centuries it was forced to pay tribute to the monarchs of Castile.

Two factors should be stressed regarding the Reconquest. First, its **unifying religious nature** – the spirit of crusade, intensified by the religious zeal of the Almoravids and Almohads, and by the wider European climate (which in 1095 gave rise to the First Crusade). This powerful religious motivation is well illustrated by the subsequent canonization of Ferdinand III, and found solid expression in the part played by the military orders of Christian knights, the most important of which were the Knights Templar and the Order of Santiago. At the same time, the Reconquest was a movement of **recolonization**. The fact that the country had been in arms for so long meant that the nobility had a major and clearly visible social role, a trend perpetuated by the redistribution of captured land in huge packages, or *latifundia*. Heirs to this tradition still remain as landlords of the great estates, most conspicuously in Andalucía. Men from the ranks were also awarded land, forming a lower, larger stratum of nobility, the *hidalgos*. It was their particular social code that provided the material for Cervantes in *Don Quixote*.

Any spirit of mutual cooperation that had temporarily united the Christian kingdoms disintegrated during the fourteenth century, and independent lines of development were once again pursued. Attempts to merge Portugal with Castile foundered at the battle of Aljubarrota (1385), and Portuguese attention turned away from Spain towards the Atlantic. Aragón experienced a similar pull towards the markets of the Mediterranean, although pre-eminence in this area was soon passed to the Genoese. It was Castile that emerged the strongest over this period: self-sufficiency in agriculture and a flourishing wool trade with the Netherlands enabled the state to build upon the prominent military role it played under Fernando III. Politically, Castilian history was a tale of dynastic conflict until the accession of the Catholic Monarchs.

Los Reyes Católicos

Los Reyes Católicos – the **Catholic Monarchs** – was the joint title given to **Fernando of Aragón and Isabel of Castile**, whose marriage in 1469 united the two largest kingdoms in Spain. Unity was in practice more symbolic than real: Castile had underlined its rights in the marriage vows and Aragón retained its old administrative structure. So, in the beginning at least, the growth of any national unity or Spanish – as opposed to local – sentiment was very much dependent on the head of state. Nevertheless, from this time on it begins to be realistic to consider Spain as a single political entity.

At the heart of Fernando and Isabel's popular appeal lay a **religious bigotry** that they shared with most of their Christian subjects. The **Inquisition** was instituted in Castile in 1480 and in Aragón seven years later. Aiming to establish the purity of the Catholic faith by rooting out heresy, it was directed mainly at Jews – resented for their enterprise in commerce and influence in high places, as well as for their faith. Expression had

711	**718**	**756**
Moors under Tariq invade and defeat Visigothic King Roderic near Jerez. Peninsula conquered in seven years	Pelayo defeats Moors at Covadonga in Asturias in northern Spain marking the start of the Reconquest	Abd-ar-Rahman I proclaims Emirate of Córdoba. Great mosque of Córdoba (Mezquita) begun

COLUMBUS AND THE CATHOLIC MONARCHS

After many frustrating years trying to find backers for his plan **to reach the Indies by sailing west**, Columbus' luck turned in 1491 when he spent a period at the Franciscan monastery of La Rabida in the province of Huelva. The abbot of La Rabida, Juan Pérez, a former confessor to Queen Isabel, was moved to write to her on Columbus' behalf. It was a timely moment as Granada had just fallen, the treasury was empty, and the promise of gold and glory for a resurgent Spain now attracted Isabel and her husband King Fernando. On August 3, 1492, Columbus set out from Palos, a port in Huelva, with three small vessels and 120 men. On October 12, he made landfall on Watling Island (aka San Salvador) in the Bahamas. After leaving a colony of men on Hispaniola (modern Haiti) he returned to Palos on March 15, 1493, to enormous acclaim. The Spanish conquest of the Americas had begun.

already been given to these feelings in a pogrom in 1391; it was reinforced by an edict issued in 1492 that forced up to 400,000 Jews to flee the country. A similar spirit was embodied in the Reconquest of the **Kingdom of Granada**, also in 1492. As the last stronghold of Muslim authority, the religious rights of its citizens were guaranteed under the treaty of surrender. Within a decade, though, those Muslims under Christian rule had been given the choice between conversion or expulsion.

The year 1492 symbolized a fresh start in another way: this was the year that Columbus (Cristóbal Colón in Spanish) discovered America, and of the papal bull that followed, entrusting Spain with the conversion of the American Indians, further entrenching Spain's sense of a mission to bring the world to the "True Faith". The next ten years saw the systematic conquest, colonization and exploitation of the **New World** as it was discovered, with new territory stretching from Labrador to Brazil, and new-found wealth pouring into the royal coffers. Important as this was for Fernando and Isabel, and especially for their prestige, their priorities remained in Europe, and strategic marriage alliances were made with Portugal, England and the Holy Roman Empire. It was not until the accession of the Habsburg dynasty that Spain could look to the activities of Cortés, Magellan and Pizarro and claim to be the world's leading power.

Habsburg Spain

Carlos I, a Habsburg, came to the throne in 1516 as a beneficiary of the marriage alliances of the Catholic Monarchs. Five years later, he was elected emperor of the Holy Roman Empire as Carlos V (**Charles V**), inheriting not only Castile and Aragón, but Flanders, the Netherlands, Artois, the Franche-Comté and all the American colonies to boot. With such responsibilities it was inevitable that attention would be diverted from Spain, whose chief function became to sustain the Holy Roman Empire with gold and silver from the Americas. It was only with the accession of **Felipe II** in 1556 that Spanish politics became more centralized. Felipe lived in the centre of Castile, near Madrid, creating a monument to the values of medieval Spain in his palace, El Escorial.

Two main themes run through his reign: the preservation of his own inheritance, and the revival of the crusade in the name of the Catholic Church. In pursuit of the former, Felipe successfully claimed the Portuguese throne (through the marriage of his mother), gaining access to the additional wealth of its empire. Plots were also woven in support of Mary

c9th century	967	1013	1037
Kingdoms of Catalunya and Navarra founded	Al-Mansur usurps Caliphal powers of Córdoba Caliphate and forces Christians back into Asturias	Caliphate disintegrates into *taifas* (petty kingdoms)	Fernando I unites kingdoms of Castile and León-Asturias

Queen of Scots' claim to the throne of England, and to that end the ill-fated **Armada** sailed in 1588, its sinking a triumph for English naval strength and for Protestantism.

This was a period of unusual religious intensity: the **Inquisition** was enforced with renewed vigour, and a rising of Moriscos (subject Moors) in the Alpujarras was fiercely suppressed. Felipe III later ordered the expulsion of half the total number of Moriscos in Spain – allowing only two families to remain in each village in order to maintain irrigation techniques. The **exodus** of both Muslim and Jew created a large gulf in the labour force and in the higher echelons of commercial life – and in trying to uphold the Catholic cause, an enormous strain was put upon resources without any clear-cut victory.

By the middle of the seventeenth century, Spain was losing international credibility. Domestically, the disparity between the wealth surrounding Crown and court and the poverty and suffering of the mass of the population was a source of perpetual tension. Discontent fuelled regional revolts in Catalunya and Portugal in 1640, and the latter had finally to be reacknowledged as an independent state in 1668.

Bourbons and the Peninsular War

The **Bourbon dynasty** succeeded to the Spanish throne in the person of **Felipe V** (1700); with him began the **War of the Spanish Succession** against the rival claim of Archduke Charles of Austria, assisted by British forces. As a result of the Treaty of Utrecht, which ended the war (1713), Spain was stripped of all territory in Belgium, Luxembourg, Italy and Sardinia, but Felipe V was recognized as king. Gibraltar was seized by the British in the course of the war. For the rest of the century, Spain fell very much under the French sphere of influence, an influence that was given political definition by an alliance with the French Bourbons in 1762.

Contact with France made involvement in the **Napoleonic Wars** inevitable and led eventually to the defeat of the Spanish fleet at Trafalgar in 1805. Popular outrage was such that the powerful prime minister, Godoy, was overthrown and King Carlos IV forced to abdicate (1808). Napoleon seized the opportunity to install his brother, Joseph, on the throne.

Fierce local resistance was eventually backed by the muscle of the British army, first under Sir John Moore, later under the Duke of Wellington, and in the course of the **Peninsular War** the French were at last driven out. Meanwhile, however, the **American colonies** had been successfully asserting their independence from a preoccupied centre and with them went Spain's last real claim of significance on the world stage. The entire nineteenth century was dominated by the struggle between an often reactionary monarchy and the aspirations of liberal constitutional reformers.

Seeds of civil war

Between 1810 and 1813 an ad-hoc Cortes (parliament) had set up a **liberal constitution** with ministers responsible to a democratically elected chamber. The first act of Ferdinand VII on being returned to the throne was to abolish this, and until his death in 1833 he continued to stamp out the least hint of liberalism. On his death, the right of succession was contested between his brother, Don Carlos, backed by the Church, conservatives and Basques, and his infant daughter, Isabel, who had the support of the liberals and the army.

1085	1086	1147	1162
Christians capture Toledo	Almoravids invade Spain from North Africa	Invasion by Almohads from Morocco; Seville becomes new Moorish capital in Spain.	Alfonso II unites kingdoms of Aragón and Catalunya

So began the **First Carlist War**, a civil war that lasted six years. Isabel II was eventually declared of age in 1843, her reign a long record of scandal, political crisis and constitutional compromise. Liberal army generals under the leadership of General Prim effected a coup in 1868 and the queen was forced to abdicate, but attempts to maintain a republican government foundered. The Cortes was again dissolved and the throne returned to Isabel's son, Alfonso XII. A new constitution was declared in 1876, limiting the power of the Crown through the institution of bicameral government, but again progress was halted by the lack of any tradition on which to base the constitutional theory.

The years preceding World War I merely heightened the discontent, finding expression in the growing **political movements** of the working class. The Socialist Workers' Party was founded in Madrid after the restoration of Alfonso XII, and spawned its own trade union, the UGT (1888), successful predominantly in areas of high industrial concentration such as the Basque Country and Asturias. Its anarchist counterpart, the CNT, was founded in 1911, gaining substantial support among the peasantry of Andalucía.

The loss of **Cuba** in 1898 emphasized the growing isolation of Spain in international affairs and added to economic problems with the return of soldiers seeking employment where there was none. A call-up for army reserves to fight in **Morocco** in 1909 provoked a general strike and the "Tragic Week" of rioting in Barcelona. Between 1914 and 1918, Spain was outwardly neutral but inwardly turbulent; inflated prices made the postwar recession harder to bear.

The general disillusionment with parliamentary government, together with the fears of employers and businessmen for their own security, gave **General Primo de Rivera** sufficient support for a military coup in 1923 in which the king, Alfonso XIII, was pushed into the background. Dictatorship did result in an increase in material prosperity, but the death of the dictator in 1930 revealed the apparent stability as a facade. New political factions were taking shape: the Liberal Republican Right was founded by Alcalá Zamora, while the Socialist Party was given definition under the leadership of Largo Caballero. The victory of antimonarchist parties in the 1931 municipal elections forced the abdication of the king, who went into exile, and the **Second Republic** was declared.

The Second Republic

Catalunya declared itself a republic independent of the central government and was ceded control of internal affairs by a statute in 1932. **Separatist movements** were powerful, too, in the Basque provinces and Galicia, each with their own demands for autonomy. Meanwhile, the government, set up on a tidal wave of hope, was hopelessly divided internally and too scared of right-wing reaction to carry out the massive tax and agrarian reforms that the left demanded, and that might have provided the resources for thoroughgoing regeneration of the economy.

The result was the increasing polarization of Spanish politics. **Anarchism**, in particular, was gaining strength among the frustrated middle classes as well as among the workers and peasantry. The **Communist Party** and left-wing **Socialists**, driven into alliance by their mutual distrust of the "moderate" socialists in government, were also forming a growing bloc. On the right, the **Falangists**, basically a youth party founded in 1923 by **José Antonio Primo de Rivera** (son of the dictator), made uneasy bedfellows with conservative traditionalists and dissident elements in the army upset by modernizing reforms.

1212	1213	1217
Almohad advance halted at Las Navas de Tolosa in Andalucía	Jaime I "El Conquistador" becomes king of Aragón and leads Christian Reconquest of Balearics (1229), Valencia (1238) and Alicante (1266)	Fernando III "El Santo" crowned king of Castile, and retakes Córdoba, Murcia (1241) and Seville (1248)

In an atmosphere of growing confusion, the left-wing Popular Front alliance won the general election of **February 1936** by a narrow margin. Normal life, though, became increasingly impossible: the economy was crippled by strikes, peasants took agrarian reform into their own hands, and the government failed to exert its authority over anyone. Finally, on July 17, 1936, the military garrison in Morocco rebelled under the leadership of **General Francisco Franco**, to be followed by risings at military garrisons throughout the country. It was the culmination of years of scheming in the army but, in the event, far from the overnight success its leaders almost certainly expected. The south and west quickly fell into Nationalist hands, but Madrid and the industrialized north and east remained loyal to the Republican government.

Civil War

The ensuing **Civil War** was undoubtedly one of the most bitter and bloody the world has seen. Violent reprisals were taken on their enemies by both sides – the Republicans shooting priests and local landowners wholesale, the Nationalists carrying out mass slaughter of the population of almost every town they took. Contradictions were legion in the way the Spanish populations found themselves divided from each other. Perhaps the greatest irony was that Franco's troops, on their "holy" mission to ensure a Catholic Spain, comprised a core of Moroccan troops from Spain's North African colony.

It was, too, the first modern war – Franco's German allies demonstrated their ability to wipe out entire civilian populations with their bombing raids on Gernika and Durango, and radio proved an important weapon, as Nationalist propagandists offered the starving Republicans "the white bread of Franco".

Despite sporadic help from Russia and thousands of volunteers in the **International Brigade**, the Republic could never compete with the professional armies and massive assistance from Fascist Italy and Nazi Germany enjoyed by the Nationalists. In addition, the left was torn by internal divisions that at times led almost to civil war within its own ranks. Nevertheless, the Republicans held out in slowly dwindling territories for nearly three years, with **Catalunya** falling in January 1939 and armed resistance in **Madrid** – which never formally surrendered – petering out over the following few months. As hundreds of thousands of refugees flooded into France, General Franco, who had long before proclaimed himself head of state, took up the reins of power.

Franco's Spain

The early reprisals taken by the victors were on a massive and terrifying scale. Executions were commonplace, and upwards of two million people were put in concentration camps until "order" had been established by authoritarian means. Only one party, the **Falange**, was permitted, and censorship was rigidly enforced. By the end of World War II, during which Spain was too weak to be anything but neutral, **Franco** was the only fascist head of state left in Europe, one responsible for sanctioning more deaths than any other in Spanish history. Spain was economically and politically isolated and, bereft of markets, suffered – almost half the population were still tilling the soil for little or no return. When General Eisenhower visited Madrid in 1953 with the offer of huge loans, it came as water to the desert, and the price, the establishment

1469	1492	1516
Castile and Aragón united by the marriage of Isabel and Fernando, los Reyes Católicos (the Catholic Monarchs)	Fall of Granada, the last Moorish kingdom. Discovery of America by Cristóbal Colón (Columbus)	Carlos V succeeds to the throne and becomes the Holy Roman Emperor (1520), inaugurating the Golden Age

of American nuclear bases, was one Franco was more than willing to pay. However belated, economic development was incredibly rapid, with Spain enjoying a growth rate second only to that of Japan for much of the 1960s, a boom fuelled by the tourist industry and the remittances of Spanish workers abroad.

Increased **prosperity**, however, only underlined the political bankruptcy of Franco's regime and its inability to cope with popular demands. Higher incomes, the need for better education, and a creeping invasion of Western culture made the anachronism of Franco ever clearer. His only reaction was to attempt to withdraw what few signs of increased liberalism had crept through, and his last years mirrored the repression of the postwar period. Trade unions remained outlawed, and the rampant inflation of the early 1970s saw striking workers across Spain hauled out of occupied mines and factories and imprisoned, or even shot in the streets. Attempts to report these events by the liberal press resulted in suspensions, fines and censorship. **Basque nationalists**, whose assassination of Admiral Carrero Blanco had effectively destroyed Franco's last hope of a like-minded successor, were singled out for particularly harsh treatment. Hundreds of so-called terrorists were tortured, and the Burgos trials of 1970, together with the executions of August 1975, provoked worldwide protest.

Franco finally died in November 1975, nominating **King Juan Carlos** as his successor. Groomed for the job and very much "in" with the army – of which he remains official commander-in-chief – the king's initial moves were cautious in the extreme, appointing a government dominated by loyal Francoists who had little sympathy for the growing opposition demands for "democracy without adjectives". In the summer of 1976, demonstrations in Madrid ended in violence, with the police upholding the old authoritarian ways.

The return of democracy

The violent events leading up to and following his mentor's death seem to have persuaded Juan Carlos that some real break with the past and a move towards **democratization** was now urgent and inevitable. Using the almost dictatorial powers he had inherited, he ousted Franco's reactionary prime minister, Carlos Arias Navarro, and replaced him with **Adolfo Suárez**, an ambitious lawyer and former apparatchik in Franco's ruling Movimiento party. Taking his cue from the king, in 1976 Suárez pushed a **Law of Political Reform** through the Cortes, reforming the legislature into two chambers elected by universal suffrage – a move massively endorsed by the Spanish people in a referendum. Suárez also passed legislation allowing the setting up of free trade unions, as well as legitimizing the Socialist Party (PSOE) and, controversially, the Communists. Several cabinet ministers resigned in protest, and an outraged military began planning their coup d'état.

When elections were held in June 1977, Suárez's own hastily formed centre-right party, the **Unión del Centro Democrático (UCD)**, was rewarded with a 34 percent share of the vote, the Socialists coming in second with 28 percent, and the Communists and Francoist **Alianza Popular** marginalized at 9 percent and 8 percent respectively. Despite the overwhelming victories in Catalunya and the Basque Country of parties appealing to regional sentiment, this was almost certainly a vote for democratic stability rather than for ideology, something reflected in the course of the parliament, with Suárez governing through "consensus politics", negotiating settlements on all important issues with the major parties.

1519	1532	1556	1588
Cortés lands in Mexico	Pizarro "discovers" Peru	Accession of Felipe II (d.1598)	British forces defeat the Spanish Armada. Marks Spain's demise as a sea power

THE LAW OF HISTORICAL MEMORY

In Spain as well as abroad the **legacy of Franco** remains controversial. In the years following the restoration of democracy there was no national debate about the dictator's thirty-five-year rule and unlike other countries, such as Germany and Argentina, Spain has never fully come to terms with its former dictatorship. Instead politicians on both sides of the divide tacitly agreed not to mention the legacy of the Franco regime and no war crimes trials were held. But many others were angry at a pact which meant that crimes committed in the Franco years not only went unpunished, but were not even recognized as having taken place. In 2007 the Spanish PSOE government – led by José Luís Rodrigo Zapatero, whose own grandfather was executed by Franco's forces – decided to address this issue and passed into law **La Ley de Memoria Histórica** (The Law of Historical Memory). This rules that sentences handed down by kangaroo courts during the regime – that led to the imprisonment or execution of thousands of Franco's opponents – were "illegitimate". It also decrees that local governments must locate, exhume from mass graves and identify the victims of the Franco regime. Historians claim that the remains of tens of thousands of Franco's opponents are buried in unmarked graves throughout the country.

The law also stipulates that all statues, plaques and symbols relating to the regime must be removed from public buildings (however, church property was excluded). It deals, too, with the dictatorship's monumental legacy – the vast basilica of the **Valle de los Caídos** near Madrid where the remains of Franco and the founder of the fascist Falange party, José Antonio Prima de Rivera, are interred. The law prohibits all political events at the site, thus preventing the traditional "Mass for the Caudillo" formerly celebrated each 20 November (the anniversary of Franco's death), and its celebration of the fascist cause.

The first parliament of the "New Spain" now embarked on the formidable task of drawing up a **constitution**, while the Suárez government applied for membership of the then EEC. One of the fundamental components of the new constitution was the concept of **autonomy** – the granting of substantial self-rule to the seventeen *autonomías* (autonomous regions) into which Spain was to be divided. In Franco's time, even speaking regional languages such as Catalan or Basque was banned, and the backlash against this policy ensured that nothing less than some form of independence would be acceptable for regions such as the Basque Country and Catalunya. Each autonomous region was also to have its own president, parliament and civil service, the costs of which have spiralled in the thirty years since. Still, on December 6, 1978, the new constitution was overwhelmingly endorsed in a national referendum and, remarkably, only three years after the death of Franco, Spain had become a full democracy.

Elections in March 1979 virtually duplicated the 1977 result, but when the UCD, a fractious coalition of moderates and extremists, started to crack, **Suárez resigned** in January 1981. This provided the trigger for a **military coup**, launched by a contingent of Guardia Civil loyal to Franco's memory and commanded by the tragi-comic Colonel Antonio Tejero. They stormed into the Cortes with Tejero brandishing a revolver, and submachine-gunned the ceiling as *diputados* (MPs) dived for cover. The crisis, for a while, was real; tanks were brought out onto the streets of Valencia, and only three of the army's ten regional commanders remained unreservedly loyal to the government. But as it became clear that the king would not support the plotters, most of the rest then affirmed their support. Juan Carlos had taken the decision of his life and emerged with immensely enhanced prestige in the eyes of most Spaniards.

1605	1609	1700	1808
Miguel de Cervantes writes *Don Quijote* (*Quixote*), considered the first modern novel	Expulsion of Moriscos, last remaining Spanish Muslims	War of Spanish Succession brings Felipe V (1713–46), a Bourbon, to the throne. British seize Gibraltar	French occupy Spain. Venezuela declares independence, others follow

The González era

On October 28, 1982, the Socialist PSOE, led by charismatic **Felipe González**, was elected with the biggest landslide victory in Spanish electoral history to rule a country that had been firmly in the hands of the right for 43 years. The Socialists captured the imagination and the votes of nearly ten million Spaniards with the simplest of appeals: "for change".

Once in power, however, the Socialist Party chose the path of pragmatism, and a relentless drift to the right followed. Four successive election victories kept the party in power for fourteen years, and by the mid-1990s the PSOE government's policies had become indistinguishable from the conservative administrations of Britain or Germany.

González himself, meanwhile, had also undergone transformation – from a radical young labour lawyer into a careworn elder statesman. Control of inflation had become a more urgent target than reducing unemployment, while loss-making heavy industries (steel and shipbuilding especially) were ruthlessly overhauled and other industries privatized. **European Union** membership came in 1986, and the pride that most Spanish people felt at this tangible proof of their acceptance by the rest of Europe bought the Socialists more valuable time.

The issue of **NATO** (or OTAN, as the Spaniards know it), perhaps more than any other, demonstrated how much González had sacrificed to pragmatism. During the 1982 election campaign, he had made an impassioned speech at a rally against Spain remaining a member of NATO, which the dying UCD administration had rushed into joining at the behest of the military. When the promised referendum was finally held four years later – which surprisingly turned out marginally in favour of staying in – his was one of the main voices in favour of continued membership.

After long years of being hopelessly divided, in the late 1980s the **Spanish right** realigned itself when former prime minister Adolfo Suárez's UCD Christian Democrats merged with the Alianza Popular to form the new right-of-centre **Partido Popular** (PP), which came a respectable runner-up in the 1989 elections; a new far-left coalition, **Izquierda Unida** (United Left), composed of the Communists and smaller leftist parties, came third, albeit with the same number of seats (18) in the Congress of Deputies as the Catalan Nationalists, barely a tenth of the PSOE's representation.

The nation's progressive disillusionment with Felipe González's government in the early 1990s saw the rise to prominence of **José María Aznar** as leader of the PP. A former tax inspector, Aznar was dogged in his criticism of government incompetence in dealing with its own sleaze and the growing economic crisis. This debilitated the PSOE's position still further in the build-up to the **1993 elections**. However, the PSOE confounded the pundits and the opinion polls to hang on to power by the skin of its teeth, albeit as a minority government. But González's victory was a poisoned chalice, for his past now began to catch up with him. As illegal financing of the PSOE and corruption and commission-taking on government projects by party officials and ministers were being exposed, the director of the Guardia Civil (appointed by González) jumped the country with millions of dollars of secret-service funds, and the governor of the Bank of Spain was caught out making a private (and illegal) fortune. But the most serious of all the scandals to beset González was the **GAL affair** (Grupo Antiterrorista de Liberación), when it was discovered that a semi-autonomous anti-terrorist unit had been carrying out a dirty war against the ETA terrorists in the 1980s, which included kidnapping and wholesale assassinations of suspected ETA members. The press – and a later judicial investigation

1812	1835	1898	1923
Liberal constitution declared in Cádiz	First Carlist War. Dissolution of the monasteries	Loss of Cuba, Spain's last American colony	Primo de Rivera dictatorship. Resigns (1930) due to ill health and popular agitation urges a republic

– exposed police participation in these crimes and a clear chain of command reaching up to the highest echelons of the PSOE government. Some Guardia Civil police officers were sent to prison for offences connected with the GAL affair, as were (briefly) two ministers for covering up the plot, before being released on appeal. But despite the efforts of prosecutors, González managed to avoid being hauled before the courts.

The swing to the right

The ailing PSOE administration, immersed in endless scandals, limped on towards what looked likely to be a crushing defeat in the **1996 elections**. The surprise result, however, was another **hung parliament**, making everyone a loser. Aznar, the narrow victor, was denied the "absolute majority" he had believed to be his throughout the campaign, and was forced to do a deal with the nationalist parties (whom he had described as "greedy parasites" on the hustings) in order to secure a workable parliamentary majority. Meanwhile, the PSOE's avoidance of the expected overwhelming defeat was proclaimed as a vindication by González, who hastily dismissed ideas of retirement. However, unable to make any significant impact on changing public opinion, and with the PSOE still in turmoil, early in 1998 **González resigned** the leadership of the party he had dominated for 23 years.

Elected on a centre-right platform, during his first term in office following his narrow 1996 victory, Aznar progressively moved his party to the centre, shifting aside the government's remaining hardliners in the hope of gaining the electorate's confidence and a working majority not dependent on alliances with the northern nationalists.

Following the resignation of Felipe González in 1998, a desperate PSOE then formed an alliance with the ex-communist Izquierda Unida, believing that their combined votes could prevent a likely Aznar victory. However, the voters turned out to support the government and the outcome of the March 2000 **general election** was a stunning **triumph for Aznar** and the PP, and for the first time since the death of Franco the right was in power with an overall majority.

The result was disaster for the left. The PSOE leader, Joaquín Almunia, resigned and a relatively unknown young politician was elected leader: **José Luis Rodríguez Zapatero**, a member of the moderate socialist "Nueva Via" (New Way) group within the PSOE. Zapatero admitted the PSOE's past mistakes, stating emphatically that any government led by him would be radically different. This seemed to go down well with the electorate, and the opinion polls began to move in the PSOE's favour.

The return of the PSOE

In 2001, José María Aznar – ever an enigma to those around him – announced that he would lead the PP up to the next general election but would then resign, and that it must seek a new leader. As leader designate (to take over following the election), the party chose Aznar's nominee, the less prickly, cigar-puffing **Mariano Rajoy**, minister for the interior and deputy prime minister. Early in 2004 all the indicators suggested the following March general election would deliver a comfortable victory for the ruling PP and its new leader, Rajoy. Then, on March 11, and three days before polling day, a series of **bombs** exploded on rush-hour commuter trains travelling into Madrid, killing 191

1931	1936	1937	1939
King Alfonso XIII is forced out and Second Republic is declared	Spanish Civil War begins	Basque town of Germika is destroyed by German bombers. Over 1500 civilians are killed	Civil War ends and Franco dictatorship begins

people and injuring almost two thousand others. The nation was thrown into shock at the most savage attack seen in Spain since the Civil War. Despite the discovery by police within hours of a van linked to the bombings containing detonators and a Koranic audiotape, the PP leadership decided that the Basque terrorist group ETA had to be the culprits. This was a high-risk tactic for the government, but it seemed convinced that by pinning the responsibility on ETA it would deflect attention away from its support for the Iraq war (ninety percent of Spaniards had been against it) just long enough for the votes to be counted. No mention was to be made of any possible link with Islamic militant groups, and at the same time the blaming of ETA would conveniently vindicate Aznar's hardline stance against Basque terrorism and separatism.

For the three days prior to the election, the heavily state-influenced media and Spanish diplomats around the world attempted to peddle the "ETA is responsible" line. But soon doubts began to surface, and in the hours before the polls opened the electorate seems to have become highly suspicious of the government's tactic of using ETA as a scapegoat to save its skin, believing that the attack – as was subsequently proved – was the work of **Islamic terrorists** and a retaliation for Spain's participation in the unpopular Iraq war.

The nation turned out in force to give its verdict – and Zapatero and the PSOE **an unexpected victory**. Two million new young voters already angered by the government's mishandling of the *Prestige* oil spill and Aznar's unwavering support for the Iraq war appear to have been pivotal to the final result. The accusations of lies and distortion hurled at the PP following the election result only intensified when it was revealed that the outgoing government had hired a specialist company to destroy all computer records dealing with the bombings before leaving office.

The first act by Zapatero as government leader was to announce the **immediate withdrawal of Spanish troops from Iraq**, an election promise. This aligned him firmly with the German and French governments in Europe to whom Aznar had been hostile, but incurred the displeasure of US president George W. Bush, who shunned Zapatero for the rest of his presidency and turned down requests by the Spanish leader for a meeting at the White House or in Madrid.

In his first four years of office leading up to elections in 2008, Zapatero's record was competent if unspectacular. It will probably be remembered more for legislation legalizing **gay marriages** than any other government innovation. He also enjoyed the benefit of a favourable economic climate with consistently high growth figures and an economy producing more jobs than any other euro-zone member. But in the latter part of 2007, the impact of the world **economic downturn** was also felt in Spain, as one of the major drivers of the Spanish economy, the huge construction industry, went into meltdown. The **general election of March 2008** took place against a backdrop of economic uncertainty, and although the result was another **PSOE victory** the reality was that they had scraped home seven seats short of the overall parliamentary majority that Zapatero had stated was the party's main campaign target.

Contemporary politics

The PSOE government's second term has been dominated by the world financial and economic crisis that started to unravel in 2007–08. The recession has caused unemployment to rise to alarming levels while an austerity programme aimed at dealing

1953	1975	1981	1986
US makes economic deal with Franco in return for military bases	Death of Franco. Spain becomes a constitutional monarchy	Attempted military coup fails; members of parliament are held hostage in the Cortes (Spanish Parliament)	Spain joins the European Union

with the government's massive debt lost it much support as civil service and teachers' salaries were cut, benefits and pensions were frozen and welfare programmes cancelled. In an effort to turn public support in the government's favour, in the autumn of 2010 prime minister Zapatero unveiled an extensive cabinet reshuffle and cut a deal with the Basque Nationalist Party's parliamentary deputies that would guarantee that the government ran its full term. In return the Basques won further transfers of power and funds to the already highly devolved Basque regional government.

Little changed, however, throughout the winter of 2010 as the economy foundered and the unemployment figure passed twenty percent, the EU's highest. The local and regional elections held in May 2011 produced a resounding victory for the opposition Partido Popular giving it control of nine of the country's 17 autonomous regions and 36 of Spain's 50 provincial capitals. The scale of the defeat was so shocking – even the PSOE bastion of Castilla La Mancha fell to the PP for the first time since democracy was restored.

Throughout the previous winter, political commentators observed that some government ministers – Zapatero in particular – appeared indecisive and weary. At the start of April 2011 Zapatero announced that he would not lead the party into the general election of 2012 and that it must seek a new leader. It appeared that while he had been a capable, if undistinguished, prime minister in times of plenty, he had little stomach for the long haul ahead to bring the Spanish economy out of deep recession. The party chose Alfredo Pérez Rubalcaba. a wily sexagenarian politician – and a minister in all the PSOE administrations since the 1990s – to succeed Zapatero and in June he assumed the title of leader designate (to take over at the start of the general election campaign). The party's clear intention was that Rubalcaba's "safe pair of hands" might be able to thwart a massacre, if not the seemingly inevitable defeat, at the approaching general election.

At the end of July 2011 Zapatero announced that he would call an early general election for the following November. If the scale of the swing in the local and regional elections is repeated in the general election the Partido Popular will win with an absolute majority, making Mariano Rajoy prime minister.

However, it remains to be seen whether a Partido Popular government will succeed in carrying out the vital reforms necessary to restore prosperity to the peninsula. During the 38 years since the end of the Franco regime the construction and tourism sectors accounted for close to 25 percent of GDP. Both industries have suffered badly in the recession and many experts now believe that Spain has no alternative but to build an advanced export-based economy.

During and after the May local and regional elections of 2011 multitudes of young people, many unemployed with little chance of finding a job, gathered in protest in makeshift campsites in the central squares and parks of major towns and cities across Spain. Their protest – coordinated via Facebook and Twitter – was against a political system they claimed is self-serving, inward-looking and oblivious to their plight. Their plight is real: unemployment averages nearly 45 percent among 16- to 29-year-olds. Whether the political establishment is capable of responding to this angry demonstration of discontent remains to be seen. Spain has come a long way since the passing of Franco's dictatorship but it now faces the greatest challenge since its democratic rebirth: to restore prosperity and jobs to a country ravaged by recession. In the struggle to achieve this, the nation's political and business classes, in particular, and society as a whole have an enormous responsibility.

2002	2004	2010
Spain adopts the euro currency as the peseta is scrapped	Madrid train bombings kill 191 and injure 2050, influencing the outcome of the general election held three days later	Spain wins the FIFA World Cup in South Africa for first time after winning the European Football championship in 2008

Wildlife

Despite its reputation as the land of the package holiday, you can't beat Spain for sheer diversity of landscape and wildlife. When the Pyrenees were squeezed from the earth's crust they created an almost impenetrable barrier stretching from the Bay of Biscay to the Mediterranean Sea. Those animals and plants already present in Spain were cut off from the rest of Europe, and have been evolving independently ever since. In the same way, the breach of the land bridge at what is now the Strait of Gibraltar, and the subsequent reflooding of the Mediterranean basin, stranded typical African species on the peninsula. The outcome was an assortment of wildlife originating from two continents, resulting in modern-day Iberia's unique flora and fauna.

Spain is the second most **mountainous** country in Europe after Switzerland. The central plateau – the *meseta* – averages 600–700m in elevation, slopes gently westwards and is surrounded and traversed by imposing *sierras* and *cordilleras*. To the north, the plateau is divided from the coast by the extensive ranges of the Cordillera Cantábrica, and in the south the towering Sierra Nevada and several lesser ranges run along the Mediterranean shore. Where these southern *sierras* continue across the Mediterranean basin, the unsubmerged peaks today form the Balearic Islands. The Pyrenean chain marks the border with France, and even along Spain's eastern shores the narrow coastal plain soon rises into the foothills of the *sierras* of Montseny, Espuña and Los Filabres, among others. The ancient *sierras* de Guadarrama and Gredos cross the *meseta* just north of Madrid, and the Sierra Morena and the Montes de Toledo rise out of the dusty southern plains. With such an uneven topography, it is not surprising to find an alpine element in the flora and fauna, with the most strictly montane species showing adaptations to high levels of ultraviolet light and prolonged winter snow cover.

   Climatic variations have produced a corresponding diversity in Spanish wildlife. The wet, humid north is populated by species typical of northern Europe, while the southern foothills of the Sierra Nevada have more in common vegetation-wise with the Atlas Mountains of Morocco. The continental weather pattern of much of the **interior** has given rise to a community of drought-resistant shrubs, together with annual herbs that flower and set seed in the brief spring and autumn rains, or more long-lived plants that possess underground bulbs or tubers to withstand the prolonged summer drought and winter cold.

Habitat

Like most of Europe, the Iberian Peninsula was once heavily forested. Today, though, following centuries of deforestation, only about ten percent of the original **woodland** remains, mostly in the north. Historically, much of the *meseta* was covered with evergreen oaks and associated shrubs such as laurustinus and strawberry tree (*madroño* – the tree in the symbol of Madrid), but the clearance of land for arable and pastoral purposes has taken its toll, as have the ravages of war. Today, tracts of Mediterranean woodland persist only in the *sierras* and some parts of Extremadura. When it was realized that much of the plateau was unsuitable for permanent agricultural use, the land was abandoned, and it is now covered with low-growing, aromatic scrub vegetation, known as *matorral* (maquis). An endangered habitat, the maquis is a haven for many rare and distinctive plant and animal species, some found nowhere else in Europe. The southeastern corner of the *meseta* is the only part of Spain that probably never supported woodland; here the arid steppe **grasslands** (*calvero*) remain basically untouched by man. In northern Spain, where vast areas are still forested, the typical tree species are more familiar: oak, beech, ash and lime on the lower slopes, grading into pine and fir at higher levels – and the appearance is distinctly northern European.

Much of the *meseta* is predominantly flat, arid and brown. Indeed, in Almería, Europe's only true **desert** is to be found, such is the lack of rainfall. But the presence of subterranean water supplies gives rise to occasional **oases** teeming with wildlife. The numerous tree-lined **watercourses** of the peninsula also attract birds and animals from the surrounding dusty plains. The great Ebro and Duero rivers of the north, and the Tajo and Guadiana in the south, have been dammed at intervals, creating **reservoirs** that attract wildfowl in winter.

The Spanish **coastline** has a little of everything: dune systems, shingle banks, rocky cliffs, salt marshes and sweeping sandy beaches. In Galicia, submerged river valleys, or *rías*, are reminiscent of the Norwegian fjords, and the offshore islands are home to noisy sea-bird colonies; the north Atlantic coast is characterized by limestone promontories and tiny, sandy coves; the Mediterranean coast, despite its reputation for wall-to-wall hotels, still boasts many undeveloped lagoons and marshes; and southwest of Seville lies perhaps the greatest of all Spain's coastal wetlands: the Coto Doñana.

While the rest of Europe strives for agricultural supremacy, in Spain much of the land is still **farmed** by traditional methods, and the **landscape** has changed little since the initial disappearance of the forests. The olive groves of the south, the extensive livestock-rearing lands of the north and even the cereal-growing and wine-producing regions of the plains, exist in relative harmony with the indigenous wildlife of the country. It is only since Spain joined the European Union that artificial pesticides and fertilizers and huge machines have made much impact. Even so, compared to its neighbours, Spain is still essentially a wild country. Apart from a few industrial areas in the northeast and around Madrid and large-scale urbanization along parts of the coast, the landscape reflects the absence of modern technology, and the low population density means that less demand is made on the wilderness areas that remain.

Flora

With such a broad range of habitats, Spain's **flora** is nothing less than superb. Excluding the Canary Islands, about eight thousand species occur on Spanish soil, approximately ten percent of – are found nowhere else in the world. The plethora of high **mountains** allows an alpine flora to persist in Spain well beyond its normal north European distribution, and because of the relative geographical isolation of the mountain ranges, plants have evolved which are specific to each. In fact, there are about 180 plants that occur only in the Pyrenees, and over forty species endemic to the Sierra Nevada.

This effect is clearly illustrated by the **buttercup** family. In the Pyrenees, endemic species include the pheasant's-eye *Adonis pyrenaica* and the meadow rue *Thalictrum macrocarpum*; the Sierra Nevada has *Delphinium nevadense* and the monkshood *Aconitum nevadense*, and of the columbines *Aquilegia nevadensis* occurs here alone. *A. discolor* is endemic to the Picos de Europa, *A. cazorlensis* is found only in the Sierra de Cazorla, and *A. pyrenaica* is unique to the Pyrenees. Other handsome montane members of this family include alpine pasqueflowers, hepatica, hellebores, clematis and a host of more obvious buttercups.

The dry Mediterranean grasslands of Spain are excellent hunting grounds for **orchids**. In spring, in the meadows of the Cordillera Cantábrica, early purple, elder-flowered, woodcock, pink butterfly, green-winged, lizard and tongue orchids are ten a penny, and a little searching will turn up sombre bee, sawfly and Provence orchids. Farther into the Mediterranean zone, exotic species to look for include Bertoloni's bee, bumblebee and mirror orchids. Lax-flowered orchids are common on the Costa Brava and high limestone areas will reveal black vanilla orchids, frog orchids and summer lady's tresses a bit later in the year.

The Mediterranean **maquis** is a delight to the eye and nose in early summer, as the cistus bushes and heaths come into flower, with wild rosemary, thyme, clary and French lavender adding to the profusion of colour. The *dehesa* grasslands of southwest Spain are carpeted with the flowers of *Dipcadi serotinum* (resembling brown bluebells), pink gladioli and twenty or so different trefoils in May. In the shade of the ancient evergreen oaks grow birthworts, with their pitcher-shaped flowers, bladder senna and a species of lupin known locally as "devil's chickpea".

Even a trip across the **northern meseta**, although reputedly through endless cereal fields, is by no means a dull experience. Arable weeds such as cornflowers, poppies, corncockle, chicory and shrubby pimpernel add a touch of colour and are sometimes more abundant than the crops themselves. Where the coastal **sand dunes** have escaped the ravages of the tourist industry you can find sea daffodils, sea holly, sea bindweed, sea squill and the large violet flowers of *Romulea clusiana*.

Mammals

The great mammalian fauna that roamed Europe in the Middle Ages today survives only as a relict population in the wildest areas of Spain. Forced to seek refuge from hunters and encroaching civilization, it is perhaps surprising that the only species to have succumbed to extinction is the little-known European beaver. Unfortunately, with elusiveness the key to their survival, the mammal species that remain can be almost impossible to see. Endangered, but common in the mountains of the north, the **wolf** (*lobo*) avoids contact with humans as much as possible. Persecuted for centuries in response to the exaggerated menace portrayed in folk tales, they are still today regarded as a major threat to livestock in some quarters, despite their dwindling numbers. Although afforded official protection, many farmers would not think twice about shooting on sight. Similarly, the omnivorous **brown bear** (*oso pardo*) shows none of the inquisitive boldness exhibited by its American cousins, and with numbers as low as a hundred in Spain, anybody catching a glimpse of one should consider themselves exceptionally fortunate.

In the **northern mountains** – the Pyrenees and the Cordillera Cantábrica – you should get at least a glimpse of chamois, roe and red deer, and possibly **wild boar** (*jabalí*), which can be seen at dusk during the winter conducting nightly raids on village potato patches. The **Spanish ibex** (*cabra montés*), the scimitar-horned wild goat, had represented the main quarry of locals since prehistoric times. However, while it was able to sustain low levels of predation, its agility was no match for modern hunters and it almost disappeared in the early years of the twentieth century. Thanks to effective conservation measures, its numbers are slowly beginning to recover and it is becoming an increasingly common sight in the *sierras* de Cazorla, Grazalema (both Andalucía) and Gredos (Castilla y León). Europe's answer to prairie dogs, **marmots** (*marmotas*) can occasionally be seen in the Pyrenees, where they graze in alpine meadows, while the surrounding pine forests support large numbers of their arboreal relatives – the **red squirrel**. Less well known, and considerably more difficult to see, is the bizarre **Pyrenean desman**, a large, shrew-like creature closely related to the mole, which inhabits mountain streams.

The typical mammals of **southern Spain** have more in common with Africa than Europe, the separation of the two continents leaving several species stranded to evolve in isolation. Specialities of African origin include the sleek, cat-like **spotted genet** and the adaptable, intelligent **Egyptian mongoose**, both of which are active mainly at night but can be glimpsed during the day. The undoubted jewel of the south, though, is the **Iberian lynx** (*lincé iberico*), paler, more heavily spotted and less heavily built than the northern-European species, in adaptation to the subtropical climate. Highly endangered, and now almost completely confined to parts of the Sierra Morena near Andújar and Parque Nacional Coto Doñana (although a small and previously unknown population has recently been discovered in Castilla-La Mancha), its haunting cries on spring nights are sadly becoming more and more infrequent. An emergency breeding programme set up in 2005 in Coto Doñana increased the population there to fifty or so individuals, which has remained roughly the same in the years reported since then. A similar programme in the Parque Natural Sierra de Andújar has had greater success and has more than doubled the 2002 population of 60 to over 150 individuals reported in 2009. It is hoped that both programmes will eventually aid the lynx's regeneration and remove it from the critically endangered species list.

In the air, no fewer than 27 species of **bat** occupy caves and woodlands throughout Spain. Highly visible and often attracted to artificial light sources by clouds of insects, they are among the easiest of wild mammals to see, although identification to species level is best left to experts. Most interesting are the four types of horseshoe bat and Europe's largest bat, the rare **greater noctule**, which, with a wingspan of 45cm, even feeds on small birds.

The most spectacular **aquatic mammals** are the twenty or so species of whale and dolphin, whose presence has encouraged the appearance of numerous boating companies to run trips out to see them. **Pilot whales** and **sperm whales** are common in the Straits of Gibraltar, and **dolphins** will often choose to accompany boat trips in all areas. Isolated and protected coves on the Mediterranean shores shelter some of the last breeding colonies of the **Mediterranean monk seal**, a severely threatened species perhaps doomed to extinction. **Fresh water** also supports a number of mammal species, perhaps the best known being the playful **European otter**, which is still fairly numerous in the north.

Birds

If any country in Europe qualifies as a paradise for **birdwatching**, then it must surely be Spain. Most twitchers head straight for the world-famous Parque Nacional Coto Doñana, where over half of all European bird species have been recorded, but other parts of the country are just as rewarding, even if you have to work a little harder to get a matching list.

Birds of prey are particularly visible, and as many as 25 species of raptor breed here, but it is during the spring and autumn migrations that you will see the most dramatic numbers. Clouds of honey buzzards, black kites and Egyptian vultures funnel across the Straits of Gibraltar, aided by warm currents, followed by less numerous but equally dramatic-looking species such as short-toed and booted eagles. Resident species include the widespread griffon vulture, the surprisingly common red kite and the Bonelli's eagle. Twitchers, though, are likely to have their sights set on four attention-grabbing species: the Eurasian black vulture, fighting against extinction in Extremadura; the bone-breaking bearded vulture of the Pyrenees; the diminutive but distinctive black-winged kite of the southern plains; and the endangered, endemic Spanish imperial eagle. The latter is most easily seen in Coto Doñana, where guides take great delight in pointing out this emblematic hunter.

There is no less variety in other types of bird. Woodpeckers are most abundant in the extensive forests of the **northern mountain ranges**. While white-backed woodpeckers are confined to the Pyrenees, other such rarities as black and middle-spotted woodpeckers may also be seen in the Cordillera Cantábrica, and the well-camouflaged wryneck breeds in the north and winters in the south of the country. Other typical breeding birds of these northern mountains are the turkey-like capercaillie, pied flycatcher, blue rock thrush, alpine accentor, citril and snow finches, and that most sought-after of all montane birds, the unique, butterfly-like wallcreeper.

In the open **grasslands** and cereal fields of the *meseta*, larks are particularly common. Look out for the calandra lark, easily identified by its chunky bill and the trailing white edge to the wing. More rewarding are great and little bustards – majestic at any time of year, but especially when the males fan out their plumage during the springtime courtship display. In a tiny area of the Mediterranean coast, strange nocturnal mooing calls from low-growing scrub betray the presence of the secretive **Andalucian buttonquail**, a tiny, quail-like bird, more closely related to the bustards than the quails. Look out also for the exotically patterned pin-tailed sandgrouse, one of only two European members of a family of **desert-dwelling birds**, as well as stone curlews and red-necked nightjars, the latter seen (and heard) mainly at dusk.

Olive groves are an ornithological treasure-trove playing host to a colourful assemblage of birds – hoopoes, azure-winged magpies, golden orioles, southern grey and woodchat shrikes, bee-eaters, rollers, great spotted cuckoos and black-eared wheatears. On a sunny summer's day, these birds are active and often easy to spot if you are patient.

Fluctuating water levels, particularly in the south, mean that there is no shortage of seasonally flooding **freshwater** habitats positively teeming with bird life. In reed beds, you may come across the vividly coloured purple gallinule, the high-stepping Bailon's crake, the thrush-sized great reed warbler or localized colonies of sociable bearded reedlings. In winter, large flocks of migrant waterfowl may gather, but it is the resident species that bring more reward: the exotic red-crested pochard, the rare ferruginous duck, the delicate marbled teal and the threatened white-headed duck among the highlights.

Coastal wetlands and **river deltas** are a must for any serious birdwatcher, with common summer occupants including black-winged stilts, avocets, greater flamingos and all but one of the European representatives of the heron family: cattle and little egrets, purple, grey, squacco and night herons, bitterns and little bitterns. In the right conditions and at the right time of year, almost all the species can be seen breeding together in vast and noisy heronries – an unforgettable sight. Wintering waders are not outstandingly distinctive, though wherever you go, even on the Atlantic coast, you should look for spoonbills. Grey phalaropes visit the northwest corner, as do whimbrels, godwits, skuas and ruffs, taking a break from their northern breeding grounds. For **sea birds**, the Illas Cíes, off the Galician coast, are unbeatable, providing breeding grounds for shags, the rare Iberian race of guillemot and the world's southernmost colony of lesser black-backed gulls.

Even **towns** have their fair share of notable species. The **white stork** (*cigüeña blanca*) is a summer visitor that has endeared itself to Andalucía and south central Spain, and few conurbations are without the unkempt nest atop a bell tower, electricity pylon or war monument. Finches such as serin and goldfinch are numerous, and the airspace above any town is usually occupied by hundreds of swifts, martins and swallows; you may be able to pick out alpine, pallid and white-rumped swifts and red-rumped swallows if you're in the southern half of the country, as well as crag martins in the north.

The **Balearic Islands** can provide you with a few more unusual cliff-nesting species, such as Eleanora's falcon, while deserted islets are ideal for hole-nesting sea birds, including Cory's shearwaters and storm petrels.

Reptiles and amphibians

Around sixty species of reptiles and amphibians occur in Spain, including some of Europe's largest and most impressive. Four species of salamander inhabit the peninsula. The brightly coloured **fire salamander**, an attractive patchwork of black and yellow, is perhaps the best known. Named for its habit of seeking solace in woodpiles and later emerging when the fire was lit, the salamander spawned the legend that it was somehow born out of the flames. The 30cm-long **sharp-ribbed salamander** of the southwest is Europe's largest, and bizarrely pierces its own skin with its ribs when attacked. The two remaining species, the drab, misnamed **golden-striped salamander** and the **Pyrenean brook salamander**, are confined to the cool, wet, mountainous north.

Closely related to the salamanders are the **newts**, of which there are only four species in Spain. If you take a trip into the high mountain pastures of the Cordillera Cantábrica, where water is present in small, peaty ponds all year round, you should see the brightly coloured **alpine newt**, while the aptly named **marbled newt** can be seen round the edges of many of Spain's inland lakes and reservoirs. Searches through tall waterside vegetation frequently turn up the tiny, lurid-green **tree frog**, striped in the north and west, but stripeless along the Mediterranean coast.

Two species of **tortoise** occur in Spain: **spur-thighed tortoises** can still be found along the southern coast and on the Balearic Islands, the latter the only Spanish locality for the other species – **Hermann's tortoise**. European **pond terrapins** and **stripe-necked terrapins** are more widely distributed, but only in freshwater habitats. Beware of confusion between these native species and the introduced North American **red-eared terrapin**, the result of the release of unwanted pets following the decline of the Teenage Mutant Ninja Turtle craze. **Marine turtles** are uncommon visitors to the Mediterranean and Atlantic coasts – perhaps the most frequently encountered is the protected **green turtle**, especially in the waters around Gibraltar, but **loggerhead** and **leathery turtles** are very occasionally reported.

The most exotic reptilian species to occur in Spain is the **chameleon**, although again this swivel-eyed creature is confined to the extreme southern shores where its camouflage skills render it difficult to find. **Lizards** are numerous, with the most handsome species being the large **ocellated lizard** – green with blue spots along the flank. Some species are very restricted in their range, such as Ibizan and Lilford's wall lizards, which live only in the Balearic Islands. In the south, the most noticeable species are **Moorish geckos**, large-eyed nocturnal creatures usually seen on the walls of buildings both inside and out. Adhesive pads on their feet enable them to cling perilously to vertical surfaces as they search for their insect prey.

Similarly, **snakes** are common, although few are venomous and even fewer are ever likely to bite. When faced with humans, evasive action is the snake's preferred option, and in most cases a snake will be long gone before the intruder even knew it was there. The **grass snake** will even play dead rather than bite, if cornered. **Asps** and **western whip snakes** occur in the Pyrenees, while the commonest species in the south is the harmless **horseshoe whip snake**, named for the distinctive horseshoe mark on the back of its head.

The most unusual Spanish reptile is undoubtedly the **amphisbaenian**, sometimes misleadingly called the blind snake. Adapted to a subterranean existence, this rarely encountered and harmless creature can sometimes be found by searching through rotten leaves and mulch in forested environments and gardens of the south.

Teresa Farino

Flamenco

Flamenco – one of the most emblematic musics of Spain and its richest musical heritage – has recently enjoyed huge exposure and today is more popular than ever before. Twenty-five years or so ago it looked like a music on the decline, preserved only in the clubs or *peñas* of its *aficionados*, or in travestied castanet-clicking form for tourists. However, prejudice vanished as flamenco went through a tremendous period of innovation in the 1980s and 90s, incorporating elements of pop, rock, jazz and Latin, and today there's a new respect for the old "pure flamenco" artists and a huge joy in the new. In line with this trend, in 2010 UNESCO added flamenco to its intangible cultural heritage list, as a world-class art form to be encouraged, protected and supported.

The initial impetus for flamenco's new-found energy came at the end of the 1960s, with the innovations of guitarist **Paco de Lucía** and, especially, the late, great singer **Camarón de la Isla**. These were musicians who had grown up learning flamenco but whose own musical tastes embraced international rock, jazz and blues.

They have been followed by groups such as **Ketama**, **Raimundo Amador** (ex Pata Negra), **La Barbería del Sur**, **Navajita Plateá** and **Niña Pastori**, who have all reached massive audiences that neither de Lucía nor de la Isla could have dreamt of decades before. At the end of the 1990s, there were even successful comebacks from such established artists as **Enrique Morente** and **José Mercé**. Morente – the established king of flamenco – experimentally revisited old styles and combined them with new moves, releasing a spectacular new album, *Omega*, in 1996, with **Lagarjita Nick**, one of the most emblematic bands of the Spanish indie rock scene. José Mercé collaborated with **Vicente Amigo** – recognized as the most gifted player of the moment, notably for his sense of syncopation – on *Del Amanecer*. Paco de Lucía acknowledges Amigo as his successor in the innovation of flamenco guitar.

Among others regarded as the best **contemporary singers** are the male singers El Cabrero, Juan Peña "El Lebrijano", the Sorderos, El Fosforito, José Menese, Duquende and El Potito. The most revered women include Fernanda and Bernarda de Utrera, Carmen Linares, Remedios Amaya, Estrella Morente (daughter of Enrique Morente, and the new "star" of Spanish flamenco), Montse Cortés, La Macanita and Carmen Amaya. Until his death **Camarón** – or more fully **Camarón de la Isla** – was by far the most popular and commercially successful singer of modern flamenco. Collaborating with the guitarists and brothers Paco de Lucía and Ramón de Algeciras, and latterly, Tomatito, Camarón raised *cante jondo* to a new art. A legend in his own lifetime, he tragically died of cancer in 1992 at the age of 42, having almost single-handedly revitalized flamenco song, inspiring and opening the way for the current generation of flamenco artists.

Origins

Flamenco evolved in southern Spain from many sources: Morocco, Egypt, India, Pakistan, Greece and other parts of the Near and Far East. Most authorities believe the roots of the music were brought to Spain by gypsies arriving in the fifteenth century. In the following century, it was fused with elements of Arab and Jewish music in the Andalucian mountains, where Jews, Muslims and "pagan" gypsies had taken refuge from the forced conversions and clearances effected by the Catholic Kings and the Church. Important flamenco centres and families are still found today in quarters and towns of *gitano* and refugee origin, such as Alcalá, Jerez, Cádiz, Utrera and the Triana *barrio* of Seville. Although flamenco is linked fundamentally to **Andalucía**, emigration from that province has long meant that flamenco thrives not only there but also in Madrid, Extremadura, the Levante and even Barcelona – wherever Andalucian migrants have settled.

Flamenco *aficionados* enjoy heated debate about the purity of their art and whether it is more validly performed by a *gitano* (gypsy) or a payo (non-gypsy). Certainly during dark times, flamenco was preserved by the oral tradition of the closed *gitano* clans. Its power, too, and the despair that its creation overcomes, seem to have emerged from the vulnerable life of a people surviving for centuries at the margins of society. These days, though, there are as many acclaimed *payo* as *gitano* flamenco artists, and the arrival on the scene of musicians from Barcelona such as Vicente Amigo – who has no Andalucian blood but grew up in a neighbourhood full of flamenco music – has de-centred the debate.

The concept of dynasty, however, remains fundamental for many. The veteran singer **Fernanda de Utrera**, one of the great voices of "pure flamenco", was born in 1923 into a *gitano* family in Utrera, one of the *cantaora* (flamenco singer) centres. The granddaughter of the legendary singer "Pinini", she and her younger sister Bernarda, also a notable singer, both inherited their flamenco with their genes. This concept of an active inheritance is crucial and has not been lost in contemporary developments: the members of Ketama, for example, the Madrid-based flamenco-rock group, come from two *gitano* clans – the Sotos and Carmonas.

While flamenco's exact origins are debated, it is generally agreed that its "laws" were established in the nineteenth century. Indeed, from the mid-nineteenth into the early twentieth century flamenco enjoyed a Golden Age, the tail end of which is preserved on some of the earliest 1930s recordings. The musicians found a first home in the **café cantantes**, traditional bars that had their own groups of performers (*cuadros*). One of the most famous was the *Café de Chinitas* in Málaga, immortalized by the poet Gabriel García Lorca in his poem *A las cinco de la tarde* (At five in the afternoon), in which he intimates the relationship between flamenco and bullfighting, both sharing root emotions and flashes of erratic genius, and both also being a way to break out of social and economic marginality.

The art of flamenco

Flamenco is played at *tablaos* and fiestas, in bars and at *juergas* (informal, more or less private parties). The fact that the Andalucian public are so knowledgeable and demanding about flamenco means that musicians, singers and dancers found at even a local club or village festival are usually very good indeed.

Flamenco songs often express pain. Generally, the voice closely interacts with improvising guitar, which keeps the *compás* (rhythm), the two inspiring each other, aided by the **jaleo** – the hand-clapping *palmas*, finger-snapping *palillos* and shouts from participants at certain points in the song. *Aficionados* will shout encouragement, most commonly ¡olé! when an artist is getting deep into a song, but also a variety of other less obvious phrases. A stunning piece of dancing may, for example, be greeted with ¡*Viva la maquina escribir!* (Long live the typewriter!), as the heels of the dancer move so fast they sound like a clicking machine; or the cry may be ¡*agua!* (water!), for the scarcity of water in Andalucía has given the word a kind of glory.

The encouragement of the audience is essential for the artists, as it lets them know they are reaching deep into the emotional psyche of their listeners. They may achieve the rare quality of **duende** – total communication with their audience, and the mark of great flamenco of any style or generation. Latterly, the word *duende* has been used to describe "innovation", which, while it is significant, does not always capture its real depth.

Flamenco songs

There is a classical repertoire of more than sixty flamenco **songs** (*cantes*) and dances (*danzas*) – some solos, some group numbers, some with instrumental accompaniment, others *a cappella*. These different styles (or *palos*) of flamenco singing are grouped in families according to more or less common melodic themes, establishing three basic types of *cante flamenco*: **cante grande** (comprising songs of the *jondo* type), **cante chico**, and **cante intermedio** between the two. Roughly speaking, the *jondo* and *chico* represent the most and the least difficult *cantes* respectively in terms of their technical and emotional interpretation, although any form, however simple, can be sung with the maximum of complexity and depth. **Cante jondo** (deep song) comprises the oldest and "purest" songs of the flamenco tradition, and is the profound flamenco of the great artists, whose *cantes* are outpourings of the soul, delivered with an intense passion, expressed through elaborate vocal ornamentation. To a large extent, however, such categories are largely arbitrary, and few flamenco musicians talk about flamenco in this way; what matters to them is whether the flamenco is good or bad.

The basic *palos* include **soleares**, **siguiriyas**, **tangos** and **fandangos**, but the variations are endless and often referred to by their place of origin: *malagueñas* (from Málaga), for example, *granaínos* (from Granada), or *fandangos de Huelva*. *Siguiriyas*, which date from the Golden Age, and whose theme is usually death, have been described as cries of despair in the form of a funeral psalm. In contrast, there are many songs and dances such as *tangos*, *Sevillanas*, *fandangos* and *alegrías* (literally "happinesses"), which capture great joy for fiestas. The **Sevillana** originated in medieval Seville as a spring country dance, with verses improvised and sung to the accompaniment of guitar and castanets (rarely used in other forms of flamenco). In the last few years, dancing *Sevillanas* has become popular in bars and clubs throughout Spain, but their great natural habitats are Seville's Feria de Abril and the annual *romería*, or pilgrimage, to El Rocio. Each year wonderful new *Sevillanas* come onto the market in time for the fiestas.

Another powerful and more seasonal form is the **saeta**, songs in honour of the Virgins that are carried on great floats in the processions of Semana Santa (Holy Week). Traditionally, they are quite spontaneous – as the float is passing, a singer will launch into a *saeta*, a sung prayer for which silence is necessary and for which the procession will therefore come to a halt while it is sung.

Flamenco guitar

The guitar used to be simply an accompanying instrument – originally, the singers themselves played – but in the early decades of last century it began developing as a solo instrument, absorbing influences from classical and Latin American traditions. The greatest of these early guitarists was **Ramón Montoya**, who revolutionized flamenco guitar with his harmonizations and introduced a whole variety of *arpeggios* – techniques of right-hand playing adapted from classical guitar playing. Along with Niño Ricardo and Sabicas, he established flamenco guitar as a solo medium, an art extended from the 1960s on by **Manolo Sanlucar**, whom most *aficionados* reckon the most technically accomplished player of his generation. Sanlucar has kept within a "pure flamenco" orbit, and not strayed into jazz or rock, experimenting instead with orchestral backing and composing for ballet.

The best known of all contemporary flamenco guitarists, however, is undoubtedly **Paco de Lucía**, who made the first moves towards "new" or "fusion" flamenco. A *payo*, he won his first flamenco prize at the age of 14, and went on to accompany many of the great singers, including a long partnership with Camarón de la Isla. He started forging new rhythms for flamenco following a trip to Brazil, where he was influenced by *bossa nova*, and in the 1970s established a sextet with electric bass, Latin percussion, flute and saxophone. Over the past twenty years, he has worked with jazz-rock guitarists such as John McLaughlin and pianist Chick Corea, while his own regular band, the Paco de Lucía Sextet featuring his other brother, the singer Pepe de Lucía, remains one of the most original and distinctive sounds on the flamenco scene.

Other modern-day guitarists have equally identifiable sounds and rhythms, and fall broadly into two camps, being known either as accompanists or soloists. The former include **Tomatito** (Camarón's last accompanist), Manolo Franco and Paco Cortés, while among the leading soloists are the brothers Pepe and Juan Habichuela; Rafael Riqueni, an astonishing player who is breaking new ground with classical influences; Enrique de Melchor; Gerardo Núñez; and Vicente Amigo. Jerónimo Maya was acclaimed by the Spanish press as the "Mozart of Flamenco" when he gave his first solo performance, aged 7, in 1984.

Nuevo flamenco

The **reinvention of flamenco** in the 1980s was initially disliked by purists, but soon gained a completely new young public. Paco de Lucía set the new parameters of innovation and commercial success, and following in his footsteps came **Lolé y Manuel** and others, updating the flamenco sound with original songs and huge success. **Jorge Pardo**, Paco de Lucía's sax and flute player, originally a jazz musician, has continued to work at the cutting edge. **Enrique Morente** and **Juan Peña "El Lebrijano"** were two of the first to work with Andalucian orchestras from Morocco, and the Mediterranean sound remains important today, together with influences from southern India.

Paco Peña's 1991 *Missa Flamenca* recording, a setting of the Catholic Mass to flamenco, with the participation of established singers including Rafael Montilla "El Chaparro" from Peña's native Córdoba and a classical academy chorus from London, has stayed a bestseller since its first appearance, remaining a benchmark for such compositions.

The encounter with rock and blues was pioneered at the end of the 1980s by Ketama and Pata Negra. **Ketama** (named after a Moroccan village famed for its hashish) were hailed by the Spanish press as creators of the music of the "New Spain" after their first album, which fused flamenco with rock and Latin salsa, adding a kind of rock–jazz sensibility, a "flamenco cool" as they put it. They then pushed the frontiers of flamenco still farther by recording the two *Songhai* albums in collaboration with Malian kora player Toumani Diabate and British bassist Danny Thompson. The group **Pata Negra**, a band led by two brothers, Raimundo and Rafael Amador, introduced a more direct rock sound with a bluesy electric guitar lead, giving a radical edge to traditional styles like *bulerías*. Their *Blues de la Frontera* album caused an equal sensation. After splitting, Raimundo Amador has continued as a solo artist.

Collectively, these young and iconoclastic musicians became known, in the 1990s, as **nuevo flamenco** – a movement associated in particular with the Madrid label Nuevos Medios. They form a challenging, versatile and at times musically incestuous scene in Madrid and Andalucía, with musicians guesting at each other's gigs and on each other's records. Ketama have gone on to have massive hits nationally, bringing flamenco fully into the mainstream.

In the 1980s and 90s, the music became the regular sound of **nightclubs**, through the appeal of young singers such as **Aurora** – whose salsa-rumba song *Besos de Caramelo*, written by Antonio Carmona of Ketama, was the first 1980s number to crack the pop charts. Pop singer **Martirio** (Isabel Quiñones Gutierrez) is one of the most flamboyant personalities on the scene, appearing dressed in lace mantilla and shades like a cameo from a Pedro Almodóvar film, recording songs with ironic, contemporary lyrics, full of local slang, about life in the cities. Martirio's producer, **Kiko Veneno**, who wrote Camarón's most popular song, *Volando Voy*, is another key artist who helped open up the scene. A rock musician originally, he has a strongly defined sense of flamenco. **Rosario**, one of Spain's top female singers, has also brought a flamenco sensibility to Spanish rock music. In the mid-1990s, **Radio Tarifa** emerged as an exciting group, leading the exploration of a flamenco-Mediterranean sound with a mix of Arabic and medieval sounds on a flamenco base. They started out as a trio, later expanding to include African musicians.

More recently, the Barcelona-based collective, **Ojos de Brujo**, have given new flamenco fusions hip credibility and a contemporary ethos, making flamenco much more integral to Spanish musical life. Their genius has been their reworking of flamenco styles to incorporate modern musical tendencies, while expressing passionate politics embedded in issues of everyday life, championing anti-corporate concerns and challenging the negative effects of global capitalism on the small community.

Other more identifiably *nuevo flamenco* bands and singers to look out for include La Barbería del Sur (who add a dash of salsa), Wili Gimenez and José el Francés.

Jan Fairly, David Loscos and Manuel Domínguez

Books

Listings below represent a highly selective reading list on Spain and matters Spanish. Most titles are in print, although we've included a few older classics, no longer in print (indicated by o/p); most of them are easy enough to find, though, in secondhand bookshops or on secondhand-book sites such as ⓦabebooks.co.uk. An excellent specialist source for books about Spain – new, used and out of print – is Paul Orssich, 2 St Stephens Terrace, London SW8 1DH (☎020/7787 0030, ⓦwww.orssich.com). Books marked ★ are particularly recommended.

TRAVEL AND GENERAL ACCOUNTS

THE BEST INTRODUCTIONS

★ **John Hooper** *The New Spaniards*. This excellent, authoritative portrait of post-Franco Spain was originally written by *The Guardian*'s former Spanish correspondent in the 1980s. A revised second edition published in 2006 is already dated, but this is still one of the best possible introductions to contemporary Spain.

Adam Hopkins *Spanish Journeys: A Portrait of Spain*. Published in the mid-1990s, this is an enjoyable and highly stimulating exploration of Spanish history and culture, weaving its considerable scholarship in an accessible and unforced travelogue form, and full of illuminating anecdotes.

★ **Michael Jacobs** *Andalusia*. A well-crafted, opinionated and wide-ranging introduction to Andalucía. It covers everything from prehistory to the Civil War and manages to cram in perceptive pieces on flamenco, gypsies and food and drink. A gazetteer at the back details major sights. Recently updated, this remains one of the best introductions to the region.

★ **Mark Kurlansky** *The Basque History of the World*. A brilliantly entertaining take on this much maligned, misunderstood and misrepresented people. Kurlansky uses history, stories, anecdotes and even recipes to concoct this heady brew.

Lucy McCauley (ed) *Spain: Travelers' Tales*. It would be hard to better this anthology of writing on Spain, which gathers its stories and journalism predominantly from the last fifteen years. Featured authors include Gabriel García Márquez, Colm Tóibín and Louis de Bernières, whose "Seeing Red", on Buñol's La Tomatina festival, is worth the purchase price alone.

★ **Cees Nooteboom** *Roads to Santiago: Detours and Riddles in the Land and History of Spain*. This is one of the most literary travel books of recent decades: an almost Shandy-esque tale (few of the roads travelled lead anywhere near Santiago), garnished from the notebooks of this quirky, architecture-obsessed Dutch writer.

★ **Giles Tremlett** *Ghosts of Spain*. Tremlett (the Madrid correspondent of *The Guardian*) digs into the untold story of Spain's Civil War dead and the collective conspiracy of silence surrounding the war's terrors, and goes on to peel away the layers of the post-Franco era to present an enthralling and often disturbing study of contemporary Spain.

RECENT TRAVELS AND ACCOUNTS

★ **Chris Stewart** *Driving Over Lemons – An Optimist in Andalucía*. A funny, insightful and very charming account of life on a remote peasant farm in the Alpujarras where Stewart and his family set up home. The sequel, *A Parrot in* *the Pepper Tree*, has more stories from the farm interspersed with accounts of some of the author's earlier adventures as a sheep shearer in Sweden, drummer with rock band Genesis and greenhorn flamenco guitarist in Seville. The saga's latest episode, *The Almond Blossom Appreciation Society*, delivers another cocktail of hilarious, improbable and poignant tales.

Ted Walker *In Spain* (o/p). Until his death in 2004, the poet Ted Walker had lived and travelled in Spain on and off since the 1950s. This is a lyrical and absorbing account of the country and people, structured around his various sorties throughout the peninsula.

TWENTIETH-CENTURY WRITERS

Alastair Boyd *The Sierras of the South: Travels in the Mountains of Andalusia*, *The Road from Ronda* and *The Essence of Catalonia*. *Sierras* is a sensitively worked portrait of the Serranía de Ronda, which describes one Englishman's continuing love affair with a region he knew as home for twenty years. His earlier *The Road from Ronda* is a 1960s view of the same landscape, while *Catalonia* is a laudable part history of, part guide to Spain's northern province: strong on art and architecture.

★ **Gerald Brenan** *South from Granada*. An enduring classic. Brenan lived in a small village in the Alpujarras in the 1920s, and records this period and the visits of his Bloomsbury contemporaries Virginia Woolf, Lytton Strachey and Bertrand Russell.

★ **Laurie Lee** *As I Walked Out One Midsummer Morning*, *A Rose for Winter* and *A Moment of War*. *One Midsummer Morning* is the irresistibly romantic account of Lee's walk through Spain – from Vigo to Málaga – and his gradual awareness of the forces moving the country towards civil war. As an autobiographical novel, of living rough and busking his way from the Cotswolds with a violin, it's a delight; as a piece of social observation, painfully sharp. In *A Rose for Winter* he describes his return, twenty years later, to Andalucía, while in *A Moment of War* he looks back again to describe a winter fighting with the International Brigade in the Civil War – by turns moving, comic and tragic.

James A. Michener *Iberia*. A bestselling, idiosyncratic and encyclopedic compendium of interviews and impressions of Spain on the brink – in 1968 – looking forward to the post-Franco years. Fascinating, still.

★ **George Orwell** *Homage to Catalonia*. Stirring account of Orwell's participation in the early exhilaration of revolution in Barcelona, and his growing disillusionment with the factional fighting among the Republican forces during the ensuing Civil War.

OLDER CLASSICS

George Borrow *The Bible in Spain* and *The Zincali* (both o/p). On first publication in 1842, Borrow subtitled *The Bible in Spain* "Journeys, Adventures and Imprisonments of an English-man"; it is one of the most famous books on Spain – slow in places but with some very amusing stories. *The Zincali* is an account of the Spanish *gitanos* (gypsies), whom Borrow got to know pretty well.

★ **Richard Ford** *A Handbook for Travellers in Spain and Readers at Home* and *Gatherings from Spain*. The *Handbook* (1845) must be the best guide ever written to any country. Massively opinionated, it is an extremely witty book in its British, nineteenth-century manner, and worth reading for the proverbs alone. *The Gatherings* is a timid – but no less entertaining – abridgement of the general pieces, intended for a female audience who wouldn't have the taste for the more cerebral stuff. A recently published biography *Richard Ford, Hispanophile, Connoisseur and Critic* by Ian Robertson places the great man in context and is also recommended.

Washington Irving *Tales of the Alhambra* (published 1832; abridged editions are on sale in Granada). Half of Irving's book consists of oriental stories, set in the Alhambra; the rest of accounts of local characters and his own residence there. A perfect read *in situ*.

George Sand *A Winter in Majorca*. Sand and Chopin spent their winter at the monastery of Valldemossa. They weren't entirely appreciated by the locals, in which lies much of the book's appeal. Local editions, including a translation by late Mallorcan resident Robert Graves, are on sale around the island.

ANTHOLOGIES

David Mitchell *Travellers in Spain: An Illustrated Anthology* (also published under the title *Here in Spain*). A well-told story of how four centuries of travellers – and most often travel writers – saw Spain. It's interesting to see Ford, Irving, Brenan, Laurie Lee and the rest set in context.

HISTORY

GENERAL

Juan Lalaguna *A Traveller's History of Spain*. A lucid (and pocketable) background history to the country, spanning the Phoenicians to Franco and the emergence of democratic Spain.

M. Vincent and R.A. Stradling *Cultural Atlas of Spain and Portugal*. A formidable survey of the Iberian Peninsula from ancient to modern times, in coffee-table format, with excellent colour maps and well-chosen photographs.

PREHISTORIC AND ROMAN SPAIN

James M. Anderson *Spain: 1001 Sights, An Archeological and Historical Guide*. A good guide and gazetteer to 95 percent of Spain's archeological sites.

María Cruz Fernandez Castro *Iberia in Prehistory*. A major study of the Iberian Peninsula prior to the arrival of the Romans, which surveys recent archeological evidence relating to the remarkable technical, economic and artistic progress of the early Iberians.

John S. Richardson *The Romans in Spain*. A new look at how Spain came to be a part of the Roman world, which also examines the influences that flowed from Spain to Rome as well as vice versa.

EARLY, MEDIEVAL AND BEYOND

J.M. Cohen *The Four Voyages of Christopher Columbus*. The man behind the myth; Columbus' astonishing voyages as described by Columbus himself in his log are interwoven with opinions of contemporaries on the great explorer, including his biographer son Hernando. A fascinating collection, superbly translated.

Roger Collins *The Arab Conquest of Spain 710–97*. Controversial study documenting the Moorish invasion and the significant influence that the conquered Visigoths had on early Muslim rule. Collins' earlier *Early Medieval Spain 400–1000* takes a broader overview of the same subject.

⭐ **J.H. Elliott** *Imperial Spain 1469–1716*. The best introduction to the "Golden Age" – academically respected, and a gripping tale.

⭐ **Richard Fletcher** *The Quest for El Cid* and *Moorish Spain*. Two of the best studies of their kind – fascinating and highly readable narratives. The latter is a masterly introduction to the story of the Moors in Spain.

L.P. Harvey *Islamic Spain 1250–1500*. Comprehensive account of its period – both the Islamic kingdoms and the Muslims living beyond their protection.

David Howarth *The Voyage of the Armada*. An account from the Spanish perspective of the personalities, from king to sailors, involved in the Armada.

⭐ **Henry Kamen** *The Spanish Inquisition*. A highly respected examination of the Inquisition and the long shadow it cast across Spanish history. *The Spanish Inquisition: An Historical Revision* returns to the subject in the light of more recent evidence, while Kamen's *Philip of Spain* is the first full biography of Felipe II, the ruler most closely associated with the Inquisition. In *Spain's Road to Empire*, Kamen skilfully dissects the conquest of the Americas and the Philippines.

Elie Kedourie *Spain and the Jews: the Sephardi Experience, 1492 and After*. A collection of essays on the three million Spanish Jews of the Middle Ages and their expulsion by Los Reyes Católicos.

John Lynch *Spain 1598–1700* and *Bourbon Spain: 1700–1808*. Two further volumes in the Blackwells project covering Spain from prehistory to modern times, written by the series' general editor and dealing with Spain's rise to empire and the critical Bourbon period.

James Reston Jr *Dogs of God*. An alternative take on the Inquisition from that of Kamen, connecting it with the epic year 1492 and linking religious intolerance to the final defeat of the Moors in Spain and Columbus' sudden widening of the Spanish Crown's sphere of influence.

Hugh Thomas *Rivers of Gold: The Rise of the Spanish Empire*. Thomas' scholarly but eminently accessible history provides a fascinating snapshot of Spain's most glorious period – its meteoric imperial rise in the late fifteenth and early sixteenth centuries, when characters such as Fernando and Isabel, Columbus and Magellan shaped the country's outlook for the next three hundred years.

THE TWENTIETH CENTURY

Phil Ball *Morbo – The Story of Spanish Football* (When Saturday Comes Books, UK). Excellent account of the history of Spanish football from its nineteenth-century beginnings with British workers at the mines of Río Tinto in Huelva to the golden years of Real Madrid and the dark days of Franco. Ever-present as a backdrop is the ferocious rivalry, or *morbo* – political, historical, regional and linguistic – that has driven the Spanish game since its birth.

⭐ **Gerald Brenan** *The Spanish Labyrinth*. First published in 1943, Brenan's account of the background to the Civil War is tinged by personal experience, yet still makes for an impressively rounded read.

⭐ **Raymond Carr** *Modern Spain 1875–1980* and *The Spanish Tragedy: the Civil War in Perspective*. Two of the best books available on modern Spanish history – concise and well-told narratives.

Ronald Fraser *Blood of Spain*. Subtitled "An Oral History of the Spanish Civil War", this is an equally impressive – and brilliantly unorthodox – piece of research allowing Spaniards to recount their experiences in their own words.

⭐ **Ian Gibson** *Federico García Lorca*, *The Assassination of Federico García Lorca* and *Lorca's Granada*. The biography is a compelling book and *The Assassination* a brilliant reconstruction of the events at the end of the writer's life, with an examination of Fascist corruption and the shaping influences on Lorca, twentieth-century Spain and the Civil War. *Granada* contains a series of walking tours around parts of the town familiar to the poet.

⭐ **Paul Preston** *Franco* and *Concise History of the Spanish Civil War*. A penetrating – and monumental – biography of Franco and his regime, which provides as clear a picture as any of how he won the Civil War and survived in power so long. *Civil War* is a more accessible than Thomas' work (below).

⭐ **Hugh Thomas** *The Spanish Civil War*. This exhaustive thousand-page study is regarded (both in Spain and abroad) as the definitive history of the Civil War.

Gamel Woolsey *Málaga Burning* (Pythia Press, US) and under its original title *Death's Other Kingdom* (Eland, UK). A long-ignored minor classic written in the late 1930s and recently reprinted (and retitled) by a US publisher, in which the American poet and wife of Gerald Brenan vividly describes the horrors of the descent of their part of Andalucía into civil war. The Eland edition includes an interesting biographical afterword by Michael Jacobs.

ART, ARCHITECTURE, PHOTOGRAPHY, FILM AND DESIGN

Marianne Barrucand and Achim Bednoz *Moorish Architecture*. A beautifully illustrated guide to the major Moorish monuments.

Bernard Bevan *History of Spanish Architecture* (o/p). Classic study of Iberian and Ibero-American architecture, including extensive coverage of the Mudéjar, Plateresque and Baroque periods.

Hugh Broughton *Madrid: A Guide to Recent Architecture*. Modern Spanish architecture is at the cutting edge of world design, and this is a fluent and pocketable guide to a hundred of the best examples in Madrid, each with its own photo and directions.

Robert Goff *The Essential Salvador Dalí*. An enjoyable and accessible introduction to Dalí and Surrealism, which examines the artist's bizarre life and obsessions (particularly his intense attachment to Gala, his wife), as well as his most enigmatic paintings.

Godfrey Goodwin *Islamic Spain*. Portable architectural guide with descriptions of virtually every significant Islamic building in Spain, and a fair amount of background.

Gijs van Hensbergen *Gaudí: the Biography*. At last, a worthy biography of one of the world's most distinctive architects. Van Hensbergen puts substantial flesh on the man while also describing the milieu in which he worked, placing his work firmly in context.

Robert Hughes *Goya*. The celebrated author of *The Shock of the New* and *Barcelona* turns his attention to one of Spain's greatest painters in this fabulous biography, a gripping account of Goya's life and work, placed within the context of turbulent eighteenth- and early nineteenth-century Spain.

Robert Irwin *The Alhambra*. A detailed tour of the building by art expert Irwin who – referring to other Islamic monuments – puts the palace in its Islamic context and attempts to determine how it functioned as a building.

★ **Michael Jacobs** *Alhambra*. Sumptuously produced volume with outstanding photographs and expert commentary. Authoritatively guides you through the history and architecture of the Alhambra, and concludes with a fascinating essay on the hold the palace has had on later artists, travellers and writers, from Irving and Ford to de Falla and Lorca.

John Richardson *A Life of Picasso*. The definitive biography of one of the twentieth century's major artistic driving forces, currently in three volumes with the final volume to come.

Gabriel Ruiz Cabrero *The Modern in Spain*. This readable book is a clear, comprehensive study of postwar Spanish architecture. The author is an architect and professor in the renowned Faculty of Architecture at Madrid's Politécnica.

Meyer Schapiro *Romanesque Art*. An excellent illustrated survey of Spanish Romanesque art and architecture – and its Visigothic and Mozarabic predecessors.

FICTION AND POETRY

SPANISH CLASSICS

Pedro de Alarcón *The Three-Cornered Hat*. Ironic nineteenth-century tales of the previous century's corruption, bureaucracy and absolutism.

Leopoldo Alas *La Regenta*. Alas' nineteenth-century novel, with its sweeping vision of the disintegrating social fabric of the period, is a kind of Spanish *Madame Bovary* (a book that it was in fact accused of plagiarizing at time of publication).

Ramón Pérez de Ayala *Belarmino and Apolonio* and *Honeymoon, Bittermoon*. A pair of tragicomic picaresque novels written around the turn of the twentieth century.

Emilia Pardo Bazán *The House of Ulloa*. Bazán was an early feminist intellectual and in this, her best-known book, she charts the decline of the old aristocracy in the time of the Glorious Revolution of 1868.

★ **Miguel de Cervantes** *Don Quixote* and *Exemplary Stories*. In 2005 Spain and the Hispanic world lavishly celebrated the four-hundredth anniversary of publication of Cervantes' work. *Quixote* (or *Quijote*) is, of course, *the* classic of Spanish literature and still an excellent and witty read, with much to inform about Spanish character and psychology. J.M. Cohen's fine Penguin translation or a new version by Edith Grossman, published by HarperCollins, are worth looking out for. If you want to try Cervantes in a more modest dose, the *Stories* are a good place to start.

Benito Pérez Galdós *Fortunata and Jacinta*. Galdós wrote in the last decades of the nineteenth century, and his novels of life in Madrid combine comic scenes and social realism; he is often characterized as a "Spanish Balzac". Other Galdós novels available in translation include *Misericordia, Nazarín* and the epic *"I"*.

★ **St Teresa of Ávila** *The Life of Saint Teresa of Ávila*. St Teresa's autobiography is said to be the most widely read Spanish classic after *Don Quixote*. It takes some wading through, but it's fascinating in parts.

MODERN FICTION

★ **Bernardo Atxaga** *Obabakoak*. This challenging novel by a Basque writer won major prizes on its Spanish publication. It is a sequence of tales of life in a Basque village and the narrator's search to give them meaning.

★ **Arturo Barea** *The Forging of a Rebel* (o/p). Superb autobiographical trilogy, taking in the Spanish war in Morocco in the 1920s, and Barea's own part in the Civil War. The books have been published in UK paperback editions under the titles *The Forge, The Track* and *The Clash*.

Camilo José Cela *The Family of Pascual Duarte* and *The Beehive*. Nobel Prize-winner Cela was considered integral to the revival of Spanish literature after the Civil War, though his reputation is compromised by his involvement with Franco's government where he worked as a censor. *Pascual Duarte*, his first novel, portrays the brutal story of a peasant murderer from Extremadura, set against the backdrop of the fratricidal Civil War, while *The Beehive*, his best-known work, is set in Madrid at the end of the same war and depicts the poverty and misery of this period through the lives of a multitude of characters.

Ildefonso Falcones *Cathedral of the Sea*. Well-researched and atmospheric historical romp tracing the life of the son of a fugitive serf who makes a new life for himself in the thriving medieval port of Barcelona. The title refers to the glorious Gothic church of Santa María del Mar, which provides the backdrop to much of the action.

★ **Juan Goytisolo** *Marks of Identity*, *Count Julian*, *Juan the Landless*, *Landscapes after the Battle* and *Quarantine*. Born in Barcelona in 1931, Goytisolo became a bitter enemy of the Franco regime, and has spent most of his life in self-exile, in Paris and Morocco. He is perhaps the most important modern Spanish novelist, confronting, above all in his great trilogy (comprising the first three titles listed above), the whole ambivalent idea of Spain and Spanishness, as well as being one of the first Spanish writers to deal openly with homosexuality. The more recent *Quarantine* documents a journey into a Dante-esque netherworld in which the torments of hell are set against reportage of the first Gulf War. Goytisolo has also written an autobiography, *Forbidden Territory*.

Carmen Laforet *Nada*. Written in 1944 but only recently translated, this is a haunting tale of a Barcelona family locked in the violence and despair of post-Civil War Spain. For all the horror, there is beauty also in the portrayal of a teenage girl's longing for consolation.

★ **Javier Marias** *Tomorrow in the Battle Think on Me*. There are many who rate Marias as Spain's finest contemporary novelist – and the evidence is here in this searching, psychological thriller, with its study of the human capacity for concealment and confession. Two other Marias novels, *A Heart So White* and *All Souls*, are also available in English translation.

Ana María Matute *School of the Sun*. The loss of childhood innocence on a Balearic island, where old enmities are redefined during the Civil War.

★ **Eduardo Mendoza** *City of Marvels* and *The Truth about the Savolta Case*. Mendoza's first and best novel, *City of Marvels*, is set in the expanding Barcelona of 1880–1920, full of rich underworld characters and riddled with anarchic and comic turns. It's a milieu repeated with flair in *The Truth about the Savolta Case*.

★ **Manuel Vázquez Montalban** *Murder in the Central Committee*, *Southern Seas*, *An Olympic Death*, *The Angst Ridden Executive*, *Off Side* and *The Man of My Life*. Montalban was, until his death in 2003, one of Spain's most influential writers. A long-time member of the Communist Party, he lived in Barcelona, like his great creation, the gourmand private detective Pepe Carvalho,

who stars in all of his wry and racy crime thrillers. The one to begin with – a classic – is *Murder in the Central Committee*.

Arturo Pérez Reverte *The Seville Communion* and *The Queen of the South*. Pérez Reverte is one of Spain's leading writers, and *Seville Communion* is an entertaining crime yarn played out against the colourfully described backdrop of Seville. Also in translation, *Queen of the South* was another Spanish bestseller and relates the story of a woman drug trafficker running narcotics between Morocco and Cádiz.

Julián Ríos *Larva*. Subtitled *Midsummer Night's Babel*, *Larva* is a large, complex, postmodern novel by a leading Spanish literary figure, published to huge acclaim in Spain.

Carlos Ruiz Zafón *The Shadow of the Wind*. A wonderfully atmospheric novel in which a young boy tries to unravel the truth behind the life and death of a forgotten writer. Set in post-Civil War Barcelona, it is beautifully written and makes for a gripping read. Its follow-up, a prequel called *The Angel's Game*, has recently been translated.

PLAYS AND POETRY

Pedro Calderón de la Barca *Life is a Dream and other Spanish Classics* and *The Mayor of Zalamea*. Some of the best works of the great dramatist of Spain's "Golden Age".

J.M. Cohen (ed) *The Penguin Book of Spanish Verse*. Spanish poetry from the twelfth century to the modern age, with (parallel text) translations from all the major names.

Lope de Vega The nation's first important playwright (b.1562) wrote literally hundreds of plays, many of which, including *Lo Cierto por lo Dudoso* (*A Certainty for a Doubt*) and *Fuenteobvejuna* (*The Sheep Well*), remain standards of classic Spanish theatre.

★ **Federico García Lorca** *Five Plays: Comedies and Tragicomedies*. Andalucía's great pre-Civil War playwright and poet.

SPAIN IN FOREIGN FICTION

★ **Ernest Hemingway** *The Sun Also Rises* and *For Whom the Bell Tolls*. Hemingway remains a big part of the American myth of Spain – *The Sun Also Rises* contains some lyrically beautiful writing, while the latter is a good deal more laboured. He also published two books on bullfighting, the enthusiastic and not very good *Death in the Afternoon* (1932), and *Dangerous Summer* (1959), an overheated account of the contest between Dominguín and Antonio Ordoñez for the title of top-dog matador.

★ **Norman Lewis** *Voices of the Old Sea*. Lewis lived in Catalunya from 1948 to 1952, just as tourism was starting to arrive. This book is an ingenious blend of novel and social record, charting the breakdown of the old ways in the face of the "new revolution".

★ **Amin Malouf** *Leo the African*. A wonderful historical

novel, re-creating the life of Leo Africanus, the fifteenth-century Moorish geographer, in the last years of the kingdom of Granada and his subsequent exile in Morocco and world travels.

SPECIALIST GUIDEBOOKS

THE PILGRIM ROUTE TO SANTIAGO

Millán Bravo Lozano *A Practical Guide for Pilgrims: The Road to Santiago* (Everest). Colourful, informative guide. Includes separate map pages so you can leave the heavy guide at home.

John Higginson *Le Puy to Santiago – A Cyclist's Guide*. A cyclist's guide to the pilgrim route, which follows as closely as possible (on tarmac) the walkers' path, visiting all the major sites en route.

Edwin Mullins *The Pilgrimage to Santiago* (o/p). This is a travelogue rather than a guide, but is by far the best book on the Santiago legend and its fascinating medieval pilgrimage industry.

Alison Raju *The Way of St James: Le Puy to the Pyrenees* (vol. I) and *Pyrenees-Santiago-Finisterre* (vol. II); *Vía de la Plata – The Way of St James* (all Cicerone, UK). Walking guide to the pilgrim route divided between the French and Spanish sections and written by an experienced Iberian hiker. Both books include detailed maps, background on sights en route as well as practical information such as where to stay. In *Vía de la Plata* Raju covers the lesser-known pilgrim route to Santiago, starting out from Seville.

David Wesson *The Camino Francés* (Confraternity of St James). Annually updated basic guide to the *camino*, with directions and accommodation. The Confraternity (⊛sj.org.uk) publishes the most accurate guides to the route, and there's also an online bookshop.

TREKKING AND CYCLING

Tony Bishop and Eva Monika Bratek *Walking in the Ronda Mountains*. Describing 30 half-day walks in the Serranía de Ronda and the Sierra de Grazalema in Andalucía, this hiking guide contains clear maps and plenty of detail (with photos) about the flora and fauna to be seen on the various routes.

David and Ros Brawn *Sierra de Aracena*. A guide covering this magnificent Andalucian *sierra* in 27 walks, with an accompanying map (sold separately), and all routes GPS waypointed.

Charles Davis *Costa del Sol Walks, Costa Blanca Walks* (both Santana, Málaga; ⊛santanabooks.com). Well-written guides to two excellent walking zones describing 34 (32 in *Costa Blanca*) walks of between 3 and 18km; each walk has its own map. The same author's *Walk! the Axarquía* (Discovery, UK; ⊛www.walking.demon.co.uk) is a reliable guide to this picturesque Andalucía region describing 30 walks between 5 and 22km, all GPS waypointed. *34 Alpujarras Walks* with similar format, details GPS waypointed treks and Mallorca's Drystone Way (both Discovery, UK) is a guide to the Balearic island's long-distance walking route. In

the latter books, each walk has its own map, or there are waterproof 1:40,000 *Axarquía/Alpujarras Tour and Trail* maps (sold separately) with all walks (and GPS points) marked.

Harry Dowdell *Cycle Touring in Spain*. Well-researched cycle-touring guide, which describes eight touring routes of varying difficulty in the north and south of Spain. Plenty of practical information on preparing your bike for the trip, transporting it, plus what to take.

★ **Teresa Farino** *Picos de Europa*. An excellent walking and touring guide in the *Landscapes* series detailing a variety of hikes in this spectacular national park, with special emphasis given to flora and fauna.

★ **Guy Hunter-Watts** *Walking in Andalucía*. First-rate walking guide to the natural parks of Grazalema, Cazorla, Los Alcornocales, Aracena and La Axarquía, as well as the Alpujarras and the Sierra Nevada, with 36 walks of various lengths, each with a colour map, and free internet updates. Regularly updated, so get the latest edition.

Jacqueline Oglesby *The Mountains of Central Spain*. Walking and scrambling guide to the magnificent *sierras* de Gredos and Guadarrama by resident author.

June Parker *Walking in Mallorca*. This popular and reliable guide is now in its fourth edition.

Jeremy Rabjohns *Holiday Walks in the Alpujarra* (Sigma, UK; ⊛ sigmapress.co.uk). Excellent, small walking guide by Alpujarras resident Rabjohns, describing 24 walks between 3 and 22km in length with clear maps (including many village street maps) and background information. Free updates and corrections available online.

Kev Reynolds *Walks and Climbs in the Pyrenees*. User-friendly guide for trekkers and walkers, though half devoted to the French side of the frontier.

Bob Stansfield *Costa Blanca Mountain Walks*. Two-volume set (sold separately) of walks in this little-known but spectacular area near Alicante. Vol. 1 covers the western Costa Blanca, Vol. 2 the eastern sector.

Douglas Streetfield-James et al *Trekking in the Pyrenees*. The best – and always the most current – English-language west-to-east guide to most of the GR11 and choice bits of the Camino de Santiago, though the GR10 and its variants is half the book. Easy-to-use sketch maps with (brisk) time courses and practical details for overnighting in villages.

Robin Walker *Walks and Climbs in the Picos de Europa* and *Walking in the Cordillera Cantábrica*. The first is a guide to walks and rock climbs in the Picos by an experienced resident mountaineer, the second expands beyond this zone to detail treks in the Cordillera mountain range.

Andy Walmsley *Walking in the Sierra Nevada*. Forty-five walks of varying distance and difficulty, from three-hour strolls in the Alpujarras to the seriously arduous Tres Mils (3000m-plus) peaks. The latest edition also caters for mountain-bikers.

The Barcelona-based map publisher **Editorial Alpina** (ⓦeditorialalpina.com) has a reliable range of 1:25,000 to 1:40,000 walking maps and guides covering Andalucía, Catalunya, the Pyrenees, the Picos de Europa, the Costa Blanca, the Balearics and other parts of Spain.

WILDLIFE

Teresa Farino and Mike Lockwood *Travellers' Nature Guides: Spain*. Excellent illustrated wildlife guide by two Spanish-based experts (one of whom contributed this guide's wildlife section); conveniently divided into regional groupings with detailed maps, it covers all the peninsula's major habitats for spotting flora and fauna.

FOOD AND WINE

Coleman Andrews *Catalan Cuisine*. The best available English-language book dealing with Spain's most adventurous regional cuisine.

Nicholas Butcher *The Spanish Kitchen*. A practical and knowledgeable guide to creating Spanish dishes when you get back. Lots of informative detail on tapas, olive oil, *jamón serrano* and herbs.

Penelope Casas *The Foods and Wines of Spain*. Superb and now classic Spanish cookbook, covering traditional and regional dishes with equal, authoritative aplomb. By the same author is the useful *Tapas: the little dishes of Spain*.

Alan Davidson *The Tio Pepe Guide to the Seafood of Spain and Portugal*. An indispensable (and pocketable) book that details and illustrates every fish and crustacean you're likely to meet in restaurants and bars along the Spanish *costas*.

★ **Julian Jeffs** *Sherry*. The story of sherry – history, production, blending and brands. Rightly a classic, and the best introduction to Andalucía's great wine. The same author's *Wines of Spain* is an erudite guide to traditional and up-and-coming wine regions, with details of vineyards, grape varieties and vintages.

Jean Claude Juston *The New Spain – Vegan and Vegetarian Restaurants* (available from ⓦvegetarianguides .co.uk). Very useful guide to vegetarian restaurants throughout Spain by the owner/chef of a vegetarian restaurant in the Alpujarras.

Jan Read *Guide to the Wines of Spain*. Encyclopedic (yet pocketable) guide to the classic and emerging wines of Spain by a leading authority. Includes maps, vintages and vineyards.

★ **Paul Richardson** *Late Dinner*. A joyous dissection of the food of Spain, region by region, season by season, nibble of ham by shoot of asparagus. He even squeezes in a meal with top chef Ferran Adrià at culinary shrine *El Bulli*. A celebration of culture and cuisine, this is the best general introduction to what Spanish food – and life – is really all about.

LIVING AND WORKING IN SPAIN

David Hampshire *Living and Working in Spain* (Survival Books, UK; ⓦsurvivalbooks.net). An excellent and comprehensive guide to moving to, and setting up home in, Spain.

LEARNING SPANISH

Breakthrough Spanish The best of the CD- and book-linked home-study courses, which aims to give you reasonable fluency within three months. The same series has advanced and business courses which are also good.

★ **Collins Spanish Dictionary** Recognized as the best single-volume bookshelf dictionary. Regularly revised and updated, so make sure you get the latest edition.

Elisabeth Smith *Teach Yourself Instant Spanish*. Good book-based (although CD is available) course that aims to get you from zero to streetwise Spanish in six weeks by studying thirty minutes per day.

★ *Get By in Spanish* (BBC Publications, UK; ⓦbbcactive .com/languages; book and CD). One of the BBC's excellent crash-course introductions (at a bargain price), which gets you to survival-level Spanish (bars, restaurants, asking the way, etc) in a couple of weeks. The CD content can be downloaded to an MP3 player to take on the trip.

Learn Spanish Now! (Transparent Language, UK/US; ⓦtransparent.com). CD-Rom-based (with facility for MP3 use) interactive course incorporating all kinds of gadgets enabling you to compare your pronunciation with a native speaker, access web-based additional learning resources and play skill-improving interactive games.

Michel Thomas Method *Foundation Course* and *Advanced Spanish*. The revolutionary "100 percent audio" CD-based learning system devised by the late polyglot Thomas has been praised by many learners (including Woody Allen and Emma Thompson) who have struggled with the more traditional "grammar grind" methods.

Rough Guide Spanish Dictionary. Good pocket-size dictionary that should help with most travel situations.

Untza Otaola Alday *Colloquial Spanish*. Excellent book-based beginner's course (supporting CDs are sold separately) with well-structured lessons and exercises. *Colloquial Spanish 2* takes you to the next level.

Language

Once you give it a try, Spanish (Castellano or Castilian) is among the easier languages to get a grip on. English is spoken, but wherever you are you'll get a far better reception if you at least try communicating with Spaniards in their own tongue. Being understood, of course, is only half the problem – getting the gist of the reply, often rattled out at a furious pace, may prove far more difficult.

The rules of **pronunciation** are straightforward and, once you get to know them, strictly observed. Unless there's an accent, words ending in d, l, r and z are **stressed** on the last syllable, all others on the second last. All **vowels** are pure and short; combinations have predictable results.

A somewhere between the A sound of "back" and that of "father".

E as in "get".

I as in "police".

O as in "hot".

U as in "rule".

C is lisped before E and I; otherwise, hard: *cerca* is pronounced "thairka" (though in Andalucía many natives pronounce the soft "c" as an "s").

G works the same way, a guttural "H" sound (like the ch in "loch") before E or I, a hard G elsewhere – *gigante* becomes "higante".

H is always silent.

J the same sound as a guttural G: *jamón* is pronounced "hamon".

LL sounds like an English Y or LY: *tortilla* is pronounced "torteeya/torteelya".

N is as in English unless it has a tilde (accent) over it, when it becomes NY: *mañana* sounds like "manyana".

QU is pronounced like an English K.

R is rolled, RR doubly so.

V sounds more like B, vino becoming "beano".

X has an S sound before consonants, normal X before vowels. More common in Catalan, Basque or Gallego words, where it's sh or zh.

Z is the same as a soft C, so *cerveza* becomes "thair-vaitha" (but again much of the south prefers the "s" sound).

The list of a few essential words and phrases overleaf should be enough to get you started, though if you're travelling for any length of time a dictionary or phrasebook is obviously a worthwhile investment. If you're using a **dictionary**, bear in mind that in Spanish CH, LL and Ñ count as separate letters and are listed after the Cs, Ls and Ns respectively.

In addition to Castilian, many Spaniards speak a second, **regional language** – we've given brief pronunciation rules and condensed glossaries for the three most widely spoken: **Catalan** (*Català*), **Basque** (*Euskara*) and **Galician** (*Galego*).

SPANISH WORDS AND PHRASES

BASICS

Yes, No, OK	Sí, No, Vale
Please, Thank you	Por favor, Gracias
Where, When	Dónde, Cuando
What, How much	Qué, Cuánto
Here, There	Aquí, Allí
This, That	Esto, Eso
Now, Later	Ahora, Más tarde
Open, Closed	Abierto/a, Cerrado/a
With, Without	Con, Sin
Good, Bad	Buen(o)/a, Mal(o)/a
Big, Small	Gran(de), Pequeño/a
Cheap, Expensive	Barato, Caro
Hot, Cold	Caliente, Frío
More, Less	Más, Menos
Today, Tomorrow	Hoy, Mañana
Yesterday	Ayer

GREETINGS AND RESPONSES

Hello, Goodbye	Hola, Adiós
Good morning	Buenos días
Good afternoon/ night	Buenas tardes/noches

See you later	Hasta luego	**the toilet**	el baño/aseo/servicio
Sorry	Lo siento/disculpéme	**Where does the bus to**	¿De dónde sale el autobús
Excuse me	perdón/Con permiso	**... leave from?**	para ...?
How are you?	¿Como está (usted)?	**Is this the train for**	¿Es este el tren para
I (don't) understand	(No) Entiendo	**Mérida?**	Mérida?
Not at all/ You're	De nada	**I'd like a (return)**	Quisiera un billete (de ida
welcome		**ticket to ...**	y vuelta) para ...
Do you speak English?	¿Habla (usted) inglés?	**What time does it leave**	¿A qué hora sale
I (don't) speak	Spanish (No) Hablo	**(arrive in ...)?**	(llega a ...)?
	español	**What is there to eat?**	¿Qué hay para comer?
My name is ...	Me llamo ...	**What's that?**	¿Qué es eso?
What's your name?	¿Como se llama usted?	**What's this called**	¿Como se llama este en
I am English/	Soy inglés(a)/	**in Spanish?**	español?
Australian/Canadian/	australiano(a)/		
American/Irish	canadiense(a)/		
	americano(a)/irlandés(a)		

NUMBERS AND DAYS

		one	un/uno/una
		two	dos
HOTELS AND TRANSPORT		**three**	tres
I want	Quiero	**four**	cuatro
I'd like	Quisiera	**five**	cinco
Do you know ...?	¿Sabe ...?	**six**	seis
I don't know	No sé	**seven**	siete
There is (is there)?	(¿)Hay(?)	**eight**	ocho
Give me ...	Deme ...(uno así)	**nine**	nueve
(one like that)		**ten**	diez
Do you have ...?	¿Tiene ...?	**eleven**	once
the time	la hora	**twelve**	doce
a room	una habitación	**thirteen**	trece
... with two beds/	... con dos camas/	**fourteen**	catorce
double bed	cama matrimonial	**fifteen**	quince
... with shower/bath	... con ducha/baño	**sixteen**	diez y seis
It's for one person	Es para una persona	**twenty**	veinte
(two people)	(dos personas)	**twenty-one**	veintiuno
for one night	para una noche	**thirty**	treinta
(one week)	(una semana)	**forty**	cuarenta
It's fine, how much is it?	¿Está bien, cuánto es?	**fifty**	cincuenta
It's too expensive	Es demasiado caro	**sixty**	sesenta
Don't you have anything	No tiene algo más barato?	**seventy**	setenta
cheaper?		**eighty**	ochenta
Can one ...? camp (near)	¿Se puede ....? ¿	**ninety**	noventa
here?	... acampar aquí (cerca)?	**one hundred**	cien(to)
Is there a hostel nearby?	¿Hay un hostal aquí	**one hundred and one**	ciento uno
	cerca?	**two hundred**	doscientos
How do I get to ...?	¿Por donde se va a ...?	**two hundred and one**	doscientos uno
Left, right,	Izquierda, derecha,	**five hundred**	quinientos
straight on	todo recto	**one thousand**	mil
Where is ...?	¿Dónde está ...?	**two thousand**	dos mil
... the bus station	... la estación de	**two thousand and one**	dos mil un
	autobuses	**two thousand and two**	dos mil dos
... the train station	... la estación de station	**two thousand and three**	dos mil tres
	ferro-carril	**first**	primero/a
... the nearest bank	... el banco mas cercano	**second**	segundo/a
... the post office	... el correos/la oficina de	**third**	tercero/a
	correos	**fifth**	quinto/a

tenth	décimo/a	**Thursday**	jueves
Monday	lunes	**Friday**	viernes
Tuesday	martes	**Saturday**	sábado
Wednesday	miércoles	**Sunday**	domingo

MENU READER

BASICS

Aceite	Oil	**Anguila/Angulas**	Eel/Elvers
Ajo	Garlic	**Atún**	Tuna
Arroz	Rice	**Bacalao**	Cod (often salt)
Azúcar	Sugar	**Bonito**	Tuna
Huevos	Eggs	**Boquerones**	Fresh anchovies
Mantequilla	Butter	**Chanquetes**	Whitebait
Miel	Honey	**Dorada**	Bream
Pan	Bread	**Lenguado**	Sole
Pimienta	Pepper	**Lubina**	Sea bass
Sal	Salt	**Merluza**	Hake
Vinagre	Vinegar	**Mero**	Grouper
		Pez espada	Swordfish
		Rape	Monkfish

MEALS

Almuerzo/Comida	Lunch	**Raya**	Ray, skate
Botella	Bottle	**Rodaballo**	Turbot
Carta	Menu	**Rosada**	Rockfish
Cena	Dinner	**Salmonete**	Mullet
Comedor	Dining room	**Sardinas**	Sardines
Cuchara	Spoon	**Trucha**	Trout
Cuchillo	Knife	**Urta**	Bream family
La cuenta	The bill		
Desayuno	Breakfast	**SEAFOOD (MARISCOS)**	
Menú del día	Fixed-price set meal	**Almejas**	Clams
Mesa	Table	**Arroz con mariscos**	Rice with seafood
Platos combinados	Mixed plate	**Calamares (en su tinta)**	Squid (in ink)
Tenedor	Fork	**Centollo**	Spider crab
Vaso	Glass	**Cigalas**	King prawns
		Conchas finas	Large scallops
		Gambas	Prawns/shrimps

SOUPS (SOPAS) AND STARTERS

Ajo blanco	Chilled almond & garlic soup	**Langosta**	Lobster
Caldillo	Clear fish soup	**Langostinos**	Crayfish
Caldo	Broth	**Mejillones**	Mussels
Caldo verde gallego	Thick cabbage-based broth	**Nécora**	Sea crab
Ensalada (mixta/verde)	(Mixed/green) salad	**Ostras**	Oysters
Gazpacho	Chilled tomato, peppers and garlic soup	**Paella**	Classic Valencian dish with saffron rice, chicken, seafood, etc
Pimientos rellenos	Stuffed peppers	**Percebes**	Goose barnacles
Sopa de ajo	Garlic soup	**Pulpo**	Octopus
Sopa de cocido	Meat soup	**Sepia**	Cuttlefish
Sopa de gallina	Chicken soup	**Vieiras**	Scallops
Sopa de mariscos	Seafood soup	**Zarzuela de mariscos**	Seafood casserole
Sopa de pescado	Fish soup		
Sopa de pasta (fideos)	Noodle soup	**COMMON TERMS**	
Verduras con patatas	Boiled potatoes with greens	**al ajillo**	in garlic
		a la brasa	grilled over embers
FISH (PESCADOS)		**a la Navarra**	stuffed with ham
Anchoas	Anchovies (fresh)	**a la parrilla/plancha**	grilled

a la Romana	fried in batter
al horno	baked
alioli	with garlic mayonnaise
asado	roasted
cazuela, cocido	stew
en salsa	in (usually tomato) sauce
frito	fried
guisado	casserole
rehogado	sautéed

MEAT (CARNE) AND POULTRY (AVES)

Callos	Tripe
Carne de buey	Beef
Cerdo	Pork
Cerdo Ibérico	Black-pig pork
Choto	Baby kid
Chuletas	Chops
Cochinillo	Suckling pig
Codorniz	Quail
Conejo	Rabbit
Cordero	Lamb
Escalopa	Escalope
Fabada asturiana/	Hotpot with butter beans,
Fabes a la catalana	black pudding, etc
Hamburguesa	Hamburger
Hígado	Liver
Jabalí	Wild boar
Lacón con grelos	Gammon with turnips
Lengua	Tongue
Lomo	Loin (of pork)
Pato	Duck
Pavo	Turkey
Perdiz	Partridge
Pollo	Chicken
Riñones	Kidneys
Solomillo	Sirloin steak
Solomillo de cerdo	Pork tenderloin
(Ibérico)	
Ternera	Beef/Veal
Venado	Venison

VEGETABLES (LEGUMBRES)

Acelga	Chard
Alcachofas	Artichokes
Arroz a la cubana	Rice with fried egg and
	tomato sauce
Berenjenas	Aubergine
Cebollas	Onions
Champiñones/Setas	Mushrooms
Coliflor	Cauliflower
Espárragos	Asparagus
Espinacas	Spinach
Garbanzos	Chickpeas
Habas	Broad/fava beans

Judías blancas	Haricot beans
Judías verdes,	Green, red, black beans
rojas, negras	
Lechuga	Lettuce
Lentejas	Lentils
Menestra/Panache de	Mixed vegetables
verduras	
Nabos/Grelos	Turnips
Patatas	Potatoes
Patatas fritas	French fries (chips)
Pepino	Cucumber
Pimientos	Peppers/capsicums
Pisto manchego	Ratatouille
Puerros	Leeks
Puré	Mashed potato
Repollo	Cabbage
Tomate	Tomato
Zanahoria	Carrot

FRUITS (FRUTAS)

Albaricoques	Apricots
Cerezas	Cherries
Chirimoyas	Custard apples
Ciruelas	Plums, prunes
Dátiles	Dates
Fresas	Strawberries
Granada	Pomegranate
Higos	Figs
Limón	Lemon
Manzanas	Apples
Melocotones	Peaches
Melón	Melon
Naranjas	Oranges
Nectarinas	Nectarines
Peras	Pears
Piña	Pineapple
Plátanos	Bananas
Sandía	Watermelon
Toronja/Pomelo	Grapefruit
Uvas	Grapes

DESSERTS (POSTRES)

Arroz con leche	Rice pudding
Crema catalana	Catalan crème brûlée
Cuajada	Cream-based dessert
	served with honey
Flan	Crème caramel
Helado	Ice cream
Melocotón en almíbar	Peaches in syrup
Membrillo	Quince paste
Nata	Whipped cream
Natillas	Custard
Pan de Calatrava	Bread pudding
Peras al vino	Pears cooked in wine

Pudín	Sweet pudding (varies nationwide)	**Costillas**	pork ribs
Tarta de almendras	Almond tart	**Empanada**	Fish/meat pasty
Tarta de manzana	Apple tart	**Ensaladilla rusa**	Russian salad (diced vegetables in mayonnaise)
Tarta de Santiago	Classic Galician almond tart		
Tocino de cielo	Syrup and egg flan (Andalucía)	**Escalibada**	Aubergine and pepper salad
Yogur	Yoghurt	**Garbanzos**	Chickpeas
		Gambas (al ajillo)	Prawns (cooked in garlic)

CHEESE

Cheeses (*quesos*) are on the whole local, though you'll get the hard, salty *queso manchego* everywhere. Mild sheep's or goat's cheese (*queso de oveja/cabra*) from León province or the Sierra de Grazalema (Cádiz) is widely distributed and worth asking for.

STANDARD TAPAS AND RACIONES

Aceitunas	Olives	**Habas**	Broad beans
Albóndigas	Meatballs	**Habas con jamón**	Broad beans with ham
Anchoas	Anchovies	**Hígado**	Liver
Berberechos	Cockles	**Hígado de pollo**	Chicken liver
Berenjenas fritas	Fried aubergine	**Huevo cocido**	Hard-boiled egg
Boquerones	Anchovies	**Jamón Serrano**	Cured ham (like Parma ham)
Cabrillas	Large snails with tomato		
Calamares	Squid	**Jamón Ibérico**	Cured black-pig ham (the best)
Callos	Tripe		
Caracolas	Whelks	**Langostinos**	Big, deep-water prawns
Caracoles	Snails	**Mejillones**	Mussels
Carne en salsa	Meat in tomato sauce	**Navajas**	Razor clams
Carne mechada	Larded meat	**Patatas alioli**	Potatoes in garlic mayonnaise
Champiñones	Mushrooms, usually fried in garlic		
		Patatas bravas	Spicy fried potatoes
Chocos	Deep-fried cuttlefish	**Pimientos**	Peppers
Chorizo	Spicy sausage	**Pincho moruno**	Kebab
Cocido	Stew	**Pintxo**	Basque tapa (on stick)
		Pisto	Ratatouille
		Pulpo	Octopus
		Riñones al Jerez	Kidneys in sherry
		Salchicha	Sausage
		Salchichón	Cured, peppery salami
		Sepia	Cuttlefish
		Tortilla española	Potato omelette
		Tortilla francesa	Plain omelette

Catalan

Catalan (Català) is spoken in Catalunya, part of Aragón, much of Valencia, the Balearic Islands and the Principality of Andorra. On paper, it looks like a cross between French and Spanish, and is generally easy to understand if you know those two, but, spoken, it has a distinct, rounded sound and is far harder to come to grips with – the language has eight vowel sounds (including three diphthongs).

The main differences from Castilian in **pronunciation** are:

A as in "hat" when stressed, as in "alone" when unstressed.

C sounds like an English S: *plaça* is pronounced "plassa".

G before E and I is like the "zh" in "Zhivago"; otherwise, hard.

J as in the French "Jean".

N is as in English, though before F or V it sometimes sounds like an M.

NY replaces the Castilian Ñ.

QU before E or I sounds like K; before A or O as in "quit".

R is rolled at the start of the word; at the end, it's often silent.

TX is like the English CH.

V sounds more like B at the start of a word; otherwise, a soft F sound.

W sounds like a B/V.

X like SH in most words, though in some it sounds like an X.

Z like the English Z.

CATALAN GLOSSARY

one	un(a)	thank you	gràcies
two	dos (dues)	today	avui
three	tres	yesterday	ahir
four	quatre	tomorrow	demà
five	cinc	day before yesterday	abans d'ahir
six	sis	day after	demà passat
seven	set	tomorrow	
eight	vuit	more	més
nine	nou	a lot, very	força
ten	deu	a little	una mica
Monday	Dilluns	left	esquerre(a)
Tuesday	Dimarts	right	dret(a)
Wednesday	Dimecres	near	(a) prop
Thursday	Dijous	far	lluny
Friday	Divendres	open	obert(a)
Saturday	Dissabte	closed	tancat
Sunday	Diumenge	town square	plaça
good morning/hello	bon dia	beach	praia
good evening	bona nit	where?	¿on?
goodbye	adéu	when?	¿quan?
please	per favor	how much?	¿quant?

Basque

Basque (Euskara) is spoken in the Basque Country and Navarra. According to the official estimates in 2008, around thirty percent of the population of the Basque Country and eleven percent of Navarra are "actively bilingual", speaking Euskara as their first language but understanding Castilian.

It's worth noting a couple of **key letter changes**: notably, the Castilian CH becomes TX (*txipirones* as opposed to *chipirones*), V becomes B and Y becomes I (Bizkaia as opposed to Vizcaya). Above all, Euskara features a proliferation of Ks: this letter replaces the Castilian C (Gipuzkoa instead of Guipúzcoa) and QU (Lekeitio instead of Lequeitio) and is also used to form the plural and the possessive (eg Bilboko means "of Bilbao").

BASQUE GLOSSARY

one	bat	good morning	egun on
two	bi	good night	gabon
three	hiru	please	mesedez
four	lau	thank you	eskerrik asko
five	bost	today	gaur
six	sei	yesterday	bihar
seven	zazpi	tomorrow	atzo
eight	zortzi	more	gehiago
nine	bederatzi	a lot	asko
ten	hamar	a little	gutxi
Monday	astelehen	left	ezker
Tuesday	astearte	right	eskuin
Wednesday	asteazken	near	hurbil
Thursday	ostegun	far	urruti
Friday	ostiral	open	ireki
Saturday	larunbat	closed	hertsi
Sunday	igande	town square	enpastantza
yes, no	bai, ez	beach	hondartza
hello	kaixo	shop	denda

| where? | ¿daude? | how much? | ¿zenbat? |
| when? | ¿noiz? | | |

Galician

While superficially similar to Castilian, **Galician** (Galego) is closer to Portuguese – in fact, both Galician and Portuguese evolved from a single ancestral tongue – and the main or only language of seventy percent of the population of Galicia.

The most obvious **characteristic** of Galician is the large number of Xs, which in Castilian might be Gs, Js or Ss; these are pronounced as a soft "sh" – thus *jamón* in Castilian becomes *xamón*, pronounced "shamon", in Galician. Similarly, LL in Castilian often becomes CH in Galician. You'll also find that the Castilian "la" becomes "a" (as in A Coruña), "el" is "o" (as in O Grove), "en la" is "na", "en el" is "no", "de la" is "da" and "del" is "do".

GALICIAN GLOSSARY

one	un	thank you	grazas
two	dous	today	hoxe
three	tres	yesterday	onte
four	catro	tomorrow	mañá
five	cinco	more	mais
six	seis	a lot	moito
seven	sete	a little	pouco
eight	oito	left	esquerda
nine	nove	right	dereita
ten	dez	near	preto
Monday	Luns	far	lonxe
Tuesday	Martes	open	aberto
Wednesday	Mécores	closed	pechado
Thursday	Xoves	town square	praza
Friday	Venres	beach	praia
Saturday	Sábado	shop	tenda
Sunday	Domingo	where?	¿onde?
good morning	bos días	when?	¿cándo?
good afternoon	boas tardes	how much?	¿cánto?
good night	boas noites		

Glossary of Spanish and architectural terms

Alameda Park or grassy promenade.
Alcazaba Moorish castle.
Alcázar Moorish fortified palace.
Apse Semicircular recess at the altar (usually eastern) end of a church.
Ayuntamiento/ajuntament Town hall.
Azulejo Glazed ceramic tilework.
Barrio Suburb or quarter.
Bodega Cellar, wine bar or warehouse.
Calle Street.
Capilla mayor Chapel containing the high altar.
Capilla real Royal chapel.
Capital Top of a column.
Cartuja Carthusian monastery.
Castillo Castle.

Chancel Part of a church containing the altar, usually at the east end.
Chiringuito Beach restaurant serving fish, seafood and paella.
Churrigueresque Extreme form of Baroque art named after José Churriguera (1650–1723) and his extended family, its main exponents.
Colegiata Collegiate (large parish) church.
Convento Monastery or convent.
Coro Central part of church built for the choir.
Coro alto Raised choir, often above west door of a church.
Correos Post office.
Corrida de toros Bullfight.
Crypt Burial place in a church, usually under the choir.

Cuadrilla A bullfighter's team of assistants.

Custodia Large receptacle for Eucharist wafers.

Dueño/a Proprietor, landlord/lady.

Ermita Hermitage.

Gitano Gypsy or Romany.

Hórreo Granary.

Iglesia Church.

Isabelline Ornamental form of Late Gothic developed during the reign of Isabel and Fernando.

Loggia Covered area on the side of a building, usually arcaded.

Lonja Stock exchange building.

Mercado Market.

Mihrab Prayer niche of Moorish mosque.

Mirador Viewing point.

Modernisme (Modernista) Catalan/Spanish form of Art Nouveau, whose most famous exponent was Antoni Gaudí.

Monasterio Monastery or convent.

Morisco Muslim Spaniard subject to medieval Christian rule – and nominally baptized.

Mozarabe Christian subject to medieval Moorish rule; normally allowed freedom of worship, they built churches in an Arab-influenced manner (Mozarabic).

Mudéjar Muslim Spaniard subject to medieval Christian rule, but retaining Islamic worship; most commonly a term applied to architecture which includes buildings built by Moorish craftsmen for the Christian rulers and later designs influenced by the Moors. The 1890s to 1930s saw a Mudéjar revival, blended with Art Nouveau and Art Deco forms.

Narthex Entrance hall of a church.

Nave Central space in a church, usually flanked by aisles.

Palacio Aristocratic mansion.

Parador State-owned luxury hotel, often (but not always) converted from minor monument.

Paseo Promenade; also the evening stroll thereon.

Patio Inner courtyard.

Plateresque Elaborately decorative Renaissance style, the sixteenth-century successor of Isabelline forms. Named for its resemblance to silversmiths' work (*platería*).

Plaza Square.

Plaza de toros Bullring.

Portico Covered entrance to a building.

Posada Old name for an inn.

Puerta Gateway, also mountain pass.

Puerto Port.

Raciones Large plate of tapas for sharing.

Reja Iron screen or grille, often fronting a window.

Reliquary Receptacle for a saint's relics, usually bones; often highly decorated.

Reredos Wall or screen behind an altar.

Retablo Altarpiece.

Ría River estuary in Galicia.

Río River.

Romería Religious procession to a rural shrine.

Sacristía, sagrario Sacristy of church – room for sacred vessels and vestments.

Sardana Catalan folk dance.

Seo, Seu, Se Ancient/regional names for cathedrals.

Sidreria Bar specializing in cider.

Sierra Mountain range.

Sillería Choir stall.

Solar Aristocratic town mansion.

Taifa Small Moorish kingdom, many of which emerged after the disintegration of the Córdoba caliphate.

Telefónica The phone company; also used for its offices in any town.

Transepts The wings of a cruciform church, placed at right angles to the nave and chancel.

Tympanum Area between lintel of a doorway and the arch above it.

Turismo Tourist office.

Vault Arched ceiling.

POLITICAL PARTIES AND ACRONYMS

CNT Anarchist trade union.

Convergencia I Unio Conservative party in power in Catalunya.

ETA Basque terrorist organization.

Falange Franco's old Fascist party; now officially defunct although a number of minor political groupings still use the name.

Fuerza Nueva Descendants of the above, also on the way out.

IU Izquierda Unida, broad-left alliance of communists and others.

MC Movimiento Comunista (Communist Movement), small radical offshoot of the PCE.

OTAN NATO.

PCE Partido Comunista de España (Spanish Communist Party).

PNV Basque Nationalist Party – in control of every post-Franco right-wing autonomous government until it lost the election in 2009.

PP Partido Popular, the centre-right alliance formed by Alianza Popular and the Christian Democrats. Currently led by Mariano Rajoy.

PSOE Partido Socialista Obrero Español, the Spanish Socialist Workers' Party. Currently led by Alfredo Pérez Rubalcaba.

UGT Unión General de Trabajadores, Spain's major union and the equivalent of Britain's Transport and General Workers' Union.

Small print and index

A ROUGH GUIDE TO ROUGH GUIDES

Published in 1982, the first Rough Guide – to Greece – was a student scheme that became a publishing phenomenon. Mark Ellingham, a recent graduate in English from Bristol University, had been travelling in Greece the previous summer and couldn't find the right guidebook. With a small group of friends he wrote his own guide, combining a highly contemporary, journalistic style with a thoroughly practical approach to travellers' needs.

The immediate success of the book spawned a series that rapidly covered dozens of destinations. And, in addition to impecunious backpackers, Rough Guides soon acquired a much broader readership that relished the guides' wit and inquisitiveness as much as their enthusiastic, critical approach and value-for-money ethos.

These days, Rough Guides include recommendations from budget to luxury and cover more than 200 destinations around the globe, as well as producing an ever-growing range of eBooks and apps.

Visit **roughguides.com** to see our latest publications.

Rough Guide credits

Editors: Edward Aves, Steve Horak, Polly Thomas
Layout: Umesh Aggarwal
Cartography: Rajesh Mishra
Picture editor: Mark Thomas
Proofreader: Diane Margolis
Managing editor: Alice Park
Assistant editor: Prema Dutta
Production: Rebecca Short
Cover design: Nicole Newman, Umesh Aggarwal
Editorial assistant: Eleanor Aldridge

Senior pre-press designer: Dan May
Design director: Scott Stickland
Travel publisher: Joanna Kirby
Digital travel publisher: Peter Buckley
Reference director: Andrew Lockett
Operations coordinator: Becky Doyle
Operations assistant: Johanna Wurm
Publishing director (Travel): Clare Currie
Commercial manager: Gino Magnotta
Managing director: John Duhigg

Publishing information

This fourteenth edition published March 2012 by
Rough Guides Ltd,
80 Strand, London WC2R 0RL
11, Community Centre, Panchsheel Park,
New Delhi 110017, India
Distributed by the Penguin Group
Penguin Books Ltd,
80 Strand, London WC2R 0RL
Penguin Group (USA)
375 Hudson Street, NY 10014, USA
Penguin Group (Australia)
250 Camberwell Road, Camberwell,
Victoria 3124, Australia
Penguin Group (NZ)
67 Apollo Drive, Mairangi Bay, Auckland 1310,
New Zealand
Rough Guides is represented in Canada by Tourmaline
Editions Inc. 662 King Street West, Suite 304, Toronto,
Ontario M5V 1M7
Printed in Singapore
© Simon Baskett, Jules Brown, Mark Ellingham, John Fisher,
Geoff Garvey, AnneLise Sorensen & Greg Ward 2012

Maps © Rough Guides, except: Madrid Metro map ©
Diseño RaRo S.L.
No part of this book may be reproduced in any form
without permission from the publisher except for the
quotation of brief passages in reviews.
944pp includes index
A catalogue record for this book is available from the
British Library
ISBN: 978-1-84836-725-8
The publishers and authors have done their best to
ensure the accuracy and currency of all the information
in **The Rough Guide to Spain**, however, they can accept
no responsibility for any loss, injury, or inconvenience
sustained by any traveller as a result of information or
advice contained in the guide.
1 3 5 7 9 8 6 4 2

MIX
Paper from
responsible sources
FSC   FSC™ C018179
www.fsc.org

Help us update

We've gone to a lot of effort to ensure that the fourteenth
edition of **The Rough Guide to Spain** is accurate
and up-to-date. However, things change – places get
"discovered", opening hours are notoriously fickle,
restaurants and rooms raise prices or lower standards. If
you feel we've got it wrong or left something out, we'd like
to know, and if you can remember the address, the price,
the hours, the phone number, so much the better.

Please send your comments with the subject line
"**Rough Guide Spain Update**" to ✉ mail@uk.roughguides
.com. We'll credit all contributions and send a copy of the
next edition (or any other Rough Guide if you prefer) for
the very best emails.
Find more travel information, connect with fellow
travellers and book your trip on ⓦ roughguides.com

ABOUT THE AUTHORS

Simon Baskett is a writer and journalist and author of the *Pocket Rough Guide to Madrid*. He lives and works in Madrid with his wife, Trini, and two children, Patrick and Laura.

Jules Brown is the author of the *Rough Guide to Barcelona*, and has also written and edited many other Rough Guides. But he's beginning to think he's left it too late to play for Huddersfield Town.

Mark Ellingham founded Rough Guides and spends time each year in the Alpujarras.

John Fisher was one of the authors of the first-ever Rough Guide and has been inextricably linked with the series ever since. The author of several other Rough Guide titles, he lives in south London with his wife and two sons.

Geoff Garvey caught the Iberian bug when hiking around Spain as a student. He now lives in Cadíz province and co-authors the *Rough Guide to Andalucía*.

AnneLise Sorensen, (ⱷannelisesorensen.com), who has Catalan-Danish roots, has penned (and wine-tasted) her way across Spain, writing and reporting for guidebooks, magazines, radio and TV. AnneLise grew up spending summers with her Catalan family, lived in Barcelona for several years, and divides her time between New York and Europe, sustained by late-night tapas and sangria on both sides of the Atlantic. AnneLise has also covered Scandinavia, Central America, India, New York and San Francisco.

Greg Ward has returned repeatedly to northern Spain since living in Galicia in the 1980s. He has also written the Rough Guides to Brittany & Normandy, the USA, Southwest USA, the Grand Canyon and Hawaii.

Acknowledgements

Simon Baskett Special thanks to Trini, Patrick and Laura for all their hard work and patience. Thanks, too, go to Antonio and Javier of the *Hostal Gonzalo*, Jorge Barrero Manzano and Maria Teresa Girón Cañas of the Metro de Madrid and to all those who gave recommendations and advice for this edition.

Jules Brown would like to thank Anna Hunt at Keytel and Paradores de Turismo de España, and Javier Lopez at Rusticae, for all their kind assistance. Thanks also to all at Rough Guides who helped give this new edition a fabulous makeover.

Geoff Garvey would like to thank Angela García, Jean-Claude Juston, Pasqual Rovira, Paco Moyano, Lola Maiztegui, Juan Carlos Ábalos, Pepa Babot, Oscar Carreño, Josefina del Castillo, Tony Bishop, Cat Gaa and Pam Lalonde for advice and assistance on the ground in Andalucía. A special "bedankt" also goes to Han for invaluable help in getting the job done.

AnneLise Sorensen Thanks to all who invited me in, wined and dined me, and shared information, travel tips and lively evenings, including: Maite Vidal, as always, for her splendid hospitality and knowledge of Spain; my entire – and ever-entertaining – Catalan family, including Anna and Miquel, Ramon and familia and all my wonderful Tietas and Tiets; Claire (and family) for being such a special best friend; Juan Peiro and the magnificent paradores, from Aiguablava to Sos del Rey Católico (cheers to Emilio Mojón); *Hotel Neptuno* and *W Hotel Barcelona*; and the top-notch turismos across Catalunya, Aragón, Valencia and Murcia. A big *gracias* also to chef Ferran Adrià and Pol Perelló, who welcomed me to *El Bulli* before it closed – an experience I'll always remember. Thanks to guapo and all the wonderful friends in New York for their support and cheery emails. A resounding thanks to my co-authors, editors Alice Park and Edward Aves, and the London and Delhi Rough Guides offices, including the excellent cartography team. Finally, a big *gracias, mange tak* and thank you to the best companion a travel-writer could ask for, Papa Kurt; and to Mama, who welcomed us back, with truita and open arms, to the home base in Cervera.

Greg Ward Thank you to Sam Cook and Pam Cook for sharing the joys of Spain; Jake, Alice and the girls for being there and going there; Polly Thomas, Ed Aves, Lara Kavanagh and Alice Park at Rough Guides, for being a pleasure to work with, as ever; Elixabete Arbe and Sara Sampedro of Basquetour, and Itziar Herrán of Lur Publicaciones, for their invaluable help in the Basque Country; and also Ane Echeverria, Desiree Fernandez, Lisa McGregor, Roberto Sousa, and José Villanueva for their generous hospitality.

Readers' letters

Thanks to all the readers who have taken the time to write in with comments and suggestions (and apologies if we've inadvertently omitted or misspelt anyone's name):

Peter Bennett, Frances Beresford, Nancy Brinton, Margaret Bullows, Iain Campbell Aird, Helena Carley, Sophia Hughes, Marjan Kuyken, Sheila MacDonald, Rocío Martín-Górriz Trillo, Joanna Mudie, Vincent Nordell, Michael Pollit, Eliza Pozzi, Mr HH Saffery, Elizabeth Washburn Joanne V Small, Marian Smith, Nick Spinks, Hilary Taylor, John White, Mark Wilcox

Photo credits

All photos © Rough Guides except the following:
(key: a-above; b-below/bottom; c-centre; l-left; r-right; t-top)

Front cover Giant Bull, Toros De Osborne, Andalucía © AWL images, Gavin Hellier
Back cover Santiago De Compostela © Alamy, Banana Pancake (t); Sagrada Família, Barcelona © Alamy, John Arnold Images (bl); Seville flamenco dancers © Axiom, Alessandra Meniconzi (br)

Title page
Getty Images, Martin Ruegner

Full page
Alamy, JLImages

Introduction
p.4 Alamy, Peter M Wilson
p.5 Getty Images, Pierre Jacques
p.9 Axiom Photographic Agency (b); Getty Images, Slow Images (t)
p.10 Getty Images, Philippe Body
p.11 Alamy, CW Images (c); SoFood (b)
p.12 4Corners, Massimo Ripani
p.13 Axiom Photographic Agency, Heidi Grassley

Things not to miss
p.14 Axiom Photographic Agency, Paul Quayle
p.15 Alamy, Ian Badley (t); Robert Harding (c); Hemis (b)
p.16 Alamy, Wilmar Photography (b); Getty Images, Juan Silva (c); Everynight Images, Jamie Baker (tr); Superstock, Rafael Campillo (tl)
p.17 4Corners, Richard Taylor (t); Getty Images, Allan Baxter (b)
p.18 Alamy, Jon Mikel Duralde; Ken Welsh (b); Robert Harding Picture Library, Rafael Jauregui (c)
p.19 Alamy, John Cancalosi (br); Mauritius images GmbH (tr); Getty Images, Harry Engels (tl)
p.20 Alamy, Pat Behnke (t); Robert Harding (b); Axiom Photographic Agency, Ian Cumming (c)
p.21 Alamy, Prisma Bildagentur AG (c); Oso Media (t); Getty Images, Jan-Pierre Lescourret (b)
p.22 Alamy, Peter Adams Photography Ltd (b); Corbis, Steven Vidler (tr); Getty Images, Oliver Benn (tl)
p.23 Alamy, LOOK Die Bildagentur der Fotografen GmbH (b)

Itineraries
p.24 4Corners, Gabriele Croppi
p.25 Alamy, Jeronimo Alba

Chapters
p.58 Getty Images, Cristina Arias
p.87 Getty Images, Jorg Greuel (t)

p.124 Alamy, Jo Chambers
p.127 Alamy, Jon Arnold Images Ltd
p.145 Alamy, Alex Segre (t); Getty Images, Maremagnum (b)
p.173 Alamy, Angela Hampton Picture Library
p.175 Alamy, Marco Cristofori
p.215 Alamy, Neil Setchfield (b); Getty Images, JMN (t)
p.222 Alamy, Ken Welsh
p.225 Alamy, Bart Pro
p.267 Axiom Photographic Agency, Anthony Webb (b); Getty Images, Maremagnum (t)
p.295 Axiom Photographic Agency, Ian Cumming (b); Peter M. Wilson (t)
p.331 Getty Images, Travel Ink (br); Visions Of Our Land (t); Hiroyuki Matsumoto (bl)
p.368 Alamy, Danita Delimont
p.371 Alamy, Jam World Images
p.381 Alamy, Jon Bower Spain (b); Hemis (t)
p.433 Alamy, Xavier Fores, Joana Roncero (t); Alberto Paredes (b)
p.444 Alamy, Hemis
p.447 Alamy, Alex Segre
p.473 Alamy, Ian Dagnall (t); Bob Masters (b)
p.496 Alamy, Prisma Bildagentur AG
p.499 Alamy, Roger Day
p.523 Alamy, Stan Kujawa (t); Gloria Latorre, Álvar Montes (b)
p.542 Getty Images, Herve Hughes
p.545 Alamy, Caroline Jones
p.555 Alamy, Hemis (br); John Norman (bl); Getty Images, Robert Frerck (t)
p.594 Alamy, Hemis
p.597 Alamy, Andalucia Plus Image bank
p.635 Alamy, Chad Ehlers
p.640 Getty Images, Sylvain Sonnet
p.675 Alamy, Kevin Foy (tr); Getty Images, Visions Of Our Land (bl)
p.704 Alamy, Wilmar Topshots
p.707 Alamy, Oso Media
p.729 Corbis, Pierre Jacques (t); Alamy, Jordi Cami Prisma Bildagentur AG (b)
p.767 Alamy, Prisma Bildagentur AG (t); Corbis Riccardo Valsecchi (b)
p.792 Alamy, Wilmar Photography
p.795 Alamy, isifa Image Service s.r.o.
p.805 Getty Images, Martin Child (b); Marco Simoni (t)
p.848 Alamy, Andrew Linscott
p.851 Alamy, Stuart Pearce
p.861 Getty Images, Dosfotos (tl)
p.890 Alamy, The Art Archive

Index

Maps are marked in grey

Map symbols

The symbols below are used on maps throughout the book

✈ Airport	✉ Post office	♨ Monastery	Rocks
★ Bus/taxi	ⓘ Information office	Spring/spa	Swamp
Ⓣ Tram stop	Ⓒ Telephone office	Swimming pool/area	Bridge
Ⓜ Metro station	♦ Museum	Waterfall	Building
⊚ Cercanías RENFE station	⊞ Hospital	⊤ Gardens	Market
Funicular	◆ Place of interest	Viewpoint	Church
●–● Cable car	Ⓜ Mosque	Cave	Stadium
— Ferry route	∴ Ruin	Campsite/ground	Park
✡ Synagogue	⊙ Statue	Mountain range	Beach
Ⓟ Parking	Castle	▲ Mountain peak	Saltpan
@ Internet café/access	Skiing	Mountain refuge	— Wall
	Lighthouse		

Listings key

- ■ Accommodation
- ● Eating and drinking
- ■ Nightlife
- ● Shop